AN INDEX
TO BOOK REVIEWS
IN THE HUMANITIES

VOLUME 15

1974

PHILLIP THOMSON

WILLIAMSTON, MICHIGAN

STANDARD BOOK NUMBER: 0-911504-15-X

INTERNATIONAL STANDARD SERIAL NUMBER:
US ISSN 0073-5892

LIBRARY OF CONGRESS CATALOG CARD NUMBER:
62-21757

PRINTED IN THE U.S.A.

THIS VOLUME OF THE INDEX CONTAINS DATA COLLECTED UP TO 31 DECEMBER
1974.
THIS IS AN INDEX TO BOOK REVIEWS IN HUMANITIES PERIODICALS. BE-
GINNING WITH VOLUME 12 OF THIS INDEX (DATED 1971), THE FORMER
POLICY OF SELECTIVELY INDEXING REVIEWS OF BOOKS IN CERTAIN SUBJECT
CATEGORIES ONLY WAS DROPPED IN FAVOR OF A POLICY OF INDEXING ALL
REVIEWS IN THE PERIODICALS INDEXED, WITH THE ONE EXCEPTION OF
CHILDREN'S BOOKS--THE REVIEWS OF WHICH WILL NOT BE INDEXED.
THE FORM OF THE ENTRIES USED IS AS FOLLOWS:

                      AUTHOR.   TITLE.
                      REVIEWER.   IDENTIFYING LEGEND.

THE AUTHOR'S NAME USED IS THE NAME THAT APPEARS ON THE TITLE-PAGE
OF THE BOOK BEING REVIEWED, AS WELL AS WE ARE ABLE TO DETERMINE,
EVEN THOUGH THIS NAME IS KNOWN TO BE A PSEUDONYM. THE TITLE ONLY
IS SHOWN; SUBTITLES ARE INCLUDED ONLY WHERE THEY ARE NECESSARY TO
IDENTIFY A BOOK IN A SERIES. THE IDENTIFYING LEGEND CONSISTS OF
THE PERIODICAL, EACH OF WHICH HAS A CODE NUMBER, AND THE DATE AND
PAGE NUMBER OF THE PERIODICAL WHERE THE REVIEW IS TO BE FOUND.
PMLA ABBREVIATIONS ARE ALSO SHOWN (WHEN A PERIODICAL HAS SUCH AN
ABBREVIATION, BUT SUCH ABBREVIATIONS ARE LIMITED TO FOUR LETTERS)
IMMEDIATELY FOLLOWING THE CODE NUMBER OF THE PERIODICAL. TO
LEARN THE NAME OF THE PERIODICAL IN WHICH THE REVIEW APPEARS, IT
IS NECESSARY TO REFER THE CODE NUMBER TO THE NUMERICALLY-ARRANGED
LIST OF PERIODICALS BEGINNING ON PAGE III. THIS LIST ALSO SHOWS
THE VOLUME AND NUMBER OF THE PERIODICALS INDEXED.
REVIEWS ARE INDEXED AS THEY APPEAR AND NO ATTEMPT IS MADE TO
HOLD THE TITLE UNTIL ALL THE REVIEWS ARE PUBLISHED. FOR THIS
REASON IT IS NECESSARY TO REFER TO PREVIOUS AND SUBSEQUENT VOLUMES
OF THIS INDEX TO BE SURE THAT THE COMPLETE ROSTER OF REVIEWS OF
ANY TITLE IS SEEN. AS AN AID TO THE USER, AN ASTERISK (*) HAS
BEEN ADDED IMMEDIATELY FOLLOWING ANY TITLE THAT WAS ALSO INDEXED
IN VOLUME 14 (1973) OF THIS INDEX.
AUTHORS WITH HYPHENATED SURNAMES ARE INDEXED UNDER THE NAME
BEFORE THE HYPHEN, AND THE NAME FOLLOWING THE HYPHEN IS NOT CROSS-
INDEXED. AUTHORS WITH MORE THAN ONE SURNAME, BUT WHERE THE NAMES
ARE NOT HYPHENATED, ARE INDEXED UNDER THE FIRST OF THE NAMES AND
THE LAST NAME IS CROSS-INDEXED. WHEN ALPHABETIZING SURNAMES CON-
TAINING UMLAUTS, THE UMLAUTS ARE IGNORED. EDITORS ARE ALWAYS
SHOWN IN THE AUTHOR-TITLE ENTRY, AND THEY ARE CROSS-INDEXED (EX-
CEPT WHERE THE EDITOR'S SURNAME IS THE SAME AS THAT OF THE
AUTHOR). TRANSLATORS ARE SHOWN ONLY WHEN THEY ARE NECESSARY TO
IDENTIFY THE BOOK BEING REVIEWED (AS IN THE CLASSICS), AND THEY
ARE NOT CROSS-INDEXED UNLESS THE BOOK BEING REVIEWED HAS NO AUTHOR
OR EDITOR. CERTAIN REFERENCE WORKS AND ANONYMOUS WORKS THAT ARE
KNOWN PRIMARILY BY THEIR TITLE ARE INDEXED UNDER THAT TITLE AND
THEIR EDITORS ARE CROSS-INDEXED.
A LIST OF ABBREVIATIONS USED IS SHOWN ON PAGE II.

ABBREVIATIONS

```
ANON ...............ANONYMOUS
APR ................APRIL
AUG ................AUGUST
BK .................BOOK
COMP(S) ............COMPILER(S)
CONT. ..............CONTINUED
DEC ................DECEMBER
ED(S) ..............EDITOR(S) [OR]
                    EDITION(S)
FASC ...............FASCICULE
FEB ................FEBRUARY
JAN ................JANUARY
JUL ................JULY
JUN ................JUNE
MAR ................MARCH
NO. (OR #) ........NUMBER
NOV ................NOVEMBER
OCT ................OCTOBER
PREV ...............PREVIOUS VOLUME OF
                    THIS INDEX
PT .................PART
REV ................REVISED
SEP ................SEPTEMBER
SER ................SERIES
SUPP ...............SUPPLEMENT
TRANS ..............TRANSLATOR(S)
VOL ................VOLUME
* (ASTERISK) ......THIS TITLE WAS ALSO
                    SHOWN IN THE VOLUME
                    OF THIS INDEX IM-
                    MEDIATELY PRECEDING
                    THIS ONE
```

THE PERIODICALS IN WHICH THE REVIEWS APPEAR ARE IDENTIFIED IN
THIS INDEX BY A NUMBER. TO SUPPLEMENT THIS NUMBER, AND TO PROMOTE
READY IDENTIFICATION, PMLA ABBREVIATIONS ARE ALSO GIVEN FOLLOWING
THIS NUMBER. EVERY ATTEMPT WILL BE MADE TO INDEX THOSE ISSUES
SHOWN HERE AS "MISSING" IN A LATER VOLUME OF THIS INDEX.
  THE FOLLOWING IS A LISTING OF THE PERIODICALS INDEXED IN VOLUME
15:

    1(ALH) - ACTA LINGUISTICA HAFNIENSIA. COPENHAGEN. TWICE YEARLY.
               VOLUME 14 COMPLETE
    5 - ARION. AUSTIN, TEXAS. QUARTERLY.
               SUMMER/AUTUMN 70 (VOL 9 # 2/3)
    9(ALAR) - ALABAMA REVIEW. UNIVERSITY, ALABAMA. QUARTERLY.
               JAN72 THRU OCT72 (VOL 25 COMPLETE)
   14 - AMERICAN ARCHIVIST. LAWRENCE, KANSAS. QUARTERLY.
               JAN72 THRU JUL/OCT72 (VOL 35 COMPLETE)
   24 - AMERICAN JOURNAL OF PHILOLOGY. BALTIMORE. QUARTERLY.
               SPRING73 THRU WINTER73 (VOL 94 COMPLETE)
   27(AL) - AMERICAN LITERATURE. DURHAM, NORTH CAROLINA. QUARTERLY.
               MAR73 THRU JAN74 (VOL 45 COMPLETE)
   31(ASCH) - AMERICAN SCHOLAR. WASHINGTON, D.C. QUARTERLY.
               WINTER73/74 THRU AUTUMN74 (VOL 43 COMPLETE)
   32 - SLAVIC REVIEW. SEATTLE, WASHINGTON. QUARTERLY.
               MAR73 THRU DEC73 (VOL 32 COMPLETE)
   35(AS) - AMERICAN SPEECH. NEW YORK. QUARTERLY.
               DEC68 (VOL 43 #4), FALL69 (VOL 44 #3) & SPRING/SUMMER
               70 AND FALL/WINTER70 (VOL 45 COMPLETE) [VOL 44
               # 1, 2 & 4 ARE MISSING]
   37 - THE AMÉRICAS. WASHINGTON, D.C. MONTHLY.
               JAN72 THRU NOV-DEC72 (VOL 24 COMPLETE)
   38 - ANGLIA. TÜBINGEN, GERMANY. QUARTERLY.
               BAND 90 COMPLETE
   39 - APOLLO. LONDON. MONTHLY.
               JAN72 THRU DEC72 (VOLS 95 & 96 COMPLETE)
   43(AR) - ANTIOCH REVIEW. YELLOW SPRINGS, OHIO. QUARTERLY.
               SPRING/SUMMER72 THRU VOL 32 #4 (VOL 32 COMPLETE)
   44 - ARCHITECTURAL FORUM. NEW YORK. MONTHLY.
               JAN/FEB72 THRU DEC72 (VOLS 136 & 137 COMPLETE)
   45 - ARCHITECTURAL RECORD. NEW YORK. MONTHLY.
               JAN72 THRU DEC72 (VOLS 151 & 152 COMPLETE) [NO
               REVIEWS INDEXED]
   46 - ARCHITECTURAL REVIEW. LONDON. MONTHLY.
               JAN72 THRU DEC72 (VOLS 151 & 152 COMPLETE)
   50(ARQ) - ARIZONA QUARTERLY. TUCSON.
               SPRING72 THRU WINTER72 (VOL 28 COMPLETE)
   52 - ARCADIA. BERLIN. THREE YEARLY.
               BAND 7 COMPLETE
   53(AGP) - ARCHIV FÜR GESCHICHTE DER PHILOSOPHIE. BERLIN. THREE
               YEARLY.
               BAND 54 COMPLETE
   54 - ART BULLETIN. NEW YORK. QUARTERLY.
               MAR72 THRU DEC72 (VOL 54 COMPLETE)
   55 - ART NEWS. NEW YORK. MONTHLY.
               JAN73 THRU DEC73 (VOL 72 COMPLETE) [MAR72 THRU DEC72
               MISSING]
   56 - ART QUARTERLY. DETROIT.
               SPRING72 THRU WINTER72 (VOL 35 COMPLETE)
   57 - ARTIBUS ASIAE. ASCONA, SWITZERLAND. QUARTERLY.
               VOLUME 34 COMPLETE
   58 - ARTS MAGAZINE. NEW YORK. MONTHLY.
               SEP/OCT72, NOV72 & FEB73 (VOL 47 # 1, 2 & 4) [DEC72/
               JAN73 ISSUE MISSING]
   59(ASOC) - ARTS IN SOCIETY. MADISON, WISCONSIN. THREE YEARLY.
               SPRING-SUMMER73 THRU FALL-WINTER73 (VOL 10 COMPLETE)
   60 - ARTS OF ASIA. HONG KONG. SIX YEARLY.
               JAN-FEB73 THRU NOV-DEC73 (VOL 3 COMPLETE)
   61 - ATLANTIC MONTHLY. BOSTON.
               JAN74 THRU DEC74 (VOLS 233 & 234 COMPLETE)
   63 - AUSTRALASIAN JOURNAL OF PHILOSOPHY. CANBERRA. THREE YEARLY.
               MAY73 THRU DEC73 (VOL 51 COMPLETE)
   67 - AUMLA [JOURNAL OF THE AUSTRALASIAN UNIVERSITIES LANGUAGE &
               LITERATURE ASSN.] CHRISTCHURCH, N.Z. TWICE YEARLY.
               MAY73 & NOV73 (#39 & #40)

                                III

69 - AFRICA. LONDON. QUARTERLY.
      JAN72 THRU OCT72 (VOL 42 COMPLETE)
70(ANQ) - AMERICAN NOTES & QUERIES. NEW HAVEN, CONN. MONTHLY.
      SEP73 THRU MAY/JUN74 (VOL 12 COMPLETE)
71(ALS) - AUSTRALIAN LITERARY STUDIES. HOBART, TASMANIA. TWICE
      YEARLY.
      MAY74 & OCT74 (VOL 6 # 3&4)
72 - ARCHIV FÜR DAS STUDIUM DER NEUEREN SPRACHEN UND LITERATUREN.
    BRAUNSCHWEIG, GERMANY. SIX YEARLY.
      BAND 210 COMPLETE
75 - BABEL. GERLINGEN, GERMANY. QUARTERLY.
      1/1972 THRU 4/1972 (VOL 18 COMPLETE)
78(BC) - BOOK COLLECTOR. LONDON. QUARTERLY.
      SPRING72 THRU WINTER72 (VOL 21 COMPLETE)
84 - THE BRITISH JOURNAL FOR THE PHILOSOPHY OF SCIENCE. CAMBRIDGE,
    ENGLAND. QUARTERLY.
      FEB72 THRU NOV72 (VOL 23 COMPLETE)
85 - THE BROWNING NEWSLETTER. WACO, TEXAS. TWICE YEARLY.
      SPRING72 & FALL72 (#8 & #9)
90 - BURLINGTON MAGAZINE. LONDON. MONTHLY.
      JAN72 THRU DEC72 (VOL 114 COMPLETE)
96 - ARTSCANADA. OTTAWA.
      FEB/MAR72 THRU DEC72/JAN73 (VOL 29 COMPLETE)
97(CQ) - THE CAMBRIDGE QUARTERLY. CAMBRIDGE, ENGLAND.
      VOL 6 #1&2
98 - CRITIQUE. PARIS. MONTHLY.
      JAN72 THRU DEC72 (VOL 28 COMPLETE)
99 - CANADIAN FORUM. TORONTO. MONTHLY.
      JAN74 THRU NOV/DEC74 (VOL 53 #636-638, VOL 54 #639-
      646) [VOL 54 BEGINS WITH APR74 ISSUE]
104 - CANADIAN-AMERICAN SLAVIC STUDIES/REVUE CANADIENNE-AMERICAINE
    D'ÉTUDES SLAVES. PITTSBURGH, PA. QUARTERLY.
      SPRING72 & SUMMER72 (VOL 6 #1&2)
111 - CAMBRIDGE REVIEW. CAMBRIDGE, ENGLAND. SIX YEARLY.
      20OCT72, 2FEB73 & 18MAY73 (VOL 94 #2209, #2211 &
      #2213) [#2210 & #2212 ARE MISSING]
114(CHIR) - CHICAGO REVIEW. QUARTERLY.
      VOL 23 #4 & VOL 24 #1 [DOUBLE ISSUE] THRU VOL 24 #4
123 - CLASSICAL REVIEW. LONDON. TWICE YEARLY.
      MAR73 & DEC73 (VOL 23 COMPLETE)
125 - CLIO. KENOSHA, WISC. THREE YEARLY.
      OCT72 THRU JUN73 (VOL 2 COMPLETE)
127 - ART JOURNAL. NEW YORK. QUARTERLY.
      FALL72 THRU SUMMER73 (VOL 32 COMPLETE)
128(CE) - COLLEGE ENGLISH. CHAMPAIGN, ILLINOIS. MONTHLY.
      JAN72 THRU MAY73 (VOL 33 #4-8, VOL 34 COMPLETE)
      [VOL 34 BEGINS WITH OCT72 ISSUE]
133 - COLLOQUIA GERMANICA. BERN, SWITZERLAND. THREE YEARLY.
      1972/1 THRU 1972/3
134(CP) - CONCERNING POETRY. BELLINGHAM, WASH. TWICE YEARLY.
      SPRING72 & FALL72 (VOL 5 COMPLETE)
135 - CONNOISSEUR. LONDON & NEW YORK. MONTHLY.
      JAN72 THRU DEC72 (VOLS 179 THRU 181 COMPLETE)
136 - CONRADIANA. ABILENE, TEXAS. THREE YEARLY.
      VOLUME 4 COMPLETE
139 - CRAFT HORIZONS. NEW YORK. BI-MONTHLY.
      DEC71 (VOL 31 #6) & FEB72 THRU DEC72 (VOL 32 COMPLETE)
145(CRIT) - CRITIQUE. ATLANTA, GEORGIA. THREE YEARLY.
      VOLUME 14 COMPLETE
149 - COMPARATIVE LITERATURE STUDIES. URBANA, ILL. QUARTERLY.
      MAR73 THRU DEC73 (VOL 10 COMPLETE)
150(DR) - DALHOUSIE REVIEW. HALIFAX, N.S., CANADA. QUARTERLY.
      SPRING72 THRU WINTER72/73 (VOL 52 COMPLETE)
151 - DANCE MAGAZINE. NEW YORK. MONTHLY.
      JAN72 THRU DEC72 (VOL 46 COMPLETE)
154 - DIALOGUE. MONTREAL. QUARTERLY.
      MAR72 THRU DEC72 (VOL 11 COMPLETE)
155 - THE DICKENSIAN. LONDON. THREE YEARLY.
      JAN72 THRU SEP72 (VOL 68 COMPLETE)
157 - DRAMA/THE QUARTERLY THEATRE REVIEW. LONDON.
      WINTER71 THRU WINTER72 (#103 THRU #107)
159(DM) - DUBLIN MAGAZINE. DUBLIN. QUARTERLY.
      AUTUMN71 THRU SUMMER72 (VOL 9 #1-3) [SUMMER71 ISSUE
      MISSING]

160 - DRAMA & THEATRE. FREDONIA, N.Y.
            FALL70 THRU SPRING72 (VOL 9 COMPLETE, VOL 10 #2&3)
165 - EARLY AMERICAN LITERATURE. AMHERST, MASS. THREE YEARLY.
            WINTER74 THRU FALL74 (VOL 8 #3, VOL 9 #1&2)
172(EDDA) - EDDA. OSLO. SIX YEARLY.
            1972/1 THRU 1972/6 (VOL 72 COMPLETE)
173(ECS) - EIGHTEENTH-CENTURY STUDIES. DAVIS, CALIF. QUARTERLY.
            FALL72 THRU SUMMER73 (VOL 6 COMPLETE)
177(ELT) - ENGLISH LITERATURE IN TRANSITION. TEMPE, ARIZ. QUARTERLY.
            VOLUME 15 COMPLETE
181 - EPOCH. ITHACA, N.Y. THREE YEARLY.
            FALL72 THRU SPRING73 (VOL 22 COMPLETE)
182 - ERASMUS. WIESBADEN, GERMANY. MONTHLY.
            VOLUME 25 COMPLETE
185 - ETHICS. CHICAGO. QUARTERLY.
            OCT72 THRU JUL73 (VOL 83 COMPLETE)
186(ETC.) - ETC. SAN FRANCISCO. QUARTERLY.
            MAR72 THRU DEC72 (VOL 29 COMPLETE)
187 - ETHNOMUSICOLOGY. ANN ARBOR, MICH. THREE YEARLY.
            JAN74 THRU SEP74 (VOL 18 COMPLETE)
188(ECR) - L'ESPRIT CRÉATEUR. LAWRENCE, KANSAS. QUARTERLY.
            SPRING72 THRU WINTER72 (VOL 12 COMPLETE)
189(EA) - ETUDES ANGLAISES. PARIS. QUARTERLY.
            JAN-MAR72 THRU OCT-DEC72 (VOL 25 COMPLETE)
190 - EUPHORION. HEIDELBERG. QUARTERLY.
            BAND 66 COMPLETE
191(ELN) - ENGLISH LANGUAGE NOTES. BOULDER, COLORADO. QUARTERLY.
            SEP72 THRU JUN73 (VOL 10 COMPLETE)
196 - FABULA. BERLIN. THREE YEARLY.
            BAND 13 COMPLETE
198 - THE FIDDLEHEAD. FREDERICTON, N.B., CANADA. QUARTERLY.
            WINTER74 THRU FALL74 (#100 THRU #103)
200 - FILMS IN REVIEW. NEW YORK. MONTHLY.
            JAN72 THRU DEC72 (VOL 23 COMPLETE)
202(FMOD) - FILOLOGÍA MODERNA. MADRID. THREE YEARLY.
            JUN72 (VOL 12 #45)
203 - FOLKLORE. LONDON. QUARTERLY.
            SPRING72 THRU WINTER72 (VOL 83 COMPLETE)
204(FDL) - FORUM DER LETTEREN. LEIDEN. QUARTERLY.
            MAR72 THRU DEC72 (VOL 13 COMPLETE)
205(FMLS) - FORUM FOR MODERN LANGUAGE STUDIES. ST. ANDREWS, SCOT-
        LAND. QUARTERLY.
            JAN72 THRU OCT72 (VOL 8 COMPLETE)
206 - FOUNDATIONS OF LANGUAGE. DORDRECHT, THE NETHERLANDS. SIX
        YEARLY.
            JAN72 THRU MAR73 (VOLS 8 & 9 COMPLETE) [VOL 9 BEGINS
                WITH SEP72 ISSUE]
207(FR) - FRENCH REVIEW. BALTIMORE. SIX YEARLY.
            OCT71 THRU MAY72 (VOL 45 COMPLETE)
208(FS) - FRENCH STUDIES. OXFORD, ENGLAND. QUARTERLY.
            JAN73 THRU OCT73 (VOL 27 COMPLETE)
209(FM) - LE FRANÇAIS MODERNE. PARIS. QUARTERLY.
            JAN72 THRU OCT72 (VOL 40 COMPLETE)
215(GL) - GENERAL LINGUISTICS. UNIVERSITY PARK, PA. QUARTERLY.
            VOLUME 12 COMPLETE
219(GAR) - GEORGIA REVIEW. ATHENS, GA. QUARTERLY.
            SPRING72 THRU WINTER72 (VOL 26 COMPLETE)
220(GL&L) - GERMAN LIFE & LETTERS. OXFORD, ENGLAND. QUARTERLY.
            OCT72 THRU JUL73 (VOL 26 COMPLETE)
221(GQ) - GERMAN QUARTERLY.
            JAN72 THRU NOV72 (VOL 45 COMPLETE)
222(GR) - GERMANIC REVIEW. NEW YORK. QUARTERLY.
            JAN72 THRU NOV72 (VOL 47 COMPLETE)
223 - GENRE. CHICAGO. QUARTERLY.
            MAR72 THRU DEC72 (VOL 5 COMPLETE)
224(GRM) - GERMANISCH-ROMANISCHE MONATSSCHRIFT. HEIDELBERG.
        QUARTERLY.
            BAND 22 COMPLETE
228(GSLI) - GIORNALE STORICO DELLA LETTERATURA ITALIANA. TORINO.
        QUARTERLY.
            VOLUME 149 COMPLETE
231 - HARPER'S MAGAZINE. NEW YORK. MONTHLY.
            JAN74 THRU DEC74 (VOLS 248 & 249 COMPLETE)

238 - HISPANIA. QUARTERLY.
          MAR72 THRU DEC72 (VOL 55 COMPLETE)
240(HR) - HISPANIC REVIEW. PHILADELPHIA. QUARTERLY.
          WINTER72 THRU AUTUMN72 (VOL 40 COMPLETE)
241 - HISPANÓFILA. CHAPEL HILL, N.C. THREE YEARLY.
          JAN72 THRU SEP72 (#44 THRU #46)
244(HJAS) - HARVARD JOURNAL OF ASIATIC STUDIES. CAMBRIDGE, MASS.
          ANNUAL.
          VOLUME 32 COMPLETE
249(HUDR) - HUDSON REVIEW. NEW YORK. QUARTERLY.
          SPRING73 THRU WINTER73/74 (VOL 26 COMPLETE)
255(HAB) - HUMANITIES ASSOCIATION BULLETIN. FREDERICTON, N.B.,
          CANADA. QUARTERLY.
          WINTER72 THRU FALL72 (VOL 23 COMPLETE)
258 - INTERNATIONAL PHILOSOPHICAL QUARTERLY. NEW YORK & HEVERLEE-
          LEUVEN, BELGIUM.
          MAR72 THRU DEC72 (VOL 12 COMPLETE)
260(IF) - INDOGERMANISCHE FORSCHUNGEN. BERLIN.
          BAND 76 COMPLETE & BAND 77 HEFT 1
262 - INQUIRY. OSLO. QUARTERLY.
          SUMMER72 THRU WINTER72 (VOL 15 COMPLETE)
263 - INTER-AMERICAN REVIEW OF BIBLIOGRAPHY. WASHINGTON, D.C.
          QUARTERLY.
          JAN-MAR73 THRU OCT-DEC73 (VOL 23 COMPLETE)
268 - THE INTERNATIONAL FICTION REVIEW. FREDERICTON, N.B., CANADA.
          TWICE YEARLY.
          JAN74 & JUL74 (VOL 1 COMPLETE)
269(IJAL) - INTERNATIONAL JOURNAL OF AMERICAN LINGUISTICS. BALTI-
          MORE. QUARTERLY.
          JAN72 THRU OCT72 (VOL 38 COMPLETE)
273(IC) - ISLAMIC CULTURE. HYDERABAD-DECCAN, INDIA. QUARTERLY.
          JAN72 THRU OCT72 (VOL 46 COMPLETE)
275(IQ) - ITALIAN QUARTERLY. RIVERSIDE, CALIFORNIA.
          FALL/WINTER72 & SPRING73 (VOL 16 #62/63 & #64)
276 - ITALICA. NEW YORK. QUARTERLY.
          SPRING72 THRU WINTER72 (VOL 49 COMPLETE)
279 - INTERNATIONAL JOURNAL OF SLAVIC LINGUISTICS & POETICS.
          'S-GRAVENHAGE, THE NETHERLANDS. ANNUAL.
          VOLUME 15 COMPLETE
285(JAPQ) - JAPAN QUARTERLY. TOKYO.
          JAN-MAR72 THRU OCT-DEC72 (VOL 19 COMPLETE)
287 - JEWISH FRONTIER. NEW YORK. MONTHLY.
          JAN72 THRU DEC72 (VOL 39 COMPLETE)
290(JAAC) - JOURNAL OF AESTHETICS & ART CRITICISM. BALTIMORE.
          QUARTERLY.
          FALL71 THRU SUMMER73 (VOLS 30 & 31 COMPLETE)
292(JAF) - JOURNAL OF AMERICAN FOLKLORE. QUARTERLY.
          JAN-MAR72 THRU OCT-DEC72 (VOL 85 COMPLETE)
293(JAST) - JOURNAL OF ASIAN STUDIES. ANN ARBOR, MICH. QUARTERLY.
          NOV71 THRU AUG72 (VOL 31 COMPLETE)
296 - JOURNAL OF CANADIAN FICTION. MONTREAL. QUARTERLY.
          VOL 3 #1-3
297(JL) - JOURNAL OF LINGUISTICS. READING, ENGLAND. TWICE YEARLY.
          FEB72 & SEP72 (VOL 8 COMPLETE)
301(JEGP) - JOURNAL OF ENGLISH & GERMANIC PHILOLOGY. URBANA, ILL.
          QUARTERLY.
          JAN73 THRU OCT73 (VOL 72 COMPLETE)
302 - JOURNAL OF ORIENTAL STUDIES. HONG KONG. TWICE YEARLY.
          JAN72 & JUL72 (VOL 10 COMPLETE)
303 - JOURNAL OF HELLENIC STUDIES. LONDON. ANNUAL.
          VOLUME 92 COMPLETE
308 - JOURNAL OF MUSIC THEORY. NEW HAVEN, CONN. TWICE YEARLY.
          VOLUMES 15 & 16 COMPLETE
311(JP) - JOURNAL OF PHILOSOPHY. NEW YORK. BI-WEEKLY.
          17JAN74 THRU 19DEC74 (VOL 71 COMPLETE)
313 - JOURNAL OF ROMAN STUDIES. LONDON. ANNUAL.
          VOLUME 62 COMPLETE
316 - JOURNAL OF SYMBOLIC LOGIC. PROVIDENCE, R.I. QUARTERLY.
          MAR72 THRU DEC72 (VOL 37 COMPLETE)
318(JAOS) - JOURNAL OF THE AMERICAN ORIENTAL SOCIETY. BALTIMORE.
          QUARTERLY.
          JAN-MAR72 THRU OCT-DEC72 (VOL 92 COMPLETE)

319 - JOURNAL OF THE HISTORY OF PHILOSOPHY. ST. LOUIS, MO.
    QUARTERLY.
        JAN74 THRU OCT74 (VOL 12 COMPLETE)
320(CJL) - CANADIAN JOURNAL OF LINGUISTICS. TORONTO. TWICE YEARLY.
        SPRING 71 (VOL 16 #2) & VOLUME 18 COMPLETE
321 - THE JOURNAL OF VALUE INQUIRY. THE HAGUE. QUARTERLY.
        WINTER72 THRU WINTER72 [SIC] (VOL 6 COMPLETE)
322(JHI) - JOURNAL OF THE HISTORY OF IDEAS. NEW YORK. QUARTERLY.
        JAN-MAR72 THRU OCT-DEC72 (VOL 33 COMPLETE)
325 - JOURNAL OF THE SOCIETY OF ARCHIVISTS. LONDON. TWICE YEARLY.
        APR72 & OCT72 (VOL 4 #5&6)
329(JJQ) - JAMES JOYCE QUARTERLY. TULSA, OKLAHOMA.
        FALL73 THRU SUMMER74 (VOL 11 COMPLETE)
342 - KANT-STUDIEN. BONN. QUARTERLY.
        BAND 63 COMPLETE
343 - KRATYLOS. WIESBADEN. TWICE YEARLY.
        BAND 14 & BAND 15 COMPLETE
350 - LANGUAGE. BALTIMORE. QUARTERLY.
        MAR73 THRU DEC73 (VOL 49 COMPLETE)
351(LL) - LANGUAGE LEARNING. ANN ARBOR, MICH. TWICE YEARLY.
        JUN72 THRU DEC73 (VOLS 22 & 23 COMPLETE)
352(LE&W) - LITERATURE EAST & WEST. AUSTIN, TEXAS. QUARTERLY.
        VOL 15 #3 AND VOL 15 #4&VOL 16 #1/2 [DOUBLE ISSUE]
353 - LINGUISTICS. THE HAGUE. EIGHTEEN YEARLY.
        JAN72 THRU 15DEC72 (#77 THRU #94)
354 - THE LIBRARY. LONDON. QUARTERLY.
        MAR72 THRU DEC72 (VOL 27 COMPLETE)
361 - LINGUA. AMSTERDAM.
        VOLUMES 28, 29 & 30 COMPLETE
362 - THE LISTENER. LONDON. WEEKLY.
        3JAN74 THRU 19/26DEC74 (VOLS 91 & 92 COMPLETE)
363 - LITURGICAL ARTS. NEW YORK. QUARTERLY.
        NOV71 THRU MAY72 (VOL 40 #1-3) [CEASED PUBLICATION
            WITH MAY72 ISSUE]
364 - LONDON MAGAZINE. LONDON. BI-MONTHLY.
        APR72 THRU FEB-MAR74 (VOLS 12 & 13 COMPLETE)
368 - LANDFALL. CHRISTCHURCH, N.Z. QUARTERLY.
        MAR72 THRU DEC72 (VOL 26 COMPLETE)
376 - THE MALAHAT REVIEW. VICTORIA, B.C., CANADA. QUARTERLY.
        APR70 (#14) & JAN72 THRU OCT72 (#21 THRU #24)
377 - MANUSCRIPTA. ST. LOUIS, MO. THREE YEARLY.
        MAR73 THRU NOV73 (VOL 17 COMPLETE)
381 - MEANJIN QUARTERLY. PARKVILLE, VICTORIA, AUSTRALIA.
        MAR72 THRU DEC72 (VOL 31 COMPLETE)
382(MAE) - MEDIUM AEVUM. OXFORD, ENGLAND. THREE YEARLY.
        1973/1 THRU 1973/3 (VOL 42 COMPLETE)
385(MQR) - MICHIGAN QUARTERLY REVIEW. ANN ARBOR.
        WINTER74 THRU FALL74 (VOL 13 COMPLETE)
390 - MIDSTREAM. NEW YORK. MONTHLY.
        JAN72 THRU DEC72 (VOL 18 COMPLETE)
391(JFI) - JOURNAL OF THE FOLKLORE INSTITUTE. BLOOMINGTON, IND.
    THREE YEARLY.
        VOLUMES 7, 8 & 9 COMPLETE
393(MIND) - MIND. LONDON. QUARTERLY.
        JAN72 THRU OCT72 (VOL 81 COMPLETE)
396(MODA) - MODERN AGE. CHICAGO. QUARTERLY.
        WINTER73 THRU FALL73 (VOL 17 COMPLETE)
397(MD) - MODERN DRAMA. TORONTO. QUARTERLY.
        MAY72 THRU MAR73 (VOL 15 COMPLETE)
398 - MODERN POETRY STUDIES. BUFFALO, N.Y. THREE YEARLY.
        SPRING74 THRU WINTER74 (VOL 5 COMPLETE)
399(MLJ) - MODERN LANGUAGE JOURNAL. MILWAUKEE, WISC. MONTHLY.
        JAN72 THRU DEC72 (VOL 56 COMPLETE)
400(MLN) - MODERN LANGUAGE NOTES. BALTIMORE. SIX YEARLY.
        JAN72 THRU DEC72 (VOL 87 COMPLETE)
401(MLQ) - MODERN LANGUAGE QUARTERLY. SEATTLE, WASH.
        MAR73 THRU DEC73 (VOL 34 COMPLETE)
402(MLR) - MODERN LANGUAGE REVIEW. LONDON. QUARTERLY.
        JAN73 THRU OCT73 (VOL 68 COMPLETE)
405(MP) - MODERN PHILOLOGY. CHICAGO. QUARTERLY.
        AUG72 THRU MAY73 (VOL 70 COMPLETE)
406 - MONATSHEFTE. MADISON, WISC. QUARTERLY.
        SPRING73 THRU WINTER73 (VOL 65 COMPLETE)

410(M&L) - MUSIC & LETTERS. LONDON. QUARTERLY.
          JAN73 THRU OCT73 (VOL 54 COMPLETE)
414(MQ) - MUSICAL QUARTERLY. NEW YORK.
          JAN72 THRU OCT72 (VOL 58 COMPLETE)
415 - MUSICAL TIMES. LONDON. MONTHLY.
          JAN73 THRU DEC73 (VOL 114 COMPLETE)
418(MR) - THE MASSACHUSETTS REVIEW. AMHERST, MASS. QUARTERLY.
          WINTER73 THRU AUTUMN73 (VOL 14 COMPLETE)
424 - NAMES. POTSDAM, N.Y. QUARTERLY.
          MAR72 THRU DEC72 (VOL 20 COMPLETE)
430(NS) - DIE NEUEREN SPRACHEN. FRANKFURT AM MAIN. MONTHLY.
          JAN72 THRU DEC72 (VOL 71 COMPLETE)
432(NEQ) - NEW ENGLAND QUARTERLY. BRUNSWICK, MAINE.
          MAR72 THRU DEC72 (VOL 45 COMPLETE)
433 - NEOPHILOLOGUS. GRONINGEN, THE NETHERLANDS. QUARTERLY.
          JAN72 THRU OCT72 (VOL 56 COMPLETE)
439(NM) - NEUPHILOLOGISCHE MITTEILUNGEN. HELSINKI. QUARTERLY.
          1972/1 THRU 1972/4 (VOL 73 COMPLETE)
441 - THE NEW YORK TIMES. DAILY.
          1JAN74 THRU 31DEC74 [SUNDAY DATES FOR THIS PERIODICAL
               REFER TO THE NEW YORK TIMES BOOK REVIEW SECTION]
442(NY) - THE NEW YORKER. WEEKLY.
          7JAN74 THRU 30DEC74 (VOL 49 #46-52 & VOL 50 #1-45)
          [VOL 50 BEGINS WITH THE 25FEB74 ISSUE]
445(NCF) - NINETEENTH-CENTURY FICTION. BERKELEY, CALIF. QUARTERLY.
          JUN72 THRU MAR73 (VOL 27 COMPLETE)
447(N&Q) - NOTES & QUERIES. LONDON. MONTHLY.
          JAN72 THRU DEC72 (VOL 19 COMPLETE)
448 - NORTHWEST REVIEW. EUGENE, OREGON. THREE YEARLY.
          FALL/WINTER71/72 THRU FALL72 (VOL 12 COMPLETE)
453 - THE NEW YORK REVIEW OF BOOKS. BI-WEEKLY.
          24JAN74 (VOL 20 #21/22) & 7FEB74 THRU 12DEC74 (VOL 21
               #1-20)
454 - NOVEL. PROVIDENCE, R.I. THREE YEARLY.
          FALL72 THRU SPRING73 (VOL 6 COMPLETE)
462(OL) - ORBIS LITTERARUM. COPENHAGEN. QUARTERLY.
          VOLUME 27 COMPLETE
470 - PAN PIPES. DES MOINES, IOWA. QUARTERLY.
          NOV71 THRU MAY72 (VOL 64 COMPLETE)
473(PR) - PARTISAN REVIEW. NEW YORK. QUARTERLY.
          WINTER73 THRU 3/1973 (VOL 40 COMPLETE)
477 - PERSONALIST. LOS ANGELES. QUARTERLY.
          WINTER72 THRU AUTUMN72 (VOL 53 COMPLETE)
478 - THE PHILOSOPHICAL JOURNAL. EDINBURGH. TWICE YEARLY.
          JAN72 & JUL72 (VOL 9 COMPLETE)
479(PHQ) - PHILOSOPHICAL QUARTERLY. ST. ANDREWS, SCOTLAND.
          JAN72 THRU OCT72 (VOL 22 COMPLETE)
480(P&R) - PHILOSOPHY & RHETORIC. UNIVERSITY PARK, PA. QUARTERLY.
          WINTER72 THRU FALL72 (VOL 5 COMPLETE)
481(PQ) - PHILOLOGICAL QUARTERLY. IOWA CITY, IOWA.
          JAN72 THRU OCT72 (VOL 51 COMPLETE)
482(PHR) - PHILOSOPHICAL REVIEW. ITHACA, N.Y. QUARTERLY.
          JAN72 THRU OCT72 (VOL 81 COMPLETE)
483 - PHILOSOPHY. LONDON. QUARTERLY.
          JAN72 THRU OCT72 (VOL 47 COMPLETE)
484(PPR) - PHILOSOPHY & PHENOMENOLOGICAL RESEARCH. BUFFALO, N.Y.
          QUARTERLY.
          SEP72 THRU JUN73 (VOL 33 COMPLETE)
485(PE&W) - PHILOSOPHY EAST & WEST. HONOLULU. QUARTERLY.
          JAN72 THRU OCT72 (VOL 22 COMPLETE)
486 - PHILOSOPHY OF SCIENCE. EAST LANSING, MICH. QUARTERLY.
          MAR72 THRU DEC72 (VOL 39 COMPLETE)
487 - PHOENIX. TORONTO. QUARTERLY.
          SPRING72 THRU WINTER72 (VOL 26 COMPLETE)
490 - POETICA. MÜNCHEN. QUARTERLY.
          JAN72 THRU JUL-OCT72 (VOL 5 COMPLETE)
491 - POETRY. CHICAGO. MONTHLY.
          OCT73 THRU SEP74 (VOLS 123 & 124 COMPLETE)
492 - POETICS. THE HAGUE, NETHERLANDS.
          #1 THRU #4
497(POLR) - POLISH REVIEW. NEW YORK. QUARTERLY.
          WINTER72 THRU AUTUMN72 (VOL 17 COMPLETE)
502(PRS) - PRAIRIE SCHOONER. LINCOLN, NEBRASKA. QUARTERLY.
          SPRING72 THRU WINTER72/73 (VOL 46 COMPLETE)

503 - THE PRIVATE LIBRARY. PINNER, MIDDLESEX, ENGLAND. QUARTERLY.
        SPRING72 & SUMMER72 (VOL 5 #1&2)
505 - PROGRESSIVE ARCHITECTURE. NEW YORK. MONTHLY.
        JAN72 THRU DEC72 (VOL 53 COMPLETE)
513 - PERSPECTIVES OF NEW MUSIC. PRINCETON. TWICE YEARLY.
        FALL-WINTER69 THRU SPRING-SUMMER72 (VOLS 8 THRU 10
        COMPLETE)
517(PBSA) - PAPERS OF THE BIBLIOGRAPHICAL SOCIETY OF AMERICA.
        NEW HAVEN, CONN. QUARTERLY.
        JAN-MAR73 THRU OCT-DEC73 (VOL 67 COMPLETE)
518 - PHILOSOPHICAL BOOKS. LEICESTER, ENGLAND. THREE YEARLY.
        JAN73 THRU OCT73 (VOL 14 COMPLETE)
529(QQ) - QUEEN'S QUARTERLY. KINGSTON, ONT., CANADA.
        SPRING72 THRU WINTER72 (VOL 79 COMPLETE)
535(RHL) - REVUE D'HISTOIRE LITTÉRAIRE DE LA FRANCE. PARIS.
        SIX YEARLY.
        JAN-FEB72 THRU SEP-DEC72 (VOL 72 COMPLETE)
536 - RATIO. OXFORD, ENGLAND. TWICE YEARLY.
        JUN72 & DEC72 (VOL 14 COMPLETE)
539(REN) - RENASCENCE. MILWAUKEE, WISCONSIN. QUARTERLY.
        AUTUMN72 THRU SUMMER73 (VOL 25 COMPLETE)
541(RES) - REVIEW OF ENGLISH STUDIES. LONDON. QUARTERLY.
        FEB72 THRU NOV72 (VOL 23 COMPLETE)
542 - REVUE PHILOSOPHIQUE DE LA FRANCE ET DE L'ÉTRANGER. PARIS.
        QUARTERLY.
        JAN-MAR72 THRU OCT-DEC72 (VOL 162 COMPLETE)
543 - REVIEW OF METAPHYSICS. NEW HAVEN, CONN. QUARTERLY.
        SEP71 THRU JUN72 (VOL 25 COMPLETE)
544 - REVIEW OF NATIONAL LITERATURES. JAMAICA, N.Y. TWICE YEARLY.
        SPRING73 & FALL73 (VOL 4 COMPLETE) [NO REVIEWS
        INDEXED]
545(RPH) - ROMANCE PHILOLOGY. BERKELEY, CALIF. QUARTERLY.
        AUG72 THRU MAY73 (VOL 26 COMPLETE)
546(RR) - ROMANIC REVIEW. NEW YORK. QUARTERLY.
        FEB72 THRU DEC72 (VOL 63 COMPLETE)
548(RCSF) - RIVISTA CRITICA DI STORIA DELLA FILOSOFIA. FIRENZE,
        ITALY. QUARTERLY.
        JAN-MAR72 THRU OCT-DEC72 (VOL 27 COMPLETE)
549(RLC) - REVUE DE LITTÉRATURE COMPARÉE. PARIS. QUARTERLY.
        JAN-MAR72 THRU OCT-DEC72 (VOL 46 COMPLETE)
550(RUSR) - RUSSIAN REVIEW. HANOVER, N.H. QUARTERLY.
        JAN72 THRU OCT72 (VOL 31 COMPLETE)
551(RENQ) - RENAISSANCE QUARTERLY. NEW YORK.
        SPRING72 THRU WINTER72 (VOL 25 COMPLETE)
555 - REVUE DE PHILOLOGIE. PARIS. TWICE YEARLY.
        VOLUME 46 COMPLETE
556(RLV) - REVUE DES LANGUES VIVANTES/TIJDSCHRIFT VOOR LEVENDE TALEN.
        BRUXELLES. SIX YEARLY.
        1972/1 THRU 1972/6 (VOL 38 COMPLETE)
557(RSH) - REVUE DES SCIENCES HUMAINES. LILLE, FRANCE. QUARTERLY.
        JAN-MAR72 THRU OCT-DEC72 (#145 THRU #148)
563(SS) - SCANDINAVIAN STUDIES. QUARTERLY.
        WINTER73 THRU AUTUMN73 (VOL 45 COMPLETE)
564 - SEMINAR. TORONTO. THREE YEARLY.
        MAR72 THRU OCT72 (VOL 8 COMPLETE)
565 - STAND. NEWCASTLE UPON TYNE, ENGLAND. QUARTERLY.
        VOLUME 13 COMPLETE
566 - THE SCRIBLERIAN. PHILADELPHIA. TWICE YEARLY.
        AUTUMN72 & SPRING73 (VOL 5 COMPLETE) [PLUS A SMALL
        GROUP DATED SPRING72 MISSED IN VOL 14]
568(SCN) - SEVENTEENTH-CENTURY NEWS. NEW YORK. QUARTERLY.
        SPRING73 THRU FALL-WINTER73 (VOL 31 COMPLETE)
569(SR) - SEWANEE REVIEW. SEWANEE, TENN. QUARTERLY.
        WINTER73 THRU AUTUMN73 (VOL 81 COMPLETE)
570(SQ) - SHAKESPEARE QUARTERLY. NEW YORK.
        WINTER72 THRU FALL72 (VOL 23 COMPLETE)
571 - THE SHAVIAN. LONDON.
        SPRING72 & WINTER72/73 (VOL 4 #5&6)
572 - SHAW REVIEW. UNIVERSITY PARK, PA. THREE YEARLY.
        JAN72 THRU SEP72 (VOL 15 COMPLETE)
573(SSF) - STUDIES IN SHORT FICTION. NEWBERRY, S.C. QUARTERLY.
        WINTER72 THRU FALL72 (VOL 9 COMPLETE)
575(SEER) - SLAVONIC & EAST EUROPEAN REVIEW. LONDON. QUARTERLY.
        JAN73 THRU OCT73 (VOL 51 COMPLETE)

576 - JOURNAL OF THE SOCIETY OF ARCHITECTURAL HISTORIANS. PHILA-
       DELPHIA. QUARTERLY.
              MAR72 THRU DEC72 (VOL 31 COMPLETE)
577(SHR) - SOUTHERN HUMANITIES REVIEW. AUBURN, ALA. QUARTERLY.
              WINTER72 THRU FALL72 (VOL 6 COMPLETE)
578 - SOUTHERN LITERARY JOURNAL. CHAPEL HILL, N.C. TWICE YEARLY.
              SPRING74 & FALL74 (VOL 6 #2 & VOL 7 #1)
579(SAQ) - SOUTH ATLANTIC QUARTERLY. DURHAM, N.C.
              WINTER73 THRU AUTUMN73 (VOL 72 COMPLETE)
581 - SOUTHERLY. SYDNEY, AUSTRALIA. QUARTERLY.
              MAR73 THRU DEC73 (VOL 33 COMPLETE)
582(SFQ) - SOUTHERN FOLKLORE QUARTERLY. GAINESVILLE, FLA.
              MAR72 THRU DEC72 (VOL 36 COMPLETE)
583 - SOUTHERN SPEECH COMMUNICATION JOURNAL. WINSTON-SALEM, N.C.
       QUARTERLY.
              FALL72 THRU SUMMER73 (VOL 38 COMPLETE)
584(SWR) - SOUTHWEST REVIEW. DALLAS, TEXAS. QUARTERLY.
              WINTER73 THRU AUTUMN73 (VOL 58 COMPLETE)
589 - SPECULUM. CAMBRIDGE, MASS. QUARTERLY.
              JAN73 THRU OCT73 (VOL 48 COMPLETE)
590 - SPIRIT. SOUTH ORANGE, N.J. TWICE YEARLY.
              SPRING/SUMMER73 & FALL/WINTER73/74 (VOL 40 #1&2)
592 - STUDIO INTERNATIONAL. LIVERPOOL. MONTHLY.
              JAN72 THRU DEC72 (VOLS 183 & 184 COMPLETE)
593 - SYMPOSIUM. SYRACUSE, N.Y. QUARTERLY.
              SPRING73 THRU WINTER73 (VOL 27 COMPLETE)
594 - STUDIES IN THE NOVEL. DENTON, TEX. QUARTERLY.
              SPRING72 THRU WINTER72 (VOL 4 COMPLETE)
595(SCS) - SCOTTISH STUDIES. EDINBURGH. TWICE YEARLY.
              VOLUME 17 COMPLETE
596(SL) - STUDIA LINGUISTICA. LUND, SWEDEN. TWICE YEARLY.
              VOLUMES 26 & 27 COMPLETE
597(SN) - STUDIA NEOPHILOLOGICA. UPPSALA, SWEDEN. TWICE YEARLY.
              VOLUME 44 COMPLETE
598(SOR) - THE SOUTHERN REVIEW. BATON ROUGE, LA. QUARTERLY.
              WINTER74 THRU AUTUMN74 (VOL 10 COMPLETE)
599 - STYLE. FAYETTEVILLE, ARK. THREE YEARLY.
              WINTER72 THRU FALL72 (VOL 6 COMPLETE)
607 - TEMPO. LONDON. QUARTERLY.
              #99 THRU #103
608 - TESOL QUARTERLY. HONOLULU.
              MAR73 THRU DEC73 (VOL 7 COMPLETE)
613 - THOUGHT. BRONX, N.Y. QUARTERLY.
              SPRING72 THRU WINTER72 (VOL 47 COMPLETE)
617(TLS) - TIMES LITERARY SUPPLEMENT. LONDON. WEEKLY.
              4JAN74 THRU 27DEC74 (#3748 THRU #3799)
618 - TRANSITION. ACCRA, GHANA. SIX YEARLY.
              #38 THRU #43
619(TC) - TWENTIETH CENTURY. LONDON. QUARTERLY.
              VOL 177 #1043 [THIS PERIODICAL CEASED PUBLICATION
                 WITH ISSUE #1049, ALREADY INDEXED]
627(UTQ) - UNIVERSITY OF TORONTO QUARTERLY.
              AUTUMN71 THRU SUMMER73 (VOLS 41 & 42 COMPLETE)
                 [ISSUES DATED SUMMER EACH YEAR ARE NOT INDEXED]
628 - UNIVERSITY OF WINDSOR REVIEW. WINDSOR, ONT. TWICE YEARLY.
              FALL72 THRU SPRING73 (VOL 8 COMPLETE)
636(VP) - VICTORIAN POETRY. MORGANTOWN, W. VA. QUARTERLY.
              SPRING72 THRU WINTER72 (VOL 10 COMPLETE)
637(VS) - VICTORIAN STUDIES. BLOOMINGTON, IND. QUARTERLY.
              SEP71 THRU JUN73 (VOLS 15 & 16 COMPLETE)
639(VQR) - VIRGINIA QUARTERLY REVIEW. CHARLOTTESVILLE, VA.
              WINTER72 THRU AUTUMN73 (VOLS 48 & 49 COMPLETE)
646(WWR) - WALT WHITMAN REVIEW. DETROIT. QUARTERLY.
              MAR72 THRU DEC72 (VOL 18 COMPLETE)
648 - WEST COAST REVIEW. BURNABY, B.C., CANADA. QUARTERLY.
              JUN72 THRU APR73 (VOL 7 COMPLETE)
649(WAL) - WESTERN AMERICAN LITERATURE. FORT COLLINS, COLORADO.
       QUARTERLY.
              SPRING72 THRU WINTER73 (VOL 7 COMPLETE)
650(WF) - WESTERN FOLKLORE. BERKELEY, CALIF. QUARTERLY.
              JAN72 THRU OCT72 (VOL 31 COMPLETE)
651(WHR) - WESTERN HUMANITIES REVIEW. SALT LAKE CITY. QUARTERLY.
              WINTER73 THRU AUTUMN73 (VOL 27 COMPLETE)

654(WB) - WEIMARER BEITRÄGE. BERLIN. MONTHLY.
         9/1971 THRU 12/1971 (VOL 17 #9-12) & 1/1972 THRU
         12/1972 (VOL 18 COMPLETE)
656(WMQ) - WILLIAM & MARY QUARTERLY. WILLIAMSBURG, VA.
         JAN72 THRU OCT73 (VOLS 29 & 30 COMPLETE)
657(WW) - WIRKENDES WORT. DUSSELDORF. SIX YEARLY.
         JAN-FEB72 THRU NOV-DEC72 (VOL 22 COMPLETE)
659 - CONTEMPORARY LITERATURE. MADISON, WISC. QUARTERLY.
         WINTER74 THRU AUTUMN74 (VOL 15 COMPLETE)
660(WORD) - WORD. NEW YORK. THREE YEARLY.
         APR/AUG/DEC69 (VOL 25 #1/2/3), APR70 & AUG70 (VOL
         26 #1&2)
676(YR) - YALE REVIEW. NEW HAVEN, CONN. QUARTERLY.
         AUTUMN72 THRU SUMMER73 (VOL 62 COMPLETE)
677 - THE YEARBOOK OF ENGLISH STUDIES. LONDON. ANNUAL.
         VOLUME 3 COMPLETE
680(ZDP) - ZEITSCHRIFT FÜR DEUTSCHE PHILOLOGIE. BERLIN. QUARTERLY.
         BAND 91 HEFT 1-3
681(ZDS) - ZEITSCHRIFT FÜR DEUTSCHE SPRACHE. BERLIN. THREE YEARLY.
         BAND 26 HEFT 3 [NO REVIEWS INDEXED]
682(ZPSK) - ZEITSCHRIFT FÜR PHONETIK, SPRACHWISSENSCHAFT UND KOMMUNI-
         KATIONSFORSCHUNG. BERLIN. SIX YEARLY.
         BAND 24 HEFT 6 & BAND 25 COMPLETE
683 - ZEITSCHRIFT FÜR KUNSTGESCHICHTE. MÜNCHEN. FIVE YEARLY.
         BAND 35 COMPLETE

     EACH YEAR WE ARE UNABLE (FOR ONE REASON OR ANOTHER) TO INDEX
THE REVIEWS APPEARING IN ALL OF THE PERIODICALS SCANNED. THE
FOLLOWING IS A LIST OF THE PERIODICALS WHOSE REVIEWS WERE NOT
INCLUDED IN THIS VOLUME OF THE INDEX. EVERY ATTEMPT WILL BE
MADE TO INDEX THESE REVIEWS IN THE NEXT VOLUME OF THE INDEX:

     2 - AFRICAN ARTS. LOS ANGELES. QUARTERLY.
    47(ARL) - ARCHIVUM LINGUISTICUM. GLASGOW. ANNUAL.
    48 - ARCHIVO ESPAÑOL DE ARTE. MADRID. QUARTERLY.
    73 - ART MAGAZINE. TORONTO. QUARTERLY.
    86(BHS) - BULLETIN OF HISPANIC STUDIES. LIVERPOOL. QUARTERLY.
    89(BJA) - THE BRITISH JOURNAL OF AESTHETICS. LONDON. QUARTERLY.
   102(CANL) - CANADIAN LITERATURE. VANCOUVER, B.C. QUARTERLY.
   109 - THE CARLETON MISCELLANY. NORTHFIELD, MINN. TWICE YEARLY.
   121(CJ) - CLASSICAL JOURNAL. TALLAHASSEE, FLORIDA. QUARTERLY.
   122 - CLASSICAL PHILOLOGY. CHICAGO. QUARTERLY.
   124 - CLASSICAL WORLD. UNIVERSITY PARK, PA. MONTHLY.
   131(CL) - COMPARATIVE LITERATURE. EUGENE, OREGON. QUARTERLY.
   141 - CRITICISM. DETROIT. QUARTERLY.
   148 - CRITICAL QUARTERLY. LONDON.
   175 - ENGLISH. LONDON. THREE YEARLY.
   179(ES) - ENGLISH STUDIES. AMSTERDAM. BI-MONTHLY.
   180(ESA) - ENGLISH STUDIES IN AFRICA. JOHANNESBURG. TWICE YEARLY.
   184(EIC) - ESSAYS IN CRITICISM. OXFORD, ENGLAND. QUARTERLY.
   214 - GAMBIT. LONDON.
   259 - IDIOMA. MUNICH. SIX YEARLY.
   270 - INTERNATIONAL P.E.N. LONDON. QUARTERLY.
   295 - JOURNAL OF MODERN LITERATURE. PHILADELPHIA. FIVE YEARLY.
   315(JAL) - JOURNAL OF AFRICAN LANGUAGES. LONDON. THREE YEARLY.
   317 - JOURNAL OF THE AMERICAN MUSICOLOGICAL SOCIETY. RICHMOND, VA.
         THREE YEARLY.
   341 - KONSTHISTORISK TIDSKRIFT. STOCKHOLM.
   349 - LANGUAGE & STYLE. CARBONDALE, ILL. QUARTERLY.
   355 - LANGUAGE IN SOCIETY. LONDON. TWICE YEARLY.
   395(MFS) - MODERN FICTION STUDIES. WEST LAFAYETTE, IND. QUARTERLY.
   412 - MUSIC REVIEW. CAMBRIDGE, ENGLAND. QUARTERLY.
   446 - NINETEENTH-CENTURY FRENCH STUDIES. FREDONIA, N.Y. QUARTERLY.
   463 - ORIENTAL ART. RICHMOND, SURREY, ENGLAND. QUARTERLY.
   488 - PHILOSOPHY OF THE SOCIAL SCIENCES. TORONTO. QUARTERLY.
   574(SEEJ) - SLAVIC & EAST EUROPEAN JOURNAL. QUARTERLY.
   591(SIR) - STUDIES IN ROMANTICISM. BOSTON. QUARTERLY.
   606(TAMR) - TAMARACK REVIEW. TORONTO. QUARTERLY.
   661 - WORKS. NEW YORK.

AACH, H. - SEE VON GOETHE, J.W.
AARON, D. THE UNWRITTEN WAR.*
    E. ROVIT, 31(ASCH):SPRING74-324
    L.P. SIMPSON, 578:FALL74-132
    C.V. WOODWARD, 453:21FEB74-26
AARON, P. TOSCANELLO IN MUSICA.
    (P. BERGQUIST, TRANS)
    C.V. PALISCA, 308:VOL16#1/2-206
    L.L. PERKINS, 551(RENQ):AUTUMN
    72-328
AARON, R.I. KNOWING & THE FUNCTION
    OF REASON.*
    A.C. EWING, 483:OCT72-379
    D.M. JOHNSON, 154:DEC72-643
    A.R. WHITE, 479(PHQ):JAN72-73
AARTS, F.G.A.M., ED. THE PATER
    NOSTER OF RICHARD ERMYTE.*
    W. RIEHLE, 38:BAND90HEFT4-525
ABASTADO, C. EXPÉRIENCE ET THÉORIE
    DE LA CRÉATION POÉTIQUE CHEZ MAL-
    LARMÉ.
    C. CHADWICK, 535(RHL):JUL-AUG72-
    736
    M. O'NEILL, 207(FR):MAY72-1188
ABBEY, B. THE COMPLETE BOOK OF
    KNITTING.
    M.W. PHILLIPS, 139:APR72-64
ABBEY, E. & P. HYDE. SLICKROCK.
    T.J. LYON, 649(WAL):SPRING72-67
ABBEY, L. FLIES [TOGETHER WITH]
    FOX, G. FLIGHT OF THE PTERODACTYL.
    M.J. EDWARDS, 99:AUG74-42
ABBOTT, H.P. THE FICTION OF SAMUEL
    BECKETT.*
    639(VQR):SPRING73-LXXIII
ABBOTT, L.W. LAW REPORTING IN ENG-
    LAND 1485-1585.
    617(TLS):15MAR74-258
ABBOUSHI, W.F. THE ANGRY ARABS.
    N. SAFRAN, 441:7APR74-4
ABDO, D.A. ON STRESS & ARABIC PHON-
    OLOGY.*
    C. KILLEAN, 297(JL):SEP72-336
ABDUL HAI, M.H.S. "ISLAMI ULUM-WA-
    FUNUN HINDUSTAN MEIN."
    Q.S.K. HUSAINI, 273(IC):APR72-
    182
ABÉ, K. THE BOX MAN.
    A. BROYARD, 441:31DEC74-19
    J. CHARYN, 441:8DEC74-6
"LA ABEJA REPUBLICANA." (A. TAURO,
    ED)
    G. LOHMANN VILLENA, 263:JAN-MAR
    73-92
ABEL, F. L'ADJECTIF DÉMONSTRATIF
    DANS LA LANGUE DE LA BIBLE LATINE.
    B. LÖFSTEDT, 72:BAND210HEFT1/3-
    202
ABELARD, P. PETER ABELARD'S "ETH-
    ICS." (D.E. LUSCOMBE, ED)
    N.M. HARING, 589:APR73-383
ABELL, T. - SEE PEARSON, D.
ABERNETHY, F.E., ED. OBSERVATIONS &
    REFLECTIONS ON TEXAS FOLKLORE.
    J.W. BYRD, 584(SWR):SPRING73-182
ABISH, W. ALPHABETICAL AFRICA.
    R. HOWARD, 441:29DEC74-19
ABOUL-FETOUH, H.M. A MORPHOLOGICAL
    STUDY OF EGYPTIAN COLLOQUIAL ARAB-
    IC.
    P.F. ABBOUD, 361:VOL28#1&2-180
ABRAHAM, H.J. JUSTICES & PRESIDENTS.
    442(NY):27MAY74-106

ABRAHAMS, R.D. DEEP DOWN IN THE JUN-
    GLE.
    J.M. VLACH, 292(JAF):APR-JUN72-
    200
ABRAHAMS, W., ED. FIFTY YEARS OF
    THE AMERICAN SHORT STORY.
    W. EASTLAKE, 50(ARQ):SPRING72-94
ABRAHAMS, W., ED. PRIZE STORIES
    1971: THE O. HENRY AWARDS.
    639(VQR):WINTER72-XIX
ABRAHAMS, W., ED. PRIZE STORIES
    1972: THE O. HENRY AWARDS.
    639(VQR):SUMMER72-CI
ABRAHAMS, W., ED. PRIZE STORIES
    1973: THE O. HENRY AWARDS.
    639(VQR):AUTUMN73-CXXXVII
ABRAHAMS, W., ED. PRIZE STORIES
    1974: THE O. HENRY AWARDS.
    P. ADAMS, 61:JUL74-100
ABRAMOWSKI, L. & A.E. GOODMAN, EDS &
    TRANS. A NESTORIAN COLLECTION OF
    CHRISTOLOGICAL TEXTS.
    J.A. EMERTON, 32:DEC73-798
ABRAMS, M.H. NATURAL SUPERNATURAL-
    ISM.*
    P.H. BUTTER, 402(MLR):JAN73-157
    F. GARBER, 401(MLQ):JUN73-206
    J.R.D. JACKSON, 627(UTQ):SPRING
    73-289
    H. LINDENBERGER, 191(ELN):DEC72-
    150
    J.J. MC GANN, 405(MP):FEB73-247
    B. WESTBURG, 290(JAAC):FALL72-
    132
ABSALOM, R.N.L. & S. PODESTÀ, EDS.
    ADVANCED ITALIAN.
    C. ROSS, 276:AUTUMN72-349
ABSE, D. FUNLAND & OTHER POEMS.*
    W.H. PRITCHARD, 249(HUDR):AUTUMN
    73-583
    L. SEARLE, 491:MAR74-353
ABSE, D. A POET IN THE FAMILY.
    E.S. TURNER, 362:19SEP74-379
    617(TLS):11OCT74-1114
ABU-LUGHOD, J.L. CAIRO.
    R. MANTRAN, 182:VOL25#17/18-590
    639(VQR):SPRING72-LXXIV
ACHEBE, C. GIRLS AT WAR & OTHER
    STORIES.*
    M. MUDRICK, 249(HUDR):AUTUMN73-
    545
    639(VQR):SUMMER73-CX
ACHER, W. JEAN-JACQUES ROUSSEAU,
    ÉCRIVAIN DE L'AMITIÉ.
    A.S. DE FABRY, 481(PQ):JUL72-754
ACHINSTEIN, P. LAW & EXPLANATION.
    R.G. SWINBURNE, 479(PHQ):OCT72-
    375
ACHINSTEIN, P. & S.F. BARKER, EDS.
    THE LEGACY OF LOGICAL POSITIVISM.*
    B.A. BRODY, 486:MAR72-102
ACHTEN, G., L. EIZENHÖFER & H. KNAUS,
    EDS. DIE LATEINISCHEN GEBETBUCH-
    HANDSCHRIFTEN DER HESSISCHEN LAND-
    ES- UND HOCHSCHULBIBLIOTHEK DARM-
    STADT.
    G. DOGAER, 182:VOL25#21-705
ACKERKNECHT, E.H. MEDICINE & ETH-
    NOLOGY.
    E.J. TRIMMER, 203:SUMMER72-167
ACKERSON, D. UA FLIGHT TO CHICAGO.
    H. GREGORY, 502(PRS):SPRING72-87
    C. WATTS, 448:SPRING72-104

ACKROYD, P. LONDON LICKPENNY.
617(TLS):3MAY74-471
ACLAND, A. THE CORSICAN LADIES.
M. MILLER, 617(TLS):13DEC74-1420
ACORN, M. MORE POEMS FOR PEOPLE.
R. ENDRES, 99:MAR74-45
"ACTA CLASSICA." (VOL 13)
J. ANDRÉ, 555:VOL46FASC1-173
"ACTA OF THE FIFTH INTERNATIONAL CON-
GRESS OF GREEK & LATIN EPIGRAPHY."
A.R. BIRLEY, 313:VOL62-189
LORD ACTON & R. SIMPSON. THE CORRES-
PONDENCE OF LORD ACTON & RICHARD
SIMPSON. (VOL 1) (J.L. ALTHOLZ &
D. MC ELRATH, EDS)
P. MARSH, 637(VS):MAR72-362
ACTON, H. TUSCAN VILLAS.
617(TLS):18JAN74-44
ACTON, H.B. KANT'S MORAL PHILOSO-
PHY.*
R.F. ATKINSON, 479(PHQ):JAN72-83
A.C. EWING, 483:APR72-173
G.J. STACK, 319:JAN74-123
ACTON, H.B. WHAT MARX REALLY SAID.
D. MC LELLAN, 32:SEP73-620
"THE ACTOR'S ANALECTS (YAKUSHA RON-
GO)."* (C.J. DUNN & BUNZO TORI-
GOE, EDS & TRANS)
J.R. BRANDON, 318(JAOS):APR-JUN
72-352
ADACHI, B. THE LIVING TREASURES OF
JAPAN.
617(TLS):12JUL74-751
ADAIR, J. CHERITON 1644.
617(TLS):11JAN74-27
ADAM DE LA HALLE. THE CHANSONS.
(J.H. MARSHALL, ED)
A.J. KENNEDY, 382(MAE):1973/3-
281
K. VARTY, 208(FS):JAN73-47
205(FMLS):JUL72-284
ADAM, A. GRANDEUR & ILLUSION.
J. GUICHARNAUD, 676(YR):AUTUMN72-
106
ADAM, A. LE THÉÂTRE CLASSIQUE.
R.C. KNIGHT, 208(FS):APR73-196
ADAM, A. - SEE DE MALHERBE, F.
ADAM, C. & G. MILHAUD - SEE DES-
CARTES, R.
ADAM, F. - SEE GLÖCKNER, E.
ADAM, H. MODERNINZING RACIAL DOMI-
NATION.*
G.M. FREDRICKSON, 453:31OCT74-29
ADAM, I. & G. PREUSS - SEE "MEYERS
HANDBUCH ÜBER DIE LITERATUR"
ADAM, S. THE TECHNIQUE OF GREEK
SCULPTURE IN THE ARCHAIC & CLASSI-
CAL PERIODS.
E.B. HARRISON, 54:DEC72-536
ADAM, T. CLEMENTIA PRINCIPIS.
M. HAMMOND, 24:FALL73-297
B. WALKER, 313:VOL62-199
ADAMOV, A. SI L'ÉTÉ REVENAIT.
D.M. CHURCH, 207(FR):OCT71-180
ADAMS, A.B. GERONIMO.
617(TLS):18JAN74-49
"ANSEL ADAMS: IMAGES 1923-1974."
H. KRAMER, 441:1DEC74-4
ADAMS, C.D. - SEE LYSIAS
ADAMS, E. FRANCIS DANBY.
617(TLS):29MAR74-309
ADAMS, E.B. BERNARD SHAW & THE
AESTHETES.
M. MEISEL, 637(VS):JUN73-483
R.S. NELSON, 572:MAY72-84

ADAMS, E.B. ISRAEL ZANGWILL.
J.O. BAYLEN, 177(ELT):VOL15#2-
174
ADAMS, H., ED. CRITICAL THEORY
SINCE PLATO.
W.L. BLIZEK, 290(JAAC):FALL72-
132
ADAMS, H. THE EDUCATION OF HENRY
ADAMS. (E. SAMUELS, ED)
H. LEIBOWITZ, 441:19MAY74-3
ADAMS, I. THE TRUDEAU PAPERS.*
P. STEVENS, 628:SPRING73-95
ADAMS, I.H., ED. DIRECTORY OF FOR-
MER SCOTTISH COMMONTIES.
J.B. CAIRD, 595(SCS):VOL17PT1-87
"JOHN ADAMS: A BIOGRAPHY IN HIS OWN
WORDS."* (J.B. PEABODY, ED)
639(VQR):AUTUMN73-CLVII
ADAMS, J.D. THE "POPULUS" OF AUGUS-
TINE & JEROME.
F.E. CRANZ, 589:OCT73-724
A.W. GODFREY, 363:MAY72-106
ADAMS, J.N., COMP. ILLINOIS PLACE
NAMES. (W.E. KELLER, ED)
E.B. VEST, 424:SEP72-214
ADAMS, L. GOVER & THE ENLIGHTENMENT.
H.T. MASON, 617(TLS):13DEC74-
1424
ADAMS, M. GOTTFRIED BENN'S CRITIQUE
OF SUBSTANCE.*
E.W. HERD, 67:MAY73-147
P. RUSSELL, 220(GL&L):APR73-265
ADAMS, R. THE NEW WEST.
S. SCHWARTZ, 441:1DEC74-101
ADAMS, R. SHARDIK.
V. GLENDINNING, 617(TLS):15NOV74-
1277
ADAMS, R. WATERSHIP DOWN.
P. ADAMS, 61:MAY74-140
R. GILMAN, 441:24MAR74-3
C. LEHMANN-HAUPT, 441:6MAR74-41
J.A. SMITH, 453:18APR74-8
442(NY):1APR74-122
ADAMS, R.F. THE OLD-TIME COWHAND.
R.H. CRACROFT, 650(WF):APR72-141
ADAMS, R.F. WESTERN WORDS.* (2ND
ED)
R.W. SORVIG, 35(AS):DEC68-302
ADAMS, S., ED. TEN ANGLO-WELSH
POETS.
617(TLS):30AUG74-932
ADAMSON, D. - SEE SENCOURT, R.
ADAMSON, J. GROUCHO, HARPO, CHICO
& SOMETIMES ZEPPO.*
B. BROWN, 617(TLS):13DEC74-1419
P. SCHJELDAHL, 441:8DEC74-35
ADAMSON, J.H. & H.F. FOLLAND. SIR
HARRY VANE.
617(TLS):19JUL74-764
ADAMSON, V. & M.J.B. LOWE. ENGLISH
STUDIES SERIES/9.
E. SCHRAEPEN, 556(RLV):1972/2-
222
ADDINGTON, R. - SEE FABER, F.W.
ADELEYE, R.A. POWER & DIPLOMACY IN
NORTHERN NIGERIA 1804-1906.
M. LAST, 69:OCT72-353
ADELMAN, B. DOWN HOME.
S. SONTAG, 453:18APR74-17
639(VQR):SPRING73-XCII
ADELMAN, I. & R. DWORKIN. THE CON-
TEMPORARY NOVEL.
J.D.Y., 145(CRIT):VOL14#3-109
ADERETH, M. - SEE RACINE, J.

ADHEMAR, J. TWENTIETH CENTURY GRA-
PHICS.
   D. THOMAS, 135:FEB72-139
ADICEAM, M.E. CONTRIBUTION À
L'ÉTUDE D'AIYANĀR-ŚĀSTĀ.
   O. VON HINÜBER, 182:VOL25#11-336
ADKINS, A.W.H. FROM THE MANY TO THE
ONE.*
   N. GULLEY, 123:DEC73-208
ADLARD, J. THE DEBT TO PLEASURE.
   S. TROTTER, 362:24OCT74-549
ADLER, A. MÖBLIERTE ERZIEHUNG.*
   E-M. KNAPP-TEPPERBERG, 224(GRM):
   BAND22HEFT3-315
ADLER, G., WITH A. JAFFÉ - SEE JUNG,
C.G.
ADLER, G.M. LAND PLANNING BY ADMIN-
ISTRATIVE REGULATION.
   L. GOOD, 529(QQ):SPRING72-121
ADLER, M.H. THE WRITING MACHINE.
   617(TLS):1MAR74-208
ADLER, M.J. THE COMMON SENSE OF
POLITICS.*
   R. NELSON, 154:SEP72-485
ADMUSSEN, R.L. LES PETITES REVUES
LITTÉRAIRES 1914-1939.
   D.M. SUTHERLAND, 208(FS):JAN73-
   108
ADORNO, T.W. MINIMA MORALIA. NEGA-
TIVE DIALECTICS. THE JARGON OF
AUTHENTICITY.
   J. SHAPIRO, 617(TLS):4OCT74-1094
ADRADOS, F.R. ESTUDIOS DE LINGUÍS-
TICA GENERAL.*
   H. GECKELER, 343:BAND14HEFT2-109
ADRADOS, F.R. LINGUÍSTICA ESTRUC-
TURAL.
   H. GECKELER, 343:BAND14HEFT2-113
ADRIANI, G., W. KONNERTZ & K. THOMAS.
JOSEPH BEUYS.
   617(TLS):12APR74-386
ADSHEAD, S.A.M. THE MODERNIZATION
OF THE CHINESE SALT ADMINISTRATION,
1900-1920.
   T.A. METZGER, 293(JAST):NOV71-
   191
ADY, P., ED. PRIVATE FOREIGN IN-
VESTMENT & THE DEVELOPING WORLD.
   M. LIPTON, 617(TLS):2AUG74-830
AEBISCHER, P. NEUF ÉTUDES SUR LE
THÉÂTRE MÉDIÉVAL.
   G. FRANK, 589:OCT73-727
AESCHYLUS. AGAMEMNON.* THE LIBA-
TION BEARERS.* (BOTH TRANS BY H.
LLOYD-JONES)
   D.W. LUCAS, 303:VOL92-195
AESCHYLUS. SEVEN AGAINST THEBES.
(A. HECHT & H. BACON, TRANS)
   H. LLOYD-JONES, 617(TLS):1NOV74-
   1221
AESCHYLUS. THE SUPPLIANTS. (VOL 1)
(H.F. JOHANSEN & O. SMITH, EDS &
TRANS)
   A.F. GARVIE, 123:MAR73-21
AFFRON, C. A STAGE FOR POETS.
   D. SICES, 207(FR):MAY72-1192
   639(VQR):SUMMER72-CV
"AFRICA SOUTH OF THE SAHARA 1971."
   B-P., 69:JUL72-261
"AFRICA SOUTH OF THE SAHARA 1974."
   617(TLS):17MAY74-534
"AFRICAN COMMUNISTS SPEAK."
   R.E. KANET, 104:SPRING72-188

AGER, D.V. THE NATURE OF THE STRATI-
GRAPHICAL RECORD.
   617(TLS):8MAR74-243
AGESTHIALINGOM, S. & N.K. RAJA, EDS.
DRAVIDIAN LINGUISTICS.
   S. VAIDYANATHAN, 318(JAOS):OCT-
   DEC72-579
AGGELER, W.F. BAUDELAIRE JUDGED BY
SPANISH CRITICS 1857-1957.*
   A.E. CARTER, 207(FR):FEB72-730
AGGERTT, O.J. & E.R. BOWEN. COMMUNI-
CATIVE READING. (3RD ED)
   P.H. GRAY, 583:WINTER72-209
AGOR, W.H. THE CHILEAN SENATE.
   F.M. NUNN, 263:APR-JUN73-214
AGRICOLA, E. SYNTAKTISCHE MEHRDEU-
TIGKEIT (POLYSYNTAKTIZITÄT) BEI
DER ANALYSE DES DEUTSCHEN UND DES
ENGLISCHEN.*
   D. KASTOVSKY, 38:BAND90HEFT1/2-
   180
"AGRICULTURAL REVOLUTION IN SOUTH-
EAST ASIA."
   B. GLASSBURNER, 293(JAST):FEB72-
   452
AGRIPPA D'AUBIGNÉ - SEE UNDER D'AUB-
IGNÉ, A.
AGUDIEZ, J.V. INSPIRACIÓN Y ESTÉT-
ICA EN "LA REGENTA" DE CLARÍN.
   O. FERNÁNDEZ DE LA VEGA, 263:
   JAN-MAR73-99
AGUIRRE, J.M. ANTONIO MACHADO,
POETA SIMBOLISTA.
   617(TLS):11OCT74-1119
AGUNG GDE AGUNG, I.A. TWENTY YEARS
OF INDONESIAN FOREIGN POLICY.
   617(TLS):17MAY74-516
AHERN, E.M. THE CULT OF THE DEAD IN
A CHINESE VILLAGE.
   617(TLS):22FEB74-188
AHLBERG, G. FIGHTING ON LAND & SEA
IN GREEK GEOMETRIC ART.*
   J. BOARDMAN, 123:DEC73-288
AHLBERG, G. PROTHESIS & EKPHORA IN
GREEK GEOMETRIC ART.
   F. BROMMER, 182:VOL25#3/4-107
AHLBORN, H. - SEE PSEUDO-HOMER & T.
PRODROMOS
AHLHEIM, K-H. WIE GEBRAUCHT MAN
FREMDWÖRTER RICHTIG?
   E. GRIEM, 399(MLJ):FEB72-117
AHLSTROM, S.E. A RELIGIOUS HISTORY
OF THE AMERICAN PEOPLE.*
   S.E. MEAD, 656(WMQ):JUL73-495
   E-R. VOLLMAR, 377:NOV73-184
AHMAD, A. ISLAMIC MODERNISM IN
INDIA & PAKISTAN: 1857-1965.*
   S. MC DONOUGH, 318(JAOS):JAN-MAR
   72-118
AHMAD, A. - SEE GHALIB
AHMAD, A. & G.E. VON GRUNEBAUM, EDS.
MUSLIM SELF-STATEMENT IN INDIA &
PAKISTAN, 1857-1968.*
   H. MALIK, 293(JAST):NOV71-214
AHMED, H. URDU WORD COUNT.
   617(TLS):19APR74-414
AHORN, M.B. THE PROBLEM OF EVIL.
   H.F., 543:DEC71-348
AI. CRUELTY.
   A. OSTRIKER, 441:17FEB74-7
   617(TLS):29MAR74-339
AIDALA, T. THE GREAT HOUSES OF SAN
FRANCISCO.
   T.B. MORTON, 441:28JUL74-4

AIKEN, C. THE CLERK'S JOURNAL.
639(VQR):SUMMER72-CII
AIKEN, C. COLLECTED POEMS.* (2ND
ED) USHANT.
F.K. SANDERS, 569(SR):WINTER73-
172
AIREY, W. A LEARNER IN CHINA.
T. HERMAN, 293(JAST):AUG72-941
AITKEN, A.J., A. MC INTOSH & H. PÁLS-
SON, EDS. EDINBURGH STUDIES IN
ENGLISH & SCOTS.
H. HARGREAVES, 541(RES):AUG72-
320
E.G. STANLEY, 447(N&Q):AUG72-305
B. STRANG, 297(JL):SEP72-346
AITMATOW, T. DER WEISSE DAMPFER.
A. LATCHINIAN, 654(WB):9/1972-
144
AJALA, A. PAN-AFRICANISM.
617(TLS):19JUL74-772
AJDUKIEWICZ, K. PROBLEMS & THEORIES
OF PHILOSOPHY.
617(TLS):5APR74-372
AJELLO, N. LO SCRITTORE E IL POTERE.
G. ALMANSI, 617(TLS):11OCT74-
1141
AKASHI, Y. THE NANYANG CHINESE
NATIONAL SALVATION MOVEMENT, 1937-
1941.*
A.P.L. LIU, 318(JAOS):OCT-DEC72-
586
AKENSON, D.H. THE CHURCH OF IRELAND.
M.J. WATERS, 637(VS):DEC72-229
AKENSON, D.H. THE UNITED STATES &
IRELAND.
617(TLS):26APR74-443
AKHMADULINA, B. FEVER & OTHER NEW
POEMS.
R. GREGG, 550(RUSR):JAN72-88
E. MORGAN, 617(TLS):11OCT74-1132
AKHMANOVA, O. & G. MIKAEL'AN. THE
THEORY OF SYNTAX IN MODERN LIN-
GUISTICS.
R. PITTMAN, 361:VOL28#1&2-143
AKHMATOVA, A. POEMS OF AKHMATOVA.*
(S. KUNITZ, WITH M. HAYWARD, EDS
& TRANS)
M. MESIC, 491:JUL74-232
617(TLS):8MAR74-225
AKIKO, Y. - SEE UNDER YOSANO AKIKO
AKIN, J. & OTHERS, EDS. LANGUAGE
BEHAVIOR.
J. PRŮCHA, 353:15OCT72-89
AKINARI, U. TALES OF MOONLIGHT &
RAIN.
639(VQR):SUMMER72-CII
AKINTOYE, S.A. REVOLUTION & POWER
POLITICS IN YORUBALAND 1840-1893.
R. SMITH, 69:JAN72-69
AKIYAMA, T. & S. MATSUBARA. ARTS OF
CHINA: BUDDHIST CAVE TEMPLES, NEW
RESEARCHES.
M. SULLIVAN, 318(JAOS):JAN-MAR72-
151
AKRIGG, G.P.V. & H.B. BRITISH COL-
UMBIA PLACE NAMES. (2ND ED)
F. TARPLEY, 424:JUN72-151
"AKTEN DES INTERNATIONALEN LEIBNIZ-
KONGRESSES, HANNOVER, 14.-19. NOV.
1966." (VOLS 3-5)
A. MERCIER, 182:VOL25#22-769

"AKTEN ZUR DEUTSCHEN AUSWÄRTIGEN
POLITIK 1918-1945." (SER B, VOL 5)
F.L. CARSTEN, 575(SEER):JAN73-
141
AL-AZM, S.J. - SEE FILED UNDER AZM
AL-FÂRÂBÎ - SEE FILED UNDER FÂRÂBÎ
AL-JAZARÎ, I.AL-R. - SEE FILED UNDER
JAZARÎ
ALAJOUANINE, T. VALERY LARBAUD SOUS
DIVERS VISAGES.
617(TLS):19JUL74-771
ALARCOS LLORACH, E. ESTUDIOS DE
GRAMÁTICA FUNCIONAL DEL ESPAÑOL.
B. FLAM, 238:SEP72-595
ALATIS, J.E., ED. BILINGUALISM &
LANGUAGE CONTACT.
J. RUBIN, 350:JUN73-517
ALATIS, J.E., ED. REPORT OF THE
TWENTY-FIRST ANNUAL ROUND TABLE
MEETING ON LINGUISTICS & LANGUAGE
STUDIES.
L.B. BUCKLIN, 399(MLJ):JAN72-56
ALAYA, F. WILLIAM SHARP - "FIONA
MACLEOD," 1855-1905.*
I. FLETCHER, 677:VOL3-324
ALAZRAKI, J. LA PROSA NARRATIVA DE
JORGE LUIS BORGES.
H.M. RASI, 399(MLJ):FEB72-112
ALBERDI, H.L. - SEE UNDER LIJERÓN
ALBERDI, H.
ALBERTI, R. THE OWL'S INSOMNIA.
(M. STRAND, ED & TRANS)
L. LIEBERMAN, 491:AUG74-280
ALBERTS, R.C. THE GOOD PROVIDER.
617(TLS):16AUG74-883
ALBERTSON, C. BESSIE.*
H. CARRUTH, 249(HUDR):WINTER
73/74-765
ALBINI, U., ED. PERI POLITEIAS.
P. LOUIS, 555:VOL46FASC2-314
ALBRAND, M. ZURICH/AZ 900.
N. CALLENDAR, 441:6OCT74-38
ALBRECHT, F. DEUTSCHE SCHRIFTSTEL-
LER IN DER ENTSCHEIDUNG.
D. ECKARDT, 654(WB):1/1972-168
ALBRECHT, J. LE FRANÇAIS LANGUE
ABSTRAITE?
K. WINN, 430(NS):MAY72-306
VON ALBRECHT, M. MEISTER RÖMISCHER
PROSA VON CATO BIS APULEIUS.
F. LASSERRE, 182:VOL25#5/6-171
ALBRIGHT, D. THE MYTH AGAINST MYTH.
H. OREL, 301(JEGP):OCT73-578
639(VQR):SPRING73-LXXII
ALCHOURRON, C.E. & E. BULYGIN. NOR-
MATIVE SYSTEMS.
D.D. TODD, 484(PPR):MAR73-437
ALCOVER, M. LA PENSÉE PHILOSOPHIQUE
ET SCIENTIFIQUE DE CYRANO DE BER-
GERAC.*
V. CROSBY, 207(FR):FEB72-741
P.M. HARRY, 402(MLR):APR73-407
E. HARTH, 551(RENQ):SUMMER72-249
R. HORVILLE, 557(RSH):OCT-DEC72-
606
ALDCROFT, D.H. STUDIES IN BRITISH
TRANSPORT HISTORY.
617(TLS):29NOV74-1351
ALDERSON, F. ENGLAND BY BICYCLE.
617(TLS):13SEP74-984
ALDERSON, W.L. & A.C. HENDERSON.
CHAUCER & AUGUSTAN SCHOLARSHIP.*
S.W. HOLTON, 597(SN):VOL44#1-171

4

ALDIS, H.G. A LIST OF BOOKS PRINTED
IN SCOTLAND BEFORE 1700.
D.W. EVANS, 354:JUN72-149
ALDISS, B. THE EIGHTY-MINUTE HOUR.
R. BLYTHE, 362:2MAY74-576
617(TLS):5APR74-357
ALDISS, B.W. FRANKENSTEIN UNBOUND.*
C. LEHMANN-HAUPT, 441:11JUN74-45
ALDRED, C. AKHENATEN & NEFERTITI.
T.G.H. JAMES, 617(TLS):18OCT74-
1170
ALDRED, C. JEWELS OF THE PHARAOHS.
J.W. THOMAS, 135:MAR72-214
ALDRIDGE, A.O., ED. COMPARATIVE
LITERATURE.*
J. FLETCHER, 447(N&Q):NOV72-436
ALEICHEM, S. INSIDE KASRILEVKE.
617(TLS):29MAR74-345
ALEKSANDROV, A.M. & OTHERS, EDS.
ISTORIIA VNESHNEI POLITIKI SSSR,
1917-1970. (VOL 2)
T. ULDRICKS, 32:SEP73-614
ALEXANDER, C.H.O. A BOOK OF CHESS.
617(TLS):29MAR74-348
ALEXANDER, C.H.O. THE PENGUIN BOOK
OF CHESS POSITIONS.
617(TLS):8MAR74-244
ALEXANDER, E. MUSEUMS & HOW TO USE
THEM.
617(TLS):9AUG74-864
ALEXANDER, E.P. - SEE FONTAINE, J.
ALEXANDER, G. THE INVISIBLE CHINA.
453:7MAR74-29
ALEXANDER, J. AFFADAVITS OF GENIUS.
R.M. ADAMS, 445(NCF):DEC72-361
M. GRIFFITHS, 150(DR):SPRING72-
147
639(VQR):WINTER72-XXVII
ALEXANDER, J. ONE SUNNY DAY.
M. LEVIN, 441:10MAR74-10
ALEXANDER, J.J.G. ANGLO-SAXON ILLUM-
INATION IN OXFORD LIBRARIES.
J. BECKWITH, 39:JUL72-84
ALEXANDER, M. MRS. FRASER ON THE
FATAL SHORE.
639(VQR):WINTER72-XVI
ALEXANDER, M. - SEE "BEOWULF"
ALEXANDER, N. POISON, PLAY, & DUEL.
M. CHARNEY, 301(JEGP):APR73-241
T. HAWKES, 676(YR):SUMMER73-561
H. LEVIN, 551(RENQ):WINTER72-498
S. WELLS, 541(RES):MAY72-199
ALEXANDER, S. LIONS & FOXES.
H. MITGANG, 441:6DEC74-35
ALEXANDER, T.B. & R.E. BERINGER.
THE ANATOMY OF THE CONFEDERATE
CONGRESS.
639(VQR):SUMMER72-XCII
ALEXIOU, M. THE RITUAL LAMENT IN
GREEK TRADITION.
617(TLS):21JUN74-672
DE ALFARO, G.G. - SEE UNDER GUARDIA
DE ALFARO, G.
ALFONSO, O.M. THEODORE ROOSEVELT &
THE PHILIPPINES, 1897-1909.*
H. SCHMIDT, 302:JUL72-218
ALFONSO, P. THE SCHOLAR'S GUIDE.*
(J.R. JONES & J.E. KELLER, EDS &
TRANS)
H.R. STONE, 238:MAR72-176
ALGAR, H. RELIGION & STATE IN IRAN
1785-1906.
N. KEDDIE, 318(JAOS):JAN-MAR72-
116

ALGER, H., JR. CAST UPON THE BREAK-
ERS.
W.M. FREEMAN, 441:26JUL74-37
ALI, MRS. M.H. OBSERVATIONS ON THE
MUSSULMANS OF INDIA.
617(TLS):1NOV74-1240
ALI-BAB. ENCYCLOPEDIA OF PRACTICAL
GASTRONOMY.
N. HAZELTON, 441:1DEC74-94
'ALĪ KHĀN, Y. THE TĀ'RĪKH-I-BANGĀLA-
I-MAHĀBATJANGĪ. (A. SUBHAN, ED)
M.N. PEARSON, 318(JAOS):OCT-DEC
72-582
ALIGHIERI, D. - SEE UNDER DANTE ALI-
GHIERI
ALINEI, M., ED. SPOGLI ELETTRONICI
DELL'ITALIANO DELLE ORIGINI E DEL
DUECENTO. (VOL 2, PT 5)
T.G. GRIFFITH, 402(MLR):JUL73-
664
ALKON, P.K. SAMUEL JOHNSON & MORAL
DISCIPLINE.
A. PARREAUX, 189(EA):OCT-DEC72-
562
ALLAND, A. HUMAN DIVERSITY.
F.W. SIXEL, 529(QQ):AUTUMN72-428
ALLARD, S. RUSSIA & THE AUSTRIAN
STATE TREATY.*
T.W. ROBINSON, 550(RUSR):JAN72-
91
ALLBEURY, T. SNOWBALL.
N. CALLENDAR, 441:2JUN74-20
617(TLS):6SEP74-960
ALLDRITT, K. THE VISUAL IMAGINATION
OF D.H. LAWRENCE.*
E. DELAVENAY, 189(EA):JAN-MAR72-
166
K. MC LEOD, 541(RES):AUG72-385
W.G.R., 502(PRS):WINTER72/73-369
M. SQUIRES, 177(ELT):VOL15#4-334
ALLEGRO, J.M. THE CHOSEN PEOPLE.
J. NEUSNER, 390:OCT72-76
ALLEMAN, G.S. & OTHERS - SEE "ENG-
LISH LITERATURE 1660-1800"
ALLEN, D.C. THE HARMONIOUS VISION.*
(NEW ED)
M.A. DI CESARE, 551(RENQ):WINTER
72-512
ALLEN, D.C. MYSTERIOUSLY MEANT.*
R.E. CARTER, 529(QQ):SUMMER72-
271
P. LEGOUIS, 189(EA):OCT-DEC72-
538
J. SEZNEC, 191(ELN):DEC72-144
J.M. STEADMAN, 405(MP):MAY73-357
ALLEN, G.W. MELVILLE & HIS WORLD.
J. DITSKY, 577(SHR):SUMMER72-301
639(VQR):SPRING72-LXI
ALLEN, H.R. WHO WON THE BATTLE OF
BRITAIN?
617(TLS):30AUG74-936
ALLEN, J.B. THE FRIAR AS CRITIC.*
M.W. BLOOMFIELD, 589:APR73-329
P. GRADON, 541(RES):MAY72-195
E. REISS, 651(WHR):AUTUMN73-425
ALLEN, J.P.B. & P. VAN BUREN - SEE
CHOMSKY, N.
ALLEN, J.S., ED. DUMBARTON OAKS BIB-
LIOGRAPHIES BASED ON "BYZANTIN-
ISCHE ZEITSCHRIFT" LITERATURE ON
BYZANTINE ART, 1892-1967. (VOL 1,
PTS 1&2)
617(TLS):26JUL74-814

ALLEN, M. E.A. BOWLES & HIS GARDEN
AT MYDDLETON HOUSE.
617(TLS):1MAR74-220
ALLEN, M. POE & THE BRITISH MAGA-
ZINE TRADITION.*
B. ROUSE, 599:FALL72-309
ALLEN, R. VALHALLA AT THE OK.
D.E. RICHARDSON, 598(SOR):WINTER
74-225
ALLEN, R.C. THE SYMBOLIC WORLD OF
FEDERICO GARCÍA LORCA.
R.L. PREDMORE, 401(MLQ):DEC73-
477
ALLEN, R.E. PLATO'S "EUTHYPHRO" &
THE EARLIER THEORY OF FORMS.*
R. ROBINSON, 393(MIND):OCT72-631
L.S., 543:MAR72-547
K.M. SAYRE, 479(PHQ):APR72-165
ALLEN, R.F. FIRE & IRON.*
G. CUBBIN, 402(MLR):OCT73-958
L. LÖNNROTH, 589:APR73-330
ALLEN, S. L'ESPACE D'UN LIVRE.
F.E. DORENLOT, 207(FR):FEB72-680
ALLEN, S.S. SAMUEL PHELPS & SAD-
LER'S WELLS THEATRE.*
H. OREL, 637(VS):SEP71-93
J.C. TREWIN, 157:SUMMER72-70
ALLEN, T. COLETTE.
H. KIRKWOOD, 99:AUG74-40
ALLEN, W.E.D., ED. RUSSIAN EMBAS-
SIES TO THE GEORGIAN KINGS, 1589-
1605.*
J. KAYALOFF, 550(RUSR):APR72-197
ALLENTUCK, M., ED. THE ACHIEVEMENT
OF ISAAC BASHEVIS SINGER.
D.P. DENEAU, 573(SSF):FALL72-422
ALLENTUCK, M.E. JOHN GRAHAM'S SYS-
TEM & DIALECTICS OF ART.
290(JAAC):SUMMER72-566
ALLEVI, F. FORTUNA ED EREDITÀ DEL
PARINI.
V.S., 275(IQ):FALL/WINTER72-121
ALLIBONE, T.E., ED. THE IMPACT OF
THE NATURAL SCIENCES ON ARCHAEOL-
OGY.
N.S. BAER, 57:VOL34#2/3-262
ALLISON, A.F. THOMAS DEKKER, C.
1572-1632.
354:DEC72-364
ALLISON, H.E., ED. THE KANT-EBER-
HARD CONTROVERSY.
617(TLS):29MAR74-348
ALLISON, K.J., ED. A HISTORY OF THE
COUNTY OF YORK: EAST RIDING. (VOL
2)
617(TLS):10MAY74-494
ALLMEN, R. STANLEY.
M. LEVIN, 441:25AUG74-31
ALLOTT, M. - SEE KEATS, J.
ALLOTT, S. PLAUDITE.
R.G. PENMAN, 123:MAR73-80
ALLROGGEN, G. E.T.A. HOFFMANNS KOM-
POSITIONEN.*
S.P.S., 191(ELN):SEP72(SUPP)-164
ALLSOPP, B. TOWARDS A HUMANE ARCHI-
TECTURE.
617(TLS):22MAR74-304
ALLSOPP, B. - SEE JONES, I.
ALLUM, P.A. POLITICS & SOCIETY IN
POST-WAR NAPLES. ITALY - REPUBLIC
WITHOUT GOVERNMENT?
617(TLS):12APR74-382

ALLWORTH, E. NATIONALITIES OF THE
SOVIET EAST.
D.S.M. WILLIAMS, 575(SEER):OCT73-
633
ALMANSI, G. L'ESTETICA DELL'OSCENO.
617(TLS):4OCT74-1082
ALONSO, D. HIJOS DE LA IRA.* (E.L.
RIVERS, ED & TRANS)
J. PALLEY, 399(MLJ):FEB72-105
ALONSO, D. OBRAS COMPLETAS. (VOL 2)
617(TLS):31MAY74-578
ALONSO, M.D.F. - SEE UNDER FERNÁNDEZ
ALONSO, M.D.
ALONSO GARCÍA, D. LITERATURA ORAL
DEL LADINO ENTRE LOS SEFARDÍES DE
ORIENTE A TRAVÉS DEL ROMANCERO.
S.G. ARMISTEAD & J.H. SILVERMAN,
240(HR):SPRING72-224
DE ALOYSIO, F. LEGGERE DEWEY.*
L.M.P., 543:SEP71-119
ALPERA, L. LOS NOMBRES TRECENTISTAS
DE BOTÁNICA VALENCIANA EN FRANCESC
EIXIMENIS.*
M.R. HARRIS, 545(RPH):AUG72-111
ALPERS, P.J. THE POETRY OF "THE
FAERIE QUEENE."*
M. MURRIN, 405(MP):MAY73-342
ALPERS, S. CORPUS RUBENIANUM LUDWIG
BURCHARD. (PT 9)
E. YOUNG, 39:MAR72-228
ALPERT, P. PARTNERSHIP OR CONFRON-
TATION?
M. LIPTON, 617(TLS):2AUG74-830
ALSAR, V. LA BALSA TO AUSTRALIA.
617(TLS):11JAN74-38
ALSDORF-BOLLÉE, A. DIE LATEINISCHEN
VERBALABSTRAKTA DER U- DEKLINATION
UND IHRE UMBILDUNGEN IM ROMANIS-
CHEN.
A.K. LEVY, 545(RPH):NOV72-412
ALSOP, S. STAY OF EXECUTION.*
L.E. SISSMAN, 442(NY):11FEB74-
125
E.S. TURNER, 362:11JUL74-60
E. WEEKS, 61:FEB74-95
617(TLS):3MAY74-482
ALSTON, R.C. A BIBLIOGRAPHY OF THE
ENGLISH LANGUAGE FROM THE INVEN-
TION OF PRINTING TO THE YEAR 1800.*
(VOLS 1-10)
617(TLS):8NOV74-1267
ALTBAUER, M., ED. PSALTERIUM SINAIT-
ICUM.
N.R. PRIBIC, 32:DEC73-799
ALTENHOFER, N. - SEE "HEINRICH HEINE"
ALTENHOFER, N. - SEE VON HOFMANNS-
THAL, H. & A. WILDGANS
ALTER, J.V. LES ORIGINES DE LA
SATIRE ANTIBOURGEOISE EN FRANCE.*
(VOL 2)
A.J. BINGHAM, 399(MLJ):FEB72-107
R. MERCIER, 557(RSH):OCT-DEC72-
607
V.W. TOPAZIO, 188(ECR):WINTER72-
330
ALTER, M.P. THE CONCEPT OF PHYSIC-
IAN IN THE WRITINGS OF HANS CAROS-
SA & ARTHUR SCHNITZLER.
K-P.W. HINZE, 221(GQ):NOV72-732
ALTHAM, J.E.J. THE LOGIC OF PLURAL-
ITY.
C. MC KNIGHT, 479(PHQ):JUL72-277
A.B.W., 543:MAR72-549

ALTHAUS, H. ÄSTHETIK, ÖKONOMIE UND GESELLSCHAFT.
   M. GSTEIGER, 301(JEGP):JAN73-111
   H.B. NISBET, 402(MLR):JUL73-693
ALTHAUS, H.P. DIE CAMBRIDGER LÖWEN-FABEL VON 1382.
   B. MURDOCH, 402(MLR):OCT73-928
ALTHOLZ, J.L. & D. MC ELRATH - SEE LORD ACTON & R. SIMPSON
ALTICK, R.D. VICTORIAN PEOPLE & IDEAS.
   617(TLS):5JUL74-731
ALTISENT, A., ED. L'ALMOINA REIAL A LA CORT DE PERE EL CERIMONIÓS.
   J.N. HILLGARTH, 589:JUL73-545
ALTMAN, H.B. & R.L. POLITZER, EDS. INDIVIDUALIZING FOREIGN LANGUAGE INSTRUCTION.
   F.M. GRITTNER, 207(FR):MAY72-1198
   D. QUILTER, 238:SEP72-601
ALTMANN, A. MOSES MENDELSSOHN.
   S.W. BARON, 319:APR74-264
ALTOMA, S.J. THE PROBLEM OF DIGLOS-SIA IN ARABIC.
   W.M. ERWIN, 350:MAR73-210
   A.S. KAYE, 318(JAOS):OCT-DEC72-538
A-LUGHOD, I., ED. THE TRANSFORMA-TION OF PALESTINE.
   A. AGES, 287:APR72-31
ALURISTA. FLORICANTO EN AZTLÁN.
   J. HANCOCK, 399(MLJ):MAR72-181
ALVAR, M. ESTRUCTURALISMO, GEOGRAF-ÍA LINGÜÍSTICA Y DIALECTOLOGÍA ACTUAL.
   J. RICCI, 241:MAY72-95
ALVAR, M. EL ROMANCERO.*
   D. EISENBERG, 400(MLN):MAR72-343
   M. FRANZBACH, 549(RLC):APR-JUN72-296
ALVAREZ, A. HERS.
   R. DAVIES, 617(TLS):8NOV74-1249
   J. MELLORS, 362:21NOV74-684
ALVAREZ, A. THE SAVAGE GOD.*
   J. GLOVER, 565:VOL13#3-68
   E. WILNER, 400(MLN):DEC72-998
   639(VQR):AUTUMN72-CLIII
ALVAREZ, G.D. THE CUBA OF NEW YORK STATE.
   E.C. SMITH, 424:JUN72-151
ALVAREZ DEL VAYO, J. THE MARCH OF SOCIALISM.
   P. PRESTON, 617(TLS):6DEC74-1366
ALVARGONZÁLEZ, R. ESTRATEGIAS DE ACTUACIÓN PARA LA SOCIEDAD ESPAÑ-OLA.
   H. MAUS, 182:VOL25#3/4-81
ALVER, B. DRAUMKVEDET.
   M. MYHREN, 172(EDDA):1972/1-52
ALVERSON, C. FIGHTING BACK.
   N. CALLENDAR, 441:13JAN74-12
AMADI, E. THE GREAT PONDS.
   J. UPDIKE, 442(NY):21JAN74-84
AMADO LEVY-VALENSI, E. LES VOIES ET LES PIÈGES DE LA PSYCHANALYSE.
   Y. BRÈS, 542:OCT-DEC72-447
AMARAL, J.V. - SEE UNDER VÁZQUEZ AMARAL, J.
AMBLER, E. DOCTOR FRIGO.
   P. ADAMS, 61:OCT74-118
   R. FULLER, 617(TLS):22NOV74-1307
   G. WALKER, 441:16NOV74-29
   442(NY):7OCT74-177

AMBLER, E. RUSSIAN JOURNALISM & POLITICS (1861-1881).
   D. BALMUTH, 32:JUN73-380
   W.E. MOSSE, 575(SEER):JUL73-479
AMBROSE, A. & M. LAZEROWITZ, EDS. G.E. MOORE: ESSAYS IN RETROSPECT.*
   A.B.W., 543:DEC71-376
AMBROSE, A. & M. LAZEROWITZ, EDS. LUDWIG WITTGENSTEIN: PHILOSOPHY & LANGUAGE.*
   J. BURNHEIM, 63:MAY73-84
AMBROSE, P. THE QUIET REVOLUTION.
   R. BLYTHE, 362:18APR74-507
   617(TLS):26JUL74-807
AMBROSOLI, L. - SEE CATTANEO, C.
"AMERICAN BOOK-PRICES CURRENT, 1967."* (E.P. HAZEN, G. MILNE & W.J. SMITH, EDS) "AMERICAN BOOK-PRICES CURRENT, 1968."* (E.P. HAZEN, G. MILNE & P.H. HEMINGSON, EDS)
   D.W. EVANS, 354:SEP72-259
"AMERICAN BOOK PRICES CURRENT." (VOL 77)
   617(TLS):1MAR74-220
"THE AMERICAN FILM INSTITUTE CATA-LOG: FEATURE FILMS 1921-1930."
   H. HART, 200:APR72-231
"AMERICA'S BIRTHDAY."
   I.R. DEE, 441:1DEC74-18
AMERIO, R. - SEE CAMPANELLA, T.
AMES, E. IN TIME LIKE GLASS.
   P. GUPTE, 441:30NOV74-29
AMES, W.E. A HISTORY OF THE NATION-AL INTELLIGENCER.
   639(VQR):AUTUMN72-CXLIV
DE AMESCUA, A.M. - SEE UNDER MIRA DE AMESCUA, A.
AMICHAI, Y. NOT OF THIS TIME, NOT OF THIS PLACE.*
   R. GARFITT, 362:14MAR74-343
AMIS, K. ENDING UP.
   A. BROYARD, 441:5OCT74-29
   L.E. SISSMAN, 442(NY):21OCT74-185
   G. STADE, 441:20OCT74-5
   J. VAIZEY, 362:30MAY74-703
   617(TLS):31MAY74-575
AMIS, K. GIRL, 20.*
   L.T. LEMON, 502(PRS):FALL72-266
   639(VQR):SPRING72-LII
AMIS, K. THE RIVERSIDE VILLAS MUR-DER.*
   R. DE FEO, 249(HUDR):WINTER73/74-781
AMIS, M. THE RACHEL PAPERS.*
   A. BROYARD, 441:19APR74-31
   G. GLUECK, 441:26MAY74-4
   J. MELLORS, 364:FEB/MAR74-133
   K. MILLER, 453:18JUL74-24
   L.E. SISSMAN, 442(NY):24JUN74-102
"JOST AMMAN'S 'KUNST UND LEHRBÜCH-LEIN'." (NOTES BY E. QUAYLE)
   W.O. HASSALL, 135:AUG72-304
AMMIANUS MARCELLINUS. AMMIEN MAR-CELLIN, "HISTOIRE." (VOL 2) (G. SABBAH, ED)
   J-P. CALLU, 555:VOL46FASC2-340
AMMON, H. JAMES MONROE.*
   B. PERKINS, 656(WMQ):JAN72-161

AMMONS, A.R. COLLECTED POEMS: 1951-
1971.*
    J.R. LINDROTH, 590:FALL/WINTER
    73/74-39
    R. PEVEAR, 249(HUDR):SPRING73-
    192
    R.B. SHAW, 491:NOV73-109
    H. VENDLER, 676(YR):SPRING73-412
AMMONS, A.R. SPHERE.
    C. BEDIENT, 441:22DEC74-2
AMMONS, A.R. TAPE FOR THE TURN OF
THE YEAR.*
    H. VENDLER, 676(YR):SPRING73-412
AMMONS, A.R. UPLANDS.*
    617(TLS):29MAR74-339
AMOR Y VÁZQUEZ, J. - SEE LOBO LASSO
DE LA VEGA, G.
AMORY, C. MAN KIND?
    E.P. DOLENSEK, 441:27OCT74-10
AMORY, H., ED. SALE CATALOGUES OF
LIBRARIES OF EMINENT PERSONS. (VOL
7)
    617(TLS):6SEP74-958
AMPE, A. DE METAMORFOZEN VAN HET
AUTHENTIEKE JAN-VAN-EYCK-KWATRIJN
OP HET LAM GODS.
    A. SMITH, 90:AUG72-562
AMPHILOCHIUS. AMPHILOCHII ICONIEN-
SIS "IAMBI AD SELEUCUM."* (E.
OBERG, ED)
    J. IRIGOIN, 555:VOL46FASC1-130
ANAND, M.R. COOLIE.
    P.K. SUNDARARAJAN, 648:OCT72-64
ANASTAPLO, G. THE CONSTITUTIONAL-
IST.*
    R.J. BISHIRJIAN, 396(MODA):WIN-
    TER73-93
"THE ANATOMY OF THE CONFEDERATE CON-
GRESS."
    H.C. BAILEY, 9(ALAR):OCT72-288
ANAYA, R.A. BLESS ME, ULTIMA.
    W. GARD, 584(SWR):SPRING73-V
ANAYA MONROY, F. & L. GORRÁEZ AR-
CAUTE, EDS. 25 ESTUDIOS DE FOLK-
LORE.
    R.J. SMITH, 292(JAF):OCT-DEC72-
    386
ANCESCHI, L., ED. L'IDEA DEL TEATRO
E LA CRISI DEL NATURALISMO.
    D.D., 275(IQ):FALL/WINTER72-124
ANDELSON, R.V. IMPUTED RIGHTS.
    W. BEACH, 577(SHR):SUMMER72-300
ANDERSCH, A. EFRAIM'S BOOK.
    G. EWART, 364:OCT/NOV72-146
ANDERSEN, J.K. & L. EMEREK. ALADDIN-
NOUREDDIN-TRADITIONEN I DET 19.
ÅRHUNDREDE.
    J.E. DE MYLIUS, 172(EDDA):1972/6-
    370
ANDERSEN, T. - SEE MALEVICH, K.S.
ANDERSEN, U.S. SUCCESS-CYBERNETICS.
    E.A. SCHMERLER, 186(ETC.):SEP72-
    322
ANDERSON, B.L., ED. CAPITAL ACCUMU-
LATION IN THE INDUSTRIAL REVOLU-
TION.
    617(TLS):17MAY74-536
ANDERSON, C.L. POE IN NORTHLIGHT.*
    W.T. BANDY, 27(AL):MAY73-305
    W. JOHNSON, 563(SS):AUTUMN73-395
ANDERSON, C.R. - SEE THOREAU, H.D.
ANDERSON, E. THIEVES LIKE US.
    M. ALWYN, 441:10FEB74-16

ANDERSON, E.M. THE DISABLED SCHOOL-
CHILD.
    617(TLS):18JAN74-46
ANDERSON, F. ALFONSO SASTRE.
    C. DE COSTER, 399(MLJ):DEC72-535
ANDERSON, J. A. PHILIP RANDOLPH.*
    639(VQR):AUTUMN73-CLVII
ANDERSON, J. & OTHERS. THE FAMILY
CIRCLE COOKBOOK.
    N. HAZELTON, 441:1DEC74-96
ANDERSON, J.K. XENOPHON.
    617(TLS):30AUG74-927
ANDERSON, J.Q. THE LIBERATING GODS.
    L. BUELL, 432(NEQ):JUN72-290
ANDERSON, L.O. & H.F. ZORNIG. BUILD
YOUR OWN LOW-COST HOME.
    505:OCT72-134
ANDERSON, M.D. HISTORY & IMAGERY IN
BRITISH CHURCHES.
    R. EDWARDS, 135:JUN72-151
    A. POWELL, 39:NOV72-460
ANDERSON, M.O. KINGS & KINGSHIP IN
EARLY SCOTLAND.
    617(TLS):22FEB74-189
ANDERSON, N. A LAWYER AMONG THE
THEOLOGIANS.
    617(TLS):25JAN74-86
ANDERSON, P. ACTIONS & PASSIONS.
    J.R. FRAKES, 441:24MAR74-36
ANDERSON, P. THE DAUGHTERS.
    E. KENDALL, 441:4AUG74-3
ANDERSON, R. THE PURPLE HEART
THROBS.
    617(TLS):15FEB74-153
ANDERSON, S. THE BUCK FEVER PAPERS.
(W.D. TAYLOR, ED)
    639(VQR):WINTER72-XXXVI
ANDERSON, S. & G. STEIN. SHERWOOD
ANDERSON/GERTRUDE STEIN: CORRES-
PONDENCE & PERSONAL ESSAYS.* (R.L.
WHITE, ED)
    639(VQR):SPRING73-LXXVI
ANDERSON, W. GAUGUIN'S PARADISE
LOST.
    W. TORTOLANO, 363:MAY72-100
ANDERSON, W. - SEE THEOPHRASTUS
ANDERSON, W.C. PENELOPE THE DAMP
DETECTIVE.
    N. CALLENDAR, 441:19MAY74-42
ANDERSSON, H. URBANISIERTE ORTSCHAF-
TEN UND LATEINISCHE TERMINOLOGIE.
    D. NICHOLAS, 589:APR73-334
ANDERSSON-SCHMIDT, M. MANUSCRIPTA
MEDIAEVALIA UPSALIENSIA.
    K.W. HUMPHREYS, 354:MAR72-59
ANDRADE, J.D. - SEE UNDER DE SOUSA
ANDRADE, J.
ANDRASSY, J. INTERNATIONAL LAW &
THE RESOURCES OF THE SEA.
    C. MC FARLAND, 639(VQR):WINTER72-
    126
ANDRÉ, J. EMPRUNTS ET SUFFIXES NOM-
INAUX EN LATIN.
    A. ERNOUT, 555:VOL46FASC2-326
    B.I. KNOTT, 123:DEC73-282
ANDRÉ, J. - SEE PLINY
ANDREAE, J.V. CHRISTIANOPOLIS 1619.
(R. VAN DÜLMAN, ED)
    W. BIESTERFELD, 182:VOL25#19/20-
    667
ANDREEV, I.D., ED. MATERIALY PO MAT-
EMATIČESKOJ LINGVISTIKE I MAŠINNO-
MU PEREVODU.
    R. RIS, 343:BAND14HEFT1-101

8

ANDREOLI, A. NEL MONDO DI L.A. MUR-
ATORI.
F. FORTI, 228(GSLI):VOL149FASC
466/467-439
ANDRESKI, S. - SEE COMTE, A.
ANDREWS, G. MOOD FOOD.
N. HAZELTON, 441:1DEC74-96
ANDREWS, T. THE STORY OF HAROLD.
R.P. BRICKNER, 441:12MAY74-6
ANDREYEV, N. STUDIES IN MUSCOVY.*
S.A. ZENKOVSKY, 550(RUSR):JAN72-
91
ANDRIEUX, M. LES FRANÇAIS À ROME.
P.F. HENNIN, 207(FR):MAY72-1173
ANDRIST, R.K. - SEE "GEORGE WASHING-
TON"
ANDRONOV, M. A STANDARD GRAMMAR OF
MODERN & CLASSICAL TAMIL.
K.V. ZVELEBIL, 361:VOL28#3-290
ANDRUS, D. DAYS WHEN THE HOUSE WAS
TOO SMALL.
M. LEVIN, 441:20OCT74-41
ANFUSO, N. & A. GIANUARIO. PREPARA-
ZIONE ALLA INTERPRETAZIONE DELLA
"POIĒSIS" MONTEVERDIANA.
D.A., 410(M&L):JAN73-96
ANGELOU, M. GATHER TOGETHER IN MY
NAME.
P. ADAMS, 61:JUN74-114
A. GOTTLIEB, 441:16JUN74-16
442(NY):15JUL74-87
ANGERMANN, N. STUDIEN ZUR LIVLAND-
POLITIK IVAN GROZNYJS.
W. KIRCHNER, 32:DEC73-802
ANGLADE, J. UN FRONT DE MARBRE.
B. KAY, 207(FR):OCT71-181
ANGLIN, J.M. THE GROWTH OF WORD
MEANING.
J.B. CARROLL, 399(MLJ):DEC72-527
L.B. CEBIK, 219(GAR):FALL72-389
E.V. CLARK, 350:MAR73-248
P.S. DALE, 399(MLJ):DEC72-529
ANGLIN, J.M. - SEE BRUNER, J.S.
ANGLO, S. MACHIAVELLI.*
F. GILBERT, 551(RENQ):SPRING72-
77
ANGOFF, C. SEASON OF MISTS.
S. KREITER, 287:JUN72-29
ANGOFF, C. & OTHERS, EDS. THE
DIAMOND ANTHOLOGY.
E.N. CHUILLEANÁIN, 159(DM):
WINTER/SPRING71/72-123
ANGRES, D. DIE BEZIEHUNGEN LUNAČAR-
SKIJS ZUR DEUTSCHEN LITERATUR.
W. BEITZ, 654(WB):9/1972-183
C.V. PONOMAREFF, 104:SUMMER72-
348
ANGULO IŃ'GUEZ, D. & A.E. PÉREZ SÁN-
CHEZ. HISTORIA DE LA PINTURA ES-
PAÑOLA: ESCUELA MADRILEÑA DEL
PRIMER TERCIO DEL SIGLO XVII.*
J. BROWN, 54:MAR72-97
ANKER, P. & A. ANDERSSON. THE ART
OF SCANDINAVIA. (VOLS 1&2)
A. POLAK, 135:APR72-290
"ANNUAIRE DE L'U.R.S.S. 1969."
J.N. HAZARD, 104:SPRING72-172
"THE ANNUAL OF THE BRITISH SCHOOL IN
ATHENS." (NO. 68, 1973)
617(TLS):13SEP74-984
ANOBILE, R.J., ED. THE MALTESE FAL-
CON.
W. FEAVER, 617(TLS):27DEC74-1471

ANSARI, K.H. JOHN WEBSTER.
B. BABINGTON, 447(N&Q):DEC72-472
R.G. HOWARTH, 402(MLR):APR73-384
ANSBACHER, L.J. PLEASE DON'T LEAVE
ME.
M. LEVIN, 441:29SEP74-40
ANSCHÜTZ, O. FRANZISKANISCHE MEN-
SCHEN.
R. MALTER, 342:BAND63HEFT4-514
ANSCOMBE, G.E.M. & G.H. VON WRIGHT -
SEE WITTGENSTEIN, L.
ANSELL, J. DYNASTY OF AIR.
M. LEVIN, 441:22DEC74-15
ANSLEY, C. THE HERESY OF WU HAN.
C.S. BURCHILL, 529(QQ):AUTUMN72-
411
J. DREYER, 293(JAST):FEB72-470
ANTAL, E. & J. HARTHAN - SEE KLING-
ENDER, F.
ANTHONY, E. THE OCCUPYING POWER.
617(TLS):18JAN74-61
ANTHONY, J.R. FRENCH BAROQUE MUSIC.
617(TLS):8MAR74-241
ANTHONY, M. CRICKET IN THE ROAD.
617(TLS):1MAR74-201
"LES ANTILLES."
D. KOENIG, 207(FR):FEB72-715
ANTON, H. MYTHOLOGISCHE EROTIK IN
KELLERS "SIEBEN LEGENDEN" UND IM
"SINNGEDICHT."*
J. SCHMIDT, 564:MAR72-66
ANTON, J.P., WITH G.L. KUSTAS, EDS.
ESSAYS IN ANCIENT GREEK PHILOSO-
PHY.*
D.Z. ANDRIOPOULOS, 484(PPR):DEC
72-276
J. DYBIKOWSKI, 154:SEP72-434
G.B. KERFERD, 123:DEC73-281
ANTONACI, A. RICERCHE SULL'ARISTO-
TELISMO DEL RINASCIMENTO: MARCAN-
TONIO ZIMARA. (VOL 1)
A. POPPI, 548(RCSF):OCT-DEC72-
467
ANTONICEK, T. MUSIK IM FESTSAAL DER
ÖSTERREICHISCHEN AKADEMIE DER WIS-
SENSCHAFTEN.
A.H. KING, 182:VOL25#21-747
ANTONIEWICZ, W. & OTHERS, EDS.
STUDIA PODHALAŃSKIE ORAZ BIBLIO-
GRAFIA PASTERSTWA TATR I PODHALA.
H. RÖSEL, 182:VOL25#12-445
ANTREASIAN, G.Z. & C. ADAMS. THE
TAMARIND BOOK OF LITHOGRAPHY.
A. FRANKENSTEIN, 55:MAR73-16
M.N. TABAK, 139:AUG72-8
ANTTILA, R. PROTO-INDO-EUROPEAN
SCHWEBEABLAUT.
F.O. LINDEMAN, 260(IF):BAND76-
254
J. SCHINDLER, 343:BAND15HEFT2-
146
AOKI, H. NEZ PERCE GRAMMAR.*
G.F. MEIER, 682(ZPSK):BAND24
HEFT6-538
M. SILVERSTEIN, 269(IJAL):JAN72-
62
AOKI, M.Y. IZUMO FUDOKI.
J. YOUNG, 293(JAST):MAY72-675
APARICIO LAURENCIO, A. JUAN CLEMEN-
TE ZENEA.
H. LINDO, 263:JAN-MAR73-100

APAT-ECHEBARNE, A. NOTICIAS Y VIE-
JOS TEXTOS DE LA "LINGUA NAVARROR-
UM."
    D. GIFFORD, 402(MLR):APR73-427
APEL, W. THE HISTORY OF KEYBOARD
MUSIC TO 1700. (TRANS & REV BY
H. TISCHLER)
    H.F., 410(M&L):JUL73-345
APOLLINAIRE, G. APOLLINAIRE ON ART.
(L.C. BREUNIG, ED)
    T. CLARK, 592:JUL/AUG72-55
    M. WILLIAMSON, 96:OCT/NOV72-86
APONTE, B.B. ALFONSO REYES & SPAIN.
    J.W. ROBB, 263:JAN-MAR73-101
APPADORAI, A. ESSAYS IN INDIAN POLI-
TICS & FOREIGN POLICY.
    N.D. PALMER, 293(JAST):AUG72-973
APPASAMY, J. ABANINDRANATH TAGORE
& THE ART OF HIS TIMES.
    R. LIPSEY, 57:VOL34#2/3-262
APPEL, B. THE DEATH MASTER.
    T. STURGEON, 441:10NOV74-50
APPIAN. APPIANI, "BELLORUM CIVILIUM
LIBER QUINTUS."* (E. GABBA, ED &
TRANS)
    P. CHANTRAINE, 555:VOL46FASC2-
313
APPLEBY, J. SKATE.
    S. O'CONNELL, 418(MR):WINTER73-
190
    639(VQR):SPRING72-XLIX
APPLEMAN, P., ED. DARWIN.
    P.A. MOODY, 637(VS):SEP71-100
APPLETON, A. MARY ANN COTTON.
    617(TLS):4JAN74-18
APTEKAR, J. ICONS OF JUSTICE.*
    W.N. KNIGHT, 128(CE):DEC72-440
    M. MURRIN, 405(MP):MAY73-342
APTER, M.J. THE COMPUTER SIMULATION
OF BEHAVIOUR.
    B.A. FARRELL, 479(PHQ):JAN72-76
APULEIUS. L'AMOUR DE CUPIDO ET DE
PSICHE.
    D. WILSON, 208(FS):JAN73-52
AQUARONE, A., ED. MEMORIE DELLA
VITA E DELLE PEREGRINAZIONI DEL
FIORENTINO FILIPPO MAZZEI.
    E.B., 228(GSLI):VOL149FASC466/
467-464
AQUILECCHIA, G., S.N. CRISTEA & S.
RALPHS, EDS. COLLECTED ESSAYS ON
ITALIAN LANGUAGE & LITERATURE PRE-
SENTED TO KATHLEEN SPEIGHT.
    400(MLN):JAN72-161
ARAGON, L. LE MOUVEMENT PERPÉTUEL.
    M·A· CAWS, 207(FR):OCT71-184
ARAKIE, M. THE BROKEN SWORD OF
JUSTICE.
    617(TLS):11JAN74-34
ARATÓ, E. KELET-EURÓPA TÖRTÉNETE A
19. SZÁZAD ELSŐ FELÉBEN.
    S. BORSODY, 32:JUN73-415
    L. PÉTER, 575(SEER):JAN73-132
ARBELECHE, J. LOS INSTANTES.
    H. LINDO, 263:APR-JUN73-206
ARBERRY, A.J., ED. RELIGION IN THE
MIDDLE EAST.
    E.J. JURJI, 318(JAOS):OCT-DEC72-
531
ARBIB, M.A. THEORIES OF ABSTRACT
AUTOMATA.
    A. SALOMAA, 316:JUN72-412
"ARBUTHNOTIANA."
    566:SPRING73-109

ARCHER, F. MUDDY BOOTS & SUNDAY
SUITS.
    617(TLS):29MAR74-348
ARCHER, M. COMPANY DRAWINGS IN THE
INDIA OFFICE LIBRARY.
    T. FALK, 135:SEP72-63
ARCHER, W.G. INDIAN PAINTINGS FROM
THE PUNJAB HILLS.
    J.K. GALBRAITH, 441:20JAN74-19
ARCHER, W.G. KALIGHAT PAINTING.
    G. EYRE, 135:JAN72-64
ARCHAIMBAULT, C. THE NEW YEAR CERE-
MONY AT BASAK (SOUTH LAOS).
    C.F. KEYES, 293(JAST):MAY72-611
ARCHIBALD, L., WITH M. SCHOLL - SEE
KLYUCHEVSKY, V.
ARCHIMEDES. ARCHIMĒDE, "DE LA
SPHÈRE ET DU CYLINDRE, LA MESURE
DU CERCLE, SUR LES CONOÏDES ET LES
SPHÉROIDES."* (C. MUGLER, ED &
TRANS)
    D.R. DICKS, 123:MAR73-28
"ARCTOS." (VOL 6)
    J. ANDRÉ, 555:VOL46FASC1-172
ARDENER, E., ED. SOCIAL ANTHROPOL-
OGY & LANGUAGE.
    A. MOULIN, 556(RLV):1972/2-219
    G·C· RUMP, 182:VOL25#1/2-59
ARDIES, T. KOSYGIN IS COMING.
    N. CALLENDAR, 441:17FEB74-33
ARDILL, J. THE NEW CITIZEN'S GUIDE
TO TOWN & COUNTRY PLANNING.
    617(TLS):9AUG74-864
ARDITI, B. DIARIO DI FIRENZE E DI
ALTRE PARTI DELLA CRISTIANITÀ
(1574-1579). (R. CANTAGALLI, ED)
    L.M. FERRARI, 276:SUMMER72-260
ARDOIN, J. & G. FITZGERALD. CALLAS.
    P. CONRAD, 617(TLS):20DEC74-1449
ARENAS, R. HALLUCINATIONS.
    J.I. CASTELEIRO, 37:OCT72-37
ARENDT, H. CRISES OF THE REPUBLIC.
    R. NISBET, 639(VQR):SUMMER72-449
ARENDT, H. ON VIOLENCE.*
    J-L. BOURGET, 98:OCT72-917
ARENDT, H. RAHEL VARNHAGEN. (REV)
    L. DICKSTEIN, 441:24NOV74-27
ARETHAS. ARETHAE "SCRIPTA MINORA."
(VOL 1) (L.G. WESTERINK, ED)
    J. IRIGOIN, 555:VOL46FASC1-132
ARGAN, G.C. THE RENAISSANCE CITY.*
    K.W. FORSTER, 576:MAR72-67
    G.L. HERSEY, 56:SUMMER72-180
ARGÜELLES, J.A. CHARLES HENRY & THE
FORMATION OF A PSYCHOPHYSICAL
AESTHETIC.
    C.E. GAUSS, 290(JAAC):SUMMER73-
554
    C. WILSON, 114(CHIR):VOL24#4-167
DEGLI ARIENTI, G.S. - SEE UNDER
SABADINO DEGLI ARIENTI, G.
ARIÈS, P. CENTURIES OF CHILDHOOD.
    L. STONE, 453:14NOV74-25
ARIÈS, P. WESTERN ATTITUDES TOWARD
DEATH.
    R. DARNTON, 453:13JUN74-11
    J. KLEIN, 31(ASCH):AUTUMN74-678
    M.G. MICHAELSON, 441:21JUL74-6
ARIOSTO, L. ORLANDO FURIOSO. (G.
WALDMAN, TRANS) ORLANDO FURIOSO.
(R. HODGENS, TRANS)
    C.P. BRAND, 362:23MAY74-668

ARP, H. GESAMMELTE GEDICHTE. (VOL
2)
R. LAST, 617(TLS):18OCT74-1160
ARP, H. & OTHERS. DADA GEDICHTE.
S. FAUCHEREAU, 98:AUG/SEP72-752
ARP, J. COLLECTED FRENCH WRITINGS.
W. FEAVER, 362:28MAR74-411
ARRABAL, F. THÉÂTRE DE GUERILLA.
R. COHN, 207(FR):OCT71-182
ARRIGHI, G. & J. SAUL. ESSAYS ON
THE POLITICAL ECONOMY OF AFRICA.
A.S. KANYA-FORSTNER, 99:MAY/JUN
74-54
ARRIGHI, M. DADDY PIG.
A. BROYARD, 441:3APR74-35
ARRIVÉ, M. & J-C. CHEVALIER. LA
GRAMMAIRE.*
A. LORIAN, 545(RPH):NOV72-407
ARROM, J.J. HISPANOAMÉRICA.
E.D. TERRY, 399(MLJ):DEC72-536
ARROYO, C.M. - SEE UNDER MORÓN ARRO-
YO, C.
ARROYO, J. DEDOS.
E. ECHEVARRÍA, 263:OCT-DEC73-468
ARSLAN, E. VENETIAN GOTHIC ARCHI-
TECTURE.
N. HALL, 135:JUN72-151
"ART PRICES CURRENT." (VOL 48)
617(TLS):15MAR74-272
"ART-LANGUAGE."
W. FEAVER, 364:DEC73/JAN74-114
ARTAUD, A. COLLECTED WORKS.* (VOLS
1-4)
A. SEYMOUR, 364:JUN/JUL72-137
"THE ARTE OF ENGLISH POESIE."
A. BONGIORNO, 551(RENQ):WINTER
72-448
ARTECHE, M. PARA UN TIEMPO TAN
BREVE.
H. LINDO, 263:APR-JUN73-207
ARTEMOV, A. & OTHERS, EDS. KAZNIMYE
SUMASSHCHESTVIEM.
C. BIRD, 550(RUSR):APR72-175
ARTIGUES, D. EL OPUS DEI EN ESPAÑA.
J. GEORGEL, 98:FEB72-183
ARTSIKHOVSKY, A.V. & OTHERS, EDS.
OCHERKI RUSSKOI KUL'TURY XIII-XV
VEKOV.
N. ANDREYEV, 32:DEC73-800
ARVON, H. LUDWIG FEUERBACH OU LA
TRANSFORMATION DU SACRÉ.
H. DUSSORT, 542:JUL-SEP72-351
ARVON, H. L'ESTHÉTIQUE MARXISTE.
D.A. GRIFFITHS, 290(JAAC):WINTER
71-270
ARVON, H. LA PHILOSOPHIE DU TRAVAIL.
C. SCHUWER, 542:OCT-DEC72-492
"AS I CROSSED A BRIDGE OF DREAMS."*
(I. MORRIS, TRANS)
M. TAHARA, 293(JAST):FEB72-407
ASCHENBRENNER, K. THE CONCEPTS OF
VALUE.
A. MERCIER, 182:VOL25#17/18-581
ASCHER, A. PAVEL AXELROD & THE DE-
VELOPMENT OF MENSHEVISM.
B. SAPIR, 32:DEC73-814
ASENJO SEDANO, J. LOS GUERREROS.
M.S. PEDEN, 238:SEP72-594
ASHBERY, J. THREE POEMS.*
639(VQR):WINTER73-XVI
ASHBERY, J., L. HARWOOD & T. RAWORTH.
PENGUIN MODERN POETS 19.
T. EAGLETON, 565:VOL13#1-76

ASHBROOK, J.B. BE/COME COMMUNITY.
R. HESS, 186(ETC.):DEC72-435
ASHBY, L. THE SPEARLESS LEADER.
B. NOGGLE, 579(SAQ):SPRING73-328
ASHBY, M.K. THE CHANGING ENGLISH
VILLAGE.
617(TLS):23AUG74-900
ASHER, J.A. A SHORT DESCRIPTIVE
GRAMMAR OF MIDDLE HIGH GERMAN.
R.N. COMBRIDGE & A.T. HATTO,
220(GL&L):JUL73-341
ASHFORD, J. THE COLOUR OF VIOLENCE.
N. CALLENDAR, 441:20OCT74-42
ASHFORTH, A. THOMAS HENRY HUXLEY.
W.J. BAKER, 577(SHR):WINTER72-91
ASHLEY, M. THE AGE OF ABSOLUTISM
1648-1775.
617(TLS):21JUN74-664
ASHLEY, M. CHARLES II.
T.W. PERRY, 656(WMQ):JAN73-178
ASHMEAD, A.H. & K.M. PHILLIPS, JR.
CORPUS VASORUM ANTIQUORUM: THE
ELLA RIEGEL MEMORIAL MUSEUM, BRYN
MAWR COLLEGE; ATTIC RED-FIGURED
VASES.
R.M. COOK, 123:DEC73-289
R. HIGGINS, 39:MAR72-231
ASHTON, D. A JOSEPH CORNELL ALBUM.
H. KRAMER, 441:29DEC74-1
ASHTON, D. THE LIFE & TIMES OF THE
NEW YORK SCHOOL.*
C. HARRISON, 592:NOV72-206
ASHTON, D. MODERN AMERICAN SCULP-
TURE.
J. DE COUX, 363:MAY72-101
ASHTON, D. THE NEW YORK SCHOOL.*
A. FRANKENSTEIN, 55:OCT73-65
B. GELFANT, 31(ASCH):WINTER73/74-
164
ASHTON, T.L. - SEE LORD BYRON
ASIEGBU, J.U.J. SLAVERY & THE POLI-
TICS OF LIBERATION 1787-1861.*
R.W. SMITH, 637(VS):MAR72-381
ASIHENE, E.V. INTRODUCTION TO TRA-
DITIONAL ART OF WEST AFRICA.
C. HARRISON, 592:JUL/AUG72-52
ASIMOV, I. ASIMOV ON ASTRONOMY.
617(TLS):27SEP74-1048
ASIMOV, I., ED. WHERE DO WE GO FROM
HERE?*
617(TLS):4JAN74-5
ASIMOV, I. & R. MC CALL. OUR
WORLD IN SPACE.
617(TLS):26JUL74-815
ASLANAPA, O. TURKISH ART & ARCHI-
TECTURE.*
M. LEVEY, 39:DEC72-562
J. WARREN, 46:OCT72-256
ASLIN, E. THE AESTHETIC MOVEMENT.*
A. BRIGGS, 637(VS):SEP71-108
ASMUTH, B. LOHENSTEIN UND TACITUS.*
P. SKRINE, 402(MLR):APR73-450
J. VON STACKELBERG, 52:BAND7
HEFT2/3-320
"ASPECTS OF SOCIOLOGY."
J. SHAPIRO, 617(TLS):4OCT74-1094
ASPEL, M. POLLY WANTS A ZEBRA.
D. THOMAS, 362:19&26DEC74-846
ASPILLERA, P.S. BASIC TAGALOG FOR
FOREIGNERS & NON-TAGALOGS.*
J.D. BOWEN, 318(JAOS):JAN-MAR72-
164
ASPINALL, A. - SEE GEORGE IV

12

AULOTTE, R., ED. PLUTARQUE EN
FRANCE AU XVIE SIÈCLE.*
C. BÉNÉ, 535(RHL):JUL-AUG72-704
I. SILVER, 551(RENQ):WINTER72-
461
AURENHAMMER, H. J.E. FISCHER VON
ERLACH.
617(TLS):24MAY74-549
AUROBINDO, S. THE MIND OF LIGHT.
N. CHOBOT, 485(PE&W):APR72-237
AUSTEN, J. MANSFIELD PARK. (J.
LUCAS, ED)
L.W. BROWN, 173(ECS):SUMMER73-
531
AUSTEN, J. SENSE & SENSIBILITY. (C.
LAMONT, ED) PRIDE & PREJUDICE.
(F.W. BRADBROOK, ED)
L.W. BROWN, 173(ECS):SUMMER73-
530
AUSTER, H. LOCAL HABITATIONS.*
S. HUDSON, 577(SHR):WINTER72-93
U.C. KNOEPFLMACHER, 445(NCF):
MAR73-484
I. MILNER, 637(VS):SEP71-99
K. WATSON, 541(RES):FEB72-96
AUSTIN, A. T.S. ELIOT.*
J. KORG, 290(JAAC):WINTER72-274
C.H. SMITH, 659:SPRING74-277
AUSTIN, C. - SEE MENANDER
AUSTIN, G. THE LIBRARY OF JEAN
GROLIER: A PRELIMINARY CATALOGUE.
H.M. NIXON, 78(BC):SPRING72-134
AUSTIN, N. THE GREEK HISTORIANS.
S.J. SIMON, 125:FEB73-201
AUSTIN, R.G. - SEE VERGIL
AUSTIN, W.B. A COMPUTER-AIDED TECH-
NIQUE FOR STYLISTIC DISCRIMINATION.
R.L. WIDMANN, 570(SQ):SPRING72-
214
AUSTIN, W.W., ED. DEBUSSY: PRELUDE
TO "THE AFTERNOON OF A FAUN."
G.W. HOPKINS, 415:DEC73-1237
AUTENRIETH, J., ED. INGELHEIM AM
RHEIN.
A. REINLE, 182:VOL25#7/8-242
"AUTHORITY, CONSCIENCE & DISSENT."
S. RAE, 368:MAR72-94
AUTY, R., J.L.I. FENNELL & J.S.G.
SIMMONS, EDS. OXFORD SLAVONIC
PAPERS. (NEW SER, VOL 3)
G. DE MALLAC, 550(RUSR):OCT72-
426
AUTY, R., J.L.I. FENNELL & J.S.G.
SIMMONS, EDS. OXFORD SLAVONIC
PAPERS. (NEW SER, VOL 4)
N.V. RIASANOVSKY, 550(RUSR):JUL
72-318
205(FMLS):JUL72-288
AVALLE-ARCE, J.B. - SEE DE CERVANTES
SAAVEDRA, M.
AVANESOV, R.I., ED. MATERIALY I
ISSLEDOVANIJA PO OBŠČESLAVJANSKOMU
LINGVISTIČESKOMU ATLASU.
M. ONATZKY-MALINE, 353:15OCT72-
121
AVERCH, H.A., J.E. KOHLER & F.H.
DENTON. THE MATRIX OF POLICY IN
THE PHILIPPINES.
42(AR):SPRING/SUMMER72-248
AVERY, C. FLORENTINE RENAISSANCE
SCULPTURE.*
J. SHAPLEY, 127:SUMMER73-466

AVERY, D. NOT ON QUEEN VICTORIA'S
BIRTHDAY.
617(TLS):7JUN74-614
AVERY, G. THE ECHOING GREEN.
442(NY):7OCT74-178
AVICENNE, P. BIBLIOGRAPHICAL SER-
VICES THROUGHOUT THE WORLD, 1960-
1964.
D.S. PADY, 14:JAN72-67
AVNI, A.A. THE BIBLE & ROMANTICISM.*
E. SHAFFER, 402(MLR):APR73-461
AVRICH, P. RUSSIAN REBELS, 1600-
1800.*
J.T. ALEXANDER, 32:JUN73-375
AWOONOR, K. THIS EARTH, MY BROTHER.
C. ACHEBE, 618:#41-69
AXELOS, K. EINFÜHRUNG IN EIN KÜNF-
TIGES DENKEN.
J.D.C., 543:DEC71-349
AXELOS, K. LE JEU DU MONDE.*
J.P. FORGET, 154:MAR72-173
AXTELL, J.L. - SEE LOCKE, J.
AXTON, R. EUROPEAN DRAMA OF THE
EARLY MIDDLE AGES.
A.C. CAWLEY, 617(TLS):1NOV74-
1232
AXTON, R. & J. STEVENS - SEE "MEDIE-
VAL FRENCH PLAYS"
AYALA, F. EL RAPTO.* (P.Z. BORING,
ED)
A.M. FAGUNDO, 399(MLJ):FEB72-102
DE AYALA, R.P. - SEE UNDER PÉREZ DE
AYALA, R.
AYANDELE, E.A. HOLY JOHNSON.
A.H.M. KIRK-GREENE, 69:JAN72-71
AYER, A.J. THE CENTRAL QUESTIONS OF
PHILOSOPHY.
D. PEARS, 362:25APR74-540
617(TLS):4JAN74-17
AYER, A.J. THE ORIGINS OF PRAGMA-
TISM.*
G.M. BRODSKY, 543:DEC71-262
AYER, A.J. PROBABILITY & EVIDENCE.
H. LOMAS, 364:OCT/NOV72-137
M. VON THUN, 63:AUG73-171
AYER, A.J. RUSSELL & MOORE.*
S.G. CLARKE, 154:DEC72-645
A.R. WHITE, 479(PHQ):JAN72-68
C.H. WHITELEY, 393(MIND):OCT72-
620
AYERS, J. THE JAMES A. DE ROTHS-
CHILD COLLECTION AT WADDESDON
MANOR: ORIENTAL PORCELAIN.
F.J.B. WATSON, 39:JUL72-86
AYERS, W. CHANG CHIH-TUNG & EDUCA-
TIONAL REFORM IN CHINA.
K. BIGGERSTAFF, 293(JAST):NOV71-
187
AYERST, D. THE MANCHESTER GUARDIAN.
J.O. BAYLEN, 637(VS):DEC72-245
AYLMER, G.E. THE STATE'S SERVANTS.
617(TLS):11JAN74-27
AYRTON, M. THE MIDAS CONSEQUENCE.
W. FEAVER, 362:29AUG74-285
617(TLS):26JUL74-813
AZAD, M. TARJUMAN-UL-QUR'AN. (VOL
4)
A.H. KHAN, 273(IC):JUL72-279
AZAÑA, M. ENSAYOS SOBRE VALERA.
(J. MARICHAL, ED)
C. DE COSTER, 238:DEC72-968
AZARPAY, G. URARTIAN ART & ARTI-
FACTS.
E.L. KOHLER, 57:VOL34#2/3-255

AZEEZ PASHA, M., COMP. UNION CATA-
LOGUE OF ARABIC & PERSIAN MEDICAL
MANUSCRIPTS IN THE LIBRARIES OF
HYDERABAD.
S. JADON, 318(JAOS):JAN-MAR72-
132
DE AZEREDO PERDIGÃO, J. CALOUSTE
GULBENKIAN - COLLECTOR.*
K. ROBERTS, 90:JUN72-405
DE AZEVEDO, F. PRINCIPIOS DE SOCIO-
LOGIA. (VOLS 9, 11 & 13)
R. LENOIR, 542:OCT-DEC72-492
DE AZEVEDO, C. UM ARTISTA ITALIANO
EM GOA, PLÁCIDO FRANCESCO RAMPONI
E O TÚMULO DE S. FR.° XAVIER. A
ARTE DE GOA, DAMÃO E DIU.
J.F. BUTLER, 576:OCT72-238
DE AZEVEDO, V.D.V. - SEE VARELA, F.
DE AZEVEDO FILHO, L.A. POESIA E
ESTILO DE CECÍLIA MEIRELES.
G.M. MOSER, 238:DEC72-973
DE AZEVEDO FILHO, L.A., J. DE DIAS
DE CARVALHO & O. GUTERRES DA SIL-
VEIRA, EDS. I CONGRESSO BRASILEI-
RO DE LÍNGUA E LITERATURA.
G. MOSER, 238:MAR72-183
AZIKIWE, N. MY ODYSSEY.
A.H.M. KIRK-GREENE, 69:JAN72-71
AZIZ, M. - SEE JAMES, H.
AL-AZM, S.J. THE ORIGINS OF KANT'S
ARGUMENTS IN THE ANTINOMIES.*
M.J. SCOTT-TAGGART, 518:JAN73-1
AZUELA, M. EPISTOLARIO Y ARCHIVO.
E. PUPO-WALKER, 240(HR):SUMMER72-
356
AZUELA, M. LOS DE ABAJO. (J.E.
ENGLEKIRK & L.B. KIDDLE, EDS)
N.F. ANGEROSA, 238:MAR72-195

VAN DEN BAAR, A.H. A RUSSIAN CHURCH
SLAVONIC KANONNIK, 1331-1332.*
J. JAHN, 353:1NOV72-122
BABB, L. THE MORAL COSMOS OF "PARA-
DISE LOST."*
D.D.C. CHAMBERS, 541(RES):MAY72-
207
W.B. HUNTER, JR., 551(RENQ):SUM-
MER72-246
B.K. LEWALSKI, 191(ELN):SEP72-46
R.H. WEST, 405(MP):MAY73-360
BABCOCK, S.S. THE SYNTAX OF SPANISH
REFLEXIVE VERBS.
J.N. GREEN, 545(RPH):AUG72-174
R.L. HADLICH, 350:JUN73-494
BABEL, I. BENYA KRIK, THE GANGSTER
& OTHER STORIES. (A. YARMOLINSKY,
ED)
C.E. LLOYD, 573(SSF)WINTER72-98
BABITZ, E. EVE'S HOLLYWOOD.
P. ADAMS, 61:APR74-120
BABLET, D. & J. JACQUOT, EDS. LES
VOIES DE LA CRÉATION THÉÂTRALE.
(VOL 3)
D. GRONAU, 182:VOL25#21-745
BABOLIN, A. ESSERE E ALTERITA IN
MARTIN BUBER.
A.M., 543:SEP71-120
BABSON, M. THE STALKING LAMB.
617(TLS):5APR74-375
BABUT, D. - SEE PLUTARCH
BACCOUCHE, T. & OTHERS. TRAVAUX DE
PHONOLOGIE.
G. INEICHEN, 260(IF):BAND76-215

BACH, R. JONATHAN LIVINGSTON SEA-
GULL.
S. O'CONNELL, 418(MR):WINTER73-
190
BACHELET, M. SYSTÈMES FONCIERS ET
RÉFORMES AGRAIRES EN AFRIQUE
NOIRE.
J. VANDERLINDEN, 69:APR72-164
BACHMANN, J. & S. VON MOOS. SWISS
ARCHITECTURE.
R. BANHAM, 54:DEC72-565
BÄCKMAN, S. THIS SINGULAR TALE.
M. GOLDEN, 481(PQ):JUL72-689
J. GURY, 549(RLC):OCT-DEC72-614
BACKUS, J. THE ACOUSTICAL FOUNDA-
TIONS OF MUSIC.
J.K. RANDALL, 513:SPRING-SUMMER
70-149
W. SLAWSON, 513:SPRING-SUMMER70-
143
BACON, E. ARCHAEOLOGY: DISCOVERIES
IN THE 1960'S.
G. DALES, 318(JAOS):OCT-DEC72-
505
"BACON, GRAND PALAIS, PARIS."
D. SOUTHALL, 592:MAR72-139
BACQUE, J. A MAN OF TALENT.*
P. STEVENS, 628:SPRING73-95
DE BADAJOZ, D.S. - SEE UNDER SÁNCHEZ
DE BADAJOZ, D.
BADALONI, N. TOMMASO CAMPANELLA.
E. NAMER, 542:JAN-MAR72-104
BADER, D. FIGHT FOR THE SKY.
617(TLS):4JAN74-18
BADER, J. CRYSTAL LAND.
639(VQR):AUTUMN73-CXLV
BADESCO, L. LA GÉNÉRATION POÉTIQUE
DE 1860.
P. MOREAU, 557(RSH):OCT-DEC72-
617
BADGER, C.R. THE REVEREND CHARLES
STRONG & THE AUSTRALIAN CHURCH.
F.B. SMITH, 381:JUN72-229
BADGLEY, J. POLITICS AMONG BURMANS.
L. PYE, 293(JAST):MAY72-723
BADIAN, E. PUBLICANS & SINNERS.*
F. LASSERRE, 182:VOL25#21-762
BADIOU, A. LE CONCEPT DE MODÈLE.
Y. GAUTHIER, 154:SEP72-460
BAENDER, P. - SEE TWAIN, M.
BAER, G., ED. ASIAN & AFRICAN STUD-
IES. (VOL 3)
C.E. FARAH, 318(JAOS):JAN-MAR72-
131
BAER, G. STUDIES IN THE SOCIAL
HISTORY OF MODERN EGYPT.
G.J. KOURY, 318(JAOS):JAN-MAR72-
122
BAERT, T. LE MOT, UNITÉ À DEUX
FACES DANS L'OPTIQUE PRÉLINGUIS-
TIQUE DES "PHILOSOPHES" ET DES
"LITTÉRATURES."
G. CLERICO, 209(FM):JAN72-62
BAETKE, W. WÖRTERBUCH ZUR ALTNORD-
ISCHEN PROSALITERATUR.
H. UECKER, 680(ZDP):BAND91HEFT3-
411
BAETZHOLD, H.G. MARK TWAIN & JOHN
BULL.*
R.B. BICKLEY, JR., 579(SAQ):
WINTER73-171
BÁEZ, C.C.R. - SEE UNDER RAMÍREZ
BÁEZ, C.C.

BAGEHOT, W. THE COLLECTED WORKS OF
WALTER BAGEHOT. (VOLS 5-8) (N.
ST. JOHN-STEVAS, ED)
A. RYAN, 617(TLS):27DEC74-1453
BAGLEY, D. THE TIGHTROPE MEN.*
N. CALLENDAR, 441:8DEC74-44
BAGULEY, D. FÉCONDITÉ D'EMILE ZOLA.
617(TLS):11OCT74-1135
BAGWELL, P.S. THE TRANSPORT REVOLU-
TION FROM 1770.
617(TLS):16AUG74-883
BAHLMAN, D.W.R. - SEE HAMILTON, E.W.
BAHM, A.J. POLARITY & ORGANICITY.
D.R.P., 543:JUN72-745
BAHNS, J. JOHANNES OTZEN 1839-1911.*
W. WEYRES, 182:VOL25#21-751
BAHR, E. DIE IRONIE IM SPÄTWERK
GOETHES "...DIESE SEHR ERNSTEN
SCHERZE..."
H.A. MAIER, 301(JEGP):JUL73-413
BAHR, E. & R.G. KUNZER. GEORG LU-
KÁCS.
R.N. BERKI, 575(SEER):OCT73-625
BAHR, E-J. A NICE NEIGHBOURHOOD.
617(TLS):1FEB74-116
BAÏCHE, A. - SEE DU DARTAS, G.S.
BAIER, K. & N. RESCHER. VALUES &
THE FUTURE.*
G.A. WELTY, 321:WINTER72[VOL6#4]-
311
DE BAÏF, J-A. POEMS. (M. QUAINTON,
ED)
W.J. BECK, 207(FR):OCT71-276
J. PINEAUX, 557(RSH):OCT-DEC72-
604
BAIGELL, M. THE AMERICAN SCENE.
THOMAS HART BENTON.
J.R. MELLOW, 441:1DEC74-103
BAILBÉ, J. AGRIPPA D'AUBIGNÉ, POÈTE
DES "TRAGIQUES."*
R. REGOSIN, 546(RR):FEB72-45
BAILBÉ, J-M. BERLIOZ, ARTISTE ET
ÉCRIVAIN DANS LES "MÉMOIRES."
H.J.M., 410(M&L):OCT73-457
BAILBÉ, J-M. LE ROMAN ET LA MUSIQUE
EN FRANCE SOUS LA MONARCHIE DE
JUILLET.*
M. MILNER, 535(RHL):MAY-JUN72-
532
N. SUCKLING, 208(FS):JAN73-86
A.J. WRIGHT, JR., 207(FR):OCT71-
258
BAILEY, A.G. THANKS FOR A DROWNED
ISLAND.
M.T. LANE, 198:WINTER74-95
BAILEY, D. IF YOU HUM ME A FEW BARS
I MIGHT REMEMBER THE TUNE.
D. DAYMOND, 296:VOL3#2-103
BAILEY, D.R.S. - SEE UNDER SHACKLE-
TON BAILEY, D.R.
BAILEY, J.O. THE POETRY OF THOMAS
HARDY.*
M. WILLIAMS, 541(RES):MAY72-231
BAILEY, R. THE EUROPEAN COMMUNITY
IN THE WORLD.
617(TLS):15FEB74-151
BAILEY, R.W. & L. DOLEŽEL, EDS. AN
ANNOTATED BIBLIOGRAPHY OF STATIS-
TICAL STYLISTICS.*
R.S. WACHAL, 599:WINTER72-66
BAILEY, T. THE PROCESSIONS OF SARUM
& THE WESTERN CHURCH.
J.H. CREHAN, 382(MAE):1973/2-195
R.W. PFAFF, 589:APR73-337

BAILY, L. GILBERT & SULLIVAN.
(BRITISH TITLE: GILBERT & SULLIVAN
& THEIR WORLD.)
H. BEVINGTON, 441:1DEC74-86
617(TLS):11JAN74-29
BAILYN, B. THE ORDEAL OF THOMAS
HUTCHINSON.
E.S. MORGAN, 453:21MAR74-7
BAINBRIDGE, B. THE BOTTLE FACTORY
OUTING.
S. CLAPP, 617(TLS):1NOV74-1217
D.A.N. JONES, 362:24OCT74-553
BAINBRIDGE, B. HARRIET SAID...* A
WEEKEND WITH CLAUD. THE DRESS-
MAKER.* ANOTHER PART OF THE WOOD.
K. MILLER, 453:16MAY74-25
BAINBRIDGE, B. THE SECRET GLASS.
P. ADAMS, 61:SEP74-103
A. BROYARD, 441:21AUG74-43
G. GODWIN, 441:15SEP74-4
BAINTON, R.H. ERASMUS OF CHRISTEN-
DOM.*
F.M. HIGMAN, 402(MLR):JUL73-649
BAIR, F.H., JR. PLANNING CITIES.
(V. CURTIS, ED)
H.H. WAECHTER, 44:SEP72-12
BAIRD, G. ALVAR AALTO.
R.F. JORDAN, 46:FEB72-129
BAIRD, I. WASTE HERITAGE.
M. HORN, 99:OCT74-36
BAIRD, M-T. A LESSON IN LOVE.
M. LEVIN, 441:24FEB74-40
BAKER, A.R.H. & R.A. BUTLIN, EDS.
STUDIES OF FIELD SYSTEMS IN THE
BRITISH ISLES.
617(TLS):15FEB74-152
BAKER, C. ERNEST HEMINGWAY.
R. ASSELINEAU, 189(EA):APR-JUN72-
334
H-J. KANN, 430(NS):NOV72-674
BAKER, D., ED. SANCTITY & SECULAR-
ITY.
617(TLS):1MAR74-221
BAKER, D.V. COMPANY OF THREE.
617(TLS):3MAY74-483
BAKER, E. POCOCK & PITT.
V. CUNNINGHAM, 617(TLS):29NOV74-
1336
BAKER, E. UNREQUITED LOVES.
M. MEWSHAW, 441:3MAR74-4
617(TLS):5APR74-357
BAKER, H., ED. FOUR ESSAYS ON
ROMANCE.
J.A. WITTREICH, JR., 223:SEP72-
307
BAKER, H. & OTHERS. NEW SHORT PLAYS:
3.
A. RENDLE, 157:AUTUMN72-84
BAKER, H.A. LONG BLACK SONG.
P.R. KLOTMAN, 659:SPRING74-283
BAKER, J.R. RACE.
617(TLS):19APR74-423
BAKER, L. JOHN MARSHALL.
K. NEWMYER, 441:6OCT74-6
A. WHITMAN, 441:3SEP74-39
BAKER, M., WITH S. BROMPTON. EXCLUS-
IVE!
J.D. SMITH, 441:17NOV74-4
BAKER, N. GOVERNMENT & CONTRACTORS.
P.G. MACKESY, 656(WMQ):JUL72-501
BAKER, R.D. JUDICIAL REVIEW IN
MEXICO.
P. KELSO, 50(ARQ):SUMMER72-179

BAKER, T.H. THE MEMPHIS COMMERCIAL-
APPEAL.
  639(VQR):SUMMER72-XCIII
BAKHTIN, M. PROBLEMS OF DOSTOEVSKY'S
POETICS.* [SHOWN IN PREV UNDER
BAKHTINE, M. & UNDER FRENCH TITLE:
PROBLÈMES DE LA POÉTIQUE DE DOS-
TOÏEVSKI.]
  617(TLS):29MAR74-346
BAKHUIZEN, S.C. SALGANEUS & THE
FORTIFICATIONS ON ITS MOUNTAINS.
  N.G.L. HAMMOND, 123:MAR73-107
BAKKER, J.J.M. CONSTANT EN VARIABEL.
  J.G. KOOIJ, 204(FDL):JUN72-120
BAKUNIN, M. SELECTED WRITINGS. (A.
LEHNING, ED)
  617(TLS):11JAN74-26
BALADI, N. LA PENSÉE DE PLOTIN.*
  J-L. POIRIER, 542:JAN-MAR72-61
BALAKIAN, A. ANDRÉ BRETON.*
  J. HILL, 290(JAAC):FALL72-126
  639(VQR):WINTER72-XV
BALAKIAN, A. SURREALISM.* (REV)
  C.A. HACKETT, 208(FS):JUL73-355
BALAWYDER, A. CANADIAN-SOVIET RELA-
TIONS BETWEEN THE WORLD WARS.
  G. ROSEME, 32:MAR73-171
BALD, R.C. JOHN DONNE.* (W. MIL-
GATE, ED)
  N. ALEXANDER, 447(N&Q):AUG72-316
  K.J. HÖLTGEN, 38(DAND90HEFT4 532
  A. LOW, 568(SCN):FALL-WINTER73-
  77
  D. NOVARR, 551(RENQ):SPRING72-
  111
BALDICK, R. DINNER AT MAGNY'S.
  639(VQR):SPRING72-XLIX
BALDINGER, K. TEORÍA SEMÁNTICA.
  A.M. BARRENECHEA, 545(RPH):NOV72-
  396
BALDINI, A.E. IL PENSIERO GIOVANILE
DI JOHN LOCKE.
  E. NAMER, 542:APR-JUN72-214
BALDRY, H.C. THE GREEK TRAGIC THE-
ATRE.
  E.W. WHITTLE, 123:DEC73-276
BALDUINO, A., ED. CANTARI DEL TRE-
CENTO.
  M.M., 228(GSLI):VOL149FASC465-
  142
BALDWIN, J. IF BEALE STREET COULD
TALK.
  A. BROYARD, 441:17MAY74-43
  T.R. EDWARDS, 453:13JUN74-37
  J.C. OATES, 441:19MAY74-1
  D. THOMAS, 362:25JUL74-125
  442(NY):8JUL74-79
  617(TLS):21JUN74-656
BALDWIN, J.W. & R.A. GOLDTHWAITE,
EDS. UNIVERSITIES IN POLITICS.
  639(VQR):AUTUMN72-CXLIX
BALFOUR, M. & J. FRISBY. HELMUTH
VON MOLTKE.*
  F.L. CARSTEN, 575(SEER):APR73-
  324
BALIMA, M.G., COMP. BOTSWANA, LESO-
THO, & SWAZILAND: A GUIDE TO OFFI-
CIAL PUBLICATIONS, 1868-1968.
  J.A. CASADA, 517(PBSA):APR-JUN73-
  208
BALKAN, L. LES EFFETS DU BILINGUAL-
ISME FRANÇAIS-ANGLAIS SUR LES APTI-
TUDES INTELLECTUELLES.
  L.G. KELLY, 320(CJL):VOL18#1-84
  J. MACNAMARA, 361:VOL28#1&2-159

BALL, H. DIE FLUCHT AUS DER ZEIT.
  S. FAUCHEREAU, 98:AUG/SEP72-752
BALL, I.M. PITCAIRN.*
  617(TLS):4JAN74-8
BALL, J. MARK ONE: THE DUMMY.
  N. CALLENDAR, 441:3NOV74-71
BALL, M.M. THE "OPEN" COMMONWEALTH.
  F. BÉDARIDA, 182:VOL25#5/6-149
BALL, P.M. THE CENTRAL SELF.*
  E. FAAS, 38:BAND90HEFT1/2-251
BALL, P.M. THE SCIENCE OF ASPECTS.*
  R. ACKERMAN, 637(VS):SEP72-117
  R.L. BRETT, 541(RES):MAY72-223
  P. FONTANEY, 189(EA):JUL-SEP72-
  441
BALLARD, J.G. CONCRETE ISLAND.
  R. BLYTHE, 362:2MAY74-576
  M. LEVIN, 441:1DEC74-78
  617(TLS):26APR74-433
BALLARD, J.G. CRASH.*
  R. DE FEO, 249(HUDR):WINTER73/74-
  782
BALLARD, J.G. VERMILION SANDS.*
  D. REED, 362:23MAY74-672
BALLET, A.H., ED. PLAYWRIGHTS FOR
TOMORROW. (VOLS 8&9)
  B.H. FUSSELL, 249(HUDR):WINTER
  73/74-753
"BALLET & MODERN DANCE."
  A. KISSELGOFF, 441:13JUL74-21
"THE BALLET GOURMET."
  M. HOROSKO, 151:MAR72-87
BALLINGER, B.S. THE CORSICAN.
  N. CALLENDAR, 441:7JUL74-19
BALLY, C. & A. SECHEHAYE, WITH A.
REIDLINGER - SEE DE SAUSSURE, F.
BALMAS, E. LA RENAISSANCE II, 1548-
1570.
  A.J. KRAILSHEIMER, 617(TLS):
  8NOV74-1265
BALME, M.G. INTELLEGENDA.
  R.G. PENMAN, 123:MAR73-80
  W.S. THURMAN, 399(MLJ):MAR72-179
BALOGH, T. & P. BALACS. FACT & FANCY
IN INTERNATIONAL ECONOMIC RELA-
TIONS.
  617(TLS):12APR74-398
BALSDON, J.P.V.D. ROME.
  J.M. CARTER, 313:VOL62-173
  M.A.R. COLLEDGE, 123:DEC73-241
BALSEIRO, J.A. & E. SUÁREZ-RIVERO -
SEE CASONA, A.
DE BALZAC, H. BALZAC'S "LE SECRET
DES RUGGIERI." (W.L. CRAIN, ED)
  D. BELLOS, 402(MLR):JAN73-178
  H.J. HUNT, 208(FS):JAN73-78
DE BALZAC, H. BEATRIX. (B. ARCHER,
TRANS)
  C.C., 191(ELN):SEP72(SUPP)-80
DE BALZAC, H. THE BLACK SHEEP. (D.
ADAMSON, TRANS)
  C.C., 191(ELN):SEP72(SUPP)-79
DE BALZAC, H. L'ILLUSTRE GAUDISSART.
LA MUSE DU DÉPARTEMENT. (B. GUYON,
ED OF BOTH)
  H.J. HUNT, 208(FS):JAN73-78
  A. MICHEL, 557(RSH):JUL-SEP72-
  459
  A.R. PUGH, 402(MLR):JAN73-179
DE BALZAC, H. OEUVRES COMPLÈTES.
(VOLS 21-23) (R. GUISE, ED)
  A. MICHEL, 557(RSH):JUL-SEP72-
  457

DE BALZAC, H. PHYSIOLOGIE DU MARI-
AGE. (M. REGARD, ED)
  B. TOLLEY, 208(FS):JAN73-80
BAMBECK, M. BODEN UND WERKWELT.
  O. JÄNICKE, 260(IF):BAND76-305
BAMBROUGH, R., ED. WISDOM.
  B. WILLIAMS, 617(TLS):30AUG74-
  922
BAMFORD, T.W. - SEE ARNOLD, T.
BANCQUART, M-C. - SEE DE MAUPASSANT,
  G.
BANDER, R.G. AMERICAN ENGLISH RHET-
ORIC.
  C.B. PAULSON, 351(LL):JUN72-137
BANDERA GOMEZ, C. EL "POEMA DE MIO
CID."*
  R.E. BARBERA, 546(RR):APR72-166
BANDINELLI, R.B. - SEE UNDER BIANCHI
BANDINELLI, R.
BANDY, W.T. - SEE POE, E.A.
BANHAM, R., ED. THE ASPEN PAPERS.
  617(TLS):24MAY74-566
BANHAM, R. LOS ANGELES.*
  T.S. HINES, 576:MAR72-75
BANKES, J. & E. KERRIDGE, EDS. THE
EARLY RECORDS OF THE BANKES FAMILY
AT WINSTANLEY.
  617(TLS):22FEB74-193
BANKS, A. A WORLD ATLAS OF MILITARY
HISTORY. (VOL 1)
  617(TLS):5APR74-370
BANKS, L.R. TWO IS LONELY.
  J. MELLORS, 362:11APR74-477
  617(TLS):22MAR74-282
BANN, S., ED. THE TRADITION OF CON-
STRUCTIVISM.
  617(TLS):8NOV74-1266
BANNERMAN, J. STUDIES IN THE HIS-
TORY OF DALRIADA.
  B.P. LENMAN, 617(TLS):29NOV74-
  1345
BÄNSCH, D. ELSE LASKER-SCHÜLER.
  H.R. KLIENEBERGER, 402(MLR):
  OCT73-952
BANTA, M. HENRY JAMES & THE OCCULT.*
  J. LYDENBERG, 27(AL):JAN74-619
BANULS, A. HEINRICH MANN.
  U. WEISSTEIN, 400(MLN):APR72-534
BAQUERO GOYANES, M. ESTRUCTURAS DE
LA NOVELA ACTUAL.*
  H. SIEBER, 400(MLN):MAR72-382
BAR-ADON, A. & W.F. LEOPOLD, EDS.
CHILD LANGUAGE.*
  D. CRYSTAL, 297(JL):SEP72-326
  V.J. ZEPS, 406:FALL73-320
BARAS, A. THE YELLOW HOUSE & OTHER
POEMS, 1933-1973.
  617(TLS):30AUG74-932
BARASCH, F.K. THE GROTESQUE.
  J.B. BENDER, 290(JAAC):WINTER72-
  275
  L. JENNINGS, 301(JEGP):JUL73-405
BARATIER, E., ED. HISTOIRE DE LA
PROVENCE.
  J. MUNDY, 589:APR73-422
BARATYNSKY, E. SELECTED LETTERS OF
EVGENIJ BARATYNSKIJ. (G.R. BAR-
RATT, ED & TRANS)
  617(TLS):18JAN74-59
BARATZ, J. & R.W. SHUY, EDS. TEACH-
ING BLACK CHILDREN TO READ.
  M.S. MIRON, 353:1JUL72-94
BARBAGLI, D.A. - SEE PATRIZI, F.

BARBARO IL VECCHIO, E. ORATIONES
CONTRA POETAS: EPISTOLAE. (G.
RONCONI, ED)
  G. TOURNOY, 568(SCN):SUMMER73-57
BARBEAU, A.T. THE INTELLECTUAL DE-
SIGN OF JOHN DRYDEN'S HEROIC
PLAYS.*
  P. LEGOUIS, 189(EA):OCT-DEC72-
  555
  C. VISSER, 627(UTQ):WINTER73-170
BARBEL, J. - SEE SAINT GREGORY OF
NYSSA
BARBER, B.R. THE DEATH OF COMMUNAL
LIBERTY.
  J. STEINBERG, 617(TLS):6SEP74-
  957
BARBER, G. COUNTRY DOCTOR.
  617(TLS):1NOV74-1240
BARBER, G., COMP. FRENCH LETTER-
PRESS PRINTING.*
  E. ARMSTRONG, 447(N&Q):DEC72-478
BARBER, N. SEVEN DAYS OF FREEDOM.
  G. MIKES, 617(TLS):29NOV74-1348
BARBER, N. THE SULTANS.
  J. UPDIKE, 442(NY):6MAY74-138
BARBER, R. THE FIGURE OF ARTHUR.
  K. JACKSON, 382(MAE):1973/2-188
BARBERI SQUAROTTI, G. & G. MARTIGNET-
TI. MANZONI.
  W.T.S., 191(ELN):SEP72(SUPP)-195
BARBERIS, P. BALZAC ET LE MAL DU
SIECLE.
  J. PELLETIER, 557(RSH):JUL-SEP72-
  461
BARBERIS, P. BALZAC, UNE MYTHOLOGIE
RÉALISTE.
  B. VANNIER, 98:JUL72-610
BARBI, M. LIFE OF DANTE. (P.G.
RUGGIERS, ED & TRANS)
  B.L., 275(IQ):FALL/WINTER72-118
BARBIER, C.P., ED. DOCUMENTS STÉ-
PHANE MALLARMÉ. (VOL 2)
  G. ZAYED, 535(RHL):JAN-FEB72-150
BARBIER, C.P., ED. DOCUMENTS STÉ-
PHANE MALLARMÉ. (VOL 3)
  E. SOUFFRIN, 208(FS):JAN73-89
BARBOUR, D. A POEM AS LONG AS THE
HIGHWAY.*
  D. BAILEY, 529(QQ):SUMMER72-242
BARBOUR, D. WHITE.
  M. ESTOK, 150(DR):WINTER72/73-
  653
BARBOUR, I.G. MYTHS, MODELS & PARA-
DIGMS.
  617(TLS):14JUN74-630
BARBOUR, P.L. POCAHONTAS & HER
WORLD.
  B.G. HOFFMAN, 656(WMQ):APR72-321
DE LA BARCA, P.C. - SEE UNDER CAL-
DERÓN DE LA BARCA, P.
BARCLAY, G.S. THE RISE & FALL OF
THE NEW ROMAN EMPIRE.
  S.J. WOOLF, 617(TLS):11OCT74-
  1118
BARDAVÍO, J. LA CRISIS.
  617(TLS):7JUN74-606
BARDÈCHE, M. MARCEL PROUST ROMAN-
CIER.* (VOL 1)
  M. GUTWIRTH, 207(FR):DEC71-508
BARDON, H. PROPOSITIONS SUR CATULLE.
  E.J. KENNEY, 123:DEC73-165
  K. QUINN, 487:AUTUMN72-312
  T.P. WISEMAN, 313:VOL62-215
BARDON, H. - SEE CATULLUS

BARDON, H. & R. VERDIÈRE. VERGILI-
ANA.
  J.R.C. MARTYN, 67:NOV73-285
BARDOS, J-P., ED. STENDHAL.*
  G. MAY, 399(MLJ):MAR72-192
BARFIELD, O. WHAT COLERIDGE THOUGHT.
  G.A. CEVASCO, 150(DR):SPRING72-
  143
  J. COLMER, 402(MLR):OCT73-894
  G.B. TENNYSON, 445(NCF):JUN72-
  117
  J.C. ULREICH, JR., 50(ARQ):
  SUMMER72-176
BARING, A. UPRISING IN EAST GERMANY:
JUNE 17, 1953.*
  M. CROAN, 32:JUN73-404
BARK, J. DER WUPPERTALER DICHTER-
KREIS.
  I. FINDLAY, 400(MLN):OCT72-800
BARK, J. & D. PFORTE, EDS. DIE
DEUTSCHSPRACHIGE ANTHOLOGIE.
  L.D. WELLS, 221(GQ):JAN72-155
BARKDULL, T. LONESOME WALLS.
  R.H. CRACROFT, 650(WF):APR72-141
BARKER, A.L. A SOURCE OF EMBARRASS-
MENT.
  R. BLYTHE, 362:21MAR74-381
  617(TLS):22MAR74-282
BARKER, C.A. AMERICAN CONVICTIONS.
  R. MIDDLEKAUFF, 656(WMQ):JAN72-
  171
  R.E. SPILLER, 27(AL):MAY73-300
BARKER, D. G.K. CHESTERTON.*
  R. NYE, 364:OCT/NOV73-143
BARKER, D. WRITER BY TRADE.
  A.J. FARMER, 189(EA):JUL-SEP72-
  442
BARKER, F. & P. JACKSON. LONDON.
  M-K. WILMERS, 617(TLS):27DEC74-
  1456
BARKER, G. POEMS OF PLACES & PEO-
PLE.*
  J. JORDAN, 159(DM):AUTUMN71-115
BARKER, K. THE THEATRE ROYAL,
BRISTOL - 1766-1966.
  617(TLS):29MAR74-349
BARKER, M.A-A-R. & A.K. MENGAL. A
COURSE IN BALUCHI.
  H. PENZL, 318(JAOS):JAN-MAR72-
  135
BARKUN, M. DISASTER & THE MILLEN-
NIUM.
  617(TLS):6SEP74-959
"ERNST BARLACH 1870/1970."
  J.M. RITCHIE, 220(GL&L):APR73-
  264
BARLOW, E. FREDERICK LAW OLMSTED'S
NEW YORK.*
  W.H. JORDY, 453:13JUN74-33
BARLOW, M. LE SOCIALISME D'EMMANUEL
MOUNIER.
  C. SCHUWER, 542:OCT-DEC72-494
BARNARD, F.M. - SEE VON HERDER, J.G.
BARNARD, H. SCHOOL ARCHITECTURE.
(J. & R. MC CLINTOCK, EDS)
  W.P. THOMPSON, 576:OCT72-246
BARNARD, J. THE DECORATIVE TRADI-
TION.
  617(TLS):5APR74-358
BARNER, W. BAROCKRHETORIK.
  G. LUTHER, 224(GRM):BAND22HEFT2-
  201

BARNES, B. PARTHENOPHIL & PARTHEN-
OPHE. (V.A. DOYNO, ED)
  J. GRUNDY, 677:VOL3-280
  J. REES, 541(RES):NOV72-529
BARNES, C. & D. BLAKE. 120 NEEDLE-
POINT DESIGN PROJECTS.
  L.J. GARTNER, JR., 441:8DEC74-49
BARNES, H.E. SARTRE.
  617(TLS):7JUN74-607
BARNES, J. THE ONTOLOGICAL ARGUMENT.
  I.M. CROMBIE, 518:MAY73-1
BARNES, J., ED. THE WRITER IN AUS-
TRALIA.
  K.L. GOODWIN, 447(N&Q):NOV72-435
BARNES, J.A. THREE STYLES IN THE
STUDY OF KINSHIP.
  G.C. RUMP, 182:VOL25#17/18-633
BARNETT, C. THE FIRST CHURCHILL.
  H. BEVINGTON, 441:1DEC74-86
BARNETT, C. MARLBOROUGH.
  A. BRETT-JAMES, 617(TLS):13DEC74-
  1425
BARNETT, F.J. & OTHERS, EDS. HIS-
TORY & STRUCTURE OF FRENCH.
  P. RICKARD, 208(FS):APR73-245
BARNETT, G.L., ED. EIGHTEENTH-CEN-
TURY BRITISH NOVELISTS ON THE
NOVEL.* NINETEENTH-CENTURY BRIT-
ISH NOVELISTS ON THE NOVEL.
  C.E. FRANK, 577(SHR):FALL72-414
BARNETT, R.D. THE CAMBRIDGE ANCIENT
HISTORY. (REV) (VOL 2, CHAPTER 28)
  M.C. ASTOUR, 318(JAOS):JUL-SEP
  72-447
BARNETT, R.D., ED. THE SEPHARDI
HERITAGE. (VOL 1)
  Y.H. YERUSHALMI, 589:OCT73-730
BARNHART, C.L., S. STEINMETZ & R.K.
BARNHART, EDS. A DICTIONARY OF
NEW ENGLISH 1963-1972.
  617(TLS):5APR74-376
BARNHART, J.E. THE BILLY GRAHAM
RELIGION.
  617(TLS):10MAY74-497
BARNIE, J. WAR IN MEDIEVAL SOCIETY.
  K. FOWLER, 617(TLS):22NOV74-1324
BARNSTONE, W., ED. EIGHTEEN TEXTS.*
  J.K. DEMETRIUS, 32:SEP73-675
BARNSTONE, W. NEW FACES OF CHINA.
  617(TLS):12APR74-386
BARNSTONE, W., WITH KO CHING-PO -
SEE MAO TSE-TUNG
BARNWELL, H.T. - SEE CORNEILLE, P.
BAROCCHI, P. TRATTATI D'ARTE DEL
CINQUECENTO FRA MANIERISMO E CON-
TRORIFORMA (1960-1962).
  M.P., 228(GSLI):VOL149FASC466/
  467-462
BAROIN, J., ED. "SIMON DE POUILLE,"
CHANSON DE GESTE.
  P.R. GRILLO, 545(RPH):FEB73-612
BAROJA, P. EL MUNDO ES ANSÍ.*
(D.L. SHAW, ED)
  J.R. AYORA, 399(MLJ):FEB72-102
  205(FMLS):JUL72-284
BAROLI, M. - SEE ZOLA, E.
BARON, F. - SEE HOEST, S.
BARON, G. & D.A. HOWELL. THE GOV-
ERNMENT & MANAGEMENT OF SCHOOLS.
  617(TLS):8MAR74-231
BARON, M. LETTERS FOR THE NEW ENG-
LAND DEAD.
  D. BROMWICH, 441:16JUN74-6
  617(TLS):30AUG74-932

BARON, R. SCIENCE ET SAGESSE CHEZ
HUGUES DE SAINT-VICTOR.
J. TROUILLARD, 542:JAN-MAR72-78
BAROOAH, N.K. DAVID SCOTT IN NORTH-
EAST INDIA, 1802-1831.
M. NAIDIS, 293(JAST):NOV71-213
BARR, J.J. THE DYNASTY.
N. WARD, 99:NOV/DEC74-41
BARR, R. THE MEASURE OF THE RULE.
J. PARR, 296:VOL3#2-94
BARRATT, D.M. & D.G. VAISEY, EDS.
OXFORDSHIRE.
617(TLS):15MAR74-272
BARRATT, G.R. - SEE BARATYNSKY, E.
BARRAULT, J-L. "JARRY SUR LA BUTTE."
T.J. REISS, 207(FR):APR72-1035
BARRAULT, J-L. MEMORIES FOR TOMOR-
ROW.
R. BRYDEN, 362:25JUL74-124
617(TLS):26JUL74-791
BARRELL, J. THE IDEA OF LANDSCAPE &
THE SENSE OF PLACE 1730-1840.
L. HERRMANN, 135:OCT72-139
BARRÈRE, J-B. L'IDÉE DE GOÛT DE
PASCAL À VALÉRY.
617(TLS):22FEB74-190
BARRET, A. FLORENCE OBSERVED.
617(TLS):26APR74-441
BARRET, L. MÉTHODE DE PRONONCIATION
DU FRANÇAIS.
M. REFFERT, 430(NS):AUG72-495
BARRETT, E.C. CLIMATOLOGY FROM
SATELLITES.
617(TLS):13SEP74-982
BARRETT, J. LIFE ON THE SEA SHORE.
617(TLS):27DEC74-1471
BARRETT, L. SONG FOR MUMU.
M. LEVIN, 441:29SEP74-40
BARRETT, M.E. AN ACCIDENT OF LOVE.*
617(TLS):31MAY74-591
BARRETTE, P. & M. FOL. UN CERTAIN
STYLE OU UN STYLE CERTAIN?*
J. CULLER, 599:FALL72-314
BARRIS, C. YOU & ME BABE.
M. LEVIN, 441:28APR74-38
BARRÓN, C.G. - SEE UNDER GARCÍA BAR-
RÓN, C.
BARRON, C.M. THE MEDIEVAL GUILDHALL
OF LONDON.
M-K. WILMERS, 617(TLS):27DEC74-
1456
BARRON, J. KGB.
H. TREVOR-ROPER, 441:21APR74-10
BARROW, G.W.S., ED. THE SCOTTISH
TRADITION.
R. MITCHISON, 617(TLS):29NOV74-
1345
BARROW, G.W.S., WITH W.W. SCOTT,
EDS. THE ACTS OF WILLIAM I, KING
OF SCOTS, 1165-1214.
W.S. REID, 589:JUL73-546
BARROW, L. & C. OLSTAD. ASPECTOS DE
LA LITERATURA ESPAÑOLA.
H.J. DENNIS, 238:SEP72-606
BARRY, B. THE LIBERAL THEORY OF
JUSTICE.
617(TLS):4JAN74-17
BARRY, F.R. TO RECOVER CONFIDENCE.
617(TLS):26JUL74-812
BARRY, J.G. DRAMATIC STRUCTURE.*
J.K. FEIBLEMAN, 290(JAAC):FALL71-
135
BARRYMAINE, N. THE TIME BOMB.
293(JAST):MAY72-754

BARSALI, I.B. GUIDA DI LUCCA.
H. HONOUR, 90:JUN72-416
BARSALI, I.B. VILLE DI ROMA.
B. FORD, 90:JUN72-412
BARSBY, J.A. - SEE OVID
BARSON, A.T. A WAY OF SEEING.
W.M. FROHOCK, 27(AL):NOV73-475
DU BARTAS, G.S. OEUVRES: LA JUDIT.
(A. BAÏCHE, ED)
K.M. HALL, 402(MLR):JUL73-653
R.A. SAYCE, 208(FS):OCT73-449
BARTH, A. PROPHETS WITH HONOR.
M.E. GALE, 441:28JUL74-2
R.R. LINGEMAN, 441:17AUG74-21
442(NY):26AUG74-92
BARTH, J. CHIMERA.*
M. ELLMANN, 676(YR):SPRING73-461
S. O'CONNELL, 418(MR):WINTER73-
190
E. ROVIT, 659:AUTUMN74-539
617(TLS):26JUL74-783
639(VQR):WINTER73-VIII
BARTH, J.R., ED. RELIGIOUS PERSPEC-
TIVES IN FAULKNER'S FICTION.
M.E. BRADFORD, 219(GAR):WINTER72-
522
639(VQR):WINTER73-XVIII
BARTHELME, D. GUILTY PLEASURES.
P. ADAMS, 61:DEC74-128
A. BROYARD, 441:2NOV74-27
W. CLEMONS, 441:3NOV74-7
BARTHELME, D. SADNESS.*
S. O'CONNELL, 418(MR):WINTER73-
190
W.H. PRITCHARD, 249(HUDR):SPRING
73-234
E. ROVIT, 659:AUTUMN74-539
N. SCHMITZ, 473(PR):3/1973-482
BARTHELME, F. RANGOON.
502(PRS):SPRING72-93
BARTHES, R. CRITICAL ESSAYS.
R. KLEIN, 473(PR):2/1973-294
BARTHES, R. L'EMPIRE DES SIGNES.
R. LAPORTE, 98:JUL72-583
BARTHES, R. MYTHOLOGIES.* (A.
LAVERS, ED & TRANS)
A.A. BERGER, 125:FEB73-192
D.P. FUNT, 249(HUDR):SUMMER73-
410
R. KLEIN, 473(PR):2/1973-294
D. LOCKE, 364:JUN/JUL72-163
G. MERLER, 648:JAN73-66
L. WELCH, 290(JAAC):SUMMER73-563
BARTHES, R. S/Z.*
F. GUENTHNER, 492:#1-113
B. VANNIER, 98:JUL72-610
BARTHES, R. SADE, FOURIER, LOYOLA.
P. DUVERNOIS, 98:JUL72-595
BARTHOLOMAY, J.A. THE SHIELD OF
PERSEUS.
L.S. DEMBO, 27(AL):JAN74-625
BARTLETT, C.J., ED. BRITAIN PRE-
EMINENT.*
D.M. SCHURMAN, 529(QQ):AUTUMN72-
432
BARTLETT, R.A. THE NEW COUNTRY.
R. SLOTKIN, 441:17NOV74-40
BARTLETT, V. I KNOW WHAT I LIKED.
E.S. TURNER, 362:11JUL74-60
617(TLS):14JUN74-628

BARTLEY, D.E. & R.L. POLITZER. PRAC-
TICE-CENTERED TEACHER TRAINING:
SPANISH. (VOL 2)
  W.J. CAMERON, 238:MAY72-396
  A. PAPALIA, 399(MLJ):MAR72-191
BARTLEY, D.E. & R.L. POLITZER. PRAC-
TICE-CENTERED TEACHER TRAINING:
STANDARD ENGLISH FOR SPEAKERS OF
NONSTANDARD DIALECTS.
  I. FEIGENBAUM, 608:SEP73-329
BARTLEY, W.W., 3D. MORALITY & RELI-
GION.*
  G. SLATER, 479(PHQ):JAN72-89
BARTLEY, W.W., 3D. WITTGENSTEIN.*
  G. STEINER & A. QUINTON, 362:
  28MAR74-399
BARTÓK, B. BÉLA BARTÓK LETTERS.*
(J. DEMÉNY, ED)
  E. RUBBRA, 607:#99-18
  H. TISCHLER, 32:JUN73-438
  639(VQR):SUMMER72-XCII
BARTON, R. CONFESSIONS OF A BIRD
WATCHER.
  G. GOLD, 441:11MAY74-29
  453:4APR74-44
BARTY-KING, H. SUSSEX IN 1839.
  617(TLS):14JUN74-647
BARUK, H. L'HYPNOSE ET LES MÉTHODES
DÉRIVÉES.
  P-M.S., 542:OCT-DEC72-447
BARZUN, J. CLIO & THE DOCTORS.
  R. SENNETT, 441:20OCT74-27
BARZUN, J. THE USE & ABUSE OF ART.
  K. BAKER, 61:DEC74-114
  H. KRAMER, 441:23JUN74-2
BASAK, A. DECISIONS OF THE UNITED
NATIONS ORGANS IN THE JUDGMENTS &
OPINIONS OF THE INTERNATIONAL
COURT OF JUSTICE.
  H. ROLIN, 182:VOL25#12-392
BASCH, F. RELATIVE CREATURES.
  A. HAYTER, 617(TLS):27DEC74-1461
BASCHE, J. THAILAND.
  B.L. FOSTER, 293(JAST):FEB72-462
  D.K. SWEARER, 318(JAOS):OCT-DEC
  72-582
BASCHIERA, K. THE TEACHING OF MOD-
ERN LANGUAGES IN SECONDARY VOCA-
TIONAL & COMMERCIAL SCHOOLS.
  D.F. BRADSHAW, 208(FS):JUL73-366
  M. HAY, 220(GL&L):OCT72-64
BASCOM, W. IFA DIVINATION.
  D.J. CROWLEY, 292(JAF):JAN-MAR72-
  87
BASDEKIS, D. - SEE DE UNAMUNO, M.
BASDEVANT, D. L'ARCHITECTURE FRAN-
ÇAISE DES ORIGINES A NOS JOURS.
  S.C., 46:SEP72-192
BAŞGÖZ, I. & H.E. WILSON. EDUCATION-
AL PROBLEMS IN TURKEY 1920-1940.
  K.H. KARPAT, 318(JAOS):APR-JUN72-
  374
BASHAM, A.L., ED. PAPERS ON THE
DATE OF KANIṢKA.*
  A.C. SOPER, 57:VOL34#1-102
BASHŌ. BACK ROADS TO FAR TOWNS.
(C. CORMAN & KAMAIKE SUSUMU, EDS
& TRANS)
  R.L. BACKUS, 318(JAOS):APR-JUN72-
  348
"BASILEON."
  E. PLAYFAIR, 617(TLS):29NOV74-
  1346

BASKOFF, F. GUIDED COMPOSITION.
  C.B. PAULSON, 351(LL):JUN72-137
BASSANI, G. BEHIND THE DOOR.*
  G. EWART, 364:OCT/NOV73-151
BASSANI, G. EPITAFFIO.
  617(TLS):4OCT74-1090
BASSANI, G. LE HÉRON.*
  N. KATTAN, 98:JAN72-95
BASTIDE, G. ESSAI D'ÉTHIQUE FONDA-
MENTALE.
  J-M. GABAUDE, 154:JUN72-267
BASTIN, J. & H.J. BENDA. A HISTORY
OF MODERN SOUTHEAST ASIA.
  L.R. WRIGHT, 302:JAN72-68
BASTIN, T., ED. QUANTUM THEORY &
BEYOND.
  N. CARTWRIGHT, 486:DEC72-558
BATAILLE, G. LITERATURE & EVIL.
  G. EWART, 364:AUG/SEP73-144
BATAILLE, M. LE CRI DANS LE MUR.
  M. NAUDIN, 207(FR):OCT71-187
BATE, S. THE ROYAL CARPET.
  H. FRANCIS, 157:WINTER72-83
BATE, W.J. & A.B. STRAUSS - SEE
JOHNSON, S.
BATES, H.E. A FOUNTAIN OF FLOWERS.
  C. SYKES, 617(TLS):13DEC74-1421
BATES, R. & H.J. POLLOCK, EDS. LIT-
TERS FROM ALOFT.
  E.A. KOPPER, JR., 339(JJQ):FALL
  73-71
BATES, R.H. UNIONS, PARTIES & POL-
ITICAL DEVELOPMENT.
  R.D. GRILLO, 69:JUL72-246
BATESON, F.W. THE SCHOLAR-CRITIC.
  R.L. BRETT, 402(MLR):JAN73-136
  W.W. ROBSON, 541(RES):NOV72-526
BATESON, F.W. & N.A. JOUKOVSKY - SEE
POPE, A.
BATESON, M.C. STRUCTURAL CONTINUITY
IN POETRY.
  G.E. VON GRUNEBAUM, 350:MAR73-
  212
  S.R. LEVIN, 361:VOL28#4-395
BATKIN, L.M. DANTE E LA SOCIETÀ
ITALIANA DELL '300.
  M. MARTI, 228(GSLI):VOL149FASC
  465-112
BATÓG, T. THE AXIOMATIC METHOD IN
PHONOLOGY.
  C.D. JOHNSON, 206:NOV72-269
BATOWSKI, H. DYPLOMACJA NIEMIECKA,
1919-1945.
  R.A. WOYTAK, 32:MAR73-188
BATTAGLIA, G. NUOVA GRAMMATICA
ITALIANA PER STRANIERI.
  M. KUITUNEN, 276:AUTUMN72-350
BATTAGLIA, S. GIOVANNI BOCCACCIO E
LA RIFORMA DELLA NARRATIVA.
  L. WHITE, 275(IQ):FALL/WINTER72-
  116
BATTAGLIA, S. L'IDEOLOGIA LETTER-
ARIA DI GIACOMO LEOPARDI.
  E.G. CASERTA, 276:SPRING72-68
BATTENHOUSE, R.W. SHAKESPEAREAN
TRAGEDY.*
  S. BARNET, 551(RENQ):SPRING72-
  109
BATTERSBY, M. ART DECO FASHION.
  617(TLS):15NOV74-1291
BATTISCOMBE, G. SHAFTESBURY.
  A. BOYLE, 362:12DEC74-785
  N. GASH, 617(TLS):8NOV74-1245

BATTISTINI, R. & P. LE BOURDIEC, EDS. ATLAS DE MADAGASCAR.
  M. URBAIN-FAUBLEE, 69:JUL72-261
BATTLES, F.L. & A.M. HUGO - SEE CALVIN, J.
BATTS, M. HOHES MITTELALTER.
  M.G. SCHOLZ, 680(ZDP):BAND91HEFT 3-445
  C. SOETEMAN, 433:APR72-233
  H. THOMKE, 182:VOL25#22-797
  E. THURNHER, 133:1972/1-102
BATTS, M.S., COMP. HANDBUCH DER DEUTSCHEN LITERATURGESCHICHTE. (2ND SECTION, VOL 2)
  P. SALMON, 220(GL&L):OCT72-78
BATTS, M.S. GOTTFRIED VON STRASSBURG.
  D. BRETT-EVANS, 564:OCT72-228
BATTS, M.S. - SEE "DAS NIBELUNGENLIED"
BAUD-BOVY, S. CHANSONS POPULAIRES DE CRETE OCCIDENTALE.
  S. CHIANIS, 187:SEP74-453
BAUDELAIRE, C. CORRESPONDANCE. (C. PICHOIS, WITH J. ZIEGLER, EDS)
  A. FAIRLIE, 617(TLS):38JUN74-688
BAUDIN, F. & N. HOEFLAKE. THE TYPE SPECIMEN OF JACQUES-FRANÇOIS ROSART.
  617(TLS):5APR74-376
BAUDOUIN, C. L'OEUVRE DE JUNG.
  C. BARDET, 542:OCT-DEC72-448
BAUER, G. STUDIEN ZUM SYSTEM UND GEBRAUCH DER "TEMPORA" IN DER SPRACHE CHAUCERS UND GOWERS.
  R. ZIMMERMANN, 72:BAND210HEFT1/3-174
BAUER, G.H. SARTRE & THE ARTIST.*
  E.F. KAELIN, 321:FALL72-237
BAUER, J. KAFKA & PRAGUE.*
  639(VQR):WINTER73-XLI
BAUM, G. VERNUNFT UND ERKENNTNIS.
  R. LAUTH, 53(AGP):BAND54HEFT1-97
BAUM, L.F. THE ANNOTATED WIZARD OF OZ. (M.P. HEARN, ED)
  A. LURIE, 453:18APR74-24
BAUM, R. RECHERCHES SUR LES OEUVRES ATTRIBUÉES À MARIE DE FRANCE.
  C. LEUBE, 224(GRM):BAND22HEFT4-452
BAUMAN, R. FOR THE REPUTATION OF TRUTH.
  J.D. MARIETTA, 656(WMQ):JUL72-510
  J.J. ZIMMERMAN, 481(PQ):JUL72-520
BAUMBACH, J. RERUNS.
  C. LEHMANN-HAUPT, 441:17OCT74-45
  M. MEWSHAW, 441:13OCT74-26
BAUMER, F. FRANZ KAFKA.
  F. JONES, 32:SEP73-670
BAUMGART, F. A HISTORY OF ARCHITECTURAL STYLES.
  C.F. OTTO, 576:MAR72-79
BAUMGART, R. DIE VERDRÄNGTE PHANTASIE.
  617(TLS):4OCT74-1082
BAUMGART, W. DER FRIEDE VON PARIS 1856.
  A. WAHL, 182:VOL25#15/16-562
BAUMGARTEN, P. SELBSTFINANZIERUNG UND EINKOMMENSVERTEILUNG.
  A. HÜFNER, 182:VOL25#19/20-652

BAUMGARTNER, H.M. & W.G. JACOBS. J.G. FICHTE - BIBLIOGRAPHIE.*
  H. OBERER, 53(AGP):BAND54HEFT1-108
BAUMWOLL, D. & R.L. SAITZ. ADVANCED READING & WRITING.
  N. ARAPOFF-CRAMER, 608:JUN73-184
BAUR, J.F. DER MISSBRAUCH IM DEUTSCHEN KARTELLRECHT.
  G. STRICKRODT, 182:VOL25#13/14-463
BAUR-HEINHOLD, M. SCHÖNE ALTE BIBLIOTHEKEN.
  617(TLS):25OCT74-1207
BAUSOLA, A. LO SVOLGIMENTO DEL PENSIERO DI SCHELLING.*
  C. CESA, 548(RCSF):JAN-MAR72-106
BAUTIER, R-H. THE ECONOMIC DEVELOPMENT OF MEDIEVAL EUROPE.
  D. HERLIHY, 589:APR73-339
  639(VQR):SPRING72-LXIX
BAWDEN, N. GEORGE BENEATH A PAPER MOON.
  J. MELLORS, 362:5DEC74-753
  J. MILLER, 617(TLS):6DEC74-1361
BAXA, J., ED. ADAM MÜLLERS LEBENSZEUGNISSE.
  H.J. KREUTZER, 224(GRM):BAND22 HEFT4-440
BAXANDALL, L., ED. RADICAL PERSPECTIVES IN THE ARTS.
  D. PECK, 418(MR):SUMMER73-641
  J. ROACHE, 128(CE):MAY73-1142
BAXANDALL, M. GIOTTO & THE ORATORS.*
  C. GILBERT, 56:WINTER72-427
  A. NEUMEYER, 127:WINTER72/73-240
  C. TRINKAUS, 589:JUL73-548
  L. VERTOVA, 39:NOV72-457
BAXANDALL, M. PAINTING & EXPERIENCE IN FIFTEENTH-CENTURY ITALY.*
  J.S. ACKERMAN, 56:WINTER72-419
  T. LASK, 55:APR73-14
  639(VQR):SPRING73-XCI
BAXTER, J. AN APPALLING TALENT.
  J. SIMON, 617(TLS):8NOV74-1253
BAXTER, J.K. RUNES.*
  R. GARFITT, 364:AUG/SEP73-118
  P. SMYTH, 491:DEC73-165
BAXTER, T.W. & E.E. BURKE. GUIDE TO THE HISTORICAL MANUSCRIPTS IN THE NATIONAL ARCHIVES OF RHODESIA.
  R. HODDER-WILLIAMS, 325:OCT72-544
BAYER, H. & M. KATSUMI. THE GRAPHIC DESIGN OF YUSAKU KAMEKURA.
  617(TLS):12JUL74-751
BAYER, W. THE GREAT MOVIES.*
  617(TLS):8MAR74-244
BAYER, W. STARDUST.
  M. LEVIN, 441:30JUN74-29
BAYES, R·H. THE CASKETMAKER.
  E. AUSTIN, 648:JAN73-82
BAYET, J. CROYANCES ET RITES DANS LA ROME ANTIQUE.
  P. GRIMAL, 98:DEC72-1045
BAYLE, P. OEUVRES DIVERSES. (A. NIDERST, ED)
  E. LABROUSSE, 535(RHL):JUL-AUG72-712
BAYLE, P. PENSIERI SULLA COMETA E DIZIONARIO STORICO E CRITICO. (G.P. BREGA, ED & TRANS)
  E. NAMER, 542:JUL-SEP72-321

BAYLEY, J. PUSHKIN.*
J.G. GARRARD, 550(RUSR):JUL72-
306
639(VQR):WINTER72-XV
639(VQR):SPRING72-LXII
BAYLEY, P. EDMUND SPENSER.
B.E.C. DAVIS, 541(RES):NOV72-478
BAYM, M.I. A HISTORY OF LITERARY
AESTHETICS IN AMERICA.
N. WRIGHT, 27(AL):NOV73-486
BAYNHAM, H. FROM THE LOWER DECK.
J.M. HAAS, 481(PQ):JUL72-521
BAZ, J.M. EL HABLA DE LA TIERRA DE
ALISTE.
R.J. PENNY, 545(RPH):FEB73-633
BAZAINE, J. EXERCICE DE LA PEINTURE.
617(TLS):4JAN74-16
BAZIN, A. JEAN RENOIR.* (F. TRUF-
FAUT, ED)
J.M. PURCELL, 290(JAAC):WINTER
72-280
BAZIN, G. THE AVANT-GARDE IN THE
HISTORY OF PAINTING.
M. VAIZEY, 135:JAN72-63
BAZIN, H. LES BIENHEUREUX DE LA
DÉSOLATION.
P. CRANT, 207(FR):OCT71-187
BAZIN, N.T. VIRGINIA WOOLF & THE
ANDROGYNOUS VISION.*
639(VQR):AUTUMN73-CXLV
BAZYLOW, L. OSTATNIE LATA ROSJI
CARSKIEJ.
E. CHMIELEWSKI, 32:SEP73-609
BEACHCROFT, T.O. THE MODEST ART.*
K.H. GÖLLER, 72:BAND210HEFT1/3-
196
BEAGLEHOLE, J.C. THE LIFE OF CAP-
TAIN JAMES COOK.
D.J. BOORSTIN, 441:24MAR74-27
J.H. PLUMB, 453:30MAY74-37
R. TRUMBULL, 441:6MAY74-39
442(NY):6MAY74-142
BEAKE, F. TEN SONGS FOR SPRING.
J. SAUNDERS, 565:VOL13#3-75
BEAMES, T. THE ROOKERIES OF LONDON.
S. GILL, 447(N&Q):NOV72-434
BEARD, J. BEARD ON FOOD.
N. HAZELTON, 441:1DEC74-94
BEARD, J.F. - SEE COOPER, J.F.
BEARDEN, R. & H. HENDERSON. 6 BLACK
MASTERS OF AMERICAN ART.
639(VQR):WINTER73-XLII
BEARDMORE, G. & J. ARNOLD BENNETT
IN LOVE.
617(TLS):9AUG74-863
BEARDSLEY, A. THE LETTERS OF AUBREY
BEARDSLEY.* (H. MAAS, J.L. DUNCAN
& W.G. GOOD, EDS)
L. ORMOND, 90:JAN72-39
BEARDSLEY, M.C. THE POSSIBILITY OF
CRITICISM.*
R.A., 502(PRS):SUMMER72-187
M. HANCHER, 290(JAAC):SPRING72-
391
M. KRIEGER, 191(ELN):SEP72-75
O.F. SIGWORTH, 50(ARQ):AUTUMN72-
282
BEARDSMORE, R.W. ART & MORALITY.*
E. ZEMACH, 290(JAAC):SPRING73-
421
BEARE, G. THE SNAKE ON THE GRAVE.
N. CALLENDAR, 441:30JUN74-32
BEARE, R.L. - SEE KUHLMANN, Q.

BEATTIE, J. THE NYORO STATE.
L.A. FALLERS, 69:JAN72-63
BEATY, F.L. LIGHT FROM HEAVEN.
D.V.E., 191(ELN):SEP72(SUPP)-25
J.O. HOGE, 219(GAR):WINTER72-526
BEATY, N.L. THE CRAFT OF DYING.*
F.L. HUNTLEY, 551(RENQ):SUMMER
72-248
P.G. STANWOOD, 405(MP):FEB73-260
BEAUCHEMIN, N. RECHERCHES SUR L'AC-
CENT D'APRÈS LES POÈMES D'ALAIN
GRANDBOIS.
P.F. CINTAS, 207(FR):DEC71-490
BEAUJOUR, E.K. THE INVISIBLE LAND.*
E. HARDEN, 648:JAN73-84
E.E. MAYER, 399(MLJ):JAN72-59
639(VQR):WINTER72-XV
BEAULIEU, A. & J. HAMELIN. LA
PRESSE QUÉBÉCOISE DES ORIGINES À
NOS JOURS. (VOL 1)
617(TLS):14JUN74-634
BEAULIEU, V-L. OH MIAMI MIAMI MIAMI.
A. POKORNY, 296:VOL3#2-102
DE BEAUMARCHAIS, P.A.C. CORRESPON-
DANCE.* (VOLS 1&2) (B.N. MORTON,
ED)
W.D. HOWARTH, 402(MLR):JAN73-176
P. MOES, 546(RR):DEC72-299
BEAUMONT, F. & J. FLETCHER. THE DRA-
MATIC WORKS IN THE BEAUMONT &
FLETCHER CANON.* (VOL 2) (F. BOW-
ERS, ED)
J. GERRITSEN, 541(RES):AUG72-385
BEAURLINE, L.A. - SEE SUCKLING, J.
BEAURLINE, L.A. & F. BOWERS - SEE
DRYDEN, J.
DE BEAUVOIR, S. ALL SAID & DONE.
P. ADAMS, 61:SEP74-103
G. ANNAN, 362:6JUN74-740
M. GALLANT, 441:21JUL74-4
C. LEHMANN-HAUPT, 441:7AUG74-39
V.S. PRITCHETT, 453:8AUG74-24
442(NY):12AUG74-99
617(TLS):24MAY74-543
BEAVER, P. THE CRYSTAL PALACE.
N. PEVSNER, 46:JUL72-64
BEAVER, P. VICTORIAN PARLOUR GAMES
FOR TODAY.
V. GLENDINNING, 617(TLS):20DEC74-
1435
BEAZLEY, E. & L. BRETT. SHELL GUIDE
TO NORTH WALES.
C. WILLIAMS-ELLIS, 46:JUN72-390
BEAZLEY, J.D. PARALIPOMENA.
R.M. COOK, 123:DEC73-289
BEBEY, F. AGATHA MOUDIO'S SON.
J. UPDIKE, 442(NY):21JAN74-90
BEC, P., ED. NOUVELLE ANTHOLOGIE DE
LA LYRIQUE OCCITANE DU MOYEN AGE.
F.R.P. AKEHURST, 207(FR):MAR72-
926
BECATTI, G. & OTHERS. MOSAICI ANTI-
CHI IN ITALIA.
E. WAYWELL, 313:VOL62-202
BECH, G. DAS GERMANISCHE REDUPLIZ-
IERTE PRÄTERITUM.*
R. HIERSCHE, 343:BAND15HEFT1-81
BECHERT, J. & OTHERS. EINFÜHRUNG IN
DIE GENERATIVE TRANSFORMATIONSGRAM-
MATIK.
R.D. CLEMENT, 297(JL):SEP72-345
U. EGLI, 343:BAND15HEFT2-198
D. KASTOVSKY, 38:BAND90HEFT3-363
W. VIERECK, 72:BAND210HEFT4/6-
335

BECHERUCCI, L. & G. BRUNETTI. IL
MUSEO DELL' OPERA DEL DUOMO A
FIRENZE. (VOL 2)
H. HONOUR, 90:JUN72-412
BECK, A. & P. RAABE, EDS. HÖLDERLIN.
C.H., 191(ELN):SEP72(SUPP)-156
BECK, E.T. KAFKA & THE YIDDISH THE-
ATRE.*
P.U. BEICKEN, 564:JUN72-142
R. LEROY, 556(RLV):1972/5-555
BECK, H. & OTHERS, EDS. REALLEXIKON
DER GERMANISCHEN ALTERTUMSKUNDE.
(VOL 1, PTS 2&3)
J. FLECK, 563(SS):AUTUMN73-376
BECK, J.H. JACOPO DELLA QUERCIA E
IL PORTALE DI S. PETRONIO A BOLOG-
NA.*
H.W. JANSON, 589:JUL73-550
R. KRAUTHEIMER, 551(RENQ):AUTUMN
72-321
BECK, L.W. EARLY GERMAN PHILOSOPHY.*
R.C.S. WALKER, 393(MIND):APR72-
306
W.H. WALSH, 536:DEC72-205
BECK, L.W., ED. PROCEEDINGS OF THE
THIRD INTERNATIONAL KANT CONGRESS.*
D.S. ROBINSON, 484(PPR):MAR73-
429
BECK, M. & E. VOSS - SEE WAGNER, R.
BECK, R.H. CHANGE & HARMONIZATION
IN EUROPEAN EDUCATION.
J.R. FISZMAN, 497(POLR):SUMMER72-
109
BECK, W. JOYCE'S "DUBLINERS."*
P.J. HURLEY, 573(SSF):SPRING72-
204
BECKER, A. "TÊTE D'OR" (1889) ET
"LA VILLE" (1890-1891).
E. BEAUMONT, 208(FS):OCT73-468
BECKER, B. BACKGAMMON FOR BLOOD.
M. WATKINS, 441:8DEC74-18
BECKER, E. THE DENIAL OF DEATH.
A. BROYARD, 441:27MAY74-15 [&
CONT. IN] 441:28MAY74-33
J.M. CAMERON, 453:31OCT74-6
M.G. MICHAELSON, 441:21JUL74-6
BECKER, H. & OTHERS. SOCIETIES
AROUND THE WORLD.
H. DUSSORT, 542:OCT-DEC72-495
BECKER, I.H. THE IRONIC DIMENSION
IN HAWTHORNE'S SHORT FICTION.
B.B. COHEN, 27(AL):MAY73-303
BECKER, J. DAS ENDE DER LANDSCHAFTS-
MALEREI.
617(TLS):9AUG74-852
BECKER, L. HENRY DE MONTHERLANT.*
R. POUILLIART, 549(RLC):OCT-DEC
72-625
BECKER, S. DOG TAGS.*
617(TLS):14JUN74-644
BECKER, W. PARIS UND DIE DEUTSCHE
MALEREI 1750-1850.
A. NEUMEYER, 54:SEP72-362
P. VAISSE, 683:BAND35HEFT4-321
BECKER, W.C. & J. SUCCESSFUL PARENT-
HOOD.
B. DE MOTT, 61:APR74-110
BECKERMAN, W. IN DEFENCE OF ECONOM-
IC GROWTH.
M. LIPTON, 617(TLS):18OCT74-1156
P. OPPENHEIMER, 362:1AUG74-155
BECKETT, L. WALLACE STEVENS.
C. RAINE, 617(TLS):6DEC74-1390

BECKETT, R.B. - SEE "JOHN CONSTA-
BLE'S DISCOURSES"
BECKETT, S. LE DÉPEUPLEUR.*
J-P. CAUVIN, 207(FR):DEC71-461
BECKETT, S. FIRST LOVE.* (FRENCH
TITLE: PREMIER AMOUR.)
E. KERN, 207(FR):DEC71-462
J.D. O'HARA, 441:15SEP74-46
BECKETT, S. MERCIER & CAMIER.
E. KERN, 207(FR):DEC71-462
T. KILROY, 617(TLS):13DEC74-1405
"SAMUEL BECKETT: AN EXHIBITION."
205(FMLS):OCT72-385
BECKFORD, W. DREAMS, WAKING
THOUGHTS & INCIDENTS. (R.J. GEM-
METT, ED)
M. JOHNSON, 481(PQ):JUL72-640
BECKHAM, B. RUNNER MACK.
S. O'CONNELL, 418(MR):WINTER73-
190
BECKSMANN, R. DIE ARCHITEKTONISCHE
RAHMUNG DES HOCHGOTISCHEN BILDFEN-
STERS.*
J. HAYWARD, 589:JAN73-110
BECKSON, K., ED. OSCAR WILDE: THE
CRITICAL HERITAGE.
K. CONNELLY, 97(CQ):VOL6#1-93
BECKWITH, J. EARLY CHRISTIAN & BYZ-
ANTINE ART.*
P.H., 90:FEB72-102
G. MATHEW, 39:JAN72-72
DUCHESS OF BEDFORD. NICOLE NOBODY.
617(TLS):19APR74-425
BEDFORD, S. ALDOUS HUXLEY.* (VOL 1)
W. PRITCHARD, 364:FEB/MAR74-110
BEDFORD, S. ALDOUS HUXLEY. (VOL 2)
R. DINNAGE, 617(TLS):20SEP74-
1017
C. SYKES, 362:17OCT74-511
BEDFORD, S. ALDOUS HUXLEY. [1-VOL
ED]
D. TRILLING, 441:24NOV74-1
BEDIENT, C. ARCHITECTS OF THE SELF.*
J. GINDIN, 401(MLQ):MAR73-108
A. JOHNSON, 177(ELT):VOL15#4-332
R. SALE, 249(HUDR):WINTER73/74-
704
G.B. TENNYSON, 445(NCF):DEC72-
365
639(VQR):WINTER73-XX
BEDIENT, C. EIGHT CONTEMPORARY
POETS.
H. VENDLER, 441:15DEC74-6
617(TLS):13SEP74-968
BEDINI, G. & G. FANELLI. LUCCA.
H. HONOUR, 90:JUN72-416
BEDINI, S.A. THE LIFE OF BENJAMIN
BANNEKER.*
639(VQR):SUMMER72-LXXXVIII
"THE BEDSIDE GUARDIAN 23."
617(TLS):22NOV74-1306
BEECHER, J. & R. BIENVENU - SEE FOUR-
IER, C.
BEECHING, W.A. CENTURY OF THE TYPE-
WRITER.
617(TLS):4OCT74-1073
BEEKES, R.S.P. THE DEVELOPMENT OF
THE PROTO-INDO-EUROPEAN LARYNGEALS
IN GREEK.*
F.R. ADRADOS, 343:BAND14HEFT2-
172
H. RIX, 343:BAND14HEFT2-176

BEEKMAN, E.M. HOMEOPATHY OF THE
ABSURD.
L. GILLET, 556(RLV):1972/5-557
BEEMAN, R.R. THE OLD DOMINION & THE
NEW NATION, 1788-1801.
H. AMMON, 656(WMQ):JUL73-510
BEER, B.L. NORTHUMBERLAND.
617(TLS):13SEP74-983
BEER, G. MEREDITH.*
S.J. SPÅNBERG, 597(SN):VOL44#1-
176
I. WILLIAMS, 541(RES):FEB72-98
I. WILLIAMS, 637(VS):SEP72-113
BEER, G. THE ROMANCE.*
N. SUCKLING, 208(FS):JAN73-107
BEER, P. THE ESTUARY.
A. CLUYSENAAR, 565:VOL13#2-72
BEER, P. AN INTRODUCTION TO THE
METAPHYSICAL POETS.
R. WILCHER, 402(MLR):JUL73-637
BEER, P. READER, I MARRIED HIM.
B. HARDY, 617(TLS):13DEC74-1408
C. TOMALIN, 362:28NOV74-714
BEERS, H.W. AN AMERICAN EXPERIENCE
IN INDONESIA.
J.L. PEACOCK, 293(JAST):MAY72-
737
BEERS, H.W., ED. INDONESIA.
J.D. CLARKSON, 293(JAST):FEB72-
457
BEESTON, A.F.L. THE ARABIC LANGUAGE
TODAY.
F. CORRIENTE, 399(MLJ):NOV72-466
BEETHAM, D. MAX WEBER & THE THEORY
OF MODERN POLITICS.
617(TLS):10MAY74-505
VAN BEETHOVEN, L. LUDWIG VAN BEE-
THOVENS KONVERSATIONSHEFTE. (VOL 1)
(K-H. KÖHLER & G. HERRE, WITH G.
BROSCHE, EDS)
A. TYSON, 415:DEC73-1239
J.A.W., 410(M&L):APR73-219
VAN BEETHOVEN, L. LUDWIG VAN
BEETHOVENS KONVERSATIONSHEFTE.
(VOL 5) (K-H. KÖHLER, G. HERRE &
P. POTSCHNER, EDS)
J.A.W., 410(M&L):APR73-219
"BEETHOVEN-STUDIEN."
A.H. KING, 182:VOL25#22-806
BEHAN, B. MY LIFE WITH BRENDAN.
617(TLS):8MAR74-230
BEHAN, B. RICHARD'S CORK LEG.
617(TLS):26APR74-440
BÉHAR, S. L'UNIVERS MÉDICAL DE
PROUST.
M-R. FINN, 207(FR):MAR72-918
BEHAR, S. PIÈCES INÉDITES.
F. TONELLI, 207(FR):MAR72-896
BEHRMAN, S.N. DUVEEN.
290(JAAC):SPRING73-422
BEHZAD, F. ADAM OLEARIUS' "PERSIAN-
ISCHER ROSENTHAL."
A. MENHENNET, 402(MLR):APR73-453
BEICKEN, P.U. FRANZ KAFKA.
617(TLS):25OCT74-1198
BEIDELMAN, T.O. THE KAGURU.
R.G. ABRAHAMS, 69:APR72-169
BEIJBOM, U. SWEDES IN CHICAGO.
W. JOHNSON, 563(SS):SPRING73-159
BEIN, A. - SEE RUPPIN, A.
BEISTER, H. UNTERSUCHUNGEN ZU DER
ZEIT DER THEBANISCHEN HEGEMONIE.
G.L. CAWKWELL, 303:VOL92-229

BEITL, K., ED. VOLKSKUNDE FAKTEN
UND ANALYSEN.
E. ETTLINGER, 203:WINTER72-346
"BEITRÄGE ZUR DEUTSCHEN VOLKS- UND
ALTERTUMSKUNDE." (VOL 15)
E. ETTLINGER, 203:AUTUMN72-259
BEJA, M. EPIPHANY IN THE MODERN
NOVEL.*
M. JOHNSON, 329(JJQ):FALL73-73
J.J. WHITE, 149:SEP73-272
BEKKER, C. HITLER'S NAVAL WAR. (F.
ZIEGLER, ED & TRANS)
617(TLS):18OCT74-1159
BEKKER, H. THE NIBELUNGENLIED.*
J.E. CREAN, JR., 406:SPRING73-76
G. MÜLLER, 597(SN):VOL44#2-422
BEKKERS, J.A.F. - SEE MORRIS, J.
BELAVAL, Y. PHILOSOPHERS & THEIR
LANGUAGE.
M. OPPENHEIMER, 186(ETC.):MAR72-
96
BELBEN, R. THE LIMIT.
617(TLS):16AUG74-877
BELFRAGE, C. THE AMERICAN INQUISI-
TION, 1945-1960.*
D. CAUTE, 473(PR):3/1973-538
BĚLIČ, O. ANÁLISIS ESTRUCTURAL DE
TEXTOS HISPANOS.*
H. HATZFELD, 240(HR):AUTUMN72-
467
BELITT, B. - SEE NERUDA, P.
BELL, A. TUDOR FOUNDATION.
617(TLS):8NOV74-1269
BELL, C. PORTUGAL & THE QUEST FOR
THE INDIES.
617(TLS):13SEP74-984
BELL, D. THE COMING OF POST-INDUS-
TRIAL SOCIETY.*
A. HACKER, 231:SEP74-72
R. NISBET, 31(ASCH):SUMMER74-506
A. RYAN, 362:14FEB74-214
R. TODD, 61:JAN74-91
BELL, J.B. THE MYTH OF THE GUERRIL-
LA.
E.F. ZIEMKE, 579(SAQ):WINTER73-
164
BELL, J.L. & A.B. SLOMSON. MODELS &
ULTRAPRODUCTS.
P. SMITH, 316:DEC72-763
BELL, M. THE ESCAPE INTO YOU.
B.M., 502(PRS):FALL72-274
639(VQR):WINTER72-XXII
BELL, M. PRIMITIVISM.
205(FMLS):OCT72-381
BELL, M.D. HAWTHORNE & THE HISTORI-
CAL ROMANCE OF NEW ENGLAND.*
J.J. MC ALEER, 613:AUTUMN72-452
J.H. MC ELROY, 50(ARQ):SPRING72-
89
B. NEVIUS, 445(NCF):SEP72-241
L. WILLSON, 401(MLQ):JUN73-215
639(VQR):WINTER72-XXVI
BELL, Q. VIRGINIA WOOLF.* (VOL 1)
D-M. MONAGHAN, 150(DR):WINTER
72/73-695
C. ROSQUI, 529(QQ):WINTER72-565
S. SPENDER, 364:FEB/MAR73-137
BELL, Q. VIRGINIA WOOLF.* (VOL 2)
S. SPENDER, 364:FEB/MAR73-137
BELL, Q. VIRGINIA WOOLF.* (VOLS
1&2 BOUND IN ONE VOL)
G. GERSH, 396(MODA):SUMMER73-325
G.S. HAIGHT, 676(YR):SPRING73-
426

[CONTINUED]

25

BENNETT, E.L., JR. & J-P. OLIVIER. THE PYLOS TABLETS TRANSCRIBED. (PT 1)
617(TLS):8MAR74-232
BENNETT, G.N. THE REALISM OF WILLIAM DEAN HOWELLS, 1889-1920.
K. VANDERBILT, 27(AL):MAY73-306
BENNETT, H. WAIT UNTIL THE EVENING.
J. YARDLEY, 441:22SEP74-14
BENNETT, H.S. ENGLISH BOOKS & READERS 1603 TO 1640.*
J.H.P. PAFFORD, 447(N&Q):MAR72-119
BENNETT, J. KANT'S DIALECTIC.
617(TLS):30AUG74-922
BENNETT, J. LOCKE, BERKELEY, HUME.*
V.M. COOKE, 258:DEC72-621
J.L. DELAPLAIN, 481(PQ):JUL72-724
J.J. JENKINS, 483:APR72-175
S. RAPPAPORT, 319:JAN74-117
D.D. TODD, 154:MAR72-115
BENNETT, J.A.W. CHAUCER'S BOOK OF FAME.*
W. WEISS, 38:BAND90HEFT1/2-227
BENNETT, J.A.W. - SEE LANGLAND, W.
BENNETT, J.A.W. & G.V. SMITHERS. EARLY MIDDLE ENGLISH VERSE & PROSE.* (2ND ED)
J.R. SIMON, 189(EA):JAN-MAR72-86
BENNETT, J.G. IS THERE "LIFE" ON EARTH? GURDJIEFF.
D.W. HARDING, 453:18JUL74-6
BENNETT, R. PHASES OF MEMORY.
617(TLS):16AUG74-879
BENNETT, S. - SEE HOWELLS, W.D.
BENOÎT, F. LE SYMBOLISME DANS LES SANCTUAIRES DE LA GAULE.*
A. ERNOUT, 555:VOL46FASC1-169
BENOT, Y. DIDEROT.*
M. DUCHET, 535(RHL):MAY-JUN72-530
R. NIKLAUS, 208(FS):JAN73-70
BENSON, C.R. THOMAS JEFFERSON AS SOCIAL SCIENTIST.
S.G. BROWN, 656(WMQ):APR72-323
BENSON, J.A. HEMINGWAY.
B. ROUSE, 599:SPRING72-207
BENSON, L.D. & T.M. ANDERSSON, EDS. THE LITERARY CONTEXT OF CHAUCER'S FABLIAUX.
H. COOPER, 382(MAE):1973/3-285
R.M. WILSON, 402(MLR):JAN73-147
BENTALL, R. MY STORE OF MEMORIES.
617(TLS):29NOV74-1351
BENTHALL, J., ED. THE LIMITS OF HUMAN NATURE.
617(TLS):4JAN74-17
BENTHALL, J. SCIENCE & TECHNOLOGY IN ART TODAY.
H. HURRELL, 592:NOV72-206
BENTHAM, J. COLLECTED WORKS OF JEREMY BENTHAM. (VOLS 3&4) (J.H. BURNS & H.L.A. HART, EDS)
D. LYONS, 483:JAN72-74
BENTLEY, E. THEATRE OF WAR.*
R. COHN, 397(MD):MAR73-459
B.H. FUSSELL, 249(HUDR):WINTER 73/74-753
BENTLEY, G.E. THE PROFESSION OF DRAMATIST IN SHAKESPEARE'S TIME, 1590-1642.*
S. BARNET, 191(ELN):DEC72-131
S.R. MAVEETY, 648:OCT72-69
[CONTINUED]

[CONTINUING]
C.H. SHATTUCK, 301(JEGP):OCT73-554
BENTLEY, G.E., JR. THE BLAKE COLLECTION OF MRS. LANDON K. THORNE.
J.E. GRANT, 481(PQ):JUL72-642
BENTLEY, N. TALES FROM SHAKESPEARE.
A. BENEDICT, 157:WINTER72-80
BENTLEY, P. MORE TALES OF THE WEST RIDING.
N. SHRAPNEL, 617(TLS):8NOV74-1248
BENTON, K. CRAIG & THE JAGUAR.
M. LEVIN, 441:23JUN74-34
BENTON, K. DEATH ON THE APPIAN WAY.
617(TLS):17MAY74-517
BENTON, K. SOLE AGENT.
N. CALLENDAR, 441:10MAR74-12
BENVENISTE, É. PROBLÈMES DE LINGUISTIQUE GÉNÉRALE. (VOL 2)
617(TLS):26JUL74-792
BENVENISTE, É. LE VOCABULAIRE DES INSTITUTIONS INDO-EUROPÉENNES.*
R. SCHMITT, 343:BAND14HEFT1-39
O. SZEMERÉNYI, 303:VOL92-215
"ROLOFF BENY IN ITALY."
W. FEAVER, 362:19&26DEC74-847
BEONIO-BROCCHIERI FUMAGALLI, M.T. DURANDO DI S. PORZIANO.
J. JOLIVET, 542:JAN-MAR72-79
"BEOWULF." (C.L. WRENN, ED; REV BY W.F. BOLTON) "BEOWULF, A VERSE TRANSLATION." (M. ALEXANDER, TRANS)
617(TLS):1FEB74-100
BÉRANGER, J. RECHERCHES SUR L'ASPECT IDÉOLOGIQUE DU PRINCIPAT.
A. VIRIEUX-REYMOND, 542:OCT-DEC 72-496
BERBEROVA, N. KURSIV MOJ.
J.D. ELSWORTH, 575(SEER):JAN73-158
DE BERCEO, G. OBRAS COMPLETAS. (VOL 2) (B. DUTTON, ED)
617(TLS):19APR74-422
DE BERCEO, G. "LA VIDA DE SAN MILLÁN DE LA CONGOLLA" DE GONZALO DE BERCEO. (B. DUTTON, ED) GONZALO DE BERCEO, "ESTORIA DE SAN MILLÁN." (G. KOBERSTEIN, ED)
J. GULSOY, 545(RPH):MAY73-719
BERCKENHAGEN, E. DIE FRANZÖSISCHEN ZEICHNUNGEN DER KUNSTBIBLIOTHEK BERLIN.
A. BLUNT, 90:MAR72-178
R. JULLIAN, 182:VOL25#5/6-169
BERCKMAN, E. WAIT, JUST YOU WAIT.
442(NY):19AUG74-92
BERCOVITCH, S. HOROLOGICALS TO CHRONOMETRICALS.
M. MC GIFFERT, 656(WMQ):APR72-324
D. SMITH, 165:WINTER74-307
BERCOVITCH, S., ED. TYPOLOGY & EARLY AMERICAN LITERATURE.*
E.H. DAVIDSON, 301(JEGP):APR73-255
J.A.L. LEMAY, 568(SCN):FALL-WINTER73-100
BERENDSOHN, W.A. DIE KÜNSTLERISCHE ENTWICKLUNG HEINES IM BUCH DER LIEDER.
J.L.S., 191(ELN):SEP72(SUPP)-148

BERENT, E. DIE AUFFASSUNG DER LIEBE
BEI OPITZ UND WECKHERLIN UND IHRE
GESCHICHTLICHEN VORSTUFEN.*
　　L. FORSTER, 220(GL&L):OCT72-84
　　H. POWELL, 220(GQ):JAN72-130
BERESFORD, M. & H.P.R. FINBERG.
ENGLISH MEDIEVAL BOROUGHS.
　617(TLS):8MAR74-244
BERESFORD-HOWE, C. THE BOOK OF EVE.*
　　R.M. BROWN, 296:VOL3#3-89
　　R. HUNT, 198:SPRING74-82
BEREZIN, F.M. OČERKI PO ISTORII
JAZYKOZNANIJA V ROSSII.
　　D.B. JOHNSON, 353:15MAR72-85
BEREZIN, F.M. SKIZZEN ZUR GESCHICH-
TE DER SPRACHWISSENSCHAFT IN RUSS-
LAND.
　　F. ERLENBUSCH, 72:BAND210HEFT1/3-
　　236
BERG, A., WITH R.J. MUSCAT. THE
NUTRITION FACTOR.
　　M. LIPTON, 617(TLS):23AUG74-912
VAN DEN BERG, J.H. THE CHANGING
NATURE OF MAN.
　　L. STONE, 453:14NOV74-25
BERG, L. SOZIAL ETHIK.
　　J. GOLDMAN, 542:OCT-DEC72-497
BERG, S. THE DAUGHTERS.*
　　L. LIEBERMAN, 676(YR):WINTER73-
　　267
BERG, W. EARLY VIRGIL.
　617(TLS):3MAY74-470
BERGAMINI, D. JAPAN'S IMPERIAL CON-
SPIRACY.*
　　S. OKAMOTO, 293(JAST):FEB72-414
BERGÉ, C. A COUPLE CALLED MOEBIUS.
　639(VQR):SPRING73-LX
BERGENS, A. PRÉVERT.*
　　L. JONES, 399(MLJ):APR72-251
BERGER, D.A. IMITATIONSTHEORIE UND
GATTUNGSDENKEN IN DER LITERATUR-
KRITIK RICHARD HURDS.
　　L.A. ELIOSEFF, 290(JAAC):SUMMER
　　73-564
BERGER, H.H. PROGRESSIVE & CONSER-
VATIVE MAN.
　　H.B. TIMOTHY, 154:SEP72-487
BERGER, J. G.*
　　M. GREEN, 364:APR/MAY73-160
BERGER, R. EXECUTIVE PRIVILEGE.
　　P. ADAMS, 61:JUL74-100
　　G. WILLS, 441:5MAY74-1
　　442(NY):3JUN74-111
BERGER, R., ED. SCIENTIFIC METHODS
IN MEDIEVAL ARCHAEOLOGY.
　　A.R. UBBELOHDE, 589:APR73-340
BERGER, R.W. ANTOINE LE PAUTRE.
　　J. LEES-MILNE, 39:AUG72-165
　　K. MERTEN, 576:MAY72-152
BERGER, T. REGIMENT OF WOMEN.*
　　J. MELLORS, 362:11JUL74-61
　　E. ROVIT, 659:AUTUMN74-539
　617(TLS):24MAY74-545
　639(VQR):AUTUMN73-CXXXVI
BERGERON, D.M. ENGLISH CIVIC PAG-
EANTRY, 1558-1642.
　　R.J. LORDI, 568(SCN):SPRING73-16
BERGERON, D.M. & H.B. CALDWELL,
COMPS. TWENTIETH-CENTURY CRITI-
CISM OF ENGLISH MASQUES, PAGEANTS,
& ENTERTAINMENTS.
　　J.A. FREEMAN, 568(SCN):FALL-
　　WINTER73-89

VAN DEN BERGHE, P.L. POWER & PRIVI-
LEGE AT AN AFRICAN UNIVERSITY.
　617(TLS):9AUG74-855
BERGMAN, A. THE BIG KISS-OFF OF
1944.
　　N. CALLENDAR, 441:31MAR74-41
BERGMAN, B. & H. SÖDERBERG. KÄRA
HJALLE KÄRA BO. (P. WÄSTBERG, ED)
　　R. JARVI, 563(SS):SPRING73-172
BERGMAN, I. SCENES FROM A MARRIAGE.
　　D. BROMWICH, 441:4AUG74-21
BERGMAN, I. & OTHERS. BERGMAN ON
BERGMAN.
　　D. BROMWICH, 441:4AUG74-21
　617(TLS):19JUL74-760
BERGMAN, J. ICH BIN ISIS.
　　R.E. WITT, 303:VOL92-222
BERGMANN, R. STUDIEN ZU ENTSTEHUNG
UND GESCHICHTE DER DEUTSCHEN PAS-
SIONSSPIELE DES 13. UND 14. JAHR-
HUNDERTS.*
　　W.F. MICHAEL, 301(JEGP):JAN73-68
BERGNER, H., ED. ENGLISH CHARACTER-
WRITING.
　568(SCN):SPRING73-22
BERGONZI, B. T.S. ELIOT.
　　D.E.S. MAXWELL, 402(MLR):OCT73-
　　897
BERGONZI, B. THE TURN OF A CENTURY.*
　　R. NYE, 364:JUN/JUL73-146
　　R. SALE, 249(HUDR):WINTER73/74-
　　704
BERGOUNIOUX, L-A. UN PRÉCURSEUR DE
LA PLÉIADE.
　　H.H. KALWIES, 207(FR):FEB72-747
BERGSTEIN, E. ADVANCING PAUL NEW-
MAN.*
　　R. TODD, 61:MAY74-130
BERGSTEN, B. - SEE NIVER, K.R.
BÉRIMONT, L. L'ÉVIDENCE MÊME.
　　T. GREENE, 207(FR):APR72-1037
BERKE, J. & C.C. HERNTON. THE CAN-
NABIS EXPERIENCE.
　　L. TAYLOR, 362:16MAY74-640
BERKELEY, G. SCHRIFTEN ÜBER DIE
GRUNDLAGEN DER MATHEMATIK UND
PHYSIK.
　　L. GÄBE, 53(AGP):BAND54HEFT3-307
BERKOV, P.N. ISTORIYA SOVETSKOGO
BIBLIOFIL'STVA (1917-1967).
　　J.S.G. SIMMONS, 78(BC):SPRING72-
　　141
BERKOWITZ, M.I. & E.K.K. POON, COMPS.
HONGKONG STUDIES.
　　A. BIRCH, 302:JUL72-213
BERKSON, W. FIELDS OF FORCE.
　617(TLS):13SEP74-982
BERLE, M., WITH H. FRANKEL. MILTON
BERLE.
　　T. BUCKLEY, 441:21DEC74-25
　　R. LASSON, 441:6OCT74-34
BERLEANT, A. THE AESTHETIC FIELD.*
　　L.L. DUROCHE, 290(JAAC):FALL71-
　　125
BERLIN, B. & P. KAY. BASIC COLOR
TERMS.*
　　G.A. COLLIER, 350:MAR73-245
BERLIN, I. FATHERS & CHILDREN.
　　P. WADDINGTON, 575(SEER):JUL73-
　　466
BERLIN, N. THE BASE STRING.*
　　B. BABINGTON, 447(N&Q):DEC72-472

BERLYNE, D.E. AESTHETICS & PSYCHO-
BIOLOGY.
W. BLIZEK, 290(JAAC):SUMMER73-
553
BERMAN, H.J. THE INTERACTION OF LAW
& RELIGION.
A.C.J. PHILLIPS, 617(TLS):22NOV
74-1323
BERMAN, L., ED. WORDS & MUSIC.
N.C.F., 410(M&L):APR73-217
BERMAN, M. THE POLITICS OF AUTHEN-
TICITY.
S.P. HALBROOK, 484(PPR):SEP72-
121
BERMAN, R.J. BROWNING'S DUKE.
M. HANCHER, 402(MLR):JUL73-643
J.W. HERRING, 85:SPRING72-62
BERMANT, C. THE LAST SUPPER.*
M. LEVIN, 441:13JAN74-14
442(NY):18FEB74-118
BERNAL, J.D. THE EXTENSION OF MAN.
M. TEICH, 111:18MAY73-161
BERNAL, O. LANGAGE ET FICTION DANS
LE ROMAN DE BECKETT.*
P.H. SOLOMON, 546(RR):FEB72-74
BERNARD OF CLAIRVAUX. THE WORKS OF
BERNARD OF CLAIRVAUX. (VOL 2)
(K. WALSH, TRANS)
J.F. KELLY, 613:WINTER72-622
BERNARD, J-P. LIBÉRALISME, NATIONAL-
ISME ET ANTICLÉRICALISME AU MILIEU
DU XIXE SIÈCLE.
J. RUEST, 154:JUN72-320
BERNARD, L. THE EMERGING CITY.*
481(PQ):JUL72-521
BERNARD, P.P. JESUITS & JACOBINS.*
J.P. SPIELMAN, 481(PQ):JUL72-521
DE BERNARDI FERRERO, D. TEATRI CLAS-
SICI IN ASIA MINORE. (VOL 3)
G.M.A. RICHTER, 303:VOL92-245
BERND, C.A. - SEE STORM, T. & P.
HEYSE
BERNDTSON, A. ART, EXPRESSION, &
BEAUTY.*
D.J. CROSSLEY, 154:JUN72-317
BERNE, E. WHAT DO YOU SAY AFTER YOU
SAY HELLO?
617(TLS):22MAR74-296
BERNE, J., ED. CAHIERS DE L'HERNE:
JEAN DUBUFFET.
R. CARDINAL, 617(TLS):6DEC74-
1364
BERNEKER, E. & M. VASMER. RUSSISCHE
GRAMMATIK. (7TH ED) (M. BRÄUER-
POSPELOVA, ED)
C.L. DAWSON, 32:SEP73-667
BERNETTI, G. SAGGI E STUDI SUGLI
SCRITTI DI ENEA SILVIO PICCOLOMINI
PAPA PIO II (1405-1464).
D.D., 275(IQ):FALL/WINTER72-119
BERNHARD, F. SANSKRITTEXTE AUS DEN
TURFANFUNDEN X: UDĀNAVARGA. (VOL
2)
W. THOMAS, 260(IF):BAND76-274
BERNHARD, H.J. DIE ROMANE HEINRICH
BÖLLS.
R.C. CONARD, 221(GQ):NOV72-754
BERNHARD, M., ED. DEUTSCHE ROMANTIK
HANDZEICHNUNGEN.
617(TLS):8MAR74-228
BERNHARDT, J. PLATON ET LE MATÉRI-
ALISME ANCIEN.
J. TROUILLARD, 542:JAN-MAR72-42

BERNINGER, H. & J-A. CARTIER. JEAN
POUGNY (IWAN PUNI) 1892-1956.*
(VOL 1)
J.E. BOWLT, 575(SEER):JAN73-129
BERNOT, D. BIBLIOGRAPHIE BIRMANE.
D.N. MARSHALL, 182:VOL25#19/20-
641
BERNSTEIN, C. & B. WOODWARD. ALL
THE PRESIDENT'S MEN.
B. BEEDHAM, 362:18JUL74-92
W. JUST, 61:JUL74-90
D. KEARNS, 441:9JUN74-1
C. LEHMANN-HAUPT, 441:14MAY74-41
R.H. ROVERE, 442(NY):17JUN74-107
J. VAIZEY, 617(TLS):28JUN74-693
G. WILLS, 453:13JUN74-6
BERNSTEIN, M.H. - SEE CHAPMAN, J.J.
BERNSTEIN, R.J. PRAXIS & ACTION.
A. MAC INTYRE, 543:JUN72-737
42(AR):SPRING/SUMMER72-245
BERNSTEIN, S. AUGUSTE BLANQUI.
P.H. AMANN, 207(FR):MAR72-893
BÉROUL. THE ROMANCE OF TRISTRAN.*
(VOL 2) (A. EWERT, ED)
I. SHORT, 545(RPH):NOV72-466
DE BERRÊDO CARNEIRO, P.E. & P. AR-
NAUD - SEE COMTE, A.
BERRIDGE, E. - SEE BROWNING, E.B.
BERRISFORD, J. WINDOW BOX & CONTAIN-
ER GARDENING.
617(TLS):15NOV74-1297
BERRY, A. THE NEXT TEN THOUSAND
YEARS.
617(TLS):7JUN74-620
BERRY, D.C. SAIGON CEMETERY.*
J.W. HEALEY, 502(PRS):WINTER72/
73-355
639(VQR):AUTUMN72-CXXIV
BERRY, L.E. - SEE STUBBS, J.
BERRY, M. MULK RAJ ANAND.
S. COWASJEE, 268:JAN74-54
BERRY, R. THE ART OF JOHN WEBSTER.
I. BROWN, 157:AUTUMN72-77
BERRY, R. SHAKESPEARE'S COMEDIES.*
T. HAWKES, 676(YR):SUMMER73-561
M. MUDRICK, 249(HUDR):SUMMER73-
375
639(VQR):SPRING73-LXVIII
BERRY, W. THE COUNTRY OF MARRIAGE.
D. ALLEN, 491:MAY74-103
J. DITSKY, 398:SPRING74-92
BERRY, W. THE MEMORY OF OLD JACK.
J.R. FRAKES, 441:31MAR74-38
BERRYMAN, J. DELUSIONS, ETC.*
J. SYMONS, 364:DEC72/JAN73-129
H. VENDLER, 676(YR):SPRING73-412
42(AR):SPRING/SUMMER72-241
639(VQR):AUTUMN72-CXXI
BERRYMAN, J. LOVE & FAME.*
E.N. CHUILLEANÁIN, 159(DM):
WINTER/SPRING71/72-123
T. EAGLETON, 565:VOL13#3-71
T.H. LANDESS, 569(SR):WINTER73-
137
E.C. STEFANIK, 539(REN):SPRING73-
115
BERRYMAN, J. RECOVERY.*
M. MUDRICK, 249(HUDR):AUTUMN73-
545
R. SALE, 418(MR):AUTUMN73-834
639(VQR):AUTUMN73-CXXXVI

BERSANI, J., ED. LES CRITIQUES DE
NOTRE TEMPS ET PROUST.*
    J. CRUICKSHANK, 208(FS):OCT73-
    472
BERSANI, J. & OTHERS, EDS. LA LIT-
TÉRATURE EN FRANCE DEPUIS 1945.
    J. CRUICKSHANK, 208(FS):OCT73-
    480
    J. DUBOIS, 556(RLV):1972/5-551
    M. HANREZ, 207(FR):DEC71-498
    R.M. MIKUS, 207(FR):MAY72-1205
BERSANI, L. BALZAC TO BECKETT.*
    R. KLEIN, 473(PR):2/1973-294
    J.C. MC LAREN, 613:SPRING72-139
BERSHADY, H.J. IDEOLOGY & SOCIAL
KNOWLEDGE.
    617(TLS):11JAN74-37
BERTAUX, P. HÖLDERLIN UND DIE FRAN-
ZÖSISCHE REVOLUTION.*
    C.H., 191(ELN):SEP72(SUPP)-156
BERTELLI, S. & G. RICUPERATI - SEE
GIANNONE, P.
BERTHE, L.N. & M. DE LANGRE - SEE
ROBESPIERRE, M.
BERTHOFF, A.E. THE RESOLVED SOUL.*
    R. ELLRODT, 189(EA):OCT-DEC70-
    551
    J.M. WALLACE, 405(MP):MAY73-364
    M. WILDING, 677:VOL3-288
BERTHOFF, R. AN UNSETTLED PEOPLE.
    B.W. SHEEHAN, 656(WMQ):JAN73-154
BERTHOFF, W. FICTIONS & EVENTS.*
    L.T. LEMON, 502(PRS):FALL72-268
BERTHOUD, E. AUGUST BACHELIN ET LE
BIBLIOPHILE JACOB.
    A. BETTEX, 182:VOL25#17/18-577
BERTINI, F. - SEE PLAUTUS
BERTO, G. ANONYMOUS VENETIAN.*
    G. EWART, 364:OCT/NOV73-152
BERTON, P. THE LAST SPIKE.
    P.B. WAITE, 150(DR):SPRING72-140
BERTON, R. REMEMBERING BIX.
    J. WIDEMAN, 441:18AUG74-6
BERTONASCO, M.F. CRASHAW & THE BAR-
OQUE.*
    R. DANIELLS, 402(MLR):APR73-388
    P.K. SUNDARARAJAN, 648:JUN72-61
BESCH, W. SPRACHLANDSCHAFTEN UND
SPRACHAUSGLEICH IM 15. JAHRHUN-
DERT.*
    W. LINDOW, 353:1JUL72-98
BESCOND, A-J. LE CHANT GRÉGORIEN.
    589:APR73-434
BESPALOFF, R. ON THE "ILIAD."
    J.B. HAINSWORTH, 123:MAR73-83
BESSETTE, G. L'INCUBATION.
    L.W. SUGDEN, 296:VOL3#2-82
BESSINGER, J.B., JR. & S.J. KAHRL,
EDS. ESSENTIAL ARTICLES FOR THE
STUDY OF OLD ENGLISH POETRY.*
    H. BERGNER, 38:BAND90HEFT1/2-208
BEST, G. MID-VICTORIAN BRITAIN,
1851-75.
    V.M. BATZEL, 637(VS):MAR73-365
    G.B. TENNYSON, 445(NCF):JUN72-
    117
    676(YR):AUTUMN72-XIV
BEST, M.R. & F.H. BRIGHTMAN, EDS.
THE BOOK OF SECRETS OF ALBERTUS
MAGNUS OF THE VIRTUES OF HERBS,
STONES & CERTAIN BEASTS. ALSO A
BOOK OF THE MARVELS OF THE WORLD.
    617(TLS):1FEB74-115

BEST, O.F. PETER WEISS.*
    H.R. PAUCKER, 221(GQ):MAY72-529
BESTERMAN, T. FIFTY YEARS A BOOKMAN.
    617(TLS):25OCT74-1207
BESTERMAN, T. SOME EIGHTEENTH-CEN-
TURY VOLTAIRE EDITIONS UNKNOWN TO
BENGESCO.
    617(TLS):26APR74-435
BESTERMAN, T., ED. STUDIES ON VOL-
TAIRE & THE EIGHTEENTH CENTURY.*
(VOL 73)
    J. LEDUC, 535(RHL):MAY-JUN72-522
BESTERMAN, T., ED. STUDIES ON VOL-
TAIRE & THE EIGHTEENTH CENTURY.
(VOL 76)
    R. NIKLAUS, 535(RHL):MAY-JUN72-
    526
BESTERMAN, T., ED. STUDIES ON VOL-
TAIRE & THE EIGHTEENTH CENTURY.
(VOL 77)
    G. BARBER, 208(FS):APR73-208
    J. VERCRUYSSE, 535(RHL):JUL-AUG
    72-721
BESTERMAN, T., ED. STUDIES ON VOL-
TAIRE & THE EIGHTEENTH CENTURY.
(VOL 79)
    R. NIKLAUS, 535(RHL):JUL-AUG72-
    723
BESTERMAN, T., ED. STUDIES ON VOL-
TAIRE & THE EIGHTEENTH CENTURY.
(VOLS 117, 118 & 120)
    H.T. MASON, 617(TLS):13DEC74-
    1424
BETH, E.W. ASPECTS OF MODERN LOGIC.*
    T.J. RICHARDS, 479(PHQ):JUL72-
    276
BETHEL, S. THE WORLD'S MISTAKE IN
OLIVER CROMWELL [1668].
    568(SCN):FALL-WINTER73-96
BETJEMAN, J. COLLECTED POEMS.*
    P. THOMAS, 651(WHR):SUMMER73-289
BETJEMAN, J. A NIP IN THE AIR.
    J. BAYLEY, 362:5DEC74-745
BETJEMAN, J. A PICTORIAL HISTORY OF
ENGLISH ARCHITECTURE. LONDON'S
HISTORIC RAILWAY STATIONS.
    H. CASSON, 46:SEP72-191
BETRIU, R.B. - SEE UNDER BORRÁS
BETRIU, R.
BETTARINI, R. - SEE VASARI, G.
BETTELHEIM, B. A HOME FOR THE HEART.
    R. DINNAGE, 617(TLS):2AUG74-829
    E. FIRST, 453:30MAY74-3
    E. JANEWAY, 441:17MAR74-27
    C. LEHMANN-HAUPT, 441:25MAR74-35
    442(NY):22APR74-155
BETTENSON, H., ED & TRANS. THE
LATER CHRISTIAN FATHERS.
    A.W. GODFREY, 363:MAY72-106
BETTEY, J.H. DORSET.
    617(TLS):21JUN74-680
BETTINI, S. & L. PUPPI. LA CHIESA
DEGLI EREMITANI DI PADOVA.
    D. ROBINSON, 90:NOV72-799
BETTONI, E. IL PROCESSO ASTRATTIVO
NELLE CONCEZIONE DI ENRICO DI GAND.
    E. NAMER, 542:JAN-MAR72-79
BETTS, D. THE RIVER TO PICKLE BEACH.
    J. YARDLEY, 473(PR):2/1973-286
    639(VQR):AUTUMN72-CXXI
BETZ, A. ÄSTHETIK UND POLITIK.
    J.L.S., 191(ELN):SEP72(SUPP)-149

BETZ, H.D. DER APOSTEL PAULUS UND
DIE SOKRATISCHE TRADITION.
F.F. BRUCE, 182:VOL25#11-338
BEUM, R. THE POETIC ART OF WILLIAM
BUTLER YEATS.
H. ADAMS, 219(GAR):FALL72-249
BEURDELEY, C. & M. A CONNOISSEUR'S
GUIDE TO CHINESE CERAMICS.
R. REIF, 441:13DEC74-41
BEURON, E., ED. VETUS LATINA. (VOL
24, PTS 2, 5 & 6)
A. ERNOUT, 555:VOL46FASC2-348
BEURON, E., ED. VETUS LATINA. (VOL
24, PTS 5, 6 & 7)
A. ERNOUT, 555:VOL46FASC2-349
BEUVE-MÉRY, H. ONZE ANS DE RÈGNE
1958-1969.
617(TLS):3MAY74-461
BEVAN, E.D., ED. A CONCORDANCE TO
THE PLAYS & PREFACES OF BERNARD
SHAW.
T.F. EVANS, 571:WINTER72/73-218
S. WEINTRAUB, 572:SEP72-117
BEVAN, H.K. LAW RELATING TO CHIL-
DREN.
617(TLS):25JAN74-88
BEVINGTON, H. BEAUTIFUL LOFTY PEO-
PLE.
J.W. JOHNSON, 441:3MAR74-6
BEYEN, R. MICHEL DE GHELDERODE OU
LA HANTISE DU MASQUE.
M. PIEMME, 556(RLV):1972/6-666
K.S. WHITE, 188(ECR):FALL72-237
205(FMLS):OCT72-379
BEYER, S. THE CULT OF TARA.
A.M. PIATIGORSKY, 617(TLS):20DEC
74-1447
VON BEYME, K. DIE POLITISCHE ELITE
IN DER BUNDESREPUBLIK DEUTSCHLAND.
G. PAULINE, 182:VOL25#11-349
BEYSSAC, M., COMP. LA VIE CULTUR-
ELLE DE L'ÉMIGRATION RUSSE EN
FRANCE: CHRONIQUE (1920-1930).
G. DONCHIN, 575(SEER):JUL73-484
DE BÈZE, T. ABRAHAM SACRIFIANT.
D. WILSON, 208(FS):JAN73-51
DE BÈZE, T. DU DROIT DES MAGISTRATS.
(R.M. KINGDON, ED)
R. BENERT, 551(RENQ):SPRING72-87
BEZZEL-DISCHNER, G. POETIK DES MOD-
ERNEN GEDICHTS.
C. HERING, 221(GQ):MAR72-369
BEZZOLA, G. - SEE MONTI, V.
BHARDWAJ, S.M. HINDU PLACES OF PIL-
GRIMAGE IN INDIA.
617(TLS):31MAY74-581
BHATIA, K. INDIRA.
P. GUPTE, 441:21SEP74-27
BHATIA, P. THE PARAMĀRAS (C. 800-
1305).
T.R. TRAUTMANN, 293(JAST):MAY72-
754
BHAṬṬA NĀRĀYAṆA. VEṆĪSAṂHĀRA. (F.
BOURGEOIS, ED & TRANS)
L. STERNBACH, 318(JAOS):OCT-DEC
72-575
BHATTACHARJI, S. THE INDIAN THEO-
GONY.
L.D. SHINN, 293(JAST):MAY72-699
BHATTACHARYA, S. A BONḌA DICTIONARY.
N.H. ZIDE, 318(JAOS):OCT-DEC72-
506

BHATTACHARYYA, B. EVOLUTION OF THE
POLITICAL PHILOSOPHY OF GANDHI.*
E.J. QUIGLEY, 485(PE&W):JAN72-
106
BHIKKHU ÑĀṆĀNANDA. CONCEPT & REAL-
ITY IN EARLY BUDDHIST THOUGHT.
S. ANACKER, 485(PE&W):OCT72-481
BIAŁOSTOCKI, J. LES MUSÉES DE POL-
OGNE (GDAŃSK, KRAKÓW, WARSZAWA).
M. HUGGLER, 182:VOL25#13/14-491
BIANCHI BANDINELLI, R. ROME, THE
LATE EMPIRE.
J.F. HEALY, 135:DEC72-291
J.M.C. TOYNBEE, 123:DEC73-260
BIANCO, L. ORIGINS OF THE CHINESE
REVOLUTION, 1915-1949.
J.K. FAIRBANK, 293(JAST):MAY72-
654
J.E. SHERIDAN, 318(JAOS):OCT-DEC
72-586
BIANCOFIORE, F. & O. TOTI. MONTE
ROVELLO.
617(TLS):8MAR74-232
BIANCONI, P. THE COMPLETE PAINTINGS
OF BRUEGEL. THE COMPLETE PAINT-
INGS OF VERMEER.
T. CROMBIE, 39:NOV72-461
BIASIN, G-P. THE SMILE OF THE GODS.
C. FANTAZZI, 593:SPRING73-91
VON BIBERACH, R. DIE SIBEN STRASSEN
ZU GOT.* (M. SCHMIDT, ED)
J. STABER, 680(ZDP):BAND91HEFT3-
470
O.F. WEBER, 680(ZDP):BAND91HEFT3-
469
"BIBLIOGRAPHIE INTERNATIONALE DE
L'HUMANISME ET DE LA RENAISSANCE."*
(VOL 4)
I.D. MC FARLANE, 208(FS):JAN73-
49
"BIBLIOGRAPHY OF THE HISTORY OF MEDI-
CINE 1964-1969."
D. VOGT, 517(PBSA):OCT-DEC73-474
"BIBLIOTHECA AMERICANA: CATALOGUE OF
THE JOHN CARTER BROWN LIBRARY IN
BROWN UNIVERSITY: BOOKS PRINTED
1675-1700." "BIBLIOTHECA AMERI-
CANA: ... SHORT-TITLE LIST OF ADDI-
TIONS: BOOKS PRINTED 1471-1700."
J.A.L. LEMAY, 165:FALL74-203
BIČANIĆ, R. ECONOMIC POLICY IN
SOCIALIST YUGOSLAVIA.
617(TLS):8MAR74-242
BICHA, K.D. THE AMERICAN FARMER &
THE CANADIAN WEST 1896-1914.
D. SWAINSON, 529(QQ):SUMMER72-
280
BICKNELL, P.J. STUDIES IN ATHENIAN
POLITICS & GENEALOGY.
F. LASSERRE, 182:VOL25#9/10-304
BIDART, F. GOLDEN STATE.
J. GALASSI, 491:NOV73-113
BIDWELL, C.E. OUTLINE OF UKRAINIAN
MORPHOLOGY. (REV) THE LANGUAGE
OF CARPATHO-RUTHENIAN PUBLICATIONS
IN AMERICA.
G.M. ERAMIAN, 104:SUMMER72-319
BIDWELL, R., ED. BIDWELL'S GUIDE TO
GOVERNMENT MINISTERS. (VOL 2)
617(TLS):29MAR74-348
BIDWELL, S. MODERN WARFARE.
617(TLS):1MAR74-197

BIEBUYCK, D.P., ED. TRADITION &
CREATIVITY IN TRIBAL ART.*
M.O. JONES, 650(WF):APR72-138
BIEDA, K. THE STRUCTURE & OPERATION
OF THE JAPANESE ECONOMY.
G.R. SAXONHOUSE, 293(JAST):NOV71-
205
BIEDENKOPF, K.H. MITBESTIMMUNG, BEI-
TRÄGE ZUR ORDNUNGSPOLITISCHEN DIS-
KUSSION.
A. PERESSIN, 182:VOL25#12-399
BIELER, L., ED. FOUR LATIN LIVES OF
ST. PATRICK.
M.L. COLKER, 589:APR73-341
BIELER, L. - SEE LOWE, E.A.
BIELFELDT, H.H. DIE ENTLEHNUNGEN
AUS DEN VERSCHIEDENEN SLAVISCHEN
SPRACHEN IM WORTSCHATZ DER NEU-
HOCHDEUTSCHEN SCHRIFTSPRACHE.
H. JELITTE, 343:BAND14HEFT2-214
BIELY, A. - SEE UNDER BELY, A.
BIEN, H. HENRIK IBSENS REALISMUS.*
E. WALTER & A. BETHKE, 654(WB):
9/1971-177
BIEN, P., J. RASSIAS & C. BIEN. DE-
MOTIC GREEK. (3RD ED)
K. KAZAZIS, 32:SEP73-676
BIENEK, H. THE CELL.
R. BLYTHE, 362:28FEB74-281
617(TLS):8MAR74-229
BIERHORST, J., ED. FOUR MASTERWORKS
OF AMERICAN INDIAN LITERATURE.
P. ADAMS, 61:SEP74-103
BIERWISCH, M. & K.E. HEIDOLPH, EDS.
PROGRESS IN LINGUISTICS.
W. ABRAHAM, 343:BAND15HEFT2-113
R.M. HOGG, 433:OCT72-493
R. LAKOFF, 350:SEP73-685
BIETENHOLZ, P.G. BASLE & FRANCE IN
THE SIXTEENTH CENTURY.
M.E. WELTI, 551(RENQ):WINTER72-
474
BIGA, D. OISEAUX MOHICANS.
A.J. ARNOLD, 207(FR):DEC71-464
BIGGS-DAVISON, J. THE HAND IS RED.
617(TLS):22FEB74-179
BIGSBY, C.W.E. DADA & SURREALISM.
205(FMLS):OCT72-381
BIHUN, Y. - SEE MOROZ, V.
BILEN, M. DIALECTIQUE CRÉATRICE ET
STRUCTURE DE L'OEUVRE LITTÉRAIRE.
J. CULLER, 208(FS):OCT73-483
BILL, V.T. INTERMEDIATE RUSSIAN.
C.L. DAWSON, 32:SEP73-667
M.K. LAUNER, 104:SUMMER72-311
BILLING, G. THE SLIPWAY.*
442(NY):7JAN74-72
617(TLS):1MAR74-219
BILLING, G. STATUES.
M.K. JOSEPH, 368:MAR72-91
BILLINGTON, R. BEAUTIFUL.
M. LEVIN, 441:18AUG74-21
617(TLS):31MAY74-591
BILLINGTON, R.A. FREDERICK JACKSON
TURNER.*
639(VQR):SUMMER73-CXVIII
DE BILLON, F. LE FORT INEXPUGNABLE
DE L'HONNEUR DU SEXE FEMENIN.
D. WILSON, 208(FS):JAN73-52
BILLS, G.D., B. VALLEJO C. & R.C.
TROIKE. AN INTRODUCTION TO SPOKEN
BOLIVIAN QUECHUA.
L.R. STARK, 269(IJAL):APR72-154

BILODEAU, F. BALZAC ET LE JEU DES
MOTS.
C.C., 191(ELN):SEP72(SUPP)-82
BINDER, A. DAS VORSPIEL AUF DEM
THEATER.
E. WEBER, 221(GQ):NOV72-703
BINDER, A.W. STUDIES IN JEWISH
MUSIC. (I. HESKES, ED)
D.W., 410(M&L):JAN73-82
BINDER, G. AENEAS UND AUGUSTUS.*
P.T. EDEN, 313:VOL62-221
BINDER, W. HÖLDERLIN-AUFSÄTZE.
C.H., 191(ELN):SEP72(SUPP)-157
BINDMAN, D., ED. WILLIAM BLAKE:
CATALOGUE OF THE COLLECTION IN THE
FITZWILLIAM MUSEUM, CAMBRIDGE.
M. BISHOP, 78(BC):SPRING72-133
K. GARLICK, 39:MAY72-426
481(PQ):JUL72-643
BINDSCHEDLER, M., R. HOTZENKÖCHERLE
& W. KOHLSCHMIDT, EDS. FEST-
SCHRIFT FÜR PAUL ZINSLI.
E. ETTLINGER, 203:AUTUMN72-258
R.E. KELLER, 402(MLR):OCT73-926
BINER, P. THE LIVING THEATRE.
B.H. FUSSELL, 249(HUDR):WINTER
73/74-753
BING, S. ARTISTIC AMERICA, TIFFANY
GLASS, & ART NOUVEAU.*
L.C. BRANTIGAN, 290(JAAC):SPRING
72-404
B. O'LOONEY, 90:JUN72-420
G.P. WEISBERG, 127:FALL72-114
BINGHAM, M. SHERIDAN.*
I. BROWN, 157:SUMMER72-69
639(VQR):SPRING73-LXXX
BINGHAM, S. THE WAY IT IS NOW.*
N.Y. HOFFMAN, 573(SSF):SUMMER72-
292
BINNI, W. - SEE RAMAT, R.
BINNS, J.W., ED. OVID.
617(TLS):8MAR74-232
BIONDI, C. & OTHERS. INTORNO A MON-
TESQUIEU. (C. ROSSO, ED)
R. SHACKLETON, 208(FS):APR73-210
BIOY CASARES, A. DIARY OF THE WAR
OF THE PIG.* (FRENCH TITLE: JOUR-
NAL DE LA GUERRE AU COCHON.)
P. CRUTTWELL & F. WESTBURG,
249(HUDR):SUMMER73-417
N. KATTAN, 98:AUG/SEP72-819
BIRCHALL, A. & P.E. CORBETT. GREEK
GODS & HEROES.
617(TLS):10MAY74-508
BIRCHER, M. JOHANN WILHELM VON STU-
BENBERG (1619-1663) UND SEIN
FREUNDESKREIS.*
A.M. HAAS, 400(MLN):APR72-518
BIRD, E.K. THE LONELIEST MAN IN THE
WORLD.
617(TLS):12JUL74-742
BIRDSALL, V.O. WILD CIVILITY.*
T.R. CLEARY, 376:APR72-130
T.H. FUJIMURA, 128(CE):APR72-845
BIRENBAUM, A. & E. SAGARIN, EDS.
PEOPLE IN PLACES.
C. DRIVER, 362:18APR74-508
BIRKENHAUER, K. DIE EIGENRHYTH-
MISCHE LYRIK BERTOLT BRECHTS.
G. STORZ, 182:VOL25#23/24-868
BIRKINSHAW, P. THE THINKING VOICE.
W. BIESTERFELD, 182:VOL25#15/16-
547

BLACKWOOD, C. FOR ALL THAT I FOUND
THERE.*
617(TLS):5APR74-361
BLADES, W. THE BIOGRAPHY & TYPOGRA-
PHY OF WILLIAM CAXTON, ENGLAND'S
FIRST PRINTER.
J. STEVENSON, 78(BC):AUTUMN72-
430
BLAINEY, G. THE STEEL MASTER.
A.A. CALWELL, 381:JUN72-226
BLAIR, P.H. - SEE UNDER HUNTER BLAIR,
P.
BLAIR, T.L. THE INTERNATIONAL URBAN
CRISIS.
617(TLS):18OCT74-1156
BLAIS, M. PARTICIPATION ET CONTES-
TATION.
T. DE KONINCK, 154:DEC72-625
BLAIS, M-C. UN JOUALONAIS SA JOUA-
LONIE.
B. GODARD, 296:VOL3#3-106
BLAIS, M-C. L'INSOUMISE.
H. MICHOT-DIETRICH, 207(FR):FEB
72-683
BLAIS, M-C. THE MANUSCRIPTS OF
PAULINE ARCHANGE.
J. KRAFT, 454:FALL72-73
BLAIS, M-C. ST. LAWRENCE BLUES.
M. ATWOOD, 441:29SEP74-4
BLAIS, M-C. DAVID STERNE.
D. CAVANAGH, 296:VOL3#3-105
BLAISE, C. A NORTH AMERICAN EDUCA-
TION.*
D. GUTTERIDGE, 99:JAN74-42
BLAISE, C. TRIBAL JUSTICE.
D. GUTTERIDGE, 99:NOV/DEC74-20
M. LEVIN, 441:29SEP74-40
BLAKE, F.M. THE STRIKE IN THE AMERI-
CAN NOVEL.
P. LISCA, 27(AL):MAR73-141
BLAKE, K. PLAY, GAMES & SPORT.
A. QUINTON, 617(TLS):20DEC74-
1436
BLAKE, N.F. - SEE "THE HISTORY OF
REYNARD THE FOX"
BLAKE, N.M. NOVELISTS' AMERICA.
J.M. SANTRAUD, 189(EA):JAN-MAR72-
180
BLAKE, R.L.V.F. THE CRIMEAN WAR.
J.S. CURTISS, 32:JUN73-379
BLAKE, W. WILLIAM BLAKE: OEUVRES 1.
(P. LEYRIS, ED & TRANS)
617(TLS):26JUL74-796
BLAKE, W. THE BOOK OF THEL. (N.
BOGEN, ED)
I.H.C., 191(ELN):SEP72(SUPP)-32
J.E. GRANT, 481(PQ):JUL72-643
639(VQR):SPRING72-LVII
BLAKE, W. DRAWINGS OF WILLIAM BLAKE.
(G. KEYNES, ED)
D.V.E., 191(ELN):SEP72(SUPP)-34
K. GARLICK, 39:MAY72-426
BLAKE, W. THE GRAVE. THE BOOK OF
AHANIA.
617(TLS):15FEB74-145
BLAKE, W. THE NOTEBOOK OF WILLIAM
BLAKE. (D.V. ERDMAN & D.K. MOORE,
EDS)
D.A.N. JONES, 362:10JAN74-54
617(TLS):15FEB74-145
"BLAKE'S WATER-COLOUR DESIGNS ILLUS-
TRATING GRAY'S POEMS."
A. FAWCUS, 135:JAN72-10

BLAKELEY, F. DREAM MILLIONS. (M.
MANSFIELD, ED)
617(TLS):22FEB74-193
BLAKEMORE, H. BRITISH NITRATES &
CHILEAN POLITICS 1886-96.
617(TLS):3MAY74-472
BLAKEMORE, K. THE BOOK OF GOLD.
R.J.L. WYNNE THOMAS, 135:AUG72-
303
BLAKISTON, G. LORD WILLIAM RUSSELL
& HIS WIFE, 1815-1846.
P. HONAN, 637(VS):JUN73-459
BLALOCK, H.M., JR. THEORY CONSTRUC-
TION.
A. ROSENBERG, 486:DEC72-572
BLAMIRES, D. DAVID JONES.*
W. BLISSETT, 627(UTQ):SPRING72-
275
S. REES, 401(MLQ):MAR73-117
BLAMIRES, H. MILTON'S CREATION.
S.S. STOLLMAN, 628:SPRING73-113
205(FMLS):APR72-194
BLAMIRES, H. WORD UNHEARD.*
H.Z. MACCOBY, 447(N&Q):SEP72-348
BLANCH, J.M.L. - SEE UNDER LOPE
BLANCH, J.M.
BLANCH, L. PAVILIONS OF THE HEART.
442(NY):24JUN74-104
BLANCHARD, D. CARTES.
A.G. RODRIGUEZ, 207(FR):FEB72-
683
BLANCHE-BENVENISTE, C. & A. CHERVEL.
L'ORTHOGRAPHE.*
J. KELEMEN, 353:1NOV72-114
BLANCHOT, M. LE PAS AU-DELÀ.
617(TLS):12APR74-389
BLANCK, J. BIBLIOGRAPHY OF AMERICAN
LITERATURE. (VOL 6)
617(TLS):26APR74-456
BLANK, W. DIE DEUTSCHE MINNEALLE-
GORIE.*
F. JACOBY, 221(GQ):NOV72-720
G.F. JONES, 400(MLN):APR72-517
BLANKENSHIP, J. PUBLIC SPEAKING.
(2ND ED)
V.R. KENNEDY, 583:SUMMER73-398
BLANKENSHIP, W.D. THE LEAVENWORTH
IRREGULARS.
M. LEVIN, 441:21APR74-40
BLÄNSDORF, J. ARCHAISCHE GEDANKEN-
GÄNGE IN DEN KOMÖDIEN DES PLAUTUS.
B. LÖFSTEDT, 260(IF):BAND76-291
BLANSHARD, B. THE USES OF A LIBERAL
EDUCATION. (E. FREEMAN, ED)
P. CAWS, 441:15SEP74-51
BLASCO, J. COMPRENDER PARA ESCRIBIR.
D.E. GULSTAD, 399(MLJ):NOV72-473
BLASS, R. DIE DICHTUNG GEORG TRAKLS.
T.J. CASEY, 220(GL&L):JUL73-324
B. SOWINSKI, 657(WW):MAR/APR72-
144
BLASSINGAME, J.W. THE SLAVE COMMUN-
ITY.*
G.W. MULLIN, 656(WMQ):JUL73-513
639(VQR):WINTER73-XXXIV
BLAXLAND, G. DESTINATION DUNKIRK.
617(TLS):4JAN74-6
BLAŽÍČEK, O.J. UMĚNÍ BAROKU V
ČECHÁCH.
M.S. FRINTA, 32:MAR73-189
BLECUA, J.M. SOBRE POESÍA DE LA
EDAD DE ORO.*
M.D. TRIWEDI, 238:MAY72-383

BLEECK, O. THE HIGHBINDERS.
N. CALLENDAR, 441:13JAN74-12
BLEIKER, J. ZUR MORPHOLOGIE UND
SPRACHGEOGRAPHIE DER VERBEN "HABEN,
SEIN, TUN" IN SCHWEIZERDEUTSCHEN.
L. SPULER, 400(MLN):APR72-515
BLEILER, E.F., ED. FIVE VICTORIAN
GHOST NOVELS.
G.B. TENNYSON, 445(NCF):JUN72-
121
BLEILER, E.F. - SEE HOFFMANN, E.T.A.
BLESSING, R.A. WALLACE STEVENS'
"WHOLE HARMONIUM."
J. PINKERTON, 128(CE):FEB72-600
BLET, P. & OTHERS, EDS. ACTES ET
DOCUMENTS DU SAINT SIÈGE RELATIFS
À LA SECONDE GUERRE MONDIALE.
(VOLS 6&7)
617(TLS):19APR74-424
BLET, P. & OTHERS, EDS. ACTES ET
DOCUMENTS DU SAINT SIÈGE RELATIFS
À LA SECONDE GUERRE MONDIALE.
(VOL 8)
617(TLS):1NOV74-1224
BLICKER, S. SCHMUCKS.*
P. STEVENS, 628:SPRING73-95
BLIER, B. GOING PLACES.
M. LEVIN, 441:22DEC74-14
BLISHEN, E. UNCOMMON ENTRANCE.
E.S. TURNER, 362:19SEP74-379
BLISS, M. A LIVING PROFIT.
T. TRAVES, 99:NOV/DEC74-45
BLISSETT, W., J. PATRICK & R.W. VAN
FOSSEN, EDS. A CELEBRATION OF BEN
JONSON.
617(TLS):20SEP74-1020
BLISTEIN, E.M., ED. THE DRAMA OF
THE RENAISSANCE.*
D. AGUZZI-BARBAGLI, 551(RENQ):
SPRING72-103
BLOCH, M. PLACING THE DEAD.
M. URBAIN-FAUBLÉE, 69:JUL72-256
BLOCH, O-R. LA PHILOSOPHIE DE GAS-
SENDI.
G. RODIS-LEWIS, 542:APR-JUN72-
203
BLOCH, R. AMERICAN GOTHIC.
N. CALLENDAR, 441:30JUN74-32
BLOCK, H.M. NATURALISTE TRIPTYCH.*
G.R. KAISER, 52:BAND7HEFT2/3-331
BLOCK, W.A. WHAT YOUR CHILD REALLY
WANTS TO KNOW ABOUT SEX - AND WHY.
D.C. ANDERSON, 441:10NOV74-47
BLOES, R. LE PLAN FOUCHET ET LE
PROBLÈME DE L'EUROPE POLITIQUE.
C. ZORGBIBE, 98:JUL72-669
BLOFELD, J. BEYOND THE GODS.
R.C. ZAEHNER, 617(TLS):6DEC74-
1389
BLOIS, J. & M. BAR. NOTRE LANGUE
FRANÇAISE.
M. LEYS, 556(RLV):1972/1-110
BLOM, Å.G. BALLADER OG LEGENDER FRA
NORSK MIDDELALDERDIKTNING.
W.E. RICHMOND, 563(SS):WINTER73-
72
BLONDEL, M. LE LIEN SUBSTANTIEL ET
LA SUBSTANCE COMPOSÉE D'APRÈS LEIB-
NIZ.
A. MERCIER, 182:VOL25#21-711
BLONDELL, J. CENTER DOOR FANCY.
R.L. BOWERS, 200:NOV72-565
BLOOM, A. - SEE KOJÈVE, A.
BLOOM, E. - SEE BURNEY, F.

BLOOM, E.A. & L.D. JOSEPH ADDISON'S
SOCIABLE ANIMAL.
L.A. ELIOSEFF, 173(ECS):SPRING73-
372
B.A. GOLDGAR, 301(JEGP):JAN73-
135
M. KELSALL, 541(RES):AUG72-360
C.J. RAWSON, 402(MLR):APR73-392
W.O.S. SUTHERLAND, 566:SPRING72-
80
M.R. ZIRKER, JR., 481(PQ):JUL72-
636
BLOOM, H. THE ANXIETY OF INFLUENCE.*
D.J. GORDON, 676(YR):SUMMER73-
583
D. HOFFMAN, 31(ASCH):AUTUMN74-
658
G. STADE, 473(PR):3/1973-494
639(VQR):SUMMER73-CXV
BLOOM, H. THE RINGERS IN THE TOWER.*
I.H.C., 191(ELN):SEP72(SUPP)-11
J.R.D. JACKSON, 627(UTQ):SPRING
73-289
J.J. MC GANN, 405(MP):FEB73-243
M. PECKHAM, 85:FALL72-59
BLOOM, H. YEATS.*
H. ADAMS, 219(GAR):FALL72-249
M. SIDNELL, 627(UTQ):SPRING72-
263
D.T. TORCHIANA, 405(MP):NOV72-
168
BLOOMFIELD, B.C. & E. MENDELSON.
W.H. AUDEN.* (2ND ED)
J. SYMONS, 364:OCT/NOV73-120
BLOOMFIELD, M.W. ESSAYS & EXPLORA-
TIONS.*
S.W. HOLTON, 597(SN):VOL44#1-170
BLOOMFIELD, M.W., ED. IN SEARCH OF
LITERARY THEORY.
J. REICHERT, 651(WHR):SPRING73-
213
W.H. YOUNGREN, 249(HUDR):AUTUMN
73-562
BLOOMFIELD, M.W., ED. THE INTERPRE-
TATION OF NARRATIVE.
F.K. SCHNEIDER, 613:SPRING72-121
BLOTNER, J. FAULKNER.
W.H. GASS, 453:27JUN74-3
C.R. LARSON, 31(ASCH):SUMMER74-
513
C. LEHMANN-HAUPT, 441:27MAR74-47
C. NEWMAN, 231:APR74-98
J. YARDLEY, 441:17MAR74-1
442(NY):9SEP74-132
BLOUNT, R. ABOUT THREE BRICKS SHY
OF A LOAD.
R.W. CREAMER, 441:1DEC74-90
BLOW, S. RHETORIC IN THE PLAYS OF
THOMAS DEKKER.
M. PFISTER, 72:BAND210HEFT4/6-
382
BLUEFARB, S. THE ESCAPE MOTIF IN
THE AMERICAN NOVEL.
P. LISCA, 27(AL):MAR73-141
639(VQR):WINTER73-XVIII
BLUHME, H. - SEE TRUBETZKOY, N.S.
BLUM, R. BIBLIOGRAPHIA.
R.A. SAYCE, 354:MAR72-55
J. VÖSS, 190:BAND66HEFT3-320
BLUM, R. OLD GLORY & THE REAL-TIME
FREAKS.
S. O'CONNELL, 418(MR):WINTER73-
190

35

BLUM, R.H. & OTHERS. DRUG DEALERS -
TAKING ACTION.
617(TLS):8MAR74-240
BLUM, S.N. EARLY NETHERLANDISH
TRIPTYCHS.*
P.W. PARSHALL, 90:APR72-247
BLUMBERG, M. JUMP FOR LOVE & MONEY
OR IS IT SEX AGAIN?
617(TLS):8FEB74-125
BLUMENFELD, H. THE MODERN METROPOL-
IS. (P.D. SPREIREGEN, ED)
505:DEC72-98
BLUMENSON, M. THE PATTON PAPERS,
1940-1945.
P. ADAMS, 61:NOV74-123
T. HIGGINS, 441:6OCT74-36
C. LEHMANN-HAUPT, 441:29OCT74-41
BLUNT, W. ON WINGS OF SONG.
442(NY):19AUG74-89
617(TLS):21JUN74-674
BLUNT, W., WITH W.T. STEARN. THE
COMPLEAT NATURALIST.
481(PQ):JUL72-560
BLUSCH, J. FORMEN UND INHALT VON
HESIODS INDIVIDUELLEM DENKEN.
J. DEFRADAS, 555:VOL46FASC2-290
BLY, R., ED. THE SEA & THE HONEY-
COMB.
W.P. ROOT, 491:OCT73-34
BLY, R. SLEEPERS JOINING HANDS.*
JUMPING OUT OF BED.
J.E. CHAMBERLIN, 249(HUDR):SUM-
MER73-398
BLY, R. - SEE NERUDA, P. & C. VAL-
LEJO
BLYTH, H. CARO.*
639(VQR):SPRING73-LXXXI
BLYTHE, R. AKENFIELD.*
J. MARSH, 97(CQ):VOL6#1-70
BLYTHE, R., ED. ALDEBURGH ANTHOLO-
GY.*
N. GOODWIN, 415:APR73-383
BLYTHE, W. THE IMPACT OF CHINESE
SECRET SOCIETIES IN MALAYA.
W.E. WILLMOTT, 318(JAOS):APR-JUN
72-360
BØ, O. & B. ALVER, EDS. RIDDER SKAU
OG JOMFRU DAME.
B. HOLBEK, 196:BAND13HEFT1/2-192
BOAK, D. ANDRÉ MALRAUX.*
C. DÉDÉYAN, 182:VOL25#22-790
W.G. LANGLOIS, 598(SOR):WINTER74-
231
BOALCH, D.H. MAKERS OF THE HARPSI-
CHORD & CLAVICHORD 1440-1840. (REV)
A. CUCKSTON, 617(TLS):27DEC74-
1465
BOARDMAN, J. ATHENIAN BLACK FIGURE
VASES.
617(TLS):23AUG74-906
BOAS, O.V. & C.V. - SEE UNDER VILLAS
BOAS, O. & C.
BOASE, A., ED. THE POETRY OF
FRANCE.* (VOL 4)
C. SCOTT, 447(N&Q):FEB72-65
BOASE, A.M. THE FORTUNES OF MON-
TAIGNE.
W.G. MOORE, 402(MLR):JUL73-654
BOASE, T.S.R. DEATH IN THE MIDDLE
AGES.
639(VQR):WINTER73-XLIII
BOBA, I. MORAVIA'S HISTORY RECON-
SIDERED.*
A.R. LEWIS, 589:JAN73-112

BOBKER, L.R. ELEMENTS OF FILM.
J.D. RAGSDALE, 583:SPRING73-303
BÕBR-TYLINGO, S. LA RUSSIE, L'ÉG-
LISE ET LA POLOGNE 1860-1866.
L.R. LEWITTER, 575(SEER):JUL73-
478
BOBROWSKI, J. LEVIN'S MILL.
G.E. EDWARDS, 220(GL&L):APR73-
269
BOCCA, G. NADINE.
M. LEVIN, 441:17NOV74-52
BOCCA, G. PALMIRO TOGLIATTI.
S.J. WOOLF, 617(TLS):18OCT74-
1152
BOCCACCIO, G. OPERE MINORI IN VOL-
GARE. (VOL 3) (M. MARTI, ED)
228(GSLI):VOL149FASC466/467-460
BOCCARDI, S. RICERCARI.
617(TLS):5APR74-371
VON BOCK, M.P. REMINISCENCES OF MY
FATHER, PETER A. STOLYPIN. (M.
PATOSKI, ED & TRANS)
G.A. HOSKING, 575(SEER):OCT73-
611
BODDE, D. TOLSTOY & CHINA.
A.F. ZWEERS, 104:SUMMER72-332
BODECHTEL, J. & H-G. GIERLOFF-EMDEN.
THE EARTH FROM SPACE.
617(TLS):8FEB74-140
BODEN, M.A. PURPOSIVE EXPLANATION
IN PSYCHOLOGY.
R. TRIGG, 518:MAY73-3
BODENHEIMER, S. POLITICAL UNION.
C. ZORGBIBE, 98:JUL72-669
BOEHNCKE, H. - SEE VON WANGENHEIM, G.
BOERNER, P. TAGEBUCH.*
P. PROCHNIK, 220(GL&L):JUL73-357
BOERSMA, J.S. ATHENIAN BUILDING
POLICY FROM 561/0 TO 405/4.
J.M. COOK, 123:MAR73-106
BOESCH, B., ED. GERMAN LITERATURE.
A.W. RILEY, 529(QQ):WINTER72-552
BOESCHENSTEIN, H. GOTTFRIED KELLER.
J. SCHMIDT, 564:MAR72-66
BOETHIUS. A.M. SEVERINO BOEZIO:
"DE HYPOTHETICIS SYLLOGISMIS."
(L. OBERTELLO, ED & TRANS)
J. JOLIVET, 542:JAN-MAR72-67
G. STRIKER, 53(AGP):BAND54HEFT3-
306
BOËTHIUS, A. & J.B. WARD-PERKINS.
ETRUSCAN & ROMAN ARCHITECTURE.*
F.E. BROWN, 54:SEP72-342
S. HAYNES, 90:JAN72-35
P. KIDSON, 46:JUL72-64
BOETIUS, H., ED. DICHTUNGSTHEORIEN
DER AUFKLÄRUNG.
I.M. KIMBER, 402(MLR):APR73-455
P. WEBER, 654(WB):6/1972-188
BOEY, C. L'ALIÉNATION DANS "LA PHÉ-
NOMÉNOLOGIE DE L'ESPRIT" DE HEGEL.
G. NOSSENT, 258:MAR72-149
BOGAN, L. WHAT THE WOMAN LIVED.*
(R. LIMMER, ED)
K. LOUCHHEIM, 61:FEB74-90
BOGARD, T. A CONTOUR IN TIME.
F.I. CARPENTER, 27(AL):MAR73-125
J.H. RALEIGH, 639(VQR):SPRING73-
306

BOGATYREV, P.G. PROBLEME DER VOLKS-
KUNSTTHEORIE.
D. TSCHIZEWSKIJ, 72:BAND210HEFT
4/6-479
BOGDAN, M. & OTHERS, EDS. DICTIONAR
ENGLEZ-ROMAN.
P.V. VEHVILAINEN, 439(NM):1972/3-
718
BOGEN, J. WITTGENSTEIN'S PHILOSOPHY
OF LANGUAGE.
J. BURNHEIM, 63:MAY73-83
C. LYAS, 518:JAN73-3
BOGEN, N. - SEE BLAKE, W.
BOGGS, J.S. THE NATIONAL GALLERY OF
CANADA.
K.R., 90:FEB72-120
M. WILLIAMSON, 96:EARLY AUTUMN72-
109
M.S. YOUNG, 39:JUL72-85
BOGLE, D. TOMS, COONS, MULATTOES,
MAMMIES & BUCKS.*
P. SCHJELDAHL, 441:8DEC74-35
441:14JUL74-36
BÖHM, R.G. GAIUSSTUDIEN. (VOL 3)
W.M. GORDON, 123:MAR73-93
BÖHME, E. & M.I. KEHDEN, EDS. FROM
THE LAW OF THE SEA TOWARDS AN
OCEAN SPACE REGIME.
A-R. WERNER, 182:VOL25#19/20-648
BÖHME, R. ORPHEUS: DER SÄNGER UND
SEINE ZEIT.*
D-A. CAMPBELL, 123:MAR73-94
BOHNE, F. - SEE BUSCH, W.
BOILEAU, N. L'ART POÉTIQUE. (A.
BUCK, ED)
G. HAINSWORTH, 208(FS):JAN73-60
BOIME, A. THE ACADEMY & FRENCH
PAINTING IN THE NINETEENTH CEN-
TURY.*
A. ALHADEFF, 54:SEP72-364
L. NOCHLIN, 90:AUG72-559
BOISSONNAS, E. INITIALES.
R.B. JOHNSON, 207(FR):FEB72-684
BOJARSKI, R. & K. BEALS, EDS. THE
FILMS OF BORIS KARLOFF.
W. FEAVER, 617(TLS):27DEC74-1471
BOJKO, S. NEW GRAPHIC DESIGN IN
REVOLUTIONARY RUSSIA.
A.C. BIRNHOLZ, 32:SEP73-668
BOKOV, V. IZBRANNOYE.
E. MORGAN, 617(TLS):11OCT74-1132
BOL, L.J. HOLLÄNDISCHE MALER DES 17.
JAHRHUNDERTS NAHE DEN GROSSEN MEIS-
TERN, STILLEBEN UND LANDSCHAFTEN.
I. BERGSTRÖM, 39:JAN72-74
BOLELLI, T. LINGUISTICA GENERALE,
STRUTTURALISMO, LINGUISTICA STOR-
ICA.
M-P., 228(GSLI):VOL149FASC465-
149
BOLELLI, T. PER UNA STORIA DELLA
RICERCA LINGUISTICA.*
L. PAP, 660(WORD):AUG70-289
BOLES, J.B. THE GREAT REVIVAL, 1787-
1805.
G.W. PILCHER, 656(WMQ):APR73-349
639(VQR):SUMMER72-XCIII
BOLGAR, R.R., ED. CLASSICAL INFLU-
ENCES ON EUROPEAN CULTURE A.D.
500-1500.
M.L. CLARKE, 123:DEC73-203
P. MC GURK, 303:VOL92-259
O. MURRAY, 447(N&Q):MAR72-109
F.J. NICHOLS, 551(RENQ):WINTER72-
444

BOLGER, P. HOBART TOWN.
617(TLS):8FEB74-140
LORD BOLINGBROKE. HISTORICAL WRIT-
INGS. (I. KRAMNICK, ED)
H.T. DICKINSON, 566:SPRING73-105
BOLINGER, D. THE PHRASAL VERB IN
ENGLISH.
B. ARTHUR, 399(MLJ):DEC72-530
A.A. HILL, 35(AS):FALL69-210
BÖLL, H. GROUP PORTRAIT WITH LADY.*
(GERMAN TITLE: GRUPPENBILD MIT
DAME.)
R. DE FEO, 249(HUDR):WINTER73/74-
777
BÖLL, H. DIE VERLORENE EHRE DER
KATHARINA BLUM.
617(TLS):11OCT74-1138
BÖLL, H., H. GOLLWITZER & C. SCHMID,
EDS. ANSTOSS UND ERMUTIGUNG GUS-
TAV W. HEINEMANN BUNDESPRÄSIDENT
1969-1974.
R. MORGAN, 617(TLS):25OCT74-1186
BOLLACHER, M. DER JUNGE GOETHE UND
SPINOZA.*
H-G. HAILE, 400(MLN):APR72-524
R.S. LUCAS, 220(GL&L):APR73-244
BOLLACK, J. EMPÉDOCLE II.* EMPÉ-
DOCLE III.*
P. VICAIRE, 555:VOL46FASC1-110
BOLLACK, J., M. BOLLACK & H. WISMANN.
LA LETTRE D'ÉPICURE.
P. BOYANCÉ, 555:VOL46FASC1-66
BOLLÈME, G. LES ALMANACHS POPU-
LAIRES AUX XVIIE ET XVIIIE SIÈC-
LES.*
R. MANDROU, 535(RHL):MAR-APR73-
307
BOLLÈME, G. LA BIBLIOTHÈQUE BLEUE.
P. AUBERY, 207(FR):FEB72-716
BOLLMANN, W.E. KAMUTI.
M. LASKI, 362:19&26DEC74-847
BOLOGNA, F. PITTORI ALLA CORTE
ANGIOINA DI NAPOLI, 1266-1414.
P. HETHERINGTON, 90:AUG72-561
BOLSTER, R. STENDHAL, BALZAC ET LE
FÉMINISME ROMANTIQUE.*
N. MOZET, 535(RHL):JUL-AUG72-726
BOLT, C. VICTORIAN ATTITUDES TO
RACE.
R. ANSTEY, 637(VS):MAR72-382
BOLTHO, A. FOREIGN TRADE CRITERIA
IN SOCIALIST ECONOMIES.*
A.H. SMITH, 575(SEER):APR73-326
BOLTON, G. BRITAIN'S LEGACY OVER-
SEAS.
617(TLS):1FEB74-116
BOLTON, G.C. A FINE COUNTRY TO
STARVE IN.
617(TLS):15FEB74-155
BOLTON, N. THE PSYCHOLOGY OF THINK-
ING.
V. RÜFNER, 182:VOL25#23/24-840
BOLTON, W.F. A HISTORY OF ANGLO-
LATIN LITERATURE 597-1066. (VOL 1)
D. SCHALLER, 38:BAND90HEFT1/2-
204
BOLTON, W.F. - SEE "BEOWULF"
BOLUS, J. RUN FOR THE ROSES.
J. MC GINNISS, 441:28APR74-10
BOMPIANI, V. VIA PRIVATA.
617(TLS):10MAY74-504
BONALD, J.M.C. - SEE UNDER CABALLERO
BONALD, J.M.

BONANSEA, B.M. TOMMASO CAMPANELLA.*
   B. MAGNUS, 275(IQ):FALL/WINTER72-
   142
   G.K. PLOCHMANN, 551(RENQ):SPRING
   72-82
   J.K.R., 543:MAR72-550
BONATH, G. UNTERSUCHUNGEN ZUR ÜBER-
LIEFERUNG ZUR PARZIVAL WOLFRAMS
VON ESCHENBACH. (VOL 1)
   V. GÜNTHER, 182:VOL25#13/14-474
   S.M. JOHNSON, 589:JAN73-113
BONATH, G. UNTERSUCHUNGEN ZUR ÜBER-
LIEFERUNG ZUR PARZIVAL WOLFRAMS
VON ESCHENBACH. (VOL 2)
   V. GÜNTHER, 182:VOL25#13/14-474
SAINT BONAVENTURE. ITINÉRAIRE DE
L'ÂME EN ELLE-MÊME.
   A. FOREST, 542:JAN-MAR72-71
SAINT BONAVENTURE. ITINÉRAIRE DE
L'ESPRIT VERS DIEU. (H. DUMÉRY,
ED & TRANS)
   A. FOREST, 542:JAN-MAR72-72
BONAVIA, D. FAT SASHA & THE URBAN
GUERILLA.*
   P. REDDAWAY, 453:12DEC74-36
BOND, E. BINGO.
   S. SCHOENBAUM, 617(TLS):30AUG74-
   920
BOND, J. A TIME TO SPEAK, A TIME TO
ACT.
   639(VQR):AUTUMN72-CLIII
BOND, M.F. GUIDE TO THE RECORDS OF
PARLIAMENT.
   J.B. CHILDS, 517(PBSA):APR-JUN73-
   197
BOND, R.P. THE TATLER.*
   E.A. & L.D. BLOOM, 481(PQ):JUL72-
   768
   R.D. SPECTOR, 301(JEGP):JUL73-
   445
   R.M. WILES, 191(ELN):JUN73-304
   C. WINTON, 566:SPRING72-83
BONDAREW, J. HEISSER SCHNEE.
   K. KANTORCZYK, 654(WB):11/1972-
   151
BONE, Q. HENRIETTA MARIA.
   617(TLS):1MAR74-202
BONHAM-CARTER, V. THE SURVIVAL OF
THE ENGLISH COUNTRYSIDE.
   R.J.S. HOOKWAY, 46:OCT72-255
BONHEIM, H. & OTHERS. THE ENGLISH
NOVEL BEFORE RICHARDSON.
   B. FABIAN, 72:BAND210HEFT1/3-189
   C.C. MISH, 551(RENQ):WINTER72-
   495
   G. ROHMANN, 430(NS):NOV72-682
   C.M. TAYLOR, 481(PQ):JUL72-509
BONHOEFFER, D. TRUE PATRIOTISM.
   (VOL 3)
   442(NY):4FEB74-110
   617(TLS):1FEB74-96
"SANCTI BONIFACII EPISTOLAE: CODEX
VINDOBONENSIS 751 DER ÖSTERREICH-
ISCHEN NATIONALBIBLIOTHEK."
   P. MEYVAERT, 589:JUL73-552
BONNER, A., ED & TRANS. SONGS OF
THE TROUBADOURS.
   L. PATERSON, 617(TLS):13DEC74-
   1411
   639(VQR):SPRING73-LXIV

BONNET, H. MARCEL PROUST DE 1907 À
1914 (AVEC UNE BIBLIOGRAPHIE GÉN-
ÉRALE). (NEW ED)
   J. CRUICKSHANK, 208(FS):OCT73-
   472
   M.R. FINN, 207(FR):APR72-1053
LE BONNIEC, H. - SEE OVID
BONNIER, H. REMBRANDT.
   M. CORMACK, 39:JAN72-71
DE BONO, E., ED. EUREKA!
   W. SULLIVAN, 441:1DEC74-6
BONOMI, P.U. A FACTIOUS PEOPLE.
   P.L. WHITE, 656(WMQ):JUL72-497
BONSAL, P.W. CUBA, CASTRO, & THE
UNITED STATES.*
   J.F. THORNING, 613:AUTUMN72-479
BONTEMPS, A., ED. THE HARLEM RENAIS-
SANCE REMEMBERED.
   P.R. KLOTMAN, 659:SPRING74-283
BONTLY, T. A YOUNG OUTLAW.
   M. LEVIN, 441:3MAR74-30
"THE BOOK OF HOURS OF THE EMPEROR OF
MAXIMILIAN THE FIRST."
   J. CANADAY, 441:1DEC74-102
"THE BOOK OF KELLS."
   J. BECKWITH, 617(TLS):1NOV74-
   1235
   J. CANADAY, 441:1DEC74-102
"THE BOOK OF THE GOONS."
   D. THOMAS, 362:9&26DEC74-846
BOOKCHIN, M. POST-SCARCITY ANAR-
CHISM.
   617(TLS):21JUN74-662
BOOMKAMP, C.V. & J.H. VAN DER MEER.
THE CAREL VAN LEEUWEN BOOMKAMP
COLLECTION OF MUSICAL INSTRUMENTS.*
   G. OLDHAM, 415:OCT73-1015
BOON, G.C. SILCHESTER.
   617(TLS):27SEP74-1032
BOON, J-P. MONTAIGNE GENTILHOMME ET
ESSAYISTE.
   W.G. MOORE, 402(MLR):APR73-405
BOONE, M. THE SEED OF THE CHURCH IN
CHINA.
   617(TLS):23AUG74-912
DE BOOR, H., H. MOSER & C. WINKLER,
EDS. SIEBS - DEUTSCHE AUSSPRACHE.*
(19TH ED)
   E.F.K. KOERNER, 221(GQ):JAN72-
   196
BOORER, M. - SEE VESELOVSKY, Z.
BOORMAN, H.L. & R.C. HOWARD, EDS.
BIOGRAPHICAL DICTIONARY OF REPUB-
LICAN CHINA.
   W. HSIEH, 293(JAST):MAY72-615
BOORMAN, S.A. THE PROTRACTED GAME.
   B.E. WALLACKER, 318(JAOS):JAN-
   MAR72-152
BOORSTIN, D.J. THE AMERICANS.*
[ALL 3 VOLS]
   S.S. WOLIN, 453:19SEP74-3
BOORSTIN, D.J. THE AMERICANS: THE
DEMOCRATIC EXPERIENCE.*
   R.H. ELIAS, 31(ASCH):SPRING74-
   308
BOORSTIN, D.J. DEMOCRACY & ITS DIS-
CONTENTS.
   A. BROYARD, 441:7MAY74-49
   S.S. WOLIN, 453:19SEP74-3
BOOTH, A. THIS ISN'T MY SCENE, MAN!
THE TRIAL.
   H. FRANCIS, 157:WINTER72-83

BOOTH, E. & W. WINTER. BETWEEN
ACTOR & CRITIC.* (D.J. WATER-
MEIER, ED)
R. DAVIES, 637(VS):JUN72-488
BOOTH, M.R., ED. ENGLISH PLAYS OF
THE NINETEENTH CENTURY.* (VOLS
1&2)
A. STRACHAN, 447(N&Q):JUL72-275
BOOTH, M.R., ED. ENGLISH PLAYS OF
THE NINETEENTH CENTURY.* (VOLS
3&4)
639(VQR):AUTUMN73-CXLIV
BOOTH, P. & N. TAYLOR. GUIDE TO
CAMBRIDGE NEW ARCHITECTURE.
P.D. O'NEILL, 46:OCT72-256
BOOTH, W.C. NOW DON'T TRY TO REASON
WITH ME.
J.A. WIGLEY, 480(P&R):SPRING72-
126
BOOTH, W.C. A RHETORIC OF IRONY.
D. DONOGHUE, 617(TLS):6DEC74-
1358
DE BOOY, J.T. - SEE DIDEROT, D.
BORCHARDT, F.L. GERMAN ANTIQUITY IN
RENAISSANCE MYTH.
W.F. MICHAEL, 125:FEB73-194
N.G. SIRAISI, 301(JEGP):JAN73-70
L.W. SPITZ, 589:OCT73-733
"BORDAS ENCYCLOPÉDIE." (VOL 8) (R.
CARATINI, ED)
A. VAN DER BIEST, 556(RLV):
1972/5-550
BORDEN, R.L. LETTERS TO LIMBO. (H.
BORDEN, ED)
C.P. STACEY, 529(QQ):SUMMER72-
276
"BORED OF THE RINGS."
617(TLS):13SEP74-975
BOREL, J. MÉDECINE ET PSYCHIATRIE
BALZACIENNES.
M. LE YAOUANC, 535(RHL):JUL-AUG
72-727
BORETZ, B. & E.T. CONE, EDS. PER-
SPECTIVES ON AMERICAN COMPOSERS.
J. CONNOLLY, 607:#99-22
M. PETERSON, 470:JAN72-32
BORG, A. ARCHITECTURAL SCULPTURE IN
ROMANESQUE PROVENCE.*
J. SEZNEC, 208(FS):OCT73-441
BORGENICHT, M. NO BAIL FOR DALTON.
N. CALLENDAR, 441:19MAY74-42
BORGER, R. & F. CIOFFI, EDS. EXPLAN-
ATION IN THE BEHAVIOURAL SCIENCES.*
R.J.B., 543:SEP71-141
C.V. BORST, 393(MIND):JUL72-471
G.R. MILLER, 480(P&R):FALL72-248
H.A. SIMON, 479(PHQ):JUL72-278
BORGES, J.L. THE ALEPH & OTHER
STORIES.* (N.T. DI GIOVANNI, WITH
J.L. BORGES, EDS & TRANS)
E. GLOVER, 565:VOL13#3-44
BORGES, J.L. DR. BRODIE'S REPORT.*
J. DITSKY, 219(GAR):FALL72-297
J. DITSKY, 529(QQ):WINTER72-575
L. MICHAELS, 473(PR):WINTER73-
121
617(TLS):14JUN74-629
BORGES, J.L. IN PRAISE OF DARKNESS.
W. BARNSTONE, 441:11AUG74-6
453:4APR74-44
BORGES, J.L. A UNIVERSAL HISTORY OF
INFAMY.
P. CRUTTWELL & F. WESTBURG,
249(HUDR):SUMMER73-417

BORGMEIER, R. SHAKESPEARES SONNETT
"WHEN FORTY WINTERS..." UND DIE
DEUTSCHER ÜBERSETZER.
V.B. HELTZEL, 570(SQ):FALL72-454
BORIE, J. ZOLA ET LES MYTHES OU DE
LA NAUSÉE AU SALUT.
C. JENNINGS, 188(ECR):WINTER72-
338
S. MAX, 207(FR):DEC71-509
BORING, P.Z. - SEE AYALA, F.
BORINSKI, L.[1] DER ENGLISCHE ROMAN
DES 18. JAHRHUNDERTS.
M. SCHULZE, 72:BAND210HEFT4/6-
394
BORINSKI, L. ENGLISCHER HUMANISMUS
UND DEUTSCHE REFORMATION.*
G. AHRENDS, 38:BAND90HEFT1/2-233
BORK, H.D. DIE FAMILIE VON LATEIN-
ISCH QUATERE IM ROMANISCHEN.
F. ABEL, 72:BAND210HEFT4/6-424
BORK, S. MISSBRAUCH DER SPRACHE.*
C.V.J. RUSS, 402(MLR):JUL73-687
BORKAR, V.V. INCOME TAX REFORM IN
INDIA.
C.P. STAELIN, 293(JAST):FEB72-
439
BORKOWSKI, J. & OTHERS. ZARYS HIS-
TORII POLSKIEGO RUCHU LUDOWEGO.
(VOL 2)
D.E. PIENKOS, 32:JUN73-405
BORKOWSKI, L. - SEE ŁUKASIEWICZ, J.
BORLAND, H.H. SWEDISH FOR STUDENTS.
D.M. MENNIE, 402(MLR):JAN73-239
BORMANN, K. PARMENIDES.*
G.B. KERFERD, 123:DEC73-129
DE BORN, E. MUTUAL OBSERVATION.
617(TLS):29MAR74-313
BORN, H. THE RARE WIT & THE RUDE
GROOM.
N. SANDERS, 677:VOL3-274
BORNECQUE, P. LE THÉÂTRE DE GEORGES
COURTELINE.
D. FREIMANIS, 207(FR):OCT71-252
BORNEMAN, E. UNSERE KINDER IM SPIE-
GEL IHRER LIEDER, REIME, VERSE UND
RÄTSEL.
617(TLS):19APR74-421
BORNEMANN, E. SEX IM VOLKSMUND.*
U. KUTTER, 196:BAND13HEFT1/2-200
BORNSCHEUER, L. - SEE BÜCHNER, G.
BORNSTEIN, G. YEATS & SHELLEY.*
H. ADAMS, 219(GAR):FALL72-249
M. SIDNELL, 627(UTQ):SPRING72-
263
BOROVOY, X.Y. KREDIT I BANKI V ROS-
SII.
O. CRISP, 575(SEER):OCT73-582
BOROWITZ, E.B. THE MASK JEWS WEAR.
A.I. WASKOW, 441:27JAN74-10
BOROWSKI, L.E., R.B. JACHMANN & A.C.
WASIANSKI. LA VITA DI IMMANUEL
KANT.*
K. OEDINGEN, 342:BAND63HEFT3-388
BORRAS, F.M. & R.F. CHRISTIAN. RUS-
SIAN SYNTAX.* (2ND ED)
205(FMLS):JAN72-86
BORRÁS BETRIU, R. EL DÍA EN QUE
MATARON A CARRERO BLANCO.
617(TLS):7JUN74-606
BORRIES, M. EIN ANGRIFF AUF HEIN-
RICH HEINE.
J.L.S., 191(ELN):SEP72(SUPP)-149

BORROT, A. & M. DIDIER. BODICO, DICTIONNAIRE DU FRANÇAIS SANS FAUTE.
   A. VAN DER BIEST, 556(RLV): 1972/1-108
BÖRSCH-SUPAN, H. CASPAR DAVID FRIEDRICH.
   J. RUSSELL, 441:1DEC74-54
BÖRSCH-SUPAN, H., ED. DIE KATALOGE DER BERLINER AKADEMIE-AUSSTELLUNGEN 1786-1850.
   G.F. KOCH, 683:BAND35HEFT3-249
BORSI, F. & P. PORTOGHESI. VICTOR HORTA.
   E. KAUFMANN, JR., 54:JUN72-227
BORTON, H. JAPAN'S MODERN CENTURY. (2ND ED)
   M.J. MAYO, 293(JAST):NOV71-157
BORY, J-F. RAOUL HAUSMANN.
   S. FAUCHEREAU, 98:AUG/SEP72-752
BOSCÁN, J. LIRICHE SCELTE.
   L. CHALON, 556(RLV):1972/6-672
BOSCH, J. REINAERT-PERSPECTIEF.
   R.W. ZANDVOORT, 382(MAE):1973/2-187
BOSCHETTO, A., WITH OTHERS, EDS. LA COLLEZIONE ROBERTO LONGHI.
   V. BLOCH, 90:APR72-252
"HENRI BOSCO À NICE."
   A. DENAT, 67:MAY73-130
BOSCO, U. REPERTORIO BIBLIOGRAFICO DELLA LETTERATURA ITALIANA, 1943-1947.*
   J.A. MOLINARO, 276:WINTER72-513
BOSCO, U. SAGGI SUL RINASCIMENTO ITALIANO.
   A. DI BENEDETTO, 228(GSLI):VOL 149FASC465-125
BOSHER, J.F. FRENCH FINANCES, 1770-1795.
   J. LOUGH, 208(FS):APR73-218
BOSL, K., ED. DAS JAHR 1945 IN DER TSCHECHOSLOWAKEI.
   A. WAHL, 182:VOL25#1/2-51
BOSLEY, K., WITH D. POSPIELOVSKY & J. SAPIETS, EDS & TRANS. RUSSIA'S UNDERGROUND POETS.
   R.D.B. THOMSON, 104:SUMMER72-339
BOSQUET, A. CHICAGO OIGNON SAUVAGE.
   H.A. BOURAOUI, 207(FR):FEB72-685
BOSQUET, A. NOTES POUR UN PLURIEL.
   617(TLS):9AUG74-852
BOSS, V. NEWTON & RUSSIA.*
   F. KAZEMZADEH, 676(YR):SUMMER73-613
   639(VQR):AUTUMN73-CLXX
BOSSAGLIA, R. IL LIBERTY IN ITALIA.
   N. PEVSNER, 54:DEC72-563
BOSSE, H. THEORIE UND PRAXIS BEI JEAN PAUL.
   M.H., 191(ELN):SEP72(SUPP)-169
   W. KOEPKE, 221(GQ):JAN72-153
BOSSE, M. THE MAN WHO LOVED ZOOS.
   N. CALLENDAR, 441:25AUG74-30
   442(NY):9SEP74-136
BOSSERMAN, P. DIALECTICAL SOCIOLOGY.
   W. SCHÄFER, 182:VOL25#5/6-150
BOSTOCK, D. LOGIC & ARITHMETIC.
   617(TLS):24MAY74-567
BOSTON, R. BRITISH CHARTISTS IN AMERICA.
   P. HOLLIS, 637(VS):DEC72-237

BOSWELL, J. DORANDO, A SPANISH TALE. (R. HUNTING, ED)
   617(TLS):26JUL74-811
BOTEY, F. LO GITANO, UNA CULTURA "FOLK" DESCONOCIDA.*
   M. LAFFRANQUE, 542:OCT-DEC72-497
BOTHA, R.P. THE FUNCTION OF THE LEXICON IN TRANSFORMATIONAL GENERATIVE GRAMMAR.
   P.G. CHAPIN, 206:MAR72-298
BOTHMER, B.V. & J.L. KEITH. BRIEF GUIDE TO THE DEPARTMENT OF ANCIENT ART. [BROOKLYN MUSEUM]
   B.A. SPARKES, 303:VOL92-252
BOTKINE, V. LETTRES SUR L'ESPAGNE.* (A. ZVIGUILSKY, ED & TRANS)
   P-J. GUINARD, 549(RLC):OCT-DEC72-616
BOTS, H. CORRESPONDANCE DE JACQUES DUPUY ET DE NICOLAS HEINSIUS (1646-56).
   B. BEUGNOT, 182:VOL25#11-321
BOTTERILL, G.S. & R.D. KEENE. THE PIRC DEFENCE.
   617(TLS):8MAR74-244
BOTTOMLEY, A.K. DECISIONS IN THE PENAL PROCESS.
   617(TLS):5APR74-364
BOTTRALL, R. DAY & NIGHT.
   617(TLS):9AUG74-852
DE BOUARD, M., ED. HISTOIRE DE LA NORMANDIE.
   J. MUNDY, 589:APR73-422
BOUCÉ, P-G. LES ROMANS DE SMOLLETT.*
   A.B. STRAUSS, 481(PQ):JUL72-765
BOUCHER, A., ED & TRANS. POEMS OF TODAY FROM TWENTY-FIVE ICELANDIC POETS.
   L. BJARNASON, 563(SS):SUMMER73-269
BOUCHER, C. LEÇONS SUR LA THÉORIE DES AUTOMATES MATHÉMATIQUES.
   A. BLIKLE, 316:DEC72-759
BOUCHER DE BOUCHERVILLE, G. UNE DE PERDUE, DEUX DE TROUVÉES.* (R. HAMEL, ED)
   617(TLS):14JUN74-634
DU BOUCHET, A. QUI N'EST PAS TOURNÉ VERS NOUS.
   P. CHAPPUIS, 98:DEC72-1074
BOUCHET, J. EPISTRES MORALES ET FAMILIERES DU TRAVERSEUR.
   D. WILSON, 208(FS):JAN73-51
BOUDJEDRA, R. LA RÉPUDIATION.
   E. SELLIN, 207(FR):OCT71-188
BOUDJEDRA, R. LA VIE QUOTIDIENNE EN ALGÉRIE.
   H.A. BOURAOUI, 207(FR):OCT71-230
BOUDON, P. LIVED-IN ARCHITECTURE.
   S.E. COHEN, 44:SEP72-14
   M. FOSTER, 46:AUG72-128
ABBÉ BOUGEANT. AMUSEMENT PHILOSOPHIQUE SUR LE LANGAGE DES BÊTES. (H. HASTINGS, ED)
   M. DAVID, 542:OCT-DEC72-449
BOUISSAC, P. LES DEMOISELLES.
   D-F. JOURLAIT, 207(FR):MAR72-898
DU BOULAY, F.R.H. & C.M. BARRON, EDS. THE REIGN OF RICHARD II.
   J.T. ROSENTHAL, 589:OCT73-741
BOULEZ, P. BOULEZ ON MUSIC TODAY.*
   R.S.J., 410(M&L):JAN73-97
   M. PETERSON, 470:MAR72-23

BOULEZ, P. RELEVÉS D'APPRENTI. (P.
THÉVENIN, ED) PENSER LA MUSIQUE
AUJOURD'HUI.
A. BANCQUART, 98:OCT72-867
BOULLE, P. DESPERATE GAMES.
442(NY):7JAN74-72
BOULNOIS, L. & H. MILLOT. BIBLIOGRA-
PHIE DU NÉPAL. (VOL 1)
D.N. MARSHALL, 182:VOL25#7/8-195
F.L. NITZBERG, 293(JAST):NOV71-
237
BOULTON, A. CAMILLE PISSARRO EN
VENEZUELA.
T. CROMBIE, 39:AUG72-169
BOULTON, J.T., ED. JOHNSON: THE
CRITICAL HERITAGE.
E.A. BLOOM, 677:VOL3-296
A. PARREAUX, 189(EA):OCT-DEC72-
560
481(PQ):JUL72-700
BOULTON, J.T. - SEE LAWRENCE, D.H.
BOUQUET, H. THE PAPERS OF HENRY
BOUQUET. (VOL 1) (S.K. STEVENS,
D.H. KENT & A.L. LEONARD, EDS)
J.R. SELLERS, 656(WMQ):JAN73-185
BOUR, J-A. EVASIONS.
V.A. LA CHARITÉ, 207(FR):FEB72-
687
BOURAOUI, H.A. ECLATE MODULE.
L. WELCH, 150(DR):WINTER72/73-
688
BOURAOUI, H.A. TREMBLÉ.
V.A. LA CHARITÉ, 207(FR):OCT71-
189
BOURGEADE, P. ORDEN.
617(TLS):24MAY74-555
BOURGEOIS, B. - SEE HEGEL, G.W.F.
BOURGEOIS, F. - SEE BHAṬṬA NĀRĀYAṆA
BOURNE, K. THE FOREIGN POLICY OF
VICTORIAN ENGLAND, 1830-1902.
J.W. CELL, 637(VS):JUN72-481
BOURNE, M.A., J.B. SILMAN & J. SOB-
RINO. EL ESPAÑOL.*
H.J. FREY, 399(MLJ):FEB72-103
BOURNIQUEL, C. SÉLINONTE OU LA
CHAMBRE IMPÉRIALE.
M. SAKHAROFF, 207(FR):FEB72-688
BOUSQUET, J. MYSTIQUE.
R. CARDINAL, 617(TLS):11OCT74-
1134
BOUTIÈRE, J. - SEE MISTRAL, F.
BOUTON, C. - SEE FLAUBERT, G.
BOUTON, C.P. LES MÉCANISMES D'AC-
QUISITION DU FRANÇAIS, LANGUE
ÉTRANGÈRE CHEZ L'ADULTE.*
J. KVAPIL, 353:1DEC72-114
BOUTROUX, E. LA PHILOSOPHIE DE KANT.
J. KOPPER, 342:BAND63HEFT1-131
BOUVERESSE, J. LA PAROLE MALHEUR-
EUSE.
Y. GAUTHIER, 154:SEP72-480
BOUZEK, J., D. KOUTECKY & E. NEUS-
TUPNY. THE KNOVÍZ SETTLEMENT OF
NORTH-WEST BOHEMIA.
U. FISCHER, 182:VOL25#12-423
BOWDEN, H.W. CHURCH HISTORY IN THE
AGE OF SCIENCE.
C.A. HOLBROOK, 432(NEQ):SEP72-
448
BOWEN, B.C. THE AGE OF BLUFF.*
D.M. FRAME, 551(RENQ):AUTUMN72-
342
É.R. VIDAL, 401(MLQ):SEP73-335
639(VQR):WINTER73-XXVI

BOWEN, C.D. THE MOST DANGEROUS MAN
IN AMERICA.
442(NY):11NOV74-213
BOWEN, E. HENRY & OTHER HEROES.
J. LEGGETT, 441:18AUG74-16
E. WEEKS, 61:JUL74-99
BOWEN, L. & R.A. BALLINGER. SIGN,
SYMBOL & FORM.
W.W. ATKIN, 505:SEP72-148
BOWERING, G. GENEVE.
D. BAILEY, 529(QQ):SUMMER72-242
BOWERING, P. ALDOUS HUXLEY.*
P. VITOUX, 677:VOL3-334
BOWERS, F. THE NEW SCRIABIN.
617(TLS):24MAY74-555
BOWERS, F. - SEE BEAUMONT, F. & J.
FLETCHER
BOWERS, F. - SEE CRANE, S.
BOWERS, F. - SEE MARLOWE, C.
BOWERS, J. THE COLONY.
M. GREEN, 364:DEC72/JAN73-145
BOWERS, J.W. & D.J. OCHS. THE RHE-
TORIC OF AGITATION & CONTROL.
N. GARVER, 480(P&R):SUMMER72-194
BOWERS, R.H. THE LEGEND OF JONAH.
J.J. ANDERSON, 382(MAE):1973/2-
181
T.D. HILL, 589:OCT73-736
BOWIE, M. HENRI MICHAUX.
G. MARTIN, 364:OCT/NOV73-139
617(TLS):15FEB74-147
BOWIE, T. & D. THIMME. THE CARREY
DRAWINGS OF THE PARTHENON SCULP-
TURES.
E.G. PEMBERTON, 127:WINTER72/73-
232
BOWKER, J. PROBLEMS OF SUFFERING IN
RELIGIONS OF THE WORLD.*
E. ANDREWS, 529(QQ):SUMMER72-281
I. WATSON, 302:JUL72-203
BOWLES, P. WITHOUT STOPPING.
N. ROREM, 364:AUG/SEP72-124
BOWMAN, F.P. - SEE LÉVI, E.
BOWMAN, L.W. POLITICS IN RHODESIA.
J. LEWIN, 617(TLS):6SEP74-957
BOWMAN, R.A. ARAMATIC RITUAL TEXTS
FROM PERSEPOLIS.
B.A. LEVINE, 318(JAOS):JAN-MAR
72-70
BOWNESS, A. GAUGUIN.
E. YOUNG, 39:AUG72-167
BOWRA, C.M. ON GREEK MARGINS.*
N.V. DUNBAR, 123:DEC73-200
BOWRA, C.M. PERICLEAN ATHENS.*
C. MOSSE, 303:VOL92-228
BOWSER, F.P. THE AFRICAN SLAVE IN
COLONIAL PERU 1524-1650.
C.R. BOXER, 617(TLS):26JUL74-787
BOWSKY, W.M. THE FINANCE OF THE
COMMUNE OF SIENA 1287-1355.
M.B. BECKER, 551(RENQ):SPRING72-
65
R. WITT, 589:JAN73-116
BOWYER, M.J.F. 2 GROUP RAF.
617(TLS):1NOV74-1240
BOX, M. ODD WOMAN OUT.
617(TLS):19JUL74-760
BOYARSKY, B. & N. BACKROOM POLITICS.
M.F. NOLAN, 441:25AUG74-21
BOYD, A. & P. PORTER. JONAH.*
R. GARFITT, 364:FEB/MAR74-102
BOYD, E. & R. PARKES. THE DARK NUM-
BER.*
N. CALLENDAR, 441:2JUN74-20

BOYD, J.P. - SEE JEFFERSON, T.
BOYD, R.H.S. INDIA & THE LATIN CAP-
TIVITY OF THE CHURCH.
    617(TLS):12JUL74-739
BOYDE, P. DANTE'S STYLE IN HIS
LYRIC POETRY.
    G. AQUILECCHIA, 382(MAE):1973/2-
    176
    T.G. BERGIN, 551(RENQ):WINTER72-
    440
    M. MARTI, 228(GSLI):VOL149FASC
    468-607
BOYDSTON, J.A., ED. GUIDE TO THE
WORKS OF JOHN DEWEY.*
    R.J.B., 543:SEP71-141
    R.J. ROTH, 258:JUN72-301
BOYER, F. LE MONDE DES ARTS EN
ITALIE ET LA FRANCE DE LA RÉVOLU-
TION ET DE L'EMPIRE.*
    205(FMLS):JAN72-86
BOYER, P. & S. NISSENBAUM. SALEM
POSSESSED.
    P. ADAMS, 61:APR74-120
    K. THOMAS, 453:8AUG74-22
BOYER, P. & S. NISSENBAUM, EDS.
SALEM-VILLAGE WITCHCRAFT.
    C. HANSEN, 656(WMQ):JUL73-528
BOYERS, R., ED. THE LEGACY OF THE
GERMAN REFUGEE INTELLECTUALS.
    R.K. ANGRESS, 406:SUMMER73-212
BOYLAN, B.R. BENEDICT ARNOLD.*
    639(VQR):AUTUMN73-CLVI
BOYLAN, J., ED. THE WORLD & THE
20'S.*
    J. SAYRE, 441:17FEB74-3
BOYLE, A. POOR, DEAR BRENDAN.
    J. GRIGG, 617(TLS):1NOV74-1219
    R. LEWIN, 362:31OCT74-581
BOYLE, E.L. CANTONESE BASIC COURSE.
    J. DEW, 293(JAST):AUG72-923
BOZEMAN, A.B. THE FUTURE OF LAW IN
A MULTICULTURAL WORLD.
    J. STARR, 293(JAST):FEB72-382
BOZZOLI, A. MANZONIANA.
    O.R., 191(ELN):SEP72(SUPP)-195
BRABEN, E. THE BEST OF MORECAMBE &
WISE.
    D. THOMAS, 362:19&26DEC74-846
DE BRACH, P. LES AMOURS D'AMYÉE.
(J. DAWKINS, ED)
    R.M. BURGESS, 551(RENQ):WINTER
    72-458
BRACHER, F. - SEE ETHEREGE, G.
BRACKMAN, A.C. THE COMMUNIST COL-
LAPSE IN INDONESIA.
    R.K. PAGET, 293(JAST):MAY72-737
BRADBROOK, F.W. - SEE AUSTEN, J.
BRADBURY, M. POSSIBILITIES.*
    R. NYE, 364:OCT/NOV73-157
BRADBURY, M. THE SOCIAL CONTEXT OF
MODERN ENGLISH LITERATURE.
    T. EAGLETON, 541(RES):MAY72-245
BRADBURY, M. & D. PALMER, EDS. THE
AMERICAN NOVEL & THE NINETEEN
TWENTIES.
    D.E.S. MAXWELL, 677:VOL3-331
    J.W. TUTTLETON, 676(YR):WINTER73-
    305
BRADBURY, M. & D. PALMER, EDS. CON-
TEMPORARY CRITICISM.
    L. LERNER, 541(RES):FEB72-109

BRADBURY, M. & D. PALMER, EDS.
SHAKESPEARIAN COMEDY.
    K. TETZELI VON ROSADOR, 72:BAND
    210HEFT4/6-374
BRADBURY, R. THE WONDERFUL ICE
CREAM SUIT & OTHER PLAYS.
    B.H. FUSSELL, 249(HUDR):WINTER
    73/74-753
BRADDOCK, J. THE GREEK PHOENIX.
    S.V. PAPACOSMA, 32:DEC73-849
BRADDY, H. MEXICO & THE OLD SOUTH-
WEST.
    R.N. ELLIS, 649(WAL):FALL72-234
BRADEN, W., ED. REPRESENTATIVE
AMERICAN SPEECHES: 1970-1971.
    G.A. YEOMANS, 583:SPRING73-298
BRADEN, W.W., ED. SPEECH METHODS &
RESOURCES. (2ND ED)
    B.M. COLLINS, 583:SPRING73-305
BRADFORD, C. - SEE YEATS, W.B.
BRADFORD, E. CHRISTOPHER COLUMBUS.*
    617(TLS):5APR74-368
BRADING, D.A. MINERS & MERCHANTS IN
BOURBON MEXICO 1763-1810.
    M.B. BERNSTEIN, 263:JUL-SEP73-
    330
BRADLEY, H.W. THE UNITED STATES:
1865 TO THE PRESENT.
    639(VQR):SPRING73-LXXXIV
BRADLEY, J. MACH'S PHILOSOPHY OF
SCIENCE.
    M. BUNGE, 486:JUN72-266
BRADY, F. HEFNER.
    P. NOBILE, 441:15DEC74-4
BRADY, F., J. PALMER & M. PRICE,
EDS. LITERARY THEORY & STRUCTURE.
    D.J. GORDON, 676(YR):SUMMER73-
    583
    639(VQR):SUMMER73-CXVI
BRADY, M. THE MONOPOLY BOOK.
    C. LEHMANN-HAUPT, 441:4DEC74-47
    M. WATKINS, 441:8DEC74-18
BRADY, V.P. LOVE IN THE THEATRE OF
MARIVAUX.*
    H. LAGRAVE, 535(RHL):MAR-APR72-
    308
    J.S. MUNRO, 402(MLR):JUL73-656
    W.H. TRAPNELL, 207(FR):OCT71-266
BRAET, H. & J. LAMBERT, COMPS. ENCY-
CLOPÉDIE DES ÉTUDES LITTÉRAIRES
ROMANES.
    D. STONE, JR., 207(FR):FEB72-739
    D.M. SUTHERLAND, 208(FS):OCT73-
    499
BRAGG, M. THE NERVE.
    R. PYBUS, 565:VOL13#2-68
BRAGG, M. THE SILKEN NET.
    J. MELLORS, 362:22AUG74-253
    617(TLS):23AUG74-897
BRAHAM, A. & P. SMITH. FRANÇOIS
MANSART.
    617(TLS):24MAY74-553
BRAIDER, C. THE GRAMMAR OF COOKING.
    N. HAZELTON, 441:1DEC74-96
BRAIN, R. & A. POLLOCK. BANGWA
FUNERARY SCULPTURE.
    G. ATKINS, 135:APR72-292
    T. HÅKANSSON, 592:MAR72-136
    M. RUEL, 69:JUL72-259
BRAINE, J. THE QUEEN OF A DISTANT
COUNTRY.*
    P. BAILEY, 364:FEB/MAR73-157
BRAINE, J. WRITING A NOVEL.
    617(TLS):26APR74-444

BRAINERD, B. INTRODUCTION TO THE
MATHEMATICS OF LANGUAGE STUDY.
M. MEPHAM, 320(CJL):VOL18#2-181
BRAISTED, W.R. THE UNITED STATES
NAVY IN THE PACIFIC, 1909-1922.
R.G. O'CONNER, 293(JAST):NOV71-
174
BRAITHWAITE, E. ISLANDS. RIGHTS OF
PASSAGE.
E. JENNINGS, 619(TC):VOL177#1043-
58
BRAKER, U. THE LIFE STORY & REAL
ADVENTURES OF THE POOR MAN OF
TOGGENBURY.
205(FMLS):JAN72-86
BRAND, G. DIE LEBENSWELT.*
R.S., 543:JUN72-745
BRAND, H.E. KLEIST UND DOSTOEVSKIJ.
A. VON GRONICKA, 221(GQ):MAY72-
539
BRAND, M. DRY SUMMER IN PROVENCE.
J. LOGAN, 628:FALL72-116
"THE BRAND NEW MONTY PYTHON PAPPER-
BOK."
D. THOMAS, 362:19&26DEC74-846
BRANDABUR, E. A SCRUPULOUS MEAN-
NESS.*
R. BOYLE, 659:SPRING74-262
C. HART, 677:VOL3-328
639(VQR):SPRING72-LVIII
BRANDEIS, L.D. LETTERS OF LOUIS D.
BRANDEIS. (VOL 1) (M.I. UROFSKY &
D.W. LEVY, EDS)
O.H. STEPHENS, 432(NEQ):MAR72-
146
BRANDELL, G. STRINDBERG IN INFERNO.
P. ADAMS, 61:AUG74-91
M. MEYER, 617(TLS):20DEC74-1443
BRANDER, M. A HUNT AROUND THE HIGH-
LANDS.
617(TLS):22FEB74-193
BRANDON, H. THE RETREAT OF AMERICAN
POWER.*
G. BARRACLOUGH, 453:27JUN74-14
BRANDON, J.R., ED. ON THRONES OF
GOLD.*
H. GEERTZ, 293(JAST):MAY72-741
J.M. VAN DER KROEF, 318(JAOS):
OCT-DEC72-554
BRANDON, S.G.F. RELIGION IN ANCIENT
HISTORY.
617(TLS):7JUN74-618
BRANDON-COX, H. SUMMER OF A MILLION
WINGS.
617(TLS):15MAR74-273
BRANDT, W. IN EXILE.
639(VQR):SUMMER72-XC
BRANIGAN, K. THE TOMBS OF MESARA.*
THE FOUNDATIONS OF PALATIAL CRETE.
P. WARREN, 303:VOL92-238
BRANSTON, B. BEYOND BELIEF.
617(TLS):19APR74-425
BRANSTON, B. THE LOST GODS OF ENG-
LAND.
617(TLS):27SEP74-1045
BRATUS, B.V. THE FORMATION & EXPRES-
SIVE USE OF DIMINUTIVES.
H.W. SCHALLER, 430(NS):NOV72-681
205(FMLS):JAN72-94
BRAUDEL, F. CAPITALISM & MATERIAL
LIFE, 1400-1800.* (FRENCH TITLE:
CIVILISATION MATÉRIELLE ET CAPITAL-
ISME. [VOL 1])
H. TREVOR-ROPER, 441:10NOV74-31

BRAUDEL, F. THE MEDITERRANEAN & THE
MEDITERRANEAN WORLD IN THE AGE OF
PHILIP II.* (VOL 1)
H.G. KOENIGSBERGER, 362:3JAN74-
10
639(VQR):SPRING73-LXXXVI
BRAUDEL, F. THE MEDITERRANEAN & THE
MEDITERRANEAN WORLD IN THE AGE OF
PHILIP II. (VOL 2)
N. BLIVEN, 442(NY):1APR74-118
H.G. KOENIGSBERGER, 362:3JAN74-
10
BRAUDY, L. NARRATIVE FORM IN HIS-
TORY & FICTION.*
M. BARIDON, 189(EA):OCT-DEC72-
559
BRAUDY, L. JEAN RENOIR.
639(VQR):AUTUMN72-CLVIII
BRAUER, H. SLAVISCHE SPRACHWISSEN-
SCHAFT. (VOLS 2&3)
F.V. MAREŠ, 260(IF):BAND77HEFT1-
141
BRÄUER, H. - SEE VASMER, M.
BRÄUER, R. LITERATURSOZIOLOGIE UND
EPISCHE STRUKTUR DER DEUTSCHEN
"SPIELMANNS" - UND HELDENDICHTUNG.
G.R. SPOHN, 654(WB):8/1972-195
BRÄUER-POSPELOVA, M. - SEE BERNEKER,
E. & M. VASMER
BRAULT, J. & B. LACROIX - SEE GAR-
NEAU, H.S-D.
BRAUN, L. DIE CANTICA DES PLAUTUS.
P.G-M. BROWN, 123:DEC73-163
BRAUN, T.E.D. LE FRANC DE POMPIGNAN.
H.A. STAVAN, 188(ECR):WINTER72-
328
BRAUNECK, M., ED. SPIELTEXTE DER
WANDERBÜHNE. (VOLS 1, 3 & 4)
D. GUTZEN, 52:BAND7HEFT2/3-323
BRAUNER, S. & J.K. BANTU. LEHRBUCH
DES SWAHILI.
G.F. MEIER, 682(ZPSK):BAND25
HEFT3-246
BRAUNSCHWEIG, D. & M. FAIN. EROS
ET ANTÉROS.
Y. BRÈS, 542:OCT-DEC72-452
BRAUTIGAN, R. THE ABORTION.* TROUT
FISHING IN AMERICA. A CONFEDERATE
GENERAL FROM BIG SUR. IN WATER-
MELON SUGAR.
P-Y. PETILLON, 98:DEC72-1054
BRAUTIGAN, R. THE HAWKLINE MONSTER.
P. ADAMS, 61:OCT74-119
J. YOHALEM, 441:8SEP74-6
BRAUTIGAN, R. REVENGE OF THE LAWN.
J. DITSKY, 219(GAR):FALL72-297
P-Y. PETILLON, 98:DEC72-1054
BRAVO, E.R. BIBLIOGRAFÍA PUERTOR-
RIQUEÑA SELECTA Y ANOTADA.
C. RIPOLL, 263:OCT-DEC73-457
BRAVO, F. THE OPERA MEDICINALIA BY
FRANCISCO BRAVO PRINTED IN MEXICO
IN 1570.
R.M. PRICE, 354:SEP72-255
BREARLEY, K.T. & R-B. MC BRIDE, EDS.
NOUVELLES DU QUÉBEC.*
W. STAAKS, 207(FR):OCT71-294
BREARS, P.C.D. THE COLLECTOR'S BOOK
OF ENGLISH COUNTRY POTTERY.
617(TLS):27DEC74-1471
BREATHNACH, B. FOLK MUSIC & DANCES
OF IRELAND.*
M. KARPELES, 203:SUMMER72-168

BREAUX, A. SAINT-EXUPÉRY IN AMERICA,
1942-1943.
C. FRANÇOIS, 207(FR):MAR72-917
BREBNER, J.A. THE DEMON WITHIN.
617(TLS):8FEB74-121
BRECH, U. - SEE KOBS, J.
BRECHER, I. & S.A. ABBAS. FOREIGN
AID & INDUSTRIAL DEVELOPMENT IN
PAKISTAN.
M. LIPTON, 617(TLS):2AUG74-830
BRECHER, K.S. - SEE VILLAS BOAS, O.
& C.
BRÉCHON, R. LE SURRÉALISME.
L. LE SAGE, 207(FR):MAR72-913
BRÉE, G. CAMUS & SARTRE.
42(AR):VOL32#3-504
617(TLS):7JUN74-607
BRÉE, G. & G. BERNAUER, EDS & TRANS.
DEFEAT & BEYOND.
F.E. DORENLOT, 207(FR):DEC71-451
BRÉE, G. & A.Y. KROFF. TWENTIETH
CENTURY FRENCH DRAMA.
A. SZOGYI, 207(FR):FEB72-770
BRÉE, G. & G. MARKOW-TOTEVY, EDS.
CONTES ET NOUVELLES. (REV)
R.E. BOSWELL, 399(MLJ):FEB72-108
BREEDON, E. THE RUSTLE OF FALLEN
LEAVES.
617(TLS):1NOV74-1240
BREEM, W. THE LEGATE'S DAUGHTER.
617(TLS):22FEB74-192
BREEN, T.H. THE CHARACTER OF THE
GOOD RULER.*
481(PQ):JUL72-561
BREGA, G.P. - SEE BAYLE, P.
BRÉHIER, É. THE HISTORY OF PHILOSO-
PHY. (VOLS 6&7)
R.C. CARROLL, 207(FR):MAR72-889
BREINES, P., ED. CRITICAL INTERRUP-
TIONS.
E.W.R., 543:JUN72-747
BREIPOHL, R. RELIGIÖSER SOZIALISMUS
UND BÜRGERLICHES GESCHICHTSBEWUSST-
SEIN ZUR ZEIT DER WEIMARER REPUB-
LIK.
A. LASSERRE, 182:VOL25#7/8-239
BREITBACH, J. DIE RABENSCHLACHT UND
ANDERE ERZÄHLUNGEN.
617(TLS):11JAN74-25
BREITBART, V. THE DAY CARE BOOK.
J. DASH, 441:21APR74-6
BREITENSTEIN, T. HÉSIODE ET ARCHIL-
OQUE.
P. WALCOT, 303:VOL92-192
BREKLE, H.E. GENERATIVE SATZSEMAN-
TIK UND TRANSFORMATIONELLE SYNTAX
IM SYSTEM DER ENGLISCHEN NOMINAL-
KOMPOSITION.
D.J. ALLERTON, 297(JL):SEP72-321
BRENAN, G. PERSONAL RECORD: 1920-
1972.
F. KERMODE, 362:5DEC74-744
H. THOMAS, 617(TLS):15NOV74-1287
BREND, R.M. A TAGMEMIC ANALYSIS OF
MEXICAN SPANISH CLAUSES.
E.L. BLANSITT, JR., 545(RPH):
AUG72-165
BRENGUES, J. CHARLES DUCLOS (1704-
1772), OU L'OBSESSION DE LA VERTU.
L.R. FREE, 188(ECR):SUMMER72-151
A.D. HYTIER, 481(PQ):JUL72-675
J. MAYER, 557(RSH):OCT-DEC72-610
BRENGUES, J. - SEE DUCLOS, C.

BRENNAN, A. THE CARBON COPY.
A. BENTLEY, 198:WINTER74-92
BRENNAN, B.P. WILLIAM JAMES.
L.B. CEBIK, 219(GAR):SPRING72-94
BRENNAN, C.J. POEMS [1913].
S.E. LEE, 581:SEP73-335
BRENNAN, M. CHRISTMAS EVE.
R. KIELY, 441:4AUG74-5
BRENT, P. LORD BYRON.
617(TLS):9AUG74-847
BRENT, P. CAPTAIN SCOTT & THE ANT-
ARCTIC TRAGEDY.
617(TLS):22MAR74-304
BRENTANO, C. BRIEFE AN EMILIE LIN-
DER. (W. FRÜHWALD, ED)
J.F.F., 191(ELN):SEP72(SUPP)-139
J.F. FETZER, 221(GQ):NOV72-777
BRENTANO, C. HISTOIRE DU BRAVE GAS-
PARD ET DE LA BELLE ANNETTE.
(J.F.A. RICCI, ED & TRANS)
R. LEROY, 556(RLV):1972/5-555
"CLEMENS BRENTANO."* (W. VORDTRIEDE,
WITH G. BARTENSCHLAGER, EDS)
G. REINHARDT, 222(GR):MAY72-228
BRENTANO, F. DIE ABKEHR VOM NICHT-
REALEN.
M.J.V., 543:SEP71-120
BRENTLINGER, J.A. - SEE PLATO
BRENTON, H. MAGNIFICENCE.
617(TLS):22MAR74-300
BRENTON, H. PLAYS FOR PUBLIC PLACES.
A. RENDLE, 157:WINTER72-80
BRESLIN, J. WORLD WITHOUT END,
AMEN.*
R. BLYTHE, 362:2MAY74-576
C.C. O'BRIEN, 453:21FEB74-13
617(TLS):3MAY74-483
BRESLIN, J.E. WILLIAM CARLOS WIL-
LIAMS.*
B. DUFFEY, 191(ELN):DEC72-138
BRETON, A. SURREALISM & PAINTING.*
R.S. SHORT, 592:NOV72-204
DE LA BRETONNE, R. - SEE UNDER RES-
TIF DE LA BRETONNE
BRETT, C.E. TOWNS & VILLAGES OF
EAST DOWN.
617(TLS):15MAR74-272
BRETT, R.L., ED. S.T. COLERIDGE.*
G. CARNALL, 402(MLR):JUL73-639
W.J.B. OWEN, 541(RES):MAY72-217
BRETTNER-MESSLER, H., ED. DIE PROTO-
KOLLE DES ÖSTERREICHISCHEN MINIS-
TERRATES (1848-1867). (PT 6, VOL
1)
F.L. CARSTEN, 575(SEER):JAN73-
136
BRETTSCHNEIDER, W. ZWISCHEN LITERAR-
ISCHER AUTONOMIE UND STAATSDIENST.
K-H. SCHOEPS, 301(JEGP):OCT73-
612
"MARCEL BREUER: NEW BUILDINGS & PRO-
JECTS 1960-70 & WORK IN RETRO-
SPECT 1921-60."
C. JENCKS, 46:MAR72-196
BREUNIG, L.C. GUILLAUME APOLLINAIRE.*
C. SCOTT, 447(N&Q):SEP72-347
BREUNIG, L.C. - SEE APOLLINAIRE, G.
BREWER, E., ED. FROM CUCHULAINN TO
GAWAIN.
M. TWYCROSS, 617(TLS):13DEC74-
1407
BRIDAHAM, L.B. - SEE MUGNIER, G.F.

BRIDENBAUGH, C. & R. THE BEGINNINGS
OF THE AMERICAN PEOPLE. (VOL 2)
E.V. GOVEIA, 656(WMQ):JAN73-149
BRIDENBAUGH, C. & R. NO PEACE BE-
YOND THE LINE.
639(VQR):SUMMER72-XCIV
BRIDGE, F.R. FROM SADOWA TO SARA-
JEVO.*
F.L. CARSTEN, 575(SEER):APR73-
315
P.F. SUGAR, 32:DEC73-839
BRIDGES, W. GATHERING OF ANIMALS.
J. O'REILLY, 441:22DEC74-4
BRIDGMAN, R. GERTRUDE STEIN IN
PIECES.*
L. CASPER, 613:SPRING72-127
BRIDGWATER, P. KAFKA & NIETZSCHE.
R. PASCAL, 617(TLS):7JUN74-611
BRIDSON, D.G. THE FILIBUSTER.
H. LOMAS, 364:DEC72/JAN73-152
BRIEGER, P., M. MEISS & C. SINGLETON.
ILLUMINATED MANUSCRIPTS OF THE
"DIVINE COMEDY."*
M.B. MC NAMEE, 377:MAR73-48
BRIEGLEB, K. - SEE HEINE, H.
BRIÈRE, E.J. A PSYCHOLINGUISTIC
STUDY OF PHONOLOGICAL INTERFERENCE.
J.A. CZOCHRALSKI, 353:1NOV72-96
BRIFFAULT, R. THE TROUBADOURS.
(L.F. KOONS, ED)
L.J. FRIEDMAN, 545(RPH):MAY73-
711
BRIGANTI, G. THE VIEW PAINTERS OF
EUROPE.*
C.F. OTTO, 576:MAR72-79
BRIGGS, A., ED. ESSAYS IN THE HIS-
TORY OF PUBLISHING.
R.K. WEBB, 617(TLS):26JUL74-802
BRIGGS, A., ED. THE NINETEENTH CEN-
TURY.
W.L. ARNSTEIN, 637(VS):SEP71-91
BRIGGS, A. & J. SAVILLE, EDS. ESSAYS
IN LABOUR HISTORY, 1886-1923.
W.H. MAEHL, JR., 637(VS):SEP72-
123
BRIGGS, J. & I. SELLERS, EDS. VIC-
TORIAN NONCONFORMITY.
617(TLS):15FEB74-152
BRIGGS, K.M. A DICTIONARY OF BRIT-
ISH FOLK-TALES IN THE ENGLISH LAN-
GUAGE.*
W.F.H. NICOLAISEN, 203:SPRING72-
70
BRILL, E. LIFE & TRADITION ON THE
COTSWOLDS.
617(TLS):11JAN74-38
BRINER, A. PAUL HINDEMITH.*
R.T.B., 410(M&L):JAN73-99
BRINER, A., P.D. MEIER & A. RUBELI -
SEE HINDEMITH, P.
BRINGLE, J.E. - SEE SHAW, G.B.
BRINITZER, C. DIE GESCHICHTE DES
DANIEL CH.
617(TLS):3MAY74-464
BRINK, A.P. LOOKING ON DARKNESS.
C.J. DRIVER, 617(TLS):15NOV74-
1278
BRINK, C.O. HORACE ON POETRY.*
(VOL 2)
O.A.W. DILKE, 313:VOL62-158
BRINKER, K. FORMEN DER HEILIGKEIT.
F.W. WENTZLAFF-EGGEBERT,
680(ZDP):BAND91HEFT3-448

BRINKERHOFF, D.M. A COLLECTION OF
SCULPTURE IN CLASSICAL & EARLY
CHRISTIAN ANTIOCH.
M.A.R. COLLEDGE, 313:VOL62-203
J.J. POLLITT, 54:JUN72-202
C.C. VERMEULE, 90:JUN72-411
BRINKMANN, H. DIE DEUTSCHE SPRACHE.
K-E. SOMMERFELDT, 682(ZPSK):
BAND25HEFT4/5-439
BRINKMANN, R. ARNOLD SCHÖNBERG:
DREI KLAVIERSTÜCKE OP. 11.
E. BARKIN, 513:SPRING-SUMMER/
FALL-WINTER71-344
BRINNIN, J.M. SKIN DIVING IN THE
VIRGINS & OTHER POEMS.*
617(TLS):13SEP74-968
BRION, M. POMPEII & HERCULANEUM.
617(TLS):29MAR74-321
BRION-GUERRY, L., ED. L'ANNÉE 1913.
(VOLS 1&2)
V.M. AMES, 290(JAAC):FALL72-133
BRION-GUERRY, L., ED. L'ANNÉE 1913.
(VOL 3)
617(TLS):24MAY74-566
BRISKIN, J. AFTERLOVE.
M. LEVIN, 441:12MAY74-12
BRISSENDEN, A. ROLF BOLDREWOOD.
A. MITCHELL, 71(ALS):MAY74-332
BRISSENDEN, R.F., ED. AUSTRALIAN
POETRY 1972.
S.E. LEE, 581:SEP73-335
BRISSON, J-P., ED. PROBLÈMES DE LA
GUERRE À ROME.*
M. MORFORD, 24:SUMMER73-210
"BRITAIN WILL WIN WITH LABOUR."
E. PYGGE, 617(TLS):4OCT74-1076
BRITTON, K. PHILOSOPHY & THE MEAN-
ING OF LIFE.*
M. FOX, 255(HAB):FALL72-53
BROADBENT, D.E. IN DEFENCE OF
EMPIRICAL PSYCHOLOGY.
617(TLS):8FEB74-129
BROADBENT, J. "PARADISE LOST:" IN-
TRODUCTION.*
R.E.C. HOUGHTON, 541(RES):NOV72-
497
BROADBENT, J. - SEE MILTON, J.
BROADBENT, J.M. WINE TASTING.
617(TLS):8MAR74-245
BROADFOOT, B. SIX WAR YEARS 1939-
1945.
J.L. GRANATSTEIN, 99:NOV/DEC74-
53
BROADFOOT, B. TEN LOST YEARS 1929-
1939.
L. GRAYSON, 99:AUG74-36
453:21MAR74-40
BROADIE, F. AN APPROACH TO DES-
CARTES' MEDITATIONS.
J.N. WRIGHT, 483:JAN72-81
BROCCIA, G. TRADIZIONE ED ESEGESI.*
É. DES PLACES, 555:VOL46FASC2-
289
BROCH, H. THE GUILTLESS.
J.D. O'HARA, 441:21APR74-4
442(NY):15APR74-150
"HERMANN BROCH - DANIEL BRODY: BRIEF-
WECHSEL 1930-1951."* (B. HACK &
M. KLEISS, EDS)
W.H. MC CLAIN, 400(MLN):OCT72-
796
G. WIENOLD, 680(ZDP):BAND91HEFT
2-302

BROCK, E. INVISIBILITY IS THE ART OF SURVIVAL.
P. COOLEY, 385(MQR):WINTER74-79
BROCK, E. THE PORTRAITS & THE POSES.*
R. GARFITT, 364:OCT/NOV73-113
BROCK, P. PACIFISM IN EUROPE TO 1914.
639(VQR):SPRING73-LXXXVI
VOM BROCKE, B. KURT BREYSIG, GE- SCHICHTSWISSENSCHAFT ZWISCHEN HIS- TORISMUS UND SOZIOLOGIE.
D. BRUNN, 182:VOL25#13/14-496
BROCKINGTON, L.H. THE HEBREW TEXT OF THE OLD TESTAMENT.
617(TLS):8FEB74-140
BROCKMAN, H.A.N. THE BRITISH ARCHI- TECT IN INDUSTRY, 1841-1940.
J.M. RICHARDS, 617(TLS):1NOV74- 1222
BROCKWAY, F. THE COLONIAL REVOLU- TION.
617(TLS):1FEB74-101
BRODER, D.S. THE PARTY'S OVER.*
S.K. BAILEY, 639(VQR):AUTUMN72- 580
BRODEUR, P. EXPENDABLE AMERICANS.
P. ADAMS, 61:NOV74-123
R. CONOT, 441:22SEP74-4
BRODIE, B. WAR & POLITICS.
M. HOWARD, 617(TLS):6SEP74-946
BRODIE, F.M. THOMAS JEFFERSON.
A. KAZIN, 441:7APR74-1
C. LEHMANN-HAUPT, 441:8APR74-39
E. WEEKS, 61:APR74-118
G. WILLS, 453:18APR74-26
BRODIN, D. MARCEL AYMÉ.*
H.T. MASON, 447(N&Q):FEB72-73
BRODIN, G. TERMINI DIMOSTRATIVI TOSCANI.*
R. STEFANINI, 545(RPH):MAY73-696
BRODSKY, J. SELECTED POEMS.*
617(TLS):15MAR74-267
BRODSKY, J. STANICA U PUSTINJI.
T.J. BUTLER, 32:DEC73-861
BRODY, A. THE ENGLISH MUMMERS & THEIR PLAYS.*
M.R. CRAIG, 650(WF):JUL72-213
N. DENNY, 677:VOL3-260
W.H. JANSEN, 582(SFQ):DEC72-399
J.H.P. PAFFORD, 447(N&Q):APR72- 141
G. WICKHAM, 541(RES):NOV72-470
BRODY, B.A., ED. MORAL RULES & PAR- TICULAR CIRCUMSTANCES.
E.S.P., 543:MAR72-551
BRODY, E. & R.A. FOWKES. THE GERMAN LIED & ITS POETRY.*
J.L.S., 191(ELN):SEP72(SUPP)-127
BRODY, E.C. THE DEMETRIUS LEGEND & ITS LITERARY TREATMENT IN THE AGE OF THE BAROQUE.
R.C. HOWES, 32:SEP73-656
BRODY, J.J. INDIAN PAINTERS & WHITE PATRONS.
A. BACIGALUPA, 363:MAY72-98
BROINOWSKI, A. TAKE ONE AMBASSADOR.
617(TLS):25JAN74-88
BROMBERG, R. THREE PASTORAL NOVELS.
D-H. DARST, 238:MAR72-176
BROMBERT, B. - SEE PONGE, F.
BROMBERT, V. FLAUBERT PAR LUI-MÊME.
L.R. FURST, 188(ECR):FALL72-231

BROMBERT, V. STENDHAL.*
H-F. IMBERT, 535(RHL):JAN-FEB72- 141
BROME, V. THE AMBASSADOR & THE SPY.
A. BROYARD, 441:4JAN74-27
BROMIGE, D. THREADS.
D. BARBOUR, 529(QQ):WINTER72-569
BROMKE, A. & T. RAKOWSKA-HARMSTONE, EDS. THE COMMUNIST STATES IN DISARRAY, 1965-1971.
R.V. BURKS, 32:MAR73-180
BROMSEN, M.A., ED. JOSÉ TORIBIO MEDINA.
E. BERNAL LABRADA, 37:OCT72-41
BRØNDSTED, M., ED. NORDENS LITTERA- TUR EFTER 1860.*
P.M. MITCHELL, 301(JEGP):OCT73- 584
BRØNDSTED, M., ED. NORDENS LITTERA- TUR FØR 1860.*
P.M. MITCHELL, 301(JEGP):APR73- 261
BRONK, W. THAT TANTALUS.
R.J. BERTHOLF, 648:JUN72-60
BRONSON, B.H. THE BALLAD AS SONG.*
J. PORTER, 650(WF):JAN72-63
BRONSON, B.H. THE TRADITIONAL TUNES OF THE CHILD BALLADS.* (VOL 4)
F. HOWES, 415:APR73-383
BRONTË, C. FIVE NOVELETTES. (W. GÉRIN, ED)
W.M. SALE, JR., 445(NCF):MAR73- 469
BRONTË, C. JANE EYRE.* (J. JACK & M. SMITH, EDS)
N. SHERRY, 402(MLR):JAN73-162
BRONZWAER, W.J.M. TENSE IN THE NOVEL.*
S. ROSSMAN, 290(JAAC):SPRING72- 404
J.G. SCHIPPERS, 204(FDL):JUN72- 113
BROOK, B.S., ED. MUSICOLOGY & THE COMPUTER.
B. VERCOE, 513:SPRING-SUMMER/ FALL-WINTER71-323
BROOK, B.S. THEMATIC CATALOGUES IN MUSIC.
J.A.W., 410(M&L):APR73-223
BROOK, G.L. THE LANGUAGE OF DICK- ENS.*
S.R. GREENBERG, 445(NCF):DEC72- 357
BROOKE, C. MEDIEVAL CHURCH & SOCI- ETY.
C-W. HOLLISTER, 125:FEB73-202
BROOKE, C. THE MONASTIC WORLD 1000- 1300.
R.B. DOBSON, 617(TLS):1NOV74- 1236
BROOKE, C.N.L. THE TWELFTH CENTURY RENAISSANCE.*
A.G. DYSON, 325:APR72-438
BROOKE, D. THE MISERABLE CHILD & HER FATHER IN THE DESERT.
617(TLS):11OCT74-1109
BROOKE, J. KING GEORGE III.
T.W. PERRY, 656(WMQ):JUL73-531
BROOKE, J. & M. SORENSEN - SEE GLAD- STONE, W.E.
BROOKE, R. RUPERT BROOKE: A REAP- PRAISAL & SELECTION. (T. ROGERS, ED)
B. BERGONZI, 541(RES):MAY72-241

BROOKE, R. FOUR POEMS. (G. KEYNES,
ED)
E. PLAYFAIR, 617(TLS):29NOV74-
1346
BROOKE, R.B., ED & TRANS. SCRIPTA
LEONIS, RUFINI ET ANGELI, SOCIORUM
S. FRANCISCI.
E.R. DANIEL, 405(MP):NOV72-157
L.K. LITTLE, 589:APR73-343
BROOKE-LITTLE, J.P. BOUTELL'S HER-
ALDRY.
617(TLS):22FEB74-189
BROOKE-LITTLE, J.P. AN HERALDIC
ALPHABET.
617(TLS):25JAN74-72
BROOKE-ROSE, C. A ZBC OF EZRA
POUND.*
D. BROWN, 376:APR72-129
BROOKES, E.H. WHITE RULE IN SOUTH
AFRICA: 1830-1910.
J. LEWIN, 617(TLS):6SEP74-957
BROOKES, G.H. THE RHETORICAL FORM
OF CARLYLE'S "SARTOR RESARTUS."*
K.J. FIELDING, 301(JEGP):JUL73-
458
BROOKHOUSE, C., ED. "SIR AMADACE" &
"THE AVOWING OF ARTHUR."*
J.R. SIMON, 189(EA):JAN-MAR72-85
BROOKNER, A. THE GENIUS OF THE
FUTURE.*
J.C. SLOANE, 54:DEC72-559
W.J. STRACHAN, 135:MAY72-64
G.P. WEISBERG, 127:FALL72-100
BROOKNER, A. GREUZE.
C. BARRETT, 592:NOV72-200
BROOKS, C. A SHAPING JOY.
A.J. FRY, 433:JAN72-115
L.T.L., 502(PRS):WINTER72/73-369
G. WATSON, 541(RES):MAY72-204
639(VQR):WINTER73-XVII
BROOKS, D. - SEE FIELDING, H.
BROOKS, H.A. THE PRAIRIE SCHOOL.*
R.L. AECK, 219(GAR):FALL72-402
L.K. EATON, 505:JUN72-120
W.R. HASBROUCK, 44:DEC72-12
T.S. HINES, 576:DEC72-332
J.F. O'GORMAN, 54:DEC72-564
BROOKS, J. THE GO-GO YEARS.*
441:10NOV74-40
BROOKS, J.R. THOMAS HARDY.*
R.O. PREYER, 637(VS):JUN72-499
W.F. WRIGHT, 594:SPRING72-93
BROOKS, P. THE NOVEL OF WORLDLI-
NESS.*
L.D. JOINER, 149:SEP73-269
J.R. LOY, 546(RR):FEB72-50
BROOM, J. JOHN MACLEAN.
617(TLS):14JUN74-631
BROOM, L. & F.L. JONES. A BLANKET
A YEAR.
617(TLS):15MAR74-263
BROPHY, B. THE ADVENTURES OF GOD IN
HIS SEARCH FOR THE BLACK GIRL.*
A. BURGESS, 441:25AUG74-4
BROSMAN, C.S. WATERING.*
639(VQR):WINTER73-XIII
BROSNAN, J. JAMES BOND IN THE CINE-
MA.
J.R. PARISH, 200:OCT72-502
BROTHERS, J. & S. HATCH. RESIDENCE
& STUDENT LIFE.
T. POOT, 182:VOL25#12-400

BROTHERSTON, G. & M. VARGAS LLOSA,
EDS. SEVEN STORIES FROM SPANISH
AMERICA.
E.D. TERRY, 399(MLJ):FEB72-115
BROWER, B. THE LATE GREAT CREATURE.
S. O'CONNELL, 418(MR):WINTER73-
190
BROWER, R., H. VENDLER & J. HOLLAN-
DER, EDS. I.A. RICHARDS.
D. YOUNG, 441:26MAY74-15
BROWER, R.A., ED. FORMS OF LYRIC.
G. DARDESS, 599:SPRING72-192
BROWER, R.A. HERO & SAINT.*
I. BROWN, 157:SPRING72-71
M. CHARNEY, 301(JEGP):APR73-241
R. GILL, 191(ELN):JUN73-300
E.A. HORSMAN, 67:MAY73-116
G. LAMBIN, 189(EA):OCT-DEC72-546
D. MEHL, 541(RES):AUG72-343
J.W. VELZ, 402(MLR):JAN73-154
P.G. WALSH, 149:DEC73-396
M. WEST, 128(CE):MAY73-1131
BROWN, A.H. SOVIET POLITICS & POL-
ITICAL SCIENCE.
M. WALLER, 617(TLS):18OCT74-1168
BROWN, A.W. SEXUAL ANALYSIS OF
DICKENS' PROPS.
M. DODSWORTH, 155:SEP72-191
S. HORTON, 637(VS):DEC72-251
G.B. TENNYSON, 445(NCF):DEC72-
369
BROWN, B.E. PROTEST IN PARIS.
F.F. RIDLEY, 617(TLS):1NOV74-
1238
BROWN, B.R. ANTICLASSICISM IN GREEK
SCULPTURE OF THE FOURTH CENTURY
B.C.
617(TLS):15FEB74-165
BROWN, C. MANDELSTAM.*
K. FITZLYON, 364:FEB/MAR74-118
S. KARLINSKY, 441:20JAN74-1
M. MESIC, 491:JUL74-232
BROWN, C. A SHADOW ON SUMMER.
J. MELLORS, 362:1AUG74-156
BROWN, C. & C.D. ROLLINS, EDS. CON-
TEMPORARY PHILOSOPHY IN AUSTRALIA.
A.B.M., 543:DEC71-374
BROWN, C.A. WILDFLOWERS OF LOUISI-
ANA & ADJOINING STATES.
R. MC VAUGH, 385(MQR):SPRING74-
169
BROWN, C.B. ALCUIN: A DIALOGUE.
N. RICE, 418(MR):AUTUMN73-802
D.A. RINGE, 165:WINTER74-310
BROWN, C.C. - SEE "SEJARAH MELAYU OR
MALAY ANNALS"
BROWN, C.H. WILLIAM CULLEN BRYANT.*
R.A. JOHNSON, 639(VQR):AUTUMN72-
630
BROWN, C.W., JR. & OTHERS. JAWS OF
VICTORY.
C. LYDON, 441:4AUG74-1
BROWN, D.D. AGRICULTURAL DEVELOP-
MENT IN INDIA'S DISTRICTS.
A.W. HESTON, 318(JAOS):OCT-DEC72-
583
BROWN, E.E. TASSAJARA COOKING.
617(TLS):10MAY74-508
BROWN, E.J., ED. MAJOR SOVIET WRIT-
ERS.
K. FITZLYON, 364:FEB/MAR74-118
BROWN, E.J. MAYAKOVSKY.
E. MORGAN, 617(TLS):11OCT74-1132
442(NY):28JAN74-103

BROWN, G.E. GEORGE BERNARD SHAW.
J-C. AMALRIC, 189(EA):OCT-DEC72-
574
BROWN, G.G. A LITERARY HISTORY OF
SPAIN: THE TWENTIETH CENTURY.
R. GUTIÉRREZ GIRARDOT, 72:BAND
210HEFT4/6-473
BROWN, G.M. FISHERMEN WITH PLOUGHS.
A. CLUYSENAAR, 565:VOL13#1-72
BROWN, G.M. GREENVOE.*
N. ROBERTS, 97(CQ):VOL6#2-181
BROWN, G.M. HAWKFALL.
617(TLS):27SEP74-1033
BROWN, G.M. POEMS NEW & SELECTED.
A. CLUYSENAAR, 565:VOL13#1-72
V. YOUNG, 249(HUDR):WINTER73/74-
732
BROWN, G.S. - SEE UNDER SPENCER
BROWN, G.
BROWN, H. EARLY TRAVELLERS IN SCOT-
LAND.
617(TLS):1FEB74-112
BROWN, H. THE WILD HUNT.*
639(VQR):SUMMER73-CV
BROWN, H.M. & J. LASCELLE. MUSICAL
ICONOGRAPHY.*
J. MONTAGU, 187:JAN74-153
M.R., 410(M&L):OCT73-493
J. ROWLANDS, 415:OCT73-1014
BROWN, J. JUSEPE DE RIBERA: PRINTS
& DRAWINGS.
617(TLS):28JUN74-696
BROWN, J.E. THE GOLDEN SEA.
D.J. BOORSTIN, 441:1DEC74-51
BROWN, J.H. - SEE DE HAAN, S.
BROWN, J.M. THE ORDEAL OF A PLAY-
WRIGHT.* (N. COUSINS, ED)
T.P. ADLER, 160:SPRING71-201
BROWN, J.R. FREE SHAKESPEARE.
617(TLS):1MAR74-209
BROWN, J.R. SHAKESPEARE'S DRAMATIC
STYLE.*
D.S. BLAND, 551(RENQ):WINTER72-
505
BROWN, J.R. THEATRE LANGUAGE.
R.J. SMITH, 157:AUTUMN72-79
BROWN, K.D., ED. ESSAYS IN ANTI-
LABOUR HISTORY.
S. KOSS, 617(TLS):23AUG74-894
BROWN, K.D. LABOUR & UNEMPLOYMENT.
W.H. MAEHL, JR., 637(VS):SEP72-
123
BROWN, L.R. IN THE HUMAN INTEREST.
E. ROTHSCHILD, 453:19SEP74-30
BROWN, L.R., WITH E.P. ECKHOLM. BY
BREAD ALONE.
J. MAYER, 441:15DEC74-19
BROWN, L.W. BITS OF IVORY.
639(VQR):AUTUMN73-CXLV
BROWN, L.W. FREE NEGROES IN THE
DISTRICT OF COLUMBIA, 1790-1846.
G.W. MULLIN, 656(WMQ):JUL73-513
BROWN, M. THE POLITICS OF IRISH
LITERATURE FROM THOMAS DAVIS TO
W.B. YEATS.*
W.R. JONES, 125:JUN73-315
M.A. KLUG, 150(DR):AUTUMN72-498
639(VQR):WINTER73-XXI
BROWN, M. - SEE PLATO
BROWN, M.E. WALLACE STEVENS.*
J. GLOVER, 565:VOL13#2-70
BROWN, M.F. ESTRANGING DAWN.
L. PERRINE, 27(AL):NOV73-468

BROWN, N.O. CLOSING TIME.*
F.D. MC CONNELL, 659:SUMMER74-
406
H.B. STAPLES, 329(JJQ):SUMMER74-
406
BROWN, O.F. & G.J. ROBERTS. PASSEN-
HAM.
617(TLS):29MAR74-348
BROWN, P. THE WORLD OF LATE ANTIQUI-
TY FROM MARCUS AURELIUS TO MUHAM-
MAD.
R. BROWNING, 123:DEC73-245
J. PERCIVAL, 313:VOL62-175
BROWN, P.L. - SEE UNDER LANCASTER
BROWN, P.
BROWN, R., ED. BETWEEN HUME & MILL.
A. THOMSON, 479(PHQ):APR72-166
BROWN, R. A FIRST LANGUAGE.
P. FARB, 453:21FEB74-24
J. GREENE, 617(TLS):9AUG74-853
BROWN, R. STREET GAMES.
A. BROYARD, 441:18JUN74-43
BROWN, R.B. & B.J. LUBY, EDS. VIS-
IONES DE HOY.
R. ANDERSON, 399(MLJ):APR72-256
S.R. WILSON, 238:MAR72-194
BROWN, R.C. & R. COOK. CANADA 1896-
1921.
M. PRANG, 99:OCT74-43
617(TLS):16AUG74-887
BROWN, R.D. REVOLUTIONARY POLITICS
IN MASSACHUSETTS.*
639(VQR):WINTER72-XXXI
BROWN, R.E. CARL BECKER ON HISTORY
& THE AMERICAN REVOLUTION.*
G.D. ROSS, 178(ECS):FALL72-122
BROWN, R.E. THE VIRGINAL CONCEPTION
& BODILY RESURRECTION OF JESUS.
617(TLS):29MAR74-347
BROWN, R.L. ROBERT BURNS'S TOUR OF
THE HIGHLANDS & STIRLINGSHIRE,
1787.
617(TLS):15FEB74-165
BROWN, S.C. DO RELIGIOUS CLAIMS
MAKE SENSE?*
M. TOOLEY, 482(PHR):OCT72-501
BROWN, T.H. LANGUE ET LITTÉRATURE.
D. NOAKES, 207(FR):OCT71-291
BROWN, T.J., ED. THE DURHAM RITUAL.
A.C. CAMPBELL, 382(MAE):1973/3-
259
BROWN, W. ON THE COAST.*
J. CAREY, 364:JUN/JUL73-120
BROWN, W.H., JR. A SYNTAX OF KING
ALFRED'S "PASTORAL CARE."*
A. CRÉPIN, 189(EA):JAN-MAR72-78
BROWN, W.N. MAN IN THE UNIVERSE.
J.P. SHARMA, 485(PE&W):JAN72-111
BROWNE, E.M. THE MAKING OF T.S.
ELIOT'S PLAYS.*
C.H. SMITH, 659:SPRING74-277
BROWNE, G.A. 11 HARROWHOUSE.
N. CALLENDAR, 441:14JUL74-39
BROWNE, G.A. HAZARD.*
N. CALLENDAR, 441:8DEC74-44
617(TLS):2AUG74-839
BROWNE, G.M., ED. DOCUMENTARY PAP-
YRI FROM THE MICHIGAN COLLECTION.
J.A.S. EVANS, 487:SUMMER72-209
N. LEWIS, 24:SUMMER73-227
BROWNE, H. YOU CAN PROFIT FROM A
MONETARY CRISIS.
A. SMITH, 441:31MAR74-7

48

BROWNE, M. - SEE CHORNOVIL, V. &
OTHERS
BROWNING, E.B. THE BARRETTS AT HOPE
END. (E. BERRIDGE, ED)
A. HAYTER, 617(TLS):6SEP74-948
BROWNING, I. PETRA.
617(TLS):27SEP74-1032
BROWNING, R. THE COMPLETE WORKS OF
ROBERT BROWNING.* (VOLS 2-4)
(R.A. KING, JR. & OTHERS, EDS)
617(TLS):22MAR74-293
BROWNING, R. JUSTINIAN & THEODORA.*
M.T.W. ARNHEIM, 313:VOL62-186
J.F. POWERS, 613:WINTER72-628
BROWNING, R. THE POETRY OF ROBERT
BROWNING. (J. KORG, ED)
M. HANCHER, 677:VOL3-318
BROWNING, R. & E.B. THE BROWNINGS
TO THE TENNYSONS. (T.J. COLLINS,
ED)
G.O. MARSHALL, JR., 85:SPRING72-
64
BROWNING, R.M. GERMAN BAROQUE POET-
RY, 1618-1723.
R.T. LLEWELLYN, 402(MLR):OCT73-
942
R.G. WARNOCK, 406:SUMMER73-197
BROWNJOHN, A. WARRIOR'S CAREER.*
J. CAREY, 364:JUN/JUL73-120
BROWNLIE, I., ED. BASIC DOCUMENTS
ON HUMAN RIGHTS. BASIC DOCUMENTS
ON AFRICAN AFFAIRS.
T.M. SHAW, 69:JUL72-252
BROWNLIE, I. PRINCIPLES OF PUBLIC
INTERNATIONAL LAW.
617(TLS):25JAN74-83
BROWNSTEIN, M. COUNTRY COUSINS.
K. ROOSEVELT, 441:17NOV74-48
BROXAP, E. THE GREAT CIVIL WAR IN
LANCASHIRE 1642-1651.
617(TLS):7JUN74-616
BROŻEK, A. ŚLĄZACY W TEKSASIE.
G.J. LERSKI, 32:SEP73-637
BRUCCOLI, M.J. - SEE CHANDLER, R.
BRUCCOLI, M.J. - SEE FITZGERALD, F.S.
BRUCCOLI, M.J. - SEE FITZGERALD,
F.S. & H. OBER
BRUCCOLI, M.J. & S.F. SMITH - SEE
FITZGERALD, F.S. & Z.
BRUCE, D. SUN PICTURES.
P. ADAMS, 61:MAY74-140
617(TLS):29MAR74-310
BRUCE, G. THE BURMA WARS 1824-1886.
617(TLS):18JAN74-61
BRUCE, G., ED. 35 SONGS FROM 35
COUNTRIES.
F. HOWES, 415:JUL73-703
BRUCE, R.V. BELL.*
H.V. NELLES, 99:MAY/JUN74-52
617(TLS):22FEB74-191
BRUCE-MITFORD, R. ASPECTS OF ANGLO-
SAXON ARCHAEOLOGY.
D.M. WILSON, 617(TLS):1NOV74-
1233
BRUCE-MITFORD, R. THE SUTTON HOO
SHIP-BURIAL. (2ND ED)
P.H. BLAIR, 382(MAE):1973/3-301
BRUCH, H. EATING DISORDERS.
S. KITZINGER, 362:28FEB74-280
617(TLS):22MAR74-280
BRUCH, J-L. - SEE KANT, I.
BRUCHAC, J. INDIAN MOUNTAIN.
E. LICHTENBERG, 114(CHIR):VOL23
#4&VOL24#1-212

BRUCHER, R. MAURICE MAETERLINCK.
E.T. DUBOIS, 182:VOL25#19/20-670
BRUCHER, R. & OTHERS, EDS. BIBLIO-
GRAPHIE DES ÉCRIVAINS FRANÇAIS DE
BELGIQUE (1881-1960).* (VOLS 3&4)
[SHOWN IN PREV UNDER CULOT, J-M.
& OTHERS]
E.T. DUBOIS, 182:VOL25#19/20-669
BRUCKNER, A., ED. HELVETIA SACRA.
(PT 1, VOL 1)
H. DUCHHARDT, 182:VOL25#11-372
BRUCKNER, J. A BIBLIOGRAPHICAL CATA-
LOGUE OF SEVENTEENTH-CENTURY GER-
MAN BOOKS PUBLISHED IN HOLLAND.*
D.L. PAISEY, 354:DEC72-342
BRÜCKNER, W., ED. FRANKFURTER WÖR-
TERBUCH. (PTS 1&2)
K. SPALDING, 182:VOL25#17/18-595
BRUDERER, G.E., COMP. PROTSESS
TSEPNOI REAKTSII.
H. ERMOLAEV, 550(RUSR):JUL72-304
BRÜGEL, J.W., ED. STALIN UND HITLER.
617(TLS):21JUN74-664
BRUGGINK, D.J. & C.H. DROPPERS.
CHRIST & ARCHITECTURE.
M. LAVANOUX, 363:MAY72-108
BRUGMANS, L.F. - SEE GIDE, A. & A.
BENNETT
BRUN, J. - SEE KIERKEGAARD, S.
BRUN, R. LE LIVRE FRANÇAIS ILLUSTRÉ
DE LA RENAISSANCE.*
E. ZIMMERMANN, 182:VOL25#17/18-
579
BRUNDAGE, J.A. RICHARD LION HEART.
442(NY):12AUG74-100
BRUNE, J.A. - SEE WOOD, M.F.
BRUNEL, P. LE MYTHE D'ELECTRE.
A. KARÁTSON, 549(RLC):OCT-DEC72-
600
BRUNER, J.S. BEYOND THE INFORMATION
GIVEN. (J.M. ANGLIN, ED)
M.D. VERNON, 617(TLS):25OCT74-
1193
BRUNI, F. SISTEMI CRITICI E STRUT-
TURE NARRATIVE.
A.L. DE GAETANO, 400(MLN):JAN72-
142
M. POZZI, 228(GSLI):VOL149FASC
466/467-424
BRÜNING, H. HEINRICH BRÜNING:
BRIEFE UND GESPRÄCHE, 1934-1945.
(C. NIX, ED)
K. VON KLEMPERER, 617(TLS):8NOV
74-1263
BRUNNER, H. DIE POETISCHE INSEL.
S.L. GILMAN, 52:BAND7HEFT1-78
BRUNNER, J. BEDLAM PLANET.
617(TLS):15FEB74-163
BRUNNER, J. THE SHEEP LOOK UP.
M. ELLMANN, 676(YR):SPRING73-461
617(TLS):23AUG74-911
BRUNNER, L. DIE GEMEINSAMEN WURZELN
DES SEMITISCHEN UND INDOGERMANIS-
CHEN WORTSCHATZES.
J.L. MALONE, 350:JUN73-495
E. NEU, 260(IF):BAND76-218
BRUNNSÅKER, S. THE TYRANT-SLAYERS
OF KRITIOS & NESIOTES.
A. BÜSING-KOLBE, 182:VOL25#9/10-
300
BRUNO, G. DES FUREURS HÉROÏQUES.
(P-H. MICHEL, ED & TRANS)
E. NAMER, 542:JAN-MAR72-93

BRUNO, G. LO SPACCIO DELLA BESTIA
TRIONFANTE. (A. NEGRI, ED)
E. NAMER, 542:JAN-MAR72-94
BRUNOT, F. HISTOIRE DE LA LANGUE
FRANÇAISE DES ORIGINES À NOS JOURS.
(VOL 11, PT 1)
M. HÖFLER, 72:BAND21OHEFT1/3-216
S. ULLMANN, 208(FS):JAN73-114
BRUNSKILL, R.W. AN ILLUSTRATED HAND-
BOOK OF VERNACULAR ARCHITECTURE.*
R.M. CANDEE, 292(JAF):JAN-MAR72-
91
BRUNSKILL, R.W. VERNACULAR ARCHI-
TECTURE OF THE LAKE COUNTIES.
617(TLS):12APR74-401
BRUNT, P.A. ITALIAN MANPOWER 225
B.C. - A.D. 14.*
K. HOPKINS, 313:VOL62-192
BRUNT, P.A. SOCIAL CONFLICTS IN THE
ROMAN REPUBLIC.
J-C. DUMONT, 555:VOL46FASC2-352
R. SEAGER, 313:VOL62-182
BRUS, W. THE ECONOMICS & POLITICS
OF SOCIALISM.
617(TLS):12APR74-398
BRUSH, C.B. - SEE GASSENDI, P.
BRUTTEN, M., S.O. RICHARDSON & C.
MANGEL. SOMETHING'S WRONG WITH MY
CHILD.
M. GANSBERG, 441:4MAY74-45
VAN DEN BRUWAENE, M. CICÉRON, DE
NATURA DEORUM, LIVRE 1ER.
A. ERNOUT, 555:VOL46FASC1-151
BRUXNER, M. MASTERING THE PIANO.
F. DAWES, 415:SEP73-900
BRYANT, A. THE GREAT DUKE.
M.E. BRADFORD, 396(MODA):FALL73-
431
BRYANT, J.H. THE OPEN DECISION.
C.E. EISINGER, 128(CE):MAY72-951
M. KLEIN, 128(CE):MAY72-955
BRYDEN, R. THE UNFINISHED HERO.
P. MÜNDER, 430(NS):FEB72-109
BRYENNIUS, M. THE HARMONICS OF
MANUEL BRYENNIUS. (G.H. JONKER,
ED & TRANS)
R.P.W-I., 410(M&L):OCT73-480
BRYER, J.R., ED. SIXTEEN MODERN
AMERICAN AUTHORS.
A. BENTLEY, 268:JUL74-158
BRZOZOWSKI, S. LISTY. (M. SROKA,
ED)
J.T. BAER, 497(POLR):WINTER72-91
BUBNER, R., K. CRAMER & R. WIEHL,
EDS. HERMENEUTIK UND DIALEKTIK.
J.J. KOCKELMANS, 480(P&R):FALL72-
261
BUCCO, M. WILBUR DANIEL STEELE.
T.J. LYON, 651(WHR):SUMMER73-318
BUCER, M. & T. CRANMER. ANNOTATIONES
IN OCTO PRIORA CAPITA EVANGELII
SECUNDUM MATTHAEUM. (H. VOGT, ED)
F.F. BRUCE, 182:VOL25#15/16-521
BUCHAN, A. CHANGE WITHOUT WAR. THE
END OF THE POSTWAR ERA.
K. KYLE, 362:29AUG74-282
E. LUTTWAK, 617(TLS):27DEC74-
1460
BUCHAN, N. & P. HALL. THE SCOTTISH
FOLKSINGER.
F. HOWES, 415:APR73-383
BUCHANAN, C. MAIDEN.
E. ROVIT, 659:AUTUMN74-539
BUCHANAN-BROWN, J. - SEE AUBREY, J.

BUCHDA, G. DIE SCHÖFFENSPRUCHSAMM-
LUNG DER STADT PÖSSNECK. (PTS 3&4)
T. KLEIN, 182:VOL25#21-729
BUCHDAHL, G. METAPHYSICS & THE PHIL-
OSOPHY OF SCIENCE.*
M.P. BRADIE & J.D. STUART, 486:
JUN72-267
D.J. O'CONNOR, 84:FEB72-79
BUCHER, A.J. MARTIN HEIDEGGER.
S. DECLOUX, 182:VOL25#7/8-197
BUCHER, F. THE PAMPLONA BIBLES.*
M.B. MC NAMEE, 377:MAR73-41
J.G. PLANTE, 363:FEB72-78
BUCHHEIM, L-G. U-BOAT.
T. SHIPPEY, 617(TLS):8NOV74-1248
BÜCHLER, F. WASSERSCHEIDE ZWEIER
ZEITALTER.
J.J. WHITE, 220(GL&L):JUL73-322
BUCHLER, J. THE MAIN OF LIGHT.
I.A. RICHARDS, 617(TLS):29NOV74-
1343
BÜCHNER, G. LEONCE & LEONA, LENZ,
WOYZECK.* (M. HAMBURGER, ED &
TRANS)
M. SONNENFELD, 160:SPRING72-187
BÜCHNER, G. THE PLAYS OF GEORG
BÜCHNER.* (V. PRICE, ED & TRANS)
G. MANDER, 157:WINTER71-71
BÜCHNER, G. WOYZECK. (L. BORN-
SCHEUER, ED)
H.J. SCHMIDT, 406:WINTER73-425
BUCHNER, H. PLOTINS MÖGLICHKEITS-
LEHRE.*
P. LOUIS, 555:VOL46FASC2-305
BÜCHNER, K. - SEE HORACE
BUCHTHAL, H. HISTORIA TROIANA.*
J.J.G. ALEXANDER, 382(MAE):
1973/2-158
BUCHWALD, W. - SEE MAAS, P.
BUCK, A., ED. RENAISSANCE UND BAR-
OCK, I UND II.
M.L. BAEUMER, 406:WINTER73-393
BUCK, A. - SEE BOILEAU, N.
BUCK, R.C. & R.S. COHEN, EDS. PSA
1970 IN MEMORY OF RUDOLF CARNAP.
A. MERCIER, 182:VOL25#9/10-257
BUCK, W. MAHABHARATA.
W. O'FLAHERTY, 617(TLS):15NOV74-
1280
BUCKE, R.M. WALT WHITMAN.
A. LOZYNSKY, 646(WWR):SEP72-104
BUCKERIDGE, N. JOURNAL & LETTER
BOOK OF NICHOLAS BUCKERIDGE 1651-
1654. (J.R. JENSON, ED)
617(TLS):19JUL74-772
BUCKLEY, M. MOTION & MOTION'S GOD.
R.S., 543:DEC71-349
BUCKLEY, W.F., JR. FOUR REFORMS.
D.P. MOYNIHAN, 441:13JAN74-5
L. SILK, 441:23MAR74-29
P. SINGER, 453:18JUL74-20
442(NY):18FEB74-119
BUCKLEY, W.F., JR. UNITED NATIONS
JOURNAL.
C. LEHMANN-HAUPT, 441:13SEP74-41
E. REDMAN, 441:6OCT74-4
442(NY):14OCT74-201
BUCKMASTER, H. WAIT UNTIL EVENING.
M. LEVIN, 441:10FEB74-8
BUCKNALL, B.J. THE RELIGION OF ART
IN PROUST.*
J. CRUICKSHANK, 208(FS):JAN73-97
E.R. JACKSON, 207(FR):OCT71-250
W.A. STRAUSS, 399(MLJ):APR72-252

BUCKRIDGE, B. AN ESSAY TOWARDS AN
ENGLISH SCHOOL OF PAINTING.
K. GARLICK, 39:JAN72-73
BUDDEN, J. THE OPERAS OF VERDI.*
(VOL 1)
W.D., 410(M&L):JUL73-341
BUDDEN, S. & J. ERNST. THE MOVABLE
AIRPORT.
J. SACK, 99:MAY/JUN74-46
BUDDICOM, J. ERIC & US.
J. VAIZEY, 362:27JUN74-839
BUDGE, I. & C. O'LEARY. BELFAST:
APPROACH TO CRISIS.
H. PATTERSON, 111:18MAY73-154
BUDICK, S. DRYDEN & THE ABYSS OF
LIGHT.*
E.J. CHIASSON, 128(CE):APR72-841
R.H. DAMMERS, 568(SCN):FALL-WIN-
TER73-66
BUEB, B. NIETZSCHES KRITIK DER PRAK-
TISCHEN VERNUNFT.*
G.J. STACK, 319:APR74-274
BUECHNER, F. THE FACES OF JESUS.
H. BEVINGTON, 441:1DEC74-86
BUECHNER, F. LOVE FEAST.
C. LEHMANN-HAUPT, 441:25SEP74-33
M. MEWSHAW, 441:22SEP74-2
442(NY):21OCT74-189
BUECHNER, F. OPEN HEART.*
L.T.L., 502(PRS):WINTER72/73-370
639(VQR):AUTUMN72-CXX
BUEHR, W. - SEE GREY, I.
BUEL, R., JR. SECURING THE REVOLU-
TION.*
L.K. KERBER, 656(WMQ):JUL73-503
BUELER, L.E. WILD DOGS OF THE WORLD.
617(TLS):27SEP74-1048
BUELL, F. W.H. AUDEN AS A SOCIAL
POET.*
R. BLOOM, 639(VQR):AUTUMN73-637
BUELL, F. THESEUS & OTHER POEMS.*
J. BULLIS, 181:FALL72-104
BUELL, T.B. THE QUIET WARRIOR.
R. TRUMBULL, 441:12OCT74-29
BUERKLE, J.V. & D. BARKER. BOURBON
STREET BLACK.*
F. CONROY, 441:3FEB74-4
BUERO VALLEJO, A. LA DOBLE HISTORIA
DEL DOCTOR VALMY.* (A.M. GIL, ED)
P.W. O'CONNOR, 399(MLJ):FEB72-
104
BUERO VALLEJO, A. EL SUEÑO DE LA
RAZÓN. (J. DOWLING, ED)
M.T. HALSEY, 238:DEC72-979
BUFFIÈRE, F., ED & TRANS. ANTHOLO-
GIE GRECQUE.* (PT 1, VOL 12)
P. CHANTRAINE, 555:VOL46FASC2-
303
A. GRIFFITHS, 303:VOL92-211
DE BUFFON, G.L.L. DE L'HOMME. (M.
DUCHET, ED)
R. MERCIER, 557(RSH):APR-JUN72-
316
BUGLIOSI, V., WITH C. GENTRY. HEL-
TER SKELTER.
C. LEHMANN-HAUPT, 441:8NOV74-43
M. ROGERS, 441:17NOV74-4
BÜHLER, C.F. - SEE DE PISAN, C.
BÜHLER, H. & OTHERS. LINGUISTIK I.
W. LEHFELDT, 353:15OCT72-101
H. LOFFLER, 343:BAND15HEFT1-1
"THE BUILDING ERECTED IN HYDE PARK
FOR THE GREAT EXHIBITION."
B. READ, 135:AUG72-302

VAN BUITENEN, J.A.B., ED & TRANS.
THE MAHABHARATA. (VOL 1)
W. O'FLAHERTY, 617(TLS):15NOV74-
1280
W. SARGEANT, 442(NY):11MAR74-131
BUITENHUIS, P. THE GRASPING IMAGI-
NATION.*
R. BELFLOWER, 541(RES):AUG72-379
R. FALK, 445(NCF):SEP72-224
BUKHSHTAB, B.I. BIBLIOGRAFICHESKIE
RAZYSKANIIA PO RUSSKOI LITERATURE
XIX VEKA. RUSSKIE POETY.
J.E. MALMSTAD, 32:JUN73-426
BUKOWSKI, C. LIFE & DEATH IN THE
CHARITY WARD.
W. FEAVER, 617(TLS):29NOV74-1336
BUKOWSKI, C. POST OFFICE.
R. BLYTHE, 362:4APR74-444
617(TLS):5APR74-375
BULGAKOV, M. DIABOLIAD & OTHER STOR-
IES. (E. & C.R. PROFFER, EDS) THE
EARLY PLAYS OF MIKHAIL BULGAKOV.
(E. PROFFER, ED)
C. BROWN, 473(PR):3/1973-533
BULL, J. BIRDS OF NEW YORK STATE.
G. GOLD, 441:20DEC74-35
BÜLL, R. VOM WACHS.
E.O. JAMES, 203:SUMMER72-160
BULL, W.E. TIME, TENSE, & THE VERB.*
H. WEINRICH, 353:JAN72-112
BULLARD, E.J. MARY CASSATT, OILS &
PASTELS.
A. FRANKENSTEIN, 55:NOV73-48
T. LASK, 55:APR73-14
BULLER, H. DAYS OF RAGE.
J.A.S. EVANS, 99:OCT74-42
BULLITT, O.H. - SEE ROOSEVELT, F.D.
& W.C. BULLITT
BULLOKAR, W. THE WORKS OF WILLIAM
BULLOKAR. (VOL 1) (B. DANIELSSON
& R.C. ALSTON, EDS)
B. SUNDBY, 597(SN):VOL44#1-195
BULLOUGH, G., ED. NARRATIVE & DRA-
MATIC SOURCES OF SHAKESPEARE.*
(VOL 7)
639(VQR):AUTUMN73-CXLIX
BULLRICH, F. LATIN AMERICAN ARCHI-
TECTURE.
R. BANHAM, 54:DEC72-565
BULMER, K., ED. NEW WRITINGS IN
SF - 24.
617(TLS):31MAY74-577
VON BÜLOW, I. DER TANZ IM DRAMA.*
G. HOFFMANN, 38:BAND90HEFT1/2-
266
BUMKE, J. DIE WOLFRAM VON ESCHEN-
BACH-FORSCHUNG SEIT 1945.*
W.T.H. JACKSON, 222(GR):NOV72-
310
BUMSTED, J.M. HENRY ALLINE, 1748-
1784.*
J.W. DAVIDSON, 656(WMQ):JUL73-
526
BUNGARTEN, J.J. MENANDERS UND GLYK-
ERAS BRIEF BEI ALKIPHRON.
C. MEILLIER, 555:VOL46FASC2-307
BUNGE, M., ED. DELAWARE SEMINAR IN
THE FOUNDATIONS OF PHYSICS. QUAN-
TUM THEORY & REALITY.
J. AGASSI, 486:JUN72-263
BUNGE, M. SCIENTIFIC RESEARCH.
W. SCHÄFER, 182:VOL25#1/2-1

BUNKER, E.C., C.B. CHATWIN & A.R.
FARKAS. "ANIMAL STYLE."
K. JETTMAR, 57:VOL34#2/3-256
BUNKER, G.E. THE PEACE CONSPIRACY.
42(AR):SPRING/SUMMER72-247
BUNTING, B. - SEE FORD, F.M.
BUNTING, J., 3D. THE ADVENT OF FRED-
ERICK GILES.
C. LEHMANN-HAUPT, 441:16MAY74-45
E. WEEKS, 61:MAY74-137
BUNTING, W.H., COMP. PORTRAIT OF A
PORT.
D.B. LITTLE, 432(NEQ):JUN72-298
BUNYAN, J. & V. BUTENKO - SEE VALEN-
TINOV, N.
BURCH, F.F. TRISTAN CORBIÈRE.
K. CORNELL, 207(FR):MAR72-920
BURCHARD, R.C. JOHN UPDIKE.*
S.I. BELLMAN, 573(SSF):SUMMER72-
293
BURCHFIELD, R.W. - SEE "A SUPPLEMENT
TO THE OXFORD ENGLISH DICTIONARY"
BURCKHARDT, C.J. RICHELIEU & HIS
AGE.
A. SEDGWICK, 639(VQR):WINTER73-
148
BURCKHARDT, C.J. & M. RYCHNER.
BRIEFE 1926-1965. (C. MERTZ-
RYCHNER, ED)
F.M. WASSERMANN, 221(GQ):JAN72-
192
BURCKHARDT, J. CONSIDÉRATIONS SUR
L'HISTOIRE UNIVERSELLE.
J. WIRTH, 98:NOV72-1006
BURDEN, D.H. - SEE MILTON, J.
VON BÜREN, E. ZUR BEDEUTUNG DER
PSYCHOLOGIE IM WERK ROBERT MUSILS.*
E. BOA, 402(MLR):APR73-472
BURFORD, L. VICE AVENGED.*
L.T.L., 502(PRS):FALL72-274
BURG, D. & G. FEIFER. SOLZHENITSYN.*
R. HAGGLUND, 32:DEC73-858
BURGER, H.O. RENAISSANCE, HUMANIS-
MUS, REFORMATION.*
M.L. BAEUMER, 406:WINTER73-393
H. ENTNER, 654(WB):3/1972-185
D. WUTTKE, 52:BAND7HEFT1-80
BURGESS, A. THE CLOCKWORK TESTAMENT.
W. PRITCHARD, 362:13JUN74-776
617(TLS):7JUN74-601
BURGESS, A. JOYSPRICK.*
J. NAREMORE, 329(JJQ):WINTER74-
175
BURGESS, A. MF.
T. WINTER, 502(PRS):SPRING72-82
BURGESS, A. NAPOLEON SYMPHONY.
J. BAYLEY, 453:19SEP74-32
S. SANBORN, 441:9JUN74-5
E. TENNANT, 362:24OCT74-552
442(NY):8JUL74-80
617(TLS):27SEP74-1033
BURGESS, F.H. A DICTIONARY FOR
YACHTSMEN.
617(TLS):1NOV74-1240
BURGESS, G.S. CONTRIBUTION À
L'ÉTUDE DU VOCABULAIRE PRÉ-COUR-
TOIS.*
R. TAYLOR, 399(MLJ):FEB72-111
BÜRGISSER, P. LA DOUBLE ILLUSION DE
L'OR ET DE L'AMOUR CHEZ VILLIERS
DE L'ISLE-ADAM.
M.G. ROSE, 546(RR):OCT72-240
BURICH, N.J. ALEXANDER THE GREAT.
G.L. CAWKWELL, 123:MAR73-103

BURKE, E. THE CORRESPONDENCE OF
EDMUND BURKE. (VOL 9) (R.B. MC
DOWELL & J.A. WOODS, EDS)
S.W. JACKMAN, 481(PQ):JUL72-651
BURKE, J.F. LOCATION SHOTS.
N. CALLENDAR, 441:3FEB74-26
BURKE, K. GOLD & SILVER.
617(TLS):12APR74-386
BURKE, S.M. PAKISTAN'S FOREIGN
POLICY.*
639(VQR):AUTUMN73-CLXIX
BURKE, T. LIMEHOUSE NIGHTS.
442(NY):20MAY74-150
BURKERT, W. HOMO NECANS.
F. LASSERRE, 182:VOL25#1/2-46
BURKERT, W. LORE & SCIENCE IN
ANCIENT PYTHAGOREANISM.
617(TLS):18JAN74-61
639(VQR):SPRING73-XCI
BURKHART, C., ED. THE ART OF I.
COMPTON-BURNETT.
C. DRESSLER, 189(EA):OCT-DEC72-
577
BURKILL, T.A. THE EVOLUTION OF
CHRISTIAN THOUGHT.*
W.C. MC CAULEY, 613:SPRING72-144
BURLAND, C.A. ECHOES OF MAGIC.
T. BROWN, 203:SUMMER72-163
BURLAS, L., ED. MUSICOLOGICA SLO-
VACA. (VOL 1)
B. KRADER, 187:JAN74-151
BURLIN, R.B. THE OLD ENGLISH ADVENT.
F.C. ROBINSON, 38:BAND90HEFT4-
516
BURLING, R. MAN'S MANY VOICES.*
J.L. FIDELHOLTZ, 269(IJAL):OCT
72-270
H. LANDAR, 215(GL):VOL12#3-172
G. SANKOFF, 350:JUN73-514
P. TRUDGILL, 297(JL):SEP72-306
BURNETT, A.P. CATASTROPHE SURVIVED.*
P.T. STEVENS, 303:VOL92-196
BURNETT, J., ED. USEFUL TOIL.
T. BARKER, 362:13JUN74-773
P.J. KEATING, 617(TLS):2AUG74-
822
BURNEY, F. EVELINA OR THE HISTORY
OF A YOUNG LADY'S ENTRANCE INTO
THE WORLD. (E. BLOOM, ED)
A. PARREAUX, 189(EA):OCT-DEC72-
557
BURNEY, F. THE JOURNALS & LETTERS
OF FANNY BURNEY (MADAME D'ARBLAY).
(VOLS 1&2) (J. HEMLOW & A. DOUGLAS,
EDS)
G.E. BENTLEY, JR., 627(UTQ):
WINTER73-177
J. GRAY, 150(DR):AUTUMN72-487
639(VQR):AUTUMN73-CLX
BURNFORD, S. ONE WOMAN'S ARCTIC.*
R. COLES, 442(NY):23SEP74-138
BURNHAM, S. THE ART CROWD.*
A. FRANKENSTEIN, 55:5OCT73-65
J. HENDRICKS, 59(ASOC):FALL-
WINTER73-95
B. SCHWARTZ, 59(ASOC):FALL-
WINTER73-96
BURNS, A. THE ANGRY BRIGADE.
V. CUNNINGHAM, 362:28MAR74-413
BURNS, A. & J. GIBBS - SEE DE CER-
VANTES SAAVEDRA, M.
BURNS, E. - SEE TOKLAS, A.B.

52

BURNS, E.L.M. A SEAT AT THE TABLE.
C.S. GRAY, 529(QQ):WINTER72-550
J. WOUK, 150(DR):AUTUMN72-515
BURNS, J. ARTHROPODS.
R. PIEROTTI, 505:NOV72-130
BURNS, J.H. & H.L.A. HART - SEE BEN-
THAM, J.
BURNS, J.M. UNCOMMON SENSE.
S.K. BAILEY, 639(VQR):AUTUMN72-
580
BURNS, J.P. - SEE LONERGAN, B.J.F.
BURNS, R. THE POEMS AND SONGS OF
ROBERT BURNS.* (J. KINSLEY, ED)
R. REITEMEIER, 38:BAND90HEFT4-
540
G.R. ROY, 405(MP):AUG72-71
BURNS, R.M., ED. ONE COUNTRY OR TWO?
D.V. SMILEY, 529(QQ):AUTUMN72-
426
BURNS, W. THE PANZAIC PRINCIPLE,
PARTS I & II.
J. DOHENY, 648:JAN73-61
BURROUGHS, W.S. EXTERMINATOR!*
R. BLYTHE, 362:21MAR74-381
617(TLS):22MAR74-282
BURROW, J.A. RICARDIAN POETRY.*
M.W. BLOOMFIELD, 589:APR73-345
D. FARLEY-HILLS, 541(RES):AUG72-
325
S. WENZEL, 382(MAE):1973/1-93
639(VQR):SPRING72-LIII
BURROW, T. & S. BHATTACHARYA. THE
PENGO LANGUAGE.
M.B. EMENEAU, 361:VOL28#1&2-197
BURROWS, J.F. JANE AUSTEN'S "EMMA."
S.F.W. JOHNSTON, 67:MAY73-117
BURSILL-HALL, G.L. SPECULATIVE
GRAMMARS OF THE MIDDLE AGES.
L.G. KELLY, 320(CJL):VOL18#2-177
R.H. ROBINS, 382(MAE):1973/3-265
BURSTIN, J. DÉSAGRÉGATION, RÉGRES-
SION ET RECONSTRUCTION DANS LA
SCHIZOPHRÉNIE.
C. BARDET, 542:OCT-DEC72-452
BURT, M.K. FROM DEEP TO SURFACE
STRUCTURE.
J.K. CHAMBERS, 320(CJL):SPRING71-
113
D.T. LANGENDOEN, 128(CE):MAY73-
1150
D.T. LANGENDOEN, 350:SEP73-714
"BURT'S LETTERS FROM THE NORTH OF
SCOTLAND."
617(TLS):29MAR74-342
BURTON, A., ED. VICTORIAN CHURCH
ART.
R. MC LEAN, 135:MAR72-216
BURTON, J.A. NATURALIST IN LONDON.
617(TLS):1NOV74-1240
BURTON, J.A., ED. OWLS OF THE WORLD.
617(TLS):22FEB74-193
BURTON, M. AN ALCOHOLIC IN THE FAM-
ILY.
617(TLS):14JUN74-628
BURTON, N., P. HART & J. LAUGHLIN -
SEE MERTON, T.
BURY, A., ED. THE OLD WATER-COLOUR
SOCIETY'S CLUB. (VOL 46)
T. CROMBIE, 39:JUN72-520
BURY, A. MAURICE QUENTIN DE LA TOUR.
B. SCOTT, 39:MAY72-426
D. THOMAS, 135:MAR72-215

BURY, J.P.T. GAMBETTA & THE MAKING
OF THE THIRD REPUBLIC.
617(TLS):15FEB74-160
BUSCH, B.C. BRITAIN, INDIA, & THE
ARABS: 1914-1921.
J. WATERBURY, 293(JAST):FEB72-
437
BUSCH, E. DES AMT DES WEHRBEAUF-
TRAGTEN DES DEUTSCHEN BUNDESTAGES.
H. RIDLEY, 220(GL&L):OCT72-72
BUSCH, F. BREATHING TROUBLE & OTHER
STORIES.
617(TLS):22FEB74-173
BUSCH, F. HAWKES.
J.H. JUSTUS, 27(AL):NOV73-477
639(VQR):SUMMER73-CXV
BUSCH, F. MANUAL LABOR.
J.C. OATES, 441:3NOV74-66
BUSCH, W. MAX UND MORITZ. GEDICHTE.
DIE FROMME HELENE. TOBIAS KNOPP.
HANS HUCKEBEIN, FIPPS DER AFFE,
PLISCH UND PLUM. BALDUIN BÄHLAMM,
MALER KLECKSEL. PROSA. (F. BOHNE,
ED) KRITISCH-ALLZUKRITISCHES. (T.
SCHLEE, ED)
617(TLS):14JUN74-633
BUSH, D. MATTHEW ARNOLD.
J.P. FARRELL, 637(VS):DEC71-238
BUSH, D. - SEE WOODHOUSE, A.S.P.
BUSH, D., J.E. SHAW & A.B. GIAMATTI,
EDS. A VARIORUM COMMENTARY ON THE
POEMS OF JOHN MILTON.* (VOL 1)
A.R. CIRILLO, 405(MP):FEB73-265
BUSH, R. - SEE KING, G.
BUSH, R. & J.B. MERIWETHER - SEE
SIMMS, W.G.
BUSH, R.C. RELIGION IN COMMUNIST
CHINA.
D.C. YU, 293(JAST):FEB72-404
BUSH, S. THE CHINESE LITERATI ON
PAINTING.
T. BOWIE, 127:SUMMER73-457
639(VQR):SPRING72-LXXVI
BUSI, F. L'ESTHÉTIQUE D'ANDRÉ
SUARÈS.*
G.W. IRELAND, 402(MLR):JUL73-662
BÜSING, H.H. DIE GRIECHISCHE HALB-
SÄULE.
H.A. THOMPSON, 54:DEC72-537
BUSSCOL, H. & M. BANAI. THE FIRST
MILLION SABRAS.
L. ELKIN, 287:MAY72-28
BUSSY, C. ANTHOLOGIE DU SURRÉALISME
EN BELGIQUE.
J.H. MATTHEWS, 593:FALL73-284
BUTCHVAROV, P. THE CONCEPT OF KNOW-
LEDGE.*
E. SOSA, 482(PHR):JUL72-364
J.M.V., 543:DEC71-350
BUTLER, C. NUMBER SYMBOLISM.*
G. GRABAND, 38:BAND90HEFT1/2-198
R. HARRÉ, 541(RES):FEB72-105
S.K. HENINGER, JR., 551(RENQ):
AUTUMN72-352
BUTLER, D. THE CANBERRA MODEL.
617(TLS):10MAY74-503
BUTLER, G. A COFFIN FOR THE CANARY.
617(TLS):6SEP74-960
BUTLER, G. SARSEN PLACE.
N. CALLENDAR, 441:27JAN74-12
BUTLER, I. THE ELDEST BROTHER.
617(TLS):25JAN74-82

BUTLER, I., COMP. THE 100 BEST
FULL-LENGTH PLAYS FOR AMATEURS.
R. STACEY, 157:SPRING72-79
BUTLER, M. MARIA EDGEWORTH.
G. WATSON, 301(JEGP):JUL73-449
A. WELSH, 676(YR):WINTER73-281
639(VQR):AUTUMN73-CLX
BUTLER, R.J., ED. CARTESIAN STUDIES.
H.B. CATON, 63:AUG73-173
G.A.J. ROGERS, 518:JAN73-7
BUTLIN, M. WILLIAM BLAKE: A COM-
PLETE CATALOGUE OF THE WORKS IN
THE TATE GALLERY.
T. CROMBIE, 39:JUN72-520
BUTOR, M. DIALOGUE AVEC 33 VARIA-
TIONS DE LUDWIG VAN BEETHOVEN SUR
UNE VALSE DE DIABELLI.
J. KOLBERT, 207(FR):MAR72-899
N. SUCKLING, 208(FS):OCT73-485
BUTOR, M. LA MODIFICATION. (J.
STURROCK, ED)
J. CRUICKSHANK, 208(FS):JAN73-
101
F. FLAGOTHIER, 556(RLV):1972/5-
553
BUTOR, M. OÙ, LE GÉNIE DU LIEU, 2.
F.S. HECK, 268:JAN74-64
J. KOLBERT, 207(FR):APR72-1038
G. RAILLARD, 98:APR72-328
BUTOR, M. PASSAGE DE MILAN.
G. RAILLARD, 98:APR72-328
BUTOR, M. RÉPERTOIRE IV.
617(TLS):17MAY74-515
BUTOR, M. LA ROSE DES VENTS.
J. KOLBERT, 207(FR):OCT71-190
BUTTEMEYER, W. ROBERTO ARDIGÒ E LA
PSICOLOGIA MODERNA.
E. NAMER, 542:OCT-DEC72-452
BUTTER, P.H. - SEE MUIR, E.
BUTTERWORTH, M. VILLA ON THE SHORE.
N. CALLENDAR, 441:30JUN74-33
BUTTS, R.E. & J.W. DAVIS, EDS. THE
METHODOLOGICAL HERITAGE OF NEW-
TON.*
A.R. HALL, 84:FEB72-80
G.A.J. ROGERS, 481(PQ):JUL72-738
BUYSSENS, E. LES DEUX ASPECTIFS DE
LA CONJUGAISON ANGLAISE AU XXE
SIÈCLE.*
J. BOURKE, 38:BAND90HEFT1/2-188
BUZO, A. MACQUARIE.
A. KRUSE, 581:JUN73-240
BYGRAVE, M. ABOUT TIME.
R. BLYTHE, 362:13JUN74-777
BYKOV, V. THE ORDEAL.
639(VQR):WINTER73-X
BYNUM, T.W. - SEE FREGE, G.
BYRNE, E. POEMS 1968-1970.
D. BARBOUR, 150(DR):SPRING72-165
BYRNE, E.F. PROBABILITY & OPINION.*
E. WINANCE, 319:JUL74-394
LORD BYRON. BYRON'S HEBREW MELO-
DIES.* (T.L. ASHTON, ED)
J. CLUBBE, 579(SAQ):SPRING73-331
J.D. JUMP, 677:VOL3-307
LORD BYRON. BYRON'S LETTERS & JOUR-
NALS.* (VOLS 1&2) (L.A. MARCHAND,
ED)
442(NY):1APR74-123
LORD BYRON. BYRON'S LETTERS & JOUR-
NALS. (VOL 3) (L.A. MARCHAND, ED)
P. ADAMS, 61:NOV74-123
P. BEER, 362:15AUG74-221
617(TLS):20SEP74-992

LORD BYRON. A CHOICE OF BYRON'S
VERSE. (D. DUNN, ED)
617(TLS):14JUN74-647
LORD BYRON. DON JUAN (1819). (B.
LEE, ED)
J.C. MAXWELL, 447(N&Q):MAR72-113
"LORD BYRON: WERNER, A TRAGEDY."
[ACTING VERSION OF W.C. MACREADY]
H. OREL, 637(VS):SEP71-93

CABALLERO BONALD, J.M., ED. NARRA-
TIVA CUBANA DE LA REVOLUCIÓN.*
S. MENTON, 238:MAY72-391
DE CABAÑAS, M.J.G. - SEE UNDER GAR-
CÍA DE CABAÑAS, M.J.
CABANNE, P. DIALOGUES WITH MARCEL
DUCHAMP.*
C. GREEN, 39:JAN72-74
CABLE, J. GUNBOAT DIPLOMACY.
J.K. EMMERSON, 550(RUSR):JUL72-
312
CABRERA, R.M. JULIÁN DEL CASAL.
F.S. STIMSON, 238:DEC72-975
CABRERA INFANTE, G. THREE TRAPPED
TIGERS.
V. DE ROZENTAL, 37:OCT72-39
CADE, R. THE FEAR DEALERS.
N. CALLENDAR, 441:21APR74-42
CADELL, E. DECK WITH FLOWERS.
M. LEVIN, 441:13JAN74-14
CADET, J.M. THE RAMAKIEN.
M. SMITHIES, 302:JAN72-69
CADOU, R.G. OEUVRES POÉTIQUES COM-
PLÈTES.
617(TLS):15MAR74-267
CADOUX, R. NOTRE MONDE.
R.J. FULTON, 207(FR):FEB72-764
H.C. TRAPANI, 399(MLJ):OCT72-410
CADOUX, R. VOUS ET MOI.*
H.C. TRAPANI, 399(MLJ):OCT72-409
CADY, E.H. THE LIGHT OF COMMON DAY.*
J.H. MAGUIRE, 649(WAL):SPRING72-
78
D. PIZER, 445(NCF):JUN72-111
CAEIRO, O.J. O DIÁRIO DE PLATEN-
HALLERMÜNDE.
J. KLEINSTÜCK, 52:BAND7HEFT2/3-
330
CAGE, J. M.*
617(TLS):8FEB74-139
"CAHIERS DE POÉSIE, 1."
617(TLS):4OCT74-1090
"CAHIERS ROMAIN ROLLAND, NO. 20."
G. GUISAN, 535(RHL):JUL-AUG72-
740
CAHILL, J. SCHOLAR PAINTERS OF
JAPAN: THE NANGA SCHOOL.
T. BOWIE, 127:SUMMER73-458
CAHM, E. POLITICS & SOCIETY IN CON-
TEMPORARY FRANCE (1789-1971).
A.R. CLARK, 67:MAY73-137
205(FMLS):OCT72-379
CAIDIN, M. THE LAST DOGFIGHT.
M. LEVIN, 441:22SEP74-41
CAILLOIS, R. LA DISSYMÉTRIE.
617(TLS):10MAY74-492
CAINE, L. WIDOW.
A. GOTTLIEB, 441:9JUN74-7
C. LEHMANN-HAUPT, 441:22MAY74-35
CAIRD, R. A GOOD & USEFUL LIFE.
COLVILLE, 362:16MAY74-640

CAIRNCROSS, J. AFTER POLYGAMY WAS
MADE A SIN.
617(TLS):6SEP74-959
CAIRNS, D. RESPONSES.*
A. JACOBS, 415:JUL73-701
CALAM, J. PARSONS & PEDAGOGUES.*
G.J. GOODWIN, 656(WMQ):JAN72-191
CALAME, C. ETYMOLOGICUM GENUINUM.
M.L. WEST, 123:MAR73-99
CALAS, N. & E. ICONS & IMAGES OF
THE SIXTIES.
C. GOTTLIEB, 58:NOV72-89
P.A. QUINLAN, 290(JAAC):FALL72-
133
CALBOLI, G., ED & TRANS. RHETORICA
AD C. HERENNIUM.
A.E. DOUGLAS, 123:DEC73-184
CALDER, N. THE WEATHER MACHINE.
T.J. CHANDLER, 617(TLS):20DEC74-
1434
CALDER, W.M. & J. STERN, EDS. PIN-
DAROS UND BAKCHYLIDES.
M.M. WILLCOCK, 123:DEC73-131
CALDERARO. NUOVI DISCORSI SULLA
PRIMA DECA DI TITO LIVIO.
E. NAMER, 542:JAN-MAR72-105
CALDERÓN, E.C. - SEE UNDER CORREA
CALDERÓN, E.
CALDERÓN DE LA BARCA, P. LA HIJA
DEL AIRE.* (G. EDWARDS, ED)
A.K.G. PATERSON, 402(MLR):JAN73-
203
V.G. WILLIAMSEN, 238:DEC72-966
CALDERÓN DE LA BARCA, P. EN LA VIDA
TODO ES VERDAD Y TODO MENTURA.
(D.W. CRUICKSHANK, ED)
G. EDWARDS, 402(MLR):JUL73-673
205(FMLS):OCT72-379
CALDERWOOD, J.L. SHAKESPEAREAN META-
DRAMA.*
L.A. BEAURLINE, 301(JEGP):JAN73-
126
N. DENNY, 541(RES):NOV72-482
G.K. HUNTER, 401(MLQ):JUN73-202
C.H. POLLACK, 529(QQ):AUTUMN72-
417
N. RABKIN, 551(RENQ):WINTER72-
500
R. WARREN, 447(N&Q):APR72-152
CALDWELL, E. ANNETTE.*
S. MILLAR, 617(TLS):15NOV74-1277
CALDWELL, H. MACHADO DE ASSIS.*
A.I. BAGBY, JR., 238:MAY72-390
CALDWELL, J. ENGLISH KEYBOARD MUSIC
BEFORE THE NINETEENTH CENTURY.
G.E.B., 410(M&L):JUL73-348
CALDWELL, O.J. A SECRET WAR.
639(VQR):SUMMER72-XCVI
CALDWELL, T. GLORY & THE LIGHTNING.
M. LEVIN, 441:15DEC74-14
"CALENDAR OF THE MANUSCRIPTS IN THE
SCHOMBURG COLLECTION OF NEGRO LIT-
ERATURE."
M.I. CRAWFORD, 14:JAN72-69
CALHOON, R.M. THE LOYALISTS IN REV-
OLUTIONARY AMERICA, 1760-1781.
P. MAIER, 441:3FEB74-32
CALHOUN, D. IS THERE LIFE AFTER
ADVERTISING?
M. LEVIN, 441:23JUN74-34
CALHOUN, J.C. THE PAPERS OF JOHN C.
CALHOUN. (VOL 5) (W.E. HEMPHILL,
ED)
J. RABUN, 579(SAQ):AUTUMN73-611

CALÍ, P. ALLEGORY & VISION IN DANTE
& LANGLAND.*
T.G. BERGIN, 275(IQ):FALL/WINTER
72-107
S.S. HUSSEY, 447(N&Q):OCT72-388
CALIN, W. - SEE "LA CHANSON DE ROL-
AND"
CALISHER, H. STANDARD DREAMING.
S. O'CONNELL, 418(MR):WINTER73-
190
639(VQR):WINTER73-VIII
CALLAGHAN, C.A. BODEGA MIWOK DIC-
TIONARY.*
H. BERMAN, 269(IJAL):JUL72-218
M. SILVERSTEIN, 215(GL):VOL12#2-
128
CALLAGHAN, W. & OTHERS - SEE ISEN-
BERG, A.
CALLAHAN, D. THE TYRANNY OF SURVIV-
AL.
J. WEIZENBAUM, 441:3MAR74-16
CALLAHAN, J.F. THE ILLUSIONS OF A
NATION.
D.M. MONAGHAN, 150(DR):SUMMER72-
325
CALLAN, R. MIGUEL ANGEL ASTURIAS.*
H.M. FRASER, 399(MLJ):MAR72-182
DE CALLATAY, V. & A. DOLLFUS. ATLAS
OF THE PLANETS.
617(TLS):8NOV74-1269
CALLISON, B. A WEB OF SALVAGE.
M. LEVIN, 441:26MAY74-19
CALVI, M.C. I VETRI ROMANI DEL
MUSEO DI AQUILEIA.
J. PRICE, 313:VOL62-204
CALVIN, J. CALVIN'S COMMENTARY ON
SENECA'S "DE CLEMENTIA." (F.L.
BATTLES & A.M. HUGO, EDS & TRANS)
R.M. KINGDON, 551(RENQ):WINTER
72-467
CALVIN, J. THREE FRENCH TREATISES.*
(F.M. HIGMAN, ED)
L. THORPE, 402(MLR):JUL73-650
CALVINO, I. IL CASTELLO DEI DESTINI
INCROCIATI.*
G. GENOT, 98:AUG/SEP72-788
CALVINO, I. INVISIBLE CITIES.*
(ITALIAN TITLE: LE CITTÀ INVISI-
BILI.)
J. MC ELROY, 441:17NOV74-35
G. VIDAL, 453:30MAY74-13
CALVINO, I. THE PATH TO THE NEST OF
SPIDERS. THE BARON IN THE TREES.
THE NONEXISTENT KNIGHT & THE CLOV-
EN VISCOUNT. COSMICOMICS. T ZERO.
THE WATCHER & OTHER STORIES.
G. VIDAL, 453:30MAY74-13
CAMBACÉRÈS. LETTRES INÉDITES À
NAPOLÉON. (J. TULARD, ED)
617(TLS):31MAY74-587
CAMBON, G. DANTE'S CRAFT.*
T.G. BERGIN, 275(IQ):FALL/WINTER
72-98
A.S. BERNARDO, 276:SPRING72-76
J.A. SCOTT, 545(RPH):MAY73-744
CAMERON, A. AGATHIAS.*
J.W. BARKER, 24:SPRING73-103
CAMERON, A. CLAUDIAN.*
O.A.W. DILKE, 487:AUTUMN72-319
CAMERON, A., R. FRANK & J. LEYERLE,
EDS. COMPUTERS & OLD ENGLISH
CONCORDANCES.*
N.C. HULTIN, 320(CJL):SPRING71-
144
M.J. PRESTON, 677:VOL3-264

CAMERON, D. THE SOCIAL THOUGHT OF
ROUSSEAU & BURKE.
617(TLS):15FEB74-150
CAMERON, D.M. SCHOOLS FOR ONTARIO.
W.G. PITMAN, 529(QQ):WINTER72-
548
CAMERON, J. AN INDIAN SUMMER.
617(TLS):25OCT74-1205
CAMERON, J.M. VICTORIAN PHOTO-
GRAPHS OF FAMOUS MEN & FAIR WOMEN.*
(REV) (T. POWELL, ED)
S. CLAPP, 362:24JAN74-118
617(TLS):22FEB74-174
CAMERON, K.N. SHELLEY: THE GOLDEN
YEARS.
P. CONRAD, 617(TLS):9AUG74-845
442(NY):15JUL74-87
CAMERON, W.J. A PERFECTIBLE MILTON
BIBLIOGRAPHY.
J.L. HARNER, 568(SCN):FALL-WIN-
TER73-76
CAMERON, W.J., ED. POEMS ON AFFAIRS
OF STATE. (VOL 5)
G.P. MAYHEW, 481(PQ):JUL72-626
E. MINER, 566:AUTUMN72-37
J.M.P., 568(SCN):FALL-WINTER73-
85
639(VQR):AUTUMN72-CXXIV
CAMERON, W.J. & D.J. CARROLL, EDS.
SHORT-TITLE CATALOGUE OF BOOKS
PRINTED IN THE BRITISH ISLES, THE
BRITISH COLONIES & THE UNITED
STATES OF AMERICA & OF ENGLISH
BOOKS PRINTED ELSEWHERE, 1700-1800,
HELD IN THE LIBRARIES OF THE AUS-
TRALIAN CAPITAL TERRITORY.
T.H. HOWARD-HILL, 354:MAR72-63
CAMES, G. ALLÉGORIES ET SYMBOLES
DANS L'"HORTUS DELICIARUM."
E. GREENHILL, 589:JUL73-553
CAMINADE, P. IMAGE ET MÉTAPHORE.
T.A. SHEALY, 188(ECR):FALL72-239
205(FMLS):JAN72-87
DE CAMÕES, L. OS LUSÍADAS. (F.
PIERCE, ED)
617(TLS):11OCT74-1137
CAMOIN, F.A. THE REVENGE CONVENTION
IN TOURNEUR, WEBSTER & MIDDLETON.
M. PFISTER, 72:BAND21OHEFT4/6-
382
CAMP, J. BELL RINGING.
617(TLS):8MAR74-245
CAMP, J. MAGIC, MYTH & MEDICINE.
617(TLS):5JUL74-731
CAMPANELLA, T. APOLOGIA PER GALILEO.
(S. FEMIANO, ED)
G. ERNST, 548(RCSF):OCT-DEC72-
471
CAMPANELLA, T. CRISTOLOGIA.
E. NAMER, 542:JAN-MAR72-101
CAMPANELLA, T. MAGIA E GRAZIA.
E. NAMER, 542:JAN-MAR72-102
CAMPANELLA, T. LA PRIMA E LA SEC-
ONDA RESURREZIONE. (R. AMERIO, ED
& TRANS)
E. NAMER, 542:APR-JUN72-167
CAMPANELLA, T. DE SANCTA MONOTRIADE.
E. NAMER, 542:JAN-MAR72-100
"CAMPANELLA E VICO."
L.M.P., 543:SEP71-139
CAMPANILE, D. POSSIBILITÀ E CONDIZ-
IONI DELLA CONOSCENZA SCIENTIFICA.
E. NAMER, 542:JAN-MAR72-113

CAMPBELL, A. KAPITI.
J.E. WEIR, 368:SEP72-263
CAMPBELL, A. SKALDIC VERSE & ANGLO-
SAXON HISTORY.
F.S. SCOTT, 382(MAE):1973/2-203
CAMPBELL, H. & C. BAUER, EDS. LA
DYNAMITE.
D. OLIVIER, 207(FR):FEB72-765
CAMPBELL, K. BODY & MIND.*
W.D., 543:SEP71-121
J. KEKES, 154:MAR72-154
D. LOCKE, 479(PHQ):JAN72-75
J. TEICHMANN, 483:JUL72-286
R.X. WARE, 393(MIND):JUL72-469
CAMPBELL, N., COMP. TENNYSON IN
LINCOLN. (VOL 1)
E.F. SHANNON, JR., 637(VS):MAR73-
363
CAMPBELL, N., COMP. TENNYSON IN
LINCOLN. (VOL 2)
617(TLS):8NOV74-1246
CAMPBELL, R.N. NOUN SUBSTITUTES IN
MODERN THAI.*
J.R. COOKE, 318(JAOS):APR-JUN72-
362
CAMPBELL, R.R. JAMES DUNCAN CAMP-
BELL.
E.H. PRITCHARD, 293(JAST):NOV71-
186
CAMPBELL, T.D. ADAM SMITH'S SCIENCE
OF MORALS.
S.A. GRAVE, 393(MIND):OCT72-632
H.J.N. HORSBURGH, 479(PHQ):JUL72-
271
J.U. LEWIS, 628:SPRING73-107
CAMPEN, R.M. ARCHITECTURE OF THE
WESTERN RESERVE.
B.F. TOLLES, 576:MAR72-78
CAMPOS, E. O TROPEL DAS COISAS.
G. SOBRAL, 263:OCT-DEC73-469
CAMPS, M. THE MANAGEMENT OF INTER-
DEPENDENCE.
G. BARRACLOUGH, 453:27JUN74-14
CAMPTON, D. THE LIFE & DEATH OF
ALMOST EVERYBODY.
A. RENDLE, 157:AUTUMN72-84
CAMUS, A. LA CHUTE. (B.G. GARNHAM,
ED)
J. CRUICKSHANK, 208(FS):JAN73-
101
F. FLAGOTHIER, 556(RLV):1972/5-
553
CAMUS, J-P. HOMÉLIES DES ÉTATS GÉN-
ÉRAUX (1614-1615).* (J. DESCRAINS,
ED)
A. LEVI, 208(FS):APR73-194
CANCALON, E.D. TECHNIQUES ET PERSON-
NAGES DANS LES RÉCITS D'ANDRÉ GIDE.
J. ONIMUS, 557(RSH):OCT-DEC72-
625
CANCRINI, A. SYNEIDESIS.
E. DES PLACES, 555:VOL46FASC1-
108
CÂNDIDO, A. TESE E ANTITESE. (2ND
ED)
G. SOBRAL, 263:JAN-MAR73-103
CANDLIN, E.S. THE BREACH IN THE
WALL.
617(TLS):8NOV74-1269
CANETTI, E. KAFKA'S OTHER TRIAL.
P. ADAMS, 61:DEC74-128
CANETTI, E. DIE PROVINZ DES MEN-
SCHEN.
617(TLS):25JAN74-66

CANFIELD, C. THE INCREDIBLE PIER-
PONT MORGAN.
H. BEVINGTON, 441:1DEC74-86
CANFORA, L. TUCIDIDE CONTINUATO.
K.J. DOVER, 123:DEC73-143
CANGIOTTI, G. PÍO BAROJA, "OSSERVA-
TORE" DEL COSTUME ITALIANO.*
E.I. FOX, 240(HR):WINTER72-101
CANNEY, M. & D. KNOTT, COMPS. CATA-
LOGUE OF THE GOLDSMITHS' LIBRARY
OF ECONOMIC LITERATURE. (VOL 1)
T.H. BOWYER, 354:MAR72-66
CANNING, J., ED. 100 GREAT ADVEN-
TURES.
617(TLS):1MAR74-221
CANNING, V. THE FINGER OF SATURN.
N. CALLENDAR, 441:17MAR74-39
617(TLS):18JAN74-61
CANNING, V. THE MASK OF MEMORY.
617(TLS):8NOV74-1248
CANNING, V. THE PAINTED TENT.
M. LEVIN, 441:6OCT74-40
CANNING, V. THE RAINBIRD PATTERN.*
N. CALLENDAR, 441:14JUL74-40
CANNON, G. - SEE JONES, W.
CANTAGALLI, R. - SEE ARDITI, B.
CANTEMIR, D. THE HISTORY OF THE
OTTOMAN EMPIRE. (ABRIDGED & ED BY
A. DUTU & P. CERNOVODEANU)
617(TLS):26APR74-435
CANTOR, N.F. & P.L. KLEIN, EDS. REN-
AISSANCE THOUGHT.
L.G., 543:SEP71-144
CANTOR, N.F. & P.L. KLEIN, EDS. SEV-
ENTEENTH CENTURY RATIONALISM.
L.G., 543:SEP71-145
CANTWELL, R. THE LAND OF PLENTY.
H. SWADOS, 454:FALL72-92
CANZONERI, R. BARBED WIRE & OTHER
STORIES.*
D.R. NOBLE, JR., 573(SSF):SPRING
72-207
CAO XUEQIN. THE STORY OF THE STONE.
(VOL 1) (D. HAWKES, TRANS)
O. HOLLOWAY, 362:5SEP74-313
617(TLS):18JAN74-59
ČAPEK, M. BERGSON & MODERN PHYSICS.
J-J. DAETWYLER, 182:VOL25#11-329
E. WINANCE, 319:JAN74-130
CAPELLANUS, A. DE AMORE DEUTSCH.
(J. HARTLIEB, TRANS; A. KARNEIN,
ED)
O. SAYCE, 220(GL&L):OCT72-83
CAPIZZI, A. SOCRATE E I PERSONAGGI
FILOSOFI DI PLATONE.*
N. GULLEY, 123:DEC73-145
CAPLAN, G. THE DILEMMA OF CANADIAN
SOCIALISM.
I. ABELLA, 99:MAR74-44
CAPLAN, H. OF ELOQUENCE.* (A. KING
& H. NORTH, EDS)
P.A. MEADOR, JR., 480(P&R):SUM-
MER72-196
P.W. ROGERS, 529(QQ):SUMMER72-
269
CAPON, R.F. HUNTING THE DIVINE FOX.
R. MATZEK, 441:31MAR74-16
CAPOTE, T. THE DOGS BARK.*
617(TLS):30AUG74-925
CAPP, B.S. THE FIFTH MONARCHY MEN.
C. HILL, 111:20OCT72-32
CAPPS, B. THE TRUE MEMOIRS OF CHAR-
LEY BLANKENSHIP.
E.W. TODD, 649(WAL):WINTER73-301

CAPUTI, A. LOVING EVIE.
M. LEVIN, 441:26MAY74-18
CARABELLESE, P. LA FILOSOFIA DELL'
ESISTENZA IN KANT.
E. NAMER, 542:JUL-SEP72-327
CARADEC, F. A LA RECHERCHE DE
ALFRED JARRY.
617(TLS):9AUG74-863
CARADEC, F., WITH A. RODRIGUEZ. ISI-
DORE DUCASSE, COMTE DE LAUTRÉAMONT.
M. BONNET, 535(RHL):MAY-JUN72-
541
CARAFA, D. DELLO OPTIMO CORTESANO.
(G. PAPARELLI, ED)
A.D.B., 228(GSLI):VOL149FASC468-
633
CARANDENTE, G. COLLECTIONS D'ITALIE.
(VOL 1: SICILE.)
M. HUGGLER, 182:VOL25#13/14-493
CARASSUS, É. BARRÈS ET SA FORTUNE
LITTÉRAIRE.*
F.J. GROVER, 207(FR):DEC71-509
P.A. OUSTON, 208(FS):JAN73-96
CARATINI, R. - SEE "BORDAS ENCYCLO-
PÉDIE"
CARDEN, M.L. ONEIDA.
K. SILBER, 182:VOL25#13/14-469
CARDEN, P. THE ART OF ISAAC BABEL.
P. BLAKE, 32:DEC73-853
R.W. HALLETT, 575(SEER):OCT73-
604
D.H. STEWART, 651(WHR):SPRING73-
202
CARDENAL, E. ANTOLOGÍA. HOMENAJE A
LOS INDIOS AMERICANOS. EN CUBA.
617(TLS):12JUL74-743
CARDINAL, R. & R.S. SHORT. SURREAL-
ISM.*
C.A. HACKETT, 208(FS):JUL73-355
CARDINI, M.T. - SEE PSEUDO-ARISTOTLE
CARDINI, R. LA CRITICA DEL LANDINO.
C.H. CLOUGH, 617(TLS):6DEC74-
1396
CARDONA, G., H.M. HOENIGSWALD & A.
SENN. INDO-EUROPEAN & INDO-EURO-
PEANS.
M. SAMILOV, 575(SEER):JAN73-128
CARDOZO, N. HELMET OF THE WIND.
J.E. CHAMBERLIN, 249(HUDR):SUM-
MER73-394
CARDUNER, J., G. MERMIER & M.K.
SPINGLER, EDS. NOUVELLES ET RÉ-
CITS DU XXE SIÈCLE.
W.W. KIBLER, 207(FR):MAY72-1203
CARDWELL, M. - SEE DICKENS, C.
CARELESS, J.M.S., ED. COLONISTS &
CANADIENS 1760-1867.*
B.T. MC CULLY, 656(WMQ):APR72-
326
CARETTI, L. T.S. ELIOT IN ITALIA.
G. SINGH, 447(N&Q):FEB72-68
CAREY, G.G. MARYLAND FOLKLORE &
FOLKLIFE.*
J.H. BRUNVAND, 650(WF):JUL72-218
CAREY, J., ED. ANDREW MARVELL.*
D.I.B. SMITH, 627(UTQ):AUTUMN71-
84
CAREY, J. THE VIOLENT EFFIGY.*
617(TLS):11JAN74-21
CARGO, R.T., COMP. CONCORDANCE TO
BAUDELAIRE'S "PETIT POÈMES EN
PROSE."
A. FAIRLIE, 208(FS):JAN73-87
[CONTINUED]

CARGO, R.T., COMP. CONCORDANCE TO
BAUDELAIRE'S "PETIT POEMES EN
PROSE." [CONTINUING]
R. GALAND, 207(FR):FEB72-731
205(FMLS):JAN72-87
CARILE, P. LOUIS-FERDINAND CÉLINE:
UN ALLUCINATO DI GENIO (SAGGI).
G. HAINSWORTH, 208(FS):JAN73-99
M. MOLINARI, 549(RLC):JAN-MAR72-
159
CARIM, E. A DREAM DEFERRED.
617(TLS):4JAN74-5
CARLES, P. & J-L. COMOLLI. FREE
JAZZ/BLACK POWER.
I. LEYMARIE, 187:JAN74-151
CARLETON, W.G. TECHNOLOGY & HUMAN-
ISM.*
C. JACKSON, 577(SHR):SUMMER72-
299
CARLING, F. SKAPENDE SINN.
L. ASKELAND, 563(SS):SPRING73-
170
CARLISLE, E.F. THE UNCERTAIN SELF.
G.W. ALLEN, 27(AL):NOV73-465
639(VQR):SPRING73-LXXII
CARLISLE, O.A. & R. STYRON, EDS &
TRANS. MODERN RUSSIAN POETRY.
S. DRIVER, 32:DEC73-855
CARLSON, H.G. - SEE LAMM, M.
CARLSON, J. NO NEUTRAL GROUND.*
G.M. FREDRICKSON, 453:31OCT74-29
CARLSSON, L. LE TYPE "C'EST LE
MEILLEUR LIVRE QU'IL AIT JAMAIS
ÉCRIT" EN ESPAGNOL, EN ITALIEN ET
EN FRANÇAIS.*
P.F. DEMBOWSKI, 545(RPH):AUG72-
139
CARLTON, C. A DESCRIPTIVE SYNTAX OF
THE OLD ENGLISH CHARTERS.*
A. CRÉPIN, 189(EA):JAN-MAR72-78
U. OOMEN, 38:BAND90HEFT4-524
CARLYLE, A. ANECDOTES & CHARACTERS
OF THE TIMES. (J. KINSLEY, ED)
617(TLS):1FEB74-114
CARLYLE, T. & J.W. THE COLLECTED
LETTERS OF THOMAS & JANE WELSH
CARLYLE.* (VOLS 1-4) (C.R. SAND-
ERS & K.J. FIELDING, EDS)
D.V.E., 191(ELN):SEP72(SUPP)-41
P. MORGAN, 627(UTQ):WINTER73-174
L. STERRENBURG, 637(VS):MAR72-
393
CARMAN, J.B. THE THEOLOGY OF RAMA-
NUJA.
R.C. ZAEHNER, 617(TLS):22NOV74-
1322
CARMER, C. RIVERS OF AMERICA: THE
HUDSON.
I.R. DEE, 441:8SEP74-30
CARMICHAEL, H. MOST DEADLY HATE.
442(NY):27MAY74-108
CARMODY, F.J. PERCEVAL LE GALLOIS.*
G.R. MERMIER, 207(FR):OCT71-278
CARNAP, R. & R.C. JEFFREY, EDS.
STUDIES IN INDUCTIVE LOGIC & PROB-
ABILITY.
H.E. KYBURG, JR., 486:DEC72-549
P. TELLER, 311(JP):17JAN74-19
CARNEIRO, P.E.D. & P. ARNAUD - SEE
UNDER DE BERRÊDO CARNEIRO, P.E. &
P. ARNAUD
CARNICELLI, D.D. - SEE PETRARCH
CARNICELLI, T.A. - SEE ST. AUGUSTINE

CARNOCHAN, W.B. LEMUEL GULLIVER'S
MIRROR FOR MAN.*
J. BÉRANGER, 189(EA):APR-JUN72-
328
CARNOT, L. - SEE UNDER ROBESPIERRE,
M.
CARO, R.A. THE POWER BROKER.
B. DE MOTT, 61:DEC74-106
G. VIDAL, 453:17OCT74-3
R.C. WADE, 441:15SEP74-1
441:9SEP74-39
CAROUTCH, Y. LE GOUVERNEMENT DES
EAUX.
S.G. STARY, 207(FR):OCT71-192
CARPANI, G. LETTERE INEDITE A ISA-
BELLA TEOTOCHI ALBRIZZI (1805-21).
(R. CIAMPINI, ED)
J.W.K., 410(M&L):JUL73-359
CARPENTER, A. - SEE STEPHENS, E.M.
CARPENTER, C.A. BERNARD SHAW & THE
ART OF DESTROYING IDEALS.*
R. DAVIES, 627(UTQ):AUTUMN71-88
A. STRACHAN, 447(N&Q):JUL72-275
CARPENTER, E. & K. HEYMAN. THEY
BECAME WHAT THEY BEHELD.*
J. BERNER, 186(ETC.):SEP72-321
CARPENTER, L.P. G.D.H. COLE.
617(TLS):22MAR74-284
CARPENTER, R. THE ARCHITECTS OF THE
PARTHENON.*
R. SCRANTON, 54:MAR72-78
I.M. SHEAR, 487:SUMMER72-192
CARPENTIER, A. THE KINGDOM OF THIS
WORLD.
J.I. CASTELEIRO, 37:APR72-42
CARPENTIER, A. WAR OF TIME.* (SPAN-
ISH TITLE: GUERRA DEL TIEMPO.)
R.T. WOODS, 573(SSF):FALL72-424
CARR, E.H. & R.W. DAVIES. A HISTORY
OF SOVIET RUSSIA.* (VOL 1) [SHOWN
IN PREV UNDER SUB-TITLE]
A. WALKER, 575(SEER):JUL73-485
CARR, F. EUROPEAN EROTIC ART.
M. YAFFE, 592:NOV72-202
CARR, J., ED. KITE-FLYING & OTHER
IRRATIONAL ACTS.
639(VQR):AUTUMN73-CXLVIII
CARR, J.D. THE THREE COFFINS.
N. CALLENDAR, 441:11AUG74-12
CARRA, M., WITH P. WALDBERG & E.
RATHKE. METAPHYSICAL ART.*
R. MC NAB, 592:NOV72-204
CARRARA, G.M.A. IOHANNIS MICHAELIS
ALBERTI CARRARIENSIS: OPERA POET-
ICA PHILOSOPHICA RHETORICA THEO-
LOGICA. (G. GIRALDI, ED)
G. BERETTA, 228(GSLI):VOL149
FASC468-610
CARRASQUER, F. "IMÁN" Y LA NOVELA
HISTÓRICA DE SENDER.
G.G. BROWN, 402(MLR):JUL73-680
LE CARRÉ, J. TINKER, TAILOR, SOL-
DIER, SPY.
A. BROYARD, 441:14JUN74-37
R. LOCKE, 441:30JUN74-1
D. MAHON, 362:4JUL74-30
K. MILLER, 453:18JUL74-24
E. WEEKS, 61:AUG74-88
442(NY):22JUL74-83
617(TLS):19JUL74-761
CARRÉ, L. A GUIDE TO OLD FRENCH
PLATE.
C. OMAN, 39:APR72-343

CARRIER, J-G. MY FATHER'S HOUSE.
G. DAVIES, 198:FALL74-91
CARRIER, R. LE DEUX-MILLIEME ETAGE.
A. POKORNY, 296:VOL3#1-97
CARRIER, R. LA GUERRE, YES SIR!*
FLORALIE, WHERE ARE YOU?
J. HARCOURT, 529(QQ):WINTER72-
567
CARRIER, R. IS IT THE SUN, PHILI-
BERT?
J. HARCOURT, 529(QQ):WINTER72-
567
A. ROBERTSON, 648:OCT72-62
CARRIER, R. THEY WON'T DEMOLISH ME.
B. GODARD, 99:MAY/JUN74-26
CARRILLO Y SOTOMAYOR, L. POESIE.
(VOL 1) (F.R. ROMANO, ED)
J.G. FUCILLA, 551(RENQ):WINTER
72-451
CARRINGTON, D. CORSICA.
442(NY):19AUG74-90
CARRINGTON, G.C., JR. - SEE HOWELLS,
W.D.
CARRINGTON, R. THE MEDITERRANEAN.
H.P. GUNDY, 529(QQ):SPRING72-125
"CARRINGTON: LETTERS & EXTRACTS FROM
HER DIARIES."* (D. GARNETT, ED)
G. MERLE, 189(EA):JAN-MAR72-172
P. MICHEL-MICHOT, 556(RLV):
1972/4-421
CARRION, A. LA LLAVE PERDIDA.
E.B. LABRADA, 37:MAR72-42
CARROLL, D. CHINUA ACHEBE.
S. MPONDO, 399(MLJ):FEB72-96
CARROLL, D.B. HENRI MERCIER & THE
AMERICAN CIVIL WAR.
R.D. CHALLENER, 377:MAR73-54
J. VIDALENC, 182:VOL25#3/4-120
639(VQR):WINTER72-XXX
CARROLL, G.H. NEXT OF KIN.
M. LEVIN, 441:15DEC74-12
CARROLL, J. BREAK-OUT FROM THE CRYS-
TAL PALACE.
A. THORLBY, 617(TLS):5JUL74-703
CARROLL, J.J. & OTHERS. PHILIPPINE
INSTITUTIONS.
C.L. HUNT, 293(JAST):FEB72-465
CARROLL, J.T. THE FRENCH. (REV)
J.J. LAKICH, 207(FR):OCT71-222
CARROLL, L. ALICE IN WONDERLAND.
THROUGH THE LOOKING-GLASS. (BOTH
ILLUSTRATED BY R. STEADMAN)
C. ROBINS, 441:6JAN74-2
CARRUBA, O. DAS PALAISCHE.
G. NEUMANN, 260(IF):BAND76-267
CARRUTH, G. & OTHERS. LE FRANÇAIS
PARTOUT 3.
P. SILBERMAN, 399(MLJ):NOV72-465
CARRUTH, H. FROM SNOW & ROCK, FROM
CHAOS.
D. ALLEN, 491:MAY74-103
CARRUTHERS, M. THE WESTERN WAY OF
DEATH.
M. DUMONT, 441:19MAY74-6
CARSANIGA, G. GESCHICHTE DER ITAL-
IENISCHEN LITERATUR VON DER RENAIS-
SANCE BIS ZUR GEGENWART.*
R.O.J. VAN NUFFEL, 549(RLC):JUL-
SEP72-462
CARSON, R. JELLY BEAN.
M. LEVIN, 441:31MAR74-40
DE CARTAGENA, A. LA RETHORICA DE M.
TULLIO CICERON. (R. MASCAGNA, ED)
C. FAULHABER, 545(RPH):NOV72-442

CARTER, A. FIREWORKS.
J. MELLORS, 362:26SEP74-416
617(TLS):23AUG74-897
CARTER, A. THE WAR OF DREAMS.
W. HJORTSBERG, 441:8SEP74-6
CARTER, A.C. THE DUTCH REPUBLIC IN
EUROPE IN THE SEVEN YEARS WAR.
S.B. BAXTER, 481(PQ):JUL72-524
CARTER, A.E. VERLAINE.*
E.M. ZIMMERMANN, 546(RR):DEC72-
311
CARTER, E. WITH TONGUE IN CHIC.
617(TLS):22NOV74-1306
CARTER, E.D., JR., ED. ANTOLOGÍA
DEL REALISMO MÁGICO.*
J.R. AYORA, 399(MLJ):DEC72-532
CARTER, H. A VIEW OF EARLY TYPOGRA-
PHY UP TO ABOUT 1600.*
P. GASKELL, 78(BC):WINTER72-561
CARTER, H.H., ED. THE PORTUGUESE
BOOK OF JOSEPH OF ARIMATHEA.
A.D. DEYERMOND, 545(RPH):NOV72-
475
CARTER, J.M. THE BATTLE OF ACTIUM.
D. STOCKTON, 123:MAR73-56
CARTER, J.R. THE NET COST OF SOVIET
FOREIGN AID.*
J.S. BERLINER, 32:MAR73-177
CARTER, K.C. - SEE GODWIN, W.
CARTER, M. A MEMBER OF THE FAMILY.
M. LEVIN, 441:5MAY74-57
CARTER, P.A. THE SPIRITUAL CRISIS
OF THE GILDED AGE.
R. FALK, 445(NCF):MAR73-497
J. LYDENBERG, 432(NEQ):SEP72-435
CARTER, R. THE SIXTEENTH ROUND.
H.J. BURROUGHS, 441:17NOV74-14
C. LEHMANN-HAUPT, 441:15OCT74-43
CARTER, S., 3D. BLAZE OF GLORY.*
639(VQR):SPRING72-LXV
CARTER, S., 3D. THE SIEGE OF ATLAN-
TA, 1864.
B.I. WILEY, 441:3FEB74-31
CARTER-RUCK, P.F. LIBEL & SLANDER.
617(TLS):25JAN74-85
CARTIER, N.R. LE BOSSU DÉSENCHANTÉ.
F.W. LANGLEY, 382(MAE):1973/2-
171
J.H. MARSHALL, 208(FS):OCT73-444
D. POIRION, 589:APR73-347
CARTIER-BRESSON, H. ABOUT RUSSIA.
E. WELTY, 441:1DEC74-28
CARTWRIGHT, A., L. HOCKEY & J.L. AN-
DERSON. LIFE BEFORE DEATH.*
C-M. PARKES, 362:4APR74-443
CARTWRIGHT, M.T. DIDEROT CRITIQUE
D'ART ET LE PROBLÈME DE L'EXPRES-
SION.*
G. MAY, 546(RR):OCT72-235
L. NEDERGAARD, 462(OL):VOL27#1-
63
CARVALHO, A.C. BUILDING UPON RAGA
"SHREE."
G. BURNS, 584(SWR):WINTER73-96
CARY, J. COCK JARVIS. (A.G. BISH-
OP, ED)
C. FYFE, 617(TLS):22NOV74-1308
CASA, F.P. EN BUSCA DE ESPAÑA.
W.R. BLUE, 238:DEC72-983
MARQUESA DE CASA VALDÉS. JARDINES
DE ESPAÑA.
617(TLS):13DEC74-1421
CASAMAYOR. LA POLICE.
617(TLS):15MAR74-258

CASARES, A.B. - SEE UNDER BIOY
  CASARES, A.
CASEY, J., ED. MORALITY & MORAL
  REASONING.*
    R.F. HOLLAND, 483:JUL72-264
    A.L. THOMAS, 479(PHQ):APR72-183
CASEY, J.B. I, KRUPSKAYA.
    J. O'REILLY, 441:29SEP74-6
CASEY, K. A SENSE OF SURVIVAL.
    R. BLYTHE, 362:21MAR74-381
CASEY, M. OBSCENITIES.*
    J.W. HEALEY, 502(PRS):WINTER72/
    73-355
    42(AR):VOL32#3-499
    639(VQR):WINTER73-X
CASH, A.H. & J.M. STEDMOND, EDS.
  THE WINGED SKULL.*
    J. SMITTEN, 541(RES):MAY72-211
CASINI, P. DIDEROT "PHILOSOPHE."
    E. NAMER, 542:JUL-SEP72-324
CASO GONZÁLEZ, J. - SEE DE JOVELLAN-
  OS, G.M.
CASONA, A. EL CABALLERO DE LAS
  ESPUELAS DE ORO. (J.A. BALSEIRO
  & E. SUÁREZ-RIVERO, EDS)
    M.T. HALSEY, 238:SEP72-612
CASSAVETES, J. MINNIE & MOSKOWITZ.
    639(VQR):AUTUMN73-CXLII
CASSELL, F.A. MERCHANT CONGRESSMAN
  IN THE YOUNG REPUBLIC.
    J. HAW, 656(WMQ):OCT72-653
CASSELS, L. CLASH OF GENERATIONS.*
    C.A. MACARTNEY, 575(SEER):OCT73-
    627
CASSERLEY, H.C. OUTLINE OF IRISH
  RAILWAY HISTORY.
    617(TLS):3MAY74-484
CASSILL, R.V. THE GOSS WOMEN.
    S. BLACKBURN, 441:21APR74-36
CASSIRER, E. KANT. (2ND SPANISH ED)
    R. MALIANDI, 342:BAND63HEFT3-388
CASSIRER, E. ROUSSEAU, KANT, GOETHE.
    K. OEDINGEN, 342:BAND63HEFT1-130
CASSIRER, H.W. A COMMENTARY OF
  KANT'S CRITIQUE OF JUDGMENT.
    J. KOPPER, 342:BAND63HEFT1-130
CASSIRER, P. DESKRIPTIV STILISTIK.*
    O. ØYSLEBØ, 172(EDDA):1972/2-125
CASSITY, T. STEEPLEJACKS IN BABEL.
    V. YOUNG, 249(HUDR):WINTER73/74-
    719
CASSOLA, C. IL TAGLIO DEL BOSCO.
  (T. O'NEILL, ED)
    Z. TILLONA, 276:AUTUMN72-357
CASSON, J. LEWIS & SYBIL.
    R. HAYMAN, 157:WINTER72-75
CASSON, L. SHIPS & SEAMANSHIP IN
  THE ANCIENT WORLD.*
    M. HAMMOND, 24:WINTER73-400
    D. KIENAST, 182:VOL25#5/6-173
CASTAGNARO, R.A. THE EARLY SPANISH
  AMERICAN NOVEL.
    M.I. LICHTBLAU, 399(MLJ):NOV72-
    468
CASTANEDA, C. TALES OF POWER.
    E. FIRST, 441:27OCT74-35
CASTANEDA, C. THE TEACHINGS OF DON
  JUAN. A SEPARATE REALITY.* JOUR-
  NEY TO IXTLAN.*
    V. CRAPANZANO, 473(PR):3/1973-
    471
CASTELAIN, D. SENTIMENTAL TALKS.
    268:JAN74-67

CASTELLI, E. CUSANO E GALILEO.
    E. NAMER, 542:JAN-MAR72-100
CASTELLI, E. & OTHERS. L'UMANESIMO
  ET "LA FOLLIA."
    W. KAISER, 551(RENQ):AUTUMN72-
    316
    J. WIRTH, 98:JAN72-92
CASTELLO, J.A. REALIDADE E ILUSÃO
  EM MACHADO DE ASSIS.
    191(ELN):SEP72(SUPP)-206
CASTIGLIONE, B. LETTERE INEDITE E
  RARE. (G. GORNI, ED)
    B.L., 275(IQ):FALL/WINTER72-120
DE CASTILHO, A.T. A SINTAXE DO
  VERBO E OS TEMPOS DO PASSADO EM
  PORTUGUÊS.
    M. SANDMANN, 545(RPH):NOV72-506
CASTLE, P. COLLECTING & VALUING OLD
  PHOTOGRAPHS.
    617(TLS):1FEB74-110
CASTORIADIS, C. LA SOCIÉTÉ BUREAU-
  CRATIQUE. L'EXPÉRIENCE DU MOUVE-
  MENT OUVRIER.
    617(TLS):11OCT74-1110
CASTORINA, E. - SEE PETRONIUS
CASTRÉN, P. & H. LILIUS. GRAFFITI
  DEL PALATINO.* (VOL 2) (V. VÄÄNÄ-
  NEN, ED)
    J.R. FEARS, 24:SPRING73-123
CASTRO, A. THE SPANIARDS.
    639(VQR):SPRING72-LXIX
CASTRO RESPOSO, E.R. THE ROLE OF
  THE UNIVERSITIES IN THE DEVELOPING
  PHILIPPINES.
    Q.S. SAMONTE, 293(JAST):AUG72-
    997
CASTRO SOROMENHO, F. A CHAGA.
    G.M. MOSER, 238:DEC72-974
CATACH, N., J. GOLFAND & R. DENUX.
  ORTHOGRAPHE ET LEXICOGRAPHIE.
  (VOL 1)
    J.P. COLIN, 209(FM):OCT72-355
CATALÁN, D. POR CAMPOS DEL ROMAN-
  CERO.*
    W. METTMANN, 72:BAND210HEFT1/3-
    217
"CATALOGUE OF BOOKS PRINTED IN THE
  XVTH CENTURY NOW IN THE BRITISH
  MUSEUM." (PT 10: SPAIN-PORTUGAL.)
    D.W. CRUICKSHANK, 354:DEC72-341
"CATALOGUE OF THE KIEV STATE MUSEUM
  OF EASTERN & WESTERN ART."
    T. CROMBIE, 39:JUL72-87
CATANOY, N. HIC ET NUNC.
    M. BACIU, 207(FR):OCT71-193
CATE, C. ANTOINE DE SAINT-EXUPÉRY.
    M. PARRY, 402(MLR):JAN73-186
CATHER, W. OBSCURE DESTINIES.
    441:13OCT74-44
CATHERINE, R. & G. THUILLER. INTRO-
  DUCTION À UNE PHILOSOPHIE DE L'AD-
  MINISTRATION.
    E.N. SULEIMAN, 98:MAR72-274 [&
    CONT IN 98:APR72-374]
CATLING, P.S. BEST SUMMER JOB.
    M. LEVIN, 441:30JUN74-29
CATO, N. BROWN SUGAR.
    617(TLS):8NOV74-1249
CATON, H. THE ORIGIN OF SUBJECTIV-
  ITY.
    617(TLS):5APR74-372
CATRYSSE, J. DIDEROT ET LA MYSTIFI-
  CATION.
    R.E. TAYLOR, 481(PQ):JUL72-667

60

CATTAN, H. PALESTINE & INTERNATION-
AL LAW.
617(TLS):25JAN74-83
CATTANEO, C. SCRITTI SCIENTIFICI E
TECNICI. (VOL 1) (C.G. LACAITA,
ED)
W.T.S., 191(ELN):SEP72(SUPP)-190
CATTANEO, C. TUTTE LE OPERE... (VOL
4) (L. AMBROSOLI, ED)
W.T.S., 191(ELN):SEP72(SUPP)-189
CATTANEO, G. ESPERIENZE INTELLET-
TUALI DEL PRIMO NOVECENTO.
F. SPACCIA, 275(IQ):FALL/WINTER
72-125
CATTANEO, G. LETTERATURA E RIBEL-
LIONE.
617(TLS):19APR74-422
CATTELL, N.R. THE NEW ENGLISH GRAM-
MAR.*
D. KASTOVSKY, 38:BAND90HEFT4-494
S. STEELE, 35(AS):FALL69-215
CATTIN, G. - SEE SAVONAROLA, G.
CATTON, B. GETTYSBURG.
E. WEEKS, 61:JUN74-109
442(NY):25MAR74-143
CATULLUS. CATULLI CARMINA.* (H.
BARDON, ED)
T.P. WISEMAN, 313:VOL62-215
CATULLUS. THE COMPLETE POEMS FOR
MODERN READERS. (R. MYERS & R.J.
ORMSBY, TRANS) THE POEMS OF CATUL-
LUS.* (P. WHIGHAM, TRANS) THE
POEMS OF CATULLUS. (J. MICHIE,
TRANS)
H.A. MASON, 97(CQ):VOL6#2-152
CATULLUS. THE POEMS.* (K. QUINN,
ED)
N.B. CROWTHER, 487:SPRING72-109
E.J. KENNEY, 123:DEC73-165
N. RUDD, 313:VOL62-212
CAUDILL, H.M. THE SENATOR FROM
SLAUGHTER COUNTY.
J.R. FRAKES, 441:31MAR74-36
CAUDWELL, C. ROMANCE & REALISM.*
(S. HYNES, ED)
T. EAGLETON, 541(RES):NOV72-499
CAULFIELD, S.F.A. HOUSE MOTTOES &
INSCRIPTIONS.
K.B. HARDER, 424:JUN72-149
CAUNEILLE, A. LES CHAANBA.
R. HERZOG, 182:VOL25#11-377
CAUTE, D. COLLISIONS.
A. RYAN, 362:9MAY74-605
617(TLS):3MAY74-467
CAUTE, D. THE FELLOW-TRAVELLERS.*
K. FITZLYON, 364(JUN/JUL73-135
CAUTE, D. THE ILLUSION.
42(AR):VOL32#3-503
CAVAFY, C.P. SELECTED POEMS.*
J.E. CHAMBERLIN, 249(HUDR):SUM-
MER73-400
639(VQR):AUTUMN73-CXLI
CAVALIERO, G. JOHN COWPER POWYS:
NOVELIST.
617(TLS):8FEB74-121
CAVE, R. THE PRIVATE PRESS.
B.C. BLOOMFIELD, 354:DEC72-351
R. MC LEAN, 135:MAR72-216
CAVE, T.C. DEVOTIONAL POETRY IN
FRANCE, C. 1570-1613.*
A.M. HARDEE, 207(FR):MAY72-1196
D.L. RUBIN, 188(ECR):FALL72-226

CAVELL, S. THE WORLD VIEWED.*
K. BAKER, 592:JUL/AUG72-57
N.H. BLUESTONE, 400(MLN):DEC72-
1003
F. FERGUSON, 128(CE):MAY73-1145
J.M. HIGHSMITH, 290(JAAC):FALL72-
134
CAVENDISH, R., ED. ENCYCLOPEDIA OF
THE UNEXPLAINED.
617(TLS):7JUN74-602
CAVETT, D. & C. PORTERFIELD. CAVETT.
G. BURNSIDE, 441:1SEP74-7
R.R. LINGEMAN, 441:7SEP74-25
CAVITCH, D. D.H. LAWRENCE & THE NEW
WORLD.*
J.E. STOLL, 219(GAR):FALL72-397
CAWLEY, R. & G. MC LACHLAN, EDS.
POLICY FOR ACTION.
617(TLS):22FEB74-176
CAWLEY, R.R. HENRY PEACHAM.
J. GRUNDY, 677:VOL3-283
J. ROBERTSON, 541(RES):NOV72-530
CAWS, M.A. ANDRÉ BRETON.*
J. HILL, 290(JAAC):FALL72-126
V.A. LA CHARITÉ, 207(FR):MAR72-
912
CAWS, M.A. THE POETRY OF DADA &
SURREALISM.*
C.A. HACKETT, 208(FS):JUL73-355
B. MORRISSETTE, 405(MP):NOV72-
174
CAYLEY, M. MOORINGS.
J. SAUNDERS, 565:VOL13#3-75
CAYRAC-BLANCHARD, F. LE PARTI COM-
MUNISTE INDONÉSIEN.
617(TLS):15FEB74-151
CAYROL, J. HISTOIRE D'UNE PRAIRIE.
Y. VELAN, 207(FR):OCT71-194
CAYROL, J. LECTURES.
617(TLS):1MAR74-220
CAZAMIAN, L. THE SOCIAL NOVEL IN
ENGLAND 1830-1850.*
G.C. SORENSEN, 651(WHR):AUTUMN73-
421
CAZDEN, R.E. GERMAN EXILE LITERA-
TURE IN AMERICA 1933-1950.
L. RIPPLEY, 221(GQ):JAN72-165
CAZENEUVE, J. MAUSS.
G. CONDOMINAS, 98:FEB72-119 [&
CONT IN 98:JUN72-487]
CAZENEUVE, J. SOCIOLOGIE DE LA
RADIOTÉLÉVISION.
C. SCHUWER, 542:OCT-DEC72-500
CAZENEUVE, J. SOCIOLOGIE DE MARCEL
MAUSS.
G. CONDOMINAS, 98:FEB72-119 [&
CONT IN 98:JUN72-487]
C. SCHUWER, 542:OCT-DEC72-503
CAZENEUVE, J. & J. OULIF. LA GRANDE
CHANCE DE LA TÉLÉVISION.
C. SCHUWER, 542:OCT-DEC72-501
CÉARD, H. UNE BELLE JOURNÉE.
F.W.J. HEMMINGS, 208(FS):APR73-
221
CÉARD, J. - SEE PARÉ, A.
CECCHETTI, G. IL VERGA MAGGIORE.*
B.L., 275(IQ):FALL/WINTER72-122
CECIL, D. VISIONARY & DREAMER.*
J.B. GORDON, 290(JAAC):WINTER71-
257
CEDERLÖF, H. JONATAN REUTER OCH
HANS SKÄRGÅRDSBERÄTTELSER.
G.C. SCHOOLFIELD, 563(SS):WINTER
73-91

CELA, C.J. SAN CAMILO, 1936.
  R.L. SHEEHAN, 238:MAY72-386
CELAN, P. SPEECH-GRILLE & SELECTED
  POEMS.*
  F.G. BLAHA, 502(PRS):SPRING72-79
CELANT, G., ED. ART POVERA.*
  D.M. SOKOL, 290(JAAC):WINTER71-
    264
  B. WRIGHT, 619(TC):VOL177#1043-
    57
CELEBONOVIC, A. SOME CALL IT KITSCH.
  J. RUSSELL, 441:1DEC74-55
"CEĻI, RAKSTU KRĀJUMS 14."
  E. HAUZENBERGA-ŠTURMA, 343:BAND
    15HEFT1-111
CÉLINE, L-F. NORTH. (R. MANHEIM,
  TRANS)
  G. EWART, 364:OCT/NOV72-146
  L.T. LEMON, 502(PRS):WINTER72/73-
    358
CÉLINE, L-F. RIGADOON.
  N. BLIVEN, 442(NY):10JUN74-129
  A. GOTTLIEB, 441:30JUN74-6
CÉLINE, L-F. ROMANS 2. (H. GODARD,
  ED)
  617(TLS):19.III.74-771
CELLIER, L. - SEE HUGO, V.
CENDRARS, B. THE ASTONISHED MAN.
  M. IVENS, 619(TC):VOL177#1043-58
CENTENO Y RILOVA, A. & D. SUTHERLAND.
  THE BLUE CLOWN, DIALOGUES.
  J.M. EDIE, 290(JAAC):SPRING73-
    418
CENTO, A. CONDORCET E L'IDEA DI
  PROGRESSO.
  E. NAMER, 542:JUL-SEP72-322
CENTO, A. STUDI DI LETTERATURA
  FRANCESE.
  G. HAINSWORTH, 208(FS):JAN73-104
CERAM, C-W. THE FIRST AMERICAN.
  639(VQR):WINTER72-XXXIII
CERULLI, E. LA LETTERATURA ETIOPICA,
  CON UN SAGGIO SULL'ORIENTE CRISTI-
  ANO. (3RD ED)
  A.K. IRVINE, 69:JUL72-255
CERUTTI, T. ANTONIO GALLENGA.
  J. RIDLEY, 617(TLS):20DEC74-1448
DE CERVANTES SAAVEDRA, M. DOS NOV-
  ELAS EJEMPLARES. (A. BURNS & J.
  GIBBS, EDS)
  205(FMLS):OCT72-380
DE CERVANTES SAAVEDRA, M. LOS TRABA-
  JOS DE PERSILES Y SIGISMUNDA.
  (J.B. AVALLE-ARCE, ED)
  O.H. GREEN, 240(HR):SPRING72-225
CÉSAIRE, A. A SEASON IN THE CONGO.
  R.L.R., 502(PRS):SPRING72-91
CÉSAIRE, A. THE TRAGEDY OF KING
  CHRISTOPHE.
  R.E. HARRIS, 207(FR):FEB72-689
CESBRON, G. CE QUE JE CROIS.
  H. FREYBURGER, 207(FR):APR72-
    1039
CHABANEIX, P. LES MATINS ET LES
  SOIRS.
  R.R. HUBERT, 207(FR):FEB72-690
CHABRUN, J-F. LES CHANTIERS CHIMÉR-
  IQUES.
  R.B. JOHNSON, 207(FR):OCT71-195
CHACE, W.M. THE POLITICAL IDENTI-
  TIES OF EZRA POUND & T.S. ELIOT.
  S. SPENDER, 453:19SEP74-18
CHACKO, D. GAGE.
  N. CALLENDAR, 441:21JUL74-18

CHACKO, D. PRICE.
  R. BLYTHE, 362:2MAY74-576
  617(TLS):3MAY74-465
CHADWICK, C. SYMBOLISM.
  J.C. EVANS, 149:DEC73-388
  M. SZEGEDY-MASZÁK, 549(RLC):APR-
    JUN72-313
CHAFE, W.H. THE AMERICAN WOMAN.
  C. SMITH-ROSENBERG, 639(VQR):
    WINTER73-132
  441:10FEB74-23
  676(YR):SUMMER73-XII
CHAFE, W.L. MEANING & THE STRUCTURE
  OF LANGUAGE.*
  D.L.F. NILSEN, 361:VOL28#1&2-124
CHAFE, W.L. A SEMANTICALLY BASED
  SKETCH OF ONONDAGA.
  P.H. MATTHEWS, 297(JL):FEB72-183
CHAGY, G. THE NEW PATRONS OF THE
  ARTS.
  M. ESTEROW, 55:NOV73-49
CHAILLEY, J. L'ART DE LA FUGUE DE
  J-S. BACH.
  B.L., 410(M&L):OCT73-497
CHAITIN, G.D. THE UNHAPPY FEW.
  R.M. ADAMS, 454:WINTER73-186
CHAIX, M. LES LAURIERS DU LAC DE
  CONSTANCE.
  617(TLS):14JUN74-643
CHAKRAVARTI, N.R. THE INDIAN MINOR-
  ITY IN BURMA.
  R.L. FELDBERG, 293(JAST):MAY72-
    719
CHAKRAVORTY, J. THE IDEA OF REVENGE
  IN SHAKESPEARE.
  M. MINCOFF, 447(N&Q):APR72-145
CHAŁASIŃSKI, J. KULTURA I NARÓD.
  F. GROSS, 32:MAR73-134
CHALKER, J. THE ENGLISH GEORGIC.*
  T.J. WINNIFRITH, 447(N&Q):JUN72-
    234
CHALKER, R.M. PIONEER DAYS ALONG
  THE OCMULGEE.
  W.S. HOOLE, 9(ALAR):APR72-152
CHALMERS, P., ED. IS.14.
  M. LUND, 198:SPRING74-95
CHAMBERLAIN, M.E. BRITAIN & INDIA.
  617(TLS):7JUN74-603
CHAMBERLAIN, N.W. THE LIMITS OF
  CORPORATE RESPONSIBILITY.
  S.B. SHEPARD, 441:24FEB74-34
CHAMBERS, D. PRIVATE PRESS BOOKS
  1972.
  617(TLS):16AUG74-880
CHAMBERS, D.S., ED. PATRONS & ART-
  ISTS IN THE ITALIAN RENAISSANCE.
  A. SMART, 39:MAY72-420
CHAMBERS, F.M. PROPER NAMES IN THE
  LYRICS OF THE TROUBADOURS.
  S.A. STOUDEMIRE, 424:SEP72-209
CHAMBERS, G. THE BONNYCLABBER.*
  J.D. BELLAMY, 114(CHIR):VOL24#3-
    144
  A. KUO, 448:FALL72-80
CHAMBERS, R. THE BOOK OF DAYS.
  K.B. HARDER, 424:MAR72-67
CHAMBERS, R. L'ANGE ET L'AUTOMATE.
  LA COMÉDIE AU CHÂTEAU.
  C. DUCKWORTH, 67:MAY73-131
CHAMBERS, W.W. & J.R. WILKIE. A
  SHORT HISTORY OF THE GERMAN LANGU-
  AGE.*
  W.C. CROSSGROVE, 222(GR):JAN72-
    76   [CONTINUED]

CHAMBERS, W.W. & J.R. WILKIE. A
SHORT HISTORY OF THE GERMAN LANGU-
AGE.*   [CONTINUING]
R.L. KYES, 399(MLJ):MAY72-340
J. MARGETTS, 402(MLR):OCT73-923
CHAMIER, G. A SOUTH-SEA SIREN. (J.
STEVENS, ED)
617(TLS):8MAR74-237
CHAMISH, B. KEEP STILLMAN - A PUN.
J. ORANGE, 296:VOL3#1-110
CHAMPA, K.S. STUDIES IN EARLY IM-
PRESSIONISM.
617(TLS):3MAY74-464
CHAMPFLEURY. LE RÉALISME. (G. & J.
LACAMBRE, EDS)
617(TLS):31MAY74-582
CHAMPIGNY, R. POUR UNE ESTHÉTIQUE
DE L'ESSAI.
F. BUSI, 207(FR):DEC71-495
CHAMPION, L.S. THE EVOLUTION OF
SHAKESPEARE'S COMEDY.*
D.L. STEVENSON, 301(JEGP):JUL73-
440
DE CHAMPSENET, P.J.D. & L. DE MERCIN.
SAINT BONAVENTURE.
A. FOREST, 542:JAN-MAR72-71
CHAN, H-L. THE HISTORIOGRAPHY OF
THE CHIN DYNASTY.
D.M. FARQUHAR, 293(JAST):FEB72-
391
CHAN, J. & OTHERS, EDS. AN ANTHOL-
OGY OF ASIAN-AMERICAN WRITERS.
J. CAREW, 441:22SEP74-16
"CHAN-KUO TS'E."* (J.I. CRUMP, JR.,
TRANS)
L.M. FUSEK, 318(JAOS):APR-JUN72-
336
F.A. KIERMAN, JR., 352(LE&W):
VOL15#3-509
CHANCE, R. THE END OF MAN.
F.R. BARRY, 617(TLS):22NOV74-
1322
CHANCELLOR, J. CHARLES DARWIN.
617(TLS):16AUG74-886
CHANCELLOR, V.E. HISTORY FOR THEIR
MASTERS.
G. SUTHERLAND, 637(VS):DEC72-250
CHANDLER, A. A DREAM OF ORDER.*
J.A.W. BENNETT, 541(RES):AUG72-
376
P. FONTANEY, 189(EA):JUL-SEP72-
435
G.P. LANDOW, 405(MP):MAY73-366
CHANDLER, D. MARLBOROUGH AS MILI-
TARY COMMANDER.
A. BRETT-JAMES, 617(TLS):13DEC74-
1425
CHANDLER, G. VICTORIAN & EDWARDIAN
MANCHESTER & EAST LANCASHIRE FROM
OLD PHOTOGRAPHS.
617(TLS):13SEP74-984
CHANDLER, R. CHANDLER BEFORE MAR-
LOWE. (M.J. BRUCCOLI, ED)
617(TLS):12APR74-391
CHANDLER, R.E. & K. SCHWARTZ, EDS.
A NEW ANTHOLOGY OF SPANISH LITERA-
TURE.
L.C. PÉREZ, 238:MAR72-200
CHANDRASEKHAR, S. ABORTION IN A
CROWDED WORLD.
617(TLS):16AUG74-878
CHANEY, W.A. THE CULT OF KINGSHIP
IN ANGLO-SAXON ENGLAND.*
R.W. HANNING, 222(GR):MAR72-141

CHANG CHUNG-YUAN, ED & TRANS. ORIG-
INAL TEACHINGS OF CH'AN BUDDHISM.
J.S. WU, 485(PE&W):OCT72-480
CHANG, H. LIANG CH'I-CH'AO & INTEL-
LECTUAL TRANSITION IN CHINA, 1890-
1907.
J.D. SPENCE, 676(YR):AUTUMN72-
136
CHANG, H-C. CHINESE LITERATURE.
617(TLS):29MAR74-346
CHANG KUO-T'AO. THE RISE OF THE
CHINESE COMMUNIST PARTY. (VOL 1)
M. MEISNER, 639(VQR):AUTUMN72-
606
T. TSOU, 31(ASCH):SUMMER74-510
CHANG KUO-T'AO. THE RISE OF THE
CHINESE COMMUNIST PARTY. (VOL 2)
T. TSOU, 31(ASCH):SUMMER74-510
CHANG, T-C. CH'ING-CHI I-KO CHING-
KUAN-TE SHENG-HUO.*
T.A. METZGER, 293(JAST):MAY72-
647
CHANG, T-T. DER KULT DER SHANG-
DYNASTIE IM SPIEGEL DER ORAKELIN-
SCHRIFTEN.
P.L-M. SERRUYS, 293(JAST):FEB72-
388
"CHANGING DIRECTIONS."
617(TLS):1NOV74-1238
"LA CHANSON DE ROLAND." (W. CALIN,
ED)
W.L. HENDRICKSON, 207(FR):OCT71-
298
CHANTRAINE, P. DICTIONNAIRE ÉTYMOL-
OGIQUE DE LA LANGUE GRECQUE.*
(VOL 1)
K. STRUNK, 260(IF):BAND76-277
CHANTRAINE, P. DICTIONNAIRE ÉTYMOL-
OGIQUE DE LA LANGUE GRECQUE.*
(VOL 2)
C.J. RUIJGH, 361:VOL28#2-162
K. STRUNK, 260(IF):BAND76-277
CHAO, K. AGRICULTURAL PRODUCTION IN
COMMUNIST CHINA, 1949-1965.
R.M. FIELD, 293(JAST):NOV71-199
CHAO, T. - SEE UNDER TS'AO CHAO
CHAO, Y.R. A GRAMMAR OF SPOKEN CHI-
NESE.
O. ŠVARNÝ, 318(JAOS):JAN-MAR72-
136
CHAO, Y.R. LANGAGE ET SYSTÈMES SYM-
BOLIQUES.
A. TROGNON, 542:OCT-DEC72-489
CHAO, Y.R., R.B. NOSS & J.K. YAMA-
GIWA, EDS. LINGUISTICS IN EAST
ASIA & SOUTH EAST ASIA.
R.A. MILLER, 318(JAOS):JAN-MAR72-
137
CHAPLAIS, P. ENGLISH ROYAL DOCU-
MENTS, KING JOHN TO HENRY VI, 1199-
1461.
N. DENHOLM-YOUNG, 382(MAE):
1973/2-193
C.A-F. MEEKINGS, 325:OCT72-526
B. WILKINSON, 589:JAN73-122
CHAPLIN, C. MY LIFE IN PICTURES.
(D. KING, ED)
617(TLS):27DEC74-1462
CHAPLIN, S. THE MINES OF ALABASTER.
E. GLOVER, 565:VOL13#3-44
AF CHAPMAN, F.H. ARCHITECTURA
NAVALIS MERCATORIA.
C. KOCH, 44:SEP72-12

63

CHAPMAN, G. THE PLAYS OF GEORGE
CHAPMAN: THE COMEDIES.* (A. HOLA-
DAY, ED)
M. EVANS, 541(RES):FEB72-73
CHAPMAN, H.W. ANNE BOLEYN.
617(TLS):12APR74-387
CHAPMAN, J.J. THE COLLECTED WORKS
OF JOHN JAY CHAPMAN.* [ALL 12
VOLS] (M.H. BERNSTEIN, ED)
W.M. WHITEHILL, 432(NEQ):JUN72-
285
CHAPMAN, J.K. - SEE PALMER, S. & A.
GORDON
CHAPMAN, K.G. TARJEI VESAAS.*
S. ARESTAD, 399(MLJ):NOV72-464
CHAPMAN, K.G. - SEE VESAAS, T.
CHAPMAN, K.M. THE POTTERY OF SAN
ILDEFONSO PUEBLO.
A. BACIGALUPA, 363:MAY72-99
CHAPMAN, R. FAITH & REVOLT.*
E.B. GREENBERGER, 541(RES):MAY72-
227
P. MARSH, 637(VS):MAR72-360
G.B. TENNYSON, 445(NCF):JUN72-
115
CHAPMAN, S. JESSE BOOT OF BOOTS THE
CHEMISTS.
C. DRIVER, 362:21FEB74-247
617(TLS):1MAR74-215
CHAPMAN, S.D., ED. THE HISTORY OF
WORKING-CLASS HOUSING.
H. HOBHOUSE, 637(VS):DEC72-254
J.N. TARN, 46:AUG72-127
CHAPPELL, F. THE GAUDY PLACE.*
E. ROVIT, 659:AUTUMN74-539
639(VQR):SUMMER73-CIV
CHAPPELOW, A. SHAW - THE "CHUCKER-
OUT."*
L. CROMPTON, 502(PRS):FALL72-257
H.F. FOLLAND, 651(WHR):AUTUMN73-
411
CHAPPLE, J.A.V. DOCUMENTARY & IMAG-
INATIVE LITERATURE, 1880-1920.
S.P. ROSENBAUM, 405(MP):FEB73-
275
CHAPPUIS, A. THE DRAWINGS OF PAUL
CÉZANNE.*
A. FRANKENSTEIN, 55:NOV73-44
CHARACHIDZÉ, G. INTRODUCTION À
L'ÉTUDE DE LA FÉODALITÉ GÉORGIENNE.
P. CHARANIS, 589:APR73-350
CHARBON, M.H., ED. HAAGS GEMEEN-
TEMUSEUM: CATALOGUS VAN DE MUZIEK-
BIBLIOTHEEK. (VOL 2)
617(TLS):10MAY74-506
CHARBONNEAU, R. ÉTUDE SUR LES VOY-
ELLES NASALES DU FRANÇAIS CANADIEN.
P.R. LÉON, 320(CJL):VOL18#1-76
CHARBONNEAUX, J., R. MARTIN & F.
VILLARD. ARCHAIC GREEK ART. (A.
MALRAUX, ED)
R. HIGGINS, 39:JAN72-70
R.J.L. WYNNE THOMAS, 135:SEP72-
63
290(JAAC):SPRING72-404
DE CHARDIN, P.T. - SEE UNDER TEIL-
HARD DE CHARDIN, P.
CHARITY, A.C. EVENTS & THEIR AFTER-
LIFE.
T.G. BERGIN, 275(IQ):FALL/WINTER
72-106
CHARLES, B.G. GEORGE OWEN OF
HENLLYS.
617(TLS):23AUG74-912

CHARLES-ROUX, E. ELLE, ADRIENNE.
L. JONES, 207(FR):MAY72-1175
CHARLESTON, R.J. THE JAMES A. DE
ROTHSCHILD COLLECTION AT WADDESDON
MANOR: MEISSEN & EUROPEAN PORCE-
LAIN.
F.J.B. WATSON, 39:JUL72-86
CHARLESWORTH, J.H., ED & TRANS. THE
ODES OF SOLOMON.
617(TLS):5JUL74-732
CHARLIER, J-M. & M. MONTARRON. STAV-
ISKY.
T. ZELDIN, 617(TLS):11OCT74-1110
CHARLTON, D.G., ED. FRANCE.
W.G. MOORE, 208(FS):APR73-232
CHARLTON, D.G. SECULAR RELIGIONS IN
FRANCE 1815-1870.
A. STERN, 542:OCT-DEC72-504
CHARLTON, D.G., J. GAUDON & A.R.
PUGH, EDS. BALZAC & THE NINE-
TEENTH CENTURY.
D.P. SCALES, 67:MAY73-127
CHARLTON, H.B. SHAKESPEARIAN TRAG-
EDY.
M. GRIVELET, 189(EA):OCT-DEC72-
543
CHARLTON, W. AESTHETICS.*
B. GIBBS, 393(MIND):JAN72-154
H. OSBORNE, 479(PHQ):JAN72-90
A. SHIELDS, 290(JAAC):FALL71-140
CHARNEY, M. STYLE IN "HAMLET."*
N.L. HARVEY, 599:WINTER72-85
H. JENKINS, 677:VOL3-277
CHARPENEL, M. LAS MINIATURAS EN EL
ARTE POPULAR MEXICANO.
J. GRIFFITH, 292(JAF):JAN-MAR72-
93
CHARTERS, A. KEROUAC.*
B.H. GELFANT, 659:SUMMER74-415
B. WEBER, 27(AL):NOV73-479
617(TLS):13SEP74-971
CHARVET, J. THE SOCIAL PROBLEMS IN
THE PHILOSOPHY OF ROUSSEAU.
617(TLS):26JUL74-786
CHARYN, J. THE TAR BABY.*
E. ROVIT, 659:AUTUMN74-539
639(VQR):SUMMER73-CV
CHASE, G. CONTEMPORARY ART IN LATIN
AMERICA.
M.S. YOUNG, 39:JUN72-523
CHASE, J.H. COME EASY - GO EASY.
N. CALLENDAR, 441:11AUG74-12
CHASINS, A. MUSIC AT THE CROSSROADS.
Y. BADER, 290(JAAC):WINTER72-275
CHASTAGNOL, A. RECHERCHES SUR L'HIS-
TOIRE AUGUSTE.*
A. CAMERON, 123:MAR73-58
CHASTAIN, K. THE DEVELOPMENT OF
MODERN-LANGUAGE SKILLS.
B.J. BUTKA, 351(LL):DEC72-309
CHATAGNIER, L.J. & G. TAGGART, EDS.
LANGUAGE LABORATORY LEARNING.
W.F. SMITH, 399(MLJ):DEC72-519
CHATAIN, J. BLICHE OU L'HERBE RANCE.
N. GREENE, 207(FR):OCT71-196
DE CHATEAUBRIAND, F.R. PAGES BRET-
ONNES. (R. LEBÈGUE, ED)
P. CHRISTOPHOROV, 535(RHL):JUL-
AUG72-726
"CHATEAUBRIAND."
P. CHRISTOPHOROV, 546(RR):DEC72-
303

CHATMAN, S. THE LATER STYLE OF
HENRY JAMES.*
B. MENIKOFF, 445(NCF):MAR73-492
CHATMAN, S., ED. LITERARY STYLE.
M.A. CAWS, 188(ECR):WINTER72-318
CHATTERJEE, B. JOHN KEATS.
J.R.D. JACKSON, 627(UTQ):SPRING
73-289
CHATTERJEE, B., ED & TRANS. THE
KHANDAKHADYAKA (AN ASTRONOMICAL
TREATISE) OF BRAHMAGUPTA, WITH
THE COMMENTARY OF BHATTOTPALA.
B.R. GOLDSTEIN, 318(JAOS):APR-
JUN72-323
CHATTERJI, N. MUDDLE OF THE MIDDLE
EAST.
617(TLS):22FEB74-179
CHATTERTON, T. THE COMPLETE WORKS
OF THOMAS CHATTERTON.* (D.S. TAY-
LOR, WITH B.B. HOOVER, EDS)
A.B. FRIEDMAN, 481(PQ):JUL72-656
A. JOHNSTON, 677:VOL3-301
R.W. KING, 541(RES):FEB72-84
173(ECS):SPRING73-400
CHAUDHURI, H. INTEGRAL YOGA. (2ND
ED)
G.E. CAIRNS, 258:JUN72-294
A.K. SARKAR, 485(PE&W):APR72-235
CHAUDHURI, K.N., ED. THE ECONOMIC
DEVELOPMENT OF INDIA UNDER THE
EAST INDIA COMPANY, 1814-58.
G. BLYN, 318(JAOS):OCT-DEC72-580
CHAUDHURI, N.C. SCHOLAR EXTRAORDI-
NARY.
M. DEAS, 362:5DEC74-751
E. STOKES, 617(TLS):27DEC74-1463
DE CHAULIAC, G. THE "CYRURGIE" OF
GUY DE CHAULIAC.* (VOL 1) (M.S.
OGDEN, ED)
P.A. CANT, 597(SN):VOL44#2-439
CHAURAND, J., ED. FOU: DIXIÈME CON-
TE DE LA "VIE DES PÈRES."
D. KELLY, 589:OCT73-737
CHAUSSERIE-LAPRÉE, J.P. L'EXPRES-
SION NARRATIVE CHEZ LES HISTORIENS
LATINS.*
R.H. MARTIN, 313:VOL62-210
CHAVANNES, E. FIVE HAPPINESSES.
617(TLS):10MAY74-508
CHAWDHARI, T.P.S., ED. SELECTED
READINGS ON COMMUNITY DEVELOPMENT.
H.A. GOULD, 293(JAST):NOV71-216
CHAZANOF, W. JOSEPH ELLICOTT & THE
HOLLAND LAND COMPANY.
H.I. COWAN, 656(WMQ):APR72-322
CHEATHAM, L. THE MARRIAGE PACT.
N. CALLENDAR, 441:27JAN74-12
CHECKLAND, S.G. THE GLADSTONES.
J. VINCENT, 637(VS):SEP72-99
CHEEVER, J. THE WORLD OF APPLES.*
M. MUDRICK, 249(HUDR):AUTUMN73-
545
617(TLS):15MAR74-253
CHEIN, I. THE SCIENCE OF BEHAVIOR
& THE IMAGE OF MAN.
P. MULLER, 182:VOL25#23/24-844
J. SHORTER, 111:18MAY73-162
CHEKHOV, A. LETTERS OF ANTON CHEK-
HOV.* (S. KARLINSKY, ED)
K. FITZLYON, 364:DEC73/JAN74-142
CHEKHOV, A. THE LETTERS OF ANTON
CHEKHOV.* (A. YARMOLINSKY, ED)
617(TLS):29MAR74-346

CHEKHOV, A. THE OXFORD CHEKHOV.
(VOLS 1, 2, 5, 6 & 8) (R. HINGLEY,
ED & TRANS)
T.G. WINNER, 32:SEP73-659
CHEN, K-I & J.S. UPPAL. COMPARA-
TIVE DEVELOPMENT OF INDIA & CHINA.
293(JAST):MAY72-753
CHEN, N-R. & W. GALENSON. THE CHI-
NESE ECONOMY UNDER COMMUNISM.
J.G. GURLEY, 318(JAOS):JAN-MAR72-
149
CHÊN, T. - SEE UNDER TAI CHÊN
CHENAKAL, V.L. WATCHMAKERS & CLOCK-
MAKERS IN RUSSIA, 1400 TO 1850.
I. DE MADARIAGA, 575(SEER):OCT73-
626
CHENEY, C.R. MEDIEVAL TEXTS & STUD-
IES.
617(TLS):15FEB74-152
CHENEY, C.R. NOTARIES PUBLIC IN
ENGLAND IN THE THIRTEENTH & FOUR-
TEENTH CENTURIES.
H. BUSZELLO, 182:VOL25#17/18-621
D.M. OWEN, 382(MAE):1973/3-299
CHENG, C-Y. THE MACHINE-BUILDING
INDUSTRY IN COMMUNIST CHINA.
293(JAST):MAY72-754
CHÊNG TÊ-K'UN. JADE FLOWERS & FLOR-
AL PATTERNS IN CHINESE DECORATIVE
ART.
J.M. HARTMAN, 57:VOL34#2/3-249
CHENOWETH, V. MELODIC PERCEPTION &
ANALYSIS.
M. HERNDON, 187:MAY74-303
CHENU, M.D. LA THÉOLOGIE AU DOUZI-
ÈME SIÈCLE.
A. FOREST, 542:JAN-MAR72-81
CHEREPNIN, L.V. & OTHERS, EDS. AK-
TUAL'NYE PROBLEMY ISTORII ROSSII
EPOKHI FEODALIZMA.
H.W. DEWEY, 32:SEP73-602
CHERMAYEFF, S. & A. TZONIS. SHAPE
OF COMMUNITY.*
M. BROADY, 46:JUN72-392
CHERNAIK, J. THE LYRICS OF SHELLEY.
D.H. REIMAN, 301(JEGP):APR73-244
L.J. ZILLMAN, 401(MLQ):JUN73-213
CHERNIAVSKY, M., ED. THE STRUCTURE
OF RUSSIAN HISTORY.
P. SCHEIBERT, 104:SPRING72-153
CHERRY, B. - SEE PEVSNER, N.
CHERRY, K. SICK & FULL OF BURNING.
P. ADAMS, 61:JUL74-100
CHERRY, M. ON HIGH STEEL.
G. BURNSIDE, 441:20OCT74-30
CHESHIRE, D.F. MUSIC HALL IN BRIT-
AIN.
617(TLS):1MAR74-221
CHESLER, P. WOMEN & MADNESS.*
L.J. KAPLAN, 473(PR):2/1973-282
CHESNEAU, M. TROISIÈME FRAGMENT DU
JOURNAL POÉTIQUE D'UNE ÂME.
M. SCHAETTEL, 557(RSH):JUL-SEP72-
482
CHESSEX, J. L'OGRE.
617(TLS):8FEB74-125
CHESTER, L. & S. BARBA, EDS. RISING
TIDES.
N. BALAKIAN, 441:15FEB74-37
CHESTERTON, G.K. GREYBEARDS AT PLAY
& OTHER COMIC VERSE. (J. SULLIVAN,
ED)
D.A.N. JONES, 362:25APR74-538
617(TLS):17MAY74-518

CHEVALIER, J-C. ALCOOLS D'APOLLI-
NAIRE.
    M. DAVIES, 402(MLR):JAN73-184
    S.I. LOCKERBIE, 208(FS):APR73-
    225
    A. NICOLAS, 557(RSH):JUL-SEP72-
    474
CHEVALLEY, S. MOLIÈRE EN SON TEMPS.
    R.T. SUSSEX, 67:NOV73-307
CHEW, A.F. AN ATLAS OF RUSSIAN
    HISTORY.* (REV)
    A. KLEIMOLA, 104:SPRING72-144
CHEW, P. THE KENTUCKY DERBY.
    J. MC GINNISS, 441:28APR74-10
    E. PERLMUTTER, 441:13APR74-23
CHI, W-S., ED. READINGS IN THE CHI-
    NESE COMMUNIST CULTURAL REVOLUTION.
    P.S.H. TANG, 293(JAST):MAY72-667
CHIAPPELLI, F. NUOVI STUDI SUL LIN-
    GUAGGIO DEL MACHIAVELLI.*
    B.L., 275(IQ):FALL/WINTER72-121
    B. LAWTON, 276:SUMMER72-255
    A. SCAGLIONE, 545(RPH):AUG72-210
CHIBNALL, M. - SEE ORDERIC VITALIS
CHICK, N., ED. ANNALS OF THE INDIAN
    REBELLION 1857-58.
    617(TLS):7JUN74-620
CHIEREGHIN, F. L'INFLUENZA DELLO
    SPINOZISMO NELLA FORMAZIONE DELLA
    FILOSOFIA HEGELIANA.
    E. NAMER, 542:JUL-SEP72-362
CHIERICI, J. IL GRIFO DANTESCO.
    T.G. BERGIN, 275(IQ):FALL/WINTER
    72-110
CHILCOTT, T. A PUBLISHER & HIS
    CIRCLE.
    R.D. ALTICK, 149:SEP73-270
CHILD, A. FARE E CONOSCERE IN
    HOBBES, VICO E DEWEY.
    E. NAMER, 542:APR-JUN72-208
CHILD, H. - SEE JOHNSTON, E.
CHILD, H. & D. COLLES. CHRISTIAN
    SYMBOLS, ANCIENT & MODERN.
    90:JUL72-508
CHIN, S.S.K. & F.H.H. KING, EDS.
    SELECTED SEMINAR PAPERS ON CONTEM-
    PORARY CHINA. (VOL 1)
    C.W. HAYFORD, 302:JUL72-208
    293(JAST):NOV71-236
"A CHINESE GLOSSARY OF INTERNATIONAL
    CONFERENCE TERMINOLOGY." (ROMAN-
    IZATION BY K. HAUN)
    D.T.Y. LEE, 293(JAST):MAY72-669
"CHINESE RHYME-PROSE." (B. WATSON,
    TRANS)
    639(VQR):SPRING72-LXXVI
CHING-CHIA, H. - SEE UNDER HUANG
    CHING-CHIA
CHIPP, H.B., ED. THEORIES OF MODERN
    ART.
    E.G. HOLT, 54:JUN72-229
DE CHIRICO, G. THE MEMOIRS OF
    GIORGIO DE CHIRICO.
    D. HYSHKA-STROSS, 290(JAAC):FALL
    72-134
    R. MC NAB, 592:NOV72-204
L.FR-CHIROVSKY, N. A HISTORY OF THE
    RUSSIAN EMPIRE. (VOL 1)
    617(TLS):19APR74-420
CHISHOLM, M. & J. OEPPEN. THE CHANG-
    ING PATTERN OF EMPLOYMENT.
    617(TLS):23AUG74-912
CHISHOLM, S. THE GOOD FIGHT.*
    639(VQR):AUTUMN73-CLXVIII

CHISSELL, J. SCHUMANN PIANO MUSIC.*
    E. SAMS, 415:JAN73-36
CHLOROS, A.G., ED. A BIBLIOGRAPHI-
    CAL GUIDE TO THE LAW OF THE UNITED
    KINGDOM, THE CHANNEL ISLANDS & THE
    ISLE OF MAN. (2ND ED)
    617(TLS):25JAN74-88
CHMIELEWSKI, E. THE POLISH QUESTION
    IN THE RUSSIAN STATE DUMA.*
    E. KUSIELEWICZ, 550(RUSR):OCT72-
    419
CHOAY, F. THE MODERN CITY.*
    G.L. HERSEY, 56:SUMMER72-180
CHOCANO, G.M. - SEE UNDER MOLINA
    CHOCANO, G.
CHODOS, R. THE CPR.
    P. BERTON, 99:MAY/JUN74-42
CHOLAKIAN, R.C., ED. THE WILLIAM P.
    SHEPARD COLLECTION OF PROVENÇALIA.
    P. BARRETTE, 207(FR):FEB72-759
CHOMSKY, C. THE ACQUISITION OF SYN-
    TAX IN CHILDREN FROM 5 TO 10.*
    J. PRŮCHA, 353:1SEP72-82
CHOMSKY, N. CARTESIAN LINGUISTICS.
    (GERMAN TITLE: CARTESIANISCHE LIN-
    GUISTIK.)
    W. VIERECK, 430(NS):AUG72-490
CHOMSKY, N. CHOMSKY: SELECTED READ-
    INGS. (J.P.B. ALLEN & P. VAN
    BUREN, EDS) PROBLEMS OF KNOWLEDGE
    & FREEDOM.
    D.T. LANGENDOEN, 35(AS):SPRING-
    SUMMER70-129
CHOMSKY, N. LANGUAGE & MIND. (REV)
    D.H., 502(PRS):WINTER72/73-370
    G. HARMAN, 350:JUN73-453
    D.T. LANGENDOEN, 35(AS):SPRING-
    SUMMER70-129
CHOMSKY, N. PEACE IN THE MIDDLE
    EAST?
    M. WALZER, 441:6OCT74-5
CHOMSKY, N. & M. HALLE. THE SOUND
    PATTERN OF ENGLISH.*
    U. EGLI, 343:BAND14HEFT1-1
CHORNOVIL, V. & OTHERS. FERMENT IN
    THE UKRAINE.* (M. BROWNE, ED)
    D. VON MOHRENSCHILDT, 550(RUSR):
    JAN72-92
CHORPENNING, C.B. THREE ADVENTURE
    PLAYS.
    A. RENDLE, 157:WINTER72-80
CHOUKRI, M. FOR BREAD ALONE.
    617(TLS):5APR74-360
CHOW TSE-TUNG, ED. WEN-LIN.
    C.N. TAY, 318(JAOS):APR-JUN72-
    329
CHOY, B-Y. KOREA.
    H.F. COOK, 293(JAST):FEB72-421
    B.H. HAZARD, 293(JAST):AUG72-905
CHRISTADLER, M. DER AMERIKANISCHE
    ESSAY 1720-1820.*
    H. WEBER, 38:BAND90HEFT1/2-246
CHRISTE, Y. LES GRANDS PORTAILS
    ROMANS.
    T.W. LYMAN, 54:MAR72-80
CHRISTENSEN, A.E. VIKINGETIDENS
    DANMARK.
    S.L. COHEN, 589:JAN73-123
CHRISTENSEN, D.E., ED. HEGEL & THE
    PHILOSOPHY OF RELIGION.
    H.A.D., 543:JUN72-747
CHRISTENSEN, T. THE DIVINE ORDER.
    617(TLS):8FEB74-140

CHRISTESEN, C.B. THE HAND OF MEMORY.
C. HADGRAFT, 381:JUN72-233
R.B.J. WILSON, 381:JUN72-221
CHRISTIAN, R. GHOSTS & LEGENDS.
J. SIMPSON, 203:WINTER72-344
CHRISTIAN, R.F. TOLSTOY.*
D. FANGER, 454:WINTER73-188
E. WASIOLEK, 594:SPRING72-86
CHRISTIAN, W.A. OPPOSITIONS OF RE-
LIGIOUS DOCTRINES.
D. BASTOW, 518:JAN73-9
CHRISTIE, A. POSTERN OF FATE.*
617(TLS):18JAN74-61
CHRISTIN, P. & P. LEFEBVRE. COMPREN-
DRE LA FRANCE.*
J. VAN BAELEN, 399(MLJ):NOV72-
469
CHRISTOUT, M-F. MAURICE BÉJART.
R. BAKER, 151:SEP72-78
CHROMATIUS. CHROMACE D'AQUILÉE,
"SERMONS." (VOL 2) (J. LEMARIÉ,
ED)
W.H.C. FREND, 123:DEC73-273
CHROUST, A-H. ARISTOTLE.
G.E.R. LLOYD, 617(TLS):23AUG74-
905
CHÜ-I, P. - SEE UNDER PO CHÜ-I
CHUANG-TZU. THE COMPLETE WORKS OF
CHUANG-TZU. (B. WATSON, TRANS)
R.B. MATHER, 318(JAOS):APR-JUN72-
334
CHUDACOFF, H.P. MOBILE AMERICANS.
639(VQR):WINTER73-XXXIX
"CHUNG-KUO HSÜEH-JEN." (VOLS 1-3)
L.Y. CHIU, 302:JAN72-75
CHUNG-YUAN, C. - SEE UNDER CHANG
CHUNG-YUAN
CHURCH, M. DON QUIXOTE.
D.G. FRICKE, 568(SCN):SPRING73-
23
CHURCH, W.F. RICHELIEU & REASON OF
STATE.*
639(VQR):SUMMER73-CXX
CHURCHILL, A. THE SPLENDOR SEEKERS.
R.C. ALBERTS, 441:19MAY74-27
CHURCHILL, P. & J. MITCHELL. JENNIE.
V. GLENDINNING, 617(TLS):22NOV74-
1309
CHURCHILL, S. ITÄ-KARJALAN KOHTALO
1917-1922.
A.F. UPTON, 563(SS):SPRING73-163
CHURCHILL, W.J. RUNNING IN PLACE.
639(VQR):SUMMER73-CV
CHURCHILL, W.S. WINSTON S. CHURCH-
ILL: HIS COMPLETE SPEECHES 1897-
1963. (R.R. JAMES, ED) GREAT CON-
TEMPORARIES.
P. STANSKY, 441:24NOV74-4
"CHUSHINGURA." (D. KEENE, TRANS)
F.T. MOTOFUJI, 293(JAST):MAY72-
677
CHÜZO, I. - SEE UNDER ICHIKO CHÜZO
CIAMPINI, R. - SEE CARPANI, G.
CIARDI, J. LIVES OF X.
639(VQR):WINTER72-XXVI
CIARDI, J. MANNER OF SPEAKING.
W.G.R., 502(PRS):WINTER72/73-371
CIBOULE, R. ÉDITION CRITIQUE DU SER-
MON "QUI MANDUCAT ME" DE ROBERT CI-
BOULE (1403-1458). (N. MARZAC, ED)
W. ROTHWELL, 208(FS):APR73-189
CICCIA, C. IL MONDO POPOLARE DI
GIOVANNI VERGA.
B.L., 275(IQ):FALL/WINTER72-123

CICCONE, S.D. - SEE UNDER DE STEFAN-
IS CICCONE S.
CICERO. MARCUS TULLIUS CICÉRO,
"BRUTUS."* (B. KYTZLER, ED &
TRANS)
J. ANDRÉ, 555:VOL46FASC1-152
A.E. DOUGLAS, 123:DEC73-181
CICERO. CICÉRON, "ACADEMICA POSTER-
IORA." (BK 1) (M. RUCH, ED)
M. TESTARD, 555:VOL46FASC2-332
CICERO. CICÉRON, "LAELIUS DE AMI-
CITIA." (R. COMBÈS, ED & TRANS)
G. SERBAT, 555:VOL46FASC2-331
CICERO. CICÉRON, "LES DEVOIRS."
(VOL 2) (M. TESTARD & ED & TRANS)
A. ERNOUT, 555:VOL46FASC1-151
CICERO. M. TULLIO CICERONE: "BRUTO."
(E.V. D'ARBELA, ED & TRANS)
A.E. DOUGLAS, 123:DEC73-181
CICERO. PHILIPPICS 4-6. (J.H.
TERRY & D.G.S. UPTON, EDS)
R.G. PENMAN, 123:MAR73-81
CICERO. RES PUBLICA.* (W.K. LACEY
& B.W.J.G. WILSON, EDS & TRANS)
R.G. PENMAN, 123:MAR73-82
CIECHANOWSKI, J. POWSTANIE WARSZAW-
SKIE.
A. POLONSKY, 575(SEER):JAN73-144
CIECHANOWSKI, J.M. THE WARSAW RIS-
ING OF 1944.
617(TLS):14JUN74-627
DE LA CIERVA, R. FRANCISCO FRANCO.
617(TLS):1NOV74-1226
CIEUTAT, V.J., L.I. KRIMERMAN & S.T.
ELDER. TRADITIONAL LOGIC & THE
VENN DIAGRAM.
T.G.N., 543:MAR72-551
ČIKOBAVA, A. MART'IVI C'INADADEBIS
P'ROBLEMA KARTULŠI. (VOL 1) (2ND
ED)
G.F. MEIER, 682(ZPSK):BAND24
HEFT6-539
CIOBANU, F. & F. HASAN. CUMPUNEREA.
M. HÖFLER, 72:BAND21OHEFT1/3-211
CIOŁKOSZ, L. & A. ZARYS DZIEJÓW SOC-
JALIZMU POLSKIEGO. (VOL 2)
Z. GROSS, 497(POLR):SUMMER72-105
CIORAN, E.M. DE L'INCONVÉNIENT
D'ÊTRE NÉ.
617(TLS):12APR74-389
CIORANESCU, A. BIBLIOGRAPHIE DE LA
LITTÉRATURE FRANÇAISE DU DIX-
SEPTIÈME SIÈCLE. (VOL 2, 2ND ED;
VOL 3, 1ST ED)
F. NIES, 224(GRM):BAND22HEFT1-
104
CIPRIANI, S., ED. CONCORDANZE DELLE
POESIE MILANESI DI CARLO PORTA.
E. BONORA, 228(GSLI):VOL149FASC
466/467-448
"CIRCLE."* (J.L. MARTIN, B. NICHOL-
SON & N. GABO, EDS)
D. IRWIN, 39:APR72-343
CIRLOT, J-E. PICASSO.*
T. HILTON, 592:NOV72-197
CIULICH, L.B. & P. BAROCCHI, EDS.
I RICORDI DI MICHELANGELO.
J.S. ACKERMAN, 551(RENQ):SPRING
72-63
CIUREANU, P. BAUDELAIRE IN ROMANIA.
N. BABUTS, 593:SUMMER73-180
CIXOUS, H. LES COMMENCEMENTS.
M.J. FRIEDMAN, 207(FR):OCT71-197

CIXOUS, H. THE EXILE OF JAMES
JOYCE.* (FRENCH TITLE: L'EXIL DE
JAMES JOYCE OU L'ART DU REMPLACE-
MENT.)
R. BOYLE, 659:SPRING74-262
D. THORBURN, 473(PR):2/1973-306
CIXOUS, H. NEUTRE.
L. FINAS, 98:OCT72-876
CIXOUS, H. LE TROISIÈME CORPS.
N. OXENHANDLER, 207(FR):APR72-
1041
CIŽEVSKIJ, D. COMPARATIVE HISTORY
OF SLAVIC LITERATURES. (S.A. ZEN-
KOVSKY, ED)
F.J. OINAS, 550(RUSR):JAN72-92
CLACK, R.J. BERTRAND RUSSELL'S
PHILOSOPHY OF LANGUAGE.*
W. SCHÄFER, 182:VOL25#7/8-198
P.A.M. SEUREN, 206:JAN73-440
CLAIBORNE, R. CLIMATE, MAN & HIS-
TORY.
617(TLS):29MAR74-316
CLAIBORNE, R. GOD OR BEAST.
J. PFEIFFER, 441:22SEP74-6
CLAIR, R. CINEMA YESTERDAY & TODAY.
639(VQR):WINTER73-XLI
CLAIRMONT, C.W. GRAVESTONE & EPI-
GRAM.*
M.B. WALLACE, 487:SUMMER72-203
A.G. WOODHEAD, 303:VOL92-236
CLANCHY, M.T., ED. CIVIL PLEAS OF
THE WILTSHIRE EYRE, 1249.
A.J. DUGGAN, 447(N&Q):JUN72-235
CLAPHAM, J. SMETANA.*
G.A., 410(M&L):JAN73-85
CLARESON, T.D., ED. SF: THE OTHER
SIDE OF REALISM.
D. SUVIN, 128(CE):MAY73-1148
CLARK, A. - SEE LEE, A.
CLARK, E. DR. HEART.
A. BROYARD, 441:17DEC74-41
CLARK, E. & N. HORROCK. CONTRABAND-
ISTA!*
R. SHERRILL, 441:7JUL74-1
CLARK, G. ENGLISH HISTORY.
639(VQR):SPRING72-LXVIII
CLARK, J. TENNESSEE HILL FOLK.
639(VQR):SPRING73-XCII
CLARK, J.G. NEW ORLEANS, 1718-1812.
J.H. SOLTOW, 656(WMQ):JAN72-179
CLARK, K. ANOTHER PART OF THE WOOD.
P. CONRAD, 617(TLS):11OCT74-1112
P. QUENNELL, 362:10OCT74-478
CLARK, K. CIVILIZATION.*
D. GERVAIS, 97(CQ):VOL6#1-64
CLARK, K. THE DRAWINGS OF HENRY
MOORE.
W. FEAVER, 362:19&26DEC74-847
J. RUSSELL, 441:1DEC74-54
CLARK, K. THE ROMANTIC REBELLION.*
P. ADAMS, 61:MAY74-139
A. BROYARD, 441:13MAR74-45
P.N. FURBANK, 362:3JAN74-21
442(NY):13MAY74-160
CLARK, K.B. PATHOS OF POWER.
M. CARROLL, 441:28SEP74-27
CLARK, L. - SEE GURNEY, I.
CLARK, L. - SEE YOUNG, A.
CLARK, L.W. HOW TO MAKE MONEY WITH
YOUR CRAFTS.
L.J. GARTNER, JR., 441:8DEC74-51
CLARK, M. LOGIC & SYSTEM.
W.H. WERKMEISTER, 319:JAN74-125

CLARK, R.W. THE SCIENTIFIC BREAK-
THROUGH.
W. SULLIVAN, 441:1DEC74-6
CLARK, T.N. PROPHETS & PATRONS.
617(TLS):4OCT74-1068
CLARKE, A. A BIBLIOGRAPHICAL DIC-
TIONARY.
P.J. KORSHIN, 481(PQ):JUL72-510
CLARKE, A. COLLECTED POEMS. (L.
MILLER, ED)
M. DODSWORTH, 617(TLS):13DEC74-
1406
CLARKE, A. WHEN HE WAS FREE & YOUNG
& HE USED TO WEAR SILKS.*
E. MC NAMARA, 529(QQ):SPRING72-
119
CLARKE, C., ED. THE PETERBOROUGH
CHRONICLE, 1070-1154. (2ND ED)
A.G. DYSON, 325:APR72-439
CLARKE, D.C. ALLEGORY, DECALOGUE, &
DEADLY SINS IN "LA CELESTINA."*
D.W. MC PHEETERS, 240(HR):SUMMER
72-312
CLARKE, D.L., ED. MODELS IN ARCHAE-
OLOGY.
K.W. BUTZER, 182:VOL25#22-809
CLARKE, L. & J. NICHOLS. ROOMMATES
CAN'T ALWAYS BE LOVERS.
C. GAISER, 231:OCT74-105
CLARKE, M. A COLONIAL CITY.* (L.T.
HERGENHAN, ED)
M. WILDING, 581:DEC73-441
CLARKE, M. HIS NATURAL LIFE.
L.T. HERGENHAN, 381:MAR72-101
CLARKE, M. & C. CRISP. BALLET.
A. KISSELGOFF, 441:13JUL74-21
CLARKE, M.L. HIGHER EDUCATION IN
THE ANCIENT WORLD.
S. USHER, 303:VOL92-214
CLARKE, M.L. PALEY.
617(TLS):7JUN74-618
CLARKE, R. LA COURSE À LA MORT.
M. SERRES, 98:MAR72-199
CLARKE, T.E.B. THIS IS WHERE I CAME
IN.
617(TLS):19JUL74-760
CLARKE WILSON, D. BRIGHT EYES.
453:4APR74-44
CLAROS, R.B. - SEE UNDER BENÍTEZ
CLAROS, R.
CLASSEN, H.G. THE TIME IS NEVER
RIPE.
H. PAGE, 150(DR):AUTUMN72-523
R. ROBERTSON, 529(QQ):WINTER72-
549
CLAUDE, H. HISTOIRE, RÉALITÉ ET DES-
TIN D'UN MONOPOLE.
J.M. LAUX, 207(FR):OCT71-232
CLAUDEL, P. FIVE GREAT ODES.
V.M. AMES, 290(JAAC):SPRING72-
400
H.A. WATERS, 207(FR):OCT71-198
CLAUDEL, P. & J-L. BARRAULT. CORRES-
PONDANCE. (M. LIOURE, ED)
617(TLS):10MAY74-504
CLAUDEL, P. & L. MASSIGNON. CORRES-
PONDANCE, 1908-1914. (M. MALICET,
ED)
617(TLS):10MAY74-504
CLAUDIAN. DE RAPTU PROSERPINAE.*
(J.B. HALL, ED)
W.S. THURMAN, 399(MLJ):MAY72-339
CLAVEL, B. LORD OF THE RIVER.
M. LEVIN, 441:13JAN74-16

CLAVEL, M. LA PERTE ET LE FRACAS.
P. CRANT, 207(FR):APR72-1042
CLAVELIN, M. - SEE GALILÉE
CLAWITER, W. & L. SANDER-HOLZMANN,
WITH E. WALDSCHMIDT. SANSKRIT-
HANDSCHRIFTEN AUS DEN TURFANFUNDEN.
(PT 2)
M.J. DRESDEN, 318(JAOS):APR-JUN
72-315
CLAYRE, A. A FIRE BY THE SEA.
617(TLS):3MAY74-471
CLAYRE, A. WORK & PLAY.
K. MINOGUE, 617(TLS):30AUG74-929
CLAYTON, B. THE SAVAGE IDEAL.*
639(VQR):SPRING73-LXXXV
CLAYTON, B., JR. THE COMPLETE BOOK
OF BREADS.
N. HAZELTON, 441:1DEC74-96
CLAYTON, M. THE COLLECTOR'S DICTION-
ARY OF THE SILVER & GOLD OF GREAT
BRITAIN & NORTH AMERICA.
J. HOUSTON, 135:APR72-290
CLAYTON, T. THE "SHAKESPEAREAN"
ADDITION IN "THE BOOKE OF SIR
THOMAS MOORE."
J.L. HALIO, 551(RENQ):AUTUMN72-
369
CLAYTON, T. - SEE SUCKLING, J.
CLAYTON, W. SELECTED PAPERS OF WILL
CLAYTON. (F.J. DOBNEY, ED)
R.A. ESTHUS, 377:MAR73-56
CLEARY, J. PETER'S PENCE.
N. CALLENDAR, 441:2JUN74-20
617(TLS):1MAR74-219
CLEBSCH, W.A. AMERICAN RELIGIOUS
THOUGHT.
617(TLS):30AUG74-935
CLECAK, P. RADICAL PARADOXES.
P. SINGER, 453:18JUL74-20
CLEGG, M. SEAL SONG.
617(TLS):9AUG74-849
CLEMEN, W. A COMMENTARY ON SHAKE-
SPEARE'S "RICHARD III."
M. GRIVELET, 189(EA):JAN-MAR72-
162
CLEMEN, W. SHAKESPEARE'S DRAMATIC
ART.
R.J.S., 570(SQ):SUMMER72-267
D.A. TRAVERSI, 401(MLQ):SEP73-
312
A.C. SPRAGUE, 402(MLR):APR73-383
CLEMENCEAU, G. LETTRES À UNE AMIE.
A. SEDGWICK, 207(FR):OCT71-231
CLÉMENT, F. & P. LAROUSSE. DICTION-
NAIRE DES OPÉRAS. (REV BY A.
POUGIN)
F.W. STERNFELD, 447(N&Q):NOV72-
436
CLEMENTS, A.L. THE MYSTICAL POETRY
OF THOMAS TRAHERNE.*
C.F. WILLIAMSON, 541(RES):FEB72-
80
CLEMO, J. THE ECHOING TIP.
A. CLUYSENAAR, 565:VOL13#2-72
CLEMOES, P. RHYTHM & COSMIC ORDER
IN OLD ENGLISH CHRISTIAN LITERA-
TURE.
H. BERGNER, 38:BAND90HEFT4-512
CLÉRY, G. ROMAN DE L'ILE.
W.V. GUGLI, 207(FR):APR72-1043
CLIFFORD, A. CUT-STEEL & BERLIN
IRON JEWELLERY.
C. BLAIR, 135:DEC72-291

CLIFFORD, D. COLLECTING ENGLISH
WATER-COLOURS.
T. CROMBIE, 39:APR72-342
CLIFFORD, F. GOODBYE & AMEN.
N. CALLENDAR, 441:15DEC74-10
CLIFFORD, F. THE GROSVENOR SQUARE
GOODBYE.
617(TLS):8NOV74-1248
CLIFFORD, J.G. THE CITIZEN SOLDIER.
R. GILLAM, 676(YR):SPRING73-472
CLIFTON-TAYLOR, A. THE PATTERN OF
ENGLISH BUILDING.
A. BARKER, 135:JUN72-150
CLIGNET, R. & P. FOSTER. THE FOR-
TUNATE FEW.
P.C.C. EVANS, 69:JUL72-253
CLINE, C.L. - SEE MEREDITH, G.
CLISSOLD, S. THE SAINTS OF SOUTH
AMERICA.
617(TLS):18JAN74-49
CLIVE, H.P. - SEE MARGUERITE DE
NAVARRE
CLIVE, M. THIS SUN OF YORK.
P. ADAMS, 61:FEB74-96
442(NY):11FEB74-127
CLIVE, W. THE TUNE THAT THEY PLAYED.
M. LEVIN, 441:17FEB74-32
CLOEREN, H-J. & S.J. SCHMIDT, EDS.
PHILOSOPHIE ALS SPRACHKRITIK IM 19.
JAHRHUNDERT. (VOLS 1 & 2)
W. BÜTTEMEYER, 548(RCSF):JUL-SEP
72-353
CLOGAN, P.M., ED. MEDIEVALIA ET
HUMANISTICA. (NEW SER 3)
639(VQR):SPRING73-LXV
CLOGG, R., ED. THE STRUGGLE FOR
GREEK INDEPENDENCE.
617(TLS):1FEB74-102
CLOSE, E. THE DEVELOPMENT OF MODERN
ROMANIAN.
617(TLS):26JUL74-792
CLOSE, R. THE BOHEME COMBINATION.
N. CALLENDAR, 441:27OCT74-56
CLOSE, R.A. THE NEW ENGLISH GRAMMAR.
(PT 2)
P. KAKIETEK, 353:15OCT72-110
CLOSE, R.A. THE NEW ENGLISH GRAMMAR.
(PTS 3&4)
B.M.H. STRANG, 206:NOV72-295
CLOSS, A. & T.P. WILLIAMS, EDS. THE
HARRAP ANTHOLOGY OF GERMAN POETRY.
(2ND ED)
K.W. MOERSCHNER, 399(MLJ):OCT72-
396
CLOUSTON, J.S. THE LUNATIC AT LARGE.
P.J. KEATING, 617(TLS):29NOV74-
1347
CLOVER, F.M. FLAVIUS MEROBAUDES.
W.R. CHALMERS, 123:DEC73-274
CLOWARD, R.A. & F.F. PIVEN. THE
POLITICS OF TURMOIL.
P.Y. SUSSMAN, 441:15SEP74-20
CLUBB, O.E. CHINA & RUSSIA.*
G.A. LENSEN, 550(RUSR):JAN72-75
S.I. LEVINE, 293(JAST):MAY72-651
R. QUESTED, 302:JUL72-206
G.R. TAYLOR, 529(QQ):SUMMER72-
277
CLUBBE, J. - SEE HOOD, T.
CLURMAN, H. ALL PEOPLE ARE FAMOUS.
M. GUSSOW, 441:25DEC74-25
I. HOWE, 441:3NOV74-8
CLURMAN, H. THE DIVINE PASTIME.
R. COHN, 441:2JUN74-48

CLYDE, P.H. & B.F. BEERS. THE FAR
EAST. (5TH ED)
  W.S.K. WAUNG, 302:JUL72-206
COATES, A. CHINA, INDIA & THE RUINS
OF WASHINGTON.
  B.B. BURCH, 639(VQR):WINTER73-
  141
COATS, A.M. THE BOOK OF FLOWERS.*
  W. FEAVER, 362:19&26DEC74-847
COBB, R.C. THE POLICE & THE PEOPLE.*
  J. GODECHOT, 182:VOL25#5/6-178
COBBAN, A.B. THE KING'S HALL WITHIN
THE UNIVERSITY OF CAMBRIDGE IN THE
LATER MIDDLE AGES.
  F.J. PEGUES, 589:JUL73-557
COBBETT, W. COBBETT'S COUNTRY BOOK.
(R. INGRAMS, ED)
  617(TLS):13DEC74-1421
COBET, J. HERODOTS EXKURSE UND DIE
FRAGE DER EINHEIT SEINES WERKES.
  F. LASSERRE, 182:VOL25#3/4-108
COBURN, A. THE TRESPASSERS.
  N. CALLENDAR, 441:17NOV74-51
COBURN, K. - SEE COLERIDGE, S.T.
COCATRE-ZILGIEN, A. DIPLOMATIC
FRANÇAISE ET PROBLÈMES INTERNA-
TIONAUX CONTEMPORAINS.
  R. FRÉCHET, 189(EA):APR-JUN72-
  339
COCHRANE, E. FLORENCE IN THE FOR-
GOTTEN CENTURIES, 1527-1800.
  J.H. ELLIOTT, 453:16MAY74-20
  J.H. PLUMB, 441:20JAN74-7
  617(TLS):26APR74-441
COCHRANE, I. GONE IN THE HEAD.
  J. MELLORS, 362:12SEP74-348
  617(TLS):18OCT74-1155
COCKBURN, C. THE DEVIL'S DECADE.*
  J. CAMERON, 441:10MAR74-6
  R.R. LINGEMAN, 441:2MAR74-29
  442(NY):20MAY74-151
COCKBURN, C. JERICHO ROAD.
  V. CUNNINGHAM, 362:9MAY74-606
  617(TLS):14JUN74-629
COCKERHAM, H. - SEE GAUTIER, T.
COCKSHUT, A.O.J. TRUTH TO LIFE.
  N. BLIVEN, 442(NY):30DEC74-62
  P. ROSENBERG, 441:22SEP74-27
  617(TLS):29MAR74-319
COCTEAU, J. BEAUTY & THE BEAST.
  639(VQR):WINTER73-XLI
COCTEAU, J. PROFESSIONAL SECRETS.*
(R. PHELPS, ED)
  J. HAMILTON, 157:WINTER72-78
CODIGNOLA, L. IL TEATRO DELLA
GUERRA FREDDA E ALTRE COSE.
  R. SCHWADERER, 52:BAND7HEFT2/3-
  339
CODY, J. AFTER GREAT PAIN.*
  S. DONALDSON, 432(NEQ):MAR72-127
  K. MC SWEENEY, 529(QQ):WINTER72-
  579
  F.L. MOREY, 613:SPRING72-124
  P. ROSENBLATT, 50(ARQ):SPRING72-
  92
CODY, J.P. TOP-SECRET KILL.
  N. CALLENDAR, 441:13OCT74-48
COE, R.N. - SEE STENDHAL
COE, T. DON'T LIE TO ME.
  617(TLS):30AUG74-933
COE, T. A JADE IN ARIES.
  617(TLS):25JAN74-88
COFFEY, B. SURROUNDED.
  N. CALLENDAR, 441:28JUL74-14

COFFEY, T.M. LION BY THE TAIL.
  H.L. MATTHEWS, 441:20OCT74-51
COFFIN, L.A., JR. & A.C. HOLDEN.
BRICK ARCHITECTURE OF THE COLONIAL
PERIOD IN MARYLAND & VIRGINIA.
  R.R., 505:SEP72-154
COGHILL, MRS. H. - SEE OLIPHANT, M.
COGHILL, N. CHAUCER'S IDEA OF WHAT
IS NODLE.
  D.S. BREWER, 382(MAE):1973/1-117
  G.C. BRITTON, 447(N&Q):JUL72-272
  R.M. WILSON, 402(MLR):JAN73-147
COGLEY, J. CATHOLIC AMERICA.*
  W. SHEED, 453:7MAR74-18
COHEN, A. TWO-DIMENSIONAL MAN.
  617(TLS):5JUL74-731
COHEN, A.A. IN THE DAYS OF SIMON
STERN.*
  E. ROVIT, 659:AUTUMN74-539
  617(TLS):15MAR74-269
COHEN, B.B., ED. THE RECOGNITION OF
NATHANIEL HAWTHORNE.*
  A. EASSON, 447(N&Q):NOV72-427
COHEN, D.S. THE RAMAPO MOUNTAIN
PEOPLE.
  M.T. KAUFMAN, 441:1NOV74-43
COHEN, D.W. & J.P. GREENE, EDS.
NEITHER SLAVE NOR FREE.
  639(VQR):SPRING73-LXXXIII
COHEN, I.B. INTRODUCTION TO NEW-
TON'S "PRINCIPIA."*
  G.A.J. ROGERS, 481(PQ):JUL72-738
COHEN, J.A., ED. CHINA'S PRACTICE
OF INTERNATIONAL LAW.
  639(VQR):AUTUMN73-CLXX
COHEN, J.A., R.F. DERABERGER & J.R.
GARSON. CHINA TRADE PROSPECTS &
U.S. POLICY. (A. ECKSTEIN, ED)
  F-H. MAH, 293(JAST):NOV71-201
COHEN, J.L. & J.A. CHINA TODAY.
  E. HAHN, 441:22DEC74-3
COHEN, L. THE ENERGY OF SLAVES.*
  M. ESTOK, 150(DR):WINTER72/73-
  653
  D. LEHMAN, 491:DEC73-173
COHEN, L.J. THE IMPLICATIONS OF
INDUCTION.*
  L.A., 543:DEC71-350
  B. CARR, 483:JAN72-85
  A.C. MICHALOS, 486:DEC72-566
COHEN, M. THE DISINHERITED.
  A. BRENNAN, 198:SUMMER74-107
COHEN, M. - SEE DOLBEN, D.M.
COHEN, P. THE GOSPEL ACCORDING TO
THE HARVARD BUSINESS SCHOOL.
  441:13OCT74-45
COHEN, R. CURRENTS IN CONTEMPORARY
DRAMA.
  J.D. ZIPES, 222(GR):JAN72-70
COHEN, R. LABOUR & POLITICS IN
NIGERIA.
  617(TLS):20SEP74-999
COHEN, R., ED. LET MY PEOPLE GO.
  J. GREENFIELD, 287:MAR72-28
COHEN, R. THE UNFOLDING OF "THE
SEASONS."*
  R. PARKIN, 173(ECS):FALL72-135
COHEN, R.J. HONORÉ DE BALZAC: "PÈRE
GORIOT."
  C.C., 191(ELN):SEP72(SUPP)-83
COHEN, R.M. & J. WITCOVER. A HEART-
BEAT AWAY.
  T. LIPPMAN, JR., 441:23JUN74-22
  442(NY):3JUN74-110

COHEN, S. & J. YOUNG, EDS. THE MANU-
FACTURE OF NEWS.
617(TLS):25JAN74-68
COHEN, S.F. BUKHARIN & THE BOLSHE-
VIK REVOLUTION.*
E.H. CARR, 617(TLS):20SEP74-989
L. SCHAPIRO, 453:7FEB74-3
442(NY):11FEB74-128
COHEN, S.P. THE INDIAN ARMY.
C.M. ELLIOTT, 293(JAST):MAY72-
703
COHEN, W.B. RULERS OF EMPIRE.
H. DESCHAMPS, 69:OCT72-345
COHN, H. THE TRIAL & DEATH OF JESUS.
A.R. ECKARDT, 390:MAR72-72
COHN, H.D. SOVIET POLICY TOWARD
BLACK AFRICA.
D.T. CATTELL, 32:DEC73-824
L.H. GANN, 550(RUSR):OCT72-420
COHN, H.W. ELSE LASKER-SCHÜLER.
617(TLS):25OCT74-1186
COHN, R.G. THE POETRY OF RIMBAUD.
617(TLS):28JUN74-690
COHN, R.G. TOWARD THE POEMS OF MAL-
LARMÉ.
L. CELLIER, 535(RHL):JAN-FEB72-
151
DE COINCI, G. - SEE UNDER GAUTIER DE
COINCI
COKE, V.D. THE PAINTER & THE PHOTO-
GRAPH FROM DELACROIX TO WARHOL.*
96:EARLY AUTUMN72-110
290(JAAC):WINTER72-280
COKER, W. MUSIC & MEANING.*
G. EPPERSON, 290(JAAC):SPRING73-
407
COLACLIDIS, P. CAVAFY ET DRECHT.
H. IOANNIDI, 98:APR72-354
COLBY, V. THE SINGULAR ANOMALY.*
P. THOMSON, 541(RES):NOV72-518
COLD, E. CHRISTUS ODER WAS IST AUF-
ERSTEHUNG.
É. DES PLACES, 555:VOL46FASC1-
130
COLE, B. MILES DAVIS.
J. WIDEMAN, 441:18AUG74-6
COLE, B. PATHETIC FALLACIES.*
R. GARFITT, 364:OCT/NOV73-114
COLE, D.C. & P.N. LYMAN. KOREAN
DEVELOPMENT.
P.W. KUZNETS, 293(JAST):NOV71-
207
COLE, H. SOUNDS & SIGNS.
617(TLS):1MAR74-216
COLE, H. THE WARS OF THE ROSES.
617(TLS):1MAR74-221
COLE, J.P. THE PROBLEMATIC SELF IN
KIERKEGAARD & FREUD.
B.S. LLAMZON, 613:AUTUMN72-472
COLE, M., ED. THE WEBBS & THEIR
WORK.
617(TLS):29NOV74-1347
COLE, R.E. JAPANESE BLUE COLLAR.
G. DE VOS, 293(JAST):MAY72-685
TAKAHASHI TAKESHI, 285(JAPQ):
JUL-SEP72-366
COLE, W.P. & C.F. MONTGOMERY - SEE
SHERATON, T.
COLE, W.S. CHARLES A. LINDBERGH &
THE BATTLE AGAINST AMERICAN INTER-
VENTION IN WORLD WAR II.
R. RADOSH, 441:29DEC74-4
COLEGATE, I. AGATHA.*
J. MELLORS, 364:FEB/MAR74-136

COLEMAN, A. OTHER VOICES.*
A.P. DEBICKI, 593:WINTER73-379
P. SILVER, 405(MP):AUG72-85
COLEMAN, D.G. RABELAIS.
B.C. BOWEN, 207(FR):MAY72-1197
D.M. FRAME, 546(RR):OCT72-229
G.M. MASTERS, 149:DEC73-395
R. WHITE, 67:MAY73-126
COLEMAN, F.X.J. THE AESTHETIC
THOUGHT OF THE FRENCH ENLIGHTEN-
MENT.*
G.C. RUMP, 182:VOL25#3/4-65
R.G. SAISSELIN, 290(JAAC):SUM-
MER72-566
481(PQ):JUL72-563
COLEMAN, J.R. BLUE-COLLAR JOURNAL.
B. DE MOTT, 61:AUG74-76
C. LEHMANN-HAUPT, 441:4APR74-45
COLEMAN, J.S. & OTHERS. YOUTH.
J. KARABEL, 441:15SEP74-48
COLEMAN, J.W., JR., ED. KENTUCKY.
639(VQR):SPRING72-LXXIV
COLEMAN, L. BEULAH LAND.*
617(TLS):15FEB74-149
COLERIDGE, S.T. COLERIDGE ON SHAKE-
SPEARE. (R.A. FOAKES, ED)
639(VQR):SPRING72-LVII
COLERIDGE, S.T. COLLECTED LETTERS
OF SAMUEL TAYLOR COLERIDGE. (VOLS
5&6) (E.L. GRIGGS, ED)
R.L. BRETT, 541(RES):AUG72-367
COLERIDGE, S.T. THE COLLECTED WORKS
OF SAMUEL TAYLOR COLERIDGE: LEC-
TURES 1795 ON POLITICS & RELIGION.*
(L. PATTON & P. MANN, EDS)
G. CARNALL, 402(MLR):JUL73-639
COLERIDGE, S.T. THE COLLECTED WORKS
OF SAMUEL TAYLOR COLERIDGE: THE
FRIEND.* (B.E. ROOKE, ED)
T.H. LANDESS, 569(SR):AUTUMN73-
847
S. PRICKETT, 447(N&Q):MAR72-116
COLERIDGE, S.T. THE COLLECTED WORKS
OF SAMUEL TAYLOR COLERIDGE: THE
WATCHMAN.* (L. PATTON, ED)
T.H. LANDESS, 569(SR):AUTUMN73-
847
COLERIDGE, S.T. THE NOTEBOOKS OF
SAMUEL TAYLOR COLERIDGE. (VOL 3)
(K. COBURN, ED)
617(TLS):24MAY74-541
COLES, J. ARCHAEOLOGY BY EXPERIMENT.
P. ADAMS, 61:DEC74-127
COLES, R. THE OLD ONES OF NEW MEXI-
CO.
442(NY):14JAN74-98
COLETTE. THE EVENING STAR.
A. BROYARD, 441:18SEP74-45
E. WEEKS, 61:SEP74-102
442(NY):11NOV74-213
COLETTE. RETREAT FROM LOVE.
S. MAITLAND, 362:12DEC74-786
E. WEEKS, 61:SEP74-102
B. WRIGHT, 617(TLS):13DEC74-1420
442(NY):26AUG74-90
COLETTE. THE THOUSAND & ONE MORN-
INGS.*
R. TONKS, 453:24JAN74-3
442(NY):14JAN74-99
COLIE, R.L. "MY ECCHOING SONG."*
R.M. CUMMINGS, 405(MP):AUG72-66
L.A. DAVIES, 402(MLR):JAN73-156
D.I.B. SMITH, 627(UTQ):AUTUMN71-
84

COLIE, R.L.   THE RESOURCES OF KIND.
  617(TLS):9AUG74-864
COLIN, J.   NEVER HAD IT SO GOOD.
  617(TLS):9AUG74-858
COLIN, J-P.   NOUVEAU DICTIONNAIRE
  DES DIFFICULTÉS DU FRANÇAIS.
  R. ARVEILLER, 209(FM):OCT72-352
COLISH, M.L.   THE MIRROR OF LANGU-
  AGE.*
  W.K. PERCIVAL, 206:MAY72-413
COLLART, J. - SEE PLAUTUS
COLLEY, C.C., COMP.   DOCUMENTS OF
  SOUTHWESTERN HISTORY.
  L.C. POWELL, 517(PBSA):OCT-DEC73-
  472
COLLIER, B.   THE AIRSHIP.
  617(TLS):25OCT74-1208
COLLIER, B.   A HISTORY OF AIR POWER.
  617(TLS):19APR74-425
COLLIER, C.   ROGER SHERMAN'S CONNEC-
  TICUT.*
  J. DANIELL, 656(WMQ):JUL72-499
  G. WEAVER, 481(PQ):JUL72-525
COLLIER, G.   ART & THE CREATIVE CON-
  SCIOUSNESS.
  H.P. RALEIGH, 290(JAAC):SUMMER
  73-553
COLLIER, J.   MILTON'S "PARADISE
  LOST."*
  639(VQR):AUTUMN73-CXLII
COLLIER, J.F.   LAW & SOCIAL CHANGE
  IN ZINACANTAN.
  L. WHITEHEAD, 617(TLS):30AUG74-
  926
COLLIER, W.   HISTORIC BUILDINGS.
  617(TLS):8MAR74-244
COLLIER, W. - SEE PARKINSON, J.
COLLIN, F.   MAURICE BLANCHOT ET LA
  QUESTION DE L'ÉCRITURE.
  J. CULLER, 208(FS):APR73-231
  R.F. ROEMING, 399(MLJ):JAN72-56
  E. ZANTS, 207(FR):APR72-1048
COLLINDER, B.   DER SPRACHFORSCHER
  "BEHIND THE LOOKING-GLASS."
  B. ROSENKRANZ, 343:BAND15HEFT1-
  104
COLLINDER, B., H. FROMM & G. GAN-
  SCHOW - SEE SCHLACHTER, W.
COLLINGE, N.E.   COLLECTANEA LINGUIS-
  TICA.
  R.H. ROBINS, 361:VOL29#1-82
COLLINGWOOD, R.G.   THE ARCHAEOLOGY
  OF ROMAN BRITAIN.*   (REV BY I.
  RICHMOND)
  C.M. WELLS, 487:SPRING72-103
COLLINS, E.J.T. - SEE WHITE, K.D.
COLLINS, F., JR.   THE PRODUCTION OF
  MEDIEVAL CHURCH MUSIC-DRAMA.*
  G. FRANK, 589:OCT73-738
  W.L.S., 410(M&L):JAN73-87
  J. STEVENS, 415:MAY73-494
COLLINS, J.   INTERPRETING MODERN
  PHILOSOPHY.*
  A.W. LEVI, 377:MAR73-51
COLLINS, K.T. & OTHERS.   KEY WORDS
  IN EDUCATION.
  617(TLS):14JUN74-636
COLLINS, L. & D. LAPIERRE.   O JERUSA-
  LEM!
  R. SANDERS, 390:NOV72-56
COLLINS, M.   CARRYING THE FIRE.
  H.S.F. COOPER, JR., 441:11AUG74-
  1
  E. WEEKS, 61:SEP74-100
  442(NY):2SEP74-84

COLLINS, P.   ARCHITECTURAL JUDGE-
  MENT.*
  C. JENCKS, 46:JAN72-65
  L.N. KREMER, 576:MAR72-78
COLLINS, P., ED.   DICKENS: THE CRITI-
  CAL HERITAGE.*
  A.P. ROBSON, 637(VS):JUN72-475
COLLINS, P. - SEE DICKENS, C.
COLLINS, T.J. - SEE BROWNING, R. &
  E.B.
COLLIS, L.   A PRIVATE VIEW OF STAN-
  LEY SPENCER.
  C. SHIELDS, 592:MAR72-138
"COLLOQUE COMMÉMORATIF DU QUATRIÈME
  CENTENAIRE DE LA NAISSANCE D'HON-
  ORÉ D'URFÉ."
  J. BAILBÉ, 535(RHL):MAR-APR72-
  304
COLODNY, R.G., ED.   ESSAYS IN CONTEM-
  PORARY SCIENCE & PHILOSOPHY.
  (VOLS 3 & 4)
  J. DORLING, 84:MAY72-181
COLODNY, R.G., ED.   THE NATURE &
  FUNCTION OF SCIENTIFIC THEORIES.*
  P. PARRINI, 548(RCSF):JAN-MAR72-
  115
COLOMBO, J.R.   THE GREAT SAN FRAN-
  CISCO EARTHQUAKE & FIRE.*
  D. BARBOUR, 150(DR):SPRING72-167
DE COLONNA, G. - SEE UNDER GUIDO DE
  COLONNA
COLONNA DI PAOLO, E. & G. COLONNA.
  CASTEL D'ASSO.
  D. RIDGWAY, 313:VOL62-201
COLTER, C.   THE HIPPODROME.
  42(AR):VOL32#4-699
COLTER, C.   THE RIVERS OF EROS.
  E. ROVIT, 659:AUTUMN74-539
COLVIN, C. - SEE EDGEWORTH, M.
COLVIN, H.M., ED.   THE BUILDING
  ACCOUNTS OF KING HENRY III.
  A.G. DYSON, 325:OCT72-537
  T.G. HASSALL, 382(MAE):1973/3-
  297
  P. KIDSON, 46:SEP72-191
  L.R. SHELBY, 589:JAN73-125
COLWIN, L.   PASSION & AFFECT.
  A. BROYARD, 441:24JAN74-41
COMBÈS, M.   FONDEMENTS DES MATHÉ-
  MATIQUES.
  Y. GAUTHIER, 154:MAR72-172
COMBÈS, R. - SEE CICERO
COMBLIN, J.   THÉOLOGIE DE LA RÉVOLU-
  TION.
  H. DECLÈVE, 154:MAR72-86
COMENIUS, J.A.   THE LABYRINTH OF THE
  WORLD & THE PARADISE OF THE HEART.
  (M. SPINKA, TRANS)
  Z.V. DAVID, 32:SEP73-641
  J.J. TOMIAK, 575(SEER):OCT73-623
COMER, J.P.   BEYOND BLACK & WHITE.
  B. DE MOTT, 441:14JUL74-29
COMMAGER, H.S., ED.   BRITAIN THROUGH
  AMERICAN EYES.
  S. KOSS, 617(TLS):27SEP74-1041
COMMONER, B.   THE CLOSING CIRCLE.
  H.B. HOUGH, 31(ASCH):WINTER73/74-
  152
  A.M. WEINBERG, 639(VQR):SPRING72-
  277
"COMMUNICATION WITH EXTRATERRESTRIAL
  INTELLIGENCE."
  A. ADLER, 61:OCT74-109

"THE COMPLETE FILMS OF EISENSTEIN."
(J. HETHERINGTON, TRANS)
617(TLS):16AUG74-882
COMPTON, D.G. THE CONTINUOUS KATH-
ERINE MORTENHOE.
617(TLS):31MAY74-591
COMPTON-BURNETT, I. THE LAST & THE
FIRST.
C. DRESSLER, 189(EA):OCT-DEC72-
577
COMTE, A. CORRESPONDANCE GÉNÉRALE
ET CONFESSIONS. (VOL 1) (P.E. DE
BERRÊDO CARNEIRO & P. ARNAUD, EDS)
617(TLS):4JAN74-1
COMTE, A. THE ESSENTIAL COMTE. (S.
ANDRESKI, ED)
617(TLS):26APR74-430
COMTE, A. OPUSCOLI DI FILOSOFIA
SOCIALE. (A. NEGRI, ED & TRANS)
E. NAMER, 542:JUL-SEP72-344
COMYN, J. THEIR FRIENDS AT COURT.
617(TLS):31MAY74-583
CONARROE, J. WILLIAM CARLOS WIL-
LIAMS' "PATERSON."*
M. NEUSSENDORFER, 613:SPRING72-
129
"CONCISE GUIDE TO THE STATE ARCHIVES
OF NEW SOUTH WALES."
M. PAMPLIN, 325:APR72-454
CONDON, R. THE VERTICAL SMILE.
C. DONNELLY, 159(DM):SUMMER72-
129
CONDON, R. WINTER KILLS.
L. BRAUDY, 441:26MAY74-5
C. LEHMANN-HAUPT, 441:24MAY74-37
617(TLS):20SEP74-993
CONE, E.T. MUSICAL FORM & MUSICAL
PERFORMANCE.
W. BERRY, 513:SPRING-SUMMER/FALL-
WINTER71-271
CONEY, M. FRIENDS COME IN BOXES.
617(TLS):10MAY74-493
CONEY, M.G. MONITOR FOUND IN ORBIT.
T. STURGEON, 441:10NOV74-50
CONEY, M.G. SYZYGY.
617(TLS):15MAR74-269
CONFINO, M., ED. DAUGHTER OF A
REVOLUTIONARY.
J. DUNN, 362:13JUN74-775
M. GALLANT, 441:6OCT74-27
CONKLIN, D.W. AN EVALUATION OF THE
SOVIET PROFIT REFORMS.*
J.R. MILLAR, 550(RUSR):JAN72-93
CONLON, D.J., ED. LE ROMMANT DE GUY
DE WARWIK ET DE HEROLT D'ARDENNE.
L. THORPE, 382(MAE):1973/1-65
CONLON, D.J. - SEE SARTRE, J-P.
CONLON, P.M. PRÉLUDE AU SIÈCLE DES
LUMIÈRES EN FRANCE. (VOLS 1&3)
R. GRIMSLEY, 402(MLR):JAN73-174
CONLON, P.M. PRÉLUDE AU SIÈCLE DES
LUMIÈRES EN FRANCE.* (VOL 2)
R. GRIMSLEY, 402(MLR):JAN73-174
P. LE CLERC, 207(FR):FEB72-740
M. LEVER, 535(RHL):JUL-AUG72-713
J. LOUGH, 208(FS):APR73-206
R. MERCIER, 557(RSH):JUL-SEP72-
452
CONN, S., ED. NEW POEMS 1973-1974.
617(TLS):23AUG74-904
CONNELL, D. THE VISION IN GOD.
P. DUBOIS, 542:APR-JUN72-215

CONNELL, E.S., JR. THE CONNOISSEUR.
G. DAVENPORT, 441:1SEP74-4
C. LEHMANN-HAUPT, 441:11SEP74-49
E. WEEKS, 61:SEP74-102
M. WOOD, 453:28NOV74-29
442(NY):14OCT74-199
CONNELL, E.S., JR. POINTS FOR A COM-
PASS ROSE.* NOTES FROM A BOTTLE
FOUND ON THE BEACH AT CARMEL.
A. DILLARD, 231:JAN74-87
CONNELLY, T.L. & A. JONES. THE
POLITICS OF COMMAND.
639(VQR):AUTUMN73-CLXIV
CONNOLLY, E. LEOPOLDO PANERO.*
B. CIPLIJAUSKAITÉ, 546(RR):OCT72-
247
M.P. PREDMORE, 240(HR):SUMMER72-
353
CONNOLLY, J. SELECTED WRITINGS.
(P.B. ELLIS, ED) SELECTED POLITI-
CAL WRITINGS. (O.D. EDWARDS & B.
RANSOM, EDS)
617(TLS):11JAN74-26
CONNOR, H.G. JOHN ARCHIBALD CAMP-
BELL, ASSOCIATE JUSTICE OF THE
UNITED STATES SUPREME COURT, 1853-
1861.
L.R. ATKINS, 9(ALAR):APR72-151
CONNOR, T. IN THE HAPPY VALLEY.*
J.W. HEALEY, 502(PRS):SUMMER72-
183
639(VQR):WINTER72-XXIII
CONNOR, T. THE MEMOIRS OF UNCLE
HARRY.
617(TLS):13SEP74-968
CONNOR, T. SEVEN LAST POEMS FROM
THE MEMOIRS OF UNCLE HENRY.
617(TLS):11OCT74-1119
CONNOR, W.D. DEVIANCE IN SOVIET
SOCIETY.
R.J. OSBORN, 32:SEP73-625
CONNOR, W.R. THE NEW POLITICIANS OF
FIFTH-CENTURY ATHENS.*
C. MOSSE, 303:VOL92-226
CONOT, R. AMERICAN ODYSSEY.
R. LOTCHIN, 441:30JUN74-3
S.R. WEISMAN, 441:30AUG74-27
CONOVER, H.F., COMP. NIGERIAN OFFI-
CIAL PUBLICATIONS, 1869-1959.
OFFICIAL PUBLICATIONS OF SOMALI-
LAND, 1941-1959. OFFICIAL PUBLI-
CATIONS OF FRENCH WEST AFRICA,
1946-1958. OFFICIAL PUBLICATIONS
OF BRITISH EAST AFRICA. (PT 1)
J.A. CASADA, 517(PBSA):APR-JUN73-
207
CONQUEST, R. V.I. LENIN.
639(VQR):SPRING73-LXXVII
CONQUEST, R., ED. THE SOVIET POLICE
SYSTEM.
R.M. SLUSSER, 32:DEC73-825
CONQUEST, R. - SEE YAKIR, P.
CONRAD, B. MY FATHER: JOSEPH CON-
RAD.*
W. ROWE, 619(TC):VOL177#1043-60
CONRAD, J. CONRAD'S MANIFESTO.
(D.R. SMITH, ED)
I. VIDAN, 136:VOL4#2-73
CONRAD, R. THE DESTRUCTION OF BRA-
ZILIAN SLAVERY, 1850-1888.
639(VQR):SUMMER73-CXXII
CONRAN, A. POEMS 1951-67.
617(TLS):4OCT74-1069

CONROW, R. FIELD DAYS.
P. ADAMS, 61:OCT74-119
"JOHN CONSTABLE'S DISCOURSES."
(R.B. BECKETT, ED)
K. GARLICK, 90:MAR72-185
"BENJAMIN CONSTANT: ACTES DU CON-
GRÈS DE LAUSANNE."*
L.M. CELLIER, 546(RR):FEB72-52
B. DIDIER, 535(RHL):MAR-APR72-
319
CONSTANTINE, K.C. THE MAN WHO LIKED
TO LOOK AT HIMSELF.*
P. ADAMS, 61:JAN74-99
CONSTANTINE, M. & A. FERN. REVOLU-
TIONARY SOVIET FILM POSTERS.
J. RUSSELL, 441:1DEC74-55
CONTINI, G. UNA LUNGA FEDELTÀ.
ESERCIZÎ DI LETTURA SOPRA AUTORI
CONTEMPORANEI CON UN'APPENDICE SU
TESTI NON CONTEMPORANEI. (NEW ED)
C. JAMES, 617(TLS):22NOV74-1312
"CONTRIBUTI DELL'ISTITUTO DI FILO-
LOGIA MODERNA." (SER FRANCESE,
VOL 6)
A. MICHEL, 557(RSH):JUL-SEP72-
460
"CONTRIBUTIONS TO INDIAN SOCIOLOGY."
(NEW SER, NO. 3)
H.A. GOULD, 293(JAST):AUG72-963
CONWAY, D. MAGIC.
H. LOMAS, 364:JUN/JUL72-149
COOK, A. THE ARMIES OF THE STREETS.
442(NY):8APR74-143
COOK, B. THE BEAT GENERATION.*
K. CONGDON, 37:APR72-42
COOK, B. LISTEN TO THE BLUES.
F. CONROY, 441:3FEB74-5
COOK, C. & J. RAMSDEN, EDS. BY-ELEC-
TIONS IN BRITISH POLITICS.
617(TLS):1FEB74-101
COOK, D. ALBERT'S MEMORIAL.
E. FEINSTEIN, 364:JUN/JUL72-166
COOK, D. HAPPY ENDINGS.
J. MELLORS, 362:12SEP74-348
617(TLS):6SEP74-945
COOK, K. BLOODHOUSE.
617(TLS):22NOV74-1308
COOK, K.J. SWINDON STEAM, 1921-1951.
617(TLS):14JUN74-647
COOK, L. THE BRIDGE.
J. BARNES, 617(TLS):13DEC74-1420
COOK, M.A., ED. STUDIES IN THE ECO-
NOMIC HISTORY OF THE MIDDLE EAST
FROM THE RISE OF ISLAM TO THE PRES-
ENT DAY.
G.T. SCANLON, 318(JAOS):APR-JUN
72-388
COOK, O. THE ENGLISH COUNTRY HOUSE.
442(NY):9DEC74-196
COOK, S. FORM PHOTOGRAPH.
J. SAUNDERS, 565:VOL13#3-75
COOK, W.A. INTRODUCTION TO TAGMEMIC
ANALYSIS.*
R.H. ROBINS, 269(IJAL):APR72-147
W.P. ROHDE, 353:MAY72-98
COOK, W.J., JR. MASKS, MODES, &
MORALS.
R.M. DAVIS, 594:SPRING72-114
COOK, W.L. FLOOD TIDE OF EMPIRE.*
639(VQR):SUMMER73-CXXI
COOK-GUMPERZ, J. SOCIAL CONTROL &
SOCIALIZATION.
617(TLS):31MAY74-580

COOKE, A.B. & J. VINCENT. THE GOV-
ERNING PASSION.
R. MITCHISON, 362:14MAR74-341
617(TLS):21JUN74-664
"ALISTAIR COOKE'S AMERICA."*
E. WEEKS, 61:JAN74-98
COOKE, J.R. PRONOMINAL REFERENCE IN
THAI, BURMESE, & VIETNAMESE.*
R.N. CAMPBELL, 318(JAOS):JAN-
MAR72-158
G.F. MEIER, 682(ZPSK):BAND25
HEFT4/5-428
COOKE, K. A.C. BRADLEY & HIS INFLU-
ENCE IN TWENTIETH-CENTURY SHAKE-
SPEARE CRITICISM.
R.W. POWELL, 67:NOV73-293
D.A. TRAVERSI, 401(MLQ):SEP73-
312
639(VQR):WINTER73-XXIV
COOKE, M.G., ED. MODERN BLACK NOV-
ELISTS.
B. BECKHAM, 454:SPRING73-266
COOKE, W. EDWARD THOMAS.*
W.J. KEITH, 627(UTQ):AUTUMN71-74
COOKRIDGE, E.H. GEHLEN.
O.J. HALE, 639(VQR):WINTER73-126
COOKSON, C. OUR JOHN WILLIE.
M. LEVIN, 441:20OCT74-41
COOKSON, W. - SEE POUND, E.
COOLIDGE, J.S. THE PAULINE RENAIS-
SANCE IN ENGLAND.*
L.H. CARLSON, 551(RENQ):AUTUMN72-
346
COOMBES, B.L. THESE POOR HANDS.
617(TLS):26JUL74-810
COOPER, B. & M. MATHESON, EDS. THE
WORLD MUSEUMS GUIDE.
617(TLS):12APR74-400
COOPER, D. THE GRAMMAR OF LIVING.
P. LOMAS, 617(TLS):25OCT74-1193
COOPER, D. THE GULLIBILITY GAP.
R. GILBERT, 362:5DEC74-750
COOPER, E. THE TENTH PLANET.
617(TLS):15FEB74-163
COOPER, G.L., 3D. ZUR SYNTAKTISCHEN
THEORIE UND TEXTKRITIK DER ATTIS-
CHEN AUTOREN.
J.W. POULTNEY, 24:FALL73-313
COOPER, I.S. THE VICTIM IS ALWAYS
THE SAME.*
R. COLES, 442(NY):29APR74-131
COOPER, J.F. THE LETTERS & JOURNALS
OF JAMES FENIMORE COOPER. (VOLS
5&6) (J.F. BEARD, ED)
K. REMMEN, 72:BAND210HEFT4/6-417
COOPER, L. A HAND UPON THE TIME.
155:MAY72-131
COOPER, M., ED. THE NEW OXFORD HIS-
TORY OF MUSIC. (VOL 10)
R. MACONIE, 617(TLS):6DEC74-1395
COOPER, R.M. LOST ON BOTH SIDES.
G.P. LANDOW, 290(JAAC):SPRING73-
422
J.L. MAHONEY, 613:SPRING72-136
COOPERMAN, S. CANNIBALS.
M. ESTOK, 150(DR):WINTER72/73-
653
COOPERSMITH, S., ED. FRONTIERS OF
PSYCHOLOGICAL RESEARCH.
M. CHASTAING, 542:OCT-DEC72-453
COOTE, A. & T. GILL. WOMEN'S RIGHTS.
617(TLS):26APR74-455

COOVER, J. MUSIC LEXICOGRAPHY.
(3RD ED)
J.A.W., 410(M&L):APR73-223
COOVER, R. A THEOLOGICAL POSITION.
B.H. FUSSELL, 249(HUDR):WINTER
73/74-753
N. SCHMITZ, 473(PR):WINTER73-131
COPE, J. ALLEY CAT.*
E. FEINSTEIN, 364:OCT/NOV73-154
COPEAU, J. APPELS. (M-H. DASTÉ,
S.M. SAINT-DENIS & C. SICARD, EDS)
R. SPEAIGHT, 617(TLS):6DEC74-
1391
COPELAND, M. WITHOUT CLOAK OR DAG-
GER.
M. BURKE, 441:18AUG74-5
R.T. WOOD, 231:JUN74-89
442(NY):23SEP74-144
COPERNICUS, N. DE REVOLUTIONIBUS.
J. NORTH, 617(TLS):22NOV74-1310
COPI, I.M. THE THEORY OF LOGICAL
TYPES.*
A. SLOMSON, 479(PHQ):JUL72-275
COPLANS, J. ELLSWORTH KELLY.*
A. FRANKENSTEIN, 55:NOV73-48
COPLESTON, F.C. A HISTORY OF PHIL-
OSOPHY. (VOL 3)
J. PUCELLE, 542:JAN-MAR72-89
COPP, T. THE ANATOMY OF POVERTY.
T. TRAVES, 99:NOV/DEC74-45
COPPARD, A.E. SELECTED STORIES.
E. FEINSTEIN, 364:AUG/SEP72-157
COPPEL, A. THIRTY-FOUR EAST.
M. LEVIN, 441:28APR74-38
CORBETT, E.P.J., ED. RHETORICAL
ANALYSES OF LITERARY WORKS.*
W.R. BROWN, 599:FALL72-311
"HELEN CORBITT COOKS FOR COMPANY."
N. HAZELTON, 441:1DEC74-94
CORDERO, F. VIENE IL RE.
617(TLS):17MAY74-517
CORDERO, H.A. VALORACIÓN DEL MARTÍN
FIERRO.
M.A. CASARTELLI, 263:APR-JUN73-
192
CORDINGLY, D. MARINE PAINTING IN
ENGLAND 1700-1900.
617(TLS):24MAY74-563
DE CÓRDOBA, S. GARCILASO A LO DIV-
INO. (G.R. GALE, ED)
B.W. WARDROPPER, 402(MLR):OCT73-
913
CORDRY, D. & D. MEXICAN INDIAN COS-
TUMES.
D. YODER, 292(JAF):APR-JUN72-196
COREN, A. THE COLLECTED BULLETINS
OF PRESIDENT AMIN.
K. KYLE, 362:4JUL74-27
CORINO, K. ROBERT MUSIL - THOMAS
MANN.
E. HILSCHER, 654(WB):2/1972-183
CORLEY, E. ACAPULCO GOLD.
617(TLS):1MAR74-219
CORLISS, R. TALKING PICTURES.
M. WOOD, 453:31OCT74-39
CORLU, A. - SEE PLUTARCH
CORMAN, C. - SEE PONGE, F.
CORMAN, C. & KAMAIKE SUSUMU - SEE
BASHŌ
CORMIER, R.J. & U.T. HOLMES, EDS.
ESSAYS IN HONOR OF LOUIS FRANCIS
SOLANO.
M.B. SPEER, 207(FR):DEC71-542

CORNATON, M. GROUPES ET SOCIÉTÉ.
E. NAMER, 542:OCT-DEC72-505
CORNEA, P. ORIGINILE ROMANTISMULUI
ROMÂNESC.
P. TEODOR, 32:SEP73-651
CORNEILLE, P. POMPÉE.* (H.T. BARN-
WELL, ED)
M-O. SWEETSER, 207(FR):DEC71-524
P.J. YARROW, 208(FS):APR73-197
CORNEILLE, P. SURÉNA, GÉNÉRAL DES
PARTHES.* (J. SANCHEZ, ED)
W.L. WILEY, 207(FR):DEC71-525
CORNEILLE, T. TIMOCRATE. (Y. GIR-
AUD, ED)
W.L. WILEY, 207(FR):DEC71-525
CORNEILLE, T. & D. DE VISÉ. LA
DEVINERESSE. (P.J. YARROW, ED)
A. NIDERST, 535(RHL):SEP-DEC72-
1097
CORNÉLIS, H. LES FONDEMENTS COSMOL-
OGIQUES DE L'ESCHATOLOGIE D'ORI-
GÈNE.
A. FOREST, 542:JAN-MAR72-64
CORNELISEN, A. VENDETTA OF SILENCE.*
D.M. KENNEDY, 385(MQR):WINTER74-
85
CORNELIUS, P. LITERARISCHE WERKE.
H.M. SCHUELLER, 290(JAAC):WINTER
71-273
CORNET, J. ART OF AFRICA: TREASURES
FROM THE CONGO.
C. HARRISON, 592:JUL/AUG72-52
E.L.R. MEYEROWITZ, 39:AUG72-165
CORNEVIN, R. LE THÉÂTRE EN AFRIQUE
NOIRE ET À MADAGASCAR.*
R.E. HARRIS, 207(FR):MAR72-907
CORREA, G. LA POESÍA MÍTICA DE FED-
ERICO GARCÍA LORCA.
H.T. YOUNG, 238:MAY72-385
CORREA CALDERÓN, E. - SEE GRACIÁN, B.
CORRIGAN, D.F. - SEE SASSOON, S.
"CORRIGENDA & ADDENDA TO THE CATA-
LOGUE OF PAINTINGS & DRAWINGS AT
56, PRINCES GATE, LONDON SW7."
K.R., 90:JUN72-444
CORRY, J.A. THE POWER OF THE LAW.
R.C. ELLSWORTH, 529(QQ):SUMMER72-
263
CORSANO, A. TOMMASO CAMPANELLA.
E. NAMER, 542:JAN-MAR72-103
CORSANO, A. SCIENZA E FILOSOFIA NEL
TARDO RINASCIMENTO.
E. NAMER, 542:JAN-MAR72-106
CORSANO, A. GIULIO CESARE VANINI.
E. NAMER, 542:JAN-MAR72-111
CORSANO, A. VANINI ED ENRICO SILVIO.
E. NAMER, 542:JAN-MAR72-110
CORTÁZAR, J. ALL FIRES THE FIRE.*
J. UPDIKE, 442(NY):25FEB74-124
CORTÁZAR, J. 62: A MODEL KIT.*
639(VQR):SPRING73-LX
DELLA CORTE, F. VARRONE. (2ND ED)
A. ERNOUT, 555:VOL46FASC1-161
CORTELAZZO, M. L'INFLUSSO LINGUIS-
TICO GRECO A VENEZIA.*
V. LUCCHESI, 402(MLR):JAN73-188
CORTI, M. METODI E FANTASMI.
B.L., 275(IQ):FALL/WINTER72-128
CORTI, M. & C. SEGRE, EDS. I METODI
ATTUALI DELLA CRITICA IN ITALIA.
B.L., 275(IQ):FALL/WINTER72-129
CORTI, W.R., ED. THE PHILOSOPHY OF
GEORGE HERBERT MEAD.
J. GOHEEN, 319:JUL74-411

75

CORY, D. A BIT OF A SHUNT UP THE
RIVER.
N. CALLENDAR, 441:7JUL74-18
COSELL, H. LIKE IT IS.
R.W. CREAMER, 441:1DEC74-90
COSER, L.A. - SEE SCHELER, M.
COSGRAVE, P. CHURCHILL AT WAR.
(VOL 1)
J. GRIGG, 362:25JUL74-123
617(TLS):23AUG74-895
COSSÍO, M.B. EL GRECO. (N. COSSÍO
DE JIMÉNEZ, ED)
617(TLS):5APR74-358
COSSÍO WOODWARD, M. SACCHARIO.
K. SCHWARTZ, 238:MAR72-186
COSTA, C.D.N., ED. HORACE.
617(TLS):8MAR74-232
COSTA, R.H. MALCOLM LOWRY.
S. GRACE, 296:VOL3#1-105
COSTA VIVA, O. PEDRO SALINAS FRENTE
A LA REALIDAD.
J. GONZÁLEZ MUELA, 240(HR):WIN-
TER72-103
COSTANZO, M. CRITICA E POETICA DEL
PRIMO SEICENTO, DEL PRIMO NOVE-
CENTO, DEI CONTEMPORANEI.
R.W. KRETSCH, 290(JAAC):SPRING72-
398
COSTE, D. POUR MON HERBE.
T. GREENE, 207(FR):OCT71-199
COSTE, D. SINK YOUR TEETH IN THE
MOON.
617(TLS):7JUN74-619
COSTONIS, J.J. SPACE ADRIFT.
P. GOLDBERGER, 441:7JUL74-5
CÔTÉ, D.G., S.N. LEVY & P. O'CONNOR.
PREMIÈRE ETAPE.
P. ARSENAULT, 207(FR):DEC71-544
COTRAN, E. & N.N. RUBIN. READINGS
IN AFRICAN LAW.
J. VANDERLINDEN, 69:OCT72-351
COTTER, J.F. INSCAPE.*
N. WHITE, 637(VS):JUN73-470
COTTERELL, A.F. THE NUTTERS & OTHER
PLAYS.
A. RENDLE, 157:WINTER71-77
COTTIN, M. - SEE GAUTIER, T.
COTTLE, T.J. BLACK CHILDREN, WHITE
DREAMS.
P. ADAMS, 61:MAR74-98
S. BLACKBURN, 441:3MAR74-10
COTTRELL, A.P. WILHELM MÜLLER'S
LYRICAL SONG-CYCLES.*
S.P. SCHER, 301(JEGP):APR73-290
F.M. WASSERMANN, 221(GQ):JAN72-
170
COTTRELL, R.D. & J.E. RÉPONDEZ-MOI!
W. STAAKS, 207(FR):OCT71-290
COUGHLAN, R. ELIZABETH & CATHERINE.
E. WEEKS, 61:MAR74-96
COULETTE, H. THE FAMILY GOLD-
SCHMITT.*
D.L. KUBAL, 50(ARQ):SUMMER72-185
COULONGES, G. LA COMMUNE EN CHAN-
TANT.
P. AUBERY, 207(FR):DEC71-454
COULSON, J. NEWMAN & THE COMMON TRA-
DITION.
D.J. DE LAURA, 637(VS):MAR72-371
COUNTS, C. COMMON CLAY.
S. PETERSON, 139:APR72-10
COUPERIE, P. PARIS THROUGH THE AGES.
(FRENCH TITLE: PARIS AU FIL DU
TEMPS.)
M. LAVANOUX, 363:FEB72-78

COUPEZ, A. & T. KAMANZI, EDS. LIT-
TÉRATURE DE COUR AU RWANDA.*
E. SELLIN, 207(FR):DEC71-541
COURLANDER, H. THE DRUM & THE HOE.
D.B. WELCH, 187:SEP74-460
COURTENS, A. ROMANESQUE ART IN
BELGIUM.
E.G. CARLSON, 54:JUN72-203
COURTHION, P. IMPRESSIONISM.
A. FRANKENSTEIN, 55:FEB73-15
COURTINE, R.J. FEASTS OF A MILITANT
GASTRONOME.
N. HAZELTON, 441:1DEC74-96
R.A. SOKOLOV, 441:27OCT74-18
COURTNEY, E. - SEE VALERIUS FLACCUS,
G.
COUSINS, N. - SEE BROWN, J.M.
COUSTILLAS, P. - SEE GISSING, G.
COUTANT, V. - SEE THEOPHRASTUS
COUTON, G. - SEE MOLIÈRE, J.B.P.
COUTON, G. & J. JEHASSE - SEE PASCAL,
B.
COUTON, G., WITH C. LONGEON - SEE
DONNET, L.J.
COVELL, J.C. MASTERPIECES OF JAPAN-
ESE SCREEN PAINTING.
A. SOPER, 57:VOL34#2/3-252
COWAN, J.C. D.H. LAWRENCE'S AMERI-
CAN JOURNEY.*
E. DELAVENAY, 189(EA):JAN-MAR72-
171
COWAN, P., N. EGLESON & N. HENTOFF.
STATE SECRETS.
R. HOLBROOKE, 441:16JUN74-4
A. KOPKIND, 453:30MAY74-21
COWASJEE, S. GOODBYE TO ELSA.
R. BLYTHE, 362:21MAR74-381
J. DREW, 99:MAY/JUN74-19
O. MURAD, 268:JUL74-151
E.J. ZINKHAN, 296:VOL3#3-97
617(TLS):22MAR74-282
COWDREY, H.E.J. THE CLUNIACS & THE
GREGORIAN REFORM.*
M.D. LEGGE, 208(FS):OCT73-441
COWDREY, H.E.J. - SEE POPE GREGORY
VII
COWELL, A. THE TRIBE THAT HIDES
FROM MAN.
617(TLS):18JAN74-58
COWEN, R.C. NEUNZEHNTES JAHRHUN-
DERT, 1830-1880.* [SHOWN IN PREV
UNDER SER TITLE: HANDBUCH DER
DEUTSCHEN LITERATURGESCHICHTE:
BIBLIOGRAPHIEN. (VOL 9)]
R. FOLTER, 301(JEGP):JAN73-107
E. MC INNES, 220(GL&L):JUL73-353
H. THOMKE, 182:VOL25#22-797
E. THURNHER, 133:1972/1-102
COWEN, R.C. - SEE GRILLPARZER, F.
COWING, C.B. THE GREAT AWAKENING &
THE AMERICAN REVOLUTION.
H.R. CEDERBERG, 481(PQ):JUL72-
564
COWLES, V. THE ROTHSCHILDS.*
442(NY):28JAN74-103
COWLEY, A. THE CIVIL WAR. (A.
PRITCHARD, ED)
C.V. WEDGWOOD, 617(TLS):15NOV74-
1286
COWLEY, M. A SECOND FLOWERING.*
A. MASSIE, 364:DEC73/JAN74-145
617(TLS):14JUN74-634
COWPER, R. THE TWILIGHT OF BRIAREUS.
617(TLS):15MAR74-269

76

COX, B.S. CRUCES OF "BEOWULF."
J.L. ROSIER, 589:OCT73-740
COX, G.S., ED. THE NIGHT-WALKER.
R. LONSDALE, 447(N&Q):MAY72-200
COX, H. THE SEDUCTION OF THE SPIR-
IT.*
J. HITCHCOCK, 31(ASCH):WINTER
73/74-173
W. SHEED, 453:7MAR74-18
617(TLS):20SEP74-1024
COX, H. & S. MC HUGH. MR. & MRS.
CHARLES DICKENS ENTERTAIN AT HOME.
G.B. TENNYSON, 445(NCF):DEC72-
369
COX, J.S., ED. UNDER MILK WOOD.
W. DAVIES, 447(N&Q):FEB72-71
COX, M. DERBY.
617(TLS):10MAY74-508
COX, R.G., ED. THOMAS HARDY: THE
CRITICAL HERITAGE.
P. GOETSCH, 430(NS):FEB72-104
A.P. ROBSON, 637(VS):JUN72-475
COX, R.T. THE ALGEBRA OF PROBABLE
INFERENCE.
D. MILLER, 316:JUN72-398
COXE, G.H. THE INSIDE MAN.
N. CALLENDAR, 441:31MAR74-41
COYSH, A.W. COLLECTING BOOKMARKERS.
617(TLS):22NOV74-1313
COYSH, V. ALDERNEY.
617(TLS):29MAR74-349
CRACRAFT, J. THE CHURCH REFORM OF
PETER THE GREAT.*
S. FEINSTEIN, 481(PQ):JUL72-564
M. RAEFF, 550(RUSR):JAN72-77
CRADDOCK, J.R. & Y. MALKIEL - SEE
GEORGES, E.S.
CRAFT, R. PREJUDICES IN DISGUISE.
D. CAIRNS, 441:7JUL74-3
CRAFT, R. STRAVINSKY.*
J.A.W., 410(M&L):JAN73-83
CRAIG, C. CHRISTOPH MARTIN WIELAND
AS THE ORIGINATOR OF THE MODERN
TRAVESTY IN GERMAN LITERATURE.*
S.E. CERNYAK, 406:FALL73-301
S.R. MILLER, 222(GR):MAR72-145
A. PHELAN, 402(MLR):JAN73-226
C. SOMMER, 52:BAND7HEFT1-96
CRAIG, D. THE REAL FOUNDATIONS.
F. KERMODE, 453:30MAY74-6
CRAIG, D. THE SQUEEZE.
N. CALLENDAR, 441:15SEP74-44
CRAIG, W. ENEMY AT THE GATES.*
617(TLS):1MAR74-197
CRAIK, W.A. THE BRONTË NOVELS.*
S. MONOD, 189(EA):JUL-SEP72-436
CRAIN, W.L. - SEE DE BALZAC, H.
CRAMER, C. AMERICAN ENTERPRISE.
617(TLS):4JAN74-18
CRAMER, T. "LOHENGRIN."*
V. GÜNTHER, 182:VOL25#7/8-216
CRANE, F. EXTANT MEDIEVAL MUSICAL
INSTRUMENTS.
A.C.B., 410(M&L):JAN73-90
J. MONTAGU, 187:JAN74-153
CRANE, H. & OTHERS. LETTERS OF HART
CRANE & HIS FAMILY. (T.S.W. LEWIS,
ED)
R.W. FLINT, 441:21JUL74-4
442(NY):21OCT74-190
CRANE, S. THE WORKS OF STEPHEN
CRANE.* (VOLS 1&2) (F. BOWERS, ED)
T.A. GULLASON, 577(SHR):SUMMER72-
295

CRANE, S. THE WORKS OF STEPHEN
CRANE.* (VOLS 4, 6 & 9) (F. BOW-
ERS, ED)
P. DAVISON, 354:DEC72-359
CRANE, S. THE WORKS OF STEPHEN
CRANE.* (VOL 5) (F. BOWERS, ED)
P. DAVISON, 354:DEC72-359
639(VQR):WINTER72-XXVII
CRANKSHAW, E. TOLSTOY.
442(NY):29APR74-135
CRAPULLI, G. MATHESIS UNIVERSALIS.*
J. BERNHARDT, 542:JAN-MAR72-109
W. RÖD, 53(AGP):BAND54HEFT1-107
CRAPULLI, G. & E. GIANCOTTI BOSCHER-
INI. RICERCHE LESSICALI SU OPERE
DI DESCARTES E SPINOZA.
E. NAMER, 542:APR-JUN72-196
W. RÖD, 53(AGP):BAND54HEFT1-106
CRARY, C.S., ED. THE PRICE OF LOYAL-
TY.
P. MAIER, 441:3FEB74-32
CRASTER, E. THE HISTORY OF ALL
SOULS COLLEGE LIBRARY. (E.F.
JACOB, ED)
J.A.W.B., 382(MAE):1973/3-297
K.W. HUMPHREYS, 447(N&Q):JUN72-
232
CRAVEN, M. I HEARD THE OWL CALL MY
NAME.
M. LEVIN, 441:3FEB74-28
CRAVEN, W.F. WHITE, RED, & BLACK.
J.B. FRANTZ, 568(SCN):SPRING73-
10
G.B. NASH, 656(WMQ):JUL72-492
W.L. ROSE, 453:17OCT74-29
639(VQR):WINTER73-XXXII
CRAWFORD, J.C. THE RELATIONSHIP OF
TEXT & MUSIC IN THE VOCAL WORKS
OF SCHOENBERG, 1908-1924.
J. LESTER, 513:SPRING-SUMMER/
FALL-WINTER71-355
CRAWLEY, W. IS IT GENUINE?
G. WILLS, 39:NOV72-461
CREAMER, R.W. BABE.
R. ANGELL, 441:13OCT74-6
C.M. CURTIS, 61:NOV74-110
C. LEHMANN-HAUPT, 441:3OCT74-47
CREEL, H.G. THE ORIGINS OF STATE-
CRAFT IN CHINA.* (VOL 1)
W. EBERHARD, 318(JAOS):OCT-DEC72-
548
CREEL, H.G. WHAT IS TAOISM? & OTHER
STUDIES IN CHINESE CULTURAL HIS-
TORY.
W.C. FINLEY, 485(PE&W):JUL72-341
CREELEY, R. THE CHARM. A QUICK
GRAPH.
P.C., 502(PRS):SPRING72-90
CREELEY, R. A DAY BOOK.*
639(VQR):SPRING73-LXII
CREELEY, R. ST. MARTIN'S.
639(VQR):WINTER72-XXIII
CREELEY, R. A SENSE OF MEASURE.
R. GARFITT, 364:JUN/JUL73-116
CREIGHTON, D. TOWARDS THE DISCOVERY
OF CANADA.
617(TLS):6SEP74-951
CRÉPIN, A. HISTOIRE DE LA LANGUE
ANGLAISE.*
J. MACHÁČEK, 353:15APR72-126
DE CRESCENZO, G. FRANCIS HUTCHESON
E IL SUO TEMPO.
E. NAMER, 542:JUL-SEP72-325

DE CRESPIGNY, R. THE LAST OF THE
HAN.
F.A. KIERMAN, JR., 293(JAST):
FEB72-389
DE CRESPIGNY, R. THE RECORDS OF THE
THREE KINGDOMS.
C. LEBAN, 318(JAOS):APR-JUN72-
344
CRESPO, R. JEAN DE MEUN TRADUTTORE
DELLA "CONSOLATIO PHILOSOPHIAE"
DI BOEZIO.
P.Y. BADEL, 545(RPH):AUG72-205
CREVEL, R. LA MORT DIFFICILE. MON
CORPS ET MOI. LES PIEDS DANS LE
PLAT.
617(TLS):11OCT74-1138
VAN CREVELD, M.L. HITLER'S STRATEGY
1940-1941.
617(TLS):1MAR74-197
CREWS, F., ED. PSYCHOANALYSIS &
LITERARY PROCESS.*
D.W. HARDING, 541(RES):FEB72-107
CREWS, H. CAR.*
S. O'CONNELL, 418(MR):WINTER73-
190
J. YARDLEY, 473(PR):2/1973-286
CREWS, H. THE GOSPEL SINGER.
J. YARDLEY, 473(PR):2/1973-286
CREWS, H. THE GYPSY'S CURSE.
J.R. FRAKES, 441:23JUN74-31
C. LEHMANN-HAUPT, 441:30APR74-45
442(NY):15JUL74-86
CREWS, H. THE HAWK IS DYING.*
617(TLS):11JAN74-25
639(VQR):SUMMER73-CV
CRICHTON SMITH, I. LOVE POEMS &
ELEGIES.*
G. EWART, 364:DEC72/JAN73-132
CRIGHTON, R.A. THE FLOATING WORLD.
617(TLS):12JUL74-751
CRISANAZ, M.P.P. - SEE UNDER PALIN
CRISANAZ, M.P.
CRISTIN, C. AUX ORIGINES DE L'HIS-
TOIRE LITTÉRAIRE.
617(TLS):26JUL74-804
CROCHET, M. LES MYTHES DANS
L'OEUVRE DE CAMUS.
617(TLS):29MAR74-314
CROCIONI, G. LE TRADIZIONI POPOLARI
NELLA LETTERATURA ITALIANA.
R.J. RODINI, 405(MP):NOV72-179
CROCKER, L.G. DIDEROT'S CHAOTIC
ORDER.
617(TLS):16AUG74-884
CROCKER, L.G. NATURE & CULTURE.
E-R. LABROUSSE, 542:JUL-SEP72-
318
CROCKER, L.G. JEAN-JACQUES ROUS-
SEAU.* (VOL 1)
R.L. FRAUTSCHI, 207(FR):OCT71-
263
CROCOMBE, R., ED. LAND TENURE IN
THE PACIFIC.
M.P. FREEDMAN, 293(JAST):MAY72-
751
CROFT, K., ED. READINGS ON ENGLISH
AS A SECOND LANGUAGE.
E.V. MOHR, 608:SEP73-341
C.A. YORIO, 351(LL):DEC72-305
CROFT, P.J., ED. AUTOGRAPH POETRY
IN THE ENGLISH LANGUAGE.
N. BARKER, 362:8AUG74-187
617(TLS):19APR74-422

CROFT-MURRAY, E. DECORATIVE PAINT-
ING IN ENGLAND 1537-1837. (VOL 2)
E. WATERHOUSE, 39:APR72-340
CROIZIER, R.C. TRADITIONAL MEDICINE
IN MODERN CHINA.
F.P. LISOWSKI, 302:JAN72-78
CROMBIE, A.C. DA S. AGOSTINO A
GALILEO.
C. VASOLI, 548(RCSF):APR-JUN72-
236
CROMPTON, L. SHAW THE DRAMATIST.*
R. DAVIES, 627(UTQ):AUTUMN71-88
CROMPTON, L., WITH H. CAVANAUGH -
SEE SHAW, G.B.
CROOK, J.M. THE BRITISH MUSEUM.
M. ROSENTHAL, 135:SEP72-64
D. WATKIN, 39:NOV72-459
CROOK, J.M., ED. VICTORIAN ARCHI-
TECTURE.
D. HINTON, 135:JUN72-152
J. LEES-MILNE, 39:AUG72-165
CROPSEY, J. - SEE HOBBES, T.
CROS, E. LITERATURAS HISPÁNICA E
HISPANOAMERICANA. (VOL 1)
J. JOSET, 556(RLV):1972/5-558
CROSBIE, J.S. THE MAYOR OF UPPER
UPSALQUITCH.
R-M., 268:JUL74-149
CROSBIE, S.K. A TACIT ALLIANCE.
617(TLS):12JUL74-740
CROSBY, A.W., JR. THE COLUMBIAN
EXCHANGE.
G.S. DUNBAR, 656(WMQ):JUL73-542
CROSBY, J. THE WHITE TELEPHONE.
617(TLS):2AUG74-839
CROSBY, S.M. THE APOSTLE BAS-RELIEF
AT SAINT-DENIS.
D. DENNY, 127:SUMMER73-462
CROSLAND, A. SOCIALISM NOW & OTHER
ESSAYS. (D. LEONARD, ED)
T. RAISON, 362:21MAR74-377
617(TLS):22MAR74-279
CROSLAND, M. COLETTE.*
R. TONKS, 453:24JAN74-3
CROSS, A., ED. RUSSIA UNDER WESTERN
EYES, 1517-1825.
J. CRACRAFT, 550(RUSR):APR72-197
I. DE MADARIAGA, 575(SEER):APR73-
311
D. WATKIN, 39:DEC72-567
205(FMLS):JAN72-93
CROSS, A.G. N.M. KARAMZIN.*
I. ELAGIN, 550(RUSR):JUL72-307
G.S. SMITH, 575(SEER):APR73-299
639(VQR):SPRING72-LXIV
CROSS, C. - SEE HASTINGS, F.
CROSS, F.L., ED. THE OXFORD DICTION-
ARY OF THE CHRISTIAN CHURCH. (2ND
ED REV BY F.L. CROSS & E.A. LIVING-
STONE)
O. CHADWICK, 617(TLS):22NOV74-
1319
CROSS, R.K. FLAUBERT & JOYCE.*
R. BOYLE, 659:SPRING74-262
CROSSETTE, G. - SEE GLEASON, H.W.
CROSSLAND, R.A. & A. BIRCHALL, EDS.
BRONZE AGE MIGRATIONS IN THE AEG-
EAN.
617(TLS):26JUL74-806
CROSSLEY-HOLLAND, K. THE RAIN-
GIVER.*
G. EWART, 364:DEC72/JAN73-132

CROTHERS, E. & P. SUPPES. EXPERI-
MENTS IN SECOND LANGUAGE LEARNING.
L. SELINKER, 351(LL):DEC72-291
CROUSE, T. THE BOYS ON THE BUS.*
T. BUCKLEY, 441:22JAN74-43
S. DARST, 441:17FEB74-14
CROUZET, F. LE CONFLIT DE CHYPRE
1946-1959.
D. HUNT, 617(TLS):20SEP74-999
CROW, C.M. PAUL VALÉRY.
C.A. HACKETT, 208(FS):OCT73-474
L. TAUMAN, 67:NOV73-310
205(FMLS):OCT72-381
CROW, D. THE VICTORIAN WOMAN.
O. BANKS, 637(VS):MAR73-369
F. BASCH, 189(EA):JUL-SEP72-437
CROW, J. - SEE "LES QUINZE JOYES DE
MARIAGE"
CROW, J.A. THE EPIC OF LATIN AMERI-
CA.* (REV)
F. HAYES, 399(MLJ):DEC72-520
CROWCROFT, P. THAT MAN BOLT.
N. CALLENDAR, 441:12MAY74-18
CROWDER, M., ED. WEST AFRICAN RESIS-
TANCE.
J. GOODY, 69:JAN72-65
CROWDER, M. & O. IKIME, EDS. WEST
AFRICAN CHIEFS.
H. DESCHAMPS, 69:APR72-159
CROWE, J. BLOODWATER.
N. CALLENDAR, 441:30JUN74-32
CROWELL, N.B. A READER'S GUIDE TO
ROBERT BROWNING.
B. LITZINGER, 301(JEGP):OCT73-
576
CROWLEY, F.G. GARCILASO DE LA VEGA
EL INCA & HIS SOURCES IN "COMEN-
TARIOS REALES DE LOS INCAS."
D. DALLA VALLE, 549(RLC):OCT-
DEC72-612
CROWLEY, F.K., ED. MODERN AUSTRALIA
IN DOCUMENTS.
617(TLS):16AUG74-875
CROWLEY, J.D., ED. HAWTHORNE: THE
CRITICAL HERITAGE.
A. EASSON, 447(N&Q):NOV72-427
CROWTHER, M.A. CHURCH EMBATTLED.
R.A. SOLOWAY, 637(VS):SEP72-104
CROXFORD, L. SOLOMON'S FOLLY.
E. KORN, 617(TLS):1NOV74-1216
CROZIER, A. THE NOVELS OF HARRIET
BEECHER STOWE.*
G.E. KENT, 405(MP):AUG72-78
CROZIER, B. DE GAULLE: THE STATES-
MAN.
F. LEWIS, 441:11MAR74-27
R.O. PAXTON, 441:27JAN74-6
442(NY):7JAN74-72
617(TLS):3MAY74-461
CRUCITTI ULLRICH, F.B. SCIPIONE
MAFFEI E LA SUA CORRISPONDENZA IN-
EDITA CON LOUIS BOURGUET.*
H. LAGRAVE, 535(RHL):MAR-APR72-
308
CRUICKSHANK, C.G. ARMY ROYAL.
N. ARONSON, 207(FR):DEC71-458
CRUICKSHANK, C.G. THE ENGLISH OCCU-
PATION OF TOURNAI, 1513-1519.
W.T. MAC CAFFREY, 551(RENQ):WIN-
TER72-485
CRUICKSHANK, D.W. - SEE CALDERÓN DE
LA BARCA, P.

CRUICKSHANK, M. CHURCH & STATE IN
ENGLISH EDUCATION 1870 TO THE
PRESENT DAY.
K. FUCHS, 430(NS):JUL72-426
CRUM, M. - SEE KING, H.
CRUMP, J.I., JR. - SEE "CHAN-KUO
TS'E"
CRUZ, F. LA CUESTIÓN HOMÉRICA.
(2ND ED)
M. LAFFRANQUE, 542:JAN-MAR72-31
CRYMES, R. SOME SYSTEMS OF SUBSTI-
TUTION CORRELATIONS IN MODERN
AMERICAN ENGLISH.*
J.E. PIERCE, 353:JUN72-115
CRYSTAL, D. LINGUISTICS.*
R.E. CALLARY, 351(LL):JUN73-155
A. CHURCH, 316:JUN72-420
CRYSTAL, D. WHAT IS LINGUISTICS?
C. GAUVIN, 189(EA):JUL-SEP72-433
A. WOLLMANN, 38:BAND90HEFT1/2-
155
CRYSTAL, D. & D. DAVY. INVESTIGAT-
ING ENGLISH STYLE.*
H. WEISS, 38:BAND90HEFT4-500
"THE CRYSTAL PALACE EXHIBITION, IL-
LUSTRATED CATALOGUE."
B. READ, 135:AUG72-302
CSAPLÁROS, I., ED. KOCHAM TWÓJ KRAJ.
G. GÖMÖRI, 497(POLR):AUTUMN72-98
CSAPODI, C. THE CORVINIAN LIBRARY.
617(TLS):31MAY74-592
CSIKÓS-NAGY, B. SOCIALIST ECONOMIC
POLICY.
617(TLS):14JUN74-646
CUÉNIN, M. - SEE MADAME DE VILLEDIEU
CUERVO, R.J. EPISTOLARIO DE RUFINO
JOSÉ CUERVO CON LOS MIEMBROS DE LA
ACADEMIA COLOMBIANA. (M.G. ROMERO,
ED)
G. SCHÜTZ, 72:BAND210HEFT4/6-442
CUESTA, P.V. & M.A. MENDES DA LUZ -
SEE UNDER VÁZQUEZ CUESTA, P. &
M.A. MENDES DA LUZ
CUFF, R. & J.L. GRANATSTEIN. CANAD-
IAN-AMERICAN RELATIONS IN WARTIME.
J. ENGLISH, 99:NOV/DEC74-52
CUISINIER, J. LE THÉÂTRE D'OMBRES
À KELANTAN.
M. DAVID, 542:OCT-DEC72-505
CULLEN, L.M. LIFE IN IRELAND.
ANGLO-IRISH TRADE.
J.P. COPE, 159(DM):WINTER/SPRING
71/72-114
CULLEN, P. SPENSER, MARVELL, & REN-
AISSANCE PASTORAL.*
A. DE RUITER, 568(SCN):FALL-WIN-
TER73-80
R.F. HILL, 677:VOL3-269
M. HUGHES, 549(RLC):APR-JUN72-
298
I.G. MAC CAFFREY, 405(MP):NOV72-
161
A.D. NUTTALL, 541(RES):NOV72-480
CULLEN, T. MAUNDY GREGORY.
J. GRIGG, 362:30MAY74-701
617(TLS):10MAY74-495
CULLER, J. FLAUBERT.
D.G. CHARLTON, 617(TLS):6DEC74-
1391
CULLINGWORTH, J.B. PROBLEMS OF AN
URBAN SOCIETY.
617(TLS):5APR74-364
CULOT, J-M. & OTHERS - SEE UNDER
BRUCHER, R. & OTHERS

CUMMINGS, E.E. COMPLETE POEMS: 1913-1962.*
   H. VENDLER, 676(YR):SPRING73-412
CUNDIFF, P.A. BROWNING'S RING META-PHOR & TRUTH.
   B.R. FRIEDMAN, 85:FALL72-53
CUNHA, G.M. & D.G. CONSERVATION OF LIBRARY MATERIALS. (VOL 1) (2ND ED)
   R.L. SCOTT, 14:JUL/OCT72-421
CUNLIFFE, B. IRON AGE COMMUNITIES IN BRITAIN.
   617(TLS):19APR74-411
CUNLIFFE, B. ROMAN BATH DISCOVERED.*
   A. FOX, 313:VOL62-229
   R.P. WRIGHT, 123:DEC73-262
CUNLIFFE, M. THE AGE OF EXPANSION 1848-1917.
   617(TLS):21JUN74-664
CUNLIFFE, M., ED. SPHERE HISTORY OF LITERATURE IN THE ENGLISH LANGUAGE. (VOL 8)
   617(TLS):17MAY74-524
CUNNINGHAM, A., ED. THE THEORY OF MYTH.
   617(TLS):7JUN74-618
CUNNINGHAM, I.C. - SEE HERODAS
CUNNINGHAM, J.P. THE COMPETITION LAW OF THE E.E.C.
   617(TLS):25JAN74-88
CUNNINGHAM, J.V. THE COLLECTED POEMS & EPIGRAMS.*
   T. EAGLETON, 565:VOL13#1-76
CUNNINGTON, P. A HANDBOOK OF ENG-LISH COSTUME IN THE EIGHTEENTH CENTURY.
   G. SQUIRE, 157:WINTER71-76
CUNNINGTON, P. & A. MANSFIELD. ENG-LISH COSTUME FOR SPORTS & RECREA-TION.
   G. WILLIS, 39:FEB72-150
CUOMO, M. FOREST HILLS DIARY.
   M. KEMPTON, 453:19SEP74-42
   S-R. WEISMAN, 441:16JUL74-39
CUPAIUOLO, F. TRAMA POETICA DELLE BUCOLICHE DI VIRGILIO.
   C. FANTAZZI, 487:SUMMER72-205
CÜPPERS, H. DIE TRIERER RÖMERBRÜCK-EN.
   E.M. WIGHTMAN, 313:VOL62-208
CURIE, M. & I. CORRESPONDANCE. (G. ZIEGLER, ED)
   T. ZELDIN, 617(TLS):5JUL74-701
CURL, J.S. THE VICTORIAN CELEBRA-TION OF DEATH.
   R.L. COLLINS, 637(VS):JUN73-468
CURLEY, D. IN THE HANDS OF OUR ENE-MIES.
   L.G., 502(PRS):SPRING72-89
CURRAN, C.A. COUNSELING-LEARNING.
   E.W. STEVICK, 351(LL):DEC73-259
CURRAN, S. SHELLEY'S "CENCI."*
   H. OREL, 637(VS):SEP71-93
CURRAN, S. & J.A. WITTREICH, JR., EDS. BLAKE'S SUBLIME ALLEGORY.
   617(TLS):15FEB74-145
CURRENT, W. & V. SCULLY. PUEBLO ARCHITECTURE OF THE SOUTHWEST.
   M. ASHTON, 576:OCT72-246
   A. BACIGALUPA, 363:MAY72-99
"CURRENT ECONOMIC POSITION & PROS-PECTS OF THE REPUBLIC OF SOUTH VIETNAM."
   W. SHAWCROSS, 453:18JUL74-16

CURRENT-GARCIA, E., WITH D.B. HAT-FIELD - SEE TUGGLE, W.O.
CURRIE, J.R.L. THE NORTHERN COUN-TIES RAILWAY. (VOL 2)
   617(TLS):11OCT74-1143
CURRIE, R. GENIUS.
   J. CAREY, 362:24OCT74-544
CURSCHMANN, M., ED. TEXTE UND MELO-DIEN ZUR WIRKUNGSGESCHICHTE EINES SPÄTMITTELALTERLICHEN LIEDES (HANS HESELLOHER: "VON ÜPPIGLICHEN DIN-GEN").*
   G.F. JONES, 221(GQ):JAN72-182
CURTEIS, I. LONG VOYAGE OUT OF WAR.
   A. RENDLE, 157:WINTER71-77
CURTI, M. & W. TILLMAN - SEE WIL-LIAMS, S.
CURTIS, A. THE PATTERN OF MAUGHAM.
   P. BLACK, 362:7FEB74-181
   617(TLS):25JAN74-67
CURTIS, A., ED. THE RISE & FALL OF THE MATINÉE IDOL.
   T. DRIBERG, 362:21MAR74-379
   617(TLS):5APR74-359
CURTIS, E.S. IN A SACRED MANNER WE LIVE.
   J.E. CHAMBERLIN, 249(HUDR):WIN-TER73/74-786
CURTIS, E.S. PORTRAITS FROM NORTH AMERICAN INDIAN LIFE.*
   639(VQR):SUMMER73-CXXIV
CURTIS, G. THE LIFE & TIMES OF QUEEN ANNE.
   566:SPRING73-110
CURTIS, G.L. ELECTION CAMPAIGNING JAPANESE STYLE.
   J. PITTAU, 293(JAST):FEB72-413
CURTIS, H.A. A NEW APPROACH TO THE DESIGN OF SWITCHING CIRCUITS.
   H.S. STONE, 316:DEC72-760
CURTIS, J-L. LE ROSEAU PENSANT.
   S. MAX, 207(FR):DEC71-465
CURTIS, J.R. WORDSWORTH'S EXPERI-MENTS WITH TRADITION.
   B.C.H., 191(ELN):SEP72(SUPP)-63
   S.M. SPERRY, JR., 301(JEGP):JAN 73-140
CURTIS, L.P., JR. APES & ANGELS.
   W.R. JONES, 125:JUN73-315
   M.J. WATERS, 637(VS):DEC72-232
CURTIS, M., ED. MARXISM.
   R.J.B., 543:SEP71-142
CURTIS, M., ED. PEOPLE & POLITICS IN THE MIDDLE EAST.
   A. AGES, 287:APR72-31
CURTIS, R. THE BERRIGAN BROTHERS.
   E.B. FISKE, 441:16JUN74-8
CURTIS, R.L. TRISTAN STUDIES.*
   R.E. ROBERTS, 545(RPH):NOV72-503
CURTIS, V. - SEE BAIR, F.H., JR.
CURTISS, T.Q. VON STROHEIM.
   C.P. REILLY, 200:JUN-JUL72-371
CURWEN, S. THE JOURNAL OF SAMUEL CURWEN, LOYALIST.* (A. OLIVER, ED)
   R.D. BROWN, 656(WMQ):OCT73-675
   639(VQR):SUMMER73-CXIX
CUSSANS, J.E. HANDBOOK OF HERALDRY. (4TH ED)
   568(SCN):SPRING73-23
DE CUSTINE, A. ALOYS OU LE RELIGI-EUX DE MONT-BERNARD. (P. SÉNART, ED)
   R.B. GRANT, 207(FR):FEB72-734

CUTLER, M.G. EVOCATIONS OF THE
EIGHTEENTH CENTURY IN FRENCH POET-
RY 1800-1869. (FRENCH TITLE:
EVOCATIONS DU DIX-HUITIÈME SIÈCLE
DANS LA POÉSIE FRANÇAISE 1800-
1869.)
F. BASSAN, 207(FR):MAY72-1189
A. CALDER, 402(MLR):JAN73-177
J. MAYER, 557(RSH):APR-JUN72-323
CUTT, T. - SEE PETRONIUS
CUTT, T. - SEE PLAUTUS
CUTT, T. & J.E. NYENHUIS - SEE PET-
RONIUS
CUTT, T. & J.E. NYENHUIS - SEE PLAU-
TUS
SAINT CYRIL. THE WORKS OF SAINT
CYRIL OF JERUSALEM. (VOL 2) (L.P.
MC CAULEY & A.A. STEPHENSON, TRANS)
H. MUSURILLO, 613:SPRING72-147

DAAKU, K.Y. TRADE & POLITICS ON THE
GOLD COAST 1600 TO 1720.
M. PRIESTLEY, 69:JAN72-73
DABBS, E.M. FACE OF AN ISLAND.
M.A. TWINING, 292(JAF):APR-JUN72-
199
DABBS, J.A. DEI GRATIA IN ROYAL
TITLES.
A.F. BERINGAUSE, 424:DEC72-287
DABBS, J.M. HAUNTED BY GOD.
639(VQR):SPRING73-XC
DABNEY, D. OLD MAN JIM'S BOOK OF
KNOWLEDGE.
617(TLS):22FEB74-192
639(VQR):AUTUMN73-CXXXVI
DABNEY, V. VIRGINIA.
A.W. MOGER, 639(VQR):SPRING72-
308
DĄBROWSCY, I. & K. CMENTARZYSKO Z
OKRESÓW PÓŹNOLATEŃSKIEGO I WPŁYWÓW
RZYMSKICH W WESÓŁKACH, POW. KALISZ.
K. TACKENBERG, 182:VOL25#22-811
DACOS, N. LA DÉCOUVERTE DE LA DOMUS
AUREA ET LA FORMATION DES GROTES-
QUES À LA RENAISSANCE.*
H-W. KRUFT, 90:FEB72-101
VON DADELSEN, G. & K. DORFMÜLLER,
EDS. QUELLENSTUDIEN ZUR MUSIK.
J.A.W., 410(M&L):APR73-228
DAEMMRICH, H.S. & D.H. HAENICKE, EDS.
THE CHALLENGE OF GERMAN LITERA-
TURE.*
K. HARRIS, 564:MAR72-61
L.J. RIPPLEY, 400(MLN):OCT72-781
L.P. WESSELL, JR., 290(JAAC):
SPRING73-423
DAETWYLER, J-J. SCIENCES ET ARTS.
U. KREMPEL, 182:VOL25#21-713
DAGOGNET, F. MÉTHODES ET DOCTRINES
DANS L'OEUVRE DE PASTEUR.
N. ROLL-HANSEN, 84:NOV72-347
DAHL, H. - SEE VON GOETHE, J.W.
DAHL, Ö. TOPIC & COMMENT.*
W. BROWNE, 206:JUL72-584
DAHL, R. SWITCH BITCH.
R.P. BRICKNER, 441:27OCT74-44
S. CLARK, 617(TLS):15NOV74-1278
DAHLBERG, C. - SEE GUILLAUME DE LOR-
RIS & JEAN DE MUEN
DAHLBERG, E. THE SORROWS OF PRIAPUS.
639(VQR):SPRING73-XCI

DAHLHAUS, C., ED. RIEMANN MUSIK
LEXIKON: ERGÄNZUNGSBAND. (PERSON-
ENTEIL, A-K)
J.A.W., 410(M&L):APR73-237
DAHLMANN, H. ZUR ARS GRAMMATICA DES
MARIUS VICTORINUS.
A.S. GRATWICK, 123:MAR73-101
DAHM, H. VLADIMIR SOLOV'EV UND MAX
SCHELER.
T.J. BLAKELEY, 32:MAR73-168
DAHRENDORF, R. PLÄDOYER FÜR DIE
EUROPÄISCHE UNION.
617(TLS):26JUL74-793
DAICHES, D. ROBERT BURNS & HIS
WORLD.
G.M. WHITE, 569(SR):AUTUMN73-870
DAICHES, D., ED. THE PENGUIN COM-
PANION TO LITERATURE: BRITAIN &
THE COMMONWEALTH.
P-G. BOUCÉ, 189(EA):OCT-DEC72-
535
B. COTTLE, 541(RES):AUG72-321
DAICHES, D. SIR WALTER SCOTT & HIS
WORLD.
G. CRONIN, JR., 613:AUTUMN72-459
G.B. TENNYSON, 445(NCF):DEC72-
369
DAIN, N. DISORDERED MINDS.
J. LEIBY, 656(WMQ):APR72-316
DAIVE, J. FUT BÂTI.
617(TLS):9AUG74-852
DAKIN, D. THE GREEK STRUGGLE FOR
INDEPENDENCE 1821-1833.
R. CLOGG, 617(TLS):19JUL74-767
DAKIN, J., B. TIFFEN & H.G. WIDDOW-
SON. LANGUAGE IN EDUCATION.
M. POLLET, 189(EA):JUL-SEP73-433
DALBOR, J.B. SPANISH PRONUNCIATION.
S. BALDWIN, 238:SEP72-612
DALBY, D., ED. LANGUAGE & HISTORY
IN AFRICA.
C. EHRET, 350:MAR73-217
DALE, A.M. METRICAL ANALYSES OF
TRAGIC CHORUSES. (VOL 1)
E.D. FLOYD, 487:WINTER72-412
DALE, F.R., G.S. THOMPSON & C.H.
CRADDOCK, EDS. LATIN ELEGY, LYRIC
& EPIGRAM.
R.G. PENMAN, 123:MAR73-81
DALE, J.B. & M.L. COURS PRÉPARA-
TOIRE DE FRANÇAIS. (CYCLES 1-3)
V.G. ALLEN, 399(MLJ):FEB72-109
DALE, J.B. & M.L. LECTURES FRAN-
ÇAISES. (BK 1)
D. DALIS, 207(FR):DEC71-544
DALE, K. NINETEENTH-CENTURY PIANO
MUSIC.
F. DAWES, 415:JUN73-604
DALE, R.R. MIXED OR SINGLE-SEX
SCHOOL? (VOL 3)
617(TLS):23AUG74-908
DALESKI, H.M. DICKENS & THE ART OF
ANALOGY.*
M. GANZ, 637(VS):DEC71-234
DALEY, J.A. SPICY LADY.
N. CALLENDAR, 441:8DEC74-44
M. LEVIN, 441:6JAN74-21
DALLAS, K., COMP. THE CRUEL WARS.*
F. HOWES, 415:JUL73-703
DALLAS, P. ITALIAN WINES.
617(TLS):25OCT74-1208

DALLIMORE, A.A. GEORGE WHITEFIELD.
(VOL 1)
H.R. CEDERBERG, 481(PQ):JUL72-
565
DALLIN, A. & G.W. BRESLAUER. POLITI-
CAL TERROR IN COMMUNIST SYSTEMS.*
R.M. SLUSSER, 32:DEC73-825
DALLIN, D.J. THE RISE OF RUSSIA IN
ASIA. SOVIET RUSSIA IN THE FAR
EAST.
D.S.M. WILLIAMS, 575(SEER):OCT73-
629
DALTON, D. JAMES DEAN.
L. BRAUDY, 441:22SEP74-6
DALVEN, R., ED & TRANS. MODERN
GREEK POETRY.
W.P. ROOT, 491:OCT73-34
DALY, D. THE YOUNG DOUGLAS HYDE.
617(TLS):5APR74-361
DALY, M. BEYOND GOD THE FATHER.*
G. GRAY, 441:3FEB74-16
DALZELL, R.F., JR. DANIEL WEBSTER
& THE TRIAL OF AMERICAN NATIONAL-
ISM, 1843-1852.*
639(VQR):SUMMER73-CXVIII
DALZIEL, M. - SEE LENNOX, C.
DAMDŽHA-PROKOP, U. QUELQUES PROPOS-
ITIONS D'ANALYSE SYNTAXIQUE DU
FRANÇAIS CONTEMPORAIN, EN APPLICA-
TION AUX ROMANS D'ALAIN ROBBE-
GRILLET.
M.G. WORTHINGTON, 545(RPH):NOV72-
448
DAMIANI, B.M. - SEE DELICADO, F.
DAMIENS, S. AMOUR ET INTELLECT CHEZ
LÉON L'HÉBREU.
B. CHEDOZEAU, 535(RHL):JUL-AUG72-
703
E. NAMER, 542:JAN-MAR72-107
DAMROSCH, L., JR. SAMUEL JOHNSON &
THE TRAGIC SENSE.*
C. CHAPIN, 301(JEGP):JUL73-447
639(VQR):SPRING73-LXIX
DANA, D. - SEE MISTRAL, G.
"DANCE INDEX."
S.J. COHEN, 290(JAAC):SUMMER72-
554
DANCHEVA, I. & M. LAZAROV, COMPS.
BŬLGARSKATA KOMUNISTICHESKA PARTI-
IA V CHUZHDATA LITERATURA, 1885-
1967.
M. PUNDEFF, 32:DEC73-847
DANCKERT, W. TONREICH UND SYMBOL-
ZAHL IN HOCHKULTUREN UND IN DER
PRIMITIVEN WELT.
B.A. BEATIE & P.H. GOTTSCHALK,
353:MAY72-106
D'ANCONA, P. & E. AESCHLIMANN. THE
ART OF ILLUMINATION.*
D.K. HAWORTH, 127:WINTER72/73-
240
DANDEKAR, R.N., ED. PROCEEDINGS OF
THE TWENTY-SIXTH INTERNATIONAL CON-
GRESS OF ORIENTALISTS. (VOL 4)
C.S. GOODRICH, 318(JAOS):OCT-DEC
72-587
D'ANDLAU, B. LA JEUNESSE DE MADAME
DE STAËL (DE 1766 À 1786).*
N. KING, 208(FS):JUL73-341
P. SAGE, 207(FR):APR72-1055
DANELSKI, D.J. & J.S. TULCHIN - SEE
HUGHES, C.E.
DANEMAN, M. A CHANCE TO SIT DOWN.
J. GALE, 151:OCT72-90

DANEŠ, F. & OTHERS. TRAVAUX LIN-
GUISTIQUES DE PRAGUE. (VOL 3)
V.M. DU FEU, 575(SEER):JUL73-459
ĐẶNG PHU'O'NG-NGHI. LES INSTITU-
TIONS PUBLIQUES DUU VIÊTNAM A
XVIIIÈME SIÈCLE.
A-G. MARSOT, 318(JAOS):APR-JUN
72-363
DANGELMAYR, S. GOTTESERKENNTNIS UND
GOTTESBEGRIFF IN DEN PHILOSOPHIS-
CHEN SCHRIFTEN DES NIKOLAUS VON
KUES.
P.J.W. MILLER, 319:JAN74-105
DANGER, P. SENSATIONS ET OBJETS
DANS LE ROMAN DE FLAUBERT.
617(TLS):3MAY74-478
DANIEL, F. - SEE MADDOX, L.G.
DANIEL, P. THE SHADOW OF SLAVERY.
639(VQR):AUTUMN72-CLIII
DANIEL, R.T. & P. LE HURAY. THE
SOURCES OF ENGLISH CHURCH MUSIC,
1549-1660.
R.B., 410(M&L):JAN73-80
DANIELL, J.R. EXPERIMENT IN REPUB-
LICANISM.*
L.R. GERLACH, 656(WMQ):JAN72-177
DANIÉLOU, J. L'ÊTRE ET LE TEMPS
CHEZ GRÉGOIRE DE NYSSE.
W. BEIERWALTES, 182:VOL25#15/16-
513
DANIELS, C. THE GARAMANTES OF
SOUTHERN LIBYA.
I.M. BARTON, 313:VOL62-207
B.H. WARMINGTON, 123:MAR73-77
DANIELS, F. DIRECT USE OF THE SUN'S
ENERGY.
S.S. ODDO, 441:10FEB74-15
DANIELS, G. THE GETTING GAME.
D. BIRD, 441:1AUG74-27
DANIELS, H. PRINTMAKING.
B. CHILDS, 363:MAY72-96
DANIELS, J.R. FIRST FLIGHT.
N. CALLENDAR, 441:20JAN74-22
DANIELSEN, N. ZUM WESEN DES KONDI-
TIONALSATZES (NICHT ZULETZT IM
INDOEUROPÄISCHEN).
W. DRESSLER, 343:BAND15HEFT1-105
DANIELSON, D. & R. HAYDEN. USING
ENGLISH.
J.G. ZUCK, 351(LL):DEC73-281
DANIELSSON, B. & R.C. ALSTON - SEE
BULLOKAR, W.
DANIELSSON, B. & D.M. VIETH - SEE
WILMOT, J. & OTHERS
DANNENBAUM, J. MENUS FOR ALL OCCA-
SIONS.
N. HAZELTON, 441:1DEC74-94
D'ANNUNZIO, G. LA VIOLANTE DALLA
BELLA VOCE. (E. DE MICHELIS, ED)
B.E. DOLD, 402(MLR):JAN73-200
DANOV, C.M. DREVNA TRAKIYA.
D.J. BLACKMAN, 303:VOL92-229
D'ANS, A-M. MATERIALES PARA EL ES-
TUDIO DEL GRUPO LINGÜISTICO PANO.
L. CHALON, 556(RLV):1972/2-221
DANTE ALIGHIERI. DANTE'S "INFERNO."
(M. MUSA, ED & TRANS)
T.G. BERGIN, 275(IQ):FALL/WINTER
72-113
M.W. BLOOMFIELD, 589:JAN73-127
D.J. DONNO, 551(RENQ):WINTER72-
442
D.G. REES, 447(N&Q):OCT72-389

DANTE ALIGHIERI. THE DIVINE COMEDY:
INFERNO.* (C.S. SINGLETON, ED &
TRANS)
M.W. BLOOMFIELD, 589:JAN73-127
DANTE ALIGHIERI. THE DIVINE COMEDY:
PURGATORIO.* (C.S. SINGLETON, ED
& TRANS)
639(VQR):SUMMER73-CXVIII
DANTE ALIGHIERI. THE PARADISO. (J.
CIARDI, TRANS)
T.G. BERGIN, 275(IQ):FALL/WINTER
72-114
DANTIN, L. FANNY.
B. GODARD, 99:NOV/DEC74-24
DANTO, A.C. MYSTICISM & MORALITY.
F. STAAL, 311(JP):28MAR74-174
D'ARBELA, E.V. - SEE CICERO
DARIO, R. SUS MEJORES PÁGINAS. (R.
GULLÓN, ED)
E.U. IRVING, 238:SEP72-609
DARLOW, C. ENCLOSED SHOPPING CEN-
TRES.
46:AUG72-128
D'ARMS, J.H. ROMANS ON THE BAY OF
NAPLES.*
A. HUS, 555:VOL46FASC1-168
L. RICHARDSON, JR., 24:SPRING73-
118
DARNELL, R., ED. LINGUISTIC DIVER-
SITY IN CANADIAN SOCIETY.
B. SAINT-JACQUES, 320(CJL):
VOL18#2-183
DARNTON, R. MESMERISM & THE END OF
THE ENLIGHTENMENT IN FRANCE.*
J.S. SPINK, 208(FS):JAN73-73
DARRACH, D. BOBBY FISCHER VS. THE
REST OF THE WORLD.
D.K. MANO, 441:13OCT74-6
DARWISH, M. SELECTED POEMS. (I.
WEDDE & F. TUQAN, EDS & TRANS)
617(TLS):11JAN74-28
DARYUSH, E. SELECTED POEMS.*
J. MATTHIAS, 491:APR74-45
DASENT, G.W. EAST O' THE SUN & WEST
O' THE MOON.
L.C. KEATING, 582(SFQ):DEC72-399
DASH, T. TRANSPLANTS.
617(TLS):11JAN74-28
DASHTI, A. IN SEARCH OF OMAR KHAY-
YAM.
A. DICKINS, 364:JUN/JUL72-169
J.D. YOHANNAN, 352(LE&W):VOL15
#4&VOL16#1/2-911
DASS, B.R. DOING YOUR OWN BEING.
617(TLS):15FEB74-162
DASSONVILLE, M. RONSARD. (VOL 2)
M.K. BÉNOUIS, 207(FR):APR72-1062
L.W. JOHNSON, 551(RENQ):SPRING
72-94
DASTÉ, M-H., S.M. SAINT-DENIS & C.
SICARD - SEE COPEAU, J.
DATTA, S. THE PROBLEM OF RELATION
IN CONTEMPORARY PHILOSOPHY.
A.M., 543:SEP71-121
D'AUBIGNÉ, A. LES TRAGIQUES.* (I.D.
MC FARLANE, ED) [SHOWN IN PREV
UNDER AGRIPPA]
F. GRAY, 207(FR):OCT71-274
L. WIERENGA, 433:JUL72-367
DAUFOUY, P. & J-P. SARTON. POP
MUSIC/ROCK.
I. LEYMARIE, 187:MAY74-305
DAULTE, F. AUGUSTE RENOIR. (VOL 1)
R. REIFF, 54:DEC72-560

DAUMAL, R. BHARATA. LE CONTRE-CIEL
[SUIVI DE] LE DERNIÈRES PAROLES DU
POÈTE.
98:JAN72-87
DAUMAL, R. TU T'ES TOUJOURS TROMPÉ.
(J. DAUMAL, ED)
98:JAN72-88
DAUMARD, A., ED. LES FORTUNES FRAN-
ÇAISES AU XIXE SIÈCLE.
617(TLS):10MAY74-496
DAUMAS, M. SCIENTIFIC INSTRUMENTS
OF THE SEVENTEENTH & EIGHTEENTH
CENTURIES.
P.L. FARBER, 173(ECS):SPRING73-
398
DAUNT, W.J.O. A LIFE SPENT FOR IRE-
LAND.
617(TLS):7JUN74-615
DAUSTER, F. XAVIER VILLAURRUTIA.
D.L. SHAW, 402(MLR):APR73-431
D'AUVERGNE, M. - SEE UNDER MARTIAL
D'AUVERGNE
DAUZAT, A. DICTIONNAIRE ÉTYMOLO-
GIQUE DES NOMS DE FAMILLE ET PRÉ-
NOMS DE FRANCE. (3RD ED REV BY
M-T. MORAT)
H-W. KLEIN, 430(NS):OCT72-619
DAUZAT, A. & C. ROSTAING. DICTION-
NAIRE ÉTYMOLOGIQUE DES NOMS DE
LIEUX EN FRANCE.
H-W. KLEIN, 430(NS):OCT72-619
DAVENANT, W. SIR WILLIAM DAVENANT:
THE SHORTER POEMS & SONGS FROM THE
PLAYS & MASQUES. (A.M. GIBBS, ED)
G.B. EVANS, 301(JEGP):OCT73-556
S. MUSGROVE, 67:NOV73-297
DAVENANT, W. SIR WILLIAM DAVENANT'S
"GONDIBERT."* (D.F. GLADISH, ED)
E. MINER, 481(PQ):JUL72-660
DAVENPORT, G. TATLIN!
A.C.J. BERGMAN, 441:20OCT74-16
I. EHRENPREIS, 453:12DEC74-42
H. KRAMER, 441:26AUG74-27
DAVENPORT, N. MEMOIRS OF A CITY
RADICAL.
R. HELLER, 362:24OCT74-543
H. STEPHENSON, 617(TLS):1NOV74-
1239
DAVID, L. JOAN.
J. O'REILLY, 441:29SEP74-6
DAVID, P. - SEE TS'AO CHAO
DAVID, P.T. PARTY STRENGTH IN THE
UNITED STATES, 1872-1970.
M.C. CUMMINGS, JR., 639(VQR):
AUTUMN72-590
DAVIDSON, B. BLACK STAR.
617(TLS):4JAN74-4
DAVIDSON, C. BIRACIAL POLITICS.
639(VQR):WINTER73-XXXIX
DAVIDSON, D. WE FEW, WE HAPPY FEW.
L. BERG, 231:AUG74-95
M. LEVIN, 441:29SEP74-40
DAVIDSON, D. & J. HINTIKKA, EDS.
WORDS & OBJECTIONS.
K.T., 543:SEP71-146
DAVIDSON, E.H. JONATHAN EDWARDS.*
B. LEE, 447(N&Q):OCT72-393
DAVIDSON, I. THESAURUS OF MEDIEVAL
HEBREW POETRY.
M.H. SCHMELZER, 318(JAOS):JAN-
MAR72-187
DAVIDSON, J.C.C. MEMOIRS OF A CON-
SERVATIVE. (R.R. JAMES, ED)
619(TC):VOL177#1043-51

DAVIDSON, M.B. HISTORY OF NOTABLE
AMERICAN HOUSES.
505:JAN72-142
DAVIDSON, R.M. - SEE UNDER FOOTE,
L.P.
DAVIE, D. COLLECTED POEMS 1950-
1970.*
J.E. CHAMBERLIN, 249(HUDR):SUM-
MER73-402
R. FULLER, 364:FEB/MAR73-131
639(VQR):SPRING73-LXI
DAVIE, D. THOMAS HARDY & BRITISH
POETRY.*
R. SALE, 249(HUDR):WINTER73/74-
704
639(VQR):SPRING73-LXXII
DAVIE, D. THE SHIRES.
J. FULLER, 362:24OCT74-545
A. THWAITE, 617(TLS):4OCT74-1069
DAVIE, E. CREATING A SCENE.
E. GLOVER, 565:VOL13#2-65
DAVIE, G.E. THE DEMOCRATIC INTELL-
ECT.
M. CHASTAING, 542:JUL-SEP72-347
DAVIES, A., ED. LANGUAGE TESTING
SYMPOSIUM.
R.W., 206:MAR72-307
DAVIES, A.M. A BOOK WITH SEVEN
SEALS.
M. LASKI, 362:22AUG74-252
617(TLS):7JUN74-616
DAVIES, G.A. A POET AT COURT.
205(FMLS):OCT72-381
DAVIES, H. THE GLORY GAME.
M. FELD, 364:JUN/JUL73-154
B. GLANVILLE, 441:24FEB74-30
DAVIES, H. A WALK ALONG THE WALL.
J. MAPPLEBECK, 362:27JUN74-842
DAVIES, J.P., JR. DRAGON BY THE
TAIL.
617(TLS):14JUN74-632
DAVIES, K.G., ED. DOCUMENTS OF THE
AMERICAN REVOLUTION 1770-1783.
(VOLS 1-3)
617(TLS):3MAY74-468
DAVIES, L. FRANCK.*
J. TREVITT, 415:JUL73-699
DAVIES, M. ROGIER VAN DER WEYDEN.*
A. FRANKENSTEIN, 55:DEC73-35
P.H. SCHABACKER, 56:WINTER72-422
DAVIES, W., ED. DYLAN THOMAS.
D. MIDDLETON, 598(SOR):SPRING74-
529
DAVIN, D. BRIDES OF PRICE.*
P. CRUTTWELL & F. WESTBURG,
249(HUDR):SUMMER73-421
DAVIS, A.R. TU FU.
C-M. CHENG, 293(JAST):MAY72-644
W. HUNG, 244(HJAS):VOL32-265
M. LOI, 549(RLC):OCT-DEC72-609
DAVIS, A.Y. ANGELA DAVIS.
F. CARNEY, 453:28NOV74-17
E. LANGER, 441:27OCT74-5
C. LEHMANN-HAUPT, 441:23OCT74-49
442(NY):11NOV74-214
DAVIS, C. TEMPTATIONS OF RELIGION.
W. DAVISON, 441:17MAR74-20
DAVIS, C., WITH J. WILLWERTH. CLIVE.
J. ROCKWELL, 441:22DEC74-10
DAVIS, C.C. THAT AMBITIOUS MR.
LEGARÉ.*
J.E. KIBLER, 219(GAR):FALL72-385

DAVIS, D.B. THE SLAVE POWER CON-
SPIRACY & THE PARANOID STYLE.
639(VQR):SPRING72-LXV
DAVIS, G. THE MOTHERLAND.
M. LEVIN, 441:30JUN74-29
DAVIS, G.N. GERMAN THOUGHT & CUL-
TURE IN ENGLAND, 1700-1770.
P.A. SHELLEY, 400(MLN):APR72-507
DAVIS, I.M. THE BLACK DOUGLAS.
617(TLS):2AUG74-837
DAVIS, J. LIFE SIGNS.*
M. MUDRICK, 249(HUDR):AUTUMN73-
545
DAVIS, J. THE PAPERS OF JEFFERSON
DAVIS. (VOL 1) (H.M. MONROE, JR.
& J.T. MC INTOSH, EDS)
C.B. DEW, 639(VQR):SUMMER72-462
J. RABUN, 14:JUL/OCT72-407
DAVIS, K.S. F.D.R.
D. PERKINS, 639(VQR):SUMMER73-
475
DAVIS, L.J. WALKING SMALL.
S. BLACKBURN, 441:6OCT74-20
DAVIS, M. THE IMAGE OF LINCOLN IN
THE SOUTH.
639(VQR):SUMMER72-XCIII
DAVIS, N., ED. PASTON LETTERS &
PAPERS OF THE FIFTEENTH CENTURY.*
(PT 1)
C.M. BARRON, 325:OCT72-530
H.S. BENNETT, 382(MAE):1973/1-
101
A.I. DOYLE, 541(RES):NOV72-468
C. GAUVIN, 189(EA):APR-JUN72-319
C. LINDBERG, 597(SN):VOL44#2-438
DAVIS, N. WILLIAM TYNDALE'S ENGLISH
OF CONTROVERSY.
S. BROOK, 402(MLR):APR73-382
DAVIS, O. THE SCENT OF APPLES.*
639(VQR):SPRING73-LX
DAVIS, O. THE STEPS OF THE SUN.
J.C. WILSON, 502(PRS):FALL72-269
639(VQR):SUMMER72-CI
DAVIS, R.B. LITERATURE & SOCIETY IN
EARLY VIRGINIA, 1608-1840.*
S. BUSH, JR., 165:WINTER74-312
DAVISON, D. DRYDEN.*
T-L. PEBWORTH, 568(SCN):FALL-
WINTER73-65
DAVISON, N.J. EDUARDO BARRIOS.*
Y.G. BARRETT, 399(MLJ):FEB72-115
R. GRASS, 238:MAR72-185
DAVISON, P. WALKING THE BOUNDARIES.
617(TLS):21JUN74-667
DAVITT, M. LEAVES FROM A PRISON
DIARY.
617(TLS):7JUN74-615
DAWE, B. CONDOLENCES OF THE SEASON.
J. TULIP, 581:JUN73-231
DAWKINS, J. - SEE DE BRACH, P.
DAWN, C.E. FROM OTTOMANISM TO ARAB-
ISM.
617(TLS):12JUL74-740
DAWSON, C., ED. MATTHEW ARNOLD: THE
POETRY.
617(TLS):4JAN74-11
DAWSON, F. THE DREAM/THUNDER ROAD.
639(VQR):WINTER73-VIII
DAWSON, F. THE GREATEST STORY EVER
TOLD.
P. CRUTTWELL & F. WESTBURG,
249(HUDR):SUMMER73-419

DAWSON, P. PROVINCIAL MAGISTRATES
& REVOLUTIONARY POLITICS IN
FRANCE, 1789-1795.
639(VQR):SUMMER73-CXXII
DAWSON, R. AN INTRODUCTION TO CLAS-
SICAL CHINESE.
H.M. STIMSON, 318(JAOS):JAN-MAR
72-141
DAWSON, S.W. DRAMA & THE DRAMATIC.*
P. GOETSCH, 430(NS):AUG72-500
DAY, A.C. THE SYNTAX OF THO, A TAI
LANGUAGE OF VIETNAM.
G.F. MEIER, 682(ZPSK):BAND25
HEFT6-525
DAY, B. SEXUAL LIFE BETWEEN BLACKS
& WHITES.
617(TLS):19JUL74-765
DAY, D. MALCOLM LOWRY.*
D.J. ENRIGHT, 362:11APR74-474
S. GRACE, 296:VOL3#1-105
617(TLS):19APR74-417
DAY, D. & A. ERSKINE - SEE FAULKNER,
W.
"THE DAYBOOKS OF EDWARD WESTON."
S. SONTAG, 453:28NOV74-35
DEACON, R. A HISTORY OF THE RUSSIAN
SECRET SERVICE.
R.M. SLUSSER, 32:DEC73-825
DEAL, B. THE OTHER ROOM.
M. LEVIN, 441:27OCT74-57
DE AMICIS, E. CUORE. (L. TAMBURINI,
ED)
617(TLS):15FEB74-153
DEAN, P.H. THE STY OF THE BLIND PIG
& OTHER PLAYS.
B.H. FUSSELL, 249(HUDR):WINTER
73/74-753
DEANE, P. THUCYDIDES' DATES 465-431
B.C.
M.F. MC GREGOR, 487:AUTUMN72-295
DEANE, S., ED. SALE CATALOGUES OF
LIBRARIES OF EMINENT PERSONS. (VOL
8)
617(TLS):6SEP74-958
DEARLOVE, J. THE POLITICS OF POLICY
IN LOCAL GOVERNMENT.
617(TLS):1MAR74-217
DEAS, S. IN DEFENCE OF HANSLICK.
(REV)
E. SAMS, 415:NOV73-1124
DEBAUVE, J-L. - SEE LAFORGUE, J.
DEBBASCH, C. & OTHERS. LES ÉCONO-
MIES MAGHRÉBINES.
P. SALMON, 182:VOL25#5/6-154
DEBENEDETTI, G. IL PERSONAGGIO
UOMO.*
400(MLN):JAN72-165
DEBICKI, A.P. DÁMASO ALONSO.
J.O. JIMÉNEZ, 238:MAR72-181
P. SILVER, 400(MLN):MAR72-380
DEBLUÉ, V. ANIMA NATURALITER IRON-
ICA.
M. FRANZBACH, 549(RLC):JAN-MAR72-
150
DEBO, A. AND STILL THE WATERS RUN.
J.E. CHAMBERLIN, 249(HUDR):WIN-
TER73/74-786
DEBRABANDERE, F. STUDIE VAN DE
PERSOONSNAMEN IN DE KASSELRIJ
KORTRIJK 1350-1400.
G.B. DROEGE, 424:JUN72-147
DEBRAY, R. THE CHILEAN REVOLUTION.
J.F. THORNING, 613:WINTER72-631
639(VQR):AUTUMN72-CLII

DEBRECZENY, P. & J. ZELDIN, EDS &
TRANS. LITERATURE & NATIONAL
IDENTITY.*
R. EKMANIS, 125:OCT72-82
B.L. WESTON, 399(MLJ):MAR72-178
DEBSKI, J. - SEE RATAJ, M.
DEBUS, A.G., ED. SCIENCE, MEDICINE
& SOCIETY IN THE RENAISSANCE.
617(TLS):16AUG74-886
DÉCAUDIN, M., ED. GUILLAUME APOLLI-
NAIRE 8.
M. DAVIES, 208(FS):JAN73-93
C. TOURNADRE, 535(RHL):MAR-APR72-
342
DÉCAUDIN, M., ED. DU MONDE EUROPÉEN
À L'UNIVERS DES MYTHES.
C.-M. BÉGUÉ, 207(FR):FEB72-726
M. DAVIES, 208(FS):JAN73-93
C. TOURNADRE, 535(RHL):MAR-APR72-
342
DECKER, D.M. LUIS DURAND.
J. HANCOCK, 399(MLJ):DEC72-524
DECKER, J.P. HANDBOOK OF TIME-ZERO.
M.W. CAMPBELL, 186(ETC.):DEC72-
437
DECLÈVE, H. HEIDEGGER ET KANT.
J.D.C., 543:MAR72-552
T. KISIEL, 484(PPR):JUN73-601
DE COMYN, T. STATE OF THE PHILIP-
PINES IN 1810 [TOGETHER WITH]
BENITEZ, C. PHILIPPINE PROGRESS
PRIOR TO 1898.
C.O. HOUSTON, 293(JAST):NOV71-
233
DE CONDE, A. HALF BITTER, HALF
SWEET.
P.J. FUNIGIELLO, 579(SAQ):SPRING
73-330
DECOTTIGNIES, J. - SEE MADAME DE
TENCIN
DE CROW, K. SEXIST JUSTICE.
P. ADAMS, 61:MAR74-97
DÉCSY, G. YURAK CHRESTOMATHY.*
G.F. MEIER, 682(ZPSK):BAND25
HEFT4/5-430
DEEMS, E.M. HOLY-DAYS & HOLIDAYS.
K.B. HARDER, 424:MAR72-67
DEESON, A.F.L. AN ILLUSTRATED HIS-
TORY OF AIRSHIPS.
617(TLS):29MAR74-348
DEEV, G.K. & OTHERS, COMPS. DOKU-
MENTY VNESHNEI POLITIKI SSSR.
(VOL 17)
R.P. BROWDER, 32:SEP73-615
DE FELICE, R., ED. LA CARTA DEL
CANARO NEI TESTI DI ALCESTE DE
AMBRIS E DI GABRIELE D'ANNUNZIO.
S.J. WOOLF, 617(TLS):11OCT74-
1118
DE FELICE, R. & E. MARIANO, EDS.
CARTEGGIO D'ANNUNZIO - MUSSOLINI
(1919-1938).
E. BONORA, 228(GSLI):VOL149FASC
466/467-456
DE FEO, N.M. ANALITICA E DIALETTICA
IN NIETZSCHE.
L.M.P., 543:SEP71-122
DEGENHART, B. & A. SCHMITT. CORPUS
DER ITALIENISCHEN ZEICHNUNGEN
1300-1450.* (PT 1)
J. GARDNER, 90:JAN72-32
DEGER, S. HERRSCHAFTSFORMEN BEI
HOMER.
J.B. HAINSWORTH, 123:DEC73-188

DEGLER, C. NEITHER BLACK NOR WHITE.
   W.L. ROSE, 453:17OCT74-29
DEGLER, C.N. THE OTHER SOUTH.
   C.V. WOODWARD, 441:10MAR74-4
   442(NY):18MAR74-150
DE GREVE, M. & F. VAN PASSEL. LIN-
GÜÍSTICA Y ENSEÑANZA DE IDIOMAS
EXTRANJERAS.* (FRENCH TITLE: LIN-
GUISTIQUE ET ENSEIGNEMENT DES
LANGUES ÉTRANGÈRES.)
   C.W. STANSFIELD, 238:DEC72-979
DEICHMANN, F.W. RAVENNA.
   C. DELVOYE, 182:VOL25#13/14-486
DEIGHTON, L. SPY STORY.
   V. CUNNINGHAM, 362:9MAY74-606
   442(NY):23SEP74-147
   617(TLS):3MAY74-465
DEININGER, J. DER POLITISCHE WIDER-
STAND GEGEN ROM IN GRIECHENLAND,
217-86 V. CHR.
   P.S. DEROW, 487:AUTUMN72-303
   J-C. RICHARD, 555:VOL46FASC2-351
DÉJEAN, J.L. LA FEUILLE À L'ENVERS.
   B.J. BUCKNALL, 207(FR):DEC71-466
DÉJEUX, J. LA LITTÉRATURE MAGHRÉ-
BINE D'EXPRESSION FRANÇAISE.
   E. SELLIN, 188(ECR):WINTER72-336
DEKKER, J.C.E. LES FONCTIONS COM-
BINATOIRES ET LES ISOLS.
   A.B. MANASTER, 316:JUN72-406
DEKKER, T. THOMAS DEKKER: OLD FOR-
TUNATUS.
   B. SALOMON, 568(SCN):FALL-WINTER
   73-90
DE KORNE, J.B. ASPEN ART IN THE NEW
MEXICO HIGHLANDS.
   J.H. BRUNVAND, 292(JAF):OCT-DEC
   72-385
DELAISEMENT, G. LES TECHNIQUES DE
L'EXPLICATION DE TEXTES.
   J.L. SHEPHERD, 3D, 207(FR):APR72-
   1070
DELAISSÉ, L.M.J. A CENTURY OF DUTCH
MANUSCRIPT ILLUMINATION.*
   J. MARROW, 382(MAE):1973/3-251
DELANEY, C.F. MIND & NATURE.
   W.A.W., 543:MAR72-552
DELANO, A. BREATHLESS DIVERSIONS.
   M. LEVIN, 441:3FEB74-28
DELANY, P. BRITISH AUTOBIOGRAPHY IN
THE SEVENTEENTH CENTURY.*
   A.H. BUFORD, 551(RENQ):SUMMER72-
   251
   J.H. SIMS, 568(SCN):SPRING73-21
DELANY, S. CHAUCER'S "HOUSE OF
FAME."
   R.A. PECK, 301(JEGP):OCT73-544
DELAS, D. - SEE RIFFATERRE, M.
DELASSUS, J-F. THE JAPANESE.
   42(AR):VOL32#3-509
   639(VQR):WINTER73-XL
DELATTRE, P. STUDIES IN FRENCH &
COMPARATIVE PHONETICS.
   P. COLLET, 660(WORD):AUG70-300
DE LAURA, D.J., ED. MATTHEW ARNOLD.
   617(TLS):4JAN74-11
DE LAURA, D.J. HEBREW & HELLENE IN
VICTORIAN ENGLAND.*
   J-C. ROJAHN, 38:BAND90HEFT1/2-
   255
   G.B. TENNYSON, 445(NCF):JUN72-
   115

DELBOUILLE, P. GENÈSE, STRUCTURE ET
DESTIN D'"ADOLPHE."*
   R. FRICKX-MONTAL, 556(RLV):
   1972/6-664
   205(FMLS):JUL72-285
DELCAMPE, A., WITH A. WIBO & B. DEL-
CAMPE. ARTS DU SPECTACLE EN BEL-
GIQUE.
   M. PIEMME, 556(RLV):1972/6-671
DELCROIX, M. LE SACRÉ DANS LES
TRAGÉDIES PROFANES DE RACINE.*
   F.R. FREUDMANN, 546(RR):DEC72-
   297
   R.C. KNIGHT, 208(FS):JAN73-61
   R.W. TOBIN, 207(FR):OCT71-269
DELDERFIELD, R.F. RETURN JOURNEY.
   M. LEVIN, 441:28JUL74-20
DELEUZE, G. & F. GUATTARI. CAPITAL-
ISME ET SCHIZOPHRÉNIE.* (VOL 1)
   R. GIRARD, 98:NOV72-957
   J-F. LYOTARD, 98:NOV72-923
DELIBES, M. CON LA ESCOPETA AL HOM-
BRO.
   E. RUGG, 238:MAY72-387
DELIBES, M. LA MORTAJA.
   L. GUINAZZO, 238:DEC72-969
DELIBES, M. SMOKE ON THE GROUND.
   42(AR):VOL32#3-496
DELICADO, F. LA LOZANA ANDALUZA.*
(B.M. DAMIANI, ED)
   D. EISENBERG, 241:SEP72-79
DELICADO, F. LA LOZANA ANDALUZA.
(L. ORIOLI, ED)
   B.M. DAMIANI, 241:MAY72-87
DELIEB, E. & M. ROBERTS. THE GREAT
SILVER MANUFACTORY.
   C. OMAN, 39:MAY72-424
   G. TAYLOR, 135:NOV72-214
DE LILLO, D. END ZONE.*
   S. O'CONNELL, 418(MR):WINTER73-
   190
   42(AR):SPRING/SUMMER72-240
DE LILLO, D. GREAT JONES STREET.*
   E. ROVIT, 659:AUTUMN74-539
   R. SALE, 418(MR):AUTUMN73-834
DELISLE, F. THE PACIFIST PILGRIMAGE
OF FRANÇOISE & HAVELOCK.
   617(TLS):26JUL74-815
DELL, E. POLITICAL RESPONSIBILITY
& INDUSTRY.
   617(TLS):11JAN74-37
DELL'ARCO, M. GIOACHINO BELLI.
   P. GIBELLINI, 228(GSLI):VOL149
   FASC466/467-400
DELLA VOLPE, G. CHIAVE DELLA DIALET-
TICA STORICA.
   E. NAMER, 542:JUL-SEP72-386
DELLEPIANE, A.B. PRESENCIA DE AMÉR-
ICA EN LA OBRA DE TIRSO DE MOLINA.
   M.A. MORÍNIGO, 240(HR):SUMMER72-
   329
DELLEPIANE, A.B. - SEE GÜIRALDES, R.
DEL MAR, N. RICHARD STRAUSS.* (VOL
3)
   D. COOKE, 415:MAY73-492
DELOFFRE, F. & J. ROUGEOT - SEE
GUILLERAGUES.
DELORIA, V., JR. BEHIND THE TRAIL
OF BROKEN TREATIES. THE INDIAN
AFFAIR.
   D. BROWN, 441:24NOV74-38
DELORT, R. LIFE IN THE MIDDLE AGES.
   D. DOUGLAS, 617(TLS):1NOV74-1237

"JOSEPH DELTEIL." (D. PELAYO, ED)
H. BONNARD, 209(FM):OCT72-359
DELTEIL, Y. LA FIN TRAGIQUE DU
VOYAGE DE VICTOR HUGO EN 1843.
P. DEGUISE, 207(FR):MAR72-922
DEL TORRE, M-A. STUDI SU CESARE
CREMONINI.
E. NAMER, 542:JAN-MAR72-108
DELUMEAU, J., ED. HISTOIRE DE LA
BRETAGNE.
J. MUNDY, 589:APR73-422
DEMANDT, A. VERFORMUNGSTENDENZEN IN
DER ÜBERLIEFERUNG ANTIKER SONNEN-
UND MONDFINSTERNISSE.
C. MUGLER, 555:VOL46FASC2-293
DE MARIA, R. THE DECLINE & FALL OF
AMERICA.
42(AR):VOL32#4-698.
DE MARIA, R. THE SATYR.
W.H. PRITCHARD, 249(HUDR):SPRING
73-231
E. ROVIT, 659:AUTUMN74-539
DE MAURO, T. PARLARE ITALIANO.
R.J. DI PIETRO, 276:AUTUMN72-337
DEMBOWSKI, P.F., ED. "AMI ET AMILE,"
CHANSON DE GESTE.*
P. MÉNARD, 545(RPH):NOV72-462
DEMELIER, J. GENS DE LA RUE.
S. MAX, 207(FR):DEC71-467
DE MENDOZA, R.G. STIMMUNG UND
TRANSZENDENZ.
J.D.C., 543:JUN72-748
DEMÉNY, J. - SEE BARTOK, B.
DEMETZ, P. POSTWAR GERMAN LITERA-
TURE.*
G. STERN, 222(GR):NOV72-302
J. STRELKA, 221(GQ):JAN72-138
DE MICHELIS, E. APPROCCI AL BELLI.
P. GIBELLINI, 228(GSLI):VOL149
FASC466/467-400
DEMING, R.H., ED. JAMES JOYCE: THE
CRITICAL HERITAGE.*
C. HART, 677:VOL3-327
DE MIRJIAN, A. NOT A CLUE.
N. CALLENDAR, 441:13OCT74-48
DEMM, E. REFORMMÖNCHTUM UND SLAWEN-
MISSION IM 12. JAHRHUNDERT.*
P.R. MC KEON, 589:JUL73-564
DE MOLEN, R.L., ED. ERASMUS OF
ROTTERDAM.
J.W. BINNS, 402(MLR):OCT73-900
DE MOLEN, R.L. - SEE "ERASMUS"
DEMOS, J., ED. REMARKABLE PROVI-
DENCES: 1600-1760.
S.J. STEIN, 432(NEQ):DEC72-593
DEMPSEY, M., ED. THE YEAR'S ART
(1968-69) & (1969-70).
T. CROMBIE, 39:MAY72-423
DEMUS, O. BYZANTINE ART & THE
WEST.*
J. BECKWITH, 39:JUL72-84
H. BELTING, 54:DEC72-542
D. GLASS, 56:SUMMER72-176
DEMUS, O. ROMANESQUE MURAL PAINT-
ING.*
J. BECKWITH, 39:JUL72-84
D'ENCAUSSE, H.C. & S.R. SCHRAM.
L'U.R.S.S. ET LA CHINE DEVANT LES
RÉVOLUTIONS DANS LES SOCIÉTÉS PRE-
INDUSTRIELLES.*
O.E. CLUBB, 104:SPRING72-186

DENECKE, L. JACOB GRIMM UND SEIN
BRUDER WILHELM.
E. KUNZE, 439(NM):1972/3-726
R. MICHAELIS-JENA, 203:SPRING72-
76
DE NEVI, D. - SEE LEWIS, O.
DENEVI, M. PARQUE DE DIVERSIONES.
D.A. YATES, 238:DEC72-972
DENHAM, A. AMO.
M. LEVIN, 441:10NOV74-22
DENISOFF, R.S., COMP. AMERICAN PRO-
TEST SONGS OF WAR & PEACE.
R.A. REUSS, 650(WF):APR72-143
DENISSOFF, E. DESCARTES, PREMIER
THÉORICIEN DE LA PHYSIQUE MATHÉ-
MATIQUE.
J. BERNHARDT, 542:APR-JUN72-191
DENKLER, H., ED. DER DEUTSCHE
MICHEL.
J. HERMAND, 406:SPRING73-80
DENNERT, J. DIE ONTOLOGISCH-ARIS-
TOTELISCHE POLITIKWISSENSCHAFT UND
DER RATIONALISMUS.
W. STEINBECK, 342:BAND63HEFT2-
266
DENNIS, B. EXPERIMENTAL MUSIC IN
SCHOOLS.
P. LANSKY, 513:SPRING-SUMMER/
FALL-WINTER71-340
DENNIS, C. THE NEXT-TO-LAST TRAIN
RIDE.
617(TLS):4OCT74-1092
DENNIS, F. & D. ATYEO. BRUCE LEE.
617(TLS):2AUG74-832
DENNIS, R. ATLANTA DEATHWATCH. THE
CHARLESTON KNIFE'S BACK IN TOWN.
N. CALLENDAR, 441:12MAY74-16
DENNIS, R. MURDER'S NOT AN ODD JOB.
N. CALLENDAR, 441:13OCT74-48
DENNIS, R.C. CONVERSATIONS WITH A
CORPSE.
N. CALLENDAR, 441:23JUN74-33
617(TLS):8NOV74-1248
DENOMMÉ, R.T. THE FRENCH PARNASSIAN
POETS.
A. FAIRLIE, 208(FS):OCT73-464
R. VERNIER, 401(MLQ):SEP73-343
DENOMMÉ, R.T. NINETEENTH-CENTURY
FRENCH ROMANTIC POETS.
J-A. BÉDÉ, 546(RR):FEB72-63
DENSMORE, F. CHIPPEWA MUSIC. TETON
SIOUX MUSIC. PAPAGO MUSIC. MUSIC
OF THE INDIANS OF BRITISH COLUMBIA.
F. HOWES, 415:JAN73-38
DENT, A. LOST BEASTS OF BRITAIN.
617(TLS):27SEP74-1048
DENT, J. CRISIS IN FINANCE.
617(TLS):19APR74-408
DENTON, J.H. ENGLISH ROYAL FREE
CHAPELS, 1100-1300.
C.E. LEWIS, 589:JAN73-129
DENZER, H. MORALPHILOSOPHIE UND
NATURRECHT BEI SAMUEL PUFENDORF.
S. DECLOUX, 182:VOL25#5/6-129
DE PAUW, L.G., WITH C.B. BICKFORD &
L.M. SIEGEL, EDS. DOCUMENTARY
HISTORY OF THE FIRST FEDERAL CON-
GRESS OF THE UNITED STATES OF AMER-
ICA, MARCH 4, 1789-MARCH 3, 1791.
(VOL 1)
P. GOODMAN, 656(WMQ):JUL73-508

DE POERCK, G., R. VAN DEYCK & R.
ZWAENEPOEL, EDS. LE CHARROI DE
NÎMES.
  W.W. KIBLER, 207(FR):DEC71-547
DEPRUN, J., R. DESNÉ & A. SOBOUL -
SEE MESLIER, J.
DERBOLAV, J. ERKENNTNIS UND ENT-
SCHEIDUNG.
  P. AUBENQUE, 542:JAN-MAR72-49
DERCSÉNYI, D., ED. THE HUNGARIAN
ILLUMINATED CHRONICLE "CHRONICON
DE GESTIS HUNGARORUM."
  W.O. HASSALL, 135:JUN72-150
DERI, O. EXPLORING TWENTIETH-CEN-
TURY MUSIC.
  D. STOCK, 513:FALL-WINTER69-141
D'ERIL, F.K.M. - SEE UNDER MELZI
D'ERIL, F.K.
DERLETH, L. DAS WERK. (D. JOST, ED)
  F. USINGER, 182:VOL25#12-409
DER NERSESSIAN, S. L'ILLUSTRATION
DES PSAUTIERS GRECS DU MOYEN AGE.
(VOL 2)
  J. BECKWITH, 39:JUL72-84
DÉROZIER, A. - SEE QUINTANA, M.J.
DERRETT, J.D.M., ED. STUDIES IN THE
LAW OF SUCCESSION IN NIGERIA.
  A.N. ALLOTT, 69:APR72-162
DERRIDA, J. "LA PHARMACIE DE PLATON"
DANS LA DISSÉMINATION.
  H. TOUBEAU, 98:AUG/SEP72-681
DERRY, J.W. CHARLES JAMES FOX.*
  J.N. MC CORD, JR., 579(SAQ):
    SPRING73-327
  639(VQR):AUTUMN72-CXL
DESAI, P. TARIFF PROTECTION & INDUS-
TRIALIZATION.
  C.P. STAELIN, 293(JAST):FEB72-
    439
DESAI, W.S. BOMBAY & THE MARATHAS
UP TO 1774.
  S.N. GORDON, 293(JAST):FEB72-433
DESANTI, J.T. LES IDÉALITÉS MATHÉ-
MATIQUES.
  Y. GAUTHIER, 154:JUN72-281
DESAUTELS, A.R. LES MÉMOIRES DE
TRÉVOUX ET LE MOUVEMENT DES IDEES
AU DIX-HUITIÈME SIÈCLE (1701-1734).
  M. DAVID, 542:JUL-SEP72-315
DESBONNETS, T. & D. VORREUX, EDS &
TRANS. SAINT FRANÇOIS D'ASSISE,
DOCUMENTS.
  L.K. LITTLE, 589:APR73-343
DESCARTES, R. CORRESPONDANCE. (C.
ADAM & G. MILHAUD, EDS)
  G. RODIS-LEWIS, 542:APR-JUN72-
    188
DESCHAMPS, J., ED. MEDIAEVAL MANU-
SCRIPTS FROM THE LOW COUNTRIES IN
FACSIMILE. (VOL 1, PT 1)
  J. BACKHOUSE, 382(MAE):1973/3-
    291
DESCHAMPS, Y. MONOLOGUES.
  R. WILLMOT, 296:VOL3#3-112
DESCOTES, M. MOLIÈRE ET SA FORTUNE
LITTÉRAIRE.*
  L. GOSSMAN, 207(FR):OCT71-270
  G. MONGRÉDIEN, 535(RHL):SEP-DEC
    72-1094
DESCOTES, M. LE PERSONNAGE DE NAPO-
LÉON III DANS LES ROUGON-MACQUART.*
  F.W.J. HEMMINGS, 208(FS):JAN73-
    88

DESCRAINS, J. BIBLIOGRAPHIE DES
OEUVRES DE JEAN-PIERRE CAMUS,
ÉVÊQUE DE BELLAY (1584-1652).
  D.M. SUTHERLAND, 208(FS):APR73-
    195
DESCRAINS, J. - SEE CAMUS, J-P.
DESGRAVES, L. LES LIVRES IMPRIMÉS
À BORDEAUX AU XVIIE SIÈCLE.
  R.A. SAYCE, 208(FS):JUL73-325
DESHPANDE, V.H. INDIAN MUSICAL TRA-
DITIONS.
  617(TLS):22FEB74-174
DESHUSSES, J. LE GRAND SOIR.
  S. MAX, 207(FR):DEC71-468
DESROCHES, H. MARXISME ET RELIGIONS.
  M. BARTHÉLEMY-MADAULE, 542:JUL-
    SEP72-386
DESSAIN, C.S. & T. GORNALL - SEE
NEWMAN, J.H.
DESSAIN, C.S. & E.E. KELLY - SEE
NEWMAN, J.H.
DESSIGANE, R. & P.Z. PATTABIRAMIN.
LA LÉGENDE DE SKANDA SELON LE
KANDAPURĀNAM TAMOUL ET L'ICONO-
GRAPHIE.
  O. VON HINÜBER, 182:VOL25#21-721
DESSOIR, M. AESTHETICS & THEORY OF
ART.*
  H. OSBORNE, 290(JAAC):WINTER71-
    262
DE STEFANIS CICCONE, S. LA QUES-
TIONE DELLA LINGUA NEI PERIODICI
LETTERARI DEL PRIMO '800.
  V. LUCCHESI, 402(MLR):JAN73-189
  O.R., 191(ELN):SEP72(SUPP)-186
DE STEFANO, J.S., ED. LANGUAGE,
SOCIETY & EDUCATION.
  L.V. ZUCK, 351(LL):DEC73-273
DESTLER, I.M. PRESIDENTS, BUREAU-
CRATS, & FOREIGN POLICY.
  R. EGGER, 639(VQR):WINTER73-118
DESVIGNES-PARENT, L. MARIVAUX ET
L'ANGLETERRE.*
  O. HAAC, 207(FR):APR72-1059
  H.T. MASON, 208(FS):JUL73-331
  D.A. TROTT, 173(ECS):WINTER72/73-
    270
  M. WACHS, 481(PQ):JUL72-730
DETHLEFSEN, D. ZU METRUM UND RHYTH-
MUS DES BLANKVERSES IN DEN DRAMEN
HEINRICH VON KLEISTS.
  M. OSSAR, 221(GQ):MAY72-512
DETIENNE, M. LES JARDINS D'ADONIS.
  C. RAMNOUX, 98:AUG/SEP72-707
  H. TOUBEAU, 98:AUG/SEP72-681
DETROY, P. WILHELM RAABE.
  V. SANDER, 221(GQ):NOV72-711
DE DEUGD, C. FROM RELIGION TO CRITI-
CISM.
  F.F. SCHWARZ, 52:BAND7HEFT2/3-
    312
  U. SIMON, 220(GL&L):JUL73-334
  P. SOMVILLE, 556(RLV):1972/3-332
DEUTSCH, H.C. HITLER & HIS GENERALS.
  617(TLS):25OCT74-1208
DEUTSCHER, I. LENIN'S CHILDHOOD.*
  C.E. BRANCOVAN, 550(RUSR):JAN72-
    85
DEUTSCHER, T. - SEE TROTSKY, L.
"DEUX SIÈCLES D'OPÉRA FRANÇAIS."
  R. LEBEGUE, 535(RHL):SEP-DEC72-
    1098
DEVA, K. TEMPLES OF NORTH INDIA.
  M.W. MEISTER, 576:OCT72-240

DEVAHUTI, D. HARSHA.
J.W. SPELLMAN, 318(JAOS):OCT-DEC
72-573
T.R. TRAUTMANN, 293(JAST):MAY72-
701
DEVEREUX, F.L. PRACTICAL NAVIGATION
FOR THE YACHTSMAN.
617(TLS):5APR74-377
DEVINE, A.M. THE LATIN THEMATIC
GENITIVE SINGULAR.
R. COLEMAN, 361:VOL30#1-72
DE VITO, J.A. THE PSYCHOLOGY OF
SPEECH & LANGUAGE.*
E. WANNER, 206:JAN73-389
DEVLIN, D.D. THE AUTHOR OF "WAVER-
LEY."*
G.B. TENNYSON, 445(NCF):DEC72-
369
DEVLIN, P. TOO PROUD TO FIGHT.
M. BELOFF, 617(TLS):25OCT74-1179
DE VOE, S.S. ENGLISH PAPIER MÂCHÉ
OF THE GEORGIAN & VICTORIAN PER-
IODS.
K.R. MARTIN, 637(VS):MAR72-380
DEVOTO, G. GESCHICHTE DER SPRACHE
ROMS.
B. WIELE, 682(ZPSK):BAND25HEFT6-
552
DEVOTO, G. & G.C. OLI. DIZIONARIO
DELLA LINGUA ITALIANA.*
G. FOLENA, 228(GSLI):VOL149FASC
466/467-416
DE VRIES, L. 'ORRIBLE MURDER.
R.B. MARTIN, 637(VS):MAR72-395
DE VRIES, P. THE GLORY OF THE HUM-
MINGBIRD.
A. BROYARD, 441:22OCT74-45
P. THEROUX, 441:27OCT74-6
442(NY):9DEC74-194
DE VRIES, P. WITHOUT A STITCH IN
TIME.
V. CUNNINGHAM, 362:24JAN74-120
DEWAR, E. A DYING BUSINESS.
617(TLS):20DEC74-1437
DEWDNEY, S. WIND WITHOUT RAIN.
J. PARR, 296:VOL3#3-102
D'EWES, S., ED. THE JOURNALS OF ALL
THE PARLIAMENTS DURING THE REIGN
OF QUEEN ELIZABETH.
617(TLS):3MAY74-484
DEWEY, D. THE THEORY OF IMPERFECT
COMPETITION.
W. SCHÄFER, 182:VOL25#1/2-29
DEWHIRST, I. MORE OLD KEIGHLEY IN
PHOTOGRAPHS.
617(TLS):1FEB74-110
DEYERMOND, A.D. EPIC POETRY & THE
CLERGY.*
R.S. PICCIOTTO, 546(RR):OCT72-
246
DEYERMOND, A.D. A LITERARY HISTORY
OF SPAIN: THE MIDDLE AGES.*
D.G. PATTISON, 382(MAE):1973/1-
115
DEYRUP, A. GETTING STARTED IN BATIK.
B. SEGAL, 139:DEC71-66
D'HARNONCOURT, A. & K. MC SHINE, EDS.
MARCEL DUCHAMP.
K. BAKER, 61:MAY74-121
C. ROBINS, 441:3MAR74-23
617(TLS):23AUG74-899

D'HAUSSY, A. POLY-OLBION OU L'ANGLE-
TERRE VUE PAR UN ÉLIZABÉTHAIN.
G.P. NORTON, 568(SCN):FALL-WIN-
TER73-83
DHAVAMONY, M. LOVE OF GOD ACCORDING
TO ŚAIVA SIDDHĀNTA.
W. HALBFASS, 318(JAOS):OCT-DEC72-
501
G.L. HART 3D, 293(JAST):NOV71-
211
D'HERTEFELT, M. LES CLANS DU RWANDA
ANCIEN.
J. MAQUET, 69:OCT72-353
D'HONDT, J. DE HEGEL À MARX.
W.H. WERKMEISTER, 319:JAN74-125
D'HONDT, J., ED. HEGEL ET LA PENSÉE
MODERNE.
H.S. HARRIS, 484(PPR):DEC72-278
DIAKIN, V.S. GERMANSKIE KAPITALY V
ROSSII.
J.P. MC KAY, 32:JUN73-382
DIAKONOVA, N. BAIRON V GODY IZGNAN-
IYA.
H. GIFFORD, 617(TLS):6DEC74-1396
DIAMENT, H. THE TOPONOMASTIC RE-
FLEXES OF CASTELLUM & CASTRUM.
H.J. WOLF, 72:BAND210HEFT4/6-428
DIAMOND, A.S. PRIMITIVE LAW, PAST &
PRESENT.
A-R. WERNER, 182:VOL25#21-729
DIAMONTE, M., COMP. FONDO ANTICO
SPAGNOLO DELLA BIBLIOTECA UNIVERSI-
TARIA DI GENOVA.
O.H. GREEN, 240(HR):WINTER72-84
DIAS, J. & M. OS MACONDES DE MOÇAM-
BIQUE. (VOL 3)
A.C. EDWARDS, 69:OCT72-347
DIAZ, F. FILOSOFIA E POLITICA NEL
SETTECENTO FRANCESE.
E. NAMER, 542:JUL-SEP72-317
DÍAZ, J.S. - SEE UNDER SIMÓN DÍAZ, J.
DÍAZ, J.W. THE MAJOR THEMES OF
EXISTENTIALISM IN THE WORK OF
JOSÉ ORTEGA Y GASSET.*
M. NOZICK, 238:MAY72-385
DIBBLE, E.F. & E.W. NEWTON, EDS.
SPAIN & HER RIVALS ON THE GULF
COAST.
R.R. REA, 9(ALAR):JUL72-236
DI BENEDETTO, A. TASSO, MINORI E
MINIMI A FERRARA.
G. STELLA, 228(GSLI):VOL149 FASC
465-127
DICK, B.F. THE HELLENISM OF MARY
RENAULT.
R.H.C., 125:FEB73-201
DICK, S. - SEE MOORE, G.
DICKASON, D.H. WILLIAM WILLIAMS.*
J.D. PROWN, 54:MAR72-101
DICKENS, A.G. THE GERMAN NATION &
MARTIN LUTHER.
617(TLS):12APR74-397
DICKENS, C. BARNABY RUDGE.
617(TLS):11JAN74-22
DICKENS, C. A CHRISTMAS CAROL - THE
PUBLIC READING VERSION. (P. COL-
LINS, ED)
L.C.S., 155:MAY72-127
DICKENS, C. DOMBEY & SON. (A. HORS-
MAN, ED)
M. SLATER, 617(TLS):20SEP74-1020

DICKENS, C. THE LETTERS OF CHARLES
DICKENS.* (VOL 2) (M. HOUSE & G.
STOREY, EDS)
    H. REINHOLD, 38:BAND90HEFT1/2-
    258
DICKENS, C. THE LETTERS OF CHARLES
DICKENS. (VOL 3) (M. HOUSE, G.
STOREY & K. TILLOTSON, EDS)
    J. CAREY, 362:22AUG74-249
    S. MONOD, 617(TLS):6DEC74-1359
DICKENS, C. THE MYSTERY OF EDWIN
DROOD. (M. CARDWELL, ED)
    D. MEHL, 72:BAND21OHEFT4/6-419
    S. MONOD, 189(EA):OCT-DEC72-567
DICKENS, C. NICHOLAS NICKLEBY.
(ADAPTED BY G. WILLIAMS)
    A. RENDLE, 157:WINTER72-80
"DICKENS STUDIES ANNUAL." (VOL 3)
(R.B. PARTLOW, JR., ED)
    617(TLS):5JUL74-733
DICKEY, G. THE JOCK EMPIRE.
    R.W. CREAMER, 441:1DEC74-90
DICKEY, R.P. RUNNING LUCKY.*
    T.H. LANDESS, 569(SR):WINTER73-
    137
DICKINSON, A.E.F. THE MUSIC OF BER-
LIOZ.*
    D. CAIRNS, 415:DEC73-1237
    H.J.M., 410(M&L):APR73-220
DICKINSON, H.T., ED. POLITICS & LIT-
ERATURE IN THE EIGHTEENTH CENTURY.
    617(TLS):21JUN74-679
DICKINSON, P. THE POISON ORACLE.
    A. BROYARD, 441:9MAY74-47
    N. CALLENDAR, 441:16JUN74-30
    617(TLS):12APR74-385
DICKINSON, P. A WINTERING TREE.*
    R. GARFITT, 364:OCT/NOV73-118
DICKINSON, T. A DISCOVERY OF CINEMA.
    639(VQR):SPRING72-LXXVI
DICKS, D.R. EARLY GREEK ASTRONOMY
TO ARISTOTLE.*
    D.E. HAHM, 24:SPRING73-121
DICKSON, K.A. - SEE LUDWIG, O.
DICKSON, L. H.G. WELLS.*
    H-J. MÜLLENBROCK, 430(NS):JAN72-
    53
DICKSON, L. WILDERNESS MAN.
    C. DRIVER, 362:14MAR74-342
    R.E. RASHLEY, 99:FEB74-38
    617(TLS):29MAR74-319
DICKSON, P. RED JOHN OF THE BATTLES.
    617(TLS):1MAR74-202
DICKSTEIN, M. KEATS & HIS POETRY.*
    J.R.D. JACKSON, 627(UTQ):SPRING
    73-289
    S.M.S., 191(ELN):SEP72(SUPP)-51
    P. ZIETLOW, 473(PR):3/1973-503
DIDERICHSEN, P. HELHED OG STRUKTUR.
    G.F. MEIER, 682(ZPSK):BAND25
    HEFT1/2-154
DIDEROT, D. CORRESPONDANCE. (VOLS
15 & 16) (G. ROTH & J. VARLOOT,
EDS)
    D.G. CREIGHTON, 207(FR):OCT71-
    265
DIDEROT, D. ECRITS INCONNUS DE
JEUNESSE. (VOL 1) (J.T. DE BOOY,
ED)
    H.T. MASON, 617(TLS):13DEC74-
    1424

DIDEROT, D. ENCYCLOPEDIA: SELECTION.
(N.S. HOYT & T. CASSIRER, EDS &
TRANS)
    M. DAVID, 542:JUL-SEP72-320
DIDEROT, D. OEUVRES COMPLÈTES.
    J. STAROBINSKI, 98:JAN72-3
DIDEROT, D. OEUVRES POLITIQUES.
(P. VERNIÈRE, ED)
    H-F. BERGERON, 542:JUL-SEP72-322
DIECKMANN, L. GOETHE'S "FAUST."
    C.E. SCHWEITZER, 301(JEGP):JAN73-
    93
DIEHL, D. SUPERTALK.
    N. LO BELLO, 441:4AUG74-22
DIEHL, G. MAX ERNST.*
    617(TLS):23AUG74-899
DIEKSTRA, F.N.M., ED. A DIALOGUE
BETWEEN REASON AND ADVERSITY.*
    P. DAMON, 545(RPH):AUG72-209
    W. RIEHLE, 38:BAND90HEFT3-390
DIERICKX, J. & Y. LEBRUN, EDS. LIN-
GUISTIQUE CONTEMPORAINE: HOMMAGE
À ERIC BUYSSENS.*
    J. GIOT, 556(RLV):1972/2-216
DIERKS, M. STUDIEN ZU MYTHOS UND
PSYCHOLOGIE BEI THOMAS MANN.*
    A.W. RILEY, 301(JEGP):JUL73-420
DIESING, P. PATTERNS OF DISCOVERY
IN THE SOCIAL SCIENCES.
    E. MATTHEWS, 518:OCT73-1
    M. ROSHWALD, 484(PPR):DEC72-288
DIETRICH, R.F. PORTRAIT OF THE
ARTIST AS A YOUNG SUPERMAN.*
    R. DAVIES, 627(UTQ):AUTUMN71-88
DIETRICHSON, J.W. THE IMAGE OF
MONEY IN THE AMERICAN NOVEL OF
THE GILDED AGE.
    E.A. HANSEN, 462(OL):VOL27#4-311
DIETZ, A.G.H. & L.S. CUTLER, EDS.
INDUSTRIALIZED BUILDING SYSTEMS
FOR HOUSING.
    R. BENDER, 505:OCT72-128
DIETZ, H. DANCING IN THE DARK.
    M. GUSSOW, 441:18MAY74-29
    H. TEICHMANN, 441:23JUN74-14
DIETZ, W. & H.F. PFANNER, EDS. OS-
KAR MARIA GRAF.
    P. LABANYI, 617(TLS):8NOV74-1263
DIGBY, G.W., WITH W. HEFFORD. THE
DEVONSHIRE HUNTING TAPESTRIES.
    S. SITWELL, 39:SEP72-249
DIGGINS, J.P. MUSSOLINI & FASCISM.*
    P. MERKLEY, 529(QQ):WINTER72-557
DIGGLE, J. - SEE EURIPIDES
VAN DIJK, T.A. MODERNE LITERATUUR-
TEORIE.
    E. KUNNE-IBSCH, 433:JUL72-364
DIKE, D.A. & D.H. ZUCKER - SEE
SCHWARTZ, D.
DIKSHIT, M.G. HISTORY OF INDIAN
GLASS.
    H. GOETZ, 318(JAOS):OCT-DEC72-
    505
DILLARD, A. PILGRIM AT TINKER CREEK.
    R. HUNT, 198:SUMMER74-113
    C. LEHMANN-HAUPT, 441:12MAR74-41
    E. WELTY, 441:24MAR74-4
DILLARD, J.L. BLACK ENGLISH.
    W. WOLFRAM, 350:SEP73-670
DILLARD, R.H.W. AFTER BORGES.
    R. PEVEAR, 249(HUDR):SPRING73-
    192
DILLARD, R.H.W. THE BOOK OF CHANGES.
    J. CHARYN, 441:25AUG74-4

DILLARD, R.H.W., G. GARRETT & J.R.
MOORE, EDS. THE SOUNDER FEW.
   639(VQR):SPRING72-LII
DILLER, E. & J.R. MC WILLIAMS. UN-
TERWEGS.
   J.B. DE VRIES, 221(GQ):MAR72-388
DILLER, H. KLEINE SCHRIFTEN ZUR
ANTIKEN LITERATUR.* (H-J. NEWIGER
& H. SEYFFERT, EDS)
   H. LLOYD-JONES, 123:DEC73-198
DILLINGHAM, W.B. AN ARTIST IN THE
RIGGING.
   F. GAIGE, 50(ARQ):SPRING72-95
   W. GILMAN, 27(AL):MAR73-120
   B. NEVIUS, 445(NCF):SEP72-241
DILLINGHAM, W.B. FRANK NORRIS.*
   F. DURHAM, 577(SHR):SPRING72-199
DILLON, E. ACROSS THE BITTER SEA.
   R. GARFITT, 362:14MAR74-343
   617(TLS):1MAR74-201
DILLON, M. & D. LEHANE. POLITICAL
MURDER IN NORTHERN IRELAND.
   617(TLS):1FEB74-101
DILLON, W.S. GIFTS & NATIONS.
   G. CONDOMINAS, 98:FEB72-119 [&
   CONT IN 98:JUN72-487]
DILMAN, I. INDUCTION & DEDUCTION.*
   J. BURNHEIM, 63:DEC73-265
DILMAN, I. & D.Z. PHILLIPS. SENSE
& DELUSION.
   R.S. DOWNIE, 479(PHQ):APR72-184
DILTS, M.R. - SEE HERAKLEIDES
DILWORTH, M. THE SCOTS IN FRANCONIA.
   617(TLS):6SEP74-951
DIMARAS, C.T. A HISTORY OF MODERN
GREEK LITERATURE.*
   617(TLS):2AUG74-824
DIMONT, M.I. THE INDESTRUCTIBLE
JEWS.
   617(TLS):22MAR74-299
DINELEY, D. EARTH'S VOYAGE THROUGH
TIME.
   617(TLS):8MAR74-243
DINESEN, I. SHADOWS ON THE GRASS.
   441:10FEB74-27
DINGWALL, W.O., ED. A SURVEY OF
LINGUISTIC SCIENCE.
   R.R. BUTTERS, 35(AS):SPRING-
   SUMMER70-122
DINTENFASS, M. FIGURE 8.
   A. BROYARD, 441:19AUG74-23
   M. MEWSHAW, 441:15SEP74-36
   442(NY):4NOV74-210
DIONNE, R., ED. PROPOS LITTÉRAIRES.
   617(TLS):14JUN74-634
DI PIETRO, R.J. LANGUAGE STRUCTURES
IN CONTRAST.*
   R.L. HADLICH, 238:DEC72-978
   B. SPOLSKY, 350:SEP73-739
DIPPLE, E. PLOT.
   P. GOETSCH, 430(NS):AUG72-500
"A DIRECTORY OF AMERICAN POETS."
   S.L. HUTCHINS, 584(SWR):AUTUMN73-
   359
"DIRECTORY OF GEOGRAPHIC NAMES IN
NEVADA."
   T.L. CLARK, 424:SEP72-208
"DIRECTORY OF SELECTED SCIENTIFIC
INSTITUTIONS IN MAINLAND CHINA."
   293(JAST):NOV71-237
DISCH, T.M., ED. BAD MOON RISING.
   617(TLS):15MAR74-269
DISCH, T.M. GETTING INTO DEATH.
   617(TLS):15FEB74-163

DISCH, T.M.   334.
   T. STURGEON, 441:8SEP74-39
DISNEY, D.M. DON'T GO INTO THE
WOODS TODAY.
   N. CALLENDAR, 441:30JUN74-33
DISQUE, R.O. APPLIED PLASTIC DESIGN
IN STEEL.
   J.B. SCALZI, 505:MAY72-140
DITTMANN, U. SPRACHBEWUSSTSEIN UND
REDEFORMEN IM WERK THOMAS MANNS.
   W. WITTE, 220(GL&L):JUL73-327
DIVOMLIKOFF, L. THE TRAITOR.
   M. LEVIN, 441:6JAN74-21
DIXON, P., ED. ALEXANDER POPE.*
   C.T. PROBYN, 566:SPRING73-102
DIXON, P. RHETORIC.
   M. WINTERBOTTOM, 123:DEC73-279
DIXON, R. CHRIST ON TRIAL.
   617(TLS):31MAY74-577
"DIZIONARIO DELLE LINGUE ITALIANA E
TEDESCA."
   G. FRANCESCATO, 361:VOL28#1&2-
   113
DJAÏT, M. LA PERSONNALITÉ ET LE
DEVENIR ARABO-ISLAMIQUES.
   617(TLS):5APR74-356
DJAMO-DIACONIŢĂ, L. LIMBA DOCUMEN-
TELOR SLAVO-ROMÂNE EMISE ÎN ŢARA
ROMÂNEASCĂ ÎN SEC. XIV ŞI XV.
   H.E. MAYER, 32:JUN73-418
DJILAS, M. MEMOIR OF A REVOLUTION-
ARY.*
   639(VQR):SUMMER73-CXX
DŁUSKA, M. STUDIA I ROZPRAWY.
   M. GIERGIELEWICZ, 497(POLR):WIN-
   TER72-87
DMYTRYSHYN, B. USSR: A CONCISE HIS-
TORY.* (2ND ED) (BRITISH TITLE: A
CONCISE HISTORY OF THE USSR.)
   J.M. THOMPSON, 32:MAR73-169
DOBBEK, W. J.G. HERDERS WELTBILD.
   W.H. BRUFORD, 220(GL&L):APR73-
   239
DOBBS, A-C. DRAMATURGIE ET LITURGIE
DANS L'OEUVRE DE JULIEN GRACQ.
   R. CHAMBERS, 67:MAY73-135
DOBBS, B. DRURY LANE.
   J.C. TREWIN, 157:AUTUMN72-77
DOBIAS, P. DAS JUGOSLAWISCHE WIRT-
SCHAFTSSYSTEM.
   L.J. BRAINARD, 32:MAR73-197
DÖBLIN, A. BRIEFE.* (H. GRABER, ED)
   J. DUYTSCHAEVER, 221(GQ):JAN72-
   144
DOBNEY, F.J. - SEE CLAYTON, W.
DOBOS, I. TARCAL TÖRTÉNETE A SZÓ-
HAGYOMÁNYBAN.
   T. DÖMÖTÖR, 196:BAND13HEFT1/2-
   189
   A. SCHEIBER, 292(JAF):APR-JUN72-
   188
DOBOSSY, L. HAŠEK VILÁGA.
   C. WOJATSEK, 104:SUMMER72-349
DOBSON, W.A.C.H. THE LANGUAGE OF
THE "BOOK OF SONGS."
   P.L. SARGENT, 318(JAOS):OCT-DEC
   72-552
DOBYNS, S. CONCURRING BEASTS.*
   M. BORROFF, 676(YR):AUTUMN72-81
   J.A. HEYNEN, 448:SPRING72-91
   42(AR):SPRING/SUMMER72-242
DOCKING, G. TWO HUNDRED YEARS OF
NEW ZEALAND PAINTING.
   A. MC CULLOCH, 381:SEP72-357

DOCTOROW, E.L. THE BOOK OF DANIEL.*
   R. BROWN, 448:FALL72-82
   E. ROVIT, 659:AUTUMN74-539
VON DODERER, H. DER GRENZWALD.
  FRÜHE PROSA. REPERTORIUM. DIE
  WIEDERKEHR DER DRACHEN.
   P. MISSAC, 98:FEB72-140
DODGE, J.W., ED. LEADERSHIP FOR
  CONTINUING DEVELOPMENT.
   E. HOCKING, 207(FR):APR72-1071
DODGSON, J.M. THE PLACE-NAMES OF
  CHESHIRE.* (PT 3)
   O. ARNGART, 597(SN):VOL44#2-435
   M. GELLING, 447(N&Q):JUL72-268
   K.B. HARDER, 424:MAR72-68
DODGSON, J.M. THE PLACE-NAMES OF
  CHESHIRE. (PT 4)
   M. GELLING, 447(N&Q):JUL72-268
   K.B. HARDER, 424:DEC72-295
DŌGEN KIGEN. A PRIMER OF SŌTŌ ZEN.
  (R. MASUNAGA, TRANS)
   R. ZEUSCHNER, 485(PE&W):APR72-
   228
DOHAN, M.H. OUR OWN WORDS.
   T. BERNSTEIN, 441:25AUG74-28
DOHERTY, F. SAMUEL BECKETT.*
   J-J. MAYOUX, 189(EA):JUL-SEP72-
   412
DOHERTY, J.E. SEIN, MENSCH UND SYM-
  BOL.
   S. DECLOUX, 182:VOL25#5/6-131
DOHNAL, B. PŘEKLADATEL A BÁSNIK.
   T. EEKMAN, 279:VOL15-219
DOLBEN, D.M. UNCOLLECTED POEMS OF
  DIGBY MACKWORTH DOLBEN. (M.
  COHEN, ED)
   617(TLS):5APR74-371
DOLBY, J.L. & H.L. RESNIKOFF. THE
  ENGLISH WORD SPECULUM.
   G.F. MEIER, 682(ZPSK):BAND25
   HEFT3-247
DOLCE, L. ARETIN: A DIALOGUE ON
  PAINTING.*
   M.R. BROWNELL, 290(JAAC):WINTER
   72-269
DOLEŽEL, L. & R.W. BAILEY, EDS. STA-
  TISTICS & STYLE.*
   G.K. MONROE, 215(GL):VOL12#1-42
DOLLINGER, P., ED. HISTOIRE DE
  L'ALSACE.
   J. MUNDY, 589:APR73-422
DOLLMAYR, V. & E. KRANZMEYER, EDS.
  BAYERISCH-ÖSTERREICHISCHES WÖR-
  TERBUCH. (VOL 1)
   G.F. MEIER, 682(ZPSK):BAND25
   HEFT4/5-425
DOLTO, F. DOMINIQUE.
   617(TLS):23AUG74-912
DÖLVERS, H. DER ERZÄHLER ROBERT
  LOUIS STEVENSON.
   S. POTTER, 182:VOL25#15/16-550
DOMANDI, M. - SEE GUICCIARDINI, F.
D'OMBRAIN, N. WAR MACHINERY & HIGH
  POLICY.
   617(TLS):8FEB74-128
DOMES, J. THE INTERNAL POLITICS OF
  CHINA 1949-1972.
   617(TLS):22FEB74-178
DOMHOFF, G.W. THE BOHEMIAN GROVE &
  OTHER RETREATS.
   D. GODDARD, 441:5MAY74-52
DOMÍNGUEZ ORTIZ, A. THE GOLDEN AGE
  OF SPAIN, 1516-1659.
   639(VQR):SPRING72-LXIX

DOMINIC, R.B. EPITAPH FOR A LOBBY-
  IST.
   N. CALLENDAR, 441:10MAR74-12
DOMINY, J. THE SERGEANT ESCAPERS.
   617(TLS):15NOV74-1297
DONALDSON, E.T. SPEAKING OF CHAU-
  CER.*
   J.R. SIMON, 189(EA):JAN-MAR73-54
DONALDSON, F. EDWARD VIII.
   A. FORBES, 617(TLS):1NOV74-1213
   J. GRIGG, 362:24OCT74-540
DONALDSON, G. SCOTTISH HISTORICAL
  DOCUMENTS.
   M. MACLAGAN, 447(N&Q):JUL72-271
DONALDSON, G. & R.S. MORPETH. WHO'S
  WHO IN SCOTTISH HISTORY.
   617(TLS):19APR74-408
DONALDSON, I. THE WORLD UPSIDE-
  DOWN.*
   B. CORMAN, 405(MP):AUG72-68
   I. HANTSCH, 72:BAND210HEFT4/6-
   387
   R. WARREN, 447(N&Q):OCT72-396
DONALDSON, S. POET IN AMERICA: WIN-
  FIELD TOWNLEY SCOTT.*
   L.S. DEMBO, 27(AL):MAY73-311
DONALDSON-EVANS, L.K. POÉSIE ET MÉD-
  ITATION CHEZ JEAN DE LA CEPPÈDE.*
   M. VAMOS, 546(RR):OCT72-232
DONATO, E. & R. MACKSEY, EDS. THE
  LANGUAGES OF CRITICISM & THE SCI-
  ENCES OF MAN.
   M.A. CAWS, 188(ECR):WINTER72-318
DONINGTON, R. A PERFORMER'S GUIDE
  TO BAROQUE MUSIC.
   617(TLS):26JUL74-788
DONLEAVY, J.P. THE ONION EATERS.
   F.G.B., 502(PRS):FALL72-276
DONLEAVY, J.P. THE PLAYS OF J.P.
  DONLEAVY.
   B.H. FUSSELL, 249(HUDR):WINTER
   73/74-753
DONNE, J. DONNE'S PREBEND SERMONS.*
  (J.M. MUELLER, ED)
   E.D. MACKERNESS, 677:VOL3-281
DONNE, J. SELECTED PROSE. (CHOSEN
  BY E. SIMPSON; H. GARDNER & T.
  HEALY, EDS)
   R. ELLRODT, 189(EA):OCT-DEC72-
   550
DONNET, L.J. LE TRIOMPHE DES BER-
  GERS PAR LOUIS JACQUEMIN DONNET.
  (G. COUTON, WITH C. LONGEON, EDS)
   H.H. CHAPMAN, JR., 568(SCN):FALL-
   WINTER73-97
DONOGHUE, D. JONATHAN SWIFT.*
   566:SPRING72-85
DONOGHUE, D. THIEVES OF FIRE.
   617(TLS):1MAR74-206
DONOHUE, J.W., JR. DRAMATIC CHARAC-
  TER IN THE ENGLISH ROMANTIC AGE.*
   A.C. SPRAGUE, 570(SQ):SPRING72-
   211
DONOHUE-GAUDET, M-L. LE VOCALISME
  ET LE CONSONANTISME FRANCAIS.*
   M. MONNOT, 207(FR):MAR72-884
DONOSO, J. THE OBSCENE BIRD OF
  NIGHT.* (SPANISH TITLE: EL OB-
  SCENO PÁJARO DE LA NOCHE.)
   D.W. FOSTER, 238:MAY72-392
   617(TLS):15MAR74-269
DONOVAN, J.C. THE COLD WARRIORS.
   R. STEEL, 453:8AUG74-37

DOOB, P.B.R. NEBUCHADNEZZAR'S CHILD-
REN.
M. TWYCROSS, 617(TLS):1NOV74-
1232
DORÉ, G. THE RARE & EXTRAORDINARY
HISTORY OF HOLY RUSSIA.
S. MONAS, 32:MAR73-165
DOREY, T.A., ED. ERASMUS.*
W.S. THURMAN, 399(MLJ):NOV72-475
DOREY, T.A., ED. LIVY.*
P.G. WALSH, 123:DEC73-183
DOREY, T.A. & D.R. DUDLEY. ROME
AGAINST CARTHAGE.*
F.W. WALBANK, 313:VOL62-181
DORFLES, G. ARTIFICIO E NATURA.*
W.A. KOCH, 52:BAND7HEFT2/3-340
DORFLES, G. SENSO E INSENSZTEZZA
NELL'ARTE D'OGGI.
R.W. KRETSCH, 290(JAAC):SPRING73-
423
DORFMAN, E. THE NARREME IN THE MEDI-
EVAL ROMANCE EPIC.*
J.L. GRIGSBY, 593:SUMMER73-172
DÖRING, B. ZU BESONDERHEITEN DER
WORTBILDUNG DES ZUSAMMENGESETZTEN
SUBSTANTIVS IN DER DEUTSCHEN
SPRACHE DER GEGENWART.
M. GAWELKO, 361:VOL29#2-177
DÖRING, K. DIE MEGARIKER.
R. SMITH, 319:OCT74-521
DORN, S.O. THE INSIDER'S GUIDE TO
ANTIQUES, ART & COLLECTIBLES.
R. REIF, 441:22JUN74-27
DORNBERG, J. BREZHNEV.
T. SHABAD, 441:19MAY74-34
617(TLS):24MAY74-551
DORSCH, T.S. & C.G. HARLOW, EDS.
THE YEAR'S WORK IN ENGLISH STUD-
IES.* (VOLS 46&47)
E.G. STANLEY, 447(N&Q):APR72-138
DORSEN, N. & S. GILLERS, EDS. NONE
OF YOUR BUSINESS.
R. HOLBROOKE, 441:16JUN74-4
DORSON, R.M. AMERICA IN LEGEND.
J. MC ELROY, 441:6JAN74-19
DORSON, R.M. AMERICAN FOLKLORE &
THE HISTORIAN.
H. FEIGENBAUM, 650(WF):JAN72-65
DORYON, J. FREUD ET LE MONOTHÉISME
HÉBREU.
P-M.S., 542:OCT-DEC72-453
DOSTOEVSKY, F.M. THE ADOLESCENT.*
(A.R. MAC ANDREW, TRANS)
R. NEUHÄUSER, 104:SUMMER72-331
DOSTOEVSKY, F.M. THE GAMBLER.* (E.
WASIOLEK, ED; V. TERRAS, TRANS)
639(VQR):SPRING73-LVII
DOSTOEVSKY, F.M. NETOCHKA NEZVANOVA.
(A. DUNNIGAN, TRANS)
R.L. JACKSON, 32:SEP73-657
DOSTOEVSKY, F.M. THE NOTEBOOKS FOR
"THE BROTHERS KARAMAZOV."* (E.
WASIOLEK, ED & TRANS)
D. FANGER, 454:WINTER73-188
H. MUCHNIC, 550(RUSR):JAN72-99
T. PACHMUSS, 399(MLJ):OCT72-395
DOTTI, U., ED. IL PROGRESSO DELLE
SCIENZE, DELLE LETTERE E DELLE
ARTI (1832-34).
M. FUBINI, 228(GSLI):VOL149FASC
465-132
DOTTI, U. - SEE PETRARCA, F.
DOTTIN, G. - SEE MARGUERITE DE NAV-
ARRE

DOTY, G.A. THE CAREER OF MRS. ANNE
BRUNTON MERRY IN THE AMERICAN THE-
ATRE.
R. MASHBURN, 583:SPRING73-302
DOTY, R., ED. PHOTOGRAPHY IN AMER-
ICA.
H. KRAMER, 441:1DEC74-34
DOUBLEDAY, N.F. HAWTHORNE'S EARLY
TALES.
N. BAYM, 301(JEGP):APR73-257
B.B. COHEN, 27(AL):MAY73-303
J.D. CROWLEY, 445(NCF):DEC72-355
DOUBROVSKY, S. LA PLACE DE LA MADE-
LEINE.
617(TLS):17MAY74-513
DOUCETTE, L. EMERY BIGOT.*
J.D. CHARRON, 207(FR):OCT71-271
C.G.S. WILLIAMS, 402(MLR):APR73-
409
DOUGAN, D. THE FOOTBALLER.
617(TLS):16AUG74-880
DOUGHTIE, E., ED. LYRICS FROM ENG-
LISH AIRS 1596-1622.
J.P. CUTTS, 551(RENQ):SUMMER72-
233
H.M. SHIRE, 405(MP):NOV72-159
DOUGLAS, A. ELECTRONIC MUSIC PRO-
DUCTION.
T. CARY, 415:MAR73-265
DOUGLAS, E. APOSTLES OF LIGHT.*
P. CRUTTWELL & F. WESTBURG,
249(HUDR):SUMMER73-421
DOUGLAS, K. & R. LAMONT, EDS. DE
VIVE VOIX.
P.A. MANKIN, 399(MLJ):MAR72-193
W. WRAGE, 207(FR):APR72-1070
DOUGLAS, M. NATURAL SYMBOLS. (1ST
ED)
D.R. BELL, 479(PHQ):JUL72-280
DOUGLAS, P.H. IN THE FULLNESS OF
TIME.
J. TOBIN, 676(YR):SPRING73-438
DOUGLAS, R. WORKING WITH R.V.W.*
A.E.F. DICKINSON, 607:#102-33
DOUGLAS, S.A. POLITICAL SOCIALIZA-
TION & STUDENT ACTIVISM IN INDO-
NESIA.
J.S. MINTZ, 293(JAST):MAY72-739
DOUGLAS, W.O. GO EAST, YOUNG MAN.
N. BLIVEN, 442(NY):8JUL74-74
N. HENTOFF, 441:14APR74-1
C. LEHMANN-HAUPT, 441:22APR74-39
DOUGLAS-WILSON, I. & G. MC LACHLAN,
EDS. HEALTH SERVICE PROSPECTS.
617(TLS):18JAN74-48
DOUGLASS, E.P. THE COMING OF AGE OF
AMERICAN BUSINESS.
639(VQR):SUMMER72-CV
DOVER, K.J. ARISTOPHANIC COMEDY.
C. MOULTON, 676(YR):AUTUMN72-127
639(VQR):AUTUMN72-CXXXIII
DOVZHENKO, A. THE POET AS FILMMAKER.
617(TLS):5JUL74-729
DOW, H. THE ART OF ALEX COLVILLE.
S. KIERAN, 99:FEB74-42
DOW, S. & J. CHADWICK. CAMBRIDGE AN-
CIENT HISTORY. (VOL 2, CHAPTER 13)
J.T. HOOKER, 303:VOL92-225
DOWDEN, W.S. JOSEPH CONRAD.*
W.J. COOK, JR., 136:VOL4#3-54
DOWLING, J. - SEE BUERO VALLEJO, A.
DOWLING, J. & R. ANDIOC - SEE FERNÁN-
DEZ DE MORATÍN, L.

93

DOWNES, K. CHRISTOPHER WREN.
J. SUMMERSON, 46:MAR72-196
J. WILTON-ELY, 39:JUN72-516
DOWNEY, J. & B. JONES, EDS. FEARFUL
JOY.
617(TLS):16AUG74-879
DOWNIE, L., JR. MORTGAGE ON AMERICA.
B. KUTTNER, 441:28APR74-4
DOWNIE, R.S. ROLES & VALUES.*
A.J.M. MC KAY, 478:JUL72-152
A. MONTEFIORE, 479(PHQ):JUL72-
283
M. SCHUMAKER, 529(QQ):SUMMER72-
262
DOWNING, G.F. DOING THEOLOGY
THOUGHTFULLY IS REALLY VERY LIKE
THOUGHTFULLY DOING ALL SORTS OF
OTHER THINGS.
617(TLS):8NOV74-1269
DOWNING, W. THE PLAYER.
N. CALLENDAR, 441:6OCT74-38
DOWNS, R.C.S. PEOPLES.
M. LEVIN, 441:12MAY74-14
LORD DOWNSHIRE. LETTERS OF A GREAT
IRISH LANDLORD. (W.A. MAGUIRE, ED)
G.E. MINGAY, 617(TLS):15NOV74-
1296
DOYÉ, P. SYSTEMATISCHE WORTSCHATZ-
VERMITTLUNG IM ENGLISCHUNTERRICHT.
O. OPPERTSHAUSER, 430(NS):DEC72-
742
DOYLE, A.C. THE ADVENTURES OF SHER-
LOCK HOLMES. THE RETURN OF SHER-
LOCK HOLMES. THE MEMOIRS OF SHER-
LOCK HOLMES. HIS LAST BOW. THE
CASE-BOOK OF SHERLOCK HOLMES.
D.A.N. JONES, 362:19&26DEC74-849
DOYLE, A.C. A STUDY IN SCARLET.
THE SIGN OF FOUR. THE HOUND OF
THE BASKERVILLES. THE VALLEY OF
FEAR.
J. CAREY, 362:10JAN74-53
617(TLS):1FEB74-113
DOYNO, V.A. - SEE BARNES, B.
DOYON, J. YOB.
N. GREENE, 207(FR):FEB72-691
DRABBLE, M. ARNOLD BENNETT.
P. GILLIATT, 442(NY):23DEC74-81
L. GRAVER, 441:1SEP74-1
F. KERMODE, 453:31OCT74-3
C. LEHMANN-HAUPT, 441:17SEP74-37
N. MAC KENZIE, 362:11JUL74-57
A. WILSON, 617(TLS):12JUL74-737
DRABBLE, M. THE NEEDLE'S EYE.*
E. FEINSTEIN, 364:JUN/JUL72-166
DRACHKOVITCH, M.M., ED. FIFTY YEARS
OF COMMUNISM IN RUSSIA.
H. HANAK, 575(SEER):OCT73-632
DRAGO, G. LA GIUSTIZIA E LE GIUS-
TIZIE.
E. NAMER, 542:JAN-MAR72-57
DRAGONETTI, R. DANTE PÈLERIN DE LA
SAINTE FACE.
J.A. SCOTT, 545(RPH):FEB73-558
DRAKE, S. GALILEO STUDIES.
V.L. BULLOUGH, 551(RENQ):AUTUMN
72-319
"DRAMA IN EDUCATION." (VOL 1) (J.
HODGSON & M. BANHAM, EDS)
C. WILLIAMS, 157:SUMMER72-73
DRAMIŃSKA-JOCZOWA, M. WPLYW IDEOLO-
GÓW NA MLODEGO STENDHALA.
K. KASPRZYK, 535(RHL):MAR-APR72-
322

DRAPER, A. SMOKE WITHOUT FIRE.
M. ZANDER, 362:5DEC74-747
DRAPER, J.A., ED. CITIZEN PARTICI-
PATION: CANADA.
H. BUCHBINDER, 529(QQ):WINTER72-
544
DRAPER, R.P., ED. D.H. LAWRENCE:
THE CRITICAL HERITAGE.*
E. DELAVENAY, 189(EA):JAN-MAR72-
170
"THE DRAWINGS OF GEORGES SEURAT."
N. LYNTON, 592:JUL/AUG72-54
"THE DRAWINGS OF MERVYN PEAKE."
W. FEAVER, 362:19&26DEC74-847
DREIZEHNTER, A. - SEE ARISTOTLE
DRESCHER, H.W. THEMEN UND FORMEN
DES PERIODISCHEN ESSAYS IM SPÄTEN
18. JAHRHUNDERT.
F. RAU, 481(PQ):JUL72-726
DRESCHER, W. VERNUNFT UND TRANSZEN-
DENZ.
W. STEINBECK, 342:BAND63HEFT2-
270
DRESNER, C. & B. LITIVINOFF - SEE
WEIZMANN, C.
DRESSENDÖRFER, P. ISLAM UNTER DER
INQUISITION.
S.B. LIEBMAN, 182:VOL25#15/16-
564
DRESSLER, W. STUDIEN ZUR VERBALEN
PLURALITÄT.
J. BECHERT, 343:BAND14HEFT2-150
DREW, P. THE POETRY OF BROWNING.*
I. ARMSTRONG, 541(RES):FEB72-90
DREWITZ, I. BETTINE VON ARNIM.
J.F.F., 191(ELN):SEP72(SUPP)-136
DREWS, R. THE GREEK ACCOUNTS OF
EASTERN HISTORY.
617(TLS):12APR74-388
DREXLER, R. TO SMITHEREENS.*
S. O'CONNELL, 418(MR):WINTER73-
190
DREYER, E-J., ED. KLEINSTE PROSA
DER DEUTSCHEN SPRACHE.
R. GILL, 220(GL&L):OCT72-74
DREYFUS, D. - SEE FREUD, S.
DREYFUSS, H. SYMBOL SOURCEBOOK.
W.W. ATKIN, 505:SEP72-148
T. CROSBY, 46:AUG72-127
F.H. FORST, 186(ETC.):JUN72-211
44:APR72-10
DRIBERG, T. "SWAFF."
W. HARDCASTLE, 362:21MAR74-378
617(TLS):5APR74-360
DRIEU LA ROCHELLE, P. THE COMEDY
OF CHARLEROI & OTHER STORIES.
617(TLS):22FEB74-190
DRIEU LA ROCHELLE, P. SECRET JOUR-
NAL & OTHER WRITINGS.* (A. HAMIL-
TON, ED & TRANS)
J. MELLORS, 364:OCT/NOV73-141
DRINNON, R. - SEE HUNTER, J.D.
DRISCOLL, P. IN CONNECTION WITH KIL-
SHAW.
N. CALLENDAR, 441:21APR74-42
617(TLS):2AUG74-825
DRIVER, C.E. A SELECTION FROM OUR
SHELVES.
617(TLS):26APR74-456
DRIVER, C.J. A MESSIAH OF THE LAST
DAYS.
J. MELLORS, 362:24OCT74-551
617(TLS):4OCT74-1092

DRONKE, P. MEDIEVAL LATIN & THE
RISE OF EUROPEAN LOVE LYRIC. (VOL
2)
    L.J. FRIEDMAN, 545(RPH):FEB73-
    599
DRONKE, P. POETIC INDIVIDUALITY IN
THE MIDDLE AGES.*
    F. RICO, 545(RPH):MAY73-673
DRONKE, U. - SEE "THE POETIC EDDA"
DROSDOWSKI, G. DER GROSSE DUDEN.
(VOL 2: STILWÖRTERBUCH.) (6TH ED)
    S. GROSSE, 657(WW):NOV/DEC72-428
DROSTE, F.G. TAAL EN BETEKENIS,
BIJDRAGE IN EEN DISCUSSIE.
    G. STORMS, 206:JAN72-145
VON DROSTE-HÜLSHOFF, A. DIE JUDEN-
BUCHE.* (H. RÖLLEKE, ED)
    E. CARE, 402(MLR):JUL73-697
DROWER, M.S. THE CAMBRIDGE ANCIENT
HISTORY. (REV) (VOL 2, CHAPTER 21)
    M.C. ASTOUR, 318(JAOS):JUL-SEP
    72-447
DROWER, M.S. & J. BOTTÉRO. THE CAM-
BRIDGE ANCIENT HISTORY. (REV)
(VOL 1, CHAPTER 17)
    M.C. ASTOUR, 318(JAOS):JUL-SEP
    72-447
DRUCKER, H.M. THE POLITICAL USES OF
IDEOLOGY.
    617(TLS):12APR74-383
DRUILLET, P. LONE SLOANE.
    P. FRESNAULT-DERUELLE, 98:MAY72-
    460
DRUMMOND, A.L. & J. BULLOCH. THE
SCOTTISH CHURCH 1688-1843.
    617(TLS):1FEB74-114
DRUMMOND, D.F. THE MOUNTAIN.*
    J.W. HEALEY, 502(PRS):SUMMER72-
    183
DRUMMOND, J. THE BOON COMPANIONS.
    617(TLS):6SEP74-960
DRURY, A. COME NINEVEH, COME TYRE.*
    D. WILSON, 617(TLS):1NOV74-1216
DRUYCKAERTS, F. LA FORMATION DU
LIEN SEXUEL.
    M. CHASTAING, 542:OCT-DEC72-454
DRYDEN, J. ALL FOR LOVE. (D.M.
VIETH, ED)
    D. COHEN, 568(SCN):SPRING73-14
    K. STURGESS, 566:SPRING73-107
DRYDEN, J. AURENG-ZEBE.* (F.M.
LINK, ED)
    K. STURGESS, 566:SPRING73-107
DRYDEN, J. JOHN DRYDEN, SELECTED
CRITICISM. (J. KINSLEY & G. PAR-
FITT, EDS)
    P. LEGOUIS, 189(EA):OCT-DEC72-
    554
DRYDEN, J. FOUR COMEDIES. FOUR
TRAGEDIES. (BOTH ED BY L.A. BEAUR-
LINE & F. BOWERS)
    T.A. BIRRELL, 433:APR72-239
DRYDEN, J. THE WORKS OF JOHN DRY-
DEN.* (VOL 2) (H.T. SWEDENBERG,
JR., ED)
    J.R. CLARK, 568(SCN):FALL-WINTER
    73-68
    G.D. LORD, 566:SPRING73-101
DRYDEN, J. THE WORKS OF JOHN DRYDEN.
(VOL 3) (E. MINER & V.A. DEARING,
EDS)
    P. HARTH, 405(MP):FEB73-236
    P. LEGOUIS, 189(EA):APR-JUN72-
    323

DRYDEN, J. THE WORKS OF JOHN DRYDEN.
(VOL 8 ED BY J.H. SMITH, D. MAC
MILLAN & V.A. DEARING; VOL 9 ED BY
J. LOFTIS & V.A. DEARING)
    W. MYERS, 541(RES):AUG72-357
DRYDEN, J. THE WORKS OF JOHN DRY-
DEN.* (VOL 10) (M.E. NOVAK &
G.R. GUFFEY, EDS)
    P. LEGOUIS, 189(EA):APR-JUN72-
    325
    W. MYERS, 541(RES):AUG72-357
DRYDEN, J. THE WORKS OF JOHN DRYDEN.
(VOL 17) (S.H. MONK, ED)
    J.R. CLARK, 568(SCN):FALL-WINTER
    73-67
    P. HARTH, 481(PQ):JUL72-672
    R.D. HUME, 566:AUTUMN72-32
DUBARLE, D. & A. DOZ. LOGIQUE ET
DIALECTIQUE.
    W.H. WERKMEISTER, 319:JAN74-125
DUBBLEDAM, L.F. THE PRIMARY SCHOOL
& THE COMMUNITY IN MWANZA DISTRICT,
TANZANIA.
    S. MILBURN, 69:JAN72-79
DUBERMAN, M. BLACK MOUNTAIN.
    J.D. MARGOLIS, 651(WHR):SPRING73-
    207
    639(VQR):SPRING73-XC
DUBIE, N. ALEHOUSE SONNETS.
    639(VQR):WINTER73-XII
DUBIN, A.D. MORE CLASSIC TRAINS.
    442(NY):9DEC74-196
DUBOIS, C-G. MYTHE ET LANGAGE AU
SEIZIÈME SIÈCLE.*
    R. BAEHR, 430(NS):MAR72-178
    L.K. DONALDSON-EVANS, 207(FR):
    FEB72-749
    M. JEANNERET, 208(FS):OCT73-448
    P. SHARRATT, 402(MLR):JUL73-651
    205(FMLS):APR72-194
DUBOIS, E.T. - SEE RAPIN, R.
DUBOIS, J. GRAMMAIRE STRUCTURALE DU
FRANÇAIS. (VOL 1: NOM ET PRONOM;
VOL 2: LE VERBE.)
    R.S. MEYERSTEIN, 545(RPH):NOV72-
    427
DUBOIS, J. & OTHERS. DICTIONNAIRE
DU FRANÇAIS CONTEMPORAIN "SPÉCIAL
ENSEIGNEMENT."
    F. HELGORSKY, 209(FM):APR72-171
DUBOIS, J. & OTHERS. RHÉTORIQUE
GÉNÉRALE.*
    S. CHATMAN, 206:MAY72-436
DUBOIS, J. & F. DUBOIS-CHARLIER.
ELÉMENTS DE LINGUISTIQUE FRANÇAISE:
SYNTAXE.
    K. WINN, 430(NS):JUL72-425
DUBOS, R. A GOD WITHIN.
    J.P. DEGNAN, 249(HUDR):AUTUMN73-
    574
    F.P. HOSKEN, 44:NOV72-20
    617(TLS):5APR74-374
DUBOS, R. LOUIS PASTEUR, FREE
LANCE OF SCIENCE.
    N. ROLL-HANSEN, 84:NOV72-347
DUBUFFET, J. L'HOMME DU COMMUN À
L'OUVRAGE.
    R. CARDINAL, 617(TLS):6DEC74-
    1364
DUBY, G. THE EARLY GROWTH OF THE
EUROPEAN ECONOMY.* (FRENCH TITLE:
GUERRIERS ET PAYSANS VII-XIIE
SIÈCLE.)
    617(TLS):15MAR74-272

DUBY, G., ED. HISTOIRE DE LA FRANCE.
D. JOHNSON, 617(TLS):27DEC74-
1468
DUCHÁČEK, O. LE CHAMP CONCEPTUEL
DE LA BEAUTÉ EN FRANÇAIS MODERNE.
H.J. WOLF, 343:BAND14HEFT2-223
DUCHAMP, M. SALT SELLER. (M. SAN-
OUILLET & E. PETERSON, EDS)
K. BAKER, 61:MAY74-121
C. ROBINS, 441:3MAR74-23
DUCHÊNE, F. THE CASE OF THE HELMET-
ED AIRMAN.*
L.S. DEMBO, 27(AL):MAR73-136
676(YR):SPRING73-XIV
DUCHÊNE, R. RÉALITÉ VÉCUE ET ART
ÉPISTOLAIRE.* (VOL 1)
L. VAN DELFT, 207(FR):DEC71-518
DUCHÊNE, R. MME. DE SÉVIGNÉ.
J. ROUGEOT, 535(RHL):MAR-APR72-
306
DUCHÊNE, R. - SEE MADAME DE SÉVIGNÉ
DUCHET, M. ANTHROPOLOGIE ET HIS-
TOIRE AU SIÈCLE DES LUMIÈRES.
R. MERCIER, 557(RSH):APR-JUN72-
316
DUCHET, M. - SEE DE BUFFON, G.L.L.
DUCKWORTH, A.M. THE IMPROVEMENT OF
THE ESTATE.
H.S. BABB, 445(NCF):SEP72-238
F.W. BRADBROOK, 191(ELN):JUN73-
307
A. WRIGHT, 454:SPRING73-273
639(VQR):AUTUMN72-CXXXII
DUCLOS, C. CORRESPONDANCE DE CHARLES
DUCLOS (1704-1772).* (J. BRENGUES,
ED)
J.C. NICHOLLS, 549(RLC):APR-JUN
72-303
DUCLOS, J. MÉMOIRES.
R. WOHL, 207(FR):OCT71-227
DUDBRIDGE, G. THE HSI-YU CHI.*
N-T. TING, 292(JAF):JUL-SEP72-
284
DUDEK, L. COLLECTED POETRY.*
C. LEVENSON, 529(QQ):SUMMER72-
272
DUDLEY, D.R. THE ROMANS.*
A.F. NORMAN, 313:VOL62-171
DUDLEY, E. & M.E. NOVAK, EDS. THE
WILD MAN WITHIN.
639(VQR):AUTUMN73-CXLVIII
DUFF, J.D. JUVENAL SATIRES. (NEW
ED)
J. ANDRÉ, 555:VOL46FASC1-160
VON DÜFFEL, P. - SEE THOMASIUS, C.
DUFFY, C. BORODINO.
639(VQR):AUTUMN73-CLXVII
DUFOUR, A. "LES VIES DES FEMMES
CÉLÈBRES," PAR ANTOINE DUFOUR.
(G. JEANNEAU, ED)
D. RUSSELL, 207(FR):DEC71-533
C.C. WILLARD, 545(RPH):AUG72-206
DUFOURCQ, N., ED. L'HISTOIRE DE
L'ORGUE FRANÇAIS AUX XVIE, XVIIE
ET XVIIIE SIÈCLES.
W.L.S., 410(M&L):JUL73-363
DUFOURNET, J. PETITE INTRODUCTION
AUX BRANCHES I, IA ET IB DU
"ROMAN DE RENARD."
E.J. MICKEL, JR., 589:JAN73-131
DUFOURNET, J. VILLON ET SA FORTUNE
LITTÉRAIRE.
J. FOX, 208(FS):OCT73-445
[CONTINUED]

[CONTINUING]
P.M. GATHERCOLE, 207(FR):FEB72-
753
DUGDALE, N. A PROSPECT OF THE WEST.
E.N. CHUILLEANÁIN, 159(DM):
WINTER/SPRING71/72-123
DUGGAN, J.J. A CONCORDANCE OF THE
"CHANSON DE ROLAND."*
F. KOENIG, 545(RPH):AUG72-204
DUGGAN, J.J. THE SONG OF ROLAND.
617(TLS):29MAR74-320
639(VQR):AUTUMN73-CLII
DUGGER, R. OUR INVADED UNIVERSITIES.
G. LEVINE, 441:15SEP74-49
DU GUILLET, P. - SEE PERNETTE DU
GUILLET
DUINTJER, O.D. DE VRAAG NAAR HET
TRANSCENDENTALE VOORAL IN VERBAND
MET HEIDEGGER EN KANT.
K. OEDINGEN, 342:BAND63HEFT3-384
DUITS, C. PTAH HOTEP.
J. ROUDAUT, 98:JUN72-576
DUKORE, B.F. BERNARD SHAW DIRECTOR.*
T.F. EVANS, 571:SPRING72-188
P.B. HETRICK, 397(MD):DEC70-337
E. SHERIN, 572:JAN72-49
DUKORE, B.F. - SEE SHAW, G.B.
DULDULAO, M.D. CONTEMPORARY PHILIP-
PINE ART.
M. CHOU, 60:JUL-AUG73-60
DULLES, A. THE SURVIVAL OF DOGMA.
R.E. BROWN, 363:FEB72-72
R. KRESS, 613:SPRING72-144
DULLES, F.R. AMERICAN POLICY TOWARD
COMMUNIST CHINA.
O.E. CLUBB, 639(VQR):WINTER73-
145
VAN DÜLMAN, R. - SEE ANDREAE, J.V.
DUMAS, H. ARK OF BONES. (E. RED-
MOND, ED)
J. DECK, 441:20OCT74-36
"DUMBARTON OAKS PAPERS, NOS. 23 &
24."
D.M. NICOL, 303:VOL92-257
"DUMBARTON OAKS PAPERS, NO. 27."
617(TLS):8NOV74-1267
DUMÉRY, H. - SEE SAINT BONAVENTURE
DUMÉZIL, G. THE DESTINY OF THE WAR-
RIOR.*
W.F. HANSEN, 292(JAF):OCT-DEC72-
378
DUMONT, J-L. MARCEL AYMÉ ET LE MER-
VEILLEUX.
B.L. KNAPP, 207(FR):DEC71-501
DUMONT, J-P. LES SOPHISTES (FRAG-
MENTS ET TÉMOIGNAGES).
J. GRENIER, 542:JAN-MAR72-34
DUMONT, R. PAYSANNERIES AUX ABOIS.
J. PIEL, 98:AUG/SEP72-818
DUMONT, R. - SEE LEBRUN, P-A.
DUNAN, E. INVENTAIRE DE LA SÉRIE
AJ37. (VOL 1) [ARCHIVES NATION-
ALES, FRANCE]
P. LEWINSON, 14:JUL/OCT72-418
DUNAWAY, V. FROM HOOK TO TABLE.
N. HAZELTON, 441:1DEC74-96
DUNBABIN, J.P.D., ED. RURAL DISCON-
TENT IN NINETEENTH-CENTURY BRITAIN.
G. RUDÉ, 617(TLS):22NOV74-1303
DUNBAR, J. J.M. BARRIE.*
J.W. STEDMAN, 637(VS):DEC71-241

DUNBAR, M.J. ENVIRONMENT & GOOD
SENSE.
    J.R. VALLENTYNE, 529(QQ): SPRING
    72-109
DUNBAR, W. THE POEMS OF WILLIAM
DUNBAR. (W.M. MACKENZIE, ED)
    H. MURPHY, 159(DM): WINTER/SPRING
    71/72-118
DUNCAN, D.D. GOODBYE PICASSO.
    A. BROYARD, 441: 28OCT74-35
    J. RUSSELL, 441: 1DEC74-54
DUNCAN, G. MARX & MILL.
    P. MC CALLUM, 99: NOV/DEC74-36
DUNCAN, I. YOUR ISADORA. (F. STEEG-
MULLER, ED)
    P. ADAMS, 61: OCT74-120
DUNCAN, J.E. MILTON'S EARTHLY PARA-
DISE.*
    D. BUSH, 401(MLQ): MAR73-78
    L.H. JACOBS, 301(JEGP): OCT73-558
DUNCAN, T. THE SKY & TOMORROW.
    M. LEVIN, 441: 21APR74-41
DUNCAN, T.B. ATLANTIC ISLANDS.*
    D. ALDEN, 656(WMQ): OCT73-671
DUNCAN-JONES, K. & J. VAN DORSTEN -
SEE SIDNEY, P.
DUNDY, E. THE INJURED PARTY.
    V. CUNNINGHAM, 362: 28MAR74-413
    617(TLS): 15FEB74-163
DUNHAM, B. ETHICS DEAD & ALIVE.
    D. RIEPE, 484(PPR): DEC72-273
DUNKLING, L. ENGLISH HOUSE NAMES.
    L.R.N. ASHLEY, 424(DEC72-288
DUNLAP, J.R. THE BOOK THAT NEVER
WAS.
    D. CHAMBERS, 503: SUMMER72-102
DUNLOP, D. MEDICINES IN OUR TIME.
    617(TLS): 22MAR74-304
DUNLOP, J.E., ED. LATIN PASTORALS.
    R.G. PENMAN, 123: MAR73-81
DUNMORE, J. FRENCH EXPLORERS IN THE
PACIFIC.* (VOL 2)
    V. CONFER, 207(FR): OCT71-232
DUNN, C.J. & BUNZO TORIGOE - SEE
"THE ACTOR'S ANALECTS"
DUNN, D. AMERICAN INDIAN PAINTING
OF THE SOUTHWEST & PLAINS AREAS.
    D.J. CROWLEY, 290(JAAC): FALL71-
    138
DUNN, D. THE HAPPIER LIFE.*
    J. SYMONS, 364: AUG/SEP72-138
DUNN, D. - SEE LORD BYRON
DUNN, E.C., T. FOTITCH & B.M.
PEEBLES, EDS. THE MEDIEVAL DRAMA
& ITS CLAUDELIAN REVIVAL.
    E. BEAUMONT, 208(FS): JUL73-318
    G.J. BRAULT, 207(FR): FEB72-756
DUNN, J. MODERN REVOLUTIONS.
    C. JOHNSON, 32: MAR73-174
DUNN, N. TEAR HIS HEAD OFF HIS
SHOULDERS.
    V. CUNNINGHAM, 362: 9MAY74-606
    617(TLS): 10MAY74-493
DUNN, R.S. SUGAR & SLAVES.*
    E.V. GOVEIA, 656(WMQ): JAN73-149
    W.L. ROSE, 453: 17OCT74-29
    639(VQR): AUTUMN72-CXLI
DUNN, S.P. - SEE ZDRAVOMYSLOV, A.G.,
V.P. ROZHIN & V.A. IADOV
DUNNE, J.G. VEGAS.
    A. BROYARD, 441: 10JAN74-41
    C. SIGAL, 617(TLS): 27DEC74-1466
    J. YARDLEY, 441: 3FEB74-6
    442(NY): 11MAR74-135

DUNNE, J.S. THE CITY OF THE GODS.
    617(TLS): 20SEP74-1024
DUNNE, J.S. THE WAY OF ALL EARTH.
    617(TLS): 15FEB74-162
DUNNING, A. DIE STAATSMOTETTE 1480-
1555.*
    L.L. PERKINS, 414(MQ): OCT72-659
DUNNING, R. LOCAL SOURCES FOR THE
YOUNG HISTORIAN.
    617(TLS): 5APR74-376
DUNNING, T.P. & A.J. BLISS - SEE
"THE WANDERER"
DUNSEATH, T.K. SPENSER'S ALLEGORY
OF JUSTICE IN BOOK FIVE OF "THE
FAERIE QUEENE."
    M. MURRIN, 405(MP): MAY73-342
DUNSTAN, G.R. THE ARTIFICE OF
ETHICS.
    617(TLS): 20SEP74-1024
DUPEUX, G. LA FRANCE DE 1945 À 1965.
    P.A. ASTIER, 207(FR): OCT71-226
DUPIRE, M. ORGANISATION SOCIALE DES
PEUL.
    P. BURNHAM, 69: APR72-170
DUPLAIX-HALL, N., ED. INTERNATIONAL
ZOO YEARBOOK. (VOL 14)
    J. O'REILLY, 441: 22DEC74-4
DUPRÉ, L. THE OTHER DIMENSION.
    A. FLEW, 518: JAN73-5
    B. MURCHLAND, 484(PPR): JUN73-592
DU PREEZ, P. THE VONTSTERN CASE.
    617(TLS): 10MAY74-508
DUPRIEZ, B. L'ÉTUDE DES STYLES OU
LA COMMUTATION EN LITTÉRATURE.*
    J. CULLER, 599: FALL72-314
DURAC, J. WINES & THE ART OF TAST-
ING.
    N. HAZELTON, 441: 8DEC74-26
DURAFFOUR, A. GLOSSAIRE DES PATOIS
FRANCOPROVENÇAUX.*
    L-F. FLUTRE, 545(RPH): AUG72-157
DURAND, G. ETATS ET INSTITUTIONS.
    481(PQ): JUL72-528
DURAND, G. L'IMAGINATION SYMBOLIQUE.
    M. CHASTAING, 542: OCT-DEC72-455
DURAND, M.M. & NGUYỄN TRẦN HUÂN.
INTRODUCTION À LA LITTÉRATURE VIET-
NAMIENNE.*
    NGUYỄN ĐINH HOA, 318(JAOS): APR-
    JUN72-364
DURANT, W. & A. INTERPRETATIONS OF
LIFE.
    D.R. BISHOP, 613: SPRING72-119
DURAS, M. DESTROY, SHE SAID.*
    502(PRS): SPRING72-93
DURDEN, R.F. THE GRAY & THE BLACK.
    639(VQR): WINTER73-XXXIV
DÜRER, A. LETTRES, ECRITS THÉOR-
IQUES. (P. VAISSE, ED & TRANS)
    J-P. ATTAL, 98: JUN72-544
"ALBRECHT DÜRER, MASTER PRINTMAKER."*
    A. FRANKENSTEIN, 55: MAR73-16
DURGNAT, R. JEAN RENOIR.
    R. MAZZOCCO, 453: 3OCT74-31
DURGNAT, R. THE STRANGE CASE OF
ALFRED HITCHCOCK.
    D. WILSON, 617(TLS): 27SEP74-1035
DURHAM, F. ELMER RICE.
    W. DORSETT, 577(SHR): WINTER72-98
DURHAM, M. THE MAN WHO LOVED CAT
DANCING.
    E.L. BULOW, 649(WAL): FALL72-238
    S. O'CONNELL, 418(MR): WINTER73-
    190

DUROCHE, L.L. ASPECTS OF CRITICISM.
E.T. LONG, 125:0CT72-70
DURR, R.A. POETIC VISION & THE PSY-
CHEDELIC EXPERIENCE.*
G. WESTLAND, 290(JAAC):FALL71-
135
DURRELL, L. THE BLACK BOOK.*
D. DUNN, 364:JUN/JUL73-151
DURRELL, L. MONSIEUR, OR THE PRINCE
OF DARKNESS.
D.J. ENRIGHT, 362:170CT74-513
617(TLS):180CT74-1155
DURRELL, L. VEGA & OTHER POEMS.*
J. CAREY, 364:AUG/SEP73-125
DURRELL, M. & OTHERS. SPRACHATLAN-
TEN.*
E. SEEBOLD, 260(IF):BAND76-254
DURZAK, M., ED. DIE DEUTSCHE EXIL-
LITERATUR 1933-1945.
T.J. REED, 617(TLS):250CT74-1199
DURZAK, M., ED. DIE DEUTSCHE LITERA-
TUR DER GEGENWART.
F.D. HIRSCHBACH, 406:SUMMER73-
215
J.J. WHITE, 402(MLR):JUL73-711
DURZAK, M. POESIE UND RATIO.
E. BAHR, 406:FALL73-302
DÜSING, K. DIE TELEOLOGIE IN KANTS
WELTBEGRIFF.
W. STEINBECK, 342:BAND63HEFT4-
511
DUSSLER, L. RAPHAEL.*
E. VERHEYEN, 54:DEC72-550
DUTOURD, J. THE SPRINGTIME OF LIFE.
L.E. SISSMAN, 442(NY):9SEP74-129
DUTTON, B. - SEE DE BERCEO, G.
DUTTON, G. WHITE ON BLACK.
P. PORTER, 617(TLS):16AUG74-874
DUTU, A. CĂRTILE DE ÎNTELEPCIUNE
IN CULTURA ROMÂNĂ.
D.J. DELETANT, 149:DEC73-391
DUTU, A. & P. CERNOVODEANU - SEE
CANTEMIR, D.
DUUS, P. FEUDALISM IN JAPAN.
W.B. HAUSER, 318(JAOS):OCT-DEC
72-545
DUVAL, J.J. WORKING WITH STAINED
GLASS.
R. SOWERS, 139:DEC72-14
DUVAL, P. FOUR DECADES.
R. AYRE, 99:FEB74-41
DUVAL, P. HIGH REALISM IN CANADA.
T.R. MAC DONALD, 99:SEP74-50
DUVAL, P-M. LA GAULE JUSQU'AU MIL-
IEU DU VE SIÈCLE.*
W.R. CHALMERS, 123:DEC73-285
DUVENECK, J.W. FRANK DUVENECK.
M.S. YOUNG, 39:AUG72-163
DUVERGER, E. & H. VLIEGHE. DAVID
TENIERS DER ÄLTERE.
F-G. PARISET, 182:VOL25#3/4-94
M. WADDINGHAM, 90:FEB72-96
DUVERT, T. LE VOYAGEUR.
H.A. BOURAOUI, 207(FR):FEB72-692
DUYTSCHAEVER, J. JAMES JOYCE.
J. BARTHELS, 556(RLV):1972/2-220
DVORETZKY, E., ED. LESSING: DOKU-
MENTE ZUR WIRKUNGSGESCHICHTE 1755-
1968.
R.C. REIMER, 406:FALL73-328
DVORNIK, F. BYZANTINE MISSIONS
AMONG THE SLAVS.*
A. VLASTO, 303:VOL92-255
D'YACHKOVA, L.S. - SEE STRAVINSKY, I.

DYCK, J. - SEE NEUMARK, G.
DYCK, J.W. BORIS PASTERNAK.
B.P. SCHERR, 32:DEC73-857
DYER, B. THE CELTIC QUEEN.
M. LEVIN, 441:29DEC74-20
DYKEMAN, W. RIVERS OF AMERICA: THE
FRENCH BROAD.
I.R. DEE, 441:8SEP74-30
DYKHUIZEN, G. THE LIFE & MIND OF
JOHN DEWEY.
J. FEATHERSTONE, 441:3FEB74-18
H.W. SCHNEIDER, 319:0CT74-541
DYOS, H.J., ED. URBAN HISTORY YEAR-
BOOK 1974.
A. BRIGGS, 617(TLS):27DEC74-1456
DYOS, H.J. & M. WOLFF, EDS. THE
VICTORIAN CITY.*
F. KERMODE, 453:30MAY74-6
DYSERINCK, H. GRAF HERMANN KEYSER-
LING UND FRANKREICH.
G.R. KAISER, 52:BAND7HEFT1-102
DYSON, A.E. THE INIMITABLE DICKENS.*
M.A. FIDO, 637(VS):SEP71-101
DZHAGAROV, G. THE PUBLIC PROSECUTOR.
I. HATTINGH, 619(TC):VOL177#1043-
60

EAGLETON, T. SHAKESPEARE & SOCIETY.
N. RABKIN, 551(RENQ):WINTER72-
500
EAMES, A. SHIPS & SEAMEN OF ANGLE-
SEY.
617(TLS):3MAY74-484
EARLE, P. ROBERT E. LEE.
617(TLS):15MAR74-270
EARLE, P.G. PROPHET IN WILDERNESS.
M.S. STABB, 399(MLJ):DEC72-536
EARLE, V., ED. ON ACADEMIC FREEDOM.
J.P.D., 543:JUN72-749
EARLY, J. THE MAKING OF "GO DOWN,
MOSES."*
P. COVICI, JR., 584(SWR):WINTER
73-87
M. MILLGATE, 27(AL):MAR73-134
G.W. RUOFF, 651(WHR):WINTER73-92
J.W. TUTTLETON, 676(YR):WINTER73-
305
639(VQR):WINTER73-XX
"'EARTHQUAKE RISK' CONFERENCE PRO-
CEEDINGS."
W. ZUK, 505:DEC72-96
EASLEA, B. LIBERATION & THE AIMS OF
SCIENCE.
617(TLS):19APR74-407
EASON, E.A. - SEE LOPE DE VEGA
EASTHOPE, G. A HISTORY OF SOCIAL
RESEARCH METHODS.
617(TLS):26JUL74-807
EASTMAN, R.M. STYLE.
S. GILL, 447(N&Q):AUG72-310
EASTON, C. STRAIGHT AHEAD.
F. CONROY, 441:3FEB74-4
EASTON, M. AUBREY & THE DYING LADY.*
M. GREEN, 364:FEB/MAR73-144
EASTON, M. & M. HOLROYD. THE ART OF
AUGUSTUS JOHN.
K. CLARK, 617(TLS):180CT74-1149
D. MAY, 362:26SEP74-407
EATON, C.E. THE GIRL FROM IPANEMA.
H.E. FRANCIS, 219(GAR):WINTER72-
524

EATON, C.E. ON THE EDGE OF THE
KNIFE.
J.T. IRWIN, 569(SR):WINTER73-158
EATON, E. THE TREES & FIELDS WENT
THE OTHER WAY.
E. FISHER, 441:7APR74-24
EATON, L.K. AMERICAN ARCHITECTURE
COMES OF AGE.*
676(YR):SPRING73-VI
EAVES, R.G. HENRY VIII'S SCOTTISH
DIPLOMACY, 1513-1524.
W.T. MAC CAFFREY, 551(RENQ):WIN-
TER72-485
EAVES, T.C.D. & B.D. KIMPEL. SAMUEL
RICHARDSON.*
R.F. BRISSENDEN, 173(ECS):SUMMER
73-518
J. CARROLL, 541(RES):NOV72-504
R.A. DAY, 72:BAND21OHEFT4/6-397
W.M. SALE, JR., 481(PQ):JUL72-
752
W.B. WARDE, JR., 577(SHR):FALL72-
417
639(VQR):SPRING72-LXI
EAYRS, J. DIPLOMACY & ITS DISCON-
TENTS.
A. BREWIN, 529(QQ):WINTER72-551
EAYRS, J. GREENPEACE & HER ENEMIES.
L. HERTZMAN, 99:APR74-33
EBACHER, R. LA PHILOSOPHIE DANS LA
CITÉ TECHNIQUE.
H. RIEFSTAHL, 182:VOL25#13/14-
453
EBERHARD, W. A HISTORY OF CHINA.
C-Y. CHEN, 318(JAOS):OCT-DEC72-
542
EBERHARD, W. STUDIES IN CHINESE
FOLKLORE & RELATED ESSAYS.*
H.H. FRANKEL, 293(JAST):FEB72-
387
EBERHARD, W. STUDIES IN TAIWANESE
FOLKTALES.*
A. YEN, 318(JAOS):OCT-DEC72-541
EBERHART, M. WHILE THE PATIENT
SLEPT.
N. CALLENDAR, 441:10FEB74-31
EBERHART, M.G. JURY OF ONE. HOUSE
OF STORM.
N. CALLENDAR, 441:12MAY74-18
EBERHART, R. FIELDS OF GRACE.*
J. CAREY, 364:AUG/SEP73-125
P. COOLEY, 398:WINTER74-289
EBERHART, R. SHIFTS OF BEING.
T.J. HINES, 448:FALL-WINTER71/72-
115
EBERLE, R.A. NOMINALISTIC SYSTEMS.
L. STEVENSON, 479(PHQ):JAN72-81
F. WILSON, 486:DEC72-556
EBERSHTEIN, I. IANTARNYI KRAI.
A.E. SENN, 32:SEP73-617
EBERSOLE, F.B. THINGS WE KNOW.
R.L.M., 543:SEP71-122
EBY, O. A COVENANT OF DESPAIR.
268:JAN74-71
LORD ECCLES. ON COLLECTING.*
J. PYM, 159(DM):WINTER/SPRING
71/72-120
ECCLES, W.J. FRANCE IN AMERICA.
T.J.A. LE GOFF, 99:APR74-18
"ECCLESIASTES, OR THE PREACHER."
(HANDWRITTEN BY B. SHAHN)
R.H. LUCK, 363:MAY72-106

ECK, W. SENATOREN VON VESPASIAN BIS
HADRIAN.
G.P. BURTON, 313:VOL62-183
J-P. CALLU, 555:VOL46FASC2-354
F. LASSERRE, 182:VOL25#3/4-110
ECKERT, A.W. THE COURT-MARTIAL OF
DANIEL BOONE.
M. LEVIN, 441:7APR74-32
ECKERT, C.W., ED. FOCUS ON SHAKE-
SPEAREAN FILMS.
J.M. HIGHSMITH, 290(JAAC):SUMMER
73-565
ECKERT, J. DIE URCHRISTLICHE VER-
KÜNDIGUNG IM STREIT ZWISCHEN PAUL-
US UND SEINEN GEGNERN NACH DEM
GALATERBRIEF.
F.F. BRUCE, 182:VOL25#7/8-211
"JACOB ECKHARD'S CHOIRMASTER'S BOOK
OF 1809."* (G.W. WILLIAMS, ED)
N. TEMPERLEY, 415:MAY73-495
ECKHART, L. DAS RÖMISCHE DONAUKAS-
TELL SCHLÖGEN IN OBERÖSTERREICH.
O. BROGAN, 313:VOL62-210
ECKSTEIN, A. - SEE COHEN, J.A., R.F.
DERABERGER & J.R. GARSON
ECO, U. IL PROBLEMA ESTETICO IN SAN
TOMASO.
A. FOREST, 542:JAN-MAR72-74
ÉCOLE, J. - SEE WOLFF, C.
"THE ECONOMIC PROMISE OF THE REPUB-
LIC OF VIETNAM."
W. SHAWCROSS, 453:18JUL74-16
ECONOMOU, G.D. THE GODDESS NATURA
IN MEDIEVAL LITERATURE.*
639(VQR):SUMMER73-CXVII
"ECRITS DU CANADA FRANÇAIS." (VOL 30)
E.J. TALBOT, 207(FR):DEC71-489
EDDINS, D. YEATS: THE NINETEENTH
CENTURY MATRIX.
T.R. HENN, 541(RES):MAY72-234
W.G.R., 502(PRS):FALL72-273
EDDY, D.D. A BIBLIOGRAPHY OF JOHN
BROWN.*
W.B. TODD, 517(PBSA):JAN-MAR73-
80
EDDY, S.L., JR. THE FOUNDING OF
"THE CORNHILL MAGAZINE."
J.O. BAYLEN, 637(VS):DEC72-245
G.B. TENNYSON, 445(NCF):JUN72-
117
EDE, C.M. CANADIAN ARCHITECTURE
1960/70.
505:SEP72-166
EDEL, L. HENRY JAMES.* (VOLS 1-4)
M. BELL, 418(MR):SPRING73-391
EDEL, L. HENRY JAMES.* (VOL 5:
THE MASTER, 1901-1916.)
Q. ANDERSON, 639(VQR):AUTUMN72-
621
M. BELL, 418(MR):SPRING73-391
M.L. KRUPNICK, 454:SPRING73-257
EDFELT, J. BIRGER SJÖBERG.
W.A. BERENDSOHN, 182:VOL25#7/8-
221
EDGAR, I.I. ESSAYS IN ENGLISH LIT-
ERATURE & HISTORY.
566:SPRING73-114
EDGAR, I.I. SHAKESPEARE, MEDICINE &
PSYCHIATRY.*
E. CLARKE, 447(N&Q):APR72-151
EDGAR, W.B. - SEE PRINGLE, R.

EDGEWORTH, M. LETTERS FROM ENGLAND,
1813-1844. (C. COLVIN, ED)
M. ALLOTT, 677:VOL3-304
J.M.S. TOMPKINS, 541(RES):NOV72-
516
EDGREN, E. TEMPORAL CLAUSES IN ENG-
LISH.
M. RYDÉN, 597(SN):VOL.44#2-450
EDIE, J.M., F.H. PARKER & C.O.
SCHRAG, EDS. PATTERNS OF THE
LIFE-WORLD.
R.S., 543:DEC71-377
EDMOND, M-P. PHILOSOPHIE POLITIQUE.
G. BRYKMAN, 542:OCT-DEC72-473
EDMUNDS, P.W. VIRGINIANS OUT FRONT.
639(VQR):SPRING73-LXXVII
EDSON, R. THE CLAM THEATER.
G. HENRY, 491:AUG74-292
EDWARDES, M. EAST-WEST PASSAGE.
H. WILHELM, 293(JAST):AUG72-921
EDWARDES, M. PLASSEY.*
R.A. CALLAHAN, 318(JAOS):JAN-MAR
72-182
EDWARDS, A. FLAWED WORDS & STUBBORN
SOUNDS.
J. CONNOLLY, 607:#99-22
EDWARDS, A. THE HESITANT HEART.
M. LEVIN, 441:31MAR74-40
EDWARDS, A. & A. ROGERS, EDS. AGRI-
CULTURAL RESOURCES.
617(TLS):10MAY74-508
EDWARDS, A.F. LIKELIHOOD.
I. HACKING, 84:MAY72-132
EDWARDS, A.S., ED. THE STATE REC-
ORDS OF SOUTH CAROLINA: JOURNALS
OF THE PRIVY COUNCIL, 1783-1789.
W. FRALEY, 14:JUL/OCT72-411
EDWARDS, D.L. IAN RAMSEY.
617(TLS):18JAN74-50
EDWARDS, E. ANECDOTES OF PAINTERS.
D. FITZ-GERALD, 90:SEP72-639
EDWARDS, G. - SEE CALDERÓN DE LA
BARCA, P.
EDWARDS, G.P. THE LANGUAGE OF
HESIOD IN ITS TRADITIONAL CONTEXT.
G. GIANGRANDE, 303:VOL92-188
W. SALE, 24:WINTER73-384
M.L. WEST, 123:MAR73-19
EDWARDS, I.E.S. THE TREASURES OF
TUTANKHAMUN.
T.G.H. JAMES, 617(TLS):18OCT74-
1170
EDWARDS, J. THE WORKS OF JONATHAN
EDWARDS. (VOL 4) (C.C. GOEN, ED)
D.D. HALL, 432(NEQ):SEP72-455
G.T. MILLER, 656(WMQ):OCT72-655
EDWARDS, O.D. & B. RANSOM - SEE CON-
NOLLY, J.
EDWARDS, P. & A. PAP, EDS. A MODERN
INTRODUCTION TO PHILOSOPHY.
D.M. ARMSTRONG, 63:DEC73-270
EDWARDS, P.D. ANTHONY TROLLOPE.
J.C. MAXWELL, 447(N&Q):FEB72-79
EDWARDS, R.B. FREEDOM, RESPONSIBIL-
ITY & OBLIGATION.
G.G.G., 543:DEC71-351
EDWARDS, R.D. AN ATLAS OF IRISH
HISTORY.
617(TLS):18JAN74-45
EDWARDS, S. THE EXPLOITERS.
M. LEVIN, 441:10NOV74-24
EDWARDS, S. REBEL.
M. CUNLIFFE, 441:4AUG74-2
A. WHITMAN, 441:6JUL74-15

EDWARDS, T. THE SONNETS OF THOMAS
EDWARDS.
617(TLS):26JUL74-810
EDWARDS, T.R. IMAGINATION & POWER.*
G.M. CRUMP, 191(ELN):JUN73-316
P.J. KORSHIN, 481(PQ):JUL72-608
A. MAC GILLIVRAY, 613:AUTUMN72-
450
P. ZIETLOW, 473(PR):3/1973-503
EFRON, A. "DON QUIXOTE" & THE DUL-
CINEATED WORLD.
E.C. RILEY, 402(MLR):JUL73-676
U. WICKS, 454:FALL72-84
J. ZASLOVE, 648:JAN73-57
EGBERT, D.D. SOCIAL RADICALISM &
THE ARTS.*
W.M. JOHNSTON, 290(JAAC):WINTER
71-271
EGERTON, C. - SEE "THE GOLDEN LOTUS"
EGERTON, J. THE AMERICANIZATION OF
DIXIE.
M. IVINS, 441:21APR74-7
EGGEBRECHT, H.H., ED. HANDWÖRTER-
BUCH DER MUSIKALISCHEN TERMINOLO-
GIE. (PT 1)
J.A.W., 410(M&L):APR73-237
EGGENSCHWILER, D. THE CHRISTIAN
HUMANISM OF FLANNERY O'CONNOR.
S.A. BLACK, 648:JAN73-81
J.E. JENSEN, 70(ANQ):SEP73-14
I. MALIN, 27(AL):MAR73-137
EGGERS, H., ED. DER VOLKSNAME
DEUTSCHE.
H-W. EROMS, 343:BAND15HEFT2-185
EGGERS, J.P. KING ARTHUR'S LAUREATE.
E.E. SMITH, 125:FEB73-198
EGGERT, H. STUDIEN ZUR WIRKUNGSGE-
SCHICHTE DES DEUTSCHEN HISTORIS-
CHEN ROMANS 1850-1875.
L.H.C. THOMAS, 402(MLR):JUL73-
700
EGROT, M. & J. MAITRON, EDS. DEUX-
IÈME PARTIE: 1864-1871.
J.T. JOUGHIN, 207(FR):DEC71-457
EHLE, J. THE JOURNEY OF AUGUST
KING.*
L. ROOKE, 376:JAN72-119
EHNINGER, D. CONTEMPORARY RHETORIC.
J. HENDRIX, 583:SPRING73-301
EHRARD, A. - SEE ZOLA, É.
EHRE, M. OBLOMOV & HIS CREATOR.
V.S. PRITCHETT, 453:7MAR74-22
617(TLS):26APR74-442
EHRENBURG, I. SELECTIONS FROM
PEOPLE, YEARS, LIFE. (C. MOODY,
ED)
205(FMLS):OCT72-382
EHRENPREIS, A.H. - SEE SMITH, C.
EHRGOTT, U. - SEE KUHN, A.
EHRISMANN, G. - SEE VON TRIMBERG, H.
EHRLICH, M. THE REINCARNATION OF
PETER PROUD.
N. CALLENDAR, 441:3NOV74-71
EHRLICH, P.R. & A.H. THE END OF
AFFLUENCE.
C. LEHMANN-HAUPT, 441:28NOV74-31
EHRMANN, J., ED. STRUCTURALISM.
L.B. CEBIK, 219(GAR):SUMMER72-
233
EICH, G. EICH. (T. SAVORY, TRANS)
C. TOMLINSON, 364:OCT/NOV72-125
EICH, G. GESAMMELTE WERKE. (H.
OHDE & OTHERS, EDS)
617(TLS):29MAR74-314

EICHELBERGER, C.L., COMP. A GUIDE
TO CRITICAL REVIEWS OF UNITED
STATES FICTION, 1870-1910.
  B. NEVIUS, 445(NCF):SEP72-241
EICHHORN, W. CHINESE CIVILIZATION.
  A. LONSDALE, 447(N&Q):JUN72-240
EICHLER, W. JAN VAN RUUSBROECS
"BRULOCHT" IN OBERDEUTSCHER ÜBER-
LIEFERUNG.*
  C.C. DE BRUIN, 433:JAN72-107
  G.B. DESOER, 382(MAE):1973/1-105
EICHNER, H., ED. "ROMANTIC" & ITS
COGNATES.
  U. WEISSTEIN, 301(JEGP):JUL73-
407
EICHNER, H. FRIEDRICH SCHLEGEL.*
  R. BELGARDT, 399(MLJ):MAY72-342
EICHWEDE, W. REVOLUTION UND INTER-
NATIONALE POLITIK.
  J.W. HULSE, 32:MAR73-173
EIDELBERG, P.G. THE GREAT RUMANIAN
PEASANT REVOLT OF 1907.
  D. CHIROT, 617(TLS):15NOV74-1295
EIFLER, G., ED. RITTERLICHES TUGEND-
SYSTEM.
  B. SCHUCHARD, 72:BAND210HEFT1/3-
153
EIFLER, M. THOMAS MANN.
  E. SCHIFFER, 221(GQ):MAY72-522
EIGHMY, J.L. CHURCHES IN CULTURAL
CAPTIVITY.
  H.S. SMITH, 579(SAQ):AUTUMN73-
614
EILERS, W. DEUTSCH-PERSISCHES WÖR-
TERBUCH. (PTS 5-7)
  M.J. DRESDEN, 318(JAOS):OCT-DEC
72-570
EIMERMACHER, K., ED. DOKUMENTE ZUR
SOWJETISCHEN LITERATURPOLITIK 1917-
1932.
  D. TSCHIŽEWSKIJ, 72:BAND210HEFT
4/6-479
EINBOND, B.L. SAMUEL JOHNSON'S
ALLEGORY.
  C. MC INTOSH, 481(PQ):JUL72-701
EIS, G. FORSCHUNGEN ZUR FACHPROSA.*
  D. BLAMIRES, 402(MLR):JUL73-688
  G.F. JONES, 400(MLN):OCT72-782
EIS, G. VOM ZAUBER DER NAMEN.*
  J.A. HUISMAN, 433:JUL72-374
  C.V.J. RUSS, 402(MLR):OCT73-923
EISELEY, L. NOTES OF AN ALCHEMIST.
  639(VQR):SPRING73-LXII
EISENBERG, A.M. & J.A. ILARDO. ARGU-
MENT.
  H. PELHAM, 583:WINTER72-210
EISENSTADT, S. THE PROPHETS.
  A.J. RAWICK, 287:NOV72-27
EISMANN, G. - SEE SCHUMANN, R.
EISNER, L.H. THE HAUNTED SCREEN.*
  G. MILLAR, 362:SEP74-542
EISSENSTAT, B.W., ED. LENIN &
LENINISM.
  M. MC CAULEY, 575(SEER):JUL73-
480
EISSFELDT, O. KLEINE SCHRIFTEN.
(VOLS 4&5) (R. SELLHEIM & F.
MAASS, EDS)
  F.F. BRUCE, 182:VOL25#22-779
EITNER, L. NEOCLASSICISM & ROMANTI-
CISM 1750-1850.
  H. HONOUR, 90:JUN72-419
  J.J. SPECTOR, 54:MAR72-102

EITREM, S., L. AMUNDSEN & R.P. WIN-
NINGTON-INGRAM. FRAGMENTS OF
UNKNOWN GREEK TRAGIC TEXTS.
  V. MOUTSOPOULOS, 542:JAN-MAR72-
66
EKAKU, H. - SEE UNDER HAKUIN EKAKU
EKEH, P.P. SOCIAL EXCHANGE THEORY.
  617(TLS):22NOV74-1304
EKELÖF, G. SELECTED POEMS.*
  R. FULTON, 565:VOL13#2-54
  639(VQR):WINTER73-XVI
EKLUND, S. THE PERIPHRASTIC, COM-
PLETIVE & FINITE USE OF THE PRES-
ENT PARTICIPLE IN LATIN.*
  A. ERNOUT, 555:VOL46FASC1-145
EKMANN, B. GESELLSCHAFT UND GEWIS-
SEN.
  E. SPEIDEL, 402(MLR):JUL73-707
EKSCHMITT, W. DIE KONTROVERSE UM
LINEAR B.*
  G. NEUMANN, 343:BAND14HEFT2-187
ELAM, Y. THE SOCIAL & SEXUAL ROLES
OF HIMA WOMEN.
  617(TLS):19APR74-423
ELBIRK, H., ED. 12 NEGRO SPIRITUALS.
  F. HOWES, 415:DEC73-1241
LORD ELCHO. THE AFFAIRS OF SCOTLAND
1744-46.
  617(TLS):1FEB74-112
ELDER, A. FOR THE RECORD.
  S.E. LEE, 581:SEP73-335
ELDERS, L. ARISTOTLE'S THEOLOGY.
  K.W. HARRINGTON, 319:OCT74-523
ELDERS, W. STUDIEN ZUR SYMBOLIK IN
DER MUSIK DER ALTEN NIEDERLÄNDER.
  J.B., 410(M&L):OCT73-489
  M.R. MANIATES, 414(MQ):JUL72-482
ELDRIDGE, P. FRANÇOIS RABELAIS.
  R.D. COTTRELL, 399(MLJ):NOV72-
471
ELEGANT, R.S. MAO'S GREAT REVOLU-
TION.
  P.H. CHANG, 293(JAST):NOV71-195
"THE ELEVENTH ANNUAL REPORT OF THE
KEEPER OF PUBLIC RECORDS." [LORD
CHANCELLOR'S OFFICE, GREAT BRIT-
AIN]
  M.H. ARNOLD, 14:JUL/OCT72-419
ELEY, L. - SEE HUSSERL, E.
ELIADE, M. FRAGMENTS D'UN JOURNAL.
  617(TLS):18JAN74-50
ELIADE, M. GODS, GODDESSES, & MYTHS
OF CREATION. MAN & THE SACRED.
DEATH, AFTERLIFE, & ESCHATOLOGY.
FROM MEDICINE MEN TO MUHAMMAD.
  H. COX, 441:11AUG74-17
ELIADE, M. LA NOSTALGIE DES ORI-
GINES.
  H. ROUSSEAU, 98:JAN72-71
ELIAS, R.H. ENTANGLING ALLIANCES
WITH NONE.
  S.N. GREBSTEIN, 27(AL):NOV73-484
  639(VQR):SUMMER73-CXXIII
ELIASON, J. FRESH MEAT/WARM WEATHER.
  M. LEVIN, 441:29DEC74-20
ELIASON, N.E. THE LANGUAGE OF CHAU-
CER'S POETRY.
  R.M. WILSON, 402(MLR):OCT73-889
ELIAV, A.L. LAND OF THE HART.
  S. HASSAN, 453:14NOV74-45
  N. SAFRAN, 441:7APR74-16

ELIOT, T.S. THE WASTE LAND.* (V.
   ELIOT, ED)
      M. MONTGOMERY, 219(GAR):WINTER72-
      415
      A.D. MOODY, 97(CQ):VOL6#1-45
      A. RIDLER, 541(RES):AUG72-380
ELIOVSON, S. NAMAQUALAND IN FLOWER.
   617(TLS):29MAR74-348
ELISSÉEFF, V. JAPAN.
   617(TLS):2AUG74-838
ELKANA, Y. THE DISCOVERY OF THE CON-
   SERVATION OF ENERGY.
   J. NORTH, 617(TLS):8NOV74-1251
ELKHADEM, S. ZUR GESCHICHTE DES
   DEUTSCHEN ROMANS.
   268:JAN74-76
ELKIN, S. THE DICK GIBSON SHOW.
   E. ROVIT, 659:AUTUMN74-539
ELKIN, S. ELIGIBLE MEN.
   S. CLAPP, 617(TLS):13DEC74-1405
ELKIN, S. SEARCHES & SEIZURES.*
   E. ROVIT, 659:AUTUMN74-539
   M. WOOD, 453:21MAR74-19
ELLENBOGEN, G. THE NIGHT UNSTONES.
   D. BARBOUR, 529(QQ):WINTER72-569
ELLINGTON, D. MUSIC IS MY MISTRESS.
   D. THOMAS, 362:22AUG74-252
   J. WIDEMAN, 441:18AUG74-6
LADY ELLIOT. THE ELLIOTS.
   617(TLS):13SEP74-984
ELLIOT, G. TWENTIETH CENTURY BOOK
   OF THE DEAD.
   W.H. AUDEN, 453:12DEC74-28
ELLIOT, R. MYTHE ET LÉGENDE DANS LE
   THÉÂTRE DE RACINE.
   C. FRANÇOIS, 207(FR):OCT71-268
   R.C. KNIGHT, 208(FS):JAN73-62
ELLIOTT, D.W. PIECES OF NIGHT.*
   J. BOOTH, 617(TLS):8NOV74-1248
ELLIOTT, J.H. THE OLD WORLD & THE
   NEW, 1492-1650.*
   J.K. GADOL, 551(RENQ):WINTER72-
   470
ELLIOTT, L. I WILL BE CALLED JOHN.
   617(TLS):3MAY74-481
ELLIOTT, R.C. THE SHAPE OF UTOPIA.*
   566:SPRING72-86
ELLIS, C. UNDER THE STONE.
   H. MURPHY, 159(DM):SUMMER72-131
ELLIS, J. ARMIES IN REVOLUTION.
   617(TLS):1MAR74-197
ELLIS, J. - SEE GILBERT, W.S.
ELLIS, J. & R. MOORE. SCHOOL FOR
   SOLDIERS.
   R. SHERRILL, 441:27OCT74-3
ELLIS, J.J. THE NEW ENGLAND MIND IN
   TRANSITION.
   617(TLS):15MAR74-270
ELLIS, J.M. KLEIST'S "PRINZ FRIED-
   RICH VON HOMBURG."
   I.F., 191(ELN):SEP72(SUPP)-173
   M. GARLAND, 220(GL&L):JUL73-338
ELLIS, J.M. NARRATION IN THE GERMAN
   NOVELLE.
   E. WRIGHT, 617(TLS):15NOV74-1292
ELLIS, J.R. & R.D. MILNS. THE SPEC-
   TRE OF PHILIP.*
   J.W. COLE, 487:SUMMER72-202
   W.K. LACEY, 67:MAY73-113
ELLIS, P.B. THE CORNISH LANGUAGE &
   ITS LITERATURE.
   A.L. ROWSE, 617(TLS):22NOV74-
   1305
ELLIS, P.B. - SEE CONNOLLY, J.

ELLIS, R.E. THE JEFFERSONIAN
   CRISIS.*
   L.R. GERLACH, 432(NEQ):MAR72-141
ELLISON, F.P. & OTHERS. MODERN POR-
   TUGUESE.
   J.L. WALKER, 238:MAY72-395
ELLISON, J. GOD ON BROADWAY.
   639(VQR):AUTUMN72-CLVIII
ELLISON, J.W. THE SUMMER AFTER THE
   WAR.
   S. O'CONNELL, 418(MR):WINTER73-
   190
ELLMAN, M. SOVIET PLANNING TODAY.
   E. AMES, 32:JUN73-398
   P.C. ROBERTS, 550(RUSR):APR72-
   198
ELLMANN, R. GOLDEN CODGERS.*
   R. NYE, 364:DEC73/JAN74-158
   S. SPENDER, 453:19SEP74-18
ELLMANN, R. ULYSSES ON THE LIFFEY.*
   R. BOYLE, 659:SPRING74-262
   K. CONNELLY, 676(YR):AUTUMN72-94
   A.A. DE VITIS, 651(WHR):WINTER73-
   90
   C. HART, 677:VOL3-330
   G. SMITH, 579(SAQ):WINTER73-175
   D. THORBURN, 473(PR):2/1973-306
   42(AR):SPRING/SUMMER72-245
   639(VQR):WINTER73-XXI
ELLMANN, R. - SEE JOYCE, J.
ELLMANN, R. - SEE WILDE, O.
ELLRICH, R.J. ROUSSEAU & HIS READ-
   ER.*
   H.M. DAVIDSON, 405(MP):AUG72-70
   J.S. SPINK, 208(FS):JAN73-68
ELLUL, J. A CRITIQUE OF THE NEW
   COMMONPLACES.
   R.L. ANDERSON, 480(P&R):WINTER72-
   61
ELLUL, J. THE FALSE PRESENCE OF THE
   KINGDOM.
   H.B. GOW, 396(MODA):SUMMER73-303
ELMAN, R. BADMEN OF THE WEST.
   A. BROYARD, 441:11DEC74-49
ELON, A. & S. HASSAN. BETWEEN
   ENEMIES.
   M. WALZER, 441:6OCT74-5
ELRINGTON, C.R., ED. A HISTORY OF
   THE COUNTY OF CAMBRIDGE & THE ISLE
   OF ELY. (VOL 5)
   617(TLS):1MAR74-217
VAN ELS, T.J.M. THE KASSEL MANU-
   SCRIPT OF BEDE'S "HISTORIA ECCLES-
   IASTICA GENTIS ANGLORUM" & ITS OLD
   ENGLISH MATERIAL.
   A. CAMPBELL, 382(MAE):1973/2-153
EL'SBERG, J.E. SOVREMENNAJA BURŽUAZ-
   NAJA LITERATURNAJA TEORIJA.
   E. REISSNER, 654(WB):10/1972-187
ELSBERRY, T. MARIE OF ROMANIA.
   617(TLS):11JAN74-38
ELSCHENBROICH, A. ROMANTISCHE SEHN-
   SUCHT UND KOSMOGONIE.
   A. CAMIGLIANO, 406:WINTER73-418
ELSEN, A., J. KIRK & T. VARNEDOE.
   THE DRAWINGS OF RODIN.*
   C. LAMPERT, 592:JUL/AUG72-53
ELSEN, A.E. PURPOSES OF ART.
   M.V. ALPER, 58:NOV72-92
ELSOM, J. EROTIC THEATRE.
   R. BRYDEN, 362:14FEB74-213
   617(TLS):1MAR74-214

ELTON, G.R. STUDIES IN TUDOR & STU-
ART POLITICS & GOVERNMENT.
S.B. CHRIMES, 617(TLS):6DEC74-
1392
ELUARD, P. LETTRES À JOË BOUSQUET.
(L. SCHÉLER, ED)
R. CARDINAL, 617(TLS):11OCT74-
1134
ELVIN, H. THE INCREDIBLE MILE.
268:JAN74-73
ELVIN, L. THE HARRISON STORY.
617(TLS):13SEP74-970
ELWERT, W.T. G.G. BELLI OSSERVATORE
DI FENOMENI LINGUISTICI.
P. GIBELLINI, 228(GSLI):VOL149
FASC466/467-400
ELWERT, W.T. STUDIEN ZU DEN ROMAN-
ISCHEN SPRACHEN UND LITERATUREN.
(VOL 5)
E.H. YARRILL, 182:VOL25#11-353
ELY, D. MR. NICHOLAS.
A. BROYARD, 441:8AUG74-37
M. LEVIN, 441:21JUL74-14
EMANUEL, J.A. & T.L. GROSS, EDS.
DARK SYMPHONY.
L.W. WAGNER, 573(SSF):WINTER72-
97
EMBREE, A.T., ED. ALBERUNI'S INDIA.
H.K. SHERWANI, 273(IC):JAN72-83
EMBREE, L.E., ED. LIFE-WORLD & CON-
SCIOUSNESS.
W. MAYS, 518:JAN73-11
EMENEAU, M.B. TODA SONGS.
P. HOCKINGS, 293(JAST):FEB72-446
EMERSON, E., ED. MAJOR WRITERS OF
EARLY AMERICAN LITERATURE.*
S. LANIER, 656(WMQ):OCT73-667
A. WARREN, 27(AL):NOV73-453
EMERSON, E.H. ENGLISH PURITANISM
FROM JOHN HOOPER TO JOHN MILTON.
H. LANDRY, 568(SCN):SPRING73-3
EMERSON, O.B., ED. ALABAMA PRIZE
STORIES - 1970.
J.E. TILFORD, JR., 573(SSF):FALL
72-426
EMERSON, R.W. THE COLLECTED WORKS
OF RALPH WALDO EMERSON. (VOL 1)
(R.E. SPILLER & A.R. FERGUSON, EDS)
G.W. ALLEN, 27(AL):MAR73-118
E.J. ROSE, 150(DR):WINTER72/73-
699
EMERSON, R.W. THE EARLY LECTURES OF
RALPH WALDO EMERSON. (VOL 3) (R.E.
SPILLER & W.E. WILLIAMS, EDS)
G.W. ALLEN, 27(AL):MAR73-118
EMERSON, R.W. THE JOURNALS & MISCEL-
LANEOUS NOTEBOOKS OF RALPH WALDO
EMERSON.* (VOL 8) (W.H. GILMAN &
J.E. PARSONS, EDS)
C. BODE, 402(MLR):JAN73-161
EMERSON, R.W. THE JOURNALS & MISCEL-
LANEOUS NOTEBOOKS OF RALPH WALDO
EMERSON.* (VOL 9) (R.H. ORTH &
A.H. FERGUSON, EDS)
E.J. ROSE, 150(DR):WINTER72/73-
699
639(VQR):SUMMER72-CIII
EMERY, A. DARTINGTON HALL.*
J. LEES-MILNE, 39:AUG72-165
EMERY, D. IN CHARACTER.*
D. THOMAS, 362:19&26DEC74-846
EMERY, F. THE OXFORDSHIRE LAND-
SCAPE.
617(TLS):7JUN74-620

EMERY, L.F. BLACK DANCE IN THE
UNITED STATES FROM 1619 TO 1970.
J.L. HANNA, 187:JAN74-155
EMERY, N. ARNOLD BENNETT (1867-
1931).
L. TILLIER, 189(EA):JUL-SEP72-
444
EMERY, R.F. THE FINANCIAL INSTITU-
TIONS OF SOUTHEAST ASIA.
F.H. GOLAY, 293(JAST):FEB72-454
"EMIGRATION IN THE VICTORIAN AGE."
617(TLS):29MAR74-343
EMMANUEL, A. UNEQUAL EXCHANGE.
M. LIPTON, 617(TLS):2AUG74-830
EMMANUEL, P. BAUDELAIRE.
L.B. HYSLOP, 207(FR):FEB72-729
EMMANUEL, P. SOPHIA.
617(TLS):24MAY74-554
EMMEL, H. GESCHICHTE DES DEUTSCHEN
ROMANS. (VOL 1)
I. SCHUSTER, 268:JUL74-160
EMMERICH, H. FEDERAL ORGANIZATION &
ADMINISTRATIVE MANAGEMENT.
639(VQR):SPRING72-LXXIII
EMMERSON, G.S. RANTIN' PIPE & TREM-
BLIN' STRING.
A. MUNRO, 595(SCS):VOL17PT1-85
P.M. SHAPIRO, 151:FEB72-86
EMMERSON, G.S. A SOCIAL HISTORY OF
SCOTTISH DANCE.
R. BAKER, 151:NOV72-86
S.J. WYNNE-EDWARDS, 529(QQ):WIN-
TER72-574
EMMERSON, J.K. ARMS, YEN & POWER.
W. BARBER, 50(ARQ):SUMMER72-188
W. BARBER, 150(DR):SPRING72-146
EMMET, D. & A. MAC INTYRE, EDS. SOC-
IOLOGICAL THEORY & PHILOSOPHICAL
ANALYSIS.
R.J.B., 543:SEP71-146
E. BARKER, 262:WINTER72-463
EMMISON, F.G., ED. EARLY ESSEX TOWN
MEETINGS: BRAINTREE 1619-1636;
FINCHINGFIELD 1626-1634.
A. CRAWFORD, 325:OCT72-542
EMMISON, F.G. ELIZABETHAN LIFE:
DISORDER.*
D.J. JOHNSON, 325:APR72-451
EMMONS, T., ED. EMANCIPATION OF THE
RUSSIAN SERFS.
G. HANSON, 104:SPRING72-157
EMSHWILLER, C. JOY IN OUR CAUSE.
A. BROYARD, 441:15MAY74-37
"ENCICLOPEDIA DANTESCA." (VOL 3)
M. MARTI, 228(GSLI):VOL149FASC
468-601
"ENCICLOPEDIA DEL ARTE EN AMÉRICA."
G. DE ZÉNDEGUI, 37:OCT72-40
"ENCYCLOPAEDIA BRITANNICA." (15TH ED)
A. BROYARD, 441:10JUN74-35
R.G. DAVIS, 441:1DEC74-98
A. QUINTON, 617(TLS):11OCT74-
1120
G. WOLFF, 61:JUN74-37
"THE ENCYCLOPEDIA OF SOCIAL DANCE."
N.M. STOOP, 151:OCT72-93
ENDELL, F. OLD TAVERN SIGNS.
K.B. HARDER, 424:JUN72-149
ENDO, S. WONDERFUL FOOL.
C. DRIVER, 362:14FEB74-215
617(TLS):25JAN74-69

ENDRESS, H-P. DIE PSYCHOLOGIE DER
EHEBRECHERIN ALS KÜNSTLERISCHES
PROBLEM BEI GUSTAVE FLAUBERT.
  A. GYERGYAI, 557(RSH):OCT-DEC72-
  613
ENGEL, J.E. ZEITALTER DER RENAIS-
SANCE, DES HUMANISMUS UND DER
REFORMATION.
  H. THOMKE, 182:VOL25#22-797
  E. THURNHER, 133:1972/1-102
ENGEL, L. THIS BRIGHT DAY.
  442(NY):29APR74-136
ENGEL, M., ED. USES OF LITERATURE.
  H. WIRTH-NESHER, 31(ASCH):AUTUMN
  74-681
ENGEL, S.M. WITTGENSTEIN'S DOCTRINE
OF THE TYRANNY OF LANGUAGE.
  A. FLEW, 518:JAN73-14
  A. LARIVE, 319:JAN74-132
  J.W.S., 543:JUN72-750
ENGELBERG, E. THE UNKNOWN DISTANCE.
  J. GINDIN, 385(MQR):SUMMER74-302
  639(VQR):SPRING73-XC
ENGELS, H-W. GEDICHTE UND LIEDER
DEUTSCHER JAKOBINER.
  F.G. DREYFUS, 182:VOL25#19/20-
  684
ENGELSING, R. ZUR SOZIALGESCHICHTE
DEUTSCHER MITTEL- UND UNTERSCHICH-
TEN.
  A. LASSERRE, 182:VOL25#23/24-887
ENGLE, E. & L. PAANANEN. THE WINTER
WAR.*
  617(TLS):1MAR74-197
ENGLEKIRK, J.E. & L.B. KIDDLE - SEE
AZUELA, M.
ENGLER, R. - SEE DE SAUSSURE, F.
ENGLER, W., ED. TEXTE ZUR FRANZÖ-
SISCHEN ROMANTHEORIE DES 19. JAHR-
HUNDERTS.*
  P.J. WHYTE, 208(FS):JAN73-85
"ENGLISCH IN DER HAUPTSCHULE."
  W. STUCK, 430(NS):JUL72-435
"ENGLISH LINGUISTICS 1500-1800."
  617(TLS):3MAY74-479
"ENGLISH LITERATURE 1660-1800: A
BIBLIOGRAPHY OF MODERN STUDIES."
(VOLS 5&6) (G.S. ALLEMAN & OTHERS,
COMPS)
  568(SCN):FALL-WINTER73-101
ENLOE, C.H. MULTI-ETHNIC POLITICS.
  C.M. TURNBULL, 302:JUL72-215
ENQUIST, P.O. THE LEGIONNAIRES.
  M. LEVIN, 441:6JAN74-20
  617(TLS):6SEP74-945
ENRIGHT, D.J. MAN IS AN ONION.*
  P. DICKINSON, 364:DEC72/JAN73-
  140
ENRIGHT, D.J. THE TERRIBLE SHEARS.*
  J. CAREY, 364:AUG/SEP73-125
ENTERLINE, J.R. VIKING AMERICA.
  J.E. KNIRK, 563(SS):AUTUMN73-391
ENTRALGO, P.L. - SEE UNDER LAÍN EN-
TRALGO, P.
"ENTRETIENS SUR L'ANTIQUITÉ CLASS-
IQUE."* (VOL 15: LUCAIN.) (O.
REVERDIN, ED)
  M. MORFORD, 313:VOL62-223
"ENTRETIENS SUR L'ANTIQUITÉ CLASS-
IQUE." (VOL 16: MÉNANDRE.) (E.G.
TURNER, ED)
  A. BILLAULT, 555:VOL46FASC2-300
  J.C.B. LOWE, 123:MAR73-23
  T.B.L. WEBSTER, 24:SUMMER73-206

ENZENSBERGER, H. BEITRÄGE ZUM KANZ-
LEI- UND URKUNDENWESEN DER NORMAN-
NISCHEN HERRSCHER UNTERITALIENS
UND SIZILIENS.
  R. SCHUMANN, 589:OCT73-743
EPPSTEIN, J. HAS THE CATHOLIC
CHURCH GONE MAD?
  J.P. BOYLE, 396(MODA):WINTER73-
  109
EPSHTEIN, S.I. INDUSTRIAL'NAIA SOT-
SIOLOGIIA V SSHA.
  M.G. FIELD, 32:DEC73-831
EPSTEIN, E.L. THE ORDEAL OF STEPHEN
DEDALUS.*
  R. BOYLE, 659:SPRING74-262
  639(VQR):SPRING72-LVII
EPSTEIN, J. DIVORCED IN AMERICA.
  M. HENTOFF, 453:8AUG74-36
  C. LEHMANN-HAUPT, 441:27JUN74-49
  S. SANBORN, 441:16JUN74-2
ERASMUS. THE COLLECTED WORKS OF
ERASMUS. (VOL 1) (R.A.B. MYNORS &
D.F.S. THOMSON, TRANS; W.K. FER-
GUSON, ED)
  E. RICE, 617(TLS):1NOV74-1223
ERASMUS. LA CORRESPONDANCE D'ERASME.
(VOL 4) (M.A. NAUWELAERTS, ED)
  W.R. GAIR, 255(HAB):SUMMER72-50
ERASMUS. OPERA OMNIA. (VOLS 1&2)
(K. KUMANIECKI & OTHERS, EDS)
  C.R. THOMPSON, 551(RENQ):SUMMER
  72-192
"ERASMUS." (R.L. DE MOLEN, ED)
  617(TLS):15FEB74-165
ERBSE, H., ED. SCHOLIA GRAECA IN
HOMERI ILIADEM (SCHOLIA VETERA).*
(VOL 1)
  P. CHANTRAINE, 555:VOL46FASC1-
  104
ERDMAN, D.V. & J.E. GRANT, EDS.
BLAKE'S VISIONARY FORMS DRAMATIC.*
  G.E. BENTLEY, JR., 39:JAN72-72
ERDMAN, D.V. & D.K. MOORE - SEE
BLAKE, W.
ERDMAN, H.L. POLITICAL ATTITUDES
OF INDIAN INDUSTRY.
  C.P. STAELIN, 293(JAST):FEB72-
  439
ERDMAN, P.E. THE SILVER BEARS.
  N. CALLENDAR, 441:18AUG74-23
  C. LEHMANN-HAUPT, 441:25JUL74-37
ERICKSON, R.J. INTERNATIONAL LAW &
THE REVOLUTIONARY STATE.
  J.N. HAZARD, 32:DEC73-831
ERICKSON, S.A. LANGUAGE & BEING.*
  J.D.C., 543:SEP71-123
  A. MANSER, 393(MIND):APR72-313
ERIKSEN, S. EARLY NEO-CLASSICISM IN
FRANCE. (P. THORNTON, ED & TRANS)
  617(TLS):15FEB74-161
ERIKSEN, S. THE JAMES A. DE ROTH-
SCHILD COLLECTION AT WADDESDON
MANOR: SÈVRES PORCELAIN.
  R.A. CECIL, 90:FEB72-105
ERIKSON, E.H. DIMENSIONS OF A NEW
IDENTITY.
  B. DE MOTT, 61:APR74-111
  G. STADE, 441:19MAY74-18
ERIKSON, E.H. ETHIQUE ET PSYCHAN-
ALYSE.
  V. THERRIEN, 154:MAR72-176
ERLER, A. AEGIDIUS ALBORNOZ ALS
GESETZGEBER DES KIRCHENSTAATES.*
  J.M. POWELL, 589:JAN73-134

ERLICH, V. GOGOL.*
V.D. MIHAILOVICH, 573(SSF):WIN-
TER72-107
ERNST, G. EINFÜHRUNGSKURS ITALIEN-
ISCH.
G.F. MEIER, 682(ZPSK):BAND25
HEFT4/5-431
EROMS, H-W. "VREUDE" BEI HARTMANN
VON AUE.*
R.C.J. ENDRES, 133:1972/3-322
ERRINGTON, R.M. PHILOPOEMEN.*
A.H. MC DONALD, 123:DEC73-235
ERSKINE-HILL, H. POPE: THE DUNCIAD.*
P. ROGERS, 566:AUTUMN72-42
ERVIN-TRIPP, S.M. LANGUAGE ACQUISI-
TION & COMMUNICATIVE CHOICE.
P. FARB, 453:21FEB74-24
ERWIN, E. THE CONCEPT OF MEANING-
LESSNESS.*
J.W.N. WATKINS, 84:FEB72-83
ERWITT, E. SON OF BITCH.
S. SCHWARTZ, 441:14DEC74-100
ESCARPIT, R., ED. LE LITTÉRAIRE ET
LE SOCIAL.
V. TASCA, 549(RLC):JAN-MAR72-135
ESCARPIT, R. LE MINISTRICULE.
617(TLS):4OCT74-1093
ESCARPIT, R. SOCIOLOGY OF LITERA-
TURE. (2ND ED)
J. GOODE, 111:18MAY73-156
ESCH, A. JAMES JOYCE UND SEIN
ULYSSES.
H. BONHEIM, 430(NS):APR72-242
ESCHAPASSE, M. L'ARCHITECTURE BENE-
DICTINE EN EUROPE.
A. LENGYEL, 576:OCT72-246
ESCOBAR GALINDO, D. EXTRAÑO MUNDO
DEL AMANECER.
H. LINDO, 263:APR-JUN73-208
ESCOTT, M. SHOW DOWN. (R. GOODMAN,
ED)
617(TLS):8MAR74-237
ESHERICK, J.W. - SEE SERVICE, J.S.
ESHLEMAN, C. ALTARS.*
639(VQR):WINTER73-XII
ESPER, E.A. MENTALISM & OBJECTIVISM
IN LINGUISTICS.
G. SCHLÖMP, 430(NS):FEB72-112
DE ESPINOSA, F. REFRANERO (1527-
1547).* (E.S. O'KANE, ED)
B.B. THOMPSON, 400(MLN):MAR72-
345
ESPMARK, K. HARRY MARTINSON ERÖVRAR
SITT SPRÅK.
C.L. ANDERSON, 563(SS):WINTER73-
85
VAN ESS, J., ED. FRÜHE MU'TAZILI-
TISCHE HÄRESIOGRAPHIE.
W.M. WATT, 182:VOL25#12-389
ESSAME, H. PATTON.
M. BLUMENSON, 441:19MAY74-33
ESSLIN, M. THE PEOPLED WOUND.*
L. BONNEROT, 189(EA):APR-JUN72-
333
ESTERMANN, C. PENTEADOS, ADORNOS E
TRABALHOS DAS MUILAS.
A.C. EDWARDS, 69:APR72-168
ESTRADA, F.L. - SEE UNDER LÓPEZ ES-
TRADA, F.
ESZTERHAS, J. CHARLIE SIMPSON'S
APOCALYPSE.
A. GOTTLIEB, 441:27JAN74-4
ESZTERHAS, J. NARK!
R. SHERRILL, 441:7JUL74-1

ETEROVICH, F.H. & C. SPALATIN, EDS.
CROATIA.
P. AUTY, 575(SEER):OCT73-631
ETHEREGE, G. SIR GEORGE ETHEREGE:
SHE WOULD IF SHE COULD. (C.M.
TAYLOR, ED)
P.E. PARNELL, 568(SCN):FALL-
WINTER73-91
ETHEREGE, G. LETTERS OF SIR GEORGE
ETHEREGE. (F. BRACHER, ED)
617(TLS):12JUL74-745
ETHERIDGE, K. COLLECTING DRAWINGS.
T. CROMBIE, 39:APR72-342
"ETHNOLOGIA SCANDINAVICA." (VOL 1)
B. GUNDA, 203:SPRING72-84
"ETHNOLOGIA SLAVICA." (VOL 1)
B. GUNDA, 203:SPRING72-84
ETIEMBLE. MES CONTRE-POISONS.
ESSAIS DE LITTÉRATURE (VRAIMENT)
GÉNÉRALE.
J. WEIGHTMAN, 617(TLS):6DEC74-
1391
"ÉTUDES SUR LE LANGAGE ENFANTIN."
M. CHASTAING, 542:OCT-DEC72-455
"ÉTUDES SUR MONTESQUIEU."
R. MERCIER, 535(RHL):JUL-AUG72-
719
ETULAIN, R.W. WESTERN AMERICAN LIT-
ERATURE.
J.H. MAGUIRE, 649(WAL):WINTER73-
308
EUCHNER, W. NATURRECHT UND POLI-
TICK BEI JOHN LOCKE.
T. MAGRI, 548(RCSF):JUL-SEP72-
346
EURIPIDES. THE BACCHAE & OTHER
PLAYS. (2ND ED) (P. VELLACOTT,
TRANS)
617(TLS):18JAN74-61
EURIPIDES. THE "BACCHAE" BY EURI-
PIDES. (G.S. KIRK, ED & TRANS)
D.J. CONACHER, 487:SPRING72-85
EURIPIDES. HELENA.* (R. KANNICHT,
ED)
P. CHANTRAINE, 555:VOL46FASC1-
121
EURIPIDES. HIPPOLYTOS. (R. BAGG,
TRANS) IPHIGENEIA IN TAURIS. (R.
LATTIMORE, TRANS)
H. LLOYD-JONES, 617(TLS):1NOV74-
1221
EURIPIDES. PHAETHON.* (J. DIGGLE,
ED)
K.J. RECKFORD, 399(MLJ):MAY72-
338
"EUROPEAN PAINTINGS FROM THE MINNE-
APOLIS INSTITUTE OF ARTS."
J. DANIELS, 135:OCT72-140
EVANS, C. CULTS OF UNREASON.
442(NY):3JUN74-112
EVANS, C.O. THE SUBJECT OF CON-
SCIOUSNESS.*
S. MUNSAT, 482(PHR):JUL72-392
W. ROSENSOHN, 484(PPR):MAR73-431
D.E. WARD, 63:AUG73-183
EVANS, D. TOMMY JOHNSON.*
W.R. FERRIS, JR., 292(JAF):JUL-
SEP72-287
EVANS, E.P. ANIMAL SYMBOLISM IN
ECCLESIASTICAL ARCHITECTURE.
J. BECKWITH, 39:JAN72-66
EVANS, G.B. - SEE SHAKESPEARE, W.
EVANS, G.E. TOOLS OF THEIR TRADES.
K. HUDSON, 637(VS):SEP72-96

EVANS, G.L. - SEE UNDER LLOYD EVANS,
G.
EVANS, H. HANDLING NEWSPAPER TEXT.
NEWS HEADLINES.
617(TLS):30AUG74-931
EVANS, H. & M. SOURCES OF ILLUSTRA-
TION, 1500-1900.
D. THOMAS, 135:FEB72-139
EVANS, J. MONASTIC ICONOGRAPHY IN
FRANCE FROM THE RENAISSANCE TO THE
REVOLUTION.
P. BARRETTE, 207(FR):OCT71-285
J. BECKWITH, 39:JAN72-66
J. MONTAGU, 54:JUN72-218
EVANS, M. BOBBY JACK SMITH YOU
DIRTY COWARD!
M. LEVIN, 441:8SEP74-43
EVANS, M. ONE-EYED SKY.
M. LEVIN, 441:29DEC74-20
EVANS, M. SPENSER'S ANATOMY OF
HEROISM.*
A.D. ISLER, 551(RENQ):SPRING72-
100
205(FMLS):APR72-194
EVANS, P. THE EARLY TROPE REPERTORY
OF SAINT MARTIAL DE LIMOGES.*
D.G. HUGHES, 589:APR73-353
T. STEMMLER, 38:BAND90HEFT3-378
EVANS, R., JR. THE LABOR ECONOMIES
OF JAPAN & THE UNITED STATES.
M. BRONFENBRENNER, 293(JAST):
MAY72-605
EVANS, S. MERITOCRATS.
J. MELLORS, 362:5DEC74-753
EVANS-PRITCHARD, E.E., ED. MAN &
WOMAN AMONG THE AZANDE.
I.M. LEWIS, 617(TLS):15NOV74-
1279
EVANS-PRITCHARD, E.E., ED. THE
ZANDE TRICKSTER.
J.D. PÉNEL, 69:APR72-167
EVENSON, N. LE CORBUSIER.*
G.L. HERSEY, 56:SUMMER72-180
EVERITT, A., ED. PERSPECTIVES IN
ENGLISH URBAN HISTORY.
617(TLS):4JAN74-3
EVERS, H-D., ED. MODERNIZATION IN
SOUTH-EAST ASIA.
617(TLS):17MAY74-516
EVRON, Y. THE MIDDLE EAST.
617(TLS):11JAN74-34
EWALD, E.B. RECIPES FOR A SMALL
PLANET.
D. ZWERDLING, 453:21FEB74-22
EWALD, K. TERMINOLOGIE EINER FRANZÖ-
SISCHEN GESCHÄFTS- UND KANZLEI-
SPRACHE VOM 13. BIS 16. JAHRHUN-
DERT.
H.J. WOLF, 72:BAND21OHEFT1/3-212
EWART, G. THE GAVIN EWART SHOW.
P. PORTER, 364:JUN/JUL72-144
EWEN, F. BERTOLT BRECHT.
K.A. DICKSON, 220(GL&L):JUL73-
330
E. SPEIDEL, 402(MLR):JUL73-707
EWER, J.R. & G. LATORRE. A COURSE
IN BASIC SCIENTIFIC ENGLISH.
B.A. BECKER, 608:JUN73-183
EWERT, A. - SEE BÉROUL
EWING, E. HISTORY OF 20TH-CENTURY
FASHION.
A. ADBURGHAM, 362:30MAY74-700

EY, H. LA CONSCIENCE. (2ND ED)
C. BARDET-GIRAUDON, 542:OCT-DEC
72-455
EY, H., P. BERNARD & C. BRISSET.
MANUEL DE PSYCHIATRIE.
H. BARUK, 542:OCT-DEC72-458
EYKMAN, C. GESCHICHTSPESSIMISMUS IN
DER DEUTSCHEN LITERATUR DES ZWAN-
ZIGSTEN JAHRHUNDERTS.*
R.W. LAST, 220(GL&L):JUL73-339
EYMERICH, N. & F. PEÑA. LE MANUEL
DES INQUISITEURS. (L. SALA-MOLINS,
ED & TRANS)
617(TLS):1MAR74-218
EYSENCK, H.J. THE INEQUALITY OF MAN.
617(TLS):3MAY74-466

FABER, F.W. FABER. (R. ADDINGTON,
ED)
617(TLS):23AUG74-901
FABER, R. PROPER STATIONS.*
B.H., 155:MAY72-130
J.M.S. TOMPKINS, 541(RES):MAY72-
225
M. VICINUS, 637(VS):JUN72-504
FABIAN, B., ED. EIN ANGLISTISCHER
GRUNDKURS ZUR EINFÜHRUNG IN DAS
STUDIUM DER LITERATURWISSEN-
SCHAFT.*
U. SCHNEIDER, 38:BAND90HEFT3-415
FABRI, C.L. DISCOVERING INDIAN
SCULPTURE.
R.A. PERRY, 293(JAST):AUG72-959
FABRO, C. LA DIALÉCTICA DE HEGEL.
Z. KOURIM, 542:JUL-SEP72-362
FABRO, C. PARTICIPATION ET CAUSAL-
ITÉ SELON SAINT THOMAS D'AQUIN.
A. FOREST, 542:JAN-MAR72-73
FACCIOLI, E. - SEE SACCHETTI, F.
FAGER, C.E. SELMA, 1965.
442(NY):9SEP74-134
FAGERENG, E. UNE FAMILLE DE DYNAS-
TIES MALGACHES.
H. DESCHAMPS, 69:OCT72-354
FAGES, J-B. COMPRENDRE JACQUES
LACAN.
Y. BRÈS, 542:OCT-DEC72-459
FAGG, W., ED. THE LIVING ARTS OF
NIGERIA.
J.B. DONNE, 135:JUL72-228
FAGYAS, M. DANCE OF THE ASSASSINS.
M. LEVIN, 441:6JAN74-20
FAHD, T. LE PANTHÉON DE L'ARABIE
CENTRALE À LA VEILLE DE L'HÉGIRE.
A. JAMME, 318(JAOS):JAN-MAR72-
111
FÄHNDERS, W. & M. RECTOR, COMPS.
LITERATUR IM KLASSENKAMPF.
T.K. BROWN, 406:WINTER73-424
FAHR, W. THEOYS NOMIZEIN.
P. CHANTRAINE, 555:VOL46FASC2-
293
DU FAIL, N. - SEE UNDER NOËL DU FAIL
FAIN, H. BETWEEN PHILOSOPHY & HIS-
TORY.*
P. PACHET, 182:VOL25#3/4-68
C-H. WHITELEY, 393(MIND):JUL72-
475
FAINLIGHT, R. TWENTY ONE POEMS.
617(TLS):24MAY74-554
FAIRBAIRN, D. SHOOT.*
617(TLS):12APR74-396

FAIRBANK, J.K. CHINA PERCEIVED.
A. AUSTIN, 441:27DEC74-29
J. LELYVELD, 441:6OCT74-32
442(NY):7OCT74-178
FAIRBANK, J.K. THE UNITED STATES &
CHINA. (3RD ED)
C.C. WOOTEN, 293(JAST):FEB72-384
FAIRBANK, W. ADVENTURES IN RETRIEV-
AL.*
LEE YU-LIN, 60:SEP-OCT73-74
FAIRCHILD, W. THE SWISS ARRANGE-
MENT.*
N. CALLENDAR, 441:1SEP74-14
FAIRHALL, D. RUSSIAN SEA POWER.*
(BRITISH TITLE: RUSSIA LOOKS TO
THE SEA.)
C.J. SMITH, 550(RUSR):JUL72-298
FAIRSERVIS, W.A., JR. THE ROOTS OF
ANCIENT INDIA.*
J.W. SPELLMAN, 293(JAST):FEB72-
430
"FAIRY TALES & LEGENDS FROM ROMANIA."
(I. STURDZA, R. VIANU & M. LĂZĂR-
ESCU, TRANS)
P.V. VEHVILAINEN, 32:JUN73-419
FALCK, C. BACKWARDS INTO THE SMOKE.
R. GARFITT, 364:FEB/MAR74-107
617(TLS):11JAN74-28
FALCK, F.J. STUTTERING LEARNED &
UNLEARNED.
L. ASHMORE, 583:WINTER72-205
DE FALCO, P. QUESTIONS DISPUTÉES
ORDINAIRES. (A-J. GONDRAS, ED)
P. BOGLIONI, 589:JUL73-558
FALDI, I. PITTORI VITERBESI DI
CINQUE SECOLI.*
A. MARTINDALE, 90:JAN72-36
FALK, E.H. TYPES OF SEMANTIC STRUC-
TURE.
B.K. BUNDY, 545(RPH):AUG72-68
FALK, J.D. JOHANN DANIEL FALKS
BEARBEITUNG DES AMPHITRYON-STOFFES.
(H. SEMBDNER, ED)
J.M. MC GLATHERY, 301(JEGP):APR
73-288
FALK, R.A. THIS ENDANGERED PLANET.
C. MC FARLAND, 639(VQR):WINTER72-
126
FALK, R.A., ED. THE VIETNAM WAR &
INTERNATIONAL LAW. (VOL 3)
639(VQR):AUTUMN72-CXLIX
FALKIRK, R. BEAU BLACKSTONE.
M. LEVIN, 441:5MAY74-57
FALKIRK, R. BLACKSTONE.*
N. CALLENDAR, 441:14JUL74-40
"THE FALL OF A PRESIDENT."
A. COCKBURN, 453:28NOV74-8
FALLANA, S. LA FEMME DE BAVE.
A. ABEL, 207(FR):APR72-1044
FALLERS, L.A. INEQUALITY.
L. MAIR, 617(TLS):1NOV74-1227
FANG, C-Y. THE ASAMI LIBRARY. (E.
HUFF, ED)
G. LEDYARD, 293(JAST):MAY72-690
P.H. LEE, 318(JAOS):APR-JUN72-
355
FANN, K.T. PEIRCE'S THEORY OF ABDUC-
TION.
F.M. WALSH, 483:OCT72-377
FANN, K.T., ED. SYMPOSIUM ON J.L.
AUSTIN.*
W. SHIBLES, 484(PPR):MAR73-443

FANN, K.T. WITTGENSTEIN'S CONCEP-
TION OF PHILOSOPHY.*
W.M. RICHARDS, 484(PPR):SEP72-
134
FANT, G. SPEECH SOUNDS & FEATURES.
J.C. WELLS, 617(TLS):29NOV74-
1337
FANTEL, H. WILLIAM PENN.
A. WHITMAN, 441:14DEC74-27
FANTINI, M.D. PUBLIC SCHOOLS OF
CHOICE.
G. LEVINE, 441:19MAY74-4
"THE FAR EAST & AUSTRALASIA."
617(TLS):17MAY74-533
AL-FĀRĀBĪ. ALFARABI'S BOOK OF LET-
TERS (KITĀB AL-ḤURŪF).* (M.
MAHDI, ED) [FILED IN PREV UNDER AL]
R.M. FRANK, 318(JAOS):APR-JUN72-
393
FARADAY, M. THE SELECTED CORRESPON-
DENCE OF MICHAEL FARADAY. (L.P.
WILLIAMS, WITH R. FITZ GERALD &
O. STALLYBRASS, EDS)
R.H. SILLIMAN, 637(VS):MAR73-364
FARAGO, L. AFTERMATH.
T. PRITTIE, 441:10NOV74-12
H.R. TREVOR-ROPER, 453:14NOV74-
15
FARAU, A. & H. SCHAFFER. LA PSY-
CHOLOGIE DES PROFONDEURS, DES
ORIGINES À NOS JOURS.
M. CHASTAING, 542:OCT-DEC72-460
FARB, P. WORD PLAY.
T. BERNSTEIN, 441:25AUG74-28
C. LEHMANN-HAUPT, 441:29JAN74-37
FARBER, B. GUARDIANS OF VIRTUE.
J.K. SOMERVILLE, 656(WMQ):APR73-
359
FARBER, M. - SEE RIEPE, D.
FARBRIDGE, M.H. STUDIES IN BIBLICAL
& SEMITIC SYMBOLISM.
D. LIEBER, 318(JAOS):OCT-DEC72-
530
FARGEAUD, M. BALZAC ET "LA RECHER-
CHE DE L'ABSOLU."*
M. HAYWARD, 402(MLR):APR73-416
FARGUE, L-P. EPAISSEURS, [SUIVI DE]
VULTURNE.
R.R. HUBERT, 207(FR):FEB72-694
FARMBOROUGH, F. NURSE AT THE RUS-
SIAN FRONT.
617(TLS):4OCT74-1080
FARMER, F. WILL THERE REALLY BE A
MORNING?
H. HART, 200:NOV72-562
617(TLS):14JUN74-628
FARMER, P.J. THE FABULOUS RIVERBOAT.
617(TLS):12APR74-385
FARMER, P.J. TARZAN ALIVE.
E. GROVE, 572:SEP72-126
FARNHAM, E. CHARLES DEMUTH.*
A.L. EISEMAN, 127:FALL72-116
S. REICH, 54:JUN72-228
FARNHAM, W. THE SHAKESPEAREAN GRO-
TESQUE.*
L.A. BEAURLINE, 301(JEGP):JAN73-
126
D.S. BLAND, 551(RENQ):WINTER72-
505
J. BUXTON, 677:VOL3-275
W. HABICHT, 72:BAND210HEFT4/6-
381

FARNOL, J. HERITAGE PERILOUS. MUR-
DER BY NAIL. THE HIGH ADVENTURE.
WAIF OF THE RIVER. THE NINTH EARL.
E.S. TURNER, 617(TLS):27DEC74-
1455
FARR, D.M. THOMAS MIDDLETON & THE
DRAMA OF REALISM.
S.G. PUTT, 617(TLS):2AUG74-833
FARR, F. O'HARA.*
617(TLS):31MAY74-576
FARRELL, E.J. DECIDING THE FUTURE.
C.A. CAMPBELL, 128(CE):DEC72-429
FARRELL, J.G. THE SIEGE OF KRISHNA-
PUR.*
J. DECK, 441:6OCT74-16
C. LEHMANN-HAUPT, 441:7OCT74-33
J. MELLORS, 364:FEB/MAR74-135
R. SALE, 453:12DEC74-18
L.E. SISSMAN, 442(NY):25NOV74-
193
FARRELL, W. THE LIBERATED MAN.
R. TODD, 61:NOV74-107
FARRIS, J. SHARP PRACTICE.
N. CALLENDAR, 441:29DEC74-21
FARSON, D. OUT OF STEP.
617(TLS):8NOV74-1269
FARSON, R. BIRTHRIGHTS.
G. LEVINE, 441:19MAY74-4
FARUKI, K.A. THE EVOLUTION OF ISLAM-
IC CONSTITUTIONAL THEORY & PRAC-
TICE, FROM 610 TO 1926.
H.K. SHERWANI, 273(IC):OCT72-363
FASANI, R. IL POETA DEL "FIORE."
M.M., 228(GSLI):VOL149FASC468-
631
FASANO, G. "LES TRAGIQUES," UN'EPO-
PEA DELLA MORTE.
J. BAILBÉ, 535(RHL):JUL-AUG72-
707
FASQUELLE, S. LES AMANTS DE KALYROS.
M.G. ROSE, 207(FR):DEC71-469
FASSKE, H., H. JENTSCH & S. MICHALK,
EDS. SORBISCHER SPRACHATLAS.*
(VOL 3)
F. HINZE, 682(ZPSK):BAND24HEFT6-
526
FAST, H. TOUCH OF INFINITY.
T. STURGEON, 441:10NOV74-50
FAST, J. BODY LANGUAGE.
E.A. SCHMERLER, 186(ETC.):JUN72-
215
FASTEAU, M.F. THE MALE MACHINE.
R. TODD, 61:NOV74-106
"THE FATHERS OF THE CHURCH." (VOLS
· 62 & 63)
A.W. GODFREY, 363:FEB72-80
FAULKNER, W. FLAGS IN THE DUST.*
(D. DAY & A. ERSKINE, EDS)
R.P. ADAMS, 598(SOR):AUTUMN74-
878
FAURE, G. LES ÉLÉMENTS DU RYTHME
POÉTIQUE EN ANGLAIS MODERNE.
J.C. BEAVER, 350:MAR73-188
E.R. MARKS, 290(JAAC):SPRING72-
399
FAURE, G. & J. CASANOVA. NOUVELLE
GRAMMAIRE ANGLAISE.
L. KUKENHEIM, 353:JUN72-101
FAURE, L. LE MALHEUR FOU.
M.G. ROSE, 207(FR):OCT71-201
FAURE-SOULET, J.F. DE MALTHUS À
MARX.
M. LAGUEUX, 154:JUN72-295

FAUST, I. FOREIGN DEVILS.*
R. SALE, 418(MR):AUTUMN73-834
FAVRE, P. & M. LES MARXISMES APRÈS
MARX.
J. BERNHARDT, 542:JUL-SEP72-387
FAVRETTI, R.F. & G.P. DE WOLF. COL-
ONIAL GARDENS.
639(VQR):WINTER73-XLIV
FAYE, J-P. LANGAGES TOTALITAIRES.
THÉORIE DU RÉCIT.
617(TLS):5APR74-353
FAYT, R. & OTHERS. BIBLIOGRAPHIE
DES ÉCRIVAINS FRANÇAIS DE BELGIQUE
1881-1960. (VOL 4)
H.C. WOODBRIDGE, 517(PBSA):OCT-
DEC73-479
FEATHER, L. FROM SATCHMO TO MILES.
D. THOMAS, 362:22AUG74-252
FEATHERSTONE, D. CAPTAIN CAREY'S
BLUNDER.
617(TLS):1MAR74-202
FEBVRE, L. AMOUR SACRÉ, AMOUR PRO-
FANE AUTOUR DE L'"HEPTAMÉRON."
N. ARONSON, 207(FR):DEC71-531
FEDER, L. ANCIENT MYTH IN MODERN
POETRY.*
639(VQR):AUTUMN72-CXXVIII
FEDERMAN, R. DOUBLE OR NOTHING.
D.M. KENNEDY, 385(MQR):WINTER74-
85
L.T. LEMON, 502(PRS):WINTER72/
73-365
E. ROVIT, 659:AUTUMN74-539
FEDERMAN, R. & J. FLETCHER. SAMUEL
BECKETT, HIS WORKS & HIS CRITICS.*
M.J. FRIEDMAN, 207(FR):OCT71-241
J. KNOWLSON, 208(FS):OCT73-486
E. SELLIN, 399(MLJ):NOV72-454
FEDERN, K. DANTE & HIS TIME.
T.G. BERGIN, 275(IQ):FALL/WINTER
72-115
FEDERSPIEL, J. PARATUGA KEHRT ZUR-
ÜCK.
617(TLS):8FEB74-125
FEDOSOV, I.A., I.I. ASTAF'EV & I.D.
KOVAL'CHENKO, EDS. ISTOCHNIKOVE-
DENIE ISTORII SSSR XIX-NACHALE XX
V.*
M. RAEFF, 104:SPRING72-149
FEDYSHYN, O.S. GERMANY'S DRIVE TO
THE EAST & THE UKRAINIAN REVOLU-
TION, 1917-1918.*
F.T. EPSTEIN, 550(RUSR):JUL72-
286
K. SAWCZUK, 497(POLR):SUMMER72-
118
FEELEY, K. FLANNERY O'CONNOR.*
J.J. QUINN, 613:WINTER72-616
FEHÉR, F. AZ ANTINÓMIÁK KÖLTŐJE.
M.D. BIRNBAUM, 32:DEC73-850
FEHL, P. THE CLASSICAL MONUMENT.
290(JAAC):WINTER72-276
FEHLBAUM, R.P. SAINT-SIMON UND DIE
SAINT-SIMONISTEN.
A. HÜFNER, 182:VOL25#9/10-270
FEHRENBACH, T.R. COMANCHES.
C. LEHMANN-HAUPT, 441:22NOV74-43
FEHRENBACHER, D.E. - SEE POTTER, D.M.
FEHRMAN, C. FORSKNING I FÖRVANDLING.
G-C. SCHOOLFIELD, 563(SS):SPRING
73-176
FEIFFER, J. THE WHITE HOUSE MURDER
CASE.
502(PRS):SPRING72-92

FEIJOO Y MONTENEGRO, B.J. THÉÂTRE
CRITIQUE. (D.H. PAGEAUX, ED)
M. BATAILLON, 549(RLC):JUL-SEP72-
465
FEINBERG, B. & R. KASRILS. BERTRAND
RUSSELL'S AMERICA. (VOL 1)
J. RICHARDSON, 231:MAR74-91
FEINBERG, J. DOING & DESERVING.*
J.L. CARAFIDES, 484(PPR):DEC72-
284
B.J. DIGGS, 311(JP):14FEB74-90
W.P.G., 543:SEP71-123
FEINSILVER, L.M. THE TASTE OF YID-
DISH.
I. RICHMAN, 292(JAF):JAN-MAR72-
90
H.R. STERN, 35(AS):FALL-WINTER70-
260
FEINSTEIN, E. THE CELEBRANTS &
OTHER POEMS.*
S. CONN, 362:28NOV74-717
FEINSTEIN, E. THE CRYSTAL GARDEN.
A. BROYARD, 441:25FEB74-25
J. DECK, 441:19MAY74-38
B. REEVE, 231:JUN74-95
442(NY):3JUN74-109
FEIS, H. FROM TRUST TO TERROR.
T.T. HAMMOND, 550(RUSR):JAN72-74
FEIX, I. & E. SCHLANT. LITERATUR
UND UMGANGSSPRACHE.
I.D. HALPERT, 399(MLJ):NOV72-475
FELD, M. HANDS OF THE PHILISTINES
& OTHER STORIES.
R. BLYTHE, 362:28FEB74-281
617(TLS):1MAR74-201
FELDER, P. JOHANN BAPTIST BABEL
1716-1799.
N. POWELL, 90:JUN72-416
FELDGES, M. GRIMMELSHAUSENS "LAND-
STÖRTZERIN COURASCHE."
G. LUTHER, 224(GRM):BAND22HEFT3-
314
J. SCHMIDT, 133:1972/2-214
FELDMAN, D.M. & W.D. KLINE. SPANISH.
C.A. MALEY, 399(MLJ):FEB72-104
FELDMAN, I. LOST ORIGINALS.*
T. WOLL, 398:AUTUMN74-203
FELDMAN, I. MAGIC PAPERS & OTHER
POEMS.*
D. JAFFE, 590:SPRING/SUMMER73-26
J. KESSLER, 390:APR72-75
FELDMAN, S.D. THE MORALITY-PAT-
TERNED COMEDY OF THE RENAISSANCE.*
J.L. LEVENSON, 551(RENQ):AUTUMN
72-362
FELDMANN, H. DIE FIABE CARLO GOZ-
ZIS.*
D. GRONAU, 182:VOL25#15/16-551
FELDMANN, H. DIE GESCHICHTLICHE ENT-
WICKLUNG DER HÖRPRÜFUNGSMETHODEN.
G.F. MEIER, 682(ZPSK):BAND25
HEFT3-248
FELL, C.E. EDWARD KING & MARTYR.
A. CAMPBELL, 447(N&Q):JUL72-270
FELLMAN, M. THE UNBOUNDED FRAME.
P. LEVINE, 99:MAY/JUN74-56
FELLOWS, O. FROM VOLTAIRE TO "LA
NOUVELLE CRITIQUE."*
R. GRIMSLEY, 402(MLR):JUL73-659
U. SCHULZ-BUSCHHAUS, 72:BAND210
HEFT4/6-465

FELLOWS, O., A. SHENKAN & M. BES-
NARD. A LIVRE OUVERT.
R.L. ADMUSSEN, 399(MLJ):FEB72-
106
B. BRAUDE, 207(FR):MAR72-875
FELMAN, S. LA "FOLIE" DANS L'OEUVRE
ROMANESQUE DE STENDHAL.
J.S.P., 191(ELN):SEP72(SUPP)-117
FELPERIN, H. SHAKESPEAREAN ROMANCE.*
T. HAWKES, 676(YR):SUMMER73-561
M. MUDRICK, 249(HUDR):SUMMER73-
375
FELS, L. PLATZANGST.
617(TLS):2AUG74-839
FEMIANO, S. - SEE CAMPANELLA, T.
FENBY, E. DELIUS.
J. CANARINA, 607:#102-35
FENELON, K.G. THE UNITED ARAB EMIR-
ATES.
617(TLS):11JAN74-34
FENGER, H. & F.J. MARKER. THE HEI-
BERGS.
T. BRUNIUS, 290(JAAC):SPRING73-
417
FENNELL, J. & A. STOKES. EARLY RUS-
SIAN LITERATURE.
617(TLS):7JUN74-605
"TÖNNIES FENNE'S LOW GERMAN MANUAL
OF SPOKEN RUSSIAN, PSKOV 1607."*
(VOL 2) (L.L. HAMMERICH & OTHERS,
EDS)
H. POULSEN, 279:VOL15-212
FENOGLIO, B. UN FENOGLIO ALLA PRIMA
GUERRA MONDIALE. (G. RIZZO, ED)
617(TLS):26APR74-442
FENTON, D., ED. SHOTS.
639(VQR):SUMMER72-CIX
FENTON, J. TERMINAL MORAINE.
J. SYMONS, 364:AUG/SEP72-138
FENYO, M.D. HITLER, HORTHY & HUN-
GARY.
C.A. MACARTNEY, 32:SEP73-646
F.T. ZSUPPAN, 575(SEER):OCT73-
614
FEREL, M. GEPREDIGTE TAUFE.
J. ATKINSON, 182:VOL25#3/4-77
FERGUSON, C. THE MOLTING SEASON.
M. LEVIN, 441:1SEP74-14
FERGUSON, J. CONTES ARDENTS DU PAYS
MAUVE.
R. WILLMOT, 296:VOL3#3-112
FERGUSON, J. THE RELIGIONS OF THE
ROMAN EMPIRE.*
M.J. BOYD, 313:VOL62-197
FERGUSON, J. SOCRATES: A SOURCE
BOOK.*
D.B. ROBINSON, 303:VOL92-212
F.M. SCHROEDER, 487:WINTER72-413
FERGUSON, M. THE BRAIN REVOLUTION.
R.M. RESTAK, 441:31MAR74-27
FERGUSON, O. THE FILM CRITICISM OF
OTIS FERGUSON. (R. WILSON, ED)
R. CAMPION, 200:AUG-SEP72-419
M. GEISMAR, 114(CHIR):VOL24#3-
151
FERGUSON, P. THE PALESTINE PROBLEM.
617(TLS):8MAR74-245
FERGUSON, S. A GUARD WITHIN.*
N. FREUD, 231:MAY74-97
J. MC ELROY, 441:31MAR74-4

FERGUSON, S. THE POETRY OF RANDALL
JARRELL.*
   J. BYER, 219(GAR):FALL72-393
   F. CHAPPELL, 579(SAQ):WINTER73-
   168
   R. SHELTON, 50(ARQ):WINTER72-374
   H.B. STAPLES, 659:SUMMER74-423
   639(VQR):AUTUMN72-CXXIX
FERGUSON, W.K. - SEE ERASMUS
FERLIN, H. NILS.
   G.C. SCHOOLFIELD, 563(SS):WINTER
   73-88
FERLITA, E. THE THEATRE OF PILGRIM-
AGE.
   J.R. MAY, 363:FEB72-76
   SISTER M. TERESA, 613:SUMMER72-
   308
FERNÁNDEZ, L. FARSAS Y ÉGLOGAS.
(J. LIHANI, ED)
   O.T. MEYERS, 238:SEP72-590
FERNÁNDEZ-SHAW, C.M. PRESENCIA ES-
PAÑOLA EN LOS ESTADOS UNIDOS.
   J.L. HELGUERA, 263:OCT-DEC73-451
FERNÁNDEZ ALONSO, M.D. AMANECER
LÍRICO DE ESPAÑA.
   L.J. FRIEDMAN, 545(RPH):MAY73-
   711
FERNÁNDEZ DE MORATÍN, L. LA COMEDIA
NUEVA Y EL SÍ DE LAS NIÑAS. (J.
DOWLING & R. ANDIOC, EDS)
   S.A. STOUDEMIRE, 241:JAN72-80
DE FERNÁNDEZ PEREIRO, N.G.B. ORIGI-
NALIDAD Y SINCERIDAD EN LA POESÍA
DE AMOR TROVADORESCA.
   F.M. CHAMBERS, 240(HR):WINTER72-
   89
FERNAU-HORN, H. DIE SPRECHNEUROSEN.
   H-J. BASTIAN, 682(ZPSK):BAND24
   HEFT6-524
FERRAND, F. - SEE PARMENTIER, J.
FERRANÉ, J-F. LE PENSIONNAIRE.
   G. SAVET, 207(FR):FEB72-695
FERRARS, E. ALIVE & DEAD.
   617(TLS):8NOV74-1248
FERRARS, E.X. HANGED MAN'S HOUSE.
   N. CALLENDAR, 441:18AUG74-24
FERRATE, J. DINÁMICA DE LA POESÍA.*
   J. FERRÁN, 593:FALL73-280
FERRER, M. BORGES Y LA NADA.*
   A. BORINSKY, 400(MLN):MAR72-387
FERRERO, D.D. - SEE UNDER DE BERNAR-
DI FERRERO, D.
FERRERS, E. HANGED MAN'S HOUSE.
   617(TLS):25JAN74-88
FERRETTI, F. THE GREAT AMERICAN
MARBLE BOOK.
   A. CORMAN, 441:17FEB74-12
FERRIER, F. WILLIAM CHALMERS (1596-
1678).
   P. DUBOIS, 542:APR-JUN72-187
FERRIS, B., JR. BLUES FROM THE
DELTA.
   B.L. PEARSON, 292(JAF):APR-JUN72-
   192
FERRIS, P. THE CURE.
   M. LEVIN, 441:13OCT74-20
   J. MELLORS, 362:22AUG74-253
   617(TLS):6SEP74-960
FERRIS, W.R., JR. MISSISSIPPI BLACK
FOLKLORE.*
   H. GLASSIE, 292(JAF):JAN-MAR72-
   98

FERRO, C.A. LAS BANDERAS CENTRO-
AMERICANAS.
   M. BARRACO MÁRMOL, 37:SEP72-40
FERRON, J. DR. COTNOIR.
   B. GODARD, 99:NOV/DEC74-24
   B. GODARD, 296:VOL3#2-107
FERRON, J. TALES FROM THE UNCERTAIN
COUNTRY.
   R. MC CARTHY, 150(DR):AUTUMN72-
   494
   A. ROBERTSON, 648:OCT72-62
FEST, J.C. HITLER.
   N. ASCHERSON, 453:18APR74-3
   O. FRIEDRICH, 441:28APR74-1
   J. JOLL, 617(TLS):26JUL74-780
   L. STOKES, 99:NOV/DEC74-31
   E. WEEKS, 61:MAY74-135
FESTUGIÈRE, A-J., ED & TRANS. VIE
DE THÉODORE DE SYKÉON.
   R. BROWNING, 589:JAN73-135
FETHERLING, D. HUGH GARNER.
   C. MAC CULLOCH, 296:VOL3#1-99
FETHERLING, D. OUR MAN IN UTOPIA.*
   D. HELWIG, 529(QQ):AUTUMN72-404
FETSCHER, I. DER MARXISMUS, SEINE
GESCHICHTE IN DOKUMENTEN.
   P. ARNAUD, 542:JUL-SEP72-388
FETTER, F.W. & D. GREGORY. MONETARY
& FINANCIAL POLICY IN NINETEENTH
CENTURY BRITAIN.
   617(TLS):22MAR74-304
FETTIG, H. GLOVE & ROD PUPPETS.
   617(TLS):20SEP74-1021
FEUCHTWANGER, E.J., ED. UPHEAVAL &
CONTINUITY.
   617(TLS):10MAY74-498
FEUER, L.S. EINSTEIN & THE GENERA-
TIONS OF SCIENCE.
   C. LEHMANN-HAUPT, 441:7JUN74-39
FICHTE, G.A. TEORIA DELLA SCIENZA,
1798 "NOVA METHODO."
   E. NAMER, 542:JUL-SEP72-354
FICHTE, J.G. OEUVRES CHOISIES DE
PHILOSOPHIE PREMIÈRE. (A. PHILO-
NENKO, TRANS)
   D. JULIA, 542:JUL-SEP72-351
FICHTELIUS, K.E. & S. SJÖLANDER.
SMARTER THAN MAN?
   42(AR):VOL32#3-511
FICHTENAU, H. DAS URKUNDENWESEN IN
ÖSTERREICH VOM 8. BIS ZUM FRÜHEN
13. JAHRHUNDERT.
   G.B. FOWLER, 589:OCT73-746
FICIN, M. THÉOLOGIE PLATONICIENNE,
DE L'IMMORTALITÉ DES AMES. (VOL 3)
   P. LOUIS, 555:VOL46FASC2-317
FIDO, M. OSCAR WILDE.
   617(TLS):22FEB74-193
VON FIEANDT, R. OMAA TIETÄÄN KULKI
VAIN.
   P.K. HAMALAINEN, 32:JUN73-402
FIEDLER, L.A. THE MESSENGERS WILL
COME NO MORE.
   R. ALTER, 441:29SEP74-5
FIEDLER, L.A. THE STRANGER IN SHAKE-
SPEARE.*
   B.H. FUSSELL, 249(HUDR):WINTER
   73/74-753
   M. GOLDMAN, 473(PR):3/1973-529
FIELD, A., COMP. THE COMPLECTION OF
RUSSIAN LITERATURE.
   R. SHELDON, 550(RUSR):APR72-198

FIELD, D. & J. NEWICK, EDS. THE
STUDY OF EDUCATION & ART.
617(TLS):15FEB74-161
FIELD, G.W. HERMANN HESSE.*
S. GITTLEMAN, 222(GR):NOV72-301
I.D. HALPERT, 399(MLJ):APR72-260
D. SCOTT, 220(GL&L):APR73-261
FIELD, L.A. & J.W., EDS. BERNARD
MALAMUD & THE CRITICS.*
D. FUCHS, 659:AUTUMN74-562
FIELD, P.J.C. ROMANCE & CHRONICLE.*
R.T. DAVIES, 382(MAE):1973/2-184
E.D. KENNEDY, 125:FEB73-196
B. VICKERS, 191(ELN):JUN73-291
FIELDHOUSE, D.K. ECONOMICS & EMPIRE
1830-1914.
617(TLS):27SEP74-1047
FIELDING, D. THE RAINBOW PICNIC.
617(TLS):12JUL74-745
FIELDING, H. THE CRITICISM OF HENRY
FIELDING.* (I. WILLIAMS, ED)
H. ERSKINE-HILL, 447(N&Q):OCT72-
391
FIELDING, H. THE HISTORY OF THE AD-
VENTURES OF JOSEPH ANDREWS & OF
HIS FRIEND MR. ABRAHAM ADAMS, & AN
APOLOGY FOR THE LIFE OF MRS. SHAM-
ELA ANDREWS. (D. BROOKS, ED)
L.W. BROWN, 173(ECS):SUMMER73-
531
J. DULCK, 189(EA):OCT-DEC72-557
FIELDING, H. A JOURNEY FROM THIS
WORLD TO THE NEXT. (C. RAWSON, ED)
617(TLS):26JUL74-811
FIELDS, J. A CRY OF ANGELS.
S.A. GRAU, 441:9JUN74-4
C. LEHMANN-HAUPT, 441:20MAY74-35
442(NY):30SEP74-130
FIELDS, K. SUNBELLY.
D. BROMWICH, 441:16JUN74-6
617(TLS):30AUG74-932
"W.C. FIELDS BY HIMSELF."
G. MILLAR, 362:25APR74-542
W. SHEED, 453:31OCT74-23
FIETZ, L. MENSCHENBILD UND ROMAN-
STRUKTUR IN ALDOUS HUXLEYS IDEEN-
ROMANEN.*
P. VITOUX, 677:VOL3-334
FIFE, A.E. & A.S. COWBOY & WESTERN
SONGS.*
J.O. WEST, 292(JAF):APR-JUN72-
195
FIFOOT, C.H.S. FREDERIC WILLIAM
MAITLAND, A LIFE.
N. GASH, 637(VS):JUN72-491
FIFOOT, R. A BIBLIOGRAPHY OF EDITH,
OSBERT & SACHEVERELL SITWELL.
(2ND ED)
D. PARKER, 503:SUMMER72-103
"50 FACTS ON ART."
W. FEAVER, 364:DEC73/JAN74-114
FIGES, E. DAYS.
V. CUNNINGHAM, 362:24JAN74-120
617(TLS):18JAN74-47
FIGUEROA, J., ED. CARIBBEAN VOICES.*
(VOLS 1&2)
S.H. GALE, 134(CP):FALL72-81
FILBY, P.W. & E.G. HOWARD, COMPS.
STAR-SPANGLED BOOKS.
639(VQR):AUTUMN72-CXLIV
FILHO, L.A.D. - SEE UNDER DE AZEVEDO
FILHO, L.A.

FILHO, L.A.D., J. DE DIAS DE CARVAL-
HO & O. GUTERRES DA SILVEIRA - SEE
UNDER DE AZEVEDO FILHO, L.A., J.
DE DIAS DE CARVALHO & O. GUTERRES
DA SILVEIRA
FILIPOVIĆ, R., ED. ZAGREB CONFER-
ENCE ON ENGLISH CONTRASTIVE PRO-
JECTS, 7-9 DECEMBER 1970.
S. ELIASSON, 596(SL):VOL27#1/2-
114
DI FILIPPO, R. SONETTI. (P.V. MEN-
GALDO, ED)
M.M., 228(GSLI):VOL149FASC468-
631
C.W., 275(IQ):FALL/WINTER72-116
DE FILITTA, F. OKTOBERFEST.
N. CALLENDAR, 441:13OCT74-48
FILLIOZAT, P-S., ED. OEUVRES POÉT-
IQUES DE NĪLAKAṆṬHA DĪKṢITA.
(VOL 1)
O. VON HINÜBER, 182:VOL25#23/24-
859
FILLMORE, C.J. & D.T. LANGENDOEN,
EDS. STUDIES IN LINGUISTIC SEMAN-
TICS.
D. LIGHTFOOT, 320(CJL):VOL18#1-
49
FILLMORE, C.J. & I. LEHISTE. WORK-
ING PAPERS IN LINGUISTICS 2.
J.W. NEY, 353:15MAR72-92
FINBERG, H.P.R., ED. THE AGRARIAN
HISTORY OF ENGLAND & WALES.*
(VOL 1, PT 2)
639(VQR):WINTER73-XXXVIII
FINBERG, H.P.R. THE FORMATION OF
ENGLAND, 550-1042.
H.R. LOYN, 617(TLS):1NOV74-1233
FINCH, C. THE ART OF WALT DISNEY.*
R. CRAFT, 453:16MAY74-3
E. WEEKS, 61:JAN74-96
FINCH, R. & E. JOLIAT, EDS. FRENCH
INDIVIDUALIST POETRY, 1686-1760.
W.H. EVANS, 529(QQ):AUTUMN72-414
FINDLAY, J.N. ASCENT TO THE ABSOL-
UTE.*
G.M.K., 543:SEP71-124
FINDLAY, J.N. AXIOLOGICAL ETHICS.*
R.F. ATKINSON, 479(PHQ):JAN72-83
FINE, W. THE MOUSECHILDREN & THE
FAMOUS COLLECTOR.
J. DITSKY, 219(GAR):FALL72-297
FINEMAN, D.A. - SEE MORGANN, M.
DE FINETTI, B. TEORIA DELLE PROBA-
BILITÀ.
D.A. GILLIES, 84:MAY72-138
FINGER, F.L. CATALOGUE OF THE IN-
CUNABULA IN THE ELMER BELT LIBRARY
OF VINCIANA.
J. WASSERMAN, 90:OCT72-723
FINGESTEN, P. THE ECLIPSE OF SYM-
BOLISM.
N. PARLAKIAN, 290(JAAC):WINTER72-
273
FINK, R.O. ROMAN MILITARY RECORDS
ON PAPYRUS.*
R.W. DAVIES, 313:VOL62-190
FINKE, U., ED. FRENCH NINETEENTH
CENTURY PAINTING & LITERATURE.
A. BROOKNER, 592:MAR72-137
M.J. ROSENTHAL, 135:OCT72-139
FINKEL, D. THE GARBAGE WARS.
D. ACKERSON, 502(PRS):SUMMER72-
176

111

FINKELPEARL, P.J. JOHN MARSTON OF
THE INNER TEMPLE.*
    G.R. HIBBARD, 447(N&Q):JAN72-39
FINLATOR, J. THE DRUGGED NATION.
    R. SHERRILL, 441:7JUL74-1
FINLEY, M.I. THE ANCIENT ECONOMY.
    617(TLS):25JAN74-79
FINLEY, M.I. DEMOCRACY ANCIENT &
MODERN.*
    617(TLS):1MAR74-205
FINLEY, M.I., ED. STUDIES IN
ANCIENT SOCIETY.
    617(TLS):12JUL74-750
FINN, M. & J. LABER. COOKING FOR
CAREFREE WEEKENDS.
    N. HAZELTON, 441:1DEC74-94
FINN, R.W. DOMESDAY BOOK: A GUIDE.
    617(TLS):5JUL74-733
FINNEGAN, R. ORAL LITERATURE IN
AFRICA.
    T.O. BEIDELMAN, 69:APR72-140
FINNERAN, R.J. - SEE YEATS, W.B.
FINNEY, C.G. THE CIRCUS OF DR. LAO.
    D.K. MANO, 441:12MAY74-27
FINNIGAN, B. & C. GONICK, EDS. MAK-
ING IT.
    R.M. PIKE, 529(QQ):AUTUMN72-431
FINOCCHIARO, M.A. HISTORY OF SCI-
ENCE AS EXPLANATION.
    617(TLS):17MAY74-535
FIORE, C. BUD.
    L. BRAUDY, 441:22SEP74-6
    M. GUSSOW, 441:6APR74-29
FIRBAS, J., WITH J. HLADKÝ, EDS.
CHARISTERIA IOSEPHO VACHEK SEXA-
GENARIO OBLATA.
    R.R.K. HARTMANN, 353:MAY72-87
FIRCHOW, P. ALDOUS HUXLEY.
    P.L. WILEY, 659:WINTER74-148
FIRPO, L. L'ICONOGRAFIA DI TOMMASO
CAMPANELLA.
    E. NAMER, 542:JAN-MAR72-102
FIRTH, J.J.F. - SEE ROBERT OF FLAM-
BOROUGH
FIRTH, J.R. SELECTED PAPERS OF J.R.
FIRTH 1952-59.* (F.R. PALMER, ED)
    K.A. SROKA, 353:FEB72-78
FIRTH, R. SYMBOLS.
    617(TLS):4JAN74-2
"FISCAL POLICY & THE ENERGY CRISIS."
    E. ROTHSCHILD, 453:24JAN74-38
FISCH, H. THE DUAL IMAGE.
    J. GOLD, 150(DR):SPRING72-152
    A.H. ROSENFELD, 390:DEC72-69
FISCH, H. HAMLET & THE WORD.
    K. MUIR, 191(ELN):JUN73-295
    H.M. RICHMOND, 149:DEC73-398
FISCHER, B. THE EVIL DAYS.
    N. CALLENDAR, 441:6JAN74-23
FISCHER, F. DIE FRÜHBRONZEZEIT-
LICHE ANSIEDLUNG IN DER BLEICHE
BEI ARBON TG.
    H-J. HUNDT, 182:VOL25#21-756
FISCHER, H. - SEE KRAUS, K.
FISCHER, H. & OTHERS - SEE KRAUS, K.
FISCHER, J., ED. SIX IN THE EASY
CHAIR.
    E. WEEKS, 61:JAN74-98
FISCHER, J.L. THE CASE OF SOCRATES.*
    C. KIRWAN, 393(MIND):JAN72-149
FISCHER, T. UNTERSUCHUNGEN ZUM PAR-
THERKRIEG ANTIOCHOS' VII IM RAHMEN
DER SELEUKIDENGESCHICHTE.*
    R.M. ERRINGTON, 303:VOL92-234

FISH, S.E. SELF-CONSUMING ARTI-
FACTS.*
    E. MINER, 301(JEGP):OCT73-536
    S. WIGLER, 568(SCN):SUMMER73-50
    639(VQR):SUMMER73-CXVI
FISH, S.E., ED. SEVENTEENTH-CENTURY
PROSE.
    T-L. PEBWORTH, 568(SCN):SPRING73-
    19
    B. VICKERS, 402(MLR):APR73-385
FISHER, A.G.B. & H.J. - SEE NACHTI-
GAL, G.
FISHER, D.E. A FEARFUL SYMMETRY.
    M. LEVIN, 441:28APR74-38
FISHER, J. PAUL KRUGER.
    617(TLS):30AUG74-924
FISHER, R. THE CUT PAGES. MATRIX.
    A. CLUYSENAAR, 565:VOL13#1-72
FISHER, R.B. & G.A. CHRISTIE. HOW
DRUGS WORK.
    617(TLS):23AUG74-907
FISHER, R.H., COMP. RECORDS OF THE
RUSSIAN-AMERICAN COMPANY: 1802,
1817-1867.
    R.A. PIERCE, 104:SPRING72-155
FISHER, S.W. ENGLISH WATER-COLOURS.
    T. CROMBIE, 39:APR72-342
FISHMAN, J.A. SOCIOLINGUISTICS.*
    R.L. LIGHT, 351(LL):JUN73-151
FISIAK, J. A SHORT GRAMMAR OF MID-
DLE ENGLISH.* (PT 1)
    H. WEINSTOCK, 38:BAND90HEFT3-367
FISKE, R. ENGLISH THEATRE MUSIC IN
THE EIGHTEENTH CENTURY.
    W. DEAN, 415:NOV73-1120
    B. TROWELL, 617(TLS):13SEP74-972
FITCH, B.T. DIMENSIONS ET STRUC-
TURES CHEZ BERNANOS.*
    P.A. FORTIER, 188(ECR):WINTER72-
    333
    A. SONNENFELD, 207(FR):DEC71-505
FITCH, J.M. AMERICAN BUILDING.
    H. WRIGHT, 505:JUL72-104
FITCH, J.M. AMERICAN BUILDING 2.
    L.K. EATON, 576:DEC72-339
    R. KNOWLES, 44:JUL/AUG72-12
FITCHEN, J. THE NEW WORLD DUTCH
BARN.*
    D.D. HENNING, 292(JAF):APR-JUN72-
    201
FITZGERALD, C.P. & M. ROPER. CHINA.
    617(TLS):1MAR74-205
FITZGERALD, F. FIRE IN THE LAKE.*
    L. HALL, 584(SWR):SPRING73-185
FITZGERALD, F.S. THE GREAT GATSBY.
(M.J. BRUCCOLI, ED)
    617(TLS):29MAR74-344
FITZGERALD, F.S. & Z. BITS OF PARA-
DISE. (M.J. BRUCCOLI & S.F. SMITH,
EDS)
    617(TLS):4JAN74-13
FITZGERALD, F.S. & H. OBER. AS EVER,
SCOTT FITZ. (M.J. BRUCCOLI, ED)
    617(TLS):4JAN74-13
    639(VQR):AUTUMN72-CXXXVII
FITZGERALD, G., ED. MODERN SATIRIC
STORIES.
    R.L. BUCKLAND, 573(SSF):SPRING72-
    203
FITZGERALD, S. & R. - SEE O'CONNOR,
F.
FITZGIBBON, T. A TASTE OF PARIS.
    N. HAZELTON, 441:1DEC74-94

FITZHUGH, G. CANNIBALS ALL!, OR,
SLAVES WITHOUT MASTERS. (C.V.
WOODWARD, ED)
617(TLS):29NOV74-1347
FITZPATRICK, J.P. PUERTO RICAN AMER-
ICANS.
R. ESTADES, 613:SUMMER72-312
FITZSIMMONS, T., ED & TRANS. JAPAN-
ESE POETRY NOW.
C. TOMLINSON, 364:OCT/NOV72-125
639(VQR):SUMMER72-CII
FITZSIMONS, R. GARISH LIGHTS.*
(BRITISH TITLE: CHARLES DICKENS'
SHOW.)
G.B. TENNYSON, 445(NCF):DEC72-
369
FLACELIÈRE, R. & E. CHAMBRY - SEE
PLUTARCH
FLAHERTY, D.H. PRIVACY IN COLONIAL
NEW ENGLAND.
J.J. WATERS, 656(WMQ):JAN73-168
FLAHERTY, J. CHEZ JOEY.
G. BURNSIDE, 441:28APR74-22
FLAKE, O. DIE VERURTEILUNG DES
SOKRATES.
Z. TAKACS, 182:VOL25#9/10-283
FLAM, J. ZOLTAN GORENCY.
617(TLS):26JUL74-813
FLANAGAN, R. INCISIONS.
S. SCOBIE, 99:MAR74-46
FLASCHE, H., ED. AUFSÄTZE ZUR POR-
TUGIESISCHEN KULTURGESCHICHTE.
(VOL 7)
E. GLASER, 400(MLN):MAR72-332
G.M. MOSER, 240(HR):WINTER72-112
FLASCHE, H., ED. HACIA CALDERÓN.
J.A. PARR, 238:MAR72-177
FLASCHE, H. DIE STRUKTUR DES AUTO
SACRAMENTAL "LOS ENCANTOS DE LA
CULPA" VON CALDERÓN.*
A.G. REICHENBERGER, 240(HR):
WINTER72-94
FLAUBERT, G. MADAME BOVARY. (C.
BOUTON, ED)
J.L. SHEPHERD, 3D, 207(FR):FEB72-
768
FLAUBERT, G. MADAME BOVARY.* (C.
GOTHOT-MERSCH, ED)
R. FRICKX-MONTAL, 556(RLV):
1972/6-670
M. VOISIN, 549(RLC):APR-JUN72-
310
FLAUBERT, G. THE SENTIMENTAL EDUCA-
TION. (P. BURLINGAME, TRANS)
A. FAIRLIE, 208(FS):JUL73-348
FLEET, B. BULLETS & CATHEDRALS.*
D. BARBOUR, 150(DR):SPRING72-165
FLEETWOOD, H. A CONDITIONAL SEN-
TENCE.
J. MELLORS, 362:11APR74-477
617(TLS):3MAY74-483
FLEETWOOD, H. FOREIGN AFFAIRS.*
N. CALLENDAR, 441:26MAY74-17
FLEISCHER, W. WORTBILDUNG DER
DEUTSCHEN GEGENWARTSSPRACHE.
D. KASTOVSKY, 260(IF):BAND76-328
FLEISHMAN, A. THE ENGLISH HISTORI-
CAL NOVEL: WALTER SCOTT TO VIR-
GINIA WOOLF.*
A. WELSH, 637(VS):SEP71-96
G.J. WORTH, 301(JEGP):OCT73-570

FLEMING, G.H. THAT NE'ER SHALL MEET
AGAIN.
R. EDWARDS, 135:JUL72-228
D. SONSTROEM, 637(VS):DEC72-235
FLEMING, J. YOU WON'T LET ME FIN-
NISH.*
N. CALLENDAR, 441:7APR74-35
FLEMING, J.V. THE "ROMAN DE LA
ROSE."*
M.A. GRELLNER, 382(MAE):1973/1-
69
FLEMING, M. THE PRICE OF PERFECT
JUSTICE.
I. SILVER, 441:16JUN74-21
FLEMING, T. THE GOOD SHEPHERD.
F. SWEENEY, 441:4AUG74-6
FLEMING, T. - SEE "BENJAMIN FRANKLIN"
FLEMING, W.G. ONTARIO'S EDUCATIVE
SOCIETY. (VOLS 1-5)
A.J.C. KING, 529(QQ):WINTER72-
546
"FLEMISH PAINTINGS & DRAWINGS AT 56,
PRINCES GATE, LONDON SW7; ADDENDA."
G. MARTIN, 90:AUG72-563
FLETCHER, A. THE PROPHETIC MOMENT.*
B.E.C. DAVIS, 541(RES):AUG72-333
R. FREEMAN, 677:VOL3-270
M. MURRIN, 405(MP):MAY73-342
FLETCHER, A. THE TRANSCENDENTAL
MASQUE.*
B. DRAKE, 401(MLQ):MAR73-102
J.A. WITTREICH, JR., 223:SEP72-
307
639(VQR):SPRING73-LXVIII
FLETCHER, D. A LOVABLE MAN.
617(TLS):8NOV74-1248
FLETCHER, I. MEREDITH NOW.
L.T. HERGENHAN, 67:NOV73-299
FLETCHER, J. & J. SPURLING. BECK-
ETT.*
J. PETER, 157:SUMMER72-72
FLETCHER, J.E. SHORT-TITLE CATA-
LOGUE OF GERMAN IMPRINTS IN AUS-
TRALIA FROM 1501 TO 1800.
J.L. FLOOD, 354:MAR72-61
FLETCHER, P. THE HELL SEEKERS.
D. BARBOUR, 150(DR):SPRING72-165
FLETCHER, R. THE AKENHAM BURIAL
CASE.
C. DRIVER, 362:4JUL74-29
617(TLS):30AUG74-919
FLETCHER, R., ED. THE CRISIS OF
INDUSTRIAL CIVILIZATION.
617(TLS):23AUG74-903
FLETCHER, R. THE POEMS & TRANSLA-
TIONS OF ROBERT FLETCHER. (D.H.
WOODWARD, ED)
B. MORRIS, 78(BC):AUTUMN72-417
FLETCHER, R., ED. THE SCIENCE OF
SOCIETY & THE UNITY OF MANKIND.
D. MAC RAE, 617(TLS):9AUG74-857
FLEURY, F. POÈMES.
L. WELCH, 150(DR):WINTER72/73-
688
FLEW, A. AN INTRODUCTION TO WESTERN
PHILOSOPHY.*
W.E.M., 543:MAR72-553
B. MAGEE, 393(MIND):APR72-312
C.H. WHITELEY, 479(PHQ):JAN72-70
FLEXNER, E. MARY WOLLSTONECRAFT.
A.F. SCOTT, 579(SAQ):AUTUMN73-
608
639(VQR):WINTER73-XXVIII

FLEXNER, J.T.   WASHINGTON.   [ONE-VOL
   ED]
      W.M. WALLACE, 441:20OCT74-7
FLEXNER, J.T.   GEORGE WASHINGTON.*
   (VOL 4)
      R.R. BEEMAN, 656(WMQ):OCT73-663
FLOECK, W.   "LAS MOCEDADES DEL CID"
   VON GUILLÉN DE CASTRO UND "LE CID"
   VON PIERRE CORNEILLE.
      E. GLASER, 240(HR):AUTUMN72-471
FLORES, J.M.   POETRY IN EAST GER-
   MANY.*
      A. HOLLIS, 565:VOL13#2-59
      H.F. PFANNER, 221(GQ):NOV72-732
      F.J. RADDATZ, 222(GR):JAN72-50
      J.J. WHITE, 402(MLR):OCT73-955
      D. WYNAND, 376:JAN72-129
FLORIOT, R.   LA VÉRITÉ TIENT À UN
   FIL.
      S.S. WEINER, 207(FR):OCT71-201
FLORIT, E. & J.O. JIMÉNEZ, EDS.   LA
   POESÍA HISPANOAMERICANA DESDE EL
   MODERNISMO.
      G.M. MOSER, 238:MAY72-403
      E.J. MULLEN, 238:SEP72-610
FLOTTES, P.   VIGNY ET SA FORTUNE
   LITTÉRAIRE.*
      P. MOREAU, 535(RHL):JAN-FEB72-
         140
      M. SCHAETTEL, 557(RSH):OCT-DEC72-
         612
      J. SUNGOLOWSKY, 207(FR):FEB72-
         733
FLOWER, J.E.   GEORGES BERNANOS: JOUR-
   NAL D'UN CURÉ DE CAMPAGNE.
      E. BEAUMONT, 208(FS):APR73-227
FLOWER, J.E., ED.   FRANCE TODAY.
      W. WRAGE, 399(MLJ):NOV72-471
      205(FMLS):JUL72-285
FLYS, M.J.   LA POESÍA EXISTENCIAL DE
   DÁMASO ALONSO.*
      B. CIPLIJAUSKAITÉ, 240(HR):WIN-
         TER72-104
      A.P. DEBICKI, 546(RR):APR72-165
      M.A. SALGADO, 241:JAN72-87
FOAKES, R.A.   SHAKESPEARE: THE DARK
   COMEDIES TO THE LAST PLAYS.*
      J.B. FORT, 189(EA):APR-JUN72-321
      J.K. WALTON, 541(RES):AUG72-338
      R. WARREN, 447(N&Q):APR72-152
FOAKES, R.A. - SEE COLERIDGE, S.T.
FODALE, S.   COMES ET LEGATUS SICIL-
   IAE.
      H. WIERUSZOWSKI, 589:JAN73-138
FODOR, J.A.   PSYCHOLOGICAL EXPLANA-
   TION.*
      T.C. CHABDACK, 486:MAR72-95
VON FOERSTER, H. & J.W. BEAUCHAMP,
   EDS.   MUSIC BY COMPUTERS.
      H.S. HOWE, JR., 513:SPRING-
         SUMMER70-151
FOERSTER, W., ED.   GNOSIS.   (VOL 2)
      617(TLS):13SEP74-984
FOGARASI, M.   BEITRÄGE ZUR GESCHICH-
   TE DER INTERNATIONALEN BILDUNGS-
   SUFFIXE DES RUSSISCHEN.
      R. RIS, 343:BAND14HEFT1-107
FOGEL, R.W. & S.L. ENGERMAN.   TIME
   ON THE CROSS.
      J.W. BLASSINGAME, 61:AUG74-78
      N. BLIVEN, 442(NY):30SEP74-128
      T.L. HASKELL, 453:19SEP74-38
      W.C. HAVARD, 598(SOR):AUTUMN74-
         835   [CONTINUED]

[CONTINUING]
      P. LASLETT, 362:4JUL74-25
      P. PASSELL, 441:28APR74-4
      C.V. WOODWARD, 453:2MAY74-3
      617(TLS):31MAY74-573
FOGLE, F. - SEE MILTON, J.
FOKKEMA, D.W.   REPORT FROM PEKING.
      J.M. GIBSON, 529(QQ):AUTUMN72-
         412
FOKKEMA, K.   NEI WIDER KIMEN.
      E.G.A. GALAMA, 433:APR72-245
FOKKEMA, K. & J.J. SPAHR VAN DER
   HOEK.   TAELATLAS FAN DE WÂLDEN.
      F. VAN COETSEM, 353:1JUL72-102
FOLENA, G. & G. PELLEGRINI - SEE
   PRATI, A.
FOLEY, A.E.   OCCULT ARTS & DOCTRINE
   IN THE THEATER OF JUAN RUIZ DE
   ALARCÓN.
      J.A. PARR, 402(MLR):OCT73-916
FOLEY, M., ED.   THE BEST AMERICAN
   SHORT STORIES: 12.
      617(TLS):6SEP74-960
FOLEY, M., ED.   THE BEST AMERICAN
   SHORT STORIES 1972.
      639(VQR):SPRING73-LX
FOLEY, M. & D. BURNETT, EDS.   THE
   BEST AMERICAN SHORT STORIES 1971.*
      639(VQR):SPRING72-XLIX
FOLEY, W.   A CHILD IN THE FOREST.
      A.L. BARKER, 362:11JUL74-59
FOLEY, W.E.   A HISTORY OF MISSOURI.
   (VOL 1)
      A.P. NASATIR, 656(WMQ):APR72-320
FOLLAIN, J.   COLLÈGE.
      617(TLS):25JAN74-82
FOLMSBEE, S.J., R.E. CORLEY & E.L.
   MITCHELL.   TENNESSEE.
      R.L. PARTIN, 9(ALAR):APR72-149
FOLZ, R.   THE CORONATION OF CHARLE-
   MAGNE 25 DECEMBER 800.
      F. YATES, 617(TLS):1NOV74-1229
FONG-TORRES, B., ED.   THE ROLLING
   STONE ROCK 'N' ROLL READER.
      J. ROCKWELL, 441:8MAY74-37
FONGARO, A., G. MOMBELLO & P. ROCCHI,
   EDS.   DEUX ANNÉES D'ÉTUDES BAUDE-
   LAIRIENNES, JUILLET 1966-JUIN 1968.
      D. SAUNDERS, 402(MLR):JUL73-659
DA FONSECA, G.   EÇA DE QUEIROZ.
      191(ELN):SEP72(SUPP)-204
FONTAINE, J.   THE JOURNAL OF JOHN
   FONTAINE.   (E.P. ALEXANDER, ED)
      P. MARAMBAUD, 656(WMQ):APR73-355
      639(VQR):AUTUMN72-CXXXVI
FONTAINE, J.   LA LITTÉRATURE LATINE
   CHRÉTIENNE.
      P. LANGLOIS, 555:VOL46FASC1-163
FONTANE, T.   BRIEFE AN WILHELM UND
   HANS HERTZ 1859-98.   (K. SCHREIN-
   ERT, ED)
      E.F. GEORGE, 182:VOL25#23/24-862
FONTANE, T.   REISEBRIEFE VOM KRIEGS-
   SCHAUPLATZ BÖHMEN 1866.
      617(TLS):5JUL74-729
FONTENROSE, J.   THE RITUAL THEORY OF
   MYTH.
      N. SIMMS, 67:NOV73-331
FONVIEILLE, R.   LE VÉRITABLE JULIEN
   SOREL.
      J.S.P., 191(ELN):SEP72(SUPP)-118
FOOT, M.   ANEURIN BEVAN.*   (VOL 2)
      J. CAMERON, 441:10FEB74-4
      442(NY):18FEB74-120

114

FOOTE, E.J. RUSSIAN & SOVIET IMPER-
IALISM.
   M. MC CAULEY, 575(SEER):OCT73-
   618
FOOTE, H.W. JOHN SMIBERT, PAINTER.
   K. GARLICK, 447(N&Q):JUN72-237
FOOTE, J.A. "PIE-POWDER:" BEING
DUST FROM THE LAW COURTS.
   617(TLS):25JAN74-86
FOOTE, L.P. VERBS OF MOTION. [TO-
GETHER WITH] DAVIDSON, R.M. THE
USE OF THE GENITIVE IN NEGATIVE
CONSTRUCTIONS.
   G.M. ERAMIAN, 104:SUMMER72-317
FOOTE, S. THE CIVIL WAR. (VOL 3)
   P. ADAMS, 61:DEC74-128
   N.K. BURGER, 441:15DEC74-2
"FOR EVERY NORTH AMERICAN INDIAN WHO
BEGINS TO DISAPPEAR I ALSO BEGIN
TO DISAPPEAR."
   M. BOWERING, 376:JUL72-137
FORBES, B. THE DISTANT LAUGHTER.
   M. FELD, 364:OCT/NOV72-152
FORBES, B. NOTES FOR A LIFE.
   617(TLS):6DEC74-1368
FORBES, C., ED. ROBERT WELCH.
   617(TLS):1MAR74-220
FORCIONE, A.K. CERVANTES, ARISTOTLE
& THE "PERSILES."*
   M. FRANZBACH, 549(RLC):JAN-MAR72-
   140
   H. SIEBER, 400(MLN):MAR72-359
FORD, F.M. RETURN TO YESTERDAY.*
   R. MC KEAN, 114(CHIR):VOL24#4-
   164
FORD, F.M. SELECTED POEMS. (B.
BUNTING, ED)
   B. BERGONZI, 565:VOL13#4-78
FORD, G.B., JR. - SEE ST. ISIDORE OF
SEVILLE
"FOREIGN LANGUAGE FRAMEWORK FOR CAL-
IFORNIA PUBLIC SCHOOLS, KINDERGAR-
TEN THROUGH GRADE TWELVE."
   D.C. SHEPPARD, 399(MLJ):DEC72-
   503
FORIN, E.M. - SEE UNDER MARTELLOZZO
FORIN, E.
FORKEL, J.N. JOHANN SEBASTIAN BACH.
   H.M. SCHUELLER, 290(JAAC):WINTER
   71-274
FORLANI, R. AU BAL DES CHIENS.
   D.M. CHURCH, 207(FR):FEB72-697
FORMIGARI, L. STUDI SULL'ESTETICA
DELL'EMPIRISMO INGLESE, 1931-1965.
   R. ADAMS, 481(PQ):JUL72-511
FORNARA, C.W. HERODOTUS.*
   J.R. GRANT, 487:SPRING72-92
   E. WILL, 555:VOL46FASC1-117
FORNER, J.P. LOS GRAMÁTICOS, HIS-
TORIA CHINESCA.* (J. JURADO, ED)
   R.P. SEBOLD, 400(MLN):MAR72-372
FORNER, J.P. LOS GRAMÁTICOS, HIS-
TORIA CHINESCA.* (J.H.R. POLT, ED)
   R.M. COX, 481(PQ):JUL72-681
   R.P. SEBOLD, 240(HR):SPRING72-
   228
FORRESTER, H. TWOPENCE TO CROSS THE
MERSEY.
   617(TLS):23AUG74-901
FORRESTER, L. DIAMOND BEACH.
   N. CALLENDAR, 441:13JAN74-12
FORRESTER, V. LE GRAND FESTIN.
   S.G. STARY, 207(FR):MAY72-1176

"FORSCHUNGEN ZUR RÖMISCHEN LITERA-
TUR."
   J-M. ANDRÉ, 555:VOL46FASC2-342
FORSEY, E. FREEDOM & ORDER.
   M.S. CROSS, 99:NOV/DEC74-43
FORSGREN, A. JOHN GAY, POET "OF A
LOWER ORDER." (VOL 2)
   S.M. ARMENS, 481(PQ):JUL72-682
   P.M. SPACKS, 566:AUTUMN72-33
FORSHAW, J.M. PARROTS OF THE WORLD.
   617(TLS):19JUL74-772
FORSTER, E.M. ALBERGO EMPEDOCLE &
OTHER WRITINGS.*
   639(VQR):SPRING72-LII
FORSTER, E.M. HOWARDS END. THE
MANUSCRIPTS OF HOWARD END. (O.
STALLYBRASS, ED OF BOTH)
   P.N. FURBANK, 362:31JAN74-153
   617(TLS):18JAN74-43
FORSTER, E.M. MAURICE.*
   D. GODFREY, 150(DR):SPRING72-136
FORSTER, G. WERKE IN VIER BÄNDEN.
(VOL 3) (G. STEINER, ED)
   E.E. REED, 221(GQ):MAY72-542
FORSTER, L. THE ICY FIRE.*
   B. CORRIGAN, 627(UTQ):AUTUMN71-
   77
   I. LEIMBERG, 38:BAND9OHEFT3-398
   P. THOMSON, 447(N&Q):JAN72-38
   S.F. WITSTEIN, 433:JUL72-363
FORSTER, L. THE POET'S TONGUES.*
   S. PRAWER, 220(GL&L):JUL73-319
   T. WEEVERS, 402(MLR):JAN73-132
   205(FMLS):JAN72-88
FORSTER, M. THE SEDUCTION OF MRS.
PENDLEBURY.
   M. JOHNSON, 617(TLS):22NOV74-
   1307
   J. MELLORS, 362:21NOV74-684
FORSTER, R. THE HOUSE OF SAULX-
TAVANES.
   J.C. RULE, 481(PQ):JUL72-530
FORSTER, R.K. WORLD POSTMARKS.
   617(TLS):8FEB74-140
FORSYTH, F. THE DOGS OF WAR.
   P. ADAMS, 61:AUG74-90
   D. GODDARD, 441:14JUL74-4
   C. LEHMANN-HAUPT, 441:3JUL74-29
   617(TLS):25OCT74-1206
FORSYTH, G.H. & K. WEITZMANN. THE
MONASTERY OF SAINT CATHERINE AT
MOUNT SINAI.*
   P. BROWN, 453:3OCT74-3
FORSYTH, I.H. THE THRONE OF WISDOM.
   617(TLS):4JAN74-16
FORSYTH, J. A GRAMMAR OF ASPECT.*
   M.S. FLIER, 297(JL):FEB72-167
   J.G. NICHOLSON, 402(MLR):JUL73-
   715
FORSYTH, J. - SEE VINOKUR, G.O.
FORSYTH, W.H. THE ENTOMBMENT OF
CHRIST.*
   J. BECKWITH, 39:JAN72-66
   C.H. KRINSKY, 551(RENQ):WINTER
   72-457
FORSYTHE, S.A. AN AMERICAN MISSION-
ARY COMMUNITY IN CHINA, 1895-1905.
   L.W. CRABTREE, 293(JAST):AUG72-
   932
FORT, C. THE BOOK OF THE DAMNED.
   C. JAMES, 617(TLS):15NOV74-1290
FORTE, A. THE STRUCTURE OF ATONAL
MUSIC.
   617(TLS):8MAR74-241

FOSCOLO, U. EPISTOLARIO. (VOL 7)
(M. SCOTTI, ED)
S. ORLANDO, 228(GSLI):VOL149FASC
466/467-443
FOSCOLO, U. SCRITTI LETTERARI E
POLITICI DAL 1796 AL 1808. (G.
GAMBARIN, ED)
M. SCOTTI, 228(GSLI):VOL149FASC
468-622
FOSKETT, D. SAMUEL COOPER 1609-1672.
617(TLS):15MAR74-261
FOSKETT, D. A DICTIONARY OF BRITISH
MINIATURE PAINTERS.
T. CROMBIE, 39:SEP72-253
J. MAYNE, 135:JUN72-150
R. WARK, 54:DEC72-555
FOSKETT, D. JOHN HARDEN OF BRATHAY
HALL, 1772-1847.
J. HARRIS, 617(TLS):27DEC74-1467
FOSS, M. THE AGE OF PATRONAGE.
C.T.P., 566:AUTUMN72-50
E. WATERHOUSE, 656(WMQ):OCT72-
663
FOSS, M. UNDREAMED SHORES.
C. HILL, 453:14NOV74-17
617(TLS):5JUL74-733
FOSTER, B. THE CHANGING ENGLISH
LANGUAGE.*
J. ALGEO, 128(CE):MAY72-936
FOSTER, D.W. & V.R., COMPS. MANUAL
OF HISPANIC BIBLIOGRAPHY.
F.M. CLARK, 241:JAN72-79
A. ESPANTOSO DE FOLEY, 240(HR):
SPRING72-216
D.S. ZUBATSKY, 399(MLJ):OCT72-
404
FOSTER, J. CLASS STRUGGLE & THE
INDUSTRIAL REVOLUTION.
D. THOMPSON, 617(TLS):27SEP74-
1039
FOSTER, J.W. FORCES & THEMES IN
ULSTER FICTION.
R. FOSTER, 617(TLS):20DEC74-1443
FOSTER, M.L. THE TARASCAN LANGUAGE.
P. FRIEDRICH, 350:MAR73-238
A.C. WARES, 297(JL):FEB72-190
FOSTER, S. THEIR SOLITARY WAY.
R.L. BUSHMAN, 432(NEQ):SEP72-457
D. LEVIN, 656(WMQ):JUL72-494
FOTHERGILL, B. THE MITRED EARL.
E.S. TURNER, 362:23MAY74-671
DE FOUCAULT, J. - SEE POLYBIUS
FOUCAULT, M. THE ARCHAEOLOGY OF
KNOWLEDGE.* (FRENCH TITLE: L'ARCH-
ÉOLOGIE DU SAVOIR.)
J. CULLER, 676(YR):WINTER73-290
FOUCAULT, M. THE BIRTH OF THE CLIN-
IC.
C. LASCH, 441:24FEB74-6
617(TLS):1FEB74-107
FOUCAULT, M. THE ORDER OF THINGS.*
G.S. ROUSSEAU, 173(ECS):WINTER
72/73-238
FOUCAULT, M. - SEE RIVIÈRE, P.
FOUCHER, L. LA PHILOSOPHIE CATHO-
LIQUE EN FRANCE AU DIX-NEUVIÈME
SIÈCLE AVANT LA RENAISSANCE THOM-
ISTE ET DANS SON RAPPORT AVEC ELLE
(1800-1880).
A. FOREST, 542:JUL-SEP72-342
FOUDRAINE, J. NOT MADE OF WOOD.
R. DINNAGE, 617(TLS):2AUG74-829

FOUGERET DE MONBRON, L-C. LE COS-
MOPOLITE OU LE CITOYEN DU MONDE,
SUIVI DE LA CAPITALE DES GAULES OU
LA NOUVELLE BABYLONE.* (R. TROUS-
SON, ED)
G. MAY, 207(FR):FEB72-737
V. MYLNE, 208(FS):JUL73-337
FOULON, C. - SEE NOËL DU FAIL
FOUQUET, D. WORT UND BILD IN DER
MITTELALTERLICHEN TRISTANTRADITION.
W.C. CROSSGROVE, 589:OCT73-748
F.P. PICKERING, 680(ZDP):BAND91
HEFT3-449
FOURCADE, M-M. NOAH'S ARK.
D. SCHOENBRUN, 441:17FEB74-29
617(TLS):5JUL74-702
FOURIER, C. THE UTOPIAN VISION OF
CHARLES FOURIER. (J. BEECHER & R.
BIENVENU, EDS)
H. LOMAS, 364:JUN/JUL72-149
FOWLER, A., ED. SILENT POETRY.*
R. HARRÉ, 541(RES):FEB72-105
FOWLER, A. TRIUMPHAL FORMS.*
J.M. KENNEDY, 541(RES):FEB72-67
P.E. MEDINE, 50(ARQ):AUTUMN72-
274
FOWLER, D.C. A LITERARY HISTORY OF
THE POPULAR BALLAD.*
N. WÜRZBACH, 38:BAND90HEFT3-393
FOWLER, J. & J. CORNFORTH. ENGLISH
DECORATION IN THE 18TH CENTURY.
W. FEAVER, 362:19&26DEC74-847
FOWLER, R. UNDERSTANDING LANGUAGE.
617(TLS):27SEP74-1037
FOWLES, J. THE EBONY TOWER.
D.A.N. JONES, 362:30OCT74-450
C. LEHMANN-HAUPT, 441:4NOV74-35
T. SOLOTAROFF, 441:10NOV74-2
E. WEEKS, 61:DEC74-126
442(NY):23DEC74-83
617(TLS):4OCT74-1061
FOWLES, J. THE FRENCH LIEUTENANT'S
WOMAN.*
P. BRANTLINGER, I. ADAM & S.
ROTHBLATT, 637(VS):MAR72-339
FOX, A. MAN MISMANAGEMENT.
617(TLS):26JUL74-807
FOX, G. BRITAIN & JAPAN, 1858-1883.*
G.K. GOODMAN, 318(JAOS):JAN-MAR
72-156
FOX, G. - SEE UNDER ABBEY, L.
FOX, I.K., ED. WATER RESOURCES LAW
& POLICY IN THE SOVIET UNION.
P.B. TAYLOR, 550(RUSR):JUL72-312
FOX, J. A LITERARY HISTORY OF
FRANCE: THE MIDDLE AGES.
617(TLS):23AUG74-894
FOX, J. THE LYRIC POETRY OF CHARLES
D'ORLÉANS.*
T. STEMMLER, 38:BAND90HEFT3-386
FOX, J.M. OPERATION DANCING DOG.
N. CALLENDAR, 441:18AUG74-24
FOX, R. ENCOUNTER WITH ANTHROPOLOGY.
442(NY):14JAN74-98
FOX, R.B. THE TABON CAVES.
W.G. SOLHEIM 2D, 293(JAST):AUG72-
999
FOX, R.G. KIN, CLAN, RAJA & RULE.
A.R. BEALS, 293(JAST):AUG72-967
FOX, R.G., ED. URBAN INDIA.
H.M. CHOLDIN, 293(JAST):FEB72-
471

FOX, R.L. ALEXANDER THE GREAT.
E. BADIAN, 453:19SEP74-8
M.I. FINLEY, 441:28APR74-16
617(TLS):15FEB74-157
FOXALL, R. BRANDY FOR THE PARSON.
N. CALLENDAR, 441:1SEP74-15
FOXALL, R. THE SILVER GOBLET. THE
DARK FOREST.
N. CALLENDAR, 441:17NOV74-52
FOXELL, N. SCHOOLBOY RISING.
617(TLS):1FEB74-97
VAN FRAASSEN, B.C. AN INTRODUCTION
TO THE PHILOSOPHY OF TIME & SPACE.*
G. NERLICH, 63:MAY73-82
FRAMERY, N.É., P-L. GINGUENÉ & J.J.
DE MOMIGNY, EDS. ENCYCLOPÉDIE
MÉTHODIQUE: MUSIQUE.*
J.A.W., 410(M&L):APR73-237
FRANCE, P. RHETORIC & TRUTH IN
FRANCE.
N. CAPALDI, 319:OCT74-535
FRANCÈS, R. LA PERCEPTION.
M. CHASTAING, 542:OCT-DEC72-461
FRANCESCO DI GIORGIO MARTINI. TRAT-
TATI DI ARCHITETTURA, INGEGNERIA E
ARTE MILITARE.* (C. MALTESE, ED)
R.J. BETTS, 576:MAR72-62
FRANCILLON, R. L'OEUVRE ROMANESQUE
DE MADAME DE LA FAYETTE.
617(TLS):26JUL74-804
FRANCIS, D. KNOCK DOWN.
617(TLS):20DEC74-1437
FRANCIS, D. SLAY-RIDE.
N. CALLENDAR, 441:17FEB74-33
442(NY):1APR74-124
617(TLS):18JAN74-61
FRANCIS, F., ED. TREASURES OF THE
BRITISH MUSEUM.*
M. ROSENTHAL, 135:SEP72-64
FRANCIS, R. - SEE FROST, R.
FRANCIS, S., ED & TRANS. LIBRARIES
IN THE USSR.
H. KUKK, 550(RUSR):APR72-199
FRANCISCONO, M. WALTER GROPIUS &
THE CREATION OF THE BAUHAUS IN
WEIMAR.*
A.C. BIRNHOLZ, 290(JAAC):SUMMER
72-552
I. GROPIUS, 44:JAN/FEB72-16
DI FRANCO, F. LE THÉÂTRE DE SALA-
CROU.
J.C. MC LAREN, 207(FR):DEC71-504
FRANCO, J. THE MODERN CULTURE OF
LATIN AMERICA.
T.O. BENTE, 37:OCT72-39
FRANÇOIS, M., ED. LA FRANCE ET LES
FRANÇAIS.
D. JOHNSON, 617(TLS):27DEC74-
1468
FRANK, H.J. GESCHICHTE DES DEUTSCH-
UNTERRICHTS.
W. BIESTERFELD, 182:VOL25#22-784
FRANK, R.W., JR. CHAUCER & THE
LEGEND OF GOOD WOMEN.
639(VQR):SUMMER73-CXVII
FRANKE, M. MORDVERLÄUFE.
617(TLS):18JAN74-59
FRANKEL, M.E. CRIMINAL SENTENCES.*
A.F. NUSSBAUM, 231:MAY74-92
FRANKFURT, H.G. DEMONS, DREAMERS,
& MADMEN.*
T.L. PRENDERGAST, 258:JUN72-303
J.N. WRIGHT, 483:JAN72-80

FRANKLIN, B. THE PAPERS OF BENJAMIN
FRANKLIN.* (VOLS 11-14) (L.W. LAB-
AREE, WITH H.C. BOATFIELD & J.H.
HUTSON, EDS)
C. CROWE, 656(WMQ):APR73-343
FRANKLIN, B. THE PAPERS OF BENJAMIN
FRANKLIN. (VOL 15) (W.B. WILLCOX,
WITH OTHERS, EDS)
C. CROWE, 656(WMQ):APR73-344
639(VQR):AUTUMN72-CXXXVI
FRANKLIN, B. THE PAPERS OF BENJAMIN
FRANKLIN. (VOL 17) (W.B. WILLCOX,
ED)
617(TLS):3MAY74-468
"BENJAMIN FRANKLIN: A BIOGRAPHY IN
HIS OWN WORDS."* (T. FLEMING, ED)
639(VQR):SPRING73-LXXVI
FRANKLIN, H. THE FLAG-WAGGER.
617(TLS):5JUL74-733
FRANKLIN, M. 99 & 44/100 DEAD.
N. CALLENDAR, 441:11AUG74-12
FRANKLIN, S. KNOWLEDGE PARK.
P. STEVENS, 628:SPRING73-95
FRANKS, L. WAITING OUT A WAR.
442(NY):12AUG74-98
FRANOLIĆ, B. LA LANGUE LITTÉRAIRE
CROATE.
R.G.A. DE BRAY, 575(SEER):APR73-
295
FRANZ, H. DAS BILD GRIECHENLANDS
UND ITALIENS IN DEN MITTELHOCH-
DEUTSCHEN EPISCHEN ERZÄHLUNGEN VOR
1250.*
B.A. BEATIE, 589:APR73-355
C. GELLINEK, 564:JUN72-137
D.H. GREEN, 402(MLR):JAN73-220
K. SMITS, 67:MAY73-140
VON FRANZ, M-L. ZAHL UND ZEIT.
R. BLANCHÉ, 542:OCT-DEC72-461
M. DE TOLLENAERE, 258:MAR72-149
FRANZEN, E. FORMEN DES MODERNEN
DRAMAS.
W.B. LEWIS, 221(GQ):MAY72-532
FRAPPIER, J. ÉTUDE SUR "YVAIN" OU
LE "CHEVALIER AU LION" DE CHRÉTIEN
DE TROYES.
K.D. UITTI, 545(RPH):AUG72-77
FRASER, A. CROMWELL.*
N. BLIVEN, 442(NY):14JAN74-95
FRASER, D. GLEN OF THE ROWAN TREES.
617(TLS):8MAR74-245
FRASER, D. VILLAGE PLANNING IN THE
PRIMITIVE WORLD.
G.L. HERSEY, 56:SUMMER72-180
FRASER, D. & H.M. COLE. AFRICAN ART
& LEADERSHIP.
J. MAQUET, 59(ASOC):SUMMER-FALL
73-297
FRASER, G.M. MC AUSLAN IN THE ROUGH.
M. LEVIN, 441:24NOV74-41
617(TLS):31MAY74-577
FRASER, G.S. METRE, RHYME & FREE
VERSE.
P. GOETSCH, 430(NS):AUG72-500
FRASER, J. VIOLENCE IN THE ARTS.
J. BEMROSE, 99:AUG74-36
J. CAREY, 362:25APR74-533
FRASER, P. LORD ESHER.
617(TLS):8FEB74-127
FRASER, R. THE DARK AGES & THE AGE
OF GOLD.
639(VQR):SUMMER73-CXVII
FRASER, R. THE MORE I LIVE.
D. BAILEY, 529(QQ):SUMMER72-242

FRASER, R. THE PUEBLO.
617(TLS):25JAN74-87
FRASER, R. THE WAR AGAINST POETRY.*
J. VAN DORSTEN, 402(MLR):JAN73-
145
D. JAVITCH, 551(RENQ):SUMMER72-
223
J.L. MURPHY, 191(ELN):DEC72-149
P. SPRIET, 189(EA):OCT-DEC72-550
FRASER, S. PANDORA.*
R. MC CARTHY, 150(DR):WINTER
72/73-701
P. STEVENS, 628:SPRING73-95
FRASER, S.E. - SEE HOLBERG, L.
FRATTI, M. 4 PLAYS BY MARIO FRATTI.
A. AMOIA, 160:SPRING72-190
FRAYN, M. CONSTRUCTIONS.
D.J. ENRIGHT, 362:21NOV74-680
FRAYN, M. SWEET DREAMS.*
M. DRABBLE, 441:13JAN74-7
442(NY):14JAN74-97
FRAYN, M. A VERY PRIVATE LIFE.
A.T. EMERSON, 159(DM):WINTER/
SPRING71/72-119
FRAYNE, J.P. - SEE YEATS, W.B.
FRAZIER, W. & I. DERKOW. ROCKIN'
STEADY.
J. KLEMESRUD, 441:24MAR74-14
FRÈCHES, C-H. LA LITTÉRATURE PORTU-
GAISE.
D. MESSNER, 430(NS):DEC72-743
FRED. LES AVENTURES DE PHILÉMON.
P. FRESNAULT-DERUELLE, 98:MAY72-
460
FREDEMAN, W.E. PRELUDE TO THE LAST
DECADE.
D. SONSTROEM, 637(VS):DEC72-235
FREDERIC, H. THE DAMNATION OF THER-
ON WARE.
617(TLS):13SEP74-975
FREDERICKS, P.G. THE SEPOY & THE
COSSACK.*
L.E. BREEZE, 637(VS):MAR72-391
FRÉDÉRIX, P. M. RENÉ DESCARTES ET
SON TEMPS.
G. RODIS-LEWIS, 542:APR-JUN72-
190
FREDRICK, W.R.N., ED. A SHAKESPEARE
BIBLIOGRAPHY.
J.G.M., 570(SQ):WINTER72-123
FREDRICKSON, G.M. THE BLACK IMAGE
IN THE WHITE MIND.
K.J. HANSEN, 529(QQ):AUTUMN72-
429
FREE, W.N. WILLIAM COWPER.
S.M. PASSLER, 577(SHR):FALL72-
416
FREEBORN, R. THE RISE OF THE RUS-
SIAN NOVEL.*
K. SANINE, 182:VOL25#22-790
FREEDMAN, M. AMERICAN DRAMA IN
SOCIAL CONTEXT.
M. MATLAW, 397(MD):DEC72-338
FREELING, N. A DRESSING OF DIAMOND.
N. CALLENDAR, 441:30JUN74-33
617(TLS):23AUG74-911
FREEMAN, C. & OTHERS. THINKING
ABOUT THE FUTURE.
G. ROYCE, 99:MAR74-39
FREEMAN, E. THE THEATRE OF ALBERT
CAMUS.*
205(FMLS):JUL72-286
FREEMAN, E. - SEE BLANSHARD, B.

FREEMAN, E. & W. SELLARS, EDS.
BASIC ISSUES IN THE PHILOSOPHY OF
TIME.
T. CHAPMAN, 154:DEC72-657
FREEMAN, L. - SEE MENNINGER, K.
FREEMAN, R.A. THE STONEWARE MONKEY
[&] THE PENROSE MYSTERY.
N. CALLENDAR, 441:30JAN74-22
FREEMAN-GRENVILLE, G.S.P. CHRONOL-
OGY OF AFRICAN HISTORY.
617(TLS):3MAY74-482
FREEMANTLE, B. FACE ME WHEN YOU
WALK AWAY.
617(TLS):12JUL74-741
FREER, C. MUSIC FOR A KING.
M.E. MASON, 568(SCN):SUMMER73-46
S.R. MAVEETY, 648:JAN73-69
FREESE, W. MYSTISCHER MOMENT UND
REFLEKTIERTE DAUER.
K. MENGES, 221(GQ):JAN72-160
FREGE, G. CONCEPTUAL NOTATION & RE-
LATED ARTICLES.* (T.W. BYNUM, ED
& TRANS)
J.E. LLEWELYN, 518:MAY73-5
FREGE, G. NACHGELASSENE SCHRIFTEN.*
(H. HERMES, F. KAMBARTEL & F.
KAULBACH, EDS)
M.D. RESNIK, 486:JUN72-269
FREGE, G. & K. GÖDEL. FREGE & GÖDEL,
TWO FUNDAMENTAL TEXTS IN MATHEMATI-
CAL LOGIC. (J. VAN HEIJENOORT, ED)
A. CHURCH, 316:JUN72-405
FREI, H.W. THE ECLIPSE OF BIBLICAL
NARRATIVE.
C.F. EVANS, 617(TLS):22NOV74-
1320
FREI-KORSUNSKY, S. GRIECHISCHE WÖR-
TER AUS LATEINISCHER ÜBERLIEFERUNG.
A. ERNOUT, 555:VOL46FASC1-143
FREIBERG, M., ED. JOURNALS OF THE
HOUSE OF REPRESENTATIVES OF MASSA-
CHUSETTS, 1763-1764 & 1764-1765.*
(VOLS 40 & 41)
J.A. SCHUTZ, 432(NEQ):MAR72-149
FREIBERG, M., ED. JOURNALS OF THE
HOUSE OF REPRESENTATIVES OF MASSA-
CHUSETTS, 1764-1765 & 1765-1766.
(VOLS 41 & 42)
R.M. CALHOON, 432(NEQ):DEC72-602
FREMLIN, C. BY HORROR HAUNTED.
617(TLS):5APR74-375
FRÉNAUD, A. DEPUIS TOUJOURS DÉJÀ.
S. MAX, 207(FR):DEC71-469
FRENCH, A., ED & TRANS. THE ATHEN-
IAN HALF-CENTURY 478-431 B.C.
J.W. COLE, 487:SUMMER72-202
FRENCH, A.L. SHAKESPEARE & THE
CRITICS.
G.M. HARVEY, 150(DR):WINTER72/73-
686
E.A. HORSMAN, 67:MAY73-116
D.A. TRAVERSI, 401(MLQ):SEP73-
312
FRENCH, D. LEAVING HOME. ON THE
FIELDS, LATELY.
E. MULLALY, 198:WINTER74-61
FRENCH, P. WESTERNS.
G. MILLAR, 362:25APR74-542
617(TLS):22MAR74-300
FRENCH, P.J. JOHN DEE.*
A.M., 125:OCT72-88
FREND, W.H.C. THE RISE OF THE MONO-
PHYSITE MOVEMENT.*
P.J. ALEXANDER, 32:DEC73-797

FRENZ, H., ED. NOBEL LECTURES, LIT-
ERATURE, 1901-1967.
J.C. MAXWELL, 447(N&Q):DEC72-480
FRÈRE, A. COMÉDIES À UNE VOIX.
J. DECOCK, 207(FR):DEC71-470
FRERE-COOK, G. THE ATTACKS ON THE
TIRPITZ.
617(TLS):19APR74-425
FREUD, S. DÉLIRE ET RÊVES DANS LA
GRADIVA DE JENSEN.
S. KOFMAN, 98:OCT72-892
FREUD, S. PSYCHANALYSE. (D. DREY-
FUS, ED)
C. BARDET, 542:OCT-DEC72-462
FREUD, S. & C.G. JUNG. THE FREUD/
JUNG LETTERS. (W. MC GUIRE, ED)
F. BROWN, 231:AUG74-88
C. RYCROFT, 453:18APR74-6
L. TRILLING, 441:21APR74-1
R. WOLLHEIM, 362:25APR74-532
442(NY):15APR74-151
617(TLS):10MAY74-489
FREUND, G. PHOTOGRAPHIE ET SOCIÉTÉ.
617(TLS):12APR74-386
FREUND, L. ZEITKRITIK IN HEINES
REISEBILDERN.
J.L.S., 191(ELN):SEP72(SUPP)-150
FREUNDLICH, E. - SEE HINSON, M.
FREY, G. SPRACHE - AUSDRUCK DES
BEWUSSTSEINS.
G. KNAUSS, 206:SEP72-147
W. KUBICEK, 182:VOL25#15/16-517
FREY, M. DER KÜNSTLER UND SEIN WERK
BEI W.H. WACKENRODER UND E.T.A.
HOFFMANN.
J.F.F., 191(ELN):SEP72(SUPP)-183
FREYTAG, H. KOMMENTAR ZUR FRÜHMIT-
TELHOCHDEUTSCHEN SUMMA THEOLOGIAE.
E. EGERT, 221(GQ):MAY72-505
FREYTAG, W. DAS OXYMORON BEI WOLF-
RAM, GOTTFRIED UND ANDERN DICHTERN
DES MITTELALTERS.
D.H. GREEN, 402(MLR):OCT73-935
FRIAR, K., ED & TRANS. MODERN
GREEK POETRY.*
V. YOUNG, 249(HUDR):WINTER73/74-
717
639(VQR):AUTUMN73-CXLI
FRIDH, Å. CONTRIBUTIONS À LA CRIT-
IQUE ET À L'INTERPRÉTATION DES
"VARIAE" DE CASSIODORE.
P. COURCELLE, 555:VOL46FASC1-165
FRIDH, Å. DER SOGENANNTE PROSPEK-
TIVE KONJUNKTIV IM LATEINISCHEN.
F. THOMAS, 555:VOL46FASC2-328
FRIED, C. AN ANATOMY OF VALUES.*
A.S.C., 543:DEC71-352
FRIED, E. GEGENGIFT.
617(TLS):4OCT74-1090
FRIED, J.J. THE MYSTERY OF HEREDITY.
42(AR):SPRING/SUMMER72-249
FRIED, J.P. HOUSING CRISIS U.S.A.
505:JUN72-128
FRIEDBERG, M. - SEE TROTSKY, L.
FRIEDENBERG, E.Z. LAING.
617(TLS):25JAN74-71
FRIEDENTHAL, R. LUTHER.*
C.F. BAYERSCHMIDT, 222(GR):MAR72-
150
FRIEDLAND, W.H. "VUTA KAMBA."
R.D. GRILLO, 69:JUL72-246
FRIEDLANDER, C.P. & E. MITCHELL.
THE POLICE.
617(TLS):14JUN74-646

FRIEDMAN, A. HERMAPHRODEITY.
S. O'CONNELL, 418(MR):WINTER73-
190
E. ROVIT, 659:AUTUMN74-539
FRIEDMAN, A. - SEE GOLDSMITH, O.
FRIEDMAN, B.H. MUSEUM.
C. LEHMANN-HAUPT, 441:17OCT74-45
M. MEWSHAW, 441:13OCT74-26
FRIEDMAN, B.H. ALFONSO OSSORIO.
A. FRANKENSTEIN, 55:MAY73-15
FRIEDMAN, B.H. JACKSON POLLOCK.*
A. FRANKENSTEIN, 55:MAY73-15
639(VQR):WINTER73-XXXII
FRIEDMAN, B.H. WHISPERS.
639(VQR):SPRING73-LVII
FRIEDMAN, B.J. ABOUT HARRY TOWNS.
J.R. FRAKES, 441:23JUN74-32
C. LEHMANN-HAUPT, 441:16MAY74-45
R. TODD, 61:MAY74-128
FRIEDMAN, D.M. MARVELL'S PASTORAL
ART.*
J.B. BROADBENT, 447(N&Q):MAY72-
194
FRIEDMAN, J.B. ORPHEUS IN THE MID-
DLE AGES.*
D. FOX, 589:JAN73-141
H. GLASSIE, 292(JAF):APR-JUN72-
202
F. JOUKOVSKY, 545(RPH):NOV72-456
FRIEDMAN, M., ED. MARTIN BUBER &
THE THEATER.
H. ZOHN, 221(GQ):MAY72-502
FRIEDMAN, M. MONETARY CORRECTION.
P. OPPENHEIMER, 362:26SEP74-410
FRIEDMAN, M. & R.H. ROSENMAN. TYPE
A BEHAVIOR & YOUR HEART.
M. DUMONT, 441:19MAY74-6
P.B. MEDAWAR, 453:4APR74-3
FRIEDMAN, P. AND IF DEFEATED ALLEGE
FRAUD.
R. LYONS, 448:FALL-WINTER71/72-
111
FRIEDMANN, W. THE FUTURE OF THE
OCEANS.
C. MC FARLAND, 639(VQR):WINTER72-
126
FRIEDRICH, O. BEFORE THE DELUGE.
R. SANDERS, 390:NOV72-56
FRIEDRICH, P. PROTO-INDO-EUROPEAN
TREES.
M. GIMBUTAS, 279:VOL15-204
P.H. SALUS, 320(CJL):SPRING71-
142
FRIEDRICHS, R.W. A SOCIOLOGY OF
SOCIOLOGY.*
A. MC LAUGHLIN, 486:SEP72-427
FRIEND, C. - SEE YASHPAL
FRIEND, J. WRITING ENGLISH AS A
SECOND LANGUAGE.
P.E. MUNSELL, 351(LL):JUN72-133
FRIESS, U. BUHLERIN UND ZAUBERIN.
G. HILLEN, 221(GQ):NOV72-747
FRIIS, E.J., ED. FIVE MODERN SCANDI-
NAVIAN PLAYS.
C. WAAL, 563(SS):AUTUMN73-393
FRINGS, M.S. PERSON UND DASEIN.
F.J. SMITH, 484(PPR):DEC72-292
VON FRISCH, K., WITH O. VON FRISCH.
ANIMAL ARCHITECTURE.
C.H. WADDINGTON, 453:28NOV74-4
FRISCH, M. SKETCHBOOK 1966-1971.
R. GILMAN, 441:28APR74-2
FRISCH, M.H. TOWN INTO CITY.
639(VQR):SPRING73-LXXXIV

FRISCHAUER, W. BEHIND THE SCENES OF
OTTO PREMINGER.
617(TLS):1MAR74-214
FRISK, H. GRIECHISCHES ETYMOLO-
GISCHES WÖRTERBUCH.* (PTS 21 & 22)
A. ERNOUT, 555:VOL46FASC1-139
FRISTEDT, S.L. THE WYCLIFFE BIBLE.
(PT 2)
B. DANIELSSON, 597(SN):VOL44#1-
188
F. STEPHAN, 260(IF):BAND77HEFT1-
124
VON FRITZ, K. GRUNDPROBLEME DER
GESCHICHTE DER ANTIKEN WISSEN-
SCHAFT.*
D.C. LEE, 319:JUL74-388
M. VEGETTI, 548(RCSF):OCT-DEC72-
401
FRITZ, P. & D. WILLIAMS, EDS. THE
TRIUMPH OF CULTURE.
566:SPRING73-112
FRIZZLE, N. THE RAPE OF MOZART.
N. BAILEY, 296:VOL3#1-107
FRODSHAM, J.D. THE MURMURING STREAM.
R.F.S. YANG, 318(JAOS):APR-JUN72-
338
FROGER, D.J. LA CRITIQUE DES TEXTES
ET SON AUTOMATISATION.
F. PAPP, 353:15MAR72-108
FROMENTIN, E. LES MAÎTRES D'AUTRE-
FOIS. (P. MOISY, ED)
M. HUGGLER, 182:VOL25#23/24-872
FROMM, E. THE ANATOMY OF HUMAN
DESTRUCTIVENESS.*
P. ADAMS, 61:JAN74-99
R. DINNAGE, 617(TLS):27DEC74-
1458
R. SENNETT, 453:18APR74-28
442(NY):28JAN74-103
FROMM, H. BERNARD SHAW & THE THEA-
TER IN THE NINETIES.
R. DAVIES, 627(UTQ):AUTUMN71-88
FROMRICH, Y. MUSIQUE ET CARICATURE
EN FRANCE AU XIXE SIÈCLE.
617(TLS):21JUN74-678
FRONCEK, T., ED. THE HORIZON BOOK
OF THE ARTS OF RUSSIA.*
N. ANDREYEV, 32:JUN73-370
FRONDIZI, R. THE NATURE OF THE SELF.
J.J.F., 543:JUN72-751
FRONDIZI, R. WHAT IS VALUE?
S.C., 543:JUN72-751
J.B. WILBUR, 484(PPR):DEC72-279
FRONING, H. DITHYRAMBOS UND VASEN-
MALEREI IN ATHEN.
T.B.L. WEBSTER, 303:VOL92-248
FROSCH, T.R. THE AWAKENING OF AL-
BION.
617(TLS):5JUL74-704
FROST, B. THE SACRED & THE SECULAR.
46:AUG72-128
FROST, P. THE BAKUMATSU CURRENCY
CRISIS.
W.C. HOEKENDORF, 293(JAST):FEB72-
470
FROST, R. ROBERT FROST: A TIME TO
TALK.* (R. FRANCIS, ED)
H. LOMAS, 364:FEB/MAR74-125
FROST, R. POETRY & PROSE. (E.C.
LATHEM & L. THOMPSON, EDS)
639(VQR):AUTUMN73-CXLI

FROST, R. & E. FAMILY LETTERS OF
ROBERT & ELINOR FROST.* (A.
GRADE, ED)
W.A. SUTTON, 598(SOR):SPRING74-
478
639(VQR):SPRING73-LXXVI
FRÜHWALD, W. - SEE BRENTANO, C.
FRUMAN, N. COLERIDGE, THE DAMNED
ARCHANGEL.*
G.A. CEVASCO, 150(DR):SPRING72-
143
D.V.E., 191(ELN):SEP72(SUPP)-43
R.H. FOGLE, 639(VQR):SUMMER72-
477
J.R.D. JACKSON, 627(UTQ):SPRING
73-289
FRUMKIN, G. ARCHAEOLOGY IN SOVIET
CENTRAL ASIA.
D.B. & E.M. SHIMKIN, 104:SPRING
72-128
FRUTAZ, A.P., ED. LE CARTE DEL
LAZIO.
617(TLS):3MAY74-470
FRUTTERO, C. & F. LUCENTINI. THE
SUNDAY WOMAN.
H. MITGANG, 441:17MAR74-37
617(TLS):15MAR74-269
FRY, A. THE BURDEN OF ADRIAN KNOWLE.
M. LEVIN, 441:3NOV74-72
FRY, D.K. BEOWULF & THE FIGHT AT
FINNSBURH.
D.C. BAKER, 191(ELN):DEC72-127
K.D. MATUSSEK, 38:BAND90HEFT1/2-
213
FRY, H.T. ALEXANDER DALRYMPLE (1737-
1808) & THE EXPANSION OF BRITISH
TRADE.
P. WHEATLEY, 293(JAST):AUG72-988
FRY, R. LETTERS OF ROGER FRY.* (D.
SUTTON, ED)
W.G. ARCHER, 39:OCT72-360
K. CLARK, 453:2MAY74-13
G. GERSH, 127:SPRING73-350
M.S. YOUNG, 55:SEP73-14
FRYE, N. THE BUSH GARDEN.
G.V. DOWNES, 376:APR74-123
S.L. DRAGLAND, 529(QQ):SUMMER72-
264
M. ROSS, 627(UTQ):WINTER72-170
FRYE, N. THE CRITICAL PATH.*
H.H. RUDNICK, 125:OCT72-72
FRYE, N. THE STUBBORN STRUCTURE.*
M.E. BROWN, 659:WINTER74-131
M. ROSS, 627(UTQ):WINTER72-170
FRYE, R.N., ED. THE PARTHIAN & MID-
DLE IRANIAN INSCRIPTIONS OF DURA-
EUROPOS.
C.J. BRUNNER, 318(JAOS):OCT-DEC
72-492
FU, M. & S. STUDIES IN CONNOISSEUR-
SHIP.
617(TLS):2AUG74-838
FUBINI, M. STUDI SULLA LETTERATURA
DEL RINASCIMENTO. (2ND ED)
228(GSLI):VOL149FASC465-143
FUCHS, A. MORPHOLOGIE DES VERBS IM
CAHUILLA.
J.F. DAVIS, 350:JUN73-510
H-J. PINNOW, 343:BAND15HEFT2-136
FUEGI, J., ED. BRECHT HEUTE -
BRECHT TODAY.
B.A. WOODS, 301(JEGP):APR73-298
DE FUENTES, Á.G. - SEE UNDER GALMÉS
DE FUENTES, Á.

FUENTES, C., J. DONOSO & S. SARDUY.
TRIPLE CROSS.*
P. CRUTTWELL & F. WESTBURG,
249(HUDR):SUMMER73-417
42(AR):VOL32#3-497
"LOUIS AGASSIZ FUERTES & THE SINGU-
LAR BEAUTY OF BIRDS." (F.G. MAR-
CHAM, ED)
639(VQR):WINTER72-XXXIV
FÜHMANN, F. 22 TAGE ODER DIE HÄLFTE
DES LEBENS.
617(TLS):29MAR74-346
FUHRMANN, J.T. THE ORIGINS OF CAPI-
TALISM IN RUSSIA.*
O. CRISP, 575(SEER):OCT73-582
639(VQR):SUMMER72-XCVIII
FUHRMANN, M., ED. TERROR UND SPIEL.
R.E. PALMER, 72:BAND21OHEFT4/6-
337
L. WELCH, 290(JAAC):SPRING73-415
FUHRMANN, M. & H. TRÄNKLE. WIE
KLASSISCH IST DIE KLASSISCHE AN-
TIKE?
W. SCHMID, 52:BAND7HEFT2/3-314
FUHRMANS, H. - SEE SCHELLING, F.W.J.
FUKUDA, H. BRITAIN IN EUROPE.
617(TLS):15FEB74-151
FUKUI, H. PARTY IN POWER.*
H.H. BAERWALD, 318(JAOS):APR-JUN
72-350
FULFORD, R. MARSHALL DELANEY AT THE
MOVIES.
M. WOLFE, 99:NOV/DEC74-16
FULFORD, R., D. GODFREY & A. ROT-
STEIN, EDS. READ CANADIAN.
H.P. GUNDY, 529(QQ):AUTUMN72-423
FULLER, J. CANNIBALS & MISSIONARIES.
J. SYMONS, 364:AUG/SEP72-138
FULLER, J. EPISTLES TO SEVERAL PER-
SONS.
P. BEER, 362:2MAY74-575
617(TLS):18JAN74-51
FULLER, J. A READER'S GUIDE TO W.H.
AUDEN.*
W. DAVIES, 447(N&Q):SEP72-345
FULLER, J.G. ARIGO.
M. GARDNER, 453:16MAY74-18
FULLER, J.O. SWINBURNE.*
B.F. FISHER 4TH, 177(ELT):VOL15
#3-236
FULLER, R. PROFESSORS & GODS.
D.W. HARDING, 362:7FEB74-182
H. LOMAS, 364:FEB/MAR74-125
FULLER, R. TINY TEARS.*
R. GARFITT, 364:DEC73/JAN74-123
FULLER, R.B. EARTH, INC. UTOPIA OR
OBLIVION.
R. SALE, 453:7FEB74-29
FULLER, R.B. & R. MARKS. THE DYMAX-
ION WORLD OF BUCKMINSTER FULLER.
R. SALE, 453:7FEB74-29
FULTON, R. THE MAN WITH THE SURBA-
HAR. THE SPACES BETWEEN THE
STONES.
A. CLUYSENAAR, 565:VOL13#1-72
FUMAGALLI, M.T.B-B. - SEE UNDER
BEONIO-BROCCHIERI FUMAGALLI, M.T.
FUMAGALLI, V. LE ORIGINI DI UNA
GRANDE DINASTIA FEUDALE ADALBERTO-
ATTO DI CANOSSA.
D. HERLIHY, 589:APR73-359

FURHAMMAR, L. & F. ISAKSSON. POLI-
TICS & FILM.
J.M. HIGHSMITH, 290(JAAC):SUMMER
72-568
FURLEY, D.J. & R.E. ALLEN, EDS.
STUDIES IN PRESOCRATIC PHILOSOPHY.*
(VOL 1)
G.B. KERFERD, 123:MAR73-47
R. LAURENTI, 548(RCSF):APR-JUN72-
233
A.A. LONG, 303:VOL92-217
FURLONG, W.B. SHAW & CHESTERTON.*
R. MASON, 571:SPRING72-193
FURNAS, J.C. GREAT TIMES.
R.C. ALBERTS, 441:17NOV74-2
FURNEAUX, R. WILLIAM WILBERFORCE.
R. MITCHISON, 362:30CT74-446
617(TLS):30AUG74-924
FURRER, D. MODUSPROBLEME BEI NOT-
KER.*
R.H. LAWSON, 301(JEGP):JAN73-64
FURST, L.R. & P.N. SKRINE. NATURAL-
ISM.
F.W.J. HEMMINGS, 208(FS):OCT73-
465
FUSS, P. & H. SHAPIRO - SEE NIETZ-
SCHE, F.W.
FUSSELL, E. LUCIFER IN HARNESS.
H.F.C. PRYCE-JONES, 590:FALL/
WINTER73/74-46
FUSSELL, P., ED. ENGLISH AUGUSTAN
POETRY.
566:AUTUMN72-48
FUSSELL, P. SAMUEL JOHNSON & THE
LIFE OF WRITING.*
P.K. ALKON, 405(MP):FEB73-268
H.D. WEINBROT, 481(PQ):JUL72-701
"THE FUTURE OF BROADCASTING."
M. WARNOCK, 362:24JAN74-113
617(TLS):25JAN74-68

GAATONE, D. ETUDE DESCRIPTIVE DU
SYSTÈME DE LA NÉGATION EN FRANÇAIS
CONTEMPORAIN.
J. REDFERN, 207(FR):MAY72-1184
VON GABAIN, A. & W. VEENKER, EDS.
VERÖFFENTLICHUNGEN DER SOCIETAS
URALO-ALTAICA. (VOL 1: "RADLOFF")
G. DOERFER, 343:BAND15HEFT1-107
GABAUDE, J-M. LIBERTÉ ET RAISON.
M. LASSÈGUE, 542:APR-JUN72-197
T. QUONIAM, 154:SEP72-437
GABBA, E. - SEE APPIAN
VON DER GABELENTZ, G. DIE SPRACHWIS-
SENSCHAFT, IHRE AUFGABEN, METHODEN
UND BISHERIGEN ERGEBNISSE. (2ND
ED)
E.F.K. KOERNER, 361:VOL28#1&2-
153
GADD, D. THE LOVING FRIENDS.
617(TLS):4OCT74-1067
GADDIS, W. THE RECOGNITIONS.
T. TANNER, 441:14JUL74-27
GADDY, J.J., COMP. TEXAS IN REVOLT.
W. GARD, 584(SWR):AUTUMN73-361
GADNEY, R. SOMETHING WORTH FIGHTING
FOR.
617(TLS):1MAR74-219
GAEDE, F. HUMANISMUS, BAROCK, AUF-
KLÄRUNG.
H. BEKKER, 406:SPRING73-84
R.T. LLEWELLYN, 402(MLR):OCT73-
941   [CONTINUED]

GAEDE, F. HUMANISMUS, BAROCK, AUF-
KLÄRUNG. [CONTINUING]
    E. LUNDING, 301(JEGP):JAN73-73
    A. MENHENNET, 220(GL&L):JUL73-
    354
GAEFFKE, P. GRUNDBEGRIFFE MODERNER
INDISCHER ERZÄHLKUNST, AUFGEZEIGT
AM WERKE JAYAŚAŃKARA PRASĀDAS
(1889-1937).
    L. LUTZE, 318(JAOS):OCT-DEC72-
    578
GAEFFKE, P. UNTERSUCHUNGEN ZUR SYN-
TAX DES HINDI.
    T. ELIZARENKOVA, 353:1APR72-108
GAENG, P.A. INTRODUCTION TO THE
PRINCIPLES OF LANGUAGE.
    A. ARLOTTO, 350:JUN73-465
    M.H. SHORT, 402(MLR):JAN73-129
GAGAN, D. THE DENISON FAMILY OF
TORONTO, 1792-1925.
    C.P. STACEY, 99:MAY/JUN74-36
GAGE, J. TURNER: RAIN STEAM &
SPEED.*
    A.C. BIRNHOLZ, 290(JAAC):SUMMER
    73-556
    A. FORGE, 592:NOV72-201
GAGE, N. BONES OF CONTENTION.
    N. CALLENDAR, 441:18AUG74-23
GAGNON, F. JEAN DUBUFFET.
    R. CARDINAL, 617(TLS):6DEC74-
    1364
GAIER, U. KRUMME REGEL.
    R. IMMERWAHR, 221(GQ):NOV72-742
    E. STOPP, 402(MLR):APR73-458
GAIKWAD, V.R. THE ANGLO-INDIANS.
    A.E. MEYERS, 352(LE&W):VOL15#4&
    VOL16#1/2-931
GAILEY, H.A. THE ROAD TO ABA.
    G.I. JONES, 69:OCT72-355
GAILLARD, P., ED. LES CRITIQUES DE
NOTRE TEMPS ET MALRAUX.
    R. GOLDTHORPE, 208(FS):OCT73-478
    W.G. LANGLOIS, 207(FR):MAR72-911
    A. VANDEGANS, 535(RHL):JAN-FEB72-
    162
GAILLARD, P. ANDRÉ MALRAUX.
    R. TARICA, 207(FR):APR72-1051
    205(FMLS):JUL72-286
GAINES, C. STAY HUNGRY.*
    T. TANNER, 364:OCT/NOV73-146
    J. YARDLEY, 473(PR):2/1973-286
GAINES, P.W. WILLIAM COBBETT & THE
UNITED STATES 1792-1835.
    617(TLS):18JAN74-41
GAJENDRAGADKAR, P.B. KASHMIR - RET-
ROSPECT & PROSPECT.
    R.A. HUTTENBACK, 293(JAST):FEB72-
    448
GAL, H. FRANZ SCHUBERT & THE
ESSENCE OF MELODY.
    617(TLS):12APR74-390
GÁL, I. BARTÓKTÓL RADNÓTIIG.
    617(TLS):19APR74-422
GALAI, S. THE LIBERATION MOVEMENT
IN RUSSIA 1900-1905.*
    A. FISCHER, 182:VOL25#22-815
GALAND, F. CORPS DE SABLE.
    R.R. HUBERT, 207(FR):MAR72-900
GALAND, R. BAUDELAIRE: POETIQUES ET
POÉSIES.*
    A. KIES, 535(RHL):MAR-APR72-332

GALANOPOULOS, A.G. & E. BACON. AT-
LANTIS.
    D.B. VITALIANO, 391(JFI):VOL8#1-
    66
GALARNEAU, C. LA FRANCE DEVANT
L'OPINION CANADIENNE (1760-1815).
    481(PQ):JUL72-530
GALAVARIS, G. THE ILLUSTRATIONS OF
THE LITURGICAL HOMILIES OF GREG-
ORY NAZIANZENUS.*
    C. MANGO, 54:SEP72-346
GALAVARIS, G. INVOCATION TO A PAGAN
DIVINITY.
    W. PROUTY, 268:JUL74-155
GALBRAITH, G. - SEE STEVENS, W.B.
GALBRAITH, J.K. ECONOMICS & THE
PUBLIC PURPOSE.*
    M. ZINKIN, 362:18APR74-505
GALBRAITH, J.K. FINANCES, FRATER-
NITÉ, FANTAISIE.
    J. ATTALI, 98:DEC72-1103
GALBRAITH, J.S. MACKINNON & EAST
AFRICA 1878-95.
    P. SALMON, 182:VOL25#13/14-499
GALBRAITH, J.S. - SEE SIMPSON, G.
GALE, G.R. - SEE DE CÓRDOBA, S.
GALE, R.M. THE LANGUAGE OF TIME.
    N.B. COCCHIARELLA, 316:MAR72-170
GALICHET, G. GRAMMAIRE STRUCTURALE
DU FRANÇAIS MODERNE.
    H.G. SCHOGT, 353:15JUN72-104
GÁLIK, M. MAO TUN & MODERN CHINESE
LITERARY CRITICISM.
    R.E. HEGEL, 318(JAOS):APR-JUN72-
    343
    P.G. PICKOWITZ, 352(LE&W):VOL15
    #3-519
GALILÉE. DIALOGUES ET LETTRES
CHOISIES. (P-H. MICHEL, TRANS)
    E. NAMER, 542:JAN-MAR72-95
GALILÉE. DISCOURS CONCERNANT DEUX
SCIENCES NOUVELLES. (M. CLAVELIN,
ED & TRANS)
    J. BERNHARDT, 542:JAN-MAR72-96
GALINDO, D.E. - SEE UNDER ESCOBAR
GALINDO, D.
GALINSKY, G.K. AENEAS, SICILY, &
ROME.*
    A. DRUMMOND, 313:VOL62-218
GALISSON, R. INVENTAIRE THÉMATIQUE
ET SYNTAGMATIQUE DU FRANÇAIS FON-
DAMENTAL.*
    H. DÜWELL, 430(NS):APR72-239
GALISSON, R. L'APPRENTISSAGE SYSTÉ-
MATIQUE DU VOCABULAIRE.*
    J. DARBELNET, 207(FR):MAY72-1186
GALLAGHER, B.G. CAMPUS IN CRISIS.
    G. LEVINE, 441:15SEP74-49
GALLAGHER, D.P. MODERN LATIN AMERI-
CAN LITERATURE.*
    D. TIPTON, 364:FEB/MAR74-142
GALLAGHER, I.J. MORALITY IN EVOLU-
TION.
    E. MOROT-SIR, 319:JUL74-410
GALLAGHER, P. THE LIFE & WORKS OF
GARCI SÁNCHEZ DE BADAJOZ.*
    C. STERN, 545(RPH):NOV72-486
GALLANT, M. THE PEGNITZ JUNCTION.*
    617(TLS):15MAR74-253
GALLANT, M. LE THÈME DE LA MORT
CHEZ ROGER MARTIN DU GARD.
    J. ONIMUS, 557(RSH):OCT-DEC72-
    627

GALLEGO MORELL, A. ESTUDIOS Y TEX-
TOS GANIVETIANOS.
A. NOUGUÉ, 182:VOL25#12-412
GALLER, M. & H.E. MARQUESS, COMPS.
SOVIET PRISON CAMP SPEECH.*
G. BROOKE, 32:MAR73-213
GALLET, M. PARIS DOMESTIC ARCHITEC-
TURE OF THE 18TH CENTURY.*
C. TADGELL, 46:NOV72-318
GALLICO, P. THE BOY WHO INVENTED
THE BUBBLE GUN.
M. LEVIN, 441:23JUN74-35
617(TLS):14JUN74-644
GALLIOT, M. - SEE VERLAINE, P.
GALLNER, S.M. PRO SPORTS.
R.W. CREAMER, 441:1DEC74-90
GALLO, E. THE "POETRIA NOVA" & ITS
SOURCES IN EARLY RHETORICAL DOC-
TRINE.
T. LAWLER, 589:OCT73-750
GALLO, I., ED. IL TEATRO GRECO.
G.M.A. RICHTER, 303:VOL92-246
GALLO, M. MUSSOLINI'S ITALY.
J. ROSSELLI, 362:21FEB74-247
617(TLS):2AUG74-828
GALLO, M. WITH THE VICTORS.
M. LEVIN, 441:6OCT74-40
GALLOWAY, D., ED. THE ELIZABETHAN
THEATRE.* (VOLS 1&2)
T.J. KING, 551(RENQ):WINTER72-
496
GALLWEY, W.T. THE INNER GAME OF
TENNIS.
A. WHITMAN, 441:20JUL74-29
GALMÉS DE FUENTES, Á., ED. HISTORIA
DE LOS AMORES DE PARÍS Y VIANA.
C. LÓPEZ-MORILLAS, 545(RPH):NOV
72-479
GALT, J. THE PROVOST. (I.A. GORDON,
ED)
617(TLS):1FEB74-112
GALTON, R. & A. SIMPSON. HANCOCK'S
HALF HOUR.
D. THOMAS, 362:19&26DEC74-846
GAMAL-ELDIN, S.M. A SYNTACTIC STUDY
OF EGYPTIAN COLLOQUIAL ARABIC.
L. DROZDÍK, 353:1MAR72-102
GAMBARIN, G. - SEE FOSCOLO, U.
GAMBARIN, G. - SEE TOMMASEO, N.
GAMBERINI, S. LO STUDIO DELL'ITAL-
IANO IN INGHILTERRA NEL '500 E NEL
'600.*
F.-J-L. MOURET, 549(RLC):JAN-MAR
72-137
GAMBINO, R. BLOOD OF MY BLOOD.
V. CRAPANZANO, 231:OCT74-102
J. MANGIONE, 441:16JUN74-26
GAMILLSCHEG, E. ROMANIA GERMANICA.
(VOL 1) (2ND ED)
D.H. GREEN, 402(MLR):APR73-440
GAMMON, S.R. STATESMAN & SCHEMER.
617(TLS):18JAN74-61
GANDON, J., JR. & T. MULVANY. THE
LIFE OF JAMES GANDON.
D. FITZ-GERALD, 90:SEP72-639
GANGULY, S. WITTGENSTEIN'S "TRAC-
TATUS."
M.M., 543:SEP71-125
GANS, H. MORE EQUALITY.
B.M. BERGER, 441:6JAN74-5
GANS, H.J. POPULAR CULTURE & HIGH
CULTURE.
C. LEHMANN-HAUPT, 441:2DEC74-31

GANZ, P.F., ED. THE DISCONTINUOUS
TRADITION.*
R.K. ANGRESS, 221(GQ):NOV72-735
M.B. BENN, 402(MLR):JAN73-221
GANZ, P.F. & W. SCHRÖDER, EDS. PROB-
LEME MITTELHOCHDEUTSCHER ERZÄHLFOR-
MEN.
D. STRAUSS, 182:VOL25#21-732
GANZGLASS, M.R. THE PENAL CODE OF
THE SOMALI DEMOCRATIC REPUBLIC.
I.M. LEWIS, 69:OCT72-343
GAPONENKO, L.S. RABOCHII KLASS
ROSSII V 1917 GODU.
F.I. KAPLAN, 32:SEP73-612
GARAB, A.M. BEYOND BYZANTIUM.*
H. ADAMS, 219(GAR):FALL72-249
GARAUDY, R. DIEU EST MORT.
M. BARTHÉLEMY-MADAULE, 542:JUL-
SEP72-362
GARBER, F. WORDSWORTH & THE POETRY
OF ENCOUNTER.
B.C.H., 191(ELN):SEP72(SUPP)-64
J.R.D. JACKSON, 627(UTQ):SPRING
73-289
J. SCOGGINS, 401(MLQ):SEP73-337
S.M. SPERRY, JR., 301(JEGP):JAN
73-140
H. VIEBROCK, 72:BAND210HEFT4/6-
412
GARCÍA, D.A. - SEE UNDER ALONSO GAR-
CÍA, D.
GARCIA, J. CORPS DE GLOIRE.
F. GALAND, 207(FR):DEC71-472
GARCÍA, S. LAS IDEAS LITERARIAS EN
ESPAÑA ENTRE 1840 Y 1850.
191(ELN):SEP72(SUPP)-211
GARCÍA-VIÑO, M. MUNDO Y TRASMUNDO
DE LAS LEYENDAS DE BÉCQUER.
P.L. ULLMAN, 238:DEC72-967
GARCÍA BARRÓN, C. LA OBRA CRÍTICA
Y LITERARIA DE DON ANTONIO ALCALÁ
GALIANO.
A.W. ASHHURST, 238:SEP72-591
191(ELN):SEP72(SUPP)-212
GARCÍA DE CABAÑAS, M.J. VOCABULARIO
DE LA ALTA ALPUJARRA.
R.J. PENNY, 545(RPH):AUG72-163
GARCÍA ICAZBALCETA, J., ED. COLEC-
CIÓN DE DOCUMENTOS PARA LA HISTOR-
IA DE MÉXICO. (VOL 1)
A. MAGAÑA-ESQUIVEL, 263:JAN-MAR
73-95
GARCÍA MÁRQUEZ, G. LEAF STORM &
OTHER STORIES.*
P. BAILEY, 364:APR/MAY73-166
GARCÍA MÁRQUEZ, G. NO ONE WRITES TO
THE COLONEL & OTHER STORIES.
A.J. CARLOS, 573(SSF):WINTER72-
101
GARCÍA MONTORO, A. & S.A. RIGOL. EN
TORNO AL POEMA.
R.C. SPIRES, 238:SEP72-610
GARCÍA PAVÓN, F. NUEVAS HISTORIAS
DE PLINIO.
J.R. STAMM, 238:DEC72-970
GARCÍA YERBA, V. - SEE ARISTOTLE
GARCILASO DE LA VEGA. POESÍAS CAS-
TELLANAS COMPLETAS. (E.L. RIVERS,
ED)
D. EISENBERG, 241:SEP72-81
GARDEN, E. TCHAIKOVSKY.*
D.C.B., 410(M&L):OCT73-472
R. MC ALLISTER, 415:SEP73-898

123

GARDET, L. DIEU ET LA DESTINÉE DE
L'HOMME.
W.C. SMITH, 318(JAOS):APR-JUN72-
377
GARDINER, F.C. THE PILGRIMAGE OF
DESIRE.
S.A. BARNEY, 589:APR73-359
GARDINER, J.R. GREAT DREAM FROM
HEAVEN.
J. YOHALEM, 441:15DEC74-26
GARDINER, M. THE WOLF-MAN & SIGMUND
FREUD.
R. JACCARD, 98:MAR72-291
GARDINER, P., ED. THE PHILOSOPHY OF
HISTORY.
617(TLS):13DEC74-1419
GARDINER, S. LE CORBUSIER.
B. BROWN, 617(TLS):1NOV74-1222
GARDNER, E.S. THE CASE OF THE CRY-
ING SWALLOW.
617(TLS):20DEC74-1437
GARDNER, E.S. THE CASE OF THE POST-
PONED MURDER.*
N. CALLENDAR, 441:12MAY74-18
GARDNER, F.F. AN ANALYSIS OF SYNTAC-
TIC PATTERNS OF OLD ENGLISH.
B. MITCHELL, 541(RES):NOV73-461
GARDNER, H., ED. A BOOK OF RELIGI-
OUS VERSE.
639(VQR):SPRING73-LXII
GARDNER, H., ED. THE NEW OXFORD
BOOK OF ENGLISH VERSE 1250-1950.*
J. MC AULEY, 67:MAY73-114
639(VQR):SUMMER73-CXI
GARDNER, H. RELIGION & LITERATURE.*
D. FORTUNA, 402(MLR):JAN73-140
P.A. LARKIN, 541(RES):MAY72-246
W.G. RICE, 385(MQR):SUMMER74-297
GARDNER, H. & T. HEALY - SEE DONNE,
J.
GARDNER, J., ED & TRANS. THE ALLIT-
ERATIVE "MORTE ARTHURE," "THE OWL
& THE NIGHTINGALE," & FIVE OTHER
MIDDLE ENGLISH POEMS.
T.H. BESTUL, 589:JAN73-142
GARDNER, J. THE CONSTRUCTION OF THE
WAKEFIELD CYCLE.
A.C. CAWLEY, 617(TLS):22NOV74-
1324
GARDNER, J. THE CORNER MEN.
617(TLS):6SEP74-960
GARDNER, J. GRENDEL.
J. DITSKY, 219(GAR):FALL72-297
639(VQR):WINTER72-XIX
GARDNER, J. JASON & MEDEIA.*
R. DE FEO, 249(HUDR):WINTER73/74-
777
GARDNER, J. THE KING'S INDIAN.
A. FRIEDMAN, 441:15DEC74-1
GARDNER, J. NICKEL MOUNTAIN.*
P. ADAMS, 61:FEB74-96
S. MILLAR, 617(TLS):13DEC74-1420
M. WOOD, 453:21MAR74-19
442(NY):21JAN74-94
GARDNER, J. THE RETURN OF MORIARTY.
617(TLS):20DEC74-1437
GARDNER, J. THE SUNLIGHT DIALOGUES.*
W.H. PRITCHARD, 249(HUDR):SPRING
73-233
E. ROVIT, 659:AUTUMN74-539
639(VQR):SPRING73-LVI

GARDNER, R.C. & W.E. LAMBERT. ATTI-
TUDES & MOTIVATION IN SECOND-LAN-
GUAGE LEARNING.
B.P. TAYLOR, 351(LL):JUN73-145
GARFIELD, B. KOLCHAK'S GOLD.
M. LEVIN, 441:17FEB74-32
617(TLS):6SEP74-945
GARFIELD, B. THE THREEPERSONS HUNT.
N. CALLENDAR, 441:5MAY74-14
GARFIELD, B. WHAT OF TERRY CONNIS-
TON?
N. CALLENDAR, 441:12MAY74-18
GARFIELD, L. THE SOUND OF COACHES.
M. LEVIN, 441:30JUN74-30
GARGAN, L. LO STUDIO TEOLOGICO E LA
BIBLIOTECA DEI DOMENICANI A PADOVA
NEL TRE E QUATTROCENTO.
K.W. HUMPHREYS, 382(MAE):1973/1-
103
R.C. TREXLER, 589:JAN73-146
GARGANI, A. LINGUAGGIO ED ESPERIEN-
ZA IN LUDWIG WITTGENSTEIN.
E. NAMER, 542:JAN-MAR72-117
GARIN, E. DAL RINASCIMENTO ALL'
ILLUMINISMO.
L. POMPA, 402(MLR):JAN73-191
GARLAND, H.B. SCHILLER: THE DRAMAT-
IC WRITER.*
F.M. FOWLER, 220(GL&L):JAN73-174
GARLAND, M. THE CHANGING FORM OF
FASHION.*
F. CRICHTON, 39:MAR72-231
GARLAND, M. THE SMALL GARDEN IN THE
CITY.
617(TLS):1FEB74-116
GARLICK, P.C. AFRICAN TRADERS &
ECONOMIC DEVELOPMENT IN GHANA.
K. HART, 69:JUL72-248
GARMIZA, V.V. KRUSHENIE ESEROV-
SKIKH PRAVITEL'STV.
A. RABINOWITCH, 32:DEC73-815
GARNEAU, H.S-D. OEUVRES. (J.
BRAULT & B. LACROIX, EDS)
P.M. GATHERCOLE, 207(FR):DEC71-
506
GARNER, H. ONE DAMN THING AFTER
ANOTHER.
C. MAC CULLOCH, 296:VOL3#1-99
GARNER, P. THE WORLD OF EDWARDIANA.
617(TLS):14JUN74-635
GARNER, W. A BIG ENOUGH WREATH.
617(TLS):30AUG74-933
GARNETT, D. - SEE "CARRINGTON"
GARNHAM, B.G. - SEE CAMUS, A.
GARNSEY, P. SOCIAL STATUS & LEGAL
PRIVILEGE IN THE ROMAN EMPIRE.
P.A. BRUNT, 313:VOL62-166
GARRAN, R.R. SCHUBERT & SCHUMANN.
E. SAMS, 415:AUG73-797
GARRARD, J.A. THE ENGLISH & IMMIGRA-
TION 1880-1910.
B. GAINER, 637(VS):SEP72-118
GARRARD, J.G., ED. THE EIGHTEENTH
CENTURY IN RUSSIA.
617(TLS):22FEB74-180
GARRATY, J.A. & J.L. STERNSTEIN, EDS.
ENCYCLOPEDIA OF AMERICAN BIOGRAPHY.
R.G. DAVIS, 441:1DEC74-100
A. WHITMAN, 441:23NOV74-29
GARRETT, A. WOOD ENGRAVINGS & DRAW-
INGS OF IAIN MACNAB OF BARACHAST-
LAIN.
617(TLS):1MAR74-220

GARRETT, G. DEATH OF THE FOX.*
639(VQR):SPRING72-XLVIII
GARRETT, P.K. SCENE & SYMBOL FROM
GEORGE ELIOT TO JAMES JOYCE.*
P.J. DE VOOGD, 433:JUL72-376
P. GOETSCH, 430(NS):JAN72-50
R.L. MORRIS, 599:WINTER72-77
U. SCHNEIDER, 38:BAND90HEFT1/2-
263
GARRETT, S. SOCIAL REFORMERS IN
URBAN CHINA.
CHAN LAU KIT-CHING, 302:JAN72-76
V.D. MEDLIN, 293(JAST):NOV71-188
GARRISON, W.L. THE LETTERS OF WIL-
LIAM LLOYD GARRISON.* (VOL 2)
(W.M. MERRILL & L. RUCHAMES, EDS)
A. ZILVERSMIT, 432(NEQ):DEC72-
609
GARRISON, W.L. THE LETTERS OF WIL-
LIAM LLOYD GARRISON. (VOL 3)
(W.M. MERRILL, ED)
J. WHITE, 617(TLS):15NOV74-1296
GARULLI, E. SAGGI SU SPINOZA.
E. NAMER, 542:APR-JUN72-225
GARVE, A. THE FILE ON LESTER.
617(TLS):25JAN74-88
GARVE, A. THE LESTER AFFAIR.
N. CALLENDAR, 441:31MAR74-41
442(NY):6MAY74-144
GARVIN, P.L., ED. METHOD & THEORY
IN LINGUISTICS.
P.H. MATTHEWS, 361:VOL29#1-67
GARY, R. THE GASP.*
N. CALLENDAR, 441:14JUL74-39
GARZETTI, A. FROM TIBERIUS TO THE
ANTONINES.
M. GRANT, 617(TLS):29NOV74-1339
GASCOIGNE, B. THE GREAT MOGHULS.
639(VQR):WINTER72-XXXII
GASCOIGNE, B. THE HEYDAY.*
M. DRABBLE, 441:13JAN74-8
GASCOIGNE, B. MURGATREUD'S EMPIRE.
M. FELD, 364:OCT/NOV72-152
GASH, N. SIR ROBERT PEEL.
P. HONAN, 637(VS):JUN73-456
GASKELL, P. A NEW INTRODUCTION TO
BIBLIOGRAPHY.
K.I.D. MASLEN, 67:NOV73-326
R.A. SAYCE, 402(MLR):JUL73-626
GASKELL, R. DRAMA & REALITY.
R.J. SMITH, 157:AUTUMN72-79
GASPARINI, L. TUNNEL BUS TO
DETROIT.*
D. BARBOUR, 150(DR):SPRING72-167
GASPAROV, M.L. SOVREMENNYY RUSSKIY
STIKH.
G.S. SMITH, 617(TLS):8NOV74-1266
GASS, W.H. FICTION & THE FIGURES OF
LIFE.
D. BARBOUR, 529(QQ):WINTER72-564
GASS, W.H. WILLIE MASTERS' LONESOME
WIFE.
J. DITSKY, 219(GAR):FALL72-297
639(VQR):WINTER72-XVIII
GASSENDI, P. THE SELECTED WORKS.
(C.B. BRUSH, ED & TRANS)
205(FMLS):OCT72-382
"PIERRE GASSENDI: SA VIE ET SON
OEUVRE (1592-1655)."
A. DE LATTRE, 542:APR-JUN72-200
GASSET, J.O. - SEE UNDER ORTEGA Y
GASSET, J.
GASSIER, P. THE DRAWINGS OF GOYA.
617(TLS):8FEB74-126

GASSIER, P. & J. WILSON. GOYA.
J. LÓPEZ-REY, 39:OCT72-358
GASSNER, J. & C. BARNES, EDS. BEST
AMERICAN PLAYS. (6TH SER: 1963-
1967)
A.E. KALSON, 160:SPRING71-199
GASSON, P.C. THEORY OF DESIGN.
617(TLS):3MAY74-484
GASTER, M. STUDIES & TEXTS IN FOLK-
LORE, MAGIC, MEDIAEVAL ROMANCE,
HEBREW APOCRYPHA & SAMARITAN
ARCHAEOLOGY.
J.E. KELLER, 582(SFQ):DEC72-401
F.L. UTLEY, 292(JAF):JUL-SEP72-
279
GASTER, T.H. MYTH, LEGEND, & CUSTOM
IN THE OLD TESTAMENT.*
D.N. FREEDMAN, 318(JAOS):JAN-MAR
72-185
GATCH, M.M. LOYALTIES & TRADITIONS.*
E.B. IRVING, JR., 589:JAN73-147
T.A. SHIPPEY, 677:VOL3-263
GATHERCOLE, P.M., ED. LAURENT DE
PREMIERFAIT'S "DES CAS DES NOBLES
HOMMES ET FEMMES." (BK 1)
H.F. WILLIAMS, 593:FALL73-282
GATHORNE-HARDY, R. - SEE MORRELL, O.
GATLEY, J.C.C. LIBEL & SLANDER.
(7TH ED) (R. MC EWAN & P. LEWIS,
EDS)
617(TLS):25JAN74-88
GATTÉGNO, J. LA SCIENCE-FICTION.
H. GODIN, 208(FS):OCT73-498
GATZ, E. KIRCHE UND KRANKENPFLEGE
IM 19. JAHRHUNDERT.
L. NORPOTH, 182:VOL25#15/16-523
GAUBIL, P.A. CORRESPONDENCE DE
PÉKIN, 1722-1759.* (R. SIMON, ED)
D.D. LESLIE, 318(JAOS):OCT-DEC72-
544
GAUGER, H-M. WORT UND SPRACHE.*
E. SCHEPPER, 430(NS):MAY72-305
GAUKSTAD, Ø. & O.M. SANDVIK, EDS.
NORSK MUSIKKGRANSKNING.
P.R. OLSEN, 187:SEP74-461
GAULDIE, E. CRUEL HABITATIONS.
F.M.L. THOMPSON, 617(TLS):2AUG74-
823
DE GAULLE, C. MEMOIRS OF HOPE.
(FRENCH TITLE: MÉMOIRES D'ESPOIR.)
R.C. MACRIDIS, 639(VQR):AUTUMN72-
600
H. PEYRE, 207(FR):OCT71-223
GAUNT, D.M. SURGE & THUNDER.*
J.B. HAINSWORTH, 123:DEC73-267
GAUNT, W. THE GREAT CENTURY OF BRIT-
ISH PAINTING.*
M. WEBSTER, 135:FEB72-139
GAUNT, W. THE RESTLESS CENTURY.
T. LASK, 55:APR73-50
GAUNT, W. TURNER.
E. YOUNG, 39:AUG72-167
GAUSTAD, E.S. DISSENT IN AMERICAN
RELIGION.
617(TLS):30AUG74-935
GAUTHIER, D.P. THE LOGIC OF "LEVIA-
THAN."*
B. MORRIS, 484(PPR):MAR73-387
GAUTIER, T. POÉSIES. (H. COCKERHAM,
ED)
617(TLS):31MAY74-590

GEORGACAS, D.J. & W.A. MC DONALD.
PLACE NAMES OF SOUTHWEST PELOPON-
NESUS: REGISTER & INDEXES.*
N.G.L. HAMMOND, 123:MAR73-110
GEORGE IV. THE CORRESPONDENCE OF
GEORGE, PRINCE OF WALES, 1770-1812.
(VOL 8) (A. ASPINALL, ED)
D.V.E., 191(ELN):SEP72(SUPP)-18
GEORGE, C. CHOIX ET APPRENTISSAGE
EN SITUATION ALÉATOIRE.
H. BALMER, 182:VOL25#3/4-75
GEORGE, C.V.R. SEGREGATED SABBATHS.
617(TLS):22FEB74-181
GEORGE, F.H. COMPUTERS, SCIENCE, &
SOCIETY.
J.M.V., 543:MAR72-554
GEORGE, R.E. A LEADER & A LAGGARD.*
R.I. MC ALLISTER, 529(QQ):WINTER
72-542
GEORGE, R.E. THE LIFE & TIMES OF
INDUSTRIAL ESTATES LIMITED.
P. MATHIAS, 99:NOV/DEC74-48
GEORGE, S. & W. ROLICZ-LIEDER. GE-
DICHTE UND ÜBERTRAGUNGEN.
H. SCHROEDER, 52:BAND7HEFT1-100
GEORGES, E.S. STUDIES IN ROMANCE
NOUNS EXTRACTED FROM PAST PARTI-
CIPLES.* (REV BY J.R. CRADDOCK
& Y. MALKIEL)
A. ALSDORF-BOLLÉE, 72:BAND210
HEFT1/3-207
A.K. LEVY, 545(RPH):NOV72-412
GEORGESCU, V. POLITICAL IDEAS &
THE ENLIGHTENMENT IN THE ROMANIAN
PRINCIPALITIES (1750-1831).
P.E. MICHELSON, 32:JUN73-417
GEORGESCU-ROEGEN, N. THE ENTROPY
LAW & THE ECONOMIC PROCESS.
L.A. BOLAND, 486:SEP72-423
GEORGI, A. DAS LATEINISCHE UND
DEUTSCHE PREISGEDICHT DES MITTEL-
ALTERS IN DER NACHFOLGE DES "GENUS
DEMONSTRATIVUM."*
W. BREUER, 680(ZDP):BAND91HEFT3-
443
GEORGIEV, L. PEN'O PENEV. (2ND ED)
E. MOŽEJKO, 32:JUN73-436
GEORGIEV, V. LA LANGUE ET L'ORIGINE
DES ÉTRUSQUES.
A. ERNOUT, 555:VOL46FASC2-322
GEORGIEV, V.I. OSNOVNI PROBLEMI NA
SLAVYANSKATA DIAKHRONNA MORFOLO-
GIYA.*
F.V. MAREŠ, 260(IF):BAND77HEFT1-
137
GEORGIEV, V.Z. ETRUSKISCHE SPRACH-
WISSENSCHAFT. (PT 2)
A. ERNOUT, 555:VOL46FASC2-322
GERAETS, T.F. VERS UNE NOUVELLE
PHILOSOPHIE TRANSCENDANTALE.
C. PANACCIO, 154:DEC72-615
R.S., 543:JUN72-752
GERALD, J.B. CONVENTIONAL WISDOM.
E. ROVIT, 659:AUTUMN74-539
639(VQR):AUTUMN72-CXX
GÉRARD, A. LES TAMBOURS DU NÉANT.*
R.A. DELATTRE, 290(JAAC):FALL71-
131
GERBER, D.E. EUTERPE.*
M.R. LEFKOWITZ, 24:SUMMER73-192
GERBER, H.E. & W.E. DAVIS, EDS.
THOMAS HARDY.
617(TLS):4JAN74-13

GERBRANDS, A.A. WOW-IPITS.
M.O. JONES, 650(WF):APR72-138
GERE, J.A. TADDEO ZUCCARO.*
L. PARTRIDGE, 54:JUN72-215
GERHARD, P. A GUIDE TO THE HISTORI-
CAL GEOGRAPHY OF NEW SPAIN.
R.E. GREENLEAF, 263:JUL-SEP73-
350
GERHARDIE, W. FUTILITY.* THE POLY-
GLOTS. OF MORTAL LOVE.
S. OLSON, 441:15SEP74-32
GERHARDT, M.I. ZEVENSLAPERS EN
ANDERE TIJD-VERLIEZERS.
F.L. UTLEY, 545(RPH):NOV72-454
GÉRIN, W. EMILY BRONTÉ.*
K. MC SWEENEY, 529(QQ):AUTUMN72-
435
R.B. MARTIN, 637(VS):SEP72-102
A.L. RUOFF, 651(WHR):WINTER73-96
W.M. SALE, JR., 445(NCF):MAR73-
469
R. SKELTON, 376:JUL72-147
639(VQR):SPRING73-LXXX
676(YR):WINTER73-XIII
GÉRIN, W. THE BRONTËS.
617(TLS):12APR74-402
GÉRIN, W. - SEE BRONTË, C.
GERLACH, H. WENN SIE ABENDS GEHEN.
S.K., 268:JUL74-150
GERLITZKI, G.J. DIE BEDEUTUNG DER
MINNE IN "MORIZ VON CRAÛN."*
H. HOMANN, 400(MLN):APR72-516
GERLO, A. & H.D.L. VERVLIET. BIBLIO-
GRAPHIE DE L'HUMANISME DES ANCIENS
PAYS-BAS.
G. TOURNOY-THOEN, 568(SCN):SUM-
MER73-58
GERMAIN, F. - SEE DE VIGNY, A.
GERMANN, G. GOTHIC REVIVAL IN EUR-
OPE & BRITAIN.*
M. BRINGMANN, 182:VOL25#23/24-
874
GERMANN, M. JOHANN JAKOB THURNEYSEN
D.J., 1754-1803.
G. NIEDHART, 182:VOL25#23/24-833
GERROLD, D. THE MAN WHO FOLDED HIM-
SELF.
617(TLS):15FEB74-163
GERROLD, D. YESTERDAY'S CHILDREN.
617(TLS):14JUN74-644
GERSBACH, M. CARLO EMILIO GADDA.
R. CRESPO, 433:OCT72-504
GERSCHENKRON, A. EUROPE IN THE RUS-
SIAN MIRROR.
M.R. DOHAN, 550(RUSR):JUL72-313
GERSON, N.B. STATE TROOPER.
N. CALLENDAR, 441:8DEC74-44
GERSON, S. SOUND & SYMBOL IN THE
DIALOGUE OF THE WORKS OF CHARLES
DICKENS.*
R.F. MOUNT, 660(WORD):AUG70-302
GERSTEIN, L. NIKOLAI STRAKHOV.*
C.A. MOSER, 550(RUSR):JAN72-94
639(VQR):WINTER72-XIV
GERSTENMAIER, C.I. THE VOICES OF
THE SILENT.* (GERMAN TITLE: DIE
STIMME DER STUMMEN.)
T. CRUMP, 32:SEP73-623
GERSTER, G. CHURCHES IN ROCK.*
J. BECKWITH, 39:JUL72-84
G. SHANE, 576:DEC72-335
GERT, B. THE MORAL RULES.
J.J. THOMSON, 311(JP):14FEB74-88

127

GERTEL, Z. LA NOVELA HISPANOAMERI-
CANA CONTEMPORÁNEA.*
  M.A. SALGADO, 241:SEP72-69
GERTZEL, C. PARTY & LOCALITY IN
NORTHERN UGANDA, 1945-62.
  K. KYLE, 362:4JUL74-27
GERVAIS, C.H. A SYMPATHY ORCHESTRA.
  D. BAILEY, 529(QQ):SUMMER72-242
GESNER, C. SHAKESPEARE & THE GREEK
ROMANCE.*
  W. VON KOPPENFELS, 72:BAND210
HEFT4/6-373
GETTENS, R.J., WITH OTHERS. THE
FREER CHINESE BRONZES.* (VOL 2)
  M. TREGEAR, 90:MAY72-337
GETTENS, R.J., R.S. CLARKE, JR. &
W.T. CHASE. TWO EARLY CHINESE
BRONZE WEAPONS WITH METEORITIC
BLADES.
  J.C.Y. WATT, 302:JUL72-211
GETTO, G. MANZONI EUROPEO.
  I.P., 275(IQ):FALL/WINTER72-123
  O.R., 191(ELN):SEP72(SUPP)-196
GEVERS, M. PLAISIR DES MÉTÉORES.
  H. KOPS, 207(FR):DEC71-472
GHALIB. GHAZALS OF GHALIB.* (A.
AHMAD, ED)
  639(VQR):AUTUMN72-CXXV
GHALIB, M.A.K. DASTANBUY.
  H. MALIK, 293(JAST):AUG72-969
GHIȘE, D. & P. TEODOR. FRAGMENTAR-
IUM ILUMINIST.
  K. HITCHINS, 32:SEP73-648
GHOSE, Z. THE INCREDIBLE BRAZILIAN.
  M. ELLMANN, 676(YR):SPRING73-461
GHOSH, K.P. THE INDIAN WAY.
  617(TLS):21JUN74-680
GHOSH, S.C. THE SOCIAL CONDITION OF
THE BRITISH COMMUNITY IN BENGAL.
  G. CANNON, 318(JAOS):OCT-DEC72-
516
GIACALONE, G. STORIA DELLA LETTERA-
TURA ITALIANA CON STORIA DELLA
CRITICA. (VOL 1)
  C. GÄNSSLE-PFEUFFER, 430(NS):
DEC72-743
GIACOMAN, H.F., ED. HOMENAJE A
ALEJO CARPENTIER.
  E.R. SKINNER, 238:MAR72-183
GIAKUMAKIS, G. THE AKKADIAN OF
ALALAḪ.
  E. REINER, 350:JUN73-500
GIANAKARIS, C.J. PLUTARCH.*
  A.J. GOSSAGE, 123:DEC73-196
GIANNANTONIO, P. DANTE E L'ALLEGOR-
ISMO.*
  F.D. MAURINO, 276:WINTER72-508
GIANNARÁS, A., ED. ÄSTHETIK HEUTE.
  617(TLS):25OCT74-1188
GIANNONE, P. OPERE DI PIETRO GIAN-
NONE. (S. BERTELLI & G. RICUPER-
ATI, EDS)
  F. DIAZ, 228(GSLI):VOL149FASC
468-617
GIANTURCO, E. A SELECTIVE BIBLIO-
GRAPHY OF VICO SCHOLARSHIP (1948-
1968).*
  C.W., 275(IQ):FALL/WINTER72-122
GIBBONS, D. THE CLOUT.
  N. CALLENDAR, 441:12MAY74-18
GIBBONS, F. DOSSO & BATTISTA DOSSI.*
  L. PUPPI, 90:APR72-251

GIBBONS, S. GREAT BRITAIN SPECIAL-
ISED STAMP CATALOGUE. (VOL 1)
(3RD ED, REV)
  617(TLS):8FEB74-140
"STANLEY GIBBONS GREAT BRITAIN SPEC-
IALISED STAMP CATALOGUE." (VOL 2)
(3RD ED)
  617(TLS):12APR74-402
GIBBS, A.M. - SEE DAVENANT, W.
GIBBS, B. THE MEETING PLACE OF THE
COLORS.
  639(VQR):WINTER73-XIII
GIBBS-SMITH, C.H. THE BAYEUX TAPES-
TRY.*
  A. FRANKENSTEIN, 55:NOV73-46
GIBBS-SMITH, C.H. FLIGHT THROUGH
THE AGES.
  W. SULLIVAN, 441:1DEC74-6
GIBIAN, G., ED & TRANS. RUSSIA'S
LOST LITERATURE OF THE ABSURD.
  P. HENRY, 575(SEER):JAN73-130
  G. DE MALLAC, 550(RUSR):JUL72-
314
GIBSON, A.M. WILDERNESS BONANZA.
  W. GARD, 584(SWR):WINTER73-V
GIBSON, C. THE PEPPER LEAF.
  P.D. EVANS, 368:SEP72-267
GIBSON, I. LA REPRESIÓN NACIONAL-
ISTA DE GRANADA EN 1936 Y LA MUER-
TE DE FEDERICO GARCÍA LORCA.*
  G. JACKSON, 400(MLN):MAR72-377
205(FMLS):OCT72-382
GIBSON, J.M. & D.M. JOHNSTON, EDS.
A CENTURY OF STRUGGLE.
  C.S. BURCHILL, 529(QQ):AUTUMN72-
411
GIBSON, M.J., COMP. PORTUGUESE
AFRICA: A GUIDE TO OFFICIAL PUBLI-
CATIONS.
  J.A. CASADA, 517(PBSA):APR-JUN73-
208
GIBSON, R. & K. ROBERTS. BRITISH
PORTRAIT PAINTERS.
  E. YOUNG, 39:AUG72-167
GIBSON, W. A SEASON IN HEAVEN.
  A. BROYARD, 441:3AUG74-21
  M. HARRIS, 441:14JUL74-5
GICOVATE, B. & A. - SEE MALLEA, E.
GIDDENS, A. THE CLASS STRUCTURE OF
THE ADVANCED SOCIETIES.
  617(TLS):8MAR74-240
GIDE, A. & J. BENNETT. CORRESPON-
DANCE ANDRÉ GIDE - ARNOLD BENNETT.
(L.F. BRUGMANS, ED)
  A.J. FARMER, 189(EA):JUL-SEP72-
445
GIDNEY, J.B. - SEE HEALD, E.T.
GIEDION, S. ARCHITECTURE & THE PHE-
NOMENA OF TRANSITION.*
  J. WILTON-ELY, 39:FEB72-147
GIELGUD, J. DISTINGUISHED COMPANY.
  J.C. TREWIN, 157:WINTER72-78
GIERGIELEWICZ, M. INTRODUCTION TO
POLISH VERSIFICATION.*
  L.L. THOMAS, 32:SEP73-669
GIES, J. CRISIS 1918.
  442(NY):3JUN74-110
GIFFORD, D. CHAPLIN.
  W. FEAVER, 617(TLS):27DEC74-1471
GIFFORD, D., WITH R.J. SEIDMAN.
NOTES FOR JOYCE.
  R.M. KAIN, 329(JJQ):SUMMER74-423

GIFFORD, P. & W.R. LOUIS, EDS.
FRANCE & BRITAIN IN AFRICA.
J.S. GALBRAITH, 637(VS):MAR73-
352
GIGLIONI, G.B. - SEE XENOPHON
GIL, A.M. HISTORIAS DE LA OTRA
ORILLA.
J.M. CARRANZA, 238:MAR72-196
GIL, A.M. LECTURAS Y RETRATOS.
G. ANTOINE, 238:DEC72-982
L.C. PÉREZ, 399(MLJ):DEC72-534
GIL, A.M. - SEE BUERO VALLEJO, A.
GILBERT, A. IMAGES OF ROSE.
M. LEVIN, 441:21JUL74-14
GILBERT, A. A NICE LITTLE KILLING.
N. CALLENDAR, 441:17MAR74-39
GILBERT, E.L. THE GOOD KIPLING.
T.A. SHIPPEY, 402(MLR):APR73-399
GILBERT, G.G., ED. THE GERMAN LAN-
GUAGE IN AMERICA.*
R.L. WELSCH, 292(JAF):JUL-SEP72-
289
GILBERT, G.G., ED. TEXAS STUDIES IN
BILINGUALISM.*
R.E. KELLER, 220(GL&L):OCT72-64
GILBERT, H. AN OFFENCE AGAINST THE
PERSONS.
617(TLS):17MAY74-517
GILBERT, M. CHURCHILL.
P. STANSKY, 441:24NOV74-4
GILBERT, M. FLASH POINT.
617(TLS):8NOV74-1248
GILBERT, M. SIR HORACE RUMBOLD.*
617(TLS):25JAN74-70
GILBERT, M. RUSSIAN HISTORY ATLAS.
R.T. FISHER, JR., 32:DEC73-808
GILBERT, S. ACTS OF ATTENTION.
A.M. BRANDABUR, 301(JEGP):JUL73-
461
GILBERT, W.S. THE BAB BALLADS OF
W.S. GILBERT.* (J. ELLIS, ED)
E.P. LAWRENCE, 637(VS):SEP72-119
GILBERT-LECOMTE, R. CORRESPONDANCE.
(P. MINET, ED)
98:JAN72-90
GILCHER, E. A BIBLIOGRAPHY OF
GEORGE MOORE.
C. BURKHART, 445(NCF):JUN72-112
J.E. DUNLEAVY, 637(VS):MAR72-376
H.E. GERBER, 78(BC):AUTUMN72-422
GILCHRIST, J. & W.J. MURRAY. THE
PRESS IN THE FRENCH REVOLUTION.
N. HAMPSON, 208(FS):OCT73-458
GILDER, G. NAKED NOMADS.
A. BROYARD, 441:3DEC74-39
GILDER, G.F. SEXUAL SUICIDE.*
P. ADAMS, 61:JAN74-99
GILES, L. THE SIEGE OF THE PEKING
LEGATIONS. (L.R. MARCHANT, ED)
J. SHRECKER, 293(JAST):MAY72-653
GILISON, J.M. BRITISH & SOVIET
POLITICS.
M. MOTE, 32:DEC73-829
GILL, B. WAYS OF LOVING.
N. BALAKIAN, 441:17JUN74-37
E. WEEKS, 61:MAY74-138
GILL, B. - SEE ZERBE, J.
GILL, E., ED. MOUNTAIN MOVING DAY.
N. BALAKIAN, 441:15FEB74-37
GILL, H.B., JR. THE APOTHECARY IN
COLONIAL VIRGINIA.
639(VQR):SUMMER73-CXXII

GILL, J. THE LAST HEROES.
A. BROYARD, 441:19MAR74-41
N. CALLENDAR, 441:7APR74-35
GILL, J.H. THE POSSIBILITY OF RELIG-
IOUS KNOWLEDGE.
R.E. SANTONI, 258:DEC72-609
GILL, M. MALLARMÉ'S POEM "LA CHEVE-
LURE VOL D'UNE FLAMME..."
205(FMLS):OCT72-383
GILL, M.L. MIND WALLS.
D. BAILEY, 529(QQ):SUMMER72-242
GILL, R., ED. WILLIAM EMPSON.
D. DONOGHUE, 617(TLS):7JUN74-597
D.A.N. JONES, 362:18JUL74-93
GILL, R. HAPPY RURAL SEAT.*
L. LERNER, 301(JEGP):OCT73-577
639(VQR):SPRING74-LXIX
GILL, R. - SEE MARLOWE, C.
GILLE, K.F. "WILHELM MEISTER" IM
URTEIL DER ZEITGENOSSEN.
H.G. HAILE, 301(JEGP):OCT73-588
GILLEN, M. THE PRINCE & HIS LADY.
639(VQR):SPRING72-LX
GILLESPIE, G. GERMAN BAROQUE
POETRY.*
R.J. ALLEN, 400(MLN):OCT72-785
GILLESPIE, G., ED & TRANS. DIE
NACHTWACHEN DES BONAVENTURA.
J.L. SAMMONS, 406:WINTER73-416
GILLESPIE, J. THE LAND IN SUNSHINE.
J. MELLORS, 362:11JUL74-61
GILLESPIE, N.C. THE COLLAPSE OF
ORTHODOXY.
L. WEEKS, 579(SAQ):SPRING73-334
639(VQR):SUMMER72-LXXXVIII
GILLETT, C. MAKING TRACKS.
J. ROCKWELL, 441:22DEC74-10
GILLHAM, D.G. - SEE KEATS, J.
GILLIAMS, M. ELIAS.
H. KOPS, 207(FR):OCT71-202
GILLIATT, P. UNHOLY FOOLS.*
R. ARMES, 364:OCT/NOV73-158
GILLIES, A. A HEBRIDEAN IN GOETHE'S
WEIMAR.*
W.D. ROBSON-SCOTT, 220(GL&L):
JAN73-178
GILLISPIE, C.C. LAZARE CARNOT,
SAVANT.
J.R.R. CHRISTIE, 481(PQ):JUL72-
569
J-J. DAETWYLER, 182:VOL25#21-715
GILLON, E.V., JR. EARLY ILLUSTRA-
TIONS & VIEWS OF AMERICAN ARCHITEC-
TURE.
R.R., 505:SEP72-154
GILLON, E.V., JR. VICTORIAN CEME-
TERY ART.
R.L. COLLINS, 637(VS):JUN73-468
GILMAN, D. A PALM FOR MRS. POLLI-
FAX.*
N. CALLENDAR, 441:10NOV74-46
GILMAN, R. THE MAKING OF MODERN
DRAMA.
A. BROYARD, 441:12SEP74-43
T.R. EDWARDS, 441:8SEP74-4
GILMAN, S. THE SPAIN OF FERNANDO DE
ROJAS.
617(TLS):5APR74-373
639(VQR):WINTER73-XXVI
GILMAN, W.H. & J.E. PARSONS - SEE
EMERSON, R.W.
GIMMESTAD, V.E. JOHN TRUMBULL.
W.D. ANDREWS, 165:FALL74-200

GIMSON, A.C. AN INTRODUCTION TO THE
PRONUNCIATION OF ENGLISH.* (2ND
ED)
  A.R. TELLIER, 189(EA):OCT-DEC72-
533
GINDIN, I. GOSUDARSTVENNYY BANK I
EKONOMICHESKAYA POLITIKA TSAR-
SKOGO PRAVITEL'STVA.
  O. CRISP, 575(SEER):OCT73-582
GINDIN, J. HARVEST OF A QUIET EYE.*
  G.B. TENNYSON, 445(NCF):DEC72-
365
GINGER, J. NOTHING & A SHADE.*
  J. MELLORS, 364(FEB/MAR74-136
GINSBERG, A. THE FALL OF AMERICA.*
  G. HENRY, 491:AUG74-292
  W.H. PRITCHARD, 249(HUDR):AUTUMN
73-592
GINSBERG, E.S. - SEE GRÉVIN, J.
GINSBERG, M. MIND & BELIEF.
  N.F. BUNNIN, 518:OCT73-6
GINZBURG, C., ED. I COSTITUTI DI
DON PIETRO MANELFI.
  A.J. SCHUTTE, 551(RENQ):AUTUMN
72-364
GINZBURG, N. NO WAY.
  M. LEVIN, 441:1SEP74-14
  L.E. SISSMAN, 442(NY):21OCT74-
185
GINZBURG, N. LE VOCI DELLA SERA.
(S. PACIFICI, ED)
  G.S. PANOFSKY, 276:AUTUMN72-352
GIOMINE, R. PROBLEMI CHRONOLOGICI E
COMPOSITIVI DEL "DE DIVINATIONE"
CICERONIANO.
  A. ERNOUT, 555:VOL46FASC2-345
GIONO, J. OEUVRES ROMANESQUES COM-
PLÈTES. (VOL 2) (R. RICATTE, WITH
P. CITRON & L. RICATTE, EDS)
  M. SCOTT, 208(FS):JUL73-359
GIORGINI, M.S., ED. SOLEB.
  G.T. MARTIN, 182:VOL25#23/24-879
DI GIOVANNI, N.T., WITH J.L. BORGES
- SEE BORGES, J.L.
GIOVENE, A. THE DICE OF WAR.
  N. BLIVEN, 442(NY):9DEC74-187
  617(TLS):8FEB74-125
GIPPER, H. & H. SCHWARZ. BIBLIO-
GRAPHISCHES HANDBUCH ZUR SPRACHIN-
HALTSFORSCHUNG. (PT 1, NOS 12&13)
  J. ANDRÉ, 555:VOL46FASC2-319
GIPPIUS, Z.N. - SEE UNDER HIPPIUS,
Z.N.
GIPSON, L.H. A BIBLIOGRAPHICAL
GUIDE TO THE HISTORY OF THE BRIT-
ISH EMPIRE, 1748-1776.* A GUIDE
TO MANUSCRIPTS RELATING TO THE HIS-
TORY OF THE BRITISH EMPIRE, 1748-
1776.*
  R.M. GEPHART, 656(WMQ):APR72-318
GIRALDI, G. - SEE CARRARA, G.M.A.
GIRARD, R. LA VIOLENCE ET LE SACRÉ.*
  P. PACHET, 98:AUG/SEP72-716
  C.A. RUBINO, 400(MLN):DEC72-986
GIRAUD, J. MANUEL DE BIBLIOGRAPHIE
LITTÉRAIRE POUR LES XVIE, XVIIE
ET XVIIIE SIÈCLES FRANÇAIS, 1946-
1955.*
  M. DASSONVILLE, 207(FR):OCT71-
286
  R. POUILLIART, 549(RLC):JAN-MAR
72-136
  R. SHACKLETON, 208(FS):APR73-190

GIRAUD, J., P. PAMART & J. RIVERAIN.
LES MOTS "DANS LE VENT."
  P. RICKARD, 208(FS):OCT73-503
GIRAUD, Y. - SEE CORNEILLE, T.
GIRAUD, Y. & M-R. JUNG. LA RENAIS-
SANCE I, 1480-1548.
  A.J. KRAILSHEIMER, 617(TLS):
8NOV74-1265
GIRAUD, Y.F-A. LA FABLE DE DAPHNÉ.*
  I.D. MC FARLANE, 402(MLR):JAN73-
170
GIRAUDOUX, J. INTERMEZZO. (E.E.
TORY, ED)
  E. RATCLIFF, 208(FS):JAN73-98
GIRDLESTONE, C. LA TRAGÉDIE EN
MUSIQUE (1673-1750) CONSIDÉRÉE
COMME GENRE LITTÉRAIRE.
  D. GRONAU, 182:VOL25#22-808
  J.G.R., 410(M&L):JUL73-335
DI GIROLAMO, N. CULTURA E COSCIEN-
ZA CRITICA NELL' "HÉRODIADE" DI
MALLARMÉ.*
  A. FONGARO, 535(RHL):MAR-APR72-
333
GIROUARD, M. THE VICTORIAN COUNTRY
HOUSE.
  H. HOBHOUSE, 46:JUN72-391
  J. LEES-MILNE, 135:MAR72-214
  M. MAC EWAN, 592:MAR72-132
  O. OVERBY, 637(VS):SEP72-120
GIROUD, F. I GIVE YOU MY WORD.
  F. LEWIS, 441:27OCT74-4
  442(NY):4NOV74-211
GIRVAN, N. FOREIGN CAPITAL & ECONOM-
IC UNDERDEVELOPMENT IN JAMAICA.
  M. LIPTON, 617(TLS):2AUG74-830
GISHFORD, A., ED. GRAND OPERA.*
  J. BUDDEN, 415:JAN73-37
GISSING, G. ESSAYS & FICTION.* (P.
COUSTILLAS, ED)
  W.V. HARRIS, 573(SSF):SPRING72-
204
GISSING, G. THE NETHER WORLD. [IN-
TRODUCTION BY W. ALLEN] THE NETH-
ER WORLD. [INTRODUCTION BY J.
GOODE]
  617(TLS):22FEB74-171
GITEAU, M. LE BORNAGE RITUEL DES
TEMPLES BOUDDHIQUES DU CAMBODGE.
  K. FISCHER, 182:VOL25#3/4-96
GITLIN, T., ED. CAMPFIRES OF THE
RESISTANCE.
  W.P. ROOT, 491:OCT73-34
  639(VQR):AUTUMN72-CXXIV
GITTLEMAN, A.I. LE STYLE ÉPIQUE
DANS "GARIN LE LOHERAIN."*
  A. FOULET, 545(RPH):MAY73-746
GIUSSO, L. SCIENZA E FILOSOFIA IN
GIORDANO BRUNO.
  E. NAMER, 542:JAN-MAR72-94
GIZYCKI, J. A HISTORY OF CHESS.
  617(TLS):1MAR74-220
VON GIZYCKI, R. HAKU MELE - DER
POET IN POLYNESIEN.
  B.F. KIRTLEY, 292(JAF):OCT-DEC72-
190
GLADISH, D.F. - SEE DAVENANT, W.
GLADSTONE, M. & G. THE NEEDLEPOINT
ALPHABET BOOK.
  L.J. GARTNER, JR., 441:8DEC74-51

GLADSTONE, W.E. THE PRIME MINIS-
TER'S PAPERS: W.E. GLADSTONE.
(VOL 1) (J. BROOKE & M. SORENSEN,
EDS)
J. VINCENT, 637(VS):SEP72-99
GLANVILLE, B. THE COMIC.
617(TLS):18OCT74-1155
GLASER, E., ED. THE CANCIONERO
"MANUEL DE FARIA."
B.N. TEENSMA, 433:OCT72-506
GLASKOW, W.G. HISTORY OF THE COS-
SACKS.
C.B. O'BRIEN, 32:JUN73-373
GLASS, A. & D. HACKETT. PITJANTJAT-
JARA GRAMMAR.
J.T. PLATT, 361:VOL29#2-192
GLASS, I. FIFTH AVENUE STORE ONLY.
M. LEVIN, 441:7APR74-32
GLASS, J.M. REFLECTIONS ON A MOUN-
TAIN SUMMER.
M. LEVIN, 441:10NOV74-22
GLASSBURNER, B., ED. THE ECONOMY OF
INDONESIA.
D.S. PAAUW, 293(JAST):FEB72-456
GLASSCO, J. THE FATAL WOMAN.
L. GARBER, 99:NOV/DEC74-21
GLASSCO, J., ED. THE POETRY OF
FRENCH CANADA IN TRANSLATION.
L. BERGERON, 565:VOL13#1-53
GLASSER, R. RETROSPEKTION UND ANTIZ-
IPATION DER SINNE.
W-D. STEMPEL, 72:BAND210HEFT1/3-
214
GLASSER, R.J. WARD 402.*
617(TLS):4OCT74-1092
GLATZER, N.N. - SEE KAFKA, F.
GLEASON, A. EUROPEAN & MUSCOVITE.*
M. BANERJEE, 32:MAR73-167
GLEASON, H.W. THE WESTERN WILDER-
NESS OF NORTH AMERICA. (TEXT BY
G. CROSSETTE)
639(VQR):WINTER73-XLIV
GLEITMAN, L.R. & H. PHRASE & PARA-
PHRASE.
K. KUIPER, 206:JAN73-438
E.H. LENNEBERG, 350:JUN73-519
GLEMSER, B. THE 60TH MONARCH.
M. LEVIN, 441:29SEP74-40
GLEN, D. A CLED SCORE.
617(TLS):24MAY74-554
GLENDAY, A. FOLLOW, FOLLOW.
617(TLS):22MAR74-281
GLENDINNING, N. A LITERARY HISTORY
OF SPAIN: THE EIGHTEENTH CENTURY.
A.O. ALDRIDGE, 402(MLR):JUL73-
677
R. GUTIÉRREZ GIRARDOT, 72:BAND
210HEFT4/6-473
GLENDINNING, N., ED. STUDIES IN
MODERN SPANISH LITERATURE & ART.
E.I. FOX, 402(MLR):OCT73-917
GLENN, J. DEUTSCHES SCHRIFTTUM DER
GEGENWART (AB 1945).
A. HOLSCHUH, 301(JEGP):JAN73-106
H. THOMKE, 182:VOL25#22-797
GLENN, J. - SEE "LESSING YEARBOOK
III"
GLENNY, M., ED. NOVY MIR: A SELEC-
TION 1925-1967.
K. FITZLYON, 364:FEB/MAR73-147
GLESSING, R.J. THE UNDERGROUND
PRESS IN AMERICA.*
H.J.L., 502(PRS):SPRING72-90

GLICK, T.F. IRRIGATION & SOCIETY IN
MEDIEVAL VALENCIA.*
G.T. SCANLON, 318(JAOS):APR-JUN
72-387
GLICKSBERG, C.I. THE IRONIC VISION
IN MODERN LITERATURE.
N. KNOX, 405(MP):AUG72-53
GLIER, I. ARTES AMANDI.*
F.H. BÄUML, 589:APR73-362
O. SAYCE, 402(MLR):APR73-444
GLIER, I. & OTHERS, EDS. WERK - TYP
- SITUATION.
W.J. JONES, 220(GL&L):JUL73-344
GLIMCHER, A.B. LOUISE NEVELSON.*
A. FRANKENSTEIN, 55:FEB73-15
GLINZ, H. LINGUISTISCHE GRUNDBE-
GRIFFE UND METHODENÜBERBLICK.
W. ABRAHAM, 343:BAND15HEFT2-199
J.B. VOYLES, 353:15DEC72-108
GLISSANT, E. L'INTENTION POÉTIQUE.
R. CHAMPIGNY, 207(FR):OCT71-203
GLOB, P.V. THE MOUND PEOPLE.
S. HEANEY, 362:6JUN74-741
617(TLS):14JUN74-633
GLÖCKNER, E. ERNST GLÖCKNER - BEGEG-
NUNG MIT STEFAN GEORGE - AUS BRIEF-
EN UND TAGEBÜCHERN 1913-1934. (F.
ADAM, ED)
B. FARRELL, 67:NOV73-316
"THE GLORY & PAGEANTRY OF CHRISTMAS."
A. BROYARD, 441:9DEC74-33
GLOTZ, S. & OTHERS. ÉCOLES ET
LIVRES D'ÉCOLE EN HAINAUT DU XVIE
AU XIXE SIÈCLE.
G. DEPLAZES, 182:VOL25#3/4-73
GLOVER, B.R. A HISTORY OF SIX SPAN-
ISH VERBS MEANING "TO TAKE, SEIZE,
GRASP."
R. POSNER, 361:VOL30#2/3-277
GLOVER, J. RESPONSIBILITY.*
M.R. AYERS, 479(PHQ):APR72-181
J. FEINBERG, 482(PHR):APR72-237
V. HAKSAR, 483:JAN72-83
N. MELCHERT, 484(PPR):SEP72-133
GLOVER, M., ED. AN ASSEMBLAGE OF
INDIAN ARMY SOLDIERS & UNIFORMS.
617(TLS):14JUN74-645
GLOVER, M. THE PENINSULAR WAR 1807-
1814.
617(TLS):16AUG74-887
GLOWKA, D. SCHULREFORM UND GESELL-
SCHAFT IN DER SOWJETUNION 1958-68.
E. SCHÜTTE, 182:VOL25#5/6-140
GLUBB, J.B. SOLDIERS OF FORTUNE.
617(TLS):26APR74-436
GLUCKSMANN, M. STRUCTURALIST ANALY-
SIS IN CONTEMPORARY SOCIAL THOUGHT.
617(TLS):24MAY74-567
GLYN, E. THREE WEEKS.
M. DAVSON, 362:14NOV74-647
P. KEATING, 617(TLS):15NOV74-
1276
GNÄDINGER, L. HIUDAN UND PETIT-
CREIU.*
D.E. LE SAGE, 220(GL&L):JUL73-
348
GNEMMI, A. IL FONDAMENTO METAFISICO.
P. DI VONA, 548(RCSF):JUL-SEP72-
344
GNEUSS, C. DER SPÄTE TIECK ALS
ZEITKRITIKER.
W.J.L., 191(ELN):SEP72(SUPP)-179
GNILKA, C. AETAS SPIRITALIS.
A. KEMMER, 182:VOL25#23/24-846

GÖBEL, H.   BILD UND SPRACHE BEI LES-
SING.*
   W.R. MAURER, 406:SPRING73-78
   H.B. NISBET, 402(MLR):APR73-456
DE GOBINEAU, A.   CE QUI EST ARRIVÉ À
LA FRANCE EN 1870.*   (A.B. DUFF,
ED)
   A.A. BAKKALČIOGLU, 207(FR):DEC71-
454
GOCHET, P.   ESQUISSE D'UNE THÉORIE
NOMINALISTE DE LA PROPOSITION.
   P. LAMARQUE, 518:JAN73-16
GÖCKENJAN, H.   HILFSVÖLKER UND
GRENZWÄCHTER IM MITTELALTERLICHEN
UNGARN.
   T. VON BOGYAY, 182:VOL25#19/20-
686
GODARD, H. - SEE CÉLINE, L-F.
GODBOLD, E.S., JR.   ELLEN GLASGOW &
THE WOMAN WITHIN.*
   C.H. HOLMAN, 639(VQR):AUTUMN72-
633
GODDARD, A.   THE VIENNA PURSUIT.
   617(TLS):20DEC74-1437
GODDARD, D.   JOEY.
   G.V. HIGGINS, 441:9JUN74-6
   E. PERLMUTTER, 441:30MAY74-41
GODENNE, R.   HISTOIRE DE LA NOUVELLE
FRANÇAISE AUX XVIIE ET XVIIIE
SIÈCLES.*
   E. LEUBE, 72:BAND21OHEFT1/3-224
   D.L. RUBIN, 207(FR):DEC71-538
   F.W. VOGLER, 546(RR):DEC72-298
GODEY, J.   THE TAKING OF PELHAM ONE
TWO THREE.*
   N. CALLENDAR, 441:8DEC74-44
GODWIN, G.   THE ODD WOMAN.
   A. BROYARD, 441:30SEP74-33
   L. DICKSTEIN, 441:20OCT74-4
   442(NY):18NOV74-234
GODWIN, W.   ENQUIRY CONCERNING POL-
ITICAL JUSTICE.   (ABRIDGED & ED
BY K.C. CARTER)
   J. STEINBERG, 481(PQ):JUL72-684
GODWIN, W.   CALEB WILLIAMS.*   (D.
MC CRACKEN, ED)
   L.W. BROWN, 173(ECS):SUMMER73-
531
GOEBEL, J., JR.   THE OLIVER WENDELL
HOLMES DEVISE HISTORY OF THE SUP-
REME COURT OF THE UNITED STATES.*
(VOL 1) [SHOWN IN PREV UNDER SUB-
TITLE]
   K. NEWMYER, 656(WMQ):OCT72-643
GOEDECKE, W., ED.   ABKÜRZUNGEN UND
KURZWÖRTER AUS TECHNIK UND NATUR-
WISSENSCHAFTEN ENGLISCH-DEUTSCH/
ABBREVIATIONS & ACRONYMS IN SCI-
ENCE & TECHNOLOGY ENGLISH-GERMAN.
   E. WEIS, 75:4/1972-36
GOEDERTIER, J.M.   A DICTIONARY OF
JAPANESE HISTORY.*
   M.V. LAMBERTI, 318(JAOS):JAN-MAR
72-153
GOEKOOP, C.   THE LOGIC OF INVARIABLE
CONCOMITANCE IN THE TATTVACINTĀ-
MANI, GANGEŚA'S ANUMITINIRŪPANA &
VYĀPTIVĀDA.
   B.K. MATILAL, 318(JAOS):JAN-MAR
72-169
   SIBAJIBAN, 316:MAR72-172
GOEN, C.C. - SEE EDWARDS, J.

VON GOETHE, J.W.   FAUST.   (B. TAYLOR,
TRANS)
   617(TLS):18OCT74-1171
VON GOETHE, J.W.   GOETHE'S ÄMTLICHE
SCHRIFTEN.   (VOL 2, PT 2) (H. DAHL,
ED)
   617(TLS):21JUN74-680
VON GOETHE, J.W.   GOETHES BRIEFE IN
DREI BÄNDEN.   (H. HOLTZHAUER, ED)
   C. STEINER, 221(GQ):MAR72-373
VON GOETHE, J.W.   GOETHE'S COLOR
THEORY.*   (R. MATTHAEI, ED; ENG-
LISH ED & TRANS BY H. AACH)
   R. SLUTZKY, 139:DEC71-12
VON GOETHE, J.W.   GOETHE'S "FAUST."*
(B. FAIRLEY, TRANS)
   L. FORSTER, 627(UTQ):WINTER72-
175
VON GOETHE, J.W.   THE SUFFERINGS OF
YOUNG WERTHER.   (H. STEINHAUER,
TRANS)
   W.V. BLOMSTER, 399(MLJ):FEB72-
118
VON GOETHE, J.W.   THEORY OF COLORS.
   P.S., 543:DEC71-352
   R. SLUTZKY, 139:DEC71-12
VON GOETHE, J.W.   DIE WAHLVERWANDT-
SCHAFTEN.   (H.B. NISBET & H.
REISS, EDS)
   E.W. HERD, 220(GL&L):JUL73-317
   D.G. LITTLE, 402(MLR):JUL73-691
GOETZ, H.   STUDIES IN THE HISTORY &
ART OF KASHMIR & THE INDIAN HIMA-
LAYA.
   E. BENDER, 318(JAOS):OCT-DEC72-
568
GOFF, P.   WILHELMINISCHES ZEITALTER.
   R. FOLTER, 301(JEGP):JAN73-110
   J. OSBORNE, 402(MLR):JAN73-237
   H. THOMKE, 182:VOL25#22-797
   E. THURNHER, 133:1972/1-102
GOFMAN, M., ED.   POETY SIMVOLIZMA.
   G. DONCHIN, 575(SEER):APR73-328
GOGARTY, P.   SNAP BOX.
   H. WILLIAMS, 364:JUN/JUL73-123
GOGOL, N.   THE COLLECTED TALES &
PLAYS OF NIKOLAI GOGOL.   (L.J.
KENT, ED)
   T.E. BIRD, 573(SSF):SPRING72-206
GOH CHENG TEIK.   THE MAY THIRTEENTH
INCIDENT & DEMOCRACY IN MALAYSIA.
   G.D. NESS, 293(JAST):MAY72-734
   C.M. TURNBULL, 302:JUL72-215
GOHEEN, J.D. & J.L. MOTHERSHEAD, JR.
- SEE LEWIS, C.I.
GÖHRUM, G.   ENGLISCHUNTERRICHT AN
HAUPT- UND REALSCHLEN.   (PT 1)
   W. STUCK, 430(NS):AUG72-497
GOITEIN, S.D.   A MEDITERRANEAN SOCI-
ETY.   (VOL 2)
   J. NEUSNER, 589:JUL73-568
GOLAN, G.   THE CZECHOSLOVAK REFORM
MOVEMENT.
   J. KREJČÍ, 575(SEER):JAN73-148
GOŁASZEWKA, M.   SWIADOMOŚĆ PIĘKNA.
   C. GEORGIADIS, 290(JAAC):SUMMER
72-563
GOLD, H.   MY LAST TWO THOUSAND
YEARS.*
   42(AR):VOL32#3-504
GOLD, H.   SWIFTIE THE MAGICIAN.
   P. ADAMS, 61:OCT74-119
   R.P. BRICKNER, 441:15SEP74-44
   M. LEVENSON, 231:NOV74-110

GOLD, J. CHARLES DICKENS.
A. FLEISHMAN, 401(MLQ):JUN73-191
N. PAGE, 150(DR):WINTER72/73-691
M. STEIG, 648:JAN73-76
L. STEVENSON, 579(SAQ):SPRING73-332
A. WELSH, 676(YR):WINTER73-281
617(TLS):25JAN74-75
GOLD, J., COMP. THE STATURE OF DICKENS.
R.D. ALTICK, 445(NCF):JUN72-107
D. DE VRIES, 155:SEP72-188
R.C. ELLSWORTH, 529(QQ):SPRING72-108
GOLDBERG, M. CARLYLE & DICKENS.*
C.R. SANDERS, 445(NCF):MAR73-490
M. STEIG, 648:JAN73-76
A. WELSH, 676(YR):WINTER73-281
639(VQR):SPRING73-LXIX
GOLDEN, H. OUR SOUTHERN LANDSMAN.
R.F. SHEPARD, 441:10JUL74-39
GOLDEN, H.H., ED. STUDIES IN HONOR OF SAMUEL MONTEFIORE WAXMAN.*
W.T. MC CREADY, 241:MAY72-85
GOLDEN, M. THE SELF OBSERVED.
T. ATTERIDGE, 579(SAQ):WINTER73-174
A. MESSENGER, 648:JAN73-72
H.E. PAGLIARO, 566:AUTUMN72-43
"THE GOLDEN HAGGADAH."*
J. BECKWITH, 39:MAR72-227
"THE GOLDEN LOTUS." (C. EGERTON, TRANS)
C. BIRCH, 453:24JAN74-46
GOLDENBERG, L.A. RUSSIAN MAPS & ATLASES AS HISTORICAL SOURCES.
R.G. JENSEN, 32:SEP73-604
GOLDFARB, S. MESSAGES.
639(VQR):WINTER72-XXII
GOLDFARB, W.D. - SEE HERBRAND, J.
GOLDIN, M.G. SPANISH CASE & FUNCTION.*
K. ADAMS, 353:1NOV72-126
GOLDING, J. DUCHAMP: THE BRIDE STRIPPED BARE BY HER BACHELORS, EVEN.*
A. FRANKENSTEIN, 55:SUMMER73-78
GOLDING, W. THE PYRAMID.
A. JOHNSTON, 145(CRIT):VOL14#2-97
GOLDING, W. THE SCORPION GOD.
L.T. LEMON, 502(PRS):FALL72-266
GOLDKNOPF, D. THE LIFE OF THE NOVEL.*
S. CORNELL, 114(CHIR):VOL24#3-159
J. GINDIN, 385(MQR):SUMMER74-302
639(VQR):AUTUMN73-CXLIV
GOLDMAN, A., WITH L. SCHILLER.
LADIES & GENTLEMEN - LENNY BRUCE!
C. LEHMANN-HAUPT, 441:31MAY74-31
W. MARKFIELD, 441:26MAY74-1
J. RICHARDSON, 453:27JUN74-12
GOLDMAN, B. READING & WRITING IN THE ARTS.
J. GUTMANN, 290(JAAC):SUMMER72-571
GOLDMAN, J. THE MAN FROM GREEK & ROMAN.
M. LEVIN, 441:1DEC74-78
GOLDMAN, L. WHEN DOCTORS DISAGREE.
617(TLS):18JAN74-48
GOLDMAN, L.L. THE CASTRATO.
617(TLS):7JUN74-619

GOLDMAN, M. SHAKESPEARE & THE ENERGIES OF DRAMA.*
T. HAWKES, 676(YR):SUMMER73-561
D.A. TRAVERSI, 401(MLQ):SEP73-312
S. WELLS, 402(MLR):OCT73-889
639(VQR):AUTUMN72-CXXXIII
GOLDMAN, M.I. THE SPOILS OF PROGRESS.
R.G. JENSEN, 32:SEP73-629
GOLDMAN, P. THE DEATH & LIFE OF MALCOLM X.*
A. SALKEY, 362:8AUG74-189
J. VAIZEY, 617(TLS):16AUG74-881
GOLDMAN, W. MARATHON MAN.
G. LYONS, 441:27OCT74-50
GOLDNER, N. THE STRAVINSKY FESTIVAL OF THE NEW YORK CITY BALLET.
A. KISSELGOFF, 441:13JUL74-21
GOLDONI, C. THE COMIC THEATRE.*
J.I. COPE, 173(ECS):SUMMER73-520
GOLDRING, P. MULTIPURPOSE MAN.
617(TLS):5JUL74-731
GOLDSCHMIDT, E.P. GOTHIC & RENAISSANCE BOOKBINDINGS.
M.M. ROMME, 78(BC):SUMMER72-279
GOLDSCHMIDT, G-A. UN CORPS DÉRISOIRE.
D. GROJNOWSKI, 98:AUG/SEP72-821
GOLDSCHMIDT, V. ESSAI SUR LE CRATYLE.
G. GENETTE, 98:DEC72-1019
GOLDSCHMIDT, V. PLATONISME ET PENSÉE CONTEMPORAINE.
J-L. POIRIER, 542:JAN-MAR72-43
GOLDSCHMIDT, W. KAMBUYA'S CATTLE.
M. RUEL, 69:APR72-161
GOLDSMITH, M.E. THE MODE & MEANING OF "BEOWULF."*
A.J. BLISS, 447(N&Q):MAR72-111
J.K. CRANE, 128(CE):APR72-830
J.B. TRAHERN, JR., 38:BAND90HEFT4-513
GOLDSMITH, O. THE VICAR OF WAKEFIELD. (A. FRIEDMAN, ED)
617(TLS):10MAY74-508
GOLDSMITH, V.F. A SHORT TITLE CATALOGUE OF SPANISH & PORTUGUESE BOOKS 1601-1700 IN THE LIBRARY OF THE BRITISH MUSEUM (THE BRITISH LIBRARY - REFERENCE DIVISION).
617(TLS):6SEP74-958
GOLDSTEIN, B.R. AL-BIṬRŪJĪ: ON THE PRINCIPLES OF ASTRONOMY.
F.J. CARMODY, 589:JAN73-150
GOLDSTEIN, J., A. FREUD & A.J. SOLNIT. BEYOND THE BEST INTERESTS OF THE CHILD.
617(TLS):25JAN74-86
GOLDSTEIN, J.A. THE LETTERS OF DEMOSTHENES.
R. WEIL, 555:VOL46FASC1-124
GOLDSTEIN, K.S. & D. BEN-AMOS, EDS. THRICE-TOLD TALES.*
F.L. UTLEY, 196:BAND13HEFT1/2-194
GOLDSTON, R. COMMUNISM.
H.K. ROSENTHAL, 32:MAR73-182
GOLDSTONE, H.H. & M. DALRYMPLE. HISTORY PRESERVED.
P. GOLDBERGER, 441:20SEP74-43
T.B. MORTON, 441:28JUL74-4

133

GÜLLER, K.H. GESCHICHTE DER ALTENG-
LISCHEN LITERATUR.
E.G. STANLEY, 72:BAND210HEFT4/6-
359
GOLLIN, J. WORLDLY GOODS.
E.T. DELANEY, 363:MAY72-109
GOMBRICH, E.H. THE STORY OF ART.
(REV)
T. LASK, 55:APR73-50
GOMBRICH, E.H. SYMBOLIC IMAGES.
R. TARR, 592:JUL/AUG72-58
GOMBRICH, E.H. ABY WARBURG.
M. WEITZ, 54:MAR72-107
GOMBROWICZ, W. A KIND OF TESTAMENT.
D. DUNN, 364:JUN/JUL73-151
GOMBROWICZ, W. OPERETTA.
A. RENDLE, 157:SPRING72-81
GOMEZ, C.B. - SEE UNDER BANDERA
GOMEZ, C.
GÓMEZ-GIL, O. HISTORIA CRÍTICA DE
LA LITERATURA HISPANOAMERICANA.
A.S. MICHALSKI, 399(MLJ):FEB72-
115
GOMME, A.H. DICKENS.
K.J. FIELDING, 155:JAN72-60
S. MONOD, 189(EA):OCT-DEC72-568
H.P. SUCKSMITH, 677:VOL3-316
GOMPERTZ, G.S.M. KOREAN POTTERY &
PORCELAIN OF THE YI PERIOD.
J.E. KIDDER, JR., 54:MAR72-77
H. TRUBNER, 318(JAOS):JAN-MAR72-
161
GOMPF, L. - SEE JOSEPH OF EXETER
GONDA, J. A CONCISE ELEMENTARY GRAM-
MAR OF THE SANSKRIT LANGUAGE.*
J.P. HUGHES, 660(WORD):APR70-149
GONDRAS, A-J. - SEE DE FALCO, P.
GONZÁLEZ, E., S. LIPP & H. PIÑERA.
SPANISH CULTURAL READER.*
A. GONZÁLEZ-PÉREZ, 399(MLJ):
FEB72-102
GONZÁLEZ, G.M.J. ESPAÑA SOL Y SOM-
BRA.
L. TARÍN TORRECILLA, 556(RLV):
1972/2-223
GONZÁLEZ, J.C. - SEE UNDER CASO GON-
ZÁLEZ, J.
GONZÁLEZ, L. SAN JOSÉ DE GRACIA.
L. WHITEHEAD, 617(TLS):8NOV74-
1254
GONZÁLEZ-GERTH, M. & G.D. SCHADE,
EDS. RUBEN DARÍO CENTENNIAL STUD-
IES.
F. DAUSTER, 238:MAR72-187
GONZÁLEZ MUELA, J. MANUAL DE COM-
POSICIÓN ESPAÑOLA.
F.G. VINSON, 399(MLJ):FEB72-105
GONZÁLEZ MUELA, J. - SEE SALINAS, P.
GOOCH, A. DIMINUTIVE, AUGMENTATIVE
& PEJORATIVE SUFFIXES IN MODERN
SPANISH.* (2ND ED)
K. ADAMS, 353:1DEC72-116
GOOD, C.M. RURAL MARKETS & TRADE IN
EAST AFRICA.
A.H.M. KIRK-GREENE, 69:JAN72-80
GOOD, R.C. UDI.
617(TLS):15FEB74-151
GOOD, T. THOMAS GOOD: SELECTED
POEMS. (M. HAMBURGER, ED)
617(TLS):5APR74-371
"GOOD FOOD GUIDE."
617(TLS):17MAY74-534
GOODALL, M.H. THE WIGHT AIRCRAFT.
617(TLS):4JAN74-18

GOODE, H.D. LA PROSA RETÓRICA DE
FRAY LUIS DE LEÓN EN "LOS NOMBRES
DE CRISTO."*
J.B. AVALLE-ARCE, 241:MAY72-89
C. FAULHABER, 545(RPH):NOV72-442
GOODE, J., ED. THE AIR OF REALITY.*
H-J. LANG, 182:VOL25#17/18-604
W.T. STAFFORD, 27(AL):JAN74-618
GOODERS, J., ED. THE BIRDWATCHER'S
BOOK.
617(TLS):8NOV74-1269
GOODERS, J. WHERE TO WATCH BIRDS.
(3RD ED)
617(TLS):25OCT74-1208
GOODERS, J. & J. BROCK. WHERE TO
WATCH BIRDS IN EUROPE. (2ND ED)
617(TLS):15NOV74-1297
GOODEY, B. WHERE YOU'RE AT.
E. WELSH, 617(TLS):15NOV74-1290
"THE GOODIES FILE."
D. THOMAS, 362:19&26DEC74-846
GOODISON, N. ORMOLU.
617(TLS):24MAY74-565
GOODKIND, H.K. VIOLIN ICONOGRAPHY
OF ANTONIO STRADIVARI 1644-1737.
617(TLS):21JUN74-678
LORD GOODMAN. NOT FOR THE RECORD.
R. FULLER, 364:JUN/JUL72-154
GOODMAN, A. THE LOYAL CONSPIRACY.
J.T. ROSENTHAL, 589:OCT73-741
GOODMAN, J. & P. PRINGLE, EDS. THE
TRIAL OF RUTH ELLIS.
617(TLS):26APR74-455
GOODMAN, K.S., ED. THE PSYCHOLIN-
GUISTIC NATURE OF THE READING PRO-
CESS.
M.S. MIRON, 353:1JUL72-94
GOODMAN, N. LANGUAGES OF ART.*
A. BARNES, 513:SPRING-SUMMER/
FALL-WINTER71-330
GOODMAN, P. ADAM & HIS WORKS. GROW-
ING UP ABSURD. FIVE YEARS. HOME-
SPUN OF OATMEAL GRAY.
H. LOMAS, 364:APR/MAY73-152
GOODMAN, P. COLLECTED POEMS.
H. CARRUTH, 441:3MAR74-6
H. SHAPIRO, 441:2FEB74-27
GOODMAN, P. SPEAKING & LANGUAGE.*
R.C. NEWTON, 128(CE):DEC72-425
P. POLSON, 648:JUN72-57
GOODMAN, R. - SEE ESCOTT, M.
GOODRICH, D.L. ART FAKES IN AMERICA.
A. FRANKENSTEIN, 55:DEC73-34
GOODRICH, L. EDWARD HOPPER.*
J. REISS, 584(SWR):WINTER73-VII
GOODRICH, L. REGINALD MARSH. RAPH-
AEL SOYER.
A. FRANKENSTEIN, 55:JAN73-13
GOODRICH, N.L. CHARLES OF ORLEANS.
T. STEMMLER, 38:BAND90HEFT3-386
GOODRICH, N.L. GIONO.*
639(VQR):AUTUMN73-CLIV
GOODSELL, C.T. AMERICAN CORPORA-
TIONS & PERUVIAN POLITICS.
M. DEAS, 617(TLS):29NOV74-1340
GOODWIN, D.W. TEXT-RESTORATION METH-
ODS IN CONTEMPORARY U.S.A. BIBLI-
CAL SCHOLARSHIP.
M. DAHOOD, 318(JAOS):JAN-MAR72-
184
GOODWIN, G. A HISTORY OF OTTOMAN
ARCHITECTURE.*
S. RUNCIMAN, 46:OCT72-256

GOODWIN, R.N. THE AMERICAN CONDI-
TION.
B. BROWER, 441:12MAY74-3
C. LEHMANN-HAUPT, 441:18MAR74-33
N.W. POLSBY, 231:JUN74-92
R. TODD, 61:MAR74-90
S.S. WOLIN, 453:2MAY74-10
GOODY, J., ED. THE CHARACTER OF KIN-
SHIP.
617(TLS):5APR74-362
GOODY, J. & S.J. TAMBIAH. BRIDE-
WEALTH & DOWRY.
617(TLS):5APR74-362
GOOLDEN, B. THE BROKEN ARC.
R. BLYTHE, 362:4APR74-444
GOOLDEN, B. MIRAGE.
617(TLS):11OCT74-1142
GOONERATNE, Y. JANE AUSTEN.
J.E.J., 191(ELN):SEP72(SUPP)-30
GOONETILEKE, H.A.I. A BIBLIOGRAPHY
OF CEYLON.
T.R. TRAUTMANN, 293(JAST):MAY72-
755
GOOSSE, M-T. UNE LECTURE DU "LAR-
RON" D'APOLLINAIRE.
S.I. LOCKERBIE, 208(FS):APR73-
225
NA GOPALEEN, M. THE POOR MOUTH.
S. MAITLAND, 362:18JUL74-93
GOPNIK, I. A THEORY OF STYLE &
RICHARDSON'S "CLARISSA."*
M. GOLDEN, 599:WINTER72-74
GORALI, M., G. ALMAGOR & M. BICK,
EDS. THE GOLDEN PEACOCK.
D. BEN-AMOS, 292(JAF):JAN-MAR72-
89
GORDAN, J.D. ARNOLD BENNETT.
L. TILLIER, 189(EA):JUL-SEP72-
443
GORDIMER, N. THE CONSERVATIONIST.
V. CUNNINGHAM, 617(TLS):1NOV74-
1217
J. MELLORS, 362:21NOV74-684
GORDIMER, N. LIVINGSTONE'S COMPAN-
IONS.
E. FEINSTEIN, 364:AUG/SEP72-157
639(VQR):SPRING72-LII
GORDON, A.L. RONSARD ET LA RHÉTOR-
IQUE.*
J. PINEAUX, 557(RSH):JUL-SEP72-
448
D. WILSON, 208(FS):JAN73-55
GORDON, A.W. DAME FLORA.
I. OGG, 617(TLS):29NOV74-1345
GORDON, C. THE GLORY OF HERA.*
J. LEWIS, 569(SR):WINTER73-185
639(VQR):SUMMER72-XCVIII
GORDON, C. THE SHORT FICTION OF
CAROLINE GORDON. (T.H. LANDESS,
ED)
A. BROWN, 569(SR):SPRING73-365
GORDON, C.H. RIDDLES IN HISTORY.
P. ADAMS, 61:APR74-120
GORDON, D.E. MODERN ART EXHIBITIONS
1900-1916.
617(TLS):23AUG74-899
GORDON, G. GIRL WITH RED HAIR.
V. CUNNINGHAM, 362:24JAN74-120
617(TLS):25JAN74-69
GORDON, G. & A. HAMILTON, EDS. FAC-
TIONS.
617(TLS):26APR74-433

GORDON, H.J., JR. HITLER & THE BEER
HALL PUTSCH.*
K.P. TAUBER, 639(VQR):WINTER73-
137
GORDON, I.A. - SEE GALT, J.
GORDON, I.A. - SEE MANSFIELD, K.
GORDON, I.L. THE DOUBLE SORROW OF
TROILUS.*
J.R. SIMON, 189(EA):APR-JUN72-
319
GORDON, P. THE VICTORIAN SCHOOL
MANAGER.
M. LASKI, 362:22AUG74-252
GORDON, R.L. THE RIVER GETS WIDER.
M. LEVIN, 441:20JAN74-24
442(NY):1APR74-123
GORE, A. LET THE GLORY OUT.
639(VQR):WINTER73-XXVIII
GORÉ, J-L. LA NOTION D'INDIFFÉRENCE
CHEZ FÉNELON ET SES SOURCES.
J. GRENIER, 542:APR-JUN72-198
GORE, K. L'IDÉE DE PROGRÈS DANS LA
PENSÉE DE RENAN.
D.G. CHARLTON, 208(FS):JUL73-349
J. POMMIER, 535(RHL):JAN-FEB72-
152
GORE, K. SARTRE: "LA NAUSÉE" & "LES
MOUCHES."
G. DANIELS, 208(FS):APR73-229
GORE, L. GAME COOKING.
617(TLS):10MAY74-508
GORE-BOOTH, P. WITH GREAT TRUTH &
RESPECT.
617(TLS):12APR74-383
GOREN, A.A. NEW YORK JEWS & THE
QUEST FOR COMMUNITY.
D.J. ELAZAR, 390:JAN72-76
GORER, R. LIVING TRADITION IN THE
GARDEN.
C. SYKES, 617(TLS):13DEC74-1421
GORES, J. DEAD SKIP.
N. CALLENDAR, 441:11AUG74-12
617(TLS):1FEB74-116
GORES, J. FINAL NOTICE.*
N. CALLENDAR, 441:10NOV74-46
617(TLS):6SEP74-960
GORES, J. INTERFACE.
N. CALLENDAR, 441:19MAY74-41
GOREY, E. THE UNSTRUNG HARP.
617(TLS):13DEC74-1401
GÖRGEMANNS, H. UNTERSUCHUNGEN ZU
PLUTARCHS DIALOG, DE FACIE IN ORBE
LUNAE.*
F.H. SANDBACH, 123:MAR73-32
GÖRGEY, L. BONN'S EASTERN POLICY,
1964-1971.
C.F. SMITH, 32:MAR73-183
GORKI, M. FRAGMENTS FROM MY DIARY.
(M. BUDBERG, TRANS)
K. FITZLYON, 364:OCT/NOV72-155
GORKI, M. THE LIFE OF A USELESS MAN.
(M. BUDBERG, TRANS)
K. FITZLYON, 364:OCT/NOV72-155
F. HOLTZMAN, 550(RUSR):JUL72-314
502(PRS):SPRING72-92
GORMAN, J.B. KEFAUVER.
639(VQR):WINTER72-XI
GORNI, G. - SEE CASTIGLIONE, B.
GORNY, L. DIDEROT.
481(PQ):JUL72-669
GORRA, M. NIEVO TRA NOI.
400(MLN):JAN72-163

135

GÓRSKI, K. & S. HRABEK, EDS. SŁOW-
NIK JĘZYKA ADAMA MICHIEWICZA.
  A. SLUPSKI, 182:VOL25#19/20-655
GOSE, E.B., JR. IMAGINATION INDULG-
ED.*
  M. ALLOTT, 637(VS):DEC72-240
  J. HALPERIN, 594:FALL72-531
  G.M. HARVEY, 150(DR):SUMMER72-
  318
  M. STEIG, 529(QQ):WINTER72-566
  G.B. TENNYSON, 445(NCF):DEC72-
  365
GOSEBRUCH, M. & OTHERS. GIOTTO DI
BONDONE.
  C. GILBERT, 56:WINTER72-427
GOSLING, J.C.B. PLATO.
  G.E.R. LLOYD, 617(TLS):23AUG74-
  905
GOSLING, J.C.B. PLEASURE & DESIRE.*
  W.P. ALSTON, 479(PHQ):JAN72-86
  R. CAMPBELL, 482(PHR):JAN72-116
GOSLING, N. GUSTAVE DORÉ.
  P. ADAMS, 61:APR74-120
  617(TLS):3MAY74-484
GOSNELL, C.F. SPANISH PERSONAL
NAMES.
  D.P. HINKLE, 424:DEC72-294
GOSSEN, C.T. FRANZÖSISCHE SKRIPTA-
STUDIEN.*
  M.S. LA DU, 545(RPH):NOV72-419
GOSSEN, C.T. GRAMMAIRE DE L'ANCIEN
PICARD.*
  B. FOSTER, 208(FS):APR73-246
GOSSMAN, L. FRENCH SOCIETY & CUL-
TURE.
  D.L. ANDERSON, 568(SCN):SPRING73-
  22
GOTHOT-MERSCH, C. - SEE FLAUBERT, G.
GOTTESMAN, R. & S. BENNETT, EDS.
ART & ERROR.*
  J. KINSLEY, 354:MAR72-56
GOTTLIEB, G. THE LOGIC OF CHOICE.
  D.P. CUSHMAN, 480(P&R):SPRING72-
  119
GOTTLIEB, N. & R. CHAPMAN - SEE TUR-
GENEV, I.S.
GOTTMANN, J. THE SIGNIFICANCE OF
TERRITORY.
  639(VQR):AUTUMN73-CLXXI
GOTTSCHALK, H.L., B. SPULER & H. KÄH-
LER. DIE KULTUR DES ISLAMS.
  S.D. GOITEIN, 589:OCT73-754
GOTTSCHALK, L.A. & G.C. GLESER. THE
MEASUREMENT OF PSYCHOLOGICAL
STATES THROUGH THE CONTENT ANALY-
SIS OF VERBAL BEHAVIOR.
  J. PRŮCHA, 353:15AUG72-103
GOTTSCHALK, L.A., C.N. WINGET & G.C.
GLESER. MANUAL OF INSTRUCTIONS
FOR USING THE GOTTSCHALK-GLESER
CONTENT ANALYSIS SCALES.
  J. PRŮCHA, 353:15AUG72-103
GOTTSCHALK, S. THE EMERGENCE OF
CHRISTIAN SCIENCE IN AMERICAN
RELIGIOUS LIFE.
  617(TLS):16AUG74-876
GOUBERT, P. L'ANCIEN RÉGIME. (VOL 2)
  C.B.A. BEHRENS, 453:21FEB74-6
GOUDIE, E. WOMAN OF LABRADOR. (D.
ZIMMERLY, ED)
  W. MITCHINSON, 99:OCT74-41

GOUGENHEIM, G. ÉTUDES DE GRAMMAIRE
ET DE VOCABULAIRE FRANÇAIS.*
  J. DARBELNET, 207(FR):OCT71-238
  A. ESKÉNAZI, 209(FM):OCT72-358
  P. RICARD, 208(FS):JAN73-111
  N.B. SPECTOR, 405(MP):NOV72-181
GOUGH, B.M. THE ROYAL NAVY & THE
NORTHWEST COAST OF NORTH AMERICA.
  R.A. PIERCE, 529(QQ):WINTER72-
  557
  P.B. WAITE, 150(DR):AUTUMN72-493
GOUGH, M. THE ORIGINS OF CHRISTIAN
ART.
  P. BROWN, 453:3OCT74-3
GOULD, J. KANGAROOS.
  617(TLS):19JUL74-772
GOULD, J.B. THE PHILOSOPHY OF
CHRYSIPPUS.*
  A.A. LONG, 123:DEC73-214
  G. WATSON, 479(PHQ):JUL72-268
GOULD, J.D. THE GREAT DEBASEMENT.
  S.A. BURRELL, 551(RENQ):SUMMER
  72-221
GOULD, L. FINAL ANALYSIS.
  C. LEHMANN-HAUPT, 441:2APR74-43
  I. OWENS, 441:14APR74-7
  R. TODD, 61:MAY74-127
  442(NY):22APR74-154
GOULD, L. NECESSARY OBJECTS.
  W.H. PRITCHARD, 249(HUDR):SPRING
  73-232
  617(TLS):12APR74-385
GOULD, L.L. PROGRESSIVES & PROHIBI-
TIONISTS.
  L.C. MILAZZO, 584(SWR):AUTUMN73-
  370
GOULD, P. & R. WHITE. MENTAL MAPS.
  617(TLS):14JUN74-630
GOULD, S.H. RUSSIAN FOR THE MATHE-
MATICIAN.
  E. HEWITT, 32:JUN73-432
GOULDNER, A.W. FOR SOCIOLOGY.
  P. STARR, 441:8SEP74-10
  617(TLS):11JAN74-37
GOULIANE, G.I. HEGEL OU LA PHILOSO-
PHIE DE LA CRISE.
  E. DIET, 542:JUL-SEP72-367
GOUNELLE, A. L'ENTRETIEN DE PASCAL
AVEC M. DE SACY.
  J-F. THOMAS, 542:APR-JUN72-220
GOW, A.S.F. & D.L. PAGE. THE GAR-
LAND OF PHILIP.
  G. GIANGRANDE, 123:DEC73-135
GOWRIE, G. A POSTCARD FROM DON GIO-
VANNI.*
  G. EWART, 364:DEC72/JAN73-132
  J. GALASSI, 491:NOV73-113
  639(VQR):SPRING73-LXI
GOYANES, M.B. - SEE UNDER BAQUERO
GOYANES, M.
GOYEN, W. SELECTED WRITINGS OF WIL-
LIAM GOYEN. COME, THE RESTORER.
  S.A. GRAU, 441:3NOV74-73
GOYTISOLO, J. COUNT JULIAN.
  C. FUENTES, 441:5MAY74-5
  V.S. PRITCHETT, 442(NY):7OCT74-
  173
  M. WOOD, 453:8AUG74-40
GOZENPUD, A. - SEE STRAVINSKY, I.
GRAB, W. & U. FRIESEL. NOCH IST
DEUTSCHLAND NICHT VERLOREN.*
  L. BORNSCHEUER, 406:SUMMER73-176
  W. FEUDEL, 654(WB):4/1972-183
GRABER, H. - SEE DÖBLIN, A.

GRACIÁN, B. AGUDEZA Y ARTE DE IN-
GENIO. (E. CORREA CALDERÓN, ED)
   M.Z. HAFTER, 240(HR):SUMMER72-
   334
GRADE, A. - SEE FROST, R. & E.
GRADE, C. THE AGUNAH.
   E. WIESEL, 441:1SEP74-5
GRADON, P. FORM & STYLE IN EARLY
ENGLISH LITERATURE.
   D. MEHL, 182:VOL25#7/8-222
   J.D.A. OGILVY, 191(ELN):DEC72-
   140
   E.G. STANLEY, 677:VOL3-265
   617(TLS):8NOV74-1265
GRADY, J. SIX DAYS OF THE CONDOR.
   N. CALLENDAR, 441:23JUN74-33
GRAF, A. L'ANGLOMANIA E L'INFLUSSO
INGLESE IN ITALIA NEL SECOLO XVIII.
   P.K., 566:AUTUMN72-10
GRAF, H., ED. DER KLEINE SALON.*
   C.E. WILLIAMS, 220(GL&L):JUL73-
   334
GRAF, L.P. & R.W. HASKINS - SEE JOHN-
SON, A.
GRAF, M. COMPOSER & CRITIC.
   M. PETERSON, 470:MAY72-32
GRAFF, G. POETIC STATEMENT & CRITI-
CAL DOGMA.*
   N.S. POBURKO, 150(DR):AUTUMN72-
   519
   V.E. VOGT, 405(MP):MAY73-372
GRAGG, G.B. - SEE UNDER SJÖBERG, Å.W.
& E. BERGMANN
GRAHAM, A. THE END OF RELIGION.
   F. KEENAN, 363:MAY72-102
GRAHAM, A. EYELIDS OF MORNING.
   J. MC ELROY, 441:26MAY74-6
GRAHAM, D. CASSINO.
   617(TLS):13SEP74-975
GRAHAM, D. KEITH DOUGLAS 1920-1944.
   617(TLS):7JUN74-600
GRAHAM, H. PASSPORT TO EARTH.
   J. SAUNDERS, 565:VOL13#3-75
GRAHAM, I. GOETHE & LESSING.
   617(TLS):15MAR74-254
GRAHAM, I. SCHILLER'S DRAMA.
   617(TLS):20SEP74-1021
GRAHAM, J. BLOODY PASSAGE.
   617(TLS):20DEC74-1437
GRAHAM, L.R. SCIENCE & PHILOSOPHY
IN THE SOVIET UNION.*
   J.P. SCANLAN, 32:DEC73-788
   617(TLS):22FEB74-175
GRAHAM, M. THE NOTEBOOKS OF MARTHA
GRAHAM.*
   617(TLS):18OCT74-1165
GRAHAM, S.F. GOVERNMENT & MISSION
EDUCATION IN NORTHERN NIGERIA 1900-
1919.
   P.C.C. EVANS, 69:APR72-168
GRAHAM, V.E. - SEE PERNETTE DE GUIL-
LET
GRAINGER, J.H. CHARACTER & STYLE IN
ENGLISH POLITICS.
   P.A. SLACK, 447(N&Q):NOV72-437
"GRAMMAIRIENS ET THÉORICIENS FRAN-
ÇAIS DE LA RENAISSANCE À LA FIN
DE L'ÉPOQUE CLASSIQUE (1521-1715)."
   R. RICKARD, 208(FS):JUL73-320
GRAMSCI, A. LETTERATURA E VITA
NAZIONALE.
   F. SPACCIA, 275(IQ):FALL/WINTER
   72-130

GRAMSCI, A. SELECTIONS FROM THE
PRISON NOTEBOOKS OF ANTONIO GRAM-
SCI. (Q. HOARE & G.N. SMITH, EDS
& TRANS) LETTERS FROM PRISON. (L.
LAWNER, ED & TRANS)
   E.J. HOBSBAWM, 453:4APR74-39
GRAN, U. & U-B. LAGERROTH, EDS. PER-
SPECTIV PÅ TEATER.
   B. FOWLER, 172(EDDA):1972/3-190
GRAÑA, C. FACT & SYMBOL.*
   290(JAAC):SUMMER72-568
   639(VQR):SUMMER72-CIV
GRANAROLO, J. D'ENNIUS À CATULLE.*
   E.D. FRANCIS, 24:WINTER73-386
GRANATSTEIN, J.L. & R.D. CUFF, EDS.
WAR & SOCIETY IN NORTH AMERICA.
   D.M. SCHURMAN, 529(QQ):AUTUMN72-
   432
"GRAND LAROUSSE DE LA LANGUE FRAN-
ÇAISE." (L. GUILBERT, R. LAGANE
& G. NIOBEY, EDS)
   J. DARBELNET, 207(FR):MAR72-887
   F. HELGORSKY, 209(FM):APR72-166
"THE GRANDES HEURES OF JEAN, DUKE OF
BERRY."* (BRITISH TITLE: LES
GRANDES HEURES DE JEAN DUC DE BER-
RY.) (M. THOMAS, ED)
   J.G. PLANTE, 363:MAY72-104
   E.P. SPENCER, 589:APR73-415
GRANEL, G. L'ÉQUIVOQUE ONTOLOGIQUE
DE LA PENSÉE KANTIENNE.
   R. MALTER, 342:BAND63HEFT3-393
GRANGE, H. LES IDÉES DE NECKER.
   617(TLS):6SEP74-944
GRANGER, G.G. - SEE WITTGENSTEIN, L.
"GRANGER'S INDEX TO POETRY." (6TH
ED) (W.J. SMITH, ED)
   617(TLS):29MAR74-348
GRANIER, J. - SEE NIETZSCHE, F.W.
GRANJARD, H. - SEE TURGENEV, I.S.
GRANT, D. REALISM.
   F.W.J. HEMMINGS, 208(FS):OCT73-
   465
GRANT, E., ED. NICOLE ORESME & THE
KINEMATICS OF CIRCULAR MOTION.
   C. WILSON, 589:JUL73-569
GRANT, E. PHYSICAL SCIENCE IN THE
MIDDLE AGES.
   N. SWERDLOW, 589:APR73-364
GRANT, G. TIME AS HISTORY.
   W.R. MATHIE, 150(DR):WINTER72/73-
   684
GRANT, M. THE ANCIENT HISTORIANS.*
   H. MUSURILLO, 613:SPRING72-153
GRANT, M. ANCIENT HISTORY ATLAS.
   E.S. STAVELEY, 303:VOL92-234
GRANT, M. HORROR.
   V. RADIN, 617(TLS):13DEC74-1419
GRANT, M. THE JEWS IN THE ROMAN
WORLD.
   617(TLS):29MAR74-321
GRANT, M. THE ROMAN FORUM.* (FRENCH
TITLE: LE FORUM ROMAIN.)
   D. REUILLARD, 98:MAY72-483
GRANT, R.M. AUGUSTUS TO CONSTAN-
TINE.*
   E.S. GRUEN, 318(JAOS):JAN-MAR72-
   190
GRANT, R.M. - SEE THEOPHILUS
GRANVILLE-BARKER, H. PREFACES TO
SHAKESPEARE. (VOL 6) (E. MOORE,
ED)
   G.W. KNIGHT, 617(TLS):26JUL74-
   794

GRASS, G. FROM THE DIARY OF A SNAIL.
D.J. ENRIGHT, 362:6JUN74-737
GRASS, N. CUSANUS UND DAS VOLKSTUM
DER BERGE.
L. CARLEN, 182:VOL25#19/20-698
GRASSI, L. TEORICI E STORIA DELLA
CRITICA D'ARTE. (VOL 1)
M. BAXANDALL, 54:MAR72-106
GRASSO, S. IL GIUOCO DELLA MEMORIA.
617(TLS):5APR74-371
GRAU, S.A. THE WIND SHIFTING WEST.*
S. CLAPP, 617(TLS):15NOV74-1278
GRAUBARD, S.R. KISSINGER.*
639(VQR):AUTUMN73-CLIV
GRAUPE, H.M. DIE ENTSTEHUNG DES
MODERNEN JUDENTUMS.
W. DE SCHMIDT, 53(AGP):BAND54
HEFT2-211
GRAVA, A. A STRUCTURAL INQUIRY INTO
THE SYMBOLIC REPRESENTATION OF
IDEAS.*
E. MARTIN, JR., 206:NOV72-268
E.P. NOLAN, 353:1NOV72-82
GRAVES, J. HARD SCRABBLE.
E. HOAGLAND, 441:19MAY74-2
E. WEEKS, 61:AUG74-88
442(NY):19AUG74-91
GRAVES, J.C. THE CONCEPTUAL FOUNDA-
TIONS OF CONTEMPORARY RELATIVITY
THEORY.*
J. EARMAN, 479(PHQ):OCT72-373
M. SACHS, 484(PPR):SEP72-122
GRAVES, R. DIFFICULT QUESTIONS,
EASY ANSWERS.*
R. BLY, 441:17MAR74-6
GRAVES, R. POEMS 1970-1972.*
J. GALASSI, 491:NOV73-113
W.H. PRITCHARD, 249(HUDR):AUTUMN
73-588
R.I. SCOTT, 648:JAN73-80
GRAVES, R. THE SPIRITUAL QUIXOTE OR
THE SUMMER'S RAMBLE OF MR. GEOFF-
REY WILDGOOSE. (C. TRACY, ED)
A. PARREAUX, 189(EA):JUL-SEP72-
434
GRAVES, R.L. THE PLATINUM BULLET.
N. CALLENDAR, 441:24NOV74-39
GRAVIL, R., ED. SWIFT: GULLIVER'S
TRAVELS.
617(TLS):21JUN74-679
GRAY, C. - SEE "HANS RICHTER BY HANS
RICHTER"
GRAY, C.S. CANADIAN DEFENCE PRIOR-
ITIES.
L. HERTZMAN, 99:APR74-33
GRAY, D. THEME & IMAGES IN THE MEDI-
EVAL ENGLISH RELIGIOUS LYRIC.
S.A. FARMER, 67:NOV73-288
A.S. MISKIMIN, 676(YR):WINTER73-
299
639(VQR):WINTER73-XXV
GRAY, E.A. THE KILLING TIME.
639(VQR):SPRING73-LXXXV
GRAY, H.P. THE ECONOMICS OF BUSI-
NESS INVESTMENT ABROAD.
M. LIPTON, 617(TLS):2AUG74-830
GRAY, J. JOHNSON'S SERMONS.
E.D. MACKERNESS, 402(MLR):JUL73-
638
GRAY, J.M. TENNYSON'S DOPPELGANGER,
"BALIN & BALAN."
C. FALL, 637(VS):SEP72-110
M.G. WIEBE, 529(QQ):SPRING72-118

GRAY, N. THE SILENT MAJORITY.
617(TLS):1FEB74-100
GRAY, R. FRANZ KAFKA.
R. PASCAL, 617(TLS):7JUN74-611
GRAY, R. & D. BIRMINGHAM, EDS. PRE-
COLONIAL AFRICAN TRADE.
R.G. ABRAHAMS, 69:APR72-172
GRAYEFF, F. ARISTOTLE & HIS SCHOOL.
617(TLS):9AUG74-850
GRAYEFF, F. KANT'S THEORETICAL PHIL-
OSOPHY.
D.P. DRYER, 482(PHR):JUL72-389
K. OEDINGEN, 342:BAND63HEFT1-129
GRAYMONT, B. THE IROQUOIS IN THE
AMERICAN REVOLUTION.
W.R. JACOBS, 656(WMQ):OCT72-652
GRAYSON, C. CINQUE SAGGI SU DANTE.
J.R. WOODHOUSE, 402(MLR):JUL73-
666
GRAZZINI, G. SOLZHENITSYN.*
K. FITZLYON, 364:AUG/SEP73-137
"GREAT SOVIET ENCYCLOPEDIA." (3RD
ED) (VOL 1)
T. SHABAD, 441:14JAN74-25
GREBE, P. & W. MÜLLER, COMPS. WAS
BEDEUTET DAS?*
H.T. BETTERIDGE, 220(GL&L):OCT72-
65
DE GREEF, E. L'HOMME ET SON JUGE.
C. SCHUWER, 542:OCT-DEC72-462
GREELEY, A.M. BUILDING COALITIONS.
R. REEVES, 441:24FEB74-5
GREELEY, A.M. THE NEW AGENDA.*
W. SHEED, 453:7MAR74-18
GREEN, A. MOTHER OF HER COUNTRY.
M. LEVIN, 441:10MAR74-10
GREEN, A. ONLY A MINER.
W.H. JANSEN, 582(SFQ):DEC72-403
GREEN, A.G. REGIONAL ASPECTS OF
CANADA'S ECONOMIC GROWTH.
R.I. MC ALLISTER, 529(QQ):WINTER
72-542
GREEN, B.K. SOME MORE HORSE TRADIN'.
W. GARD, 584(SWR):WINTER73-V
GREEN, D. QUEEN ANNE.
H.T. DICKINSON, 566:SPRING72-84
GREEN, D. BLENHEIM.
A. BRETT-JAMES, 617(TLS):13DEC74-
1425
GREEN, D. ULYSSES BOUND.*
K. STEWART, 71(ALS):MAY74-320
GREEN, D.E. LAND OF THE UNDERGROUND
RAIN.
W. GARD, 584(SWR):AUTUMN73-361
GREEN, F.M. THE RÔLE OF THE YANKEE
IN THE OLD SOUTH.
639(VQR):WINTER73-XXXIV
GREEN, G.D. FINANCE & ECONOMIC DE-
VELOPMENT IN THE OLD SOUTH.
M.E. REED, 14:JUL/OCT72-405
GREEN, H. GUIDE TO THE BATTLEFIELDS
OF BRITAIN & IRELAND.
617(TLS):15MAR74-260
GREEN, J., ED. CAMERA WORK.
H. KRAMER, 441:21APR74-3
GREEN, J. OEUVRES COMPLÈTES. (VOL
3) (J. PETIT, ED)
617(TLS):7JUN74-607
GREEN, J., ED. THE SNAPSHOT.
S. SCHWARTZ, 441:1DEC74-101
GREEN, J.R. & N.A POULIN. FRENCH
PHONOLOGY FOR TEACHERS.
R.W. NEWMAN, 207(FR):DEC71-551

GREEN, M. THE VON RICHTHOFEN SIS-
TERS.
C. LEHMANN-HAUPT, 441:22FEB74-37
G. LEVINE, 441:10MAR74-1
A. QUINTON, 617(TLS):13SEP74-977
442(NY):25MAR74-142
GREEN, O.H. THE LITERARY MIND OF
MEDIEVAL & RENAISSANCE SPAIN.*
(J.E. KELLER, ED)
A.V. EBERSOLE, 241:SEP72-70
V. MASSON DE GÓMEZ, 545(RPH):
FEB73-628
GREEN, P. ARMADA FROM ATHENS.*
K.J. DOVER, 487:AUTUMN72-297
GREEN, R.L. & W. HOOPER. C.S. LEWIS.
J. BAYLEY, 617(TLS):12JUL74-747
P. BEER, 362:11JUL74-61
442(NY):4NOV74-210
GREEN, R.P.H. THE POETRY OF PAULIN-
US OF NOLA.
A. ERNOUT, 555:VOL46FASC2-348
GREEN, W.M. THE SALISBURY MANU-
SCRIPT.
N. CALLENDAR, 441:13JAN74-12
442(NY):4MAR74-115
GREENBAUM, S. STUDIES IN ENGLISH
ADVERBIAL USAGE.*
J. MACHÁČEK, 353:JUN72-104
P.A. SCHREIBER, 361:VOL29#3/4-
347
S.A. THOMPSON, 350:JUN73-489
GREENBAUM, S. VERB-INTENSIFIER COL-
LOCATIONS IN ENGLISH.*
J.W. NEY, 353:JUN72-108
GREENBERG, J. RITES OF PASSAGE.*
S. O'CONNELL, 418(MR):WINTER73-
190
GREENBERG, J.H. & OTHERS. LINGUIS-
TICS IN THE 1970'S.
R.R. BUTTERS, 35(AS):SPRING-
SUMMER70-122
GREENBERGER, E.B. ARTHUR HUGH
CLOUGH.*
K. ALLOTT, 541(RES):FEB72-94
GREENBLATT, S.J. SIR WALTER RALEGH.
J.H. PLUMB, 441:10MAR74-5
GREENE, B. BILLION DOLLAR BABY.
C. LEHMANN-HAUPT, 441:14NOV74-51
J. ROCKWELL, 441:22DEC74-10
442(NY):9DEC74-194
GREENE, G. THE HONORARY CONSUL.*
R. DE FEO, 249(HUDR):WINTER73/74-
783
A. ROTHBERG, 584(SWR):AUTUMN73-
VIII
GREENE, G. THE PLEASURE-DOME.*
(J.R. TAYLOR, ED)
P. BAILEY, 364:JUN/JUL73-157
GREENE, G. LORD ROCHESTER'S MONKEY.
P. ADAMS, 61:OCT74-118
A. BROYARD, 441:10SEP74-45
W. CLEMONS, 441:15SEP74-3
V.S. PRITCHETT, 453:3OCT74-17
G. STEINER, 442(NY):28OCT74-185
J. SUTHERLAND, 617(TLS):20SEP74-
992
S. TROTTER, 362:24OCT74-549
GREENE, G. A SORT OF LIFE.*
R.M. KEILS, 150(DR):SPRING72-159
R. LÓPEZ ORTEGA, 202(FMOD):JUN72-
340
P. WOLFE, 502(PRS):SPRING72-83
639(VQR):WINTER72-VIII

GREENE, G. TRIPLE PURSUIT!
P. WOLFE, 502(PRS):SPRING72-83
GREENE, H., ED. THE CROOKED COUN-
TIES.
617(TLS):18JAN74-61
GREENE, J. PSYCHOLINGUISTICS.*
F. SMITH, 320(CJL):VOL18#1-87
GREENE, T.M. RABELAIS.*
A. GLAUSER, 551(RENQ):AUTUMN72-
340
GREENE, T.P. AMERICA'S HEROES.*
B. POLI, 189(EA):JUL-SEP72-453
GREENE, T.W. THE DESCENT FROM HEAV-
EN.
D.G. FRICKE, 568(SCN):FALL-WIN-
TER73-75
GREENFELD, J. & P. MAZURSKY. HARRY
& TONTO.
A. BROYARD, 441:6JUN74-41
M. LEVIN, 441:19MAY74-40
GREENFIELD, J. WILHELM REICH VS.
THE U.S.A.
P. ADAMS, 61:AUG74-90
N.G. HALE, JR., 441:11AUG74-2
GREENFIELD, R. S.T.P.
J. ROCKWELL, 441:27JUL74-27
GREENFIELD, T.N. THE INDUCTION IN
ELIZABETHAN DRAMA.
C.R. FORKER, 405(MP):AUG72-63
A. GRIFFIN, 551(RENQ):SUMMER72-
226
GREENHALGH, P.A.L. EARLY GREEK WAR-
FARE.
617(TLS):21JUN74-672
GREENHOOD, D. THE WRITER ON HIS OWN.
W. LEUBA, 584(SWR):SPRING73-184
GREENLEE, D. PEIRCE'S CONCEPT OF
SIGN.
617(TLS):19APR74-412
GREENWAY, J. DOWN AMONG THE WILD
MEN.
617(TLS):15MAR74-263
GREENWAY, J., ED. FOLKLORE OF THE
GREAT WEST.
R.M. DORSON, 292(JAF):OCT-DEC72-
383
GREER, S. THE URBANE VIEW.
639(VQR):WINTER73-XXXIX
GREGOR, A. SELECTED POEMS.*
P. DACEY, 502(PRS):WINTER72/73-
366
GREGOR, I. & W. STEIN, EDS. THE
PROSE FOR GOD.
617(TLS):12APR74-397
GREGOROVIUS, F. ROME & MEDIEVAL
CULTURE.* (K.F. MORRISON, ED)
A.W. GODFREY, 363:MAY72-100
LADY GREGORY. COOLE. (C. SMYTHE,
ED)
R. SKELTON, 376:JAN72-132
LADY GREGORY, ED & TRANS. GODS &
FIGHTING MEN.*
E. ETTLINGER, 203:WINTER72-340
LADY GREGORY, COMP. VISIONS & BE-
LIEFS IN THE WEST OF IRELAND.*
(2ND ED)
E. ETTLINGER, 203:SUMMER72-171
POPE GREGORY VII. THE EPISTOLAE
VAGANTES OF POPE GREGORY VII.*
(H.E.J. COWDREY, ED & TRANS)
C.R. CHENEY, 382(MAE):1973/3-261

SAINT GREGORY OF NYSSA. GREGOR VON
NYSSA, DIE GROSSE KATECHETISCHE
REDE. (J. BARBEL, ED)
A. KEMMER, 182:VOL25#9/10-266
GREGORY, P. SOCIALIST & NONSOCIAL-
IST INDUSTRIALIZATION PATTERNS.
G. GROSSMAN, 550(RUSR):JAN72-95
GREGORY, R. THE TROMBONE.
A. LUMSDEN, 415:JUN73-602
J.A.W., 410(M&L):JUL73-368
GREGORY, R.G. INDIA & EAST AFRICA.
G.W. HARTWIG, 579(SAQ):WINTER73-
165
GREGORY, R.L. CONCEPTS & MECHANISMS
OF PERCEPTION.
T.G.R. BOWER, 617(TLS):6DEC74-
1362
GREGORY, R.L. & E.H. GOMBRICH.
ILLUSION IN NATURE & ART.
617(TLS):22MAR74-302
GREGORY, T. ANIMA MUNDI, LA FILOSO-
FIA DI GUGLIELMO DI CONCHES E LA
SCUOLA DI CHARTRES.
E. NAMER, 542:JAN-MAR72-85
GREIFF, C.M., ED. LOST AMERICA.*
505:JAN72-142
GREINER, W.F. STUDIEN ZUR ENTSTE-
HUNG DER ENGLISCHEN ROMANTHEORIE
AN DER WENDE ZUM 18. JAHRHUNDERT.*
L. FIETZ, 38:BAND90HEFT1/2-239
R. SCHÖWERLING, 72:BAND210HEFT
4/6-391
GRENDEL, F. BEAUMARCHAIS, OU LA
CALOMNIE.
617(TLS):19APR74-415
GRENE, M. SARTRE.
617(TLS):11OCT74-1136
GRENET, A. & C. JODRY. LA LITTÉRA-
TURE DE SENTIMENT AU XVIIIE SIÈCLE.
A.D. HYTIER, 481(PQ):JUL72-610
GRENET, P. LE THOMISME.
A. FOREST, 542:JAN-MAR72-72
GRENIER, J. RÉFLEXIONS SUR QUELQUES
ÉCRIVAINS.
617(TLS):16AUG74-884
GRENIER, R. AVANT UND GUERRE.
C. FRANÇOIS, 207(FR):DEC71-473
GRENVILLE, J.A.S. THE MAJOR INTER-
NATIONAL TREATIES 1914-1973.
617(TLS):19JUL74-772
GRETTON, P. CRISIS CONVOY.
617(TLS):23AUG74-912
GRÉVIN, J. CÉSAR. (E.S. GINSBERG,
ED)
W.J. BECK, 207(FR):FEB72-743
R.M. BURGESS, 551(RENQ):WINTER
72-458
F. GRAY, 399(MLJ):NOV72-470
J. PINEAUX, 557(RSH):OCT-DEC72-
605
GRÉVISSE, M. PROBLÈMES DE LANGAGE.*
(VOL 4)
F.M. JENKINS, 545(RPH):MAY73-707
GRÉVISSE, M. PROBLÈMES DE LANGAGE.*
(VOL 5)
G. GOUGENHEIM, 209(FM):APR72-173
GREWAL, J.S. MUSLIM RULE IN INDIA.
F.F. CONLON, 293(JAST):FEB72-431
H.K. SHERWANI, 273(IC):JUL72-275
GREY, H. & G. STUART, EDS. THE VIC-
TORIANS BY THE SEA.
F. KERMODE, 453:30MAY74-6

GREY, I. THE HORIZON HISTORY OF
RUSSIA.* (W. BUEHR, ED)
N. ANDREYEV, 32:JUN73-370
GRIBBIN, J. & S. PLAGEMANN. THE
JUPITER EFFECT.
617(TLS):27DEC74-1471
GRIBBIN, W. THE CHURCHES MILITANT.*
639(VQR):SPRING73-LXXXIII
GRICE, G.R. THE GROUNDS OF MORAL
JUDGEMENT.
M. SCHUMAKER, 154:JUN72-309
GRIECO, V. GENESI E SVILUPPO DEL
CRITICISMO.
K. OEDINGEN, 342:BAND63HEFT3-388
GRIEG, E.H. GRIEG THE WRITER. (VOL
1) (B. KORTSEN, ED)
J. HORTON, 415:SEP73-903
GRIEG, E.H. GRIEG THE WRITER. (VOL
2) (B. KORTSEN, ED)
J.H., 410(M&L):JUL73-351
GRIERSON, E. KING OF TWO WORLDS.
617(TLS):11OCT74-1139
GRIESBACH, H. DEUTSCH FÜR FORTGE-
SCHRITTENE.
M. TRIESCH & E. WERNER, 221(GQ):
MAY72-551
GRIESER, H. DIE SOWJETPRESSE ÜBER
DEUTSCHLAND IN EUROPA 1922-32.
P. KOVALEVSKY, 182:VOL25#23/24-
889
GRIEST, G.L. MUDIE'S CIRCULATING
LIBRARY & THE VICTORIAN NOVEL.*
H. LUKE, 502(PRS):SPRING72-78
V.L. TOLLERS, 577(SHR):SPRING72-
201
GRIEVE, M. A MODERN HERBAL. (MRS.
C.F. LEYELL, ED)
617(TLS):26JUL74-810
GRIEVE, M. & A. SCOTT - SEE MAC DIAR-
MID, H.
GRIFFIN, C.C., ED. LATIN AMERICA.
A.B. EDWARDS, 37:APR72-43
GRIFFIN, J. - SEE PESSOA, F.
GRIFFIN, R. CORONATION OF THE POET.*
R.C. LA CHARITÉ, 207(FR):OCT71-
277
W.L. WILEY, 546(RR):DEC72-294
GRIFFIN, R.A. HIGH BAROQUE CULTURE
& THEATRE IN VIENNA.
G. KAHAN, 583:SUMMER73-403
GRIFFING, R.P., JR. THE ART OF THE
KOREAN POTTER.
J.E. KIDDER, JR., 54:MAR72-77
GRIFFITH, A.J. PETER TAYLOR.
D.B. KESTERSON, 573(SSF):WINTER
72-113
GRIFFITH, D.W. THE MAN WHO INVENTED
HOLLYWOOD. (J. HART, ED)
R. GIROUX, 200:MAY72-299
GRIFFITH, J. & L.E. MINER, EDS. THE
FIRST LINCOLNLAND CONFERENCE ON
DIALECTOLOGY.
G. BAUER, 72:BAND210HEFT1/3-151
W. VIERECK, 430(NS):AUG72-491
GRIFFITH, P. MY STILLNESS.*
639(VQR):SPRING73-LVI
GRIFFITH, T. HOW TRUE.
M. ARNOLD, 441:8JUL74-27
GRIFFITH, T.G. ITALIAN WRITERS &
THE "ITALIAN" LANGUAGE.
D.D., 275(IQ):FALL/WINTER72-126
GRIFFITHS, B. THE DARK CONVOYS.
617(TLS):11OCT74-1119
GRIFFITHS, J.G. - SEE PLUTARCH

GRIFFITHS, R., ED. CLAUDEL.*
V.M. AMES, 290(JAAC):SPRING72-
400
GRIFFITHS, R. PÉTAIN.
N. HAMPSON, 208(FS):APR73-242
B.H. SMITH, 396(MODA):SUMMER73-
312
GRIGG, D.B. THE AGRICULTURAL SYS-
TEMS OF THE WORLD.
617(TLS):22NOV74-1303
GRIGGS, E.L. - SEE COLERIDGE, S.T.
GRIGSON, G. THE CONTRARY VIEW.
617(TLS):19APR74-410
GRIGSON, G. A DICTIONARY OF ENGLISH
PLANT NAMES.
M. LASKI, 362:19&26DEC74-847
GRIGSON, G. DISCOVERIES OF BONES &
STONES.
A. CLUYSENAAR, 565:VOL13#2-72
GRILLI, E. THE ART OF THE JAPANESE
SCREEN.
A. SOPER, 57:VOL34#2/3-252
GRILLO, V. CHARLES DICKENS' SKET-
CHES BY BOZ.
617(TLS):23AUG74-902
GRILLPARZER, F. DES MEERES UND DER
LIEBE WELLEN.* (R.C. COWEN, ED)
B. MURDOCH, 221(GQ):MAR72-390
GRILLPARZER, F. PLAYS ON CLASSIC
THEMES. (S. SOLOMON, TRANS)
B. MURDOCH, 221(GQ):NOV72-780
"FRANZ GRILLPARZER."* (K. PÖRNBACH-
ER, ED)
G. REINHARDT, 222(GR):MAY72-228
"GRILLPARZER-FORUM FORCHTENSTEIN."
[1969]
I.V. MORRIS, 220(GL&L):JAN73-181
GRIMAL, P. GUIDE DE L'ÉTUDIANT LAT-
INISTE.
J. ANDRÉ, 555:VOL46FASC1-140
"THE GRIMANI BREVIARY." (TEXT BY M.
SALMI)
J. CANADAY, 441:1DEC74-102
GRIMBLE, I. SCOTTISH CLANS & TAR-
TANS.
617(TLS):12APR74-399
GRIMES, W.F. THE EXCAVATION OF
ROMAN & MEDIAEVAL LONDON.*
C.M. WELLS, 487:SPRING72-103
GRIMM, G. DIE ZEUGNISSE ÄGYPTISCHER
RELIGION UND KUNSTELEMENTE IM RÖM-
ISCHEN DEUTSCHLAND.
J.G. GRIFFITHS, 123:DEC73-247
GRIMM, R., ED. DEUTSCHE DRAMENTHE-
ORIEN.
T.G. REBER, 406:SUMMER73-209
G. RODGER, 402(MLR):JUL73-712
G.L. TRACY, 564:OCT72-222
GRIMM, R. & J. HERMAND, EDS. EXIL
UND INNERE EMIGRATION.
T.J. REED, 617(TLS):25OCT74-1199
GRIMM, R. & J. HERMAND, EDS. DIE
KLASSIK-LEGENDE.*
H.B. NISBET, 402(MLR):JUL73-693
GRIMSHAW, P. WOMEN'S SUFFRAGE IN
NEW ZEALAND.
C. BOLLINGER, 368:DEC72-355
GRIMSLEY, L. GUERILLA IN THE KIT-
CHEN.
M. LEVIN, 441:17MAR74-38
GRIMSLEY, R. JEAN D'ALEMBERT (1717-
1783).
E. LABROUSSE, 542:JUL-SEP72-320
GRIMSLEY, R. - SEE ROUSSEAU, J-J.

GRIMSTAD, K. & S. RENNIE, EDS. THE
NEW WOMAN'S SURVIVAL CATALOG.
A. NELSON, 441:6JAN74-2
GRIMSTED, P.K. ARCHIVES & MANU-
SCRIPT REPOSITORIES IN THE USSR:
MOSCOW & LENINGRAD.
W.F. RYAN, 575(SEER):OCT73-599
GRINDEA, C. & OTHERS. WE MAKE OUR
OWN MUSIC.
F. DAWES, 415:SEP73-900
GRINDEL, C., ED. GOD, MAN, & PHIL-
OSOPHY.
J.M.V., 543:MAR72-555
GRINSPOON, L. MARIHUANA RECONSIDER-
ED.
J. BUCKMAN, 639(VQR):WINTER72-
149
GRIPP, R.C. THE POLITICAL SYSTEM OF
COMMUNISM.
617(TLS):8FEB74-124
GRISAY, A., G. LAVIS & M. DUBOIS-
STASSE. LES DÉNOMINATIONS DE LA
"FEMME" DANS LES ANCIENS TEXTES
LITTÉRAIRES FRANÇAIS.*
P.F. DEMBOWSKI, 545(RPH):MAY73-
701
GRISEZ, G.G. ABORTION.*
J.V. DOLAN, 613:SPRING72-140
GRISI, F. & C. MARTINI. INCONTRI
CON I CONTEMPORANEI.
C. FANTAZZI, 276:AUTUMN72-361
GRISWOLD, W.S. THE BOSTON TEA PARTY
16 DECEMBER 1773.
617(TLS):3MAY74-468
GROB, A. THE PHILOSOPHIC MIND.
617(TLS):24MAY74-560
GROD, W.O. EINFÜHRUNG IN DIE DURCH-
SCHAUENDE KUNSTUNTERSUCHUNG.
H. TRUBNER, 57:VOL34#2/3-258
GROMOV, P. O STILE L'VA TOLSTOGO.
R.F. GUSTAFSON, 32:MAR73-205
GROMYKO, A.A. & OTHERS, EDS. SSSR V
BOR'BE ZA MIR NAKANUNE VTOROI MIR-
OVOI VOINY (SENTIABR' 1938 G. -
AVGUST 1939 G.).
M. BELOFF, 32:SEP73-617
VON GRONICKA, A. THOMAS MANN.
H. HATFIELD, 222(GR):NOV72-314
K.W. JONAS, 221(GQ):MAR72-348
H.W. REICHERT, 406:SUMMER73-205
GRÖNING, C-H. UNTERHALTUNGSMUSIK IN
DER SCHULE.
P. MICHEL, 654(WB):2/1972-181
GROPIUS, W. & OTHERS. TOWN PLAN FOR
THE DEVELOPMENT OF SELB.
C.B. LEACH, 505:JAN72-132
GROSHEIM, G.C. DAS LEBEN DER KÜNST-
LERIN MARA.
J.A.W., 410(M&L):JUL73-370
GROSS, M. GRAMMAIRE TRANSFORMATION-
NELLE DU FRANÇAIS. SYNTAXE DU
VERBE.*
M.E. LONG, 207(FR):FEB72-717
GROSS, T.L. THE HEROIC IDEAL IN
AMERICAN LITERATURE.*
R. SLOTKIN, 128(CE):MAY72-941
GROSSER, A. GERMANY IN OUR TIME.*
(FRENCH TITLE: L'ALLEMAGNE DE
NOTRE TEMPS.)
639(VQR):SUMMER72-XCVI

GROSSMAN, A.R. POETIC KNOWLEDGE IN
THE EARLY YEATS.*
  H. ADAMS, 219(GAR):FALL72-249
  M. SIDNELL, 627(UTQ):SPRING72-
  263
GROSSMAN, H. GROSSMAN'S GUIDE TO
WINES, SPIRITS & BEERS. (5TH ED)
  N. HAZELTON, 441:8DEC74-26
GROSSMAN, M.L. DADA.
  L.W. ROSENFIELD, 125:OCT72-81
GROSSMAN, R. MEINONG.
  G. RYLE, 617(TLS):27SEP74-1043
GROSSMANN, R. REFLECTIONS ON
FREGE'S PHILOSOPHY.*
  P.T. GEACH, 482(PHR):OCT72-498
  K.J.W., 543:SEP71-125
GROSSVOGEL, D.I. LIMITS OF THE
NOVEL.*
  B.K. BUNDY, 545(RPH):AUG72-68
GROSZ, G. LOVE ABOVE ALL, & OTHER
DRAWINGS.
  I. BREAKWELL, 592:MAR72-137
GROTH, A.J. PEOPLE'S POLAND.
  A. BROMKE, 32:JUN73-407
  A. KATZ, 497(POLR):SUMMER72-114
GROULX, L. ROLAND-MICHEL BARRIN DE
LA GALISSONIÈRE 1693-1756.
  481(PQ):JUL72-531
GROVE, F.P. A SEARCH FOR AMERICA.
  H. SMITH, 376:JAN72-126
GROVER, P. HENRY JAMES & THE FRENCH
NOVEL.
  617(TLS):3MAY74-478
GRUA, G. LA JUSTICE HUMAINE SELON
LEIBNIZ.
  A. ROBINET, 542:APR-JUN72-209
GRUBE, O.W. INDUSTRIAL BUILDINGS &
FACTORIES.
  M. MANSER, 46:JUN72-392
GRUBER, H.E. DARWIN ON MAN.
  R. DINNAGE, 617(TLS):8NOV74-1251
  S.J. GOULD, 441:14JUL74-7
  442(NY):13MAY74-158
GRUBER, I.D. THE HOWE BROTHERS &
THE AMERICAN REVOLUTION.
  P. MACKESY, 656(WMQ):JAN73-158
  639(VQR):WINTER73-XXXV
GRUCZA, F. SPRACHLICHE DIAKRISE IM
BEREICH DER AUSDRUCKSEBENE DES
DEUTSCHEN.
  G. MEINHOLD, 682(ZPSK):BAND25
  HEFT6-549
GRUENING, E. MANY BATTLES.
  N. VON HOFFMAN, 453:7MAR74-16
GRUMBERG, J-C. AMORPHE D'OTTENBURG.
  F. TONELLI, 207(FR):MAY72-1177
GRÜNBAUM, A. GEOMETRY & CHRONOMETRY
IN PHILOSOPHICAL PERSPECTIVE.*
  E.W. ADAMS, 486:DEC72-553
  L. SKLAR, 482(PHR):OCT72-506
GRUNFELD, F.V. THE ART & TIMES OF
THE GUITAR.
  K.J., 410(M&L):JAN73-86
  E.F. STANTON, 582(SFQ):DEC72-404
GRUNFELD, F.V. THE HITLER FILE.
  A. BROYARD, 441:25NOV74-29
GRUNWALD, S., ED. OSTEN UND WESTEN.
  A. OTTEN, 399(MLJ):MAY72-337
GRUNWALD, S.F.L. A BIOGRAPHY OF
JOHANN MICHAEL MOSCHEROSCH (1601-
1669).
  R.F. AMBACHER, 221(GQ):MAR72-363
GRUPP, S.E. THE MARIHUANA MUDDLE.
  617(TLS):8MAR74-240

GRYAZNOV, G.V. SOTSIALISTICHESKAYA
INDUSTRIALIZATSIYA V KNDR (1945-
1960GG.).
  G. GINSBURGS, 293(JAST):FEB72-
  425
GRZYBOWSKI, K. SOVIET PUBLIC INTER-
NATIONAL LAW, DOCTRINES & DIPLO-
MATIC PRACTICE.
  P. MAGGS, 550(RUSR):APR72-184
GSTEIGER, M. FRANZÖSISCHE SYMBOLIS-
TEN IN DER DEUTSCHEN LITERATUR DER
JAHRHUNDERTWENDE (1869-1914).
  O. BOECK, 406:SPRING73-89
  U.K. GOLDSMITH, 301(JEGP):OCT73-
  607
GUARDI, R. AFRICAN CRAFTS & CRAFTS-
MEN.
  K. CURTIS, 290(JAAC):SPRING72-
  404
GUARDIA DE ALFARO, G. ESTUDIO SOBRE
EL PENSAMIENTO POÉTICO DE PABLO
ANTONIO CUADRA.
  R.O. FLORIPE, 263:JUL-SEP73-338
GUDIOL, J. EL GRECO 1541-1614.*
  A. FRANKENSTEIN, 55:NOV73-44
  617(TLS):26JUL74-815
GUENTHER, H.V., ED & TRANS. THE
ROYAL SONG OF SARAHA.*
  T.V. WYLIE, 318(JAOS):JAN-MAR72-
  157
GUÉRIN, M. L'OEUVRE GRAVÉ DE MANET.
  A.C. HANSON, 90:JUL72-481
GUÉRIN, Y. UNE OEUVRE ANGLO-INDI-
ENNE ET SES VISAGES FRANÇAIS.
  F. LÉAUD, 189(EA):JUL-SEP72-451
  T.A. SHIPPEY, 402(MLR):APR73-399
GUERINOT, J.V. PAMPHLET ATTACKS ON
ALEXANDER POPE 1711-1744.*
  R. LONSDALE, 447(N&Q):JUN72-238
GUERINOT, J.V., ED. POPE.
  566:SPRING73-108
GUERRA, F. THE PRE-COLUMBIAN MIND.
  A.M. PADILLA & D. MACIEL, 263:
  OCT-DEC73-455
"LA GUERRE EN MÉDITERRANÉE 1939-45."
  H.R. KURZ, 182:VOL25#15/16-566
GUEST, B. MOSCOW MANSIONS.
  J. MATTHIAS, 491:APR74-45
GUEST, H. & L. AND KAJIMA SHOZO, EDS
& TRANS. POST-WAR JAPANESE POETRY.*
  V. YOUNG, 249(HUDR):WINTER73/74-
  719
GUETTEL, C. MARXISM & FEMINISM.
  V. HUNTER, 99:OCT74-39
DE GUEVARA, J.V. - SEE UNDER VÉLEZ
DE GUEVARA, J.
GUFFEY, G.R., COMP. TRAHERNE & THE
SEVENTEENTH-CENTURY ENGLISH PLATON-
ISTS 1900-1966.
  568(SCN):FALL-WINTER73-84
GUGUSI, P. EPISTOLOGRAPHI LATINI
MINORES. (VOL 1)
  J. ANDRÉ, 555:VOL46FASC2-330
GUIBERT, R. SEVEN VOICES.*
  639(VQR):SPRING73-LXXXI
GUICCIARDINI, F. THE HISTORY OF
FLORENCE. (M. DOMANDI, ED & TRANS)
  F. GILBERT, 551(RENQ):SPRING72-
  77
GUICHARD, L. - SEE RENARD, J.
"GUIDE TO CARTOGRAPHIC RECORDS IN
THE NATIONAL ARCHIVES."
  P. BRYANT, 14:APR72-222

142

GUIDO DE COLONNA. "LA CORÓNICA
TROYANA."* (F.P. NORRIS 2D, ED)
R.E. BARBERA, 238:DEC72-964
B. DUTTON, 405(MP):NOV72-158
GUIETTE, R. D'UNE POÉSIE FORMELLE
EN FRANCE AU MOYEN AGE.
M. FRANÇON, 382(MAE):1973/3-278
GUILBERT, L., R. LAGANE & G. NIOBEY
- SEE "GRAND LAROUSSE DE LA LANGUE
FRANÇAISE"
GUILLAND, H.F. EARLY AMERICAN FOLK
POTTERY.
J. TROY, 139:APR72-10
GUILLAUME DE LORRIS & JEAN DE MUEN.
THE ROMANCE OF THE ROSE.* (C.
DAHLBERG, ED & TRANS)
A. DAVID, 589:JUL73-560
M.A. GRELLNER, 382(MAE):1973/1-
69
W.W. KIBLER, 207(FR):DEC71-536
GUILLAUME LE VINIER. LES POÉSIES DE
GUILLAUME LE VINIER.* (P. MÉNARD,
ED)
T. NEWCOMBE, 402(MLR):JUL73-647
GUILLAUME, G. RÉCRÉATIONS ET RE-
CHERCHES LINGUISTIQUES ET STYLIS-
TIQUES. (VOL 2)
J. MAZALEYRAT, 535(RHL):MAY-JUN
72-547
GUILLÉN, C. LITERATURE AS SYSTEM.*
M.E. NOVAK, 594:SPRING72-75
P. THEINER, 72:BAND21OHEFT4/6-
342
B.W. WARDROPPER, 402(MLR):JAN73-
138
A.P. WEBER, 149:DEC73-392
639(VQR):AUTUMN72-CXXVIII
GUILLERAGUES. LETTRES PORTUGAISES.
(F. DELOFFRE & J. ROUGEOT, EDS)
E.T. DUBOIS, 182:VOL25#22-792
GUILLERM-CURUTCHET, L. & OTHERS, EDS.
LA FEMME DANS LA LITTÉRATURE FRAN-
ÇAISE ET LES TRADUCTIONS EN FRAN-
ÇAIS DU XVIE SIÈCLE.
R. MERCIER, 557(RSH):OCT-DEC72-
603
GUILLEVIC. ENCOCHES. DE L'HIVER.
R. MUNIER, 98:JUL72-623
GUILLEVIC. INCLUS.
617(TLS):24MAY74-554
GUILLEVIC. PAROI.
S. LÉVY, 207(FR):MAY72-1178
R. MUNIER, 98:JUL72-623
GUIMOND, J. THE ART OF WILLIAM CAR-
LOS WILLIAMS.
A. STEAD, 447(N&Q):SEP72-357
GUINNESS, D. & W. RYAN. IRISH
HOUSES & CASTLES.*
M. CRAIG, 90:OCT72-723
GUINNESS, D. & J.T. SADLER, JR.
MR. JEFFERSON, ARCHITECT.*
639(VQR):AUTUMN73-CLXXII
GÜIRALDES, R. DON SEGUNDO SOMBRA.
(A.B. DELLEPIANE, ED)
J.D. DANIELSON, 238:MAR72-198
L. LORENZO-RIVERO, 399(MLJ):
OCT72-402
GUIRAUD, P. ESSAIS DE STYLISTIQUE.
G. GORCY, 209(FM):JAN72-64
GUIRAUD, P. LE JARGON DE VILLON OU
LE GAI SAVOIR DE LA COQUILLE.*
A. GRAUR, 353:1NOV72-124

GUIRAUD, P. LA SÉMIOLOGIE.
J. CULLER, 208(FS):OCT73-497
M-J. HANOULLE, 209(FM):JUL72-259
GUIRAUD, P. & P. KUENTZ. LA STYLIS-
TIQUE.
G. GORCY, 209(FM):JAN72-64
GUISE, R. - SEE DE BALZAC, H.
GUIZOT, F. HISTORICAL ESSAYS & LEC-
TURES. (S. MELLON, ED)
D. JOHNSON, 617(TLS):27DEC74-
1468
GULBRANSSON, O. SPRÜCHE UND WAHR-
HEITEN.
617(TLS):25OCT74-1188
GULDAN, E. EVA UND MARIA.
P. MOISY, 182:VOL25#3/4-99
GULLBERG, E. & P. ÅSTRÖM. THE
THREAD OF ARIADNE.*
B.A. SPARKES, 303:VOL92-250
GULLIVER, H. KILL WITH STYLE.
N. CALLENDAR, 441:4AUG74-26
GULLIVER, P.H., ED. TRADITION &
TRANSITION IN EAST AFRICA.
A.I. RICHARDS, 69:JUL72-244
GULLIVER, S. THE VULCAN BULLETINS.
N. CALLENDAR, 441:24MAR74-40
617(TLS):5APR74-375
GULLÓN, R. TÉCNICAS DE GALDÓS.
R.M. FEDORCHEK, 399(MLJ):APR72-
268
M.C. PEÑUELAS, 593:WINTER73-380
GULLÓN, R. EL ÚLTIMO JUAN RAMÓN.
G. PALAU DE NEMES, 240(HR):
SPRING72-231
GULLÓN, R. - SEE DARÍO, R.
GULYA, J. EASTERN OSTYAK CHRESTO-
MATHY.
H. KATZ, 260(IF):BAND76-361
L. SCHIEFER, 343:BAND15HEFT2-212
GUMILEV, N.S. SELECTED WORKS OF
NIKOLAI S. GUMILEV. (B. RAFFEL &
A. BURAGO, EDS & TRANS)
S. DRIVER, 32:DEC73-855
D. RAYFIELD, 575(SEER):OCT73-624
GUMPERZ, J.J. & D. HYMES, EDS. DIR-
ECTIONS IN SOCIOLINGUISTICS.
J. BOSCO, 608:SEP73-327
GUNDEL, H.G. WELTBILD UND ASTROLO-
GIE IN DIE GRIECHISCHEN ZAUBER-
PAPYRI.
D. PINGREE, 318(JAOS):JAN-MAR72-
183
GUNDERMANN, H. DIE BERUFSDYSPHONIE.
I. KOSSEL, 682(ZPSK):BAND25HEFT3-
245
GUNDERMANN, H. MEIN KIND LERNT
SPRECHEN.
L. KACZMAREK, 682(ZPSK):BAND25
HEFT1/2-143
GUNDERSHEIMER, W.L. FERRARA.
617(TLS):29MAR74-318
GUNDERSHEIMER, W.L. THE LIFE &
WORKS OF LOUIS LE ROY.
L.J. FRIEDMAN, 545(RPH):AUG72-
196
GUNDERSHEIMER, W.L. - SEE SABADINO
DEGLI ARIENTI, G.
GUNDERSON, K. MENTALITY & MACHINES.
L.J. COHEN, 84:AUG72-292
GUNE, V.T. ANCIENT SHRINES OF GOA.
J.F. BUTLER, 576:OCT72-238
GUNN, E. A DARING COIFFEUR.
K. FEUER, 32:JUN73-425
E. WASIOLEK, 594:SPRING72-86

GUNN, G.B. LITERATURE & RELIGION.
H.A.D., 543:MAR72-555
GUNN, T. MOLY [&] MY SAD CAPTAINS.*
D. ALLEN, 491:MAY74-103
GUNN, T. TO THE AIR.
D. BROMWICH, 441:16JUN74-6
617(TLS):30AUG74-932
GUNSTON, B. ATTACK AIRCRAFT OF THE
WEST.
E.C. SHEPHERD, 617(TLS):13DEC74-
1416
GUNTER, P.A.Y., ED & TRANS. BERGSON
& THE EVOLUTION OF PHYSICS.*
L.G., 543:SEP71-140
GUNTHER, E. INDIAN LIFE ON THE
NORTHWEST COAST OF NORTH AMERICA
AS SEEN BY THE EARLY EXPLORERS &
FUR TRADERS DURING THE LAST DEC-
ADES OF THE EIGHTEENTH CENTURY.
639(VQR):SPRING73-XCIII
GÜNTZSCHEL, D. BEITRÄGE ZUR DATIER-
UNG DES CULEX.
A.A. BARRETT, 487:WINTER72-416
GUNZENHÄUSER, M. DIE PARISER FRIED-
ENSKONFERENZ 1919 UND DIE FRIEDENS-
VERTRÄGE 1919-20.
R. ALBRECHT-CARRIÉ, 182:VOL25
#5/6-185
GUPPY, N. A YOUNG MAN'S JOURNEY.
617(TLS):18JAN74-58
GUPTA, G.R. MARRIAGE, RELIGION &
SOCIETY.
617(TLS):17MAY74-516
GUPTA, S. KASHMIR.
R.A. HUTTENBACK, 293(JAST):FEB72-
449
GURNEY, A.R., JR. THE GOSPEL ACCORD-
ING TO JOE.
M. LEVIN, 441:26MAY74-18
GURNEY, I. POEMS OF IVOR GURNEY
1890-1937.* (L. CLARK, ED)
P. DICKINSON, 364:FEB/MAR74-121
J. FULLER, 362:7MAR74-310
GURR, A. THE SHAKESPEAREAN STAGE,
1574-1642.*
T.J. KING, 551(RENQ):WINTER72-
496
GURR, E. POPE.
566:AUTUMN72-11
GUSAROVA, A. MIR ISKUSSTVA.
J.E. BOWLT, 32:MAR73-200
GUSDORF, G. L'AVÈNEMENT DES SCI-
ENCES HUMAINES AU SIÈCLE DES LUM-
IÈRES.
617(TLS):22MAR74-286
GUSTAFSON, R. FIRE ON STONE.
J. ROSENBLATT, 99:NOV/DEC74-20
GUSTIN, M.M. TONALITY.
A. KOMAR, 513:FALL-WINTER69-146
GUTCH, J. BEYOND THE REEFS.
617(TLS):15NOV74-1297
GUTCHEON, B. THE PERFECT PATCHWORK
PRIMER.
L.J. GARTNER, JR., 441:8DEC74-51
GUTHEIM, F. RIVERS OF AMERICA: THE
POTOMAC.
I.R. DEE, 441:8SEP74-30
GUTHKE, K.S. DIE MODERNE TRAGIKOMÖ-
DIE.
T. MEYER, 657(WW):JUL/AUG72-287
GUTHKE, K.S. DIE MYTHOLOGIE DER ENT-
GÖTTERTEN WELT.
P. SALM, 301(JEGP):JUL73-409
GUTHKE, K.S. - SEE VON HALLER, A.

GUTHRIE, G.M. THE PSYCHOLOGY OF
MODERNIZATION IN THE RURAL PHILIP-
PINES.
D.J. SCHEANS, 293(JAST):MAY72-
745
GUTHRIE, W.K.C. A HISTORY OF GREEK
PHILOSOPHY.* (VOL 3)
A.W.H. ADKINS, 479(PHQ):OCT72-
357
GUTIÉRREZ, G. A THEOLOGY OF LIBERA-
TION.* (C. INDA & J. EAGLESON,
EDS & TRANS)
617(TLS):14JUN74-647
GUTKNECHT, C. & P. KERNER. SYSTEM-
ATISIERTE STRUKTURMODELLE DES
ENGLISCHEN.
G. SCHLÖMP, 430(NS):FEB72-110
A. SCHOPF, 38:BAND90HEFT4-497
GUTMANN, J., ED. BEAUTY IN HOLI-
NESS.*
E. ORING, 292(JAF):JAN-MAR72-88
GUTNOV, A. & OTHERS. THE IDEAL COM-
MUNIST CITY.*
K. FRAMPTON, 44:MAR72-13
B.S. PUSHKAREV, 550(RUSR):APR72-
189
GUTSCHE, W. AUFSTEIG UND FALL EINES
KAISERLICHEN REICHSKANZLERS.
617(TLS):9AUG74-862
GUTTERIDGE, D. COPPERMINE.
D. CAVANAGH, 198:WINTER74-102
GUTTERIDGE, D. DEATH AT QUEBEC.
D. BAILEY, 529(QQ):SUMMER72-242
D. BARBOUR, 150(DR):SPRING72-167
GUTTMANN, A. THE JEWISH WRITER IN
AMERICA.*
D. FUCHS, 659:AUTUMN74-562
A.H. ROSENFELD, 390:DEC72-66
639(VQR):WINTER72-XXVII
GUTWIRTH, M. JEAN RACINE.
F.R. FREUDMANN, 546(RR):DEC72-
296
R.C. KNIGHT, 208(FS):APR73-198
GUY, A. EL PENSAMIENTO FILOSÓFICO
DE FRAY LUIS DE LEÓN.
542:JAN-MAR72-105
GUYET, F. LE ROMAN SATIRIQUE DE
GAEOMEMPHION DU CANTAL. (J. DES-
JARDINS, TRANS)
L.V.R., 568(SCN):SPRING73-33
GUYON, B. PÉGUY DEVANT DIEU.
617(TLS):14JUN74-628
GUYON, B. - SEE DE BALZAC, H.
GVISHIANI, L. SOVETSKAIA ROSSIIA I
SSHA (1917-1920).
P. ROLEY, 32:MAR73-170
GWALTNEY, F.I. IDOLS & AXLE GREASE.
M. LEVIN, 441:15DEC74-12
GWALTNEY, J.L. THE THRICE SHY.
J. PHILIPS, 37:SEP72-43
GYBBON-MONYPENNY, G.B., ED. "LIBRO
DE BUEN AMOR" STUDIES.*
R. AYERBE-CHAUX, 593:SUMMER73-
176
P.L. ULLMAN, 400(MLN):MAR72-336
GYSIN, H.P. STUDIEN ZUM VOKABULAR
DER MUSIKTHEORIE IM MITTELALTER.
J.A.W., 410(M&L):JUL73-366

H.D. HERMETIC DEFINITION.
F.D. REEVE, 491:JUN74-162
639(VQR):AUTUMN73-CXLI

H.D. TRILOGY.
F.D. REEVE, 491:JUN74-162
617(TLS):15MAR74-267
DE HAAN, S. ABENTEUER IM WATTEN-
MEER. (J.H. BROWN, ED)
D.D. HOOK, 221(GQ):NOV72-796
HAARMANN, H. DIE INDIREKTE ERLEBNIS-
FORM ALS GRAMMATISCHE KATEGORIE.
P. AALTO, 343:BAND15HEFT2-133
M. SAMILOV, 575(SEER):JAN73-156
HAAS, A. TEILHARD DE CHARDIN-LEXI-
KON.
A. GUGGENBERGER, 182:VOL25#23/24-
836
HAAS, B. DAISY CANFIELD.*
N. CALLENDAR, 441:12MAY74-18
HAAS, D. FLUCHT AUS DER WIRKLICH-
KEIT.
D. MESSNER, 430(NS):APR72-242
D.J. MOSSOP, 208(FS):JAN73-91
HAAS, E. THE CREATION.
M. LAVANOUX, 363:MAY72-104
HAAS, G. ESSAY.
P. PROCHNIK, 220(GL&L):JUL73-357
HAAS, R.B. - SEE STEIN, G.
HAAS, W., ED. ALPHABETS FOR ENGLISH.
J. VACHEK, 350:MAR73-190
HAAS, W. PHONO-GRAPHIC TRANSLATION.
J. VACHEK, 350:MAR73-190
HABE, H. PROUD ZION.
D. PRYCE-JONES, 441:21APR74-20
HABERMAS, J. ERKENNTNIS UND INTER-
ESSE.* LEGITIMATIONSPROBLEME IM
SPÄTKAPITALISMUS.
J. SHAPIRO, 617(TLS):4OCT74-1094
HABERMAS, J. KNOWLEDGE & HUMAN IN-
TERESTS.
D. MISGELD, 154:DEC72-639
H.L. PARSONS, 484(PPR):DEC72-281
HABERMAS, J. TECHNIK UND WISSEN-
SCHAFT ALS IDEOLOGIE. TOWARD A
RATIONAL SOCIETY.*
D. MISGELD, 154:MAR72-155
HACK, B. & M. KLEISS - SEE "HERMANN
BROCH - DANIEL BRODY: BRIEFWECHSEL
1930-1951"
HACKER, P.M.S. INSIGHT & ILLUSION.
H.O. MOUNCE, 518:JAN73-18
HACKETT, J. THE LETTERS OF SIR JOHN
HACKETT 1526-1534. (E.F. ROGERS,
ED)
D.S. BERKOWITZ, 551(RENQ):WINTER
72-486
HACKETT, M.B. THE ORIGINAL STATUTES
OF CAMBRIDGE UNIVERSITY.*
A.J. DUGGAN, 447(N&Q):MAY72-184
HACKETT, W.M. LA LANGUE DE GIRART
DE ROUSSILLON.
W.G. VAN EMDEN, 208(FS):JAN73-45
HACKING, I. THE LOGIC OF STATISTI-
CAL INFERENCE.
G.A. BARNARD, 84:MAY72-123
HADDOX, J.H. ANTONIO CASO.*
A. DONOSO, 258:SEP72-464
HADLEY, D. STRANDS OF RAWHIDE. THE
SPIRIT BY THE DEEP WELL TANK.
G. BURNS, 584(SWR):WINTER73-96
HADLICH, R.L. A TRANSFORMATIONAL
GRAMMAR OF SPANISH.*
W.E. BULL, 399(MLJ):APR72-254
HADOT, P. PLOTIN OU LA SIMPLICITÉ
DU REGARD.
J. BRUNSCHWIG, 542:JAN-MAR72-59

HAENY, G. BASILIKALE ANLAGEN IN DER
ÄGYPTISCHEN BAUKUNST DES NEUEN
REICHES.
A.M. BADAWY, 318(JAOS):APR-JUN72-
306
DE HAES, F. IMAGES DE LAUTRÉAMONT.*
M. BONNET, 535(RHL):MAY-JUN72-
541
M.A. CAWS, 207(FR):OCT71-251
VON HAGEN, E. ABSTRACTION UND KON-
KRETION BEI HEGEL UND KIERKEGAARD.
A.M. FINNEMANN, 542:JUL-SEP72-
368
VON HAGEN, V.W. THE GOLDEN MAN.
617(TLS):1NOV74-1240
VON HAGEN, V.W. SEARCH FOR THE MAYA.
617(TLS):26APR74-448
HAGER, F-P. DER GEIST UND DAS EINE.
G.B. KERFERD, 123:DEC73-209
HAGER, F-P. DIE VERNUNFT UND DAS
PROBLEM DES BÖSEN IM RAHMEN DER
PLATONISCHEN ETHIK UND METAPHYSIK.
H.J. EASTERLING, 123:MAR73-89
HÄGG, T. NARRATIVE TECHNIQUE IN
ANCIENT GREEK ROMANCES.*
B.P. REARDON, 487:SUMMER72-207
F. VIAN, 555:VOL46FASC2-305
HAGGARD, W. THE KINSMEN.
617(TLS):8NOV74-1248
HAGGIN, B.H. A DECADE OF MUSIC.
D. CAIRNS, 441:17FEB74-23
HAGIWARA SAKUTARŌ. FACE AT THE BOT-
TOM OF THE WORLD & OTHER POEMS.
SHINODA HAJIME, 285(JAPQ):OCT-
DEC72-487
HAGSTRUM, J.H. SAMUEL JOHNSON'S LIT-
ERARY CRITICISM.* (2ND ED)
A. PARREAUX, 189(EA):OCT-DEC72-
562
HAHL, W. REFLEXION UND ERZÄHLUNG.
B. DEDNER, 481(PQ):JUL72-611
HAHN, E. ONCE UPON A PEDESTAL.
E.R. LIPSON, 441:29SEP74-20
442(NY):19AUG74-89
HAHN, E.A. NAMING-CONSTRUCTIONS IN
SOME INDO-EUROPEAN LANGUAGES.*
T. BURROW, 318(JAOS):JAN-MAR72-
166
K.H. SCHMIDT, 343:BAND15HEFT2-
218
W. THOMAS, 260(IF):BAND76-245
HAHN, K-H. - SEE SCHILLER, F.
HAHN, R. THE ANATOMY OF A SCIEN-
TIFIC INSTITUTION.*
S.A. SHAPIN, 481(PQ):JUL72-571
HAHNLOSER-INGOLD, M. DAS ENGLISCHE
THEATER UND BERT BRECHT.*
D. BATHRICK, 221(GQ):JAN72-178
P. GOETSCH, 430(NS):MAY72-303
HAI, M.H.S.A. - SEE UNDER ABDUL HAI,
M.H.S.
HAIG, A. PERUVIAN PRINTOUT.
N. CALLENDAR, 441:7JUL74-18
617(TLS):1MAR74-219
HAIG, S. MADAME DE LAFAYETTE.
A.R. PUGH, 188(ECR):SPRING72-68
J.W. SCOTT, 208(FS):APR73-199
HAIGHT, G.S., ED. THE PORTABLE VIC-
TORIAN READER.
G.B. TENNYSON, 445(NCF):JUN72-
117
HAIKEN, P. LIFESCAPE PACK 1.
K. WHEELER, 46:DEC72-385

HALLE, L.J. THE IDEOLOGICAL IMAGINA-
TION.
W. BERNS, 639(VQR):SPRING72-297
HALLE, L.J. THE SEA & THE ICE.*
617(TLS):27DEC74-1471
VON HALLER, A. HALLERS LITERATUR-
KRITIK. (K.S. GUTHKE, ED)
W. LEPPMANN, 221(GQ):JAN72-162
HALLER, R.S. - SEE DE MÉZIÈRES, P.
HALLIBURTON, D. EDGAR ALLAN POE.*
S.P. MOSS, 27(AL):NOV73-462
639(VQR):SUMMER73-CXIV
HALLIDAY, J. & P. FULLER, EDS. THE
PSYCHOLOGY OF GAMBLING.
J. COHEN, 617(TLS):18OCT74-1151
HALLIDAY, J. & G. MC CORMACK. JAPAN-
ESE IMPERIALISM TODAY.*
H. SCOTT-STOKES, 441:17FEB74-4
HALLIDAY, M.A.K., A. MC INTOSH & P.
STREVENS. THE LINGUISTIC SCIENCES
& LANGUAGE TEACHING.
H.J. FREY, 399(MLJ):MAR72-186
HALLIG, R. SPRACHERLEBNIS UND
SPRACHFORSCHUNG. (H.P. SCHWANKE,
ED)
Å. GRAFSTRÖM, 597(SN):VOL44#1-
164
B. SCHLIEBEN-LANGE, 224(GRM):
BAND22HEFT2-207
HALLS, G. THE COBRA KITE.
E. FEINSTEIN, 364:APR/MAY72-142
HALLS, G. THE VOICE OF THE CRAB.
617(TLS):13SEP74-969
HALLS, W.D. FOREIGN LANGUAGES &
EDUCATION IN WESTERN EUROPE.
D.F. BRADSHAW, 208(FS):JUL73-366
M. HAY, 330(GL&L):OCT72-63
HALLS, Z. WOMEN'S COSTUMES, 1600-
1750.
G. WILLIS, 39:FEB72-150
HALLSTEIN, W. DIE EUROPÄISCHE GE-
MEINSCHAFT.
617(TLS):26APR74-454
HALPERIN, M.H. BUREAUCRATIC POLI-
TICS & FOREIGN POLICY.
R. REEVES, 441:11AUG74-4
HALPERN, D. TRAVELING ON CREDIT.
P. COOLEY, 385(MQR):WINTER74-79
42(AR):VOL32#3-500
HALPERT, H. & G.M. STORY, EDS.
CHRISTMAS MUMMING IN NEWFOUND-
LAND.*
F. GILLMOR, 50(ARQ):WINTER72-370
HALPERT, I.D. & E. VON NARDROFF. IN
WORT UND SCHRIFT.
H. KAISER, 221(GQ):MAY72-552
HALSBAND, R. LORD HERVEY.*
442(NY):11MAR74-134
HALSBAND, R. - SEE MONTAGU, M.W.
HALTER, C. LES PALESTINIENS DU
SILENCE.
S. HASSAN, 453:14NOV74-45
HAMBURGER, A., A. SUDMANN & B. NOLDE,
EDS. SPRÅK I NORDEN 1971.
S.R. SMITH, 563(SS):AUTUMN73-379
HAMBURGER, M., ED. EAST GERMAN
POETRY.
E. OSERS, 364:FEB/MAR73-133
HAMBURGER, M. A MUG'S GAME.
617(TLS):25OCT74-1205
HAMBURGER, M. OWNERLESS EARTH.*
J. CAREY, 364:AUG/SEP73-125
D. DAVIE, 441:28APR74-30
J. MATTHIAS, 491:APR74-45

HAMBURGER, M. - SEE BÜCHNER, G.
HAMBURGER, M. - SEE GOOD, T.
HAMBY, A.L. BEYOND THE NEW DEAL.
R. RADOSH, 441:1SEP74-3
HAMEL, R. - SEE BOUCHER DE BOUCHER-
VILLE, G.
HAMER, C. ECSTASY & VENDETTA.
617(TLS):1MAR74-218
HAMER, D.A. LIBERAL POLITICS IN THE
AGE OF GLADSTONE & ROSEBERRY.
P. STANSKY, 637(VS):DEC72-253
HAMER, P.M. & G.C. ROGERS, JR. - SEE
LAURENS, H.
HAMER, W.S. THE BRITISH ARMY: CIVIL-
MILITARY RELATIONS, 1885-1905.
K.G. LAREW, 637(VS):MAR72-386
HAMEROW, T.S. THE SOCIAL FOUNDA-
TIONS OF GERMAN UNIFICATION, 1858-
1871.
639(VQR):SUMMER73-CXXIII
HAMILTON, A. THE PAPERS OF ALEXAN-
DER HAMILTON.* (VOLS 16 & 17)
(H.C. SYRETT, ED)
639(VQR):SPRING73-LXXVI
HAMILTON, A. THE XANDER PURSUIT.
N. CALLENDAR, 441:8DEC74-44
HAMILTON, A. - SEE DRIEU LA ROCHELLE,
P.
HAMILTON, A.C., ED. ESSENTIAL AR-
TICLES FOR THE STUDY OF EDMUND
SPENSER.
J. MULRYAN, 568(SCN):FALL-WINTER
73-79
HAMILTON, C.D., ED. LÍRICA HISPÁN-
ICA DEL SIGLO XIII AL XX.
G. SABAT DE RIVERS, 400(MLN):
MAR72-350
HAMILTON, D. & C. MURLAND. LA DANSE.
617(TLS):10MAY74-500
HAMILTON, E. WHAT'S IT LIKE OUT
THERE?
T. STURGEON, 441:10NOV74-50
HAMILTON, E. WILLIAM'S MARY.
H.T.D., 566:AUTUMN72-46
HAMILTON, E.W. THE DIARY OF SIR
EDWARD WALTER HAMILTON. (D.W.R.
BAHLMAN, ED)
P. STANSKY, 637(VS):JUN73-482
HAMILTON, G.H. 19TH & 20TH CENTURY
ART.
J.K. NELSON, 290(JAAC):FALL71-
140
A. WERNER, 127:FALL72-106
HAMILTON, I. A POETRY CHRONICLE.*
R. GARFITT, 364:JUN/JUL73-116
J.M. NEWTON, 97(CQ):VOL6#2-178
HAMILTON, J.R. ALEXANDER THE GREAT.
617(TLS):25JAN74-80
HAMILTON, O. PARADISE OF EXILES.
M. GRANT, 617(TLS):20DEC74-1448
HAMILTON, P. KNOWLEDGE & SOCIAL
STRUCTURE.
617(TLS):3MAY74-473
HAMILTON, R. POEMS.
617(TLS):16AUG74-879
HAMLIN, J.D., WITH J.E. HALEY & W.C.
HOLDEN. THE FLAMBOYANT JUDGE,
JAMES D. HAMLIN.
L.C. MILAZZO, 584(SWR):SUMMER73-
283
HAMMACHER, A.M. MAGRITTE.
J. RUSSELL, 441:1DEC74-55

HAMMER, K. DEUTSCHE KRIEGSTHEOLOGIE
(1870 BIS 1918).
D.H.R. JONES, 182:VOL25#1/2-11
HAMMERICH, L.L. & OTHERS - SEE "TÖN-
NIES FENNE'S LOW GERMAN MANUAL OF
SPOKEN RUSSIAN"
HAMMERSTRÖM, G. LINGUISTISCHE EIN-
HEITEN IM RAHMEN DER MODERNEN
SPRACHWISSENSCHAFT.*
G.F. MEIER, 682(ZPSK):BAND25
HEFT4/5-431
HAMMETT, D. THE CONTINENTAL OP. (S.
MARCUS, ED)
C. LEHMANN-HAUPT, 441:16DEC74-31
L. MICHAELS, 441:8DEC74-1
HAMMETT, D. THE DAIN CURSE. RED
HARVEST. THE MALTESE FALCON. THE
GLASS KEY.
617(TLS):29MAR74-344
HAMMOND, B. SOVEREIGNTY & AN EMPTY
PURSE.*
H. JAEGER, 182:VOL25#7/8-240
HAMMOND, D. & A. JABLOW. THE AFRICA
THAT NEVER WAS.
J.C. MESSENGER, 292(JAF):APR-JUN
72-185
HAMMOND, L.D., ED. NEWS FROM NEW
CYTHERA.
N. SUCKLING, 208(FS):APR73-214
HAMMOND, M. THE CITY IN THE ANCIENT
WORLD.
617(TLS):25JAN74-80
HAMMOND, M., A.W. MACK & W. MOSKALEW
- SEE PLAUTUS
HAMMOND, N.G.L. STUDIES IN GREEK
HISTORY.
617(TLS):29MAR74-321
HAMMOND-TOOKE, W.D., ED. THE BANTU-
SPEAKING PEOPLES OF SOUTHERN
AFRICA.
J. BLACKING, 617(TLS):1NOV74-
1227
HAMPARES, K.J. SPANISH 2400.
G.L. JACKSON, 238:MAR72-192
J.J. KINCAID, 399(MLJ):APR72-266
HAMPDEN-TURNER, C. RADICAL MAN.
H. LOMAS, 364:APR/MAY72-135
HAMPSHIRE, S. FREEDOM OF MIND &
OTHER ESSAYS.*
R.J.B., 543:SEP71-125
C. BARRETT, 518:MAY73-7
HAMSUN, K. BREV TIL MARIE. (T.
HAMSUN, ED)
C. WALL, 563(SS):SUMMER73-270
HAMSUN, K. HUNGER.
R. BLYTHE, 362:28FEB74-281
617(TLS):29MAR74-313
HAMSUN, K. MYSTERIES.*
R. BLYTHE, 362:10JAN74-56
R.D. SPECTOR, 563(SS):WINTER73-
79
HAMSUN, K. VICTORIA.
A. MACLEAN, 617(TLS):8NOV74-1249
HAN, P. - SEE DE LA TAILLE, J.
HAN, W-K. THE HISTORY OF KOREA.*
(G.K. MINTZ, ED)
B.H. HAZARD, 293(JAST):AUG72-905
HANAN, P. THE CHINESE SHORT STORY.
617(TLS):22MAR74-304
HANCE, W.A. POPULATION, MIGRATION &
URBANIZATION IN AFRICA.
J.W. GREGORY, 69:JAN72-70

HAND, W.D., ED. AMERICAN FOLK LEG-
END.
K.M. BRIGGS, 203:SPRING72-72
G. CAREY, 292(JAF):OCT-DEC72-380
"HANDBOOK OF THE BYZANTINE COLLEC-
TION: DUMBARTON OAKS, WASHINGTON,
D.C."
P. BROWN, 453:3OCT74-3
HANDEL, M.I. ISRAEL'S POLITICAL-
MILITARY DOCTRINE.
N. SAFRAN, 441:7APR74-4
HANDKE, P. KASPAR.
A. RENDLE, 157:SUMMER72-75
HANDKE, P. SHORT LETTER, LONG FARE-
WELL.
J. ROCKWELL, 441:15SEP74-5
HANDLER, J.S. A GUIDE TO SOURCE
MATERIALS FOR THE STUDY OF BARBA-
DOS HISTORY, 1627-1834.
R.S. MAXWELL, 14:JUL/OCT72-414
R.M. PIERSON, 517(PBSA):APR-JUN
73-212
HANDSCHUR, E. DIE FARB- UND GLANZ-
WÖRTER BEI HOMER UND HESIOD, IN
DEN HOMERISCHEN HYMNEN UND DEN
FRAGMENTEN DES EPISCHEN KYKLOS.
M.M. WILLCOCK, 303:VOL92-192
HANDY, R.T. A CHRISTIAN AMERICA.
C.A. HOLBROOK, 432(NEQ):SEP72-
448
HANE, M. JAPAN.
639(VQR):AUTUMN72-CXLVIII
HANFF, H. THE DUCHESS OF BLOOMSBURY
STREET.
617(TLS):10MAY74-508
HANKE, H., ED. ZU TENDENZEN UND
ERFORDERNISSEN EINES KULTURVOLLEN
FREIZEITVERHALTENS.
R. ZIMMERMANN, 654(WB):10/1972-
175
HANKINS, J.E. SOURCE & MEANING IN
SPENSER'S ALLEGORY.
H. MACLEAN, 301(JEGP):OCT73-548
HANLE, Z. COOKING WILD GAME.
N. HAZELTON, 441:1DEC74-98
HANLEY, J. ANOTHER WORLD.
P. BAILEY, 364:FEB/MAR73-157
HANLEY, J. A WOMAN IN THE SKY.*
A. BROYARD, 441:13FEB74-43
J. MELLORS, 364:DEC73/JAN74-154
M. MEWSHAW, 441:3MAR74-4
HANLEY, T.O. THE AMERICAN REVOLU-
TION & RELIGION.
639(VQR):SPRING73-LXXXII
HANLEY, T.O. CHARLES CARROLL OF
CARROLLTON.*
F.X. CURRAN, 613:SPRING72-155
W.S. ROBINSON, 481(PQ):JUL72-532
HANN, R.G. & OTHERS, EDS. PRIMARY
SOURCES IN CANADIAN WORKING CLASS
HISTORY, 1860-1930.
P. BASKERVILLE, 99:NOV/DEC74-46
HANNA, W.J. & J.L. URBAN DYNAMICS
IN BLACK AFRICA.
K. LITTLE, 69:OCT72-349
HANNAH, B. GERONIMO REX.
E. ROVIT, 659:AUTUMN74-539
HANNAY, A. MENTAL IMAGES.
G. BRYKMAN, 542:OCT-DEC72-463
HANNING, R.W. THE VISION OF HISTORY
IN EARLY BRITAIN.
K.H. GÖLLER, 38:BAND90HEFT1/2-
200

HANSEN, B. FOLKEEVENTYR.
W.E. RICHMOND, 563(SS):WINTER73-75

HANSEN, H.H. COSTUME CAVALCADE.
G. SQUIRE, 157:AUTUMN72-82

HANSEN, H.J., ED. ARCHITECTURE IN WOOD.
D. HINTON, 135:APR72-292
P.F. NORTON, 576:MAY72-156

HANSEN, H.J., ED. LATE NINETEENTH CENTURY ART.
E.D.H. JOHNSON, 637(VS):MAR73-351

HANSEN, W.F. THE CONFERENCE SEQUENCE.
B.A. ROSENBERG, 292(JAF):OCT-DEC72-379

HANSFORD, S.H. JADE.*
J.M. HARTMAN, 57:VOL34#2/3-247

HANSON, K. SPINE.
E. LICHTENBERG, 114(CHIR):VOL23 #4&VOL24#1-212

HANSON, K.O. THE UNCORRECTED WORLD.
X.J. KENNEDY, 441:17FEB74-6
J. PARISI, 491:SEP74-343
617(TLS):29MAR74-339

HANSON, R.M. VIRGINIA PLACE NAMES.
E. GREEN, 424:SEP72-207

HANTSCHK, R. DIE GESCHICHTE DER KARTAUSE MAUERBACH.
G. CONSTABLE, 589:JUL73-545

HÄNTZSCHEL, G. - SEE HEINE, H.

HANZELI, V.E. MISSIONARY LINGUISTICS IN NEW FRANCE.*
W.L. WONDERLY, 361:VOL30#2/3-280

HAPP, H. HYLE, STUDIEN ZUM ARISTOTELISCHEN MATERIEBEGRIFF.
C. MUGLER, 555:VOL46FASC2-298
R.S., 543:JUN72-753

HARASZTI, E.H. TREATY-BREAKERS OR "REALPOLITIKER."
617(TLS):13DEC74-1422

HARBAGE, A. SHAKESPEARE WITHOUT WORDS & OTHER ESSAYS.*
P. EDWARDS, 447(N&Q):APR72-150
A. YOUNG, 150(DR):AUTUMN72-491

HARBAGE, A. - SEE SHAKESPEARE, W.

HARBAUGH, W.H. LAWYER'S LAWYER.*
W. BROCK, 617(TLS):27DEC74-1470

HARBUTT, C. TRAVELOG.
S. SCHWARTZ, 441:1DEC74-101

HARCOURT, P. SIX EUROPEAN DIRECTORS.
D.A.N. JONES, 362:6JUN74-745

HARDIE, F. THE ABYSSINIAN CRISIS.
617(TLS):2AUG74-828

HARDIE, F. THE POLITICAL INFLUENCE OF THE BRITISH MONARCHY, 1868-1952.
B. SACKS, 637(VS):DEC71-239

HARDIN, H. A NATION UNAWARE.
H.V. NELLES, 99:NOV/DEC74-49

HARDING, D.W. THE IRON AGE IN LOWLAND BRITAIN.
617(TLS):26JUL74-806

HARDING, F.J.W. JEAN-MARIE GUYAU (1854-1888).
617(TLS):31MAY74-582

HARDING, J. THE OX ON THE ROOF.*
639(VQR):SUMMER73-CXX

HARDING, T.D. BISHOP'S OPENING.
617(TLS):25OCT74-1208

HARDING, W., G. BRENNER & P.A. DOYLE, EDS. HENRY DAVID THOREAU.
M.I. LOWANCE, JR., 432(NEQ): DEC72-604

HARDISON, O.B., ED. THE QUEST FOR IMAGINATION.
W.L. BLIZEK, 290(JAAC):FALL72-132

HARDISON, O.B., JR., ED. MEDIEVAL & RENAISSANCE STUDIES.
639(VQR):SPRING72-LIII

HARDISON, O.B., JR. TOWARD HUMAN FREEDOM & DIGNITY.*
H.M. CURTLER, 396(MODA):SUMMER73-301

HARDON, J.A. CHRISTIANITY IN THE TWENTIETH CENTURY.
R. KRESS, 613:WINTER72-623

HARDOY, J. URBAN PLANNING IN PRE-COLUMBIAN AMERICA.*
G.L. HERSEY, 56:SUMMER72-180

HARDWICK, E. SEDUCTION & BETRAYAL.
R. DINNAGE, 617(TLS):29NOV74-1333
S. HAMPSHIRE, 453:27JUN74-21
J. RICHARDSON, 231:JUL74-87
B.P. SOLOMON, 441:5MAY74-4
C. TOMALIN, 362:28NOV74-714

HARDWICK, M. THE OSPREY GUIDE TO ANTHONY TROLLOPE.
617(TLS):18JAN74-43

HARDY, A., R. HARVIE & A. KOESTLER. THE CHALLENGE OF CHANCE.
B. BROPHY, 362:3JAN74-22

HARDY, B., ED. CRITICAL ESSAYS ON GEORGE ELIOT.*
I. MILNER, 637(VS):SEP71-99

HARDY, B. THE EXPOSURE OF LUXURY.
R. AP ROBERTS, 579(SAQ):AUTUMN73-612
L. STEVENSON, 637(VS):MAR73-359
639(VQR):WINTER73-XXI

HARDY, B. THE MORAL ART OF DICKENS.*
T.J. CRIBB, 541(RES):AUG72-372
K. CUSHMAN, 405(MP):NOV72-166
J.M.S. TOMPKINS, 597(SN):VOL44#1-175

HARDY, J.E. KATHERINE ANNE PORTER.
L. HARTLEY, 578:SPRING74-139

HARDY, J.P. REINTERPRETATIONS.
C.T.P., 566:AUTUMN72-12

HARDY, T. JUDE THE OBSCURE. (F.R. SOUTHERINGTON, ED)
F.B. PINION, 447(N&Q):NOV72-430

HARDY, T. ONE RARE FAIR WOMAN. (E. HARDY & F.B. PINION, EDS)
J.O. BAILEY, 594:WINTER72-656
P. DICKINSON, 364:AUG/SEP72-149

HARE, D. SLAG.
L. RUSSELL, 376:JAN72-121

HARE, J., ED. CONTES ET NOUVELLES DU CANADA FRANÇAIS 1778-1859. (VOL 1)
L.S. RODEN, 529(QQ):SUMMER72-267
A. VIATTE, 549(RLC):JUL-SEP72-468

HARE, R.M. APPLICATIONS OF MORAL PHILOSOPHY.*
J. RACHELS, 311(JP):14FEB74-84

HARE, R.M. ESSAYS ON PHILOSOPHICAL METHOD.
H. RUJA, 484(PPR):JUN73-584

HARGREAVES, R. SUPERPOWER.
617(TLS):19JUL74-758

HARICH-SCHNEIDER, E. A HISTORY OF JAPANESE MUSIC.*
L. PICKEN, 415:DEC73-1240

149

HARIG, L. ALLSEITIGE BESCHREIBUNG
DER WELT ZUR HEIMKEHR DES MENSCHEN
IN EINE SCHÖNERE ZUKUNFT.
617(TLS):25OCT74-1188
HARING, B. SIN IN THE SECULAR AGE.
617(TLS):26JUL74-812
HARLAN, L.R. BOOKER T. WASHINGTON.*
639(VQR):AUTUMN73-CLVI
HARLAN, L.R. - SEE WASHINGTON, B.T.
HARLEY, R.D. ARTISTS' PIGMENTS C.
1600-1835.
R.L. FELLER, 90:MAY72-341
HARLFINGER, D. DIE TEXTGESCHICHTE
DER PSEUDO-ARISTOTELISCHEN SCHRIFT
"PERI ATOMŌN GRAMMŌN."
D. BARGRAVE-WEAVER, 123:DEC73-
153
HARLING, R. THE ATHENIAN WIDOW.
617(TLS):7JUN74-601
HARLING, R., ED. DICTIONARY OF
DESIGN & DECORATION.
617(TLS):11JAN74-24
HARLOW, C.G. & J. REDMOND, EDS. THE
YEAR'S WORK IN ENGLISH STUDIES.
(VOLS 48&49)
E.G. STANLEY, 447(N&Q):APR72-138
HARLOW, R. SCANN.*
G. ELLIOTT, 648:JAN73-54
HARMAND, J. LES CELTES AU SECOND
ÂGE DU FER.
T.G.E. POWELL, 313:VOL62-206
HARMON, W. LEGION: CIVIC CHORUSES.
P. SMYTH, 491:DEC73-165
HARMS, R.T. INTRODUCTION TO PHONOL-
OGICAL THEORY.*
M. MURAKI, 206:NOV72-254
F.C.C. PENG, 361:VOL30#2/3-262
HARNER, M.J., ED. HALLUCINOGENS &
SHAMANISM.
617(TLS):15FEB74-162
HAROOTUNIAN, H.D. TOWARD RESTORA-
TION.*
J.C. LEBRA, 318(JAOS):APR-JUN72-
349
HARPER, H.M., JR. & C. EDGE, EDS.
THE CLASSIC BRITISH NOVEL.
639(VQR):AUTUMN72-CXXXII
HARPER, J.R., ED. PAUL KANE'S
FRONTIER.*
T.A. HEINRICH, 96:FEB/MAR72-48
HARPER, J.W. - SEE MARLOWE, C.
HARPER, M.S. DEBRIDEMENT.
D. LEHMAN, 491:DEC73-173
HARR, B. THE MORTGAGED WIFE.*
W.G.R., 502(PRS):WINTER72/73-370
"HARRAP'S STANDARD GERMAN & ENGLISH
DICTIONARY." (PT 1, VOL 3) (T.
JONES, ED)
G.P. BUTLER, 617(TLS):8NOV74-
1262
HARRAUER, H. A BIBLIOGRAPHY TO THE
CORPUS TIBULLIANUM.
A.R. & R.J. LITTLEWOOD, 487:SUM-
MER72-205
HARRÉ, R. THE PRINCIPLES OF SCIEN-
TIFIC THINKING.*
R. JONES, 393(MIND):APR72-300
D. MILLER, 84:FEB72-69
HARRÉ, R. & P.F. SECORD. THE EXPLAN-
ATION OF SOCIAL BEHAVIOUR.
Q. GIBSON, 63:MAY73-87

HARRELL, D.E., JR. WHITE SECTS &
BLACK MEN IN THE RECENT SOUTH.
F.N. BONEY, 219(GAR):SUMMER72-
227
HARRELL, J. & C. BARRETT - SEE TATAR-
KIEWICZ, W.
HARRINGTON, A. PSYCHOPATHS.
J.P. BOYLE, 396(MODA):SUMMER73-
328
HARRINGTON, M. FRAGMENTS OF THE
CENTURY.
M. DUBERMAN, 441:27JAN74-2
C. LEHMANN-HAUPT, 441:23JAN74-41
W. SHEED, 453:7MAR74-18
HARRIS, A. THE JOSEPH FILE.
N. CALLENDAR, 441:29DEC74-21
HARRIS, B. CONFESSIONS OF CHERUBINO.
639(VQR):SUMMER72-C
HARRIS, B. - SEE VANBRUGH, J.
HARRIS, C. ISLINGTON.
617(TLS):17MAY74-520
HARRIS, C.B. CONTEMPORARY AMERICAN
NOVELISTS OF THE ABSURD.*
J. KLINKOWITZ, 454:SPRING73-268
HARRIS, C.D. CITIES OF THE SOVIET
UNION.
D.B. & E.M. SHIMKIN, 550(RUSR):
JUL72-294
HARRIS, E.E. HYPOTHESIS & PERCEP-
TION.*
D. LOCKE, 479(PHQ):JAN72-77
E.L. MASCALL, 483:APR72-176
HARRIS, F.J. ANDRÉ GIDE & ROMAIN
ROLLAND.
617(TLS):22FEB74-190
HARRIS, H.J. - SEE "THE TALES OF ISE"
HARRIS, I. THE PRICE GUIDE TO VIC-
TORIAN SILVER.
D. COOMBS, 135:MAY72-63
HARRIS, J. A CATALOGUE OF BRITISH
DRAWINGS FOR ARCHITECTURE, DECORA-
TION, SCULPTURE & LANDSCAPE GAR-
DENING, 1550-1900, IN AMERICAN
COLLECTIONS.
G. BEARD, 90:AUG72-564
H. COLVIN, 135:JUN72-108
M. HECKSCHER, 481(PQ):JUL72-595
J. LEES-MILNE, 39:MAY72-423
HARRIS, J. THE INDIAN MUTINY.
617(TLS):3MAY74-484
HARRIS, J. - SEE WILLIAMSON, H.N.H.
HARRIS, J.C. ÉDOUARD MANET: GRAPHIC
WORKS.*
A.C. HANSON, 90:JUL72-481
A. ROBISON, 54:JUN72-224
HARRIS, J.F. & R.H. SEVENENS, EDS.
ANALYTICITY.
M.S., 543:SEP71-139
HARRIS, L. THE ANGUISH OF CHANGE.
442(NY):1APR74-123
HARRIS, M. COWS, PIGS - WARS &
WITCHES.
P. ADAMS, 61:JUN74-115
HARRIS, M. KILLING EVERYBODY.*
E. ROVIT, 659:AUTUMN74-539
HARRIS, M., WITH OTHERS. THE BLACK
BOOK.
G. DAVIS, 441:31MAR74-22
HARRIS, R. NOR EVIL DREAMS.
N. CALLENDAR, 441:3FEB74-26
HARRIS, W. BLACK MARSDEN.
P. BAILEY, 364:FEB/MAR73-157
HARRIS, W.G. GABLE & LOMBARD.
J. SAYRE, 441:15DEC74-22

HARRIS, W.V. ARTHUR HUGH CLOUGH.*
E.B. GREENBERGER, 636(VP):WINTER
72-379
HARRIS, Z.S. PAPERS IN STRUCTURAL &
TRANSFORMATIONAL LINGUISTICS.*
M.B. KAC, 350:JUN73-466
HARRISON, B. DRINK & THE VICTOR-
IANS.*
J.F.C. HARRISON, 637(VS):DEC71-
231
G.B. TENNYSON, 445(NCF):JUN72-
117
HARRISON, B. FORM & CONTENT.
617(TLS):6SEP74-956
HARRISON, B. MEANING & STRUCTURE.
H.A. LEWIS, 518:OCT73-8
HARRISON, C. MAKE OUT WITH MURDER.
N. CALLENDAR, 441:13OCT74-48
HARRISON, G. EARTHKEEPING.
A.M. WEINBERG, 639(VQR):SPRING72-
277
HARRISON, G.B., ED. ELIZABETHAN
JOURNALS.
617(TLS):26JUL74-809
HARRISON, H. QUEEN VICTORIA'S
REVENGE.
N. CALLENDAR, 441:15SEP74-45
HARRISON, J.A. THE FOUNDING OF THE
RUSSIAN EMPIRE IN ASIA & AMERICA.*
J.A. WHITE, 293(JAST):AUG72-957
HARRISON, J.A. LATIN READING COURSE.
(PT 1)
R.G. PENMAN, 123:MAR73-80
HARRISON, J.F.C. THE EARLY VICTOR-
IANS, 1832-1861.
V.M. BATZEL, 637(VS):MAR73-365
HARRISON, M. THE ROOTS OF WITCH-
CRAFT.
617(TLS):15FEB74-162
HARRISON, M. THE WORLD OF SHERLOCK
HOLMES.
617(TLS):1FEB74-113
HARRISON, R. GALLIC SALT.
N. MANN, 617(TLS):1NOV74-1221
HARRISON, R. REX.
A. FORBES, 617(TLS):20DEC74-1439
HARRISON, R. - SEE "THE SONG OF ROL-
AND"
HARRISON, W. EXPRESSION OF THE PAS-
SIVE VOICE. [TOGETHER WITH] MULLEN,
J. AGREEMENT OF THE VERB-PREDI-
CATE WITH A COLLECTIVE SUBJECT.
G.M. ERAMIAN, 104:SUMMER72-317
HARRISON, W., Y. CLARKSON & S. LE
FLEMING. COLLOQUIAL RUSSIAN.*
B. COMRIE, 575(SEER):OCT73-596
HARRISON, W. & S. LE FLEMING. RUS-
SIAN-ENGLISH & ENGLISH-RUSSIAN
DICTIONARY.*
B. COMRIE, 575(SEER):OCT73-597
HARRISSON, T. & S. O'CONNOR. GOLD &
MEGALITHIC ACTIVITY IN PREHISTORIC
& RECENT WEST BORNEO.
W. WATSON, 57:VOL34#4-356
HARROLD, W.E. THE VARIANCE & THE
UNITY.
617(TLS):22MAR74-293
HARSENT, D. AFTER DARK.
R. GARFITT, 364:FEB/MAR74-104
617(TLS):11JAN74-28
HARSENT, D. TRUCE.
R. GARFITT, 364:FEB/MAR74-106
617(TLS):11JAN74-28

HART, C. THE HIDATION OF CAMBRIDGE-
SHIRE.
617(TLS):5APR74-376
HART, D.V. BISAYAN FILIPINO &
MALAYAN HUMORAL PATHOLOGIES.
R.W. LIEBAN, 293(JAST):FEB72-468
HART, E.L. - SEE NICHOLS, J.
HART, F.R. LOCKHART AS ROMANTIC
BIOGRAPHER.*
O.M. BRACK, JR., 481(PQ):JUL72-
613
J. KINSLEY,¹ 677:VOL3-310
J.H. RALEIGH, 637(VS):DEC72-248
HART, H.L.A. PUNISHMENT & RESPONSI-
BILITY.
J.A. WEISS, 543:MAR72-527
HART, J. AID & LIBERATION.
M. LIPTON, 617(TLS):2AUG74-830
HART, J. - SEE GRIFFITH, D.W.
HART-DAVIS, D. PETER FLEMING.
M. LINDSAY, 362:28NOV74-717
M. MUGGERIDGE, 617(TLS):8NOV74-
1247
HARTE, N.B. & K.G. PONTING, EDS.
TEXTILE HISTORY & ECONOMIC HISTORY.
617(TLS):5APR74-365
HARTH, D. PHILOLOGIE UND PRAKTISCHE
PHILOSOPHIE.*
P. SKRINE, 402(MLR):APR73-446
HARTH, E. CYRANO DE BERGERAC & THE
POLEMICS OF MODERNITY.*
A.M. BEICHMAN, 546(RR):OCT72-233
P.M. HARRY, 402(MLR):APR73-407
M. LAUGAA, 557(RSH):OCT-DEC72-
606
V. RAMOS, 207(FR):DEC71-523
HARTH, K-L. GESPROCHENES DEUTSCH.
S. ŽEPIĆ, 206:JUL72-598
HARTH, P. CONTEXTS OF DRYDEN'S
THOUGHT.*
T.A. BIRRELL, 433:APR72-239
HARTLEY, L.P. MRS. CARTERET RE-
CEIVES.
E. GLOVER, 565:VOL13#2-65
HARTLIB, S. SAMUEL HARTLIB & THE
ADVANCEMENT OF LEARNING. (C. WEB-
STER, ED)
C. HILL, 447(N&Q):OCT72-399
HÄRTLING, P. EINE FRAU.
617(TLS):4OCT74-1093
HARTMAN, G.H. BEYOND FORMALISM.*
A. FLETCHER, 128(CE):DEC72-414
M. KRIEGER, 659:WINTER74-141
HARTMAN, G.H., ED. NEW PERSPECTIVES
ON COLERIDGE & WORDSWORTH.
H. LUKE, 502(PRS):WINTER72/73-
368
HARTMANN VON AUE. DER ARME HEINRICH.
(H. PAUL, ED; 14TH ED REV BY L.
WOLFF)
J.S. GROSECLOSE, 406:SUMMER73-
214
HARTMANN, H. WALLENSTEIN.*
H-J. GEERDTS, 654(WB):2/1972-185
HARTMANN, P. SYNTAX UND BEDEUTUNG.
(PT 1)
R. RADVILA, 343:BAND15HEFT2-207
HARTMANN, P. & C. HUSBAND. RACISM
& THE MASS MEDIA.
617(TLS):26APR74-439
HARTMANN, W. - SEE MANEGOLD VON LAU-
TENBACH
HARTSHORNE, C. BORN TO SING.
639(VQR):AUTUMN73-CLXXIV

HARTSHORNE, C. CREATIVE SYNTHESIS
& PHILOSOPHIC METHOD.*
R.L.C., 543:JUN72-754
D.S. ROBINSON, 484(PPR):DEC72-
271
HARTT, F. A HISTORY OF ITALIAN
RENAISSANCE ART.*
J.T. PAOLETTI, 56:SPRING72-76
A. SMART, 39:MAY72-420
HARTT, F. & D. FINN. DONATELLO.*
J. POPE-HENNESSY, 453:24JAN74-7
HARTUNG, A.E., ED. A MANUAL OF THE
WRITINGS IN MIDDLE ENGLISH 1050-
1500. (VOL 3)
M.W.B., 589:JAN73-186
HARTVIGSON, H.H. ON THE INTONATION
& POSITION OF THE SO-CALLED SEN-
TENCE MODIFIERS IN PRESENT-DAY
ENGLISH.*
P.A. SCHREIBER, 361:VOL29#3/4-
347
H. WODE, 38:BAND90HEFT1/2-191
HARTWIG, J. SHAKESPEARE'S TRAGI-
COMIC VISION.
G.M. HARVEY, 150(DR):SUMMER72-
322
S. WELLS, 677:VOL3-279
"RUSSELL HARTY PLUS."
D. THOMAS, 362:19&26DEC74-846
HARVARD, J. & F. ROSE. BILINGUAL
GUIDE TO BUSINESS & PROFESSIONAL
CORRESPONDENCE/GUIDE BILINGUE DE
LA CORRESPONDANCE COMMERCIALE ET
PROFESSIONNELLE. (REV)
F.W. VOGLER, 399(MLJ):MAR72-180
HARVARD, S. ORNAMENTAL INITIALS.
J. DREYFUS, 617(TLS):29NOV74-
1338
HARVESTER, S. FORGOTTEN ROAD.
N. CALLENDAR, 441:29SEP74-41
HARVEY, D. SOCIAL JUSTICE & THE
CITY.
617(TLS):22FEB74-172
HARVEY, E.B. & J.L. LENNARDS. KEY
ISSUES IN HIGHER EDUCATION.
W. PITMAN, 99:JUL74-32
HARVEY, J. CONSERVATION OF BUILD-
INGS.
A. CLIFTON-TAYLOR, 135:DEC72-290
HARVEY, J.R. VICTORIAN NOVELISTS &
THEIR ILLUSTRATORS.*
R. GRAHAM, 503:SUMMER72-104
P.A. HOLCOMB, 191(ELN):SEP72-54
R.A. VOGLER, 637(VS):SEP71-102
HARVEY, L.E. SAMUEL BECKETT.*
M.J. FRIEDMAN, 207(FR):DEC71-499
J-J. MAYOUX, 189(EA):JUL-SEP72-
412
HARVEY, N.L. ELIZABETH OF YORK.
617(TLS):4JAN74-18
HARVOR, B. WOMEN & CHILDREN.
R.M. BROWN, 296:VOL3#3-89
617(TLS):21JUN74-656
HARWOOD, M. & M. DURANT. A COUNTRY
JOURNAL.
442(NY):9SEP74-135
HARWOOD, R. ARTICLES OF FAITH.*
R. BLYTHE, 362:10JAN74-56
HARWOOD, R. SIR DONALD WOLFIT.
E. SHORTER, 157:WINTER71-73
HASAN, S.Y. - SEE UNDER YAQUB HASAN,
S.

HASENHÜTTL, G. CHARISMA, ORDNUNGS-
PRINZIP DER KIRCHE.
J. RICHES, 182:VOL25#23/24-849
HASKELL, M. FROM REVERENCE TO RAPE.
A. BROYARD, 441:5MAR74-37
J. WILSON, 441:24MAR74-6
HASLINGER, A. EPISCHE FORMEN IM
DEUTSCHEN BAROCKROMAN.
H.G. HAILE, 221(GQ):JAN72-159
HASLIP, J. THE CROWN OF MEXICO.
V. DE ROZENTAL, 37:NOV-DEC72-38
HASLIP, J. THE SULTAN.
J. UPDIKE, 442(NY):6MAY74-141
HASLUCK, A. ROYAL ENGINEER.
617(TLS):18JAN74-61
HASS, R. FIELD GUIDE.
V. YOUNG, 249(HUDR):WINTER73/74-
723
639(VQR):AUTUMN73-CXL
HASSAN, I. CONTEMPORARY AMERICAN
LITERATURE 1945-1972.
S. STEPANCHEV, 27(AL):JAN74-626
HASSAN, I. THE DISMEMBERMENT OF
ORPHEUS.*
L. CASPER, 613:WINTER72-618
HASSÁN, I.M., ED. ACTAS DEL PRIMER
SIMPOSIO DE ESTUDIOS SEFARDÍES.
R. HABOUCHA, 400(MLN):MAR72-330
I.J. LÉVY, 238:SEP72-595
HASSELL, J.W., JR. SOURCES & ANA-
LOGUES OF THE "NOUVELLES RÉCRÉA-
TIONS ET JOYEUX DEVIS" OF BONAVEN-
TURE DES PÉRIERS.* (VOL 2)
M. BENSIMON, 545(RPH):MAY73-738
W.F.J. DE JONGH, 546(RR):OCT72-
231
HASTINGS, F. THE LETTERS OF SIR
FRANCIS HASTINGS, 1574-1609. (C.
CROSS, ED)
D. PENNINGTON, 447(N&Q):MAY72-
197
HASTINGS, H. - SEE ABBÉ BOUGEANT
HATCH, A. BUCKMINSTER FULLER.
E. WEEKS, 61:JUL74-97
HATCHER, J. ENGLISH TIN PRODUCTION
& TRADE BEFORE 1550.
617(TLS):5APR74-365
HATCHER, W.S. FOUNDATIONS OF MATHE-
MATICS.
J. CORCORAN, 486:MAR72-88
Y. GAUTHIER, 154:MAR72-167
HATFIELD, G.W. HENRY FIELDING & THE
LANGUAGE OF IRONY.*
U. DENECKE, 38:BAND90HEFT1/2-244
HATFIELD, H. CRISIS & CONTINUITY IN
MODERN GERMAN FICTION.
D. LATIMER, 385(MQR):FALL74-421
HATHAWAY, B. A TRANSFORMATIONAL
SYNTAX.
J.K. CHAMBERS, 320(CJL):SPRING71-
113
HATHAWAY, W. TRUE CONFESSIONS &
FALSE ROMANCES.
D.E. RICHARDSON, 598(SOR):WINTER
74-225
HATJE, G. & E. KASPAR, EDS. NEW
FURNITURE 10.
505:SEP72-166
HATTEMER, H. DENKMALE DES MITTEL-
ALTERS.
H. STOPP, 680(ZDP):BAND91HEFT3-
414
HATTERSLEY, R. NELSON.
617(TLS):31MAY74-592

HATTO, A.T. - SEE NORMAN, F.
HATTON, R. & M.S. ANDERSON, EDS.
 STUDIES IN DIPLOMATIC HISTORY.
 H.A. BARTON, 563(SS):SUMMER73-
 265
HATTON, R.W. - SEE DE LERA, A.M.
HATZFELD, H. INITIATION À L'EXPLI-
 CATION DE TEXTES FRANÇAIS.
 P. DELBOUILLE, 556(RLV):1972/1-
 108
HATZFELD, H.A. ANALISI E INTERPRE-
 TAZIONI STILISTICHE.
 A. SCAGLIONE, 545(RPH):NOV72-440
HAUBRICHS, W. ORDO ALS FORM.*
 P. OCHSENBEIN, 680(ZDP):BAND91
 HEFT3-418
HAUCK, P. OVERCOMING DEPRESSION.
 617(TLS):22NOV74-1314
HAUCK, R.B. A CHEERFUL NIHILISM.*
 L. CASPER, 613:AUTUMN72-456
HAUDRICOURT, A. & A. JUILLAND.
 ESSAI POUR UNE HISTOIRE STRUCTUR-
 ALE DU PHONÉTISME FRANÇAIS. (2ND
 ED)
 W. ZWANENBURG, 361:VOL29#3/4-382
HAUFRECHT, H. FOLKSONGS IN SETTINGS
 BY MASTER COMPOSERS.
 W.K. MC NEIL, 292(JAF):JAN-MAR72-
 95
HAUGEN, E., ED & TRANS. FIRST GRAM-
 MATICAL TREATISE.
 E. LORENZO, 202(FMOD):JUN72-343
HAUGEN, E. THE NORWEGIAN LANGUAGE
 IN AMERICA.
 K. KAZAZIS, 269(IJAL):JUL72-219
 J. MEY, 353:10CT72-125
HAUGEN, E. & A.E. SANTANIELLO - SEE
 KOHT, H.
HAUN, K. - SEE "A CHINESE GLOSSARY
 OF INTERNATIONAL CONFERENCE TERMIN-
 OLOGY"
HAUPT, G. SOCIALISM & THE GREAT WAR.
 W.D. MC CLELLAN, 32:JUN73-384
HAUPT, J. DER TRUCHSESS KEIE IM
 ARTUSROMAN.
 E.S. DICK, 406:FALL73-324
 D.H. GREEN, 402(MLR):0CT73-939
HAUPTMANN, H. & V. MILOJČIČ. DIE
 FUNDE DER FRÜHEN DIMINI-ZEIT AUS
 DER ARAPI-MAGULA, THESSALIEN.
 M.S.F. HOOD, 303:VOL92-237
HAUSER, A. KUNST UND GESELLSCHAFT.
 617(TLS):3MAY74-466
HAUSER, A. SOZIOLOGIE DER KUNST.
 P. BURKE, 617(TLS):27DEC74-1467
HAUSER, O. ENGLAND UND DAS DRITTE
 REICH. (VOL 1)
 617(TLS):21JUN74-664
HAUSER, W.B. ECONOMIC INSTITUTIONAL
 CHANGE IN TOKUGAWA JAPAN.
 617(TLS):20SEP74-1023
HAUSIUS, K.G. MATERIALIEN ZUR GES-
 CHICHTE DER KRITISCHEN PHILOSOPHIE.
 R. MALTER, 342:BAND63HEFT2-278
HÄUSLER, F. DAS PROBLEM PHONETIK
 UND PHONOLOGIE BEI BAUDOUIN DE
 COURTENAY UND IN SEINER NACHFOLGE.
 E.F.K. KOERNER, 353:JAN72-63
HÄUSLER, F. RUSSISCHE AUSSPRACHE.
 W. SCHAMSCHULA, 430(NS):NOV72-
 680
HAUSMAN, G. CIRCLE MEADOW.
 G. MALANGA, 491:JAN74-236

HAVARD, W.C., ED. THE CHANGING POLI-
 TICS OF THE SOUTH.
 T.W. ROGERS, 396(MODA):FALL73-
 438
 639(VQR):SPRING73-LXXXVI
HAVELOCK, C.M. HELLENISTIC ART.*
 S. HOWARD, 127:WINTER72/73-236
 B.S. RIDGWAY, 54:SEP72-341
 G.B. WAYWELL, 303:VOL92-246
HAVELOCK, E.A. PROMETHEUS.
 L.P.E. PARKER, 447(N&Q):NOV72-
 439
HAVERKAMP, A. HERRSCHAFTSFORMEN DER
 FRÜHSTAUFER IN REICHSITALIEN.
 H.S. OFFLER, 182:VOL25#9/10-310
HAVERKAMP-BEGEMANN, E. & A-M.S.
 LOGAN. EUROPEAN DRAWINGS & WATER-
 COLOURS IN THE YALE UNIVERSITY ART
 GALLERY 1500-1900.
 K. ANDREWS, 39:JAN72-68
HAVIGHURST, A.F. RADICAL JOURNALIST.
 S. KOSS, 362:12DEC74-784
 F.M. LEVENTHAL, 617(TLS):22NOV74-
 1306
HAWES, J.J. THE LEGACY OF JOSIAH
 JOHNSON HAWES. (R.J. HOMER, ED)
 639(VQR):SUMMER73-CXXV
HAWES, J.M. CHILDREN IN URBAN SOCI-
 ETY.*
 639(VQR):SPRING72-LXVIII
HAWKE, D.F. PAINE.
 M. CUNLIFFE, 441:4AUG74-2
 A. WHITMAN, 441:6JUL74-15
 442(NY):20MAY74-152
HAWKE, D.F. BENJAMIN RUSH, REVOLU-
 TIONARY GADFLY.
 J.H. HUTSON, 656(WMQ):APR72-309
 639(VQR):WINTER72-X
HAWKE, G.R. RAILWAYS & ECONOMIC
 GROWTH IN ENGLAND & WALES, 1840-
 1870.
 J. GINARLIS, 637(VS):MAR72-389
HAWKES, C. & S., EDS. GREEKS, CELTS
 & ROMANS.
 617(TLS):12APR74-388
HAWKES, J. THE BLOOD ORANGES.
 S.A. BLACK, 648:0CT72-76
 J. DITSKY, 219(GAR):FALL72-297
 639(VQR):WINTER72-XVIII
HAWKES, J. DEATH, SLEEP & THE TRAV-
 ELER.
 D. BROMWICH, 441:21APR74-5
 A. BROYARD, 441:11APR74-39
 R. TODD, 61:MAY74-130
 M. WOOD, 453:8AUG74-40
HAWKEY, R. & R. BINGHAM. WILD CARD.
 N. CALLENDAR, 441:18AUG74-24
HAWKINS, F. CANADA & IMMIGRATION.
 H. TROPER, 99:FEB74-37
HAWKINS, G.S. BEYOND STONEHENGE.*
 617(TLS):17MAY74-535
HAWKINS, H. LIKENESSES OF TRUTH IN
 ELIZABETHAN & RESTORATION DRAMA.*
 D. COHEN, 568(SCN):SPRING73-14
 T. HAWKES, 676(YR):SUMMER73-561
 B.R. SCHNEIDER, 566:SPRING73-112
HAWTHORNE, N. THE AMERICAN NOTE-
 BOOKS. (C.M. SIMPSON, ED) TRUE
 STORIES FROM HISTORY & BIOGRAPHY.
 A WONDER BOOK & TANGLEWOOD TALES.
 T. MARTIN, 27(AL):JAN74-613

VON HAXTHAUSEN, A. STUDIES ON THE
INTERIOR OF RUSSIA.* (S.F. STARR,
ED)
N.V. RIASANOVSKY, 32:SEP73-605
HAY, J. ANCIENT CHINA.
617(TLS):19JUL74-772
HAY, J. BORN 1900.
P. IGNOTUS, 617(TLS):15NOV74-
1289
HAY, J. MASTERPIECES OF CHINESE ART.
617(TLS):11OCT74-1108
HAYAKAWA, S.I., ED. MODERN GUIDE TO
SYNONYMS.
G.H. BLANKE, 430(NS):OCT72-614
G.F. MEIER, 682(ZPSK):BAND24
HEFT6-545
HAYDEN, D.E., E.P. ALLWORTH & G.
TATE, EDS. CLASSICS IN LINGUIS-
TICS.
K.E. ZIMMER, 545(RPH):FEB73-592
HAYDEN, J.M. FRANCE & THE ESTATES
GENERAL OF 1614.
R. BRIGGS, 617(TLS):13DEC74-1422
HAYDEN, J.O., ED. ROMANTIC BARDS &
BRITISH REVIEWERS.
J.R.D. JACKSON, 627(UTQ):SPRING
73-289
HAYDEN, J.O., ED. SCOTT: THE CRITI-
CAL HERITAGE.*
A.P. ROBSON, 637(VS):JUN72-475
HAYDN, H. WORDS & FACES.
M. COWLEY, 441:3NOV74-10
G. WALKER, 441:19OCT74-29
442(NY):14OCT74-202
HAYEN, A. L'INTENTIONNEL SELON
SAINT THOMAS. (2ND ED)
A. FOREST, 542:JAN-MAR72-73
HAYES, A. THE STOCKBROKER, THE BIT-
TER YOUNG MAN, & THE BEAUTIFUL
GIRL.*
P. BAILEY, 364:APR/MAY73-166
HAYES, A.S. LANGUAGE LABORATORY
FACILITIES.*
W.J. MEYS, 206:SEP72-129
HAYES, D. QUITE A GOOD ADDRESS.*
J. MELLORS, 364:DEC73/JAN74-155
HAYES, J. CATALOGUE OF THE OIL
PAINTINGS IN THE LONDON MUSEUM.*
D. PIPER, 90:JUL72-484
HAYES, J. THE DRAWINGS OF THOMAS
GAINSBOROUGH.*
W. AMES, 54:SEP72-360
L. HERRMANN, 90:DEC72-874
R. PAULSON, 173(ECS):FALL72-106
HAYES, J. GAINSBOROUGH AS PRINT-
MAKER.
R. EDWARDS, 39:JUN72-518
HAYES, J. THE LONG DARK NIGHT.
N. CALLENDAR, 441:28JUL74-14
617(TLS):27DEC74-1466
HAYES, J. ROWLANDSON: WATERCOLOURS
& DRAWINGS.
F.W. HILLES, 676(YR):SPRING73-
443
HAYES, P. FASCISM.
617(TLS):25JAN74-87
HAYES, P.M. QUISLING.
M. SCHIFF, 563(SS):SPRING73-160
HAYIT, B. TURKESTAN ZWISCHEN RUSS-
LAND UND CHINA.
D.S.M. WILLIAMS, 575(SEER):APR73-
309
HAYMAN, D. ULYSSES.
R. BOYLE, 659:SPRING74-262

HAYMAN, R. IONESCO.
J. PETER, 157:SUMMER72-72
HAYMAN, R. THE SET-UP.
R. BRYDEN, 362:14FEB74-213
617(TLS):5APR74-359
HAYNES, S. ETRUSCAN SCULPTURE.
F.R. SERRA RIDGWAY, 313:VOL62-
227
HAYTER, T. AID AS IMPERIALISM.
M. LIPTON, 617(TLS):2AUG74-830
HAYTER, W. A DOUBLE LIFE.
617(TLS):24MAY74-551
HAYWARD, C.H. ANTIQUE OR FAKE?
G. WILLS, 39:NOV72-461
HAZELTON, N. I COOK AS I PLEASE.
A. YOUNGMAN, 441:1DEC74-98
HAZEN, A.T. A CATALOGUE OF HORACE
WALPOLE'S LIBRARY.*
R.R. ALLEN, 173(ECS):FALL72-118
J.D. FLEEMAN, 78(BC):SUMMER72-
275
HAZEN, E.P., G. MILNE & P.H. HEMING-
SON - SEE "AMERICAN BOOK-PRICES
CURRENT, 1968"
HAZEN, E.P., G. MILNE & W.J. SMITH -
SEE "AMERICAN BOOK-PRICES CURRENT,
1967"
HAZLEHURST, C. & C. WOODLAND. A
GUIDE TO THE PAPERS OF BRITISH
CABINET MINISTERS, 1900-1951.
617(TLS):11OCT74-1143
HAZLITT, W. THE SPIRIT OF THE AGE.
(E.D. MACKERNESS, ED)
J.C. MAXWELL, 447(N&Q):MAR72-113
HEAD, B. A QUESTION OF POWER.*
J. MELLORS, 364:FEB/MAR74-134
HEAD, C. JUSTINIAN II OF BYZANTIUM.
J.M. HUSSEY, 575(SEER):APR73-329
HEAD, L. THE FIRST OF JANUARY.
M. LEVIN, 441:27JAN74-14
HEADINGTON, C. THE BODLEY HEAD HIS-
TORY OF WESTERN MUSIC.
617(TLS):18OCT74-1165
HEALD, E.T. WITNESS TO REVOLUTION.
(J.B. GIDNEY, ED)
W.E. MOSSE, 575(SEER):APR73-317
R.H. ULLMAN, 32:SEP73-613
J.L. WIECZYNSKI, 550(RUSR):OCT72-
427
HEALD, T. BLUE BLOOD WILL OUT.
N. CALLENDAR, 441:20OCT74-42
HEANEY, S. WINTERING OUT.*
J.E. CHAMBERLIN, 249(HUDR):SUM-
MER73-393
G. EWART, 364:DEC72/JAN73-132
J. GALASSI, 491:NOV73-113
HEAP, J. EVERYBODY'S CANADA.
J.P. GRAYSON, 99:NOV/DEC74-50
HEAPS, L. LOG OF THE CENTURION.
617(TLS):21JUN74-680
HEARD, K.A. GENERAL ELECTIONS IN
SOUTH AFRICA 1943-1970.
J. LEWIN, 617(TLS):6SEP74-957
"HEARINGS BEFORE THE SELECT COMMIT-
TEE ON NUTRITION & HUMAN NEEDS."
(PTS 2-4)
D. ZWERDLING, 453:21FEB74-22
HEARN, M.P. - SEE BAUM, L.F.
HEARSEY, J.E.N. YOUNG MR. PEPYS.
442(NY):22JUL74-84

HEATER, D.B., ED. THE TEACHING OF
POLITICS.
S. MC KNIGHT, 619(TC):VOL177
#1043-49
HEATH, P. THE PHILOSOPHER'S ALICE.
A. QUINTON, 617(TLS):20DEC74-
1436
HEATH, R.A.K. A MAN COME HOME.
F. PIKE, 617(TLS):27DEC74-1466
HEATH, S. THE NOUVEAU ROMAN.*
F.S. HECK, 268:JUL74-161
HEATH, S. LE VERTIGE DU DÉPLACEMENT.
J. CULLER, 617(TLS):30AUG74-934
HEATH, W. WORDSWORTH & COLERIDGE.*
J. COLMER, 402(MLR):APR73-394
M. JACOBUS, 541(RES):FEB72-86
K.K., 191(ELN):SEP72(SUPP)-65
H. VIEBROCK, 72:BAND210HEFT4/6-
414
"MAIDA HEATTER'S BOOK OF GREAT DES-
SERTS."
N. HAZELTON, 441:1DEC74-96
HEBER, R. BISHOP HEBER IN NORTHERN
INDIA. (M.A. LAIRD, ED)
N.G. BARRIER, 293(JAST):AUG72-
968
D.C. ELLINWOOD, 302:JUL72-223
HÉBERT, A. THE TORRENT.
B. GODARD, 99:NOV/DEC74-24
F.M. MACRI, 296:VOL3#2-105
HEBERT, A. & F. SCOTT. DIALOGUE SUR
LAS TRADUCTION.
E.J. TALBOT, 207(FR):OCT71-243
HECHT, M.B. JOHN QUINCY ADAMS.
P.P. HILL, 656(WMQ):OCT73-683
R. KETCHAM, 639(VQR):SPRING73-
290
HECHT, W. AUFSÄTZE ÜBER BRECHT.
J. FUEGI, 221(GQ):MAY72-508
C. TRILSE, 654(WB):9/1971-182
HECKSCHER, A. ALIVE IN THE CITY.
H. POST, 441:7APR74-6
HEDAYAT, D. LE BLEU LE BLEU.
S. MAX, 207(FR):MAY72-1179
HEENAN, J.C. A CROWN OF THORNS.
P. HEBBLETHWAITE, 617(TLS):
4OCT74-1064
BISHOP OF SOUTHWARK, 362:12SEP74-
347
HEER, N.W. POLITICS & HISTORY IN
THE SOVIET UNION.*
L. HOLMES, 125:OCT72-84
HEERS, J. LE CLAN FAMILIAL AU MOYEN
ÂGE.
J.K. HYDE, 617(TLS):22NOV74-1324
HEESTERMAN, J.C., G.H. SCHOKKER &
V.I. SUBRAMONIAM, EDS. PRATIDĀNAM.
M.J. DRESDEN, 318(JAOS):APR-JUN
72-312
HEEZEN, B.C. & C.D. HOLLISTER. THE
FACE OF THE DEEP.
C. MC FARLAND, 639(VQR):WINTER72-
126
HEFTING, V. JONGKIND D'APRÈS SA
CORRESPONDANCE.*
R.L. HERBERT, 54:MAR72-104
HEFTRICH, E. NOVALIS.
H. EICHNER, 221(GQ):NOV72-762
HEGEL, G.W.F. ENCYCLOPÉDIE DES SCI-
ENCES PHILOSOPHIQUES. (VOL 1)
(B. BOURGEOIS, ED & TRANS)
J. BERNHARDT, 542:JUL-SEP72-356

HEGEL, G.W.F. ENCYCLOPÉDIE DES SCI-
ENCES PHILOSOPHIQUES EN ABRÉGÉ
(1830). (M. DE GANDILLAC, TRANS)
J. BERNHARDT, 542:JUL-SEP72-358
HEGEL, G.W.F. FENOMENOLOGIA DELLO
SPIRITO.
E. NAMER, 542:JUL-SEP72-356
HEGEL, G.W.F. GESAMMELTE WERKE.*
(VOL 7) (R-P. HORSTMANN & J.H.
TREDE, EDS)
T.M. KNOX, 479(PHQ):JUL72-274
HEGEL, G.W.F. HEGEL'S PHILOSOPHY OF
NATURE.* (A.V. MILLER, TRANS)
G. BUCHDAHL, 84:AUG72-257
J.A. DOULL, 154:SEP72-379
K. HARTMANN, 53(AGP):BAND54HEFT1-
93
HEGEL, G.W.F. HEGEL'S PHILOSOPHY OF
NATURE.* (M.J. PETRY, ED & TRANS)
R.J.B., 543:SEP71-126
G. BUCHDAHL, 84:AUG72-257
J.A. DOULL, 154:SEP72-379
W.P.D. WIGHTMAN, 479(PHQ):JUL72-
272
HEGEL, G.W.F. PHILOSOPHY OF MIND.
(W. WALLACE, TRANS)
K. HARTMANN, 53(AGP):BAND54HEFT1-
93
HEGER, H. DAS LEBENSZEUGNIS WAL-
THERS VON DER VOGELWEIDE.
M.E. GIBBS, 220(GL&L):JUL73-345
HEGER, K. DIE BISHER VERÖFFENTLICH-
TEN HARGAS UND IHRE DEUTUNGEN.
L.J. FRIEDMAN, 545(RPH):MAY73-
711
HEGER, K. MONEM, WORT UND SATZ.
E.H. YARRILL, 182:VOL25#7/8-219
"THE HEIBONSHA SURVEY OF JAPANESE
ART." (VOLS 2, 10, 12, 17-19 & 22)
617(TLS):2AUG74-838
HEIDEGGER, G. MYTHOSCOPIA ROMANTICA
ODER DISCOURS VON DEN SO BENANNTEN
ROMANS. (W.E. SCHÄFER, ED)
W. BENDER, 222(GR):MAR72-132
K. HABERKAMM, 657(WW):JUL/AUG72-
285
HEIDEGGER, M. ON THE WAY TO LANGU-
AGE.
J.D.C., 543:DEC71-353
K. HARRIES, 482(PHR):JUL72-387
J.J. KOCKELMANS, 215(GL):VOL12#3-
176
L. & C. WELCH, 290(JAAC):FALL72-
117
HEIDEGGER, M. PHÄNOMENOLOGIE UND
THEOLOGIE.
J.D.C., 543:DEC71-353
HEIDEGGER, M. POETRY, LANGUAGE,
THOUGHT.
J.D.C., 543:JUN72-755
R.H.C., 125:OCT72-86
L. & C. WELCH, 290(JAAC):FALL72-
117
HEIDEGGER, M. SÔBRE A ESSÊNCIA DA
VERDADE.
R. MALIANDI, 342:BAND63HEFT3-389
HEIDEGGER, M. WHAT IS A THING?
(W.B. BARTON, JR. & V. DEUTSCH,
TRANS)
C.M. SHEROVER, 480(P&R):SUMMER
72-191
HEIDEGGER, M. & E. FINK. HERAKLIT.
J.D.C., 543:SEP71-126

HEIDENREICH, C. HURONIA.
H.V. NELLES, 99:OCT74-44
HEIDENREICH, H. THE LIBRARIES OF
DANIEL DEFOE & PHILLIPS FAREWELL.*
K.J. HÖLTGEN, 38:BAND9OHEFT1/2-
243
HEIDSIECK, A. DAS GROTESKE UND DAS
ABSURDE IM MODERNEN DRAMA.*
S. MELCHINGER, 52:BAND7HEFT1-112
HEIDUK, F. DIE DICHTER DER GALANTEN
LYRIK.
A.G. DE CAPUA, 301(JEGP):JAN73-
81
A. MENHENNET, 402(MLR):APR73-452
HEIER, E. L.H. NICOLAY (1737-1820)
& HIS CONTEMPORARIES.
M. DAVID, 542:JUL-SEP72-331
HEIER, E. RELIGIOUS SCHISM IN THE
RUSSIAN ARISTOCRACY: 1890-1900.
P.D. STEEVES, 550(RUSR):JAN72-95
HEIFERMAN, R. WORLD WAR II.
617(TLS):8FEB74-128
VAN HEIJENOORT, J. - SEE FREGE, G. &
K. GÖDEL
HEILBRONER, R.L. AN INQUIRY INTO
THE HUMAN PROSPECT.
G. BARRACLOUGH, 453:27JUN74-14
J. FALLOWS, 441:12MAY74-5
A. HACKER, 231:SEP74-72
442(NY):22APR74-155
HEILBRUN, C. TOWARD A RECOGNITION
OF ANDROGYNY.* (BRITISH TITLE:
TOWARDS ANDROGYNY.)
676(YR):SUMMER73-VIII
HEILMAN, R.B. TRAGEDY & MELODRAMA.*
A.V.C. SCHMIDT, 447(N&Q):DEC72-
471
HEILMANN, L. GRAMMATICA STORICA
DELLA LINGUA GRECA, CON CENNI DI
SINTASSI STORICA DI ALFREDO GHI-
SELLI.
H. RIX, 343:BAND14HEFT2-169
HEIMAN, L. PORVOON VAIHEITA.
G.C. SCHOOLFIELD, 563(SS):SPRING
73-180
HEIMSATH, C.H. & S. MANSINGH. A DIP-
LOMATIC HISTORY OF MODERN INDIA.
M.W. FISHER, 293(JAST):AUG72-972
HEIMSOETH, H. STUDIEN ZUR PHILOSO-
PHIE IMMANUEL KANTS. (VOL 1) (2ND
ED)
R. MALTER, 342:BAND63HEFT2-278
HEINE, H. SÄMTLICHE SCHRIFTEN.
(VOL 4) (K. BRIEGLEB, ED)
J.L.S., 191(ELN):SEP72(SUPP)-150
HEINE, H. SÄMTLICHE WERKE: DÜSSEL-
DORFER AUSGABE. (VOL 6) (J. HER-
MAND, ED) SÄMTLICHE SCHRIFTEN.
(VOL 2) (G. HÄNTZSCHEL, ED)
617(TLS):25JAN74-65
HEINE, H. ÜBER DIE FRANZÖSISCHE
BÜHNE UND ANDERE SCHRIFTEN ZUM THÉ-
ATER. (C. TRILSE, ED)
J.L.S., 191(ELN):SEP72(SUPP)-154
HEINE, H. WERKE, BRIEFE, LEBENS-
ZEUGNISSE: SÄKULARAUSGABE.* (VOL
7: ÜBER FRANKREICH 1831-1837.) (F.
MENDE & K.H. HAHN, EDS)
M. MANN, 400(MLN):APR72-529
617(TLS):25JAN74-65
"HEINRICH HEINE."* (N. ALTENHOFER,
ED)
J.A. KRUSE, 182:VOL25#5/6-157
J.L.S., 191(ELN):SEP72(SUPP)-148

HEINEKAMP, A. DAS PROBLEM DES GUTEN
BEI LEIBNIZ.
J. FREUND, 542:APR-JUN72-212
HEINER, H-J. DAS GANZHEITSDENKEN
FRIEDRICH SCHLEGELS.*
M.H., 191(ELN):SEP72(SUPP)-178
HEINESEN, W. THE LOST MUSICIANS.
R.D. SPECTOR, 563(SS):SPRING73-
169
HEINEY, D. THREE ITALIAN NOVELISTS.
C. FANTAZZI, 593:SPRING73-91
HEINLEIN, R.A. TIME ENOUGH FOR
LOVE.*
617(TLS):14JUN74-644
HEINRICHS, H., ED. LEXIKON DER
AUDIO-VISUELLEN BILDUNGSMITTEL.
O. ALLENDORF, 430(NS):JUN72-370
HEINSIUS, D. ON PLOT IN TRAGEDY.*
(P.R. SELLIN & J.J. MC MANMON,
TRANS)
C.Z. OREOVICZ, 568(SCN):SPRING73-
19
HEINZLE, J. STELLENKOMMENTAR ZU
WOLFRAMS "TITUREL."
H.B. WILLSON, 301(JEGP):APR73-
273
HEIRMAN, L.J.R. - SEE PLUTARCH
HEIRON, G.F. THE MAJESTY OF BRITISH
STEAM.
617(TLS):8FEB74-140
HEISENBERG, W. PHYSICS & BEYOND.*
H.W. BRANN, 258:SEP72-466
HEISEY, A. THE GREAT CANADIAN STAM-
PEDE.
A.M. RUGMAN, 99:SEP74-47
HEISSIG, W. GESCHICHTE DER MONGOL-
ISCHEN LITERATUR.
617(TLS):18JAN74-59
HEITSCH, E. GEGENWART UND EVIDENZ
BEI PARMENIDES.
P.M. HUBY, 123:MAR73-84
HEITZ, G. BRÈVES NOUVELLES NÉES.
M. SCHAETTEL, 557(RSH):JUL-SEP72-
480
HEJINIAN, J. EXTREME REMEDIES.
R. JAFFE, 441:4AUG74-4
C. LEHMANN-HAUPT, 441:11JUN74-45
HEJZLAR, J. THE ART OF VIETNAM.
617(TLS):12APR74-401
HELBIG, G. & W. SCHENKEL. WÖRTER-
BUCH ZUR VALENZ UND DISTRIBUTION
DEUTSCHER VERBEN.*
G. FISCHER, 353:10CT72-114
HELD, J.S. & D. POSNER. 17TH & 18TH
CENTURY ART.
E. LARSEN, 127:SUMMER73-474
HELD, V. THE PUBLIC INTEREST & INDI-
VIDUAL INTERESTS.
P.M.S. HACKER, 393(MIND):APR72-
311
HELLEINER, K.F. FREE TRADE & FRUS-
TRATION.
617(TLS):5APR74-365
HELLER, E. & J. BORN - SEE KAFKA, F.
HELLER, J. CATCH-22: A DRAMATIZA-
TION.
B.H. FUSSELL, 249(HUDR):WINTER
73/74-753
HELLER, J. PRINTMAKING TODAY.
96:EARLY AUTUMN72-111

HELLER, J. SOMETHING HAPPENED.
C. BLACKWOOD, 617(TLS):25OCT74-
1183
B. DE MOTT, 61:OCT74-106
C. LEHMANN-HAUPT, 441:1OCT74-39
J. MELLORS, 362:24OCT74-551
L.E. SISSMAN, 442(NY):25NOV74-
193
J. THOMPSON, 453:17OCT74-24
K. VONNEGUT, JR., 441:6OCT74-1
HELLER, L.G. & J. MACRIS. PARAMET-
RIC LINGUISTICS.*
W.P. LEHMANN, 660(WORD):APR70-
139
HELLER, L.G. & J. MACRIS. TOWARD A
STRUCTURAL THEORY OF LITERARY
ANALYSIS.
J.P. STANLEY, 219(GAR):SUMMER72-
229
HELLER, R. EDVARD MUNCH: THE
SCREAM.*
A. FRANKENSTEIN, 55:SUMMER73-78
HELLIE, R. ENSERFMENT & MILITARY
CHANGE IN MUSCOVY.*
W. KIRCHNER, 550(RUSR):OCT72-423
HELLMAN, L. PENTIMENTO.*
G. ANNAN, 362:25APR74-535
J. SIMON, 249(HUDR):WINTER73/74-
743
617(TLS):26APR74-440
HELLSTERN, D. DER RITTERKANTON
NECKAR-SCHWARZWALD 1560-1805.
H. LEI, 182:VOL25#11-374
HELM, A., ED. EIGHT MUMMERS' PLAYS.
A. GAILEY, 203:SUMMER72-165
A. RENDLE, 157:AUTUMN72-84
HELM, E. BÉLA BARTÓK.*
J.S. WEISSMANN, 607:#99-20
HELMCKE, H., K. LUBBERS & R. SCHMIDT-
VON BARDELEBEN, EDS. LITERATUR
UND SPRACHE DER VEREINIGTEN STAAT-
EN.
H. PRIESSNITZ, 430(NS):SEP72-552
HELMERS, H. LYRISCHER HUMOR.
L. THOMAS, 182:VOL25#3/4-84
HELMS, E. DIE HOCHSCHULREFORM IN
DEN USA UND IHRE BEDEUTUNG FÜR DIE
BRD.
M. SCHELER, 430(NS):NOV72-684
HELMS, S., ED. SCHLAGER IN DEUTSCH-
LAND.
E. SAMS, 415:SEP73-904
HELSA, D.H. THE SHAPE OF CHAOS.
G. SZANTO, 149:DEC73-387
HELWIG, D. THE BEST NAME OF SILENCE.
M. ESTOK, 150(DR):WINTER72/73-
653
HELWIG, D. & T. MARSHALL, EDS. FOUR-
TEEN STORIES HIGH.*
E. MC NAMARA, 529(QQ):SPRING72-
119
HEMINGWAY, E. THE NICK ADAMS STOR-
IES.* (P. YOUNG, ED)
K. MC SWEENEY, 150(DR):SUMMER72-
309
G. MONTEIRO, 219(GAR):WINTER72-
518
D. WILSON, 651(WHR):SUMMER73-295
639(VQR):AUTUMN72-CXXI
HEMINGWAY, J. & P. BONNECARRÈRE.
ROSEBUD.
J. FLAHERTY, 441:23JUN74-12
HEMLOW, J. & A. DOUGLAS - SEE BURNEY,
F.

HEMMERLE, K. GOTT UND DAS DENKEN
NACH SCHELLINGS SPÄTPHILOSOPHIE.
M.J.V., 543:JUN72-755
HEMMING, J. THE CONQUEST OF THE
INCAS.
A.B. EDWARDS, 37:JAN72-40
HEMMINGS, F.W.J. CULTURE & SOCIETY
IN FRANCE, 1848-1898.
C. BECKER, 535(RHL):JUL-AUG72-
736
HEMPEL, W. PHILIPP II. UND DER
ESCORIAL IN DER ITALIENISCHEN LIT-
ERATUR DES CINQUECENTO.
F. MEREGALLI, 52:BAND7HEFT2/3-
317
HEMPEL, W. ÜBERMUOT DIU ALTE...*
G.P. KNAPP, 680(ZDP):BAND91HEFT3-
446
S. WENZEL, 589:APR73-366
HEMPHILL, P. THE GOOD OLD BOYS.
A. MURRAY, 441:22SEP74-18
M. WATKINS, 441:24JUL74-45
HEMPHILL, W.E. - SEE CALHOUN, J.C.
HEMPHILL, W.E., W.A. WATES & R.N.
OLSBERG, EDS. THE STATE RECORDS
OF SOUTH CAROLINA: JOURNALS OF THE
GENERAL ASSEMBLY & HOUSE OF REPRE-
SENTATIVES, 1776-1780.
W. FRALEY, 14:JUL/OCT72-411
HEMSCHEMEYER, J. I REMEMBER THE
ROOM WAS FILLED WITH LIGHT.
V. YOUNG, 249(HUDR):WINTER73/74-
728
HENDERSON, D. DITCH VALLEY.
R.D. KELLER, 649(WAL):WINTER73-
303
HENDERSON, H.B., 3D. VERSIONS OF
THE PAST.
C. LEHMANN-HAUPT, 441:9OCT74-41
HENDERSON, J.A. THE FIRST AVANT-
GARDE (1887-1894).
B.L. KNAPP, 397(MD):MAY72-107
J. PETER, 157:SUMMER72-72
HENDERSON, P. SWINBURNE.
P. ADAMS, 61:OCT74-120
N. ANNAN, 453:28NOV74-19
442(NY):16SEP74-148
HENDERSON, R., ED. THE IMAGE MAKER.
W. ALEXANDER, 385(MQR):SPRING74-
180
HENDERSON, R.M. D.W. GRIFFITH.*
C.P. REILLY, 200:MAY72-300
639(VQR):WINTER73-XXIX
HENDIN, J. THE WORLD OF FLANNERY
O'CONNOR.*
D. GREGORY, 502(PRS):FALL72-259
W. LEAMON, 219(GAR):FALL72-381
HENDRICKS, G. THE LIFE & WORK OF
THOMAS EAKINS.
J. RUSSELL, 441:1DEC74-54
HENDRIKS, A.L. MADONNA OF THE UN-
KNOWN NATION.
617(TLS):11OCT74-1119
HENFREY, C. MANSCAPES.
M. GREEN, 364:AUG/SEP73-156
HENISSART, P. NARROW EXIT.
N. CALLENDAR, 441:20JAN74-22
HENKIN, L. FOREIGN AFFAIRS & THE
CONSTITUTION.*
C.P. IVES, 396(MODA):SUMMER73-
314
HENLE, J. GREEK MYTHS.
617(TLS):5APR74-376
HENLE, M. - SEE KÖHLER, W.

157

HENN, T.R. THE LIVING IMAGE.
  J. BUXTON, 402(MLR):JUL73-634
  G. LAMBIN, 189(EA):OCT-DEC72-542
HENNEMAN, J.B. ROYAL TAXATION IN
  FOURTEENTH CENTURY FRANCE.
  G. BEECH, 377:MAR73-47
HENNESSEY, J. & V. PAPANEK. NOMADIC
  FURNITURE 2.
  S. STEPHENS, 441:8DEC74-42
HENNESSY, J.P. - SEE UNDER POPE
  HENNESSY, J.
HENNESSY, M. THE WILD GEESE.
  617(TLS):18JAN74-45
HENNING, H., ED. FAUST-BIBLIOGRAPH-
  IE. (PT 2, VOL 2)
  D.F. BUB, 221(GQ):MAR72-371
HENNING, H. DAS WESTDEUTSCHE BÜR-
  GERTUM IN DER EPOCHE DER HOCHINDUS-
  TRIALISIERUNG 1860-1914. (PT 1)
  A. LASSERRE, 182:VOL25#9/10-314
HENNING, H. & S. SEIFERT, COMPS.
  INTERNATIONALE BIBLIOGRAPHIE ZUR
  DEUTSCHEN KLASSIK 1750-1850.
  (FOLGE 11-13)
  G. SEIDEL, 654(WB):4/1972-174
  J. TRAINER, 220(GL&L):APR73-273
HENNING, H. & S. SEIFERT, COMPS.
  INTERNATIONALE BIBLIOGRAPHIE ZUR
  DEUTSCHEN KLASSIK 1750-1850.
  (FOLGE 14 & 15)
  G. SEIDEL, 654(WB):4/1972-174
HENRETTA, J.A. "SALUTARY NEGLECT."*
  C.R. RITCHESON, 173(ECS):SUMMER
  73-509
  J. SOSIN, 656(WMQ):APR73-329
  639(VQR):AUTUMN72-CXLI
HENRIQUES, F. CHILDREN OF CALIBAN.
  M. BANTON, 617(TLS):13DEC74-1402
  A. SALKEY, 362:26SEP74-408
HENRY, A. C'ÉTAIT "IL Y A" DES
  LUNES.
  M. SANDMANN, 545(RPH):MAY73-705
HENRY, A. LES OEUVRES D'ADENET LE
  ROI. (VOL 5)
  R. O'GORMAN, 589:OCT73-756
  M. THIRY-STASSIN, 556(RLV):
  1972/4-441
HENRY, D.P. MEDIEVAL LOGIC & META-
  PHYSICS.
  P.A. CLARKE, 518:OCT73-10
  P.T. GEACH, 382(MAE):1973/3-269
HENRY, J. THE PAPERS OF JOSEPH
  HENRY. (VOL 1) (N. REINGOLD, ED)
  M.F. GIBBONS, JR., 70(ANQ):SEP73-
  13
HENRY, P. ON THE TRACK.
  J. SAUNDERS, 565:VOL13#3-75
HENRY, R. - SEE PHOTIUS
HENSLEY, J.L. THE POISON SUMMER.
  N. CALLENDAR, 441:24MAR74-40
HENSMAN, C.R. RICH AGAINST POOR.
  M. LIPTON, 617(TLS):2AUG74-830
HENSON, H. BRITISH SOCIAL ANTHRO-
  POLOGISTS & LANGUAGE.
  E. LEACH, 617(TLS):19JUL74-759
HENTHORN, W.E. A HISTORY OF KOREA.
  B.H. HAZARD, 293(JAST):AUG72-905
HENZ, R. UNTERNEHMEN LEONARDO.
  617(TLS):2AUG74-825
HENZEN, W. DIE BEZEICHNUNG VON RICH-
  TUNG UND GEGENRICHTUNG IM DEUT-
  SCHEN.*
  J. GÖSCHEL, 260(IF):BAND76-338
HEPBURN, J. - SEE BENNETT, A.

HEPPENSTALL, R. BLUEBEARD & AFTER.
  R. GADNEY, 364:APR/MAY72-144
HERAKLEIDES. HERACLIDIS LEMBI EX-
  CERPTA POLITIARUM. (M.R. DILTS,
  ED & TRANS)
  P. HARDING, 487:WINTER72-414
HERBERT, F. HELLSTROM'S HIVE.
  T. STURGEON, 441:8SEP74-39
HERBERT, F. UNDER PRESSURE.
  T. STURGEON, 441:8SEP74-40
HERBERT, J., ED. CHRISTIE'S REVIEW
  OF THE SEASON 1973.
  617(TLS):22MAR74-304
HERBERT, M. THE SNOW PEOPLE.
  617(TLS):4JAN74-8
HERBERT, R.L. DAVID, VOLTAIRE,
  "BRUTUS," & THE FRENCH REVOLUTION.
  A. FRANKENSTEIN, 55:SUMMER73-78
HERBRAND, J. LOGICAL WRITINGS.
  (W.D. GOLDFARB, ED)
  D. VAN DALEN, 311(JP):5SEP74-544
HERD, D., COMP. ANCIENT & MODERN
  SCOTTISH SONGS.*
  F. HOWES, 415:SEP73-903
HERDE, H. JOHANN GEORG HAMANN.
  J.C. O'FLAHERTY, 222(GR):NOV72-
  307
HERDE, P. AUDIENTIA LITTERARUM CON-
  TRADICTARUM.
  L.E. BOYLE, 589:APR73-368
HERDEN, W. GEIST UND MACHT.
  U. BASTIAN, 654(WB):7/1972-188
VON HERDER, J.G. J.G. HERDER ON
  SOCIAL & POLITICAL CULTURE.* (F.M.
  BARNARD, ED & TRANS)
  R. MAYO, 125:JUN73-313
HEREN, L. & OTHERS. CHINA'S THREE
  THOUSAND YEARS.*
  A. AUSTIN, 441:27DEC74-29
HERGENHAN, L.T. - SEE CLARKE, M.
HERINGER, H-J. DEUTSCHE SYNTAX.
  C.V.J. RUSS, 402(MLR):OCT73-922
HERINGTON, C.J. THE AUTHOR OF THE
  "PROMETHEUS BOUND."
  A.J. PODLECKI, 24:FALL73-305
HERMAN, J. & M.S. THE CORNUCOPIA.
  M.F.K. FISHER, 442(NY):27MAY74-
  95
HERMAND, J. LITERATURWISSENSCHAFT
  UND KUNSTWISSENSCHAFT. SYNTHET-
  ISCHES INTERPRETIEREN.
  D. KLICHE, 654(WB):10/1972-165
HERMAND, J. UNBEQUEME LITERATUR.*
  B. PESCHKEN, 564:OCT72-220
  H. RIDLEY, 402(MLR):OCT73-947
HERMAND, J. - SEE HEINE, H.
HERMANNS, M. SCHAMANEN.
  R. BASTIDE, 182:VOL25#7/8-247
HERMASSI, E. LEADERSHIP & NATIONAL
  DEVELOPMENT IN NORTH AFRICA.
  617(TLS):29MAR74-312
HERMES, H., F. KAMBARTEL & F. KAUL-
  BACH - SEE FREGE, G.
HERMET, G. THE COMMUNISTS IN SPAIN.
  P. PRESTON, 617(TLS):18OCT74-
  1152
HERMET, G. LA POLITIQUE DANS L'ES-
  PAGNE FRANQUISTE.
  J. BÉCARUD, 98:JUN72-575
HERMLIN, S. SCARDANELLI.
  C.H., 191(ELN):SEP72(SUPP)-160
HERMS, D. ENGLISCH-DEUTSCHE ÜBER-
  SETZUNG.
  H.O. THIEME, 430(NS):DEC72-745

HERN, N. PETER HANDKE.
  M. ESSLIN, 397(MD):MAR73-464
  G. MANDER, 157:WINTER71-71
  J.J. WHITE, 402(MLR):OCT73-957
HERNDL, G.C. THE HIGH DESIGN.*
  W.N. KNIGHT, 128(CE):DEC72-440
HERNDON, J.H. A SURVEY OF MODERN
  GRAMMARS.
  J. BALABAN, 215(GL):VOL12#1-59
HERNDON, V. JAMES DEAN.
  L. BRAUDY, 441:22SEP74-6
HERODAS. MIMIAMBI.* (I.C. CUNNING-
  HAM, ED)
  F. WILLIAMS, 303:VOL92-201
HERODIAN. HISTORY.* (LOEB, VOL 2,
  BKS 5-8) (C.R. WHITTAKER, ED &
  TRANS)
  T.F. CARNEY, 123:DEC73-159
HEROLD, C.P. THE MORPHOLOGY OF KING
  ALFRED'S TRANSLATION OF THE "OROS-
  IUS."*
  A. CRÉPIN, 189(EA):JAN-MAR72-78
HERRE, F. FREIHERR VOM STEIN.
  617(TLS):22FEB74-180
HERRERO, J. LOS ORÍGENES DEL PENSA-
  MIENTO REACCIONARIO ESPAÑOL.
  I.L. MC CLELLAND, 402(MLR):APR73-
  429
HERRING, J. BROWNING'S OLD SCHOOL-
  FELLOW.
  617(TLS):22MAR74-293
HERRING, P.F. - SEE JOYCE, J.
HERRING, P.J. & M.R. CLARKE, EDS.
  DEEP OCEANS.
  C. MC FARLAND, 639(VQR):WINTER72-
  126
HERRIOT, J. ALL CREATURES GREAT &
  SMALL.*
  P. ADAMS, 61:AUG74-91
HERRIOT, J. ALL THINGS BRIGHT &
  BEAUTIFUL.
  A. BROYARD, 441:24SEP74-45
  P. SHOWERS, 441:3NOV74-60
  E. WEEKS, 61:OCT74-114
HERRIOT, P. AN INTRODUCTION TO THE
  PSYCHOLOGY OF LANGUAGE.*
  J. HEWSON, 320(CJL):VOL18#1-63
HERRLINGER, R. HISTORY OF MEDICAL
  ILLUSTRATION FROM ANTIQUITY TO A.D.
  1600.
  W. LE FANU, 354:SEP72-254
HERRLITZ, W. HISTORISCHE PHONOLOGIE
  DES DEUTSCHEN. (PT 1)
  G.J. METCALF, 221(GQ):MAR72-380
HERRMANN, F. THE ENGLISH AS COLLEC-
  TORS.
  D. SUTTON, 39:DEC72-564
  135:JUN72-77
HERRMANN, L. CHRESTOS.
  A. ERNOUT, 555:VOL46FASC1-164
HERRMANN, R-D. DER KÜNSTLER IN DER
  MODERNEN GESELLSCHAFT.
  H. UHR, 290(JAAC):SUMMER73-567
HERRNSTEIN, R.J. I.Q. IN THE MERIT-
  OCRACY.*
  617(TLS):29MAR74-317
HERRON, S. THE BIRD IN LAST YEAR'S
  NEST.
  J. HAMILTON-PATERSON, 617(TLS):
  13DEC74-1420
  M. LEVIN, 441:24NOV74-40

HERSEY, G.L. ALFONSO II & THE ARTIS-
  TIC RENEWAL OF NAPLES, 1485-1495.*
  D.R. COFFIN, 576:MAR72-64
  C. PEDRETTI, 551(RENQ):SPRING72-
  69
HERSEY, G.L. HIGH VICTORIAN GOTHIC.
  N. PEVSNER, 56:AUTUMN72-315
HERSEY, J. MY PETITION FOR MORE
  SPACE.
  G. HICKS, 441:22SEP74-2
HERSEY, J., ED. THE WRITER'S CRAFT.
  C. LEHMANN-HAUPT, 441:6FEB74-41
HERTEL, H. - SEE MØLLER, P.L.
HERTZ, K.V. EURETHREA.
  J. ORANGE, 296:VOL3#1-110
HERTZBERG, A. THE FRENCH ENLIGHTEN-
  MENT & THE JEWS.*
  M.H. WADDICOR, 208(FS):APR73-204
VON HERTZEN, H. & P.D. SPREIREGEN.
  BUILDING A NEW TOWN.
  M.B. LAPPING, 576:OCT72-245
HERWIG, H.H. THE GERMAN NAVAL
  OFFICER CORPS.
  617(TLS):14JUN74-645
HERZFELD, A. & L.D.C. MILLS. NOTAS
  Y EJERCICIOS DE COMPOSICIÓN.
  I.E. STANISLAWCZYK, 238:MAR72-
  201
HERZOG, A. THE SWARM.
  M. LEVIN, 441:7APR74-32
HERZOG, M.I., W. RAVID & U. WEIN-
  REICH, EDS. THE FIELD OF YIDDISH.
  (VOL 3)
  A.S. KAYE, 353:1OCT72-127
HERZOG, V. IRONISCHE ERZÄHLFORMEN
  BEI CONRAD FERDINAND MEYER, DAR-
  GESTELLT AM "JÜRG JENATSCH."*
  W.A. COUPE, 402(MLR):JAN73-234
HERZOG ZU MECKLENBURG, C.G. 1970
  SUPPLEMENT TO INTERNATIONAL JAZZ
  BIBLIOGRAPHY & INTERNATIONAL DRUM
  & PERCUSSION BIBLIOGRAPHY.
  F.J. GILLIS, 187:SEP74-460
HERZOGENRATH, W. OSKAR SCHLEMMER.
  617(TLS):24MAY74-566
HESCHEL, A.J. A PASSION FOR TRUTH.
  E.B. BOROWITZ, 441:13JAN74-22
HESELTINE, H. XAVIER HERBERT.
  C. HADGRAFT, 71(ALS):OCT74-437
HESELTINE, J.E., ED. THE OXFORD
  BOOK OF FRENCH PROSE.*
  E.L. DUTHIE, 208(FS):APR73-234
HESIOD. THEOGONIA, OPERA ET DIES,
  SCUTUM. (FR. SOLMSEN, ED) [TOGETH-
  ER WITH] FRAGMENTA SELECTA. (R.
  MERKELBACH & M.L. WEST, EDS)
  P. CHANTRAINE, 555:VOL46FASC2-
  287
  D. YOUNG, 24:SUMMER73-188
HESKES, I. - SEE BINDER, A.W.
HESLA, D.H. THE SHAPE OF CHAOS.*
  A.W. BRINK, 529(QQ):SUMMER72-265
  R. COHN, 397(MD):MAY72-105
HESS, G. DEUTSCH-LATEINISCHE NARREN-
  ZUNFT.*
  P. SCHÄFFER, 182:VOL25#9/10-274
HESS, H. GEORGE GROSZ.
  W. FEAVER, 362:19&26DEC74-847
  J. WILLETT, 617(TLS):13DEC74-
  1410

HESS, H-J. DIE OBERSTEN GRUNDSÄTZE
KANTISCHER ETHIK UND IHRE KONKRET-
ISIERBARKEIT.
W. STEINBECK, 342:BAND63HEFT2-
273
HESS, J.L. THE GRAND ACQUISITORS.
B. HILLIER, 441:7APR74-5
E. WEEKS, 61:JUL74-99
HESS, R., M. FRAUENRATH & G. SIEBEN-
MANN. LITERATURWISSENSCHAFTLICHES
WÖRTERBUCH FÜR ROMANISTEN.
U. SCHULZ-BUSCHHAUS, 72:BAND210
HEFT4/6-452
HESS, T.B. WILLEM DE KOONING DRAW-
INGS.*
A. FRANKENSTEIN, 55:MAR73-16
HESS, T.B. & J. ASHBERY, EDS. PAINT-
ERLY PAINTING.
639(VQR):SUMMER72-CVIII
HESSE, H. AUTOBIOGRAPHICAL WRIT-
INGS.* (T. ZIOLKOWSKI, ED)
H. LOMAS, 364:DEC73/JAN74-132
639(VQR):SPRING73-LXXXI
HESSE, H. MY BELIEF.
453:7MAR74-29
HESSE, H. STORIES OF FIVE DECADES.*
(T. ZIOLKOWSKI, ED)
617(TLS):20SEP74-993
639(VQR):SPRING73-LX
HESSE, H. STRANGE NEWS FROM ANOTHER
STAR & OTHER TALES.*
42(AR):VOL32#3-498
HESSE, H. WANDERING.*
639(VQR):SUMMER72-CVI
HESSE, M. THE STRUCTURE OF SCIEN-
TIFIC INFERENCE.
617(TLS):26APR74-450
HESTER, R.M., ED. TEACHING A LIVING
LANGUAGE.*
J.E. CREAN, JR., 221(GQ):MAR72-
383
HETHERINGTON, J. NORMAN LINDSAY.
(3RD ED)
K.L. GOODWIN, 447(N&Q):SEP72-359
C. HADGRAFT, 71(ALS):MAY74-328
HETHERINGTON, J. - SEE "THE COMPLETE
FILMS OF EISENSTEIN"
HEUER, H., ED. DEUTSCHE SHAKESPEARE-
GESELLSCHAFT WEST: JAHRBUCH 1966.
V.B. HELTZEL, 570(SQ):FALL72-451
HEUER, H., ED. DEUTSCHE SHAKESPEARE-
GESELLSCHAFT WEST: JAHRBUCH 1967.
DEUTSCHE SHAKESPEARE-GESELLSCHAFT
WEST: JAHRBUCH 1968.
V.B. HELTZEL, 570(SQ):FALL72-452
K. OTTEN, 430(NS):JUL72-427
HEUER, H., ED. DEUTSCHE SHAKESPEARE-
GESELLSCHAFT WEST: JAHRBUCH 1969.
V.B. HELTZEL, 570(SQ):FALL72-452
HEUER, H., ED. DEUTSCHE SHAKESPEARE-
GESELLSCHAFT WEST: JAHRBUCH 1970.
V.B. HELTZEL, 570(SQ):FALL72-454
HEUER, H., ED. DEUTSCHE SHAKESPEARE-
GESELLSCHAFT WEST: JAHRBUCH 1971.
V.B. HELTZEL, 570(SQ):FALL72-455
HEURGON, J. THE RISE OF ROME TO 264
B.C.* (FRENCH TITLE: ROME ET LA
MÉDITERRANÉE OCCIDENTALE JUSQU'AUX
GUERRES PUNIQUES.)
A.H. MC DONALD, 313:VOL62-172
HEWARD, B. & D.V. GAT. SOME ARE
CALLED CLOWNS.
R.W. CREAMER, 441:1DEC74-90

HEWETT, C. ENGLISH CATHEDRAL CAR-
PENTRY.
617(TLS):21JUN74-680
HEWETT, D. THE CHAPEL PERILOUS.
A. KRUSE, 581:JUN73-240
HEWISH, J. EMILY BRONTË.*
R.B. MARTIN, 637(VS):SEP72-102
HEWITT, J., ED. EYE WITNESSES TO
IRELAND IN REVOLT.
617(TLS):12APR74-402
HEWITT, M., ED. GOOD TIME.
E. WELSH, 617(TLS):15NOV74-1290
HEY, D. THE RURAL METALWORKERS OF
THE SHEFFIELD REGION.
617(TLS):8FEB74-140
HEY, D.G. AN ENGLISH RURAL COMMUN-
ITY.
617(TLS):9AUG74-859
HEYDENREICH, L.H. LEONARDO: THE
LAST SUPPER.
J. RUSSELL, 441:1DEC74-54
HEYDENREICH, L.H. & W. LOTZ. ARCHI-
TECTURE IN ITALY 1400-1600.
617(TLS):5JUL74-729
HEYDENREICH, T. TADEL UND LOB DER
SEEFAHRT.
H-J. LOPE, 52:BAND7HEFT1-76
HEYERDAHL, T. FATU-HIVA.
C. NEWBURY, 362:21NOV74-679
HEYERDAHL, T. RA.
L.S. THOMPSON, 263:OCT-DEC73-465
"GEORG HEYM." (K.L. SCHNEIDER & G.
MARTENS, EDS)
R.W. LAST, 402(MLR):JUL73-702
H. SCHER, 406:SUMMER73-200
D. SCOTT, 220(GL&L):APR73-260
HEYM, S. THE QUEEN AGAINST DEFOE.
IONEL, 441:8SEP74-22
HEYNEN, W.J., COMP. CARTOGRAPHIC
RECORDS OF THE BUREAU OF AGRICUL-
TURAL ECONOMICS.
J.M. KINNEY, 14:JUL/OCT72-415
HEYWOOD, P. PLANNING & HUMAN NEED.
617(TLS):26APR74-455
HEYWORTH, P., ED. CONVERSATIONS
WITH KLEMPERER.*
E. SAMS, 415:JUL73-700
J.A.W., 410(M&L):OCT73-486
HEYWORTH, P.L. "JACK UPLAND," "FRI-
AR DAW'S REPLY" & "UPLAND'S RE-
JOINDER."*
J.R. SIMON, 189(EA):JAN-MAR72-84
HIBBARD, H. CARLO MADERNO & ROMAN
ARCHITECTURE 1580-1630.*
D. LEWIS, 127:SPRING73-356
HIBBARD, H. POUSSIN: THE HOLY FAM-
ILY ON THE STEPS.
J. RUSSELL, 441:1DEC74-54
617(TLS):24MAY74-564
HIBBERD, J. A STRETCH OF THE IMAGI-
NATION.
A. KRUSE, 581:JUN73-240
HIBBERT, C. GEORGE IV: PRINCE OF
WALES, 1762-1811.
E. WEEKS, 61:FEB74-95
442(NY):25FEB74-126
HIBBERT, C. THE PERSONAL HISTORY OF
SAMUEL JOHNSON.
R.E. KELLEY, 481(PQ):JUL72-703
HICHENS, P. WINE MAN'S BLUFF.
617(TLS):4JAN74-18

HICK, J. ARGUMENTS FOR THE EXIS-
TENCE OF GOD.*
  S.M. NAJM, 154:MAR72-148
  R.C. WALLACE, 479(PHQ):OCT72-380
HICK, J. GOD & THE UNIVERSE OF
FAITHS.
  617(TLS):22MAR74-299
HICKEY, K., ED. THE LIGHT OF OTHER
DAYS.
  617(TLS):18JAN74-45
HICKMAN, P. TWO CENTURIES OF SIL-
HOUETTES.
  F.G. ROE, 135:FEB72-139
HICKMANN, H. & W. STAUDER. ORIENTAL-
ISCHE MUSIK.
  B. NETTL, 187:MAY74-307
HIEBERT, P.G. KONDURU.
  A.R. BEALS, 293(JAST):MAY72-709
HIENGER, J. & R. KNAUF, EDS. DEUT-
SCHE GEDICHTE VON ANDREAS GRYPHIUS
BIS INGEBORG BACHMANN.
  T.J. CASEY, 220(GL&L):JUL73-323
HIERSCHE, A. & E. KOWALSKI, EDS.
KONTUREN UND PERSPEKTIVEN.
  J.D. SIMONS, 104:SUMMER72-347
HIERSCHE, R. GRUNDZÜGE DER GRIECH-
ISCHEN SPRACHGESCHICHTE BIS ZUR
KLASSISCHEN ZEIT.
  P. CHANTRAINE, 555:VOL46FASC2-
  283
  A. SCHERER, 343:BAND15HEFT1-57
HIETSCH, O., ED. ÖSTERREICH UND DIE
ANGELSACHSISCHE WELT.* (VOL 2)
  A. CLOSS, 433:APR72-237
HIGGINBOTHAM, D. THE WAR OF AMERI-
CAN INDEPENDENCE.
  M.A. JONES, 656(WMQ):JAN73-166
HIGGINS, A. THE BALCONY OF EUROPE.*
  P. CRUTTWELL & F. WESTBURG,
  249(HUDR):SUMMER73-421
  M. GREEN, 364:APR/MAY73-160
HIGGINS, A. IMAGES OF AFRICA.
  P. HARDING, 159(DM):AUTUMN71-118
HIGGINS, C. HAROLD & MAUDE.
  502(PRS):SPRING72-92
HIGGINS, G.V. COGAN'S TRADE.
  P. ADAMS, 61:APR74-120
  O.L. BAILEY, 441:31MAR74-10
  C. LEHMANN-HAUPT, 441:10APR74-41
  442(NY):24JUN74-103
  617(TLS):16AUG74-877
HIGGINS, J. A PRAYER FOR THE DYING.
  N. CALLENDAR, 441:3MAR74-33
HIGHAM, C. CECIL B. DE MILLE.*
  617(TLS):30AUG74-925
HIGHET, G. EXPLORATIONS.*
  E. CONSTANTINIDES, 613:WINTER72-
  617
HIGHFILL, P.H., JR., K.A. BURNIM &
E.A. LANGHANS. A BIOGRAPHICAL
DICTIONARY OF ACTORS, ACTRESSES,
MUSICIANS, DANCERS, MANAGERS &
OTHER STAGE PERSONNEL IN LONDON,
1660-1800. (VOLS 1&2)
  617(TLS):18OCT74-1165
HIGHSMITH, P. RIPLEY'S GAME.
  N. CALLENDAR, 441:7JUL74-19
  C. LEHMANN-HAUPT, 441:25JUL74-37
  442(NY):27MAY74-107
  617(TLS):22MAR74-282
HIGMAN, F.M. - SEE CALVIN, J.
HIGONNET, P.L-R. PONT-DE-MONTVERT.*
  481(PQ):JUL72-533

HILDER, G. DER SCHOLASTISCHE WORT-
SCHATZ BEI JEAN DE MEUN.
  W. ROTHWELL, 182:VOL25#9/10-279
HILEN, A. - SEE LONGFELLOW, H.W.
HILEY, M. FRANK SUTCLIFFE.
  M. HAWORTH-BOOTH, 617(TLS):
  27DEC74-1457
LORD HILL. BEHIND THE SCREEN.
  O. WHITLEY, 362:19SEP74-354
HILL, A. A CAGE OF SHADOWS.
  617(TLS):5APR74-360
HILL, A.A., ED. LINGUISTICS TODAY.*
  W. DRESSLER, 206:SEP72-146
  J. KRÁMSKY, 353:FEB72-72
HILL, B. JULIA MARGARET CAMERON.*
  S. CLAPP, 362:24JAN74-118
HILL, C. LET'S FALL IN LOVE.
  A. GOTTLIEB, 441:14APR74-6
  C. LEHMANN-HAUPT, 441:18APR74-45
  M. LEVENSON, 231:SEP74-78
  R. SALE, 453:27JUN74-24
  442(NY):13MAY74-157
HILL, C. SCORPION.
  N. CALLENDAR, 441:24NOV74-39
  442(NY):23SEP74-147
HILL, C. THE WORLD TURNED UPSIDE
DOWN.*
  T.W. HAYES, 568(SCN):SPRING73-5
  639(VQR):SUMMER73-CXXIII
HILL, C. ZWEIHUNDERT JAHRE DEUTSCH-
ER KULTUR.
  K.G. KNIGHT, 220(GL&L):OCT72-69
HILL, D.R. - SEE AL-JAZARĪ, I.AL-R.
HILL, E. QUIETLY CRUSH THE LIZARD.
  M. ELLMANN, 676(YR):SPRING73-461
HILL, E. THE TRINIDAD CARNIVAL.*
  L. KING, 263:JAN-MAR73-90
HILL, E.L. - SEE UNDER LEÓN HILL, E.
HILL, G. MERCIAN HYMNS.
  M. DODSWORTH, 565:VOL13#1-61
HILL, L.A. PREPOSITIONS & ADVERBIAL
PARTICLES.*
  B. FRASER, 206:MAR72-294
HILL, M. THE RELIGIOUS ORDER.
  617(TLS):29MAR74-347
HILL, N. HOW TO SOLVE CROSSWORD
PUZZLES.
  P. SHOWERS, 441:3NOV74-62
HILL, O. HOMES OF THE LONDON POOR
[TOGETHER WITH] MEARNS, A. THE
BITTER CRY OF OUTCAST LONDON.
  S. GILL, 447(N&Q):NOV72-434
HILL, P.G. THE LIVING ART.
  W.H. SHAW, 583:FALL72-114
HILL, P.P. WILLIAM VANS MURRAY,
FEDERALIST DIPLOMAT.
  A. DE CONDE, 656(WMQ):JAN72-184
HILL, R., ED. ON THE FRONTIERS OF
ISLAM.
  T. ASAD, 69:APR72-169
HILL, R.T. & T.G. BERGIN, EDS. AN-
THOLOGY OF THE PROVENÇAL TROUBA-
DOURS. (2ND ED)
  L. PATERSON, 617(TLS):13DEC74-
  1411
HILL, S. THE BIRD OF NIGHT.*
  M. GREEN, 364:APR/MAY73-160
HILL, S. A BIT OF SINGING & DANC-
ING.*
  E. FEINSTEIN, 364:OCT/NOV73-154
HILL, S. IN THE SPRINGTIME OF THE
YEAR.
  M. ATWOOD, 441:5MAY74-7
                        [CONTINUED]

HILL, S. IN THE SPRINGTIME OF THE
YEAR. [CONTINUING]
V. CUNNINGHAM, 362:24JAN74-120
442(NY):16SEP74-147
617(TLS):25JAN74-69
HILL, T.E. THE CONCEPT OF MEANING.
617(TLS):8NOV74-1250
HILLACH, A. & K-D. KRABIEL. EICHEN-
DORFF-KOMMENTAR. (VOL 1)
J.F.F., 191(ELN):SEP72(SUPP)-142
HILLEBRAND, B. THEORIE DES ROMANS.
S.K., 268:JUL74-161
HILLENAAR, H. FÉNELON ET LES JÉSU-
ITES.
J-R. ARMOGATHE, 182:VOL25#15/16-
552
HILLER, F. FORMGESCHICHTLICHE UNTER-
SUCHUNGEN ZUR GRIECHISCHEN STATUE
DES SPÄTEN 5. JAHRHUNDERTS V. CHR.
J.M. COOK, 123:DEC73-290
HILLIARD, N. MAORI WOMAN.
617(TLS):2AUG74-825
HILLIER, J., COMP. THE HARARI COL-
LECTION OF JAPANESE PAINTINGS &
DRAWINGS. (VOL 3)
617(TLS):1MAR74-200
HILLIER, J. THE UNINHIBITED BRUSH.
617(TLS):2AUG74-838
HILLING, J.B. CARDIFF & THE VALLEYS.
617(TLS):1FEB74-116
HILLS, G. ROCK OF CONTENTION.
C.E. CARRINGTON, 362:30MAY74-702
617(TLS):6SEP74-951
HILLS, P. EASTMAN JOHNSON.
F. MURPHY, 432(NEQ):DEC72-584
HILSCHER, E. GERHART HAUPTMANN.*
W.R. MAURER, 221(GQ):NOV72-713
HILTON, I. PETER WEISS.
J.J. WHITE, 220(GL&L):JUL73-325
HILTON, R. BOND MEN MADE FREE.
617(TLS):22FEB74-189
HILTON, T. THE PRE-RAPHAELITES.*
R.M. BISANZ, 127:SPRING73-352
HIMES, C. BLACK ON BLACK.
639(VQR):SUMMER73-CV
HIMES, C. THE QUALITY OF HURT.
639(VQR):SUMMER72-LXXXIX
HIMMELFARB, G. ON LIBERTY & LIBERAL-
ISM.
R. DWORKIN, 453:31OCT74-21
D. SPITZ, 441:28JUL74-15
HIMMELHEBER, G. BIEDERMEIER FURNI-
TURE.
617(TLS):9AUG74-851
HINA, H. NIETZSCHE UND MARX BEI
MALRAUX.
R. RÜTTEN, 52:BAND7HEFT1-108
HINCHCLIFF, P. CYPRIAN OF CARTHAGE
& THE UNITY OF THE CHRISTIAN
CHURCH.
617(TLS):20SEP74-1024
HINCKLE, W., 3D. IF YOU HAVE A
LEMON, MAKE LEMONADE.
J. O'REILLY, 441:15DEC74-4
HINDE, R.A., ED. NON-VERBAL COMMUNI-
CATION.
R.J. SMITH, 157:WINTER72-74
HINDE, T. AGENT.
E. TENNANT, 362:20JUN74-808
617(TLS):21JUN74-656

HINDEMITH, P. ÜBUNGSBUCH FÜR DEN
DREISTIMMIGEN SATZ. (A. BRINER,
P.D. MEIER & A. RUBELI, EDS)
C. SHACKFORD, 308:VOL16#1/2-238
S. SLATIN, 414(MQ):JAN72-141
HINE, D. THE HOMERIC HYMNS & THE
BATTLE OF THE FROGS & THE MICE.
M. RUDICK, 651(WHR):SUMMER73-319
639(VQR):SUMMER73-CXII
HINES, T.S. BURNHAM OF CHICAGO.
P. GOLDBERGER, 441:10NOV74-7
HINGLEY, R. THE RUSSIAN SECRET POL-
ICE.*
N. GRANT, 550(RUSR):APR72-199
HINGLEY, R. JOSEPH STALIN.
R. PIPES, 617(TLS):14JUN74-625
HINGLEY, R. - SEE CHEKHOV, A.
HINMAN, C. - SEE SHAKESPEARE, W.
HINSKE, N. KANTS WEG ZUR TRANSZEN-
DENTALPHILOSOPHIE.*
A. PHILONENKO, 542:JUL-SEP72-328
HINSON, M. GUIDE TO THE PIANIST'S
REPERTOIRE. (E. FREUNDLICH, ED)
F. DAWES, 415:OCT73-1015
HINTIKKA, J. LOGIC, LANGUAGE-GAMES,
& INFORMATION.*
S. READ, 518:OCT73-12
HINTIKKA, J. TIME & NECESSITY.
617(TLS):8FEB74-136
HINTIKKA, J. & P. SUPPES, EDS. IN-
FORMATION & INFERENCE.
A.C. MICHALOS, 486:JUN72-271
HINTON, D.A. A CATALOGUE OF THE
ANGLO-SAXON ORNAMENTAL METALWORK
700-1100 IN THE DEPARTMENT OF AN-
TIQUITIES, ASHMOLEAN MUSEUM.
D.M. WILSON, 617(TLS):1NOV74-
1233
HINTON, J. THE FIRST SHOP STEWARDS'
MOVEMENT.
617(TLS):4JAN74-18
HINZ, W. ALTIRANISCHE FUNDE UND
FORSCHUNGEN.
R. SCHMITT, 343:BAND14HEFT1-54
HIPPIUS, Z.N. SELECTED WORKS OF ZIN-
AIDA HIPPIUS.* (T. PACHMUSS, ED
& TRANS)
639(VQR):AUTUMN73-CXXXVIII
HIPPIUS, Z.N. STIKHOTVORENIYA I
POEMY. (T. PACHMUSS, ED)
G. DONCHIN, 575(SEER):JUL73-469
HIPPIUS, Z.N. ZHIVYYE LITSA.
G. DONCHIN, 575(SEER):JUL73-468
HIPPOCRATES. HIPPOCRATE.* (VOL 11)
(R. JOLY, ED & TRANS)
P. CHANTRAINE, 555:VOL46FASC2-
297
E.D. PHILLIPS, 123:DEC73-141
HIRAI, K. FEUDAL ARCHITECTURE OF
JAPAN.
617(TLS):24MAY74-553
HIRO, D. BLACK BRITISH, WHITE BRIT-
ISH.
S. KEECH, 441:26MAY74-10
HIRSCH, W. PLATONS WEG ZUM MYTHOS.
É. DES PLACES, 555:VOL46FASC1-
123
HIRSCH, W. ÜBER DER GRUNDLAGEN
EINER UNIVERSALEN METHODE DER
PHILOSOPHIE.
S. DECLOUX, 182:VOL25#22-773
HIRSCHMAN, A.O. A BIAS FOR HOPE.
D. CARNEIRO, 263:OCT-DEC73-461

HIRSH, M. & P. LOUBERT. THE GREAT
CANADIAN COMIC BOOKS.
G. CURNOE, 99:APR74-38
HIRST, P.H. & R.S. PETERS. THE
LOGIC OF EDUCATION.*
G. LANGFORD, 483:OCT72-371
Ž.R. PRVULOVICH, 479(PHQ):APR72-
188
HISAKO, M. - SEE UNDER MARUYAMA
HISAKO
HISCOCK, E.C. SOU'WEST IN WANDERER
IV.
617(TLS):15MAR74-260
HISCOCKS, R. THE SECURITY COUNCIL.
617(TLS):10MAY74-498
HISLOP, J. STEEPLECHASING.
617(TLS):29MAR74-348
"HISTORIC BRITISH NEWSPAPERS." (SER
1, 1689-1866)
P. COLLINS, 155:MAY72-129
"HISTORICAL RELICS UNEARTHED IN
CHINA."
B. LORD, 99:SEP74-26
"THE HISTORY OF REYNARD THE FOX."*
(W. CAXTON, TRANS; N.F. BLAKE, ED)
R. BREUER, 38:BAND90HEFT4-527
HITCHCOCK, G., ED. FOLK-SONGS OF
THE WEST COUNTRY.
617(TLS):5APR74-376
HITCHCOCK, H-R. ROCOCO ARCHITECTURE
IN SOUTHERN GERMANY.*
H. ERNST, 683:BAND35HEFT4-316
HITCHCOCK, H-R. & OTHERS. THE RISE
OF AN AMERICAN ARCHITECTURE.* (E.
KAUFMANN, JR., ED)
M. WHIFFEN, 46:FEB72-130
HITCHCOCK, H.W. MUSIC IN THE UNITED
STATES.
C. HANSEN, 290(JAAC):SUMMER73-
560
HITCHCOCK, J. THE DECLINE & FALL OF
RADICAL CATHOLICISM.*
J.P. BOYLE, 396(MODA):FALL73-435
HITNER, J.M. BROWNING'S ANALYSIS OF
A MURDER.*
A.B. CROWDER, 637(VS):MAR72-385
HIX, J. THE GLASS HOUSE.
617(TLS):9AUG74-851
HIXSON, W.B., JR. MOORFIELD STOREY
& THE ABOLITIONIST TRADITION.*
G.W. GAWALT, 432(NEQ):SEP72-451
HJELHOLT, H. GREAT BRITAIN, THE
DANISH-GERMAN CONFLICT & THE DAN-
ISH SUCCESSION 1850-1852.
E. ANDERSON, 563(SS):SUMMER73-
263
HJELMSLEV, L. ESSAIS LINGUISTIQUES.
A. ERNOUT, 555:VOL46FASC2-319
HJORTH, A. & OTHERS. LEVA BLAND
MÄNNISKOR.
R-M.G. OSTER, 563(SS):AUTUMN73-
400
HJORTSBERG, W. TORO! TORO! TORO!
C. LEHMANN-HAUPT, 441:5SEP74-41
G. STADE, 441:25AUG74-4
442(NY):7OCT74-175
HOARE, Q. & G.N. SMITH - SEE GRAMSCI,
A.
HOBAN, R. KLEINZEIT.
617(TLS):29MAR74-345
HOBBES, T. CRITIQUE DU "DE MUNDO"
DE THOMAS WHITE. (J. JACQUOT &
H.W. JONES, EDS)
617(TLS):1FEB74-115

HOBBES, T. A DIALOGUE BETWEEN A
PHILOSOPHER & A STUDENT OF LAW OF
THE COMMON LAWS OF ENGLAND. (J.
CROPSEY, ED)
A.S.C., 543:DEC71-354
H.J. JOHNSON, 185:APR73-261
HOBBES, T. THOMAS HOBBES: LÉVIATHAN.
(F. TRICAUD, ED & TRANS)
568(SCN):FALL-WINTER73-95
HOBERG, H., ED. DIE EINNAHMEN DER
APOSTOLISCHEN KAMMER UNTER INNO-
ZENZ VI. (PT 2)
R. FOLZ, 182:VOL25#15/16-568
HOBHOUSE, H. THOMAS CUBITT, MASTER
BUILDER.
J. SUMMERSON, 46:APR72-259
HOBSBAUM, P. A THEORY OF COMMUNI-
CATION.
A.J. FRY, 433:OCT72-514
HOBSON, A. FULL CIRCLE.
T.W. CRAIK, 541(RES):NOV72-484
H.M. RICHMOND, 149:DEC73-398
HOCHHUTH, R. LYSISTRATE UND DIE
NATO.
617(TLS):26APR74-440
HOCHMAN, S. WALKING PAPERS.*
J. HURLBERT, 648:JAN73-82
639(VQR):WINTER72-XVIII
HOCKETT, C.F. LANGUAGE, MATHEMATICS
& LINGUISTICS.*
H. SCHNELLE, 206:JAN72-147
HOCKIN, T.A., ED. APEX OF POWER.
J.L. MC DOUGALL, 529(QQ):SPRING
72-122
HOCKING, M. DANIEL COME TO JUDGE-
MENT.
V. CUNNINGHAM, 362:18APR74-509
617(TLS):12APR74-396
HODDER, B.W. & U.I. UKWU. MARKETS
IN WEST AFRICA.
A.H.M. KIRK-GREENE, 69:JAN72-80
HODDER-WILLIAMS, C. COWARDS' PARA-
DISE.
617(TLS):14JUN74-644
HODGE, F. PLAY DIRECTING.
G. DOTY, 583:FALL72-110
HODGE, J.A. ONLY A NOVEL.
S. WOOD, 569(SR):SPRING73-380
A. WRIGHT, 445(NCF):MAR73-495
HODGES, C.W. SHAKESPEARE'S SECOND
GLOBE.
617(TLS):4JAN74-14
HODGETTS, J.E. THE CANADIAN PUBLIC
SERVICE.
C. ARMSTRONG, 99:JAN74-40
HODGKINSON, T. THE JAMES A. DE
ROTHSCHILD COLLECTION AT WADDESDON
MANOR: THE SCULPTURE.
D. THOMAS, 135:MAY72-65
HODGSON, D.H. CONSEQUENCES OF UTILI-
TARIANISM.
P. SINGER, 482(PHR):JAN72-94
HODGSON, J., ED. THE USES OF DRAMA.
R. WHITELEY, 157:AUTUMN72-81
HODGSON, J. & M. BANHAM - SEE "DRAMA
IN EDUCATION"
HODNETT, E. ENGLISH WOODCUTS 1480-
1535.
617(TLS):1FEB74-110
HODSON, H.V. THE GREAT DIVIDE.
W.H. MORRIS-JONES, 293(JAST):
AUG72-915

HOEST, S. REDEN UND BRIEFE. (F.
BARON, ED)
   H.O. BURGER, 182:VOL25#13/14-479
HOF, W. PESSIMISTISCH-NIHILISTISCHE
STRÖMUNGEN IN DER DEUTSCHEN LITERA-
TUR VOM STURM UND DRANG BIS ZUM
JUNGEN DEUTSCHLAND.*
   P. ROUBICZEK, 220(GL&L):OCT72-75
   J.L.S., 191(ELN):SEP72(SUPP)-128
HÖFER, W., ED. DEUTSCHE NOBEL GAL-
ERIE.
   M. BRÄNDLE, 67:NOV73-314
HOFF, U. THE NATIONAL GALLERY OF
VICTORIA.
   617(TLS):22FEB74-193
HOFF, U. & M. DAVIES. LES PRIMITIFS
FLAMANDS. (SER 1, VOL 12: CORPUS
DE LA PEINTURE DES ANCIENS PAYS-
BAS MERIDIONAUX AU QUINZIEME
SIÈCLE; THE NATIONAL GALLERY OF
VICTORIA, MELBOURNE.)
   L. CAMPBELL, 39:NOV72-460
HOFFMAN, D. THE CENTER OF ATTENTION.
   C. BEDIENT, 441:11AUG74-6
HOFFMAN, D. POE POE POE POE POE POE
POE.*
   B. ALLEN, 249(HUDR):WINTER73/74-
   735
   R.P. BENTON, 445(NCF):MAR73-480
   G. EWART, 364:FEB/MAR74-140
   R.D. JACOBS, 578:SPRING74-107
   P.F. QUINN, 219(GAR):FALL72-379
   W.G. REGIER, 502(PRS):SUMMER72-
   180
   P. ZIETLOW, 473(PR):3/1973-503
   639(VQR):SUMMER72-CIV
HOFFMAN, E.B. & F.J. FLERON, EDS.
THE CONDUCT OF SOVIET FOREIGN POLI-
CY.
   H. HANAK, 575(SEER):OCT73-630
HOFFMAN, F. ROOKS.
   A. RENDLE, 157:WINTER72-80
HOFFMAN, G.W., ED. EASTERN EUROPE.
   F.W. CARTER, 575(SEER):JAN73-153
HOFFMAN, G.W. REGIONAL DEVELOPMENT
STRATEGY IN SOUTHEAST EUROPE.
   J.M. MONTIAS, 32:JUN73-401
HOFFMAN, H. & H. PICKER. HITLER
CLOSE-UP. (J. VON LANG, COMP)
   N. ASCHERSON, 453:18APR74-3
HOFFMAN, J. MINK COAT.
   A. OSTRIKER, 441:17FEB74-7
HOFFMAN, M.J. THE SUBVERSIVE VISION.
   D. PIZER, 27(AL):JAN74-616
HOFFMAN, R. LANGUAGE, MINDS, &
KNOWLEDGE.
   M. KOHL, 484(PPR):DEC72-282
HOFFMAN, S. SOLOMON'S TEMPLE.
   J.R. FRAKES, 441:24MAR74-37
HOFFMANN, E.T.A. THE BEST TALES OF
HOFFMANN. (E.F. BLEILER, ED)
   P.R. GRAHAM, 220(GL&L):APR73-247
HOFFMANN, E.T.A. LIEBE UND EIFER-
SUCHT (DIE SCHÄRPE UND DIE BLUME).
TAGEBUCHER.* (F. SCHNAPP, ED OF
BOTH)
   S.P.S., 191(ELN):SEP72(SUPP)-167
HOFFMANN, E.T.A. PRINZESSIN BRAM-
BILLA. (W. NEHRING, ED)
   S.P.S., 191(ELN):SEP72(SUPP)-166
HOFFMANN, H. COLLECTING GREEK AN-
TIQUITIES.
   R. HIGGINS, 39:MAY72-426

HOFFMANN, K. DER INJUNKTIV IM VEDA.
   G. CARDONA, 343:BAND15HEFT1-47
HOFFMANN, K. TAUFSYMBOLIK IM MITTEL-
ALTERLICHEN HERRSCHERBILD.
   C. DAVIS-WEYER, 54:DEC72-540
HOFFMANN, L., ED. FACHWORTSCHATZ
MEDIZIN.
   G.F. MEIER, 682(ZPSK):BAND25
   HEFT1/2-156
HOFFMANN, S. DECLINE OR RENEWAL?
   T. ZELDIN, 453:27JUN74-22
HOFFMANN, S. GULLIVER EMPÊTRÉ.
   C. ZORGBIBE, 98:DEC72-1091
HOFFMEISTER, J., ED. BRIEFE VON UND
AN HEGEL.
   R. MINDER, 542:JUL-SEP72-359
HÖFLER, O. HOMUNCULUS - EINE SATIRE
AUF A.W. SCHLEGEL.
   N.H. SMITH, 182:VOL25#23/24-864
HOFMANN, D., WITH W. LANGE & K. VON
SEE - SEE KUHN, H.
HOFMANN, W. GUSTAV KLIMT.
   F. WHITFORD, 592:NOV72-200
VON HOFMANNSTHAL, H. & A. WILDGANS.
BRIEFWECHSEL. (N. ALTENHOFER, ED)
   E.E. THEOBALD, 406:WINTER73-433
HOFSTADTER, A. AGONY & EPITAPH.*
   M. WEITZ, 482(PHR):JAN72-110
HOFSTADTER, R. AMERICA AT 1750.
   639(VQR):WINTER72-XXXI
HOGARTH, J. SENTENCING AS A HUMAN
PROCESS.
   J. HAGAN, 99:NOV/DEC74-36
HOGARTH, W. THE ANALYSIS OF BEAUTY.*
   J. GUTMANN, 290(JAAC):WINTER72-
   276
HOGG, J. DIE ÄLTESTEN CONSUETUDINES
DER KARTÄUSER. MITTELALTERLICHE
CAERIMONIALIA DER KARTÄUSER. (VOL
1) LATE FIFTEENTH CENTURY CARTHUS-
IAN RUBRICS FOR THE DEACON & THE
SACRISTAN FROM THE MS. VALSAINTE
42/T.I.8.
   G. CONSTABLE, 589:JUL73-545
HÖGSTRAND, O. THE GAMBLER.
   N. CALLENDAR, 441:13JAN74-12
HOHENBERG, J. THE PULITZER PRIZES.
   D. DEMPSEY, 441:29DEC74-12
HOHENDAHL, P.U., ED. BENN - WIRKUNG
WIDER WILLEN.
   A. HUYSSEN, 406:WINTER73-434
HOHENDAHL, P.U. & E. SCHWARZ, EDS.
EXIL UND INNERE EMIGRATION II.
   T.J. REED, 617(TLS):250CT74-1199
HÖHFELD, T.H. DIE FUNKTION DER
STEINKOHLENREVIERE DER BUNDESRE-
PUBLIK DEUTSCHLAND IM WESTEUROP-
ÄISCHEN WIRTSCHAFTSRAUM.
   G. MERTINS, 182:VOL25#22-827
HÖHLER, G. UNRUHIGE GÄSTE.
   V. SANDER, 221(GQ):NOV72-711
HÖHNE, H. & H. ZOLLING. THE GENERAL
WAS A SPY.
   O.J. HALE, 639(VQR):WINTER73-126
HOLADAY, A. - SEE CHAPMAN, G.
HOLBEIN THE YOUNGER, H. THE DANCE
OF DEATH.
   J.E. KELLER, 582(SFQ):DEC72-408
HOLBERG, L. LUDVIG HOLBERG'S MEM-
OIRS. (S.E. FRASER, ED)
   B.G. MADSEN, 563(SS):SUMMER73-
   267
   P. RIES, 402(MLR):APR73-475

HOLBROOK, D. DYLAN THOMAS.
    A.W. BRINK, 529(QQ):WINTER72-572
    D. MIDDLETON, 598(SOR):SPRING74-
    529
HOLBROOK, S.H. RIVERS OF AMERICA:
    THE COLUMBIA.
    I.R. DEE, 441:8SEP74-30
HOLCOMBE, L. VICTORIAN LADIES AT
    WORK.
    617(TLS):26APR74-443
HOLDEN, A. THE GIRL ON THE BEACH.*
    N. CALLENDAR, 441:6JAN74-23
HOLDEN, D. GREECE WITHOUT COLUMNS.*
    639(VQR):WINTER73-XL
HOLDEN, F. AU PAS DES ARBRES -
    POÈMES.
    A.J. ARNOLD, 207(FR):DEC71-474
HOLDEN, M. AIR & CHILL EARTH.
    J. SYMONS, 364:AUG/SEP72-138
HOLDEN, M., COMP. THE STAGE GUIDE.
    W. LUCAS, 157:SPRING72-83
HÖLDERLIN, F. HÖLDERLIN: SÄMTLICHE
    GEDICHTE. (D. LÜDERS, ED) FRIED-
    RICH HÖLDERLIN: SÄMTLICHE WERKE
    UND BRIEFE. (G. MIETH & OTHERS,
    EDS)
    C.H., 191(ELN):SEP72(SUPP)-161
HOLDREN, J. & P. HERRERA. ENERGY.
    42(AR):SPRING/SUMMER72-250
HOLGATE, D. NEW HALL & ITS IMITAT-
    ORS.
    G.E.A. GREY, 90:APR72-251
HOLGER, R., ED. NORSKE RELIGIOSE
    FØLKETONER.
    F. HOWES, 415:DEC73-1241
HOLLAENDER, A.E.J. & W. KELLAWAY,
    EDS. STUDIES IN LONDON HISTORY
    PRESENTED TO PHILIP EDMUND JONES.
    J.F.A. MASON, 447(N&Q):FEB72-62
HOLLAND, C. THE DEATH OF ATTILA.
    S. MARCUS, 231:MAR74-88
    617(TLS):1FEB74-97
HOLLAND, M. OLD COUNTRY SILVER.
    G.T., 90:AUG72-576
HOLLAND, T. BETTER BACKGAMMON.
    M. WATKINS, 441:8DEC74-18
HOLLANDER, A. DECORATIVE PAPERS &
    FABRICS.
    P. LADA-MOCARSKI, 139:APR72-64
DEN HOLLANDER, A.N.J., ED. DIVERG-
    ING PARALLELS.
    K-J. POPP, 182:VOL25#7/8-228
HOLLANDER, G.D. SOVIET POLITICAL
    INDOCTRINATION.
    E.P. HOFFMANN, 32:SEP73-624
HOLLANDER, J., ED. AMERICAN SHORT
    STORIES SINCE 1945.
    D. ROBILLARD, 573(SSF):WINTER72-
    108
HOLLANDER, J. THE HEAD OF THE BED.
    D. BROMWICH, 441:16JUN74-6
    617(TLS):30AUG74-932
HOLLANDER, J. THE NIGHT MIRROR.
    M. BORROFF, 676(YR):AUTUMN72-81
    T.P., 502(PRS):SUMMER72-186
HOLLANDER, J. SELECTED POEMS.*
    H. WILLIAMS, 364:JUN/JUL73-123
HOLLANDER, J. TOWN & COUNTRY MAT-
    TERS.
    W.H. PRITCHARD, 249(HUDR):AUTUMN
    73-588

HOLLANDER, R. ALLEGORY IN DANTE'S
    "COMMEDIA."*
    T.G. BERGIN, 275(IQ):FALL/WINTER
    72-104
    J.M. FERRANTE, 276:SUMMER72-252
    J.A. SCOTT, 545(RPH):FEB73-558
HOLLINGDALE, R.J. NIETZSCHE.
    617(TLS):5APR74-373
HOLLINGSWORTH, T.H. HISTORICAL DEM-
    OGRAPHY.
    D. BARNES, 325:APR72-452
HOLLIS, C. THE SEVEN AGES.
    S. HOGGART, 362:16MAY74-639
    617(TLS):14JUN74-628
HOLLIS, P., ED. CLASS & CONFLICT IN
    NINETEENTH-CENTURY ENGLAND 1815-
    1850.
    617(TLS):26APR74-443
HOLLIS, P. THE PAUPER PRESS.
    A.T. PEACOCK, 637(VS):SEP71-104
HOLLON, W.E. FRONTIER VIOLENCE.
    M. ROGIN, 441:7JUL74-15
HOLLOWAY, G. RHINE JUMP.
    617(TLS):9AUG74-852
HOLM, I. DRAMA PÅ SCEN.
    S. SWAHN, 172(EDDA):1972/3-186
HOLM, S., ED. THE DEVIL'S INSTRU-
    MENT & OTHER DANISH STORIES.
    268:JAN74-74
HOLMAN, C.H. THE ROOTS OF SOUTHERN
    WRITING.
    639(VQR):SUMMER73-CXII
HOLMES, A.F. CHRISTIAN PHILOSOPHY
    IN THE TWENTIETH CENTURY.
    H.F., 543:MAR72-555
HOLMES, C.M. ALDOUS HUXLEY & THE
    WAY TO REALITY.*
    R. HOPE, 541(RES):MAY72-250
    P. VITOUX, 677:VOL3-334
HOLMES, D.M. THE ART OF THOMAS MID-
    DLETON.*
    D. CRAWLEY, 529(QQ):SPRING72-117
    M. ECCLES, 191(ELN):DEC72-128
    R. GILL, 541(RES):FEB72-75
    R.B. PARKER, 677:VOL3-284
HOLMES, J. ON TARGET.
    J. ORANGE, 296:VOL3#2-100
HOLMES, J.S., ED. THE NATURE OF
    TRANSLATION.
    H. ZOHN, 399(MLJ):NOV72-466
HOLMES, M. SHAKESPEARE & HIS PLAY-
    ERS.*
    T. HAWKES, 676(YR):SUMMER73-561
HOLMES, M. TWO FROM GALILEE.
    M. PHILLIPS, 441:14APR74-10
HOLMES, R. BIR HACHEIM.
    617(TLS):13SEP74-975
HOLMES, R. SHELLEY: THE PURSUIT.
    P. CONRAD, 617(TLS):9AUG74-845
HOLMES, U.T. CHRÉTIEN DE TROYES.*
    G.J. BRAULT, 207(FR):FEB72-755
HOLROYD, M. AUGUSTUS JOHN. (VOL 1)
    K. CLARK, 617(TLS):18OCT74-1149
    D. MAY, 362:26SEP74-407
HOLROYD, M. UNRECEIVED OPINIONS.*
    R. NYE, 364:OCT/NOV73-157
HOLROYD, M. - SEE KINGSMILL, H.
HOLROYD, M. - SEE STRACHEY, L.
HÖLSCHER, T. VICTORIA ROMANA.
    A.R. BIRLEY, 313:VOL62-195
    R. BRILLIANT, 54:MAR72-79

HOLST, G. LETTERS TO W.G. WHITTAKER.
(M. SHORT, ED)
J. WARRACK, 617(TLS):27DEC74-
1465
HOLST, I. HOLST.* A THEMATIC CATA-
LOGUE OF GUSTAV HOLST'S MUSIC.
J. WARRACK, 617(TLS):27DEC74-
1465
HOLSTEIN, H. - SEE KANT, I.
HOLSTI, O.R. CRISIS ESCALATION WAR.
K.E. MC VICAR, 529(QQ):SUMMER72-
282
HOLT, J. ESCAPE FROM CHILDHOOD.
G. LEVINE, 441:19MAY74-4
HOLT, M., ED. THE MODERN SPANISH
STAGE.
V.A. WARREN, 399(MLJ):FEB72-101
HOLT, V. THE HOUSE OF A THOUSAND
LANTERNS.
M. LEVIN, 441:13OCT74-22
HOLTAN, O.I. MYTHIC PATTERNS IN
IBSEN'S LAST PLAYS.*
S. ARESTAD, 397(MD):SEP72-215
HOLTHUSEN, J. TWENTIETH-CENTURY
RUSSIAN LITERATURE.
V. SETCHKAREV, 32:SEP73-663
HOLTON, G. THEMATIC ORIGINS OF
SCIENTIFIC THOUGHT.
617(TLS):25JAN74-76
HOLTON, L. THE DEVIL TO PLAY.
N. CALLENDAR, 441:17FEB74-33
HOLTON, M. CYLINDER OF VISION.*
R. FALK, 445(NCF):MAR73-497
H.S. WHITTIER, 150(DR):AUTUMN72-
502
HOLTZ, W.V. IMAGE & IMMORTALITY.*
H. MOGLEN, 128(CE):APR72-847
T.A. OLSHIN, 556(RLV):1972/3-333
HOLTZHAUER, H. GOETHE-MUSEUM.
W. KARALUS, 654(WB):2/1972-190
HOLTZHAUER, H. - SEE VON GOETHE, J.W.
HOLTZMAN, J., ED. NO CHEERING IN
THE PRESS BOX.
C. LEHMANN-HAUPT, 441:23JUL74-31
R. LIPSYTE, 441:22SEP74-32
D. WAKEFIELD, 61:AUG74-82
HOMANN, H. STUDIEN ZUR EMBLEMATIK
DES 16. JAHRHUNDERTS.
E. ZIMMERMANN, 182:VOL25#7/8-193
HOMER. THE ILIAD. (R. FITZGERALD,
TRANS)
P. ADAMS, 61:NOV74-123
D.S. CARNE-ROSS, 453:12DEC74-3
HOMER, R.J. - SEE HAWES, J.J.
HOMER, W.I., WITH V. ORGAN. ROBERT
HENRI & HIS CIRCLE.*
J.H. BAKER, 90:JAN72-38
"HOMMAGE À HENRI BOSCO."
R.T. SUSSEX, 67:MAY73-129
"HOMMAGES À MARIE DELCOURT."
A. ERNOUT, 555:VOL46FASC1-171
HONE, W. THE EVERY-DAY BOOK. THE
TABLE BOOK. THE YEAR BOOK.
K.B. HARDER, 424:MAR72-67
HONEYCOMBE, G. ADAM'S TALE.
J. BARNES, 617(TLS):1NOV74-1216
HONG, H.V. & E.H. - SEE MELANTSCHUCK,
G.
HONIG, E. CALDERÓN & THE SEIZURES
OF HONOR.
639(VQR):SPRING73-LXXVI

HONIG, E. FOUR SPRINGS. SHAKE A
SPEAR WITH ME, JOHN BERRYMAN.
L. GOLDSTEIN, 385(MQR):FALL74-
427
HONOUR, H. CHINOISERIE.
617(TLS):18OCT74-1171
HONOUR, H. GOLDSMITHS & SILVER-
SMITHS.
C. OMAN, 39:MAR72-230
HOOD, G. AMERICAN SILVER.
C. OMAN, 135:MAY72-63
HOOD, G. BONNIN & MORRIS OF PHILA-
DELPHIA.
B. LIGGETT, 656(WMQ):OCT73-673
HOOD, H. THE FRUIT MAN, THE MEAT
MAN & THE MANAGER.*
E. MC NAMARA, 529(QQ):SPRING72-
119
HOOD, H. THE GOVERNOR'S BRIDGE IS
CLOSED.*
E.J. DEVEREUX, 99:APR74-37
HOOD, H. YOU CAN'T GET THERE FROM
HERE.*
P. STEVENS, 628:SPRING73-95
HOOD, M. THE ETHNOMUSICOLOGIST.*
W. RHODES, 414(MQ):JAN72-136
HOOD, S. IN & OUT THE WINDOWS.
J. MELLORS, 362:1AUG74-156
617(TLS):19JUL74-761
HOOD, S. THE MINOANS.
J. BOARDMAN, 123:DEC73-283
HOOD, T. SELECTED POEMS OF THOMAS
HOOD.* (J. CLUBBE, ED)
M.S., 155:MAY72-125
HOOKER, J. WRITERS OF WALES: JOHN
COWPER POWYS.
617(TLS):8FEB74-121
HOOKHAM, H. A SHORT HISTORY OF
CHINA.
C.S. GOODRICH, 318(JAOS):OCT-DEC
72-588
HOOLE, K. A REGIONAL HISTORY OF THE
RAILWAYS OF GREAT BRITAIN. (VOL 4)
617(TLS):29MAR74-349
HOOLE, W.S. ACCORDING TO HOOLE.
I.H. HERRON, 584(SWR):SUMMER73-
280
HOOPER, W. - SEE LEWIS, C.S.
HOOPES, D.F. THE AMERICAN IMPRES-
SIONISTS.
A. FRANKENSTEIN, 55:FEB73-15
A. FRANKENSTEIN, 55:NOV73-46
HOOPES, D.F. SARGENT WATERCOLOURS.
M.S. YOUNG, 39:MAY72-423
HOOPES, T. THE DEVIL & JOHN FOSTER
DULLES.*
R.D. ACCINELLI, 99:NOV/DEC74-38
M. HOWARD, 617(TLS):19JUL74-757
R. O'RORKE, 362:19SEP74-379
G. WILLS, 453:7FEB74-7
HOPE, A.D. DUNCIAD MINOR.*
C. MC INTOSH, 481(PQ):JUL72-745
HOPE, A.D. A MIDSUMMER EVE'S DREAM.*
D. FOX, 447(N&Q):JAN72-31
HOPE, C. CAPE DRIVES.
617(TLS):21JUN74-667
HOPE, N.M. THE ALTERNATIVE TO GER-
MAN UNIFICATION.
617(TLS):23AUG74-909
HOPE, T. HOUSEHOLD FURNITURE & IN-
TERIOR DECORATION.
D. IRWIN, 39:OCT72-367

HOPE, T.E. LEXICAL BORROWINGS IN
THE ROMANCE LANGUAGES.*
R.A. HALL, JR., 275(IQ):FALL/
WINTER72-135
HOPF, D. ÜBERGANGSAUSLESE UND
LEISTUNGSDIFFERENZIERUNG.
K. FUCHS, 430(NS):JUL72-432
HOPKINS, B. - SEE WÖRNER, K.H.
HOPKINS, E.J. & E.F. RIMBAULT. THE
ORGAN.*
P. WILLIAMS, 415:NOV73-1125
HOPKINS, H. GRAND ROUNDS.
M. LEVIN, 441:24NOV74-40
HOPKINS, J. TANGIER BUZZLESS FLIES.
639(VQR):SUMMER72-XCVIII
HOPKINS, K., ED. HONG KONG.
P. LUEY, 293(JAST):AUG72-948
M. TOPLEY, 302:JUL72-214
A.K. WONG, 302:JAN72-70
HOPKINS, M.W. MASS MEDIA IN THE
SOVIET UNION.
J. CRITCHLOW, 550(RUSR):OCT72-
428
HOPKINS, R.F. POLITICAL ROLES IN A
NEW STATE.
L. MAIR, 69:JUL72-245
HOPKINS, T.J. THE HINDU RELIGIOUS
TRADITION.
J.P. SHARMA, 318(JAOS):OCT-DEC
72-576
HÖPP, G. EVOLUTION DER SPRACHE UND
VERNUNFT.
L.F. BROSNAHAN, 361:VOL30#2/3-
274
E. PULGRAM, 297(JL):FEB72-156
E.H. YARRILL, 182:VOL25#19/20-
644
HORACE. Q. HORATIUS FLACCUS: "EPIS-
TULAE" LIBER PRIMUS. (J. PRÉAUX,
ED)
O. HILTBRUNNER, 182:VOL25#5/6-
175
HORACE. HORAZ: "DIE SATIREN." (K.
BÜCHNER, ED)
F. LASSERRE, 182:VOL25#9/10-306
N. RUDD, 123:DEC73-171
HORACEK, B. KUNSTPRINZIPIEN DER
SATZ- UND VERSGESTALTUNG.*
S. KLEYE, 682(ZPSK):BAND24HEFT6-
528
O. LUDWIG, 343:BAND14HEFT2-218
HORGAN, P. ENCOUNTERS WITH STRAVIN-
SKY.*
G. MARTIN, 676(YR):WINTER73-296
639(VQR):WINTER73-XXXII
HORKHEIMER, M. & T.W. ADORNO. DIA-
LECTIC OF ENLIGHTENMENT.
J. SHAPIRO, 617(TLS):4OCT74-1094
42(AR):VOL32#3-507
HORL, S. LEIDENSCHAFTEN UND AFFEKTE
IM DRAMATISCHEN WERK TIRSO DE MOL-
INAS.*
M. WILSON, 240(HR):SPRING72-226
HÖRMANN, H. PSYCHOLINGUISTICS.*
A. DABIJA, 353:1SEP72-85
L.A. JAKOBOVITS, 399(MLJ):APR72-
254
B.J. KOEKKOEK, 399(MLJ):DEC72-
537
HORN, J.M. - SEE LE NEVE, J.
HORNBACK, B.G. THE METAPHOR OF
CHANCE.*
R.O. PREYER, 637(VS):JUN72-499
W.F. WRIGHT, 594:SPRING72-93

HORNBACK, B.G. "NOAH'S ARKITEC-
TURE."*
A. FLEISHMAN, 401(MLQ):JUN73-191
G.J. WORTH, 301(JEGP):APR73-246
HORNER, D. THE TREASURE GALLEONS.
639(VQR):SUMMER72-CIX
HORNER, J. STUDIES IN INDUSTRIAL
DEMOCRACY.
617(TLS):26APR74-454
HORNSBY, R.A. PATTERNS OF ACTION IN
THE "AENEID."*
A.G. MC KAY, 24:FALL73-315
HORNSEY, A.W. - SEE MANN, T.
HOROVITZ, I. CAPPELLA.*
42(AR):VOL32#4-697
HOROWITZ, A. FROM MORPHY TO FISCHER.
617(TLS):29MAR73-349
HOROWITZ, I.A. CHESS: GAMES TO
REMEMBER.
617(TLS):15MAR74-272
HOROWITZ, I.A. & G. MOTT-SMITH.
POINT COUNT CHESS.
617(TLS):1MAR74-220
HORROCKS, B. A FULL LIFE.
E.S. TURNER, 362:7MAR74-310
617(TLS):8MAR74-230
HORRY, R.N. PAUL CLAUDEL & SAINT-
JOHN PERSE.
J.P. HOUSTON, 207(FR):FEB72-727
HORSKÁ-VRBOVÁ, P. KAPITALISTICKÁ
INDUSTRIALIZACE A STŘEDOEVROPSKÁ
SPOLEČNOST.
R.L. RUDOLPH, 32:DEC73-835
HORSMAN, A. - SEE DICKENS, C.
TER HORST, J.F. GERALD FORD & THE
FUTURE OF THE PRESIDENCY.
B. KOVACH, 441:28DEC74-21
HORSTMANN, R-P. & J.H. TREDE - SEE
HEGEL, G.W.F.
HORTEN, H.E. EXPORT-IMPORT-KORRES-
PONDENZ IN VIER SPRACHEN - DEUTSCH-
ENGLISCH-FRANZÖSISCH-SPANISCH.
M. REFFET, 430(NS):OCT72-613
HORTON, J. GRIEG.
617(TLS):23AUG74-907
HORTON, J.A.B. LETTERS ON THE POLIT-
ICAL CONDITION OF THE GOLD COAST.
A.H.M. KIRK-GREENE, 69:JAN72-71
HORVAT, B. BUSINESS CYCLES IN YUGO-
SLAVIA.
G. MACESICH, 32:JUN73-422
HORVATH, V.M. ANDRÉ MALRAUX.*
W.G. LANGLOIS, 598(SOR):WINTER74-
231
HORWITZ, H. - SEE LUTTRELL, N.
HORWITZ, J. THE MARRIED LOVERS.*
D.A.N. JONES, 617(TLS):13DEC74-
1405
HOSILLOS, L.V. PHILIPPINE-AMERICAN
LITERARY RELATIONS, 1898-1941.
C.O. HOUSTON, 293(JAST):NOV71-
235
HOSKINS, W.G. THE MAKING OF THE
ENGLISH LANDSCAPE.
A. CLIFTON-TAYLOR, 46:JAN72-66
HOSKYNS, C. CASE STUDIES IN AFRICAN
DIPLOMACY: 2.
I.M. LEWIS, 69:OCT72-343
HOSMON, R.S., ED. THE GERM.
W.E. FREDEMAN, 636(VP):SPRING72-
87
HOSPERS, J. LIBERTARIANISM.
J.H. WELLBANK, 484(PPR):SEP72-
139

HOTTEL, H.C. & J.B. HOWARD. NEW
ENERGY TECHNOLOGY.
42(AR):SPRING/SUMMER72-250
HOTTON, J.C. THE SLANG DICTIONARY.
J. SIMPSON, 203:AUTUMN72-257
HOTZENKÖCHERLE, R. & R. BRUNNER.
SCHWEIZER DIALEKTE IN TEXT UND TON.
(VOL 1, PT 5)
R.E. KELLER, 402(MLR):JAN73-207
HOUGH, R. FIGHTING SHIPS.
G. WILLS, 39:MAR72-231
HOUGH, R. LOUIS & VICTORIA.
G. BATTISCOMBE, 617(TLS):22NOV74-
1309
HOUGH, S.B. FEAR FORTUNE, FATHER.
617(TLS):8NOV74-1248
HOULDEN, J.L. ETHICS & THE NEW
TESTAMENT.
617(TLS):5JUL74-732
HOURANI, G.F. ISLAMIC RATIONALISM.*
F. SHEHADI, 484(PPR):MAR73-434
HOURS, M. COROT.
A. FRANKENSTEIN, 55:FEB73-15
HOUSE, M. & G. STOREY - SEE DICKENS,
C.
HOUSE, M., G. STOREY & K. TILLOTSON
- SEE DICKENS, C.
HOUSEHOLD, G. THE LIVES & TIMES OF
BERNARDO BROWN.*
M. LEVIN, 441:3MAR74-28
HOUSEHOLDER, F.W. LINGUISTIC SPECU-
LATIONS.
205(FMLS):OCT72-383
HOUSMAN, A.E. THE LETTERS OF A.E.
HOUSMAN.* (H. MAAS, ED)
C.K. HYDER, 636(VP):SUMMER72-185
639(VQR):WINTER72-X
HOUSTON, J. & B.A. KING. OJIBWA
SUMMER.
J.E. CHAMBERLIN, 249(HUDR):WIN-
TER73/74-786
HOUSTON, J.P. THE DEMONIC IMAGINA-
TION.*
A. DU BRUCK, 546(RR):DEC72-310
HOUSTON, J.P. FICTIONAL TECHNIQUE
IN FRANCE: 1802-1927.
R.T. DENOMMÉ, 188(ECR):FALL72-
233
HOUSTON, J.W. & J.D. FAREWELL TO
MANZANAR.*
441:13JAN74-31
HOUTART, F. & A. ROUSSEAU. THE
CHURCH & REVOLUTION.
A.W. GODFREY, 363:FEB72-77
HOVANNISIAN, R.G. THE REPUBLIC OF
ARMENIA.* (VOL 1)
D.S.M. WILLIAMS, 575(SEER):APR73-
319
HOVDHAUGEN, E. TRANSFORMASJONELL
GENERATIV GRAMMATIKK.
M. DURBIN, 353:1NOV72-89
HÖVER, W. THEOLOGIA MYSTICA IN ALT-
BAIRISCHER ÜBERTRAGUNG.
E. BAUER, 597(SN):VOL44#2-428
HOWARD, C. BRITAIN & THE "CASUS
BELLI," 1822-1902.
617(TLS):27SEP74-1047
HOWARD, D. THE DEVELOPMENT OF THE
MARXIAN DIALECTIC.*
L.H. LEGTERS, 32:SEP73-619
M. VADÉE, 182:VOL25#17/18-583
HOWARD, D. & K.E. KLARE, EDS. THE
UNKNOWN DIMENSION.
L.H. LEGTERS, 32:SEP73-619

HOWARD, D.S. CHINESE ARMORIAL POR-
CELAIN.
R. REIF, 441:13DEC74-41
M. SULLIVAN, 617(TLS):1NOV74-
1222
HOWARD, E. RATTLIN THE REEFER. (A.
HOWSE, ED)
A. EASSON, 155:SEP72-196
HOWARD, M.S. JONATHAN CAPE, PUB-
LISHER.
H.P. GUNDY, 529(QQ):AUTUMN72-425
HOWARD, R., ED. PREFERENCES.
W.H. PRITCHARD, 441:17NOV74-42
HOWARD, R.R. THE DARK GLASS.
G.P. LANDOW, 290(JAAC):SPRING73-
422
D. SONSTROEM, 637(VS):DEC72-235
HOWARD-HILL, T.H., ED. OXFORD SHAKE-
SPEARE CONCORDANCES: THE MERCHANT
OF VENICE; AS YOU LIKE IT; ALL'S
WELL THAT ENDS WELL; THE WINTER'S
TALE; TWELFTH NIGHT; THE TAMING OF
THE SHREW; A MIDSUMMER NIGHT'S
DREAM; LOVE'S LABOUR'S LOST; MUCH
ADO ABOUT NOTHING; KING JOHN; I
HENRY VI; II HENRY VI.*
J.G. MC MANAWAY, 551(RENQ):
AUTUMN72-366
HOWARD-HILL, T.H. SHAKESPEARIAN BIB-
LIOGRAPHY & TEXTUAL CRITICISM.
P. DAVISON, 354:JUN72-155
HOWARTH, R.G. DIARY, DRAMA & POETRY.
T.G.H., 581:JUN73-247
HOWARTH, W.D. & C.L. WALTON. EXPLI-
CATIONS.
E.C. KNOX, 207(FR):FEB72-761
HOWAT, G., ED. WHO DID WHAT.
617(TLS):25OCT74-1208
HOWAT, G.M.D., GENERAL ED. DICTION-
ARY OF WORLD HISTORY.
617(TLS):18JAN74-56
HOWAT, J.K. THE HUDSON RIVER & ITS
PAINTERS.
J. ROTHENSTEIN, 58:NOV72-92
HOWATCH, S. APRIL'S GRAVE.
N. CALLENDAR, 441:17MAR74-39
HOWATCH, S. CASHELMARA.
M. LEVIN, 441:28JUL74-20
HOWE, E. THE MAGICIANS OF THE GOLD-
EN DAWN.
M. GREEN, 364:FEB/MAR73-144
HOWE, F. & E. BASS, EDS. NO MORE
MASKS!
V. YOUNG, 249(HUDR):WINTER73/74-
725
HOWE, I. THE CRITICAL POINT.*
R. SALE, 441:6JAN74-7
HOWE, I. & C. GERSHMAN, EDS. ISRAEL,
THE ARABS & THE MIDDLE EAST.
M.S. CHERTOFF, 287:SEP72-29
HOWE, I. & M. HARRINGTON, EDS. THE
SEVENTIES.
42(AR):VOL32#3-502
HOWELL, B. THE RED FOX.*
D. BARBOUR, 150(DR):SPRING72-169
HOWELL, W.S. EIGHTEENTH-CENTURY
BRITISH LOGIC & RHETORIC.
P.K. ALKON, 566:AUTUMN72-47
V.M. BEVILACQUA, 481(PQ):JUL72-
613
W.J. ONG, 656(WMQ):OCT72-637
J.V. PRICE, 319:JUL74-397

HOWELLS, W. THE PACIFIC ISLANDERS.
B.M. BLACKWOOD, 617(TLS):20DEC74-
1431
HOWELLS, W.D. INDIAN SUMMER. (S.
BENNETT, ED) THE KENTONS. (G.C.
CARRINGTON, JR., ED)
J. SCHIFFMAN, 27(AL):MAR73-121
HOWER, A. & R.A. PRETO-RODAS, EDS.
CRÔNICAS BRASILEIRAS.
T. BROWN, 399(MLJ):DEC72-523
L. LOCKETT, 263:JAN-MAR73-104
M. SILVERMAN, 238:MAY72-399
HOWES, A.B., ED. STERNE: THE CRITI-
CAL HERITAGE.
617(TLS):9AUG74-863
HOWES, B. THE BLUE GARDEN.*
639(VQR):SUMMER73-CX
HOWLAND, B. W-3.
A. BROYARD, 441:2SEP74-13
D. RABINOWITZ, 441:6OCT74-22
HOWSE, A. - SEE HOWARD, E.
HOY, P.C. JULIEN GREEN I (PREMIÈRE
LIVRAISON).
R.B. JOHNSON, 207(FR):FEB72-725
A. LAVERS, 208(FS):JAN73-100
HOYLES, J. THE WANING OF THE RENAIS-
SANCE 1640-1740.*
D.G. FRICKE, 568(SCN):FALL-WIN-
TER73-85
HOYT, N.S. & T. CASSIRER - SEE
DIDEROT, D.
HRABAL, B. TRAINS ÉTROITEMENT
SURVEILLÉS.
A. LIEHM, 98:OCT72-841
HRABEC, S. & OTHERS, EDS. SYMBOLAE
PHILOLOGICAE IN HONOREM VITOLDI
TASZYCKI.
M.Z. BROOKS, 353:JAN72-97
HRBEK, R. & W. KEUTSCH. GESELL-
SCHAFT UND STAAT IN GROSSBRITAN-
NIEN.
L. BORINSKI, 38:BAND90HEFT4-551
HRUBÝ, A. DER "ACKERMANN" UND SEINE
VORLAGE.
L.L. HAMMERICH, 301(JEGP):APR73-
274
HRUBÝ, F. ETUDIANTS TCHÈQUES AUX
ÉCOLES PROTESTANTES DE L'EUROPE
OCCIDENTALE À LA FIN DU XVIe ET AU
DÉBUT DU XVIIe SIÈCLE.
O. ODLOZILIK, 551(RENQ):AUTUMN72-
343
HSIA, C.T., WITH J.S.M. LAU, EDS.
TWENTIETH-CENTURY CHINESE STORIES.*
W.L. MAC DONALD, 352(LE&W):VOL15
#3-518
639(VQR):SPRING72-LII
HSIANG-LIN, L. - SEE UNDER LO HSIANG-
LIN
HSIAO, K.H. MONEY & MONETARY POLICY
IN COMMUNIST CHINA.
D.C. COLE, 293(JAST):MAY72-662
HSIEH, C-M. ATLAS OF CHINA.* (C.L.
SALTER, ED)
T. SHABAD, 441:5APR74-35
HSIEN-CHANG, L. - SEE UNDER LI
HSIEN-CHANG
HSIN-NUNG, Y. - SEE UNDER YAO HSIN-
NUNG
HSU, F.L.K. THE CHALLENGE OF AMERI-
CAN DREAM.
C-T. WU, 293(JAST):MAY72-671

HSÜ-BALZER, E., R.L. BALZER & F.L.K.
HSU. CHINA DAY BY DAY.
E. HAHN, 441:22DEC74-3
HSÜEH YÜN-SHENG, COMP. TU-LI TS'UN-I
CH'UNG-K'AN PEN. (HUANG CHING-
CHIA, ED)
D. BODDE, 293(JAST):MAY72-650
HUAN, M. - SEE UNDER MA HUAN
HUANG CHING-CHIA - SEE HSÜEH YÜN-
SHENG
HUANG, P.P-F. CANTONESE DICTIONARY.*
C.N. LI, 318(JAOS):OCT-DEC72-564
HUANG, R. MANDARIN PRONUNCIATION.
C.N. LI, 318(JAOS):OCT-DEC72-566
HUBBARD, G. QUAKER BY CONVINCEMENT.
617(TLS):7JUN74-618
HUBBARD, P.M. A THIRSTY EVIL.
A. BROYARD, 441:1APR74-35
617(TLS):5APR74-375
HUBBELING, H.G. INLEIDING TOT HET
DENKEN VAN WITTGENSTEIN.
W.A. DE PATER, 206:JUL72-601
HUBBELING, H.G. SPINOZA'S METHODOLO-
GY.
J. BRUNSCHWIG, 542:APR-JUN72-223
HUBBELL, J.B. WHO ARE THE MAJOR
AMERICAN WRITERS?*
D.K. KIRBY, 432(NEQ):SEP72-446
L.T.L., 502(PRS):FALL72-274
J.H. MAGUIRE, 649(WAL):SUMMER72-
157
639(VQR):SUMMER72-CIII
HUBER, B. & J-C. STEINEGGER, EDS.
JEAN PROUVÉ.
R. BANHAM, 46:FEB72-130
R. LE RICOLAIS, 505:APR72-128
HUBER, W. HELIAND UND MATTHÄUSEXE-
GESE.
D.H. GREEN, 402(MLR):APR73-441
HUBERMAN, E.L. THE POETRY OF EDWIN
MUIR.*
B. QUINN, 613:AUTUMN72-462
C. WISEMAN, 150(DR):SPRING72-154
639(VQR):WINTER72-XXX
HUBERT, J., J. PORCHER & W.F. VOL-
BACH. CAROLINGIAN ART.* (A.
MALRAUX & A. PARROT, EDS)
P. HETHERINGTON, 90:JUN72-411
HUBERT, R.R. ENCHAÎNEMENT.
H.A. BOURAOUI, 207(FR):OCT71-205
HÜBNER, F. DIE PERSONENDARSTELLUNG
IN DEN DRAMEN ANTON P. ČECHOVS.
J.L. CONRAD, 32:MAR73-207
A.B. MC MILLIN, 575(SEER):OCT73-
624
HÜBSCHER, A. - SEE "ARTHUR SCHOPEN-
HAUER: GESPRÄCHE"
HÜBSCHMANN, H. DIE ALTARMENISCHEN
ORTSNAMEN.
R. SCHMITT, 343:BAND15HEFT2-222
HUBSCHMID, J. THESAURUS PRAEROMANI-
CUS.* (FASC 1&2)
G.F. MEIER, 682(ZPSK):BAND25
HEFT6-526
HUBY, P. PLATO & MODERN MORALITY.
R.C. CROSS, 518:MAY73-10
HUDDLESTON, R.D. THE SENTENCE IN
WRITTEN ENGLISH.
R. SINGH, 206:JAN73-406
A.R. TELLIER, 189(EA):OCT-DEC72-
531
HUDSON, G.W., COMP. "PARADISE LOST:"
A CONCORDANCE.
J.C. MAXWELL, 447(N&Q):MAY72-185

HUDSON, L. THE CULT OF THE FACT.
H. LOMAS, 364:AUG/SEP72-144
HUDSON, W.D. REASON & RIGHT.
P.S. ARDAL, 479(PHQ):JAN72-65
HUDSON, W.M., ED. DIAMOND BESSIE &
THE SHEPHERDS.
J.W. BYRD, 584(SWR):WINTER73-99
HUFF, E. - SEE FANG, C-Y.
HUFFMAN, F.E., WITH C-R.T. LAMBERT &
I. PROUM. CAMBODIAN SYSTEM OF
WRITING & BEGINNING READER.
P.N. JENNER, 318(JAOS):OCT-DEC72-
556
HUFFMAN, F.E., WITH C. PROMCHAN &
C-R.T. LAMBERT. MODERN SPOKEN CAM-
BODIAN.*
P.N. JENNER, 318(JAOS):OCT-DEC72-
556
HUGGINS, N.I. HARLEM RENAISSANCE.*
C.T. DAVIS, 27(AL):MAR73-138
L. GURKO, 191(ELN):DEC72-135
P.R. KLOTMAN, 659:SPRING74-283
HUGHES, C.E. THE AUTOBIOGRAPHICAL
NOTES OF CHARLES EVANS HUGHES.
(D.J. DANELSKI & J.S. TULCHIN, EDS)
H.S. HUGHES, 453:30MAY74-30
HUGHES, D., ED. THE MAN OF WAX.
J.E. DUNLEAVY, 637(VS):MAR72-376
HUGHES, E.J. THE LIVING PRESIDENCY.*
R. EGGER, 639(VQR):AUTUMN73-612
W.V. SHANNON, 441:18JAN74-37
HUGHES, G. FIFTY FAMOUS COMPOSERS.
A. JACOBS, 415:SEP73-904
HUGHES, G. TOWARDS THE SUN.
J. SAUNDERS, 565:VOL13#3-75
HUGHES, H.S. THE SEA CHANGE.
C. LEHMANN-HAUPT, 441:26DEC74-35
HUGHES, J.L. TOM JONES SLEPT HERE.
E. GLOVER, 565:VOL13#3-44
HUGHES, L. THE DRAMA'S PATRONS.*
H.W. PEDICORD, 481(PQ):JUL72-615
HUGHES, L., ED. THE OLD MAN OF THE
MIST & OTHER STORIES.
617(TLS):12APR74-396
HUGHES, M. - SEE MUMFORD, L. & F.J.
OSBORN
HUGHES, P. & D. WILLIAMS, EDS. THE
VARIED PATTERN.
F. BRADY, 566:AUTUMN72-34
205(FMLS):OCT72-386
HUGHES, R. THE FOX IN THE ATTIC.
R. DE FEO, 249(HUDR):WINTER73/74-
779
HUGHES, R. HEAVEN & HELL IN WESTERN
ART.
P. FINGESTEN, 363:FEB72-80
HUGHES, R. THE WOODEN SHEPHERDESS.*
R. DE FEO, 249(HUDR):WINTER73/74-
780
HUGHES, R.P., S. KARLINSKY & V. MAR-
KOV, EDS. CALIFORNIA SLAVIC STUD-
IES. (VOL 6)
R.E. MATLAW, 550(RUSR):JUL72-310
HUGHES, T. ANTIQUES.
90:JUN72-440
HUGHES, T. CROW.*
M. MARCUS, 502(PRS):FALL72-272
HUGHES, T. THE IRON GIANT.
K. MILLER, 453:7MAR74-3
HUGHES, T. SELECTED POEMS 1957-1967.
C. BEDIENT, 441:13JAN74-3
K. MILLER, 453:7MAR74-3
HUGHES, Z. THE LEGEND OF MIAREE.
T. STURGEON, 441:8SEP74-39

HUGHEY, R. JOHN HARINGTON OF STEP-
NEY, TUDOR GENTLEMAN.
J.A. EPPERSON, 551(RENQ):WINTER
72-488
G.A. HOAR, 377:JUL73-117
J. ROBERTSON, 541(RES):AUG72-331
HUGLO, M. LES TONARIES.
R. STEINER, 414(MQ):OCT72-672
HUGNET, G. L'AVENTURE DADA.
S. FAUCHEREAU, 98:AUG/SEP72-752
HUGO, L. BERNARD SHAW - PLAYWRIGHT
& PREACHER.
T.F. EVANS, 571:SPRING72-188
C. HARRISON, 157:SPRING72-74
HUGO, R. THE LADY IN KICKING HORSE
RESERVOIR.*
D. ALLEN, 491:MAY74-103
W.H. PRITCHARD, 249(HUDR):AUTUMN
73-584
639(VQR):AUTUMN73-CXL
HUGO, V. LES CONTEMPLATIONS.* (L.
CELLIER, ED)
A.R.W. JAMES, 208(FS):JAN73-82
HUGO, V. LA LÉGENDE DES SIÈCLES
(FRAGMENTS). (F. LAMBERT, ED)
B. LEUILLIOT, 535(RHL):MAR-APR72-
323
HUGUET, L., COMP. BIBLIOGRAPHIE
ALFRED DÖBLIN.
H.D. OSTERLE, 301(JEGP):OCT73-
609
HULL, F., ED. CATALOGUE OF ESTATE
MAPS 1590-1840 IN THE KENT COUNTY
ARCHIVES OFFICE.
617(TLS):10MAY74-508
HÜLLEN, W. LINGUISTIK UND ENGLISCH-
UNTERRICHT.
A. DIGESER, 72:BAND210HEFT4/6-
357
H. HEUER, 430(NS):APR72-237
"HUMANISTICA LOVANIENSIA." (VOLS
18 & 19) (J. IJSEWIJN, ED)
M. MARCOVICH, 52:BAND7HEFT2/3-
315
HUMBERT-DROZ, J. LE COURONNEMENT
D'UNE VIE DE COMBAT.
617(TLS):26APR74-454
HUMBLE, R. HITLER'S GENERALS.
617(TLS):4JAN74-6
VON HUMBOLDT, W. LINGUISTIC VARI-
ABILITY & INTELLECTUAL DEVELOPMENT.
E.F-K. KOERNER, 350:SEP73-682
HUME, B. INSIDE STORY.
S.R. WEISMAN, 441:11AUG74-4
HUME, R.D. DRYDEN'S CRITICISM.*
P. LEGOUIS, 189(EA):OCT-DEC72-
553
E.R. MARKS, 290(JAAC):WINTER71-
264
O.F. SIGWORTH, 173(ECS):FALL72-
127
HUMMEL, C.F. WITH HAMMER IN HAND.
G. WILLS, 39:SEP72-254
HUMMERT, P.A. BERNARD SHAW'S MARX-
IAN ROMANCE.
H.F. FOLLAND, 651(WHR):AUTUMN73-
411
639(VQR):AUTUMN73-CXLV
HUMPHREY, G.R. L'ESTHÉTIQUE DE LA
POÉSIE DE GÉRARD DE NERVAL.*
W. BEAUCHAMP, 188(ECR):SUMMER72-
153

HUMPHREY, W. D'UN TEMPS ET D'UN
LIEU.
P-Y. PETILLON, 98:MAR72-288
HUMPHREYS, C. EXPLORING BUDDHISM.
R.C. ZAEHNER, 617(TLS):6DEC74-
1389
HUMPHREYS, E. FLESH & BLOOD.
J. MELLORS, 362:22AUG74-253
HUMPHRIES, R. COAT ON A STICK.
J.T. IRWIN, 569(SR):WINTER73-158
HUND, F. THE HISTORY OF QUANTUM
THEORY.
617(TLS):13SEP74-982
HUNDSNURSCHER, F. NEUERE METHODEN
DER SEMANTIK.
J.A. HAWKINS, 220(GL&L):JUL73-
358
HUNT, D. PARENTS & CHILDREN IN HIS-
TORY.
L. STONE, 453:14NOV74-25
HUNT, E.H. UNDERCOVER.
N.W. ALDRICH, JR., 231:DEC74-102
A. COCKBURN, 453:28NOV74-8
HUNT, E.M. NEW HAMPSHIRE TOWN NAMES
& WHENCE THEY CAME.
S.A. STOUDEMIRE, 424:JUN72-140
HUNT, J., WITH P. HARBISON. IRISH
MEDIEVAL FIGURE SCULPTURE 1200-
1600.
R. CAMBER, 617(TLS):1NOV74-1235
HUNT, J.W. FORMS OF GLORY.
617(TLS):19APR74-425
HUNT, P., ED. THE BOOK OF GARDEN
ORNAMENT.
617(TLS):26JUL74-815
HUNT, R. & R. CAMPBELL. K.C. IRVING.
D. CAMERON, 99:MAY/JUN74-49
HUNT, S. FROM BOTTLE CREEK.*
P. CRISP, 368:DEC72-347
HUNTER, A. GENTLY WITH THE INNO-
CENTS.
N. CALLENDAR, 441:18AUG74-24
HUNTER, A. GENTLY WITH THE LADIES.
N. CALLENDAR, 441:3NOV74-71
"BEATRICE TRUM HUNTER'S FAVORITE
NATURAL FOODS."
N. HAZELTON, 441:1DEC74-96
HUNTER, G. METALOGIC.*
M.J. CRESSWELL, 479(PHQ):JAN72-
79
E.M.F., 543:SEP71-127
HUNTER, G. MODERNIZING PEASANT
SOCIETIES.
W. ELKAN, 69:APR72-166
HUNTER, J., ED. MODERN POETS ONE,
TWO, THREE, FOUR.
W. STUCK, 430(NS):JUL72-437
HUNTER, J.D. MEMOIRS OF A CAPTIVITY
AMONG THE INDIANS OF NORTH AMERICA.
(R. DRINNON, ED)
442(NY):4MAR74-113
HUNTER, J.F.M. ESSAYS AFTER WITTGEN-
STEIN.
617(TLS):9AUG74-850
HUNTER, L.H. BUDDHISM IN HAWAII.
H. CONROY, 293(JAST):MAY72-638
HUNTER, R. THE STORMING OF THE MIND.
R. ROBERTSON, 529(QQ):SUMMER72-
261
HUNTER, R.E. & J.E. RIELLY, EDS.
DEVELOPMENT TODAY.
M. LIPTON, 617(TLS):2AUG74-830

HUNTER, R.H. & T.H.C. BROWN. BATTLE
COAST.
617(TLS):5APR74-356
HUNTER, S. AMERICAN ART OF THE
TWENTIETH CENTURY.*
A. FRANKENSTEIN, 55:FEB73-14
HUNTER, W.B., C.A. PATRIDES & J.H.
ADAMSON. BRIGHT ESSENCE.*
H.A.D., 543:JUN72-756
M. KELLEY, 577(SHR):FALL72-418
J.R. MC ADAMS, 568(SCN):FALL-
WINTER73-70
S.P. REVARD, 301(JEGP):JAN73-128
639(VQR):SPRING72-LVI
HUNTER BLAIR, P. THE WORLD OF BEDE.*
639(VQR):SPRING72-LX
HUNTFORD, R. THE NEW TOTALITARIANS.
P.C. ROBERTS, 396(MODA):SPRING73-
219
HUNTING, R. - SEE BOSWELL, J.
HUNTLEY, H.R. THE ALIEN PROTAGONIST
OF FORD MADOX FORD.*
M. ALLOTT, 402(MLR):JAN73-165
HUPPE, B.F. THE WEB OF WORDS.*
J.K. CRANE, 128(CE):APR72-834
P.W. ROGERS, 529(QQ):SUMMER72-
270
HUPPERT, G. THE IDEA OF PERFECT
HISTORY.*
B.C. BOWEN, 125:OCT72-78
H. DURANTON, 557(RSH):APR-JUN72-
302
HUQ, A.M.A. A STUDY OF BENGALI MUS-
LIM PERSONAL NAMES TO ASCERTAIN
THE FEASIBILITY OF APPLICATION OF
A MECHANISTIC RULE FOR THEIR
ARRANGEMENT.
M.L. SHARMA, 424:JUN72-139
HURD, M. VAUGHAN WILLIAMS.
A.E.F. DICKINSON, 607:#102-33
HURLEY, F.J. PORTRAIT OF A DECADE.
M. ORVELL, 31(ASCH):AUTUMN74-671
639(VQR):SPRING73-XCII
HURLEY, N.P. THEOLOGY THROUGH FILM.*
E.V. WYATT, 363:FEB72-75
HURT, J. CATILINE'S DREAM.*
639(VQR):SPRING73-LXXIII
HURT, J. EDUCATION IN EVOLUTION.
G.J. CLIFFORD, 637(VS):JUN72-502
HUSAIN, Q.T. SAHEBUL MATHNAWI.
Q.S.K. HUSAINI, 273(IC):JUL72-
278
HUSSEIN, E.N. KINJEKETILE.
A. RENDLE, 157:SPRING72-81
HUSSEIN, M. CLASS CONFLICT IN EGYPT
1945-1970.
617(TLS):26APR74-436
HUSSERL, E. PHILOSOPHIE DER ARITH-
METIK. (L. ELEY, ED)
J.D.C., 543:SEP71-127
HUSSEY, M. THE WORLD OF SHAKESPEARE
& HIS CONTEMPORARIES.
I. BROWN, 157:WINTER71-68
639(VQR):AUTUMN72-CLVI
HUSSEY, S.S. CHAUCER.
G.C. BRITTON, 447(N&Q):JUL72-272
H. COOPER, 382(MAE):1973/2-205
P.W. ROGERS, 529(QQ):AUTUMN72-
416
R.M. WILSON, 402(MLR):JAN73-147
C.K. ZACHER, 589:OCT73-757
HUSSON, G. - SEE LUCIAN

HUTCHENS, J.K. & G. OPPENHEIMER, EDS.
THE BEST IN THE WORLD.*
  J. SAYRE, 441:17FEB74-3
  442(NY):28JAN74-104
HUTCHESON, F. ILLUSTRATIONS ON THE
MORAL SENSE. (B. PEACH, ED)
  A.S.C., 543:MAR72-556
HUTCHINGS, A. SCHUBERT.* (4TH ED)
  M.J.E. BROWN, 415:JUN73-600
HUTCHINSON, T. HORROR & FANTASY IN
THE CINEMA.
  W. FEAVER, 617(TLS):27DEC74-1471
HUTCHINSON, W.T. & W.M.E. RACHAL -
SEE MADISON, J.
HUTCHISON, R.A. VESCO.
  C. WELLES, 441:29DEC74-2
HUTSCHNECKER, A.A. THE DRIVE FOR
POWER.
  J. O'REILLY, 441:3NOV74-20
HUTSON, J.H. PENNSYLVANIA POLITICS,
1746-1770.
  R. KETCHAM, 656(WMQ):APR73-327
  639(VQR):AUTUMN72-CXLI
VON HUTTEN, U. DEUTSCHE SCHRIFTEN.
(P. UKENA, ED)
  R. STAMBAUGH, 400(MLN):OCT72-783
HUTTENBACK, R.A. GANDHI IN SOUTH
AFRICA.
  A.J. GREENBERGER, 293(JAST):MAY
  72-706
HUTTON, J.B. HESS.
  639(VQR):WINTER72-XI
HUWS, D. NOTH.*
  H. WILLIAMS, 364:JUN/JUL73-123
HUXLEY, A. THE COLLECTED POETRY OF
ALDOUS HUXLEY. (D. WATT, ED)
  R. WAJC-TENENBAUM, 556(RLV):
  1972/4-438
HUXLEY, A. LETTERS OF ALDOUS HUX-
LEY.* (G. SMITH, ED)
  N. BRAYBROOKE, 619(TC):VOL177
  #1043-57
HUXLEY, A. PLANT & PLANET.
  M. LASKI, 362:19&26DEC74-847
HUXLEY, E. LIVINGSTONE & HIS AFRI-
CAN JOURNEYS.
  A. BROYARD, 441:15AUG74-37
  442(NY):18NOV74-235
  617(TLS):11OCT74-1143
HUXLEY, F. THE WAY OF THE SACRED.
  W. FEAVER, 362:19&26DEC74-847
HUXLEY, J. EVOLUTION. (3RD ED)
  C.D. DARLINGTON, 617(TLS):20DEC
  74-1434
HUXLEY, J. MEMORIES. (VOL 1)
  C. STEPHEN, JR., 502(PRS):SUM-
  MER72-184
HUXTABLE, A.L. WILL THEY EVER
FINISH BRUCKNER BOULEVARD?
  W.P. THOMPSON, 576:MAR72-75
HUYGHE, R. WATTEAU.
  M. CORMACK, 39:JAN72-71
HYAMS, E. PRINCE HABIB'S ICEBERG.
  S. MAITLAND, 362:12DEC74-786
HYDE, F.E. LIVERPOOL & THE MERSEY.
  J.G. CLARK, 481(PQ):JUL72-535
HYDE, G. THE SOVIET HEALTH SERVICE.
  E. DUNN, 617(TLS):29NOV74-1348
HYDE, H.M. STALIN.*
  H.F. FIRESIDE, 550(RUSR):OCT72-
  414
  639(VQR):AUTUMN72-CXL

HYDE, H.M. THE TRIALS OF OSCAR
WILDE.
  617(TLS):13SEP74-975
HYDE, M. THE IMPOSSIBLE FRIENDSHIP.*
  617(TLS):8MAR74-244
  639(VQR):AUTUMN73-CLX
HYDE, R. THE GODWITS FLY. (G.
RAWLINSON, ED)
  617(TLS):8MAR74-237
HYDER, C.K., ED. SWINBURNE: THE
CRITICAL HERITAGE.*
  L. ORMOND, 677:VOL3-321
  A.P. ROBSON, 637(VS):JUN72-475
HYDER, C.K. - SEE SWINBURNE, A.C.
HYMAN, H.M. A MORE PERFECT UNION.*
  639(VQR):AUTUMN73-CLXV
HYMAN, L.W. THE QUARREL WITHIN.
  D. BUSH, 401(MLQ):MAR73-78
  639(VQR):SPRING73-LXV
HYMAN, R., ED. A DICTIONARY OF
FAMOUS QUOTATIONS.
  617(TLS):3MAY74-484
HYMAN, R. THE WORKERS' UNION.
  R. HOLTON, 637(VS):JUN72-483
HYMAN, S.E. IAGO.
  K. MUIR, 677:VOL3-278
HYMES, D., ED. REINVENTING ANTHRO-
POLOGY.
  E. LEACH, 453:4APR74-33
HYNES, S. - SEE CAUDWELL, C.
HYSLOP, L.B., ED. BAUDELAIRE AS A
LOVE POET & OTHER ESSAYS.*
  L. WELCH, 150(DR):SPRING72-150

IAKOVIDIS, S.E. PERATĒ: TO NEKROTA-
PHEION.
  H. WATERHOUSE, 303:VOL92-244
IANNI, F.A.J. BLACK MAFIA.
  J. KRAMER, 441:1SEP74-13
IATRIDES, J.O. REVOLT IN ATHENS.
  639(VQR):SUMMER73-CXXIII
  676(YR):SUMMER73-XV
IBÁÑEZ, F.S. - SEE UNDER SOPEÑA
IBÁÑEZ, F.
IBN GARCÍA. THE SHU'ŪBIYYA IN AL-
ANDALUS. (J.T. MONROE, ED & TRANS)
  A.G. CHEJNE, 318(JAOS):APR-JUN72-
  381
  H.T. STURCKEN, 238:MAY72-382
IBN KAMMŪNA, S.M. SA'D B. MANṢŪR
IBN KAMMŪNA'S EXAMINATION OF THE
INQUIRIES INTO THE THREE FAITHS.*
(M. PERLMANN, ED & TRANS)
  L.E. GOODMAN, 485(PE&W):OCT72-
  487
ICAZBALCETA, J.G. - SEE UNDER GARCÍA
ICAZBALCETA, J.
ICHIKO CHŪZŌ. KINDAI CHŪGOKU NO
SEIJI TO SHAKAI.
  R.H. MYERS, 293(JAST):AUG72-931
IDE, H., ED. BESTANDSAUFNAHME DEUT-
SCHUNTERRICHT.
  H-C. KAYSER, 221(GQ):NOV72-788
IDE, H., H. IVO & V. MERKELBACH, EDS.
DISKUSSION DEUTSCH.
  S. MEWS, 221(GQ):NOV72-794
"LES IDÉOLOGIES DANS LE MONDE
ACTUEL."
  A. VACHET, 154:DEC72-627
IDINOPULOS, T.A. THE EROSION OF
FAITH.
  B.M.B., 543:JUN72-757

IGGERS, G.G. THE GERMAN CONCEPTION
OF HISTORY.
M. ERMARTH, 125:FEB73-203
IGGERS, W.A. KARL KRAUS.*
D. JOST, 182:VOL25#21-740
IGNOTUS, P. HUNGARY.
G.F. CUSHING, 575(SEER):JUL73-
477
IHDE, D. HERMENEUTIC PHENOMENOLOGY.
P.J. BOSSERT, 484(PPR):JUN73-588
R.D. SWEENEY, 258:MAR73-140
IHIMAERA, W. TANGI.
617(TLS):12JUL74-741
IHLAU, T. & L. RALL. DIE MESSUNG
DES TECHNISCHEN FORTSCHRITTS.
A. HÜFNER, 182:VOL25#9/10-272
IHWE, J., ED. LITERATURWISSENSCHAFT
UND LINGUISTIK.
G. WIENOLD, 680(ZDP):BAND91HEFT2-
311
II-GYO, S. - SEE UNDER SǑ II-GYO
IJSEWIJN, J. - SEE "HUMANISTICA
LOVANIENSIA"
IKEDA, D. THE HUMAN REVOLUTION.
(VOL 2)
R.C. ZAEHNER, 617(TLS):6DEC74-
1389
IKEDA, H. A TYPE & MOTIF INDEX OF
JAPANESE FOLK-LITERATURE.
F.H. MAYER, 293(JAST):MAY72-674
IKELER, A.A. PURITAN TEMPER &
TRANSCENDENTAL FAITH.*
R.J. DUNN, 301(JEGP):JUL73-456
ILIE, P., ED. DOCUMENTS OF THE
SPANISH VANGUARD.*
J.W. DÍAZ, 241:JAN72-81
ILLICH, I.D. TOOLS FOR CONVIVIAL-
ITY.* ENERGY & EQUITY.
617(TLS):19APR74-413
"ILLUSTRATED CATALOGUE OF THE INTER-
NATIONAL EXHIBITION, 1862."
617(TLS):1FEB74-110
IMBERT, H-F. STENDHAL ET LA TENTA-
TION JANSÉNISTE.*
F.W. SAUNDERS, 208(FS):JAN73-75
IMBODEN, M. STAAT UND RECHT.
A. FAVRE, 182:VOL25#11-343
IMBS, P. - SEE "TRÉSOR DE LA LANGUE
FRANÇAISE"
IMMERMANN, K. WERKE IN FÜNF BÄNDEN.
(VOLS 1&2) (B. VON WIESE, ED)
W.H. MC CLAIN, 406:SPRING73-103
INADA, K.K. - SEE "NĀGĀRJUNA, A
TRANSLATION OF HIS MŪLAMADHYAMAKAK-
ĀRIKĀ"
INADA KŌJI. MUKASHIBANASHI WA IKITE
IRU.
F.H. MAYER, 293(JAST):AUG72-911
INADA KŌJI & FUKUDA AKIRA, EDS.
DAISEN HOKUROKU NO MUKASHIBANASHI.
F.H. MAYER, 293(JAST):AUG72-911
INBER, V. LENINGRAD DIARY.
L. GOURE, 32:JUN73-391
639(VQR):AUTUMN72-CXLI
INDA, C. & J. EAGLESON - SEE GUTIÉR-
REZ, G.
INFANTE, G.C. - SEE CABRERA INFANTE,
G.
INFIELD, G.B. EVA & ADOLF.
J. O'REILLY, 441:29SEP74-6
INGALLS, D.H.H. - SEE MATILAL, B.K.

INGALLS, R. THE MAN WHO WAS LEFT
BEHIND.
R. GARFITT, 362:21FEB74-248
617(TLS):15FEB74-149
INGATE, M. THE SOUND OF THE WEIR.
617(TLS):31MAY74-591
INGE, M.T. - SEE WADE, J.D.
VAN INGEN, F. PHILIPP VON ZESEN.
G. HOFFMEISTER, 221(GQ):NOV72-
745
INGLIS, A., ED. DOCUMENTS ON CANAD-
IAN EXTERNAL RELATIONS. (VOL 5)
J. ENGLISH, 99:MAY/JUN74-48
INGLIS, B. ROGER CASEMENT.*
N. ANNAN, 453:21MAR74-23
P. JOHNSON, 441:27JAN74-5
INGRAM, J.C. ECONOMIC CHANGE IN
THAILAND: 1850-1970.
J.A. HAFNER, 293(JAST):MAY72-728
INGRAM, R. YORIS.
617(TLS):30AUG74-933
INGRAM, W. & K. SWAIM, EDS. A CON-
CORDANCE TO MILTON'S ENGLISH
POETRY.
J.C. MAXWELL, 447(N&Q):MAY72-185
J.M. PATRICK, 568(SCN):FALL-WIN-
TER73-76
INGRAMS, R. - SEE COBBETT, W.
IÑIGUEZ, D.A. & A.E. PÉREZ SÁNCHEZ -
SEE UNDER ANGULO IÑIGUEZ, D. & A.E.
PÉREZ SÁNCHEZ
INNES, C.D. ERWIN PISCATOR'S POLITI-
CAL THEATRE.
D. GRONAU, 182:VOL25#5/6-163
INNES, M. APPLEBY'S OTHER STORY.
A. BROYARD, 441:1APR74-35
N. CALLENDAR, 441:26MAY74-17
617(TLS):25JAN74-88
INNES, M. THE MYSTERIOUS COMMISSION.
617(TLS):8NOV74-1248
"INNOCENT ART."
W. FEAVER, 362:19&26DEC74-847
INOUE, K. A STUDY OF JAPANESE SYN-
TAX.*
S-Y. KURODA, 318(JAOS):APR-JUN72-
353
"INSIGHT ON THE MIDDLE EAST WAR."
617(TLS):8MAR74-227
INSINGEL, M. REFLECTIONS.*
268:JAN74-68
"INTERNATIONAL DISPUTES: THE LEGAL
ASPECTS."
617(TLS):25JAN74-83
"THE INTERNATIONAL WHO'S WHO 1974-
75."
617(TLS):18OCT74-1168
"INTERNATIONALE BIBLIOGRAPHIE ZUR
GESCHICHTE DER DEUTSCHEN LITERA-
TUR."* (PTS 1&2)
G. WENZEL, 654(WB):11/1972-173
INTISAR-UL-HAQUE. A CRITICAL STUDY
OF LOGICAL PARADOXES.
T.G.N., 543:DEC71-354
"INTRODUCTION 5."
617(TLS):18JAN74-47
"AN INTRODUCTION TO THE NATIONAL LAN-
GUAGE RESEARCH INSTITUTE." [TOKYO]
G.F. MEIER, 682(ZPSK):BAND24
HEFT6-537
"AN INVENTORY OF HISTORICAL MONU-
MENTS IN THE COUNTY OF CAMBRIDGE."
(VOL 2: NORTH-EAST CAMBRIDGE-
SHIRE.)
617(TLS):18JAN74-44

"INVENTORY OF RESEARCH IN PROGRESS
IN THE HUMANITIES/INVENTAIRE DES
RECHERCHES EN COURS DANS LES HUM-
ANITÉS."*
   R. MERCIER, 557(RSH):OCT-DEC72-
603
"AN INVENTORY OF THE HISTORICAL MONU-
MENTS IN THE COUNTY OF DORSET."
(VOL 3)
   J. LEES-MILNE, 39:JUN72-522
"AN INVENTORY OF THE HISTORICAL MONU-
MENTS IN THE COUNTY OF DORSET: CEN-
TRAL DORSET."
   A. CLIFTON-TAYLOR, 135:JAN72-62
IONESCO, E. CE FORMIDABLE BORDEL!
   617(TLS):24MAY74-555
IONESCO, E. THE HERMIT.
   P. ADAMS, 61:NOV74-123
   N. BLIVEN, 442(NY):9DEC74-187
   A. BROYARD, 441:7NOV74-49
   E. WHITE, 441:27OCT74-6
IONESCO, E. VICTIMES DU DEVOIR [&]
UNE VICTIME DU DEVOIR. (V. LEE,
ED)
   L. MINOR, 160:SPRING72-190
IORDAN, I. & J. ORR. AN INTRODUC-
TION TO ROMANCE LINGUISTICS.*
(REV BY R. POSNER)
   E.P. HAMP, 269(IJAL):JAN72-78
   G. PRICE, 208(FS):JAN73-113
   H.G. SCHOGT, 320(CJL):SPRING71-
139
IRELAND, D. FROM THE JUNGLE OF BEL-
FAST.
   617(TLS):22FEB74-179
IRELAND, R.M. THE COUNTY COURTS IN
ANTEBELLUM KENTUCKY.
   C.T. CULLEN, 656(WMQ):APR73-334
IRESON, J.C. LAMARTINE.*
   A.J. STEELE, 208(FS):JUL73-342
IRIARTE, V.R. - SEE UNDER RUIZ
IRIARTE, V.
IRISH, L. TIME OF THE DOLPHINS.
   D. GILBEY, 581:MAR73-83
IRIZARRY, E. TEORÍA Y CREACIÓN LIT-
ERARIA EN FRANCISCO AYALA.
   K. ELLIS, 238:DEC72-970
   E. GUILLERMO, 263:JAN-MAR73-106
IRMSCHER, H.D. ADALBERT STIFTER.
   I.M. GOESSL, 406:WINTER73-429
   C.O. SJÖGREN, 301(JEGP):JUL73-
415
IRVINE, W. & P. HONAN. THE BOOK,
THE RING & THE POET.
   P. ADAMS, 61:APR74-120
   A. BURGESS, 441:24FEB74-1
   R. EDER, 441:23APR74-35
   V.S. PRITCHETT, 453:2MAY74-20
IRVING, C. TRUE BRIT.
   617(TLS):19JUL74-765
IRVING, D. THE RISE & FALL OF THE
LUFTWAFFE.
   617(TLS):15MAR74-255
IRVING, E.B., JR. A READING OF
"BEOWULF."*
   G. NICKEL, 38:BAND9OHEFT3-381
IRVING, J. THE 158-POUND MARRIAGE.
   A. BROYARD, 441:8OCT74-39
   M. LEVIN, 441:3NOV74-72
IRVING, L. THE PRECARIOUS CRUST.
   B. DEAN, 157:SPRING72-72
IRVING, M., WITH C. SOPKIN. THE
BANK BOOK.*
   G. GOLD, 441:5JAN74-25

IRVING, W. WASHINGTON IRVING, JOUR-
NALS & NOTEBOOKS.* (VOL 1) (N.
WRIGHT, ED) MAHOMET & HIS SUCCES-
SORS. (H.A. POCHMANN & E.N. FELT-
SKOG, EDS) WASHINGTON IRVING &
THE HOUSE OF MURRAY.* (B.H.
MC CLARY, ED)
   A. HOOK, 447(N&Q):AUG72-311
IRWIN, C. GUDRID'S SAGA.
   M. LEVIN, 441:17NOV74-53
IRWIN, D. - SEE WINCKELMANN, J.J.
IRWIN, G. SAMUEL JOHNSON.
   L. DAMROSCH, JR., 481(PQ):JUL72-
703
   L.C. MC HENRY, JR., 173(ECS):
WINTER72/73-257
   639(VQR):SUMMER72-LXXXIX
ISAAC, K. HOW TO BUILD YOUR OWN
LIVING STRUCTURES.
   S. STEPHENS, 441:8DEC74-42
ISAACS, N.D. STRUCTURAL PRINCIPLES
IN OLD ENGLISH POETRY.*
   J.K. CRANE, 128(CE):APR72-837
ISAACS, N.D. & R.A. ZIMBARDO, EDS.
TOLKIEN & THE CRITICS.*
   K. DUNCAN-JONES, 447(N&Q):SEP72-
353
ISAACS, S.D. JEWS & AMERICAN POLI-
TICS.
   P. HAMILL, 441:10NOV74-5
ISAACSON, B. & D. WIGODER. THE POPU-
LAR JEWISH ENCYCLOPEDIA.
   617(TLS):19APR74-424
ISAACSON, J. MONET: LE DÉJEUNER SUR
L'HERBE.
   A.C. BIRNHOLZ, 290(JAAC):SUMMER
73-556
   A. FORGE, 592:NOV72-201
ISAČENKO, A. & H-J. SCHÄDLICH. A
MODEL OF STANDARD GERMAN INTONA-
TION.
   W. JASSEM, 350:JUN73-482
ISAJIW, W.W. CAUSATION & FUNCTION-
ALISM IN SOCIOLOGY.
   A.C. MICHALOS, 486:MAR72-86
ISBELL, H. - SEE "THE LAST POETS OF
IMPERIAL ROME"
ISCHBOLDIN, B. HISTORY OF THE RUS-
SIAN NON-MARXIAN SOCIAL-ECONOMIC
THOUGHT.*
   J.M. HARVEY, 550(RUSR):OCT72-428
ISENBERG, A. AESTHETICS & THE THE-
ORY OF CRITICISM. (W. CALLAGHAN &
OTHERS, EDS)
   C.L. STEVENSON, 311(JP):19DEC74-
821
ISHIDA, T. JAPANESE SOCIETY.
   D.W. PLATH, 293(JAST):FEB72-416
ISHIGURO, H. LEIBNIZ'S PHILOSOPHY
OF LOGIC & LANGUAGE.*
   B. MATES, 319:JAN74-106
ISHIHARA, A. & H.S. LEVY. THE TAO
OF SEX.
   M. PORKERT, 318(JAOS):JAN-MAR72-
142
ISICHEI, E. VICTORIAN QUAKERS.*
   P. MARSH, 637(VS):MAR72-366
ST. ISIDORE OF SEVILLE. THE LETTERS
OF ST. ISIDORE OF SEVILLE.* (G.B.
FORD, JR., ED & TRANS) ISIDORE OF
SEVILLE'S HISTORY OF THE GOTHS,
VANDALS & SUEVI. (G. DONINI &
G.B. FORD, JR., TRANS)
   Á.P. ORBÁN, 433:OCT72-505

ISLAMOV, T.M. POLITICHESKAIA BOR'BA
V VENGRII NAKANUNE PERVOI MIROVOI
VOINY, 1906-14.
G. VERMES, 32:DEC73-841
ISLER, G. DIE SENNENPUPPE.*
H. LIXFELD, 196:BAND13HEFT1/2-
188
ISRAEL, P. HUSH MONEY.
N. CALLENDAR, 441:20OCT74-42
ISSACHAROFF, M. J-K. HUYSMANS DE-
VANT LA CRITIQUE EN FRANCE, 1874-
1960.*
J. BIRKETT, 402(MLR):JUL73-661
P. WALDNER, 535(RHL):MAR-APR72-
340
"ISTORIA LIMBII ROMÂNE."* (VOL 2)
W. ROTHE, 260(IF):BAND76-299
"ISTORIA TOU ELLINIKOU ETHNOUS."
(VOL 4)
617(TLS):17MAY74-530
"ISTORIKO-FILOLOGICHESKIE ISSLEDOV-
ANIYA, SBORNIK STATEY K SEMIDES-
YATILETIYU AKADEMIKA N.I. KONRADA."
D. BODDE, 318(JAOS):OCT-DEC72-
560
ITENBERG, B.S. ROSSIIA I PARIZH-
SKAIA KOMMUNA.
A. KIMBALL, 32:MAR73-168
ITKONEN, K. DIE SHAKESPEARE-ÜBER-
SETZUNG WIELANDS (1762-1766).
E. ERÄMETSÄ, 439(NM):1972/4-895
A.R. SCHMITT, 301(JEGP):APR73-
282
IVANOV, L.M., ED. PROBLEMY SOTSIAL'-
NO-EKONOMICHESKOI ISTORII ROSSII.
W.L. BLACKWELL, 32:DEC73-807
IVANOV, M. THE ASSASSINATION OF HEY-
DRICH.
617(TLS):1MAR74-207
IVANOV, V. SOBRANIE SOCHINENII.
(VOL 1) (D.V. IVANOV & O. DESHART,
EDS)
V. TERRAS, 32:SEP73-661
IVASK, I. & J. MARICHAL, EDS. LUMI-
NOUS REALITY.*
P.R. OLSON, 240(HR):SPRING72-233
IVENS, M. & C. BRADLEY, EDS. "WHICH
WAY?"
M. HARRINGTON, 619(TC):VOL177
#1043-48
IVIĆ, M. WEGE DER SPRACHWISSEN-
SCHAFT.
W. HERRLITZ, 361:VOL29#2-173
IVINS, W.M., JR. PRINTS & BOOKS.*
PRINTS & VISUAL COMMUNICATION.*
C. ELLIS, 447(N&Q):JUL72-277
IVŠIĆ, S. IZABRANA DJELA IZ SLAVEN-
SKE AKCENTUACIJE (GESAMMELTE
SCHRIFTEN ZUM SLAVISCHEN AKZENT).
T.F. MAGNER, 32:SEP73-674
IYER, R.N. THE MORAL & POLITICAL
THOUGHT OF MAHATMA GANDHI.
617(TLS):19APR74-414
"IZISTORJI-SOVYETSKOY ARKHITEKTURI
1926-1932: DOKUMENTI I MATERYALI."
A. KROLL, 46:NOV72-319

JABÈS, E. EL, OU LE DERNIER LIVRE.
617(TLS):19JUL74-771
JABÈS, E. JE BÂTIS MA DEMEURE. LE
LIVRE DES QUESTIONS. (VOLS 1-3)
YAËL. ELYA.
J. GUGLIELMI, 98:JAN72-32

JACCOTTET, P. LA SEMAISON.
J. SOJCHER, 98:AUG/SEP72-781
JACK, I. BROWNING'S MAJOR POETRY.
617(TLS):22MAR74-293
JACK, J. & M. SMITH - SEE BRONTË, C.
JACK, R.D.S. THE ITALIAN INFLUENCE
ON SCOTTISH LITERATURE.
M.P. MC DIARMID, 149:SEP73-263
JACKS, O. MAN ON A SHORT LEASH.
N. CALLENDAR, 441:23JUN74-33
JACKSON, A.A. SEMI-DETACHED LONDON.
617(TLS):4JAN74-7
JACKSON, B. OPERATION BURNING
CANDLE.
M. WATKINS, 441:17FEB74-31
JACKSON, B. RAGE UNDER THE ARCTIC.
M. LEVIN, 441:10FEB74-8
JACKSON, B. WAKE UP, DEAD MAN.*
F. HOWES, 415:JUN73-604
JACKSON, D. INTERMARRIAGE IN IRE-
LAND 1550-1650.
P. SLACK, 447(N&Q):SEP72-360
JACKSON, D.D. JUDGES.
I. SILVER, 441:16JUN74-21
JACKSON, G. A CONCISE HISTORY OF
THE SPANISH CIVIL WAR.
617(TLS):5APR74-363
JACKSON, G. THE MAKING OF MEDIEVAL
SPAIN.
639(VQR):SUMMER72-XCVII
JACKSON, G. SURVIVING THE LONG
NIGHT.
A. BROYARD, 441:4OCT74-37
J.D. SMITH, 441:17NOV74-4
442(NY):11NOV74-212
JACKSON, G.B. - SEE JONSON, B.
JACKSON, G.S. MUSIC IN DURBAN.
W. KOLNEDER, 182:VOL25#21-748
JACKSON, J.C. SARAWAK.
D.J. DWYER, 302:JUL72-217
JACKSON, J.R.D., ED. COLERIDGE:
THE CRITICAL HERITAGE.*
C. RAINE, 447(N&Q):MAR72-118
JACKSON, S. MONSIEUR BUTTERFLY.
D. ARNOLD, 362:2MAY74-575
L.F. LOVEDAY, 441:27OCT74-22
JACKSON, W.A.D., ED. AGRARIAN POLI-
CIES & PROBLEMS IN COMMUNIST & NON-
COMMUNIST COUNTRIES.*
E. STRAUSS, 575(SEER):JAN73-149
JACKSON, W.T.H. THE ANATOMY OF
LOVE.*
D.H. GREEN, 402(MLR):JAN73-215
R. HENNIG, 401(MLQ):SEP73-331
639(VQR):SPRING72-LIII
JACKSON, W.T.H. DIE LITERATUREN DES
MITTELALTERS.*
W. BREUER, 680(ZDP):BAND91HEFT3-
431
JACOB, A. LES EXIGENCES THÉORIQUES
DE LA LINGUISTIQUE SELON GUSTAVE
GUILLAUME.*
K. TOGEBY, 1(ALH):VOL14#1-153
JACOB, A. & P. HOGARTH. A RUSSIAN
JOURNEY FROM SUZDAL TO SAMARKAND.
E. YOUNG, 39:SEP72-254
JACOB, D. DAS KAFKA-BILD IN ENGLAND.
S. CORNGOLD, 406:WINTER73-436
JACOB, E.F. - SEE CRASTER, E.
JACOB, F. THE LOGIC OF LIFE.*
(FRENCH TITLE: LA LOGIQUE DU VIV-
ANT.)
L. THOMAS, 231:APR74-100
S. TOULMIN, 453:18JUL74-30

JACOB, L.A. & OTHERS, COMPS. SOUTH
ASIA.*
    R.I. CRANE, 293(JAST):MAY72-697
JACOBI, K. DIE METHODE DER CUSAN-
ISCHEN PHILOSOPHIE.
    R.S., 543:DEC71-355
JACOBIUS, A.J. CARL ZUCKMAYER.
    S. MEWS, 221(GQ):NOV72-768
JACOBS, A., ED. THE MUSIC YEARBOOK.
(1972-73)
    J.A.W., 410(M&L):JAN73-99
JACOBS, E. EUROPEAN TRADE UNIONISM.
    617(TLS):10MAY74-498
JACOBS, E.P. L'ÉNIGME DE L'ATLAN-
TIDE.
    P. FRESNAULT-DERUELLE, 98:MAY72-
    460
JACOBS, H. THE EGG OF THE GLAK &
OTHER STORIES.
    A.L. ELLER, 573(SSF):SPRING72-
    208
JACOBS, L. A JEWISH THEOLOGY.
    K. SUTTON, 362:11APR74-476
    G. VERMES, 617(TLS):18OCT74-1169
JACOBS, R.A. & P.S. ROSENBAUM. ENG-
LISH TRANSFORMATIONAL GRAMMAR.*
    J.K. CHAMBERS, 320(CJL):SPRING71-
    113
    R. STANLEY, 206:MAR72-288
JACOBS, R.A. & P.S. ROSENBAUM, EDS.
READINGS IN ENGLISH TRANSFORMATION-
AL GRAMMAR.
    P.H. MATTHEWS, 297(JL):FEB72-125
JACOBS, R.A. & P.S. ROSENBAUM.
TRANSFORMATIONS, STYLE & MEANING.
    J.K. CHAMBERS, 320(CJL):SPRING71-
    113
JACOBS, R.L. & G. SKELTON - SEE
WAGNER, R.
JACOBS, W.R. DISPOSSESSING THE AMER-
ICAN INDIAN.
    R.N. ELLIS, 651(WHR):WINTER73-98
    N.O. LURIE, 656(WMQ):JAN73-179
JACOBSEN, H-A., ED. HANS STEINACHER.
    F.T. EPSTEIN, 32:SEP73-631
JACOBSON, D. THE WONDER-WORKER.*
    C. LEHMANN-HAUPT, 441:2APR74-43
    J. MELLORS, 364:FEB/MAR74-136
    K. MILLER, 453:18JUL74-24
    L.E. SISSMAN, 442(NY):24JUN74-
    101
    R.A. SOKOLOV, 441:21APR74-4
JACOBSON, M. NUTRITION SCOREBOARD.
    D. ZWERDLING, 453:21FEB74-22
JACOBSON, N.P. BUDDHISM.*
    D.W. MITCHELL, 485(PE&W):JAN72-
    117
JACOBSON, R., ED. STUDIES IN ENG-
LISH TO SPEAKERS OF OTHER LANGU-
AGES & STANDARD ENGLISH TO SPEAK-
ERS OF A NON-STANDARD DIALECT.
    B. ARTHUR, 351(LL):JUN72-143
JACOBUS, J. MATISSE.
    P. ADAMS, 61:MAR74-99
JACOBY, D. LA FÉODALITÉ EN GRÈCE
MÉDIÉVALE.
    P. TOPPING, 589:OCT73-760
JACOBY, F.R. VAN DEN VOS REINAERDE.
    T.L. MARKEY, 589:JAN73-153
JACOBY, N.H. CORPORATE POWER &
SOCIAL RESPONSIBILITY.
    S.B. SHEPARD, 441:24FEB74-34

JACOMUZZI, A. UNA POETICA STRUMEN-
TALE.
    G. ALMANSI, 617(TLS):20DEC74-
    1448
DI JACOPO, M. [TACCOLA] MARIANO
TACCOLA DE MACHINIS. (G. SCAGLIA,
ED)
    P.L. ROSE, 377:NOV73-182
JACOT, M. THE LAST BUTTERFLY.*
    A. BROYARD, 441:7MAR74-43
    E. WEEKS, 61:APR74-119
JACQUET, C. JOYCE ET RABELAIS.
    N. SILVERSTEIN, 329(JJQ):SUMMER
    74-414
JACQUET-GORDON, H. - SEE PIANKOFF, A.
JACQUOT, J., ED. DRAMATURGIE ET
SOCIÉTÉ.
    J. MOREL, 535(RHL):MAY-JUN72-511
JACQUOT, J. & D. BABLET, EDS. LES
VOIES DE LA CRÉATION THÉÂTRALE.*
    J. MOLINO, 549(RLC):JUL-SEP72-
    445
JACQUOT, J. & H.W. JONES - SEE
HOBBES, T.
JAEGER, H. HEIDEGGER UND DIE SPRACHE.
    A. BORGMANN, 301(JEGP):APR73-302
    I. SOLL, 406:WINTER73-438
JAEGER, P.L. - SEE SCHRÖER, M.M.A.
JAEGGI, U. LITERATUR UND POLITIK.
    H.U. GUMBRECHT, 490:APR72-233
    D.C. WIXSON, 125:FEB73-180
JAFFE, I.B. JOSEPH STELLA.*
    D.M. SOKOL, 290(JAAC):SUMMER72-
    568
JAFFE, R. FAMILY SECRETS.
    G. LYONS, 441:27OCT74-50
JAFFE, R. THE OTHER WOMAN.
    S. O'CONNELL, 418(MR):WINTER73-
    190
JÄGER, H-W. POLITISCHE KATEGORIEN
IN POETIK UND RHETORIK DER ZWEITEN
HÄLFTE DES 18. JAHRHUNDERTS.
    K. KENKEL, 481(PQ):JUL72-617
JAHN, E.K. DIE DEUTSCHEN IN DER
SLOWAKEI IN DEN JAHREN 1918-29.*
    E. WINTER, 182:VOL25#11-376
JAHN, J. INTERREGNUM UND WAHLDIKTA-
TUR.*
    J. BRISCOE, 313:VOL62-187
"JAHRBUCH DER AUKTIONSPREISE FÜR
BÜCHER, HANDSCHRIFTEN UND AUTO-
GRAPHEN, ERGEBNISSE DER AUKTIONEN
IN DEUTSCHLAND, HOLLAND, ÖSTER-
RECIH UND DER SCHWEIZ." (VOL 20)
    D.W. EVANS, 354:SEP72-259
JAHSS, M. & B. INRO & OTHER MINIA-
TURE FORMS OF JAPANESE LACQUER ART.
    M. HILLIER, 135:FEB72-140
JAIMES-FREYRE, M. MODERNISMO Y 98
A TRAVÉS DE RICARDO JAIMES FREYRE.
    M.A. SALGADO, 241:JAN72-88
JAIN, R.C. ETHNOLOGY OF ANCIENT
BHÁRATA.
    F. WILHELM, 318(JAOS):OCT-DEC72-
    573
JAIN, R.K. SOUTH INDIANS ON THE
PLANTATION FRONTIER IN MALAYA.
    C. JAYAWARDENA, 293(JAST):NOV71-
    225
JAIRAZBHOY, N.A. THE RÁGS OF NORTH
INDIAN MUSIC.*
    D.W., 410(M&L):JAN73-82

JAKÓBCZYK, W. BISMARCK.
H.K. ROSENTHAL, 497(POLR):SUMMER
72-117
JAKOBSON, R. SELECTED WRITINGS, I.
(2ND ED)
R.H. WHITMAN, 350:SEP73-679
JAKOBSON, R. SELECTED WRITINGS, II.
D. WARD, 575(SEER):JUL73-452
R.H. WHITMAN, 350:SEP73-679
JAKOBSON, R. STUDIES IN VERBAL ART.
R.B. PYNSENT, 575(SEER):JUL73-
472
"ROMAN JAKOBSON: A BIBLIOGRAPHY OF
HIS WRITINGS."
R.H. WHITMAN, 350:SEP73-679
JAKUBAITE, T. & OTHERS, EDS. LATVI-
EŠU VALODAS BIEŽUMA VARDNĪCA.
T.G. FENNELL, 353:15JUN72-106
JAL, P. - SEE LIVY
JAMES OF VITERBO. JACOBI DE VITER-
BIO O.E.S.A. DISPUTATIO PRIMA DE
QUOLIBET. JACOBI DE VITERBIO
O.E.S.A. DISPUTATIO SECUNDA DE
QUOLIBET. (E. YPMA, ED OF BOTH)
E.P. MAHONEY, 319:APR74-257
JAMES I OF SCOTLAND. THE KINGIS
QUAIR. (J. NORTON-SMITH, ED)
T.W. CRAIK, 382(MAE):1973/1-98
T.A. SHIPPEY, 677:VOL3-267
J.M. TEMPLETON, 597(SN):VOL44#2-
442
JAMES, C. THE METROPOLITAN CRITIC.
617(TLS):31MAY74-585
JAMES, E.T., WITH J.W. JAMES & P.S.
BOYER, EDS. NOTABLE AMERICAN
WOMEN, 1607-1950.
M.F. GUTHEIM, 432(NEQ):JUN72-281
B. WELTER, 656(WMQ):JUL73-518
JAMES, F.G. IRELAND IN THE EMPIRE,
1688-1770.
617(TLS):18JAN74-45
JAMES, H. THE TALES OF HENRY JAMES.
(VOL 1) (M. AZIZ, ED)
617(TLS):11JAN74-36
JAMES, M. FAMILY, LINEAGE, & CIVIL
SOCIETY.
617(TLS):23AUG74-900
JAMES, M.H., ED. BENTHAM & LEGAL
THEORY.
D.D. RAPHAEL, 617(TLS):27SEP74-
1036
JAMES, M.K. STUDIES IN THE MEDIEVAL
WINE TRADE. (E.M. VEALE, ED)
S.L. THRUPP, 589:APR73-369
JAMES, P.D. A MIND TO MURDER.
F. WYNDHAM, 617(TLS):13DEC74-
1419
JAMES, P.E. ON GEOGRAPHY. (D.W.
MEINIG, ED)
P. VOSSELER, 182:VOL25#1/2-61
JAMES, R. STORM'S END.
M. LEVIN, 441:17NOV74-52
JAMES, R.R. - SEE CHURCHILL, W.S.
JAMES, R.R. - SEE DAVIDSON, J.C.C.
JAMES, T. LETTERS TO A STRANGER.
617(TLS):29MAR74-339
JAMESON, F. MARXISM & FORM.*
C. BANERJEE, 648:JAN73-63
M.E. BROWN, 659:WINTER74-131
B. LANGE, 125:FEB73-174
H. SUSSMAN, 400(MLN):DEC72-1009
Z. TAKACS, 182:VOL25#5/6-160
R. WELLEK, 676(YR):AUTUMN72-119

JAMESON, F. THE PRISON-HOUSE OF
LANGUAGE.*
A. BOURMEYSTER, 182:VOL25#12-403
M.E. BROWN, 659:WINTER74-131
J. CULLER, 676(YR):WINTER73-290
V. ERLICH, 401(MLQ):SEP73-344
S. FISH, 454:SPRING73-283
D.P. FUNT, 249(HUDR):SUMMER73-
413
A. SHUKMAN, 575(SEER):OCT73-602
639(VQR):SPRING73-XC
JAMESON, J.D., ED. AGRICULTURE IN
UGANDA. (2ND ED)
J. MIDDLETON, 69:JUL72-258
JAMMES, A. WILLIAM H. FOX TALBOT.
S. SONTAG, 453:28NOV74-35
JAMMES, A. & R. SOBIESZEK. FRENCH
PRIMITIVE PHOTOGRAPHY.
S. SONTAG, 453:28NOV74-35
JANEWAY, E. BETWEEN MYTH & MORNING.
J. WILSON, 441:29SEP74-7
JANIK, A. & S. TOULMIN. WITTGEN-
STEIN'S VIENNA.*
G. STEINER & A. QUINTON, 362:
28MAR74-399
42(AR):VOL32#4-710
JANIS, I.L. VICTIMS OF GROUPTHINK.*
T.H. ETZOLD, 396(MODA):SUMMER73-
331
D. YERGIN, 676(YR):SUMMER73-594
JANKUHN, H. DIE PASSIVE BEDEUTUNG
MEDIALER FORMEN UNTERSUCHT AN DER
SPRACHE HOMERS.
J. BECHERT, 260(IF):BAND76-283
P. FLOBERT, 343:BAND15HEFT2-153
JANKUHN, H. & OTHERS, EDS. REALLEX-
IKON DER GERMANISCHEN ALTERTUMS-
KUNDE. (VOL 1, PT 1)
J. FLECK, 563(SS):AUTUMN73-376
JANNI, P. IL MONDO DI OMERO.
J.B. HAINSWORTH, 123:DEC73-268
JANNINI, P-A. LE AVANGUARDIE LETTER-
ARIE NELL'IDEA CRITICA DI GUIL-
LAUME APOLLINAIRE.
M. SCHAETTEL, 557(RSH):JUL-SEP72-
477
JANOSSY, L. THEORY OF RELATIVITY
BASED ON PHYSICAL REALITY.
M. KOSOK, 484(PPR):SEP72-124
JANOTA, P. PERSONAL CHARACTERISTICS
OF SPEECH.
G.F. MEIER, 682(ZPSK):BAND24
HEFT6-540
JANOUCH, G. CONVERSATIONS WITH
KAFKA.* (2ND ED)
F. JONES, 32:SEP73-670
JANOUCH, G. JAROSLAV HAŠEK.
C. DEDEYAN, 182:VOL25#22-795
JANSEN, F.J.B. & P.M. MITCHELL, EDS.
ANTHOLOGY OF DANISH LITERATURE.*
J.L. GREENWAY, 563(SS):AUTUMN73-
397
JANSSEN, P. GESCHICHTE UND LEBENS-
WELT.*
R.S., 543:JUN72-758
JANSSENS, G.A.M. THE AMERICAN LIT-
ERARY REVIEW.*
U. BRUMM, 38:BAND90HEFT1/2-272
JAQUETTE, J.S., ED. WOMEN IN POLI-
TICS.
L. SHERR, 441:24NOV74-34
JARDÍ, E. NONELL.
P. BRAFF, 54:SEP72-367
JAREÑO, E. - SEE SAMANIEGO, F.M.

JENKINS, G. A BRIDGE OF MAGPIES.
617(TLS):20DEC74-1437
JENKINS, J.G., ED. THE WOOL TEXTILE
INDUSTRY IN GREAT BRITAIN.
E.M. SIGSWORTH, 637(VS):MAR73-
356
JENKINS, R. A FAR CRY FROM BOWMORE.*
E. FEINSTEIN, 364:OCT/NOV73-154
JENKINS, R. NINE MEN OF POWER.
E. IONS, 362:31OCT74-582
JENNINGS, W.D. THE SINKING OF THE
SARAH DIAMOND.
M. LEVIN, 441:7APR74-32
JENNISON, C. WAIT 'TIL NEXT YEAR.
R.W. CREAMER, 441:1DEC74-90
JENNISON, P.S. & R.M. SHERIDAN, EDS.
THE FUTURE OF GENERAL ADULT BOOKS
& READING IN AMERICA.
P.H. ENNIS, 128(CE):DEC72-436
JENS, I. DICHTER ZWISCHEN RECHTS
UND LINKS.*
A. CLOSS, 402(MLR):OCT73-953
JENSEN, A.C. THE COD.
639(VQR):AUTUMN72-CLVIII
JENSEN, A.R. EDUCATIONAL DIFFER-
ENCES.
617(TLS):3MAY74-466
JENSEN, F. THE ITALIAN VERB.
G.C. LEPSCHY, 402(MLR):APR73-427
M.T. NAVARRO, 202(FMOD):JUN72-
347
JENSEN, H. MOTIVATION & THE MORAL
SENSE IN FRANCIS HUTCHESON'S ETHI-
CAL THEORY.*
D.D. RAPHAEL, 319:APR74-263
JENSEN, H. SIGN, SYMBOL & SCRIPT.*
(3RD ED)
V. ŠEVOROŠKIN, 353:1NOV72-110
JENSEN, H.J. & M.R. ZIRKER, EDS.
THE SATIRIST'S ART.*
566:AUTUMN72-47
JENSEN, J.S. SUBJONCTIF ET HYPOTAXE
EN ITALIEN.
G.C. LEPSCHY, 361:VOL29#3/4-371
P.A.M. SEUREN, 433:JUL72-370
JENSEN, M.K. SPRÅKLYDLAERE.
G.F. MEIER, 682(ZPSK):BAND25
HEFT6-532
H.W. WODARZ, 353:FEB72-120
JENSON, J.R. - SEE BUCKERIDGE, N.
JEPHCOTT, P., WITH H. ROBINSON.
HOMES IN HIGH FLATS.
C. MC KEAN, 46:JUN72-392
SAINT JÉRÔME. TEXTES SUR LA VIE
MONASTIQUE. (P. ANTIN, TRANS)
A. ERNOUT, 555:VOL46FASC1-165
JEROME, J. CULTURE OUT OF ANARCHY.
E.W.R., 543:JUN72-759
JERROLD, D. THE BEST OF MR. PUNCH.
(R.M. KELLY, ED)
M.S., 155:MAY72-125
JERSTAD, L. MANI-RIMDU.*
T. RICCARDI, JR., 318(JAOS):OCT-
DEC72-578
JESSOP, B. TRADITIONALISM, CONSER-
VATISM & BRITISH POLITICAL CULTURE.
C. CROUCH, 617(TLS):13SEP74-974
JESSUP, P.C. THE BIRTH OF NATIONS.
R. EMERSON, 441:19MAY74-32
JESSUP, R. THE HOT BLUE SEA.
M. LEVIN, 441:17FEB74-32
JEUNE, S. MUSSET ET SA FORTUNE LIT-
TÉRAIRE.*
R. MULHAUSER, 207(FR):DEC71-513

JEUNE, S. POÉSIE ET SYSTÈME.*
A. EUSTIS, 546(RR):FEB72-66
"JEUNESSE DE RACINE."
B. CHEDOZEAU, 535(RHL):JAN-FEB72-
131
JEVONS, F.R., ED. SCIENCE OBSERVED.
617(TLS):31MAY74-579
"THE JEWS OF CZECHOSLOVAKIA." (VOL 2)
S.B. WINTERS, 497(POLR):AUTUMN72-
100
JEZIORKOWSKI, K. - SEE "GOTTFRIED
KELLER"
JHABVALA, R.P. AN EXPERIENCE OF
INDIA.
E. FEINSTEIN, 364:APR/MAY72-142
JHABVALA, R.P. A NEW DOMINION.*
E. FEINSTEIN, 364:AUG/SEP73-148
JHABVALA, R.P. A STRONGER CLIMATE.
J.K. CRANE, 573(SSF):WINTER72-
100
JIDEJIAN, N. TYRE THROUGH THE AGES.
J.M. SASSON, 318(JAOS):APR-JUN72-
300
JILES, P. WATERLOO EXPRESS.
M.J. EDWARDS, 99:AUG74-42
JIMÉNEZ, J.O., ED. ANTOLOGÍA DE LA
POESÍA HISPANOAMERICANA CONTEMPOR-
ÁNEA 1914-1970.*
A. BORINSKY, 400(MLN):MAR72-385
M.E. RUIZ, 238:MAY74-388
JO, Y-H., ED. KOREA'S RESPONSE TO
THE WEST.
S.C. YANG, 293(JAST):FEB72-423
JOBST, W. DIE HÖHLE IM GRIECHISCHEN
THEATER DES 5. UND 4. JAHRHUNDERTS
V. CHR.
C. GARTON, 24:FALL73-310
E.W. WHITTLE, 123:DEC73-194
JOCHUM, K.P. DIE DRAMATISCHE STRUK-
TUR DER SPIELE VON W.B. YEATS.
R. HALBRITTER, 38:BAND90HEFT4-
548
JOERGES, C. ZUM FUNKTIONSWANDEL
DES KOLLISIONSRECHTS.
E.J. COHN, 182:VOL25#12-396
JOFEN, J. DAS LETZTE GEHEIMNIS.
W.A. REICHART, 301(JEGP):OCT73-
599
JOHANNESEN, R.L., R. STRICKLAND &
R.T. EUBANKS - SEE WEAVER, R.M.
JOHANNSEN, R.W. STEPHEN A. DOUGLAS.*
617(TLS):18JAN74-49
639(VQR):AUTUMN73-CLIV
JOHANSEN, H.F. & O. SMITH - SEE AES-
CHYLUS
JOHANSEN, J.D. NOVELLETEORI EFTER
1945.*
M. NØJGAARD, 462(OL):VOL27#1-64
JOHANSEN, K. & W. DAHL. KONFRONTAS-
JONER.
H. RØNNING, 172(EDDA):1972/1-59
JOHN OF GARLAND. JOHANNES DE GAR-
LANDIA: DE MENSURABILI MUSICA.
(E. REIMER, ED)
A.H. KING, 182:VOL25#15/16-559
JOHN OF PARIS. ON ROYAL & PAPAL
POWER. (J.A. WATT, TRANS)
J.L. NELSON, 382(MAE):1973/3-289
ST. JOHN OF THE CROSS. POEMS OF ST.
JOHN OF THE CROSS. (W. BARNSTONE,
TRANS)
R. PEVEAR, 249(HUDR):SPRING73-
192

JOHNSTON, E. FORMAL PENMANSHIP &
OTHER PAPERS.* (H. CHILD, ED)
  J.P. ASCHERL, 363:MAY72-96
JOHNSTON, G. HAPPY ENOUGH.
  J. GALASSI, 491:NOV73-113
JOHNSTON, J. THE CAPTAINS & THE
KINGS.
  E. FEINSTEIN, 364:JUN/JUL72-166
JOHNSTON, J. THE GATES.*
  P. BAILEY, 364:APR/MAY73-166
JOHNSTON, J. HOW MANY MILES TO
BABYLON?
  R. BLYTHE, 362:28FEB74-281
  H. ROGAN, 441:27OCT74-46
  617(TLS):1MAR74-201
JOHNSTON, J. WILDERNESS WOMEN.
  W. MITCHINSON, 99:OCT74-41
JOHNSTON, N. SONGS OF MY SEASONS.
  K. THOMPSON, 198:SUMMER74-1
JOHNSTON, R. & OTHERS. MON-KHMER
STUDIES III.
  G.F. DIFFLOTH, 350:MAR73-233
JOHNSTON, W. CHRISTIAN ZEN.
  R.B. ZEUSCHNER, 485(PE&W):JUL72-
  336
JOHNSTON, W.M. THE AUSTRIAN MIND.
  E.E. KRAEHE, 639(VQR):SPRING72-
  293
  G. WILLIAMS, 484(PPR):JUN73-589
JOHNSTONE, H.W., JR. THE PROBLEM OF
THE SELF.
  D.M. BURKS, 480(P&R):SPRING72-
  124
  A.S.C., 543:DEC71-356
JOLY, A. NEGATION & THE COMPARATIVE
PARTICLE IN ENGLISH.
  J.P. HUGHES, 660(WORD):AUG70-297
JOLY, A. - SEE THUROT, F.
JOLY, R. DEUX ÉTUDES SUR LA PRÉ-
HISTOIRE DU RÉALISME.*
  C.A. PORTER, 546(RR):OCT72-236
JOLY, R. - SEE HIPPOCRATES
JONAS, G. CITIES.
  K. THOMPSON, 198:SPRING74-79
JONAS, I.B. THOMAS MANN UND ITAL-
IEN.*
  C.B. EVANS, 399(MLJ):FEB72-121
  J. HÖSLE, 52:BAND7HEFT2/3-336
  W. WITTE, 220(GL&L):JUL73-327
JONAS, K.W., ED. DIE THOMAS-MANN-
LITERATUR. (VOL 1)
  H. WEBER, 182:VOL25#12-414
JONDORF, G. ROBERT GARNIER & THE
THEMES OF POLITICAL TRAGEDY IN THE
SIXTEENTH CENTURY.*
  M. GRAS, 546(RR):OCT72-228
JONES, A. THE POLITICS OF REFORM,
1884.
  P. STANSKY, 637(VS):DEC72-252
JONES, A.H.M. AUGUSTUS.
  J.M. CARTER, 123:MAR73-54
  A.S. HALL, 313:VOL62-229
  J-C. RICHARD, 555:VOL46FASC1-168
JONES, A.H.M., ED. A HISTORY OF
ROME THROUGH THE FIFTH CENTURY.
(VOL 2)
  B.M. LEVICK, 123:MAR73-68
  R. TOMLIN, 313:VOL62-174
JONES, A.H.M., J.R. MARTINDALE & J.
MORRIS. THE PROSOPOGRAPHY OF THE
LATER ROMAN EMPIRE.* (VOL 1)
  A.R. BIRLEY, 313:VOL62-185
  J-P. CALLU, 555:VOL46FASC2-357

JONES, B. FOLLIES & GROTTOES.
  J. BARNES, 617(TLS):13DEC74-1421
JONES, B.Z. & L.G. BOYD. THE HAR-
VARD COLLEGE OBSERVATORY.
  E.H. TAVES, 432(NEQ):JUN72-314
JONES, C.A. & A. PAYNE, EDS. AD-
VANCED SPANISH PROSE COMPOSITION.
  205(FMLS):JAN72-86
JONES, C.P. PLUTARCH & ROME.
  O. MURRAY, 487:WINTER72-404
  D.A. RUSSELL, 313:VOL62-226
JONES, C.R. & B.T. KATHAKALI.
  F. RICHMOND, 318(JAOS):APR-JUN
  72-322
  D.L. SWANN, 293(JAST):AUG72-980
JONES, D. THE SLEEPING LORD & OTHER
FRAGMENTS.
  617(TLS):10MAY74-507
JONES, D. & D. WARD. THE PHONETICS
OF RUSSIAN.*
  W. SCHAMSCHULA, 430(NS):NOV72-
  680
  R. SUSSEX, 67:MAY73-157
JONES, D.G. BUTTERFLY ON ROCK.*
  D. LE PAN, 627(UTQ):AUTUMN71-90
JONES, D.M. & N.G. WILSON, EDS.
SCHOLIA IN ARISTOPHANEM.* (PT 1,
FASC 2)
  P. CHANTRAINE, 555:VOL46FASC2-
  295
JONES, E. BARLOW COMES TO JUDGE-
MENT.
  617(TLS):20DEC74-1437
JONES, E. KENNETH MACKENZIE.
  K.L. GOODWIN, 447(N&Q):SEP72-359
JONES, E. SCENIC FORM IN SHAKES-
PEARE.*
  P. BEMENT, 541(RES):AUG72-341
  J.P. ROCHE, 67:NOV73-295
JONES, E.B. LAW OF THE SEA.
  A.J. THOMAS, JR., 584(SWR):
  SPRING73-179
JONES, G. KINGS, BEASTS, & HEROES.*
  D.W. EVANS, 402(MLR):OCT73-884
  V.M. LAGORIO, 377:MAR73-37
  R.P.M. LEHMANN, 301(JEGP):JUL73-
  438
  A.S. MISKIMIN, 676(YR):WINTER73-
  299
  J.D.A. OGILVY, 191(ELN):JUN73-
  290
  639(VQR):WINTER73-XXV
JONES, G.F. SPÄTES MITTELALTER
[1300-1450].
  D. BLAMIRES, 402(MLR):APR73-445
  J.W. MARCHAND, 301(JEGP):APR73-
  265
  H. THOMKE, 182:VOL25#22-797
JONES, G.F. - SEE URLSPERGER, S.
JONES, G.F. & M. HAHN - SEE URLSPER-
GER, S.
JONES, G.S. OUTCAST LONDON.
  A.S. WOHL, 637(VS):MAR73-349
JONES, H. DE L'ESTHÉTIQUE CLASSIQUE.
  S. FOISY, 154:SEP72-482
  R. MERCIER, 557(RSH):APR-JUN72-
  309
JONES, H.E. KANT'S PRINCIPLE OF PER-
SONALITY.
  W.H. WERKMEISTER, 319:JUL74-405
JONES, H.M. THE AGE OF ENERGY.*
  M. CURTI, 639(VQR):WINTER72-139

JONES, H.M. REVOLUTION & ROMANTI-
CISM.
R. ALTER, 441:8SEP74-14
JONES, I. INIGO JONES ON PALLADIO.*
(B. ALLSOPP, ED)
J. HARRIS, 90:JUN72-415
J. WILTON-ELY, 39:FEB72-147
R. WITTKOWER, 576:MAR72-61
JONES, J. VIET JOURNAL.
P. ADAMS, 61:MAY74-140
C. LEHMANN-HAUPT, 441:14MAR74-41
J. REED, 441:17MAR74-4
442(NY):8APR74-142
JONES, J.A. POPE'S COUPLET ART.*
E.G. BEDFORD, 599:SPRING72-198
JONES, J.B., ED. W.S. GILBERT.
E.P. LAWRENCE, 637(VS):SEP72-119
JONES, J.C. DESIGN METHODS.
K. BAYNES, 46:NOV72-319
JONES, J.R. & J.E. KELLER - SEE
ALFONSO, P.
JONES, J.W. THE SHATTERED SYNTHESIS.
617(TLS):10MAY74-497
JONES, L. BLACK MUSIC.
V. THOMSON, 453:17OCT74-14
JONES, M. A CRY OF ABSENCE.*
F.C. WATKINS, 577(SHR):SUMMER72-
304
J. YARDLEY, 473(PR):2/1973-286
JONES, M. DUCAL BRITTANY 1364-1399.
C.C. BAYLEY, 551(RENQ):WINTER72-
469
JONES, M. LORD RICHARD'S PASSION.
T.R. FYVEL, 362:5DEC74-752
K. MILLER, 453:18JUL74-24
617(TLS):25OCT74-1206
JONES, M., ED. PRIVACY.
617(TLS):19JUL74-765
JONES, M. STRANGERS.
617(TLS):5JUL74-705
JONES, M.E. ENGLISH CREWEL DESIGNS.
L.J. GARTNER, JR., 441:8DEC74-50
JONES, M.E.W. THE LITERARY WORLD OF
ANA MARÍA MATUTE.
L. ALPERA, 238:MAR72-182
J.W. DÍAZ, 241:JAN72-83
JONES, N. THE ORIGINS OF STRATEGIC
BOMBING.
617(TLS):4JAN74-6
JONES, O.R., ED. THE PRIVATE LAN-
GUAGE ARGUMENT.
L. THIRY, 154:DEC72-662
JONES, P., ED. IMAGIST POETRY.*
C. FALCK, 473(PR):3/1973-490
JONES, P.E. EDUCATION IN AUSTRALIA.
617(TLS):14JUN74-646
JONES, P.E., ED. THE FIRE COURT.*
(VOL 2)
W.M. STERN, 325:APR72-444
JONES, P.J. THE MALATESTA OF RIMINI
& THE PAPAL STATE.
617(TLS):31MAY74-588
JONES, R. THE NINETEENTH-CENTURY
FOREIGN OFFICE.
J.W. CELL, 637(VS):JUN72-481
JONES, R. THE THEME OF LOVE IN THE
ROMANS D'ANTIQUITÉ.
H.C.R. LAURIE, 382(MAE):1973/2-
166
JONES, R.E. PANORAMA DE LA NOUVELLE
CRITIQUE EN FRANCE DE GASTON BACHE-
LARD À JEAN-PAUL WEBER.
M.A. CAWS, 546(RR):FEB72-75

JONES, R.F. BLOOD SPORT.
M. MEWSHAW, 441:19MAY74-4
JONES, R.H. DISRUPTED DECADES.
639(VQR):AUTUMN73-CLXIV
JONES, R.M. SYSTEM IN CHILD LAN-
GUAGE.
J. HEWSON, 350:SEP73-745
JONES, S. MEN OF INFLUENCE IN NUR-
ISTAN.
617(TLS):6DEC74-1360
JONES, T. - SEE "HARRAP'S STANDARD
GERMAN & ENGLISH DICTIONARY"
JONES, W. THE LETTERS OF SIR WIL-
LIAM JONES.* (G. CANNON, ED)
R. ROCHER, 318(JAOS):OCT-DEC72-
514
JONES, W.D. THE AMERICAN PROBLEM IN
BRITISH DIPLOMACY, 1841-1861.
617(TLS):3MAY74-468
JONES, W.R.D. THE MID-TUDOR CRISIS
1539-1563.
617(TLS):1FEB74-116
JONES, Y.P. THE FORMAL EXPRESSION
OF MEANING IN JUAN CARLOS ONETTI'S
NARRATIVE ART.
V. CABRERA, 263:JAN-MAR73-107
JONG, E. FEAR OF FLYING.*
R. BLYTHE, 362:2MAY74-576
M. WOOD, 453:21MAR74-19
617(TLS):26JUL74-813
JONG, E. HALF-LIVES.*
R.K. MORRIS, 398:SPRING74-93
L. SEARLE, 491:MAR74-353
617(TLS):19JUL74-762
DE JONGE, C.H. DUTCH TILES.
O. VAN OSS, 135:APR72-292
JONIN, P. PAGES ÉPIQUES DU MOYEN
AGE FRANÇAIS. (VOL 2)
L. VAN DELFT, 207(FR):MAR72-925
JONKER, G.H. - SEE BRYENNIUS, M.
JÓNSDÓTTIR, S. ILLUMINATION IN A
MANUSCRIPT OF STJÓRN.
P.A. JORGENSEN, 589:APR73-370
JONSON, B. EPICOENE. (E. PARTRIDGE,
ED)
A. RENDLE, 157:SUMMER72-75
JONSON, B. EVERY MAN IN HIS HUMOUR.*
(G.B. JACKSON, ED)
R. GILL, 447(N&Q):JUL72-279
JONSON, B. BEN JONSON: THE COMPLETE
MASQUES.* (S. ORGEL, ED)
E. TIEDJE, 430(NS):FEB72-105
JONSON, B. BEN JONSON: SELECTED
WORKS. (D. MC PHERSON, ED)
J.H. SIMS, 568(SCN):SPRING73-13
JONSSON, I. EMANUEL SWEDENBORG.
T. FRÄNGSMYR, 172(EDDA):1972/6-
377
JOPLING, C.F., ED. ART & AESTHETICS
IN PRIMITIVE SOCIETIES.
M.O. JONES, 650(WF):APR72-138
JORAVSKY, D. THE LYSENKO AFFAIR.*
A. VUCINICH, 550(RUSR):JAN72-87
JORAVSKY, D. & G. HAUPT - SEE MEDVE-
DEV, R.A.
JORDAN, B. POOR PARENTS.
J. VAIZEY, 362:15AUG74-222
JORDAN, D. NILE GREEN.*
N. CALLENDAR, 441:17MAR74-39
JORDAN, D.P. GIBBON & HIS ROMAN
EMPIRE.*
J.T. BOULTON, 677:VOL3-299
P. FUSSELL, 191(ELN):DEC72-133

JORDAN, R.D. THE TEMPLE OF ETERNITY.
B. KING, 628:SPRING73-118
JORDAN, W.D. THE WHITE MAN'S BURDEN.
G.M. FREDRICKSON, 453:7FEB74-23
M. KILSON, 441:19MAY74-16
JÖRG, H. UNTERRICHTSPRAXIS.
B. MEISER, 430(NS):APR72-238
JØRGENSEN, A. H.C. ANDERSEN-LITTERA-
TUREN 1875-1968.*
B.G. MADSEN, 222(GR):NOV72-300
JØRGENSEN, J.C. LITTERAER VURDER-
INGSTEORI OG VURDERINGSANALYSE.
LITTERAER METODELAERE.
H.J. CHRISTENSEN, 172(EDDA):
1972/3-188
JORIO, C. NIEVO MORALE.
A.D.B., 228(GSLI):VOL149FASC466/
467-465
JOSEPH OF EXETER. JOSEPH ISCANUS:
WERKE UND BRIEFE. (L. GOMPF, ED)
P.G. WALSH, 123:MAR73-72
JOSEPH, B.L. SHAKESPEARE'S EDEN.
J. HURSTFIELD, 402(MLR):JAN73-
148
K. MUIR, 541(RES):MAY72-203
JOSEPHSON, H. JEANNETTE RANKIN.
S. BROWNMILLER, 441:3NOV74-14
JOSHI, K.N. & B.S. RAO. STUDIES IN
ANGLO-INDIAN LITERATURE.
S. COWASJEE, 268:JAN74-54
JOSHI, L.M. BRAHMANISM, BUDDHISM &
HINDUISM.
S.C. CRAWFORD, 485(PE&W):JAN72-
114
JOSHI, S.D. - SEE "PATAÑJALI'S 'VYĀ-
KARAṆA-MAHĀBHĀṢYA'"
JUSIPOVICI, G. MOBIUS THE STRIPPER.
S. CLARK, 617(TLS):6DEC74-1361
JOSIPOVICI, G. THE WORLD & THE
BOOK.*
G. CLIFFORD, 541(RES):NOV72-520
H. LEVIN, 208(FS):JUL73-369
JOST, D. - SEE DERLETH, L.
JOUANNY, R.A. JEAN MORÉAS, ÉCRIVAIN
FRANÇAIS.*
L. FORESTIER, 535(RHL):JUL-AUG72-
738
JOUDRY, P. THE DWELLER ON THE
THRESHOLD.
K. O'DONNELL, 296:VOL3#2-106
JOUHANDEAU, M. JEUX DE MIROIRS.
617(TLS):11OCT74-1134
JOUHANDEAU, M. UN SECOND SOLEIL.
617(TLS):22FEB74-190
JOUKOVSKY, F. ORPHÉE ET SES DISCI-
PLES DANS LA POÉSIE FRANÇAISE ET
NÉO-LATINE DU XVIE SIÈCLE.*
I.D. MC FARLANE, 402(MLR):JAN73-
170
JOUVE, P.J. "DIADÈME" SUIVI DE
"MÉLODRAME."
W. ALBERT, 207(FR):OCT71-206
DE JOVELLANOS, G.M. OBRAS EN PROSA.
(J. CASO GONZÁLEZ, ED)
J.H.R. POLT, 240(HR):SUMMER72-
342
JOVINE, D.B. LA SCUOLA ITALIANA DAL
1870 AI NOSTRI GIORNI. (2ND ED)
L. TOSCHI, 275(IQ):FALL/WINTER72-
131
JOY, T. THE BOOKSELLING BUSINESS.
617(TLS):1MAR74-220

JOYAUX, G.J. & A. TUKEY. LECTURES
DE FRANCE ET D'OUTRE-MER.
W. STAAKS, 207(FR):OCT71-293
JOYCE, J. GIACOMO JOYCE. (R. ELL-
MANN, ED)
P. RECONDO, 202(FMOD):JUN72-337
JOYCE, J. JOYCE'S "ULYSSES" NOTE-
SHEETS IN THE BRITISH MUSEUM.*
(P.F. HERRING, ED)
R. BOYLE, 659:SPRING74-262
639(VQR):SUMMER73-CXVI
JOYNER, C.W. FOLK SONG IN SOUTH
CAROLINA.
H. GLASSIE, 292(JAF):APR-JUN72-
202
JOYNSON, R.B. PSYCHOLOGY & COMMON
SENSE.
617(TLS):18OCT74-1151
JUCKER, I. AUS DER ANTIKENSAMMLUNG
DES BERNISCHEN HISTORISCHEN MUSE-
UMS.
B.A. SPARKES, 303:VOL92-251
JUDD, D. THE HOUSE OF WINDSOR.
617(TLS):18JAN74-61
JUDEN, B. TRADITIONS ORPHIQUES ET
TENDANCES MYSTIQUES DANS LE ROMAN-
TISME FRANÇAIS (1800-1855).
D.G. CHARLTON, 208(FS):OCT73-461
JUDSON, J.R. DIRCK BARENDSZ, 1534-
1592.
M. ROETHLISBERGER, 54:DEC72-553
JUHÁSZ, J. PROBLEME DER INTERFERENZ.
H. HÖRMANN, 343:BAND15HEFT2-203
JUILLAND, A., ED. LINGUISTIC STUD-
IES PRESENTED TO ANDRÉ MARTINET
UN THE OCCASION OF HIS SIXTIETH
BIRTHDAY.* (VOL 1)
B. CARSTENSEN, 430(NS):AUG72-500
JUILLAND, A., D. BRODIN & C. DAVIDO-
VITCH. FREQUENCY DICTIONARY OF
FRENCH WORDS.
G. ENGWALL, 597(SN):VOL44#2-455
W. MARTIN, 361:VOL29#3/4-374
JUILLAND, A. & P.M.H. EDWARDS. THE
RUMANIAN VERB SYSTEM.
J.E. AUGEROT, 350:MAR73-200
R.L. RANKIN, 32:MAR73-197
JUILLAND, A. & H.H. LIEB. "KLASSE"
UND KLASSIFIKATION IN DER SPRACH-
WISSENSCHAFT.
G.F. MEIER, 682(ZPSK):BAND25
HEFT1/2-157
JULESZ, B. FOUNDATIONS OF CYCLOPEAN
PERCEPTION.
H.R. WILSON, 114(CHIR):VOL24#3-
146
JULIARD, P. PHILOSOPHIES OF LAN-
GUAGE IN EIGHTEENTH-CENTURY
FRANCE.*
R.E. BARTLETT, 399(MLJ):DEC72-
526
JULLIAN, P. D'ANNUNZIO.
G. GERSH, 396(MODA):SUMMER73-326
JULLIAN, P. DREAMERS OF DECADENCE.*
M. CORMACK, 617(TLS):15NOV74-
1290
J. DANIELS, 135:MAR72-215
JULLIAN, P. JEAN LORRAIN OU LE
SATIRICON 1900.
617(TLS):10MAY74-504
JULLIAN, P. THE SYMBOLISTS.
617(TLS):15FEB74-161

JULLIAN, P. THE TRIUMPH OF ART NOU-
VEAU.
A. BROYARD, 441:5DEC74-51
JULLIARD, J. FERNAND PELLOUTIER ET
LES ORIGINES DU SYNDICALISME
D'ACTION DIRECTE.
M. PERROT, 98:MAY72-467
JUMP, J.D. BURLESQUE.*
205(FMLS):OCT72-381
JUNEAU, M. CONTRIBUTION À L'HISTOIRE
DE LA PRONONCIATION FRANÇAISE AU
QUÉBEC.
N. BEAUCHEMIN, 320(CJL):VOL18#2-
199
JUNG, C.G. LETTERS.* (GERMAN TITLE:
BRIEFE.) (VOL 1) (G. ADLER, WITH
A. JAFFÉ, EDS)
V. VON DER HEYDT, 182:VOL25#19/
20-647
639(VQR):AUTUMN73-CLXIV
JUNG, M-R. ÉTUDES SUR LE POÈME ALLÉ-
GORIQUE EN FRANCE AU MOYEN AGE.*
W.T.H. JACKSON, 546(RR):OCT72-
222
JUNG, M.R. HERCULE DANS LA LITTÉRA-
TURE FRANÇAISE DU XVIE SIÈCLE.
I.D. MC FARLANE, 402(MLR):JAN73-
170
JUNG, T. - SEE UNDER TSOU JUNG
JUNGBLUTH, G., ED. INTERPRETATIONEN
MITTELHOCHDEUTSCHER LYRIK.
M.G. SCHOLZ, 680(ZDP):BAND91HEFT
3-453
JÜNGER, E. ANNÄHERUNGEN.
G. LOOSE, 400(MLN):APR72-536
JÜNGER, H., ED. THE LITERATURES OF
THE SOVIET PEOPLES.*
M. FRIEDBERG, 32:DEC73-862
JÜNGER, H., ED. DAS MENSCHENBILD IN
DER SOWJETLITERATUR.
U. RIESE, 654(WB):1/1972-175
JUNGK, R. & OTHERS. CHINA & THE
WEST.
W-T. CHAN, 293(JAST):NOV71-179
JUNGRAITHMAYR, H. DIE RON-SPRACHEN.*
C-T. HODGE, 350:DEC73-948
JUN'ICHI, N. & K. - SEE UNDER NOMURA
JUN'ICHI & KEIKO
JUNIPER, D. MAN AGAINST MORTALITY.
617(TLS):14JUN74-647
JUNKER, H. DRAMA UND "PSEUDODRAMA."
V.W. HILL, 406:SUMMER73-204
JUNKIN, H. & C. ORNADEL. THE PIANO
CAN BE FUN.
F. DAWES, 415:SEP73-900
JUPP, P. BRITISH & IRISH ELECTIONS
1784-1831.
617(TLS):12APR74-402
JURADO, J. - SEE FORNER, J.P.
JUST, W. STRINGER.
C. LEHMANN-HAUPT, 441:20FEB74-43
J.D. O'HARA, 441:3MAR74-5
442(NY):27MAY74-105
JUSTICE, D. DEPARTURES.*
617(TLS):29MAR74-339
JÜTTNER, S. GRUNDTENDENZEN DER
THEATERKRITIK VON FRIEDRICH MEL-
CHIOR GRIMM (1753-1773).
R. BAUER, 52:BAND7HEFT2/3-327
JUYNBOLL, G.H.A. THE AUTHENTICITY
OF THE TRADITION LITERATURE.
C.E. FARAH, 318(JAOS):APR-JUN72-
390

AL-KABIR, 'A.A. AL-SOLLAM AL-ROK-
HAMI.
S.K., 268:JUL74-154
KABUZAN, V.M. IZMENENIIA V RAZMESH-
CHENII NASELENIIA ROSSII V XVIII-
PERVOI POLOVINE XIX V. (PO MATER-
IALAM REVIZII).
R.N. TAAFFE, 32:DEC73-805
KABWASA, A. & M.M. KAUNDA, EDS. COR-
RESPONDENCE EDUCATION IN AFRICA.
617(TLS):12APR74-402
KACHRU, Y. AN INTRODUCTION TO HINDI
SYNTAX.*
A. DEBRECZENI, 353:1APR72-106
KADE, G., H-J. ZUBROD & R. HUJER.
ORGANISATIONSPROBLEME DER WIRT-
SCHAFTSREFORMEN IN DER UDSSR UND
DER DDR IM LICHTE DER KYBERNETIK
UND GRAPHENTHEORIE.
J.M. MONTIAS, 32:MAR73-178
KADISH, M.R. REASON & CONTROVERSY
IN THE ARTS.
A. GOLDIN, 290(JAAC):FALL71-120
KADLER, E.H. LINGUISTICS & TEACHING
FOREIGN LANGUAGES.*
W.W. DERBYSHIRE, 399(MLJ):JAN72-
60
KADUSHIN, C. THE AMERICAN INTELLEC-
TUAL ELITE.
P. STARR, 441:15SEP74-6
617(TLS):6SEP74-952
KAEGI, W. JACOB BURCKHARDT. (VOL 5)
617(TLS):14JUN74-632
KAEMPFERT, M. SÄKULARISATION UND
NEUE HEILIGKEIT.
H. REICHERT, 301(JEGP):JUL73-419
KAFITZ, D. LOHENSTEINS "ARMINIUS."*
V. MEID, 221(GQ):NOV72-738
KAFKA, F. THE COMPLETE STORIES.
(N.N. GLATZER, ED)
S. FRIEBERT, 573(SSF):SUMMER72-
291
KAFKA, F. I AM A MEMORY COME ALIVE.
(N.N. GLATZER, ED)
P. ADAMS, 61:DEC74-128
KAFKA, F. SHORTER WORKS. (VOL 1)
(M. PASLEY, ED & TRANS) LETTERS
TO FELICE.* (GERMAN TITLE: BRIEFE
AN FELICE.) (E. HELLER & J. BORN,
EDS)
R. PASCAL, 617(TLS):7JUN74-611
KAGAN, N. THE WAR FILM.
P. SCHJELDAHL, 441:8DEC74-36
KAGEYAMA, H. THE ARTS OF SHINTO.
617(TLS):26APR74-434
KAHANE, H. & R. AND L. BREMNER.
GLOSSARIO DEGLI ANTICHI PORTOLANI
ITALIANI.
F.E. DE ROOVER, 589:JAN73-155
KAHANE, M. NEVER AGAIN!
J. RIEMER, 287:JAN72-24
KAHANE, M. OUR CHALLENGE.
A.I. WASKOW, 441:21JUL74-15
KAHIL, R. INFLATION & ECONOMIC DEV-
ELOPMENT IN BRAZIL 1946-1963.
617(TLS):8MAR74-242
KAHLE, G. BARTOLOMÉ DE LAS CASAS.
M.E. GILES, 545(RPH):AUG72-208
KAHLER, E. THE GERMANS. (R. & R.
KIMBER, EDS)
442(NY):23SEP74-145
KAHLER, E. THE INWARD TURN OF NAR-
RATIVE.
J. UPDIKE, 442(NY):25MAR74-133

KÄHLER, R. VARIANTEN OHNE PERSPEK-
TIVE.
H. PIETSCH, 654(WB):11/1972-178
KAHMEN, V. EROTIC ART TODAY.
W.D. CASE, 58:NOV72-90
KAHMEN, V. EROTICISM IN CONTEMPOR-
ARY ART.
M. YAFFÉ, 592:NOV72-202
KAHN, E.A. JOURNAL OF A NEUROSUR-
GEON.
M.C. BROMAGE, 385(MQR):FALL74-
425
KAHN, E.J., JR. THE AMERICAN PEOPLE.
R. KLUGER, 441:10MAR74-2
S.R. WEISMAN, 441:1JUN74-27
KAHN, H.L. MONARCHY IN THE EMPER-
OR'S EYES.
F. WAKEMAN, JR., 293(JAST):FEB72-
393
639(VQR):WINTER72-XXXVI
KAHN, R. HOW THE WEATHER WAS.
P. SHOWERS, 441:6JAN74-10
KAHN-WALLERSTEIN, C. DIE FRAU IM
SCHATTEN.
W.H. BRUFORD, 220(GL&L):JUL73-
321
KAHNWEILER, D-H., WITH F. CRÉMIEUX.
MY GALLERIES & PAINTERS.*
C. GREEN, 39:JAN72-74
KAHRL, S.J. TRADITIONS OF MEDIEVAL
ENGLISH DRAMA.
A.C. CAWLEY, 617(TLS):1NOV74-
1232
KAHRMANN, B. DIE IDYLLISCHE SZENE
IM ZEITGENÖSSISCHEN ENGLISCHEN
ROMAN.
K-H. STOLL, 430(NS):FEB72-104
KAIKO, T. DARKNESS IN SUMMER.
A. BROYARD, 441:28JAN74-31
P. THEROUX, 441:17MAR74-41
442(NY):4FEB74-109
KAIMIO, M. THE CHORUS OF GREEK
DRAMA WITHIN THE LIGHT OF THE
PERSON & NUMBER USED.*
L. GOLDEN, 24:SUMMER73-195
KAINZ, F. PHILOSOPHISCHE ETYMOLOGIE
UND HISTORISCHE SEMANTIK.*
W. THÜMMEL, 343:BAND14HEFT2-206
KAINZ, F. PSYCHOLOGIE DER SPRACHE.
(VOL 5, PT 2)
W. KUBICEK, 343:BAND15HEFT1-9
K.H. SCHMIDT, 260(IF):BAND76-210
KAINZ, F. DIE "SPRACHE" DER TIERE.
G.F. MEIER, 682(ZPSK):BAND24
HEFT6-541
KAISER, F.B. DIE RUSSISCHE JUSTIZ-
REFORM VON 1864.
M. MANELI, 32:DEC73-829
KAISER, G. GEORG KAISER: FIVE PLAYS.
(B.J. KENWORTHY, R. LAST & J.M.
RITCHIE, TRANS)
R. FURNESS, 402(MLR):JUL73-703
KAISER, M. ADALBERT STIFTER.
H.R. KLIENEBERGER, 402(MLR):
JUL73-699
KAKRIDIS, I.T. MELETES KAI ARTHRA.
R.B., 303:VOL92-260
KAKRIDIS, J.T. HOMER REVISITED.
J.B. HAINSWORTH, 123:DEC73-267
KALB, M. & B. KISSINGER.
J. CHACE, 441:25AUG74-1
W. LAQUEUR, 617(TLS):1NOV74-1225
F. LEWIS, 441:22AUG74-37
[CONTINUED]

[CONTINUING]
R. STEEL, 453:19SEP74-24
442(NY):26AUG74-91
KALEMBKA, S. WIELKA EMIGRACJA.
P. BROCK, 497(POLR):SPRING72-99
KALGHATGI, T.G. JAINA VIEW OF LIFE.
J.P. SHARMA, 485(PE&W):APR72-234
KALIDASA. THE DIVINE MARRIAGE.
L. ROCHER, 293(JAST):NOV71-210
KALLENBERGER, J. RELIGIOUS DISCOV-
ERY, FAITH & KNOWLEDGE.
H. MEYNELL, 518:MAY73-11
KALLICH, M. THE ASSOCIATION OF
IDEAS & CRITICAL THEORY IN EIGHT-
EENTH-CENTURY ENGLAND.*
R. HARRÉ, 541(RES):MAY72-213
R.W. UPHAUS, 290(JAAC):FALL71-
141
KALLICH, M. HORACE WALPOLE.
R.A. BARRELL, 125:JUN73-323
KALLICH, M.I. HEAV'N'S FIRST LAW.*
R. PARKIN, 599:WINTER72-82
KALMYKOW, A.D. MEMOIRS OF A RUS-
SIAN DIPLOMAT.* (A. KALMYKOW, ED)
A. PARRY, 550(RUSR):JUL72-315
D.S.M. WILLIAMS, 575(SEER):JAN73-
139
KALNYN', L.E. TIPOLOGIJA ZVUKOVYX
DIALEKTNYX RAZLIČIJ V NIŽNELUŽIC-
KOM JAZYKE.
K. HELTBERG, 353:1JUL72-111
KAMANIN, N.P. - SEE RIABCHIKOV, E.
KAMATCHINATHAN, A. THE TIRUNELVELI
TAMIL DIALECT.
K. RAJA, 318(JAOS):OCT-DEC72-513
J.W. SCHUBERT, 350:MAR73-220
KAMBER, G. MAX JACOB & THE POETICS
OF CUBISM.
L.C. BREUNIG, 546(RR):APR72-162
J. MC CLELLAND, 529(QQ):WINTER72-
554
KAMMEN, M. PEOPLE OF PARADOX.
C. BRIDENBAUGH, 676(YR):WINTER73-
287
J.M. MURRIN, 656(WMQ):JUL73-491
639(VQR):SPRING73-LXXXVIII
KAMMEN, M. - SEE SMITH, W., JR.
KAMMENHUBER, A. DIE ARIER IM VORD-
EREN ORIENT.*
A. GOETZE, 318(JAOS):APR-JUN72-
284
KAMMENHUBER, A. HETHITISCH, PALAI-
SCH, LUWISCH, HIEROGLYPHENLUWISCH
UND HATTISCH.
E. NEU, 260(IF):BAND76-259
KAMPF, L. & P. LAUTER, EDS. THE
POLITICS OF LITERATURE.*
639(VQR):WINTER73-XX
KAMPHAUS, F. THE GOSPEL FOR PREACH-
ERS & TEACHERS.
617(TLS):9AUG74-864
KAMSTRA, J. WEED.
R. SHERRILL, 441:7JUL74-1
KANDELL, A. SIKKIM.
M. SLIVKA, 139:DEC71-66
KÄNDLER, K. DRAMA UND KLASSENKAMPF.
K. PFÜTZNER, 654(WB):11/1971-189
KANDUTH, E. WESENSZÜGE DER MODERNEN
ITALIENISCHEN ERZÄHLLITERATUR.
R. CRESPO, 433:OCT72-504
KANE, G.F. WHAT'S THE NEXT MOVE?
M. WATKINS, 441:8DEC74-16

KARKOSCHKA, E. NOTATION IN NEW
MUSIC.
    B. DENNIS, 415:FEB73-146
    A. GILBERT, 607:#103-46
    J.A.W., 410(M&L):APR73-226
KARLINSKY, S. - SEE CHEKHOV, A.
KARMI, H.S. AL-MANAR.
    M.A. MU'ID KHAN, 273(IC):JAN72-
    88
KARNEIN, A. - SEE CAPELLANUS, A.
KARP, W. INDISPENSABLE ENEMIES.*
    42(AR):VOL32#4-703
KARPELES, M., ED. FOLK SONGS FROM
NEWFOUNDLAND.* (NEW ED)
    M.D-S., 410(M&L):JAN73-107
KARPELES, M. AN INTRODUCTION TO
ENGLISH FOLK SONG.
    P. CROSSLEY-HOLLAND, 187:SEP74-
    454
    F. HOWES, 415:SEP73-903
KARPELES, M. - SEE SHARP, C.
KARST, R. THOMAS MANN ODER DER
DEUTSCHE ZWIESPALT.*
    I. FEUERLICHT, 221(GQ):JAN72-163
KARVE, I. HINDU SOCIETY.
    P. KOLENDA, 293(JAST):MAY72-700
KASACK, W. DER STIL KONSTANTIN
GEORGIEVIČ PAUSTOVSKIJS.
    B.P. SCHERR, 32:JUN73-428
KASHAP, P.S., ED. STUDIES IN SPIN-
OZA.
    R.S. WALTERS, 63:DEC73-269
KASHTANOV, S.M. OCHERKI RUSSKOI DIP-
LOMATIKI.
    D.C. WAUGH, 32:MAR73-158
KASSEL, N. DAS GROTESKE BEI FRANZ
KAFKA.
    C.B. EVANS, 221(GQ):NOV72-764
KATIČIĆ, R. A CONTRIBUTION TO THE
GENERAL THEORY OF COMPARATIVE LIN-
GUISTICS.
    M. FAUST, 343:BAND15HEFT2-140
KATKOV, G. & OTHERS, EDS. RUSSIA
ENTERS THE TWENTIETH CENTURY.*
(GERMAN TITLE: RUSSLANDS AUFBRUCH
INS 20. JAHRHUNDERT.)
    T. HUNCZAK, 104:SPRING72-160
KATO, S. FORM STYLE TRADITION.*
    C.D. WEBER, 293(JAST):AUG72-949
KATONA, A. A VALÓSÁGÁBRÁZOLÁS PROB-
LÉMÁI GEORGE ELIOT REGÉNYEIBEN.
    P.W. SCHRAMM, 445(NCF):MAR73-488
KATZ, A. POLAND'S GHETTOS.
    Z. GROSS, 497(POLR):SUMMER72-116
KATZ, E. & D.R. HALL. EXPLICATING
FRENCH TEXTS.*
    J.L. SHEPHERD, 3D, 207(FR):APR72-
    1070
KATZ, J. STEPHEN CRANE IN TRANSI-
TION.
    W.B. DILLINGHAM, 27(AL):NOV73-
    467
KATZ, J. OUT OF THE GHETTO.*
    C. ABRAMSKY, 453:12DEC74-22
KATZ, S. BATTLEGROUND.
    N. SAFRAN, 441:7APR74-4
KATZ, S. SAW.
    W.H. PRITCHARD, 249(HUDR):SPRING
    73-229
KATZ, W.L. THE BLACK WEST.
    P. DURHAM, 649(WAL):SPRING72-65
KATZMAN, D.M. BEFORE THE GHETTO.
    639(VQR):AUTUMN73-CLXVI

KAU, W. THEORIE UND ANWENDUNG RAUM-
WIRTSCHAFTLICHER POTENTIALMODELLE.
    P. BRAUCH, 182:VOL25#11-351
KAUFELT, D.A. THE BRADLEY BEACH
RUMBA.
    M. LEVIN, 441:18AUG74-20
KAUFFMANN, L. A PLOT OF GRASS.
    617(TLS):29MAR74-313
KAUFMAN, G.D. GOD THE PROBLEM.*
    676(YR):WINTER73-XII
KAUFMAN, P. LIBRARIES & THEIR
USERS.*
    W.G. DAY, 447(N&Q):AUG72-308
KAUFMAN, S. FALLING BODIES.
    L. DICKSTEIN, 441:3FEB74-7
    C. LEHMANN-HAUPT, 441:7JAN74-35
    B. REEVE, 231:JUN74-95
    R. TODD, 61:MAY74-128
    442(NY):11FEB74-126
KAUFMANN, E., JR. - SEE HITCHCOCK,
H-R. & OTHERS
KAUL, A.N. THE ACTION OF ENGLISH
COMEDY.*
    R. WARREN, 447(N&Q):OCT72-396
KAUNE, F.J. SELBSTVERWIRKLICHUNG.
    M.S., 543:JUN72-759
KAUVAR, G.B. THE OTHER POETRY OF
KEATS.
    S.M.S., 191(ELN):SEP72(SUPP)-53
KAVAN, A. JULIA & THE BAZOOKA.
    J.L. ABBOTT, 573(SSF):WINTER72-
    105
KAVAN, A. LET ME ALONE.
    R. GARFITT, 362:21FEB74-248
    617(TLS):14JUN74-644
KAVANAGH, P. NOT COMIN' HOME TO YOU.
    M. LEVIN, 441:14JUL74-20
KAVANAGH, P.J. EDWARD THOMAS IN
HEAVEN.
    617(TLS):24MAY74-554
KAVANAGH, T. THE ITMA YEARS.
    D. THOMAS, 362:19&26DEC74-846
KAVOLIS, V. HISTORY ON ART'S SIDE.
    W.M. JOHNSTON, 290(JAAC):SUMMER
    73-554
KAWABATA, Y. THE HOUSE OF THE
SLEEPING BEAUTIES.*
    617(TLS):23AUG74-911
KAWABATA, Y. THE LAKE.
    E. WHITE, 441:23JUN74-7
KAWIN, B.F. TELLING IT AGAIN &
AGAIN.
    C. GEDULD, 659:WINTER74-123
    R. STUDING, 290(JAAC):WINTER72-
    277
KAY, G. RHODESIA.
    D.J. SIDDLE, 69:APR72-171
KAY, M. - SEE RIGAUT, J.
KAY, R. THE PAINTER'S GUIDE TO
STUDIO METHODS & MATERIALS.
    M. WILLIAMSON, 96:OCT/NOV72-86
KAY-ROBINSON, D. HARDY'S WESSEX
REAPPRAISED.
    S. HYNES, 401(MLQ):SEP73-325
    W.J. KEITH, 637(VS):MAR73-367
KAYE, E. XAVIER FORNERET DIT
"L'HOMME NOIR" (1809-1884).
    F.P. BOWMAN, 207(FR):APR72-1054
    P. MOREAU, 557(RSH):OCT-DEC72-
    621
    F.R. SMITH, 208(FS):APR73-220
    J-L. STEINMETZ, 535(RHL):JUL-AUG
    72-729

KAYE, H.E. MALE SURVIVAL.
R. TODD, 61:NOV74-104
KAYE, M. THE GRAND OLE OPRY MURDERS.
N. CALLENDAR, 441:28JUL74-14
KAYSER, W. & H. GRONEMEYER. MAX
BROD.
H. THOMKE, 182:VOL25#7/8-232
KAZAN, E. THE UNDERSTUDY.
A. BROYARD, 441:19DEC74-43
KAZIN, A. BRIGHT BOOK OF LIFE.*
S.V. DANIELS, 584(SWR):AUTUMN73-
363
J. HENDIN, 31(ASCH):WINTER73/74-
168
R. SALE, 453:21MAR74-36
R.E. SPILLER, 27(AL):JAN74-622
441:10NOV74-39
617(TLS):14JUN74-634
KEARNEY, R.N. THE POLITICS OF CEY-
LON (SRI LANKA).
617(TLS):5APR74-377
KEAST, W.R., ED. SEVENTEENTH-CEN-
TURY ENGLISH POETRY.
B. VICKERS, 402(MLR):APR73-385
KEATING, H.R.F. BATS FLY UP FOR
INSPECTOR GHOTE.
N. CALLENDAR, 441:20OCT74-42
617(TLS):19JUL74-761
KEATING, H.R.F. THE UNDERSIDE.
617(TLS):9AUG74-849
KEATING, P.J., ED. WORKING-CLASS
STORIES OF THE 1890S.
P. COUSTILLAS, 189(EA):OCT-DEC72-
572
J. KORG, 445(NCF):SEP72-219
S.M. SMITH, 155:JAN72-61
S.M. SMITH, 541(RES):AUG72-374
M. VICINUS, 637(VS):JUN72-504
KEATING, P.J. THE WORKING CLASSES
IN VICTORIAN FICTION.*
P. COUSTILLAS, 189(EA):OCT-DEC72-
572
J. KORG, 445(NCF):SEP72-219
S.M. SMITH, 155:JAN72-61
M. VICINUS, 637(VS):JUN72-504
KEATS, J. POEMS OF 1820. (D.G.
GILLHAM, ED)
J.C. MAXWELL, 447(N&Q):MAR72-113
KEATS, J. THE POEMS OF JOHN KEATS.*
(M. ALLOTT, ED)
S.M.S., 191(ELN):SEP72(SUPP)-50
KEČKEMET, D. IVAN MEŠTROVIĆ.
V. MOLÈ, 32:JUN73-434
KEDDIE, N.R. RELIGION & REBELLION
IN IRAN.
T.C. YOUNG, 318(JAOS):JAN-MAR72-
115
KEE, R. THE GREEN FLAG.*
P. BEW, 111:18MAY73-152
KEEGAN, W. CONSULTING FATHER WIN-
TERGREEN.
617(TLS):11OCT74-1109
KEELEY, E. & P. BIEN, EDS. MODERN
GREEK WRITERS.*
J.K. DEMETRIUS, 32:SEP73-675
KEEN, B. THE AZTEC IMAGE IN WESTERN
THOUGHT.*
R. HILTON, 322(JHI):APR-JUN72-
337
KEEN, M.H. ENGLAND IN THE LATER
MIDDLE AGES.*
A. LEGUAI, 182:VOL25#12-429

KEENAN, E.L. THE KURBSKII-GROZNYI
APOCRYPHA.*
639(VQR):SUMMER72-XCVIII
KEENE, D. THE JAPANESE DISCOVERY OF
EUROPE, 1720-1830. (REV)
R.P. DORE, 318(JAOS):JAN-MAR72-
154
KEENE, D. - SEE "CHUSHINGURA"
KEENE, D., WITH R. TYLER, EDS. TWEN-
TY PLAYS OF THE NŌ THEATRE.*
J. RUBIN, 244(HJAS):VOL32-289
KEENE, R. ARON NIMZOWITSCH 1886-
1935.
617(TLS):8NOV74-1269
KEENE, R. & D. LEVY. CHESS OLYMPIAD
SKOPJE 1972.
617(TLS):22FEB74-193
KEGLEY, C.W., ED. THE PHILOSOPHY &
THEOLOGY OF ANDERS NYGREN.
J.M.V., 543:DEC71-379
KEHL, D.G. LITERARY STYLE OF THE
OLD BIBLE & THE NEW.
W. ALLEN, 599:SPRING72-185
KEIL, G. "KURZE HARNTRAKTAT" DES
BRESLAUER "CODEX SALERNITANUS" UND
SEINE SIPPE.
B. HAAGE, 680(ZDP):BAND91HEFT3-
471
KEINEG, P. LIEUX COMMUNS [SUIVI DE]
DAHUT.
617(TLS):9AUG74-852
KEITER, F., ED. VERHALTENSFORSCHUNG
IM RAHMEN DER WISSENSCHAFTEN VOM
MENSCHEN.
V. RÜFNER, 182:VOL25#17/18-586
KEITH-SMITH, B. JOHANNES BOBROWSKI.*
G.E. EDWARDS, 220(GL&L):APR73-
269
KELCH, R.A. NEWCASTLE.
617(TLS):29MAR74-319
KELDER, D. THE FRENCH IMPRESSION-
ISTS & THEIR CENTURY.
J. ISAACSON, 207(FR):OCT71-233
KELE, M.H. NAZIS & WORKERS.
617(TLS):1FEB74-93
KELF-COHEN, R. BRITISH NATIONALISA-
TION 1945-1973.
617(TLS):3MAY74-472
KELLER, E. NATIONALISMUS UND LITERA-
TUR.
H.E. HOLTHUSEN, 301(JEGP):APR73-
270
H. RIDLEY, 402(MLR):APR73-469
"GOTTFRIED KELLER."* (K. JEZIORKOW-
SKI, ED)
G. REINHARDT, 222(GR):MAY72-228
KELLER, J.E. - SEE GREEN, O.H.
KELLER, M. JOHANN KLAJS WEIHNACHTS-
DICHTUNG.*
J.L. GELLINEK, 301(JEGP):APR73-
281
P. SKRINE, 402(MLR):APR73-449
KELLER, W. THE ETRUSCANS.
P. ADAMS, 61:JUN74-115
442(NY):23SEP74-146
KELLER, W.E. - SEE ADAMS, J.N.
KELLEY, D.R. FOUNDATIONS OF MODERN
HISTORICAL SCHOLARSHIP.*
J. DENT, 551(RENQ):AUTUMN72-334
H. DURANTON, 535(RHL):JAN-FEB72-
127
P. FERRUA, 125:OCT72-76

KELLEY, R.E. & O.M. BRACK, JR. SAM-
UEL JOHNSON'S EARLY BIOGRAPHERS.*
E.A. BLOOM, 677:VOL3-296
W.R. KEAST, 481(PQ):JUL72-706
KELLOGG, A. CHAUCER, LANGLAND,
ARTHUR.
639(VQR):SPRING73-LXV
KELLOGG, M. LIKE THE LION'S TOOTH.*
639(VQR):WINTER73-VIII
KELLS, J.H. - SEE SOPHOCLES
KELLY, G. CLINICAL PSYCHOLOGY &
PERSONALITY. (B. MAHER, ED)
J.S. BOIS, 186(ETC.):MAR72-98
KELLY, H. PRELUDE.
617(TLS):24MAY74-554
KELLY, H.A. DIVINE PROVIDENCE IN
THE ENGLAND OF SHAKESPEARE'S HIS-
TORIES.*
J. BRITTON, 613:SPRING72-131
T.W. CRAIK, 541(RES):MAY72-198
P. EDWARDS, 447(N&Q):APR72-150
M.H. FLEISCHER, 551(RENQ):SUMMER
72-228
KELLY, L.G., ED. THE DESCRIPTION &
MEASUREMENT OF BILINGUALISM.*
V. ROZENCVEJG, 353:1NOV72-100
G.R. TUCKER, 399(MLJ):APR72-253
KELLY, M. THAT GIRL IN THE ALLEY.
617(TLS):6SEP74-960
KELLY, R.J., COMP. JOHN BERRYMAN.
639(VQR):SPRING73-LXXIII
KELLY, R.M. - SEE JERROLD, D.
KELSAY, L.E. & C.M. ASHBY, COMPS.
CARTOGRAPHIC RECORDS RELATING TO
THE TERRITORY OF WISCONSIN, 1836-
1848.
J.M. KINNEY, 14:JUL/OCT72-415
KELSAY, L.E. & F.W. PERNELL, COMPS.
CARTOGRAPHIC RECORDS RELATING TO
THE TERRITORY OF IOWA, 1838-1846.
J.M. KINNEY, 14:JUL/OCT72-415
KELSEY, D.P., ED. FARMING IN THE
NEW NATION.
G.M. HERNDON, 656(WMQ):APR73-358
KEMAL, Y. IRON EARTH, COPPER SKY.
R. BLYTHE, 362:13JUN74-777
617(TLS):3MAY74-465
KEMBLE, J.M. & J. GRIMM. JOHN MIT-
CHELL KEMBLE & JAKOB GRIMM: A COR-
RESPONDENCE 1832-1852. (R.A.
WILEY, ED & TRANS)
M. PEPPARD, 301(JEGP):JAN73-96
KEMELMAN, H. TUESDAY THE RABBI SAW
RED.
N. CALLENDAR, 441:3MAR74-32
442(NY):18MAR74-152
KEMÉNY, G.G., COMP. IRATOK A NEM-
ZETISÉGI KÉRDÉS TÖRTÉNETÉHEZ MAG-
YARORSZÁGON A DUALIZMUS KORÁBAN,
1867-1918. (VOL 5)
R.E. ALLEN, 32:DEC73-840
KEMILÄINEN, A. "L'AFFAIRE D'AVIGNON"
(1789-91) FROM THE VIEWPOINT OF
NATIONALISM.
J. GODECHOT, 182:VOL25#22-816
KEMMNER, E. SPRACHSPIEL UND STIL-
TECHNIK IN RAYMOND QUENEAUS ROMAN-
EN.
H.D. BORK, 72:BAND210HEFT4/6-475
KEMP, J. ETHICAL NATURALISM.
R.F. ATKINSON, 479(PHQ):JAN72-83
KEMP, J.A. - SEE WALLIS, J.
KEMP, P. MURIEL SPARK.
G. ANNAN, 617(TLS):15NOV74-1277

KEMPER, H-G. GEORG TRAKLS ENTWÜRFE.
B. KÖNNEKER, 224(GRM):BAND22
HEFT4-444
H. WETZEL, 406:SPRING73-96
KEMPF, R. HOW NICE TO SEE YOU!
Y. VELAN, 207(FR):MAY72-1180
KEMPF, R. - SEE KANT, I.
KENDALL, K.E. LEIGH HUNT'S "REFLEC-
TOR."*
S.I. TUCKER, 541(RES):MAY72-219
KENDRICK, A. THE WOUND WITHIN.
H. MITGANG, 441:24AUG74-23
KENDRICK, G. EROSIONS.
J. SAUNDERS, 565:VOL13#3-75
KENEALLY, T. BLOOD RED, SISTER ROSE.
617(TLS):11OCT74-1142
KENEALLY, T. THE CHANT OF JIMMIE
BLACKSMITH.
B. KIERNAN, 381:DEC72-489
T. STURM, 581:SEP73-261
KENEZ, P. CIVIL WAR IN SOUTH RUSSIA,
1918.*
V.D. MEDLIN, 550(RUSR):JAN72-86
KENG-WANG, Y. - SEE UNDER YEN KENG-
WANG
KEN'ICHI, M. - SEE UNDER MIZUSAWA
KEN'ICHI
KENNA, P. THE SLAUGHTER OF ST.
TERESA'S DAY.
A. KRUSE, 581:JUN73-240
KENNAN, G.F. THE MARQUIS DE CUSTINE
& HIS "RUSSIA IN 1839."*
P. AVRICH, 550(RUSR):JAN72-96
A.G. CROSS, 575(SEER):APR73-313
191(ELN):SEP72(SUPP)-91
KENNAN, G.F. MEMOIRS, 1950-1963.*
W.M. FRANKLIN, 639(VQR):SPRING73-
287
KENNEDY, G. THE ART OF RHETORIC IN
THE ROMAN WORLD 300 B.C. - A.D.
300.*
E. TIFFOU, 487:WINTER72-408
KENNEDY, G. QUINTILIAN.
A.E. DOUGLAS, 123:MAR73-92
H. NORTH, 480(P&R):WINTER72-65
KENNEDY, L. PURSUIT.
C. LEHMANN-HAUPT, 441:2AUG74-25
E.S. TURNER, 362:4APR74-443
E. WEEKS, 61:AUG74-87
617(TLS):26JUL74-782
KENNEDY, M. MAHLER.
D. MITCHELL, 617(TLS):29NOV74-
1349
KENNEDY, M. THE WORKS OF RALPH
VAUGHAN WILLIAMS.*
A.E.F. DICKINSON, 607:#102-33
KENNEDY, M. - SEE HALLÉ, C.
KENNEDY, M.L. THE JACOBIN CLUB OF
MARSEILLES, 1790-1794.
617(TLS):15FEB74-160
KENNEDY, R.F. TIMES TO REMEMBER.
P. BLACK, 362:4APR74-442
C. LEHMANN-HAUPT, 441:8MAR74-37
M.F. NOLAN, 441:31MAR74-1
617(TLS):29MAR74-311
KENNEDY, X.J. EMILY DICKINSON IN
SOUTHERN CALIFORNIA.
D. BROMWICH, 441:16JUN74-6
J. PARISI, 491:SEP74-343
617(TLS):30AUG74-932
KENNEDY, X.J. GROWING INTO LOVE.*
K. SKINNER, 448:SPRING72-94
KENNER, H. BUCKY.*
R. SALE, 453:7FEB74-29

KENNER, H. DAS MÄDCHEN VON ANTIUM.
A. HUS, 555:VOL46FASC2-360
KENNER, H. THE POUND ERA.*
P. EDWARDS, 111:20OCT72-29
W. HARMON, 125:OCT72-79
W.W. ROBSON, 473(PR):WINTER73-
136
639(VQR):AUTUMN73-CXLVIII
KENNETT, A. THE PALACES OF LENIN-
GRAD.
617(TLS):1FEB74-103
KENNEY, E.J. - SEE LUCRETIUS
KENNY, A. THE ANATOMY OF THE SOUL.
617(TLS):8FEB74-136
KENNY, A.J.P. & OTHERS. THE DEVEL-
OPMENT OF MIND.
617(TLS):12JUL74-739
KENNY, H.A. LITERARY DUBLIN.
P. ADAMS, 61:JUN74-115
P. MAC MANUS, 441:24NOV74-20
KENNY, S.S. - SEE STEELE, R.
KENRICK, T. TWO FOR THE PRICE OF
ONE.
N. CALLENDAR, 441:21JUL74-18
KENT, A. COMMAND A KING'S SHIP.
M. LEVIN, 441:27JAN74-18
KENT, C. CHARLES DICKENS AS A
READER.
J.G., 155:MAY72-130
KENT, G. BLACKNESS & THE ADVENTURE
OF WESTERN CULTURE.
441:13JAN74-31
KENT, L.J. - SEE GOGOL, N.
KENTFIELD, C. THE GREAT GREEN.
E. CAPOUYA, 441:24FEB74-32
KENYON, M. A SORRY STATE.
N. CALLENDAR, 441:21JUL74-18
KENYON, P. HARD-CORE MURDER.
N. CALLENDAR, 441:12MAY74-16
KENYON, P. OPERATION DOOMSDAY.
N. CALLENDAR, 441:11AUG74-12
KENYON, P. THE SONIC SLAVE.
N. CALLENDAR, 441:8DEC74-44
KEPLER, C.F. THE LITERATURE OF THE
SECOND SELF.
G.B. TENNYSON, 445(NCF):DEC72-
365
KEPPEL, S. THE SOVEREIGN LADY.
617(TLS):12JUL74-750
KER, N.R. RECORDS OF ALL SOULS COL-
LEGE LIBRARY 1473-1600.
K.W. HUMPHREYS, 447(N&Q):JUN72-
232
A.G. WATSON, 382(MAE):1973/3-295
KERBY, R.L. KIRBY SMITH'S CONFED-
ERACY.
639(VQR):SPRING73-LXXXIII
KERENSKY, O. ANNA PAVLOVA.*
A. KISSELGOFF, 441:20APR74-29
KERENYI, C. & OTHERS. EVIL.
M. VETÖ, 321:WINTER72[VOL6#1]-72
KERMODE, F. D.H. LAWRENCE.
C. RICKS, 453:24JAN74-43
KERMODE, F. SHAKESPEARE, SPENSER,
DONNE.*
T.R. EDWARDS, 149:DEC73-401
G. WATSON, 541(RES):MAY72-204
KERMODE, F. & J. HOLLANDER, EDS.
THE OXFORD ANTHOLOGY OF ENGLISH
LITERATURE.*
J. BAYLEY, 362:3JAN74-24
KERN, P. TRINITÄT, MARIA, INKARNA-
TION.*
O. SAYCE, 402(MLR):APR73-445

KERN, P.C. ZUR GEDANKENWELT DES
SPÄTEN HOFMANNSTHAL.*
P. GOFF, 400(MLN):APR72-533
R.T. LLEWELLYN, 220(GL&L):APR73-
263
KERNDL, R. STÜCKE.
617(TLS):29MAR74-314
KEROUAC, J. MAGGIE CASSIDY.
617(TLS):13SEP74-971
KEROUAC, J. VISIONS OF CODY.*
J. TYTELL, 473(PR):2/1973-301
639(VQR):SPRING73-LVI
KERR, E.M. & R.M. ADERMAN, EDS. AS-
PECTS OF AMERICAN ENGLISH. (2ND ED)
A.H. MARCKWARDT, 399(MLJ):DEC72-
522
KERR, H. MEDIUMS, & SPIRIT-RAPPERS,
& ROARING RADICALS.*
M. GRIFFITHS, 150(DR):SUMMER72-
339
639(VQR):AUTUMN72-CXXIX
KERR, W. THIRTY PLAYS HATH NOVEMBER.
J. SCHWARTZ, 160:SPRING71-202
KERSCHENSTEINER, J. DIE MYKENISCHE
WELT IN IHREN SCHRIFTLICHEN ZEUG-
NISSEN.
J. CHADWICK, 123:DEC73-222
KERSH, C. THE SOHO SUMMER OF MR.
GREEN.
617(TLS):27SEP74-1033
KERSHAW, I. BOLTON PRIORY.
617(TLS):5APR74-365
KERTÉSZ, A. J'AIME PARIS.
E. WELTY, 441:1DEC74-22
KERTESZ, S.D., ED. THE TASK OF UNI-
VERSITIES IN A CHANGING WORLD.
G.W. SHEA, 613:SPRING72-156
KESSEL, J. KISLING.
A. FRANKENSTEIN, 55:NOV73-48
KESSEL, J. STAVISKY.
T. ZELDIN, 617(TLS):11OCT74-1110
KESSINGER, T.G. VILYATPUR 1848-1968.
617(TLS):27SEP74-1038
KESSLER, E. IMAGES OF WALLACE STEV-
ENS.*
H. TAYLOR, 651(WHR):WINTER73-100
KESSLER, H.L. - SEE WEITZMANN, K.
KESSLER, J. AN EGYPTIAN BONDAGE.
K.T. WOLMAN, 573(SSF):WINTER72-
110
KESSLER, M-C. LE CONSEIL D'ETAT.
E.N. SULEIMAN, 98:MAR72-274 [&
CONT IN 98:APR72-374]
KETCHAM, R. FROM COLONY TO COUNTRY.
442(NY):30SEP74-132
KETCHAM, R. JAMES MADISON.
R.A. RUTLAND, 656(WMQ):JAN72-169
A.F. YOUNG, 639(VQR):SUMMER72-
467
KETCHUM, B., ED. THE WATER'S EDGE.
42(AR):VOL32#4-711
KETCHUM, W.C., JR. EARLY POTTERS &
POTTERIES OF NEW YORK STATE.
P. PASSLOF, 139:DEC71-66
KEUDEL, U. POETISCHE VORLÄUFER UND
VORBILDER IN CLAUDIANS DE CONSU-
LATU STILICHONIS.
J.B. HALL, 123:DEC73-179
KEYES, R.S. & K. MIZUSHIMA. THE THE-
ATRICAL WORLD OF OSAKA PRINTS.*
P.G. O'NEILL, 617(TLS):29NOV74-
1341

KINCAID, J.R. DICKENS & THE RHETOR-
IC OF LAUGHTER.
G.B. TENNYSON, 445(NCF):DEC72-
369
K. TETZELI VON ROSADOR, 72:BAND
210HEFT4/6-420
A. WELSH, 676(YR):WINTER73-281
KINDLEBERGER, C.P. THE WORLD IN
DEPRESSION, 1929-1939.*
G. BARRACLOUGH, 453:27JUN74-14
KING, A. & H. NORTH - SEE CAPLAN, H.
KING, A.L. LOUIS T. WIGFALL.*
L.R. ATKINS, 9(ALAR):OCT72-289
KING, B., ED. TWENTIETH CENTURY IN-
TERPRETATIONS OF "ALL FOR LOVE."
P. LEGOUIS, 189(EA):APR-JUN72-
327
KING, B.J., WITH K. CHAPIN. BILLIE
JEAN.
A. BROYARD, 441:20JUN74-43
KING, C. A SPACE ON THE FLOOR.
R. WHITELEY, 157:AUTUMN72-81
KING, D. - SEE CHAPLIN, C.
KING, E. PETERBOROUGH ABBEY 1086-
1310.
617(TLS):28JUN74-696
KING, F. FLIGHTS.*
E. FEINSTEIN, 364:FEB/MAR74-137
KING, F. A GAME OF PATIENCE.
J. MELLORS, 362:12SEP74-348
617(TLS):13SEP74-969
KING, G. HARROWVALE.
M. LEVIN, 441:1SEP74-14
KING, G. GRACE KING OF NEW ORLEANS.
(R. BUSH, ED)
C.M. SIMPSON, JR., 578:SPRING74-
130
KING, H. THE POEMS OF HENRY KING.
(M. CRUM, ED)
R. ELLRODT, 189(EA):JAN-MAR72-
164
KING, J.C. - SEE NOTKER DER DEUTSCHE
KING, L.L. THE OLD MAN.
C. LEHMANN-HAUPT, 441:31JAN74-37
KING, P. THE IDEOLOGY OF ORDER.
617(TLS):26JUL74-786
KING, P.K. DAWN POETRY IN THE
NETHERLANDS.
J. VAN DORSTEN, 402(MLR):APR73-
473
KING, R. THE PARTY OF EROS.
S. HOOK, 639(VQR):SPRING73-274
S. PAUL, 301(JEGP):APR73-252
D. YERGIN, 676(YR):AUTUMN72-147
KING, R.A., JR. & OTHERS - SEE BROWN-
ING, R.
KING, R.D. HISTORICAL LINGUISTICS &
GENERATIVE GRAMMAR.*
J. KLAUSENBURGER, 399(MLJ):MAR72-
188
KING, S. CARRIE.
N. CALLENDAR, 441:26MAY74-17
KING, T.J. SHAKESPEAREAN STAGING,
1599-1642.*
M. JONES, 541(RES):NOV72-491
KING, W., ED. BLACK SPIRITS.
639(VQR):WINTER73-XVI
KING, W. & R. MILNER, EDS. BLACK
DRAMA ANTHOLOGY.
O. OWOMOYELA, 502(PRS):FALL72-
262
KINGDON, R.M. - SEE DE BÈZE, T.

KINGSFORD, P.W. VICTORIAN RAILWAY-
MEN.
T. COLEMAN, 637(VS):SEP71-95
KINGSMILL, H. HUGH KINGSMILL: SELEC-
TIONS FROM HIS WRITINGS. (M. HOL-
ROYD, ED)
G. MERLE, 189(EA):JAN-MAR72-178
KININMONTH, C. MAZE.
617(TLS):8MAR74-229
KINKADE, R.P., ED. LOS "LUCIDARIOS"
ESPANOLES.*
F. MÁRQUEZ VILLANUEVA, 545(RPH):
NOV72-483
KINKEAD-WEEKES, M. SAMUEL RICHARD-
SON.
617(TLS):25JAN74-75
KINNAMON, K. THE EMERGENCE OF
RICHARD WRIGHT.*
D. AARON, 27(AL):NOV73-474
J.M. REILLY, 301(JEGP):OCT73-581
639(VQR):SUMMER73-CXV
KINNEAVY, J.L. A THEORY OF DIS-
COURSE.
D.C. BRYANT, 480(P&R):SUMMER72-
188
KINSELLA, T. NEW POEMS 1973.*
R. GARFITT, 364:DEC73/JAN74-127
KINSELLA, T. NOTES FROM THE LAND OF
THE DEAD & OTHER POEMS.
C. BEDIENT, 441:16JUN74-7
KINSLEY, J. - SEE BURNS, R.
KINSLEY, J. - SEE CARLYLE, A.
KINSLEY, J. & G. PARFITT - SEE DRY-
DEN, J.
KINTNER, W.R. & W. KLAIBER. EASTERN
EUROPE & EUROPEAN SECURITY.
A.R. JOHNSON, 32:MAR73-181
KINTNER, W.R. & R.L. PFALTZGRAFF,
EDS. SALT.
639(VQR):AUTUMN73-CLXIX
KINYAPINA, N.S. POLITIKA RUSSKOGO
SAMODERZHAVIYA V OBLASTI PROMYSH-
LENNOSTI (20-50-YE GODY XIX V.).
O. CRISP, 575(SEER):OCT73-582
KIPARSKY, V. GIBT ES EIN FINNOU-
GRISCHES SUBSTRAT IM SLAVISCHEN?
H.W. SCHALLER, 260(IF):BAND77
HEFT1-152
KIRCHHOFF, U. DIE DARSTELLUNG DES
FESTES IM ROMAN UM 1900.
T.A. SCHEUFELE, 400(MLN):APR72-
531
KIRCHNER, G. FORTUNA IN DICHTUNG
UND EMBLEMATIK DES BAROCK.*
E. SOBEL, 221(GQ):NOV72-710
D. SULZER, 182:VOL25#9/10-285
KIRCHNER, J. AUSGEWÄHLTE AUFSÄTZE
AUS PALÄOGRAPHIE, HANDSCHRIFTEN-
KUNDE, ZEITSCHRIFTENWESEN UND
GEISTESGESCHICHTE.
J.L. FLOOD, 354:MAR72-69
KIRCHNER, W. COMMERCIAL RELATIONS
BETWEEN RUSSIA & EUROPE 1400-1800.
O. CRISP, 575(SEER):OCT73-582
KIR'IANOV, I.I. RABOCHIE IUGA
ROSSII.
F.I. KAPLAN, 32:SEP73-612
KIRK, E.D. THE DREAM THOUGHT OF
PIERS PLOWMAN.
D. PEARSALL, 301(JEGP):OCT73-543
639(VQR):AUTUMN73-CLII
KIRK, G.S. MYTH.*
G. STEINER, 24:SPRING73-107
KIRK, G.S. - SEE EURIPIDES

KIRK, H.L. PABLO CASALS.
R. EDER, 441:14APR74-2
D. HENAHAN, 441:29APR74-37
KIRK, R. THE CONSERVATIVE MIND.
(5TH ED)
D.A. ZOLL, 396(MODA):FALL73-413
KIRK, R. ELIOT & HIS AGE.*
W.W. ROBSON, 473(PR):WINTER73-
136
639(VQR):SUMMER72-LXXXIX
KIRK-GREENE, A.H.M. CRISIS & CON-
FLICT IN NIGERIA.
W. GUTTERIDGE, 69:APR72-156
KIRKENDALE, W. L'ARIA DI FIORENZA,
ID EST IL BALLO DEL GRAN DUCA.
N. FORTUNE, 415:FEB73-147
J.R., 410(M&L):JAN73-98
KIRKHAM, M. THE POETRY OF ROBERT
GRAVES.*
G. STEBNER, 430(NS):APR72-240
KIRKMAN, J. FORT JESUS.
617(TLS):16AUG74-887
KIRKNESS, W.J. LE FRANÇAIS DU THÉ-
ÂTRE ITALIAN.
A.C. KEYS, 67:MAY73-133
KIRKPATRICK, R. - SEE "DOMENICO SCAR-
LATTI: COMPLETE KEYBOARD WORKS"
KIRKPATRICK, S. THE SUN'S GOLD.
M. LEVIN, 441:17MAR74-38
KIRKUP, J. A BEWICK BESTIARY. THE
BODY SERVANT.
A. CLUYSENAAR, 565:VOL13#2-72
KIRKWOOD, G.M. EARLY GREEK MONODY.
617(TLS):21JUN74-672
KIRSCH, A. JACOBEAN DRAMATIC PER-
SPECTIVES.
639(VQR):AUTUMN72 CXXXIII
KIRSCHENMANN, P.P. INFORMATION &
REFLECTION.*
A. YAKUSHEV, 258:SEP72-453
KIRSHNER, S. - SEE SCHILLER, F.
KIRSOP, W. BIBLIOGRAPHIE MATÉRIELLE
ET CRITIQUE TEXTUELLE: VERS UNE
COLLABORATION.
D. SHAW, 354:DEC72-353
KIRST, H.H. A TIME FOR TRUTH.
N. CALLENDAR, 441:17NOV74-51
KIRSTEN, W. - SEE VON KEYSERLING, E.
KIRWAN, C. - SEE ARISTOTLE
KISH, G. NORTH-EAST PASSAGE.
617(TLS):3MAY74-483
KISHI, A.H. SPIRITUAL CONSCIOUSNESS
IN ZEN FROM A THOMISTIC THEOLOGI-
CAL POINT OF VIEW.
H.V. RAPPARD, 485(PE&W):JAN72-
116
KISS, S. LES TRANSFORMATIONS DE LA
STRUCTURE SYLLABIQUE EN LATIN TAR-
DIF.
C.W. ASPLAND, 67:NOV73-333
KISSINGER, H.A. A WORLD RESTORED.
617(TLS):5APR74-356
KISTLER, M.O. DRAMA OF THE STORM &
STRESS.*
A. BLUNDEN, 220(GL&L):APR73-240
KIVIMAA, K. & L. LEHTO. THE GREAT
VOWEL SHIFT - A COMBINATORY
CHANGE?
K. DIETZ, 38:BAND90HEFT1/2-168
H. WEINSTOCK, 597(SN):VOL44#2-
444

KIYOSHI KOJIMA. JAPAN & A PACIFIC
FREE TRADE AREA.
P. DRYSDALE, 285(JAPQ):JUL-SEP72-
363
KJAMILEV, S.X. MAROKKANSKIJ DIALEKT
ARABSKOGO JAZYKA.
E.T. ABDEL-MASSIH, 353:1MAR72-
112
KJØRUP, S. ESTETISKE PROBLEMER.
L. AAGAARD-MOGENSEN, 290(JAAC):
SUMMER73-544
KLAKOWICZ, B. LA COLLEZIONE DEI
CONTI FAINA IN ORVIETO.*
B.A. SPARKES, 303:VOL92-251
KLAPP, O. BIBLIOGRAPHIE DER FRANZÖ-
SISCHEN LITERATURWISSENSCHAFT.
(VOL 7)
D. STONE, JR., 207(FR):FEB72-739
KLAPPER, C. THE GOLDEN AGE OF TRAM-
WAYS. (2ND ED)
617(TLS):12APR74-402
KLAPPERT, P. LUGGING VEGETABLES TO
NANTUCKET.*
M. BORROFF, 676(YR):AUTUMN72-81
KLATT, H. DIE ALTERSVERSORGUNG DER
ABGEORDNETEN.
V. VON BETHUSY-HUC, 182:VOL25
#17/18-593
KLAUDER, F.J. ASPECTS OF THE
THOUGHT OF TEILHARD DE CHARDIN.
H.J. BIRX, 484(PPR):SEP72-120
KLÄUI, E. GESTALTUNG UND FORMEN DER
ZEIT IM WERK ADALBERT STIFTERS.
A. STILLMARK, 220(GL&L):APR73-
254
KLAUSER, T., ED. REALLEXIKON FÜR
ANTIKE UND CHRISTENTUM. (FASC 61
& 62)
A. ERNOUT, 555:VOL46FASC2-349
KLAUSER, T., ED. DAS REALLEXIKON
FÜR ANTIKE UND CHRISTENTUM UND DAS
F.J. DÖLGER-INSTITUT IN BONN. (2ND
ED)
P. COURCELLE, 555:VOL46FASC1-166
KLEBERG, T. MEDELTIDA UPPSALABIBLIO-
TEK. (VOLS 1&2)
R.C. ELLSWORTH, 517(PBSA):JUL-
SEP73-361
KLEE, P. FORM- UND GESTALTUNGS-
LEHRE. (VOL 2)
R. JULLIAN, 182:VOL25#5/6-170
KLEE, P. PAUL KLEE NOTEBOOKS. (VOL
2) (J. SPILLER, ED)
D.A.N. JONES, 362:10JAN74-54
617(TLS):19APR74-411
KLEIN, A. DIE KRISE DES UNTERHALT-
UNGSROMANS IM 19. JAHRHUNDERT.
D.L. ASHLIMAN, 221(GQ):NOV72-752
KLEIN, A.M. THE COLLECTED POEMS OF
A.M. KLEIN. (M. WADDINGTON, ED)
F.W. WATT, 99:NOV/DEC74-18
KLEIN, D.E. A HISTORY OF SCIENTIFIC
PSYCHOLOGY.
R.S. PETERS, 479(PHQ):APR72-176
KLEIN, D.W. & A.B. CLARK. BIOGRA-
PHIC DICTIONARY OF CHINESE COMMUN-
ISM 1921-1965.*
C-T. HSÜEH, 293(JAST):FEB72-405
KLEIN, E., ED. A COMPREHENSIVE ETY-
MOLOGICAL DICTIONARY OF THE ENG-
LISH LANGUAGE.*
G. BAUER, 343:BAND15HEFT1-93
G.F. MEIER, 682(ZPSK):BAND25
HEFT6-530

KLEIN, H-W. PHONETIK UND PHONOLOGIE
DES HEUTIGEN FRANZÖSISCH.
G.F. MEIER, 682(ZPSK):BAND25
HEFT1/2-159
KLEIN, K.L. VORFORMEN DES ROMANS IN
DER ENGLISCHEN ERZÄHLENDEN PROSA
DES 16. JAHRHUNDERTS.
W. VON KOPPENFELS, 72:BAND210
HEFT4/6-389
G. ROHMANN, 430(NS):NOV72-675
KLEIN, K.L., ED. WEGE DER SHAKE-
SPEARE-FORSCHUNG.
M. PFISTER, 72:BAND210HEFT4/6-
370
KLEIN, K.W. THE PARTISAN VOICE.
H. HEINEN, 589:OCT73-763
KLEIN, R. COMPLAINTS AGAINST DOC-
TORS.
617(TLS):18JAN74-48
KLEIN, R. SYMMACHUS.*
W.H.C. FREND, 123:DEC73-286
KLEINBAUER, W.E. MODERN PERSPEC-
TIVES IN ART HISTORY.
J. MOFFITT, 127:FALL72-108
KLEINT, B.H. BILDLEHRE.
D. HELMS, 182:VOL25#13/14-489
VON KLEIST, E.C. SÄMTLICHE WERKE.
(J. STENZEL, ED)
R.P. BAREIKIS, 481(PQ):JUL72-715
KLEM, K. TOUCH THE SUN.
P. MORROW, 649(WAL):SUMMER72-155
KLEMKE, E.D., ED. ESSAYS ON WITTGEN-
STEIN.*
H. MOUNCE, 393(MIND):OCT72-618
W.M. RICHARDS, 484(PPR):SEP72-
VON KLEMPERER, K. IGNAZ SEIPEL.*
C.A. MACARTNEY, 32:JUN73-410
KLESSMANN, R. THE BERLIN GALLERY.
J. DANIELS, 135:NOV72-215
KLEVER, W.N.A. "ANAMNĒSIS" EN "AYA-
GŌGĒ."
P. SOMVILLE, 542:JAN-MAR72-53
KLIENEBERGER, H.R. THE CHRISTIAN
WRITERS OF THE INNER EMIGRATION.
E. FRIEDRICHSMEYER, 222(GR):MAY
72-238
KLIGMAN, R. LOVE AFFAIR.
M. ENGEL, 441:17MAR74-30
KLIMOV, G.A. DIE KAUKASISCHEN
SPRACHEN.*
M. JOB, 343:BAND15HEFT2-216
K.H. SCHMIDT, 260(IF):BAND77HEFT
1-154
KLINCK, R. DIE LATEINISCHE ETYMOLO-
GIE DES MITTELALTERS.*
M. SCHMIDT, 133:1972/2-203
KLINE, M. WHY JOHNNY CAN'T ADD.
441:10FEB74-29
KLINE, T.J. ANDRÉ MALRAUX & THE
METAMORPHOSIS OF DEATH.
639(VQR):AUTUMN73-CLIII
KLINEFELTER, W. LEWIS EVANS & HIS
MAPS.
W.P. CUMMING, 656(WMQ):APR73-366
KLINGENDER, F. ANIMALS IN ART &
THOUGHT TO THE END OF THE MIDDLE
AGES. (E. ANTAL & J. HARTHAN, EDS)
L. DE PAOR, 592:MAR72-133
290(JAAC):SUMMER72-569
KLOCKARS, C.B. THE PROFESSIONAL
FENCE.
T. PLATE, 441:8DEC74-3

KLONSKY, M. THE FABULOUS EGO.
A. BROYARD, 441:19NOV74-47
KLOSE, K. & P.A. MC COMBS. THE
TYPHOON SHIPMENTS.
N. CALLENDAR, 441:1SEP74-15
KLOSS, H. LES DROITS LINGUISTIQUES
DES FRANCO-AMÉRICAINS AUX ÉTATS-
UNIS.
M.R. MILLER, 351(LL):DEC73-277
KLOSSOWSKI DE ROLA, S. ALCHEMY.
D.J. ENRIGHT, 362:17JAN74-87
KLOTZ, V. DIE ERZÄHLTE STADT.
H. HERTING, 654(WB):10/1972-173
G. MÜLLER, 597(SN):VOL44#1-218
KLUGE, R., ED. LANCELOT.
C. MINIS, 433:OCT72-507
KLÜVER, B., J. MARTIN & B. ROSE,
EDS. EXPERIMENTS IN ART & TECH-
NOLOGY.
A. BERLEANT, 290(JAAC):SUMMER73-
567
KLYUCHEVSKY, V. THE RISE OF THE
ROMANOVS. (L. ARCHIBALD, WITH M.
SCHOLL, EDS & TRANS)
R.T. FISHER, JR., 32:JUN73-374
KNAPP, B.L. JEAN RACINE.*
A. AMOIA, 207(FR):DEC71-519
L. LE SAGE, 397(MD):MAY72-108
R.J. NELSON, 149:DEC73-408
R.W. TOBIN, 188(ECR):SPRING72-70
KNAPP, F.P. RENNEWART.
D.H. GREEN, 402(MLR):JAN73-218
C. LOFMARK, 220(GL&L):OCT72-81
KNAPP, G. MENSCH UND KRANKHEIT.
M. DE TOLLENAERE, 258:MAR72-148
KNAPP, J.G. TORTURED SYNTHESIS.
205(FMLS):JAN72-90
KNAPP, L.M. - SEE SMOLLETT, T.
KNAPP-TEPPERBERG, E-M. ROBERT CHAL-
LES "ILLUSTRES FRANÇOISES."*
G. HAINSWORTH, 208(FS):APR73-201
P. SCHUNCK, 224(GRM):BAND22HEFT1-
108
KNAPPERT, J., ED. AN ANTHOLOGY OF
SWAHILI LOVE POETRY.
639(VQR):AUTUMN72-CXXV
KNEALE, W. & M. THE DEVELOPMENT OF
LOGIC.
J. MYHILL, 53(AGP):BAND54HEFT3-
284
KNECHT, D., ED. CIRIS.
J. ANDRÉ, 555:VOL46FASC1-154
R.O.A.M. LYNE, 123:DEC73-168
KNEISSL, P. DIE SIEGESTITULATUR
DER RÖMISCHEN KAISER.
A.R. BIRLEY, 313:VOL62-195
"KNIGA: ISSLEDOVANIYA I MATERIALY."
(VOLS 22 & 23)
J.S.G. SIMMONS, 78(BC):AUTUMN72-
433
KNIGHT, C. JIMI.
J. ROCKWELL, 441:22DEC74-10
KNIGHT, D., ED. ORBIT 8.
617(TLS):23AUG74-911
KNIGHT, D.W. SOME STUDIES IN ATHEN-
IAN POLITICS IN THE FIFTH CENTURY
B.C.
E. WILL, 555:VOL46FASC1-117
KNIGHT, I.F. THE GEOMETRIC SPIRIT.
A. VARTANIAN, 546(RR):FEB72-49
KNIGHT, K.G., ED. DEUTSCHE ROMANE
DER BAROCKZEIT.*
W.F. SCHERER, 399(MLJ):FEB72-120
KNIGHT, R.C. - SEE RACINE, J.

KOHLS, E-W. LUTHERS ENTSCHEIDUNG IN
WORMS.
U. SIMON, 220(GL&L):JUL73-334
KOHNSTAMM, M. & W. HAGER, EDS. A
NATION WRIT LARGE?
617(TLS):10MAY74-498
KOHR, L. DEVELOPMENT WITHOUT AID.
M. LIPTON, 617(TLS):2AUG74-830
KOHT, H. LIFE OF IBSEN.* (E. HAUG-
EN & A.E. SANTANIELLO, EDS & TRANS)
L.A. MUINZER, 159(DM):AUTUMN71-
110
KOIZUMI, F., A. HOSHI & O. YAMAGUCHI,
EDS. NIHON ONGAKU TO SONO SHŪHEN.
R.K. WINSLOW, JR., 187:MAY74-306
KOJ, P. DIE FRÜHE REZEPTION DER
FAZETIEN POGGIOS IN FRANKREICH.
R. SCHWADERER, 52:BAND7HEFT1-85
KOJECKY, R. T.S. ELIOT'S SOCIAL
CRITICISM.*
A.J. KOPPENHAVER, 27(AL):MAY73-
308
W.W. ROBSON, 473(PR):WINTER73-
136
KOJÈVE, A. INTRODUCTION TO THE
READING OF HEGEL. (A. BLOOM, ED)
M. FOX, 154:SEP72-444
KŌJI, I. - SEE UNDER INADA KŌJI
KŌJI, I. & FUKUDA AKIRA - SEE UNDER
INADA KŌJI & FUKUDA AKIRA
KOJIMA, K. - SEE UNDER KIYOSHI KO-
JIMA
KOKOSCHKA, O. MY LIFE.
P. CAMPBELL, 362:30CT74-447
KOKOSCHKA, O. SAUL & DAVID.
617(TLS):4JAN74-18
"OSKAR KOKOSCHKA, LONDON VIEWS, BRIT-
ISH LANDSCAPES."
A. FRANKENSTEIN, 55:DEC73-35
KOLASKY, J. - SEE MOROZ, V.
KOLB, E. PHONOLOGICAL ATLAS OF THE
NORTHERN REGION.*
K. DIETZ, 38:BAND90HEFT3-372
KOLB, E., ED. VOM KAISERREICH ZUR
WEIMARER REPUBLIK.
F.T. EPSTEIN, 182:VOL25#13/14-
500
KOLB, E. & J. HASLER, EDS. FEST-
SCHRIFT RUDOLF STAMM.
E. EISENBACH, 430(NS):0CT72-616
KOLB, K. NIGHT CROSSING.
M. LEVIN, 441:24NOV74-40
KOLB, P. - SEE PROUST, M.
KOLENDA, K. IN DEFENSE OF PRACTICAL
REASON.
A.S.C., 543:MAR72-558
KOLINSKY, E. ENGAGIERTER EXPRESSION-
ISMUS.
J.M. RITCHIE, 220(GL&L):APR73-
257
KOLKO, G. THE POLITICS OF WAR.
H. HANAK, 575(SEER):JUL73-487
KOLKO, J. & G. THE LIMITS OF POWER.*
W.M. FRANKLIN, 639(VQR):AUTUMN72-
594
KOLNEDER, W. DAS BUCH DER VIOLINE.
C.D.S.F., 410(M&L):0CT73-487
KÖLVER, B. TULU TEXTS WITH GLOSSARY.
K. DE VREESE, 318(JAOS):APR-JUN
72-317
KOMAR, A. THEORY OF SUSPENSIONS.
J. ROTHGEB, 308:VOL16#1/2-210
KONEV, I. BELETRISTUT KARAVELOV.
C.A. MOSER, 104:SUMMER72-350

KONEVSKOY, I. SOBRANIYE SOCHINENIY.
G. DONCHIN, 575(SEER):APR73-328
KÖNIG, E. ADJECTIVAL CONSTRUCTION
IN ENGLISH & GERMAN.
C. JAMES, 399(MLJ):DEC72-510
KÖNIG, H. HEINRICH MANN.
H.B. GARLAND, 182:VOL25#21-742
U. WEISSTEIN, 301(JEGP):JUL73-
423
KÖNIG, R. THE RESTLESS IMAGE.
617(TLS):12APR74-384
KONIGSBERG, I., ED. THE CLASSIC
SHORT STORY.
D.B. KESTERSON, 573(SSF):FALL72-
412
KONIGSON, E. LA REPRÉSENTATION D'UN
MYSTÈRE DE LA PASSION À VALENCIEN-
NES EN 1547.
R. LEBÈGUE, 182:VOL25#9/10-288
KONING, H. DEATH OF A SCHOOLBOY.
P. ADAMS, 61:AUG74-91
M. TUCKER, 441:7APR74-30
442(NY):6MAY74-142
KONITZER, E. LARRA UND DER COSTUM-
BRISMO.
W. VOGT, 430(NS):0CT72-618
KONRAD, A.N. RUSSIA & BYZANTIUM.
W.F. RYAN, 575(SEER):APR73-307
KONRÁD, G. THE CASE WORKER.
N. ASCHERSON, 453:8AUG74-14
I. HOWE, 441:27JAN74-1
C. LEHMANN-HAUPT, 441:25JAN74-37
442(NY):11MAR74-134
KONRÁD, G. A LÁTOGATÓ.
P. VARNAI, 268:JAN74-57
KONVITZ, M.R., ED. JUDAISM & HUMAN
RIGHTS.
M.S. SHAPIRO, 287:MAY72-26
KONVITZ, M.R., ED. THE RECOGNITION
OF RALPH WALDO EMERSON.
639(VQR):WINTER73-XVIII
KOOL, F., ED. DIE LINKE GEGEN DIE
PARTEIHERRSCHAFT.
A. LASSERRE, 182:VOL25#5/6-183
KOOL, F. & E. OBERLÄNDER, EDS. AR-
BEITERDEMOKRATIE ODER PARTEIDIKTA-
TUR.
A. LASSERRE, 182:VOL25#5/6-181
KOONS, L.F. - SEE BRIFFAULT, R.
KOOPMANN, H. DAS JUNGE DEUTSCHLAND.
R. LEROY, 556(RLV):1972/4-445
C-P. MAGILL, 220(GL&L):APR73-249
J.L.S., 191(ELN):SEP72(SUPP)-151
J.L. SAMMONS, 221(GQ):NOV72-716
W.E. YUILL, 402(MLR):JAN73-230
KOOPS, W.R.H., E.H. KOSSMAN & G. VAN
DER PLAAT, EDS. JOHAN HUIZINGA
1872-1972.
P. BURKE, 617(TLS):13DEC74-1423
KOOSER, T. GRASS COUNTY.
H. GREGORY, 502(PRS):SPRING72-87
KOPCZYK, H. NIEMIECKA DZIAŁALNOŚĆ
WYWIADOWCZA NA POMORZU, 1920-1933.
R.A. WOYTAK, 32:MAR73-188
KÖPECZI, B. LA FRANCE ET LA HONGRIE
AU DÉBUT DU XVIIIE SIÈCLE.
M. BRAUBACH, 52:BAND7HEFT2/3-325
KOPPER, J. DIE METAPHYSIK MEISTER
ECKHARTS.
M. DE GANDILLAC, 542:JAN-MAR72-
86
KORDIG, C.R. THE JUSTIFICATION OF
SCIENTIFIC CHANGE.
W.R. SHEA, 154:SEP72-464

KORG, J. - SEE BROWNING, R.
KORN, F. BUENOS AIRES.
A. ANGELL, 617(TLS):13DEC74-1403
KÖRNER, S. KANT.
R. MALTER, 342:BAND63HEFT1-129
KÖRNER, S. WHAT IS PHILOSOPHY?*
H. SKOLIMOWSKI, 84:NOV72-366
KÖRNER, W.H. KATT IM GLÜCK.
617(TLS):2AUG74-839
KORNEXL, E. BEGRIFF UND EINSCHÄT-
ZUNG DER GESUNDHEIT DES KÖRPERS IN
DER GRIECHISCHEN LITERATUR VON
IHREN ANFÄNGEN BIS ZUM HELLENISMUS.
É. DES PLACES, 555:VOL46FASC2-
290
KORNWOLF, J.D. M.H. BAILLIE SCOTT &
THE ARTS & CRAFTS MOVEMENT.
D. ROBERTSON, 637(VS):JUN73-474
KOROLENKO, V.G. THE HISTORY OF MY
CONTEMPORARY. (TRANS & ABRIDGED
BY N. PARSONS)
R.H.W. THEEN, 32:JUN73-389
KORSHIN, P.J. FROM CONCORD TO DIS-
SENT.
617(TLS):8MAR74-235
KORSHIN, P.J., ED. STUDIES IN
CHANGE & REVOLUTION.*
566:SPRING73-111
KORT, W. ALFRED DÖBLIN.
J. DUYTSCHAEVER, 221(GQ):JAN72-
144
K. MÜLLER-SALGET, 680(ZDP):BAND
91HEFT2-295
A.W. RILEY, 564:MAR72-69
KORTEPETER, C.M. OTTOMAN IMPERIAL-
ISM DURING THE REFORMATION.*
S. FISCHER-GALATI, 32:JUN73-416
KORTSEN, B. FOUR UNKNOWN CANTATAS
BY GRIEG.
J. HORTON, 415:JUN73-603
KORTSEN, B. - SEE GRIEG, E.H.
KORZHAN, V.V. YESENIN I NARODNAYA
POEZIYA.
G. MC VAY, 402(MLR):JUL73-717
KOS-RABCEWICZ-ZUBKOWSKI, L. EAST
EUROPEAN RULES ON THE VALIDITY OF
INTERNATIONAL COMMERCIAL ARBITRA-
TION AGREEMENTS.*
W.E. BUTLER, 104:SPRING72-185
KOSAČ-KRYVYNJUK, O. LESJA UKRAJINKA.
D. TSCHIŽEWSKIJ, 72:BAND21OHEFT
1/3-237
KOSHECHKIN, S. - SEE YESENIN, S.
KOSINSKI, J. THE DEVIL TREE.*
P. CRUTTWELL & F. WESTBURG,
249(HUDR):SUMMER73-419
E. ROVIT, 659:AUTUMN74-539
R. SALE, 418(MR):AUTUMN73-834
639(VQR):SUMMER73-CIV
KOSKENNIEMI, H. DER NOMINALE NUMER-
US IN DER SPRACHE UND IM STIL DES
CURTIUS RUFUS.
B. LÖFSTEDT, 260(IF):BAND76-293
P.G. WALSH, 123:MAR73-100
KOSKENNIEMI, I. REPETITIVE WORD
PAIRS IN OLD & EARLY MIDDLE ENG-
LISH PROSE.*
F.C. ROBINSON, 38:BAND90HEFT1/2-
166
KOSKOFF, D.E. JOSEPH P. KENNEDY.
M.F. NOLAN, 441:31MAR74-1
KOSMA, S.A. KEPHALAIA APO TĒN
CHRĒSE TOY EPITHETOY STON PINDARO.
D.C. INNES, 123:MAR73-84

KOSOK, H. SEAN O'CASEY.
G. ROHMANN, 38:BAND90HEFT4-553
KOSS, S.E. SIR JOHN BRUNNER.
K. TRACE, 637(VS):SEP71-98
KOSSOFF, A.D. & J. AMOR VÁZQUEZ, EDS.
HOMENAJE A WILLIAM L. FICHTER.
J. LOWE, 402(MLR):JUL73-668
KOST, K. MUSAIOS, "HERO UND LEAN-
DER."
G. GIANGRANDE, 123:DEC73-138
KOSTELANETZ, R., ED. JOHN CAGE.
R.T.B., 410(M&L):JAN73-92
KOSTELANETZ, R. THE END OF INTELLI-
GENT WRITING.
T. POWERS, 231:NOV74-97
R. SALE, 441:29DEC74-12
KÖSTER, P. - SEE MANLEY, M.D.
KOSTER, S. ANTIKE EPOSTHEORIEN.
J.B. HAINSWORTH, 123:DEC73-186
KOSTOF, S. CAVES OF GOD.
J. FOLDA, 32:SEP73-601
G. SHANE, 576:DEC72-335
KOTARSKA, J. POETYKA POPULARNEJ
LIRYKI MIŁOSNEJ XVII WIEKU W
POLSCE.
D. WELSH, 104:SUMMER72-344
KOTT, J. THE EATING OF THE GODS.*
J. BAYLEY, 362:21NOV74-681
B.H. FUSSELL, 249(HUDR):WINTER
73/74-753
H. LLOYD-JONES, 617(TLS):29NOV74-
1339
441:10FEB74-24
KOTZIN, M.C. DICKENS & THE FAIRY
TALE.
K.M. BRIGGS, 203:AUTUMN72-258
KOTZWINKLE, W. THE FAN MAN.
M. LEVIN, 441:10FEB74-8
F. PIKE, 617(TLS):22NOV74-1308
R. TODD, 61:MAY74-128
442(NY):25MAR74-142
KOTZWINKLE, W. NIGHTBOOK.
M. LEVIN, 441:17MAR74-38
KOUTAISSOFF, E. THE SOVIET UNION.
H.F. FIRESIDE, 550(RUSR):JAN72-
97
KOUTRAS, D.N. HĒ ENNOIA TOY PHŌTOS
EIS TĒN AISTHĒTIKEN TOY PLŌTINOY.
A.H. ARMSTRONG, 123:MAR73-91
KOVACCI, O. TENDENCIAS ACTUALES DE
LA GRAMÁTICA. (2ND ED)
N.P. SACKS, 263:APR-JUN73-213
KOWALCZYK, S. & OTHERS. ZARYS HIS-
TORII POLSKIEGO RUCHU LUDOWEGO.
(VOL 1)
D.E. PIENKOS, 32:JUN73-405
KOWZAN, T. LITTÉRATURE ET SPECTACLE
DANS LEURS RAPPORTS ESTHÉTIQUES,
THEMATIQUES ET SÉMIOLOGIQUES.*
M. CORVIN, 535(RHL):MAY-JUN72-
545
M. RIESER, 290(JAAC):SPRING72-
399
KOYAMA, F. THE HERITAGE OF JAPANESE
CERAMICS.
617(TLS):12JUL74-751
KOYRÉ, A. ETUDES GALILÉENNES.
E. NAMER, 542:JAN-MAR72-98
KOZIOL, H. GRUNDZÜGE DER GESCHICHTE
DER ENGLISCHEN SPRACHE.
H. WEINSTOCK, 38:BAND90HEFT1/2-
163

KREKIĆ, B. DUBROVNIK IN THE 14TH & 15TH CENTURIES.
  B.A. STOLZ, 32:JUN73-421
KREMEN, B. DATELINE: AMERICA.
  D. WAKEFIELD, 441:31MAR74-18
KREMER, K. GOTT UND WELT IN DER KLASSISCHEN METAPHYSIK.
  W.J. HOYE, 258:JUN72-295
KREMER-MARIETTI, A. WILHELM DILTHEY ET L'ANTHROPOLOGIE HISTORIQUE.
  C. LOCAS, 154:JUN72-302
KRENN, H. & K. MÜLLNER. BIBLIOGRAPHIE ZUR TRANSFORMATIONSGRAMMATIK.
  E.F.K. KOERNER, 343:BAND14HEFT1-7
KRESSING, H. MARRIED LIVES.
  R. BLYTHE, 362:13JUN74-777
  617(TLS):7JUN74-619
KRETSCHMAR, R.S., JR. & R. FOOR. THE POTENTIAL FOR JOINT VENTURES IN EASTERN EUROPE.
  J. WILCZYNSKI, 32:JUN73-400
KRETZENBACHER, L. KYNOKEPHALE DÄMONEN SÜDOSTEUROPÄISCHER VOLKSDICHTUNG.
  R. GRAMBO, 196:BAND13HEFT1/2-202
KREUDER, H-D. MILTON IN DEUTSCHLAND.
  M.K. TORBRUEGGE, 406:FALL73-325
KREUTZBERGER, M., ED. LEO BAECK INSTITUTE, NEW YORK: BIBLIOTHEK UND ARCHIV: KATALOG. (VOL 1)
  J. STRELKA, 222(GR):JAN72-57
KREUTZER, E. SPRACHE UND SPIEL IM "ULYSSES" VON JAMES JOYCE.
  K. SPINNER, 38:BAND9HEFT1/2-270
KREUTZER, H.J. DIE DICHTERISCHE ENTWICKLUNG HEINRICHS VON KLEIST.*
  R. KOESTER, 221(GQ):JAN72-141
KREUTZER, L. ALFRED DÖBLIN.
  J. DUYTSCHAEVER, 221(GQ):JAN72-144
  K. MÜLLER-SALGET, 680(ZDP):BAND91HEFT2-295
KREUTZER, L. HEINE UND DER KOMMUNISMUS.
  J.L.S., 191(ELN):SEP72(SUPP)-151
KREUZER, H. DIE BOHEME.
  G.P. KNAPP, 657(WW):MAR/APR72-142
KRIEGER, G. SCHÖNBERGS WERKE FÜR KLAVIER.
  E. BARKIN, 513:SPRING-SUMMER/FALL-WINTER71-344
KRIEGER, M. THE CLASSIC VISION.
  M.K. SPEARS, 191(ELN):JUN73-310
KRIM, S. YOU & ME.
  S. MALOFF, 441:13OCT74-16
KRISPYN, E. GÜNTER EICH.
  P. STEINER, 406:SUMMER73-177
KRISPYN, E. GEORG HEYM.
  T.J. CASEY, 220(GL&L):JUL73-325
  E. SPEIDEL, 447(N&Q):FEB72-66
KRISTENSSON, G. STUDIES ON MIDDLE ENGLISH TOPOGRAPHICAL TERMS.*
  H. VOITL, 72:BAND210HEFT1/3-177
KRISTENSSON, G. A SURVEY OF MIDDLE ENGLISH DIALECTS 1290-1350: THE SIX NORTHERN COUNTIES & LINCOLNSHIRE.
  H. WEINSTOCK, 224(GRM):BAND22HEFT4-448
KRISTEVA, J. LA RÉVOLUTION DU LANGAGE POÉTIQUE.
  J. CULLER, 617(TLS):30AUG74-934

KRISTEVA, J. LE TEXTE DU ROMAN.
  J. CULLER, 402(MLR):OCT73-900
  L.S. ROUDIEZ, 546(RR):FEB72-76
KROEBER, K. STYLES IN FICTIONAL STRUCTURE.*
  A.M. DUCKWORTH, 191(ELN):MAR73-233
  P. JENKINS, 541(RES):NOV72-514
  G. LEVINE, 637(VS):DEC71-245
KROETSCH, R. GONE INDIAN.
  G. STOW, 296:VOL3#1-93
KROHN, K. FOLKLORE METHODOLOGY FORMULATED BY JULIUS KROHN & EXPANDED BY NORDIC RESEARCHERS.
  M.E. BARRICK, 292(JAF):JUL-SEP72-288
KROHN, R. & OTHERS. ENGLISH SENTENCE STRUCTURE.
  P.J. ANGELIS, 608:JUN73-175
  C.W. KREIDLER, 399(MLJ):NOV72-467
KROLL, J. IN THE TEMPERATE ZONE.
  A. OSTRIKER, 441:17FEB74-7
KROLL, M. SOPHIE.
  617(TLS):18JAN74-56
KROLL, U. TM.
  617(TLS):16AUG74-876
KRÖMER, W. ZUR WELTANSCHAUUN, ÄSTHETIK UND POETIK DES NEOKLASSIZISMUS UND DER ROMANTIK IN SPANIEN.*
  J.H.R. POLT, 240(HR):WINTER72-96
KRONENBERGER, L. THE EXTRAORDINARY MR. WILKES.
  P. ADAMS, 61:MAR74-99
  C. LEHMANN-HAUPT, 441:8FEB74-29
  J.H. PLUMB, 441:10FEB74-4
  J. RICHARDSON, 231:MAR74-90
KRONHAUSEN, P. & E. EROTIC ART.
  M. YAFFE, 592:NOV72-202
KRÖNIG, W. IL DUOMO DI MONREALE E L'ARCHITETTURA NORMANNA IN SICILIA.
  D.T. RICE, 90:MAY72-338
KROOS, R. NIEDERSÄCHSISCHE BILDSTIKKEREIEN DES MITTELALTERS.
  L. VON WILCKENS, 683:BAND35HEFT4-307
KROPOTKIN, P.A. MEMOIRS OF A REVOLUTIONIST. (N. WALTER, ED)
  A.V. KNOWLES, 575(SEER):JAN73-140
KRÜGER, M.L. DIE RELIEFS DES STADTGEBIETES VON CARNUNTUM. (PT 1)
  J.M.C. TOYNBEE, 123:MAR73-72
KRÜGER-LÖWENSTEIN, U. RUSSLAND, FRANKREICH UND DAS REICH 1801-03.
  W. KIRCHNER, 182:VOL25#17/18-624
KRUMMEL, D.W. BIBLIOTHECA BOLDUANIANA.
  H.M. BROWN, 415:NOV73-1124
KRUTCH, J.W. HENRY DAVID THOREAU.
  441:10MAR74-32
KRZYŻANOWSKA, A. MONNAIES COLONIALES D'ANTIOCHE DE PISIDIE.
  A.S. ROBERTSON, 123:MAR73-109
KUBIAK, H. POLSKI NARODOWY KOSCIOL W STANACH ZJEDNOCZONYCH AMERYKI W LATACH 1897-1965.
  T.L. ZAWISTOWSKI, 497(POLR):WINTER72-95
KUBIJOVYČ, V., ED. UKRAINE, A CONCISE ENCYCLOPEDIA.* (VOL 2)
  Y. BILINSKY, 550(RUSR):APR72-194
  W. STOJKO, 497(POLR):SUMMER72-121

KUBIK, G. NATUREZA E ESTRATURA DE
ESCALAS MUSICAIS AFRICANAS. MUSI-
CA TRADICIONAL E ACULTURADA DOS
!KUNG DE ANGOLA.
A.M. JONES, 69:JAN72-82
KÜBLER-ROSS, E. QUESTIONS & ANSWERS
ON DEATH & DYING.
M.G. MICHAELSON, 441:21JUL74-6
KUBLIN, H., COMP. JEWS IN OLD CHINA.
STUDIES OF THE CHINESE JEWS.
D. LESLIE, 318(JAOS):OCT-DEC72-
584
KUBOVA, M. BIBLIOGRAFIA SLOVENSKEJ
ETNOGRAFIE A FOLKLORISTIKY ZA
ROKY 1960-1969.
B. GUNDA, 203:SPRING72-83
KUČERA, H. & W.N. FRANCIS. COMPUTA-
TIONAL ANALYSIS OF PRESENT-DAY
AMERICAN ENGLISH.*
B. GORODECKIJ, 353:JUN72-118
KUCHAREK, C. THE BYZANTINE-SLAV
LITURGY OF ST. JOHN CHRYSOSTOM.
J. MEYENDORFF, 32:SEP73-602
M.H. SHEPHERD, JR., 589:OCT73-
764
KUCHEROV, S. THE ORGANS OF SOVIET
ADMINISTRATION OF JUSTICE.
P.B. TAYLOR, 550(RUSR):APR72-182
KUCHLING, H. - SEE SCHLEMMER, O.
KUCZYŃSKI, A. SYBERYJSKIE SZLAKI.
S.D. WATROUS, 32:MAR73-164
KUDĚLKA, M. & Z. ŠIMEČEK, EDS. ČES-
KOSLOVENSKÉ PRÁCE O JAZYCE, DĚJIN-
ÁCH A KULTUŘE SLOVANSKÝCH NÁRODŮ
OD ROKU 1760.
O. JOSEK, 575(SEER):JUL73-462
KUGLER, M. DIE TASTENMUSIK IM CODEX
FAENZA.
J.A.C., 410(M&L):APR73-227
KUHL, E.P. STUDIES IN CHAUCER &
SHAKESPEARE.
G. STILLWELL, 481(PQ):APR72-491
KUHLMANN, C. SCHULREFORM UND GESELL-
SCHAFT IN DER BUNDESREPUBLIK
DEUTSCHLAND 1946-66.
E. SCHÜTTE, 182:VOL25#5/6-139
KUHLMANN, Q. DER KÜHLPSALTER. (R.L.
BEARE, ED)
F. VAN INGEN, 433:JAN72-108
KUHLMANN, S. KNAVE, FOOL, GENIUS.
617(TLS):8MAR74-235
KÜHLWEIN, W., ED. LINGUISTICS IN
GREAT BRITAIN. (VOL 1)
C. GAUVIN, 189(EA):OCT-DEC72-530
KÜHLWEIN, W., ED. LINGUISTICS IN
GREAT BRITAIN. (VOL 2)
C. GAUVIN, 189(EA):OCT-DEC72-530
E.F.K. KOERNER, 297(JL):SEP72-
342
KUHN, A., ED. POEMA DEL CID. (2ND
ED REV BY U. EHRGOTT)
S.G. ARMISTEAD, 545(RPH):AUG72-
208
KUHN, D. BIRD SONGS AT EVENTIDE.
H. FRANCIS, 157:WINTER72-83
KUHN, H. DAS ALTE ISLAND.*
T.M. ANDERSSON, 589:JAN73-157
E. ETTLINGER, 203:SUMMER72-170
KUHN, H. KLEINE SCHRIFTEN. (VOL 1)
(D. HOFMANN, WITH W. LANGE & K.
VON SEE, EDS)
J. GÖSCHEL, 260(IF):BAND76-319

KUHN, S.M. & J. REIDY, EDS. MIDDLE
ENGLISH DICTIONARY. (LETTER "H"
[5 PTS])
B.D.H. MILLER, 382(MAE):1973/1-
73
KÜHNEL, E. ISLAMIC ARTS.*
G. FEHÉRVÁRI, 39:JUN72-517
KUHNS, R. STRUCTURES OF EXPERIENCE.*
(BRITISH TITLE: LITERATURE & PHIL-
OSOPHY.)
M.A. CAWS, 188(ECR):WINTER72-318
A.W.J. HARPER, 154:MAR72-131
R.A. OAKES, 484(PPR):MAR73-433
D. WALSH, 479(PHQ):JAN72-93
M. WEITZ, 290(JAAC):SPRING72-405
KUIC, V. - SEE SIMON, Y.
KUIPERS, A.H. THE SQUAMISH LANGU-
AGE.* (VOLS 1&2)
B.S. EFRAT, 350:MAR73-235
K.C. KELLER, 353:1JUL72-113
KŪKAI. KŪKAI: MAJOR WORKS. (Y.S.
HAKEDA, ED & TRANS)
E. PUTZAR, 352(LE&W):VOL15#4&
VOL16#1/2-928
639(VQR):WINTER73-XXXII
KUKLICK, B. AMERICAN POLICY & THE
DIVISION OF GERMANY.
R.M. SLUSSER, 32:JUN73-393
KULKE, H. CIDAMBARAMĀHĀTMYA.
L. ROCHER, 318(JAOS):OCT-DEC72-
571
KÜLP, B. & W. SCHREIBER, EDS. AR-
BEITSÖKONOMIK.
K. MELLEROWICZ, 182:VOL25#15/16-
533
KULSKI, W.W. THE SOVIET UNION IN
WORLD AFFAIRS.
639(VQR):AUTUMN73-CLXIX
KULTERMANN, U. AFRICAN ARCHITECTURE.
R. BANHAM, 54:DEC72-565
KULTERMANN, U. ART EVENTS & HAPPEN-
INGS.
W. FEAVER, 364:FEB/MAR73-124
KULTERMANN, U. NEW REALISM.
W. FEAVER, 364:FEB/MAR73-124
C. NEMSER, 58:NOV72-90
KUMANIECKI, K. & OTHERS - SEE ERAS-
MUS
KUMAR, R., ED. ESSAYS ON GANDHIAN
POLITICS.
H. SPODEK, 293(JAST):MAY72-707
KUMARASWAMI RAJA, N. POST-NASAL
VOICELESS PLOSIVES IN DRAVIDIAN.
J.W. SCHUBERT, 350:MAR73-220
KUMIN, M. THE DESIGNATED HEIR.
A. BROYARD, 441:26JUN74-33
J. HOWARD, 441:23JUN74-10
KUMIN, M. UP COUNTRY.
639(VQR):SUMMER73-CXI
KUNCEWICZ, M. TRISTAN.
M. LEVIN, 441:3MAR74-28
KUNDERA, M. LAUGHABLE LOVES.
N. ASCHERSON, 453:8AUG74-14
A. BROYARD, 441:10AUG74-27
P. THEROUX, 441:28JUL74-7
KUNDERA, M. LIFE IS ELSEWHERE.
N. ASCHERSON, 453:8AUG74-14
P. THEROUX, 441:28JUL74-7
KUNDERA, M. RISIBLES AMOURS. LA
PLAISANTERIE.
A. LIEHM, 98:OCT72-841
KUNER, M.C. THORNTON WILDER.
J.T. FLANAGAN, 27(AL):MAR73-135

KÜNG, H. INFALLIBLE?*
  R.E. BROWN, 363:FEB72-72
KUNIO, Y. - SEE UNDER YANAGITA KUNIO
KUNISCH, H. HANDBUCH DER DEUTSCHEN
GEGENWARTSLITERATUR. (2ND ED)
  H. DENKLER, 221(GQ):MAR72-356
  W. SCHUMANN, 399(MLJ):NOV72-458
  T. ZIOLKOWSKI, 222(GR):MAY72-220
KUNITZ, S. THE TERRIBLE THRESHOLD.
  617(TLS):13SEP74-968
KUNITZ, S., WITH M. HAYWARD - SEE
AKHMATOVA, A.
KUNTZ, P.G. - SEE SANTAYANA, G.
KUNZ, H. BILDERSPRACHE ALS DASEIN-
SERSCHLIESSUNG.*
  F. WASSERMANN, 221(GQ):MAR72-362
KUNZ, J. DIE DEUTSCHE NOVELLE IM
19. JAHRHUNDERT.*
  D. LO CICERO, 221(GQ):NOV72-704
KUNZE, K. STUDIEN ZUR LEGENDE DER
HEILIGEN MARIA AEGYPTIACA IM
DEUTSCHEN SPRACHGEBIET.
  S.C. HARRIS, 220(GL&L):OCT72-82
KUO, L.T.C. THE TECHNICAL TRANSFOR-
MATION OF AGRICULTURE IN COMMUNIST
CHINA.
  293(JAST):AUG72-1001
KUO MING-K'UN. CHŪGOKU NO KAZOKUSEI
OYOBI GENGO NO KENKYŪ. (LI HSIEN-
CHANG, COMP)
  293(JAST):FEB72-470
KUO-T'AO, C. - SEE UNDER CHANG KUO-
T'AO
KUO-WEI, W. - SEE UNDER WANG KUO-WEI
KUPER, A. KALAHARI VILLAGE POLITICS.
  P.H. GULLIVER, 69:APR72-161
KUPER, Y. HOLY FOOLS IN MOSCOW.
  H.E. SALISBURY, 441:8JUN74-29
KUPER, Y. MOSCOW STILL LIFE.
  J. MILLER, 617(TLS):29NOV74-1336
KUPFERBERG, H. THE MENDELSSOHNS.
  S. CAIN, 390:OCT72-51
KUPFERBERG, T. & S. TOPP. AS THEY
WERE.
  S. SONTAG, 453:18APR74-17
KÜPPER, P. - SEE MILCH, W.
KUPPERMAN, J.J. ETHICAL KNOWLEDGE.*
  M.M. AHMAD, 185:JUL73-346
  M. SCHUMAKER, 529(QQ):AUTUMN72-
412
  R.K. SHOPE, 311(JP):31JAN74-46
KURASZKIEWICZ, W., ED. WYRAZY POL-
SKIE W SŁOWNIKU ŁACIŃSKO-POLSKIM
JANA MĄCZYŃSKIEGO.
  H. RÖSEL, 182:VOL25#19/20-660
KURIHARA, K.K. THE GROWTH POTENTIAL
OF THE JAPANESE ECONOMY.
  M. BRONFENBRENNER, 293(JAST):
FEB72-412
KURIYAGAWA, F., ED. THE MIDDLE ENG-
LISH ST. BRENDAN'S CONFESSION &
PRAYER.
  J.R. SIMON, 189(EA):JAN-MAR72-87
KURLANSKY, M. & J. NAAR. THE FAITH
OF GRAFFITI. (BRITISH TITLE:
WATCHING MY NAME GO BY.) (TEXT BY
N. MAILER)
  A. BROYARD, 441:1MAY74-49
  C. ROBINS, 441:5MAY74-51
  617(TLS):21JUN74-655
KURMANN, P. LA CATHÉDRALE SAINT-
ÉTIENNE DE MEAUX.
  C.F. BARNES, JR., 54:MAR72-84

KURSCHAT, A. LITAUISCH-DEUTSCHES
WÖRTERBUCH. (VOLS 2&3)
  V. RUKE-DRAVINA, 182:VOL25#11-
356
KURTÉN, B. NOT FROM THE APES.
  639(VQR):SPRING72-LXXVI
KURTZ, S.A. WASTELAND.
  P. GOLDBERGER, 441:7JUL74-5
KURTZ, S.G. & J.H. HUTSON, EDS.
ESSAYS ON THE AMERICAN REVOLUTION.
  639(VQR):SPRING73-LXXXII
KURTZMAN, J. SWEET BOBBY.
  M. LEVIN, 441:24FEB74-39
KURYŁOWICZ, J. INDOGERMANISCHE
GRAMMATIK.* (VOL 2)
  R. ANTTILA, 343:BAND15HEFT1-37
KURYŁOWICZ, J. DIE SPRACHLICHEN
GRUNDLAGEN DER ALTGERMANISCHEN
METRIK.
  A.J. BLISS, 38:BAND90HEFT4-510
KURYŁOWICZ, J. - SEE WATKINS, C.
KURZ, R. LETHAL GAS.
  N. CALLENDAR, 441:15DEC74-10
KUSCH, E. PERU IM BILD.
  L.S. THOMPSON, 263:OCT-DEC73-453
KUSENBERG, K. THE SUNFLOWERS.
  E. FEINSTEIN, 364:AUG/SEP72-157
KUSHEV, E. OGRYZKOM KARANDASHA.
  H. ERMOLAEV, 550(RUSR):JUL72-304
KUSIN, V. THE INTELLECTUAL ORIGINS
OF THE PRAGUE SPRING.
  D. VINEY, 575(SEER):JAN73-145
KUSIN, V.V. POLITICAL GROUPING IN
THE CZECHOSLOVAK REFORM MOVEMENT.*
  J.P. SHAPIRO, 32:DEC73-837
KUSS, O. PAULUS.
  F.F. BRUCE, 182:VOL25#5/6-147
KUTATELADZE, L. - SEE STRAVINSKY, I.
KUUSINEN, A. BEFORE & AFTER STALIN.
  617(TLS):16AUG74-887
KUXDORF, M. DIE SUCHE NACH DEM
MENSCHEN IM DRAMA GEORG KAISERS.*
  H. HESS, 654(WB):11/1972-169
  I. SCHUSTER, 564:MAR72-73
KUZMA, G. GOOD NEWS.
  V. YOUNG, 249(HUDR):WINTER73/74-
721
KUZMA, G. SONG FOR SOMEONE GOING
AWAY.
  E. LICHTENBERG, 114(CHIR):VOL23
#4&VOL24#1-212
  D.E. RICHARDSON, 598(SOR):WINTER
74-225
KUZNETSOV, I. WEST-EUROPEAN STILL-
LIFE PAINTING IN RUSSIAN COLLEC-
TIONS.
  T. CROMBIE, 39:JUL72-87
KUZNETSOVA, N.A. & L.M. KULAGINA.
IZ ISTORII SOVETSKOVO VOSTOKOVE-
DENIYA.
  D.N. JACOBS, 293(JAST):NOV71-174
KVIDELAND, R., ED. PRINSESSENE SOM
DANSA I ÅKEREN. KONGSDOTTERA I
KOPPARTÅRNET.
  B. HOLBEK, 196:BAND13HEFT1/2-192
KWEI, C-G. THE KUOMINTANG-COMMUNIST
STRUGGLE IN CHINA 1922-1949.
  R.H. YANG, 396(MODA):SPRING73-
216
KWILECKA, I., ED. PERYKOPY WIELKO-
POSTNE W PRZEKŁADZIE TOMASZA ŁY-
SEGO ZE ZBRUDZEWA.
  H. RÖSEL, 182:VOL25#12-390

LAGRAVE, H. MARIVAUX ET SA FORTUNE
LITTÉRAIRE.*
O. HAAC, 207(FR):APR72-1059
H.T. MASON, 208(FS):JUL73-331
LA GUMA, A. IN THE FOG OF THE
SEASON'S END.
J. UPDIKE, 442(NY):21JAN74-89
LAHR, J. ACTING OUT AMERICA.
A. SEYMOUR, 364:DEC72/JAN73-127
LAHR, J. ASTONISH ME.
B.H. FUSSELL, 249(HUDR):WINTER
73/74-753
LAHR, J. HOT TO TROT.
A. BROYARD, 441:21NOV74-51
G. LYONS, 441:15DEC74-26
LAIDMAN, H. THE COMPLETE BOOK OF
DRAWING & PAINTING.
617(TLS):12APR74-401
LAÍN ENTRALGO, P. MALADIE ET CULPA-
BILITÉ.
M. ADAM, 542:OCT-DEC72-464
LAÍN ENTRALGO, P. THE THERAPY OF
THE WORD IN CLASSICAL ANTIQUITY.
(L.J. RATHER & J.M. SHARP, EDS &
TRANS)
E.D. PHILLIPS, 123:MAR73-95
LAING, A. SEAFARING AMERICA.
I.R. DEE, 441:1DEC74-12
LAING, R.D. & D.G. COOPER. REASON
& VIOLENCE. (FRENCH TITLE: RAISON
ET VIOLENCE.) (2ND ED)
G. BRYKMAN, 542:OCT-DEC72-466
P. TROTIGNON, 542:OCT-DEC72-465
LAIRD, M.A. - SEE HEBER, R.
LAIRD, R.D. THE SOVIET PARADIGM.
J.G. GREENSLADE, 104:SPRING72-
169
LAKATOS, I., ED. THE PROBLEM OF
INDUCTIVE LOGIC.
A.C. MICHALOS, 486:MAR72-90
LAKATOS, I. & A. MUSGRAVE, EDS.
CRITICISM & THE GROWTH OF KNOWL-
EDGE.*
H. LEHMAN, 486:MAR72-92
J.J.C. SMART, 84:AUG72-266
LAKOFF, R.T. ABSTRACT SYNTAX &
LATIN COMPLEMENTATION.*
W. BOEDER, 343:BAND15HEFT1-24
D.H. KELLY, 215(GL):VOL12#2-106
LALLY, M. SOUTH ORANGE SONNETS.
G. BURNS, 584(SWR):SUMMER73-278
LALONDE, R. LES CONTES DU PORTAGE.
R. WILLMOT, 296:VOL3#3-112
LAMANNA, E.P. LA RELIGIONE NELLA
VITA DELLO SPIRITO. (2ND ED)
(D. PESCE & A. SCIVOLETTO, EDS)
B.M.B., 543:MAR72-559
DE LAMARTINE, A.M.L.D. LE LIVRE DU
CENTENAIRE. (P. VIALLANEIX, ED)
M. SCHAETTEL, 557(RSH):JUL-SEP72-
454
"LAMARTINE: LE POÈTE ET L'HOMME
D'ÉTAT."
A.J. STEELE, 208(FS):JUL73-342
DE LA MAZIÈRE, C. THE CAPTIVE
DREAMER.
442(NY):19AUG74-90
LAMB, A. LA ESTILÍSTICA APLICADA.
E.R. MULVIHILL, 399(MLJ):NOV72-
456
LAMB, A. THE MANDARIN ROAD TO OLD
HUÉ.
J.F. CADY, 293(JAST):NOV71-229

LAMB, G. PEASANT POLITICS.
617(TLS):30AUG74-926
LAMB, K.A. AS ORANGE GOES.
R. REEVES, 441:15SEP74-6
LAMB, W.K. - SEE MACKENZIE, A.
LAMBERT, A. TU ME FAIS CHAUD.
M. CRANSTON, 207(FR):OCT71-207
LAMBERT, D. THE YERMAKOV TRANSFER.
N. CALLENDAR, 441:27OCT74-56
LAMBERT, F. - SEE HUGO, V.
LAMBERT, H.M. GUJARATI LANGUAGE
COURSE.
L. DEROY, 556(RLV):1972/3-335
LAMBERT, J. & J. PEARSON. ADVENTURE
PLAYGROUNDS.
617(TLS):5JUL74-731
LAMBERT, K. & G.G. BRITTAN, JR. AN
INTRODUCTION TO THE PHILOSOPHY OF
SCIENCE.*
G.J. MASSEY, 486:DEC72-561
LAMBERT, S. BILLS & ACTS.*
H.L. SNYDER, 481(PQ):JUL72-538
LAMBERT, W.E. & G.R. TUCKER. BILIN-
GUAL EDUCATION OF CHILDREN.
B. SPOLSKY, 608:SEP73-321
LAMBERTS, J.J. A SHORT INTRODUCTION
TO ENGLISH USAGE.
T. PYLES, 35(AS):FALL-WINTER70-
252
LAMBRECHTS, R. LES INSCRIPTIONS
AVEC LE MOT "TULAR" ET LE BORNAGE
ÉTRUSQUE.
A. HUS, 555:VOL46FASC1-142
LAMBRICK, H.T. SIND BEFORE THE MUS-
LIM CONQUEST. (VOL 2)
617(TLS):31MAY74-592
LAME DEER, J. & R. ERDOES. LAME
DEER, SEEKER OF VISIONS.*
J.E. CHAMBERLIN, 249(HUDR):WIN-
TER73/74-786
LAMÉRAND, R. SYNTAXE TRANSFORMATION-
NELLE DES PROPOSITIONS HYPOTHÉ-
TIQUES DU FRANÇAIS PARLÉ.*
H. BONNARD, 209(FM):JAN72-71
LAMM, M. AUGUST STRINDBERG.* (H.G.
CARLSON, ED & TRANS)
E. SPRINCHORN, 397(MD):SEP72-209
LAMMER, J. THE RHEINHOLD BOOK OF
NEEDLECRAFT.
L.J. GARTNER, JR., 441:8DEC74-50
LÄMMERT, E. REIMSPRECHERKUNST IM
SPÄTMITTELALTER.
P. KERN, 680(ZDP):BAND91HEFT3-
463
LAMMICH, S. DAS SOZIALISTISCHE PAR-
LAMENT POLENS.
A. KORBONSKI, 32:SEP73-636
LAMMING, G. WATER WITH BERRIES.
NATIVES OF MY PERSON.
M. COOKE, 676(YR):SUMMER73-616
LAMONT, C. - SEE AUSTEN, J.
L'AMOUR, L. SACKETT'S LAND.
M. LEVIN, 441:24NOV74-40
LAMPERT, E. SONS AGAINST FATHERS.
M. MATTMÜLLER, 182:VOL25#19/20-
689
LAMPL, P. CITIES & PLANNING IN THE
ANCIENT NEAR EAST.
G.L. HERSEY, 56:SUMMER72-180
LANATA, G. POETICA PRE-PLATONICA,
TESTIMONIANZE E FRAMMENTI.
P. SOMVILLE, 542:JAN-MAR72-33

LANCASTER BROWN, P. COMETS, METEOR-
ITES & MEN.
617(TLS):4JAN74-18
LANCE, A. LES GENS PERDUS DEVIEN-
NENT FRAGILES.
E. MARKS, 207(FR):OCT71-208
LANCOUR, H., A. KENT & W.Z. NASRI,
EDS. ENCYCLOPEDIA OF LIBRARY SCI-
ENCE & INFORMATION RETRIEVAL.
(VOLS 4&5)
H.C. WOODBRIDGE, 517(PBSA):JAN-
MAR73-81
LAND, S.K. FROM SIGNS TO PROPOSI-
TIONS.
L.J. COHEN, 617(TLS):11OCT74-
1136
"LAND OF THE REED PLAINS." (K. YAS-
UDA, TRANS)
A. CHAMBERS, 352(LE&W):VOL15#4&
VOL16#1/2-921
LANDAU, D. KISSINGER.
617(TLS):5APR74-356
LANDAU, J.M. JEWS IN NINETEENTH-
CENTURY EGYPT.
A.A. KUDSI-ZADEH, 318(JAOS):JAN-
MAR72-126
LANDAUER, C. GERMANY.
H. RIDLEY, 220(GL&L):OCT72-73
LANDAY, J.M. SILENT CITIES, SACRED
STONES.
E.M. GEINZER, 363:MAY72-110
LANDESMAN, C. DISCOURSE & ITS PRE-
SUPPOSITIONS.
M. DURRANT, 518:MAY73-12
LANDESS, T.H. - SEE GORDON, C.
LANDOLT, E. GELASSENHEIT DE M. HEI-
DEGGER.
A.M., 543:JUN72-761
LANDON, H.C.R. HAYDN.
R. HUGHES, 415:JUN73-601
LANDOW, G.P. THE AESTHETIC & CRITI-
CAL THEORIES OF JOHN RUSKIN.*
Q. BELL, 90:NOV72-799
J.L. BRADLEY, 637(VS):DEC71-236
V.A. BURD, 290(JAAC):SPRING72-
405
F.G. TOWNSEND, 405(MP):FEB73-273
LANDSBERG, M. DOS PASSOS' PATH TO
"U.S.A."*
B. GELFANT, 27(AL):JAN74-621
"LANDSEER."
617(TLS):12APR74-386
LANDSTRÖM, B. SAILING SHIPS.
G. WILLS, 39:MAR72-231
LANDWEHR, J. EMBLEM BOOKS IN THE
LOW COUNTRIES, 1554-1949.
D.W. EVANS, 354:JUN72-150
LANDWEHR, J. GERMAN EMBLEM BOOKS
1531-1888.
E. ZIMMERMANN, 182:VOL25#7/8-195
LANDWEHRMANN, F. INDUSTRIELLE FÜH-
RUNG UNTER FORTSCHREITENDER AUTO-
MATISIERUNG.
A. HÜFNER, 182:VOL25#15/16-535
LANE, F.C. VENICE.
J.H. ELLIOTT, 453:16MAY74-20
J.H. PLUMB, 441:20JAN74-7
LANE, P. BEWARE THE MONTHS OF FIRE.
L. HICKS, 99:MAY/JUN74-20
LANG, B. & F. WILLIAMS, EDS. MARX-
ISM & ART.
D. PECK, 418(MR):SUMMER73-640

LANG, D.M., ED. GUIDE TO EASTERN
LITERATURES.
F. RICHTER, 293(JAST):MAY72-633
VON LANG, J. - SEE HOFFMAN, H. & H.
PICKER
LANG, P.H., ED. THE CREATIVE WORLD
OF BEETHOVEN.
M. PETERSON, 470:MAY72-32
LANG, P.H. THE EXPERIENCE OF OPERA.*
A. JACOBS, 415:JUL73-701
M.F.R., 410(M&L):JUL73-340
LANG, T. THE WORD & THE SWORD.
J. KEATES, 617(TLS):27DEC74-1466
LANG, W. PROBLEME DER ALLGEMEINEN
SPRACHTHEORIE.
F. HUNDSNURSCHER, 353:15DEC72-
110
LANGBAUM, R. THE MODERN SPIRIT.*
P. VEYRIRAS, 189(EA):APR-JUN72-
339
LANGBEIN, J.H. PROSECUTING CRIME IN
THE RENAISSANCE.
G.R. ELTON, 617(TLS):20SEP74-991
LANGDON, M. A GRAMMAR OF DIEGUEÑO,
THE MESA GRANDE DIALECT.
J.M. CRAWFORD, 361:VOL30#1-88
LANGE, D.L., ED. BRITANNICA REVIEW
OF FOREIGN LANGUAGE EDUCATION.*
(VOL 2)
H. LEDERER, 221(GQ):JAN72-199
D.C. SHEPPARD, 399(MLJ):APR72-
246
LANGE, H. DIE REVOLUTION ALS GEIS-
TERSCHIFF.
617(TLS):25OCT74-1188
LANGE, J. THE COGNITIVITY PARADOX.*
W.G. BYWATER, JR., 484(PPR):
SEP72-137
LANGE, J. - SEE LEWIS, C.I.
LANGE, M. A BEACH IN SPAIN.
E. GLOVER, 565:VOL13#2-65
LANGE, O. PAPERS IN ECONOMICS & SOC-
IOLOGY, 1930-1960. (P.F. KNIGHTS-
FIELD, ED & TRANS)
F. GROSS, 32:MAR73-134
A. ZAUBERMAN, 497(POLR):SUMMER72-
101
LANGE, O. & A. BANASIŃSKI. INTRODUC-
TION TO ECONOMIC CYBERNETICS.
A. ZAUBERMAN, 497(POLR):SUMMER72-
101
LANGE, W-D. EL FRAILE TROBADOR.
D. BRIESEMEISTER, 72:BAND210
HEFT4/6-462
LANGELLIER, A. & A.N. LEVY. CE
MONDE DES FRANÇAIS.
P. ARSENAULT, 207(FR):FEB72-766
LANGENDOEN, D.T. ESSENTIALS OF ENG-
LISH GRAMMAR.*
J.K. CHAMBERS, 320(CJL):SPRING71-
113
LANGENDOEN, D.T. THE LONDON SCHOOL
OF LINGUISTICS.*
J. KRÁMSKÝ, 353:JAN72-58
LANGENDOEN, D.T. THE STUDY OF SYN-
TAX.*
J.K. CHAMBERS, 320(CJL):SPRING71-
113
J.M. SADOCK, 269(IJAL):JUL72-209
"LANGENSCHEIDT'S ENCYCLOPAEDIC DIC-
TIONARY OF THE ENGLISH & GERMAN
LANGUAGES." (PT 2, VOL 1) (O.
SPRINGER, ED)
G.P. BUTLER, 617(TLS):8NOV74-
1262

VON LANGENSTEIN, H. ERCHANTNUZZ DER
SUND. (R. RAINER, ED)
A. VAN DER LEE, 433:APR72-234
VON LANGENSTEIN, H. ERCHANTNUZZ DER
SUND.* (P.R. RUDOLF, ED)
A. VAN DER LEE, 433:OCT72-511
LANGER, P.F. & J.J. ZASLOFF. NORTH
VIETNAM & THE PATHET LAO.
J. BADGLEY, 293(JAST):NOV71-232
LANGGUTH, A.J. MARKSMAN.
N. CALLENDAR, 441:28JUL74-14
LANGHORNE, E. NANCY ASTOR & HER
FRIENDS.
E. WEEKS, 61:MAY74-136
617(TLS):11OCT74-1143
LANGLAND, W. PIERS PLOWMAN. (J.A.W.
BENNETT, ED)
617(TLS):4JAN74-9
LANGO, J.W. WHITEHEAD'S ONTOLOGY.
W. MAYS, 518:OCT73-16
LANGONE, J. VITAL SIGNS.
M.G. MICHAELSON, 441:21JUL74-6
LANGOSCH, K. LYRISCHE ANTHOLOGIE
DES LATEINISCHEN MITTELALTERS, MIT
DEUTSCHEN VERSEN.
H. NAUMANN, 680(ZDP):BAND91HEFT3-
438
LANGOSCH, K., ED. MITTELLATEINISCHE
DICHTUNG.
H. NAUMANN, 680(ZDP):BAND91HEFT3-
434
LANGOSCH, K., ED. MITTELLATEINIS-
CHES JAHRBUCH. (VOLS 5&6)
R. DÜCHTING, 680(ZDP):BAND91HEFT
3-436
LANHAM, R.A. A HANDLIST OF RHETORI-
CAL TERMS.*
A.E. DOUGLAS, 123:MAR73-99
M.E. GILES, 545(RPH):MAY73-743
LANHAM, R.A. STYLE.
T. BERNSTEIN, 441:25AUG74-28
J. RICHARDSON, 231:APR74-94
LANING, E. THE SKETCHBOOKS OF REGI-
NALD MARSH.
H. ROSENBERG, 442(NY):13MAY74-
155
LANLY, A. - SEE VILLON, F.
"L'ANNÉE BALZACIENNE 1970."*
J. DECOTTIGNIES, 557(RSH):JUL-
SEP72-471
"L'ANNÉE PHILOLOGIQUE." (VOL 39)
A. ERNOUT, 555:VOL46FASC1-170
"L'ANNÉE PHILOLOGIQUE." (VOL 40)
A. ERNOUT, 555:VOL46FASC2-360
LANNING, J.T. PEDRO DE LA TORRE.
617(TLS):30AUG74-924
LANSBURY, C. ARCADY IN AUSTRALIA.
T.I. MOORE, 381:MAR72-99
D.H. SIMPSON, 155:MAY72-119
G.B. TENNYSON, 445(NCF):JUN72-
117
LANTÉRI-LAURA, G. LA PSYCHIATRIE
PHÉNOMÉNOLOGIQUE.
C. BARDET, 542:OCT-DEC72-467
LANTZEFF, G.V. & R.A. PIERCE. EAST-
WARD TO EMPIRE.
617(TLS):24MAY74-550
LANZA, D. & M. VEGETTI - SEE ARIS-
TOTLE
LAO SHE. CAT COUNTRY.* (A. LYELL,
JR., TRANS)
M. LOI, 549(RLC):OCT-DEC72-620
LAPASSADE, G. L'ENTRÉE DANS LA VIE.
L. ARÉNILLA, 542:OCT-DEC72-468

LAPATINE, K.A. THE TRIALS & TRIBU-
LATIONS OF AARON AMSTED.
M. LEVIN, 441:23JUN74-34
LAPIDUS, I.M., ED. MIDDLE EASTERN
CITIES.
R.S. HUMPHREYS, 318(JAOS):JAN-
MAR72-119
LAPLANCHE, J. HÖLDERLIN ET LA QUES-
TION DU PÈRE.
C. BARDET, 542:OCT-DEC72-470
LAPOINTE, C. SUR UNE ÉTUDE PROBABIL-
ISTE EN THÉORIE DE LA GRAMMAIRE EN
CHAÎNES DU FRANÇAIS.
W. ZWANENBURG, 206:JAN73-403
LAPORTA, R.L. LA LIBERTÀ NEL PEN-
SIERO DI VINCENZO CUOCO.
E. NAMER, 542:JUL-SEP72-346
LAPORTE, J. LA DOCTRINE DE PORT-
ROYAL. (PTS 2&3)
J-F. THOMAS, 542:APR-JUN72-221
LAPORTE, R. FUGUE.
J-N. VUARNET, 98:MAY72-430
LAPP, J.C. THE ESTHETICS OF NEGLI-
GENCE.*
F.S. HOWARD, 188(ECR):SUMMER72-
147
J. MARMIER, 535(RHL):JUL-AUG72-
711
H. MYDLARSKI, 149:DEC73-407
P.A. WADSWORTH, 207(FR):MAR72-
924
LAPPE, C. STUDIEN ZUM WORTSCHATZ
EMPFINDSAMER PROSA.
J. WHITON, 564:JUN72-140
LAPPÉ, F.M. DIET FOR A SMALL PLANET.
D. ZWERDLING, 453:21FEB74-22
LAQUEUR, W. CONFRONTATION.
617(TLS):12JUL74-740
LAQUEUR, W. A HISTORY OF ZIONISM.*
B. HALPERN, 390:DEC72-63
LAQUEUR, W. THE STRUGGLE FOR THE
MIDDLE EAST.
C.D. SMITH, 318(JAOS):APR-JUN72-
383
LAQUEUR, W. WEIMAR.
J. JOLL, 617(TLS):25OCT74-1185
LAQUIAN, A.A. SLUMS ARE FOR PEOPLE.
W.F. ARCE, 293(JAST):MAY72-748
LARDNER, R. THE BEST SHORT STORIES
OF RING LARDNER.
J. BRESLIN, 441:14APR74-8
LARDNER, R., JR. THE ECSTASY OF
OWEN MUIR.
42(AR):VOL32#4-696
LARGEAULT, J. LOGIQUE ET PHILOSO-
PHIE CHEZ FREGE.*
N. LACHARITÉ, 154:SEP72-456
LARKIN, D., ED. THE FANTASTIC KING-
DOM.
M.F. O'CONNELL, 441:8DEC74-48
LARKIN, J.F. & P.L. HUGHES, EDS.
STUART ROYAL PROCLAMATIONS. (VOL
1)
617(TLS):22MAR74-280
LARKIN, M. CHURCH & STATE AFTER THE
DREYFUS AFFAIR.
M. RICHARDS, 617(TLS):22NOV74-
1322
LARKIN, P. HIGH WINDOWS.
J. BAYLEY, 617(TLS):21JUN74-653
P. BEER, 362:6JUN74-742

LARKIN, P., ED. THE OXFORD BOOK OF
TWENTIETH-CENTURY ENGLISH VERSE.*
W.H. PRITCHARD, 249(HUDR):AUTUMN
73-588
639(VQR):AUTUMN73-CXLII
LARN, R. DEVON SHIPWRECKS.
617(TLS):11OCT74-1143
LARNER, J. CULTURE & SOCIETY IN
ITALY, 1290-1420.
D. HERLIHY, 589:APR73-375
LA ROCHELLE, P.D. - SEE DRIEU LA
ROCHELLE, P.
LAROUI, A. LA CRISE DES INTELLEC-
TUELS ARABES.
617(TLS):5APR74-356
LARSON, G.J. CLASSICAL SĀMKHYA.*
K.N. UPADHYAYA, 485(PE&W):JUL72-
333
LARTÉGUY, J. LES LIBERTADORS.
D. O'CONNELL, 207(FR):OCT71-209
LARTIGUE, J.H. LES FEMMES.
S. SCHWARTZ, 441:1DEC74-101
LARY, N.M. DOSTOEVSKY & DICKENS.*
D.H. STEWART, 651(WHR):AUTUMN73-
418
LASCELLES, M. - SEE JOHNSON, S.
LASKI, A. NIGHT MUSIC.
617(TLS):5APR74-357
LASKY, J.L., JR. WHATEVER HAPPENED
TO HOLLYWOOD?
M. WOOD, 453:31OCT74-39
LASOCKI, A-M. SIMONE DE BEAUVOIR OU
L'ENTREPRISE D'ÉCRIRE.
R. GOLDTHORPE, 208(FS):OCT73-479
Z. TAKACS, 182:VOL25#1/2-37
LAST, R.W., ED. AFFINITIES.
K. BULLIVANT, 402(MLR):JUL73-713
R.H. FARQUHARSON, 564:OCT72-219
"THE LAST POETS OF IMPERIAL ROME."
(H. ISBELL, TRANS)
A.W. GODFREY, 363:MAY72-106
DE LA TAILLE, J. JEAN DE LA TAILLE,
DRAMATIC WORKS. (K.M. HALL & C.N.
SMITH, EDS)
E.C. FORSYTH, 67:NOV73-302
LATHAM, A. CRAZY SUNDAYS.
L. CASPER, 613:SPRING72-130
A. MASSIE, 364:DEC72/JAN73-149
H.A. WYCHERLEY, 70(ANQ):MAY/JUN
74-170
LATHAM, R. & W. MATTHEWS - SEE PEPYS,
S.
LATHEM, E.C. & L. THOMPSON - SEE
FROST, R.
LATHEN, E. DEATH SHALL OVERCOME.
N. CALLENDAR, 441:10NOV74-45
LATHEN, E. SWEET & LOW.
N. CALLENDAR, 441:22SEP74-41
442(NY):9SEP74-135
617(TLS):20DEC74-1437
LATHUILLÈRE, R. "GUIRON LE COUR-
TOIS."
J.L. GRIGSBY, 545(RPH):MAY73-726
"LATINITAS."
A. ERNOUT, 555:VOL46FASC2-361
LATO, S. & W. STANKIEWICZ, EDS. PRO-
GRAMY STRONNICTW LUDOWYCH.
D.E. PIENKOS, 32:JUN73-405
DE LA TOUR DU PIN, P. PSAUMES DE
TOUS MES TEMPS.
617(TLS):19JUL74-771
LA TOURRETTE, J. THE MADONNA CREEK
WITCH.
M. LEVIN, 441:20JAN74-24

LATTIMORE, R. POEMS FROM THREE
DECADES.*
R. PEVEAR, 249(HUDR):SPRING73-
192
639(VQR):SPRING73-LXI
LAU, D.C. - SEE "MENCIUS"
LAUBE, H.L. HOW TO HAVE AIR CONDI-
TIONING & STILL BE COMFORTABLE.
W.J. MC GUINNESS, 505:APR72-140
"L'AUBRAC." (VOL 2)
P. VOSSELER, 182:VOL25#19/20-695
LAUDE, J. THE ARTS OF BLACK AFRICA.*
J.L. LEAHY, 290(JAAC):FALL72-136
LAUER, Q. HEGEL'S IDEA OF PHILOSO-
PHY.
J.E. SMITH, 613:AUTUMN72-468
W.H. WERKMEISTER, 319:JAN74-125
LAUFER, R. LESAGE OU LE MÉTIER DU
ROMANCIER.
A. CIORANESCU, 549(RLC):APR-JUN
72-300
J.S. SPINK, 208(FS):JAN73-66
LAUFER, R. - SEE LESAGE, A-R.
LAUFHÜTTE, H. WIRKLICHKEIT UND
KUNST IN GOTTFRIED KELLERS ROMAN
"DER GRÜNE HEINRICH."*
C. FISCHER, 654(WB):1/1972-182
B.G. THOMAS, 222(GR):MAR72-135
"CLARENCE JOHN LAUGHLIN."
S. SCHWARTZ, 441:1DEC74-101
LAUGHTON, B. PHILIP WILSON STEER.
D. FARR, 39:OCT72-362
E.D.H. JOHNSON, 637(VS):MAR73-
351
P. SKIPWITH, 135:JUL72-226
LAUMER, K. THE HOUSE IN NOVEMBER.
617(TLS):1MAR74-219
LAUMER, K. THE STAR TREASURE.
617(TLS):14JUN74-644
LAUNAY, A. THE INNOCENCE HAS GONE,
DADDY.
R. BLYTHE, 362:13JUN74-777
617(TLS):20SEP74-993
LAURENCE, D.H. - SEE SHAW, G.B.
LAURENCE, M. THE DIVINERS.
P. BRUCE, 99:MAY/JUN74-15
B. LEVER, 296:VOL3#3-93
M. PIERCY, 441:23JUN74-6
E. WEEKS, 61:JUN74-108
442(NY):8JUL74-79
LAURENCIO, A.A. - SEE UNDER APARICIO
LAURENCIO, A.
"ANDRÉ LAURENDEAU: WITNESS FOR QUÉ-
BEC." (P. STRATFORD, ED)
B. NEATBY, 99:MAY/JUN74-34
LAURENS, H. THE PAPERS OF HENRY
LAURENS. (VOLS 2&3) (P.M. HAMER &
G.C. ROGERS, JR., EDS)
R.M. WEIR, 656(WMQ):APR73-351
LAURENSON, D.T. & A. SWINGEWOOD.
THE SOCIOLOGY OF LITERATURE.
J. GOODE, 111:18MAY73-156
D. LA BOTZ, 114(CHIR):VOL24#4-
174
LAURENT, V. LES REGESTES DES ACTES
DU PATRIARCAT DE CONSTANTINOPLE.
(VOL 1, PT 4)
A.E. LAIOU, 589:OCT73-767
LAURENTI, J.L. ESTUDIOS SOBRE LA
NOVELA PICARESCA ESPAÑOLA.*
S-A. STOUDEMIRE, 238:DEC72-964
LAURENTIN, A. DOXA.
A. KEMMER, 182:VOL25#22-781

LAURIE, J., ED. COSMOLOGY NOW.
617(TLS):11JAN74-38
LAURY, J.R. NEW USES FOR OLD LACES.
L.J. GARTNER, JR., 441:8DEC74-50
VON LAUTENBACH, M. - SEE UNDER MANE-
GOLD VON LAUTENBACH
LAUTERBACH, J.Z. STUDIES IN JEWISH
LAW, CUSTOM & FOLKLORE.
E. ORING, 292(JAF):JAN-MAR72-88
LAUTERPACHT, H. INTERNATIONAL LAW.
(VOL 1) (E. LAUTERPACHT, ED)
617(TLS):25JAN74-83
COMTE DE LAUTRÉAMONT. LAUTRÉAMONT'S
"MALDOROR." (A. LYKIARD, TRANS)
639(VQR):WINTER73-XXVI
LAUWAARS, R.M. LAWFULNESS & LEGAL
FORCE OF COMMUNITY DECISIONS.
617(TLS):25JAN74-88
LA VALLEY, A.J., ED. FOCUS ON HITCH-
COCK.
J. SPEARS, 200:AUG-SEP72-417
LAVERS, A. - SEE BARTHES, R.
LAVERYCHEV, V.I. TSARIZM I RABOCHII
VOPROS V ROSSII (1861-1917 GG.).
R.A. ROOSA, 32:JUN73-381
LAVIN, M. HAPPINESS & OTHER STOR-
IES.*
J.M. MELLARD, 573(SSF):FALL72-
411
LAVIN, M. THE STORIES. (VOL 2)
J. ALEXANDER, 617(TLS):8NOV74-
1249
J. MELLORS, 362:26SEP74-416
LAVIN, M.A. PIERO DELLA FRANCESCA:
THE FLAGELLATION.*
A.C. BIRNHOLZ, 290(JAAC):SUMMER
73-556
A. FORGE, 592:NOV72-201
LAVINE, R.A. BENJAMIN DISRAELI.
W.J. BAKER, 577(SHR):WINTER72-91
LAW, S.A. & OTHERS. BLUE CROSS.
H.J. GEIGER, 441:23JUN74-23
LAWLESS, R. AN EVALUATION OF PHIL-
IPPINE CULTURE-PERSONALITY RE-
SEARCH.
D.J. SCHEANS, 293(JAST):MAY72-
747
LAWN, B. I QUESITI SALERNITANI.
F. ALESSIO, 548(RCSF):APR-JUN72-
240
LAWNER, L. - SEE GRAMSCI, A.
LAWRENCE, D. BLACK MIGRANTS: WHITE
NATIVES.
N. DEAKIN, 617(TLS):15NOV74-1281
LAWRENCE, D.H. LAWRENCE IN LOVE.
(J.T. BOULTON, ED)
M. ALLOTT, 447(N&Q):FEB72-69
LAWRENCE, D.H. "LA PRINCESSE," SUIVI
DE "LA FILLE DU MARCHAND DE CHE-
VAUX." (P. LEYRIS, TRANS)
E. DELAVENAY, 189(EA):OCT-DEC72-
576
LAWRENCE, D.H. THE QUEST FOR RANA-
NIM.* (G.J. ZYTARUK, ED)
S. GILL, 447(N&Q):SEP72-354
LAWRENCE, D.H. JOHN THOMAS & LADY
JANE.*
639(VQR):SPRING73-LVII
LAWRENCE, F.L. MOLIÈRE.*
F. WYNNE, 593:SPRING73-93
LAWRENCE, V. AN END TO FLIGHT.*
J. MELLORS, 364:DEC73/JAN74-154
LAWRY, J.S. SIDNEY'S TWO "ARCADIAS."*
G. HILLER, 67:NOV73-292

LAWSON, E.L. VERY SURE OF GOD.
M. ROBERTS, 617(TLS):25OCT74-
1184
LAWSON, H. HENRY LAWSON: SHORT STOR-
IES & SKETCHES 1888-1922.* HENRY
LAWSON: AUTOBIOGRAPHICAL & OTHER
WRITINGS 1887-1922.* HENRY LAWSON:
LETTERS 1890-1922.* (C. RODERICK,
ED OF ALL)
G.A.W., 581:SEP73-346
LAXER, J. CANADA'S ENERGY CRISIS.
W.O. TWAITS, 99:NOV/DEC74-58
LAXER, R., ED. (CANADA) LTD.
C. TAYLOR, 99:MAY/JUN74-28
LAYCOCK, D.C., ED. LINGUISTIC
TRENDS IN AUSTRALIA.
L.A. HERCUS, 361:VOL29#1-91
LAYTON, I. THE COLLECTED POEMS OF
IRVING LAYTON.*
C. LEVENSON, 529(QQ):SUMMER72-
272
S. MAYNE, 648:OCT72-59
LAYTON, I. THE POLE VAULTER.
S. NAMJOSHI, 99:NOV/DEC74-19
LAZAR, M., ED. THE SEPHARDIC TRADI-
TION.
287:JUN72-28
LAZAREV, V.N. RUSSKAIA SREDNEVEKOV-
AIA ZHIVOPIS'.
A. FARKAS, 54:MAR72-83
LAZARUS, M. A TALE OF TWO BROTHERS.
P. COLLINS, 617(TLS):25OCT74-
1184
LAZENBY, W. ARTHUR WING PINERO.
A. LEGGATT, 397(MD):MAR73-461
LAZERE, D. THE UNIQUE CREATION OF
ALBERT CAMUS.
617(TLS):29MAR74-314
LAZITCH, B., WITH M.M. DRACHKOVITCH.
BIOGRAPHICAL DICTIONARY OF THE
COMINTERN.
617(TLS):26APR74-456
LAZITCH, B. & M.M. DRACHKOVITCH.
LENIN & THE COMINTERN.* (VOL 1)
H. GRUBER, 32:SEP73-611
G.P. HOLMAN, JR., 396(MODA):
WINTER73-98
LAZZARINI, V. SCRITTI DI PALEOGRAF-
IA E DIPLOMATICA.
G.F., 228(GSLI):VOL149FASC466/
467-459
LEACH, B.A. GERMAN STRATEGY AGAINST
RUSSIA 1939-1941.
617(TLS):1MAR74-197
LEACH, C. THE EVERYTHING MAN.
617(TLS):14JUN74-629
LEACH, C. THE SEND-OFF.*
N. CALLENDAR, 441:7JUL74-18
LEACH, E. & S.N. MUKHERJEE, EDS.
ELITES IN SOUTH ASIA.
M.F. FRANDA, 318(JAOS):APR-JUN72-
326
LEACH, J. BRIGHT PARTICULAR STAR.*
S.L. POWERS, 570(SQ):SPRING72-
215
LEACOCK, S. & R. SPIRITS OF THE
DEEP.
K.L. COTHRAN, 292(JAF):OCT-DEC72-
391
LEAKEY, F.W. BAUDELAIRE & NATURE.*
A. FAIRLIE, 535(RHL):JAN-FEB72-
144
E.J. KEARNS, 402(MLR):APR73-415

LEAKEY, L.S.B. BY THE EVIDENCE.
S.J. GOULD, 441:17NOV74-18
LEAL, L. MARIANO AZUELA.
D. KADIR, 399(MLJ):DEC72-526
D.L. SHAW, 402(MLR):APR73-431
LEAL, L. BREVE HISTORIA DE LA LIT-
ERATURA HISPANOAMERICANA.
R. ROSALDO, 50(ARQ):AUTUMN72-276
LEARMONTH, A. & N., EDS. ENCYCLO-
PAEDIA OF AUSTRALIA. (REV)
617(TLS):8FEB74-140
LEARY, L. SOUTHERN EXCURSIONS.
R. FALK, 445(NCF):MAR73-497
R.S. MOORE, 219(GAR):SUMMER72-
237
LEARY, L., WITH C. BARTHOLET & C.
ROTH. ARTICLES ON AMERICAN LIT-
ERATURE 1950-1967.
R. ASSELINEAU, 189(EA):JAN-MAR72-
181
R. ASSELINEAU, 189(EA):APR-JUN72-
340
LEASE, B. THAT WILD FELLOW JOHN
NEAL & THE AMERICAN LITERARY
REVOLUTION.*
M.D. BELL, 27(AL):NOV73-458
639(VQR):SUMMER73-CXIX
LEASKA, M.A. VIRGINIA WOOLF'S
"LIGHTHOUSE."*
N. FRIEDMAN, 599:SPRING72-212
LEATHERBARROW, J.S. WORCESTERSHIRE.
617(TLS):26JUL74-815
LEAVIS, F.R. LETTERS IN CRITICISM.
(J. TASKER, ED)
617(TLS):31MAY74-585
LEAVIS, F.R. NOR SHALL MY SWORD.
H. LOMAS, 364:OCT/NOV72-137
G.A. PANICHAS, 396(MODA):SUMMER
73-321
LEAVIS, F.R. & Q.D. DICKENS THE
NOVELIST.*
J.R. HARVEY, 97(CQ):VOL6#1-77
LEAVITT, J.F. WAKE OF THE COASTERS.
J.J. SAFFORD, 432(NEQ):MAR72-151
LEBANO, E. - SEE PIRANDELLO, L.
LEBEAU, A. & J. MÉTAYER. COURS DE
GREC ANCIEN À L'USAGE DES GRANDS
DÉBUTANTS.
M. CASEVITZ, 555:VOL46FASC1-139
LEBECK, A. THE ORESTEIA.
H. LLOYD-JONES, 303:VOL92-193
LEBÈGUE, R. LE THÉÂTRE COMIQUE EN
FRANCE DE PATHELIN À "MÉLITE."
J. MOREL, 535(RHL):SEP-DEC72-
1094
LEBÈGUE, R. - SEE DE CHATEAUBRIAND,
F.R.
LEBER, E. DAS BILD DES MENSCHEN IN
SCHILLERS UND KLEISTS DRAMEN.
A. CAMIGLIANO, 406:FALL73-300
LE BIDOIS, R. LES MOTS TROMPEURS OU
LE DÉLIRE VERBAL.
R. ARVEILLER, 209(FM):APR72-172
LE BONHEUR, A. LA SCULPTURE INDO-
NÉSIENNE AU MUSÉE GUIMET.
U. BATES, 293(JAST):MAY72-740
H. GOETZ, 318(JAOS):OCT-DEC72-
574
LE BONNIEC, H. - SEE OVID
LEBOWITZ, A. PROGRESS INTO SILENCE.*
B.C. BACH, 613:SPRING72-126
P. MC CARTHY, 594:SPRING72-98
D. TIMMS, 402(MLR):JUL73-645

LEBRUN, F. LES HOMMES ET LA MORT EN
ANJOU AUX 17E ET 18E SIÈCLES.*
481(PQ):JUL72-539
LEBRUN, G. KANT ET LA FIN DE LA
MÉTAPHYSIQUE.
J. KOPPER, 342:BAND63HEFT1-123
LE BRUN, J. BOSSUET.
E. STOPP, 208(FS):OCT73-451
LEBRUN, P-A. MARIE STUART. (R.
DUMONT, ED)
J. VOISINE, 549(RLC):OCT-DEC72-
615
LECERCLE, J-L. ROUSSEAU ET L'ART DU
ROMAN.*
J.S. SPINK, 208(FS):JAN73-68
LECH, K., ED. DAS MONGOLISCHE WELT-
REICH.
D.P. LITTLE, 318(JAOS):APR-JUN72-
357
LECLAIR, S. DÉMASQUER LE RÉEL.
F. GRAMAT, 98:APR72-369
LECLERC, I. THE NATURE OF PHYSICAL
EXISTENCE.*
A. MERCIER, 182:VOL25#21-716
LECLERC, I., ED. THE PHILOSOPHY OF
LEIBNIZ & THE MODERN WORLD.
K. CLATTERBAUGH, 319:APR74-260
LE CLERC, P.O. VOLTAIRE & CRÉBILLON
PÈRE.
617(TLS):26APR74-435
LE CLÈRE, M. L'ASSASSINAT DE JEAN
JAURÈS.
L. SEIGEL, 207(FR):MAR72-891
LE CLÉZIO, J.M.G. THE BOOK OF
FLIGHTS.* (FRENCH TITLE: LE
LIVRE DES FUITES.)
M. CAGNON, 98:FEB72-158
LE CLÉZIO, J.M.G. WAR.*
G. EWART, 364:OCT/NOV73-151
"L'ÉCOLE DE FONTAINEBLEAU." "L'ÉCOLE
DE FONTAINEBLEAU: GUIDE."
E. ARMSTRONG, 208(FS):OCT73-446
LECOMTE, G. GRAMMAIRE DE L'ARABE.
K. PETRÁČEK, 353:1MAR72-99
LECONTE DE LISLE, C.M. LA DERNIÈRE
ILLUSION DE LECONTE DE LISLE. (I.
PUTTER, ED)
R.T. DENOMMÉ, 207(FR):FEB72-727
LECONTE DE LISLE, C.M. LECONTE DE
LISLE, ARTICLES, PRÉFACES, DIS-
COURS. (E. PICH, ED)
P. FLOTTES, 557(RSH):OCT-DEC72-
623
LE CORBEILLER, C. CHINA TRADE POR-
CELAIN.
R. REIF, 441:13DEC74-41
LECROMPE, R. VIRGILE, "BUCOLIQUES:"
INDEX VERBORUM, RELEVÉS STATIS-
TIQUES.
D.A. MALCOLM, 123:MAR73-92
"LECTURES ON THE HISTORY & ART OF
MUSIC."
F.W. STERNFELD, 447(N&Q):AUG72-
307
LÉCUYER, M. & P. VIREY. ADVANCED
NON-LITERARY TEXTS FOR TRANSLATION
FROM & INTO FRENCH.
N.C.W. SPENCE, 208(FS):JUL73-365
LE DANTEC, Y-G. - SEE POE, E.A.
LEDDERHOSE, L. DIE SIEGELSCHRIFT
(CHUAN-SHU) IN DER CH'ING-ZEIT.
R. BARNHART, 54:JUN72-202

LEDER, L.H., ED. THE COLONIAL LEG-
ACY.
   M.B. NORTON, 656(WMQ):OCT72-666
LEDÉSERT, R.P.L. & M. - SEE MANSION,
J.E.
LEDNICKI, W. REMINISCENCES.
   I. NAGURSKI, 497(POLR):AUTUMN72-
95
LEDUC, V. LA CHASSE À L'AMOUR.
   617(TLS):26APR74-442
LEDYARD, G. THE DUTCH COME TO KOREA.
   H.F. COOK, 293(JAST):FEB72-420
LEDYARD, P. 'UTULEI, MY TONGAN HOME.
   617(TLS):9AUG74-864
LEE, A. A GOOD INNINGS. (A. CLARK,
ED)
   E.S. TURNER, 362:15AUG74-220
   617(TLS):9AUG74-848
LEE, A.A. THE GUEST-HALL OF EDEN.
   S.B. GREENFIELD, 301(JEGP):JAN73-
122
   D. WILLIAMS, 529(QQ):AUTUMN72-
415
   639(VQR):SUMMER72-CV
LEE, A.G. FLY PAST.
   617(TLS):13SEP74-984
LEE, B. - SEE LORD BYRON
LEE, B.A. BRITAIN & THE SINO-JAPAN-
ESE WAR, 1937-1939.*
   617(TLS):22FEB74-178
LEE, C-J. COMMUNIST CHINA'S POLICY
TOWARD LAOS.
   A.P.L. LIU, 318(JAOS):OCT-DEC72-
585
"ELSIE LEE'S PARTY COOKBOOK."
   N. HAZELTON, 441:1DEC74-94
LEE, G.J. SELECTED FAR EASTERN ART
IN THE YALE UNIVERSITY ART GALLERY.
   J. HILLIER, 135:DEC72-292
LEE, J., COMP. THE GOLDEN MOUNTAIN.
(P. RADIN, ED)
   N-T. TING, 292(JAF):OCT-DEC72-
382
LEE, J.N. SWIFT & SCATOLOGICAL SAT-
IRE.*
   W.P. JONES, 481(PQ):JUL72-774
   P.J. KORSHIN, 173(ECS):SPRING73-
399
LEE, L. AS I WALKED OUT ONE MIDSUM-
MER MORNING.
   C. CHAUMEIL, 189(EA):JUL-SEP72-
448
LEE, L. CIDER WITH ROSIE.
   C. CHAUMEIL, 189(EA):JUL-SEP72-
447
LEE, M-G. & H.R. BARRINGER, EDS. A
CITY IN TRANSITION.
   H.N. KIM, 293(JAST):AUG72-955
LEE, R.A. ORWELL'S FICTION.*
   J. GRADY, 447(N&Q):FEB72-72
LEE, S.E. THE COLORS OF INK.
   P. ADAMS, 61:JUN74-115
LEE, T-H. INTERSECTORAL CAPITAL
FLOWS IN THE ECONOMIC DEVELOPMENT
OF TAIWAN, 1895-1960.
   R.H. MYERS, 293(JAST):MAY72-670
LEE, V. - SEE IONESCO, E.
LEE, W. REFERENCE GUIDE TO FANTAS-
TIC FILMS.
   T. STURGEON, 441:10NOV74-49
LEE YONG LENG. POPULATION & SETTLE-
MENT IN SARAWAK.
   A. MORRISON, 293(JAST):FEB72-460

LEE-ASKINS, A., ED. CANCIONERO DE
CORTE E DE MAGNATES.
   E. GLASER, 240(HR):SUMMER72-315
LEECH, C. THE DRAMATIST'S EXPERI-
ENCE.
   R.A. FOAKES, 627(UTQ):AUTUMN71-
86
   E. SALMON, 529(QQ):WINTER72-561
LEECH, C. & J.M.R. MARGESON, EDS.
SHAKESPEARE 1971.
   T. HAWKES, 676(YR):SUMMER73-561
   M. MUDRICK, 249(HUDR):SUMMER73-
387
LEECH, G. SEMANTICS.
   617(TLS):9AUG74-853
LEECH, G.N. A LINGUISTIC GUIDE TO
ENGLISH POETRY.*
   H. PRIESSNITZ, 430(NS):FEB72-113
LEECH, G.N. TOWARDS A SEMANTIC DES-
CRIPTION OF ENGLISH.*
   H. KRAUS, 38:BAND9OHEFT1/2-171
   G. SAMPSON, 206:NOV72-249
LEES-MILNE, J. ENGLISH COUNTRY
HOUSES: BAROQUE 1685-1715.*
   S. MILLIKIN, 90:SEP72-635
VAN LEEUWEN, A.T. CRITIQUE OF
HEAVEN.
   H. CHAMBRE, 32:SEP73-618
LEFEBURE, M. SAMUEL TAYLOR COLER-
IDGE.
   J. BEER, 617(TLS):6SEP74-949
LEFEBVE, M-J. STRUCTURE DU DISCOURS
DE LA POÉSIE ET DU RÉCIT.
   F. EDELINE, 556(RLV):1972/6-669
LEFEBVRE, H. AU DELÀ DU STRUCTURAL-
ISME.
   J. CULLER, 208(FS):OCT73-484
LEFFLAND, E. LOVE OUT OF SEASON.
   C. LEHMANN-HAUPT, 441:5SEP74-41
LEFKOWITZ, M., ED. TROIS MASQUES À
LA COUR DE CHARLES IER D'ANGLE-
TERRE.*
   A.J. SABOL, 551(RENQ):AUTUMN72-
331
LEFTWICH, A., ED. SOUTH AFRICA.
   J. LEWIN, 617(TLS):6SEP74-957
LE GALL, A. & R. BRUN. LES MALADES
ET LES MÉDICAMENTS.
   L. JERPHAGNON, 542:OCT-DEC72-472
LE GALL, B. - SEE DE SENANCOUR, E.P.
LEGEZA, I.L. A DESCRIPTIVE & ILLUS-
TRATED CATALOGUE OF THE MALCOLM
MAC DONALD CHINESE CERAMICS IN THE
GULBENKIAN MUSEUM OF ART & ARCHAE-
OLOGY, SCHOOL OF ORIENTAL STUDIES,
UNIVERSITY OF DURHAM.*
   J. RAWSON, 135:DEC72-290
LEGGETT, B.J. HOUSMAN'S LAND OF
LOST CONTENT.*
   J.N. WYSONG, 529(QQ):AUTUMN72-
419
LEGGETT, J. ROSS & TOM.
   P. ADAMS, 61:SEP74-103
   I. EHRENPREIS, 453:31OCT74-19
   R.R. LINGEMAN, 441:28AUG74-35
   J. YARDLEY, 441:18AUG74-1
   442(NY):16SEP74-148
"LEGIO VII GEMINA."
   R.W. DAVIES, 313:VOL62-195
LEGLER, P. THE INTRUDER.
   P. COOLEY, 385(MQR):WINTER74-79
   639(VQR):SUMMER73-CXI
LEGOUIS, P. ASPECTS DU XVIIE SIÈCLE.
   617(TLS):21JUN74-679

LEGOUIS, P., WITH E.E. DUNCAN-JONES
- SEE MARVELL, A.
LEGRAND, G. LA PENSÉE DES PRÉSOCRA-
TIQUES.
J-L. POIRIER, 542:JAN-MAR72-32
LE GUILLOU, L. LAMENNAIS.*
A. VIATTE, 549(RLC):JAN-MAR72-
147
LEHAN, R. THEODORE DREISER.*
C. LAUN, 594:SPRING72-117
LE HIR, Y. - SEE MARTIAL D'AUVERGNE
LEHISTE, I. SUPRASEGMENTALS.
A.K. LOJKINE, 67:NOV73-324
LEHMAN, F.K., ED. OCCASIONAL PAPERS
OF THE WOLFENDEN SOCIETY ON TIBETO-
BURMAN LINGUISTICS. (VOL 2)
K. CHANG, 293(JAST):AUG72-987
LEHMANN, G. CONVERSATION WITH A
RIDER.
J. TULIP, 581:JUN73-231
LEHMANN, W.C. HENRY HOME, LORD KAMES,
& THE SCOTTISH ENLIGHTENMENT.*
[SHOWN IN PREV UNDER LEHMAN]
J.J. ELLIS, 656(WMQ):OCT73-669
A.E. MC GUINNESS, 173(ECS):SUM-
MER73-514
LEHMANN, W.P. EINFÜHRUNG IN DIE
HISTORISCHE LINGUISTIK.*
G. PLANGG, 430(NS):AUG72-500
LEHMANN, W.P., ED & TRANS. A READER
IN NINETEENTH-CENTURY HISTORICAL
INDO-EUROPEAN LINGUISTICS.*
O. PANAGL, 353:15APR72-124
LEHMBERG, S.E. THE REFORMATION PAR-
LIAMENT 1529-36.*
F.O. EDWARDS, 325:APR72-440
M. LEVINE, 551(RENQ):AUTUMN72-
345
LEHNING, A. - SEE BAKUNIN, M.
LEIBER, F. NIGHT MONSTERS.
617(TLS):31MAY74-591
LEIBFRIED, E. KRITISCHE WISSEN-
SCHAFT VOM TEXT.*
R.E. PALMER, 72:BAND21OHEFT4/6-
346
J.J. WHITE, 220(GL&L):OCT72-59
LEIDEN, C., ED. THE CONFLICT OF TRA-
DITIONALISM & MODERNISM IN THE MUS-
LIM MIDDLE EAST.
C.E. FARAH, 318(JAOS):JAN-MAR72-
113
LEIFER, M., ED. NATIONALISM, REVOLU-
TION & EVOLUTION IN SOUTH-EAST
ASIA.
R.K. PAGET, 293(JAST):AUG72-985
LEIKINA-SVIRSKAIA, V.R. INTELLIGENT-
SIIA V ROSSII VO VTOROI POLOVINE
XIX VEKA.
P. POMPER, 32:MAR73-166
LEIMBACH, R. EURIPIDES ION.
E.W. WHITTLE, 123:DEC73-269
LEINER, J. LE DESTIN LITTÉRAIRE DE
PAUL NIZAN ET SES ÉTAPES SUCCES-
SIVES.
S. SULEIMAN, 207(FR):OCT71-245
LEIPEN, N. ATHENA PARTHENOS.
A.J.N.W. PRAG, 303:VOL92-247
LEITCH, M., ED. GREAT SONGS OF
WORLD WAR II.
R. DAVIES, 617(TLS):13DEC74-1419
LEITH-ROSS, S., COMP. NIGERIAN POT-
TERY.
G.I. JONES, 69:OCT72-357

LEIVE, D.M. INTERNATIONAL TELECOM-
MUNICATIONS & INTERNATIONAL LAW.
A-R. WERNER, 182:VOL25#21-731
LEJEUNE, M. LEPONTICA.
A. ERNOUT, 555:VOL46FASC2-324
LEKOMCEVA, M.I. TIPOLOGIJA STRUKTUR
SLOGA V SLAVJANSKIX JAZYKAX.
P. GARDE, 353:15OCT72-122
LELCHUK, A. AMERICAN MISCHIEF.*
M. MUDRICK, 249(HUDR):AUTUMN73-
545
R. SALE, 418(MR):AUTUMN73-834
T. TANNER, 364:OCT/NOV73-146
639(VQR):SPRING73-LVI
LELCHUK, A. MIRIAM AT THIRTY-FOUR.
S. BLACKBURN, 441:17NOV74-50
A. BROYARD, 441:13NOV74-47
B. DE MOTT, 61:OCT74-104
LEM, S. MEMOIRS FOUND IN A BATHTUB.*
617(TLS):15FEB74-163
LEMAIRE, C., ED & TRANS. LE CERCLE
DES CHOSES.
P. AQUILON, 549(RLC):JUL-SEP72-
455
LEMARCHAND, E. NO VACATION FROM
MURDER.
N. CALLENDAR, 441:10MAR74-12
LEMARIÉ, J. - SEE CHROMATIUS
LEMAY, J.A.L. A CALENDAR OF AMERI-
CAN POETRY IN THE COLONIAL NEWS-
PAPERS & MAGAZINES & IN THE MAJOR
ENGLISH MAGAZINES THROUGH 1765.
E. WOLF 2D, 432(NEQ):DEC72-587
LEMAY, J.A.L. MEN OF LETTERS IN
COLONIAL MARYLAND.*
A.O. ALDRIDGE, 568(SCN):FALL-
WINTER73-99
E. EMERSON, 27(AL):MAY73-302
L.P. SIMPSON, 656(WMQ):OCT73-665
LEMERLE, P. LE PREMIER HUMANISME
BYZANTIN.
P.J. ALEXANDER, 589:OCT73-770
LEMERLE, P., A. GUILLOU & N. SVORO-
NOS, EDS. ACTES DE LAVRA. (VOL 1)
J.L. TEALL, 589:JAN73-158
LEMEUNIER, F., ED. SARTHOIS PENDANT
L'ANNÉE TERRIBLE 1870-71.
E. KESSEL, 182:VOL25#17/18-626
LEMIRE, M. LES GRANDS THÈMES NATION-
ALISTES DU ROMAN HISTORIQUE CANAD-
IEN-FRANÇAIS.
D.M. HAYNE, 208(FS):APR73-239
D.M. HAYNE, 535(RHL):MAY-JUN72-
546
A. VIATTE, 207(FR):DEC71-541
LEMMER, M. - SEE SCHERNBERG, D.
LEMMON, S.M., ED. THE PETTIGREW
PAPERS. (VOL 1)
J.H. SMYLIE, 656(WMQ):APR73-363
LEMON, J.T. THE BEST POOR MAN'S
COUNTRY.
J.H. WOOD, JR., 656(WMQ):OCT72-
645
LENAGHAN, J.O. A COMMENTARY ON CIC-
ERO'S ORATION "DE HARUSPICUM RES-
PONSO."*
A.E. DOUGLAS, 313:VOL62-216
LENAGHAN, R.T., ED. CAXTON'S AESOP.
W. RIEHLE, 38:BAND90HEFT3-392
LENARD, Y. PAROLE ET PENSÉE.
B. EBLING, 207(FR):APR72-1068

LENČEK, R.L. THE VERB PATTERN OF
CONTEMPORARY STANDARD SLOVENE.*
B. PANZER, 260(IF):BAND77HEFT1-
150
LENCZOWSKI, G. SOVIET ADVANCES IN
THE MIDDLE EAST.
R.M. DE VORE, 497(POLR):SUMMER72-
124
LE NEVE, J. FASTI ECCLESIAE ANGLI-
CANAE, 1541-1857. (J.M. HORN, ED)
617(TLS):19JUL74-772
LENG, L.Y. - SEE UNDER LEE YONG LENG
LENGYEL, J. CONFRONTATION.* (HUN-
GARIAN TITLE: SZEMBESITÉS.)
I. HOWE, 441:24MAR74-34
LENIN, W.I. ÜBER WISSENSCHAFT UND
HOCHSCHULWESEN.
U. LEHMANN, 654(WB):10/1971-180
LENK, H. KRITIK DER LOGISCHEN KON-
STANTEN.
W. FLACH, 53(AGP):BAND54HEFT2-
208
LENNIG, R. TRAUM UND SINNESTÄUS-
CHUNG BEI AISCHYLOS, SOPHOKLES,
EURIPIDES.*
A.F. GARVIE, 123:MAR73-85
G. RONNET, 555:VOL46FASC1-120
E.W. WHITTLE, 303:VOL92-196
LENNOX, C. THE FEMALE QUIXOTE. (M.
DALZIEL, ED)
L.W. BROWN, 173(ECS):SUMMER73-
531
LENSEN, G.A. THE D'ANETHAN DISPAT-
CHES FROM JAPAN 1894-1910.
H.J. JONES, 293(JAST):FEB72-411
LENSEN, G.A. THE STRANGE NEUTRALITY.
J.A. WHITE, 32:JUN73-391
LENTIN, A. RUSSIA IN THE EIGHTEENTH
CENTURY.
617(TLS):1FEB74-116
LENTIN, A. VOLTAIRE & CATHERINE THE
GREAT.
617(TLS):9AUG74-850
LENZ, S. THE GERMAN LESSON.* (GER-
MAN TITLE: DEUTSCHSTUNDE.)
G. EWART, 364:OCT/NOV72-146
LEON, G.B. GREECE & THE GREAT
POWERS, 1914-1917.
C.M. WOODHOUSE, 617(TLS):6DEC74-
1366
DE LEÓN, L. LA POESÍA DE FRAY LUIS
DE LEÓN. (O. MACRÍ, ED)
P.M. KOMANECKY, 400(MLN):MAR72-
358
DE LEÓN, L.S.P. - SEE UNDER PONCE DE
LEÓN, L.S.
LÉON, M. L'ACCENTUATION DES PRONOMS
PERSONNELS EN FRANÇAIS STANDARD.
M. FREEMAN, 320(CJL):VOL18#2-166
LÉON, P.R., ED. APPLIED LINGUISTICS
& THE TEACHING OF FRENCH.
N.A. POULIN, 207(FR):MAR72-886
LÉON, P.R. ESSAIS DE PHONOSTYLIS-
TIQUE.
F. CARTON, 209(FM):JUL72-258
C. TATILON, 320(CJL):VOL18#2-196
LÉON, P.R., ED. RECHERCHES SUR LA
STRUCTURE PHONIQUE DU FRANÇAIS
CANADIEN.*
L. CHALON, 556(RLV):1972/1-109
LÉON, P.R., G. FAURE & A. RIGAULT.
PROSODIC FEATURE ANALYSIS/ANALYSE
[CONTINUED]

[CONTINUING]
DES FAITS PROSODIQUES.
N. BEAUCHEMIN, 320(CJL):VOL18#2-
163
A.W. GRUNDSTROM, 207(FR):OCT71-
239
LÉON, P.R. & P. MARTIN. PROLÉGOMÈNES
A L'ETUDE DES STRUCTURELLES INTON-
ATIVES.*
L. SANTERRE, 320(CJL):VOL18#2-
190
LEÓN HILL, E. MIGUEL ÁNGEL ASTURIAS.
E. ARDURA, 263:APR-JUN72-209
LEONARD, D. - SEE CROSLAND, A.
LEONARD, E. FIFTY-TWO PICKUP.
N. CALLENDAR, 441:23JUN74-33
LEONARD, J.N. & OTHERS. THE WORLD
OF GAINSBOROUGH (1727-1788).
E. WATERHOUSE, 39:DEC72-569
LEONARDO DA VINCI. THE MADRID CO-
DICES OF LEONARDO DA VINCI. (L.
RETI, ED & TRANS)
P. ADAMS, 61:DEC74-127
K. CLARK, 453:12DEC74-12
E. COCHRANE, 441:1DEC74-2
"LEONARDO DA VINCI." (WITH AN ESSAY
BY W. PATER)
E. YOUNG, 39:AUG72-167
LEONHARD, W. THREE FACES OF MARXISM.
453:7MAR74-29
LEONT'EV, A.A. PSIXOLINGVISTIČESKIE
EDINICY I POROŽDENIE REČEVOGO VYS-
KAZYVANIJA.
J. PRŮCHA, 353:1SEP72-91
LEONT'EV, A.A., ED. TEORIJA REČEVOJ
DEJATEL'NOSTI (PRODLEMY PSIXOLING-
VISTIKI).
K. HELTBERG, 353:15MAR72-106
LEONT'EV, A.A. & T.V. RJABOVA, EDS.
PSIXOLOGIJA GRAMMATIKI.
J. PRŮCHA, 353:JAN72-108
"LEOPARDI E L'OTTOCENTO."
E. BIGI, 228(GSLI):VOL149FASC
468-585
G. CARSANIGA, 402(MLR):JAN73-194
LEOPOLD, J.H. THE ALMANUS MANU-
SCRIPT.
H. ELKHADEM, 182:VOL25#21-707
LE PATOUREL, H.E.J. THE MOATED
SITES OF YORKSHIRE.
617(TLS):10MAY74-508
"L'ÉPIGRAMME GRECQUE" - SEE UNDER
RAUBITSCHEK, I.K. & OTHERS
LEPPMANN, W. WINCKELMANN.*
J.M. COOK, 123:DEC73-291
S. HOWARD, 173(ECS):WINTER72/73-
266
LEPSCHY, G.C. A SURVEY OF STRUCTUR-
AL LINGUISTICS.*
H.J. HERINGER, 343:BAND15HEFT2-
118
E.F.K. KOERNER, 353:15OCT72-93
DE LERA, A.M. LOS CLARINES DEL
MIEDO. (R.W. HATTON, ED)
I. MOLINA, 238:MAR72-197
LERCH, W. PROBLEME DER SCHREIBUNG
BEI SCHWEIZERDEUTSCHEN MUNDART-
SCHRIFTSTELLERN.
R.E. KELLER, 402(MLR):OCT73-925
DE LERMA, D-R. REFLECTIONS ON AFRO-
AMERICAN MUSIC.
V. THOMSON, 453:17OCT74-14
LERMAN, E. ARMED LOVE.
X.J. KENNEDY, 441:17FEB74-6

LERNER, G. BLACK WOMEN IN WHITE
AMERICA.
  639(VQR):SUMMER72-XCIV
LERNER, L. THE USES OF NOSTALGIA.
  P. DICKINSON, 364:DEC72/JAN73-
  140
  H. TOLIVER, 401(MLQ):JUN73-200
LERNER, W. KARL RADEK.*
  P.J. BEST, 497(POLR):WINTER72-
  100
LE ROY, G. PASCAL SAVANT ET CROYANT.
  G. RODIS-LEWIS, 542:APR-JUN72-
  220
LEROY, M. LES GRANDS COURANTS DE LA
LINGUISTIQUE MODERNE. (2ND ED)
  A. ERNOUT, 555:VOL46FASC1-61
  V. HOŘEJŠÍ, 353:15MAR72-91
  D. MESSNER, 430(NS):APR72-242
  R. ROCHER, 318(JAOS):OCT-DEC72-
  577
LEROY, M. MAIN TRENDS IN MODERN
LINGUISTICS.
  P.H. SALUS, 206:SEP72-126
LESAGE, A-R. LE DIABLE BOITEUX.
(R. LAUFER, ED)
  F. LAUGAA, 557(RSH):APR-JUN72-
  307
LESER, H. LANDSCHAFTSÖKOLOGISCHE
STUDIEN IM KALAHARISANDGEBIET UM
AUOB UND NOSSOB (ÖSTLICHES SÜD-
WESTAFRIKA).
  P. VOSSELER, 182:VOL25#19/20-699
LESER, H.G. - SEE RABEL, E.
LESIEUTRE, A. THE SPIRIT & SPLEN-
DOUR OF ART DECO.
  W. FEAVER, 362:19&26DEC74-847
LESLIE, R.C. - SEE ROGERS, W.
LESSING, D. THE MEMOIRS OF A SUR-
VIVOR.
  V. GLENDINNING, 617(TLS):13DEC74-
  1405
LESSING, D. A SMALL PERSONAL VOICE.
(P. SCHLUETER, ED)
  R. SALE, 441:22SEP74-4
LESSING, D. THE SUMMER BEFORE THE
DARK.*
  E. JONG, 473(PR):3/1973-500
  M. MUDRICK, 249(HUDR):AUTUMN73-
  545
LESSING, D. THE TEMPTATION OF JACK
ORKNEY.*
  W-H. PRITCHARD, 249(HUDR):SPRING
  73-234
  441:10NOV74-39
"LESSING YEARBOOK I, 1969."* (G.
STERN, G. MERKEL & J. GLENN, EDS)
  P. HERNADI, 399(MLJ):MAR72-185
"LESSING YEARBOOK II, 1970."* (G.
STERN, G. MERKEL & J. GLENN, EDS)
  S. ATKINS, 400(MLN):APR72-523
  J. FUEGI, 221(GQ):MAR72-352
"LESSING YEARBOOK III." (J. GLENN,
ED)
  J.R. FREY, 173(ECS):WINTER72/73-
  273
LESTER, J. TWO LOVE STORIES.
  J. MELLORS, 362:26SEP74-416
LESTER, M., ED. READINGS IN APPLIED
TRANSFORMATIONAL GRAMMAR.*
  W. RUTHERFORD, 350:JUN73-474
LESURE, F. L'OPÉRA CLASSIQUE FRAN-
ÇAIS.
  J.G.R., 410(M&L):OCT73-476
  617(TLS):21JUN74-678

LESURE, M. LES SOURCES DE L'HIS-
TOIRE DE RUSSIE AUX ARCHIVES
NATIONALES.*
  P.K. GRIMSTED, 104:SPRING72-147
  N.V. RIASANOVSKY, 550(RUSR):APR
  72-201
LESY, M. WISCONSIN DEATH TRIP.*
  S. SONTAG, 453:18APR74-17
  42(AR):VOL32#4-709
  639(VQR):AUTUMN73-CLXXII
LESZL, W. LOGIC & METAPHYSICS IN
ARISTOTLE.*
  A. EDEL, 319:JAN74-103
  C. GEORGIADIS, 154:MAR72-135
  D.W. HAMLYN, 123:DEC73-212
  M. VEGETTI, 548(RCSF):JAN-MAR72-
  98
LESZNAI, L. BARTÓK.
  617(TLS):29MAR74-347
LEUBE, E. FORTUNA IN KARTHAGO.*
  D.W. GUERIN, 546(RR):FEB72-43
  B. KÖNIG, 72:BAND21OHEFT4/6-455
LEUILLIOT, B. VICTOR HUGO PUBLIE
"LES MISÉRABLES" (CORRESPONDANCE
AVEC ALBERT LACROIX, AOÛT 1861-
JUILLET 1862).*
  R. POUILLIART, 549(RLC):JAN-MAR
  72-151
LEUTSCHER, A. EPPING FOREST.
  M-K. WILMERS, 617(TLS):27DEC74-
  1456
LE VAILLANT, Y. SAINTE MAFFIA.
  J. GEORGEL, 98:FEB72-183
LEVENSON, C. STILLS.
  D. BARBOUR, 529(QQ):WINTER72-571
LEVENSON, J.R. REVOLUTION & COSMO-
POLITANISM.
  D. KEENE, 293(JAST):AUG72-939
LEVENSON, J.R. & F. SCHURMANN.
CHINA.
  C-Y. CH'EN, 318(JAOS):JAN-MAR72-
  145
LEVENTHAL, A.R. WAR.*
  617(TLS):22FEB74-177
LEVENTHAL, F.M. RESPECTABLE RADI-
CAL.
  R.N. PRICE, 637(VS):SEP72-108
LÉVÊQUE, P. & P. VIDAL-NAQUET.
CLISTHÈNE L'ATHÉNIEN.
  R. WEIL, 542:JAN-MAR72-35
LEVER, J.W. THE TRAGEDY OF STATE.*
  D.J. PALMER, 541(RES):NOV72-495
  C.H. POLLACK, 529(QQ):AUTUMN72-
  417
LEVERTOV, D. FOOTPRINTS.*
  R. PEVEAR, 249(HUDR):SPRING73-
  192
LEVERTOV, D. THE POET IN THE WORLD.
  S. HOERCHNER, 659:SUMMER74-435
LEVERTOV, D. TO STAY ALIVE.*
  M. BORROFF, 676(YR):AUTUMN72-81
  S. COOPERMAN, 648:APR73-12
LÉVESQUE, J. LE CONFLIT SINO-SOVI-
ÉTIQUE ET L'EUROPE DE L'EST.
  R.E. KANET, 104:SPRING72-168
LEVEY, M. NATIONAL GALLERY CATA-
LOGUES: THE SEVENTEENTH & EIGHT-
EENTH CENTURY ITALIAN SCHOOLS.*
  E. YOUNG, 39:JUL72-85
LEVEY, M. PAINTING AT COURT.*
  290(JAAC):WINTER71-274

LEVI, A. IL PROBLEMA DELL'ERRORE
NELLA METAFISICA E NELLA GNOSEOLO-
GIA DI PLATONE.* (G. REALE, ED)
M. ISNARDI PARENTE, 548(RCSF):
JAN-MAR72-96
LEVI, A.H.T., ED. HUMANISM IN
FRANCE AT THE END OF THE MIDDLE
AGES & IN THE EARLY RENAISSANCE.
A. CIORANESCU, 549(RLC):OCT-DEC
72-611
H. DALE, 402(MLR):APR73-400
LÉVI, E. ELIPHAS LÉVI, VISIONNAIRE
ROMANTIQUE.* (F.P. BOWMAN, ED)
E.L. BAGNALL, 402(MLR):JAN73-183
R.T. DENOMMÉ, 207(FR):DEC71-512
LEVI, P. THE ENGLISH BIBLE, 1534-
1859.
617(TLS):30AUG74-936
LEVI, P. LIFE IS A PLATFORM. DEATH
IS A PULPIT.
A. CLUYSENAAR, 565:VOL13#2-72
LEVI, P. THE LIGHT GARDEN OF THE
ANGEL KING.*
639(VQR):SUMMER73-CXXVI
LEVI, R. RÉFLEXIONS SUR LA SCIENCE
ET L'EXISTENCE DE DIEU.
M. ADAM, 542:APR-JUN72-232
LÉVI-STRAUSS, C. ANTHROPOLOGIE
STRUCTURALE DEUX.
617(TLS):22FEB74-188
LÉVI-STRAUSS, C. MYTHOLOGIQUES.
(VOLS 1-4)
A.R. KING, 187:JAN74-101
LÉVI-STRAUSS, C. TRISTES TROPIQUES.*
P. ADAMS, 61:APR74-120
A. BROYARD, 441:21FEB74-37
G. STEINER, 442(NY):3JUN74-100
617(TLS):22FEB74-188
LEVIN, A. THE THIRD DUMA, ELECTION
& PROFILE.
G. HOSKING, 617(TLS):13DEC74-
1409
LEVIN, D.M. APOLLONIUS' ARGONAUTICA
RE-EXAMINED. (VOL 1)
A. GRIFFITHS, 303:VOL92-203
LEVIN, H., ED. VEINS OF HUMOR.
639(VQR):SPRING73-LXIV
LEVIN, I. THE STEPFORD WIVES.
S. O'CONNELL, 418(MR):WINTER73-
190
LEVIN, M. THE OBSESSION.
V.S. NAVASKY, 441:3FEB74-5
LEVIN, M. THE SPELL OF TIME.
M. LEVIN, 441:1DEC74-78
LEVIN, R. THE MULTIPLE PLOT IN ENG-
LISH RENAISSANCE DRAMA.*
J. ARNOLD, 568(SCN):FALL-WINTER
73-88
B. BABINGTON, 447(N&Q):DEC72-472
N.A. BRITTIN, 577(SHR):FALL72-
420
C. LEECH, 401(MLQ):MAR73-100
LEVIN, S. THE INDO-EUROPEAN & SEM-
ITIC LANGUAGES.
J.L. MALONE, 350:MAR73-204
LEVINE, A. PROPHECY IN BRIDGEPORT &
OTHER POEMS.
D. OFFEN, 114(CHIR):VOL24#4-165
LEVINE, B. THE DISSOLVING IMAGE.*
H. ADAMS, 219(GAR):FALL72-249
T.R. HENN, 541(RES):FEB72-100
M. SIDNELL, 627(UTQ):SPRING72-
263

LEVINE, G.R. HENRY FIELDING & THE
DRY MOCK.
J. DULCK, 189(EA):OCT-DEC72-558
LEVINE, P. THEY FEED THEY LION.*
M. BORROFF, 676(YR):AUTUMN72-81
639(VQR):AUTUMN72-CXXIV
LEVINE, S. EDGAR POE.
R.D. JACOBS, 27(AL):NOV73-461
LEVINSON, A. THE WORKING-CLASS
MAJORITY.
G. BURNSIDE, 441:20OCT74-30
LEVINSON, C., ED. INDUSTRY'S DEMO-
CRATIC REVOLUTION.
617(TLS):26APR74-454
LEVINSON, H., WITH J. MOLINARI & A.
SPOHN. ORGANIZATIONAL DIAGNOSIS.
P.B. BUCHAN, 529(QQ):WINTER72-
541
LEVIS, L. WRECKING CREW.*
J. ANDERSON, 502(PRS):FALL72-264
LÉVIS-MANO, G. LOGER LA SOURCE.
H.A. BOURAOUI, 207(FR):FEB72-698
LEVITINE, G. THE SCULPTURE OF FAL-
CONET.
A.B. WEINSHENKER, 127:SUMMER73-
468
LEVITT, J. THE "GRAMMAIRE DES GRAM-
MAIRES" OF GIRAULT-DUVIVIER.*
G. LEPSCHY, 545(RPH):AUG72-148
LEVITT, P. J.M. SYNGE.
617(TLS):19APR74-410
LEVTZION, N. ANCIENT GHANA & MALI.
P. KRÜGER, 182:VOL25#23/24-891
LEVY, A. ÉTUDES SUR LE CONTE ET LE
ROMAN CHINOIS.
P. HANAN, 244(HJAS):VOL32-293
LEVY, A. GOOD MEN STILL LIVE!
N. ASCHERSON, 453:8AUG74-14
LEVY, B. LEGACY OF DEATH.
E. BRAWLEY, 441:24MAR74-35
617(TLS):1NOV74-1220
LÉVY, C-F. CAPITALISTES ET POUVOIR
AU SIÈCLE DES LUMIÈRES.
R. HOWELL, JR., 182:VOL25#15/16-
569
LEVY, D. & R. KEENE. HOW TO PLAY
THE OPENING IN CHESS.
617(TLS):1NOV74-1240
LEVY, D.N.L. SACRIFICES IN THE
SICILIAN.
617(TLS):11OCT74-1143
LEVY, J.D. THE ILLUSTRATED HERBAL
HANDBOOK.
617(TLS):5APR74-376
LEVY, K.L. & K. ELLIS, EDS. EL
ENSAYO Y LA CRÍTICA LITERARIA EN
IBEROAMERICA.*
M.S. STABB, 238:DEC72-971
LEVY, L.S. FLASHES OF MERRIMENT.
J.H. BRUNVAND, 292(JAF):JUL-SEP
72-290
LEVY-VALENSI, E.A. - SEE UNDER AMADO
LEVY-VALENSI, E.
LEVYTSKY, B. THE USES OF TERROR.
R.M. SLUSSER, 32:DEC73-825
LEWALD, H.E. ARGENTINA.
S.R. WILSON, 240(HR):WINTER72-
111
LEWALD, H.E. BUENOS AIRES.
H.D. OBERHELMAN, 238:SEP72-613
LEWALD, H.E., ED. THE CRY OF HOME.
W.P. FRIEDERICH, 67:NOV73-325

LI YU-NING. THE INTRODUCTION OF
SOCIALISM INTO CHINA.
Y.J. CHIH, 293(JAST):AUG72-933
LIANG, C-T. GENERAL STILWELL IN
CHINA, 1942-1944.
P.K.T. SIH, 396(MODA):WINTER73-
100
LIBAL, M. JAPAN WEG IN DEN KRIEG.
F.W. IKLÉ, 293(JAST):AUG72-953
LIBBRECHT, U. CHINESE MATHEMATICS
IN THE THIRTEENTH CENTURY.
617(TLS):23AUG74-907
LIBERMAN, A.S. ISLANDSKAJA PROSO-
DIKA.
E.H. ANTONSEN, 301(JEGP):JUL73-
403
LIBERMAN, E.G. ECONOMIC METHODS &
THE EFFECTIVENESS OF PRODUCTION.
S. MARKOWSKI, 575(SEER):OCT73-
620
LIBERMAN, M.M. KATHERINE ANNE POR-
TER'S FICTION.*
L. HARTLEY, 578:SPRING74-139
LIBERTELLA, H. AVENTURAS DE LOS
MITICISTAS.
268:JAN74-69
"ALEXIS LICHINE'S NEW ENCYCLOPEDIA
OF WINE & SPIRITS."
N. HAZELTON, 441:8DEC74-26
LICHTENBERG, G.C. HOGARTH ON HIGH
LIFE.* (A.S. WENSINGER & W.B.
COLEY, EDS & TRANS)
F.H. MAUTNER, 406:SPRING73-100
LICHTENSTEIN, G. A LONG WAY, BABY.
A. WHITMAN, 441:20JUL74-29
LICHTHEIM, G. EUROPE IN THE TWENTI-
ETH CENTURY.*
P. GAY, 473(PR):3/1973-461
639(VQR):AUTUMN73-CLXVI
LICHTHEIM, G. MARXISM. MARXISM IN
MODERN FRANCE. FROM MARX TO HEGEL
& OTHER ESSAYS.* IMPERIALISM.
GEORGE LUKÁCS.* THE CONCEPT OF
IDEOLOGY & OTHER ESSAYS. THE ORI-
GINS OF SOCIALISM. A SHORT HIS-
TORY OF SOCIALISM. COLLECTED ES-
SAYS.*
P. GAY, 473(PR):3/1973-461
LICHTIGFELD, A. ASPECTS OF JASPER'S
PHILOSOPHY. (2ND ED)
J.D.C., 543:MAR72-560
LIDA, C.E. & I.M. ZAVALA, EDS. LA
REVOLUCIÓN DE 1868.
S.G. PAYNE, 400(MLN):MAR72-379
LIDSKY, P. LES ÉCRIVAINS CONTRE LA
COMMUNE.*
P. AUBERY, 207(FR):DEC71-455
LIEB, H-H. COMMUNICATION COMPLEXES
& THEIR STAGES.*
B. GORODECKIJ, 353:JAN72-98
LIEB, M. THE DIALECTICS OF CREA-
TION.*
R.H. WEST, 405(MP):MAY73-360
LIEBER, T.M. ENDLESS EXPERIMENTS.
S. PAUL, 27(AL):NOV73-487
LIEBERMAN, A. FARM BOY.
S. SCHWARTZ, 441:1DEC74-101
LIEBERMAN, F. CHINESE MUSIC.
L. PICKEN, 187:JAN74-157
LIEBERMAN, L. THE OSPREY SUICIDES.
J.R. COOLEY, 398:WINTER74-295
V. YOUNG, 249(HUDR):WINTER73/74-
729

LIEBERMAN, M.A. & OTHERS. ENCOUNTER
GROUPS: FIRST FACTS.
E. KURZWEIL, 473(PR):3/1973-512
LIEBERMAN, R. PARADISE REZONED.
M. LEVIN, 441:15DEC74-12
LIEBERSON, S. LANGUAGE & ETHNIC RE-
LATIONS IN CANADA.*
J.B. RUDNYCKYJ, 361:VOL29#2-188
LIEFRINK, F. SEMANTICO-SYNTAX.
617(TLS):26JUL74-792
LIEHM, A.J. THE POLITICS OF CULTURE.
E.J. CZERWINSKI, 32:MAR73-190
LIETZ, J. STUDIEN ZU DEN NOVELLEN
ALFRED DE MUSSETS.*
P.J. WHYTE, 208(FS):JUL73-347
LIEVSAY, J.L. THE ENGLISHMAN'S
ITALIAN BOOKS, 1550-1700.*
K.M. LEA, 447(N&Q):MAY72-192
LIEVSAY, J.L., ED. MEDIEVAL & REN-
AISSANCE STUDIES.*
W.K. FERGUSON, 551(RENQ):SUMMER
72-209
LIEVSAY, J.L. - SEE TUVILL, D.
LIEW, K.S. STRUGGLE FOR DEMOCRACY.
E.P. YOUNG, 293(JAST):AUG72-934
LIFTON, R.J. HISTORY & HUMAN SUR-
VIVAL.*
W.P. IRVINE, 529(QQ):SUMMER72-
260
LIFTON, R.J. & E. OLSON. LIVING &
DYING.
J.M. CAMERON, 453:31OCT74-6
M.G. MICHAELSON, 441:21JUL74-6
LIGGETT, J. THE HUMAN FACE.
D. PIPER, 617(TLS):15NOV74-1275
LIGHTFOOT, K. THE PHILIPPINES.
617(TLS):19JUL74-758
LIHANI, J. LUCAS FERNÁNDEZ.
C. STERN, 240(HR):SUMMER72-317
LIHANI, J. - SEE FERNÁNDEZ, L.
LIJERÓN ALBERDI, H. UNAMUNO Y LA
NOVELA EXISTENCIALISTA.
J.A. HERNÁNDEZ, 263:JAN-MAR73-
109
LIKHACHEV, D.S. CHELOVEK V LITERA-
TURE DREVNEI RUSI.
H. MC LEAN, 32:MAR73-129
LILES, B.L. AN INTRODUCTORY TRANS-
FORMATIONAL GRAMMAR.
J.K. CHAMBERS, 320(CJL):SPRING71-
113
J.L. FIDELHOLTZ, 350:SEP73-726
LILJA, S. THE TREATMENT OF ODOURS
IN THE POETRY OF ANTIQUITY.
F. LASSERRE, 182:VOL25#21-764
LILLI, M.C.D. LA BIBLIOTECA MANO-
SCRITTA DI CELSO CITTADINI.
F. CERRETA, 551(RENQ):SUMMER72-
212
M.P., 228(GSLI):VOL149FASC468-
634
LILLY, M. SICKERT.*
J. HOBHOUSE, 592:JUL/AUG72-57
R. PICKVANCE, 135:MAR72-216
A. POWELL, 39:MAR72-226
LIMA, J.L. - SEE UNDER LEZAMA LIMA,
J.
LIMA, R. RAMÓN DEL VALLE-INCLÁN.
E.G. NEGLIA, 397(MD):MAR73-463
DE LIMA, R.T. ROMANCEIRO FOLCLÓRICO
DO BRASIL. FOLCLORE DAS FESTAS
CÍCLICAS.
G. BÉHAGUE, 187:MAY74-310
LIMMER, R. - SEE BOGAN, L.

LIMOGES, C. LA SÉLECTION NATURELLE.
F.B. CHURCHILL, 637(VS):DEC72-
257
LIMOUZY, P. & J. BOURGEACQ. MANUEL
DE COMPOSITION FRANÇAISE.
M.M. CELLER, 207(FR):DEC71-549
LIN, J.C. MODERN CHINESE POETRY.*
T.A. ROSS, 134(CP):FALL72-79
LINCOLN, H.B., ED. THE COMPUTER &
MUSIC.*
B. VERCOE, 513:SPRING-SUMMER/
FALL-WINTER71-323
LIND, J. THE TRIP TO JERUSALEM.
617(TLS):12JUL74-745
LINDBECK, J.M.H., ED. CHINA, MANAGE-
MENT OF A REVOLUTIONARY SOCIETY.
M. GOLDMAN, 293(JAST):MAY72-665
LINDBERG, D.C., ED & TRANS. JOHN
PECHAM & THE SCIENCE OF OPTICS.*
S.Y. EDGERTON, JR., 54:SEP72-349
LINDBERGH, A.M. LOCKED ROOMS & OPEN
DOORS.
C.R. STIMPSON, 441:24MAR74-28
E. WEEKS, 61:JUN74-111
A. WHITMAN, 441:30MAR74-29
442(NY):25MAR74-143
LINDEMAN, F.O. EINFÜHRUNG IN DIE
LARYNGALTHEORIE.
R.S.P. BEEKES, 343:BAND15HEFT1-
40
LINDFORS, B. FOLKLORE IN NIGERIAN
LITERATURE.
617(TLS):30AUG74-934
LINDSAY, I.G. & M. COSH. INVERARAY
& THE DUKES OF ARGYLL.*
617(TLS):12APR74-399
LINDSAY, J. GUSTAVE COURBET.
617(TLS):25JAN74-73
LINDSAY, R.O. & J. NEU, COMPS.
FRENCH POLITICAL PAMPHLETS, 1547-
1648.*
D.A. WATTS, 208(FS):JAN73-57
LINDSAY, R.O. & J. NEU. MAZARINADES.
W. GOLDWATER, 517(PBSA):APR-JUN
73-214
LINDSAY, T.F. & M. HARRINGTON. THE
CONSERVATIVE PARTY 1918-1970.
617(TLS):22MAR74-279
LINE, M.B., A. ETTLINGER & J.M. GLAD-
STONE. BIBLIOGRAPHY OF RUSSIAN
LITERATURE IN ENGLISH TRANSLATION
TO 1945.
C.C. HOFFMEISTER, 517(PBSA):OCT-
DEC73-476
LINEHAN, P. THE SPANISH CHURCH &
THE PAPACY IN THE THIRTEENTH CEN-
TURY.*
R.H. TRAME, 377:MAR73-45
639(VQR):SUMMER72-XCVII
LING MENGCHU. THE LECHEROUS ACADEM-
ICIAN & OTHER TALES.
617(TLS):22FEB74-178
LING, T. A HISTORY OF RELIGION EAST
& WEST.
R.T. BOBILIN, 485(PE&W):JAN72-
112
"THE LINGUISTIC ATLAS OF JAPAN
(NIHON GENGO TIZU)." (1ST 5 VOLS)
K.V. TEETER, 350:JUN73-506
LINHART, S. SOZIALER WANDEL IN LAND-
LICHEN SIEDLUNGEN AUF HOKKAIDO.
293(JAST):NOV71-237
LINHARTOVA, V. CANON À L'ÉCREVISSE.
A. LIEHM, 98:OCT72-841

LINK, A.S. THE HIGHER REALISM OF
WOODROW WILSON & OTHER ESSAYS.
F.C. ROSENBERGER, 639(VQR):
SPRING72-304
LINK, A.S. & OTHERS - SEE WILSON, W.
LINK, A.S., D.W. HIRST & J.E. LITTLE
- SEE WILSON, W.
LINK, F.M. - SEE DRYDEN, J.
LINKS, J.G. TOWNSCAPE PAINTING &
DRAWING.
R. EDWARDS, 39:OCT72-366
LINN, B. PLANNING THE ENVIRONMENT.
E. DE MARE, 46:NOV72-320
LINN, E. THE ADVERSARIES.
N. CALLENDAR, 441:27JAN74-12
LINNEY, R. THE LOVE SUICIDE AT SCHO-
FIELD BARRACKS & DEMOCRACY & EST-
HER.
B.H. FUSSELL, 249(HUDR):WINTER
73/74-753
LINO, R. & L. SILVEIRA. DOCUMENTOS
PARA A HISTÓRIA DA ARTE EM PORTU-
GAL.
H. WOHL, 54:MAR72-99
LINTOTT, A.W. VIOLENCE IN REPUBLI-
CAN ROME.
A.H. MC DONALD, 123:DEC73-239
LINZ, M. THE PHILOSOPHY OF LAW.
W. ROSENSOHN, 484(PPR):JUN73-597
LIOTTA, F. LA CONTINENZA DEI CHIER-
ICI NEL PENSIERO CANONISTICO CLAS-
SICO DA GRATIANO A GREGORIO IX.
J.A. BRUNDAGE, 589:APR73-376
M.B. HACKETT, 382(MAE):1973/1-59
LIOU, B. PRAETORES ETRURIAE XV
POPULORUM.*
R.P. DUNCAN-JONES, 313:VOL62-228
LIOURE, M. - SEE CLAUDEL, P. & J-L.
BARRAULT
LIPATOW, W. DIE MÄR VOM DIREKTOR P.
H. CONRAD, 654(WB):10/1972-142
LIPCHITZ, J., WITH H.H. ARNASON. MY
LIFE IN SCULPTURE.* [SHOWN IN PREV
UNDER LIPSCHITZ]
M. WILLIAMSON, 96:OCT/NOV72-86
290(JAAC):WINTER72-280
LIPKING, L. THE ORDERING OF THE
ARTS IN EIGHTEENTH-CENTURY ENG-
LAND.*
L. BRAUDY, 128(CE):FEB72-616
W.J. HIPPLE, JR., 290(JAAC):WIN-
TER72-263
LIPMAN, J. & A. WINCHESTER. THE
FLOWERING OF AMERICAN FOLK ART,
1776-1876.
A. BROYARD, 441:19FEB74-31
LIPPARD, L.R. CHANGING.*
B. REISE, 592:MAR72-131
LIPPARD, L.R., ED. SIX YEARS.
A. FRANKENSTEIN, 55:MAY73-14
LIPPINCOTT, D. THE VOICE OF ARMA-
GEDDON.
N. CALLENDAR, 441:7JUL74-18
LIPSCHITZ, J., WITH H.H. ARNASON -
SEE LIPCHITZ, J., WITH H.H. ARNA-
SON
LIPSIUS, F. ALEXANDER THE GREAT.
E.V.C. PLUMPTRE, 617(TLS):29NOV
74-1339
LIPSYTE, R. LIBERTY TWO.
J. YARDLEY, 441:28APR74-36
LISH, G., ED. THE SECRET LIFE OF
OUR TIMES.*
J. KOSINSKI, 441:13JAN74-26

DE LISLE, C.M.L. - SEE UNDER LECONTE DE LISLE, C.M.

LISOVSKII, N.M., COMP. RUSSKAIA PERIODICHESKAIA PECHAT' 1703-1900 GG.
M. RAEFF, 104:SPRING72-150

LISPECTOR, C. FAMILY TIES.
P. CRUTTWELL & F. WESTBURG, 249(HUDR):SUMMER73-417

LISSITZKY, L. RUSSIA: AN ARCHITEC-TURE FOR WORLD REVOLUTION.*
B.S. PUSHKAREV, 550(RUSR):APR72-189

LISSITZKY-KÜPPERS, S. EL LISSITZKY.*
K.C. LINDSAY, 54:SEP72-369

LISTER, M. A JOURNEY TO PARIS IN THE YEAR 1698. (R.P. STEARNS, ED)
G. RODIS-LEWIS, 542:APR-JUN72-231

LISTER, S. A SMELL OF BRIMSTONE.
617(TLS):11OCT74-1142

LITTELL, R. SWEET REASON.
C. LEHMANN-HAUPT, 441:20FEB74-43

LITTLE, K. AFRICAN WOMEN IN TOWNS.
617(TLS):5JUL74-731

LITTLE, S.W. ENTER JOSEPH PAPP.
R. BERKVIST, 441:6AUG74-37
M. GUSSOW, 441:4AUG74-20

LITTLEJOHN, B. & J. PEARCE, EDS. MARKED BY THE WILD.
B. GODARD, 296:VOL3#1-108

LITTLEJOHN, D. DR. JOHNSON & NOAH WEBSTER.
W. KUPERSMITH, 481(PQ):JUL72-707

LITTLETON, H.K. GLASSBLOWING.
P. PERROT, 139:JUN72-10

LITTMAN, R.J. THE GREEK EXPERIMENT.
617(TLS):8MAR74-232

DEL LITTO, V. - SEE STENDHAL

LITVAK, B.G. RUSSKAIA DEREVNIA V REFORME 1861 GODA (CHERNOZEMNYI TSENTR, 1861-1895 GG.).
F. WATTERS, 32:SEP73-607

LITVAK, I. & C. MAULE. CULTURAL SOVEREIGNTY.
P.C. NEWMAN, 99:OCT74-11

LITVINOFF, E. A DEATH OUT OF SEAS-ON.*
442(NY):19AUG74-89

LITVINOV, P., COMP. THE TRIAL OF THE FOUR. (P. REDDAWAY, ED)
J.B. DUNLOP, 32:SEP73-622

LITZ, A.W., ED. ELIOT IN HIS TIME.*
S. SPENDER, 453:19SEP74-18
617(TLS):3MAY74-471

LITZ, A.W. INTROSPECTIVE VOYAGER.*
J.N. RIDDEL, 27(AL):MAR73-128

LITZEN, V. A WAR OF ROSES & LILIES.
M.J. WILKS, 382(MAE):1973/1-114

LITZINGER, B. & D. SMALLEY, EDS. BROWNING: THE CRITICAL HERITAGE.*
A.P. ROBSON, 637(VS):JUN72-475

LIU, A.P.L. COMMUNICATIONS & NATION-AL INTEGRATION IN COMMUNIST CHINA.
Y. KURODA, 293(JAST):MAY72-664

LIU, J-C. CHINA'S FERTILIZER ECON-OMY.
293(JAST):FEB72-470

LIU, J.J.Y. THE POETRY OF LI SHANG-YIN, NINTH-CENTURY BAROQUE CHINESE POET.
LI CHI, 318(JAOS):APR-JUN72-340

LIU, J.T.C. & W-M. TU, EDS. TRADI-TIONAL CHINA.
A.Y-C. LUI, 302:JAN72-74

LIVERSIDGE, J. BRITAIN IN THE ROMAN EMPIRE.*
C.M. WELLS, 487:SPRING72-103

LIVESAY, D. PLAINSONGS. (REV)
D. BAILEY, 529(QQ):SUMMER72-242
D. BARBOUR, 150(DR):SPRING72-169

LIVESAY, D. A WINNIPEG CHILDHOOD.*
F.W. WATT, 99:APR74-39

LIVET, G., ED. RECUEIL DES INSTRUC-TIONS DONNÉES AUX AMBASSADEURS ET MINISTRES DE FRANCE DEPUIS LES TRAITÉS DE WESTPHALIE JUSQU'À LA RÉVOLUTION FRANÇAISE.
H. DUCHHARDT, 182:VOL25#1/2-53

LIVINGSTON, B. ZOO.
J. O'REILLY, 441:22DEC74-4

LIVINGSTON, D.M. THE MASTER OF LIGHT.
P. ADAMS, 61:MAR74-98

LIVINGSTON, J., J. MOORE & F. OLD-FATHER, EDS. THE JAPAN READER 1. THE JAPAN READER 2.
H. SCOTT-STOKES, 441:17FEB74-4

LIVINGSTONE, L. TEMA Y FORMA EN LAS NOVELAS DE AZORÍN.
J. PALLEY, 238:MAR72-180

LIVY. TITE-LIVE, "HISTOIRE ROMAINE." (VOL 31) (P. JAL, ED & TRANS)
A. ERNOUT, 555:VOL46FASC2-335

LJUNG, M. ENGLISH DENOMINAL ADJEC-TIVES.
R.B. LEES, 350:SEP73-704

LLAMAZON, T.A. A SUBGROUPING OF NINE PHILIPPINE LANGUAGES.
J.U. WOLFF, 318(JAOS):APR-JUN72-368

LLEWELLYN, A. THE DECADE OF REFORM.
V.M. BATZEL, 637(VS):MAR73-365

LLEWELLYN, P. ROME IN THE DARK AGES.*
H.A. CALLAHAN, 613:AUTUMN72-475

LLEWELLYN SMITH, M. IONIAN VISION.
617(TLS):8FEB74-133

LLINARÈS, A. - SEE LULLE, R.

LLORACH, E.A. - SEE UNDER ALARCOS LLORACH, E.

LLOSA, M.V. - SEE UNDER VARGAS LLOSA, M.

LLOYD, A.L. FOLK SONG IN ENGLAND.
L.L. DANIELSON, 650(WF):JAN72-61

LLOYD, A.L., ED. DER MÜNCHENER PSALTER DES 14. JAHRHUNDERTS.*
A. VAN DER LEE, 433:APR72-233

LLOYD, G.E.R. EARLY GREEK SCIENCE.
C. MUGLER, 555:VOL46FASC2-292

LLOYD, H.A. THE ROUEN CAMPAIGN 1590-1592.
617(TLS):1FEB74-102

LLOYD, J. THE FURTHER ADVENTURES OF CAPTAIN GREGORY DANGERFIELD.
M. LEVIN, 441:7JUL74-19

LLOYD, P.M. VERB-COMPLEMENT COM-POUNDS IN SPANISH.*
W. BÖRNER, 260(IF):BAND76-311

LLOYD EVANS, G. SHAKESPEARE III, 1599-1604.
I. BROWN, 157:SPRING72-71
R. WARREN, 447(N&Q):APR72-155

LLOYD-JONES, H., ED. MAURICE BOWRA.
J.B. BAMBOROUGH, 617(TLS):1NOV74-
1218
G. REES, 362:24OCT74-548
LLOYD-JONES, H. THE JUSTICE OF
ZEUS.*
C.J. HERINGTON, 24:WINTER73-395
C. MOULTON, 676(YR):AUTUMN73-127
S. SHUCARD, 125:FEB73-193
P.L. SMITH, 376:APR72-127
639(VQR):SPRING72-LXXV
LO HSIANG-LIN. CHUNG-KUO TSU-P'U
YEN-CHIU.
L.Y. CHIU, 302:JAN72-76
LO, I.Y. HSIN CH'I-CHI.
H.K. JOSEPHS, 293(JAST):MAY72-
646
LO, K.H.C. CHINESE VEGETARIAN COOK-
ING.
N. HAZELTON, 441:1DEC74-94
LOBATO, M. OS OUTROS SÃO DIFERENTES.
G. SOBRAL, 263:JUL-SEP73-340
LOBO LASSO DE LA VEGA, G. MEXICANA.
(J. AMOR Y VÁZQUEZ, ED)
S.L. ARORA, 238:MAR72-186
LO CASCIO, V. STRUTTURE PRONOMINALI
E VERBALI ITALIANE.
R.J. DI PIETRO, 276:AUTUMN72-336
G.C. LEPSCHY, 361:VOL29#3/4-368
LO CASTRO, A. DANTE E LA SOCIETÀ.*
T.G. BERGIN, 275(IQ):FALL/WINTER
72-111
H. RHEINFELDER, 430(NS):OCT72-
619
LOCHER, J.L., ED. THE WORLD OF M.C.
ESCHER.
M. HANCOCK, 58:NOV72-91
LOCHMAN, J.M. CHURCH IN A MARXIST
SOCIETY.
N. HURLEY, 363:FEB72-74
LOCK, A.H. SURREY IN 1815.
617(TLS):14JUN74-647
LOCKE, D. MEMORY.*
A.J. HOLLAND, 483:JUL72-285
F. JACKSON, 63:DEC73-265
J.D. RABB, 154:SEP72-472
LOCKE, D. MYSELF & OTHERS.
D.D. TODD, 154:SEP72-469
LOCKE, J. THE EDUCATIONAL WRITINGS
OF JOHN LOCKE. (J.L. AXTELL, ED)
R.J. BAUER, 568(SCN):FALL-WINTER
73-94
LOCKE, M. POWER & POLITICS IN THE
SCHOOL SYSTEM.
P. BUCKMAN, 362:23MAY74-670
LOCKE, R. MAYDAY 747.
M. LEVIN, 441:20OCT74-41
LOCKE, R.R. FRENCH LEGITIMISTS &
THE POLITICS OF MORAL ORDER IN THE
EARLY THIRD REPUBLIC.
J.P.T. BURY, 617(TLS):27DEC74-
1469
LOCKHART, R.B. THE DIARIES OF SIR
ROBERT BRUCE LOCKHART.* (VOL 1)
(K. YOUNG, ED)
C. COCKBURN, 441:25AUG74-6
LOCKIE, D.M. - SEE TAPIÉ, V-L.
LOCKLEY, R. SEAL WOMAN.
P. CAMPBELL, 617(TLS):13DEC74-
1405
LOCKRIDGE, R. DEATH ON THE HOUR.
N. CALLENDAR, 441:4AUG74-26

LOCKSPEISER, E. MUSIC & PAINTING.*
A. FITZLYON, 364:AUG/SEP73-146
C.P., 410(M&L):OCT73-465
LOCKWOOD, C. BRICKS & BROWNSTONE.
639(VQR):SUMMER73-CXXV
LOCKWOOD, J.G. WORLD CLIMATOLOGY.
617(TLS):16AUG74-886
LOCKWOOD, S.B., COMP. NIGERIA: A
GUIDE TO OFFICIAL PUBLICATIONS.
J.A. CASADA, 517(PBSA):APR-JUN73-
208
LOCKWOOD, S.C. AUGUSTINE HEARD &
COMPANY, 1858-1862.
F.W. DRAKE, 293(JAST):NOV71-185
LOCKWOOD, W.B. HISTORICAL GERMAN
SYNTAX.*
R.G. FINCH, 220(GL&L):OCT72-66
LOCKWOOD, W.B. INDO-EUROPEAN PHILOL-
OGY.*
O. PANAGL, 353:1OCT72-97
LOENERTZ, R-J. BYZANTINA ET FRANCO-
GRAECA. (P. SCHREINER, ED)
P. TOPPING, 589:JAN73-160
LOERZER, E. EHESCHLIESSUNG UND WER-
BUNG IN DER "KUDRUN."
H. HEINEN, 589:APR73-377
LOEWEN, J.W. THE MISSISSIPPI CHIN-
ESE.
D.M. CHALMERS, 293(JAST):AUG72-
922
LOFMARK, C. RENNEWART IN WOLFRAM'S
"WILLEHALM."
D. BLAMIRES, 382(MAE):1973/3-276
LOFTIS, J. & V.A. DEARING - SEE DRY-
DEN, J.
LOGAN, J. THE ANONYMOUS LOVER.*
E. BUTSCHER, 398:WINTER74-284
617(TLS):29MAR74-339
LOH, P.P.Y. THE EARLY CHIANG KAI-
SHEK.
H-M. TIEN, 293(JAST):MAY72-658
LOHMANN, D. DIE KOMPOSITION DER
REDEN IN DER ILIAS.*
J.B. HAINSWORTH, 303:VOL92-187
M.M. WILLCOCK, 123:MAR73-15
LOHMEIER, D. - SEE OLEARIUS, A.
LOHRLI, A., COMP. HOUSEHOLD WORDS.
617(TLS):19APR74-410
LOIZE, J. ALAIN-FOURNIER, SA VIE ET
"LE GRAND MEAULNES."
R. GIANNONI, 535(RHL):MAR-APR72-
344
LOMAS, P. TRUE & FALSE EXPERIENCE.
617(TLS):8FEB74-129
LOMBARD, M. MONNAIE ET HISTOIRE
D'ALEXANDRE À MAHOMET.
A.R. LEWIS, 589:APR73-379
LOMIENTO, G. IL DIALOGO DI ORIGENE
CON ERACLIDE ED I VESCOVI SUOI
COLLEGHI SUL PADRE, IL FIGLIO E
L'ANIMA.
É. DES PLACES, 555:VOL46FASC2-
315
LOMMEL, H. DIE GATHAS DES ZARATHUS-
TRA. (B. SCHLERATH, ED)
M.J. DRESDEN, 318(JAOS):OCT-DEC
72-571
"A LONDON BIBLIOGRAPHY OF THE SOCIAL
SCIENCES, SEVENTH SUPPLEMENT, 1969-
72." (VOLS 22-28)
617(TLS):6SEP74-958

"LONDON'S LIBERTIES OR A LEARNED
  ARGUMENT OF LAW & REASON [1651;
  I.E. DEC. 1650]."
    568(SCN):FALL-WINTER73-96
LONERGAN, B.J.F. GRACE & FREEDOM.
  (J.P. BURNS, ED)
    H.B. GOW, 613:AUTUMN72-464
LONERGAN, B.J.F. INSIGHT.
    W.F.J. RYAN, 484(PPR):MAR73-435
LONG, A.A. HELLENISTIC PHILOSOPHY.
    G.E.R. LLOYD, 617(TLS):23AUG74-
    905
LONG, A.A. LANGUAGE & THOUGHT IN
  SOPHOCLES.*
    M. FAUST, 260(IF):BAND76-288
LONG, A.A., ED. PROBLEMS IN STOI-
  CISM.*
    P.M. HUBY, 479(PHQ):JUL72-267
    C. MUGLER, 555:VOL46FASC2-299
    T.V.U., 543:DEC71-380
LONG, E. "THE MAID" & "THE HANG-
  MAN."*
    E.B. LYLE, 203:SUMMER72-169
LONG, G. THE FOLKLORE CALENDAR.
    K.B. HARDER, 424:JUN72-149
LONG, J.H., ED. MUSIC IN ENGLISH
  RENAISSANCE DRAMA.
    D. GREER, 570(SQ):SPRING72-212
LONG, M. AT THE PIANO WITH RAVEL.
    617(TLS):6SEP74-950
LONGEON, C. LES ÉCRIVAINS FORÉZIENS
  DU XVIE SIÈCLE.*
    I.D. MC FARLANE, 208(FS):APR73-
    193
LONGFELLOW, H.W. THE LETTERS OF
  HENRY WADSWORTH LONGFELLOW.* (VOLS
  3&4) (A. HILEN, ED) [ENTRY IN PREV
  WAS OF VOLS 1-4]
    C.M. SIMPSON, JR., 639(VQR):
    SPRING73-312
LORD LONGFORD. THE LIFE OF JESUS
  CHRIST.
    D. CUPITT, 362:7NOV74-611
    P. HEBBLETHWAITE, 617(TLS):
    11OCT74-1115
LONGFORD, E. WINSTON CHURCHILL.
    THE BISHOP OF SOUTHWARK, 362:
    7NOV74-610
    P. STANSKY, 441:24NOV74-4
LONGFORD, E. THE ROYAL HOUSE OF
  WINDSOR.
    THE BISHOP OF SOUTHWARK, 362:
    7NOV74-610
LONGFORD, E. WELLINGTON: PILLAR OF
  STATE.*
    M.E. BRADFORD, 396(MODA):FALL73-
    431
    J.F.C. HARRISON, 639(VQR):SUMMER
    73-468
LONGFORD, E. WELLINGTON: THE YEARS
  OF THE SWORD.*
    M.E. BRADFORD, 396(MODA):FALL73-
    431
LONGFORD, F. THE GRAIN OF WHEAT.
    E.S. TURNER, 362:7MAR74-310
    617(TLS):8MAR74-230
LONGHI, P. PAINTING & DRAWINGS.
  (T. PIGNATTI, ED)
    G. KNOX, 481(PQ):JUL72-598
LONGLEY, M. AN EXPLODED VIEW.*
    R. GARFITT, 364:OCT/NOV74-119
LONGLEY, M. NO CONTINUING CITY.*
    D. JAFFE, 590:SPRING/SUMMER73-26

LONGMATE, N. THE WORKHOUSE.
    A. BROYARD, 441:16OCT74-47
    M. LASKI, 362:22AUG74-252
    442(NY):25NOV74-194
    617(TLS):30AUG74-919
LONGYEAR, R.M. NINETEENTH-CENTURY
  ROMANTICISM IN MUSIC. (2ND ED)
    J.A.W., 410(M&L):OCT73-467
LONSDALE, R., ED. HISTORY OF LITERA-
  TURE IN THE ENGLISH LANGUAGE: DRY-
  DEN TO JOHNSON.
    J. MOWAT, 566:AUTUMN72-45
LOORY, S.H. DEFEATED.*
    J.W. FINNEY, 441:9FEB74-27
    442(NY):7JAN74-74
LOOS, A. GENTLEMEN PREFER BLONDES.
  BUT GENTLEMEN MARRY BRUNETTES.
    W. CLEMONS, 441:10FEB74-13
LOOS, A. KISS HOLLYWOOD GOOD-BY.
    M. GUSSOW, 441:31AUG74-17
    R. MAYNE, 617(TLS):6DEC74-1368
    J. SAYRE, 441:18AUG74-3
LOOS, B. MYTHOS, ZEIT UND TOD.*
    W. MOHR, 680(ZDP):BAND91HEFT2-
    305
LOPE BLANCH, J.M. - SEE DE VALDÉS, J.
LOPE DE VEGA. A CRITICAL EDITION OF
  LOPE DE VEGA'S AUTOGRAPH PLAY "EL
  PODER EN EL DISCRETO." (H. ZIOMEK,
  ED)
    R.W. TYLER, 238:DEC72-965
LOPE DE VEGA. EL DUQUE DE VISEO.*
  (E.A. EASON, ED)
    M.A. PEYTON, 238:DEC72-967
LOPE DE VEGA. LA FIANZA SATISFECHA.*
  (W.M. WHITBY & R.R. ANDERSON, EDS)
    P.J. POWERS, 399(MLJ):DEC72-525
    G.E. WADE, 238:SEP72-590
LÖPELMANN, M. ETYMOLOGISCHES WÖRTER-
  BUCH DER BASKISCHEN SPRACHE.*
    W. DIETRICH, 343:BAND14HEFT1-86
LOPEZ, R.S. THE COMMERCIAL REVOLU-
  TION OF THE MIDDLE AGES, 950-1350.
    R.D. FACE, 589:APR73-381
LÓPEZ ESTRADA, F. RUBÉN DARÍO Y LA
  EDAD MEDIA.*
    M. VOISIN, 549(RLC):JAN-MAR72-
    152
LORAINE, P. VOICES IN AN EMPTY ROOM.
    M. LEVIN, 441:16JUN74-28
    617(TLS):25JAN74-88
LORANT, S. SIEG HEIL!
    N. ASCHERSON, 453:18APR74-3
LORCH, M.D. - SEE UNDER DE PANIZZA
  LORCH, M.
LORD, B. THE HISTORY OF PAINTING IN
  CANADA.
    K. MULHALLEN, 99:NOV/DEC74-14
LORD, M. HAL PORTER.
    C. HADGRAFT, 71(ALS):OCT74-437
LORD, R.T. DOSTOEVSKY.*
    E. WASIOLEK, 594:SPRING72-86
LORD, W. THE DAWN'S EARLY LIGHT.*
    F.A. CASSELL, 656(WMQ):OCT73-682
    639(VQR):SPRING73-LXXXII
LOREAU, M. JEAN DUBUFFET.
    R. CARDINAL, 617(TLS):6DEC74-
    1364
    M. RICHIR, 98:MAR72-228
LORENZ, A.L. HUGH GAINE.
    R.A. BROWN, 656(WMQ):OCT73-680

LUCAS, A.T. TREASURES OF IRELAND.
P. BROWN, 453:3OCT74-3
LUCAS, J., ED. LITERATURE & POLI-
TICS IN THE NINETEENTH CENTURY.*
P. BRANTLINGER, 637(VS):SEP72-
106
P. MEIER, 189(EA):APR-JUN72-336
LUCAS, J. THE MELANCHOLY MAN.*
T.J. CRIBB, 541(RES):AUG72-372
M. GANZ, 637(VS):DEC71-234
LUCAS, J. - SEE AUSTEN, J.
LUCAS, J.R. THE CONCEPT OF PROBA-
BILITY.
L.J. COHEN, 393(MIND):OCT72-625
D. EDGINGTON, 483:OCT72-375
C. HOWSON, 84:MAY72-157
LUCAS, J.R. THE FREEDOM OF THE
WILL.*
D.M. MAC KAY, 483:APR72-180
LUCAS, N. THE SEX KILLERS.
617(TLS):22MAR74-304
LUCAS, T.E. ELDER OLSON.
R.H.C., 125:OCT72-87
J.C. DE VANY, 590:FALL/WINTER
73/74-42
R. KIRSCHTEN, 114(CHIR):VOL24#4-
177
LUCCIONI, J. LA PENSÉE POLITIQUE
DE PLATON.
P. AUBENQUE, 542:JAN-MAR72-41
LUCE, A.A. BERKELEY & MALEBRANCHE.
P. DUBOIS, 542:APR-JUN72-218
LUCE, G.H. OLD BURMA - EARLY PAGÁN.*
J. LOWRY, 39:AUG72-170
E. LYONS, 318(JAOS):OCT-DEC72-
518
J.G. MAHLER, 54:JUN72-201
W.M. SPINK, 293(JAST):MAY72-717
LUCE, J.V. LOST ATLANTIS.
D.B. VITALIANO, 391(JFI):VOL8#1-
66
LUCIAN. LUCIEN: LE NAVIRE OU LES
SOUHAITS.* (G. HUSSON, ED & TRANS)
B.P. REARDON, 487:SUMMER72-201
LUCID, R.F. NORMAN MAILER.*
639(VQR):SUMMER72-CIV
LUCIE-SMITH, E. EROTICISM IN WEST-
ERN ART.
M. YAFFÉ, 592:NOV72-202
90:AUG72-576
LUCIE-SMITH, E. LATE MODERN.
D.M. SOKOL, 290(JAAC):FALL71-141
LUCIE-SMITH, E. SYMBOLIST ART.
B. PETRIE, 592:JUL/AUG72-49
LUCK, R. GOTTFRIED KELLER ALS LIT-
ERATURKRITIKER.*
H. BOESCHENSTEIN, 182:VOL25#17/
18-607
LUCKETT, R. THE WHITE GENERALS.*
G.A. BRINKLEY, 550(RUSR):JUL72-
300
LUCKHAM, R. THE NIGERIAN MILITARY.
W. GUTTERIDGE, 69:APR72-156
T.M. SHAW, 150(DR):SUMMER72-327
LUCRETIUS. DE RERUM NATURA.* (BK 3)
(E.J. KENNEY, ED)
D. WEST, 313:VOL62-211
LUDAT, H. AN ELBE UND ODER UM DAS
JAHR 1000.*
J.M. BAK, 32:DEC73-832
LÜDEKE, D. EIN ÖKONOMETRISCHES VIER-
TELJAHRESMODELL FÜR DIE BUNDESRE-
PUBLIK DEUTSCHLAND.
A. OCKER, 182:VOL25#3/4-83

LÜDERS, D. - SEE HÖLDERLIN, F.
LUDLUM, R. THE MATLOCK PAPER.*
N. CALLENDAR, 441:12MAY74-18
LUDLUM, R. THE RHINEMANN EXCHANGE.
N. CALLENDAR, 441:27OCT74-56
442(NY):14OCT74-202
LÜDTKE, H. GESCHICHTE DES ROMANIS-
CHEN WORTSCHATZES.
D. MESSNER, 430(NS):DEC72-741
LUDWIG, J. A WOMAN OF HER AGE.*
A. BRENNAN, 198:WINTER74-83
R.M. BROWN, 296:VOL3#3-89
LUDWIG, O. ZWISCHEN HIMMEL UND
ERDE. (K.A. DICKSON, ED)
H.R. KLIENEBERGER, 402(MLR):JAN
73-234
LUGINBÜHL, E. STUDIEN ZU NOTKERS
ÜBERSETZUNGSKUNST.
E.S. FIRCHOW, 343:BAND15HEFT2-
188
LUGT, F. MUSÉE DU LOUVRE - INVEN-
TAIRE GÉNÉRAL DES DESSINS DES
ÉCOLES DU NORD: MAÎTRES DES AN-
CIENS PAYS-BAS NÉS AVANT 1550.
J. SNYDER, 54:MAR72-88
LUGTON, R.C., ED. ENGLISH AS A
SECOND LANGUAGE: CURRENT ISSUES.
R.N. CAMPBELL, 399(MLJ):OCT72-
405
J. ROSS, 608:SEP73-335
LUGTON, R.C., ED. PREPARING THE EFL
TEACHER.
W.J. CAMERON, 238:SEP72-605
R.L. LIGHT, 399(MLJ):OCT72-407
LUKÁCS, G. HISTORY & CLASS CON-
SCIOUSNESS.*
H.B., 543:SEP71-129
J. BIEN, 154:DEC72-637
A. VUCINICH, 550(RUSR):JUL72-315
LUKÁCS, G. EL JOVEN HEGEL Y LOS
PROBLEMAS DE LA SOCIEDAD CAPITAL-
ISTA.
H.B., 543:SEP71-129
LUKÁCS, G. SOLZHENITSYN.
P. BLAKE, 550(RUSR):JUL72-316
42(AR):SPRING/SUMMER72-245
639(VQR):WINTER72-XIV
LUKÁCS, G. THEORY OF THE NOVEL.*
(FRENCH TITLE: LA THÉORIE DU
ROMAN.)
G. GOOD, 454:WINTER73-175
LUKAS, J. STUDIEN ZUR SPRACHE DER
GISIGA (NORDKAMERUN).
D. CRABB, 350:MAR73-218
LUKAS, S.R. FAT EMILY.
A. BROYARD, 441:1FEB74-27
M. LEVIN, 441:7APR74-33
ŁUKASIEWICZ, J. SELECTED WORKS.*
(L. BORKOWSKI, ED)
W. KNEALE, 393(MIND):JAN72-144
LUKES, S. ÉMILE DURKHEIM.*
A. MAC INTYRE, 453:7MAR74-25
LULLE, R. LE LIVRE DU GENTIL ET DES
TROIS SAGES. (A. LLINARÈS, ED &
TRANS)
L. SALA-MOLINS, 542:JAN-MAR72-83
LUMBROSO, M.M., ED. PROVERBI E MODI
DI DIRE.
S.F. SANDERSON, 203:SUMMER72-161
LUMPP, H-M. PHILOLOGIA CRUCIS.*
S-A. JØRGENSEN, 301(JEGP):JAN73-
87
H.B. NISBET, 402(MLR):JAN73-227
[CONTINUED]

LUMPP, H-M. PHILOLOGIA CRUCIS.*
[CONTINUING]
J.C. O'FLAHERTY, 221(GQ):MAR72-
367
LUMSDEN, D. - SEE ROBINSON, T.
LUNDEN, S.S. THE TRONDHEIM RUSSIAN-
GERMAN MS VOCABULARY.
Λ.E. PENNINGTON, 575(SEER):OCT73-
594
LUNELLI, A. AERIUS.
J. ANDRÉ, 555:VOL46FASC2-329
LUNENFIELD, M. THE COUNCIL OF THE
SANTA HERMANDAD.
R.L. KAGAN, 551(RENQ):SUMMER72-
214
LUNN, E. PROPHET OF COMMUNITY.
617(TLS):8NOV74-1250
LUNN, J.E. & U. VAUGHAN WILLIAMS.
RALPH VAUGHAN WILLIAMS.*
A.E.F. DICKINSON, 607:#102-33
LUONGO, E.P. AMERICAN MEDICINE IN
CRISIS.
J.S. BOIS, 186(ETC.):MAR72-94
LUPORINI, C. SPAZIO E MATERIA IN
KANT.
E. NAMER, 542:JUL-SEP72-329
LUR'E, I.S., ED. ISTOKI RUSSKOI BEL-
LETRISTIKI.
R.W.F. POPE, 32:SEP73-654
LURIA, A.R. THE WORKING BRAIN. THE
MAN WITH A SHATTERED WORLD.* THE
NATURE OF HUMAN CONFLICTS.
D. JORAVSKY, 453:16MAY74-22
LURIA, S.E. LIFE.
G.S. STENT, 441:8SEP74-27
C.H. WADDINGTON, 453:28NOV74-4
LURIE, A. THE WAR BETWEEN THE TATES.
P. ADAMS, 61:SEP74-103
C. LEHMANN-HAUPT, 441:19JUL74-39
D. MAY, 362:20JUN74-808
R. SALE, 453:8AUG74-32
S. SANBORN, 441:28JUL74-1
442(NY):19AUG74-89
617(TLS):21JUN74-657
LURIE, L. THE RUNNING OF RICHARD
NIXON.
639(VQR):WINTER73-XXXIX
LUSCHEI, M. THE SOVEREIGN WAYFARER.
C.H. HOLMAN, 27(AL):NOV73-476
LUSCOMBE, D.E. - SEE ABELARD, P.
LUTHER, W. SPRACHPHILOSOPHIE ALS
GRUNDWISSENSCHAFT.
H. PRIESSNITZ, 430(NS):JAN72-47
E.H. YARRILL, 182:VOL25#1/2-32
LÜTHI, M. VOLKSLITERATUR UND HOCH-
LITERATUR.
H. BOESCHENSTEIN, 182:VOL25#21-
743
F.P. PICKERING, 220(GL&L):JUL73-
341
LÜTT, J. HINDU-NATIONALISMUS IN
UTTAR PRADÉS, 1867-1900.*
T.P. THORNTON, 293(JAST):AUG72-
978
LUTTRELL, C. THE CREATION OF THE
FIRST ARTHURIAN ROMANCE.
617(TLS):21JUN74-679
LUTTRELL, N. THE PARLIAMENTARY
DIARY OF NARCISSUS LUTTRELL, 1691-
1693.* (H. HORWITZ, ED)
H.T.D., 566:SPRING73-114
LUTYENS, E. A GOLDFISH BOWL.*
R.H.M., 410(M&L):APR73-235
P.J. PIRIE, 415:MAY73-492

LUTYENS, M. CLEO.*
M. LEVIN, 441:21APR74-40
LUTZ, J.G. CHINA & THE CHRISTIAN
COLLEGES 1850-1950.
R. LUND, 293(JAST):MAY72-655
LUXENBURG, N. - SEE SKRJABINA, E.
LUXMOORE, C.F.C. ENGLISH SALT-
GLAZED EARTHENWARE.
J.P. CUSHION, 135:JUN72-151
LYALL, G. BLAME THE DEAD.*
N. CALLENDAR, 441:12MAY74-18
LYDON, J. IRELAND IN THE LATER
MIDDLE AGES.
617(TLS):18JAN74-45
LYDON, J.G. PIRATES, PRIVATEERS, &
PROFITS.
L.M. MALONEY, 656(WMQ):APR73-356
LYLES, A.M. & J. DOBSON, COMPS. THE
JOHN C. HODGES COLLECTION OF WIL-
LIAM CONGREVE IN THE UNIVERSITY OF
TENNESSEE LIBRARY.
J. BARNARD, 354:MAR72-65
LYNCH, K.M. JACOB TONSON.*
R.P. BOND, 566:SPRING72-82
J.T. BOULTON, 354:JUN72-153
O.M. BRACK, JR., 481(PQ):JUL72-
513
C.J. RAWSON, 677:VOL3-296
LYNCH, M. CUENTOS DE COLORES.
J.C. MC KEGNEY, 238:DEC72-972
LYNCH, W.F. CHRIST & PROMETHEUS.
B.B. GILLIGAN, 613:SUMMER72-316
LYNEN, J.F. THE DESIGN OF THE PRE-
SENT.*
A. HOOK, 447(N&Q):NOV72-425
B. ROUSE, 599:WINTER72-79
LYNES, R. GOOD OLD MODERN.*
A. FRANKENSTEIN, 55:NOV73-49
LYNN, K.S. WILLIAM DEAN HOWELLS.*
W.M. GIBSON, 445(NCF):SEP72-228
LYON, J.K. & C. INGLIS. KONKORDANZ
ZUR LYRIK GOTTFRIED BENNS.*
P.M. DALY, 564:OCT72-224
H. WETZEL, 406:SUMMER73-201
LYON, P. EISENHOWER.
D. MIDDLETON, 441:28JUN74-37
W.V. SHANNON, 441:21JUL74-3
LYONS, A. THE DEAD ARE DISCREET.
N. CALLENDAR, 441:16JUN74-31
LYONS, B.G. VOICES OF MELANCHOLY.
J. ARNOLD, 568(SCN):FALL-WINTER
73-92
LYONS, C.R. HENRIK IBSEN.
I. DEER, 290(JAAC):WINTER72-277
LYONS, D. IN THE INTEREST OF THE
GOVERNED.
D.D. RAPHAEL, 617(TLS):27SEP74-
1036
R. SARTORIUS, 311(JP):21NOV74-
779
LYONS, F.S. IRELAND SINCE THE FAM-
INE.
M.J. WATERS, 637(VS):DEC72-224
LYONS, J. NOAM CHOMSKY.*
A. BAMMESBERGER, 430(NS):DEC72-
746
LYONS, J. EINFÜHRUNG IN DIE MODERNE
LINGUISTIK.
W. LANGE, 406:SPRING73-101
LYONS, J., ED. NEW HORIZONS IN LIN-
GUISTICS.
L.A. BORSAY, 399(MLJ):MAR72-191
LYONS, L.M. NEWSPAPER STORY.
E.D. CANHAM, 432(NEQ):MAR72-125

LYONS, M. NICHOLAS II.
  617(TLS):29NOV74-1351
LYONS, N. FISHING WIDOWS.
  C. LEHMANN-HAUPT, 441:24APR74-45
LYSIAS. SELECTED SPEECHES.* (C.D.
  ADAMS, ED)
  D.M. MAC DOWELL, 123:MAR73-87
LYS'KO, Z., ED. UKRAJINS'KI NARODNI
  MELODIJI.
  R.B. KLYMASZ, 187:SEP74-455
LYTTELTON, A., ED. ITALIAN FAS-
  CISMS.
  617(TLS):25JAN74-87
LYTTELTON, A. THE SEIZURE OF POWER.
  617(TLS):25JAN74-87
LYUBLINSKII, V.S. KNIGA V ISTORII
  CHELOVECHESKOGO OBSHCHESTVA.
  J.S.G. SIMMONS, 78(BC):WINTER72-
  569

MA HUAN. YING-YAI SHENG-LAN, THE
  OVERALL SURVEY OF THE OCEAN'S
  SHORES [1433]. (J.V.G. MILLS, ED
  & TRANS)
  J-P. LO, 293(JAST):NOV71-181
MA, L.J.C. COMMERCIAL DEVELOPMENT &
  URBAN CHANGE IN SUNG CHINA (960-
  1279).
  P.J. GOLAS, 293(JAST):AUG72-928
MAAS, H. - SEE HOUSMAN, A.E.
MAAS, H., J.L. DUNCAN & W.G. GOOD -
  SEE BEARDSLEY, A.
MAAS, P. KLEINE SCHRIFTEN. (W.
  BUCHWALD, ED)
  F. LASSERRE, 182:VOL25#22-812
MABEY, R. ROADSIDE WILDLIFE BOOK.
  617(TLS):13DEC74-1421
MABEY, R. THE UNOFFICIAL COUNTRY-
  SIDE.
  617(TLS):15MAR74-260
MC ALEAVEY, D. STERLING 403.
  E. LICHTENBERG, 114(CHIR):VOL23
  #4&VOL24#1-212
  D.E. RICHARDSON, 598(SOR):WINTER
  74-225
MACALPINE, I. & R. HUNTER. GEORGE
  III & THE MAD-BUSINESS.*
  M. COOK, 325:APR72-448
MC ARTHUR, D.G.M. LES CONSTRUCTIONS
  VERBALES DU FRANÇAIS CONTEMPORAIN.
  A.C. KEYS, 67:MAY73-134
  M. WILMET, 556(RLV):1972/6-671
MACAULAY, D.B. ALLERGIES.
  617(TLS):12APR74-402
MACAULAY, T.B. THE LETTERS OF THOM-
  AS BABINGTON MACAULAY. (VOLS 1&2)
  (T. PINNEY, ED)
  R. MITCHISON, 362:8AUG74-186
  617(TLS):7JUN74-603
MC BAIN, E. HAIL TO THE CHIEF.*
  G. WALKER, 441:1JAN74-17
  617(TLS):1FEB74-116
MACBEATH, I. CLOTH CAP & AFTER.
  617(TLS):12APR74-396
MAC BETH, G. COLLECTED POEMS 1958-
  1970.*
  J. ANDERSON, 502(PRS):WINTER72/
  73-360
  A. CLUYSENAAR, 565:VOL13#2-72
MAC BETH, G. THE ORLANDO POEMS.
  A. CLUYSENAAR, 565:VOL13#2-72
MAC BETH, G. A POET'S YEAR.*
  R. GARFITT, 364:OCT/NOV73-119

MAC BETH, G. SHRAPNEL.*
  J. CAREY, 364:JUN/JUL73-120
MC BRIDE, R.M., ED. MORE LANDMARKS
  OF TENNESSEE HISTORY.
  R. PARTIN, 9(ALAR):JAN72-78
MC BRIDE, W.L. FUNDAMENTAL CHANGE
  IN LAW & SOCIETY.
  G.G.G., 543:DEC71-360
MAC CAIG, N. THE WHITE BIRD.*
  R. GARFITT, 364:AUG/SEP73-122
MC CALL, D. JACK THE BEAR.
  L. MC MURTRY, 441:28APR74-6
  442(NY):29APR74-134
  617(TLS):11OCT74-1109
MC CALL, D.K. THE THEATRE OF JEAN-
  PAUL SARTRE.*
  A. DEMAITRE, 207(FR):DEC71-503
  R. LORRIS, 546(RR):OCT72-244
MC CALL, S. ARISTOTLE'S MODAL SYL-
  LOGISMS.
  I. THOMAS, 316:JUN72-418
MC CARTHY, A. BIG BAND JAZZ.
  R. DAVIES, 617(TLS):2AUG74-826
  D. THOMAS, 362:22AUG74-252
MC CARTHY, C. CHILD OF GOD.*
  R.P. BRICKNER, 441:13JAN74-6
  R. COLES, 442(NY):26AUG74-87
  R. TODD, 61:MAY74-128
MC CARTHY, C. THE DECADE OF UP-
  HEAVAL.
  617(TLS):12APR74-396
MC CARTHY, C. OUTER DARK.
  J. YARDLEY, 473(PR):2/1973-286
MC CARTHY, E. OTHER THINGS & THE
  AARDVARK.*
  D. JAFFE, 590:SPRING/SUMMER73-26
MAC CARTHY, F. ALL THINGS BRIGHT &
  BEAUTIFUL.
  S. GARDINER, 592:JUL/AUG72-59
  J.M.R., 46:SEP72-192
MC CARTHY, M. BIRDS OF AMERICA.*
  S.A. BLACK, 648:OCT72-76
MC CARTHY, M. THE MASK OF STATE.
  B. BEEDHAM, 362:18JUL74-92
  R. GOODWIN, 441:30JUN74-5
  H. ROSENBERG, 453:31OCT74-16
MC CARTHY, M. THE SEVENTEENTH
  DEGREE.
  H. ROSENBERG, 453:31OCT74-16
MC CARTY, C. FILM COMPOSERS IN
  AMERICA.
  K. THOMPSON, 415:JUL73-705
MAC CAY, W. LITTLE NEMO IN SLUMBER-
  LAND.
  P. FRESNAULT-DERUELLE, 98:MAY72-
  460
MACCIOCCHI, M.A. LETTERS FROM IN-
  SIDE THE ITALIAN COMMUNIST PARTY
  TO LOUIS ALTHUSSER.
  617(TLS):12APR74-382
MC CLARY, B.H. - SEE IRVING, W.
MC CLELLAN, E. TWO JAPANESE NOVEL-
  ISTS.*
  C.F. TAEUSCH, 285(JAPQ):APR-JUN
  72-237
MC CLELLAN, J. JOSEPH STORY & THE
  AMERICAN CONSTITUTION.*
  T.P. CAMPBELL, JR., 432(NEQ):
  SEP72-439
  K. PREYER, 656(WMQ):JAN73-172
MC CLELLAND, C.E. THE GERMAN HISTOR-
  IANS & ENGLAND.
  Z. STEINER, 637(VS):DEC72-247

MC CLELLAND, I.L. BENITO JERÓNIMO
FEIJÓO.*
E. HELMAN, 240(HR):AUTUMN72-474
MC CLELLAND, I.L. SPANISH DRAMA OF
PATHOS, 1750-1808.
R.M. COX, 481(PQ):JUL72-620
J. DOWLING, 400(MLN):MAR72-367
G.E. MAZZEO, 238:MAR72-178
MC CLINTOCK, J. & R. - SEE BARNARD,
H.
MC CLINTOCK, R. MAN & HIS CIRCUM-
STANCES.
G. BÖHME, 182:VOL25#7/8-201
MC CLOSKEY, D.N. ECONOMIC MATURITY
& ENTREPRENEURIAL DECLINE.
617(TLS):16AUG74-883
MC CLOSKEY, H.J. META-ETHICS & NOR-
MATIVE ETHICS.*
F.A. OLAFSON, 482(PHR):JAN72-105
MC CLOSKEY, H.J. JOHN STUART MILL.*
K. BRITTON, 483:JUL72-280
MC CLOY, H. THE SLEEPWALKER.
N. CALLENDAR, 441:10MAR74-12
617(TLS):6SEP74-960
MC CLURE, J. THE CATERPILLAR COP.*
N. CALLENDAR, 441:10NOV74-46
MC CLURE, J. THE GOOSEBERRY FOOL.
P. ADAMS, 61:AUG74-91
N. CALLENDAR, 441:1SEP74-14
617(TLS):6SEP74-960
MC CLURE, J. THE STEAM PIG.
N. CALLENDAR, 441:13OCT74-48
MC CLUSKEY, J. LOOK WHAT THEY DONE
TO MY SONG.
M. LEVIN, 441:17NOV74-52
442(NY):25NOV74-194
MACCOBY, H. REVOLUTION IN JUDAEA.
617(TLS):3MAY74-481
MC COLLOM, W.G. THE DIVINE AVERAGE.*
K. MUIR, 447(N&Q):APR72-157
MAC CORKLE, S.A. AUSTIN'S THREE
FORMS OF GOVERNMENT.
W. GARD, 584(SWR):SUMMER73-272
MC CORMACK, J.R., ED. GUI DE NAN-
TEUIL: CHANSON DE GESTE.*
A. IKER-GITTLEMAN, 545(RPH):
FEB73-615
MAC CORMACK, J.R. REVOLUTIONARY
POLITICS IN THE LONG PARLIAMENT.
617(TLS):10MAY74-494
MC CORMICK, D. ISLANDS OF ENGLAND &
WALES. ISLANDS OF IRELAND. IS-
LANDS OF SCOTLAND.
617(TLS):5APR74-377
MC COY, F.N. ROBERT BAILLIE & THE
SECOND SCOTS REFORMATION.
617(TLS):2AUG74-837
MC CRACKEN, D. - SEE GODWIN, W.
MC CROSKEY, J.C. AN INTRODUCTION TO
RHETORICAL COMMUNICATION. (2ND ED)
J.J. CONNER, 583:SUMMER73-399
MC CULLERS, C. THE MORTGAGED HEART.
(M.G. SMITH, ED)
N. GORDIMER, 364:OCT/NOV72-134
MC CULLIN, D. IS ANYONE TAKING ANY
NOTICE?*
617(TLS):12APR74-386
MC CULLOCH, J., ED. UNDER BOW BELLS.
P. HEBBLETHWAITE, 617(TLS):
20DEC74-1447
MC CULLOH, W.E. LONGUS.
B.P. REARDON, 399(MLJ):FEB72-99

MC CULLOUGH, C. STRANGER IN CHINA.*
W.O. DOUGLAS, 31(ASCH):SUMMER74-
490.
P. MITCHELL, 99:JAN74-41
MC CULLOUGH, C. TIM.
M. LEVIN, 441:21APR74-41
MC CULLOUGH, W.S. JEWISH & MANDAEAN
INCANTATION BOWLS IN THE ROYAL ON-
TARIO MUSEUM.
J. STRUGNELL, 318(JAOS):JAN-MAR
72-191
MC CURDY, H.G. THE CHASTENING OF
NARCISSUS.
E. KRICKEL, 219(GAR):SPRING72-71
MAC CURDY, R.R. FRANCISCO DE ROJAS
ZORRILLA.
W.M. WHITBY, 240(HR):SUMMER72-
331
MAC CURDY, R.R., ED. SPANISH DRAMA
OF THE GOLDEN AGE.
E. RUIZ-FORNELLS, 238:MAR72-193
MC CUTCHAN, P. CALL FOR SIMON SHARD.
617(TLS):5APR74-375
MAC DIARMID, H. A DRUNK MAN LOOKS
AT THE THISTLE. (J.C. WESTON, ED)
A. WATT, 376:JAN72-128
MAC DIARMID, H. THE HUGH MAC DIAR-
MID ANTHOLOGY. (M. GRIEVE & A.
SCOTT, EDS) LUCKY POET.
R. PEVEAR, 249(HUDR):SPRING73-
192
MC DONAGH, D. MARTHA GRAHAM.*
617(TLS):18OCT74-1165
MC DONAGH, D. THE RISE & FALL &
RISE OF MODERN DANCE.*
A. PAGE, 290(JAAC):SPRING72-406
MACDONALD, C. AMPUTATIONS.
R. PINSKY, 491:JAN74-241
MACDONALD, D. DISCRIMINATIONS.
R. SALE, 441:3NOV74-3
442(NY):16DEC74-168
MAC DONALD, G. THE GIFTS OF THE
CHILD CHRIST. (G.E. SADLER, ED)
R.L. WOLFF, 617(TLS):15NOV74-
1282
MACDONALD, J.A. THE LETTERS OF SIR
JOHN A. MACDONALD, 1836-1857.
(J.K. JOHNSON, ED) THE LETTERS OF
SIR JOHN A. MACDONALD, 1858-1861.
(J.K. JOHNSON & C.B. STOLMACK,
EDS)
D. HARRISON & J. WALLACE, 14:
APR72-226
MACDONALD, J.D. BIRDS OF AUSTRALIA.
617(TLS):23AUG74-912
MAC DONALD, J.D. THE TURQUOISE
LAMENT.
N. CALLENDAR, 441:6JAN74-22
G. WALKER, 441:1JAN74-17
MAC DONALD, M. HAVERGAL BRIAN.*
J. CANARINA, 607:#102-35
MAC DONALD, M. THE SYMPHONIES OF
HAVERGAL BRIAN. (VOL 1)
617(TLS):5JUL74-706
MACDONALD, R. ON CRIME WRITING.
G. WALKER, 441:1JAN74-17
MAC DONALD, R. SLEEPING BEAUTY.*
R. SALE, 418(MR):AUTUMN73-834
617(TLS):18JAN74-61
MACDONNELL, K. EADWEARD MUYBRIDGE.*
G. MILLAR, 362:25APR74-542
MC DONOUGH, S. THE AUTHORITY OF THE
PAST.
M. SALAHUDDIN, 273(IC):JAN72-85

MC DOUGALL, B.S. THE INTRODUCTION
OF WESTERN LITERARY THEORIES INTO
MODERN CHINA, 1919-1925.
    M. LOI, 549(RLC):OCT-DEC72-623
    P.G. PICKOWITZ, 352(LE&W):VOL15
    #3-519
MAC DOWELL, D.M. - SEE ARISTOPHANES
MC DOWELL, J. - SEE PLATO
MC DOWELL, R.B. & J.A. WOODS - SEE
BURKE, E.
MACE, C.E. TWO SPANISH-QUICHÉ DANCE-
DRAMAS OF RABINAL.
    J. GRIFFITH, 292(JAF):OCT-DEC72-
    388
    P.F. HOGGARTH, 402(MLR):OCT73-
    920
MC ELRATH, D., WITH OTHERS. LORD
ACTON, THE DECISIVE DECADE, 1864-
1874.
    P. MARSH, 637(VS):MAR72-361
MC ELROY, T.P., JR. THE HABITAT
GUIDE TO BIRDING.
    G. GOLD, 441:11MAY74-29
MC EWAN, R. & P. LEWIS - SEE GATLEY,
J.C.C.
MC EWEN, G.D. THE ORACLE OF THE
COFFEE HOUSE.
    F.H. ELLIS, 568(SCN):FALL-WINTER
    73-93
    566:AUTUMN72-50
MAC EWEN, M. CRISIS IN ARCHITECTURE.
    P. NUTTGENS, 362:16MAY74-637
MC FADDEN, D. INTENSE PLEASURE.
    D. HELWIG, 529(QQ):AUTUMN72-404
MC FARLAND, D.T. WILLA CATHER.
    J. WOODRESS, 27(AL):MAR73-123
MC FARLAND, T. COLERIDGE & THE PAN-
THEIST TRADITION.*
    S. PRICKETT, 447(N&Q):MAR72-116
MC FARLAND, T. SHAKESPEARE'S PAS-
TORAL COMEDY.*
    T. HAWKES, 676(YR):SUMMER73-561
    M. MUDRICK, 249(HUDR):SUMMER73-
    375
    639(VQR):SUMMER73-CXVII
MAC FARLANE, A. THE FAMILY LIFE OF
RALPH JOSSELIN, A SEVENTEENTH-
CENTURY CLERGYMAN.*
    J.J. WATERS, 432(NEQ):JUN72-316
MC FARLANE, I.D. A LITERARY HISTORY
OF FRANCE: RENAISSANCE FRANCE 1470-
1589.
    A.J. KRAILSHEIMER, 617(TLS):
    8NOV74-1265
MC FARLANE, I.D. - SEE AGRIPPA D'AUB-
IGNÉ
MC FARLANE, J., ED. HENRIK IBSEN.*
    R-M.G. OSTER, 563(SS):SPRING73-
    167
MC FARLANE, K.B. HANS MEMLING.*
(E. WIND, WITH G.L. HARRISS, EDS)
    L. CAMPBELL, 39:DEC72-563
MAC FARQUHAR, R. THE ORIGINS OF THE
CULTURAL REVOLUTION. (VOL 1)
    J.F. MELBY, 99:SEP74-43
    617(TLS):3MAY74-463
MAC GAFFEY, W. CUSTOM & GOVERNMENT
IN THE LOWER CONGO.
    A. KUPER, 69:JAN72-82
MC GAHERN, J. NIGHTLINES.
    J.M. PURCELL, 573(SSF):FALL72-
    417

MC GANN, J.J. SWINBURNE.*
    C. DAHL, 637(VS):JUN73-480
    L. STEVENSON, 301(JEGP):APR73-
    249
    P. ZIETLOW, 473(PR):3/1973-503
MC GILL, G. ARTHUR.
    617(TLS):30AUG74-933
MC GINNISS, J. THE DREAM TEAM.
    A. ROSS, 364:AUG/SEP73-157
    639(VQR):SUMMER72-CI
MC GIRR, E. BARDEL'S MURDER.
    617(TLS):1FEB74-116
MC GIVERN, W. REPRISAL.*
    617(TLS):6SEP74-960
MC GOVERN, E., WITH M.F. HOYT. UP-
HILL.
    J. O'REILLY, 441:29SEP74-6
MC GOVERN, J.R., ED. ANDREW JACKSON
& PENSACOLA.
    W.S. HOOLE, 9(ALAR):APR72-150
MC GOWAN, M.M. MONTAIGNE'S DECEITS.
    617(TLS):23AUG74-902
MC GRADE, A.S. THE POLITICAL
THOUGHT OF WILLIAM OF OCKHAM.
    G. LEFF, 617(TLS):2AUG74-827
MC GRADY, D. MATEO ALEMÁN.*
    G. SOBEJANO, 240(HR):SUMMER72-
    325
MC GRATH, R.L. EARLY VERMONT WALL
PAINTINGS, 1790-1850.
    M.A. MC CORISON, 432(NEQ):DEC72-
    605
MC GRATH, W.J. DIONYSIAN ART & POPU-
LIST POLITICS IN AUSTRIA.
    R.H. THOMAS, 617(TLS):6DEC74-
    1394
"MC GRAW-HILL DICTIONARY OF ART."*
(B.S. MYERS, ED)
    L. MURRAY, 54:SEP72-372
MC GREEVEY, W.P. AN ECONOMIC HIS-
TORY OF COLOMBIA, 1845-1930.
    H. BERNSTEIN, 263:JUL-SEP73-334
MC GREGOR, C. DON'T TALK TO ME
ABOUT LOVE.
    E. GLOVER, 565:VOL13#3-44
MC GREGOR, R.S., ED. EXERCISES IN
SPOKEN HINDI.*
    E. BENDER, 318(JAOS):OCT-DEC72-
    570
MAC GREGOR, S. THE SINNER.*
    R. GARFITT, 362:21FEB74-248
MC GREW, J.H. - SEE "STURLUNGA SAGA"
MC GUANE, T. THE BUSHWHACKED PIANO.*
    E. ROVIT, 659:AUTUMN74-539
MC GUANE, T. NINETY-TWO IN THE
SHADE.*
    R. DE FEO, 249(HUDR):WINTER73/74-
    775
    617(TLS):2AUG74-825
MC GUINNESS, B.F., T. NYBERG & G.H.
VON WRIGHT - SEE WITTGENSTEIN, L.
MC GUINNESS, R. ENGLISH COURT ODES,
1660-1820.*
    H.L. CLARKE, 414(MQ):JUL72-479
    C.T.P., 566:AUTUMN72-49
MC GUIRE, W. - SEE FREUD, S. & C.G.
JUNG
MACHADO DE ASSIS, J.M. & M. DE AZER-
EDO. CORRESPONDÊNCIA DE MACHADO
DE ASSIS COM MAGALHÃES DE AZEREDO.
(C. VIRGILLO, ED)
    O. FERNÁNDEZ, 399(MLJ):NOV72-462

MC HALE, T. ALINSKY'S DIAMOND.
T. LE CLAIR, 441:20OCT74-38
M. LEVENSON, 231:NOV74-110
L.E. SISSMAN, 442(NY):21OCT74-185
DE MACHAUT, G. LA LOUANGE DES
DAMES.* (N. WILKINS, ED)
F.D., 410(M&L):JUL73-365
MC HENRY, R., WITH C. VAN DOREN, EDS.
A DOCUMENTARY HISTORY OF CONSERVA-
TION IN AMERICA.
H.B. HOUGH, 31(ASCH):WINTER73/74-152
"NICCOLO MACHIAVELLI, THE FIRST 'DE-
CENNALE,' A FACSIMILE OF THE FIRST
EDITION OF FEBRUARY, 1506."
I.F. MAXTED, 325:OCT72-540
MC HUGH, P. & OTHERS. ON THE BEGIN-
NING OF SOCIAL INQUIRY.
617(TLS):3MAY74-473
MC HUGH, R. - SEE YEATS, W.B. & M.
RUDDOCK
MC HUGH, T. THE TIME OF THE BUFFALO.
W. GARD, 584(SWR):SPRING73-V
MACIEJEWSKI, F., ED. THEORIE DER
GESELLSCHAFT ODER SOZIALTECHNOLO-
GIE.
617(TLS):25OCT74-1188
MAC INNES, C. OUT OF THE GARDEN.
V. CUNNINGHAM, 362:7MAR74-311
617(TLS):22FEB74-173
MAC INNES, H. THE SNARE OF THE HUNT-
ER.
N. CALLENDAR, 441:17MAR74-39
MC INNES, N. THE WESTERN MARXISTS.
T. MOLNAR, 396(MODA):SUMMER73-317
MC INTOSH, A. & M.A.K. HALLIDAY.
PATTERNS OF LANGUAGE.* (2ND ED)
M. GRADY, 599:SPRING72-216
MC INTOSH, C. THE CHOICE OF LIFE.
617(TLS):8MAR74-244
MC INTYRE, J., COMP. MIND IN THE
WATERS.
A. GOTTLIEB, 441:3NOV74-68
MACK, D. ANSICHTEN ZUM TRAGISCHEN
UND ZUR TRAGÖDIE.
W.B. LEWIS, 221(GQ):MAY72-519
MACK, M. THE GARDEN & THE CITY.*
P. BRÜCKMANN, 627(UTQ):FALL72-84
MACK, M., ED. THE TWICKENHAM EDI-
TION OF POPE. (VOL 11: INDEX)
R. LONSDALE, 447(N&Q):JUN72-238
MACK, M., JR. KILLING THE KING.
T. HAWKES, 676(YR):SUMMER73-561
639(VQR):AUTUMN73-CXLIX
MC KAIN, D.W., ED. THE WHOLE EARTH.
R. BEUM, 396(MODA):WINTER73-104
MACKAY, A. HIGHLAND PIPE MUSIC.
F. HOWES, 415:APR73-383
MC KAY, A.G. VERGIL'S ITALY.*
R.M. OGILVIE, 123:MAR73-41
K. WELLESLEY, 313:VOL62-220
MC KAY, C. BANANA BOTTOM.
441:14JUL74-30
MACKAY, J. A SOURCE BOOK OF STAMPS.
617(TLS):12APR74-402
MACKAY, J.A. THE DICTIONARY OF
STAMPS IN COLOUR.
617(TLS):15MAR74-273
MACKAY, R.F. FISHER OF KILVERSTONE.
J. GRIGG, 362:21FEB74-245
617(TLS):15MAR74-255

MC KEE, A. KING HENRY VIII'S MARY
ROSE.
442(NY):9SEP74-134
MAC KENDRICK, P. THE ATHENIAN ARIS-
TOCRACY, 399-31 B.C.*
J.K. DAVIES, 123:DEC73-228
MAC KENDRICK, P. ROMAN FRANCE.*
639(VQR):WINTER73-XLIV
MC KENNA, G., ED. AMERICAN POPULISM.
M. NOVAK, 441:4AUG74-16
MACKENZIE, A. THE JOURNALS & LET-
TERS OF SIR ALEXANDER MACKENZIE.*
(W.K. LAMB, ED)
D. SWAINSON, 529(QQ):AUTUMN72-430
MAC KENZIE, A. RIDDLE OF THE FUTURE.
R. HAYNES, 617(TLS):20DEC74-1438
MACKENZIE, D. ZALESKI'S PERCENTAGE.
N. CALLENDAR, 441:7APR74-34
617(TLS):6SEP74-960
MACKENZIE, D.A. THE MIGRATION OF
SYMBOLS & RELATIONS TO BELIEFS &
CUSTOMS.
K.B. HARDER, 424:JUN72-149
MAC KENZIE, D.N. A CONCISE PAHLAVI
DICTIONARY.
M.J. DRESDEN, 361:VOL29#3/4-384
MAC KENZIE, J.P. THE APPEARANCE OF
JUSTICE.
I. SILVER, 441:16JUN74-21
MACKENZIE, K. THE POEMS OF KENNETH
MACKENZIE.
S.E. LEE, 581:SEP73-335
MACKENZIE, O. A HUNDRED YEARS IN
THE HIGHLANDS.
I. FRASER, 595(SCS):VOL17PT2-169
MAC KENZIE, R. THE WINE OF ASTONISH-
MENT.
A. BROYARD, 441:21MAY74-35
M. LEVIN, 441:16JUN74-28
442(NY):3JUN74-108
MACKENZIE, W.M. - SEE DUNBAR, W.
MACKERNESS, E.D. - SEE HAZLITT, W.
MACKEY, F. BILINGUAL EDUCATION IN A
BINATIONAL SCHOOL.
G.R. TUCKER, 608:SEP73-325
MC KIE, D. & C. COOK. THE GUARDIAN/
QUARTET ELECTION GUIDE.
617(TLS):13SEP74-974
MACKIE, J.L. TRUTH, PROBABILITY &
PARADOX.*
J.E. LLEWELYN, 518:OCT73-17
J.J.C. SMART, 63:DEC73-258
MACKIE, P. THE ORGANIZATION.
617(TLS):4OCT74-1092
MACKIE, T.T. & R. ROSE. THE INTER-
NATIONAL ALMANAC OF ELECTORAL
HISTORY.
P. PULZER, 617(TLS):6DEC74-1366
MACKIN, R. & D. CARVER. A HIGHER
COURSE OF ENGLISH STUDY: 2.*
E. SCHRAEPEN, 556(RLV):1972/2-222
MC KINNEY, J.P. THE STRUCTURE OF
MODERN THOUGHT.
M.A. STEWART, 479(PHQ):OCT72-365
MC KINNON, A. FALSIFICATION & BE-
LIEF.*
R.E. SANTONI, 258:MAR72-145
MC KINNON, A. THE KIERKEGAARD IN-
DICES. (VOLS 1&2)
J. COLLINS, 154:SEP72-450

MACKINNON, D.M.   THE PROBLEM OF META-
PHYSICS.
   617(TLS):5APR74-372
MAC KINNON, J.   IN SEARCH OF THE RED
APE.
   442(NY):23SEP74-145
MAC KINNON, S.   SKYDECK.
   D. HELWIG, 529(QQ):AUTUMN72-404
MC KINNON, W.T.   APOLLO'S BLENDED
DREAM.*
   E. MACKENZIE, 541(RES):MAY72-242
MC KINZIE, R.D.   THE NEW DEAL FOR
ARTISTS.
   639(VQR):AUTUMN73-CLXXIII
MC KISACK, M.   MEDIEVAL HISTORY IN
THE TUDOR AGE.*
   R.I. JACK, 325:APR72-439
   C.E. WRIGHT, 382(MAE):1973/2-196
MC KNIGHT, B.E.   VILLAGE & BUREAU-
CRACY IN SOUTHERN SUNG CHINA.
   J.T.C. LIU, 293(JAST):AUG72-927
MACKRELL, J.Q.C.   THE ATTACK ON
"FEUDALISM" IN 18TH CENTURY FRANCE.
   617(TLS):15FEB74-160
MACKSEY, R. & E. DONATO, EDS.   THE
LANGUAGES OF CRITICISM & THE SCI-
ENCES OF MAN.*
   R.H.C., 125:OCT72-86
   J. KOLBERT, 207(FR):OCT71-279
MACKWORTH, C.   ENGLISH INTERLUDES.
   L. ALLEN, 362:1AUG74-153
   617(TLS):11OCT74-1140
MC LANE, J.R., ED.   THE POLITICAL
AWAKENING IN INDIA.
   E.D. CHURCHILL, 293(JAST):NOV71-
   212
MAC LAREN, A.A.   RELIGION & SOCIAL
CLASS.
   617(TLS):30AUG74-935
MACLAREN, D.   LITTLE BLUE ROOM.
   J. MELLORS, 362:11JUL74-61
   617(TLS):6SEP74-960
MC LAUGHLIN, J.C.   ASPECTS OF THE
HISTORY OF ENGLISH.*
   J. ALGEO, 128(CE):MAY72-936
   C.J.E. BALL, 297(JL):SEP72-340
MC LAUGHLIN, P.D., COMP.   PRE-
FEDERAL MAPS IN THE NATIONAL AR-
CHIVES.
   J.M. KINNEY, 14:JUL/OCT72-415
MC LAUGHLIN, T.   MUSIC & COMMUNICA-
TION.
   G. EPPERSON, 290(JAAC):SPRING72-
   405
MACLAY, J.H. & T.O. SLOAN.   INTERPRE-
TATION.
   F. MERRITT, 583:SUMMER73-396
MACLEAN, A.   BREAKHEART PASS.
   617(TLS):31MAY74-591
MACLEAN, A.   FROM THE WILDERNESS.*
   R. GARFITT, 364:FEB/MAR74-108
MACLEAN, A.D., ED.   WINTER'S TALES
20.
   D.A.N. JONES, 617(TLS):20DEC74-
   1437
MACLEAN, M.   LE JEU SUPRÊME.
   617(TLS):23AUG74-902
MC LEAN, R.   VICTORIAN BOOK DESIGN &
COLOUR PRINTING.*   (2ND ED)
   639(VQR):WINTER73-XLII
MC LEAN, R.   VICTORIAN PUBLISHERS'
BOOK-BINDINGS IN CLOTH & LEATHER.
   617(TLS):1MAR74-200

MAC LEAN, S. & OTHERS.   FOUR POINTS
OF A SALTIRE.
   A. WATT, 376:JAN72-123
MACLEAN, V., COMP.   MUCH ENTERTAIN-
MENT.
   M.F.K. FISHER, 442(NY):27MAY74-
   97
MC LEAVE, H.   THE DAMNED DIE HARD.*
   617(TLS):21JUN74-680
MC LEAVE, H.   ONLY GENTLEMEN CAN
PLAY.
   N. CALLENDAR, 441:26MAY74-17
MAC LEISH, A.   THE HUMAN SEASON.
   L. LIEBERMAN, 676(YR):WINTER73-
   267
MAC LEISH, A.   THE MIDDLE ENGLISH
SUBJECT-VERB CLUSTER.
   J.R. SIMON, 189(EA):JAN-MAR72-59
   R. ZIMMERMANN, 38:BAND90HEFT3-
   370
MC LELLAN, D.   KARL MARX.*
   C. LEHMANN-HAUPT, 441:4FEB74-33
   J.E. SEIGEL, 453:31OCT74-35
   S.S. WOLIN, 441:13JAN74-23
MC LELLAN, D. - SEE MARX, K.
MAC LENNAN, H.   CROSS-COUNTRY.
   K. MC SWEENEY, 529(QQ):AUTUMN72-
   438
MC LEOD, A.L. - SEE SMUTS, J.C.
MACLEOD, A.M.   PAUL TILLICH.
   617(TLS):7JUN74-618
MC LEOD, E.   CHARLES OF ORLEANS.
   J.R. SIMON, 189(EA):JAN-MAR72-55
   T. STEMMLER, 38:BAND90HEFT3-386
MAC LEOD, M.J.   SPANISH CENTRAL
AMERICA.
   617(TLS):26APR74-448
MC LEOD, W.H.   GURŪ NĀNAK & THE SIKH
RELIGION.
   G.R. WELBON, 318(JAOS):JAN-MAR72-
   175
MAC LIAMMÓIR, M.   AN OSCAR OF NO
IMPORTANCE.
   J. STREATHER, 159(DM):WINTER/
   SPRING71/72-122
MC LOUGHLIN, J.B.   CONTROL & URBAN
PLANNING.
   617(TLS):13SEP74-984
MC LOUGHLIN, P.F.M., ED.   AFRICAN
FOOD PRODUCTION SYSTEMS.
   A.H.M. KIRK-GREENE, 69:JAN72-80
MC LUHAN, T.C., COMP.   TOUCH THE
EARTH.
   S. LORANT, 639(VQR):SUMMER72-472
MC MAHON, J.J.   THE WORLD OF JEAN-
PAUL SARTRE.
   C.M. DOHERTY, 188(ECR):SPRING72-
   61
MC MANNERS, J.   THE FRENCH REVOLU-
TION & THE CHURCH.
   481(PQ):JUL72-577
MC MASTER, J.   THACKERAY: THE MAJOR
NOVELS.
   S. MONOD, 189(EA):APR-JUN72-330
   S.M. SMITH, 402(MLR):APR73-396
   L. STEVENSON, 637(VS):MAR73-359
   H.P. SUCKSMITH, 150(DR):AUTUMN72-
   507
   M.G. SUNDELL, 594:FALL72-513
   J. SUTHERLAND, 401(MLQ):MAR73-
   105
   J.H. WHEATLEY, 445(NCF):DEC72-
   352

MC MICHAEL, J. AGAINST THE FALLING
EVIL.*
P. COOLEY, 385(MQR):WINTER74-79
MC MILLAN, D., ED. LE CHARROI DE
NÎMES.
J.C. PAYEN, 382(MAE):1973/3-279
MACMILLAN, H. AT THE END OF THE DAY,
1961-1963.*
J. CAMERON, 441:10FEB74-4
MACMILLAN, H. RIDING THE STORM,
1956-1959.*
639(VQR):SUMMER72-XC
MC MILLAN, J.B. ANNOTATED BIBLIOGRA-
PHY OF SOUTHERN AMERICAN ENGLISH.
G.R. WOOD, 35(AS):SPRING-SUMMER
70-138
MAC MULLEN, R. ROMAN SOCIAL RELA-
TIONS.
617(TLS):12APR74-388
MC MULLEN, R. VICTORIAN OUTSIDER.*
D. COOPER, 453:8AUG74-10
H. KRAMER, 441:3MAR74-1
617(TLS):15MAR74-249
MC MURTRY, L. ALL MY FRIENDS ARE
GOING TO BE STRANGERS.*
A.F. CROOKS, 649(WAL):SUMMER72-
151
S. O'CONNELL, 418(MR):WINTER73-
190
MC MURTRY, L. MOVING ON.
A.F. CROOKS, 649(WAL):SUMMER72-
151
MC NALLY, R.T. CHAADAYEV & HIS
FRIENDS.*
M. BANERJEE, 32:DEC73-809
MC NAMARA, E. DILLINGER POEMS.
D. BAILEY, 529(QQ):SUMMER72-242
MC NASPY, C.J. A GUIDE TO CHRISTIAN
EUROPE.
M. LAVANOUX, 363:FEB72-78
MC NAUGHTON, A., COMP. THE BOOK OF
KINGS.*
617(TLS):25JAN74-72
MC NAUGHTON, W. THE BOOK OF SONGS.
A.A. RICKETT, 651(WHR):WINTER73-
93
639(VQR):SPRING73-LXIV
MAC NEIL, D. THE RED DANIEL.
M. LEVIN, 441:7APR74-33
MAC NEIL, D. SUBALTERN'S CHOICE.
M. LEVIN, 441:6OCT74-41
MC NEILL, D. THE ACQUISITION OF
LANGUAGE.*
S.D. FISCHER, 206:NOV72-288
MC NEILL, M. VERE FOSTER.
M.J. WATERS, 637(VS):DEC72-228
MC NEILL, M.R. GUIDELINES TO PROB-
LEMS OF EDUCATION IN BRAZIL.*
M.B. VAUGHAN, 399(MLJ):DEC72-523
MC NEILL, W.H. THE RISE OF THE WEST.
H. STRETTON, 381:MAR72-87
MC NEILL, W.H. THE SHAPE OF EURO-
PEAN HISTORY. VENICE: THE HINGE
OF EUROPE, 1081-1797.
J.H. ELLIOTT, 453:16MAY74-20
MC PHEE, J. THE CURVE OF BINDING
ENERGY.
C. LEHMANN-HAUPT, 441:9JUL74-41
S.S. ODDO, 441:23JUN74-4
MC PHEE, J. ENCOUNTERS WITH THE
ARCHDRUID.
639(VQR):WINTER72-XXXIV

MC PHEETERS, D.W. CAMILO JOSÉ CELA.*
J. DÍAZ, 241:MAY72-92
D.W. FOSTER, 240(HR):SUMMER72-
349
R.L. PREDMORE, 546(RR):APR72-167
MACPHERSON, C.B. LA THÉORIE POLI-
TIQUE DE L'INDIVIDUALISME POSSES-
SIF, DE HOBBES À LOCKE.
J. FREUND, 98:JUN72-555
MC PHERSON, D. - SEE JONSON, B.
MC PHERSON, H. HAWTHORNE AS MYTH-
MAKER.*
J.F. LYNEN, 627(UTQ):WINTER72-
163
MC PHERSON, S. RADIATION.
D. CAVITCH, 441:17NOV74-46
MC PHERSON, T. SOCIAL PHILOSOPHY.
S.S. KLEINBERG, 479(PHQ):JUL72-
283
MACQUARRIE, J. THE CONCEPT OF PEACE.
617(TLS):1MAR74-218
MC QUEEN, I. SHERLOCK HOLMES
DETECTED.
617(TLS):31MAY74-592
MAC QUEEN, J., ED. BALLATIS OF
LUVE.*
D. FOX, 447(N&Q):JAN72-32
K. WITTIG, 38:BAND90HEFT1/2-230
MAC QUEEN, J. ALEXANDER SCOTT &
SCOTTISH COURT POETRY OF THE MID-
DLE SIXTEENTH CENTURY.*
D. FOX, 447(N&Q):JAN72-32
MACRÍ, O. - SEE DE LEÓN, L.
MC SEVENEY, S.T. THE POLITICS OF
DEPRESSION.
639(VQR):SPRING73-LXXXV
676(YR):SPRING73-XII
MC SHEA, R.J. THE POLITICAL PHILOSO-
PHY OF SPINOZA.
S. ZAC, 542:APR-JUN72-225
MC SHERRY, J.E. KHRUSHCHEV & KEN-
NEDY IN RETROSPECT.
A. PARRY, 550(RUSR):JAN72-81
MACSWEENEY, B. OUR MUTUAL SCARLET
BOULEVARD.
J. SAUNDERS, 565:VOL13#3-75
MAC VICAR, A. HEATHER IN MY EARS.
617(TLS):29MAR74-348
MC VICAR, J. MC VICAR BY HIMSELF.
(G. REES, ED)
Z. BARTEK, 362:17OCT74-512
MC WHIRTER, G. CATALAN POEMS.
D. BAILEY, 529(QQ):SUMMER72-242
MC WILLIAMS, W.C. THE IDEA OF FRA-
TERNITY IN AMERICA.*
R.H. ELIAS, 31(ASCH):SPRING74-
308
A.P. GRIMES, 639(VQR):SUMMER73-
477
DE MADARIAGA, S. MORNING WITHOUT
NOON.
442(NY):27MAY74-106
617(TLS):8FEB74-127
MADDEN, D. BIJOU.
S. BLACKBURN, 441:21APR74-35
R. SALE, 453:27JUN74-24
442(NY):27MAY74-105
MADDEN, D., ED. REMEMBERING JAMES
AGEE.
E. WENSBERG, 441:29DEC74-7
MADDEN, L. HOW TO FIND OUT ABOUT
THE VICTORIAN PERIOD.
R.D. ALTICK, 155:JAN72-62

MADDOW, B. EDWARD WESTON: FIFTY
YEARS.
H. KRAMER, 441:1DEC74-34
J. MALCOLM, 442(NY):18NOV74-226
MADDOX, J. THE DOOMSDAY SYNDROME.
J.P. DEGNAN, 249(HUDR):AUTUMN73-
574
J.W. FORRESTER, 111:2FEB73-70
MADDOX, L.G. ADDRESSES OF LESTER
GARFIELD MADDOX, GOVERNOR OF GEOR-
GIA 1967-1971. (F. DANIEL, ED)
E.L. HILL, 14:JUL/OCT72-413
MADDOX, R.J. THE NEW LEFT & THE
ORIGINS OF THE COLD WAR.*
C.B. MARSHALL, 639(VQR):AUTUMN
73-626
MADDY, P.A. OBASAI & OTHER PLAYS.
A. RENDLE, 157:SPRING72-81
MADELUNG, A.M.A. THE LAXDOELA SAGA.
M.E. KALINKE, 563(SS):AUTUMN73-
388
MADGWICK, D. & T. SMYTHE. THE IN-
VASION OF PRIVACY.
617(TLS):19JUL74-765
MADISON, J. THE PAPERS OF JAMES
MADISON. (VOL 7) (W.T. HUTCHINSON
& W.M.E. RACHAL, EDS)
639(VQR):WINTER72-X
MADISON, J. THE PAPERS OF JAMES
MADISON. (VOL 8) (R.A. RUTLAND &
W.M.E. RACHAL, EDS)
639(VQR):AUTUMN73-CLVI
MADSEN, S.A., D. MOWAT & J.M. HENE-
GAN. NEW WRITERS XI.
S. CLAPP, 617(TLS):8NOV74-1248
MAEDA, R.J. TWO TWELFTH CENTURY
TEXTS ON CHINESE PAINTING.
T. LAWTON, 57:VOL34#4-349
MAEHLER, H., ED. URKUNDEN RÖMISCHER
ZEIT.*
H. CADELL, 555:VOL46FASC1-134
MAERTH, O.K. THE BEGINNING WAS THE
END.*
P. ADAMS, 61:APR74-120
MAFFEI, D. IL GIOVANE MACHIAVELLI
BANCHIERE CON BERTO BERTI A ROMA.
617(TLS):14JUN74-632
MAGARSHACK, D. THE REAL CHEKHOV.
N. MARSHALL, 157:WINTER72-76
MAGEE, B. ASPECTS OF WAGNER. (REV)
R. DONINGTON, 415:OCT73-1012
MAGEE, B. MODERN BRITISH PHILOSOPHY.
A. BROADIE, 478:JUL72-150
MAGEE, B. KARL POPPER.*
P. SINGER, 453:2MAY74-22
MAGILL, C.P. GERMAN LITERATURE.
S.S. PRAWER, 617(TLS):13DEC74-
1408
MAGIRIUS, H. DER FREIBERGER DOM.
A. REINLE, 182:VOL25#17/18-614
MAGIS, C.H. LA LÍRICA POPULAR CON-
TEMPORÁNEA.*
P. GALLAGHER, 402(MLR):JUL73-682
M.E. SIMMONS, 240(HR):SPRING72-
235
MAGNE, É. & A. NIDERST - SEE MADAME
DE LAFAYETTE
MAGNER, J.A., JR. JOHN CROWE RAN-
SOM.
L.T. LEMON, 290(JAAC):SUMMER72-
569
MAGNER, T.F. & L. MATEJKA. WORD
ACCENT IN MODERN SERBO-CROATIAN.
T.J. BUTLER, 215(GL):VOL12#2-94

MAGNER, T.F. & W.R. SCHMALSTIEG,
EDS. BALTIC LINGUISTICS.*
E. HOFMANN, 343:BAND15HEFT2-165
J. MARVAN, 279:VOL15-205
J.I. PRESS, 575(SEER):JAN73-125
MAGNUS, B. HEIDEGGER'S METAHISTORY
OF PHILOSOPHY.*
S.A. ERICKSON, 319:APR74-278
R.J.G., 543:DEC71-358
MAGNUS, O. DE GENTIBUS SEPTENTRION-
ALIBUS.
617(TLS):5APR74-368
MAGNUSON, J. WITHOUT BARBARIANS.
J. DECK, 441:60CT74-18
R. TODD, 61:NOV74-107
MAGNUSSON, M. THE CLACKEN & THE
SLATE.
A. BELL, 617(TLS):29NOV74-1344
MAGNY, C-E. THE AGE OF THE AMERICAN
NOVEL.
C. GEDULD, 659:WINTER74-123
DE MAGNY, O. LES CENT DEUX SONNETS
DES "AMOURS" DE 1553.* (M.S.
WHITNEY, ED)
B. BRAUNROT, 207(FR):FEB72-744
M. QUAINTON, 402(MLR):APR73-404
L. TERREAUX, 535(RHL):MAR-APR72-
300
MAGRO, H.S. & P. DE PAULA. PORTU-
GUÊS.
R. HAMILTON, 238:DEC72-985
R.A. PRETO-RODAS, 238:DEC72-985
MAGRUDER, J.S. AN AMERICAN LIFE.
W.S. COFFIN, JR., 231:AUG74-94
B. DE MOTT, 61:AUG74-74
J. GREENFIELD, 441:30JUN74-4
C. LEHMANN-HAUPT, 441:25JUN74-41
442(NY):24JUN74-104
MAGUIRE, D.C. DEATH BY CHOICE.
M.G. MICHAELSON, 441:21JUL74-6
MAGUIRE, W.A. - SEE LORD DOWNSHIRE
MAH, F-H. THE FOREIGN TRADE OF
MAINLAND CHINA.
293(JAST):MAY72-754
MAHAJANI, U. PHILIPPINE NATIONALISM.
P.W. STANLEY, 293(JAST):AUG72-
993
MAHATHIR BIN MOHAMAD. THE MALAY
DILEMMA.
G.D. NESS, 293(JAST):NOV71-223
MAHDI, M. - SEE AL-FÂRÂBÎ
MAHER, B. - SEE KELLY, G.
MAHFÛZ, N. HOB TAHT AL-MATAR.
268:JAN74-68
MAHGOUB, F.M. A LINGUISTIC STUDY OF
CAIRENE PROVERBS.*
E.T. ABDEL-MASSIH, 353:1MAR72-
109
MAHGOUB, M.A. DEMOCRACY ON TRIAL.
G.N. SANDERSON, 617(TLS):18OCT74-
1170
MAHLER, A. GUSTAV MAHLER. (3RD ED)
(D. MITCHELL, ED)
617(TLS):8MAR74-241
MAHMOUDIAN, M. LES MODALITÉS NOMI-
NALES EN FRANÇAIS.
W. ZWANENBURG, 361:VOL29#2-182
MAHON, D. ECCLESIASTES.
J. SAUNDERS, 565:VOL13#3-75
MAHON, D. LIVES.
J. GALASSI, 491:NOV73-113
H. MURPHY, 159(DM):SUMMER72-131

MAHONEY, M.S. THE MATHEMATICAL
CAREER OF PIERRE DE FERMAT (1601-
1665).
617(TLS):12APR74-401
MAHR, J. ÜBERGANG ZUM ENDLICHEN.*
I. LOTZE, 222(GR):MAR72-154
MAI, J. DAS DEUTSCHE KAPITAL IN
RUSSLAND 1850-1894.
E.C. HELMREICH, 104:SPRING72-158
MAIA, P.A., ED. DICIONÁRIO CRÍTICO
DO MODERNO ROMANCE BRASILEIRO.
191(ELN):SEP72(SUPP)-201
MAIBERGER, P. "DAS BUCH DER KOST-
BAREN PERLE" VON SEVERUS IBN AL-
MUQAFFA'.
M. CRAMER, 182:VOL25#11-339
MAIER, A. ZWEI UNTERSUCHUNGEN ZUR
NACHSCHOLASTISCHEN PHILOSOPHIE.
(2ND ED)
R. MALTER, 342:BAND63HEFT2-277
MAIER, P. FROM RESISTANCE TO REVO-
LUTION.*
R. BUEL, JR., 432(NEQ):DEC72-599
G. RUDÉ, 656(WMQ):JAN73-152
MAIER, W. LEBEN, TAT UND REFLEXION.*
H. TUCKER, JR., 221(GQ):NOV72-
763
MAILER, N. MARILYN.*
S.P. LEE & L. ROSS, 42(AR):VOL
32#4-714
G. WEALES, 249(HUDR):WINTER73/74-
769
MAILER, N. - SEE KURLANSKY, M. & J.
NAAR
MAILHOT, L. LA LITTÉRATURE QUÉBÉC-
OISE.
617(TLS):2AUG74-824
MAILING, A. DING-DONG.
N. CALLENDAR, 441:2JUN74-20
MAILLET, A. LES CRASSEUX. GAPI ET
SULLIVAN. MARIAAGÉLAS.
A. POKORNY, 296:VOL3#3-108
MAILLOUX, K.F. & H.P. LENIN.
B.D. WOLFE, 32:JUN73-385
MAILS, T.E. THE PEOPLE CALLED
APACHE.
I.R. DEE, 441:1DEC74-18
MAIN, J.T. POLITICAL PARTIES BEFORE
THE CONSTITUTION.
E.J. FERGUSON, 656(WMQ):OCT73-
661
J.P. GREENE, 639(VQR):SPRING73-
295
MAINUSCH, H. ROMANTISCHE ÄSTHETIK.
H. OPPEL, 430(NS):JAN72-47
H.M. SCHUELLER, 290(JAAC):FALL71-
128
MAINWARING, M., ED & TRANS. THE
PORTRAIT GAME.*
442(NY):21JAN74-96
MAISEL, E.M. CHARLES T. GRIFFES.
C. PALMER, 415:SEP73-899
MAÎTRE, H.J. THOMAS MANN.
R. NÄGELE, 221(GQ):MAY72-516
G. WENZEL, 654(WB):12/1971-185
MAJAULT, J. VIRGINIE, OR THE DAWN-
ING OF THE WORLD.
M. LEVIN, 441:19MAY74-40
MAJED KHAN, A. THE TRANSITION IN
BENGAL 1756-1775.
R.A. CALLAHAN, 318(JAOS):JAN-MAR
72-182

MAJOR, M. & T.M. PEARCE, EDS. SOUTH-
WEST HERITAGE. (3RD ED)
W. GARD, 584(SWR):SPRING73-V
"MAJOR ACQUISITIONS OF THE PIERPONT
MORGAN LIBRARY 1924-1974."
617(TLS):26JUL74-814
MAKAEV, È.A. STRUKTURA SLOVA V INDO-
EVROPEJSKIX I GERMANSKIX JAZYKAX.
R. ANTTILA, 350:SEP73-701
MAKAI, M. THE DIALECTICS OF MORAL
CONSCIOUSNESS.
A. FLEW, 518:JAN73-22
MAKARIUS, R. & L. STRUCTURALISME
OU ETHNOLOGIE.
617(TLS):18JAN74-58
MAKECHNIE, S. JACOB SPORNBERG.
F.G. ROE, 135:JUL72-227
MAKONNEN, R. PAN-AFRICANISM FROM
WITHIN.
617(TLS):21JUN74-665
MAKSIMOV, V. SEM' DNEI TVORENIIA.
D. POSPIELOVSKY, 550(RUSR):APR72-
195
MALAGÓN, J., ED. LAS ACTAS DE INDE-
PENDENCIA DE AMÉRICA. (2ND ED)
S.R. ROSS, 263:OCT-DEC73-465
MALAGÓN, J. & S. ZAVALA. RAFAEL AL-
TAMIRA Y CREVEA.
G. DE ZÉNDEGUI, 37:FEB72-40
MALAMUD, B. REMBRANDT'S HAT.*
E. FEINSTEIN, 364:FEB/MAR74-137
M. MUDRICK, 249(HUDR):AUTUMN73-
545
MALAMUD, B. THE TENANTS.*
E. FEINSTEIN, 364:JUN/JUL72-166
M.M., 502(PRS):FALL72-275
639(VQR):WINTER72-XIX
MALANTSCHUK, G. DIALECTIQUE ET EXIS-
TENCE CHEZ SØREN KIERKEGAARD.
A.M. FINNEMANN, 542:JUL-SEP72-
381
MALANTSCHUK, G. KIERKEGAARD'S
THOUGHT.
G.J. STACK, 319:OCT74-538
MALANTSCHUK, G. LE PROBLÈME DE LA
LIBERTÉ DANS LE CONCEPT DE L'AN-
GOISSE DE KIERKEGAARD.
A.M. FINNEMANN, 542:JUL-SEP72-
380
MALCOLM, A. THE TYRANNY OF THE
GROUP.
M. WOLFE, 99:JUL74-37
MALCOLM, H. GENERATION OF NARCIS-
SUS.
G. FORBES, 376:JUL72-141
MALCOLM, N. PROBLEMS OF MIND.
C.H. WHITELEY, 479(PHQ):OCT72-
367
MALE, D.J. RUSSIAN PEASANT ORGANI-
ZATION BEFORE COLLECTIVIZATION.
R. TOWBER, 550(RUSR):JAN72-97
MALEVICH, K.S. ESSAYS ON ART 1915-
1933. (T. ANDERSEN, ED)
A.C. BIRNHOLZ, 290(JAAC):FALL72-
128
P. SLOANE, 127:FALL72-110
MALGONKAR, M. THE DEVIL'S WIND.
Y.J. DAYANANDA, 352(LE&W):VOL15
#3-523
42(AR):VOL32#3-497
DE MALHERBE, F. OEUVRES. (A. ADAM,
ED)
O. DE MOURGUES, 208(FS):JAN73-58

MALICET, M. - SEE CLAUDEL, P. & L.
MASSIGNON
MALIK, H., ED. IQBAL.
M.U. MEMON, 293(JAST):AUG72-982
R.J. NELSON, 485(PE&W):OCT72-483
MALIK, S.C. INDIAN CIVILIZATION -
THE FORMATIVE PERIOD.
L. ROCHER, 318(JAOS):OCT-DEC72-
572
MALIN, I., ED. CONTEMPORARY AMERI-
CAN-JEWISH LITERATURE.
D. FUCHS, 659:AUTUMN74-562
MALING, A. DINGDONG.
442(NY):27MAY74-108
MALINS, E. YEATS AND MUSIC.
G. HOFFMANN, 38:BAND90HEFT1/2-
266
MALITA, M. AURUL CENUSIU.
617(TLS):15MAR74-252
MALKIEL, Y. ESSAYS ON LINGUISTIC
THEMES.*
W.P. LEHMANN, 206:MAR72-280
MALKIEL, Y. LINGUISTICA GENERALE,
FILOLOGIA ROMANZA, ETIMOLOGIA.*
A. BOHNET, 320(CJL):VOL18#1-81
MALKIEL, Y. PATTERNS OF DERIVATION-
AL AFFIXATION IN THE CABRANIEGO
DIALECT OF EAST-CENTRAL ASTURIAN.
J.R. CRADDOCK, 361:VOL28#4-383
MALKOFF, K. CROWELL'S HANDBOOK OF
CONTEMPORARY AMERICAN POETRY.
I. MALIN, 31(ASCH):SUMMER74-502
DE MALLAC, G. & M. EBERBACH. BAR-
THES.
M.A. CAWS, 188(ECR):WINTER72-318
MALLÉ, L. INCONTRI CON GAUDENZIO.
T.S.R. BOASE, 54:MAR72-94
MALLEA, E. CHAVES.* (B. & A. GICO-
VATE, EDS)
M.I. LICHTBLAU, 399(MLJ):MAR72-
184
MALLET, J. THEY CAN'T HANG ME!
442(NY):14OCT74-203
MALLETT, M. MERCENARIES & THEIR
MASTERS.
617(TLS):1FEB74-102
MALLORY, K. & A. OTTAR. ARCHITEC-
TURE OF AGGRESSION.
617(TLS):1MAR74-199
MALMBERG, B. LES DOMAINES DE LA
PHONÉTIQUE.
G.F. MEIER, 682(ZPSK):BAND25
HEFT6-534
MALMBERG, B., ED. MANUAL OF PHONET-
ICS. (2ND ED)
K. WODARZ-MAGDICS, 353:JAN72-77
MALMBERG, B. PHONÉTIQUE FRANÇAISE.
P.R. LEON, 207(FR):FEB72-718
B. ROCHET, 320(CJL):VOL18#1-68
MALMSTROM, J. & J. LEE. TEACHING
ENGLISH LINGUISTICALLY.
F. GOMES DE MATOS, 351(LL):DEC72-
301
MALONE, D. JEFFERSON THE PRESIDENT:
SECOND TERM, 1805-1809.
J.M. BANNER, JR., 441:5MAY74-2
G. WILLS, 453:2MAY74-15 [& CONT.
IN] 453:16MAY74-9
MALONEY, R. FISH IN A STREAM IN A
CAVE.
S. O'CONNELL, 418(MR):WINTER73-
190

MALORY, T. THE WORKS OF SIR THOMAS
MALORY.* (2ND ED) (E. VINAVER, ED)
J.M. COWEN, 447(N&Q):JAN72-30
MALOUF, D. BICYCLE, & OTHER POEMS.*
J. SAUNDERS, 565:VOL13#3-75
MALRAUX, A. FELLED OAKS.
R.C. MACRIDIS, 639(VQR):AUTUMN72-
600
MALRAUX, A. LA TÊTE D'OBSIDIENNE.
THE VOICES OF SILENCE.
617(TLS):24MAY74-552
MALRAUX, A. - SEE CHARBONNEAUX, J.,
R. MARTIN & F. VILLARD
MALRAUX, A. & A. PARROT - SEE HUBERT,
J., J. PORCHER & W.F. VOLBACH
MALTBY, A. THE GOVERNMENT OF NORTH-
ERN IRELAND, 1922-72.
617(TLS):12APR74-402
MALTESE, C. - SEE FRANCESCO DI GIOR-
GIO MARTINI
VON MALTITZ, H. THE EVOLUTION OF
HITLER'S GERMANY.
N. ASCHERSON, 453:18APR74-3
MALTZ, A. AFTERNOON IN THE JUNGLE.
G.O. CAREY, 573(SSF):SUMMER72-
287
MALTZ, M. PSYCHO-CYBERNETICS.
E.A. SCHMERLER, 186(ETC.):SEP72-
322
MALZBERG, B.N. BEYOND APOLLO.
617(TLS):23AUG74-911
MAMATEY, V.S. & R. LUŽA, EDS. A
HISTORY OF THE CZECHOSLOVAK REPUB-
LIC, 1918-1948.
617(TLS):12APR74-401
MAMCZARZ, I. LES INTERMÈDES COM-
IQUES ITALIENS AU XVIIIE SIÈCLE EN
FRANCE ET EN ITALIE.
D. GRONAU, 182:VOL25#23/24-865
DE MAN, P. BLINDNESS & INSIGHT.*
M.A. CAWS, 188(ECR):WINTER72-318
MANCALL, M. RUSSIA & CHINA.*
G.A. LENSEN, 550(RUSR):JAN72-75
E. WIDMER, 293(JAST):NOV71-208
MANCHESTER, W. THE GLORY & THE
DREAM.
A. BROYARD, 441:15NOV74-41
A. KAZIN, 441:17NOV74-2
E. WEEKS, 61:DEC74-123
MANCINI, A.N. IL ROMANZO NEL SEI-
CENTO.
D. CONRIERI, 228(GSLI):VOL149
FASC468-613
MANCINO, L. LA BELLA SCIENZA.
617(TLS):4OCT74-1090
MANCROFT, L. A CHINAMAN IN MY BATH
& OTHER PIECES.
617(TLS):7JUN74-620
MANCUSI-UNGARO, H.R., JR. THE
BRUGES MADONNA & THE PICCOLOMINI
ALTAR.
J. SHAPLEY, 127:WINTER72/73-248
MAŃCZAK, W. LE DÉVELOPPEMENT PHONÉT-
IQUE DES LANGUES ROMANES ET LE FRÉ-
QUENCE.*
G. FRANCESCATO, 353:1DEC72-95
MANDEL, A.S. "LA CELESTINA" STUDIES.
D.P. TESTA, 593:SUMMER73-182
MANDEL, E., ED. CONTEXTS OF CAN-
ADIAN CRITICISM.*
S. DJWA, 648:JAN73-46
G.V. DOWNES, 376:APR72-123
S.L. DRAGLAND, 529(QQ):AUTUMN72-
408

MANDEL, J. & B.A. ROSENBERG, EDS.
MEDIEVAL LITERATURE & FOLKLORE
STUDIES.
 C.G. ZUG 3D, 292(JAF):JUL-SEP72-
 278
MANDELBAUM, D.G. SOCIETY IN INDIA.
 O.M. LYNCH, 293(JAST):FEB72-429
MANDELBAUM, M. HISTORY, MAN, &
REASON.
 R.P.M., 543:JUN72-761
 H.L. PARSONS, 484(PPR):SEP72-119
MANDELSTAM, N. HOPE ABANDONED.
 J. BRODSKY, 453:7FEB74-13
 B. DE MOTT, 61:FEB74-87
 S. KARLINSKY, 441:20JAN74-1
 C. LEHMANN-HAUPT, 441:15JAN74-41
 M. MESIC, 491:JUL74-232
 C. NEWMAN, 231:FEB74-83
 P. WINDSOR, 362:21MAR74-371
MANDELSTAM, N. HOPE AGAINST HOPE.*
 M. MESIC, 491:JUL74-232
 T. PACHMUSS, 399(MLJ):MAR72-177
 G. STEINER, 442(NY):18FEB74-113
MANDELSTAM, O. COMPLETE POETRY OF
OSIP EMILIEVICH MANDELSTAM. (B.
RAFFEL & A. BURAGO, TRANS; S.
MONAS, ED)
 J. BRODSKY, 453:7FEB74-13
 S. KARLINSKY, 441:20JAN74-1
MANDELSTAM, O. OSIP MANDEL'SHTAM,
SELECTED POEMS.* (D. MC DUFF,
TRANS)
 J. BRODSKY, 453:7FEB74-13
MANDELSTAM, O. SELECTED POEMS.*
(C. BROWN & W.S. MERWIN, TRANS)
 J. BRODSKY, 453:7FEB74-13
 B. DE MOTT, 61:FEB74-86
 S. KARLINSKY, 441:20JAN74-1
 M. MESIC, 491:JUL74-232
MANDER, J. ALLEN ADAIR. (D. TUR-
NER, ED)
 617(TLS):8MAR74-237
MANDER, J. OUR GERMAN COUSINS.
 617(TLS):2AUG74-828
MANDER, R. & J. MITCHENSON. REVUE.
 N. MARSHALL, 157:SPRING72-76
MANDERS, F.W.D. A HISTORY OF GATES-
HEAD.
 617(TLS):12APR74-402
DE MANDIARGUES, A.P. - SEE UNDER
PIEYRE DE MANDIARGUES, A.
MANDL, H. KOMPENDIUM DEUTSCHSPRACH-
IGER SCHULREIFETESTS.
 K. SAMSTAG, 182:VOL25#5/6-137
MANE, R. HENRY ADAMS ON THE ROAD TO
CHARTRES.*
 M.I. BAYM, 613:WINTER72-612
 J.W. CROWLEY, 432(NEQ):JUN72-292
 C.H. HOLMAN, 189(EA):OCT-DEC72-
 579
 639(VQR):SPRING72-LXII
MANEGOLD VON LAUTENBACH. LIBER CON-
TRA WOLFELMUM. (W. HARTMANN, ED)
 R. FOLZ, 182:VOL25#21-727
MANÉN, L. THE ART OF SINGING.
 W. GRUNER, 617(TLS):13DEC74-1411
MANET, E. LES NONNES.
 F. TONELLI, 207(FR):DEC71-477
"MANET/MONET/DEGAS."
 R.M. QUINN, 50(ARQ):AUTUMN72-288
MANETTI, A.D. THE LIFE OF BRUNEL-
LESCHI. (H. SAALMAN, ED)
 J.S. ACKERMAN, 54:JUN72-208

MANEY, A.S. & R.L. SMALLWOOD, EDS.
MHRA STYLE BOOK.
 R. SHACKLETON, 208(FS):APR73-243
MANGANELLI, G. LUNARIO DELL'ORFANO
SANNITA.
 617(TLS):3MAY74-478
MANGELSDORF, P.C. CORN.
 617(TLS):27SEP74-1048
MANGIONE, J. THE DREAM & THE DEAL.*
 M. ORVELL, 31(ASCH):AUTUMN74-671
 W. THORP, 27(AL):NOV73-480
 441:14JUL74-34
MANGO, C. THE ART OF THE BYZANTINE
EMPIRE, 312-1453 A.D.
 P. BROWN, 453:30CT74-3
MANGOLD, M.M., ED. LA CAUSA CHICANA.
 W. GARD, 584(SWR):AUTUMN73-361
MANGUM, D. THE FARGUS TECHNIQUE.*
 639(VQR):AUTUMN73-CXXXVI
MANKIEWICZ, J.L. & G. CAREY. MORE
ABOUT "ALL ABOUT EVE."*
 P. SCHJELDAHL, 441:8DEC74-36
MANKIN, P. & A. SZOGYI, EDS. ANTHOL-
OGIE D'HUMOUR FRANÇAIS.
 N. OXENHANDLER, 207(FR):DEC71-
 546
MANLEY, M.D. THE NOVELS OF MARY
DELARIVIERE MANLEY.* (P. KÖSTER,
ED)
 H.L. SNYDER, 481(PQ):JUL72-729
MANN, E. COMRADE GEORGE.
 F. CARNEY, 453:28NOV74-17
MANN, E.A. THE PORTALS.
 N. CALLENDAR, 441:19MAY74-42
MANN, F.A. STUDIES IN INTERNATIONAL
LAW.
 617(TLS):25JAN74-83
MANN, G. ZWÖLF VERSUCHE.
 617(TLS):10MAY74-498
MANN, J. THE STICKING PLACE.
 617(TLS):22NOV74-1308
MANN, M. HEINRICH HEINES MUSIKKRIT-
IKEN.
 J.L.S., 191(ELN):SEP72(SUPP)-152
MANN, P. & R. KLÜGER. THE LAST
ESCAPE.
 441:10NOV74-41
MANN, T. DER TOD IN VENEDIG.*
(A.W. HORNSEY, ED)
 W.D. WETZELS, 399(MLJ):FEB72-118
MANN, T. DER TOD IN VENEDIG. (T.J.
REED, ED)
 D.G. LITTLE, 402(MLR):JUL73-691
 205(FMLS):JUL72-287
MANNES, M. LAST RIGHTS.
 D. CALLAHAN, 441:3MAR74-14
 C. LEHMANN-HAUPT, 441:11JAN74-29
MANNHEIM, K. FROM KARL MANNHEIM.
(K.H. WOLFF, ED)
 639(VQR):SPRING72-LXXVI
MANNING, O. THE RAIN FOREST.
 V. CUNNINGHAM, 362:18APR74-509
 617(TLS):5APR74-357
MANNING, S.B. DICKENS AS SATIRIST.*
 R.J. ALLEN, 637(VS):JUN72-492
 G.B. TENNYSON, 445(NCF):DEC72-
 369
 R. TRICKETT, 155:JAN72-54
MANNIX, D.P. DRIFTER.
 M. LEVIN, 441:23JUN74-34
"MAN'S IMPACT ON THE GLOBAL ENVIRON-
MENT."
 C. MC FARLAND, 639(VQR):WINTER72-
 126

MANSERGH, N. & E.W.R. LUMBY, EDS.
CONSTITUTIONAL RELATIONS BETWEEN
BRITAIN & INDIA: THE TRANSFER OF
POWER 1942-7. (VOLS 1&2)
M. COOK, 325:APR72-433
MANSERGH, N. & E.W.R. LUMBY, EDS.
CONSTITUTIONAL RELATIONS BETWEEN
BRITAIN & INDIA: THE TRANSFER OF
POWER 1942-7. (VOL 4)
617(TLS):18JAN74-57
MANSFIELD, J. THE PSEUDO-HIPPOCRAT-
IC TRACT "PERI HEBDOMADON" CH.
1-11 & GREEK PHILOSOPHY.*
M. VEGETTI, 548(RCSF):APR-JUN72-
234
MANSFIELD, K. UNDISCOVERED COUNTRY.
(I.A. GORDON, ED)
P. BEER, 617(TLS):22NOV74-1307
MANSFIELD, M. - SEE BLAKELEY, F.
MANSFIELD, P. THE BRITISH IN EGYPT.
M.S. CHERTOFF, 287:NOV72-29
MANSION, J.E., COMP. HARRAP'S NEW
STANDARD FRENCH & ENGLISH DICTION-
ARY.* (PT 1: FRENCH-ENGLISH)
(REV & ED BY R.P.L. & M. LEDÉSERT)
P. RICKARD, 208(FS):OCT73-489
205(FMLS):OCT72-383
MANSUY, M. ETUDES SUR L'IMAGINATION
DE LA VIE.*
J-P. CAUVIN, 207(FR):DEC71-497
MANSUY, M., ED. POSITIONS ET OPPOSI-
TIONS SUR LE ROMAN CONTEMPORAIN.
J. CRUICKSHANK, 208(FS):OCT73-
482
M. PICARD, 535(RHL):JUL-AUG72-
741
MANTE, A., ED. EINE NIEDERDEUTSCHE
BIRGITTA-LEGENDE AUS DER MITTE DES
XV. JAHRHUNDERTS.
L. HERMODSSON, 597(SN):VOL44#2-
433
MANTHORPE, J. THE POWER & THE TOR-
IES.
G.L. CAPLAN, 99:NOV/DEC74-42
MANTOY, J. LES 50 MOTS CLÉS DE LA
PSYCHOLOGIE DE L'ENFANT.
M. ADAM, 542:OCT-DEC72-473
MANUEL, F.E. FREEDOM FROM HISTORY.
R.H.C., 125:JUN73-328
MANUWALD, B. DAS BUCH H DER ARIS-
TOTELISCHEN PHYSIK.
P.M. HUBY, 123:DEC73-270
MANVELL, R. SHAKESPEARE & THE FILM.
639(VQR):AUTUMN72-CLVI
676(YR):AUTUMN72-XX
MANVELL, R. & H. FRAENKEL. THE GER-
MAN CINEMA.
J.M. HIGHSMITH, 290(JAAC):SUMMER
72-571
MANZALAOUI, M., ED. ARABIC WRITING
TODAY: THE SHORT STORY.
G.M. WICKENS, 352(LE&W):VOL15#4
&VOL16#1/2-908
MAO TSE-TUNG. THE POEMS OF MAO TSE-
TUNG.* (W. BARNSTONE, WITH KO
CHING-PO, EDS & TRANS)
639(VQR):AUTUMN72-CXXV
MAQUET, J. AFRICANITY.*
639(VQR):SPRING73-LXXXVII
MAQUET, J. POWER & SOCIETY IN AFRI-
CA.
L. MAIR, 69:OCT72-346

MARAMBAUD, P. WILLIAM BYRD OF WEST-
OVER, 1674-1744.
C.R. DOLMETSCH, 639(VQR):WINTER
72-145
L.B. WRIGHT, 481(PQ):JUL72-653
MARANDA, P. & E.K., EDS. STRUCTURAL
ANALYSIS OF ORAL TRADITION.*
W.H. JANSEN, 582(SFQ):MAR72-96
MARAWILLE, S. FOOL'S GOLD.
M. LEVIN, 441:19MAY74-40
MARBY, H. TEA IN CEYLON.
P. VOSSELER, 182:VOL25#12-446
MARC-LIPIANSKY, M. LA NAISSANCE DU
MONDE PROUSTIEN DANS "JEAN SAN-
TEUIL."
617(TLS):17MAY74-513
MARCADÉ, V. LE RENOUVEAU DE L'ART
PICTURAL RUSSE.
J.E. BOWLT, 32:JUN73-433
MARCEL, G. COLERIDGE ET SCHELLING.
E. JOOS, 154:DEC72-602
MARCH, L. & P. STEADMAN. GEOMETRY
OF ENVIRONMENT.
P. PURCELL, 46:JUN72-391
MARCHAM, F.G. - SEE "LOUIS AGASSIZ
FUERTES & THE SINGULAR BEAUTY OF
BIRDS"
MARCHAND, H. THE CATEGORIES & TYPES
OF PRESENT-DAY ENGLISH WORD-FORMA-
TION.* (2ND ED)
L. MOESSNER, 343:BAND14HEFT2-199
W. VIERECK, 430(NS):AUG72-493
MARCHAND, L.A. - SEE LORD BYRON
MARCHANT, L.R. - SEE GILES, L.
MARCHANT, R.A. THE CHURCH UNDER THE
LAW.
P. SLACK, 447(N&Q):MAY72-189
MARCHE, A. LUZON & PALAWAN.
M.S. MC LENNAN, 293(JAST):AUG72-
998
MARCHETEAU, M. & J. TARDIEU. BUSI-
NESS & ECONOMICS.
A. MOULIN, 556(RLV):1972/4-448
MARCHETTI, V.L. & J.D. MARKS. THE
C.I.A. & THE CULT OF INTELLIGENCE.
R.J. BARNET, 453:30CT74-29
W. MILLER, 441:18AUG74-5
C. WHEELER, 362:26SEP74-409
MARCIC, R. HEGEL UND DAS RECHTS-
DENKEN.
W. SCHMIED-KOWARZIK, 53(AGP):
BAND54HEFT1-95
MARCONI, D. IL MITO DEL LINGUAGGIO
SCIENTIFICO.
E. NAMER, 542:JAN-MAR72-116
MARCOTTE, P.J. PRIAPUS UNBOUND.
J.B. FORT, 189(EA):OCT-DEC72-541
MARCOVALDI, G. ASPETTI DELLO SPIR-
ITO DI DANTE.
E. NAMER, 542:APR-JUN72-169
MARCUCCI, S. L'IDEALISMO SCIENTIF-
ICO DI WILLIAM WHEWELL.
A.M., 543:SEP71-130
MARCUCCI, S. HENRY L. MANSEL.*
R. BLANCHÉ, 542:JUL-SEP72-384
MARCUS, J.R. THE COLONIAL AMERICAN
JEW, 1492-1776.
M. RISCHIN, 656(WMQ):APR73-353
MARCUS, M. FIVE MINUTES TO NOON.
C. WATTS, 448:SPRING72-104

MARCUS, P.L. YEATS & THE BEGINNINGS
OF THE IRISH RENAISSANCE.*
H. ADAMS, 219(GAR):FALL72-249
M. SIDNELL, 627(UTQ):SPRING72-
263
MARCUS, S. ENGELS, MANCHESTER, &
THE WORKING CLASS.
A. BRIGGS, 441:28APR74-27
F. KERMODE, 453:30MAY74-6
A.J.P. TAYLOR, 617(TLS):25OCT74-
1181
MARCUS, S. MINDING THE STORE.
L. SLOANE, 441:22NOV74-35
MARCUS, S. - SEE HAMMETT, D.
MARCUSE, H. COUNTERREVOLUTION &
REVOLT.
D. YERGIN, 676(YR):AUTUMN72-147
MARCUSE, H. STUDIES IN CRITICAL
PHILOSOPHY.
W.V. DONIELA, 63:DEC73-267
MARDER, A.J. FROM THE DARDANELLES
TO ORAN.
S. ROSKILL, 617(TLS):13DEC74-
1415
DE LA MARE, A., COMP. CATALOGUE OF
THE COLLECTION OF MEDIAEVAL MANU-
SCRIPTS BEQUEATHED TO THE BODLEIAN
LIBRARY, OXFORD, BY JAMES P.R.
LYELL.
J. BACKHOUSE, 382(MAE):1973/3-
293
DE MARE, E. LONDON 1851.
617(TLS):8MAR74-244
DE MARE, E. THE NAUTICAL STYLE.
617(TLS):12APR74-401
MARECHAL, E.R. - SEE UNDER ROSBACO
MARECHAL, E.
MARECHAL, L. LA BATALLA DE JOSÉ
LUNA.
G.E. SMITH, 238:MAR72-185
MAREIN, S. STITCHERY NEEDLEPOINT
APPLIQUE & PATCHWORK.
L.J. GARTNER, JR., 441:8DEC74-51
MAREN-GRISEBACH, M. METHODEN DER
LITERATURWISSENSCHAFT.
O. CHRISTIANSEN, 597(SN):VOL44#2-
420
M. ZUTSHI, 402(MLR):JAN73-225
MARGALEF, R. PERSPECTIVES IN ECOLOG-
ICAL THEORY.
L.G., 543:SEP71-131
MARGARIS, A. FIRST ORDER MATHEMATI-
CAL LOGIC.
A.H. LIGHTSTONE, 316:SEP72-616
DE MARGERIE, B. LE CHRIST POUR LE
MONDE.
H. MUSURILLO, 613:AUTUMN72-463
MARGOLIN, J-C. DOUZE ANNÉES DE BIB-
LIOGRAPHIE ÉRASMIENNE (1950-1961).
A. DE LATTRE, 542:APR-JUN72-169
MARGOLIOUTH, H.W. - SEE MARVELL, A.
MARGOLIS, J.D. T.S. ELIOT'S INTEL-
LECTUAL DEVELOPMENT, 1922-1939.*
W.W. ROBSON, 473(PR):WINTER73-
136
C.H. SMITH, 659:SPRING74-277
E. WEBB, 648:JAN73-79
MARGOLIUS, H. I DO NOT WANT TO
REMEMBER.
E.S. TURNER, 362:11JUL74-60
617(TLS):3MAY74-482
MARGOTTA, R. AN ILLUSTRATED HISTORY
OF MEDICINE. (P. LEWIS, ED)
E. YOUNG, 39:MAY72-426

MARGUERITE DE NAVARRE. CHANSONS
SPIRITUELLES.* (G. DOTTIN, ED)
J.L. ALLAIRE, 207(FR):FEB72-748
J. GELERNT, 551(RENQ):WINTER72-
464
K.M. HALL, 208(FS):JUL73-323
M. SOULIÉ, 535(RHL):MAR-APR72-
300
MARGUERITE DE NAVARRE. LA COCHE.
(R. MARICHAL, ED)
J.L. ALLAIRE, 207(FR):FEB72-748
G. DOTTIN, 535(RHL):JUL-AUG72-
703
J. GELERNT, 551(RENQ):WINTER72-
464
K.M. HALL, 208(FS):JUL73-323
MARGUERITE DE NAVARRE. MARGUERITES
DE LA MARGUERITE DES PRINCESSES.
J.L. ALLAIRE, 207(FR):FEB72-748
D. WILSON, 208(FS):JAN73-51
MARGUERITE DE NAVARRE. TALES FROM
THE HEPTAMÉRON.* (H.P. CLIVE, ED)
J. GELERNT, 551(RENQ):WINTER72-
464
A.T. HARRISON, 207(FR):DEC71-531
DE MARIA, A. ANTROPOLOGIA E TEODI-
CEA DI MALEBRANCHE.
E. NAMER, 542:APR-JUN72-218
MARIAH, P. PERSONAE NON GRATAE.
G. MALANGA, 491:JAN74-236
MARIANI, G. IL PRIMO MARINETTI.
P. ZOCCOLA, 228(GSLI):VOL149
FASC466/467-452
MARIANI, P.L. A COMMENTARY ON THE
COMPLETE POEMS OF GERARD MANLEY
HOPKINS.*
M. BOWEN, 405(MP):AUG72-80
MARÍAS, J. AMERICA IN THE FIFTIES
& SIXTIES. (M.A. ROCKLAND, ED)
R. KIRK, 676(YR):AUTUMN72-142
MARÍAS, J. METAPHYSICAL ANTHROPOLO-
GY.
A. DONOSO, 258:SEP72-462
MARIATEGUI, J.C. SEVEN INTERPRETIVE
ESSAYS ON PERUVIAN REALITY.
V. DE ROZENTAL, 37:AUG72-41
MARICHAL, J. - SEE AZAÑA, M.
MARICHAL, R. - SEE MARGUERITE DE
NAVARRE
DE MARICHAL, S.S. - SEE UNDER SALI-
NAS DE MARICHAL, S.
MARÍN, D. LITERATURA ESPAÑOLA.
(VOL 1)
W. WOODHOUSE, 238:DEC72-983
MARIN, P. IN A MAN'S TIME.
M. LEVENSON, 231:SEP74-78
M. ROSENTHAL, 441:5MAY74-55
MARINELLI, P.V. PASTORAL.
P.A. MC CARTHY, 399(MLJ):NOV72-
463
MARIO, T. PLAYBOY'S WINE & SPIRITS
COOKBOOK.
N. HAZELTON, 441:8DEC74-26
MARION, F. OFF WITH THEIR HEADS!
G. RINGGOLD, 200:NOV72-563
MARISSEL, A. SAUVÉ DES EAUX.
R.R. HUBERT, 207(FR):FEB72-699
MARITAIN, J. APPROCHES SANS EN-
TRAVES.
617(TLS):5APR74-374
MARITAIN, J. & E. MOUNIER. MARITAIN-
MOUNIER. (J. PETIT, ED)
617(TLS):5APR74-374

MARKAKIS, J. ETHIOPIA.
E. ULLENDORFF, 617(TLS):20SEP74-
998
MARKANDAYA, K. THE NOWHERE MAN.*
J. MELLORS, 364:AUG/SEP73-150
MARKANDAYA, K. TWO VIRGINS.*
617(TLS):17MAY74-517
VAN MARKEN, A. KNUT HAMSUN EN DE
VROUWENFIGUREN IN ZIJN WERK.
A. BOLCKMANS, 172(EDDA):1972/3-
179
MARKER, F.J. HANS CHRISTIAN ANDER-
SEN & THE ROMANTIC THEATRE.
E. BREDSDORFF, 301(JEGP):JAN73-
116
J.E. DE MYLIUS, 563(SS):AUTUMN73-
398
E. SPRINCHORN, 627(UTQ):SPRING73-
297
MARKFIELD, W. YOU COULD LIVE IF
THEY LET YOU.
R. ALTER, 441:3NOV74-6
MARKOV, D. GENEZIS SOCIALISTIČE-
SKOGO REALIZMA.
E. BAYER, M. JÄHNICHEN & H. JÜN-
GER, 654(WB):12/1971-179
MARKS, J., WITH G.A. MARKS & A.J.
FARMER. HARRAP'S FRENCH-ENGLISH
DICTIONARY OF SLANG & COLLOQUIAL-
ISMS.*
V. GUILLOTON, 207(FR):DEC71-492
M. PIRON, 209(FM):OCT72-368
N.C.W. SPENCE, 208(FS):JUL73-362
MARKSTEIN, G. THE COOLER.
617(TLS):31MAY74-591
MARLOWE, C. THE COMPLETE WORKS OF
CHRISTOPHER MARLOWE. (F. BOWERS,
ED)
617(TLS):8FEB74-130
639(VQR):AUTUMN73-CXLIX
MARLOWE, C. THE PLAYS OF CHRISTO-
PHER MARLOWE.* (R. GILL, ED)
M. HATTAWAY, 402(MLR):JAN73-153
MARLOWE, C. TAMBURLAINE. (J.W.
HARPER, ED)
J. GURY, 549(RLC):JAN-MAR72-139
MARLOWE, D. SOMEBODY'S SISTER.
N. CALLENDAR, 441:24NOV74-39
MARLOWE, S. THE MAN WITH NO SHADOW.
M. LEVIN, 441:30JUN74-31
MARNELL, W.H. THE GOOD LIFE OF
WESTERN MAN.
H. STRETTON, 381:MAR72-87
MAROSÁN, G. AZ ÚTON VÉGIG KELL
MENNI.
A. FELKAY, 32:JUN73-413
MAROT, C. LES EPIGRAMMES.* (C.A.
MAYER, ED)
R.M. BURGESS, 551(RENQ):SPRING
72-91
S.M. CARRINGTON, 207(FR):FEB72-
752
I.D. MC FARLANE, 402(MLR):APR73-
403
MARQUARDT, H. HENRY CRABB ROBINSON
UND SEINE DEUTSCHEN FREUNDE.
J. BOURKE, 38:BAND90HEFT3-406
MARQUARDT, W.F. & OTHERS. ENGLISH
AROUND THE WORLD.
A.M. MALKOÇ, 608:JUN73-167
MARQUES, A.H.D. - SEE UNDER DE OLI-
VEIRA MARQUES, A.H.
MÁRQUEZ, G.G. - SEE UNDER GARCÍA
MÁRQUEZ, G.

MARR, D. & J. WERNER - SEE VIEN, N.K.
MARR-JOHNSON, D. TAKE A GOLDEN
SPOON.
M. LEVIN, 441:27JAN74-18
MARRA, N. VIETNAM SE DIVIERTE.
J. RICCI, 241:SEP72-69
MARRIOTT, A. COUNTRIES.
D. BARBOUR, 150(DR):SPRING72-167
MARRIS, P. LOSS & CHANGE.
M.P. DUMONT, 441:24NOV74-3
617(TLS):13SEP74-966
MARRIS, P. & A. SOMERSET. AFRICAN
BUSINESSMEN.
M. PEIL, 69:JAN72-84
MARSDEN, B.M. THE EARLY BARROW-
DIGGERS.
617(TLS):9AUG74-864
MARSH, A.I. & E.O. EVANS. THE DIC-
TIONARY OF INDUSTRIAL RELATIONS.
617(TLS):4JAN74-18
MARSH, F.B. A HISTORY OF THE ROMAN
WORLD FROM 146 TO 30 B.C. (REV BY
H.H. SCULLARD)
J-C. RICHARD, 555:VOL46FASC2-350
MARSH, N. BLACK AS HE'S PAINTED.
N. CALLENDAR, 441:25AUG74-29
442(NY):5AUG74-88
617(TLS):31MAY74-591
MARSHACK, A. THE ROOTS OF CIVILIZA-
TION.*
G. DAVENPORT, 249(HUDR):SPRING73-
248
MARSHALL, A. GIRLS WILL BE GIRLS.
N. ANNAN, 617(TLS):13SEP74-967
MARSHALL, B. OPERATION ISCARIOT.
617(TLS):30AUG74-933
MARSHALL, D. INDUSTRIAL ENGLAND,
1776-1851.*
639(VQR):AUTUMN73-CLXVI
MARSHALL, J. BEARINGS.
J. MATTHIAS, 491:APR74-45
MARSHALL, J.H. - SEE ADAM DE LA
HALLE
MARSHALL, J.H. - SEE VIDAL, R.
MARSHALL, P.J., ED. THE BRITISH
DISCOVERY OF HINDUISM IN THE
EIGHTEENTH CENTURY.
F.F. CONLON, 293(JAST):FEB72-431
R. ROCHER, 318(JAOS):APR-JUN72-
319
MARSHALL, R. THE HAUNTED MAJOR.
617(TLS):17MAY74-529
MARSHALL, R.G., C.J. SCHMITT & P.E.
WOODFORD. LA FUENTE HISPANA.
S.I. ARELLANO, 238:SEP72-602
G.E.A. SCAVNICKY, 399(MLJ):APR72-
267
MARSHALL, R.H., JR., WITH T.E. BIRD
& A.Q. BLANE, EDS. ASPECTS OF
RELIGION IN THE SOVIET UNION, 1917-
1967.*
J.S. CURTISS, 550(RUSR):JAN72-98
E. DUNN, 104:SPRING72-138
MARSHALL, R.K. THE DAYS OF DUCHESS
ANNE.
617(TLS):12APR74-399
MARSHALL, R.L. THE COMPOSITIONAL
PROCESS OF J.S. BACH.*
W. EMERY, 415:APR73-380
F. SALZER, 308:VOL16#1/2-220
J.A.W., 410(M&L):JUL73-362
MARSHALL, S.L.A. CRIMSONED PRAIRIE.*
639(VQR):SPRING73-LXXXIV

MARSHALL, T. THE PSYCHIC MARINER.*
K. MC SWEENEY, 529(QQ):AUTUMN72-
438
MARSHALL-CORNWALL, J. HAIG AS MILI-
TARY COMMANDER.
617(TLS):1MAR74-197
MARTELL, G. THE POLITICS OF THE
CANADIAN PUBLIC SCHOOL.
D. MYERS, 99:NOV/DEC74-27
MARTELLO, P.J. RIME PER LA MORTE
DEL FIGLIO. (G. SPAGNOLETTI, ED)
M. FUBINI, 228(GSLI):VOL149FASC
466/467-431
MARTELLOZZO FORIN, E., ED. ISTITUTO
PER LA STORIA DELL'UNIVERSITÀ DI
PADOVA: ACTA GRADUUM ACADEMICORUM
AD ANNO 1501 AD ANNUM 1525; AB
ANNO 1526 AD ANNUM 1538; AB ANNO
1538 AD ANNUM 1550.
P. ZAMBELLI, 548(RCSF):JUL-SEP72-
342
MARTÍ, J. LUCÍA JEREZ.
M.A. SALGADO, 241:MAY72-95
MARTI, M. CON DANTE FRA I POETI DEL
SUO TEMPO. (2ND ED)
228(GSLI):VOL149FASC466/467-459
MARTI, M. - SEE BOCCACCIO, G.
MARTIAL D'AUVERGNE. MATINES DE LA
VIERGE. (Y. LE HIR, ED)
P.M.F. KUNSTMANN, 207(FR):APR72-
1065
C.C. WILLARD, 545(RPH):MAY73-736
MARTIENSSEN, A. QUEEN KATHERINE
PARR.
617(TLS):22FEB74-193
MARTÍN, C. AMÉRICA EN RUBÉN DARÍO.
S.J. SWINYARD, 263:OCT-DEC73-470
MARTIN, C., ED. ANDRÉ GIDE I.
J. ONIMUS, 557(RSH):OCT-DEC72-
624
MARTIN, C. THE SAGA OF THE BUFFALO.
639(VQR):AUTUMN73-CLXXIV
MARTIN, D. GENERAL AMIN.
K. KYLE, 362:4JUL74-27
MARTIN, D. TRACTS AGAINST THE
TIMES.*
617(TLS):1FEB74-98
MARTIN, F.D. ART & THE RELIGIOUS
EXPERIENCE.
C.W. KEGLEY, 290(JAAC):SUMMER73-
546
MARTIN, G. THE DURHAM REPORT &
BRITISH POLICY.
G. PATTERSON, 99:MAR74-43
MARTIN, G., ED. ELIOT IN PERSPEC-
TIVE.*
C.H. SMITH, 659:SPRING74-277
S. SPENDER, 453:19SEP74-18
MARTIN, G. THE RED SHIRT & THE
CROSS OF SAVOY.
E. ZAPPULLA, 276:SPRING72-92
MARTIN, G.D., ED & TRANS. ANTHOLOGY
OF CONTEMPORARY FRENCH POETRY.
205(FMLS):OCT72-379
MARTIN, G.D. - SEE VALÉRY, P.
MARTIN, H. ARMAN.
A. FRANKENSTEIN, 55:NOV73-49
MARTIN, H.H. RALPH MC GILL, REPOR-
TER.*
G. MC MILLAN, 453:18APR74-32
MARTIN, H-J. LIVRE, POUVOIRS ET
SOCIÉTÉ À PARIS AU XVIIE SIÈCLE
(1598-1701).*
W. FLOECK, 72:BAND210HEFT1/3-221

MARTIN, J-C. MOODS.
A. ABEL, 207(FR):MAR72-902
MARTIN, J.H. LOVE'S FOOLS.
K. WHINNOM, 402(MLR):JAN73-144
MARTIN, J.L., B. NICHOLSON & N. GABO
- SEE "CIRCLE"
MARTIN, J.S. RAGNARÖK.
J. SIMPSON, 203:WINTER72-342
MARTIN, K. DIE ALEXANDERSCHLACHT
VON ALBRECHT ALTDORFER.
E. YOUNG, 39:JUN72-518
MARTIN, L. ARMS & STRATEGY.
617(TLS):1MAR74-197
MARTIN, M. THREE POPES & THE CARDI-
NAL.*
J.P. BOYLE, 396(MODA):FALL73-435
MARTIN, P. SHAKESPEARE'S SONNETS.
J. MC AULEY, 67:MAY73-114
MARTIN, R. RECHERCHES SUR LES AGRO-
NOMES LATINS ET LEUR CONCEPTIONS
SOCIALES ET ÉCONOMIQUES.
K.D. WHITE, 313:VOL62-194
MARTIN, R. TEMPS ET ASPECT.
J. CHAURAND, 209(FM):OCT72-360
T.B.W. REID, 208(FS):OCT73-501
MARTIN, R.G. THE WOMAN HE LOVED.
C. CURTIS, 441:25AUG74-7
A. FORBES, 617(TLS):1NOV74-1213
MARTIN, R.M. BELIEF, EXISTENCE, &
MEANING.*
J. BACON, 258:JUN72-279
MARTIN, R.M. LOGIC, LANGUAGE & META-
PHYSICS.
J.M.B. MOSS, 479(PHQ):OCT72-371
MARTINDALE, A. THE RISE OF THE
ARTIST IN THE MIDDLE AGES & EARLY
RENAISSANCE.
639(VQR):SPRING73-XCI
MARTINEAU, H. A DESCRIPTION OF THE
ENGLISH LAKES.
617(TLS):29MAR74-342
MARTINET, A. GRUNDZÜGE DER ALLGE-
MEINEN SPRACHWISSENSCHAFT.
K. DETTWILER, 343:BAND14HEFT1-
102
MARTINET, A., ED. LA LINGUISTIQUE.*
L. MOESSNER, 260(IF):BAND76-203
W.G. MOULTON, 350:MAR73-161
MARTINET, A. LA LINGUISTIQUE SYN-
CHRONIQUE.
P.A.M. SEUREN, 353:FEB72-109
MARTINET, A. SYNCHRONISCHE SPRACH-
WISSENSCHAFT.
D. MESSNER, 430(NS):DEC72-747
MARTÍNEZ NADAL, R. "EL PÚBLICO."*
C. DE COSTER, 397(MD):DEC72-341
MARTINI, F.D. - SEE UNDER FRANCESCO
DI GIORGIO MARTINI
MARTINS, W. THE MODERNIST IDEA.
M.L. DANIEL, 399(MLJ):FEB72-97
MARTY, S. HEADWATERS.
L. HICKS, 99:MAY/JUN74-20
M.T. LANE, 198:SUMMER74-125
MARTZ, L.L. THE WIT OF LOVE.*
R. FREEMAN, 541(RES):FEB72-70
MARUYAMA HISAKO, ED. SADO KUNINAKA
NO MUKASHIBANASHI.
F.H. MAYER, 293(JAST):AUG72-911
MARVELL, A. THE POEMS & LETTERS OF
ANDREW MARVELL. (H.W. MARGOLIOUTH,
ED; 3RD ED REV BY P. LEGOUIS WITH
E.E. DUNCAN-JONES)
R. ELLRODT, 189(EA):OCT-DEC72-
552

MARVELL, A. THE POEMS OF ANDREW
MARVELL. (J. REEVES & M. SEYMOUR-
SMITH, EDS)
N.W. BAWCUTT, 447(N&Q):MAY72-198
MARVELL, A. THE REHEARSAL TRANS-
POS'D [&] THE REHEARSAL TRANSPOS'D
THE SECOND PART.* (D.I.B. SMITH,
ED)
P. LEGOUIS, 189(EA):APR-JUN72-
326
L.A. DAVIES, 677:VOL3-286
H. KELLIHER, 541(RES):AUG72-355
MARX, G. & R.J. ANOBILE. THE MARX
BROS. SCRAPBOOK.*
P. SCHJELDAHL, 441:8DEC74-35
MARX, K. CRITIQUE OF HEGEL'S "PHIL-
OSOPHY OF RIGHT." (J. O'MALLEY,
ED)
R.J.B., 543:SEP71-131
A. HOLLOWAY, 479(PHQ):APR72-168
J.A. SCHWANDT, 613(AUTUMN72-471
MARX, K. GRUNDRISSE.* (M. NICOLAUS,
ED & TRANS)
J.E. SEIGEL, 453:31OCT74-35
MARX, K. MARX'S GRUNDRISSE.* (D.
MC LELLAN, ED & TRANS)
R.J.B., 543:SEP71-132
MARX, K. & F. ENGELS. ERGÄNZUNS-
BAND.
F. MARKOVITS, 98:JAN72-53
MARX, W. HEIDEGGER & THE TRADITION.
J.D.C., 543:DEC71-359
MARX, W. OILSPILL.
42(AR):SPRING/SUMMER72-250
MARY, A. - SEE VILLON, F.
MARZAC, N. - SEE CIBOULE, R.
MASARYK, T.G. THE MEANING OF CZECH
HISTORY.
617(TLS):15NOV74-1289
MASCAGNA, R. - SEE DE CARTAGENA, A.
MASCALL, E.L. THE OPENNESS OF BEING.
G.A. MC COOL, 613:WINTER72-632
MASCHNER, H. NATURE, MORALITY &
INDIVIDUAL.
K. OEDINGEN, 342:BAND63HEFT1-128
MASEFIELD, J. CAPTAIN MARGARET.
P.J. KEATING, 617(TLS):29NOV74-
1347
MASER, W. HITLER.
N. ASCHERSON, 453:18APR74-3
MASIELLO, V. VERGA TRA IDEOLOGIA E
REALTÀ.
400(MLN):JAN72-163
MASIH, Y. INTRODUCTION TO RELIGIOUS
PHILOSOPHY.
A.B. CREEL, 485(PE&W):OCT72-482
MASINTON, C.G. CHRISTOPHER MAR-
LOWE'S TRAGIC VISION.
R.E. KNOLL, 401(MLQ):DEC73-462
C.J. SUMMERS, 568(SCN):SPRING73-
10
K. TETZELI VON ROSADOR, 72:BAND
21OHEFT4/6-369
MASKALERIS, T. KOSTIS PALAMAS.
P. BIEN, 32:DEC73-864
MASKELL, D. THE HISTORICAL EPIC IN
FRANCE 1500-1700.
617(TLS):19JUL74-771
MASON, A.E.W. AT THE VILLA ROSA.
P.J. KEATING, 617(TLS):29NOV74-
1347

MASON, G. THE PAPERS OF GEORGE
MASON, 1725-1792.* (R.A. RUTLAND,
ED)
J.P. GREENE, 579(SAQ):WINTER73-
159
MASON, H.A. TO HOMER THROUGH POPE.*
W. FROST, 566:SPRING73-99
MASON, P. PATTERNS OF DOMINANCE.*
G.D. BERREMAN, 318(JAOS):APR-JUN
72-325
MASON, R.H.P. JAPAN'S FIRST GENERAL
ELECTION, 1890.
G. AKITA, 244(HJAS):VOL32-256
MASSANO, R. ROMANTICISMO ITALIANO E
CULTURA EUROPEA.
O.R., 191(ELN):SEP72(SUPP)-187
MASSAR, I. THE ILLUSTRATED WORLD OF
THOREAU.
H. BEVINGTON, 441:1DEC74-82
MASSAUT, J-P. JOSSE CLICHTOVE,
L'HUMANISME ET LA RÉFORME DU
CLERGÉ.
M.J. KRAUS, 551(RENQ):AUTUMN72-
337
MASSET, P. LES 50 MOTS CLÉS DU
MARXISME.
M. ADAM, 542:JUL-SEP72-388
MASSEY, I. THE UNCREATING WORD.*
I.F., 191(ELN):SEP72(SUPP)-13
MASSIE, S., ED. THE LIVING MIRROR.
E. MORGAN, 617(TLS):11OCT74-1132
MASSINGHAM, B. TURN ON THE FOUN-
TAINS.
A. BELL, 617(TLS):13DEC74-1421
M. LASKI, 362:19&26DEC74-847
MASSIOT, M. LES INSTITUTIONS POLI-
TIQUES ET ADMINISTRATIVES DE LA
RÉPUBLIQUE MALGACHE.
J. VANDERLINDEN, 69:APR72-164
MASSO, R. & A. SÅ SNAKKER VI NORSK.
S.R. SMITH, 563(SS):WINTER73-76
MASSON, A. LE DÉCOR DES BIBLIO-
THÈQUES DU MOYEN AGE À LA RÉVOLU-
TION.
617(TLS):25OCT74-1207
MASSON, A. MASSACRES ET AUTRES DES-
SINS.
D. HOLLIER, 98:JAN72-23
MASSON, E. ÉTUDE DE VINGT-SIX BOUL-
ES D'ARGILE INSCRITES TROUVÉES À
ENKOMI ET HALA SULTAN TEKKE (CHY-
PRE).
J.T. HOOKER, 303:VOL92-243
MASSON, J.L. & M.V. PATWARDHAN.
ŚĀNTARASA & ABHINAVAGUPTA'S PHIL-
OSOPHY OF AESTHETICS.*
E. GEROW & A. AKLUJKAR,
318(JAOS):JAN-MAR72-80
MASSON, V.M. & V.I. SARIANIDI. CEN-
TRAL ASIA. (R. TRINGHAM, ED &
TRANS)
C.S. CHARD, 32:MAR73-156
MASTERMAN, J.C. THE DOUBLE-CROSS
SYSTEM IN THE WAR OF 1939 TO 1945.
R. CONQUEST, 364:JUN/JUL72-157
639(VQR):SUMMER72-XCVI
MASTERS, A. BAKUNIN.
617(TLS):9AUG74-864
MASTERS, B. MOLIÈRE.
J.H. PHILLIPS, 188(ECR):SPRING72-
71
MASTERS, G.M. RABELAISIAN DIALECTIC
& THE PLATONIC-HERMETIC TRADITION.*
J.C. LAPP, 546(RR):FEB72-44

MASTERS, J. THUNDER AT SUNSET.
M. LEVIN, 441:4AUG74-27
617(TLS):7JUN74-619
MASTERS, R.D. THE POLITICAL PHILOSO-
PHY OF ROUSSEAU.
D.A. DAY, 321:SUMMER72-158
MASTERS, R.E.L. THE HIDDEN WORLD OF
EROTICA.
G. EWART, 364:AUG/SEP73-144
MASTERSON, P. ATHEISM & ALIENATION.*
J. HEJJA, 613:WINTER72-627
MASTERSON, W. THE MAN WITH TWO
CLOCKS.
N. CALLENDAR, 441:27OCT74-56
MASUMI, S.H. - SEE AL-RAZI, I.F.A.
MATANOVIC, A. & B. RABAR, EDS. THE
ENCYCLOPAEDIA OF CHESS OPENINGS.
(VOL C)
617(TLS):29NOV74-1351
MATCZAK, S.A. PHILOSOPHY.*
H.F., 543:MAR72-561
MATEJKA, L. INTRODUCTORY BIBLIOGRA-
PHY OF SLAVIC PHILOLOGY.
G.E. CONDOYANNIS, 660(WORD):
APR70-150
MATEJKA, L. & K. POMORSKA, EDS.
READINGS IN RUSSIAN POETICS.*
L.T.L., 502(PRS):SUMMER72-187
G.S. SMITH, 575(SEER):OCT73-602
"MATEMATIČESKIE METODY V JAZYKOZ-
NANII."
W. LEHFELDT, 353:15AUG72-108
MATER, E. DEUTSCHE VERBEN. (PTS
7&8)
M.H. FOLSOM, 353:FEB72-125
MATER, E. RÜCKLÄUFIGES WÖRTERBUCH
DER DEUTSCHEN GEGENWARTSSPRACHE.
S. KLEYE, 682(ZPSK):BAND24HEFT6-
529
MATER, E. & J. ŠTINDLOVÁ, EDS. LES
MACHINES DANS LA LINGUISTIQUE.
G.F. MEIER, 682(ZPSK):BAND25
HEFT3-249
MATES, B. ELEMENTARE LOGIK (PRÄDI-
KATENLOGIK DER ERSTEN STUFE).
A. CHURCH, 316:SEP72-615
MATES, B. ELEMENTARY LOGIC. (2ND
ED)
A. CHURCH, 316:JUN72-419
MATHER, B. THE WHITE DACOIT.
M. LEVIN, 441:10NOV74-22
MATHER, C. SELECTED LETTERS OF COT-
TON MATHER. (K. SILVERMAN, ED)
D.B. RUTMAN, 432(NEQ):JUN72-305
S.J. STEIN, 173(ECS):FALL72-137
MATHERS, M. RIDING THE RAILS.*
P. ADAMS, 61:JAN74-99
MATHERS, P. THE WORT PAPERS.
N. KEESING, 581:SEP73-345
MATHESON, W. - SEE MORISON, R.
MATHEWS, J. - SEE VALÉRY, P.
MATHEWS, T.F. THE EARLY CHURCHES OF
CONSTANTINOPLE.*
P. BROWN, 453:3OCT74-3
I.E. ELLINGER, 127:WINTER72/73-
238
MATHIAS, R. ABSALOM IN THE TREE.
A. CLUYSENAAR, 565:VOL13#2-72
MATHIAS, R. VERNON WATKINS.
A. YOUNG, 617(TLS):27DEC74-1461
MATHIEU, V. - SEE KANT, I.
MATICH, O. PARADOX IN THE RELIGIOUS
POETRY OF ZINAIDA GIPPIUS.
T. PACHMUSS, 32:DEC73-854

MATILAL, B.K. THE NAVYA-NYĀYA DOC-
TRINE OF NEGATION. (D.H.H. IN-
GALLS, ED)
I.M. COPI, 485(PE&W):APR72-221
MATISSE, H. ÉCRITS ET PROPOS SUR
L'ART.*
J. SEZNEC, 208(FS):OCT73-488
MATORÉ, G., WITH J. CADIOT-CUEILLER-
ON, EDS. MÉLANGES DE LINGUISTIQUE
ET DE PHILOLOGIE ROMANES DÉDIÉS À
LA MÉMOIRE DE PIERRE FOUCHÉ (1891-
1967). ᵀ
N.C.W. SPENCE, 208(FS):JUL73-364
MATORÉ, G. & I. MECZ. MUSIQUE ET
STRUCTURE ROMANESQUE DANS LA
"RECHERCHE DU TEMPS PERDU."
R.H-M., 410(M&L):OCT73-460
MATSUMOTO, S. MOTOORI NORINAGA,
1730-1801.*
R.L. BACKUS, 318(JAOS):OCT-DEC
72-561
MATSUNAGA, A. THE BUDDHIST PHILOSO-
PHY OF ASSIMILATION.*
I. WATSON, 302:JUL72-210
MATTAUCH, H. DIE LITERARISCHE KRIT-
IK IN FRÜHEN FRANZÖSISCHEN ZEIT-
SCHRIFTEN (1665-1748).*
N. SUCKLING, 182:VOL25#1/2-39
MATTENKLOTT, G. BILDERDIENST.
C. KRÖLL, 52:BAND7HEFT2/3-334
MATTER, H., ED. DIE LITERATUR ÜBER
THOMAS MANN.
I.B. JONAS, 182:VOL25#17/18-609
MATTES, J. DER WAHNSINN IM GRIECH-
ISCHEN MYTHOS UND IN DER DICHTUNG
BIS ZUM DRAMA DES FÜNFTEN JAHRHUN-
DERTS.*
A.F. GARVIE, 123:DEC73-190
MATTESINI, F. LA CRITICA LETTERARIA
DI GIACOMO DEBENEDETTI.
P.Z., 228(GSLI):VOL149FASC466/
467-467
MATTHAEI, R. - SEE VON GOETHE, J.W.
MATTHEWS, B. THE RECEDING WAVE.*
A.A. PHILLIPS, 381:DEC72-486
MATTHEWS, C.M. PLACE NAMES OF THE
ENGLISH-SPEAKING WORLD.
R.I. MC DAVID, JR., 579(SAQ):
AUTUMN73-617
MATTHEWS, D.J. & C. SHACKLE, EDS &
TRANS. AN ANTHOLOGY OF CLASSICAL
URDU LOVE LYRICS.
L.A. FLEMMING, 352(LE&W):VOL15
#4&VOL16#1/2-914
MATTHEWS, G.M., ED. KEATS: THE
CRITICAL HERITAGE.
M. ALLOTT, 677:VOL3-312
MATTHEWS, J. THE CHARISMA CAMPAIGNS.
639(VQR):SUMMER72-C
MATTHEWS, J. OVER MY SHOULDER.
E.S. TURNER, 617(TLS):25OCT74-
1191
MATTHEWS, J. PICTURES OF THE JOUR-
NEY BACK.*
P. CRUTTWELL & F. WESTBURG,
249(HUDR):SUMMER73-419
639(VQR):SUMMER73-CIV
MATTHEWS, J.F. GEORGE BERNARD SHAW.
J-C. AMALRIC, 189(EA):OCT-DEC72-
574
MATTHEWS, J.H. SURREALISM & FILM.
J.M. WHITE, 593:SUMMER73-165

MATTHEWS, J.H. THEATRE IN DADA & SURREALISM.
  J. PLAUT, 31(ASCH):AUTUMN74-688
MATTHEWS, M., ED. SOVIET GOVERN-MENT.
  617(TLS):15MAR74-273
MATTHEWS, P.H. MORPHOLOGY.
  617(TLS):29NOV74-1337
MATTHEWS, R.A. INDUSTRIAL VIABILITY IN A FREE TRADE ECONOMY.
  J.L. MC DOUGALL, 529(QQ):SPRING 72-111
MATTHEWS, T.S. GREAT TOM.
  D.J. ENRIGHT, 362:15AUG74-218
  L. GRAVER, 441:3MAR74-7
  D.W. HARDING, 617(TLS):18OCT74-1154
  S. SPENDER, 453:19SEP74-18
  J. UPDIKE, 442(NY):8APR74-137
MATTHEWS, W. SLEEK FOR THE LONG FLIGHT.*
  R. PINSKY, 491:JAN74-241
MATTHEWS, W., F. SMITH & E. GOLDBERG, EDS. MAN'S IMPACT ON TERRESTRIAL & OCEANIC ECOSYSTEMS.
  42(AR):VOL32#3-511
MATTHIESSEN, P. & E. PORTER. THE TREE WHERE MAN WAS BORN.*
  639(VQR):SPRING73-XCIII
MATURO, G. CLAVES SIMBÓLICAS DE GABRIEL GARCÍA MÁRQUEZ.
  268:JAN74-76
MATUTE, A.M. LA TORRE VIGÍA.
  J.W. DÍAZ, 238:SEP72-593
MATUTE, A.M. LA TRAMPA.
  J.W. DÍAZ, 241:SEP72-71
MATVEJEVITCH, P. LA POÉSIE DE CIR-CONSTANCE.
  M. SCHAETTEL, 557(RSH):JUL-SEP72-481
MAUCHLINE, M. HAREWOOD HOUSE.
  R. FULFORD, 617(TLS):6DEC74-1363
MAUGHAM, R. THE BARRIER.*
  M. LEVIN, 441:26MAY74-19
MAUGHAM, R. THE SIGN.
  617(TLS):23AUG74-911
MAULNIER, T. & G. PROUTEAU. L'HON-NEUR D'ÊTRE JUIF.
  J. SUNGOLOWSKY, 207(FR):DEC71-450
MAUNG, M. BURMA & PAKISTAN.
  R.L. FELDBERG, 293(JAST):MAY72-719
DE MAUPASSANT, G. "BOULE DE SUIF" ET AUTRES CONTES NORMANDS. (M-C. BANCQUART, ED)
  P. COGNY, 535(RHL):MAR-APR72-339
  G. HAINSWORTH, 208(FS):OCT73-467
MAURENS, J. - SEE DE VOLTAIRE, F.M.A.
MAURER, C.B. CALL TO REVOLUTION.
  J. GODFREY, 150(DR):SPRING72-155
MAURER, F. DICHTUNG UND SPRACHE DES MITTELALTERS. (2ND ED)
  D. BLAMIRES, 402(MLR):JUL73-688
MAURER, F., ED. DIE RELIGIÖSEN DICH-TUNGEN DES 11. UND 12. JAHRHUN-DERTS.* (VOL 3)
  D.A. WELLS, 220(GL&L):OCT72-79
MAURER, F. - SEE WALTHER VON DER VOGELWEIDE.
MAURER, W.R. THE NATURALIST IMAGE OF GERMAN LITERATURE.
  J.A. KRUSE, 182:VOL25#17/18-611

MAURIAC, C. THE OTHER DE GAULLE.*
  R.O. PAXTON, 441:27JAN74-6
  442(NY):21JAN74-94
MAURIAC, C. LE TEMPS IMMOBILE.
  617(TLS):5JUL74-730
MAURIAC, F. LA PHARISIENNE. (A.M.C. WILCOX, ED)
  205(FMLS):OCT72-383
DU MAURIER, D. THE INFERNAL WORLD OF BRANWELL BRONTË.
  441:10MAR74-33
MAUROIS, A. MEMOIRS 1885-1967.* (FRENCH TITLE: MÉMOIRES.)
  J. KOLBERT, 207(FR):DEC71-478
"CHARLES MAURRAS ET LA VIE FRANÇAISE SOUS LA TROISIÈME RÉPUBLIQUE."
  617(TLS):14JUN74-631
MAURY, C. FOLK ORIGINS OF INDIAN ART.*
  W.M. SPINK, 54:SEP72-338
DE MAUSE, L., ED. THE HISTORY OF CHILDHOOD.
  L. STONE, 453:14NOV74-25
MAUSS, M. OEUVRES DE MARCEL MAUSS.* (VOLS 1-3) (V. KARADY, ED) SOCI-OLOGIE ET ANTHROPOLOGIE. MANUEL D'ETHNOGRAPHIE. ESSAIS DE SOCIO-LOGIE.
  G. CONDOMINAS, 98:FEB72-118 [& CONT IN 98:JUN72-487]
MAUTNER, F.H. - SEE NESTROY, J.
MAVES, C. SENSUOUS PESSIMISM.
  C. WEGELIN, 27(AL):NOV73-466
MAVOR, J.W., JR. VOYAGE TO ATLANTIS.
  D.B. VITALIANO, 391(JFI):VOL8#1-66
MAVRIYANNAKI, C. RECHERCHES SUR LES LARNAKES MINOENNES DE LA CRÈTE OCCIDENTALE.
  617(TLS):8MAR74-232
MAXFIELD, H.S. ANOTHER SPRING.
  N. CALLENDAR, 441:25AUG74-29
  M. LEVIN, 441:21JUL74-14
MAXWELL, J.C. - SEE WORDSWORTH, W.
MAXWELL, K.R. CONFLICTS & CONSPIRA-CIES.
  C.R. BOXER, 617(TLS):25OCT74-1180
MAY, D. THE LAUGHTER IN DJAKARTA.*
  J. MELLORS, 364:FEB/MAR74-135
MAY, E.R. "LESSONS" OF THE PAST.
  R. STEEL, 453:8AUG74-37
MAY, E.R. & J.C. THOMSON, JR., EDS. AMERICAN-EAST ASIAN RELATIONS.
  639(VQR):SPRING73-LXXXV
MAY, G. MADAME ROLAND & THE AGE OF REVOLUTION.*
  B. GUY, 207(FR):APR72-1056
  S. PITOU, 188(ECR):FALL72-227
MAY, J.R. TOWARD A NEW EARTH.
  J.E. MILLER, JR., 27(AL):MAY73-314
LE MAY, R. A CONCISE HISTORY OF BUDDHIST ART IN SIAM.
  R.H. LEARY, 60:NOV-DEC73-60
MAY, W. REPORTS.
  639(VQR):SUMMER73-CX
"THE MAY 13 TRAGEDY: A REPORT."
  G.D. NESS, 293(JAST):MAY72-734
MAYBAUM, I. TRIALOGUE BETWEEN JEW, CHRISTIAN & MUSLIM.
  617(TLS):30AUG74-936
LADY MAYER. ANGELICA KAUFFMANN.
  T. CROMBIE, 39:OCT72-367

MAYER, C.A. - SEE MAROT, C.
MAYER, H. STEPPENWOLF & EVERYMAN.
    D. BATHRICK, 406:SPRING73-87
    A. HUYSSEN, 125:FEB73-182
    J.L. SAMMONS, 222(GR):MAR72-127
MAYER, J. MISCHFORMEN BAROCKER
ERZÄHLKUNST.
    K.G. KNIGHT, 402(MLR):APR73-454
MAYFIELD, S. EXILES FROM PARADISE.*
    D. AARON, 639(VQR):WINTER72-157
MAYHALL, J. GIVERS & TAKERS 2.
    W.H. PRITCHARD, 249(HUDR):AUTUMN
    73-585
MAYHEW, H. THE UNKNOWN MAYHEW.*
(E.P. THOMPSON & E. YEO, EDS)
    A. HUMPHERYS, 637(VS):DEC71-243
    A. THOMAS, 627(UTQ):WINTER72-176
MAYLE, P. "WHERE DID I COME FROM?"
    617(TLS):11OCT74-1122
MAYO, R.S. HERDER & THE BEGINNINGS
OF COMPARATIVE LITERATURE.*
    H.M. BLOCK, 301(JEGP):JAN73-90
    P. SALM, 222(GR):JAN72-59
    F.M. WASSERMANN, 221(GQ):MAR72-
    360
MAYOR, A.H. POPULAR PRINTS OF THE
AMERICAS.
    442(NY):11MAR74-136
MAYOR, A.H. PRINTS & PEOPLE.*
    A. FRANKENSTEIN, 55:MAR73-16
    D. THOMAS, 135:JUL72-227
MAYRHOFER, M. KURZGEFASSTES ETYMOLO-
GISCHES WÖRTERBUCH DES ALTINDIS-
CHEN.* (PT 19)
    T. BURROW, 343:BAND15HEFT1-51
MAYRHOFER, M. KURZGEFASSTES ETYMOLO-
GISCHES WÖRTERBUCH DES ALTINDIS-
CHEN.* (PTS 20-22)
    T. BURROW, 343:BAND15HEFT1-51
    M.B. EMENEAU, 350:MAR73-162
MAYS, S. LAST POST.
    617(TLS):15FEB74-165
MAYSER, E. GRAMMATIK DER GRIECHIS-
CHEN PAPYRI AUS DER PTOLEMÄERZEIT.
(2ND ED) (VOL 1, PT 1) (H. SCHMOLL,
ED)
    P. CHANTRAINE, 555:VOL46FASC2-
    312
    E.G. TURNER, 123:DEC73-219
MAYUYAMA, J. GUIDE TO ART IN JAPAN.
    P.M. SCULL, 57:VOL34#4-350
MAZEAUD, P. NAKED BEFORE THE MOUN-
TAIN.
    617(TLS):4OCT74-1080
DE LA MAZIÈRE, C. THE CAPTIVE
DREAMER.
    B. GIQUEL, 231:JUN74-93
MAZLISH, B. IN SEARCH OF NIXON.*
    639(VQR):AUTUMN72-CXXXVII
MAZOUR, A.G. THE WRITING OF HISTORY
IN THE SOVIET UNION.*
    J. BARBER, 575(SEER):JAN73-151
MAZZAMUTO, P. CULTURA E POESIA.
    M.M., 228(GSLI):VOL149FASC465-
    147
MAZZAOUI, M.M. THE ORIGINS OF THE
ŞAFAWIDS.
    J. VAN ESS, 182:VOL25#12-434
MAZZARELLA, P. METAFISICA E GNOSE-
OLOGIA NEL PENSIERO DI TEODORICO
DI VRIBERG.
    N. PALLINI, 548(RCSF):APR-JUN72-
    244

MAZZARO, J. CHANGING THE WINDOWS.
    J. LOGAN, 628:FALL72-116
MAZZARO, J. TRANSFORMATIONS IN THE
RENAISSANCE ENGLISH LYRIC.*
    D.L. PETERSON, 191(ELN):DEC72-
    147
MAZZARO, J. WILLIAM CARLOS WILLIAMS:
THE LATER POEMS.
    S. PAUL, 301(JEGP):OCT73-580
MAZZOLENI, J. PALEOGRAFIA E DIPLO-
MATICA E SCIENZE AUSILIARIE. (NEW
ED)
    L.E. BOYLE, 589:APR73-385
MAZZONI, F. - SEE DA PISA, G.
MBAMBIYIOTĒS, G.D. HO DIA SYNTHE-
SEŌS YPOKORISMOS EIS TĒN HELLĒN-
IKĒN.
    E. TRAPP, 260(IF):BAND76-289
MBITI, J.S. AFRICAN RELIGIONS &
PHILOSOPHIES.*
    J.D. ROBERTS, SR., 485(PE&W):
    JUL72-340
MBITI, J.S. NEW TESTAMENT ESCHATOL-
OGY IN AN AFRICAN BACKGROUND.
    A.C. EDWARDS, 69:OCT72-358
MEAD, M. RUTH BENEDICT.
    J. ZORN, 441:17NOV74-20
MEAD, M. BLACKBERRY WINTER.
    C. DRIVER, 362:3JAN74-24
    617(TLS):1MAR74-213
MEADOWS, A.J. SCIENCE & CONTROVER-
SY.
    42(AR):VOL32#3-510
MEADOWS, D.H. & OTHERS. LIMITS TO
GROWTH.
    G.S. SCHATZ, 37:MAY72-38
MEANLEY, B. SWAMPS, RIVER BOTTOMS,
& CANEBREAKS.
    639(VQR):WINTER73-XLIV
MEANS, G.P. MALAYSIAN POLITICS.
    A.A. SHANTZ, 293(JAST):NOV71-221
MEARNS, A. - SEE UNDER HILL, O.
MEATYARD, R.E. RALPH EUGENE MEAT-
YARD. THE FAMILY ALBUM OF LUCY-
BELLE CRATER.
    S. SCHWARTZ, 441:1DEC74-100
VON MECK, G. AS I REMEMBER THEM.*
    J. WARRACK, 415:JUL73-699
MECKEL, C. MANIFEST DER TOTEN.
    O.W. TETZLAFF, 221(GQ):NOV72-748
MECKIER, J. ALDOUS HUXLEY.*
    J. GINDIN, 594:SPRING72-119
MECKLENBURG, C.G.H. - SEE UNDER HER-
ZOG ZU MECKLENBURG, C.G.
MEDICI, M. & R. SIMONE, EDS. GRAM-
MATICA TRASFORMAZIONALE ITALIANA.
    R.J. DI PIETRO, 276:AUTUMN72-335
MEDICI, M. & R. SIMONE, EDS. L'IN-
SEGNAMENTO DELL'ITALIANO IN ITALIA
E ALL'ESTERO.
    R.J. DI PIETRO, 276:AUTUMN72-336
"MEDIEVAL COMIC TALES." (P. RICKARD
& OTHERS, TRANS)
    M. TWYCROSS, 617(TLS):13DEC74-
    1407
"MEDIEVAL FRENCH PLAYS."* (R. AXTON
& J. STEVENS, TRANS)
    B.M. CRAIG, 399(MLJ):NOV72-468
    T.B.W. REID, 382(MAE):1973/2-163
    G.A. RUNNALLS, 208(FS):OCT73-443
MEDLEY, J. THE MIDNIGHT TIDE.
    H. FRANCIS, 157:WINTER72-83

MEDLICOTT, W.N., D. DAKIN & M.E.
LAMBERT, EDS. DOCUMENTS ON BRIT-
ISH FOREIGN POLICY 1919-1939.
(2ND SER, VOL 13)
617(TLS):12JUL74-742
MEDLIN, W.K. & C.G. PATRINELIS. REN-
AISSANCE INFLUENCES & RELIGIOUS
REFORMS IN RUSSIA.*
M. SAMILOV, 575(SEER):APR73-329
MEDVEDEV, R. KNIGA O SOTSIALISTICH-
ESKOI DEMOKRATII.
F.C. BARGHOORN, 32:SEP73-590
MEDVEDEV, R.A. LET HISTORY JUDGE.*
(D. JORAVSKY & G. HAUPT, EDS)
M. FRIEDBERG, 390:MAY72-76
R.H. MC NEAL, 550(RUSR):APR72-
179
I. STEVENSON, 639(VQR):SPRING72-
280
MEDVEDEV, Z.A. THE MEDVEDEV PAPERS.*
B.S. ALMGREN, 550(RUSR):OCT72-
411
I. STEVENSON, 639(VQR):SPRING72-
280
MEDVEDEV, Z.A. THE RISE & FALL OF
T.D. LYSENKO.
A. VUCINICH, 550(RUSR):JAN72-87
MEDVEDEV, Z.A. TEN YEARS AFTER
IVAN DENISOVICH.*
B. DE MOTT, 61:FEB74-89
C. NEWMAN, 231:FEB74-83
P. REDDAWAY, 453:12DEC74-36
T. SHABAD, 441:17MAR74-10
617(TLS):22FEB74-187
MEDVEDEV, Z.A. & R.A. A QUESTION OF
MADNESS.
C. BIRD, 550(RUSR):APR72-175
M. FRIEDBERG, 390:MAY72-76
I. STEVENSON, 639(VQR):SPRING72-
280
MEDVIN, N. THE ENERGY CARTEL.
M. GREEN, 441:6OCT74-10
MEDZINI, M. FRENCH POLICY IN JAPAN
DURING THE CLOSING YEARS OF THE
TOKUGAWA REGIME.
H.J. JONES, 293(JAST):MAY72-681
MEEK, C.K. THE NORTHERN TRIBES OF
NIGERIA.
A.H.M.K-G., 69:JUL72-262
MEEKER, J.W. THE COMEDY OF SURVIVAL.
A. BROYARD, 441:24JUN74-33
MEGARRY, R. A SECOND MISCELLANY-AT-
LAW.
617(TLS):10MAY74-508
MEGAS, G.A., ED. FOLKTALES OF
GREECE.
R.A. GEORGES, 650(WF):JUL72-211
G. GIZELIS, 292(JAF):JAN-MAR72-
86
MEGGS, B. SATURDAY GAMES.
N. CALLENDAR, 441:19MAY74-41
VON DER MEHDEN, F.R. & D.A. WILSON,
EDS. LOCAL AUTHORITY & ADMINISTRA-
TION IN THAILAND.
B. NUSSBAUM, 293(JAST):NOV71-228
MEHENDALE, M.A. SOME ASPECTS OF
INDO-ARYAN LINGUISTICS.*
B. SCHLERATH, 343:BAND14HEFT2-
212
MEHEUST, J. - SEE STATIUS
MEHL, D. DIE MITTELENGLISCHEN ROMAN-
ZEN DES 13. UND 14. JAHRHUNDERTS.
J. FINLAYSON, 38:BAND90HEFT1/2-
220

MEHLINGER, H.D. & J.M. THOMPSON.
COUNT WITTE & THE TSARIST GOVERN-
MENT IN THE 1905 REVOLUTION.
B. HOLLINGSWORTH, 575(SEER):
APR73-303
S.G. PUSHKAREV, 32:JUN73-383
MEHNERT, K-H. SAL ROMANUS UND ES-
PRIT FRANÇAIS.*
G. HAINSWORTH, 208(FS):JUL73-321
52:BAND7HEFT1-87
MEHRA, J., ED. THE PHYSICIST'S
CONCEPTION OF NATURE.
617(TLS):9AUG74-861
MEID, W. DAS GERMANISCHE PRÄTERITUM.
A.L. LLOYD, 350:JUN73-479
E. SEEBOLD, 343:BAND15HEFT2-169
MEID, W. INDOGERMANISCH UND KEL-
TISCH.
E. NEU, 260(IF):BAND76-241
MEID, W. - SEE KRAHE, H.
MEIER, A. & E.M. RUDWICK. CORE.
639(VQR):AUTUMN73-CLXVIII
MEIJER, M.J. MARRIAGE LAW & POLICY
IN THE CHINESE PEOPLE'S REPUBLIC.
A.K. WONG, 302:JAN72-77
MEIJER, R.P. LITERATURE OF THE LOW
COUNTRIES.
P.K. KING, 402(MLR):JUL73-714
205(FMLS):OCT72-384
MEILAND, J.W. THE NATURE OF INTEN-
TION.*
S.S.C., 543:SEP71-132
MEILAND, J.W. TALKING ABOUT PARTIC-
ULARS.*
A.F. MAC KAY, 482(PHR):JUL72-376
MEILLASSOUX, C. THE DEVELOPMENT OF
INDIGENOUS TRADE & MARKETS IN
WEST AFRICA.
P.C. LLOYD, 69:JUL72-254
MEILLER, A. - SEE JEAN DU PRIER
MEILLET, A. GENERAL CHARACTERISTICS
OF THE GERMANIC LANGUAGES.
W.P. LEHMANN, 215(GL):VOL12#1-38
MEIN, M. A FORETASTE OF PROUST.
M. TURNELL, 617(TLS):13DEC74-
1408
MEINECKE, D. WORT UND NAME BEI PAUL
CELAN.
K. WEISSENBERGER, 133:1972/2-211
MEINIG, D.W. - SEE JAMES, P.E.
MEISE, E. UNTERSUCHUNGEN ZUR GE-
SCHICHTE DER JULISCH-CLAUDISCHEN
DYNASTIE.
M.T. GRIFFIN, 313:VOL62-184
MEISEL, P. THOMAS HARDY.
W.J. KEITH, 637(VS):MAR73-367
M. STEIG, 529(QQ):WINTER72-566
MEISS, M. & E.H. BEATSON - SEE "THE
BELLES HEURES OF JEAN, DUKE OF
BERRY"
MEISS, M. & E.W. KIRSCH - SEE "THE
VISCONTI HOURS"
MEISS, M. & M. THOMAS - SEE "THE
ROHAN BOOK OF HOURS"
MEISSBURGER, G. GRUNDLAGEN ZUM VER-
STÄNDIS DER DEUTSCHEN MÖNCHSDICH-
TUNG IM 11. UND 12. JAHRHUNDERT.*
N. HUNT, 589:JAN73-162
MEISSNER, B., ED. SOCIAL CHANGE IN
THE SOVIET UNION.
J.R. AZRAEL, 32:JUN73-395
D. LANE, 575(SEER):OCT73-629

MEIXNER, H. ROMANTISCHER FIGURALIS-
MUS.
    W. KUDSZUS, 406:WINTER73-437
MELA, P. POMPONII MELAE, "DE CHORO-
GRAPHIA LIBRI TRES." (G. RAND-
STRAND, ED)
    J. ANDRÉ, 555:VOL46FASC2-336
MELADA, I. THE CAPTAIN OF INDUSTRY
IN ENGLISH FICTION, 1821-1871.*
    P.J. KEATING, 637(VS):JUN72-484
    J.M.S. TOMPKINS, 541(RES):MAY72-
    225
MELANDER, I. THE POETRY OF SYLVIA
PLATH.
    B. LINDBERG-SEYERSTED, 172(EDDA):
    1972/1-54
"MÉLANGES DE LANGUE ET DE LITTÉRA-
TURE DU MOYEN AGE ET DE LA RENAIS-
SANCE."
    L.P.G. PECKHAM, 546(RR):OCT72-
    219
"MÉLANGES DE LINGUISTIQUE, DE PHILO-
LOGIE ET DE MÉTHODOLOGIE DE L'EN-
SEIGNEMENT DES LANGUES ANCIENNES
OFFERTS À M. RENÉ FOHALLE À L'OC-
CASION DE SON SOIXANTE-DIXIÈME
ANNIVERSAIRE."
    J. KNOBLOCH, 343:BAND15HEFT2-209
    K.H. SCHMIDT, 260(IF):BAND76-213
"MÉLANGES MARCEL DURRY."
    A. ERNOUT, 555:VOL46FASC1-171
MELANTSCHUCK, G. KIERKEGAARD'S
THOUGHT. (H.V. & E.H. HONG, EDS
& TRANS)
    H. KASSIM, 484(PPR):DEC72-286
MELCHINGER, S. ANTON CHEKHOV.
    K.D. KRAMER, 32:DEC73-852
MELCHIORI, G. L'UOMO E IL POTERE.
    617(TLS):22MAR74-288
MELDOLESI, C. GLI STICOTTI.
    W.D. HOWARTH, 208(FS):JAN73-67
MELESKI, P.F. ECHOES OF THE PAST.
    W. GARD, 584(SWR):WINTER73-V
MELLAART, J. THE CHALCOLITHIC &
EARLY BRONZE AGES IN THE NEAR EAST
& ANATOLIA.
    R.D. BARNETT, 39:JUN72-521
MELLANBY, K. HUMAN GUINEA-PIGS.
    617(TLS):8MAR74-243
MELLEN, J. WOMEN & THEIR SEXUALITY
IN THE NEW FILM.
    J. WILSON, 441:24MAR74-6
MELLEN, P. JEAN CLOUET.
    A. MONGAN, 39:DEC72-560
    D. THOMAS, 135:OCT72-139
MELLERS, W. TWILIGHT OF THE GODS.
    H. KELLER, 362:7FEB74-183
    R. REYNOLDS, 441:22SEP74-39
    J. ROCKWELL, 441:4JUL74-17
    617(TLS):12APR74-390
MELLING, E. CRIME & PUNISHMENT:
KENTISH SOURCES. (VOL 6)
    P.E. JONES, 325:APR72-450
MELLINKOFF, R. THE HORNED MOSES IN
MEDIEVAL ART AND THOUGHT.*
    J. BECKWITH, 39:JAN72-66
    A.S. CALARCO, 127:SPRING73-364
    J. GUTMANN, 290(JAAC):WINTER71-
    275
    K. LANGEDIJK, 54:DEC72-544
MELLON, S. - SEE GUIZOT, F.
MELLOR, D.H. THE MATTER OF CHANCE.
    L. SKLAR, 311(JP):18JUL74-418

MELLOR, R.E.H. COMECON.
    M. GAMARNIKOW, 32:MAR73-179
MELLORS, J. SHOTS IN THE DARK.
    E.S. TURNER, 362:19SEP74-379
    617(TLS):4OCT74-1080
MELLOW, J.R. CHARMED CIRCLE.
    P. BEER, 617(TLS):8NOV74-1252
    A. BROYARD, 441:30JAN74-39
    H. LEIBOWITZ, 441:3FEB74-1
    D. SUTHERLAND, 453:30MAY74-28
    442(NY):25FEB74-127
MELNICK, A. KANT'S ANALOGIES OF
EXPERIENCE.
    617(TLS):20SEP74-1022
MELSON, R. & H. WOLPE, EDS. NIGERIA.
    A.H.M.K-G., 69:OCT72-356
MELTON, W. NINE LIVES TO POMPEII.
    N. CALLENDAR, 441:28APR74-39
MELVILLE, H. ISRAEL POTTER.
    441:10FEB74-18
MELVILLE, H. SELECTED POEMS OF HER-
MAN MELVILLE. (R.P. WARREN, ED)
    J. GRIMSHAW, 598(SOR):SPRING74-
    504
MELVILLE, J. NUN'S CASTLE.
    617(TLS):12APR74-385
MELVILLE, R. HENRY MOORE.*
    J. PIPER, 46:MAR72-195
MELZI D'ERIL, F.K. CARTEGGIO MON-
TALEMBERT-CANTÙ (1842-1868).
    L. LE GUILLOU, 535(RHL):MAR-APR
    72-326
MENANDER. MENANDRI, "ASPIS ET SAM-
IA." (VOL 1) (C. AUSTIN, ED)
    P. CHANTRAINE, 555:VOL46FASC1-
    129
MENANDER. MENANDRI, "ASPIS ET SAM-
IA." (VOL 2) (C. AUSTIN, ED)
    P. CHANTRAINE, 555:VOL46FASC1-
    129
    R.K. SHERK, 24:SPRING73-93
MÉNARD, J. LA VIE LITTÉRAIRE AU
CANADA FRANÇAIS.
    L.S. RODEN, 529(QQ):SUMMER72-267
MÉNARD, J-É. L'ÉVANGILE SELON
PHILIPPE.
    F. WISSE, 318(JAOS):JAN-MAR72-
    188
MÉNARD, P. LE RIRE ET LE SOURIRE
DANS LE ROMAN COURTOIS EN FRANCE
AU MOYEN ÂGE (1150-1250).
    A. FOULET, 545(RPH):AUG72-187
MÉNARD, P. - SEE GUILLAUME LE VINIER
MENASHE, S. FRINGE OF FIRE.*
    617(TLS):25JAN74-77
MENASHE, S. NO JERUSALEM BUT THIS.*
    J. KESSLER, 390:APR72-79
"MENCIUS."* (D.C. LAU, TRANS)
    E.J. COLEMAN, 485(PE&W):JAN72-
    113
MENDE, F. HEINRICH HEINE: CHRONIK
SEINES LEBENS UND WERKES.*
    M. MANN, 400(MLN):APR72-531
MENDE, F. & K.H. HAHN - SEE HEINE, H.
MENDE, K-D. SCHULREFORM UND GESELL-
SCHAFT IN DER DEUTSCHEN DEMOKRAT-
ISCHEN REPUBLIK 1945-65.
    E. SCHÜTTE, 182:VOL25#5/6-140
MENDE, T. FROM AID TO RE-COLONIZA-
TION.*
    M. LIPTON, 617(TLS):2AUG74-830
MENDELOFF, H. A MANUAL OF COMPARA-
TIVE ROMANCE LINGUISTICS.*
    J.R. ALLERS, 207(FR):FEB72-719

MENDELSON, E. - SEE AUDEN, W.H.
MENDELSON, M.A. TENDER LOVING GREED.
S. CURTIN, 441:28APR74-12
MENDELSSOHN, F. FELIX MENDELSSOHN
BARTHOLDY: BRIEFE AUS LEIPZIGER
ARCHIVEN. (H-J. ROTHE & R. SZES-
KUS, EDS)
J.A.W., 410(M&L):JAN73-91
MENDELSSOHN, K. THE RIDDLE OF THE
PYRAMIDS.
P. ADAMS, 61:MAY74-140
442(NY):24JUN74-104
MENEN, A. FONTHILL.
P. ADAMS, 61:OCT74-118
MENGALDO, P.V. - SEE DI FILIPPO, R.
MENGCHU, L. - SEE UNDER LING MENGCHU
MENHENNET, D. THE JOURNALS OF THE
HOUSE OF COMMONS.
J.B. CHILDS, 517(PBSA):APR-JUN73-
197
MENNEMEIER, F.N. FRIEDRICH SCHLEG-
ELS POESIEBEGRIFF DARGESTELLT
ANHAND DER LITERATURKRITISCHEN
SCHRIFTEN.
R. BELGARDT, 301(JEGP):JAN73-94
R. IMMERWAHR, 406:SUMMER73-191
MENNINGER, K. SPARKS. (L. FREEMAN,
ED)
E. TAYLOR, 584(SWR):AUTUMN73-367
MENON, R.R. DISCOVERING INDIAN
MUSIC.
617(TLS):22FEB74-174
MENTON, S., ED. EL CUENTO HISPANO-
AMERICANO. (3RD ED)
T.O. BENTE, 238:SEP72-596
MENUHIN, Y. VIOLIN.
42(AR):SPRING/SUMMER72-243
MERCER, P. SYMPATHY & ETHICS.*
W. LYONS, 479(PHQ):OCT72-363
MERCHANT, M. COMEDY.
205(FMLS):OCT72-381
MERCIER, L-S. L'AN DEUX MILLE
QUATRE CENT QUARANTE. (R. TROUS-
SON, ED)
R. AGGÉRI, 535(RHL):JUL-AUG72-
725
A. VIATTE, 549(RLC):JAN-MAR72-
146
205(FMLS):JAN72-90
MERCIER, V. THE NEW NOVEL FROM
QUENEAU TO PINGET.*
E. MOROT-SIR, 546(RR):DEC72-314
R.Z. TEMPLE, 207(FR):FEB72-724
MEREDITH, G. THE LETTERS OF GEORGE
MEREDITH.* (C.L. CLINE, ED)
B. HARDY, 637(VS):SEP71-107
J.W. MORRIS, 636(VP):AUTUMN72-
283
MEREDITH, M.C. POETS & THEIR POETRY:
ROBERT BROWNING.
W. BARNES, 85:FALL72-66
MEREDITH, S. GEORGE S. KAUFMAN &
HIS FRIENDS.
H. CLURMAN, 441:24NOV74-12
MEREDITH, W. EARTH WALK.*
T.H. LANDESS, 569(SR):WINTER73-
137
MÉRIDIER, L. - SEE PLATO
MERIWETHER, J.B. JAMES GOULD COZ-
ZENS.
J.S. CRANE, 517(PBSA):OCT-DEC73-
469

MERK, F. SLAVERY & THE ANNEXATION
OF TEXAS.*
L.C. MILAZZO, 584(SWR):WINTER73-
102
MERK, F., WITH L.B. MERK. FRUITS OF
PROPAGANDA IN THE TYLER ADMINISTRA-
TION.
J.H. SILBEY, 432(NEQ):SEP72-442
639(VQR):WINTER72-XXXI
MERKEL, H. DIE WIDERSPRÜCHE ZWIS-
CHEN DEN EVANGELIEN.
F.F. BRUCE, 182:VOL25#1/2-15
MERKEL, I. BAROCK.
R.T. LLEWELLYN, 402(MLR):OCT73-
941
H. THOMKE, 182:VOL25#22-797
MERKELBACH, R. & M.L. WEST - SEE
HESIOD
MERKUR, D. AROUND & ABOUT SALLY'S
SHACK.
L. SHIRINIAN, 296:VOL3#1-102
MERLE, R. LES HOMMES PROTÉGÉS.
617(TLS):5JUL74-705
MERLE, R. MALEVIL.
C. LEHMANN-HAUPT, 441:9JAN74-39
D.K. MANO, 441:13JAN74-6
617(TLS):17MAY74-517
MERLI, F.J. GREAT BRITAIN & THE
CONFEDERATE NAVY.
E.J. DOYLE, 637(VS):MAR72-374
MERRIFIELD, D.F. DAS BILD DER FRAU
BEI MAX FRISCH.*
E. SCHÜRER, 301(JEGP):JUL73-431
MERRILEES, B.S. - SEE "LE PETIT PLET"
MERRILL, J. BRAVING THE ELEMENTS.*
J. CAREY, 364:AUG/SEP73-125
R. PEVEAR, 249(HUDR):SPRING73-
192
J. VERNON, 651(WHR):WINTER73-107
MERRILL, J.S. - SEE RUIZ IRIARTE, V.
MERRILL, W.M. - SEE GARRISON, W.L.
MERRILL, W.M. & L. RUCHAMES - SEE
GARRISON, W.L.
MERRY, H.J. MONTESQUIEU'S SYSTEM OF
NATURAL GOVERNMENT.*
J.R. LOY, 481(PQ):JUL72-734
MERSENNE, M. CORRESPONDANCE DU PÈRE
MARIN MERSENNE, RELIGIEUX MINIME.*
(VOL 11) (C. DE WAARD, ED)
R. LEBÈGUE, 535(RHL):MAR-APR72-
305
MERSMANN, W. DER BESITZWECHSEL UND
SEINE BEDEUTUNG IN DEN DICHTUNGEN
WOLFRAMS VON ESCHENBACH UND GOTT-
FRIEDS VON STRASSBURG.
W.C. CROSSGROVE, 301(JEGP):JAN73-
66
D.H. GREEN, 402(MLR):OCT73-937
MERTON, R.K. THE SOCIOLOGY OF SCI-
ENCE.* (N.W. STORER, ED)
617(TLS):26APR74-438
MERTON, T. THE ASIAN JOURNAL OF
THOMAS MERTON.* (N. BURTON, P.
HART & J. LAUGHLIN, EDS)
J.Y. GLIMM, 569(SR):AUTUMN73-845
617(TLS):12JUL74-739
MERTON, T. THE GEOGRAPHY OF LOG-
RAIRE.*
J.T. IRWIN, 569(SR):WINTER73-158
MERTZ-RYCHNER, C. - SEE BURCKHARDT,
C.J. & M. RYCHNER
MERWIN, W.S. (ASIAN FIGURES).*
G. HENRY, 491:AUG74-292

MERWIN, W.S. WRITINGS TO AN UNFIN-
ISHED ACCOMPANIMENT.*
    D. BLAZEK, 491:JUN74-167
    J.E. CHAMBERLIN, 249(HUDR):SUM-
    MER73-391
    L. LIEBERMAN, 676(YR):SUMMER73-
    602
    D.H. ZUCKER, 398:SPRING74-87
    639(VQR):SUMMER73-CX
MÉRY, M., ED. LETTRES DE RENOUVIER
À HENNEGUY (1861-1899).
    M. ADAM, 542:JUL-SEP72-390
MEŠČERSKIJ, N.A., ED. RUSSISCHE
SPRACHWISSENSCHAFT AN DER PETERS-
BURGER-LENINGRADER UNIVERSITÄT.
    D. TSCHIŽEWSKIJ, 72:BAND21OHEFT
    1/3-236
MESERVE, W.J. & R.I., EDS. MODERN
DRAMA FROM COMMUNIST CHINA.*
    D.S.P. YANG, 397(MD):MAY72-104
MESLIER, J. OEUVRES COMPLÈTES.*
(VOL 1) (J. DEPRUN, R. DESNÉ & A.
SOBOUL, EDS)
    G. BESSE, 542:JUL-SEP72-330
    J.S. SPINK, 208(FS):JAN73-64
MESLIER, J. OEUVRES COMPLÈTES.*
(VOL 2) (J. DEPRUN, R. DESNÉ &
A. SOBOUL, EDS)
    G. BESSE, 542:JUL-SEP72-330
    R. MERCIER, 557(RSH):OCT-DEC72-
    609
MESLIER, J. OEUVRES COMPLÈTES.*
(VOL 3) (J. DEPRUN, R. DESNÉ &
A. SOBOUL, EDS)
    R. MERCIER, 557(RSH):OCT-DEC72-
    609
MESLIN, M. LA FÊTE DES KALENDES DE
JANVIER DANS L'EMPIRE ROMAIN.*
    E.N. LANE, 24:SUMMER73-223
MESSERLI, J. HORACE MANN.
    D.W. HOWE, 432(NEQ):DEC72-589
    42(AR):SPRING/SUMMER72-244
MESSICK, H. & B. GOLDBLATT. THE
MOBS & THE MAFIA.
    617(TLS):22FEB74-181
METCALF, P. VICTORIAN LONDON.
    639(VQR):SPRING73-XCII
METHVIN, E.H. THE RISE OF RADICAL-
ISM.
    L.W. BEILENSON, 396(MODA):FALL73-
    419
METTAS, O. LES TECHNIQUES DE LA
PHONÉTIQUE INSTRUMENTALE ET L'IN-
TONATION.
    E.T. ULDALL, 361:VOL29#2-199
METZ, C. ESSAIS SUR LA SIGNIFICA-
TION AU CINÉMA. (VOL 2) FILM
LANGUAGE.
    G. NOWELL-SMITH, 617(TLS):8NOV74-
    1268
METZELTIN, M. DIE TERMINOLOGIE DES
SEEKOMPASSES IN ITALIEN UND AUF
DER IBERISCHEN HALBINSEL BIS 1600.
    H. KAHANE, 545(RPH):NOV72-435
METZGER, A. FREIHEIT UND TOD. (2ND
ED)
    W. SCHWARZ, 484(PPR):MAR73-445
METZGER, C.H. THE PRISONER IN THE
AMERICAN REVOLUTION.
    I.D. GRUBER, 656(WMQ):JUL72-506
METZGER, M.M. & E.A. STEFAN GEORGE.
    P. GOFF, 406:SUMMER73-213

METZGER, T.A. THE INTERNAL ORGANI-
ZATION OF CH'ING BUREAUCRACY.
    M. FREEDMAN, 617(TLS):27SEP74-
    1038
MEUS, K. & S. SCHOENBAUM, EDS. A
NEW COMPANION TO SHAKESPEARE STUD-
IES.
    J.C. MAXWELL, 447(N&Q):AUG72-318
MEUVRET, J. ETUDES D'HISTOIRE ÉCON-
OMIQUE.
    617(TLS):18JAN74-56
MEWS, H. FRAIL VESSELS.*
    O. BANKS, 637(VS):MAR73-369
    I.Z. SHERWOOD, 648:JAN73-71
    R. WIEMANN, 430(NS):JUN72-367
MEWS, S., ED. STUDIES IN GERMAN LIT-
ERATURE OF THE NINETEENTH & TWEN-
TIETH CENTURIES.
    M. BOULBY, 564:MAR72-63
    R.C. COWEN, 221(GQ):JAN72-136
MEWSHAW, M. THE TOLL.
    A. BROYARD, 441:19MAR74-41
    J.R. FRAKES, 441:24MAR74-36
    J. MELLORS, 362:12SEP74-348
    442(NY):8APR74-140
    617(TLS):6SEP74-960
MEWSHAW, M. WAKING SLOW.*
    S. O'CONNELL, 418(MR):WINTER73-
    190
    T. TANNER, 364:OCT/NOV73-146
    639(VQR):SUMMER72-C
MEYER, A., ED. RED SALMON, BROWN
BEAR.
    639(VQR):SPRING72-LXXVII
MEYER, A.G. MARXISM.
    A. WALKER, 575(SEER):OCT73-631
MEYER, C. DERRIÈRE LE SOURIRE KHMER.
    D.P. CHANDLER, 293(JAST):MAY72-
    730
MEYER, C. DIE URKUNDEN IM GE-
SCHICHTSWERK DES THUKYDIDES. (2ND
ED)
    H.D. WESTLAKE, 123:MAR73-25
    A.G. WOODHEAD, 303:VOL92-199
MEYER, C.S., ED. SIXTEENTH CENTURY
ESSAYS & STUDIES. (VOL 1)
    K.A. STRAND, 551(RENQ):WINTER72-
    479
MEYER, H. DIESE SEHR ERNSTEN
SCHERZE.
    I.A. WHITE, 220(GL&L):APR73-272
MEYER, K.E. THE PLUNDERED PAST.*
    A. FRANKENSTEIN, 55:DEC73-34
MEYER, K.M., ED. DETROIT ARCHITEC-
TURE.
    505:FEB72-112
MEYER, M. IBSEN.*
    R.M. QUINN, 50(ARQ):SUMMER72-180
MEYER, M. HENRIK IBSEN. (VOLS 2&3)
    J. WARD, 157:WINTER71-70
MEYER, M.C. HUERTA.
    G. DE BEER, 263:APR-JUN73-201
    C.J. FLEENER, 377:NOV73-183
MEYER, M.W. SOUTHEAST ASIA.
    L.R. WRIGHT, 302:JAN72-68
MEYER, N. THE SEVEN-PER-CENT SOLU-
TION.
    A. BROYARD, 441:27AUG74-37
    N. CALLENDAR, 441:29SEP74-41
MEYER, N. TARGET PRACTICE.
    N. CALLENDAR, 441:28APR74-39
MEYER, P. PRECISION JOURNALISM.
    42(AR):VOL32#4-704

MEYER, U. CONCEPTUAL ART.*
  D. HYSHKA-STROSS, 290(JAAC):
    FALL72-136
  J. STEZAKER, 592:JUL/AUG72-51
MEYER, W. DIE OXFORDER GEDICHTE DES
  PRIMAS (DES MAGISTERS HUGO VON OR-
  LEANS). DIE ARUNDEL-SAMMLUNG MIT-
  TELLATEINISCHER LIEDER.
  H. NAUMANN, 680(ZDP):BAND91HEFT3-
    437
MEYER-EHLERS, G., ED. RAUMPROGRAMME
  UND BEWOHNERERFAHRUNGEN.
  H. LUDMANN, 182:VOL25#15/16-537
"MEYERS HANDBUCH ÜBER DIE LITERATUR."
  (2ND ED REV BY I. ADAM & G. PREUSS)
  P. OCHSENBEIN, 657(WW):JUL/AUG72-
    288
  G. SCHULZ, 67:MAY73-144
MEYERSTEIN, R.S. FUNCTIONAL LOAD.
  J. VACHEK, 361:VOL28#1&2-137
  W.S-Y. WANG, 297(JL):SEP72-338
MEYLAN, J-P. LA REVUE DE GENÈVE.*
  I. STEMPEL, 52:BAND7HEFT1-106
MEYNELL, F. MY LIVES.*
  639(VQR):WINTER72-X
MEYNELL, L. THE FORTUNATE MISS EAST.
  M. LEVIN, 441:26MAY74-19
MEYNELL, L. THE THIRTEEN TRUMPETERS.
  617(TLS):18JAN74-61
MEZIÈRES, J.C. & P. CHRISTIN. LA
  CITÉ DES EAUX MOUVANTES. L'EMPIRE
  DES MILLE PLANÈTES.
  P. FRESNAULT-DERUELLE, 98:MAY72-
    460
DE MÉZIÈRES, P. FIGURATIVE REPRESEN-
  TATION OF THE PRESENTATION OF THE
  VIRGIN MARY IN THE TEMPLE. (R.S.
  HALLER, ED & TRANS)
  S.J. KAHRL, 589:APR73-351
MEZU, S.O. & R. DESAI, EDS. BLACK
  LEADERS OF THE CENTURY.
  J. MFOULOU, 207(FR):OCT71-229
MICHAEL, F. THE TAIPING REBELLION.
  (VOLS 2&3)
    YUJI MURAMATSU, 293(JAST):AUG72-
      929
MICHAEL, H.N. - SEE OKLADNIKOV, A.P.
MICHAEL, I. ENGLISH GRAMMATICAL
  CATEGORIES & THE TRADITION TO 1800.
  J. ALGEO, 128(CE):MAY72-936
  N. DAVIS, 541(RES):FEB72-63
  W. HARSH, 301(JEGP):JUL73-435
  A.R. TELLIER, 189(EA):JUL-SEP72-
    432
  205(FMLS):APR72-195
MICHAEL, I. THE TREATMENT OF CLASSI-
  CAL MATERIAL IN THE "LIBRO DE ALEX-
  ANDRE."*
  A.D. DEYERMOND, 402(MLR):JAN73-
    202
MICHAEL, W.F. DAS DEUTSCHE DRAMA
  DES MITTELALTERS.*
  E. SIMON, 589:OCT73-776
MICHAELIS-JENA, R. THE BROTHERS
  GRIMM.*
  E.V.K. BRILL, 220(GL&L):APR73-
    246
MICHALOS, A.G. IMPROVING YOUR
  REASONING.
  T.G.N., 543:MAR72-561
MICHAUD-QUANTIN, P. ARISTOTELIS
  POETICA, TRANSLATIO PRIOR IMPER-
  FECTA. (BKS 1&2, 11)
  O. THILLET, 542:JAN-MAR72-54

MICHAUD-QUANTIN, P. UNIVERSITAS.
  G. POST, 589:JAN73-165
MICHAUD-QUANTIN, P., WITH M. LEMOINE.
  ETUDES SUR LE VOCABULAIRE PHILOSO-
  PHIQUE DU MOYEN AGE.*
  J. JOLIVET, 542:JAN-MAR72-77
MICHAUX, H. MOMENTS.
  617(TLS):15FEB74-147
MICHAUX, H. POTEAUX D'ANGLE.
  R.R. HUBERT, 207(FR):FEB72-701
MICHEL, C. ERLÄUTERUNGEN ZUM "N"
  DER ILIAS.*
  J.B. HAINSWORTH, 123:DEC73-266
MICHEL, G. LA PROMENADE DU DIMANCHE.
  (C.A. PRENDERGAST, ED)
  J. CRUICKSHANK, 208(FS):JAN73-
    101
  F. FLAGOTHIER, 556(RLV):1972/5-
    553
MICHEL, J. - SEE DEL VALLE-INCLÁN, R.
MICHEL, L. THE THING CONTAINED.*
  D.J. CAHILL, 613:SPRING72-120
MICHEL, P-H. - SEE BRUNO, G.
MICHEL, S. & P-H. RÉPERTOIRE DES
  OUVRAGES IMPRIMÉS EN LANGUE ITAL-
  IENNE AU XVIIE SIÈCLE. (VOL 1)
  RÉPERTOIRE DES OUVRAGES IMPRIMÉS
  EN LANGUE ITALIENNE AU XVIIE
  SIÈCLE, CONSERVÉS DANS LES BIBLIO-
  THÈQUES DE FRANCE. (VOLS 1-3)
  E. ZIMMERMANN, 182:VOL25#11-325
"MICHELIN GUIDE TO GREAT BRITAIN &
  IRELAND."
  617(TLS):17MAY74-534
DE MICHELIS, E. - SEE D'ANNUNZIO, G.
MICHELS, V. HERMANN HESSE.
  617(TLS):15MAR74-254
MICHELS, V., ED. MATERIALIEN ZU
  HERMANN HESSES "DAS GLASPERLEN-
  SPIEL."
  617(TLS):15MAR74-254
MICHENER, J.A. CENTENNIAL.
  J. BARNES, 617(TLS):22NOV74-1308
  J.R. FRAKES, 441:8SEP74-6
  C. LEHMANN-HAUPT, 441:27SEP74-45
  E. WEEKS, 61:NOV74-118
MICHENER, J.A. RETURN TO PARADISE.
  441:10FEB74-22
MICHIE, J., ED. THE BODLEY HEAD
  BOOK OF LONGER SHORT STORIES.
  J. MELLORS, 362:26SEP74-416
MICHIO, N. - SEE UNDER NAGAI MICHIO
MICKEL, E.J., JR. THE ARTIFICIAL
  PARADISES IN FRENCH LITERATURE.*
  (VOL 1)
  A. FAIRLIE, 535(RHL):JAN-FEB72-
    143
  C.B. OSBORN, 546(RR):OCT72-237
  J.S. PATTY, 399(MLJ):OCT72-397
MICZKA, G. DAS BILD DER KIRCHE BEI
  JOHANNES VON SALISBURY.
  G.B. FOWLER, 589:JAN73-166
MIDDELHAUVE, G., ED. DICHTER EURO-
  PAS ERZÄHLEN KINDERN.
  268:JAN74-74
MIDDENDORF, J.H., ED. ENGLISH WRIT-
  ERS OF THE EIGHTEENTH CENTURY.*
  P-G. BOUCÉ, 189(EA):OCT-DEC72-
    564
  C.J. RAWSON, 402(MLR):APR73-391
  566:SPRING72-85
  639(VQR):SPRING72-LVI
"THE MIDDLE EAST & NORTH AFRICA."
  617(TLS):22FEB74-193

MIDDLEBROOK, M. THE NUREMBERG RAID.
617(TLS):4JAN74-6
MIDDLEKAUFF, R. THE MATHERS.*
H.R. CEDERBERG, 481(PQ):JUL72-
543
M.G. HALL, 656(WMQ):JAN72-165
J.A. SCHUTZ, 613:SUMMER72-310
MIDDLEMAS, K. LIFE & TIMES OF
GEORGE VI.
617(TLS):13SEP74-983
MIDDLEMAS, K. & J. BARNES. BALDWIN.
619(TC):VOL177#1043-51
MIDDLETON, B.C. THE RESTORATION OF
LEATHER BINDINGS.
G. BAER, 517(PBSA):JUL-SEP73-359
MIDDLETON, C. WIE WIR GROSSMUTTER
ZUM MARKT BRINGEN.
O.W. TETZLAFF, 221(GQ):NOV72-748
MIDDLETON, D. RETREAT FROM VICTORY.
L.C. GARDNER, 441:17MAR74-16
MIDDLETON, D. WHERE HAS LAST JULY
GONE?
442(NY):18MAR74-151
MIDDLETON, S. HOLIDAY.
J. MELLORS, 362:1AUG74-156
617(TLS):19JUL74-761
MIDELFORT, H.C.E. WITCH HUNTING IN
SOUTHWESTERN GERMANY 1562-1684.*
L.F. BARMANN, 377:MAR73-38
J.W. CLARK, JR., 568(SCN):FALL-
WINTER73-97
MIETH, G. & OTHERS - SEE HÖLDERLIN,
F.
MIETHKE, J. OCKHAMS WEG ZUR SOZIAL-
PHILOSOPHIE.
A.S. MC GRADE, 589:JAN73-168
MIGLIORINI, E. - SEE KANT, I.
MIGNOT, X. LES VERBES DÉNOMINATIFS
LATINS.
D.M. JONES, 123:DEC73-220
MIHAILOVICH, V.D., ED. MODERN SLAV-
IC LITERATURES. (VOL 1)
R. SHELDON, 32:SEP73-665
MIHORDEA, V. MAÎTRES DU SOL ET PAY-
SANS DANS LES PRINCIPAUTÉS ROU-
MAINES AU XVIIIE SIÈCLE.
K. HITCHINS, 575(SEER):JAN73-134
MIKES, G. THE SPY WHO DIED OF BORE-
DOM.*
N. CALLENDAR, 441:21APR74-42
MIKHAIL, E.H. COMEDY & TRAGEDY.
354:DEC72-369
MIKKOLA, E. DAS KOMPOSITUM.* (VOL
1)
R. HARWEG, 343:BAND14HEFT1-103
MIKKOLA, E. DIE KONZESSIVITÄT DES
ALTLATEINS IM BEREICH DES SATZGAN-
ZEN.*
H. HAPP, 343:BAND15HEFT2-155
MIKO, S.J. TOWARD "WOMEN IN LOVE."
W.G.R., 502(PRS):WINTER72/73-369
J.E. STOLL, 219(GAR):FALL72-397
MIKUŠ, R.F. LA STRUCTURE PHONÉTIQUE
DU FRANÇAIS.
G.F. MEIER, 682(ZPSK):BAND25
HEFT1/2-161
MILCH, W. DIE JUNGE BETTINE 1785-
1811. (P. KÜPPER, ED)
J. TRAINER, 402(MLR):JAN73-229
MILDE, W. DER BIBLIOTHEKSKATALOG
DES KLOSTERS MURBACH AUS DEM 9.
JAHRHUNDERT.*
P.W. TAX, 589:JUL73-575

MILES, D.H. HOFMANNSTHAL'S NOVEL
"ANDREAS."
R.E. LORBE, 301(JEGP):OCT73-603
MILES, J. THE BLACKMAILER.
N. CALLENDAR, 441:17NOV74-52
MILES, J. THE SILVER BULLET GANG.
N. CALLENDAR, 441:28APR74-39
MILEWSKI, T. INDOEUROPEJSKIE IMIONA
OSOBOWE.
Z. GOŁĄB, 353:1OCT72-106
MILGATE, W. - SEE BALD, R.C.
MILGRAM, S. OBEDIENCE TO AUTHORITY.
P. ADAMS, 61:FEB74-96
C. LEHMANN-HAUPT, 441:3JAN74-39
S. MARCUS, 441:13JAN74-1
617(TLS):7JUN74-602
MILHAUD, D. MA VIE HEUREUSE.
617(TLS):1NOV74-1239
MILIBAND, R. & J. SAVILLE, EDS. THE
SOCIALIST REGISTER 1973.
617(TLS):3MAY74-467
MILIĆ, D. STRANI KAPITAL U RUDAR-
STVU SRBIJE DO 1918.
J.R. LAMPE, 32:SEP73-653
MILIC, L.T. STYLISTS ON STYLE.
J. LEED, 599:WINTER72-71
MILIN, G. - SEE NOËL DU FAIL
"THE MILITARY BALANCE 1973-74."
J. GELLNER, 99:OCT74-47
MILL, J.S. L'UTILITARISME. (G.
TANESSE, TRANS)
A-L. LEROY, 542:JUL-SEP72-389
MILLÁN, R. LECTURAS DEL SUBURBIO.
G. ANTOINE, 238:DEC72-981
MILLAND, R. WIDE-EYED IN BABYLON.
M. WOOD, 453:31OCT74-39
MILLAR, G. THE BRUNEVAL RAID.
617(TLS):26JUL74-782
MILLAR, M. VANISH IN AN INSTANT.
N. CALLENDAR, 441:12MAY74-18
MILLAR, O., ED. THE INVENTORIES &
VALUATIONS OF THE KING'S GOODS:
1649-1651.
R. EDWARDS, 39:NOV72-453
MILLAR, O. THE QUEENS GALLERY,
BUCKINGHAM PALACE, DUTCH PICTURES
FROM THE ROYAL COLLECTION.
E. LARSEN, 127:SPRING73-364
"MILLE."* [CIRCOLO LINGUISTICO
FLORENTINO]
400(MLN):JAN72-160
MILLER, A.R. THE ASSAULT ON PRIVACY.
R.H. LYTLE, 14:JUL/OCT72-403
MILLER, B., N.J. PINNEY & W.S. SAS-
LOW. INNOVATION IN NEW COMMUNI-
TIES.
505:DEC72-98
MILLER, B.S. PHANTASIES OF A LOVE-
THIEF.
D.B. LEVINE, 293(JAST):FEB72-446
F. WILSON, 318(JAOS):OCT-DEC72-
502
MILLER, C.W. BENJAMIN FRANKLIN'S
PHILADELPHIA PRINTING, 1728-1766.
617(TLS):27SEP74-1042
MILLER, D. THE CHINESE JADE AFFAIR.
617(TLS):18JAN74-61
MILLER, D.W. CHURCH, STATE & NATION
IN IRELAND 1898-1921.
617(TLS):17MAY74-525
MILLER, E. THAT NOBLE CABINET.
LORD RADCLIFFE, 362:21MAR74-376
617(TLS):25OCT74-1196

MILLER, G.M., ED. BBC PRONOUNCING
DICTIONARY OF BRITISH NAMES.*
  A.R. TELLIER, 189(EA):OCT-DEC72-
  532
MILLER, H.H. GREECE THROUGH THE
AGES.
  639(VQR):SUMMER72-CIX
MILLER, H.K., E. ROTHSTEIN & G.S.
ROUSSEAU, EDS. THE AUGUSTAN MIL-
IEU.*
  V.M. HAMM, 613:SPRING72-134
  P.J. KORSHIN, 72:BAND21OHEFT1/3-
  192
MILLER, H.T., ED. LOUDON SAINTHILL.
  617(TLS):4JAN74-14
MILLER, J., ED. THE ARIZONA RANGERS.
  W. GARD, 584(SWR):SUMMER73-272
MILLER, J. THE LIFE & TIMES OF WIL-
LIAM & MARY.
  617(TLS):6SEP74-951
MILLER, J. MARSHALL MC LUHAN.*
  K. MC SWEENEY, 529(QQ):SPRING72-
  115
MILLER, J.B., ED. PSYCHOANALYSIS &
WOMEN.
  C. LASCH, 453:30OCT74-12
MILLER, J.H., ED. ASPECTS OF NARRA-
TIVE.
  G.B. TENNYSON, 445(NCF):DEC72-
  365
MILLER, J.H. THOMAS HARDY.*
  W.F. WRIGHT, 594:SPRING72-93
MILLER, J.H. & D. BOROWITZ. CHARLES
DICKENS & GEORGE CRUIKSHANK.
  J.R. COHEN, 155:JAN72-58
  S. MONOD, 189(EA):JUL-SEP72-436
  H.P. SUCKSMITH, 677:VOL3-316
MILLER, K.B. IDEOLOGY & MORAL PHIL-
OSOPHY.
  R. FRONDIZI, 484(PPR):DEC72-275
MILLER, L. - SEE CLARKE, A.
MILLER, M. PLAIN SPEAKING.
  M. KEMPTON, 453:4APR74-24
  C. LEHMANN-HAUPT, 441:21JAN74-25
  R. SHERRILL, 441:10FEB74-2
  R. TODD, 61:MAR74-89
  442(NY):11FEB74-127
MILLER, M. WHAT HAPPENED.
  S. O'CONNELL, 418(MR):WINTER73-
  190
MILLER, R.A. JAPANESE & THE OTHER
ALTAIC LANGUAGES.
  C.F. CARLSON, 293(JAST):MAY72-
  673
  G.B. MATHIAS, 244(HJAS):VOL32-
  284
  J. STREET, 350:DEC73-950
MILLER, R.D. SCHILLER & THE IDEAL
OF FREEDOM.*
  A.J. CAMIGLIANO, 406:SPRING73-82
  H.B. GARLAND, 220(GL&L):JAN73-
  175
MILLER, R.L. THE ECONOMICS OF
ENERGY.
  M. GREEN, 441:6OCT74-10
MILLER, S. THE PICARESQUE NOVEL.
  M.E. NOVAK, 594:SPRING72-75
  G. SOBEJANO, 240(HR):SUMMER72-
  319
MILLER, S., E. MASLEN & K. WRIGHT.
TREBLE POETS I.
  617(TLS):8NOV74-1265

MILLER, S.R. DIE FIGUR DES ERZÄHL-
ERS IN WIELANDS ROMANEN.
  E.E. REED, 221(GQ):JAN72-173
MILLER, V.B. SIEGE. REQUIEM FOR A
COP.
  N. CALLENDAR, 441:10NOV74-45
MILLER, W.C. AN ARMED AMERICA.
  W.R. MC DONALD, 128(CE):MAY72-
  947
MILLER, W.D. A HARSH & DREADFUL
LOVE.
  617(TLS):11JAN74-26
MILLER, W.R., ED. CONTEMPORARY AMER-
ICAN PROTESTANT THOUGHT.
  639(VQR):AUTUMN73-CLXXI
MILLET, J. LA BELLE MÉTHODE, OU
L'ART DE BIEN CHANTER.
  D. SCOTT, 415:NOV73-1127
MILLET, L. PERCEPTION, IMAGINATION,
MÉMOIRE.
  G. BRYKMAN, 542:OCT-DEC72-473
MILLETT, K. FLYING.
  C. LEHMANN-HAUPT, 441:15JUL74-29
  J. WILSON, 441:23JUN74-2
  442(NY):26AUG74-92
MILLGATE, M. THOMAS HARDY.*
  J.O. BAILEY, 637(VS):DEC71-242
  J. GINDIN, 639(VQR):WINTER72-152
  K. WILSON, 529(QQ):SUMMER72-266
MILLHAUSER, S. EDWIN MULLHOUSE.*
  S. O'CONNELL, 418(MR):WINTER73-
  190
  W.H. PRITCHARD, 249(HUDR):SPRING
  73-233
  E. ROVIT, 659:AUTUMN74-539
MILLS, A.D., ED. THE DORSET LAY
SUBSIDY ROLL OF 1332.
  A.J. DUGGAN, 447(N&Q):JUN72-236
MILLS, D.E. A COLLECTION OF TALES
FROM UJI.
  C. BLACKER, 203:SPRING72-79
  B. RUCH, 293(JAST):NOV71-167
  M. URY, 318(JAOS):OCT-DEC72-563
MILLS, E.S. STUDIES IN THE STRUC-
TURE OF THE URBAN ECONOMY.
  505:SEP72-178
MILLS, J. THE OCTOBER MEN.
  M. FOSTER, 296:VOL3#2-97
MILLS, J.P. THE AO NAGAS.
  617(TLS):13SEP74-984
MILLS, J.V.G. - SEE MA HUAN
MILLS, R. YOUNG OUTSIDERS.
  P. DELANY, 441:13JAN74-32
MILLSTEIN, G. THE LATE HARVEY GROS-
BECK.
  A. BROYARD, 441:28MAR74-43
  J.R. FRAKES, 441:19MAY74-4
  L.E. SISSMAN, 442(NY):9SEP74-130
MILOSZ, C. SELECTED POEMS.
  D.J. ENRIGHT, 453:4APR74-29
  P. ZWEIG, 441:7JUL74-6
MILTON, D.S. PARADISE ROAD.
  M. LEVIN, 441:28APR74-37
MILTON, J. THE HISTORY OF BRITAIN.
(F. FOGLE, ED)
  L. MILLER, 447(N&Q):AUG72-320
MILTON, J. A MASKE. (S.E. SPROTT,
ED)
  617(TLS):19JUL74-770
MILTON, J. THE MILTONIC STATE PAP-
ERS, 1649-1659. (J.M. PATRICK, ED)
  L. MILLER, 447(N&Q):DEC72-474

247

MILTON, J. PARADISE LOST.* (BKS
1&2) (J. BROADBENT, ED)
R.E.C. HOUGHTON, 541(RES):NOV72-
497
MILTON, J. THE SHORTER POEMS OF
JOHN MILTON. (D.H. BURDEN, ED)
N.W. BAWCUTT, 447(N&Q):MAY72-198
MILTON, J.R., ED. CONVERSATIONS
WITH FRANK WATERS.
M. BUCCO, 649(WAL):FALL72-230
MILTON, N. JOHN MACLEAN.
617(TLS):14JUN74-631
MILTON, P. THE JOLLY CORNER.
W.D. CASE, 58:SEP/OCT72-69
MINARIK, E. LES 50 MOTS CLÉS DE LA
PSYCHOSOCIOLOGIE.
M. ADAM, 542:OCT-DEC72-474
MINEAR, R.H. VICTOR'S JUSTICE.*
639(VQR):SUMMER72-XCVI
MINEO, N. PROFETISMO E APOCALITTICA
IN DANTE.
T.G. BERGIN, 275(IQ):FALL/WINTER
72-109
MINER, E. THE CAVALIER MODE FROM
,JONSON TO COTTON.*
A. FLETCHER, 149:SEP73-266
MINER, E., ED. JOHN DRYDEN.*
W. MYERS, 566:SPRING73-104
MINER, E. JAPANESE POETIC DIARIES.
D.E. MILLS, 318(JAOS):APR-JUN72-
351
MINER, E. THE METAPHYSICAL MODE
FROM DONNE TO COWLEY.*
W. VON KOPPENFELS, 38:BAND90
HEFT3-401
MINER, E., ED. STUART & GEORGIAN
MOMENTS.
D.G. LOUGEE, 566:SPRING73-113
J.D. WOOLLEY, 568(SCN):FALL-WIN-
TER73-87
MINER, E. & V.A. DEARING - SEE DRY-
DEN, J.
MINERS, N.J. THE NIGERIAN ARMY 1956-
66.
W. GUTTERIDGE, 69:APR72-156
MINET, P. - SEE GILBERT-LECOMTE, R.
MING-K'UN, K. - SEE UNDER KUO MING-
K'UN
MINKOFF, H., ED. TEACHING ENGLISH
LINGUISTICALLY.
R. WARDHAUGH, 399(MLJ):NOV72-463
MINNEY, R.J. - SEE "THE GEORGE BER-
NARD SHAW VEGETARIAN COOK BOOK"
MINTEER, C. UNDERSTANDING IN A
WORLD OF WORDS.
M.J. FLAX, 186(ETC.):SEP72-324
MINTER, D.L. THE INTERPRETED DESIGN
AS A STRUCTURAL PRINCIPLE IN AMERI-
CAN PROSE.
B. LEE, 447(N&Q):OCT72-393
MINTON, H.G. BLIND MAN'S BUFF.
617(TLS):15FEB74-165
MINTZ, G.K. - SEE HAN, W-K.
MINTZ, M.M. GOUVERNEUR MORRIS & THE
AMERICAN REVOLUTION.*
B. MASON, 656(WMQ):JUL72-508
MIRA DE AMESCUA, A. NO HAY DICHA NI
DESDICHA HASTA LA MUERTE.* (V.G.
WILLIAMSEN, ED)
V. DIXON, 402(MLR):JUL73-672
P.P. MITCHELL, 400(MLN):MAR72-
363
J.A. PARR, 399(MLJ):APR72-257

MIRAMBEL, A. GRAMMAIRE DU GREC
MODERNE.
W.J. AERTS, 206:SEP72-131
MIRANDOLA, G. LA "GAZZETTA LETTER-
ARIA" E LA FRANCIA.
F.J. JONES, 402(MLR):JAN73-198
205(FMLS):JUL72-287
DELLA MIRANDOLA, G.P. - SEE UNDER
PICO DELLA MIRANDOLA, G.
MIRSKY, M. BLUE HILL AVENUE.
42(AR):VOL32#4-699
MISCHEL, T., ED. UNDERSTANDING
OTHER PERSONS.
617(TLS):16AUG74-885
MISEREZ-SCHIRA, G. THE ART OF PAINT-
ING ON PORCELAIN.
L.J. GARTNER, JR., 441:8DEC74-50
MISHIMA, Y. THE DECAY OF THE ANGEL.
P. ADAMS, 61:JUL74-100
A. FRIEDMAN, 441:12MAY74-1
MISHIMA, Y. RUNAWAY HORSES.*
C. DRIVER, 362:14FEB74-215
639(VQR):AUTUMN73-CXXXVII
MISHIMA, Y. THE TEMPLE OF DAWN.*
617(TLS):26JUL74-783
MISKIMIN, A. - SEE "'SUSANNAH,' AN
ALLITERATIVE POEM OF THE FOURTEENTH
CENTURY"
MISRA, B.B. THE ADMINISTRATIVE HIS-
TORY OF INDIA, 1834-1947.
N.G. BARRIER, 293(JAST):FEB72-
434
MISRA, G. ANALYTICAL STUDIES IN
INDIAN PHILOSOPHICAL PROBLEMS.
K.H. POTTER, 485(PE&W):JUL72-337
MISRA, L. BHARATIYA SANGEET VADYA.
L.G. TEWARI, 187:SEP74-458
MISTRAL, F. LIS ISCLO D'OR.* (J.
BOUTIÈRE, ED)
A.V. ROCHE, 545(RPH):NOV72-473
MISTRAL, G. SELECTED POEMS OF GAB-
RIELA MISTRAL. (D. DANA, ED &
TRANS)
A. BORINSKY, 400(MLN):MAR72-387
G. BROWER, 399(MLJ):NOV72-461
R.B. HENDERSON, 37:MAY72-40
J. WALKER, 529(QQ):WINTER72-576
639(VQR):WINTER72-XXVI
MITCHELL, A. A FIELD GUIDE TO THE
TREES OF BRITAIN & NORTHERN EUROPE.
617(TLS):1NOV74-1240
MITCHELL, A. RIDE THE NIGHTMARE.
A. CLUYSENAAR, 565:VOL13#2-72
MITCHELL, B. THE JUSTIFICATION OF
RELIGIOUS BELIEF.
617(TLS):3MAY74-481
MITCHELL, B., ED. THE PHILOSOPHY OF
RELIGION.
H.F., 543:MAR72-562
G.M. PATERSON, 154:DEC72-668
MITCHELL, D. FOUR-STROKE.
C. LEHMANN-HAUPT, 441:18APR74-45
M. LEVIN, 441:28APR74-38
MITCHELL, D. - SEE MAHLER, A.
MITCHELL, G. BLOW MY BLUES AWAY.
B.L. PEARSON, 292(JAF):APR-JUN72-
192
MITCHELL, H. THE SPICE OF LIFE.
H. D'AVIGDOR-GOLDSMID, 617(TLS):
6DEC74-1363
MITCHELL, J. DEATH & BRIGHT WATER.
617(TLS):8NOV74-1248
MITCHELL, J. THOMAS HOCCLEVE.*
P.J. GALLACHER, 599:SPRING72-195

MOLÈ, G. THE T'U-YÜ-HUN FROM THE
NORTHERN WEI TO THE TIME OF THE
FIVE DYNASTIES.
T. CONNOR, 244(HJAS):VOL32-240
MOLE, J. THE INSTRUMENTS.
J. SAUNDERS, 565:VOL13#3-75
MOLE, J. THE LOVE HORSE.
617(TLS):22MAR74-895
MOLHO, A. FLORENTINE PUBLIC FINAN-
CES IN THE EARLY RENAISSANCE,
1400-1433.
R. WITT, 589:JAN73-116
MOLHO, M. LINGUISTIQUES ET LAN-
GAGES.*
M. SANDMANN, 545(RPH):MAY73-740
MOLHO, R. - SEE SAINTE-BEUVE, C-A.
MOLIÈRE, J.B.P. LES FOURBERIES DE
SCAPIN. (J.T. STOKER, ED)
205(FMLS):JAN72-91
MOLIÈRE, J.B.P. OEUVRES COMPLÈTES.
(G. COUTON, ED)
A.C. KEYS, 67:MAY73-124
R. ZUBER, 535(RHL):SEP-DEC72-
1098
DE MOLINA, T. - SEE UNDER TIRSO DE
MOLINA
MOLINA CHOCANO, G. INTEGRACIÓN
CENTROAMERICANA Y DOMINACIÓN IN-
TERNACIONAL.
D.G. ROSS, 263:JUL-SEP73-389
MÖLK, U., ED. FRANZÖSISCHE LITERAR-
ÄSTHETIK DES 12. UND 13. JAHRHUN-
DERTS.*
M. JACKSON, 545(RPH):NOV72-470
MOLLAT, M. & P. WOLFF. THE POPULAR
REVOLUTIONS OF THE LATE MIDDLE
AGES.
617(TLS):15MAR74-268
MOLLAY, K., ED. DIE DENKWÜRDIGKEI-
TEN DER HELENE KOTTANERIN (1439-
1440).
A. CLOSS, 433:OCT72-512
MØLLER, P.L. KRITISKE SKIZZER FRA
AARENE 1840-47. (H. HERTEL, ED)
N. INGWERSEN, 563(SS):SUMMER73-
269
MOLLET, G. QUINZE ANS APRÈS.
617(TLS):3MAY74-461
MOLNÁR, J. A MAGYAR BESZÉDHANGOK
ATLASZA.
G. MEINHOLD, 682(ZPSK):BAND25
HEFT3-252
MOLNAR, J.W., ED. SONGS FROM THE
WILLIAMSBURG THEATRE.*
J.A.W., 410(M&L):OCT73-500
639(VQR):SUMMER73-CXXVI
MOLNÁR, M. BUDAPEST 1956.
B.K. KIRÁLY, 32:DEC73-842
MOLNAR, T. SARTRE PHILOSOPHE DE LA
CONTESTATION.
E. MOROT-SIR, 207(FR):DEC71-502
MOLONEY, B. FLORENCE & ENGLAND.*
H.S. NOCE, 276:SPRING72-90
K. SPEIGHT, 402(MLR):JAN73-192
MOLONY, J.N. AN ARCHITECT OF FREE-
DOM.
617(TLS):15MAR74-263
MOLTMANN, J. THE CRUCIFIED GOD.
D. JENKINS, 617(TLS):22NOV74-
1320
MOMADAY, N.S. ANGLE OF GEESE &
OTHER POEMS.
D. BROMWICH, 441:16JUN74-6
617(TLS):30AUG74-932

MOMADAY, N.S. HOUSE MADE OF DAWN.*
M.W. HYLTON, 145(CRIT):VOL14#2-
60
MOMIGLIANO, A. POLYBIUS BETWEEN THE
ENGLISH & THE TURKS.
O. MURRAY, 617(TLS):18OCT74-1158
MOMMSEN, W.A. DIE NACHLÄSSE IN DEN
DEUTSCHEN ARCHIVEN. (VOL 1, PT 1)
C.G. ANTHON, 14:APR72-221
MOMMSEN, W.J. THE AGE OF BUREAU-
CRACY.
617(TLS):10MAY74-505
MONAS, S. - SEE MANDELSTAM, O.
DE MONBRON, L-C.F. - SEE UNDER FOU-
GERET DE MONBRON, L-C.
MONCK, F.E.O.C. MONCK LETTERS &
JOURNALS 1863-1868.* (W.L. MORTON,
ED)
D. SWAINSON, 529(QQ):WINTER72-
555
MÖNCKEBERG, V. DAS MÄRCHEN UND
UNSERE WELT.
E. ETTLINGER, 203:WINTER72-341
MONDOLFO, R. EL MATERIALISMO HISTOR-
ICO EN F. ENGELS.
G. FABRE, 542:JUL-SEP72-347
MONDRAGÓN, M. PORQUE ME DA LA GANA!
(J. SARNACKI, ED)
J. ALMEIDA, 238:MAY72-403
MONÉSI, I. L'AMOUR ET LE DÉDAIN.
617(TLS):2AUG74-839
MONÉSI, I. UN PEUPLE DE COLOMBES.
B. KAY, 207(FR):DEC71-479
MONEY, K. FONTEYN.
617(TLS):1FEB74-104
MONGRÉDIEN, G. LA QUERELLE DE
"L'ÉCOLE DES FEMMES."
J. MOREL, 535(RHL):SEP-DEC72-
1095
MONIER-WILLIAMS, R. THE TALLOW
CHANDLERS OF LONDON. (VOL 3)
617(TLS):1MAR74-221
MONK, S.H. - SEE DRYDEN, J.
MONOD, J. CHANCE & NECESSITY.*
(FRENCH TITLE: LE HASARD ET LA
NÉCESSITÉ.)
J. BELOFF, 639(VQR):SPRING72-289
A. COMFORT, 381:SEP72-351
E. DOWLING, 63:MAY73-90
H. LOMAS, 364:AUG/SEP72-144
R. MONRO, 111:20OCT72-20
MONOGATARI, O. - SEE UNDER OCHIKUBO
MONOGATARI
MONROE, H.M., JR. & J.T. MC INTOSH -
SEE DAVIS, J.
MONROE, J. THE BARE FACTS.
H. FRANCIS, 157:WINTER72-83
MONROE, J.T. - SEE IBN GARCÍA
MONROY, F.A. & L. GORRÁEZ ARCAUTE -
SEE UNDER ANAYA MONROY, F. & L.
GORRÁEZ ARCAUTE
MONSARRAT, A. AND THE BRIDE WORE...
617(TLS):15MAR74-273
MONSARRAT, N. THE KAPPILLAN OF
MALTA.*
W. SCHOTT, 441:7APR74-28
MONTAGU, M.W. THE COMPLETE LETTERS
OF LADY MARY WORTLEY MONTAGU.*
(VOLS 2&3) (R. HALSBAND, ED)
A. PARREAUX, 189(EA):OCT-DEC72-
563
MONTAGUE, J. THE CAVE OF NIGHT.
617(TLS):16AUG74-879

MONTAGUE, J., ED. THE FABER BOOK
OF IRISH VERSE.
F.S.L. LYONS, 617(TLS):19JUL74-
763
MONTAGUE, R. FORMAL PHILOSOPHY.
(R.H. THOMASON, ED)
L.J. COHEN, 617(TLS):22NOV74-
1310
MONTALE, E. LA POESIA NON ESISTE.
E. SACCONE, 400(MLN):JAN72-166
MONTEFIORE, A., ED. PHILOSOPHY &
PERSONAL REALTIONS.
617(TLS):8FEB74-136
MONTEIL, V. INDONÉSIE.
R. VAN NIEL, 293(JAST):NOV71-220
MONTELL, W.L. THE SAGA OF COE
RIDGE.*
W.H. JANSEN, 582(SFQ):MAR72-93
MONTENEGRO, B.J.F. - SEE UNDER FEI-
JOO Y MONTENEGRO, B.J.
MONTENEGRO, T.H. TUBERCULOSE E
LITERATURA.
R.A. MAZZARA, 263:JAN-MAR73-110
MONTESINOS, J.F. ENSAYOS Y ESTUDIOS
DE LITERATURA ESPAÑOLA. (J.H.
SILVERMAN, ED)
E.L. RIVERS, 400(MLN):MAR72-349
MONTESINOS, J.F. PEREDA O LA NOVELA
IDILIO.
J.B. AVALLE-ARCE, 241:SEP72-75
MONTGOMERIE, J. IMPLOSION.
617(TLS):5APR74-375
MONTGOMERY, B. A FIELD-MARSHAL IN
THE FAMILY.*
C.P. STACEY, 99:NOV/DEC74-33
MONTGOMERY, C.F. - SEE MOXON, J.
MONTGOMERY, C.F. & W.P. COLE - SEE
SHERATON, T.
MONTGOMERY, C.F. & B.M. FORMAN - SEE
SMITH, G.
MONTGOMERY, E.D., JR., ED. LE CHAS-
TOIEMENT D'UN PÈRE À SON FILS.*
R. HARDEN, 589:APR73-385
MONTGOMERY, F.M. PRINTED TEXTILES.*
P. IRWIN, 90:MAR72-182
S. ROBINSON, 39:AUG72-167
MONTGOMERY, M. T.S. ELIOT.
C.H. SMITH, 659:SPRING74-277
MONTGOMERY, M. FUGITIVE.
S.A. GRAU, 441:9JUN74-4
MONTGOMERY, S. SHABBY SUNSHINE.
617(TLS):15FEB74-148
DE MONTHERLANT, H. UN ASSASSIN EST
MON MAÎTRE.
M. ROSENBERG, 207(FR):MAY72-1182
DE MONTHERLANT, H. THE BOYS.
V. CUNNINGHAM, 362:18APR74-509
DE MONTHERLANT, H. LE FICHIER PARIS-
IEN.
617(TLS):4OCT74-1060
MONTI, F. PRE-COLUMBIAN TERRACOTTAS.
M.S. YOUNG, 39:AUG72-170
MONTI, V. POESIE.* (G. BEZZOLA, ED)
W.T.S., 191(ELN):SEP72(SUPP)-199
MONTORO, A.G. & S.A. RIGOL - SEE
UNDER GARCÍA MONTORO, A. & S.A.
RIGOL
MONTY, J.R. LES ROMANS DU L'ABBÉ
PRÉVOST.*
V. MYLNE, 208(FS):JUL73-330
J. SGARD, 535(RHL):MAY-JUN72-527
MOODY, C. SOLZHENITSYN.
617(TLS):22FEB74-187
MOODY, C. - SEE EHRENBURG, I.

MOODY, H.L.B. VARIETIES OF ENGLISH.
E. QUENON-PAQUES, 556(RLV):
1972/3-334
MOODY, R. LILLIAN HELLMAN.*
L-L. MARKER, 397(MD):DEC72-344
T.F. MARSHALL, 27(AL):MAY73-312
MOON, M.J. BYGONE WHITEHAVEN.
617(TLS):15MAR74-273
MOONEY, C.F. THE MAKING OF MAN.
W.C. MC CAULEY, 613:WINTER72-625
MOORCOCK, M. BREAKFAST IN THE RUINS.
J. DECK, 441:19MAY74-38
MOORCOCK, M. THE LAND LEVIATHAN.
617(TLS):31MAY74-577
MOORCRAFT, C. MUST THE SEAS DIE?
H.B. HOUGH, 31(ASCH):WINTER73/74-
152
MOORE, B., ED. BLACK THEOLOGY.
K. SUTTON, 362:11APR74-476
MOORE, B. CATHOLICS.*
P. BAILEY, 364:FEB/MAR73-157
K. MC SWEENEY, 529(QQ):WINTER72-
581
M. MUDRICK, 249(HUDR):AUTUMN73-
545
W. SHEED, 453:7MAR74-18
MOORE, B. HARD ON THE ROAD.
M. LEVIN, 441:25AUG74-31
MOORE, C. DANIEL H. BURNHAM.
P. BRENIKOV, 447(N&Q):FEB72-64
MOORE, D.K. MESSAGES, ADDRESSES, &
PUBLIC PAPERS OF DANIEL KILLIAN
MOORE, GOVERNOR OF NORTH CAROLINA,
1965-1969. (M.F. MITCHELL, ED)
E.L. HILL, 14:JUL/OCT72-413
MOORE, D.L., ED. LORD BYRON.
P. ADAMS, 61:JUN74-115
MOORE, D.L. FASHION THROUGH FASHION
PLATES 1771-1970.
D. COOMBS, 135:MAR72-215
F. CRICHTON, 39:MAR72-231
MOORE, E. - SEE GRANVILLE-BARKER, H.
MOORE, F.C.T. THE PSYCHOLOGY OF
MAINE DE BIRAN.
M.S., 543:JUN72-763
MOORE, G. CONFESSIONS OF A YOUNG
MAN. (S. DICK, ED)
K. MC SWEENEY, 529(QQ):WINTER72-
583
MOORE, G. WILLIAM JEMISON MIMS.
L. ALLEN, 9(ALAR):APR72-148
MOORE, G.E. PRINCIPIA ETHICA. (B.
WISSER, ED & TRANS)
H. NELLES, 53(AGP):BAND54HEFT2-
208
MOORE, H.T. TWENTIETH-CENTURY GER-
MAN LITERATURE.*
R.W. LAST, 220(GL&L):JUL73-329
J.J. WHITE, 402(MLR):OCT73-949
MOORE, J. TIMECHARTS, 1-6.
R.G. PENMAN, 123:MAR73-80
MOORE, J.N. ELGAR.
D. MC VEAGH, 415:JUN73-599
J.A.W., 410(M&L):APR73-237
MOORE, J.N. LAW & THE INDO-CHINA
WAR.
F.O. WILCOX, 639(VQR):SPRING73-
265
MOORE, J.R. MASKS OF LOVE & DEATH.*
A. PARKIN, 397(MD):SEP72-211
H. PYLE, 541(RES):MAY72-249
M. SIDNELL, 627(UTQ):SPRING72-
263

MOORE, K. VICTORIAN WIVES.
617(TLS):26JUL74-785
MOORE, L.H., JR. ROBERT PENN WARREN
& HISTORY.
J. GRIMSHAW, 598(SOR):SPRING74-
504
MOORE, P. WATCHERS OF THE STARS.
W. SULLIVAN, 441:1DEC74-46
617(TLS):15NOV74-1297
MOORE, R. WORD FROM THE HILLS.*
639(VQR):SPRING73-LXII
MOORE, S. & K. MAGUIRE. THE DREAMER
NOT THE DREAM.
F. KEENAN, 363:FEB72-75
MOORE, W. THE THIN YELLOW LINE.
617(TLS):5APR74-370
MOORE, W.G. THE CLASSICAL DRAMA OF
FRANCE.*
205(FMLS):APR72-195
MOORE, W.G. FRENCH ACHIEVEMENT IN
LITERATURE.
C.G.S. WILLIAMS, 399(MLJ):MAR72-
194
MOORE, W.G. LA ROCHEFOUCAULD.*
N. GROSS, 546(RR):FEB72-47
MOORHOUSE, F. THE AMERICANS, BABY.
C. HARRISON-FORD, 581:JUN73-167
MOORHOUSE, G. THE FEARFUL VOID.
P. ZWEIG, 441:31MAR74-32
453:4APR74-44
MOORMAN, C. KINGS & CAPTAINS.
T.R. HENN, 402(MLR):JAN73-141
E.G. STANLEY, 447(N&Q):NOV72-440
J. TURVILLE-PETRE, 382(MAE):
1973/2-204
MOORMAN, M. - SEE WORDSWORTH, D.
MOQUIN, W., WITH C. VAN DOREN, EDS.
GREAT DOCUMENTS IN AMERICAN INDIAN
HISTORY.
J.E. CHAMBERLIN, 249(HUDR):WIN-
TER73/74-786
MOQUIN, W., WITH C. VAN DOREN &
F.A.J. IANNI, EDS. A DOCUMENTARY
HISTORY OF THE ITALIAN AMERICANS.
F. FERRETTI, 441:22JUL74-27
J. MANGIONE, 441:16JUN74-26
MORAES, D. A MATTER OF PEOPLE.
617(TLS):30AUG74-926
MORAES, J. - SEE DE SOUSA ANDRADE, J.
MORAES, J. & F.G. WILLIAMS - SEE DE
SOUSA ANDRADE, J.
MORAIN, M.S., ED. TEACHING GENERAL
SEMANTICS.
C. HAMBRO, 186(ETC.):MAR72-91
MORAMARCO, F. EDWARD DAHLBERG.
J. CHAMETZKY, 651(WHR):SUMMER73-
313
MORAN, L., COMP. THE CRAFTSMAN'S
COOKBOOK.
D. HARE, 139:DEC72-14
MORAN, R. LOUIS SIMPSON.
P. STITT, 598(SOR):SPRING74-517
MORANTE, E. LA STORIA.
617(TLS):4OCT74-1062
MORAT, M-T. - SEE DAUZAT, A.
DE MORATÍN, L.F. - SEE UNDER FERNÁN-
DEZ DE MORATÍN, L.
MORAUX, P. & D. HARLFINGER, EDS.
UNTERSUCHUNGEN ZUR EUDEMISCHEN
ETHIK.*
P.M. HUBY, 123:DEC73-149
P. LOUIS, 555:VOL46FASC1-126
F.E. SPARSHOTT, 487:AUTUMN72-300

MORAVIA, A. BOUGHT & SOLD.*
268:JAN74-74
MORAVIA, A. TWO.*
42(AR):SPRING/SUMMER72-239
MORAVIA, A. THE TWO OF US.
G. EWART, 364:OCT/NOV72-146
MORAVIA, A. UN' ALTRA VITA.*
A.M. KINSELLA, 268:JUL74-156
MORAVIA, A. WHICH TRIDE DO YOU
BELONG TO?
A. BROYARD, 441:5NOV74-39
P. THEROUX, 441:8DEC74-7
617(TLS):19JUL74-759
MORAVIA, S. LA SCIENZA DELL'UOMO
NEL SETTECENTO.
A. VARTANIAN, 173(ECS):SPRING73-
382
MÖRCHEN, H. DIE EINBILDUNGSKRAFT
BEI KANT. (2ND ED)
R. MALTER, 342:BAND63HEFT2-278
MORE, T. THE COMPLETE WORKS OF ST.
THOMAS MORE. (VOL 8) (L.A.
SCHUSTER & OTHERS, EDS)
617(TLS):19JUL74-770
MOREAU, J. DICTIONNAIRE DE GÉOGRA-
PHIE HISTORIQUE DE LA GAULE ET DE
LA FRANCE.*
G.C., 589:JAN73-187
MOREAU, J. SPINOZA ET LE SPINOZISME.
G. BRYKMAN, 542:JAN-JUN72-228
MOREL, J. LA RENAISSANCE III, 1570-
1624.
A.J. KRAILSHEIMER, 617(TLS):
8NOV74-1265
MOREL, J-P. LE MURAL.
J. CARDUNER, 207(FR):DEC71-480
MORELL, A.G. - SEE UNDER GALLEGO
MORELL, A.
MORENO, A. JUNG, GODS, & MODERN MAN.
617(TLS):5APR74-374
MORENZ, S. EGYPTIAN RELIGION.
617(TLS):12APR74-397
MORETTI, B. LA LINGUA DI FRANCESCO
DE SANCTIS.
W.T.S., 191(ELN):SEP72(SUPP)-190
MORETTI, W. CORTESIA E FURORE NEL
RINASCIMENTO ITALIANO.
400(MLN):JAN72-162
MOREWEDGE, P. THE METAPHYSICA OF
AVICENNA (IBN SĪNĀ).
R.E.A. SHANAB, 319:JUL74-392
MORGAN, A. ANCHORWOMAN.
M. LEVIN, 441:16JUN74-28
MORGAN, A.M., ED. BRITISH GOVERN-
MENT PUBLICATIONS: AN INDEX TO
CHAIRMEN & AUTHORS, 1941-1966.
J.B. CHILDS, 517(PBSA):APR-JUN73-
197
MORGAN, B. THE MYSTIC ADVENTURES OF
ROXIE STONER.
P. ADAMS, 61:SEP74-103
M. WOOD, 453:28NOV74-29
MORGAN, D. DELIA.
617(TLS):13SEP74-969
MORGAN, D. PHOENIX OF FLEET STREET.
617(TLS):4JAN74-7
MORGAN, E. THE DESCENT OF WOMAN.
N. WEYL, 396(MODA):SUMMER73-333
MORGAN, E. FROM GLASGOW TO SATURN.*
R. GARFITT, 364:OCT/NOV73-115
J. MATTHIAS, 491:APR74-45
MORGAN, I. PURITAN SPIRITUALITY.
617(TLS):5JUL74-732

MORGAN, K.O. LLOYD GEORGE.
617(TLS):12JUL74-742
MORGAN, M.C. LENIN.
R.D. WARTH, 32:JUN73-386
MORGAN, M.M. THE SHAVIAN PLAY-
GROUND.*
D. GRONAU, 182:VOL25#11-359
C. HARRISON, 157:SPRING72-74
R.J. JORDAN, 67:MAY73-120
K. MUIR, 677:VOL3-325
F.L. RADFORD, 401(MLQ):JUN73-217
MORGAN, P. THE GREY MARE BEING THE
BETTER STEED.
617(TLS):11JAN74-28
MORGAN, R. MONSTER.
D. LEHMAN, 491:DEC73-173
MORGAN, R. RED OWL.
R. PEVEAR, 249(HUDR):SPRING73-
192
MORGAN, W.J., ED. NAVAL DOCUMENTS
OF THE AMERICAN REVOLUTION. (VOL 5)
F.L. OWSLEY, JR., 9(ALAR):JUL72-
235
H.B. ZOBEL, 432(NEQ):SEP72-444
MORGANN, M. SHAKESPEARIAN CRITICISM.
(D.A. FINEMAN, ED)
T. HAWKES, 676(YR):SUMMER73-561
R.W. UPHAUS, 290(JAAC):SUMMER73-
565
639(VQR):SPRING73-LXVIII
MORHANGE-BÉGUÉ, C. "LA CHANSON DU
MAL AIMÉ" D'APOLLINAIRE.*
M. DAVIES, 402(MLR):JAN73-184
S.I. LOCKERBIE, 208(FS):APR73-
225
MORICE, A. DEATH & THE DUTIFUL
DAUGHTER.
N. CALLENDAR, 441:24FEB74-41
MORIGUCHI TARI. KOGANE NO UMA.
F.H. MAYER, 293(JAST):AUG72-911
MORIN, E. PLODEMET.
J. MARSH, 97(CQ):VOL6#1-70
MORIN, E. RUMOUR IN ORLÉANS.
S.A. WEINSTOCK, 390:NOV72-73
MORISON, R. THE BLIND HARPER (AN
CLARSAIR DALL). (W. MATHESON, ED)
C. Ó BAOILL, 595(SCS):VOL17PT1-
81
MORISON, S. & N. BARKER, EDS. POLI-
TICS & SCRIPT.
V. BROWN, 377:JUL73-115
MORISON, S.E. THE EUROPEAN DISCOV-
ERY OF AMERICA: THE NORTHERN VOY-
AGES A.D. 500-1600.*
K.R. ANDREWS, 656(WMQ):JAN72-167
F.X. CURRAN, 613:SUMMER72-310
B.B. SOLNICK, 37:JUN-JUL72-42
MORISON, S.E. THE EUROPEAN DISCOV-
ERY OF AMERICA: THE SOUTHERN VOY-
AGES A.D. 1492-1616.
D.J. BOORSTIN, 441:13OCT74-1
R. DAVIS, 617(TLS):20DEC74-1430
C. HILL, 453:14NOV74-17
M.M. MOONEY, 231:DEC74-97
R.F. SHEPARD, 441:24DEC74-17
E. WEEKS, 61:NOV74-122
442(NY):14OCT74-200
MORITZ, K.P. ANDREAS HARTKNOPF.
(H.J. SCHRIMPF, ED)
C.P. MAGILL, 220(GL&L):APR73-242
MORLAND, D. ALBION! ALBION!
617(TLS):20DEC74-1441

MORLAND, J.K., ED. THE NOT SO SOLID
SOUTH.
H. GLASSIE, 292(JAF):JAN-MAR72-
97
MORLEY, F. THE POWER IN THE PEOPLE.
(4TH ED)
F.G. WILSON, 396(MODA):SPRING73-
204
MORLEY, J. DEATH, HEAVEN & THE VIC-
TORIANS.*
G.W. STOCKING, JR., 637(VS):
DEC72-242
639(VQR):SUMMER72-CVIII
MORLEY, J.W., ED. DILEMMAS OF
GROWTH IN PREWAR JAPAN.
H.J. JONES, 293(JAST):AUG72-951
MORLEY, J.W., ED. FORECAST FOR
JAPAN.
639(VQR):AUTUMN72-CXLIX
MORLEY, P.A. THE MYSTERY OF UNITY.*
J.B. BESTON, 67:MAY73-121
MORLEY-PEGGE, R. THE FRENCH HORN.
(2ND ED)
N. O'LOUGHLIN, 415:SEP73-903
MORÓN ARROYO, C. EL SISTEMA DE
ORTEGA Y GASSET.
G. SOBEJANO, 240(HR):AUTUMN72-
476
MOROZ, V. REPORT FROM THE BERIA RE-
SERVE. (J. KOLASKY, ED & TRANS)
BOOMERANG. (Y. BIHUN, ED)
B.W. HUDSON, 617(TLS):13DEC74-
1409
P. REDDAWAY, 453:12DEC74-36
MORPURGO-TAGLIABUE, G. I PROCESSI
DI GALILEO E L'EPISTEMOLOGIA.
E. NAMER, 542:APR-JUN72-169
MORREALE, M. PARA UNA ANTOLOGÍA DE
LITERATURA CASTELLANA MEDIEVAL.
J. GULSOY, 545(RPH):AUG72-199
MORRELL, O. OTTOLINE AT GARSINGTON.
(R. GATHORNE-HARDY, ED)
A. BELL, 617(TLS):13SEP74-978
E. TENNANT, 362:26SEP74-408
MORRESSY, J. A LONG COMMUNION.
M. LEVIN, 441:14JUL74-20
MORRILL, J.S. CHESHIRE 1630-1660.
V. PEARL, 617(TLS):23AUG74-900
MORRIS, A.J.A. RADICALISM AGAINST
WAR, 1906-1914.
617(TLS):1MAR74-202
MORRIS, A.K. WALLACE STEVENS.
C. RAINE, 617(TLS):6DEC74-1390
MORRIS, B., ED. WILLIAM CONGREVE.
M.E. NOVAK, 566:SPRING73-105
D.A. SAMUELSON, 568(SCN):FALL-
WINTER73-90
MORRIS, C. WRITINGS ON THE GENERAL
THEORY OF SIGNS.
H.W. JOHNSTONE, JR., 484(PPR):
JUN73-579
MORRIS, C.B. SURREALISM & SPAIN
1920-1936.
A. BENSOUSSAN, 182:VOL25#12-419
A.P. DEBICKI, 401(MLQ):DEC73-475
617(TLS):25JAN74-77
639(VQR):SUMMER73-CXXVI
MORRIS, C.W. THE PRAGMATIC MOVEMENT
IN AMERICAN PHILOSOPHY.
P. TIBBETTS, 477:AUTUMN72-448
MORRIS, D.B. THE RELIGIOUS SUBLIME.
J.M. ARMISTEAD, 579(SAQ):AUTUMN
73-616
639(VQR):SPRING73-LXIX

MORRIS, H. BIRTH & COPULATION &
DEATH.
J.T. IRWIN, 569(SR):WINTER73-158
MORRIS, I. - SEE "AS I CROSSED A
BRIDGE OF DREAMS"
MORRIS, J. AGAINST NATURE & GOD.
R. HILL, 617(TLS):22NOV74-1323
MORRIS, J. CONUNDRUM.
P. BEER, 362:25APR74-534
A. BROYARD, 441:9APR74-35
J. RICHARDSON, 453:2MAY74-7
M. RICHIE, 231:AUG74-91
R. WEST, 441:14APR74-5
617(TLS):26APR74-431
MORRIS, J. CORRESPONDENCE OF JOHN
MORRIS WITH JOHANNES DE LAET, 1634-
1649.* (J.A.F. BEKKERS, ED)
A.E.C. SIMONI, 354:JUN72-151
MORRIS, J. DESCARTES DICTIONARY.
P. DUBOIS, 542:APR-JUN74-189
MORRIS, J. HEAVEN'S COMMAND.*
617(TLS):4JAN74-3
MORRIS, J. THE NUDE IN CANADIAN
PAINTING.*
M. GREENWOOD, 96:DEC72/JAN73-89
MORRIS, J. PLACES.*
639(VQR):SUMMER73-CXXVI
MORRIS, J. THE PREACHERS.*
M. GARDNER, 453:21FEB74-29
MORRIS, J. VENICE. (NEW ED)
617(TLS):29MAR74-342
MORRIS, J. & T. JONES - SEE TREPTOW,
O.
MORRIS, M. THE ART OF J.D. FERGUS-
SON.
617(TLS):26JUL74-789
MORRIS, R.K. CONTINUANCE & CHANGE.
T.L. ASHTON, 454:SPRING73-276
MORRIS, S. & E.O. FURBER, EDS. HERE-
DITAS.
R.G. PENMAN, 123:MAR73-81
MORRIS, W. FIRE SERMON.
J.K. FOLSOM, 649(WAL):SPRING72-
72
C. ROOKE, 376:JAN72-117
639(VQR):WINTER72-XVI
MORRIS, W. THE LAST OF THE SOUTHERN
GIRLS.*
617(TLS):8MAR74-229
639(VQR):AUTUMN73-CXXXVI
MORRIS, W. TOWARD A NEW HISTORICISM.
R. COHEN, 639(VQR):WINTER73-157
V.A. KRAMER, 290(JAAC):FALL72-
137
L. LEARY, 125:FEB73-208
MORRIS, W. WAR GAMES.
C. ROOKE, 376:JUL72-143
639(VQR):SUMMER72-XCVIII
MORRISON, B.M. POLITICAL CENTERS &
CULTURAL REGIONS IN EARLY BENGAL.
K.K. SARKAR, 318(JAOS):APR-JUN
72-324
MORRISON, D.E. & R.E. HENKEL, EDS.
THE SIGNIFICANCE TEST CONTROVERSY.
R.N. GIERE, 84:MAY72-170
MORRISON, J.C. MEANING & TRUTH IN
WITTGENSTEIN'S "TRACTATUS."*
R. BLANCHÉ, 542:JAN-MAR72-116
MORRISON, J.L. GOVERNOR O. MAX
GARDNER.
D.C. ROLLER, 579(SAQ):SPRING73-
329

MORRISON, K. ROBERT FROST.
H. BEVINGTON, 441:1DEC74-82
E. WEEKS, 61:OCT74-115
MORRISON, K.F. - SEE GREGOROVIUS, F.
MORRISON, T. CHAUTAUQUA.
E. WEEKS, 61:JUL74-97
MORRISON, T. SULA.*
C. LEHMANN-HAUPT, 441:7JAN74-35
617(TLS):4OCT74-1062
MORRISSON, C. CATALOGUE DES MON-
NAIES BYZANTINES DE LA BIBLIO-
THÈQUE NATIONALE.
J.M. FAGERLIE, 589:APR73-386
MORSE, E.L. FOREIGN POLICY & INTER-
DEPENDENCE IN GAULLIST FRANCE.
H. SIMMONS, 99:NOV/DEC74-35
617(TLS):3MAY74-461
MORSE, J., ED. BEN SHAHN.
639(VQR):WINTER73-XLII
MORSE, J.M. THE IRRELEVANT ENGLISH
TEACHER.*
O. JENKINS, 128(CE):APR73-1014
MORSE, P. JOHN SLOAN'S PRINTS.*
J.H. BAKER, 90:JAN72-38
MORTIER, R. DIFFICULTÉS SUR LA RE-
LIGION PROPOSÉE AU PÈRE MALE-
BRANCHE PAR MR. ..., OFFICIER
MILITAIRE DANS LA MARINE.
J. MAYER, 557(RSH):APR-JUN72-320
G. MENANT-ARTIGAS, 535(RHL):MAY-
JUN72-515
MORTIMER, P. LONG DISTANCE.
D. BROMWICH, 441:22SEP74-3
I. EHRENPREIS, 453:12DEC74-42
E. TENNANT, 362:20JUN74-808
617(TLS):28JUN74-687
MORTIMER, R., ED. SHOWCASE STATE.
617(TLS):17MAY74-516
MORTIMORE, M.J., ED. ZARIA & ITS
REGIONS.
A.H.M.K-G., 69:JUL72-260
MORTON, A.Q. & OTHERS. IT'S GREEK
TO THE COMPUTER.
L. BRANDWOOD, 487:WINTER72-402
MORTON, A.S. A HISTORY OF THE CAN-
ADIAN WEST TO 1870-1. (L.G. THOM-
AS, ED)
D. MORTON, 99:APR74-36
MORTON, B.N. LA DERNIÈRE AVENTURE
DE BEAUMARCHAIS.
E. STURM, 207(FR):OCT71-262
MORTON, B.N. - SEE DE BEAUMARCHAIS,
P.A.C.
MORTON, D. THE CANADIAN GENERAL.
J.L. GRANATSTEIN, 99:MAY/JUN74-
38
MORTON, D. NDP: THE DREAM OF POWER.
N. PENNER, 99:SEP74-45
MORTON, W.L. - SEE MONCK, F.E.O.C.
MORTON, W.S. JAPAN.*
M.J. MAYO, 293(JAST):NOV71-157
MORTUREUX, B. L. ANNAEI SENECAE
OPERUM MORALIUM CONCORDANTIA.
(VOL 4)
J. ANDRÉ, 555:VOL46FASC1-156
MOSCATI, S. THE WORLD OF THE PHOENI-
CIANS.
E.C. KINGSBURY, 318(JAOS):APR-
JUN72-312
MOSEDALE, J. THE GREATEST OF ALL.
C. LEHMANN-HAUPT, 441:23JUL74-31
MOSER, C.A. A HISTORY OF BULGARIAN
LITERATURE, 856-1944.
V. PINTO, 575(SEER):APR73-297

MOSER, G.M. PENN STATE STUDIES:
ESSAYS IN PORTUGUESE-AFRICAN LIT-
ERATURE.*
N. ANDREWS, JR., 240(HR):SPRING
72-239
MOSER, H., ED. SATZ UND WORT IM
HEUTIGEN DEUTSCH.
M. KOLIWER & I. RAHNENFÜHRER,
682(ZPSK):BAND24HEFT6-530
MOSER, H. & I. SCHRÖBLER - SEE PAUL,
H.
MOSER, T. LEHRJAHRE AUF DER COUCH.
617(TLS):25OCT74-1193
MOSÈS, A. - SEE PHILO
MOSHIER, W.F. THE FILMS OF ALICE
FAYE.
D. MC CLELLAND, 200:AUG-SEP72-
418
MOSKOWITZ, H. LECTURAS MADRILEÑAS.*
F.A. BUTLER, 399(MLJ):OCT72-402
MOSLEY, N. IMPOSSIBLE OBJECT.
E.C. BUFKIN, 219(GAR):SPRING72-
100
MOSLEY, O. MY LIFE.
P.W. FILBY, 396(MODA):SUMMER73-
310
MOSS, H. INSTANT LIVES.
442(NY):3JUN74-112
MOSS, H., ED. THE POET'S STORY.
J. MELLORS, 362:26SEP74-416
MOSS, H. SELECTED POEMS.*
E. WHITE, 491:MAR74-350
MOSS, J. PATTERNS OF ISOLATION IN
ENGLISH-CANADIAN FICTION.
T.D. MAC LULICH, 198:SUMMER74-
120
P.C. NOEL-BENTLEY, 296:VOL3#3-
116
MOSS, R. CHILE'S MARXIST EXPERIMENT.
617(TLS):8FEB74-124
MOSS, R. THE FAMILY REUNION.
M. LEVIN, 441:7APR74-32
MOSSE, C. ATHENS IN DECLINE, 404-86
B.C.
617(TLS):26APR74-445
MOSSE, F. A HANDBOOK OF MIDDLE ENG-
LISH.* (REV)
J. VOISINE, 549(RLC):APR-JUN72-
297
MOSSNER, E.C. THE LIFE OF DAVID
HUME.
J. VOISINE, 189(EA):JAN-MAR72-
165
MOSSOP, D.J. PURE POETRY.*
A.B. EYRE, 67:NOV73-305
MOSSUZ, J. ANDRÉ MALRAUX ET LE
GAULLISME.*
W.G. LANGLOIS, 207(FR):OCT71-225
MOSTERT, N. SUPERSHIP.
T. FERRIS, 231:DEC74-99
C. LEHMANN-HAUPT, 441:6NOV74-49
E. REDMAN, 441:17NOV74-1
E. WEEKS, 61:NOV74-117
MOTE, F.W. INTELLECTUAL FOUNDATIONS
OF CHINA.
A.S. CUA, 485(PE&W):JUL72-335
MOTTO, S. OLD HOUSES OF NEW MEXICO
& THE PEOPLE WHO BUILT THEM.
W. GARD, 584(SWR):WINTER73-V
MOTYKOVÁ-ŠNEIDROVÁ, K. WEITERENT-
WICKLUNG UND AUSKLANG DER ÄLTEREN
RÖMISCHEN KAISERZEIT IN BÖHMEN.
U. FISCHER, 182:VOL25#12-425

MOULD, C. THE MUSICAL MANUSCRIPTS
OF ST. GEORGE'S CHAPEL, WINDSOR
CASTLE.*
R.B., 410(M&L):JUL73-360
D. SCOTT, 415:SEP73-901
MOULTON, P.P. - SEE WOOLMAN, J.
MOUNIN, G. INTRODUCTION À LA SÉMIO-
LOGIE.
J. CULLER, 208(FS):OCT73-497
MOUNIN, G. LA LINGUISTIQUE DU XXE
SIÈCLE.
E.H. YARRILL, 182:VOL25#22-786
MOUNTFIELD, D. A HISTORY OF POLAR
EXPLORATION.
D.J. BOORSTIN, 441:1DEC74-7
617(TLS):9AUG74-864
MOURELATOS, A.P.D. THE ROUTE OF
PARMENIDES.*
G.B. KERFERD, 53(AGP):BAND54
HEFT1-89
MOUSNIER, R. THE ASSASSINATION OF
HENRY IV.*
R.J. KNECHT, 617(TLS):6DEC74-
1392
MOUSNIER, R. PEASANT UPRISINGS IN
SEVENTEENTH-CENTURY FRANCE, RUSSIA,
& CHINA.*
639(VQR):WINTER72-XXXII
MOUSSA-MAHMOUD, F. THE ARABIC
NOVEL IN EGYPT (1914-1970).
S.K., 268:JUL74-159
MOUSTIERS, P. HERVÉ BAZIN OU LE
ROMANCIER EN MOUVEMENT.
617(TLS):22FEB74-190
MOWAT, F. SIBIR.
R.A. PIERCE, 529(QQ):SUMMER72-
278
MOWAT, F. WAKE OF THE GREAT SEALERS.
P. O'FLAHERTY, 99:JUL74-35
MOWAT, F. A WHALE FOR THE KILLING.*
R.L. RAYMOND, 150(DR):WINTER
72/73-682
MOWAT, R.C. CREATING THE EUROPEAN
COMMUNITY.
617(TLS):26APR74-454
MOWATT, D.G., ED. FRIDERICH VON
HÜSEN.*
H. HEINEN, 589:JUL73-578
S.J. KAPLOWITT, 399(MLJ):FEB72-
116
K.J. NORTHCOTT, 221(GQ):MAY72-
511
205(FMLS):JAN72-89
MOWATT, I. JUST SHEAFFER OR STORMS
IN THE TROUBLED HEIR.*
M. MUDRICK, 249(HUDR):AUTUMN73-
545
MOXON, J. MECHANICK EXERCISES OR
THE DOCTRINE OF HANDY-WORKS.*
(C.F. MONTGOMERY, ED)
N. GOODISON, 90:JAN72-37
MOYA, M. LE POESIE.* (L. STEGAGNO
PICCHIO, ED)
W. METTMANN, 240(HR):SPRING72-
217
MOYNIHAN, D.P. COPING.
N. BLIVEN, 442(NY):22APR74-151
W.C. MC WILLIAMS, 441:27JAN74-2
R. TODD, 61:MAR74-90
MOYNIHAN, M., ED. PEOPLE AT WAR
1939-1945.
617(TLS):26APR74-455

MPAGIONA, A. Ē ENNOIA TĒS PROODOY
CHAI Ē METHODOLOGIA TĒS HISTORIAS,
ATHĒNAI, ECHDOSEIS PAPAZĒOĒ.
K. KATSIMANIS, 542:JAN-MAR72-113
MPAGIONA, A. HĒ POLITICHĒ PHILOSO-
PHIA TŌN KYNICHŌN.
K. KATSIMANIS, 542:JAN-MAR72-64
MPHAHLELE, E. THE AFRICAN IMAGE.
K. SUTTON, 362:11APR74-476
MROZEK, S. THREE PLAYS.
639(VQR):SUMMER73-CXII
MUDFORD, P. BIRDS OF A DIFFERENT
PLUMAGE.
M. EGREMONT, 617(TLS):22NOV74-
1318
MUECKE, D.C. THE COMPASS OF IRONY.*
N. KNOX, 405(MP):AUG72-53
D. WYKES, 447(N&Q):AUG72-308
MUELA, J.G. - SEE UNDER GONZÁLEZ
MUELA, J.
MUELLER, J.M. - SEE DONNE, J.
MUELLER, K.H. TWENTY-SEVEN MAJOR
AMERICAN SYMPHONY ORCHESTRAS.
B. CARR, 415:SEP73-902
MÜFFELMANN, F. ALTHOCHDEUTSCH.
H. STOPP, 680(ZDP):BAND91HEFT3-
418
MUGGERIDGE, M. CHRONICLES OF WASTED
TIME.* (VOL 1)
C. LEHMANN-HAUPT, 441:11JUL74-35
MUGGERIDGE, M. CHRONICLES OF WASTED
TIME.* (VOL 2)
P. ADAMS, 61:AUG74-91
J.K. GALBRAITH, 441:14JUL74-1
C. LEHMANN-HAUPT, 441:11JUL74-35
MUGGERIDGE, M. JESUS REDISCOVERED.
441:10FEB74-26
MUGLER, C. - SEE ARCHIMEDES
MUGLIONI, J. PROUDHON, JUSTICE ET
LIBERTÉ.
C. SCHUWER, 542:JUL-SEP72-390
MUGNIER, G.F. NEW ORLEANS & BAYOU
COUNTRY. (L.B. BRIDAHAM, ED)
639(VQR):AUTUMN73-CLXXII
MUGRUZIN, A.S. AGRARNYE OTNOSHENIIA
V KITAE V 20-40-KH GODAKH XXV.
V.D. MEDLIN, 293(JAST):MAY72-660
ZUR MÜHLEN, K-H. NOS EXTRA NOS.
J-D. BURGER, 182:VOL25#9/10-268
MUIR, E. SELECTED LETTERS OF EDWIN
MUIR. (P.H. BUTTER, ED)
R. FULLER, 362:29AUG74-284
S. SPENDER, 617(TLS):21JUN74-666
MUIR, F. & D. NORDEN. UPON MY WORD!
D. THOMAS, 362:19&26DEC74-846
MUIR, J. STICKEEN.
E. HOAGLAND, 441:14APR74-18
MUIR, K., ED. SHAKESPEARE SURVEY
21.*
P.A. JORGENSEN, 570(SQ):SUMMER72-
267
MUIR, K., ED. SHAKESPEARE SURVEY
23.*
E.J. DOBSON, 447(N&Q):APR72-143
R.K. TURNER, JR., 570(SQ):FALL72-
457
MUIR, K., ED. SHAKESPEARE SURVEY 24.
I. BROWN, 157:SPRING72-71
R. HARRIER, 570(SQ):FALL72-458
MUIR, K., ED. SHAKESPEARE SURVEY 26.
617(TLS):1MAR74-209
MUIR, K. SHAKESPEARE'S TRAGIC SE-
QUENCE.*
A.C. SPRAGUE, 402(MLR):OCT73-891

MUIR, K. & S. SCHOENBAUM, EDS. A
NEW COMPANION TO SHAKESPEARE STUD-
IES.*
R. GILL, 541(RES):NOV72-485
MUIR, P. VICTORIAN ILLUSTRATED
BOOKS.
M. STEIG, 637(VS):MAR72-392
G.B. TENNYSON, 445(NCF):JUN72-
117
MUIR, P.H. - SEE JOHNSON, A.F.
MUIRDEN, R. STAMMERING.
L. ASHMORE, 583:WINTER72-205
MUIRDEN, S.J., R.M. PEEL & S. ARROM.
CARTAS DE LUIS.
R.L. JIMÉNEZ, 238:SEP72-611
AL MUJAHID, S. INDIAN SECULARISM.
T.P. WRIGHT, JR., 293(JAST):MAY
72-702
MUJEEB, M. ISLAMIC INFLUENCE ON
INDIAN SOCIETY.
B-U-D. TYABJI, 273(IC):JUL72-273
MUKENDI WA NSANGA, K. ENTWICKLUNG
UND PERSPEKTIVEN DER GROSSEN BERG-
BAU-SIEDLUNGEN IN OBER-KATANGA.
Y. VERHASSELT-VAN WETTERE, 182:
VOL25#19/20-700
MUKHERJEE, B. THE TIGER'S DAUGHTER.*
J. MELLORS, 364:DEC73/JAN74-154
MULAS, U. CALDER.
J.R. MAY, 363:FEB72-76
MULCOCK, A. LANDSCAPE WITH FIGURES.
P.D. EVANS, 368:SEP72-267
MULDER, J.W.F. SETS & RELATIONS IN
PHONOLOGY.*
A.M. ZWICKY, 206:SEP72-133
MULDOON, P. NEW WEATHER.*
H. WILLIAMS, 364:JUN/JUL73-123
MULDROW, G.M. MILTON & THE DRAMA OF
THE SOUL.
W.B. HUNTER, JR., 551(RENQ):
AUTUMN72-373
MULHAUSER, R.E. SAINTE-BEUVE &
GRECO-ROMAN ANTIQUITY.*
R.M. CHADBOURNE, 399(MLJ):DEC72-
516
M.J. PRETINA, JR., 188(ECR):SUM-
MER72-155
MULJAČIĆ, Ž. FONOLOGIA GENERALE E
FONOLOGIA DELLA LINGUA ITALIANA.*
D.D., 275(IQ):FALL/WINTER72-127
E. PULGRAM, 353:1DEC72-118
MULJAČIĆ, Ž. INTRODUZIONE ALLO
STUDIO DELLA LINGUA ITALIANA.
R.J. DI PIETRO, 276:AUTUMN72-336
M. ULLELAND, 597(SN):VOL44#1-166
MULLEN, J. - SEE UNDER HARRISON, W.
MÜLLENBROCK, H-J. LITERATUR UND
ZEITGESCHICHTE IN ENGLAND ZWISCH-
EN DEM ENDE DES 19. JAHRHUNDERTS
UND DEM AUSBRUCH DES ERSTEN WELT-
KRIEGES.*
G. STILZ, 224(GRM):BAND22HEFT4-
450
MULLER, A.V., ED & TRANS. THE "SPIR-
ITUAL REGULATION" OF PETER THE
GREAT.*
R. STUPPERICH, 32:DEC73-804
MULLER, C. INITIATION À LA STATIS-
TIQUE LINGUISTIQUE.
J. JAHN, 353:JAN72-105
MULLER, G.H. NIGHTMARES & VISIONS.*
S.A. BLACK, 648:JAN73-81
639(VQR):SPRING73-LXXIII

MÜLLER, H. & G. HAHN, EDS. ASPEKTE
ZUR KUNSTGESCHICHTE VON MITTELAL-
TER UND NEUZEIT.
A. REINLE, 182:VOL25#9/10-295
MÜLLER, J-D. WIELANDS SPÄTE ROMANE.*
W.H. CLARK, 221(GQ):NOV72-725
J.A. MC CARTHY, 481(PQ):JUL72-
785
MÜLLER, O. DAS PROBLEM DER SENTI-
MENTALITÄT IN GOTTHELFS HISTORIS-
CHEN NOVELLEN.
F. WASSERMANN, 221(GQ):MAR72-362
MÜLLER, O.W. INTELLIGENCIJA.*
P. POMPER, 32:MAR73-166
MULLER, P.E. JEWELS IN SPAIN, 1500-
1800.
C. OMAN, 39:NOV72-462
MÜLLER, T. SCULPTURE IN THE NETHER-
LANDS, GERMANY, FRANCE & SPAIN:
1400-1500.
D.L. EHRESMANN, 56:SUMMER72-178
MÜLLER, U., ED. HEINRICH VON MORUN-
GEN.
D. BLAMIRES, 402(MLR):APR73-443
H. TERVOOREN, 680(ZDP):BAND91
HEFT3-456
MÜLLER-GINDULLIS, D. DAS INTERNA-
TIONALE PRIVATRECHT IN DER RECHTS-
PRECHUNG DES BUNDESGERICHTSHOFS.
E-J. COHN, 182:VOL25#19/20-650
MÜLLER-LAUTER, W. NIETZSCHE.*
P. PREUSS, 154:JUN72-299
MÜLLER-SEIDEL, W., ED. KLEIST UND
FRANKREICH.
M. GARLAND, 220(GL&L):JUL73-336
P. HORWATH, 221(GQ):JAN72-179
MULLIGAN, J.J. VON STUFE ZU STUFE.
J.E. BOURGEOIS, 399(MLJ):DEC72-
533
MULLIN, D.C. THE DEVELOPMENT OF THE
PLAYHOUSE.*
A.S. GILLETTE, 551(RENQ):SUMMER
72-232
MULLIN, G.W. FLIGHT & REBELLION.*
H.S. KLEIN, 656(WMQ):APR73-337
W.L. ROSE, 453:17OCT74-29
639(VQR):SPRING72-LXV
MULLINS, E. THE PILGRIMAGE TO SAN-
TIAGO.
617(TLS):9AUG74-864
MUMBY, F.A. & I. NORRIE. PUBLISHING
& BOOKSELLING.
617(TLS):9AUG74-861
MUMFORD, L. INTERPRETATIONS & FORE-
CASTS: 1922-1972.*
R. SALE, 453:7FEB74-29
MUMFORD, L. & F.J. OSBORN. THE LET-
TERS OF LEWIS MUMFORD & FREDERIC H.
OSBORN. (M. HUGHES, ED)
639(VQR):AUTUMN72-CXXXVII
MUMFORD, L. & F.J. OSBORN. TRANS-
ATLANTIC DIALOGUE.
R. MADGE, 46:JUL72-63
MUNBY, A.N.L. CONNOISSEURS & MEDIE-
VAL MINIATURES.
M. ROSENTHAL, 135:NOV72-216
MUNBY, A.N.L., ED. SALE CATALOGUES
OF LIBRARIES OF EMINENT PERSONS.
(VOLS 1&2)
S.C., 191(ELN):SEP72(SUPP)-17
L. MADDEN, 637(VS):MAR72-373
S. NOWELL-SMITH, 354:DEC72-350
MÜNCHOW, U. DEUTSCHER NATURALISMUS.*
P. WRUCK, 654(WB):10/1971-183

MÜNCHOW, U., ED. NATURALISMUS 1885-
1899.
P. WRUCK, 654(WB):10/1971-183
MUNDLE, C.W.K. A CRITIQUE OF LIN-
GUISTIC PHILOSOPHY.
D. HOCKNEY, 154:MAR72-164
H.D. LEWIS, 393(MIND):APR72-303
D. POLE, 483:APR72-170
M. SHORTER, 479(PHQ):APR72-172
MUNDLE, C.W.K. PERCEPTION.
G.J. WARNOCK, 479(PHQ):APR72-175
MUNGO, R. TROPICAL DETECTIVE STORY.
639(VQR):AUTUMN72-CXXI
MUNHALL, E. MASTERPIECES OF THE
FRICK COLLECTION.*
K. ROBERTS, 90:JUN72-406
MUNI, S.D. FOREIGN POLICY OF NEPAL.
617(TLS):1FEB74-116
MUNITZ, M.K., ED. IDENTITY & INDI-
VIDUATION.
G. ENGLEBRETSEN, 154:DEC72-660
MUNN, A.M. FROM NOUGHT TO RELATIV-
ITY.
617(TLS):30AUG74-936
MUNN, H.W. MERLIN'S RING.
T. STURGEON, 441:8SEP74-40
MUNOZ, A.N. THE FILIPINOS IN AMERI-
CA.
D.V. HART, 293(JAST):MAY72-749
MUNRO, A. DANCE OF THE HAPPY
SHADES.*
R. BLYTHE, 362:13JUN74-777
617(TLS):10MAY74-493
MUNRO, A. SOMETHING I'VE BEEN MEAN-
ING TO TELL YOU.
F. BUSCH, 441:27OCT74-54
R. HUNT, 198:SUMMER74-113
MUNRO, D.G. THE UNITED STATES & THE
CARIBBEAN REPUBLICS 1921-1933.
M. DEAS, 617(TLS):29NOV74-1340
MUNRO, I.S. THE ISLAND OF BUTE.
617(TLS):29MAR74-342
MUNRO, J., ED. DOCUMENTS ON CANAD-
IAN EXTERNAL RELATIONS. (VOL 6)
J. ENGLISH, 99:MAY/JUN74-48
MUNRO, J.A. & A.I. INGLIS - SEE
PEARSON, L.B.
MUNRO, T. FORM & STYLE IN THE ARTS.
A. BERLEANT, 484(PPR):JUN73-581
M. RIESER, 319:JAN74-134
MUNTHE, L. NY KOLEJY LOTERANA MALA-
GASY NANDRITRA NY 100 TAONA.
M. URBAIN-FAUBLÉE, 69:JUL72-261
MUNZ, P. FREDERICK BARBAROSSA.
H. WIERUSZOWSKI, 589:JAN73-170
MUNZ, P. WHEN THE GOLDEN BOUGH
BREAKS.
617(TLS):4JAN74-2
MÜNZEL, F. STRAFRECHT IM ALTEN
CHINA NACH DEN STRAFRECHTSKAPITELN
IN DEN MING-ANNALEN.
K. MÄDING, 318(JAOS):APR-JUN72-
345
MURAMATSU YŪJI. KINDAI KŌNAN NO
SOSAN.
R.H. MYERS, 293(JAST):FEB72-397
MURARO, M. PALAZZO CONTARINI A SAN
BENETO.
J. MC ANDREW, 54:JUN72-212
MURATA, K. JAPAN'S NEW BUDDHISM.*
G. BERNSTEIN, 352(LE&W):VOL15#4
&VOL16#1/2-933

MURDOCH, I.   AN ACCIDENTAL MAN.*
    J. HARCOURT, 529(QQ):AUTUMN72-
        420
    L.T. LEMON, 502(PRS):FALL72-266
    M. PAGE, 648:OCT72-75
    639(VQR):SUMMER72-C
MURDOCH, I.   THE BLACK PRINCE.*
    R. DE FEO, 249(HUDR):WINTER73/74-
        784
    639(VQR):AUTUMN73-CXXXVI
MURDOCH, I.   A FAIRLY HONOURABLE
    DEFEAT.*
    J. WATRIN, 556(RLV):1972/1-46
MURDOCH, I.   THE NICE & THE GOOD.
    E.C. BUFKIN, 219(GAR):SPRING72-
        100
MURDOCH, I.   THE SACRED & PROFANE
    LOVE MACHINE.
    C. LEHMANN-HAUPT, 441:19SEP74-47
    R. SALE, 453:12DEC74-18
    J. VAIZEY, 362:21MAR74-379
    J. WAIN, 441:22SEP74-1
    E. WEEKS, 61:NOV74-120
    617(TLS):22MAR74-281
MURDOCH, I.   THE SOVEREIGNTY OF
    GOOD.*
    R.J.B., 543:SEP71-133
    H.O. MOUNCE, 483:APR72-178
MURDOCH, I.   THE THREE ARROWS [AND]
    THE SERVANTS & THE SNOW.*
    M. DRABBLE, 362:17JAN74-89
MURE, G.R.G.   A STUDY OF HEGEL'S
    LOGIC.
    E. AMADO-LÉVI-VALENSI, 542:JUL-
        SEP72-369
MURENA, H.A.   POLISPUERCÓN.
    T.E. LYON, 238:SEP72-596
MURPHY, B.   THE BUSINESS OF SPYING.
    617(TLS):4JAN74-6
MURPHY, F. - SEE WINTERS, Y.
MURPHY, J.   THE EL GRECO PUZZLE.
    N. CALLENDAR, 441:4AUG74-24
MURPHY, J.B.   L.Q.C. LAMAR.
    639(VQR):AUTUMN73-CLVI
MURPHY, J.G.   KANT: THE PHILOSOPHY
    OF RIGHT.*
    A.C. EWING, 483:APR72-173
MURPHY, J.J., ED.   A SYNOPTIC HIS-
    TORY OF CLASSICAL RHETORIC.
    R.L. HENDREN, 583:SPRING73-299
MURPHY, J.J., ED.   THREE MEDIEVAL
    RHETORICAL ARTS.
    T. LAWLER, 589:APR73-388
    A.B. SCOTT, 382(MAE):1973/3-262
    639(VQR):WINTER72-XXX
MURRAY, A.   TRAIN WHISTLE GUITAR.
    T.R. EDWARDS, 453:13JUN74-37
    J.A. MC PHERSON, 61:DEC74-118
    J. WIDEMAN, 441:12MAY74-7
    442(NY):22JUL74-83
MURRAY, E.   THE CINEMATIC IMAGINA-
    TION.
    C. GEDULD, 659:WINTER74-123
MURRAY, F.   THE BURNING LAMP.
    M. LEVIN, 441:20JAN74-24
MURRAY, G.   VOLTAIRE'S "CANDIDE."*
    C. THACKER, 402(MLR):JUL73-657
MURRAY, I. - SEE WILDE, O.
MURRAY, J.   THE KINGS & QUEENS OF
    ENGLAND.
    P. ADAMS, 61:OCT74-120
MURRAY, L.A.   POEMS AGAINST ECONOM-
    ICS.
    J. TULIP, 581:JUN73-231

MURRAY, L.S.   BAYLOR AT INDEPENDENCE.
    W. GARD, 584(SWR):SPRING73-V
MURRAY, P.   BRAMANTE'S TEMPIETTO.
    J. LEES-MILNE, 39:DEC72-569
MURRAY, P.   PIRANESI & THE GRANDEUR
    OF ANCIENT ROME.
    J. LEES-MILNE, 39:OCT72-364
    M. ROSENTHAL, 135:APR72-291
MURRAY, P. - SEE NEWMAN, J.H.
MURRAY, W.   THE KILLING TOUCH.
    N. CALLENDAR, 441:19MAY74-42
MURRAY, W.C.   A LONG WAY FROM HOME.
    A. BROYARD, 441:1MAR74-27
    M. LEVIN, 441:10MAR74-10
MUSA, M. - SEE DANTE ALIGHIERI
MUSCATINE, C.   CHAUCER & THE FRENCH
    TRADITION.
    J.R. SIMON, 189(EA):JAN-MAR72-53
MUSCATINE, C.   POETRY & CRISIS IN
    THE AGE OF CHAUCER.
    J.H. FISHER, 579(SAQ):AUTUMN73-
        609
    639(VQR):WINTER73-XXV
MUSCHG, W.   DIE DICHTERISCHE PHAN-
    TASIE.
    R. PEACOCK, 402(MLR):JAN73-223
MUSGRAVE, S.   GRAVE-DIRT & SELECTED
    STRAWBERRIES.
    M.J. EDWARDS, 99:AUG74-42
MUSHKAT, J.   TAMMANY.
    M-L. FRINGS, 182:VOL25#23/24-892
MUSIL, R.   THREE SHORT STORIES.   (H.
    SACKER, ED)
    J.J. WHITE, 220(GL&L):APR73-274
MÜSSENER, H.   DIE DEUTSCHSPRACHIGE
    EMIGRATION IN SCHWEDEN NACH 1933.
    E. HILSCHER, 654(WB):11/1972-188
DE MUSSET, A.   CONTES D'ESPAGNE ET
    D'ITALIE.   (M.A. REES, ED)
    617(TLS):31MAY74-590
MUSSOLINI, R., WITH A. ZARCA.   MUS-
    SOLINI.
    L. BARZINI, 453:17OCT74-22
MUSSULMAN, J.A.   MUSIC IN THE CUL-
    TURED GENERATION.*
    C.H., 414(MQ):APR72-322
MUSURILLO, H., ED & TRANS.   THE ACTS
    OF THE CHRISTIAN MARTYRS.
    T. HALTON, 613:WINTER72-620
MUTHESIUS, S.   THE HIGH VICTORIAN
    MOVEMENT IN ARCHITECTURE 1850-
    1870.*
    N. PEVSNER, 56:AUTUMN72-315
    B. READ, 135:NOV72-215
MUTISO, G-C.M.   SOCIO-POLITICAL
    THOUGHT IN AFRICAN LITERATURE.
    617(TLS):11OCT74-1106
MYERHOFF, B.G.   PEYOTE HUNT.
    P. RIVIÈRE, 617(TLS):6DEC74-1360
MYERS, B.S. - SEE "MC GRAW-HILL
    DICTIONARY OF ART"
MYERS, D. & F. REID.   EDUCATING
    TEACHERS.
    J. MACDONALD, 99:NOV/DEC74-25
MYERS, J.M.   THE ALAMO.   THE LAST
    CHANCE.
    W. GARD, 584(SWR):SPRING73-V
MYERS, N.   THE LONG AFRICAN DAY.*
    617(TLS):22FEB74-191
MYERS, R.   CLAUDE DEBUSSY.
    G.W. HOPKINS, 415:DEC73-1237

MYERS, R.L. RÉMOND DE SAINT-MARD.*
S. MENANT, 535(RHL):MAY-JUN72-
523
M.H. WADDICOR, 208(FS):APR73-202
MYERS, R.M., ED. THE CHILDREN OF
PRIDE.*
F.N. BONEY, 219(GAR):WINTER72-
528
F.M. BRODIE, 639(VQR):AUTUMN72-
616
R.F. DURDEN, 579(SAQ):WINTER73-
162
W.C. HAVARD, 598(SOR):AUTUMN74-
823
J.M. LALLEY, 396(MODA):WINTER73-
83
J.P. WELDON, 14:JUL/OCT72-408
MYERS, W. DRYDEN.
617(TLS):12APR74-394
MYINT, H. SOUTHEAST ASIA'S ECONOMY.
42(AR):SPRING/SUMMER72-247
MYLETT, A. - SEE BENNETT, A.
MYRDAL, J. & G. KESSLE. GATES TO
ASIA.
639(VQR):WINTER72-XIV

NABOKOV, V. LOOK AT THE HARLEQUINS!
A. BROYARD, 441:10OCT74-45
R. POIRIER, 441:13OCT74-2
V.S. PRITCHETT, 453:28NOV74-3
P. STEGNER, 61:NOV74-98
J. UPDIKE, 442(NY):11NOV74-209
NABOKOV, V. POEMS & PROBLEMS.
A. DICKINS, 364:DEC72/JAN73-157
V. SETCHKAREV, 550(RUSR):APR72-
201
NABOKOV, V. A RUSSIAN BEAUTY &
OTHER STORIES.*
M. MUDRICK, 249(HUDR):AUTUMN73-
545
639(VQR):AUTUMN73-CXXXVIII
NABOKOV, V. STRONG OPINIONS.*
P. ADAMS, 61:JAN74-99
V.S. PRITCHETT, 453:28NOV74-3
NABOKOV, V. TRANSPARENT THINGS.*
J. GATHORNE-HARDY, 364:AUG/SEP73-
152
S. O'CONNELL, 418(MR):WINTER73-
190
W.H. PRITCHARD, 249(HUDR):SPRING
73-227
NACCI, C.N. ALTAMIRANO.
J.S. BRUSHWOOD, 593:SUMMER73-187
P. QUARGNALI, 399(MLJ):MAR72-183
R.M. REEVE, 238:MAY72-392
NACHT, S. GUÉRIR AVEC FREUD.
Y. BRÈS, 542:OCT-DEC72-474
NACHTIGAL, G. SAHARA & SUDAN. (VOL
4) (A.G.B. & H.J. FISHER, EDS &
TRANS)
A.H.M. KIRK-GREENE, 69:JUL72-256
NADAL, R.M. - SEE UNDER MARTÍNEZ
NADAL, R.
NADEAU, M. GUSTAVE FLAUBERT ÉCRI-
VAIN.*
E. ZAPPULLA, 546(RR):OCT72-239
NADEL, M.H. & C.G., EDS. THE DANCE
EXPERIENCE.*
A. PAGE, 290(JAAC):SPRING72-406
NADER, R., L. DODGE & R. HOTCHKISS.
WHAT TO DO WITH YOUR BAD CAR.
42(AR):VOL32#4-712

NADLER, H. & OTHERS. AMERICAN ENG-
LISH.
C.W. STANSFIELD, 399(MLJ):OCT72-
398
NAGAI MICHIO. HIGHER EDUCATION IN
JAPAN.
D.J. CALISTA, 285(JAPQ):APR-JUN
72-233
"NĀGĀRJUNA, A TRANSLATION OF HIS
MŪLAMADHYAMAKAKĀRIKĀ."* (K.K.
INADA, TRANS)
F.J. STRENG, 485(PE&W):JAN72-105
NAGEL, E. THE STRUCTURE OF SCIENCE.
L. NOWAK, 486:DEC72-533
NAGEL, E., S. BROMBERGER & A. GRÜN-
BAUM. OBSERVATION & THEORY IN
SCIENCE.*
C.G. MORGAN, 154:DEC72-651
NAGEL, I. DIE BEZEICHNUNG FÜR
"DUMM" UND "VERRÜCKT" IM SPAN-
ISCHEN.
W. BEINHAUER, 182:VOL25#17/18-
599
NAGEL, P.C. THIS SACRED TRUST.
639(VQR):WINTER72-XXXI
NAGEL, T. THE POSSIBILITY OF ALTRU-
ISM.
J. BENSON, 479(PHQ):JAN72-82
R. KRAUT, 482(PHR):JUL72-351
NAGELS, J. REPRODUCTION DU CAPITAL
SELON KARL MARX, BOISGUILLEBERT,
QUESNAY, LEONTIEV.
M. LAGUEUX, 154:DEC72-633
NAGUIB, N. ROBERT WALSER.*
G.B. PICKAR, 406:FALL73-309
J.D. ZIPES, 000(GR):MAR72-152
NAGY, G. GREEK DIALECTS & THE TRANS-
FORMATION OF AN INDO-EUROPEAN PRO-
CESS.*
A. SIHLER, 350:MAR73-167
O. SZEMERÉNYI, 343:BAND14HEFT2-
157
NAGY, L. LOVE OF THE SCORCHING
WIND.
617(TLS):15MAR74-267
NAIK, M.K. MULK RAJ ANAND.
S. COWASJEE, 268:JAN74-54
NAIPAUL, S. THE CHIP-CHIP GATHER-
ERS.*
J. MELLORS, 364:AUG/SEP73-150
NAIPAUL, V.S. THE OVERCROWDED BAR-
RACOON.*
T. HARRISON, 364:DEC72/JAN73-135
NAIRN, B., G. SERLE & R. WARD - SEE
PIKE, D.
NAJARIAN, P. VOYAGES.
E. ROVIT, 659:AUTUMN74-539
NAKANE, C. JAPANESE SOCIETY.*
R.H. BROWN, 318(JAOS):OCT-DEC72-
546
NAKATA, Y. THE ART OF JAPANESE
CALLIGRAPHY.
617(TLS):26APR74-434
NAKHNIKIAN, G., ED. BERTRAND RUS-
SELL'S PHILOSOPHY.
617(TLS):8NOV74-1250
NALBACH, D. THE KING'S THEATRE 1704-
1867.*
O. BALDWIN & T. WILSON, 415:
OCT73-1012
NAMIER, J. LEWIS NAMIER.
C.R. RITCHESON, 656(WMQ):JAN73-
174

ÑĀÑĀNANDA, B. - SEE UNDER BHIKKHU
ÑĀÑĀNANDA
NANAVATI, J.M. & M.A. DHAKY. THE
MAITRAKA & THE SAINDHAVA TEMPLES
OF GUJARAT.
M.W. MEISTER, 576:OCT72-240
NAPIER, P. REVOLUTION & THE NAPIER
BROTHERS 1820-1840.
R. CROSSMAN, 362:24JAN74-119
617(TLS):19APR74-420
NARAIN, P. PRESS & POLITICS IN
INDIA: 1885-1905.
C. FUREDY, 293(JAST):FEB72-435
NARANJO, C. THE HEALING JOURNEY.
E. FIRST, 441:3MAR74-3
NARAYAN, R.K. MY DAYS.
P. ADAMS, 61:JUL74-100
A. BROYARD, 441:12JUN74-49
P. THEROUX, 441:30JUN74-16
J. UPDIKE, 442(NY):2SEP74-80
NĀRĀYAṆA, B. - SEE UNDER BHAṬṬA
NĀRĀYAṆA
NARAZAKI, M. MASTERWORKS OF UKIYO-E.
P. HARDIE, 39:JUN72-522
DE NARDIS, L. L'USIGNOLO E IL FAN-
TASMA, SAGGI FRANCESI SULLA CIVIL-
TÀ LETTERARIA DELL'OTTOCENTO.
L. GUICHARD, 535(RHL):JUL-AUG72-
730
NARDO, D. IL "COMMENTARIOLUM PETI-
TIONIS."
J. HELLEGOUARC'H, 555:VOL46FASC1-
153
A.W. LINTOTT, 313:VOL62-218
NAREMORE, J. THE WORLD WITHOUT A
SELF.*
639(VQR):AUTUMN73-CXLIV
NARKISS, B. - SEE ROTH, C.
NARSKI, I.S. THE PHILOSOPHY OF
DAVID HUME.
P.K. CROSSER, 484(PPR):JUN73-590
NASH, R.H. THE LIGHT OF THE MIND.
H.F., 543:DEC71-361
NASH, W. OUR EXPERIENCE OF LANGU-
AGE.
S. POTTER, 677:VOL3-259
NASLIN, P. CIRCUITS À RELAIS ET
AUTOMATISMES À SÉQUENCES. CIR-
CUITS LOGIQUES ET AUTOMATISMES À
SEQUENCES. (2ND ED)
J. KUNTZMANN, 316:SEP72-627
NASSAR, E.P. THE RAPE OF CINDERELLA.
J. PINKERTON, 128(CE):FEB72-600
NATAN, A. & O. WOLFF. SWISS MEN OF
LETTERS.*
V. FÄSSLER, 221(GQ):MAR72-358
NATANSON, M., ED. PHENOMENOLOGY &
SOCIAL REALITY.
W. ROSENSOHN, 484(PPR):SEP72-117
NATANSON, M. - SEE STRAUS, E.W., M.
NATANSON & H. EY
NATH, R. COLOURED DECORATION IN
MOGHUL ARCHITECTURE.
M. FAYAZUDDIN, 273(IC):JAN72-85
NATHAN, J. MISHIMA.
A. BROYARD, 441:29NOV74-43
H. CLURMAN, 441:29DEC74-6
NATHHORST, B. FORMAL OR STRUCTURAL
STUDIES OF TRADITIONAL TALES.
D. BEN-AMOS, 292(JAF):JAN-MAR72-
82

"THE NATIONAL UNION CATALOGUE OF MAN-
USCRIPT COLLECTIONS, 1970 & INDEX
1970."
O.M. FREDERICK & C.C. HAY, 3D,
517(PBSA):JAN-MAR73-79
NAUDEAU, O. LA PENSÉE DE MONTAIGNE
ET LA COMPOSITION DES "ESSAIS."
R.A. SAYCE, 208(FS):APR73-192
NAUERT, C.G., JR. AGRIPPA & THE
CRISIS OF RENAISSANCE THOUGHT.
E. NAMER, 542:APR-JUN72-163
NAUGLE, H.H., WITH P.B. SHERRY, EDS.
A CONCORDANCE TO THE POEMS OF
SAMUEL JOHNSON.
617(TLS):8MAR74-244
NAUMANN, B. WORTBILDUNG IN DER
DEUTSCHEN GEGENWARTSSPRACHE.
L. SEPPÄNEN, 439(NM):1972/4-898
NAUMANN, H-P. GOETHES "FAUST" IN
SCHWEDISCHER ÜBERSETZUNG.
H.H. BORLAND, 402(MLR):JUL73-689
NAUWELAERTS, M.A. - SEE ERASMUS
DE NAVARRE, M. - SEE UNDER MARGUER-
ITE DE NAVARRE
NAVARRO TOMÁS, T., G. HAENSCH & B.
LECHNER. SPANISCHE AUSSPRACHE-
LEHRE.
M. FRANZBACH, 430(NS):DEC72-744
H. SCHNEIDER, 430(NS):JAN72-49
NAVEH, J. THE DEVELOPMENT OF THE
ARAMAIC SCRIPT.
J. TEIXIDOR, 318(JAOS):OCT-DEC72-
529
NAYLOR, G. THE ARTS & CRAFTS MOVE-
MENT.*
D. ROBERTSON, 637(VS):JUN73-474
NEBENZAHL, K. & D. HIGGINBOTHAM.
ATLAS OF THE AMERICAN REVOLUTION.
I.R. DEE, 441:1DEC74-12
NECTOUX, J-M. FAURÉ.
N.S., 410(M&L):OCT73-462
NEEDHAM, J. CLERKS & CRAFTSMEN IN
CHINA & THE WEST.*
E.H. SCHAFER, 318(JAOS):JAN-MAR
72-150
NEEDHAM, J. THE GRAND TITRATION.*
R. CROIZIER, 318(JAOS):APR-JUN
72-333
NEEDHAM, J., WITH LU GWEI-DJEN.
SCIENCE & CIVILIZATION IN CHINA.
(VOL 5, PT 2)
P. MORRISON, 453:12DEC74-8
NEEDHAM, J., WITH WANG LING & LU
GWEI-DJEN. SCIENCE & CIVILISATION
IN CHINA. (VOL 4, PT 3)
D.N. KEIGHTLEY, 293(JAST):FEB72-
367
NEEDHAM, R. BELIEF, LANGUAGE, &
EXPERIENCE.*
G.C. RUMP, 182:VOL25#22-828
NEEDHAM, R. REMARKS & INVENTIONS.
F. EGGAN, 617(TLS):13DEC74-1402
NEEDHAM, R., ED. RETHINKING KINSHIP
& MARRIAGE.
G.C. RUMP, 182:VOL25#17/18-633
NEEDLER, H. SAINT FRANCIS & SAINT
DOMINIC IN THE DIVINE COMEDY.
G. MAZZOTTA, 276:WINTER72-506
NEF, E. DER ZUFALL IN DER ERZÄHL-
KUNST.*
N.H. SMITH, 182:VOL25#3/4-91
NEGRI, A. AUGUSTE COMTE E L'UMANE-
SIMO POSITIVISTICO.
E. NAMER, 542:JUL-SEP72-345

NEGRI, A. LA PRESENZA DI HEGEL.
E. NAMER, 542:JUL-SEP72-372
NEGRI, A. SCHILLER E LA MORALE DI
KANT.
E. NAMER, 542:JUL-SEP72-329
K. OEDINGEN, 342:BAND63HEFT3-386
NEGRI, A. - SEE BRUNO, G.
NEGRI, A. - SEE COMTE, A.
DE NEGRI, E. LA TEOLOGIA DI LUTERO.
E. NAMER, 542:APR-JUN72-170
NEGRI, R. INTERPRETAZIONE DELL'
"ORLANDO FURIOSO."
E. SACCONE, 400(MLN):JAN72-147
NEGRIOLLI, C. LA SYMBOLIQUE DE
D-H. LAWRENCE.
E. DELAVENAY, 189(EA):JAN-MAR72-
168
NEHRING, W. - SEE HOFFMANN, E.T.A.
NEIDER, C., ED. ANTARCTICA.
617(TLS):4JAN74-8
NEIDER, C. EDGE OF THE WORLD.
W.F. BUCKLEY, JR., 441:23JUN74-5
NEIHARDT, J.G. ALL IS BUT A BEGIN-
NING.
M.R. BENNETT, 649(WAL):FALL72-
231
NEIL, J.M. PARADISE IMPROVED.
A. GOWANS, 576:DEC72-337
NEILD, M. THE HORRIBLE THING IN THE
GARDEN.
H. FRANCIS, 157:WINTER72-83
NEILL, P. MOCK TURTLE SOUP.
639(VQR):SUMMER72-CI
NEILL, W.T. TWENTIETH-CENTURY INDO-
NESIA.
617(TLS):17MAY74-516
NELLES, H.V. THE POLITICS OF DEVEL-
OPMENT.
D.C. MAC DONALD, 99:MAY/JUN74-39
NELMS, H. SCENE DESIGN.
G. SQUIRE, 157:AUTUMN72-82
NÉLOD, G. PANORAMA DU ROMAN HISTOR-
IQUE.*
H. GODIN, 208(FS):APR73-235
NELSON, B. AZRAQ.
617(TLS):3MAY74-482
NELSON, D.F. PORTRAIT OF THE ARTIST
AS HERMES.
H.S. DAEMMRICH, 301(JEGP):JAN73-
101
L. VOSS, 406:SUMMER73-208
NELSON, J.G. THE EARLY NINETIES.*
J. BATCHELOR, 354:DEC72-347
L. ORMOND, 402(MLR):APR73-398
R.H. ROSS, 636(VP):WINTER72-373
G.B. TENNYSON, 445(NCF):JUN72-
117
NELSON, P. CARGO.
R. PEVEAR, 249(HUDR):SPRING73-
192
NELSON, R.J. IMMANENCE & TRANSCEN-
DENCE.*
J. MOREL, 535(RHL):JAN-FEB72-131
NELSON, W. FACT OF FICTIONS.
617(TLS):16AUG74-884
NEME, M. FÓRMULAS POLÍTICAS NO
BRASIL HOLANDÊS.
G. SOBRAL, 263:APR-JUN73-203
NEMEROV, H. GNOMES & OCCASIONS.
W.H. PRITCHARD, 249(HUDR):AUTUMN
73-581
P. SMYTH, 491:DEC73-165

NEMEROV, H. REFLEXIONS ON POETRY &
POETICS.
639(VQR):WINTER73-XVII
NEMEROV, H. STORIES, FABLES & OTHER
DIVERSIONS.
D.M. KENNEDY, 385(MQR):WINTER74-
85
NEMESKÜRTY, I. ELFELEJTETT ÉVTIZED
1542-1552.
617(TLS):4OCT74-1091
NÉMETH, J. DIE TÜRKISCHE SPRACHE IN
UNGARN IM SIEBZEHNTEN JAHRHUNDERT.
P. ZIEME, 682(ZPSK):BAND25HEFT3-
253
NEMIROVSKIĬ, E.L. NACHALO SLAVYAN-
SKOGO KNIGOPECHATANIYA.
J.S.G. SIMMONS, 78(BC):SUMMER72-
280
DER NERSESSIAN, S., ED. ARMENIAN
MANUSCRIPTS IN THE WALTERS ART GAL-
LERY.
J. CANADAY, 441:1DEC74-102
NERSOYAN, H.J. ANDRÉ GIDE.*
C.S. BROSMAN, 546(RR):FEB72-67
NERUDA, P. THE CAPTAIN'S VERSES.
R. PEVEAR, 249(HUDR):SPRING73-
192
639(VQR):SPRING73-LXIV
NERUDA, P. EXTRAVAGARIA. RESIDENCE
ON EARTH.
M. WOOD, 453:3OCT74-8
NERUDA, P. FIVE DECADES. (B. BEL-
ITT, ED & TRANS)
P. ADAMS, 61:SEP74-103
M. WOOD, 453:3OCT74-8
NERUDA, P. NEW POEMS (1968-1970).
639(VQR):SPRING73-LXIV
NERUDA, P. SPLENDOR & DEATH OF
JOAQUÍN MURIETA.
H.J. NUWER, 649(WAL):WINTER73-
306
R. PEVEAR, 249(HUDR):SPRING73-
192
639(VQR):SUMMER73-CXII
NERUDA, P. & C. VALLEJO. NERUDA &
VALLEJO: SELECTED POEMS. (R.
BLY, ED)
D. ACKERSON, 134(CP):SPRING72-79
NESBITT, B., ED. EARLE BIRNEY.
K. MULHALLEN, 99:OCT74-19
NESBITT, B. & S. HADFIELD, COMPS.
AUSTRALIAN LITERARY PSEUDONYMS.
W. STONE, 71(ALS):OCT74-442
NESSEN, M. ORANGE POWER, BLACK
JUICE.
M. LEVIN, 441:28JUL74-20
NESTROY, J. KOMÖDIEN.* (F.H. MAUT-
NER, ED)
W.H. GRILK, 301(JEGP):APR73-291
NETTELBECK, C.W. LES PERSONNAGES DE
BERNANOS ROMANCIER.
E. BEAUMONT, 208(FS):OCT73-477
J. ONIMUS, 557(RSH):OCT-DEC72-
626
NETTESHEIM, J. WILHELM JUNKMANN.
E. CARE, 402(MLR):JUL73-698
NETTING, R.M. THE HILL FARMERS OF
NIGERIA.
F.P. CONANT, 69:APR72-152
NETTL, B. FOLK & TRADITIONAL MUSIC
OF THE WESTERN CONTINENTS. (2ND
ED)
C.L. BOILÈS, 187:MAY74-312

NEWMAN, P.C. HOME COUNTRY.
T. HOCKIN, 99:AUG74-35
NEWMAN, W.M. LES SEIGNEURS DE NESLE
EN PICARDIE (XIIE - XIIIE SIÈCLE).
R. HOWELL, JR., 182:VOL25#22-821
NEWTON, H.P., WITH J.H. BLAKE. REV-
OLUTIONARY SUICIDE.*
617(TLS):24MAY74-551
NEWTON, I. THE MATHEMATICAL PAPERS
OF ISAAC NEWTON. (VOL 5) (D.T.
WHITESIDE, ED) THE UNPUBLISHED
FIRST VERSION OF ISAAC NEWTON'S
CAMBRIDGE LECTURES ON OPTICS 1670-
1672.
617(TLS):26APR74-451
NEWTON, N.T. DESIGN ON THE LAND.
42(AR):SPRING/SUMMER72-251
NEWTON, R.P. FORM IN THE "MENSCH-
HEITSDÄMMERUNG."
R. FURNESS, 402(MLR):JUL73-702
H.G. HERMANN, 406:SPRING73-85
NIALL, B. MARTIN BOYD.
C. HADGRAFT, 71(ALS):OCT74-437
NIALL, I. A LONDON BOYHOOD.
617(TLS):15NOV74-1297
"DAS NIBELUNGENLIED." (M.S. BATTS,
ED)
D.H. GREEN, 402(MLR):JAN73-209
NIČEV, A. L'ÉNIGME DE LA CATHARSIS
TRAGIQUE DANS ARISTOTE.*
P. LOUIS, 555:VOL46FASC1-127
NICHOLAS, D.M. TOWN & COUNTRYSIDE.
J.B. HENNEMAN, 589:OCT73-779
NICHOLAS, R.L. EL MUNDO DE HOY.
F.H. NUESSEL, JR., 399(MLJ):DEC
72-534
NICHOLLS, K. GAELIC & GAELICISED
IRELAND IN THE MIDDLE AGES.
C. Ó BAOILL, 595(SCS):VOL17PT2-
168
NICHOLLS, R.A. THE DRAMAS OF CHRIS-
TIAN FRIEDRICH GRABBE.*
L. JENNINGS, 221(GQ):NOV72-741
NICHOLS, B. DOWN THE KITCHEN SINK.
617(TLS):25OCT74-1205
NICHOLS, J. THE MILAGRO BEANFIELD
WAR.
F. BUSCH, 441:27OCT74-53
NICHOLS, J. MINOR LIVES.* (E.L.
HART, ED)
R.E. KELLEY, 481(PQ):JUL72-741
R. LONSDALE, 541(RES):AUG72-365
NICHOLS, J.B., ED. ANECDOTES OF
WILLIAM HOGARTH.*
D. FITZ-GERALD, 90:SEP72-639
NICHOLS, P. ITALIA, ITALIA.
J. ROSSELLI, 362:21FEB74-247
442(NY):13MAY74-159
617(TLS):12APR74-381
NICHOLS, R. DEBUSSY.
G.W. HOPKINS, 415:DEC73-1237
NICHOLSON, A. ESPRIT DE LAW.
617(TLS):25JAN74-86
NICHOLSON, G.W.L. MORE FIGHTING
NEWFOUNDLANDERS.
D.M. SCHURMAN, 529(QQ):AUTUMN72-
432
NICHOLSON, N. A LOCAL HABITATION.
R. GARFITT, 364:AUG/SEP73-120
NICHOLSON, R. THE EDINBURGH HISTORY
OF SCOTLAND. (VOL 2)
B.P. LENMAN, 617(TLS):1NOV74-
1234

NICKEL, G., ED. PAPERS IN CONTRAS-
TIVE LINGUISTICS.*
G.C. LEPSCHY, 402(MLR):JUL73-622
NICKL, T. & H. SCHNITZLER - SEE
SCHNITZLER, A. & O. WAISSNIX
NICOLAUS, M. - SEE MARX, K.
NICOLSON, B. THE TREASURES OF THE
FOUNDLING HOSPITAL.
D. COOMBS, 135:SEP72-62
R. EDWARDS, 39:SEP72-250
NICOLSON, H. PUBLIC FACES.
441:10NOV74-39
NICOLSON, N. PORTRAIT OF A MARRI-
AGE.*
W. PLOMER, 364:DEC73/JAN74-129
441:10NOV74-43
NICULESCU, A. & F. DIMITRESCU, EDS.
TESTI ROMENI ANTICHI (SECOLI XVI-
XVIII).
A. LOMBARD, 597(SN):VOL44#2-462
NIDA, E.A. & C.R. TABER. THE THEORY
& PRACTICE OF TRANSLATION.
G. LEPSCHY, 353:MAY72-102
NIDERST, A., ED. L'AME MATÉRIELLE
(OUVRAGE ANONYME).
J. MAYER, 557(RSH):APR-JUN72-321
NIDERST, A. - SEE BAYLE, P.
NIDERST, A. - SEE SAINT-ÉVREMOND
NIEL, H. KARL MARX.
Q. LAUER, 258:DEC72-635
NIELSEN, K. CONTEMPORARY CRITIQUES
OF RELIGION.
A. FLEW, 393(MIND):OCT72-629
NIELSEN, K. SCEPTICISM.
H. MEYNELL, 518:OCT73-20
NIEMEYER, G. DECEITFUL PEACE.
J.C. CAMPBELL, 550(RUSR):OCT72-
429
NIERENBERG, G.I. & H. CALERO. HOW
TO READ A PERSON LIKE A BOOK.
E.A. SCHMERLER, 186(ETC.):JUN72-
215
NIETZSCHE, F.W. NIETZSCHE: A SELF-
PORTRAIT FROM HIS LETTERS.* (P.
FUSS & H. SHAPIRO, EDS & TRANS)
R.J.G., 543:MAR72-554
W.H. WERKMEISTER, 319:JAN74-129
NIETZSCHE, F.W. NIETZSCHE: VIE ET
VÉRITÉ. (J. GRANIER, ED)
R.J.G., 543:DEC71-377
"NIETZSCHE AUJOURD'HUI."
617(TLS):5APR74-373
"NIHON GENGO TIZU" - SEE UNDER "THE
LINGUISTIC ATLAS OF JAPAN"
"NIHON RIKU-KAIGUN NO SEIDO, SOSHIKI,
JINJI."
M.R. PEATTIE, 293(JAST):MAY72-
688
NIKAM, N.A. VEDANTA.
W. HALBFASS, 318(JAOS):OCT-DEC
72-576
NIKIPROWETZKY, V. LA TROISIÈME
SIBYLLE.*
J.G. GRIFFITHS, 123:MAR73-97
A. PELLETIER, 555:VOL46FASC2-310
NIKLAUS, R. A LITERARY HISTORY OF
FRANCE: THE EIGHTEENTH CENTURY
1715-1789.*
L.G. CROCKER, 207(FR):OCT71-282
R. GRIMSLEY, 402(MLR):JAN73-174
J. VERCRUYSSE, 535(RHL):MAY-JUN
72-529
NIKLAUS, R. - SEE SEDAINE, M-J.

NILSEN, D.L.F. & A.P. PRONUNCIATION
CONTRASTS IN ENGLISH.
   J.D. BOWEN, 399(MLJ):MAR72-190
NILSSON, L., WITH J. LINDBERG. BE-
HOLD MAN.
   I. GEIS, 441:3NOV74-4
NIMS, J.F., ED & TRANS. SAPPHO TO
VALÉRY.
   B. GHISELIN, 569(SR):SPRING73-
371
NIN, A. DIARY OF ANAÏS NIN, 1944-
1947. (G. STUHLMANN, ED)
   R. ZALLER, 59(ASOC):SUMMER-FALL
73-308
   R. ZALLER, 502(PRS):SUMMER72-181
NIN, A. THE DIARY OF ANAÏS NIN.
(VOL 5: 1947-1955.) (G. STUHLMANN,
ED)
   W. GOYEN, 441:14APR74-4
442(NY):13MAY74-159
NIN, A. WINTER OF ARTIFICE & HOUSE
OF INCEST.
   S. MAITLAND, 362:12DEC74-786
617(TLS):11OCT74-1142
NINYOLES, R.L. CONFLICTE LINGÜÍSTIC
VALENCIÀ. IDIOMA I PREJUDICI.
   M.M. AZEVEDO, 350:SEP73-733
NIRENBERG, M. THE RECEPTION OF AMER-
ICAN LITERATURE IN GERMAN PERIODI-
CALS, 1820-1850.
   G.N. DAVIS, 399(MLJ):FEB72-120
NISBET, A. & B. NEVIUS, EDS. DICK-
ENS CENTENNIAL ESSAYS.*
   J.R. KINCAID, 155:SEP72-186
NISBET, H.B. & H. REISS - SEE VON
GOETHE, J.W.
NISBET, R. THE DEGRADATION OF THE
ACADEMIC DOGMA.
   H. REGNERY, 396(MODA):SUMMER73-
298
NISBET, R. THE SOCIAL PHILOSOPHERS.
   617(TLS):26JUL74-786
NISBET, R. THE SOCIOLOGY OF EMILE
DURKHEIM.
   L.A. COSER, 441:21APR74-29
617(TLS):20SEP74-1022
NISBET, R.G.M. & M. HUBBARD. A COM-
MENTARY ON HORACE: "ODES," BOOK
I.*
   K. QUINN, 5:SUMMER/AUTUMN70-264
NISSEN, C. DIE ZOOLOGISCHE BUCHILL-
USTRATION. (VOL 2, PT 10)
   H. LEHMANN-HAUPT, 517(PBSA):JUL-
SEP73-360
NISSENBAUM, S., ED. THE GREAT AWAK-
ENING AT YALE COLLEGE.
   R.W. BEALES, JR., 656(WMQ):JUL73-
530
NITCHIE, G.W. MARIANNE MOORE.*
   W.D. SHERMAN, 447(N&Q):SEP72-356
NITZ, H-J. FORMEN DER LANDWIRT-
SCHAFT UND IHRE RÄUMLICHE ORDNUNG
IN DER OBEREN GANGESEBENE.
   M. SCHICK, 182:VOL25#17/18-637
NIVAT, G. & M. AUCOUTURIER, EDS.
L'HERNE SOLJÉNITSYNE.
   L. KOEHLER, 104:SUMMER72-340
NIVELLE, A. FRÜHROMANTISCHE DICH-
TUNGSTHEORIE.
   R.M., 191(ELN):SEP72(SUPP)-130

NIVELLE, A. KUNST- UND DICHTUNGS-
THEORIEN ZWISCHEN AUFKLÄRUNG UND
KLASSIK.* (2ND ED)
   H.M. SCHUELLER, 290(JAAC):SUM-
MER72-569
NIVEN, J. GIDEON WELLES.*
   617(TLS):15MAR74-270
NIVER, K.R. D.W. GRIFFITH'S "THE
BATTLE AT ELDERBUSH GULCH." (B.
BERGSTEN, ED)
   R. GIROUX, 200:NOV72-563
NIVETTE, J. PRINCIPES DE GRAMMAIRE
GÉNÉRATIVE.*
   H. BONNARD, 209(FM):JUL72-269
   M.E. LONG, 207(FR):FEB72-720
   C. ROHRER, 399(MLJ):OCT72-399
   W. VIERECK, 72:BAND210HEFT4/6-
335
NIWA, T. FIRST COURSE IN JAPANESE.
   E. PUTZAR, 293(JAST):MAY72-689
NIX, C. - SEE BRÜNING, H.
NIXON, H.M. ENGLISH RESTORATION
BOOKBINDINGS.
   A. HOBSON, 617(TLS):23AUG74-910
NIZAN, P. THE WATCHDOGS.
   A. AHMAD, 128(CE):APR73-1026
NOAKES, J. THE NAZI PARTY IN LOWER
SAXONY 1921-1933.
   617(TLS):1FEB74-93
NOBILE, P. INTELLECTUAL SKYWRITING.
   C. LEHMANN-HAUPT, 441:4MAR74-33
   J. SIMON, 441:24MAR74-6
NOBLE, C.A.M. KRANKHEIT, VERBRECHEN
UND KÜNSTLERISCHES SCHAFFEN BEI
THOMAS MANN.
   R. DUMONT, 549(RLC):JAN-MAR72-
155
NOBLE, J., E. FOUAD & J. LACASA.
SPANISH - A BASIC COURSE.
   D.A. KLEIN, 238:MAR72-195
   F.H. NUESSEL, JR., 399(MLJ):FEB
72-94
NOBLE, J.R., ED. RECOLLECTIONS OF
VIRGINIA WOOLF BY HER CONTEMPOR-
ARIES.*
   G.S. HAIGHT, 676(YR):SPRING73-
426
   N. HALE, 639(VQR):SPRING73-309
NOCHLIN, L. REALISM.
   A.C. BIRNHOLZ, 127:WINTER72/73-
232
   C. NEMSER, 58:SEP/OCT72-70
NOËL DU FAIL. LES BALIVERNERIES
D'EUTRAPEL. (C. FOULON, ED; NEWLY
ED BY G. MILIN)
   N. CAZAURAN, 535(RHL):MAY-JUN72-
508
NOEL, G. PRINCESS ALICE.
   G. ANNAN, 362:5DEC74-748
   G. BATTISCOMBE, 617(TLS):15NOV74-
1276
NOGALES, L.G., ED. THE MEXICAN
AMERICAN.* (2ND ED)
   H. GLASSIE, 292(JAF):JAN-MAR72-
98
NOHL, H. DIE DEUTSCHE BEWEGUNG.
   H.B. GARLAND, 220(GL&L):OCT72-70
NOLAN, F. THE OSHAWA PROJECT.
   617(TLS):31MAY74-591
NOLEN, W.A. A SURGEON'S WORLD.
   441:10FEB74-28
NOLTE, H-H. RELIGIÖSE TOLERANZ IN
RUSSLAND, 1600-1725.*
   W. LEITSCH, 32:SEP73-603

NOMURA JUN'ICHI & KEIKO, EDS. HAG-
INO SAIHEI MUKASHIBANASHI SHŪ.
F.H. MAYER, 293(JAST):AUG72-911
NOON, P.W. THE INTEGRITY OF WOR-
SHIP.
T.P. HILL, 363:FEB72-73
NOONE, J. THE NIGHT OF ACCOMPLISH-
MENT.
J. MELLORS, 362:21NOV74-684
NORBERG-SCHULZ, C. EXISTENCE, SPACE
& ARCHITECTURE.
C. HEIMSATH, 363:MAY72-101
NORBU, T.J. & R.B. EKVALL. THE
YOUNGER BROTHER DON YOD.
T.V. WYLIE, 318(JAOS):JAN-MAR72-
158
NORDENFALK, C. DIE SPÄTANTIKEN
ZIERBUCHSTABEN.
H.L. KESSLER, 54:SEP72-344
NORDENSTAM, T. EMPIRICISM & THE
ANALYTIC-SYNTHETIC DISTINCTION.
R. KIRK, 518:JAN73-24
NORGE. LES CERVEAUX BRÛLÉS.
M. CRANSTON, 207(FR):APR72-1045
NORMAN, A.V.B. THE MEDIEVAL SOLDIER.
C.T. WOOD, 589:JUL73-582
NORMAN, D. ALFRED STIEGLITZ.
H. KRAMER, 441:21APR74-3
J. MALCOLM, 442(NY):18NOV74-223
NORMAN, E. A HISTORY OF MODERN IRE-
LAND.
M.J. WATERS, 637(VS):DEC72-231
NORMAN, F. MUCH ADO ABOUT NUFFINK.
J. MELLORS, 362:22AUG74-253
NORMAN, F. THREE ESSAYS ON THE HIL-
DEBRANDSLIED. (A.T. HATTO, ED)
617(TLS):11OCT74-1119
NORMAN, J. HUNTERS OF GOR.
T. STURGEON, 441:8SEP74-39
NORMAN, P. LONDON SIGNS & INSCRIP-
TIONS.
K.B. HARDER, 424:JUN72-149
NORMAN, R. REASONS FOR ACTIONS.*
G.R. GRICE, 479(PHQ):OCT72-377
J. NARVESON, 154:MAR72-140
NORRIS, F.P. 2D - SEE GUIDO DE COL-
ONNA
NORRIS, H.T. SHINQĪṬĪ FOLK LITERA-
TURE & SONG.
L.A. ANDERSON, 187:JAN74-158
NORRIS, L. MOUNTAINS, POLECATS,
PHEASANTS.
617(TLS):22MAR74-295
NORTH, A. STRIKE DEEP.
N. CALLENDAR, 441:15SEP74-45
NORTH, D.C. & R.P. THOMAS. THE RISE
OF THE WESTERN WORLD.
617(TLS):18JAN74-56
NORTH, M. BODY MOVEMENT FOR CHILD-
REN.
B. KING, 151:NOV72-85
NORTON, F.J. & E.M. WILSON. TWO
SPANISH VERSE CHAP-BOOKS.*
R.H. WEBBER, 240(HR):WINTER72-92
NORTON, M.B. THE BRITISH-AMERICANS.*
E.R. FINGERHUT, 656(WMQ):JUL73-
506
NORTON-SMITH, J. - SEE JAMES I OF
SCOTLAND
NORWOOD, C. ABOUT PATERSON.
B. BROWER, 441:15SEP74-16
S.R. WEISMAN, 441:30AUG74-27

NOSSACK, H.E. TO THE UNKNOWN HERO.
P. ADAMS, 61:OCT74-118
V. CUNNINGHAM, 362:28MAR74-413
E. PAWEL, 441:29SEP74-22
NOTEHELFER, F.G. KŌTOKU SHŪSUI.
G.R. FALCONERI, 293(JAST):MAY72-
683
A. HIRAI, 244(HJAS):VOL32-261
NOTKER DER DEUTSCHE. DIE WERKE NOT-
KER DER DEUTSCHE. (VOL 5 ED BY
J.C. KING; VOL 8A ED BY P.W. TAX)
H. TIEFENBACH, 182:VOL25#15/16-
540
NOTT, D.O. & J.E. TRICKEY. ACTUAL-
ITÉS FRANÇAISES.
205(FMLS):JAN72-91
NOURRISSIER, F. LA CRÈVE.
R. MERKER, 207(FR):OCT71-210
NOVA, C. TURKEY HASH.
W.H. PRITCHARD, 249(HUDR):SPRING
73-229
639(VQR):WINTER73-IX
NOVAK, B. AMERICAN PAINTING OF THE
NINETEENTH CENTURY.*
J.H. BAKER, 90:JAN72-38
NOVAK, M. ASCENT OF THE MOUNTAIN,
FLIGHT OF THE DOVE.
H.F., 543:DEC71-362
NOVAK, M. CHOOSING OUR KING.
H.S. PARMET, 441:7APR74-26
NOVAK, M. THE RISE OF THE UNMELT-
ABLE ETHNICS.*
D. BERLINSKI, 390:DEC72-72
K. GLASER, 396(MODA):FALL73-414
W. SHEED, 453:7MAR74-18
NOVAK, M.F. WILLIAM CONGREVE.*
A. BARTON, 677:VOL3-291
G. MARSHALL, 568(SCN):SPRING73-
15
A.H. SCOUTEN, 481(PQ):JUL72-658
NOVAK, M.E. & G.R. GUFFEY - SEE DRY-
DEN, J.
NOVE, A. EFFICIENCY CRITERIA FOR
NATIONALISED INDUSTRIES.
617(TLS):12APR74-398
NOVOSEL'SKY, A.A. & L.V. CHEREPNIN,
EDS. RELAŢIILE ISTORICE DINTRE
POPOARELE U.R.S.S. ŞI ROMÎNIA ÎN
VEACURILE XV-ÎNCEPUTUL CELUI DE
AL XVIII-LEA. (VOL 3)
D.L. RANSEL, 32:MAR73-196
NOVOZHILOV, V.V. PROBLEMY IZMEREN-
IIA ZATRAT I REZUL'TATOV PRI OPTI-
MAL'NOM PLANIROVANII. (2ND ED)
R. CAMPBELL, 32:SEP73-628
NOWAK, A. HEGELS MUSIKÄSTHETIK.
J.S.W., 410(M&L):JAN73-73
NOWICKI, A. VANINI E IL PARADOSSO
DI EMPEDOCLE.
E. NAMER, 542:APR-JUN72-230
NOWINSKI, J. BARON DOMINIQUE VIVANT
DENON (1747-1825).
T.E.D. BRAUN, 207(FR):DEC71-514
NOWLAN, A. VARIOUS PERSONS NAMED
KEVIN O'BRIEN.*
D. GUTTERIDGE, 99:OCT74-45
268:JAN74-66
NOY, D. & I. BEN-AMI, EDS. FOLKLORE
RESEARCH CENTER STUDIES. (VOL 1)
F.L. UTLEY, 292(JAF):OCT-DEC72-
389
WA NSANGA, K.M. - SEE UNDER MUKENDI
WA NSANGA, K.

O'KONOR, L. VIKING EGGELING.
　　H. RICHTER, 290(JAAC):SUMMER72-
　　545
ØKSENHOLT, S., ED. DEUTSCH DER
　GEGENWART.
　　J. HIEBLE, 399(MLJ):FEB72-121
OKUDZHAVA, B. PROZA I POEZIIA. DVA
　ROMANA.
　　O. SOROKIN, 550(RUSR):JAN72-89
OKULOV, A.F. SOVETSKAIA FILOSOF-
　SKAIA NAUKA I EE PROBLEMY.
　　T.J. BLAKELEY, 32:SEP73-622
OKUN, M., ED. SOMETHING TO SING
　ABOUT!
　　M. PETERSON, 470:MAY72-35
OLBRICHT, P., ED. ZUM UNTERGANG
　ZWEIER REICHE. (E. HAENISCH,
　TRANS)
　　H. SERRUYS, 318(JAOS):OCT-DEC72-
　　555
"OLD MASTER DRAWINGS."
　　H. MACANDREW, 135:MAY72-64
OLDENBURG, H. THE CORRESPONDENCE OF
　HENRY OLDENBURG. (VOL 9) (A.R. &
　M.B. HALL, EDS)
　　617(TLS):26APR74-451
OLDERMAN, R.M. BEYOND THE WASTE
　LAND.
　　J. KLINKOWITZ, 454:SPRING73-268
　　B. WEBER, 27(AL):MAR73-142
　　639(VQR):AUTUMN72-CXXXII
OLEARIUS, A. VERMEHRTE NEWE BESCH-
　REIBUNG DER MUSCOWITISCHEN UND
　PERSISCHEN REYSE.* (D. LOHMEIER,
　ED)
　　V. MEID, 221(GQ):NOV72-776
OLIPHANT, M. AUTOBIOGRAPHY & LET-
　TERS OF MRS. MARGARET OLIPHANT.
　(MRS. H. COGHILL, ED)
　　617(TLS):7JUN74-616
OLITSKAIA, E. MOI VOSPOMINANIYA.
　　D. POSPIELOVSKY, 550(RUSR):JUL72-
　　317
OLIVECRONA, K. LAW AS FACT.
　　T. MAUTNER, 479(PHQ):APR72-179
DE OLIVEIRA MARQUES, A.H. HISTORY
　OF PORTUGAL.*
　　639(VQR):SUMMER73-CXXI
OLIVER, A. PORTRAITS OF JOHN QUINCY
　ADAMS & HIS WIFE.*
　　S.W. JACKMAN, 432(NEQ):JUN72-310
OLIVER, A. - SEE CURWEN, S.
OLIVER, J.H. MARCUS AURELIUS: AS-
　PECTS OF CIVIC & CULTURAL POLICY
　IN THE EAST.
　　M.A.R. COLLEDGE, 123:MAR73-63
OLIVER, R. POEMS WITHOUT NAMES.*
　　J.R. SIMON, 189(EA):JAN-MAR72-49
　　T.A. VAN, 128(CE):APR72-839
OLIVER, R.T. COMMUNICATION & CUL-
　TURE IN ANCIENT INDIA & CHINA.*
　　O. VON HINÜBER, 182:VOL25#9/10-
　　307
OLIVER, W.I., ED & TRANS. VOICES OF
　CHANGE IN THE SPANISH AMERICAN THE-
　ATER.
　　F. DONAHUE, 584(SWR):WINTER73-
　　100
　　H.L. JOHNSON, 263:JAN-MAR73-111
　　G.W. WOODYARD, 263:JUL-SEP73-341
OLIVIER, D. ALEXANDRE IER.
　　617(TLS):24MAY74-550

OLIVOVÁ, V. THE DOOMED DEMOCRACY.
　　H. HANAK, 575(SEER):OCT73-608
　　J. KORBEL, 32:JUN73-408
OLKEN, I.T. - SEE PRATOLINI, V.
OLLARD, R. PEPYS.
　　J. SUTHERLAND, 617(TLS):4OCT74-
　　1063
OLLIER, C. LAW & ORDER.
　　268:JAN74-71
OLLIER, C. OUR, OU VINGT ANS APRÈS.
　　617(TLS):11OCT74-1138
OLLMAN, B. ALIENATION.
　　T.R.F., 543:JUN72-764
　　D. MC LELLAN, 32:JUN73-394
　　R. SCHACHT, 319:APR74-268
OLMSTED, F.L. CIVILIZING AMERICAN
　CITIES.* (S.B. SUTTON, ED)
　　D.J. COOLIDGE, 432(NEQ):MAR72-
　　129
　　505:AUG72-98
OLMSTED, F.L., JR. & T. KIMBALL, EDS.
　FORTY YEARS OF LANDSCAPE ARCHITEC-
　TURE: CENTRAL PARK.
　　W.H. JORDY, 453:13JUN74-33
OLNEY, J. METAPHORS OF SELF.
　　J. BISHOP, 639(VQR):WINTER73-152
　　B.J. MANDEL, 579(SAQ):SPRING73-
　　326
　　R.F. SAYRE, 454:WINTER73-190
OLNEY, J. TELL ME AFRICA.
　　617(TLS):21JUN74-665
OLNEY, R. SIMPLE FRENCH FOOD.
　　N. HAZELTON, 441:1DEC74-94
OLSCAMP, P.J. THE MORAL PHILOSOPHY
　OF GEORGE BERKELEY.
　　H.M. BRACKEN, 173(ECS):SPRING73-
　　396
　　S. GREAN, 319:JUL74-398
OLSCHAK, B.C. & G.T. WANGYAL. MYSTIC
　ART OF ANCIENT TIBET.
　　617(TLS):15MAR74-272
OLSEN, T. YONNONDIO.
　　A. GOTTLIEB, 441:31MAR74-5
　　442(NY):25MAR74-140
OLSHEWSKY, T.M., ED. PROBLEMS IN
　THE PHILOSOPHY OF LANGUAGE.
　　D. SMITH, 320(CJL):SPRING71-148
OLSON, A.G. ANGLO-AMERICAN POLITICS
　1660-1775.
　　617(TLS):3MAY74-468
OLSON, J.R. ULZANA.
　　M. LEVIN, 441:20JAN74-24
OLUJIC, G. WILD SEED.
　　J. MELLORS, 362:12SEP74-348
"OMAGGIO A VICO."*
　　E. NAMER, 542:JUL-SEP72-338
O'MALLEY, J. - SEE MARX, K.
OMARI, T.P. KWAME NKRUMAH.
　　A.H.M. KIRK-GREENE, 69:JAN72-71
OMASREITER, R. NATURWISSENSCHAFT
　UND LITERATURKRITIK IM ENGLAND DES
　18. JAHRHUNDERTS.
　　P.H. MEYER, 173(ECS):SPRING73-
　　386
OMRCANIN, M.S., JR. RUTH SUCKOW.
　　L. GURKO, 27(AL):MAR73-146
O'NAN, M. THE ROLE OF MIND IN HUGO,
　FAULKNER, BECKETT & GRASS.*
　　W.G. CUNLIFFE, 546(RR):OCT72-240
ONDAATJE, M. THE COLLECTED WORKS OF
　BILLY THE KID.*
　　P. ADAMS, 61:NOV74-124
　　K. ROOSEVELT, 441:17NOV74-48

"100 NINETEENTH-CENTURY RHYMING AL-
PHABETS IN ENGLISH FROM THE LIB-
RARY OF RUTH M. BALDWIN."
 F. MERRITT, 583:SUMMER73-396
 G.B. TENNYSON, 445(NCF):DEC72-
 373
O'NEIL, R. THE NEED.
 M. LEVIN, 441:3NOV74-72
O'NEILL, J., ED. CRITICS ON JANE
AUSTEN.
 F. MC COMBIE, 447(N&Q):AUG72-314
O'NEILL, J. PERCEPTION, EXPRESSION,
& HISTORY.
 J. BIEN, 154:MAR72-162
O'NEILL, J. SOCIOLOGY AS A SKIN
TRADE.
 K-P. MARKL, 111:20OCT72-24
O'NEILL, K. ANDRÉ GIDE & THE "ROMAN
D'AVENTURE."*
 C.S. BROSMAN, 188(ECR):FALL72-
 234
O'NEILL, P.G. ESSENTIAL KANJI.
 617(TLS):26APR74-434
O'NEILL, T. - SEE CASSOLA, C.
O'NEILL, W.F. WITH CHARITY TOWARD
NONE.
 H.F., 543:MAR72-562
ONG, W.J. RETROUVER LA PAROLE.
 J. LANGLOIS, 154:DEC72-620
ONG, W.J. RHETORIC, ROMANCE, &
TECHNOLOGY.
 R.A. LANHAM, 149:DEC73-389
ONIMUS, J. CAMUS.
 J-M. KLINKENBERG, 556(RLV):
 1972/5-553
ONIMUS, J. LA COMMUNICATION LITTÉR-
AIRE.
 J-M. PIEMME, 556(RLV):1972/1-109
ONORATO, R.J. THE CHARACTER OF THE
POET.*
 K.K., 191(ELN):SEP72(SUPP)-67
 L. WALDOFF, 301(JEGP):JAN73-144
 639(VQR):WINTER72-XXVII
OPIE, I. & P. THE CLASSIC FAIRY
TALES.
 W. GOLDING, 362:14NOV74-646
OPITZ, M. MARTIN OPITZ: GESAMMELTE
WERKE. (VOL 3, PT 1) (G. SCHULZ-
BEHREND, ED)
 D.A. FLEMING, 551(RENQ):SUMMER
 72-241
 G. GILLESPIE, 222(GR):MAR72-143
 P. SKRINE, 402(MLR):APR73-447
OPITZ, M. MARTIN OPITZ: GESAMMELTE
WERKE. (VOL 3, PT 2) (G. SCHULZ-
BEHREND, ED)
 F. VAN INGEN, 433:JAN72-108
 P. SKRINE, 402(MLR):APR73-447
OPPEL, H. ENGLISCHE-DEUTSCHE LITERA-
TURBEZIEHUNGEN.*
 F. JOST, 301(JEGP):JAN73-113
"OPUSCULES D'AMOUR PAR HEROET, LA
BORDERIE ET AUTRES DIVINS POÈTES."
 D. WILSON, 208(FS):JAN73-51
ORBÁN, Á.P. LES DÉNOMINATIONS DU
MONDE CHEZ LES PREMIERS AUTEURS
CHRÉTIENS.*
 C.W. MACLEOD, 123:MAR73-102
ORCIBAL, J. LA RENCONTRE DU CARMEL
THÉRÉSIEN AVEC LES MYSTIQUES DU
NORD.
 A. FOREST, 542:APR-JUN72-180

ORDERIC VITALIS. THE ECCLESIASTICAL
HISTORY OF ORDERIC VITALIS. (VOL
3, BKS 5&6) (M. CHIBNALL, ED &
TRANS)
 F. BARLOW, 382(MAE):1973/2-156
OREA, T.R. - SEE UNDER RAMOS OREA,
T.
OREN, N. BULGARIAN COMMUNISM.
 W.S. VUCINICH, 32:DEC73-848
ORGA, A. THE PROMS.
 617(TLS):8NOV74-1268
ORGAMBIDE, P. LA BUENA GENTE.
 G.I. CASTILLO, 238:MAY72-390
ORGEL, S. - SEE JONSON, B.
ORGEL, S. & R. STRONG. INIGO JONES.
 J. HOLLANDER, 441:20JAN74-5
 617(TLS):15MAR74-257
ORIEUX, J. TALLEYRAND.
 P. ADAMS, 61:MAR74-97
 N. BLIVEN, 442(NY):20MAY74-146
 A.J.P. TAYLOR, 453:13JUN74-15
 A. WHITMAN, 441:27APR74-29
 T. ZELDIN, 441:28APR74-18
 617(TLS):6DEC74-1363
ORIGO, I. IMAGES & SHADOWS.
 639(VQR):WINTER72-VIII
ORIOLI, G. - SEE BELLI, G.G.
ORIOLI, L. - SEE DELICADO, F.
ORKIN, H. SCUFFLER.
 F. BUSCH, 441:29DEC74-22
 442(NY):25NOV74-194
ORLOFF, K. ROCK 'N' ROLL WOMAN.
 J. ROCKWELL, 441:22DEC74-10
ORLOFSKY, P. & M. QUILTS IN AMERICA.
 R. REIF, 441:13DEC74-41
ORLOW, D. THE HISTORY OF THE NAZI
PARTY.* (VOL 1)
 617(TLS):1FEB74-93
ORLOW, D. THE HISTORY OF THE NAZI
PARTY. (VOL 2)
 A.J. NICHOLLS, 617(TLS):8NOV74-
 1264
ORME, N. ENGLISH SCHOOLS IN THE MID-
DLE AGES.
 617(TLS):19APR74-421
ORMOND, R. JOHN SINGER SARGENT.*
 H.H. RHYS, 54:MAR72-105
ORNATO, E. JEAN MURET ET SES AMIS
NICOLAS DE CLAMANGES ET JEAN DE
MONTREUIL.
 J. CROW, 382(MAE):1973/1-67
ORNSTEIN, R. A KINGDOM FOR A STAGE.
 J.A. BRYANT, JR., 579(SAQ):
 SPRING73-335
 T. HAWKES, 676(YR):SUMMER73-561
 D.A. TRAVERSI, 401(MLQ):SEP73-
 312
 A.R. YOUNG, 150(DR):AUTUMN72-503
ORNSTEIN, R.E. THE PSYCHOLOGY OF
CONSCIOUSNESS.
 A. HISS, 442(NY):7JAN74-65
O'ROURKE, W. THE MEEKNESS OF ISAAC.
 C.D.B. BRYAN, 441:22DEC74-6
ORR, D. ITALIAN RENAISSANCE DRAMA
IN ENGLAND BEFORE 1625.*
 D.C. BOUGHNER, 551(RENQ):SUMMER
 72-225
ORR, G. BURNING THE EMPTY NESTS.*
 D. LEHMAN, 491:DEC73-173
ORR, M. THE TEJERA SECRETS.
 M. LEVIN, 441:18AUG74-21
ORREN, K. CORPORATE POWER & SOCIAL
CHANGE.
 S.B. SHEPARD, 441:24FEB74-34

ORSZÁGH, L., ED. ANGOL FILOLÓGIAI
TANULMÁNYOK.
   G.F. CUSHING, 575(SEER):JUL73-
463
ORTEGA, J. MEDIODÍA.
   B. DULSEY, 238:MAY72-394
ORTEGA Y GASSET J. ORTEGA Y GASSET.
   D. SUTTON, 39:JUL72-2
ORTH, R.H. & A.H. FERGUSON - SEE
EMERSON, R.W.
ORTIZ, A.D. - SEE UNDER DOMÍNGUEZ
ORTIZ, A.
DE ORTIZ, S.R. UNCERTAINTIES IN
PEASANT FARMING.
   L. WHITEHEAD, 617(TLS):30AUG74-
926
ORTON, G. EYVIND JOHNSON.
   M. MAZZARELLA, 563(SS):SUMMER73-
273
ORTZEN, L. STORIES OF FAMOUS SHIP-
WRECKS.
   617(TLS):11OCT74-1143
ORVELL, M. INVISIBLE PARADE.
   M.J. FRIEDMAN, 27(AL):MAY73-313
   G.W. RUOFF, 651(WHR):SUMMER73-
312
OSBORN, D. OPEN SEASON.
   N. CALLENDAR, 441:28APR74-39
OSBORN, J.M. YOUNG PHILIP SIDNEY.
   639(VQR):AUTUMN72-CXL
OSBORN, J.M. - SEE SPENCE, J.
OSBORN, R.J. SOVIET SOCIAL POLICIES.
   B. MADISON, 104:SPRING72-175
OSBORNE, C. - SEE WAGNER, R.
OSBORNE, H., ED. THE OXFORD COMPAN-
ION TO ART.*
   T. CROMBIE, 39:MAY72-423
OSBORNE, J. THE NATURALIST DRAMA IN
GERMANY.*
   R. HINTON-THOMAS, 402(MLR):APR73-
467
   S. HOEFERT, 564:MAR72-67
   E. MC INNES, 205(FMLS):JUL72-261
   G. MANDER, 157:WINTER71-71
OSBORNE, J. ROMANTIK.
   E. STOPP, 402(MLR):JUL73-695
   H. THOMKE, 182:VOL25#22-797
OSBORNE, J. A SENSE OF DETACHMENT.
A PLACE CALLING ITSELF ROME.
   617(TLS):4JAN74-14
OSBORNE, J. - SEE WILDE, O.
OSBURN, C.B., ED. THE PRESENT
STATE OF FRENCH STUDIES.
   A. CIORANESCU, 549(RLC):OCT-DEC
72-604
   R. MERCIER, 557(RSH):JUL-SEP72-
447
OSBURN, C.B. RESEARCH & REFERENCE
GUIDE TO FRENCH STUDIES.
   H.C. WOODBRIDGE, 545(RPH):NOV72-
497
OSCHINSKY, D. WALTER OF HENLEY &
OTHER TREATISES ON ESTATE MANAGE-
MENT & ACCOUNTING.
   N. DENHOLM-YOUNG, 382(MAE):
1973/1-57
   J.A. RAFTIS, 589:JAN73-174
OSSOWSKA, M. SOCIAL DETERMINANTS OF
MORAL IDEAS.
   H. MEYNELL, 479(PHQ):APR72-185
OST, H. EIN SKIZZENBUCH ANTONIO
CANOVAS 1796-1799.
   M.F. FISCHER, 683:BAND35HEFT1/2-
145

[CONTINUED]

[CONTINUING]
   F. LICHT, 54:SEP72-362
OSTENDORF, B. DER MYTHOS IN DER
NEUEN WELT.
   L. BRUST, 27(AL):MAR73-140
OSTERWALDER, C. DIE MITTLERE BRONZE-
ZEIT IM SCHWEIZERISCHEN MITTELLAND
UND JURA.
   M. GIMBUTAS, 183:VOL25#19/20-676
OSTOLOPOV, N.F. SLOVAR DREVNEJ I
NOVOJ POÉZII.
   H-J. ZUM WINKEL, 72:BAND21OHEFT
1/3-234
OSTROUMOFF, I.N. THE HISTORY OF THE
COUNCIL OF FLORENCE.
   D.J. GEANAKOPLOS, 32:JUN73-372
OSTROVSKY, E. VOYEUR VOYANT.*
   D. HAYMAN, 659:SPRING74-257
   J.H. MATTHEWS, 207(FR):MAY72-
1187
   J. MILLS, 648:OCT72-67
   639(VQR):SUMMER72-XC
   676(YR):SPRING73-XVI
OSTWALD, M. NOMOS & THE BEGINNINGS
OF THE ATHENIAN DEMOCRACY.*
   J.K. DAVIES, 123:DEC73-224
O'SULLIVAN, L. PARTISANS.
   E. ROVIT, 659:AUTUMN74-539
OTERO, R. FOREVER PICASSO.
   A. BROYARD, 441:28OCT74-35
   J. RUSSELL, 441:1DEC74-55
OTIS, B. OVID AS AN EPIC POET.*
(2ND ED)
   R. COLEMAN, 123:DEC73-177
OTT, L. DIE LEHRE DES DURANDUS DE
S. PORCIANO O.P. VOM WIEHESAKRA-
MENT.
   J. GALOT, 182:VOL25#13/14-459
OTT, P. ZUR SPRACHE DER JÄGER IN
DER DEUTSCHEN SCHWEIZ.*
   R.E. KELLER, 402(MLR):JAN73-207
OTTAWAY, H. VAUGHAN WILLIAMS SYM-
PHONIES.
   C. PALMER, 415:JUN73-600
OTTE, G. DIALEKTIK UND JURISPRUDENZ.
   G. MAY, 182:VOL25#15/16-526
OTTEN, H. EIN HETHITISCHES FESTRIT-
UAL (KBO XIX 128).
   G. NEUMANN, 260(IF):BAND76-272
   G. WILHELM, 343:BAND15HEFT2-223
OTTEN, H. SPRACHLICHE STELLUNG UND
DATIERUNG DES MADDUWATTA-TEXTES.
   G. NEUMANN, 260(IF):BAND76-267
OTTEN, H. & W. VON SODEN. DAS
AKKADISCH-HETHITISCHE VOKABULAR
KBO I 44 + KBO XIII 1.
   G. NEUMANN, 260(IF):BAND76-260
OTTEN, H. & V. SOUČEK. EIN ALTHETH-
ITISCHES RITUAL FÜR DAS KÖNIGSPAAR.
   G. NEUMANN, 260(IF):BAND76-263
OTTO, E. AUS DER SAMMLUNG DES ÄGYP-
TOLOGISCHEN INSTITUTES DER UNIVER-
SITÄT HEIDELBERG.
   J. LECLANT, 182:VOL25#19/20-677
OUELLETTE, F. EDGARD VARÈSE.
   R.H.M., 410(M&L):JUL73-338
OUSPENSKY, P.D. THE PSYCHOLOGY OF
MAN'S POSSIBLE EVOLUTION. TALKS
WITH A DEVIL.
   D.W. HARDING, 453:18JUL74-6
OUSTON, P. THE IMAGINATION OF MAUR-
ICE BARRÈS.
   R. GRIFFITHS, 617(TLS):13DEC74-
1420

OVENDEN, G., ED. HILL & ADAMSON
PHOTOGRAPHS.
  617(TLS):29MAR74-310
OVENDEN, G., ED. THE ILLUSTRATORS
OF ALICE.
  C. ROBINS, 441:6JAN74-2
OVERMAN, M. SIR MARC BRUNEL & THE
TUNNEL.
  K. HUDSON, 637(VS):SEP72-97
OVID. OVIDE: "LES FASTES." (VOL 2)
(H. LE BONNIEC, ED & TRANS)
  E.J. KENNEY, 123:DEC73-175
OVID. P. OVIDIUS NASO: "FASTORUM"
LIBER SECUNDUS. (H. LE BONNIEC,
ED)
  O. HILTBRUNNER, 182:VOL25#5/6-
  176
OVID. OVID'S AMORES. (BK 1) (J.A.
BARSBY, ED & TRANS)
  617(TLS):11JAN74-38
OVIEDO, J.M. MARIO VARGAS LLOSA.*
  G.R. MC MURRAY, 238:SEP72-600
OWEN, D.D.R., ED. ARTHURIAN ROMANCE.*
  J. LAWLOR, 541(RES):MAY72-248
OWEN, D.D.R. THE EVOLUTION OF THE
GRAIL LEGEND.
  H. NEWSTEAD, 546(RR):DEC72-293
OWEN, D.D.R. THE LEGEND OF ROLAND.
  617(TLS):29MAR74-320
OWEN, D.D.R. THE VISION OF HELL.*
  L. POLAK, 208(FS):APR73-188
OWEN, D.F. MAN'S ENVIRONMENTAL
PREDICAMENT.
  617(TLS):8MAR74-243
OWEN, D.M. CHURCH & SOCIETY IN MEDI-
EVAL LINCOLNSHIRE.
  E.G. KIMBALL, 589:APR73-396
OWEN, G. THE WHITE STALLION & OTHER
POEMS.
  N.A. BRITTIN, 577(SHR):SPRING72-
  197
OWEN, G.D., ED. CALENDAR OF THE
MANUSCRIPTS OF THE MARQUESS OF
SALISBURY, PRESERVED AT HATFIELD
HOUSE. (PT 21)
  A.G.R. SMITH, 325:APR72-443
OWEN, H., ED. THE NEXT PHASE IN
FOREIGN POLICY.*
  639(VQR):AUTUMN73-CLXVIII
OWEN, H.P. CONCEPTS OF DEITY.*
  K. WARD, 479(PHQ):JUL72-285
OWEN, L.J. & N.H., EDS. MIDDLE
ENGLISH POETRY.
  E. SHORB, 399(MLJ):APR72-248
  J.R. SIMON, 189(EA):JAN-MAR72-82
OWENS, G., ED. GEORGE MOORE'S MIND
& ART.*
  J.E. DUNLEAVY, 637(VS):MAR72-376
OWENS, L.L. SAINTS OF CLAY.
  B. MENKUS, 14:JAN72-72
OWENS, W.A. A SEASON OF WEATHERING.*
  L.C. MILAZZO, 584(SWR):SPRING73-
  181
"OXFORD LATIN DICTIONARY." (FASC 3)
  A. ERNOUT, 555:VOL46FASC3-327
OXLEY, G.W. POOR RELIEF IN ENGLAND
& WALES 1601-1834.
  617(TLS):8NOV74-1269
OZ, A. ELSEWHERE, PERHAPS.*
  R. GARFITT, 362:14MAR74-343
  M. WOOD, 453:7FEB74-10
  617(TLS):22FEB74-173
OZ, A. MY MICHAEL. UNTO DEATH.
  B. HOCHMAN, 390:NOV72-63

OZ, A. TOUCH THE WATER TOUCH THE
WIND.
  A. FRIEDMAN, 441:24NOV74-7
  442(NY):18NOV74-233

PAAP, A.H.R.E. THE XENOPHON PAPYRI.
  B.E. DONOVAN, 24:SUMMER73-225
  E.G. TURNER, 123:DEC73-144
VAN DER PAARDT, R.T. L. APULEIUS
MADAURENSIS, "THE METAMORPHOSES."
  H.J. MASON, 487:AUTUMN72-314
  P.G. WALSH, 123:DEC73-158
PABST, W., ED. DAS MODERNE FRANZÖ-
SISCHE DRAMA.*
  K. BAHNERS, 430(NS):JUL72-434
PABST, W. NOVELLENTHEORIE UND NOV-
ELLENDICHTUNG. (2ND ED)
  A. SCAGLIONE, 545(RPH):MAY73-717
PACE, E. ANY WAR WILL DO.*
  617(TLS):8NOV74-1248
PACEY, D., ED. FREDERICK PHILIP
GROVE.
  H. SMITH, 376:JAN72-126
PACHMAN, L. JAK TO BYLO.
  617(TLS):7JUN74-606
PACHMUSS, T. ZINAÏDA HIPPIUS.*
  S.D. CIOREN, 104:SUMMER72-336
  S.A. ZENKOVSKY, 550(RUSR):APR72-
  190
PACHMUSS, T. - SEE HIPPIUS, Z.N.
PÄCHT, O. & J.J.G. ALEXANDER. ILLU-
MINATED MANUSCRIPTS IN THE BODLEI-
AN LIBRARY, OXFORD.* (VOL 2)
  W.O. HASSALL, 135:APR72-291
PACI, E. IL NULLA E IL PROBLEMA
DELL'UOMO. (3RD ED)
  A.M., 543:SEP71-133
"THE PACIFIC RIVALS."
  F.W. MARTIN, 285(JAPQ):OCT-DEC72-
  484
PACIFICI, S., ED. FROM "VERISMO" TO
EXPERIMENTALISM.*
  R. KOFFLER, 276:WINTER72-511
PACIFICI, S. - SEE GINZBURG, N.
PACK, R. NOTHING BUT LIGHT.
  R. PINSKY, 491:JAN74-241
PACK, S.W.C. THE BATTLE FOR CRETE.
  617(TLS):29MAR74-349
PACKER, E. STRESS IN YOUR LIFE.
  617(TLS):27SEP74-1048
PADFIELD, P. THE GREAT NAVAL RACE.
  617(TLS):8NOV74-1264
PADHI, S. SERPENT & COLUMBINE.
  S. DEVONS, 551(RENQ):SUMMER72-
  243
PADUANO, G. LA FORMAZIONE DEL MONDO
IDEOLOGICO E POETICO DI EURIPIDE.
  A.F. GARVIE, 123:MAR73-86
PAFFORD, M. INGLORIOUS WORDSWORTHS.
  617(TLS):15FEB74-162
PAGANELLI, S. MUSICAL INSTRUMENTS
FROM THE RENAISSANCE TO THE 19TH
CENTURY.
  G. OLDHAM, 415:OCT73-1013
PAGANI, W. REPERTORIO TEMATICO
DELLA SCUOLA POETICA SICILIANA.*
  R. CRESPO, 433:JUL72-372
PAGANO, R., L. BIANCHI & G. ROSTIR-
OLLA. ALESSANDRO SCARLATTI.
  C.M.B., 410(M&L):OCT73-474
PAGE, D. FOLKTALES IN HOMER'S
"ODYSSEY."
  617(TLS):17MAY74-530

PAGE, J.F., ED. PENGUIN GERMAN
READER.
C.B. CAPLES, 399(MLJ):DEC72-517
PAGE, N., ED. WILKIE COLLINS: THE
CRITICAL HERITAGE.
J.I.M. STEWART, 617(TLS):6SEP72-
953
PAGE, N. THE LANGUAGE OF JANE
AUSTEN.
K. KROEBER, 301(JEGP):JUL73-454
PAGE, P.K. POEMS, SELECTED & NEW,
1942-1973.
A. PEARSON, 99:MAY/JUN74-17
PAGE, R. THE DECLINE OF AN ENGLISH
VILLAGE.
R. BLYTHE, 362:18APR74-507
617(TLS):14JUN74-647
PAGE, S.R. FAULKNER'S WOMEN.
W. TAYLOR, 27(AL):MAY73-310
PAGEARD, R. LE DROIT PRIVÉ DES
MOSSI.
D. ZAHAN, 69:APR72-158
PAGEAUX, D.H. - SEE FEIJOO Y MONTE-
NEGRO, B.J.
PAGEL, W. PARACLESE.
M. CLAVELIN, 542:APR-JUN72-170
PAGETTI, C. IL SENSO DEL FUTURO, LA
FANTASCIENZA NELLA LETTERATURA
AMERICANA.
G. CORDESSE, 189(EA):JAN-MAR72-
182
PAGIS, D. SELECTED POEMS.
G. EWART, 364:DEC72/JAN73-132
PAGLIARO, H.E., ED. STUDIES IN
EIGHTEENTH-CENTURY CULTURE. (VOL 2)
566:SPRING73-111
PAHLEN, K. GREAT SINGERS FROM THE
17TH CENTURY TO THE PRESENT DAY.
617(TLS):8FEB74-139
PAI, G.B. COCHIN POSTMARKS & CANCEL-
LATIONS.
617(TLS):15FEB74-165
PAIGE, H.W. SONGS OF THE TETON
SIOUX.
T.L. DWORSKY, 187:JAN74-161
PAINTER, C. GONJA.
E.A. GREGERSEN, 350:JUN73-504
PAL, P. THE ART OF TIBET.*
P. HARDIE, 39:JUN72-522
PALA, D. TRUMPET FOR A WALLED CITY.
617(TLS):11OCT74-1142
DE PALACIO, J. MARY SHELLEY DANS
SON OEUVRE.*
S. JEUNE, 557(RSH):APR-JUN72-322
PALANDRI, A.J., ED & TRANS. MODERN
VERSE FROM TAIWAN.
J. ISMAIL, 648:OCT72-65
PALEK, B. CROSS-REFERENCE.
G. FISCHER, 353:15AUG72-93
PALÉOLOGUE, M. AN AMBASSADOR'S
MEMOIRS 1914-1917.*
E.C. THADEN, 32:JUN73-388
PALEY, G. ENORMOUS CHANGES AT THE
LAST MINUTE.
P. ADAMS, 61:APR74-120
L. HARRIS, 441:17MAR74-3
C. LEHMANN-HAUPT, 441:28FEB74-41
B. REEVE, 231:JUN74-95
M. WOOD, 453:21MAR74-19
PALEY, M.D. ENERGY & THE IMAGINA-
TION.*
G.S. ROUSSEAU, 72:BAND210HEFT4/6-
407

PALEY, M.D. & M. PHILLIPS, EDS.
WILLIAM BLAKE.
617(TLS):15FEB74-145
PALIN CRISANAZ, M.P. FAVOLA E MITO
NELLA POESIA DI SERGEJ ESENIN.
J. BAINES, 402(MLR):APR73-478
PALLISTER, J.L. THE WORLD VIEW OF
BÉROALDE DE VERVILLE.
R.D. COTTRELL, 207(FR):MAR72-923
D.L. RUBIN, 188(ECR):WINTER72-
327
PALLUCCHINI, R. TIZIANO.*
P. HENDY, 54:SEP72-350
PALMER, A. ALEXANDER I.
617(TLS):24MAY74-550
PALMER, A. FREDERICK THE GREAT.
617(TLS):13DEC74-1423
PALMER, A. METTERNICH.
639(VQR):SPRING73-LXXX
PALMER, C. IMPRESSIONISM IN MUSIC.*
P. GRIFFITHS, 415:OCT73-1011
PALMER, F. GRAMMAR.
A. CHURCH, 316:JUN72-420
PALMER, F.R., ED. PROSODIC ANALYSIS.
G. BROWN, 361:VOL29#1-84
PALMER, F.R. - SEE FIRTH, J.R.
PALMER, J.J.N. ENGLAND, FRANCE &
CHRISTENDOM, 1377-99.
639(VQR):WINTER73-XXXVIII
PALMER, L. DICKE LILLI, GUTES KIND.
A. FORBES, 617(TLS):1NOV74-1213
PALMER, R., ED. THE PAINFUL PLOUGH.
F. HOWES, 415:MAR73-264
PALMER, R. SONGS OF THE MIDLANDS.
F. HOWES, 415:APR73-383
PALMER, R., ED. THE VALIANT SAILOR.*
F. HOWES, 415:DEC73-1241
PALMER, R.B. & R. HAMERTON-KELLY,
EDS. PHILOMATHES.
J.M. RIST, 487:AUTUMN72-322
PALMER, R.E. HERMENEUTICS.*
L. NATHAN, 206:NOV72-262
L. WELCH, 290(JAAC):WINTER71-260
PALMER, R.E., JR. THOMAS WHY-
THORNE'S SPEECH.
A.J. BLISS, 447(N&Q):JAN72-36
T. SÖDERHOLM, 597(SN):VOL44#2-
448
PALMER, R.E.A. THE ARCHAIC COMMUN-
ITY OF THE ROMANS.
A. DRUMMOND, 313:VOL62-176
E.T. SALMON, 24:WINTER73-388
E.J. WEINRIB, 487:SPRING72-95
PALMER, R.E.A. THE KING & THE COMI-
TIUM.
A. DRUMMOND, 313:VOL62-176
PALMER, R.R. TWELVE WHO RULED.
N. HAMPSON, 208(FS):APR73-239
PALMER, S. & A. GORDON. A POLITICAL
CORRESPONDENCE OF THE GLADSTONE
ERA. (J.K. CHAPMAN, ED)
J. VINCENT, 637(VS):SEP72-99
PALMER, S.E., JR. & R.R. KING. YUGO-
SLAV COMMUNISM & THE MACEDONIAN
QUESTION.
I. AVAKUMOVIC, 32:SEP73-652
PALMIER, L. COMMUNISTS IN INDONESIA.
617(TLS):19APR74-414
PÁLSSON, H. ART & ETHICS IN HRAFN-
KEL'S SAGA.
C.F. BAYERSCHMIDT, 222(GR):NOV72-
316
H. BESSASON, 563(SS):WINTER73-65

PALTER, R., ED. THE "ANNUS MIRABIL-
IS" OF SIR ISAAC NEWTON 1666-1966.*
G.A.J. ROGERS, 481(PQ):JUL72-738
PAMLÉNYI, E., ED. SOCIAL-ECONOMIC
RESEARCHES ON THE HISTORY OF EAST-
CENTRAL EUROPE.
P.F. SUGAR, 575(SEER):JUL73-481
PANA, S. - SEE TZARA, T.
PANCAKE, J.S. SAMUEL SMITH & THE
POLITICS OF BUSINESS: 1752-1839.
R.A. OVERFIELD, 656(WMQ):OCT73-
678
PANFILOV, V.Z. VZAIMOOTNOŠENIE
JAZYKA I MYŠLENIJA.
E. ALBRECHT & K. KRÜGER,
682(ZPSK):BAND25HEFT4/5-419
LAYMAN P'ANG. THE RECORDED SAYINGS
OF LAYMAN P'ANG. (R.F. SASAKI, Y.
IRIYA & D.R. FRASER, TRANS)
WONG KAI-CHEE, 302:JUL72-209
PANGANIBAN, J.V. CONCISE ENGLISH-
TAGALOG DICTIONARY.*
J.D. BOWEN, 318(JAOS):JAN-MAR72-
163
PANICHAS, G.A. THE REVERENT DISCI-
PLINE.
617(TLS):13SEP74-968
DE PANIZZA LORCH, M. - SEE VALLA, L.
PANNONIUS, J. JANUS PANNONIUS VER-
SEI. (T. KARDOS, ED)
M.D. BIRNBAUM, 32:SEP73-672
PANOFSKY, E. PROBLEMS IN TITIAN.
M. MURARO, 54:SEP72-353
"PANORAMA DE LA ACTUAL LITERATURA
LATINOAMERICANA."
E. ECHEVARRÍA, 240(HR):WINTER72-
109
PANTIN, C.F.A. THE RELATIONS BE-
TWEEN THE SCIENCES. (A.M. PANTIN
& W.H. THORPE, EDS)
M. MARTIN, 154:JUN72-312
M.E. RUSE, 486:MAR72-91
PANTIN, W.A. OXFORD LIFE IN OXFORD
ARCHIVES.
C.R.H. COOPER, 325:OCT72-540
PANUNZIO, S. - SEE ROBERT OF GRETHAM
PAOLETTI, M. CIVILISATION FRAN-
ÇAISE CONTEMPORAINE.
J. VAN BAELEN, 207(FR):FEB72-772
DI PAOLO, E.C. & G. COLONNA - SEE
UNDER COLONNA DI PAOLO, E. & G.
COLONNA
PAOLUCCI, A. FROM TENSION TO TONIC.
C.J. GIANAKARIS, 397(MD):DEC72-
339
R.J. SMITH, 157:AUTUMN72-79
PAPADEMETRIOU, P.C. HOUSTON: AN
ARCHITECTURAL GUIDE.
505:AUG72-98
PAPAIOANNOU, K. HEGEL.
F. HEIDSIECK, 542:JUL-SEP72-373
PAPALIA, A. & J.A. MENDOZA. LECTUR-
AS DE AHORA Y DEL MAÑANA.
A. EISENHARDT, 238:SEP72-607
PAPARELLI, G. - SEE CARAFA, D.
PAPE, H. KLOPSTOCKS AUTORENHONORARE
UND SELBSTVERLAGSGEWINNE.*
G. FRIESEN, 400(MLN):OCT72-790
"PAPER & WOOD PACKAGING IN SOLID
WASTE."
42(AR):VOL32#4-712
PAPI, F. ANTHROPOLOGIA E CIVILTÀ
NEL PENSIERO DI GIORDANO BRUNO.
E. NAMER, 542:APR-JUN72-166

PAPIĆ, M. L'EXPRESSION ET LA PLACE
DU SUJET DANS LES "ESSAIS" DE MON-
TAIGNE.
P. CLIFFORD, 208(FS):JUL73-324
PAPMEHL, K.A. FREEDOM OF EXPRESSION
IN EIGHTEENTH CENTURY RUSSIA.*
J.T. ALEXANDER, 481(PQ):JUL72-
546
PÂQUES, G. ...COMME UN VOLEUR.
J. SARELL, 207(FR):FEB72-703
PARAIN-VIAL, J. LE SENS DU PRÉSENT.
DE L'ETRE MUSICAL. GABRIEL MARCEL
OU LES NIVEAUX DE L'EXPÉRIENCE.
LA NATURE DU FAIT DANS LES SCI-
ENCES HUMAINES. ANALYSES STRUC-
TURALES ET IDÉOLOGIES STRUCTURAL-
ISTES.
A. MERCIER, 262:AUTUMN72-355
PARDO, R. LA CIENCIA Y LA FILOSOFÍA
COMO SABER SIN SER.
A. LLINARES, 263:OCT-DEC73-475
PARDUE, P.A. BUDDHISM.
J. HALVERSON, 293(JAST):MAY72-
637
PARÉ, A. DES MONSTRES ET PRODIGES.
(J. CÉARD, ED)
R. SCHENDA, 182:VOL25#12-385
PAREDES, A., ED & TRANS. FOLKTALES
OF MEXICO.
T.L. HANSEN, 650(WF):APR72-137
R.J. SMITH, 292(JAF):JAN-MAR72-
84
PAREKH, B., ED. BENTHAM'S POLITICAL
THOUGHT. JEREMY BENTHAM.
D.D. RAPHAEL, 617(TLS):27SEP74-
1036
PAREKH, B., ED. COLOUR, CULTURE &
CONSCIOUSNESS.
M. ABRAMS, 617(TLS):13SEP74-974
PARENT, G. SHEILA LEVINE IS DEAD &
LIVING IN NEW YORK.
S. O'CONNELL, 418(MR):WINTER73-
190
PARENT, M. COHÉRENCE ET RÉSONANCE
DANS LE STYLE DE "CHARMES" DE
P. VALÉRY.
D. BOUVEROT, 209(FM):JUL72-265
W.N. INCE, 208(FS):JUL73-352
D.L. PARRIS, 402(MLR):APR73-424
N. WING, 207(FR):APR72-1052
PAREYSON, L. VERITÀ E INTERPRETA-
ZIONE.*
M. RIESER, 290(JAAC):SUMMER72-
570
PARIS, J. RABELAIS AU FUTUR.*
Y. VELAN, 207(FR):DEC71-530
PARISH, J.R. & R.L. BOWERS. THE MGM
STOCK COMPANY.
G. MILLAR, 362:25APR74-542
PARK, R. HAZLITT & THE SPIRIT OF
THE AGE.*
L.A. ELIOSEFF, 290(JAAC):WINTER
72-278
J.O. HAYDEN, 677:VOL3-306
J.E.J., 191(ELN):SEP72(SUPP)-48
R.W. KING, 541(RES):AUG72-370
D. MAJDIAK, 301(JEGP):OCT73-572
PARKER, A.A. LITERATURE & THE DELIN-
QUENT.*
M.E. NOVAK, 594:SPRING72-75
PARKER, A.A. LOS PÍCAROS EN LA LIT-
ERATURA.
B.W. IFE, 402(MLR):JUL73-671

PARKER, F. GEORGE PEABODY.
R. MERIDETH, 432(NEQ):JUN72-302
639(VQR):SPRING72-LVIII
PARKER, F.D., ED. TRAVELS IN CEN-
TRAL AMERICA, 1820-1840.
M.H. BRENNAN, 37:SEP72-42
PARKER, H., ED. THE RECOGNITION OF
HERMAN MELVILLE.
H. KERR, 573(SSF):WINTER72-103
PARKER, H.J. VIEW FROM THE BOYS.
617(TLS):15NOV74-1297
PARKER, J.H. & OTHERS, COMPS. CAL-
DERÓN DE LA BARCA STUDIES, 1951-
69.
A.V. EBERSOLE, 238:DEC72-965
J.A. PARR, 399(MLJ):NOV72-460
B.W. WARDROPPER, 400(MLN):MAR72-
364
PARKER, P.S. GOOD GIRLS DON'T GET
MURDERED.
N. CALLENDAR, 441:15DEC74-10
PARKER, R. COTTAGE ON THE GREEN.
617(TLS):1MAR74-221
PARKER, R. THE MYTH OF THE MIDDLE
CLASS.
441:10FEB74-26
PARKER, R.B. GOD SAVE THE CHILD.
N. CALLENDAR, 441:15DEC74-10
PARKER, R.B. THE GODWULF MANUSCRIPT.
N. CALLENDAR, 441:13JAN74-12
617(TLS):30AUG74-933
PARKER, W.H. THE SUPERPOWERS.
P. HOLLANDER, 32:SEP73-626
PARKER, W.O. & H.K. SMITH. SCENE
DESIGN & STAGE LIGHTING. (2ND ED)
H.W. POE, 583:FALL72-113
PARKES, M.B. ENGLISH CURSIVE BOOK
HANDS 1250-1500.*
P.D.A. HARVEY, 325:OCT72-539
PARKES, R. THE GUARDIANS.*
N. CALLENDAR, 441:6OCT74-38
PARKIN, M. LOVE: ALL.
J. MELLORS, 362:11JUL74-61
617(TLS):3MAY74-465
PARKINSON, C.N. THE LIFE & TIMES OF
HORATIO HORNBLOWER.
639(VQR):WINTER72-XVI
PARKINSON, J. A TOUR OF RUSSIA, SI-
BERIA & THE CRIMEA, 1792-1794. (W.
COLLIER, ED)
J.T. ALEXANDER, 481(PQ):JUL72-
546
W. KIRCHNER, 32:SEP73-606
I. DE MADARIAGA, 575(SEER):APR73-
311
PARKINSON, R. A DAY'S MARCH NEARER
HOME.
442(NY):12AUG74-99
617(TLS):7JUN74-599
PARKS, E.D. EARLY ENGLISH HYMNS.
N. TEMPERLEY, 415:MAY73-495
PARKS, S., ED. SALE CATALOGUES OF
LIBRARIES OF EMINENT PERSONS. (VOL
5)
617(TLS):6SEP74-958
PARLATORE, A. PROVISIONS.
R. JORGENSEN, 181:WINTER73-220
PARMENTIER, J. OEUVRES POÉTIQUES.
(F. FERRAND, ED)
R.M. BURGESS, 551(RENQ):WINTER
72-458
G. GUEUDET, 535(RHL):JUL-AUG72-
706

PARRA, N. EMERGENCY POEMS.*
S. COOPERMAN, 648:APR73-12
PARRISH, S.M. THE ART OF "THE LYRI-
CAL BALLADS."
617(TLS):1MAR74-206
PARRY, B. DELUSIONS & DISCOVERIES.
M.M. LAGO, 637(VS):MAR73-361
G. WOODCOCK, 401(MLQ):MAR73-111
PARRY, J.H. THE DISCOVERY OF THE
SEA.
D.J. BOORSTIN, 441:1DEC74-7
C. HILL, 453:14NOV74-17
M.M. MOONEY, 231:DEC74-97
PARRY, J.H. TRADE & DOMINION.
C.R. RITCHESON, 173(ECS):SUMMER
73-509
PARRY, M. THE MAKING OF HOMERIC
VERSE.* (A. PARRY, ED)
C.A. TRYPANIS, 24:FALL73-302
PARRY-JONES, W.L. THE TRADE IN LUN-
ACY.
A. ROOK, 637(VS):DEC72-244
PARSONS, C.S. THE DUNLAPS & THEIR
FURNITURE.
W. GARRETT, 432(NEQ):DEC72-595
PARSONS, H.L. HUMANISM & MARX'S
THOUGHT.
T.S. CLEMENTS, 484(PPR):JUN73-
586
PARSONS, J.B. PEASANT REBELLIONS OF
THE LATE MING DYNASTY.*
R. TAYLOR, 318(JAOS):OCT-DEC72-
541
PARSONS, N. - SEE KOROLENKO, V.G.
PARSONS, T. & G.M. PLATT, WITH N.J.
SMELSER. THE AMERICAN UNIVERSITY.*
S.S. WOLIN, 453:24JAN74-40
PARTLOW, R.B., JR. - SEE "DICKENS
STUDIES ANNUAL"
PARTRIDGE, E. THE ROUTLEDGE DICTION-
ARY OF HISTORICAL SLANG. (ABRIDG-
ED BY J. SIMPSON)
617(TLS):5APR74-376
PARTRIDGE, E. - SEE JONSON, B.
PASCAL, B. OEUVRES COMPLÈTES. (L.
LAFUMA, ED)
J.A. MOREAU, 98:AUG/SEP72-810
PASCAL, B. PENSÉES DE M. PASCAL SUR
LA RELIGION ET SUR QUELQUES AUTRES
SUJETS. (G. COUTON & J. JEHASSE,
EDS)
H.H. CHAPMAN, JR., 568(SCN):FALL-
WINTER73-95
PASCAL, P. LA RÉVOLTE DE POUGAT-
CHÉV.*
P. AVRICH, 550(RUSR):APR72-202
PASCAL, R. FROM NATURALISM TO EX-
PRESSIONISM.
617(TLS):1FEB74-105
PASHA, M.A. - SEE UNDER AZEEZ PASHA,
M.
PASLEY, J.M.S., ED. OXFORD GERMAN
STUDIES. (VOL 2)
R.G. FINCH, 220(GL&L):OCT72-61
PASLEY, M., ED. GERMANY.
R.E. KELLER & OTHERS, 402(MLR):
APR73-432
PASLEY, M. - SEE KAFKA, F.
PASOLI, R. A BOOK ON THE OPEN
THEATRE.
T.P. ADLER, 160:WINTER71/72-123
PASQUAZI, S. AGGIORNAMENTI DI
CRITICA DANTESCA.
D.D., 275(IQ):FALL/WINTER72-118

PAUL, W.H. THE GRAY-FLANNEL PIGSKIN.
R.W. CREAMER, 441:1DEC74-90
PAULHART, H. DIE KARTAUSE GAMING
ZUR ZEIT DES SCHISMAS UND DER
REFORMKONZILIEN.
G. CONSTABLE, 589:JUL73-545
PAULIN, H.W., ED. HIER SPUKT ES.
G. GILLHOFF, 221(GQ):JAN72-205
PAULME, D., ED. CLASSES ET ASSOCIA-
TIONS D'ÂGE EN AFRIQUE DE L'OUEST.
R. BRAIN, 69:OCT72-346
PAULSEN, W., ED. DER DICHTER UND
SEINE ZEIT.*
E.W. HERD, 67:MAY73-146
H.D. OSTERLE, 399(MLJ):NOV72-457
H. RIDLEY, 220(GL&L):JUL73-357
D.C. WIXSON, 125:FEB73-180
PAULSEN, W., ED. DAS NACHLEBEN DER
ROMANTIK IN DER MODERNEN DEUTSCHEN
LITERATUR.*
R.M., 191(ELN):SEP72(SUPP)-131
PAULSEN, W., ED. PSYCHOLOGIE IN DER
LITERATURWISSENSCHAFT.
F.J. BEHARRIELL, 406:FALL73-321
PAULSON, R. HOGARTH.* (VOLS 1&2)
M. KITSON, 592:MAR72-134
L. LIPKING, 481(PQ):JUL72-694
D. SUTTON, 39:JAN72-2
P. TOMORY, 54:DEC72-557
PAULSON, R. ROWLANDSON.
F.W. HILLES, 676(YR):SPRING73-
443
R.W. UPHAUS, 290(JAAC):SUMMER73-
559
639(VQR):SPRING73-XCI
PAUSTOVSKY, K. STORY OF A LIFE.
(VOL 6)
617(TLS):12APR74-391
PAUTRAT, B. VERSIONS DU SOLEIL.
M. SERVIÈRE, 542:JUL-SEP72-297
PAUWELS, J.M. RÉPERTOIRE DE DROIT
COUTUMIER CONGLAIS, JURISPRUDENCE
ET DOCTRINE, 1954-1967.
J. VANDERLINDEN, 69:OCT72-350
PAVESE, C. AMERICAN LITERATURE.
R.S. DOMBROSKI, 191(ELN):SEP72-
65
PAVLOWITCH, S.K. YUGOSLAVIA.
D. WILSON, 575(SEER):JAN73-133
PAVÓN, F.G. - SEE UNDER GARCÍA PAVÓN,
F.
PAWLEY, M. LE CORBUSIER. MIES VAN
DER ROHE.
R.F. JORDAN, 46:FEB72-129
PAWLEY, M. THE PRIVATE FUTURE.
B. DE MOTT, 61:OCT74-108
617(TLS):20SEP74-1022
PAXTON, J., ED. THE STATESMAN'S
YEARBOOK 1974-1975.
617(TLS):29NOV74-1340
PAXTON, N. THE DEVELOPMENT OF MAL-
LARMÉ'S PROSE STYLE.
A.H. GREET, 207(FR):OCT71-254
A. STREIFF, 535(RHL):MAR-APR72-
337
PAYEN, J.C. LES ORIGINES DE LA
RENAISSANCE.
J.M. FERRANTE, 545(RPH):AUG72-
200
PAYNE, A. SCHOENBERG.
E. BARKIN, 513:FALL-WINTER69-139
PAYNE, P.L. BRITISH ENTREPRENEUR-
SHIP IN THE NINETEENTH CENTURY.
617(TLS):5JUL74-733

PAYNE, R. THE GREAT MAN.
P. STANSKY, 441:24NOV74-4
PAYNTER, J. & P. ASTON. SOUND &
SILENCE.
P. LANSKY, 513:SPRING-SUMMER/
FALL-WINTER71-340
PAZ, O. ALTERNATING CURRENT.*
L-B. HALL, 584(SWR):AUTUMN73-V
PAZ, O. THE BOW & THE LYRE.
H. VENDLER, 441:30JUN74-23
M. WOOD, 453:16MAY74-12
PAZ, O. CHILDREN OF THE MIRE.
EARLY POEMS 1935-1955.
M. WOOD, 453:16MAY74-12
PAZ, O. CONJUNCTIONS & DISJUNCTIONS.
H. VENDLER, 31(ASCH):AUTUMN74-
686
M. WOOD, 453:16MAY74-12
PAZ, O. & OTHERS. RENGA.
G. BURNS, 584(SWR):WINTER73-96
PAZZI, R. L'ESPERIENZA ANTERIORE.
617(TLS):5APR74-371
PEABODY, J.B. - SEE "JOHN ADAMS"
PEACE, R. DOSTOYEVSKY.*
T. PACHMUSS, 399(MLJ):FEB72-98
E. WASIOLEK, 594:SPRING72-86
205(FMLS):JAN72-91
PEACH, B. - SEE HUTCHESON, F.
PEAKE, M. THE DRAWINGS OF MERVYN
PEAKE.
617(TLS):29NOV74-1329
PEARCE, D. DYING IN THE SUN.
P. ADAMS, 61:JUN74-115
S. CURTIN, 441:28APR74-12
PEARCE, R. WILLIAM STYRON.
R. ASSELINEAU, 189(EA):JUL-SEP72-
450
PEARCE, T.M. OLIVER LA FARGE.
W. GARD, 584(SWR):WINTER73-V
PEARCE-HIGGINS, J.D. & G.S. WHITBY,
EDS. LIFE, DEATH & PSYCHICAL
RESEARCH.
617(TLS):5JUL74-733
PEARL, A. THE ATROCITY OF EDUCATION.
P. PICCONE, 484(PPR):SEP72-131
PEARLMAN, D.D. THE BARB OF TIME.*
E.N. CHUILLEANÁIN, 159(DM):
WINTER/SPRING71/72-117
PEARLMAN, M. THE MACCABEES.
617(TLS):11OCT74-1143
PEARN, V.A. ALICE'S ADVENTURES IN
WONDERLAND.
A. RENDLE, 157:SUMMER72-75
PEARS, D. LUDWIG WITTGENSTEIN.
R. BLANCHÉ, 542:JAN-MAR72-118
S.A.M. BURNS, 154:SEP72-478
J. CORCORAN, 660(WORD):AUG70-294
PEARSALL, D. JOHN LYDGATE.*
P.J. FRANKIS, 541(RES):NOV72-472
D. MEHL, 38:BAND90HEFT3-383
M.C. SEYMOUR, 439(NM):1972/3-729
PEARSALL, D.A. & R.A. WALDRON, EDS.
MEDIEVAL LITERATURE & CIVILIZA-
TION.*
M. GRETSCH, 72:BAND210HEFT4/6-
363
J.R. SIMON, 189(EA):JAN-MAR72-51
PEARSALL, R. COLLECTING & RESTORING
SCIENTIFIC INSTRUMENTS.
617(TLS):23AUG74-907
PEARSALL, R. EDWARDIAN LIFE & LEI-
SURE.
442(NY):9SEP74-133
617(TLS):25JAN74-72

PEARSALL, R. VICTORIAN POPULAR
MUSIC.
A. LAMB, 415:MAR73-264
PEARSALL, W.H. & W. PENNINGTON, EDS.
THE LAKE DISTRICT.
617(TLS):4JAN74-8
PEARSE, P.H., ED. THE MACKENZIE
PIPELINE.
J.C. RUSSELL, 99:NOV/DEC74-57
PEARSON, D. DREW PEARSON DIARIES,
1949-1959. (T. ABELL, ED)
W.V. SHANNON, 441:17MAR74-5
442(NY):25FEB74-127
PEARSON, J. JAMES BOND.*
617(TLS):25JAN74-67
PEARSON, L.B. MIKE. (VOL 2) (BRIT-
ISH TITLE: MEMOIRS. [VOL 2]) (J.A.
MUNRO & A.I. INGLIS, EDS)
H.V. NELLES, 99:AUG74-25
R.F. SWANSON, 441:22SEP74-36
617(TLS):5JUL74-707
PEARSON, M. THE AGE OF CONSENT.
K. NIELD, 637(VS):JUN73-475
PEARSON, M. THOSE DAMNED REBELS.
E.J. BERBUSSE, 396(MODA):WINTER
73-90
PEAVY, C.D. GO SLOW NOW.
C.H. HOLMAN, 27(AL):MAR73-132
PECCORINI, F. A METHOD OF SELF-
ORIENTATION TO THINKING.
K. OEDINGEN, 342:BAND63HEFT1-127
PECK, J. SHAGBARK.*
L. LIEBERMAN, 676(YR):WINTER73-
267
L. SEARLE, 491:MAR74-353
639(VQR):SPRING73-LXI
PECKHAM, M. THE TRIUMPH OF ROMANTI-
CISM.
G. MC NIECE, 50(ARQ):WINTER72-
367
PECKHAM, M. - SEE SWINBURNE, A.C.
PECORARO, M. SAGGI VARI DA DANTE AL
TOMMASEO.*
M. SHAPIRO, 545(RPH):FEB73-622
PÉDECH, P. - SEE POLYBIUS
PEDEN, W. TWILIGHT AT MONTICELLO.*
639(VQR):SUMMER73-CV
PEDERSEN, J., E. SPANG-HAASEN & C.
VIKNER. FRANSK SYNTAKS.
P. HÖYBYE, 209(FM):OCT72-367
PEDERSEN, O. & M. PIHL. EARLY PHYS-
ICS & ASTRONOMY.
J. NORTH, 617(TLS):20DEC74-1434
PEDERSON, D.M. SOME TECHNIQUES FOR
COMPUTER-AIDED ANALYSIS OF MUSI-
CAL SCORES.
H.S. HOWE, JR., 513:SPRING-
SUMMER/FALL-WINTER71-350
DE PÉDERY-HUNT, D. & E. FREY. MED-
ALS.
R. DESMEULES, 99:SEP74-48
PEDLER, K. & G. DAVIS. BRAINRACK.
D. REED, 362:23MAY74-672
617(TLS):15MAR74-269
PEDLEY, J.G. ANCIENT LITERARY
SOURCES ON SARDIS.
639(VQR):AUTUMN73-CLXXIV
PEDREIRA, A.S. OBRAS.
L.S. THOMPSON, 263:JUL-SEP73-343
PEDRETTI, C. LEONARDO: A STUDY IN
CHRONOLOGY & STYLE.
617(TLS):9AUG74-851

PEDRETTI, C. LEONARDO DA VINCI: THE
ROYAL PALACE AT ROMORANTIN.
639(VQR):SUMMER73-CXXVI
PEEL, J.D.Y. HERBERT SPENCER.
R.L. SCHOENWALD, 637(VS):MAR72-
379
PEETERS, L. HISTORISCHE UND LITERAR-
ISCHE STUDIEN ZUM DRITTEN TEIL DES
KUDRUNEPOS.*
D.E. LE SAGE, 402(MLR):APR73-442
PEHLKE, M. & N. LINGFELD. ROBOTER
UND GARTENLAUBE.
D. WESSELS, 205(FMLS):OCT72-372
PEHNT, W. EXPRESSIONIST ARCHITEC-
TURE.
617(TLS):19APR74-425
PEI, M. WORDS IN SHEEP'S CLOTHING.*
A.R. TELLIER, 189(EA):JUL-SEP72-
433
PEIFER, J. THE CONCEPT IN THOMISM.
A. FOREST, 542:APR-JUN72-176
PEIGNOT, J. LA TOUR.
S.G. STARY, 207(FR):DEC71-481
PEIRCE, N.R. THE DEEP SOUTH STATES
OF AMERICA.
M. IVINS, 441:21APR74-7
PEKKANEN, J. THE AMERICAN CONNEC-
TION.
R. SHERRILL, 441:7JUL74-1
PÉLADEAU, M.B. - SEE TYLER, R.
PELAYO, D. - SEE "JOSEPH DELTEIL"
PELC, J., ED. PROBLEME DER ALTPOL-
NISCHEN LITERATUR. (VOL 1)
D. TSCHIŽEWSKIJ, 72:BAND210HEFT
4/6-478
PELCZYNSKI, Z.A., ED. HEGEL'S POL-
ITICAL PHILOSOPHY.
W.V. DONIELA, 63:AUG73-176
G.A. KELLY, 479(PHQ):OCT72-364
Q. LAUER, 613:WINTER72-635
PELEKANIDES, S. KALLIERGIS.
617(TLS):8FEB74-126
PELEKANIDIS, S.M. & OTHERS. THE
TREASURES OF MOUNT ATHOS.
617(TLS):14JUN74-646
PÉLIEU, C. EMBRUNS D'EXIL TRADUITS
DU SILENCE.
R. LORRIS, 207(FR):APR72-1046
PELIKAN, J. THE EMERGENCE OF THE
CATHOLIC TRADITION (100-600).
A.W. GODFREY, 363:MAY72-106
639(VQR):AUTUMN72-CXLIV
PELIKAN, J. HISTORICAL THEOLOGY.
P. SCHRODT, 613:WINTER72-621
PELLEGRINI, C., ED. IL BOCCACCIO
NELLA CULTURA FRANCESE.
M.M., 228(GSLI):VOL149FASC465-
148
PELLETIER, G. THE OCTOBER CRISIS.
R. SIMEON, 529(QQ):SPRING72-100
R.H. WAGENBERG, 628:SPRING73-122
PELLETIER, W. & T. POOLE. NO FOREIGN
LAND.
P. ADAMS, 61:FEB74-96
PELLING, H. WINSTON CHURCHILL.
J. GRIGG, 362:25JUL74-123
S. KOSS, 617(TLS):26JUL74-781
P. STANSKY, 441:24NOV74-4
PEMBERTON, J.E. BRITISH OFFICIAL
PUBLICATIONS.
J.B. CHILDS, 517(PBSA):APR-JUN73-
197

PEÑA, H.S. RUMBOS DE ESPAÑA.
  F.H. NUESSEL, JR., 399(MLJ):APR
  72-256
PENDERS, C.L.M. THE LIFE & TIMES OF
  SUKARNO.
  617(TLS):17MAY74-516
PENICK, J. & OTHERS, EDS. THE POLI-
  TICS OF AMERICAN SCIENCE.
  42(AR):VOL32#3-510
PENN, I. WORLDS IN A SMALL ROOM.
  S. SCHWARTZ, 441:1DEC74-101
PENNACCHIETTI, F.A. STUDI SUI PRO-
  NOMI DETERMINATIVI SEMITICI.
  G. BUCCELLATI, 318(JAOS):APR-JUN
  72-296
PENNAR, J. THE U.S.S.R. & THE ARABS.
  617(TLS):11JAN74-34
PENNAR, J., I.I. BAKALO & G.Z.F.
  BEREDAY. MODERNIZATION & DIVER-
  SITY IN SOVIET EDUCATION.
  G.S. COUNTS, 550(RUSR):APR72-188
PENNATI, C. EROSAGONIE.
  617(TLS):5APR74-371
PENNINGTON, R.R. STANNARY LAW.
  617(TLS):25JAN74-88
PENNY, R.J. EL HABLA PASIEGA.*
  C. BLAYLOCK, 350:SEP73-729
PENNYCUICK, J. IN CONTACT WITH THE
  PHYSICAL WORLD.
  P. DUBOIS, 542:OCT-DEC72-475
  D.L.C. MACLACHLAN, 154:SEP72-466
PENOYRE, M. BREACH OF SECURITY.
  617(TLS):27SEP74-1033
PENROSE, R. PICASSO.
  E. YOUNG, 39:AUG72-167
PENROSE, R. & J. GOLDING, EDS.
  PICASSO 1881-1973.
  617(TLS):11JAN74-24
"LES 'PENSÉES' DE PASCAL ONT TROIS
  CENTS ANS."
  P. SELLIER, 535(RHL):JUL-AUG72-
  709
PENTECOST, H. BARGAIN WITH DEATH.
  N. CALLENDAR, 441:16JUN74-30
PENTTILÄ, A. ZUR GRUNDLAGENFOR-
  SCHUNG DER GESCHRIEBENEN SPRACHE.
  G.F. MEIER, 682(ZPSK):BAND25
  HEFT4/5-437
PEÑUELAS, M.C. & W.E. WILSON. INTRO-
  DUCCIÓN A LA LITERATURA ESPAÑOLA.
  D.H. DARST, 238:DEC72-986
PENZL, H. LAUTSYSTEM UND LAUTWANDEL
  IN DEN ALTHOCHDEUTSCHEN DIALEKTEN.*
  T.W. JUNTUNE, 320(CJL):VOL18#1-
  45
  A.L. LLOYD, 399(MLJ):NOV72-472
  W. SANDERS, 680(ZDP):BAND91HEFT3-
  427
  P. VALENTIN, 343:BAND15HEFT2-172
PENZL, H. METHODEN DER GERMANISCHEN
  LINGUISTIK.
  M.G. CLYNE, 67:MAY73-150
PÉPIN, J. DANTE ET LA TRADITION DE
  L'ALLÉGORIE.
  D.J. DONNO, 551(RENQ):WINTER72-
  442
PEPPER, S.C. THE SOURCES OF VALUE.
  A.S.C., 543:DEC71-364
PEPYS, S. THE DIARY OF SAMUEL
  PEPYS.* (VOLS 1-3) (R. LATHAM &
  W. MATTHEWS, EDS)
  P.E. JONES, 325:APR72-446

PEPYS, S. THE DIARY OF SAMUEL
  PEPYS.* (VOLS 4&5) (R. LATHAM &
  W. MATTHEWS, EDS)
  P.E. JONES, 325:APR72-446
  D. UNDERDOWN, 639(VQR):SPRING72-
  311
PEPYS, S. THE DIARY OF SAMUEL
  PEPYS.* (VOLS 6&7) (R. LATHAM &
  W. MATTHEWS, EDS)
  D. UNDERDOWN, 639(VQR):SPRING73-
  302
PEPYS, S. THE DIARY OF SAMUEL PEPYS.
  (VOL 8)`(R. LATHAM & W. MATTHEWS,
  EDS)
  H. TREVOR-ROPER, 362:27JUN74-837
  617(TLS):2AUG74-837
PERCEVAL-MAXWELL, M. THE SCOTTISH
  MIGRATION TO ULSTER IN THE REIGN
  OF JAMES I.
  617(TLS):17MAY74-525
PERCIVAL, A.C. THE ORIGINS OF THE
  HEADMASTERS' CONFERENCE.
  J.R.D. HONEY, 637(VS):SEP72-111
PERCIVAL, J. THE WORLD OF DIAGHILEV.
  M.G. SWIFT, 32:MAR73-203
PERCY, W. LOVE IN THE RUINS.*
  M.E. BRADFORD, 569(SR):AUTUMN73-
  839
  J. YARDLEY, 473(PR):2/1973-286
PERDIGÃO, J.D. - SEE UNDER DE AZER-
  EDO PERDIGÃO, J.
PEREIRO, N.G.B.D. - SEE UNDER DE FER-
  NÁNDEZ PEREIRO, N.G.B.
PERELESHIN, V. IUZHNYI DOM. STIKHI
  NA VEERE.
  G. IVASK, 550(RUSR):JAN72-99
PERELLA, N.J. NIGHT & THE SUBLIME
  IN GIACOMO LEOPARDI.*
  W.T.S., 191(ELN):SEP72(SUPP)-194
  R.O.J. VAN NUFFEL, 549(RLC):JUL-
  SEP72-472
PERELLI, L. ANTOLOGIA DELLA LETTERA-
  TURA LATINA.*
  E.J. KENNEY, 123:DEC73-280
PERELMAN, C. LE CHAMP DE L'ARGUMEN-
  TATION.
  P. BRANDES, 480(P&R):FALL72-255
PERELMAN, C. & L. OLBRECHTS-TYTECA.
  THE NEW RHETORIC.*
  D.S.S., 543:DEC71-363
PEREMANS, N. ÉRASME ET BUCER
  D'APRÈS LEUR CORRESPONDANCE.
  J-C. MARGOLIN, 535(RHL):JAN-FEB
  72-130
PERÉNYI, E. LISZT.
  R. HOWARD, 441:24NOV74-6
  C. LEHMANN-HAUPT, 441:10DEC74-43
PÉREZ-GÁLLEGO, C. NIVELES EN EL
  DRAMA DE MARLOWE.
  R. VIDÁN, 202(FMOD):JUN72-349
PÉREZ DE AYALA, R. BELARMINO &
  APOLONIO.
  D. HENN, 376:JUL72-144
  42(AR):SPRING/SUMMER72-239
PÉREZ DE AYALA, R. HONEYMOON, BIT-
  TERMOON.
  42(AR):SPRING/SUMMER72-239
PERICOLI, U. 1815 THE ARMIES AT
  WATERLOO.
  617(TLS):15FEB74-165
PERIN, C. WITH MAN IN MIND.*
  J. FREEMAN, 505:MAY72-132
PERKINS, G.C. EXPRESSIONISMUS.
  H.G. HERMANN, 406:FALL73-311

PERKINS, J.A. THE CONCEPT OF SELF
IN THE FRENCH ENLIGHTENMENT.*
P. DUBOIS, 542:JUL-SEP72-315
PERKINS, J-G. SIMÉON LA ROQUE,
POÈTE DE L'ABSENCE (1550-1615).*
L. DONALDSON-EVANS, 207(FR):OCT
71-273
J. PINEAUX, 557(RSH):JUL-SEP72-
449
PERLIS, V. CHARLES IVES REMEMBERED.
N. HENTOFF, 441:20OCT74-3
PERLMANN, M. - SEE IBN KAMMŪNA, S.M.
PERLMUTTER, D.M. DEEP & SURFACE
STRUCTURE CONSTRAINTS IN SYNTAX.
M-L. RIVERO, 350:SEP73-697
PERLMUTTER, T. WAR MOVIES.
W. FEAVER, 617(TLS):27DEC74-1471
PERLO, V. THE UNSTABLE ECONOMY.
G. BARRACLOUGH, 453:27JUN74-14
PERLOFF, M. RHYME & MEANING IN THE
POETRY OF YEATS.*
H. ADAMS, 219(GAR):FALL72-249
M. SIDNELL, 627(UTQ):SPRING72-
263
PERLOFF, M.G. THE POETIC ART OF
ROBERT LOWELL.
T. PARKINSON, 659:SUMMER74-432
PERMAN, M. REUNION WITHOUT COMPROM-
ISE.
D.T. CARTER, 639(VQR):AUTUMN73-
629
PERNETTE DE GUILLET. RYMES. (V.E.
GRAHAM, ED)
R.A. KATZ, 546(RR):OCT72-232
PERNIOLA, M. L'ALIENAZIONE ARTIS-
TICA.*
R.W. KRETSCH, 290(JAAC):SUMMER72-
570
PÉROUSE, G.A. L'EXAMEN DES ESPRITS
DU DOCTEUR JUAN HUARTE DE SAN
JUAN.
M. FRANZBACH, 549(RLC):JAN-MAR72-
142
PEROWNE, B. A SINGULAR CONSPIRACY.
M. LEVIN, 441:19MAY74-41
PEROWNE, S. THE CAESARS' WIVES.
617(TLS):31MAY74-592
PEROWNE, S. ROME FROM ITS FOUNDA-
TION TO THE PRESENT.
J. LEES-MILNE, 39:MAR72-228
639(VQR):AUTUMN72-CXLIX
PERREN, G.E. & J.L.M. TRIM, EDS.
APPLICATIONS OF LINGUISTICS.
J.R. BERNARD, 67:NOV73-321
G.C. LEPSCHY, 402(MLR):JUL73-622
PERRETT, G. DAYS OF SADNESS, YEARS
OF TRIUMPH.*
441:12MAY74-36
PERRETT, G. EXECUTIVE PRIVILEGE.
N. CALLENDAR, 441:28APR74-39
PERRIER, M. RIMBAUD.*
617(TLS):28JUN74-690
PERRINS, C. BIRDS.
617(TLS):27DEC74-1471
PERROUX, F. "INDÉPENDANCE" DE
L'ÉCONOMIE NATIONALE ET INTERDÉ-
PENDANCE DES NATIONS.
R.F. KUISEL, 207(FR):FEB72-713
PERRY, G. BLACK SWANS AT BERRIMA.
J.E. CHAMBERLIN, 249(HUDR):SUM-
MER73-389
J. TULIP, 581:JUN73-231

PERRY, G. THE GREAT BRITISH PICTURE
SHOW.
R. MAYNE, 617(TLS):6DEC74-1368
PERRY, K.I. - SEE SAGAN, F.
PERRY, P.J. BRITISH FARMING IN THE
GREAT DEPRESSION 1870-1914.
617(TLS):19APR74-408
PERRY, R. CHANGES.
M. MEWSHAW, 441:15SEP74-37
PERRY, R. LIFE AT THE SEA'S FRON-
TIERS.
617(TLS):30AUG74-936
PERRY, R. TICKET TO RIDE.
N. CALLENDAR, 441:22SEP74-42
PERSE, S-J. OEUVRES COMPLÈTES.
R. LITTLE, 208(FS):JUL73-358
PERSONÈ, L.M. IL TEATRO ITALIANO
DELLA "BELLE ÉPOQUE."
J. DAVIES, 402(MLR):OCT73-908
PERTWEE, I. TOGETHER.
J. MELLORS, 362:11APR74-477
PESCE, D. & A. SCIVOLETTO - SEE
LAMANNA, E.P.
PESCHLOW-KONDERMANN, A. REKONSTRUK-
TION DES WESTLETTNERS UND DER
OSTCHORANLAGE DES 13. JAHRHUNDERTS
IM MAINZER DOM.
H. REINHARDT, 182:VOL25#17/18-
618
PESHTICH, S.L. RUSSKAIA ISTORIO-
GRAFIIA XVIII VEKA.
J. AFFERICA, 32:JUN73-377
PESKETT, S.J. GRIM GRUESOME & GRIS-
LY.
617(TLS):29NOV74-1334
PESSOA, F. SIXTY PORTUGUESE POEMS.
(F.E.G. QUINTANILHA, ED & TRANS)
SELECTED POEMS. (P. RICKARD, ED &
TRANS) SELECTED POEMS. (J. GRIF-
FIN, ED & TRANS)
R. BURRISS, 617(TLS):18OCT74-
1160
PESTALOZZI, K. DIE ENTSTEHUNG DES
LYRISCHEN ICH.*
E. MASON, 402(MLR):JAN73-224
PETERLEY, D. PETERLEY HARVEST.
A.R. CHISHOLM, 381:DEC72-497
PETERS, A.K. JEAN COCTEAU & ANDRÉ
GIDE.
G. BRÉE, 441:24FEB74-22
PETERS, E. THE HORN OF ROLAND.
617(TLS):6SEP74-960
PETERS, E. THE MURDERS OF RICHARD
III.
N. CALLENDAR, 441:25AUG74-30
PETERS, E. THE SHADOW KING.*
D.H. GREEN, 402(MLR):OCT73-929
M.J. WILKS, 382(MAE):1973/1-111
PETERS, E.H. HARTSHORNE & NEOCLASSI-
CAL METAPHYSICS.
D.S. ROBINSON, 484(PPR):DEC72-
271
PETERS, F.E. GREEK PHILOSOPHICAL
TERMS.
W.E.W.S. CHARLTON, 123:MAR73-98
PETERS, F.E. THE HARVEST OF HELLEN-
ISM.
O. MURRAY, 123:DEC73-237
639(VQR):WINTER72-XXXII
PETERS, J. & A. SUTCLIFFE. MAKING
COSTUMES FOR SCHOOL PLAYS.
G. SQUIRE, 157:WINTER71-76
PETERS, L.T. THE 11TH PLAGUE.
M. LEVIN, 441:20JAN74-24

PFANNER, H.F. HANNS JOHST.
R. GRIMM, 221(GQ):NOV72-727
J.M. RITCHIE, 220(GL&L):APR73-
262
PFEFFER, J.A. GRUNDDEUTSCH: BASIC
(SPOKEN) GERMAN DICTIONARY FOR
EVERYDAY USAGE.*
E.A. METZGER, 399(MLJ):JAN72-61
PFEFFER, J.A. GRUNDDEUTSCH: BASIC
(SPOKEN) GERMAN WORD LIST: MITTEL-
STUFE. (PRELIMINARY ED)
E.A. METZGER, 399(MLJ):APR72-261
H. VARDAMAN, 221(GQ):JAN72-213
PFEILSCHIFTER, G., ED. ACTA REFOR-
MATIONIS CATHOLICAE. (VOL 4, PT 2)
R. STUPPERICH, 182:VOL25#3/4-123
PFIFFIG, A.J. DIE ETRUSKISCHE
SPRACHE.
A. HUS, 555:VOL46FASC2-320
C. DE SIMONE, 343:BAND14HEFT1-91
PFIFFIG, A.J. EIN OPFERGELÜBDE AN
DIE ETRUSKISCHE MINERVA.
H. RIX, 343:BAND14HEFT2-210
PHELPS, R. - SEE COCTEAU, J.
PHILIPP, E. ZUR FUNKTION DES WORTES
IN DEN GEDICHTEN GEORG TRAKLS.
R.D. SCHIER, 301(JEGP):APR73-305
PHILIPP, M. PHONOLOGIE DE L'ALLE-
MAND.
C.V.J. RUSS, 402(MLR):APR73-439
PHILIPP, M. LE SYSTÈME PHONOLOGIQUE
DU PARLER DE BLAESHEIM.*
P. WIESINGER, 680(ZDP):BAND91
HEFT3-473
PHILIPS, C.H. & M.D. WAINWRIGHT.
THE PARTITION OF INDIA.
W.H. MORRIS-JONES, 293(JAST):
AUG72-915
PHILIPS, J. THE LARKSPUR CONSPIR-
ACY.*
617(TLS):6SEP74-960
PHILIPS, J. THE POWER KILLERS.
N. CALLENDAR, 441:20OCT74-42
PHILLIPS, A. & H.F. MORRIS. MARRI-
AGE LAWS IN AFRICA.
J. VANDERLINDEN, 69:JUL72-252
PHILLIPS, A.A. HENRY LAWSON.*
B. KIERNAN, 381:SEP72-346
PHILLIPS, C.H. THE SINGING CHURCH.
W. TORTOLANO, 363:MAY72-106
PHILLIPS, D.Z. DEATH & IMMORTALITY.*
G. SLATER, 479(PHQ):JAN72-89
PHILLIPS, J. THE REFORMATION OF
IMAGES.
F. YATES, 453:30MAY74-23
PHILLIPS, M.W. CREATIVE KNITTING.
M. SONDAY, 139:DEC71-12
PHILLIPS, W. & R. KEALLEY. CHINA:
BEHIND THE MASK.*
W.O. DOUGLAS, 31(ASCH):SUMMER74-
490
PHILMUS, R.M. INTO THE UNKNOWN.*
E. KIRK, 454:FALL72-93
PHILO. PHILON D'ALEXANDRIE. (VOL
17 ED & TRANS BY E. STAROBINSKI-
SAFRAN; VOL 25 ED & TRANS BY A.
MOSES)
É. DES PLACES, 555:VOL46FASC2-
309
"PHILOLOGIA FRISICA ANNO 1969."
E.G.A. GALAMA, 433:OCT72-516
"PHONÉTIQUE ET LINGUISTIQUE ROMANES."
W. ROTHWELL, 208(FS):JAN73-115

PHOTIUS. BIBLIOTHÈQUE. (VOL 6)
(R. HENRY, ED & TRANS)
N.G. WILSON, 123:DEC73-275
PHU'O'NG-NGHI, Đ. - SEE UNDER ĐẶNG
PHU'O'NG-NGHI
PHYSICK, J. THE WELLINGTON MONU-
MENT.*
K. GARLICK, 39:JUN72-520
PIAGET, J. THE PRINCIPLES OF GEN-
ETIC EPISTEMOLOGY. INSIGHTS &
ILLUSIONS OF PHILOSOPHY. BIOLOGY
& KNOWLEDGE.
M. MORGAN, 111:20OCT72-16
PIAGET, J. STRUCTURALISM.* (FRENCH
TITLE: LE STRUCTURALISME.)
F.M. BERENSON, 483:JUL72-283
R.H.C., 125:OCT72-86
PIAGET, J., ED. LES THÉORIES DE LA
CAUSALITÉ.
Y. GAUTHIER, 154:MAR72-170
PIAMENTA, M. STUDIES IN THE SYNTAX
OF PALESTINIAN ARABIC.
R.L. CLEVELAND, 660(WORD):APR70-
142
PIANKOFF, A. THE WANDERING OF THE
SOUL. (COMPLETED BY H. JACQUET-
GORDON)
617(TLS):18OCT74-1170
PICARD, B.L. THREE ANCIENT KINGS.
R.L. GREEN, 203:AUTUMN72-259
PICARD, H.R. DIE ILLUSION DER WIRK-
LICHKEIT IM BRIEFROMAN DES ACHT-
ZEHNTEN JAHRHUNDERTS.
P-E. KNABE, 72:BAND210HEFT1/3-
228
PICARD, R. GÉNIE DE LA LITTÉRATURE
FRANÇAISE (1600-1800).*
V. RAMOS, 188(ECR):SUMMER72-150
T.G. ROOT, 207(FR):OCT71-284
PICCARD, G. DER MAGDALENENALTAR DES
"LUCAS MOSER" IN TIEFENBRONN.
W. KÖHLER, 683:BAND35HEFT3-228
PICCHIO, L.S. - SEE UNDER STEGAGNO
PICCHIO, L.
PICCOLO, L. COLLECTED POEMS OF
LUCIO PICCOLO. (B. SWANN & R.
FELDMAN, EDS & TRANS)
A. BURGESS, 385(MQR):WINTER74-74
J.E. CHAMBERLIN, 249(HUDR):SUM-
MER73-397
PICH, E. - SEE LECONTE DE LISLE, C.M.
PICHL, W.J. SHERBRO-ENGLISH DICTION-
ARY.
K.L. BAUCOM, 353:1JUL72-112
PICHOIS, C., WITH V. PICHOIS, EDS.
LETTRES À CHARLES BAUDELAIRE.
A. FAIRLIE, 617(TLS):28JUN74-688
PICHOIS, C. & A-M. ROUSSEAU. LA
LITTÉRATURE COMPARÉE.* (SPANISH
TITLE: LA LITERATURA COMPARADA;
GERMAN TITLE: VERGLEICHENDE LIT-
ERATURWISSENSCHAFT.)
J. BALDRAN & J. VOISINE,
549(RLC):OCT-DEC72-597
P. WEBER, 654(WB):11/1972-182
PICHOIS, C., WITH J. ZIEGLER - SEE
BAUDELAIRE, C.
PICKARD, R.A.E. DICTIONARY OF 1,000
BEST FILMS.
R. CAMPION, 200:AUG-SEP72-418
PICKARD, T. THE ORDER OF CHANCE.
J. SAUNDERS, 565:VOL13#3-75

281

PICKER, F. RAPA NUI.
B.M. BLACKWOOD, 617(TLS):20DEC74-
1431
PICKERING, F.P. LITERATURE & ART IN
THE MIDDLE AGES.*
R.J. BAUER, 577(SHR):FALL72-413
J. EBEL, 188(CE):FEB72-609
PICKETT, K.G. & D.K. BOULTON. MIGRA-
TION & SOCIAL ADJUSTMENT.
P. WILLMOTT, 617(TLS):15NOV74-
1281
PICKFORD, C.E., ED. THE SONG OF
SONGS.
617(TLS):30AUG74-936
PICKFORD, R.W. PSYCHOLOGY & VISUAL
AESTHETICS.
M. BORNSTEIN, 290(JAAC):SUMMER
73-552
PICKVANCE, R. DRAWINGS OF GAUGUIN.
B. LAUGHTON, 39:JAN72-68
PICO DELLA MIRANDOLA, G. ON THE
DIGNITY OF MAN, ON BEING & THE ONE,
HEPTAPLUS. (C.G. WALLIS, P.J.W.
MILLER & D. CARMICHAEL, TRANS)
P. DUBOIS, 542:APR-JUN72-173
PICON, G. LE TRAVAIL DE JEAN DUBUF-
FET.
R. CARDINAL, 617(TLS):6DEC74-
1364
PICOZZI, R. A HISTORY OF TRISTAN
SCHOLARSHIP.
W.T.H. JACKSON, 222(GR):NOV72-
310
"PICTURESQUE AMERICA."
I.R. DEE, 441:1DEC74-18
PIDHAINY, O.S. & I. OLEXANDRA, EDS.
THE UKRAINIAN REPUBLIC IN THE
GREAT EAST-EUROPEAN REVOLUTION.
V.D. MEDLIN, 550(RUSR):APR72-202
PIÉDOUE, M. LA MENACE.
F. APPEL, 207(FR):FEB72-704
PIEHLER, P. THE VISIONARY LAND-
SCAPE.*
O. BARFIELD, 382(MAE):1973/1-84
A.C. CAWLEY, 191(ELN):DEC72-142
R.O. IREDALE, 541(RES):MAY72-194
PIEKALKIEWICZ, J.A. PUBLIC OPINION
POLLING IN CZECHOSLOVAKIA, 1968-69.
J.P. SHAPIRO, 32:DEC73-837
PIEPE, A. KNOWLEDGE & SOCIAL ORDER.
R.C. ELLSWORTH, 529(QQ):SPRING72-
122
PIERCE, F. - SEE DE CAMÕES, L.
PIERCE, J-R. SYMBOLS, SIGNALS, &
NOISE.* (FRENCH TITLE: SYMBOLES,
SIGNAUX ET BRUIT.)
R.C. DOUGHERTY, 206:SEP72-150
PIERCE, O.W. THE WEDDING GUEST.
M. LEVIN, 441:5MAY74-57
PIERCE, R.B. SHAKESPEARE'S HISTORY
PLAYS.*
T.L. BERGER, 579(SAQ):WINTER73-
172
J.C. MAXWELL, 447(N&Q):APR72-159
PIERETTI, A. L'ARGOMENTAZIONE NEL
DISCORSO FILOSOFICO.
D.A. LA RUSSO, 480(P&R):FALL72-
257
PIERIDES, A. JEWELLERY IN THE
CYPRUS MUSEUM.
J. BOARDMAN, 123:DEC73-289
PIERRARD, P. LA VIE OUVRIÈRE À
LILLE SOUS LE 2ND EMPIRE.
A. LASSERRE, 182:VOL25#19/20-691

PIERRE-NOEL, A.V. NOMENCLATURE POLY-
GLOTTE DES PLANTES HAÏTIENNES ET
TROPICALES (EN 4 LANGUES).
M.A. LUBIN, 263:APR-JUN73-216
PIERREPOINT, A. EXECUTIONER: PIERRE-
POINT.
D. CANNAN, 617(TLS):29NOV74-1334
PIETTRE, A. MARX ET MARXISME.
C. SCHUWER, 542:JUL-SEP72-389
PIEYRE DE MANDIARGUES, A. MASCARETS.
S. MAX, 207(FR):FEB72-705
PIEYRE DE MANDIARGUES, A. TROISIÈME
BELVÉDÈRE.
S. MAX, 207(FR):FEB72-707
PIGGOTT, P. THE LIFE & MUSIC OF
JOHN FIELD 1782-1837.
617(TLS):25JAN74-74
PIGHI, G.B. STUDI DI RITMICA E MET-
RICA.
J. SOUBIRAN, 555:VOL46FASC1-146
PIGNATTI, T. - SEE LONGHI, P.
PIIRAINEN, I.T. GRAPHEMATISCHE
UNTERSUCHUNGEN ZUM FRÜHNEUHOCH-
DEUTSCHEN.*
W. ABRAHAM, 206:JUL72-594
W. LINDOW, 353:1OCT72-111
O. WERNER, 343:BAND14HEFT2-194
PIKE, D., GENERAL ED. AUSTRALIAN
DICTIONARY OF BIOGRAPHY. (VOL 4)
(B. NAIRN, G. SERLE & R. WARD, EDS)
617(TLS):15FEB74-155
PIKE, E.R., ED. GOLDEN TIMES.
G.B. TENNYSON, 445(NCF):DEC72-
373
PIKE, E.R., ED. HUMAN DOCUMENTS OF
ADAM SMITH'S TIME.
617(TLS):29MAR74-348
PIKE, K.L. LANGUAGE IN RELATION TO
A UNIFIED THEORY OF THE STRUCTURE
OF HUMAN BEHAVIOR. (2ND ED)
K.A. SROKA, 353:15JUN72-72
PIKE, N. GOD & TIMELESSNESS.*
W.L. ROWE, 482(PHR):JUL72-372
PIKE, R.L. BANK JOB.
N. CALLENDAR, 441:6JAN74-23
PILCH, H. ALTENGLISCHE GRAMMATIK.*
A.R. TELLIER, 189(EA):JAN-MAR72-
81
R. ZIMMERMANN, 343:BAND15HEFT2-
191
PILCH, H. ALTENGLISCHER LEHRGANG.*
A.R. TELLIER, 189(EA):JAN-MAR72-
81
PILCHER, G.W. SAMUEL DAVIES.
R. ISAAC, 656(WMQ):OCT72-657
639(VQR):WINTER72-X
PILCHER, R. ANOTHER VIEW.
M. LEVIN, 441:6OCT74-40
PILCHER, R. SLEEPING TIGER.
M. LEVIN, 441:6OCT74-41
PILLEMENT, G. PARIS POUBELLE.
R. COBB, 617(TLS):4OCT74-1058
PILLIN, W. EVERYTHING FALLING.
S. GRANGER, 448:SPRING72-101
PILLING, C. IN ALL THE SPACES ON
ALL THE LINES.
J. SAUNDERS, 565:VOL13#3-75
PILLSBURY, P.W. DESCRIPTIVE ANALY-
SIS OF DISCOURSE IN LATE WEST
SAXON TEXTS.*
A. CRÉPIN, 189(EA):JAN-MAR72-78

PIMSLEUR, P. & T. QUINN, EDS. THE
PSYCHOLOGY OF SECOND LANGUAGE
LEARNING.
J.B. DALBOR, 238:SEP72-603
G.C. LEPSCHY, 402(MLR):JUL73-622
DU PIN, P.D.L.T. - SEE UNDER DE LA
TOUR DU PIN, P.
PINCHBECK, I. & M. HEWITT. CHILDREN
IN ENGLISH SOCIETY. (VOL 2)
617(TLS):31MAY74-580
PINCKNEY, E.L. THE LETTERBOOK OF
ELIZA LUCAS PINCKNEY, 1739-1762.
(E. PINCKNEY, ED)
H.P. WILLIAMS, 579(SAQ):SPRING73-
333
639(VQR):SUMMER72-LXXXVIII
PINDER-WILSON, R., ED. PAINTINGS
FROM ISLAMIC LANDS.
D.N. WILBER, 318(JAOS):JAN-MAR72-
133
PINEAS, R. THOMAS MORE & TUDOR POL-
EMICS.*
F. CASPARI, 551(RENQ):AUTUMN72-
350
PINEDA, R. AMORES DE BOLĪVAR Y
MANUELA, POEMA.
A.A. CARSON, 37:FEB72-41
PINERO, A. THE COLLECTED LETTERS OF
SIR ARTHUR PINERO. (J.P. WEARING,
ED)
617(TLS):4OCT74-1063
PINES, M. THE BRAIN CHANGERS.
R.M. RESTAK, 441:31MAR74-27
PINGET, R. AUTOUR DE MORTIN. (A.C.
PUGH, ED)
J. CRUICKSHANK, 208(FS):JAN73-
101
F. FLAGOTHIER, 556(RLV):1972/5-
553
205(FMLS):JUL72-288
PINGET, R. FABLE. IDENTITÉ [SUIVI
DE] ABEL ET BELA.
J. ROUDAUT, 98:AUG/SEP72-729
PINGET, R. L'INQUISITOIRE.
R. HENKELS, JR., 207(FR):FEB72-
707
PINGET, R. PARALCHIMIE.
617(TLS):1MAR74-214
PINGET, R. PASSACAILLE.*
P. BROOME, 268:JUL74-135
PINGREE, D. THE THOUSANDS OF ABŪ
MA'SHAR.
S.H. NASR, 318(JAOS):OCT-DEC72-
568
PINNEY, T. - SEE MACAULAY, T.B.
PINSENT, G. THE ROWDYMAN.
A. BRENNAN, 268:JUL74-152
PINSKER, S. THE SCHLEMIEL AS META-
PHOR.
D. FUCHS, 659:AUTUMN74-562
PINTER, H. LANDSCAPE, SILENCE [&]
NIGHT.* C'ÉTAIT HIER.
D. SALEM, 189(EA):OCT-DEC72-578
PINTER, H. OLD TIMES.
R.J. NELSON, 502(PRS):SPRING72-
81
D. SALEM, 189(EA):OCT-DEC72-578
PINTNER, W.M. RUSSIAN ECONOMIC POL-
ICY UNDER NICHOLAS I.
O. CRISP, 575(SEER):OCT73-582
PINTO, E.H. & E.R. TUNBRIDGE &
SCOTTISH SOUVENIR WOODWARE.
E.T. JOY, 135:MAR72-215

PINTO, O. NUPTIALIA.
E. ZIMMERMANN, 182:VOL25#23/24-
834
617(TLS):4OCT74-1070
PIOVANI, P. PER GLI STUDI VICHIANI.
E. NAMER, 542:JUL-SEP72-341
PIPER, D.G.B. V.A. KAVERIN.*
R.D.B. THOMSON, 575(SEER):APR73-
301
PIPES, R. STRUVE.*
T. EMMONS, 104:SPRING72-161
639(VQR):WINTER72-XIV
PIRAGES, D.C. MODERNIZATION & POLI-
TICAL-TENSION MANAGEMENT.
J.R. FISZMAN, 32:SEP73-639
PIRANDELLO, L. ENRICO IV. (M.
TETEL, ED) PENSACI, GIACOMINO!
(E. LĒBANO, ED)
O. RAGUSA, 276:AUTUMN72-359
PIRE, G. LE LATIN EN QUESTION.
G. SERBAT, 555:VOL46FASC2-325
PIRENNE, M.H. OPTICS, PAINTING &
PHOTOGRAPHY.
M. BORNSTEIN, 290(JAAC):FALL72-
137
PIROMALLI, A. STUDI SUL NOVECENTO.
G. ALMANSI, 276:SPRING72-94
PIRON, H.T. ENSOR, EEN PSYCHOANAL-
YTISCHE STUDIE.
P. SOMVILLE, 542:OCT-DEC72-476
PIRSIG, R.M. ZEN & THE ART OF MOTOR-
CYCLE MAINTENANCE.
R.M. ADAMS, 453:13JUN74-22
C. LEHMANN-HAUPT, 441:16APR74-43
G. STEINER, 442(NY):15APR74-147
R. TODD, 61:SEP74-92
617(TLS):19APR74-405
DA PISA, G. DECLARATIO SUPER COME-
DIAM DANTIS. (F. MAZZONI, ED)
M.M., 228(GSLI):VOL149FASC468-
633
DE PISAN, C. THE EPISTLE OF OTHEA.*
(S. SCROPE, TRANS; C.F. BÜHLER, ED)
[SHOWN IN PREV UNDER BOTH DE PISAN
& SCROPE]
F.C. DE VRIES, 541(RES):AUG72-
327
PISANI, E. LE GÉNÉRAL INDIVIS.
617(TLS):3MAY74-461
PISANI, V. LINGUE E CULTURE.
A. ERNOUT, 555:VOL46FASC1-141
J. GONDA, 353:1OCT72-88
PITCAIRNE, A. THE ASSEMBLY. (T.
TOBIN, ED)
P.E. PARNELL, 568(SCN):SPRING73-
15
PITCHER, G. A THEORY OF PERCEPTION.*
M.S. GRAM, 486:SEP72-388
F. JACKSON, 63:MAY73-85
R.L.M., 543:SEP71-134
C.W.K. MUNDLE, 479(PHQ):JAN72-74
W.P. WARREN, 484(PPR):SEP72-136
PITCHER, H. THE CHEKHOV PLAY.
617(TLS):8FEB74-122
PITCHFORD, K. COLOR PHOTOS OF THE
ATROCITIES.
D. BLAZEK, 491:JUN74-167
J.J. MC GANN, 385(MQR):FALL74-
416
PITMAN, J.H. GOLDSMITH'S ANIMATED
NATURE.*
P.L. FARBER, 173(ECS):SUMMER73-
524

PITTERI, L. LA PERSONA UMANA, SUA
STRUTTURA ONTOLOGICA, NELLA FILO-
SOFIA DI TOMMASO D'AQUINO.
E. NAMER, 542:APR-JUN72-176
PITZ, E. PAPSTRESKRIPT UND KAISER-
RESKRIPT IM MITTELALTER.
L.E. BOYLE, 589:OCT73-780
PIVČEVIĆ, E. HUSSERL & PHENOMENOL-
OGY.
M.S.H., 543:SEP71-134
PIZER, M. TIDES FLOW.
S.E. LEE, 581:SEP73-335
PIZZEY, E. SCREAM QUIETLY OR THE
NEIGHBOURS WILL HEAR.
T. BROWN, 617(TLS):15NOV74-1290
PIZZORUSSO, A. DA MONTAIGNE A BAUDE-
LAIRE.
A. LANAPOPPI, 481(PQ):JUL72-625
PLACE, E.B., ED. AMADÍS DE GAULA.*
(VOL 4)
A. REY, 240(HR):SUMMER72-310
PLAIDY, J. A HEALTH UNTO HIS MAJES-
TY.
639(VQR):WINTER73-IX
"THE PLANETS TODAY."
617(TLS):14JUN74-646
PLANT, H.R. SYNTAKTISCHE STUDIEN ZU
DEN MONSEER FRAGMENTEN.*
W. ABRAHAM, 343:BAND14HEFT1-73
PLANTE, D. THE DARKNESS OF THE BODY.
V. CUNNINGHAM, 362:7FEB74-183
617(TLS):1FEB74-97
PLANTE, D. RELATIVES.
T. LE CLAIR, 441:20OCT74-38
PLANTIER, T. C'EST MOI DIÉGO.
J. GREENLEE, 207(FR):APR72-1047
VON PLATEN, M., ED. BERÖMDA SVENSKA
BÖCKER.
G.C. SCHOOLFIELD, 563(SS):SPRING
73-174
PLATH, S. THE BELL JAR.*
J. HURLBERT, 648:JAN73-82
PLATH, S. CROSSING THE WATER.*
T. EAGLETON, 565:VOL13#1-76
639(VQR):WINTER72-XXII
PLATH, S. WINTER TREES.*
R. PEVEAR, 249(HUDR):SPRING73-
192
PLATO. EUTHYDEMUS. (R.K. SPRAGUE,
TRANS)
P. SOMVILLE, 542:JAN-MAR72-39
PLATO. LACHES & CHARMIDES. (R.K.
SPRAGUE, ED & TRANS)
G. ANAGNOSTOPOULOS, 319:JAN74-
102
PLATO. THE LAWS. (T.J. SAUNDERS,
TRANS)
N. GULLEY, 123:MAR73-88
J.B. SKEMP, 303:VOL92-200
PLATO. THE MENO. (W.K.C. GUTHRIE,
TRANS; M. BROWN, ED)
L.S., 543:MAR72-563
PLATO. PLATON, "CRATYLE." (L.
MÉRIDIER, ED)
G. GENETTE, 98:DEC72-1019
PLATO. PLATON, "PHÉDON."* (P. VIC-
AIRE, ED & TRANS)
P. CHANTRAINE, 555:VOL46FASC2-
296
PLATO. THE "SYMPOSIUM" OF PLATO.
(S.Q. GRODEN, TRANS; J.A. BRENT-
LINGER, ED)
A.R.C. DUNCAN, 529(QQ):SUMMER72-
268

PLATO. THEAETETUS. (J. MC DOWELL,
ED & TRANS)
617(TLS):24MAY74-567
PLATONOV, A. THE FOUNDATION PIT.
P. THEROUX, 441:17MAR74-40
PLATONOV, S.F. MOSCOW & THE WEST.
(J.L. WIECZYNSKI, ED & TRANS)
R. UROFF, 32:MAR73-161
PLATONOV, S.F. THE TIME OF TROUBLES.
T. ESPER, 32:MAR73-160
PLATT, D.C.M. THE CINDERELLA SER-
VICE.
J.W. CELL, 637(VS):JUN72-481
PLATT, J.T. GRAMMATICAL FORM & GRAM-
MATICAL MEANING.
W.A. COOK, 35(AS):FALL-WINTER70-
262
PLATT, K. THE GIANT KILL.
N. CALLENDAR, 441:31MAR74-41
PLATT, V.B. & D.C. SKAGGS, EDS. OF
MOTHER COUNTRY & PLANTATIONS.
J.A. ERNST, 656(WMQ):APR73-364
PLAUTUS. AMPHITRUO.* (T. CUTT &
J.E. NYENHUIS, EDS)
R.G. PENMAN, 123:MAR73-81
PLAUTUS. AMPHITRUO.* (REV) (T.
CUTT, ED)
A. ERNOUT, 555:VOL46FASC1-149
PLAUTUS. MILES GLORIOSUS. (2ND ED)
(M. HAMMOND, A.W. MACK & W. MOSKA-
LEW, EDS)
J.G. GRIFFITH, 123:MAR73-91
PLAUTUS. PLAUTI "ASINARIA." (F.
BERTINI, ED)
M.M. WILLCOCK, 123:DEC73-160
PLAUTUS. T. MACCIUS PLAUTUS, "MOS-
TELLARIA."* (J. COLLART, ED)
M.M. WILLCOCK, 123:MAR73-36
PLAYFORD, J. AN INTRODUCTION TO THE
SKILL OF MUSICK BY JOHN PLAYFORD.
(12TH ED REV BY H. PURCELL)
D. SCOTT, 415:JUL73-704
J.A.W., 410(M&L):JUL73-368
PLEASANTS, H. THE GREAT AMERICAN
POPULAR SINGERS.
J. ROCKWELL, 441:7JUL74-2
J.S. WILSON, 441:29JUN74-27
PLEPELITS, K. DIE FRAGMENTE DER
DEMEN DES EUPOLIS.*
G. ARNOTT, 303:VOL92-198
PLEUSER, C. DIE BENENNUNGEN UND DER
BEGRIFF DES LEIDES BEI J. TAULER.*
F.W. WENTZLAFF-EGGEBERT,
680(ZDP):BAND91HEFT3-466
PLEVICH, M. & C.S. LICHTMAN. HOJAS
LITERARIAS.
J.L. MARTIN, 238:DEC72-980
PLEWNIA, M. AUF DEM WEG ZU HITLER.
H. RIDLEY, 220(GL&L):OCT72-71
PLIMPTON, G. MAD DUCKS & BEARS.*
B.G. HARRISON, 441:6JAN74-24
W. PHILLIPS, 453:7FEB74-17
PLIMPTON, G. ONE FOR THE RECORD.
R.W. CREAMER, 441:1DEC74-90
PLINY. PLINE L'ANCIEN, "HISTOIRE
NATURELLE."* (BKS 22 & 23) (J.
ANDRÉ, ED)
A. ERNOUT, 555:VOL46FASC2-337
PLOMER, W. CELEBRATIONS.
P. PORTER, 364:JUN/JUL72-144
PLOMER, W. COLLECTED POEMS.
J. FULLER, 362:7MAR74-310
617(TLS):11JAN74-28

PLOSS, E.E., ED. WALTHARIUS UND WALTHERSAGE.
C. MINIS, 680(ZDP):BAND91HEFT3-440
PLOSS, S.I., ED. THE SOVIET POLITICAL PROCESS.
J.A. ARMSTRONG, 104:SPRING72-171
J.H. HODGSON, 550(RUSR):JAN72-100
PLOTINUS. PLOTINS SCHRIFTEN. (R. HARDER, TRANS)
M. BALTES, 53(AGP):BAND54HEFT3-297
PLOURDE, M. PAUL CLAUDEL: UNE MUSIQUE DU SILENCE.*
; M. DEUEL, 402(MLR):JUL73-663
PLOWDEN, D. BRIDGES.
E.E. MORISON, 441:10NOV74-6
PLUMB, J.H. IN THE LIGHT OF HISTORY.*
566:SPRING73-110
PLUMER, J.M. TEMMOKU, A STUDY OF THE WARE OF CHIEN.
LI CHI, 385(MQR):FALL74-423
PLUMLY, S. IN THE OUTER DARK.*
H. CARLILE, 134(CP):SPRING72-81
A. PICCIONE, 577(SHR):FALL72-406
PLUMMER, A. BRONTERRE.
P. HOLLIS, 637(VS):DEC72-237
PLUTARCH. PLUTARCH'S "DE ISIDE ET OSIRIDE."* (J.G. GRIFFITHS, ED & TRANS)
H. MARTIN, JR., 24:SPRING73-98
PLUTARCH. PLUTARCHUS "DE AUDIENDIS POETIS." (L.J.R. HEIRMAN, ED & TRANS)
E.G. BERRY, 487:WINTER72-417
PLUTARCH. PLUTARQUE, "DE LA VERTU ÉTHIQUE."* (D. BABUT, ED & TRANS)
G.J.P. O'DALY, 123:DEC73-156
F.H. SANDBACH, 303:VOL92-207
PLUTARCH. PLUTARQUE, "LE DÉMON DE SOCRATE."* (A. CORLU, ED & TRANS)
G.J.P. O'DALY, 123:DEC73-155
F.H. SANDBACH, 303:VOL92-208
PLUTARCH. PLUTARQUE, "VIES."* (VOL 5) (R. FLACELIÈRE & E. CHAMBRY, EDS & TRANS)
A.J. GOSSAGE, 303:VOL92-206
PLUTARCH. PLUTARQUE, "VIES."* (VOL 6) (R. FLACELIÈRE & E. CHAMBRY, EDS & TRANS)
R.M. ERRINGTON, 123:DEC73-271
PO CHÜ-I. TRANSLATIONS FROM PO CHÜ-I'S COLLECTED WORKS. (H.S. LEVY, TRANS)
R. MC LEOD, 293(JAST):FEB72-392
POCELUEVSKIJ, E.A. TJURKSKIJ TREXČLEN.
L. HŘEBÍČEK, 353:1MAR72-123
POCHMANN, H.A. & E.N. FELTSKOG - SEE IRVING, W.
POCHODA, E.T. ARTHURIAN PROPAGANDA.*
P.J.C. FIELD, 541(RES):NOV72-466
E.D. KENNEDY, 589(APR73-397
L. MITCHELL, 382(MAE):1973/3-286
POCOCK, D.F. MIND, BODY & WEALTH.
617(TLS):8FEB74-131
PODDAR, A. RENAISSANCE IN BENGAL.
D. KOPF, 293(JAST):AUG72-971
PODRO, M. THE MANIFOLD IN PERCEPTION.*
J.G. HARRELL, 319:OCT74-537
E. SCHAPER, 518:MAY73-15

PODULKA, F. THE WONDER JUNGLE.
M. LEVIN, 441:3FEB74-30
POE, E.A. OEUVRES EN PROSE. (C. BAUDELAIRE, TRANS; Y-G. LE DANTEC, ED)
H. CIXOUS, 98:APR72-299
POE, E.A. SEVEN TALES. (C. BAUDELAIRE, TRANS; W.T. BANDY, ED)
R.M. ADAMS, 445(NCF):DEC72-361
"POEMA DE MIO CID." (C. SMITH, ED)
L.P. HARVEY, 382(MAE):1973/3-273
E.B. PLACE, 402(MLR):JUL73-670
"POEMS OF THE VIKINGS: THE ELDER EDDA." (P. TERRY, TRANS)
J.B. CONANT, 221(GQ):NOV72-782
"THE POETIC EDDA."* (VOL 1) (U. DRONKE, ED & TRANS)
R.J. GLENDINNING, 563(SS):AUTUMN 73-383
L.M. HOLLANDER, 222(GR):JAN72-73
"POETRY INTRODUCTION 2."
J. SAUNDERS, 565:VOL13#3-75
POGGI SALANI, T. IL LESSICO DELLA "TANCIA" DI MICHELANGELO BUONARROTI IL GIOVANE.
A. ALSDORF-BOLLÉE, 72:BAND210 HEFT4/6-463
M.P., 228(GSLI):VOL149FASC466/467-463
POHL, F.J. LIKE TO THE LARK.*
T. HAWKES, 676(YR):SUMMER73-561
POHL, F.J. PRINCE HENRY SINCLAIR.
A.N. RYAN, 617(TLS):13DEC74-1422
POHL, F.J. THE VIKING SETTLEMENTS OF NORTH AMERICA.
P.K. SUBLETT, 656(WMQ):OCT72-665
POINTON, M.R. MILTON & ENGLISH ART.*
D. IRWIN, 39:JAN72-72
POIRIER, R. NORMAN MAILER.*
D. FUCHS, 659:AUTUMN74-562
POIRIER, R. THE PERFORMING SELF.*
J.C. SHERWOOD, 648:OCT72-74
W. WASSERSTROM, 191(ELN):SEP72-74
POIROT-DELPECH, B. LA FOLLE DE LITUANIE.
N.L. GOODRICH, 207(FR):DEC71-482
"POLAROID PORTRAITS." (VOL 1)
E. GLAZEBROOK, 592:NOV72-198
POLE, J.R. FOUNDATIONS OF AMERICAN INDEPENDENCE, 1763-1815.
639(VQR):WINTER73-XXXV
POLIAKOV, L. THE ARYAN MYTH.
442(NY):16SEP74-149
POLIN, R. LA POLITIQUE DE LA SOLITUDE.
D.L. SCHALK, 481(PQ):JUL72-757
POLIŠENSKÝ, J.V. THE THIRTY YEARS WAR.*
639(VQR):SUMMER72-XCVII
POLITZER, R.L. ACTIVE REVIEW OF GERMAN.
R. DETSCH, 399(MLJ):NOV72-473
POLITZER, R.L. PRACTICE-CENTERED TEACHER TRAINING: FRENCH. (VOL 1)
G.C. LIPTON, 207(FR):MAR72-881
A. PAPALIA, 399(MLJ):MAR72-191
POLITZER, R.L. TEACHING GERMAN.
D.P. LOTZE, 221(GQ):NOV72-797
POLITZER, R.L. & F.N. TEACHING ENGLISH AS A SECOND LANGUAGE.
D. MAJOR, 608:SEP73-337

POLITZER, R.L. & L. WEISS. IMPROV-
ING ACHIEVEMENT IN FOREIGN LAN-
GUAGE.*
  W.J. CAMERON, 238:MAY72-397
  G.C. LIPTON, 207(FR):MAR72-881
POLITZER, R.L. & L. WEISS. THE SUC-
CESSFUL FOREIGN-LANGUAGE TEACHER.*
  W.J. CAMERON, 238:SEP72-606
  G.C. LIPTON, 207(FR):MAR72-881
POLK, J.K. CORRESPONDENCE OF JAMES
K. POLK. (VOL 2) (H. WEAVER & P.H.
BERGERON, EDS)
  639(VQR):WINTER73-XXVIII
POLLACK, H. JEWISH FOLKWAYS IN GER-
MANIC LANDS (1648-1806).
  E.R. SAMUEL, 203:SPRING72-85
  G. WARSHAVER, 292(JAF):JUL-SEP
  72-282
POLLARD, D.E. A CHINESE LOOK AT
LITERATURE.
  617(TLS):14JUN74-634
POLLARD, G. A CATALOGUE OF THE
GREEK COINS IN THE COLLECTION OF
SIR STEPHEN COURTAULD AT THE UNI-
VERSITY COLLEGE OF RHODESIA.
  J.F. HEALY, 123:DEC73-256
POLLARD, R. THE CREAM MACHINE.
  617(TLS):12JUL74-741
POLLARD, S. EUROPEAN ECONOMIC INTE-
GRATION 1815-1970.
  617(TLS):27SEP74-1048
POLLARD, S. THE IDEA OF PROGRESS.
  H.A. BARTON, 125:OCT72-89
POLLIN, B.R. DICTIONARY OF NAMES &
TITLES IN POE'S COLLECTED WORKS.
  P. DISKIN, 447(N&Q):AUG72-315
POLLIN, B.R. DISCOVERIES IN POE.*
  J.M. FLORA, 573(SSF):SPRING72-
  211
  R.G. THOMAS, 541(RES):NOV72-530
POLLIN, B.R. GODWIN CRITICISM.*
  H-J. LANG, 38:BAND90HEFT1/2-249
POLLINI, F. DUBONNET.
  617(TLS):5APR74-375
POLLITT, J.J. ART & EXPERIENCE IN
CLASSICAL GREECE.*
  639(VQR):SUMMER72-CVIII
POLLMANN, L. "TROBAR CLUS."
  L.J. FRIEDMAN, 545(RPH):MAY73-
  711
POLOMÉ, E.C., ED. OLD NORSE LITERA-
TURE & MYTHOLOGY.*
  M. CIKLAMINI, 222(GR):JAN72-68
POLOMÉ, E.C. SWAHILI LANGUAGE HAND-
BOOK.
  R. OHLY, 353:1MAR72-124
POLONSKY, A. POLITICS IN INDEPEN-
DENT POLAND 1921-39.*
  N. DAVIES, 575(SEER):APR73-321
POLT, J.H.R. - SEE FORNER, J.P.
POLT, J.R. GASPAR MELCHOR DE JOVEL-
LANOS.
  R.M. COX, 481(PQ):JUL72-711
  I.L. MC CLELLAND, 402(MLR):OCT73-
  915
POLYBIUS. HISTOIRES. (BK 3) (J. DE
FOUCAULT, ED & TRANS)
  F.W. WALBANK, 303:VOL92-205
POLYBIUS. POLYBE, "HISTOIRES." (BK
2) (P. PÉDECH, ED & TRANS)
  F.W. WALBANK, 123:MAR73-30

POMEAU, R. L'AGE CLASSIQUE, III,
1680-1720.
  R. MERCIER, 557(RSH):APR-JUN72-
  310
POMMER, R. EIGHTEENTH-CENTURY
ARCHITECTURE IN PIEDMONT.
  H.A. MILLON, 54:SEP72-357
POMONTI, J-C. & S. THION. DES COUR-
TISANS AUX PARTISANS.
  D.P. CHANDLER, 293(JAST):MAY73-
  730
POMORSKA, K., ED. FIFTY YEARS OF
RUSSIAN PROSE.*
  639(VQR):SUMMER72-CVI
POMPER, P. PETER LAVROV & THE RUS-
SIAN REVOLUTIONARY MOVEMENT.*
  A.P. MENDEL, 32:DEC73-812
POMYALOVSKY, N.G. SEMINARY SKETCHES.
  617(TLS):18JAN74-59
PONCÉ, C. KABBALAH.
  617(TLS):1NOV74-1240
PONCE DE LEÓN, L.S. LA NOVELA ESPAÑ-
OLA DE LA GUERRA CIVIL (1936-1939).
  F. SEDWICK, 238:DEC72-969
PONCHON, R. LA MUSE FRONDEUSE.
  M. SCHAETTEL, 557(RSH):JUL-SEP72-
  478
POND, K.S. FRENCH BY DEGREES.
  G.R. DANNER, 207(FR):OCT71-288
PONDROM, C.N. THE ROAD FROM PARIS.
  617(TLS):11OCT74-1135
PONGE, F. LA FABRIQUE DU PRÉ.
  C. PRIGENT, 98:JUN72-505
PONGE, F. THINGS.* (C. CORMAN, ED
& TRANS)
  G. BURNS, 584(SWR):WINTER73-96
PONGE, F. THE VOICE OF THINGS. (B.
ARCHER, TRANS)
  R. PEVEAR, 249(HUDR):SPRING73-
  192
PONGE, F. THE VOICE OF THINGS. (B.
BROMBERT, ED & TRANS)
  639(VQR):SPRING73-LXII
PONS, M. MADEMOISELLE B.
  P. ADAMS, 61:NOV74-124
PONTANO, G. DE MAGNANIMITATE. (F.
TATEO, ED)
  D. AGUZZI-BARBAGLI, 276:SUMMER72-
  264
PONTING, K.G. THE WOOLLEN INDUSTRY
OF SOUTHWEST ENGLAND.
  J.L. NEVINSON, 135:JAN72-64
  E.M. SIGSWORTH, 637(VS):MAR73-
  356
PONZALLI, R. AVERROIS IN LIBRUM V
(Δ) METAPHYSICORUM ARISTOTELIS COM-
MENTARIUS.
  J. JOLIVET, 182:VOL25#11-331
POOLE, P.A. THE VIETNAMESE IN THAI-
LAND.*
  M. SMITHIES, 302:JUL72-221
POPE, A. ALEXANDER POPE: A CRITICAL
ANTHOLOGY. (F.W. BATESON & N.A.
JOUKOVSKY, EDS)
  566:SPRING72-87
POPE, A.U., ED. A SURVEY OF PERSIAN
ART. (VOL 14)
  P. HARPER, 57:VOL34#4-354
POPE, D. RAMAGE'S PRIZE.
  617(TLS):16AUG74-877
POPE, J.A. & OTHERS. THE FREER
CHINESE BRONZES.* (VOL 1)
  M. TREGEAR, 90:MAY72-337
POPE, M.K. - SEE THOMAS

POPE-HENNESSY, J. FRA ANGELICO.
W. FEAVER, 362:19&26DEC74-847
J. RUSSELL, 441:1DEC74-54
POPE-HENNESSY, J. ITALIAN RENAIS-
SANCE SCULPTURE. (2ND ED) ITAL-
IAN HIGH RENAISSANCE & BAROQUE
SCULPTURE.* (2ND ED)
P. CANNON-BROOKES, 39:JAN72-71
POPE-HENNESSY, J. RAPHAEL.*
K.W. FORSTER, 56:WINTER72-423
E. VERHEYEN, 54:DEC72-550
J. WISE, 290(JAAC):FALL71-142
POPE-HENNESSY, J. ROBERT LOUIS
STEVENSON.
B. CHATWIN, 617(TLS):25OCT74-
1195
M. LASKI, 362:31OCT74-585
POPE-HENNESSY, J. THE VICTORIA &
ALBERT MUSEUM YEARBOOK, 4.
617(TLS):19JUL74-772
POPE-HENNESSY, J. & A.J. RADCLIFFE.
THE FRICK COLLECTION.* (VOL 3)
J. MONTAGU, 90:JUN72-410
POPE-HENNESSY, J., A.J. RADCLIFFE &
T.W.I. HODGKINSON. THE FRICK COL-
LECTION.* (VOLS 1 & 2)
K. ROBERTS, 90:JUN72-405
POPE-HENNESSY, J., A.J. RADCLIFFE &
T.W.I. HODGKINSON. THE FRICK COL-
LECTION.* (VOL 4)
J. MONTAGU, 90:JUN72-410
POPE HENNESSY, J. ANTHONY TROLLOPE.*
N.J. HALL, 445(NCF):MAR73-477
D. SKILTON, 637(VS):JUN72-485
J. SYMONS, 364:APR/MAY72-133
POPHAM, A.E. CATALOGUE OF THE DRAW-
INGS OF PARMIGIANINO.
C. GOULD, 39:AUG72-163
R.W. LIGHTBOWN, 135:MAY72-62
POPHAM, M. A BLANK BOOK.
M. LEVIN, 441:19MAY74-41
POPOVIČ, A. ŠTRUKTURALIZMUS V SLOV-
ENSKEJ VEDE (1931-1949).
H-J. SCHLEGEL, 490:APR72-238
POPPER, K.R. OBJECTIVE KNOWLEDGE.*
P. SINGER, 453:2MAY74-22
R.G. SWINBURNE, 518:MAY73-17
POPPERWELL, R.G. THE PRONUNCIATION
OF NORWEGIAN.
G.F. MEIER, 682(ZPSK):BAND25
HEFT6-541
POPPERWELL, R.G., ED. THE YEAR'S
WORK IN MODERN LANGUAGE STUDIES.
(VOL 31, 1969)
M.P., 228(GSLI):VOL149FASC465-
148
POPS, M.L. THE MELVILLE ARCHETYPE.*
P. MC CARTHY, 594:SPRING72-98
"POPULATION PROBLEMS IN THE VICTOR-
IAN AGE."
617(TLS):29MAR74-343
PORCELLI, B. STUDI SULLA "DIVINA
COMMEDIA."*
M.M., 228(GSLI):VOL149FASC465-
141
PORIET, M. BODYTALK.
E.A. SCHMERLER, 186(ETC.):JUN72-
215
PÖRKSEN, U. DER ERZÄHLER IM MITTEL-
HOCHDEUTSCHEN EPOS.*
F.H. BÄUML, 564:OCT72-223
D.H. GREEN, 402(MLR):OCT73-932
B. HAUPT, 72:BAND210HEFT1/3-163
[CONTINUED]

[CONTINUING]
D.A. HOWARD, 220(GL&L):JUL73-346
W.H. JACKSON, 382(MAE):1973/1-62
H. REINITZER, 182:VOL25#11-362
PÖRNBACHER, K. - SEE "FRANZ GRILLPAR-
ZER"
PORPHYRY. PORPHYRII, "QUAESTIONUM
HOMERICARUM." (BK 1) (A.R. SODANO,
ED)
F. BUFFIÈRE, 555:VOL46FASC1-106
R.R. SCHLUNK, 24:SPRING73-101
PORSET, C., ED. VARIA LINGUISTICA.*
R. POSNER, 208(FS):APR73-216
PORTER, A. A MUSICAL SEASON.
J. YOHALEM, 441:7JUL74-2
PORTER, D., ED. EARLY NEGRO WRITING
1760-1837.
M.L. FISHER, 432(NEQ):JUN72-296
G. FULKERSON, 583:FALL72-112
PORTER, E. THE FOLKLORE OF EAST
ANGLIA.
617(TLS):4OCT74-1075
PORTER, G. & R. CUFF, EDS. ENTER-
PRISE & NATIONAL DEVELOPMENT.
T. TRAVES, 99:MAY/JUN74-40
PORTER, H. SELECTED STORIES. (L.
KRAMER, ED)
R.B.J. WILSON, 381:JUN72-224
PORTER, J. ONLY WITH A BARGEPOLE.
N. CALLENDAR, 441:24MAR74-41
PORTER, M. & OTHERS. DOES MONEY
MATTER?
P. AXELROD, 99:NOV/DEC74-29
PORTER, P. AFTER MARTIAL.*
J.E. CHAMBERLIN, 249(HUDR):SUM-
MER73-401
S.E. LEE, 581:SEP73-335
639(VQR):AUTUMN73-CXLI
PORTER, P. PREACHING TO THE CON-
VERTED.*
J.E. CHAMBERLIN, 249(HUDR):SUM-
MER73-401
J. GALASSI, 491:NOV73-113
S.E. LEE, 581:SEP73-335
639(VQR):AUTUMN73-CXLI
PORTER, R.J. & J.D. BROPHY, EDS.
MODERN IRISH LITERATURE.
R.J. FINNERAN, 329(JJQ):SPRING74-
293
PORTERFIELD, A.L. THE NEW GENERA-
TION.
C. JACKSON, 577(SHR):FALL72-410
"A PORTFOLIO OF THOMAS BEWICK WOOD
ENGRAVINGS."
N. BARKER, 78(BC):SPRING72-138
PORTIER, L. DANTE.
G. VANWELKENHUYZEN, 549(RLC):
JUL-SEP72-453
DE LA PORTILLA, M. & T. COLCHIE.
TEXTBOOKS IN SPANISH & PORTUGUESE.
H.C. WOODBRIDGE, 399(MLJ):OCT72-
410
PORTOGHESI, P. THE ROME OF BORRO-
MINI.
H.A. MILLON, 576:OCT72-243
PORTOGHESI, P. ROME OF THE RENAIS-
SANCE.
T. LASK, 55:APR73-14
617(TLS):29MAR74-318
"POSITIONS DES THÈSES DE TROISIÈME
CYCLE SOUTENUES DEVANT LA FACULTÉ
EN 1969."
J. DECREUS, 208(FS):APR73-237

POSNER, D. ANNIBALE CARRACCI.*
  G. MARTIN, 39:APR72-338
  E. WATERHOUSE, 90:AUG72-562
POSNER, R. - SEE IORDAN, I. & J. ORR
POSPESEL, H. ARGUMENTS.
  T.G.N., 543:DEC71-364
POSPIELOVSKY, D. RUSSIAN POLICE
  TRADE UNIONISM.*
  A.G. MAZOUR, 550(RUSR):OCT72-430
VAN DER POST L. A FAR OFF PLACE.
  K. GRAHAM, 362:19SEP74-381
  M. LEVIN, 441:22SEP74-40
POST, S. PLAYING IN THE FM BAND.
  A. KOPKIND, 453:8AUG74-33
POSTAL, P.M. ASPECTS OF PHONOLOGI-
  CAL THEORY.*
  E.C. FUDGE, 297(JL):FEB72-136
  O.F. KRIVNOVA & S.V. KODZASOV,
  353:15DEC72-111
  R. POSNER, 545(RPH):MAY73-664
POSTAN, M.M. FACT & REFERENCE.
  M. MARTIN, 486:DEC72-569
POSTAN, M.M. THE MEDIEVAL ECONOMY
  & SOCIETY.*
  639(VQR):AUTUMN73-CLXVI
POSTEL, R. JOHANN MARTIN LAPPENBERG.
  C.E. MC CLELLAND, 182:VOL25#15/
  16-571
POSTER, M. THE UTOPIAN THOUGHT OF
  RESTIF DE LA BRETONNE.*
  D. COWARD, 208(FS):JUL73-340
POSTGATE, J. A PLAIN MAN'S GUIDE TO
  JAZZ.
  617(TLS):5JUL74-706
POSTGATE, J.N. NEO-ASSYRIAN ROYAL
  GRANTS & DECREES.
  R.A. HENSHAW, 318(JAOS):APR-JUN
  72-291
POSTL, B. DIE BEDEUTUNG DES NIL IN
  DER RÖMISCHEN LITERATUR.
  J.G. GRIFFITHS, 123:DEC73-278
POSTMAN, N. & C. WEINGARTNER. TEACH-
  ING AS A SUBVERSIVE ACTIVITY. THE
  SOFT REVOLUTION.
  G. KUNZMAN, 186(ETC.):SEP72-326
POSTON, E. & P. ARMA. THE FABER
  BOOK OF FRENCH FOLK SONGS.
  F. HOWES, 415:JUL73-703
POTHOLM, C.P. & R. DALE, EDS.
  SOUTHERN AFRICA IN PERSPECTIVE.
  K. GLASER, 396(MODA):SPRING73-
  210
  639(VQR):SPRING73-LXXXVII
POTOK, C. MY NAME IS ASHER LEV.
  M. ABRAMS, 287:NOV72-29
POTONNIER, G.E. & B. WÖRTERBUCH FÜR
  WIRTSCHAFT, RECHT UND HANDEL.
  (VOL 2)
  E. WEIS, 75:3/1972-35
PÖTSCHER, W. STRUKTURPROBLEME DER
  ARISTOTELISCHEN UND THEOPHRASTIS-
  CHEN GOTTESVORSTELLUNG.
  P.M. HUBY, 123:MAR73-52
POTTER, D. & P. SARRE, EDS. DIMEN-
  SIONS OF SOCIETY.
  617(TLS):15NOV74-1279
POTTER, D.M. HISTORY & AMERICAN
  SOCIETY.* (D.E. FEHRENBACHER, ED)
  639(VQR):AUTUMN73-CLXIV
  676(YR):SUMMER73-X
POTTER, D.M. THE SOUTH & THE CONCUR-
  RENT MAJORITY.
  639(VQR):WINTER73-XXXIV

POTTER, J.M. CAPITALISM & THE CHI-
  NESE PEASANT.
  J. WONG, 302:JAN72-72
POTTER, K.H., COMP. BIBLIOGRAPHY OF
  INDIAN PHILOSOPHIES.
  L. ROCHER, 293(JAST):AUG72-960
POTTER, L. A PREFACE TO MILTON.
  R.E.C. HOUGHTON, 541(RES):NOV72-
  497
POTTHAST, A., ED. REPERTORIUM FON-
  TIUM HISTORIAE MEDII AEVI. (VOLS
  1-3)
  U. DIRLMEIER, 182:VOL25#15/16-
  572
POTTIER, B. GRAMÁTICA DEL ESPAÑOL.
  D.N. CARDENAS, 238:MAR72-198
POUCET, J. RECHERCHES SUR LA LÉG-
  ENDE SABINE DES ORIGINES DE ROME.
  J. PINSENT, 313:VOL62-178
POUGIN, A. - SEE CLÉMENT, F. & P.
  LAROUSSE
POULET, G. & R. KOPP. BAUDELAIRE.
  E.M. LEVITINE, 127:FALL72-102
POULIN, A., JR. IN ADVENT.*
  B. MATHIEU, 134(CP):FALL72-74
POULTON, D. JOHN DOWLAND.*
  M.H. FRANK, 568(SCN):FALL-WINTER
  73-98
POUND, E. SELECTED PROSE, 1909-
  1965.* (W. COOKSON, ED)
  J.C. DE VANY, 590:FALL/WINTER
  73/74-42
  H. LOMAS, 364:JUN/JUL73-141
  639(VQR):AUTUMN73-CXLVIII
POUND, R. ALBERT.
  442(NY):18MAR74-151
POW-KEY, S., KIM CHOL-CHOON & HONG
  YI-SUP - SEE UNDER SOHN POW-KEY,
  KIM CHOL-CHOON & HONG YI-SUP
POWE, B. THE LAST DAYS OF THE AMERI-
  CAN EMPIRE.
  M. LEVIN, 441:6OCT74-41
POWELL, J.M., ED & TRANS. THE LIBER
  AUGUSTALIS OR CONSTITUTIONS OF
  MELFI.*
  D.R. KELLEY, 377:MAR73-40
  W.A. PERCY, 589:APR73-402
POWELL, L.C. CALIFORNIA CLASSICS.*
  M.L. HARTLEY, 584(SWR):SPRING73-
  190
POWELL, N. FUSELI: THE NIGHTMARE.*
  A. FRANKENSTEIN, 55:SUMMER73-78
POWELL, P.W. TREE OF HATE.
  D.E. WORCESTER, 263:APR-JUN73-
  204
POWELL, T. - SEE CAMERON, J.M.
POWELL, V. A COMPTON-BURNETT COMPEN-
  DIUM.*
  J. GINGER, 364:JUN/JUL73-148
POWELL, W.R., ED. A HISTORY OF THE
  COUNTY OF ESSEX. (VOL 6)
  617(TLS):1MAR74-217
POWELL, W.S. THE FIRST STATE UNIVER-
  SITY.
  639(VQR):AUTUMN72-CLVI
POWER, E.T. CATHOLIC HIGHER EDUCA-
  TION IN AMERICA.
  C.A. HANGARTNER, 377:JUL73-118
POWERS, J.R. THE LAST CATHOLIC IN
  AMERICA.*
  W. SHEED, 453:7MAR74-18
POWERSCOURT, S. SUN TOO FAST.
  617(TLS):1MAR74-215

POWNALL, D. THE RAINING TREE WAR.
617(TLS):2AUG74-825
POWYS, J.C. WEYMOUTH SANDS. ROD-
MOOR.
617(TLS):8FEB74-121
POZDNEYEV, A.M. MONGOLIA & THE MON-
GOLS.
D.M. FARQUHAR, 293(JAST):AUG72-
958
"PRACHUM SILA CHARUK, PHAK THI 4."
D.K. WYATT, 293(JAST):NOV71-227
PRADINES, M. TRATADO DE PSICOLOGIA
GENERAL.
A. GRAPPE, 542:OCT-DEC72-478
PRAGER, F.D. & G. SCAGLIA. BRUNEL-
LESCHI.
H. SAALMAN, 576:OCT72-241
PRASSE, L.E. LYONEL FEININGER, A
DEFINITIVE CATALOGUE OF HIS GRAPH-
IC WORK.
A. FRANKENSTEIN, 55:MAR73-16
PRATER, D.A. EUROPEAN OF YESTERDAY.
E. BURGSTALLER, 67:NOV73-317
D.G. DAVIAU, 406:SUMMER73-180
H. ZOHN, 301(JEGP):APR73-300
205(FMLS):OCT72-384
PRATI, A. ETIMOLOGIE VENETE. (G.
FOLENA & G. PELLEGRINI, EDS)
G.P. CLIVIO, 405(MP):AUG72-90
PRATOLINI, V. CRONACA FAMILIARE.
(I.T. OLKEN, ED)
E.A. LEBANO, 276:AUTUMN72-354
PRATT, J.C. THE LAOTIAN FRAGMENTS.
M. LEVIN, 441:14JUL74-20
PRATT, V. RELIGION & SECULARISATION.
G. SLATER, 479(PHQ):JAN72-89
PRAUSS, G. ERSCHEINUNG BEI KANT.*
R.B. PIPPIN, 319:JUL74-403
PRAWER, J. THE LATIN KINGDOM OF
JERUSALEM. THE WORLD OF THE CRU-
SADERS.
617(TLS):5APR74-367
PRAWER, S. HEINE & SHAKESPEARE.
C.P. MAGILL, 220(GL&L):APR73-248
PRAWER, S., ED. THE ROMANTIC PERIOD
IN GERMANY.*
L.R. FURST, 220(GL&L):JUL73-333
PRAWER, S., ED. SEVENTEEN MODERN
GERMAN POETS.
J.C. MIDDLETON, 220(GL&L):JAN73-
180
205(FMLS):JUL72-289
PRAWER, S.S. COMPARATIVE LITERARY
STUDIES.
617(TLS):1FEB74-105
PRAY, B.R. TOPICS IN HINDI-URDU
GRAMMAR.
P.E. HOOK, 293(JAST):FEB72-444
PRAZ, M. CONVERSATION PIECES.
R. EDWARDS, 135:FEB72-138
PRAZ, M. MNEMOSYNE.*
E.H. GOMBRICH, 90:MAY72-345
J.B. GORDON, 290(JAAC):WINTER71-
257
PREAUX, J. - SEE HORACE
PRENDERGAST, C.A. - SEE MICHEL, G.
PRENTICE, R.P. THE BASIC QUIDDITA-
TIVE METAPHYSICS OF DUNS SCOTUS AS
SEEN IN HIS "DE PRIMO PRINCIPIO."
A.B.W., 543:MAR72-565
PREOBRAZHENSKY, A.A. URAL I ZAPAD-
NAIA SIBIR' V KONTSE XVI-NACHALE
XVIII VEKA.
G. HANSON, 32:DEC73-806

PRESCOTT, P.S. A DARKENING GREEN.
C. TRILLIN, 441:5MAY74-54
442(NY):6MAY74-143
PRESS, A.R., ED & TRANS. ANTHOLOGY
OF TROUBADOUR LYRIC POETRY.
J.H. MARSHALL, 382(MAE):1973/2-
162
205(FMLS):APR72-194
PRESS, J. THE LENGTHENING SHADOWS.*
A. RODWAY, 541(RES):AUG72-383
PRESSAT, R. A WORKBOOK IN DEMOGRA-
PHY.
617(TLS):23AUG74-908
PRESSMAN, E. LA CHASSE.
D.M. CHURCH, 207(FR):MAY72-1183
PRESSMAN, J.L. & A.B. WILDAVSKY.
IMPLEMENTATION.*
H.W. CHASE, 639(VQR):AUTUMN73-
617
PREST, J. LORD JOHN RUSSELL.
P. HONAN, 637(VS):JUN73-455
PREST, T.P. VARNEY THE VAMPYRE.
N. KIRBY, 651(WHR):SPRING73-210
PREST, T.P. - SEE UNDER RYMER, J.M.
PRESTHUS, R. ELITE ACCOMMODATION IN
CANADIAN POLITICS.
J. MEISEL, 99:MAY/JUN74-44
PRESTON, A., ED. WARSHIPS IN PRO-
FILE. (VOL 3)
617(TLS):31MAY74-592
PRESTON, N., ED. WISDEN CRICKETERS'
ALMANACK.
617(TLS):17MAY74-533
PRESTWICH, M. WAR, POLITICS & FIN-
ANCE UNDER EDWARD I.
617(TLS):15MAR74-268
PREVOST, A. THOMAS MORE ET LA CRISE
DE LA PENSEE EUROPEENNE.
G. MARC'HADOUR, 551(RENQ):
AUTUMN72-348
PREVOST, G. & K. DUNLOP. LA FRANCE
EN MARCHE.
P. SIEGEL, 207(FR):MAY72-1201
PREZZOLINI, G. CRISTO E/O MACHIA-
VELLI.
G.P. BARRICELLI, 275(IQ):FALL/
WINTER72-133
PRICE, A. OCTOBER MEN.
N. CALLENDAR, 441:29SEP74-41
617(TLS):18JAN74-61
PRICE, A. OTHER PATHS TO GLORY.
617(TLS):20DEC74-1437
PRICE, C. - SEE SHERIDAN, R.B.
PRICE, G. THE FRENCH LANGUAGE.*
205(FMLS):JUL72-288
PRICE, H.H. BELIEF.*
J.R.H., 543:SEP71-135
K. MARC-WOGAU, 482(PHR):APR72-
246
PRICE, H.H. ESSAYS IN THE PHILOSO-
PHY OF RELIGION.
D.Z. PHILLIPS, 311(JP):14MAR74-
151
PRICE, J.L. CULTURE & SOCIETY IN
THE DUTCH REPUBLIC DURING THE 17TH
CENTURY.
617(TLS):23AUG74-909
PRICE, L.B., ED. MARCEL PROUST.
617(TLS):17MAY74-515
639(VQR):AUTUMN73-CLIII
PRICE, R. AN IMPERIAL WAR & THE
BRITISH WORKING CLASS.*
A.P. HAYDON, 637(VS):JUN73-472

PRICE, R. PERMANENT ERRORS.* A
LONG & HAPPY LIFE.
J. YARDLEY, 473(PR):2/1973-286
PRICE, R. THE WANDERERS.
C. LEHMANN-HAUPT, 441:20MAR74-45
R. SALE, 453:27JUN74-24
H. SELBY, JR., 441:21APR74-38
442(NY):20MAY74-150
PRICE, V. - SEE BÜCHNER, G.
PRIDE, J.B. THE SOCIAL MEANING OF
LANGUAGE.
W.J. SAMARIN, 320(CJL):VOL18#1-
86
PRIDHAM, G. HITLER'S RISE TO POWER.
A.J. NICHOLLS, 617(TLS):8NOV74-
1264
DU PRIER, J. - SEE UNDER JEAN DU
PRIER
PRIEST, C. INVERTED WORLD.
R. BLYTHE, 362:13JUN74-777
PRIESTLAND, G. THE FUTURE OF VIO-
LENCE.
J. NAUGHTON, 362:12SEP74-349
PRIESTLEY, F.E.L. LANGUAGE & STRUC-
TURE IN TENNYSON'S POETRY.
617(TLS):15MAR74-267
PRIESTLEY, J.B. OUTCRIES & ASIDES.
P. CAMPBELL, 362:19SEP74-381
PRIESTLEY, J.B. VICTORIA'S HEYDAY.
A.B., 155:SEP72-194
PRIESTLEY, J.B. A VISIT TO NEW ZEA-
LAND.
P. CAMPBELL, 362:19SEP74-381
617(TLS):20SEP74-1019
PRIMMER, B. THE BERLIOZ STYLE.
H.J.M., 410(M&L):OCT73-457
PRIN, C. CÉRÉMONIAL POUR UN COMBAT.
J. DECOCK, 207(FR):MAR72-894
PRINCE, H. CONTRADICTIONS.
B. ATKINSON, 441:24NOV74-16
PRINCE, P. DOGCATCHER.
V. CUNNINGHAM, 362:28MAR74-413
617(TLS):29MAR74-313
PRINGLE, J.D. HAVE PEN: WILL
TRAVEL.*
E.J.B. ROSE, 364:DEC73/JAN74-151
PRINGLE, L. WILD RIVER.
639(VQR):WINTER73-XLIV
PRINGLE, R. THE LETTERBOOK OF ROB-
ERT PRINGLE.* (W.B. EDGAR, ED)
P.M. VAN EE, 656(WMQ):APR73-362
PRINGLE, R. RAJAHS & REBELS.*
C. CRISSWELL, 302:JUL72-217
PRINZ, W. DIE SAMMLUNG DER SELBST-
BILDNISSE IN DEN UFFIZIEN. (VOL 1)
D. HEIKAMP, 90:FEB72-98
PRIOR, A.N. OBJECTS OF THOUGHT.
(P.T. GEACH & A.J.P. KENNY, EDS)
T.R. BALDWIN, 479(PHQ):APR72-174
M. CLARK, 483:JUL72-278
C.G. PRADO, 154:MAR72-150
K.T., 543:DEC71-364
PRIOR, M. THE LITERARY WORKS OF MAT-
THEW PRIOR.* (2ND ED) (H.B.
WRIGHT & M.K. SPEARS, EDS)
L.C. BONNEROT, 189(EA):APR-JUN72-
329
PRIP-MOLLER, J. CHINESE BUDDHIST
MONASTERIES.
M. CHOU, 60:MAY-JUN73-68
PRITCHARD, A. - SEE COWLEY, A.
PRITCHARD, R.E. D.H. LAWRENCE.
V. MAHON, 541(RES):MAY72-239
J.E. STOLL, 219(GAR):FALL72-397

PRITCHETT, V.S. THE CAMBERWELL BEAU-
TY.
P. ADAMS, 61:NOV74-123
A. BROYARD, 441:16SEP74-33
D.A.N. JONES, 617(TLS):25OCT74-
1182
P. MORTIMER, 441:15SEP74-31
PRITCHETT, V.S. LONDON PERCEIVED.
(NEW ED)
D.A.N. JONES, 617(TLS):25OCT74-
1182
PRITCHETT, V.S. GEORGE MEREDITH &
ENGLISH COMEDY.*
I. WILLIAMS, 637(VS):SEP72-113
PRITCHETT, W.K. STUDIES IN ANCIENT
GREEK TOPOGRAPHY.* (PT 2)
B. HELLY, 555:VOL46FASC2-275
PRITTIE, T. WILLY BRANDT.
B. CONNELL, 362:4JUL74-28
617(TLS):23AUG74-901
"PRIVATE REALITIES."
S. SCHWARTZ, 441:1DEC74-100
PRIVITERA, G.A. DIONISO IN OMERO E
NELLA POESIA GRECA ARCAICA.
J. DEFRADAS, 555:VOL46FASC2-286
J.B. HAINSWORTH, 123:MAR73-95
"PROBLÈMES ET MÉTHODES D'HISTOIRE
DES RELIGIONS."
H. ROUSSEAU, 98:JAN72-71
"PROCEEDINGS OF THE ROYAL MUSICAL
ASSOCIATION." (1971-72)
R.L.S., 410(M&L):JUL73-353
"PROCEEDINGS OF THE SIXTH INTERNA-
TIONAL CONGRESS OF PHONETIC SCI-
ENCES, PRAGUE 1967."
H. MOL, 353:15MAR72-111
PROCTOR, D. HANNIBAL'S MARCH IN
HISTORY.
G. DE BEER, 313:VOL62-180
PROCTOR, M. & P. YEO. THE POLLINA-
TION OF FLOWERS.
617(TLS):18JAN74-61
PRODAN, D. SUPPLEX LIBELLUS VALA-
CHORUM, OR THE POLITICAL STRUGGLE
OF THE ROMANIANS IN TRANSYLVANIA
DURING THE 18TH CENTURY.
F. KELLOGG, 32:SEP73-650
PROFFER, C.R., ED & TRANS. SOVIET
CRITICISM OF AMERICAN LITERATURE
IN THE SIXTIES.*
L. WALLEK, 114(CHIR):VOL24#4-172
PROFFER, C.R. - SEE PUSHKIN, A.S.
PROFFER, E. - SEE BULGAKOV, M.
PROFFER, E. & C.R. - SEE BULGAKOV, M.
PROFITLICH, U. EITELKEIT.
M.H., 191(ELN):SEP72(SUPP)-170
PROHASKA, D. RAIMUND & VIENNA.*
L. BODI, 67:MAY73-149
C.E. WILLIAMS, 220(GL&L):JUL73-
335
PROKOSCH, F. AMERICA, MY WILDERNESS.
R.C. CHURCHILL, 385(MQR):SPRING
74-175
639(VQR):SUMMER72-C
PROKUSHEV, Y.L., ED. NA RODINE
YESENINA.
G. MC VAY, 402(MLR):JUL73-717
PROMYSLOV, V. MOSCOW IN CONSTRUC-
TION.
L.A. KOSINSKI, 104:SPRING72-177
PRONZINI, B. SNOWBOUND.
N. CALLENDAR, 441:23JUN74-33
PRONZINI, B. UNDERCURRENT.*
N. CALLENDAR, 441:11AUG74-12

PRONZINI, B. THE VANISHED.*
N. CALLENDAR, 441:12MAY74-18
PROPERTIUS. THE POEMS OF PROPER-
TIUS.* (J. WARDEN, TRANS)
639(VQR):AUTUMN72-CXXV
PROPES, S. THOSE OLDIES BUT GOODIES.
F.J. GILLIS, 187:SEP74-462
PROSE, F. THE GLORIOUS ONES.
P. ADAMS, 61:MAR74-99
PROSE, F. JUDAH THE PIOUS.*
P. CRUTTWELL & F. WESTBURG,
249(HUDR):SUMMER73-419
PROSSER, E. HAMLET & REVENGE.*
M. GRIVELET, 189(EA):OCT-DEC72-
547
"PROSTITUTION IN THE VICTORIAN AGE."
617(TLS):29MAR74-343
PROU, S. THE PAPERHANGER.
M. LEVIN, 441:6OCT74-40
442(NY):4NOV74-208
PROUST, M. CORRESPONDANCE DE MARCEL
PROUST.* (VOL 1) (P. KOLB, ED)
G. BRÉE, 207(FR):DEC71-507
PRUCHA, F.P., ED. AMERICANIZING THE
AMERICAN INDIANS.
617(TLS):18JAN74-49
PRULHIÈRE, C. QUÉBEC.
617(TLS):14JUN74-634
PRUNER, F. L'UNITÉ SECRÈTE DE
"JACQUES LE FATALISTE."
J-L. LEUTRAT, 535(RHL):JAN-FEB72-
139
V. MYLNE, 208(FS):JAN73-72
J.N. PAPPAS, 207(FR):DEC71-517
PRUS, B. THE DOLL.
B. CZAYKOWSKI, 575(SEER):JUL73-
468
PRŮŠEK, J. CHINESE HISTORY & LITERA-
TURE.*
E.O. EIDE, 293(JAST):NOV71-176
PRUSSIN, L. ARCHITECTURE IN NORTH-
ERN GHANA.*
R.A. BRAVMANN, 54:SEP72-371
PRYCE-JONES, D., ED. EVELYN WAUGH
& HIS WORLD.*
G. GLUECK, 441:10FEB74-6
L.E. SISSMAN, 442(NY):4FEB74-107
PRZELECKI, M. THE LOGIC OF EMPIRI-
CAL THEORIES.
M.D. RESNIK, 486:SEP72-421
PRZYGODA, J. TEXAS PIONEERS FROM
POLAND.
G.J. LERSKI, 32:SEP73-637
M. STARCZEWSKA, 497(POLR):SPRING
72-108
PSEUDO-ARISTOTLE. PSEUDO-ARISTOTELE:
"DE LINEIS INSECABILIBUS." (M.T.
CARDINI, ED & TRANS)
D. BARGRAVE-WEAVER, 123:DEC73-
153
PSEUDO-HOMER & T. PRODROMOS. PSEUDO-
HOMER, "DER FROSCHMÄUSEKRIEG;" THE-
ODOROS PRODROMOS, "DER KATZENMÄUSE-
KRIEG." (H. AHLBORN, ED & TRANS)
J. DEFRADAS, 555:VOL46FASC2-314
"PSYCHOLOGIE ET ÉPISTÉMOLOGIE GÉNÉT-
IQUES."
Y. HATWELL, 542:OCT-DEC72-475
"THE PUBLIC & PREPARATORY SCHOOLS
YEAR BOOK." (84TH ED)
617(TLS):17MAY74-534
PUCCETTI, R. PERSONS.
M. FOX, 255(HAB):SUMMER72-52

PUCCIANI, O. - SEE ROBBE-GRILLET, A.
PUDNEY, J. BRUNEL & HIS WORLD.
617(TLS):8MAR74-244
PUECH, H-C., ED. HISTOIRE DES RE-
LIGIONS. (VOL 1)
H. ROUSSEAU, 98:JAN72-71
PUGH, A.C. - SEE PINGET, R.
PUGH, M. A DREAM OF TREASON.
N. CALLENDAR, 441:21APR74-42
617(TLS):13SEP74-969
PUGH, P.D.G. STAFFORDSHIRE PORTRAIT
FIGURES.
G. WILLS, 39:JUN72-523
PUGH, R.B., ED. COURT ROLLS OF THE
WILTSHIRE MANORS OF ADAM DE STRAT-
TON.*
P.D.A. HARVEY, 325:OCT72-537
PUGH, R.B., ED. THE VICTORIA HIS-
TORY OF THE COUNTIES OF ENGLAND:
GENERAL INTRODUCTION.
A.G. DYSON, 325:OCT72-536
PUGH, T.B., ED. GLAMORGAN COUNTY
HISTORY. (VOL 3)
R.W. HAYS, 589:OCT73-781
PUGLIELLI, A. STRUTTURE SINTATTICHE
DEL PREDICATO IN ITALIANO.
R.J. DI PIETRO, 276:AUTUMN72-335
G.C. LEPSCHY, 402(MLR):JAN73-187
PUHARICH, A. URI.
M. GARDNER, 453:16MAY74-18
PUHVEL, J., ED. MYTH & LAW AMONG
THE INDO-EUROPEANS.
J. FONTENROSE, 24:SUMMER73-214
PUHVEL, J., ED. SUBSTANCE & STRUC-
TURE OF LANGUAGE.*
R.H. ROBINS, 206:JAN72-135
E. ROULET, 343:BAND14HEFT2-133
PUIG, M. BETRAYED BY RITA HAYWORTH.
(SPANISH TITLE: LA TRAICIÓN DE
RITA HAYWORTH.)
A.B. EDWARDS, 37:OCT72-38
DEL PULGAR, F. CLAROS VARONES DE
CASTILLA.* (R.B. TATE, ED)
R.L. KAGAN, 551(RENQ):SUMMER72-
214
PULGRAM, E. SYLLABLE, WORD, NEXUS,
CURSUS.
M.A.G. GARMAN, 297(JL):SEP72-333
PULMAN, M.B. THE ELIZABETHAN PRIVY
COUNCIL IN THE FIFTEEN-SEVENTIES.
J.A. EPPERSON, 551(RENQ):WINTER
72-488
A.J. LOOMIE, 377:MAR73-50
PULS, H., R. KIWITTER & E. DEHNKE.
PARLONS FRANÇAIS, FRANZÖSISCHES
UNTERRICHTSWERK FÜR HAUPTSCHULEN.
(PT 1)
R. SCHÜTTE, 430(NS):JUL72-429
PULVER, J. A BIOGRAPHICAL DICTION-
ARY OF OLD ENGLISH MUSIC.
D. SCOTT, 415:JUL73-705
PUNDT, H.G. SCHINKEL'S BERLIN.
617(TLS):11JAN74-24
639(VQR):AUTUMN73-CLXXI
PUNNETT, R.M. FRONT-BENCH OPPOSI-
TION.
617(TLS):11JAN74-23
PUNYODYANA, B. CHINESE-THAI DIFFER-
ENTIAL ASSIMILATION IN BANGKOK.
J.M. & S.H. POTTER, 293(JAST):
FEB72-464
PUNZO, V.C. REFLECTIVE NATURALISM.
R.D.L., 543:DEC71-366
PURCELL, H. - SEE PLAYFORD, J.

PURDY, A. SELECTED POEMS.
D. HELWIG, 529(QQ):AUTUMN72-404
PURDY, J. I AM ELIJAH THRUSH.*
P. BAILEY, 364:FEB/MAR73-157
S. O'CONNELL, 418(MR):WINTER73-
190
639(VQR):AUTUMN72-CXX
PURDY, J. JEREMY'S VERSION.*
502(PRS):SPRING72-91
PURKAYASTHA, J. FIVE ESSAYS ON HAM-
LET.
617(TLS):15MAR74-272
PURNELL, R. THE SOCIETY OF STATES.
617(TLS):22FEB74-179
PURRINGTON, P.F. FOUR YEARS A-WHAL-
ING.
639(VQR):SUMMER73-CXXIV
PURSER, P. THE LAST GREAT TRAM RACE,
& OTHER MEMOIRS.
E.S. TURNER, 362:22AUG74-253
PURTELL, J. THE TIFFANY CAPER.
N. CALLENDAR, 441:SEP74-45
PURTILL, R.L. LOGIC FOR PHILOSOPH-
ERS.
T.G.N., 543:DEC71-365
PUSEY, M.J. EUGENE MEYER.
R. REEVES, 441:8DEC74-4
PUSHHAREV, S., COMP. DICTIONARY OF
RUSSIAN HISTORICAL TERMS FROM THE
ELEVENTH CENTURY TO 1917. (G. VER-
NADSKY & R.T. FISHER, JR., EDS)
N.E. EVANS & G.M. PHIPPS, 325:
OCT72-546
A. KLEIMOLA, 104:SPRING72-145
PUSHKIN, A.S. THE CRITICAL PROSE OF
ALEXANDER PUSHKIN.* (C.R. PROFFER,
ED & TRANS)
L. MAJHANOVICH, 628:SPRING73-115
PUSHKIN, A.S. PUSHKIN ON LITERA-
TURE.* (T. WOLFF, ED & TRANS)
G. DONCHIN, 575(SEER):JAN73-156
L. MAJHANOVICH, 628:SPRING73-115
N.P. POLTORATZKY, 550(RUSR):OCT
72-424
205(FMLS):JAN72-92
PUSHKIN, A.S. PUSHKIN THREEFOLD.*
(W. ARNDT, ED & TRANS)
A. BOYER, 550(RUSR):OCT72-426
639(VQR):WINTER73-XVII
PUTNAM, H. PHILOSOPHY OF LOGIC.*
A.B.W., 543:MAR72-565
PUTNAM, M.C.J. VIRGIL'S PASTORAL
ART.*
C. WITKE, 24:SPRING73-96
PUTTER, I. - SEE LECONTE DE LISLE,
C.M.
"PUTTING BRITAIN FIRST."
E. PYGGE, 617(TLS):4OCT74-1076
PÜTZ, P., ED. THOMAS MANN UND DIE
TRADITION.
T.J. REED, 402(MLR):JUL73-704
L. VOSS, 406:SUMMER73-206
PÜTZ, P. DIE ZEIT IM DRAMA.*
H. KNUST, 301(JEGP):JAN73-103
G.F. PROBST, 221(GQ):JAN72-170
VAN PUYVELDE, L. FLEMISH PAINTING
FROM THE VAN EYCK TO MATSYS.
K.R., 90:JAN72-52
PYE, J. PATRONAGE OF BRITISH ART.*
D. FITZ-GERALD, 90:SEP72-639
PYE, L.W. CHINA.
T-L. LEE, 396(MODA):SPRING73-213

PYE, L.W. WARLORD POLITICS.
S.R. MAC KINNON, 293(JAST):AUG72-
935
PYLE, H. JACK B. YEATS.
M. SIDNELL, 627(UTQ):SPRING72-
263
PYLE, K.B. THE NEW GENERATION IN
MEIJI JAPAN.*
H.J. JONES, 293(JAST):MAY72-688
PYNCHON, T. GRAVITY'S RAINBOW.*
R. DE FEO, 249(HUDR):WINTER73/74-
773
A.J. FRIEDMAN & M. PUETZ, 659:
SUMMER74-345
G. LEVINE, 473(PR):3/1973-517
E. MENDELSON, 676(YR):SUMMER73-
624
E. ROVIT, 659:AUTUMN74-539
R. SALE, 418(MR):AUTUMN73-834
639(VQR):SUMMER73-CIV

QUACKENBUSH, J. CALCIUM & OTHER
PLAYS.
A. RENDLE, 157:SPRING72-81
QUACQUARELLI, A. SAGGI PATRISTICI.
P. COURCELLE, 555:VOL46FASC2-347
QUAGLINO. THE COMPLETE HOSTESS.
617(TLS):29NOV74-1347
QUAINTON, M. - SEE DE BAÏF, J-A.
QUAM, A. - SEE "THE ZUÑIS"
QUAYLE, E. THE COLLECTOR'S BOOK OF
BOOKS.
J. COTTON, 503:SUMMER72-106
QUAYLE, E. THE COLLECTOR'S BOOK OF
BOY'S STORIES.
617(TLS):17MAY74-529
QUAYLE, E. THE COLLECTOR'S BOOK OF
CHILDREN'S BOOKS.
J. COTTON, 503:SUMMER72-106
P.H. MUIR, 78(BC):SPRING72-149
QUAYLE, E. - SEE "JOST AMMAN'S
'KUNST UND LEHRBÜCHLEIN'"
DE QUELJOE, D.H. A PRELIMINARY
STUDY OF MALAY/INDONESIAN ORTHOG-
RAPHY.
A.M. STEVENS, 293(JAST):AUG72-
991
QUELLET, H. LES DÉRIVÉS LATINS EN
"-OR."*
V. LEINIEKS, 353:1DEC72-101
F. PICCOLI, 343:BAND15HEFT1-65
QUENEAU, R. LES FLEURS BLEUES.
(B. WRIGHT, ED)
J. CRUICKSHANK, 208(FS):JAN73-
101
F. FLAGOTHIER, 556(RLV):1972/5-
553
QUENEAU, R. THE FLIGHT OF ICARUS.*
G. EWART, 364:OCT/NOV73-151
J. UPDIKE, 442(NY):25FEB74-122
QUENEAU, R. QUENEAU. (T. SAVORY,
TRANS)
C. TOMLINSON, 364:OCT/NOV72-125
QUENNELL, P., WITH H. JOHNSON. A
HISTORY OF ENGLISH LITERATURE.
617(TLS):21JUN74-680
QUENNELL, P. & H. JOHNSON. WHO'S
WHO IN SHAKESPEARE.
617(TLS):8FEB74-138
DE QUESADA, G. PÁGINAS ESCOGIDAS.
E. BERNAL LABRADA, 263:JAN-MAR73-
89

"A QUESTION OF AUTHENTICITY."
K.W. HUMPHREYS, 354:SEP72-261
QUILIS, A. FONÉTICA Y FONOLOGÍA DEL
ESPAÑOL.
G.F. MEIER, 682(ZPSK):BAND25
HEFT4/5-437
QUILLET, J. LA PHILOSOPHIE POLI-
TIQUE DE MARSILE DE PADOUE.
A. FOREST, 542:JAN-MAR72-82
G. POST, 589:JUL73-583
QUIMBY, I.M.G., ED. AMERICAN PAINT-
ING TO 1776.
639(VQR):SUMMER72-CVIII
QUIMBY, I.M.G., ED. CERAMICS IN
AMERICA.
639(VQR):AUTUMN73-CLXXIV
QUIN, A. TRIPTICKS.
M. FELD, 364:OCT/NOV72-152
QUINE, W.V. ONTOLOGICAL RELATIVITY
& OTHER ESSAYS.
G.B. OLIVER, 321:WINTER72[VOL6
#1]-74
QUINE, W.V. PHILOSOPHY OF LOGIC.
J. CORCORAN, 486:MAR72-97
L. STEVENSON, 479(PHQ):JAN72-80
QUINE, W.V. SET THEORY & ITS LOGIC.
(1ST & 2ND EDS)
G.T. KNEEBONE, 316:DEC72-768
QUINLAN, P.M.H. & W.V. COMPTON.
ESPAÑOL RÁPIDO.
T.E. HAMILTON, 238:MAR72-199
QUINLAN, S.R. THE HUNDRED MILLION
DOLLAR LUNCH.
K. COONEY, 441:22SEP74-30
A. KOPKIND, 453:8AUG74-33
QUINN, B. EZRA POUND.
R.H. PEARCE, 27(AL):JAN74-620
QUINN, D.B. ENGLAND & THE DISCOVERY
OF AMERICA, 1481-1620.
C. HILL, 453:14NOV74-17
G.V. SCAMMELL, 617(TLS):20DEC74-
1431
QUINN, K., ED. APPROACHES TO CATUL-
LUS.
H.A. MASON, 97(CQ):VOL6#2-152
QUINN, K. CATULLUS: AN INTERPRETA-
TION.*
H.A. MASON, 97(CQ):VOL6#2-152
H.D. RANKIN, 67:NOV73-286
QUINN, K. - SEE CATULLUS
QUINONES, R.J. THE RENAISSANCE
DISCOVERY OF TIME.*
R.E. CARTER, 529(QQ):WINTER72-
560
M. MUDRICK, 249(HUDR):SPRING73-
219
G.F. WALLER, 150(DR):AUTUMN72-
469
639(VQR):WINTER73-XXIV
QUINTANA, M.J. POESÍAS COMPLETAS.
(A. DÉROZIER, ED)
R.M. COX, 240(HR):SUMMER72-343
QUINTANILHA, F.E.G. - SEE PESSOA, F.
QUINTERO, J. IF YOU DON'T DANCE
THEY BEAT YOU.
B. ATKINSON, 441:24NOV74-16
C. LEHMANN-HAUPT, 441:18NOV74-37
QUINTILIAN. QUINTILIANI INSTITUTION-
IS ORATORIAE LIBRI DUODECIM.* (M.
WINTERBOTTOM, ED)
J. ANDRÉ, 555:VOL46FASC1-158
F.R.D. GOODYEAR, 123:MAR73-37
QUINTON, A. THE NATURE OF THINGS.*
P. JONES, 518:OCT73-22

"LES QUINZE JOYES DE MARIAGE."* (J.
CROW, ED)
P.B. FAY & P.F. DEMBOWSKI,
545(RPH):FEB73-620
QUIRARTE, J. MEXICAN AMERICAN AR-
TISTS.
C.T. WHALEY, 584(SWR):SUMMER73-V
QUIRINO, C. QUEZON.
M. CULLINANE, 293(JAST):AUG72-
995
QUIRK, L.J. THE GREAT ROMANTIC
FILMS.
W. FEAVER, 617(TLS):27DEC74-1471
QUIRK, R. & OTHERS. A GRAMMAR OF
CONTEMPORARY ENGLISH.*
H.V. KING, 351(LL):JUN73-119
QUIRK, R. & J. SVARTVIK. INVESTI-
GATING LINGUISTIC ACCEPTABILITY.
R.D. EAGLESON, 353:15AUG72-90
QURESHI, Q. PESSIMISMUS UND FORT-
SCHRITTSGLAUBE BEI BERT BRECHT.
R. GRIMM, 406:FALL73-326

RAAB, L. MYSTERIES OF THE HORIZON.*
42(AR):VOL32#3-499
639(VQR):WINTER73-X
RAABE, P. EINFÜHRUNG IN DIE QUELLEN-
KUNDE ZUR NEUEREN DEUTSCHEN LITERA-
TURGESCHICHTE. QUELLENREPERTORIUM
ZUR NEUEREN DEUTSCHEN LITERATUR-
GESCHICHTE.
P.W. TAX, 400(MLN):APR72-506
RABAN, J. THE SOCIETY OF THE POEM.
J. GLOVER, 565:VOL13#3-68
205(FMLS):OCT72-384
RABAN, J. SOFT CITY.
R. SENNETT, 441:10NOV74-7
E.S. TURNER, 362:31JAN74-152
617(TLS):22MAR74-303
RABB, T.K. & J.E. SEIGEL, EDS.
ACTION & CONVICTION IN EARLY MOD-
ERN EUROPE.
R.B. WERNHAM, 447(N&Q):MAY72-191
RABEL, E. GESAMMELTE AUFSÄTZE.
(VOLS 1-3 ED BY H.G. LESER, VOL 4
ED BY H.J. WOLFF)
E.J. COHN, 182:VOL25#1/2-20
RABEL, L. KHASI, A LANGUAGE OF
ASSAM.
A. WEIDERT, 343:BAND14HEFT2-137
RABIKAUSKAS, P., ED. RELATIONES
STATUS DIOECESIUM IN MAGNO DUCATU
LITUANIAE. (VOL 1)
H. DUCHHARDT, 182:VOL25#5/6-187
RABKIN, N. SHAKESPEARE & THE COMMON
UNDERSTANDING.
F.M. DICKEY, 551(RENQ):WINTER72-
508
RACHELS, J., ED. A COLLECTION OF
PHILOSOPHICAL ESSAYS.
J.W.S., 543:MAR72-566
RACHET, M. ROME ET LES BERBÈRES.
I.M. BARTON, 313:VOL62-207
A. ERNOUT, 555:VOL46FASC1-169
B.H. WARMINGTON, 123:MAR73-65
DE RACHEWILTZ, I. INDEX TO THE SEC-
RET HISTORY OF THE MONGOLS.
N. POPPE, 32:JUN73-372
DE RACHEWILTZ, J. PAPAL ENVOYS TO
THE GREAT KHANS.
J.A. BOYLE, 293(JAST):MAY72-636

RACINE, J. BRITANNICUS. (M. ADER-
ETH, ED)
B. CHEDOZEAU, 535(RHL):MAY-JUN
72-514
RACINE, J. PHAEDRA OF RACINE.* (R.
LOWELL, TRANS)
J. JORDAN, 159(DM):AUTUMN71-115
RACINE, J. PHÈDRE. (R.C. KNIGHT,
ED & TRANS)
205(FMLS):OCT72-384
RADCLIFF-UMSTEAD, D. UGO FOSCOLO.
O.R., 191(ELN):SEP72(SUPP)-192
RADER, D. BLOOD DUES.*
617(TLS):5JUL74-707
RADILLO, C.M.S. - SEE UNDER SUÁREZ
RADILLO, C.M.
RADIN, P. - SEE LEE, J.
RADKE, D. CHEESE MAKING AT HOME.
N. HAZELTON, 441:1DEC74-96
RADŁOWSKI, M. ENCHIRIDION VANDALI-
CUM ANDREAE THARAEI.
H. RÖSEL, 182:VOL25#12-407
RADNER, L. EICHENDORFF.*
J.F.F., 191(ELN):SEP72(SUPP)-144
J.M. RITCHIE, 220(GL&L):APR73-
251
RADNER, M. & S. WINOKUR, EDS. ANAL-
YSES OF THEORIES & METHODS OF
PHYSICS & PSYCHOLOGY.
R. ACKERMANN, 311(JP):18JUL74-
424
R.J.B., 543:SEP71-140
N. KOERTGE, 84:AUG72-274
RADNITZKY, G. CONTEMPORARY SCHOOLS
OF METASCIENCE. (2ND ED)
R.C. NEVILLE, 258:MAR72-131
RADVÁNYI, J. HUNGARY & THE SUPER-
POWERS.
S.D. KERTESZ, 32:SEP73-647
RAE, H.C. THE ROOKERY.
617(TLS):14JUN74-644
RAE, I. CHARLES CAMERON, ARCHITECT
TO THE COURT OF RUSSIA.
D. HINTON, 135:MAY72-64
D. WATKIN, 39:DEC72-567
RAEDER, T. JOHAN BOJER OG HEIM-
BYGDA RISSA.
P. AMDAM, 172(EDDA):1972/6-377
RAEFF, M. IMPERIAL RUSSIA, 1682-
1825.*
D.L. RANSEL, 32:JUN73-376
RAFFEL, B. THE FORKED TONGUE.
D. BOWMAN, 402(MLR):JUL73-628
RAFFEL, B., ED & TRANS. RUSSIAN
POETRY UNDER THE TSARS.*
W. ARNDT, 32:MAR73-141
RAFFEL, B. - SEE "SIR GAWAIN & THE
GREEN KNIGHT"
RAFFEL, B. & A. BURAGO - SEE GUMILEV,
N.S.
RAGHAVAN, V. MALAYAMĀRUTA, A COL-
LECTION OF MINOR WORKS IN SANSKRIT.
(PT 2)
L. STERNBACH, 318(JAOS):OCT-DEC
72-574
RAGHAVAN, V. NEW CATALOGUS CATALOG-
ORUM. (VOL 1) (REV)
L. STERNBACH, 318(JAOS):JAN-MAR
72-178
RAHMAN, T.A. MAY 13.
G.D. NESS, 293(JAST):MAY72-734
RAHMANI, L. SOVIET PSYCHOLOGY.
D. JORAVSKY, 453:16MAY74-22

RAHNER, K. SCHRIFTEN ZUR THEOLOGIE.
(VOLS 10&11) THEOLOGICAL INVESTI-
GATIONS. (VOLS 10&11) THE SHAPE
OF THE CHURCH TO COME.
617(TLS):6SEP74-959
RAHUL, R. THE HIMALAYA BORDERLAND.
L.E. ROSE, 293(JAST):AUG72-984
RAHUL, R. MODERN BHUTAN.
W.O. DOUGLAS, 31(ASCH):SUMMER74-
490
RAHUL, R. POLITICS OF CENTRAL ASIA.
W.O. DOUGLAS, 31(ASCH):SUMMER74-
490
617(TLS):3MAY74-484
RAIMONDI, E. METAFORA E STORIA.
K.O., 275(IQ):FALL/WINTER72-117
RAINE, K. WILLIAM BLAKE.*
D.V.E., 191(ELN):SEP72(SUPP)-35
RAINE, K. FAREWELL HAPPY FIELDS.*
C. DRIVER, 362:3JAN74-24
RAINE, K. ON A DESERTED SHORE.
617(TLS):3MAY74-471
RAINER, R. - SEE VON LANGENSTEIN, H.
RAINES, J.C., ED. CONSPIRACY.
J.A. LUKAS, 441:16JUN74-5
RAINEY, S. WALL HANGINGS.
B. WASSERMAN, 139:DEC71-66
RAISTRICK, A. WEST RIDING OF YORK-
SHIRE.
A. CLIFTON-TAYLOR, 46:JAN72-66
RAITIÈRE, A. L'ART DE L'ACTEUR
SELON DORAT ET SAMSON.*
T. LAWRENSON, 208(FS):OCT73-457
RAITT, A.W. PROSPER MÉRIMÉE.
J.S.P., 191(ELN):SEP72(SUPP)-104
S. PITOU, 613:SPRING72-137
RAITT, J. MADAME DE LAFAYETTE & "LA
PRINCESSE DE CLÈVES."
N.M. LEOV, 67:NOV73-307
RAIZIS, M.B. DIONYSIOS SOLOMOS.
P. BIEN, 32:DEC73-864
RAJA, N.K. - SEE UNDER KUMARASWAMI
RAJA, N.
RAKNEM, I. JOAN OF ARC IN HISTORY,
LEGEND & LITERATURE.
D. GRONAU, 182:VOL25#11-366
RAKOSI, C. ERE-VOICE.
W.G. REGIER, 502(PRS):SPRING72-
85
RAKOTO, I. LE MARIAGE MERINA.
M. BLOCH, 69:JUL72-259
RALBOVSKY, M. LORDS OF THE LOCKER
ROOM.
R.W. CREAMER, 441:1DEC74-90
RALEGH, W. - SEE UNDER RALEIGH, W.
RALEIGH, W. A CHOICE OF SIR WALTER
RALEGH'S VERSE. (R. NYE, ED)
H. MURPHY, 159(DM):SUMMER72-127
RALLIDES, C. THE TENSE ASPECT SYS-
TEM OF THE SPANISH VERB, AS USED
IN CULTIVATED BOGOTÁ SPANISH.
M. SANDMANN, 545(RPH):NOV72-505
RALSTON, G. THE DEADLY, DEADLY ART.
N. CALLENDAR, 441:8DEC74-44
RAMACHANDRAN, T.P. THE CONCEPT OF
THE VYĀVAHĀRIKA IN ĀDVAITA VEDĀN-
TA.*
I.T. WEIERHOLT, 485(PE&W):APR72-
229
RAMAGE, E.S. URBANITAS.
617(TLS):12APR74-388

RASMO, N. MICHAEL PACHER.
C.M. KAUFFMANN, 39:APR72-342
M. ROSENTHAL, 135:JUN72-152
RASMUSSEN, K. DIE LIVLÄNDISCHE
KRISE 1554-1561.
D. KIRBY, 575(SEER):OCT73-605
RATAJ, M. PAMIĘTNIKI. (J. DĘBSKI,
ED)
A.M. CIENCIALA, 32:MAR73-185
RATCLIFF, C. FEVER COAST.
G. HENRY, 491:AUG74-292
RATH, F.L., JR. & M.R. O'CONNELL,
COMPS. GUIDE TO HISTORIC PRESER-
VATION, HISTORICAL AGENCIES, &
MUSEUM PRACTICES.
J.C. WRIGHT, 14:APR72-224
RATHER, D. & G.P. GATES. THE PALACE
GUARD.
A. COCKBURN, 453:28NOV74-8
S.R. WEISMAN, 441:8DEC74-4
RATHER, L.J. & J.M. SHARP - SEE LAÍN
ENTRALGO, P.
RATKOŠ, P., J. BUTVIN & M. KROPILÁK,
EDS. NAŠE DEJINY V PARMEŇOCH.
V.S. MAMATEY, 32:MAR73-192
RATTUNDE, E. "LI PROVERBES AU VIL-
AIN."
J.L. GRIGSBY, 545(RPH):AUG72-192
RAUBITSCHEK, I.K. & OTHERS. L'ÉPI-
GRAMME GRECQUE.*
P. CHANTRAINE, 555:VOL46FASC1-
115
RAUCH, E.M. ARKANSAS ADIOS.
E. ROVIT, 659:AUTUMN74-539
VON RAUCH, G. THE BALTIC STATES.
J.W. HIDEN, 617(TLS):15NOV74-
1295
RAUCHER, H. A GLIMPSE OF TIGER.
M.M., 502(PRS):SUMMER72-185
RAUF, A. WEST PAKISTAN.
H.M. RAULET, 293(JAST):AUG72-981
RAUPACH, H. & OTHERS, EDS. JAHRBUCH
DER WIRTSCHAFT OSTEUROPAS. (VOL 2)
G.R. FEIWEL, 32:SEP73-633
RAUPACH, H., E. FELS & E. BOETTCHER,
EDS. JAHRBUCH DER WIRTSCHAFT OST-
EUROPAS. (VOL 1)
G.R. FEIWEL, 32:SEP73-633
RAVEN, S. BRING FORTH THE BODY.
D.A.N. JONES, 617(TLS):1NOV74-
1216
J. MELLORS, 362:21NOV74-684
RAVENSDALE, J.R. LIABLE TO FLOODS.
W.G. HOSKINS, 617(TLS):1NOV74-
1234
RAVETZ, A. MODEL ESTATE.
J. NAUGHTON, 617(TLS):23AUG74-
908
RAVITCH, D. THE GREAT SCHOOL WARS.
G. LEVINE, 441:12MAY74-4
442(NY):15APR74-151
RAVIZZA, V., ED. FESTSCHRIFT ARNOLD
GEERING ZUM 70. GEBURTSTAG.
J.A.W., 410(M&L):APR73-228
RAWLINS, R. FOUR HUNDRED YEARS OF
BRITISH AUTOGRAPHS.
J.H.P. PAFFORD, 447(N&Q):DEC72-
479
F. RANGER, 325:APR72-449
RAWLINSON, G. - SEE HYDE, R.
RAWLS, J. A THEORY OF JUSTICE.*
M.T. DALGARNO, 518:JAN73-26
R.J. REGAN, 613:WINTER72-634
[CONTINUED]

[CONTINUING]
A. SCHWARTZ, 185:JUL73-294
42(AR):VOL32#3-509
RAWNSLEY, H.D. REMINISCENCES OF
WORDSWORTH AMONG THE PEASANTRY OF
WESTMORELAND.
H. VIEBROCK, 72:BAND210HEFT4/6-
411
RAWSON, C. - SEE FIELDING, H.
RAWSON, C.J. HENRY FIELDING & THE
AUGUSTAN IDEAL UNDER STRESS.*
C.T.P., 566:SPRING73-109
R. PAULSON, 401(MLQ):DEC73-470
RAWSON, C.J., ED. FOCUS: SWIFT.*
A.H. SCOUTEN, 481(PQ):JUL72-775
RAWSON, P. INTRODUCING ORIENTAL ART.
617(TLS):12APR74-401
RAWSON, P. TANTRA.
D.J. ENRIGHT, 362:17JAN74-87
RAWSON, P. & L. LEGEZA. TAO.
D.J. ENRIGHT, 362:17JAN74-87
RAY, G.N. H.G. WELLS & REBECCA WEST.
L. HELLMAN, 441:13OCT74-4
N. MAC KENZIE, 362:21NOV74-676
D. TRILLING, 617(TLS):22NOV74-
1301
RAY, N. AN ARTIST IN LIFE.
R.E. TEELE, 352(LE&W):VOL15#4&
VOL16#1/2-917
RAY, P.C. THE SURREALIST MOVEMENT
IN ENGLAND.
F. BERRY, 541(RES):NOV72-523
J. HILL, 290(JAAC):FALL72-126
A. RODWAY, 402(MLR):JAN73-166
RAY, S., ED. GANDHI, INDIA & THE
WORLD.
B. STEIN, 485(PE&W):OCT72-483
RAYBOULD, T.J. THE ECONOMIC EMER-
GENCE OF THE BLACK COUNTRY.
617(TLS):1MAR74-217
RAYFIELD, J.R. THE LANGUAGES OF A
BILINGUAL COMMUNITY.*
E. HAUGEN, 361:VOL29#1-78
RAYMOND, D. INCIDENT ON A SUMMER'S
DAY.
617(TLS):14JUN74-629
RAYMOND, E. UNDER WEDGERY DOWN.
617(TLS):11OCT74-1142
RAYMOND, E. & J.S. MARTIN. A PIC-
TURE HISTORY OF EASTERN EUROPE.
P.J. BEST, 497(POLR):SPRING72-
103
P.F. SUGAR, 32:SEP73-630
RAYMOND, M., ED. LA POÉSIE FRAN-
ÇAISE ET LE MANIÉRISME 1546-
1610(?).
R.A. SAYCE, 402(MLR):OCT73-904
RAYMOND, M.B. SWINBURNE'S POETICS.
L. ORMOND, 677:VOL3-321
RAYMOND, P. THE LAST SOLDIER.
R. BLYTHE, 362:4APR74-444
617(TLS):12APR74-385
RAYNOR, H. A SOCIAL HISTORY OF
MUSIC FROM THE MIDDLE AGES TO
BEETHOVEN.*
42(AR):VOL32#4-708
RAYNOR, J. A WESTMINSTER CHILDHOOD.
617(TLS):1FEB74-104
AL-RAZI, I.F.A. KITAB AL-NAFS WAL-
RUH WA SHARH QUWAHUMA. (S.H.
MASUMI, ED)
S.A. AKBARABADI, 273(IC):JUL72-
278

RAZZELL, P.E. & R.W. WAINWRIGHT, EDS. THE VICTORIAN WORKING CLASS.
F. KERMODE, 453:30MAY74-6
617(TLS):17MAY74-520
READ, D., ED. DOCUMENTS FROM ED-WARDIAN ENGLAND 1901-1915.
617(TLS):25JAN74-72
READ, G. MUSIC NOTATION.
617(TLS):10MAY74-508
READ, H. THE CONTRARY EXPERIENCE.
617(TLS):1FEB74-104
READ, H. EDUCATION THROUGH ART.
L. NOCHLIN, 441:13OCT74-36
READ, H., ED. SURREALISM.
R. PENROSE, 46:JUN72-390
READ, J. WARNINGS FROM THE LEFT.
Z. BARTEK, 362:17OCT74-512
READ, J. THE WINES OF SPAIN & POR-TUGAL.
617(TLS):1FEB74-116
READ, P.P. ALIVE.
P. ADAMS, 61:MAY74-140
C. LEHMANN-HAUPT, 441:12APR74-35
D.K. MANO, 441:7APR74-2
G. MOORHOUSE, 362:9MAY74-604
442(NY):22APR74-154
617(TLS):10MAY74-500
READ, P.P. THE PROFESSOR'S DAUGHTER.
J.C. OATES, 473(PR):WINTER73-143
READ, P.P. THE UPSTART.*
J. MELLORS, 364:DEC73/JAN74-154
READ, S. TRAVELLING ACTORS.
617(TLS):16AUG74-879
REALE, G. - SEE LEVI, A.
REANEY, P.H. THE ORIGIN OF ENGLISH SURNAMES.
R. LASS, 206:JAN73-392
REARDON, B.M.G. FROM COLERIDGE TO GORE.
R.A. SOLOWAY, 637(VS):SEP72-104
REARICK, J.C. THE DRAWINGS OF PON-TORMO.
J. SHEARMAN, 54:JUN72-209
REASON, J. MAN IN MOTION.
617(TLS):24MAY74-544
REBHOLZ, R.A. THE LIFE OF FULKE GRE-VILLE, FIRST LORD BROOKE.*
W.R. DAVIS, 568(SCN):FALL-WINTER 73-78
J. GRUNDY, 541(RES):AUG72-335
H. MACLEAN, 551(RENQ):WINTER72-492
J. REES, 402(MLR):JAN73-149
639(VQR):AUTUMN72-CXL
REBOUL, O. KANT ET LE PROBLÈME DU MAL.
P.M., 543:JUN72-764
W.H. WERKMEISTER, 319:JUL74-405
RÉBUFFAT, G. MEN & THE MATTERHORN.*
442(NY):4FEB74-110
RÉBUFFAT, G. ON ICE & SNOW & ROCK.
639(VQR):SUMMER72-CIX
"'RECHERCHES' SUR LA MUSIQUE FRAN-ÇAISE CLASSIQUE." (VOL 12)
W. KOLNEDER, 182:VOL25#21-750
RECK, R.D. LITERATURE & RESPONSI-BILITY.*
W.G. LANGLOIS, 598(SOR):WINTER74-231
RECKOW, F. DIE COPULA.
G.A.A., 410(M&L):OCT73-453

"RECORDS RETENTION AND DISPOSAL SCHEDULE FOR NEW JERSEY SCHOOL DIS-TRICTS."
R.H. POTTER, JR., 14:JAN72-70
"RECUEIL LINGUISTIQUE DE BRATISLAVA." (VOL 2)
H. GALTON, 353:JAN72-81
REDCLIFFE-MAUD, J.P. & B. WOOD. ENG-LISH LOCAL GOVERNMENT REFORMED.
617(TLS):27SEP74-1047
REDDAWAY, P., ED. UNCENSORED RUSSIA.
B.M. COHEN, 584(SWR):AUTUMN73-353
V. CONOLLY, 575(SEER):JAN73-152
V.S. DUNHAM, 32:SEP73-595
D. POSPIELOVSKY, 550(RUSR):OCT 72-416
REDDAWAY, P. - SEE LITVINOV, P.
RÉDEI, K., ED. NORD-OSTJAKISCHE TEXTE (KAZYM-DIALEKT) MIT SKIZZE DER GRAMMATIK.
I. FUTAKY, 260(IF):BAND76-373
RÉDEI, K. NORTHERN OSTYAK CHRESTO-MATHY.
E. SCHIEFER, 343:BAND15HEFT2-215
REDFERN, J. A GLOSSARY OF FRENCH LITERARY EXPRESSIONS.*
H. GODIN, 208(FS):JAN73-106
REDFERN, J. A LEXICAL STUDY OF RAETO-ROMANCE & CONTIGUOUS ITALIAN DIALECT AREAS.
J. KRAMER, 72:BAND21OHEFT4/6-437
REDFERN, W.D. PAUL NIZAN.*
J. KOLBERT, 188(ECR):WINTER72-331
REDGROVE, P. DR. FAUST'S SEA-SPIRAL SPIRIT.*
G. EWART, 364:DEC72/JAN73-132
REDGROVE, P. & P. SHUTTLE. THE TER-RORS OF DR. TREVILES.
617(TLS):25OCT74-1206
REDMON, A. EMILY STONE.
J. MELLORS, 362:11JUL74-61
617(TLS):7JUN74-601
REDMOND, E. - SEE DUMAS, H.
REDWAY, M.W. MARKS OF LEE ON OUR LAND.
W. GARD, 584(SWR):SUMMER73-272
RÉE, H. EDUCATOR EXTRAORDINARY.
617(TLS):4JAN74-4
REED, I. CHATTANOOGA.
N. SCHMITZ, 398:AUTUMN74-205
REED, I. CONJURE.*
639(VQR):WINTER73-XVI
REED, I. THE LAST DAYS OF LOUISIANA RED.
C. LEHMANN-HAUPT, 441:21OCT74-31
R. SALE, 453:12DEC74-18
R. SCHOLES, 441:10NOV74-2
442(NY):4NOV74-208
REED, I. MUMBO JUMBO.
S. O'CONNELL, 418(MR):WINTER73-190
E. ROVIT, 659:AUTUMN74-539
639(VQR):WINTER73-VIII
REED, J. SCHUBERT: THE FINAL YEARS.*
A.H., 410(M&L):APR73-213
REED, J.R. PERCEPTION & DESIGN IN THE "IDYLLS OF THE KING."
C. FALL, 637(VS):SEP72-110
REED, J.S. THE ENDURING SOUTH.
639(VQR):SPRING73-LXXXVII

REED, J.W., JR. FAULKNER'S NARRA-
TIVE.*
    H.H. WAGGONER, 27(AL):NOV73-471
REED, T.J. THOMAS MANN.
    E. HELLER, 617(TLS):11OCT74-1103
REED, T.J. - SEE MANN, T.
REEDY, G.E. THE PRESIDENCY IN FLUX.
    R. EGGER, 639(VQR):AUTUMN73-612
REEMAN, D. THE DESTROYERS.
    M. LEVIN, 441:20OCT74-41
REES, B.R. & M.E. JERVIS. LAMPAS.
    R.G. PENMAN, 123:MAR73-80
REES, D. HARRY DEXTER WHITE.
    617(TLS):10MAY74-497
REES, G. A CHAPTER OF ACCIDENTS.
    R. CONQUEST, 364:JUN/JUL72-157
REES, G. - SEE MC VICAR, J.
REES, J. FULKE GREVILLE, LORD
BROOKE, 1554-1628.*
    N.K. FARMER, JR., 551(RENQ):SUM-
MER72-237
    J. GRUNDY, 541(RES):AUG72-335
    M.R. MAHL, 191(ELN):SEP72-42
REES, M.A. ALFRED DE MUSSET.
    205(FMLS):JUL72-289
REES, M.A. - SEE DE MUSSET, A.
REES, P.M. THE MIRACULOUS YEAR &
OTHER PLAYS.*
    H. FRANCIS, 157:WINTER72-83
REES, R.A. & E.N. HARBERT, EDS.
FIFTEEN AMERICAN AUTHORS BEFORE
1900.
    L. LEARY, 445(NCF):SEP72-235
REES, V. SHELL GUIDE TO MID-WESTERN
WALES.
    C. WILLIAMS-ELLIS, 46:JUN72-390
REESE, S. I'M WAITING.
    M. LEVIN, 441:7APR74-32
REEVES, J. & M. SEYMOUR-SMITH - SEE
MARVELL, A.
REEVES, N. HEINRICH HEINE.
    D.J. ENRIGHT, 617(TLS):25OCT74-
1187
REEVES, P.D. - SEE SLEEMAN, W.H.
REFEROVSKAJA, E.A. FRANCUZSKIJ
JAZYK V KANADE.
    H.G. SCHOGT, 320(CJL):VOL18#2-
193
REFEROVSKAJA, E.A. SINMAKSIS SOGRE-
MENNOGO FRANIUZSKOGO JAZYKA.
    J. KELEMEN, 353:1DEC71-102
REGALADO, N.F. POETIC PATTERNS IN
RUTEBEUF.*
    G. LAFEUILLE, 546(RR):OCT72-225
REGARD, M. - SEE DE BALZAC, H.
REGEN, F. APULEIUS PHILOSOPHUS
PLATONICUS.
    J. BEAUJEU, 555:VOL46FASC2-346
"LA RÉGENCE."
    A.D. HYTIER, 207(FR):OCT71-237
    R. MERCIER, 557(RSH):APR-JUN72-
313
    J. VERCRUYSSE, 535(RHL):JAN-FEB
72-133
    M.H. WADDICOR, 208(FS):APR73-200
"RÉGI MAGYARORSZÁGI NYOMTATVÁNYOK
1473-1600."
    W. HAMMER, 551(RENQ):SUMMER72-
210
REGINA, U. HEIDEGGER, DAL NICHILIS-
MO ALLA DIGNITÀ DELL'UOMO.*
    A.M., 543:JUN72-766
REGNAULT, M. 66-67.
    F. GALAND, 207(FR):DEC71-483

REGOSIN, R.L. THE POETRY OF INSPIRA-
TION.
    J. BAILBÉ, 535(RHL):JUL-AUG72-
707
    J.H. CAULKINS, 207(FR):DEC71-527
    M. JEANNERET, 208(FS):JAN73-56
    S. SMITH, 399(MLJ):FEB72-112
REGUEIRA, M.S. - SEE UNDER SÁNCHEZ
REGUEIRA, M.
REGULA, M. KURZGEFASSTE ERKLÄRENDE
SATZKUNDE DES NEUHOCHDEUTSCHEN.*
    E.H. HOFMANN, 133:1972/2-213
    G. KOLDE, 260(IF):BAND76-350
REGUSH, N.M. PIERRE VALLIÈRES.
    B. COOPER, 99:MAY/JUN74-35
REIBSTEIN, E. VOLKSSOUVERÄNITÄT UND
FREIHEITSRECHTE.
    C.J. FRIEDRICH, 182:VOL25#15/16-
529
REICH-RANICKI, M., ED. ERFUNDENE
WAHRHEIT.
    H.W. NIESCHMIDT, 67:MAY73-145
REICHARD, R. THE FIGURE FINAGLERS.
    G. GOLD, 441:15JUN74-29
REICHARDT, D. VON QUEVEDOS "BUSCÓN"
ZUM DEUTSCHEN "AVANTURIER."
    M. FRANZBACH, 52:BAND7HEFT1-93
REICHARDT, J., ED. CYBERNETICS,
ART & IDEAS.
    C. NEMSER, 58:SEP/OCT72-69
REID, B.L. TRAGIC OCCASIONS.
    L. HARTLEY, 219(GAR):SPRING72-
112
REID, C. HILBERT.
    J. CORCORAN, 486:MAR72-106
REID, C.L. BASIC PHILOSOPHICAL
ANALYSIS.
    H.A.D., 543:MAR72-567
REID, J.C. BUCKS & BRUISERS.*
    G.B. TENNYSON, 445(NCF):JUN72-
117
REID, L.A. MEANING IN THE ARTS.*
    R.A. SMITH, 290(JAAC):SPRING72-
395
REID, L.A., ED. PHILIPPINE MINOR
LANGUAGES.
    C.O. FRAKE, 293(JAST):MAY72-750
REID, P. THE FUN HOUSE.
    N. CALLENDAR, 441:23JUN74-33
REID, R. MARIE CURIE.
    A. WHITMAN, 441:19JUN74-37
    T. ZELDIN, 617(TLS):5JUL74-701
REID, T.B.W. THE "TRISTRAN" OF
BEROUL.
    B. BLAKEY, 208(FS):JUL73-316
REID, T.B.W. - SEE THOMAS
REID, W. & A. DE MENIL. OUT OF THE
SILENCE.
    639(VQR):SPRING72-LXXIV
REID, W.S. TRUMPETER OF GOD.
    N.K. BURGER, 441:4AUG74-7
REIFFEN, D. THE JUVENILE COURT IN A
CHANGING SOCIETY.
    T. MORRIS, 617(TLS):18OCT74-1157
REIGSTAD, P. RÖLVAAG.*
    R.W. ETULAIN, 649(WAL):WINTER73-
305
REILLY, A.P. AMERICA IN CONTEMPOR-
ARY SOVIET LITERATURE.*
    E.J. BROWN, 550(RUSR):OCT72-431
REILLY, R. WEDGWOOD PORTRAIT MEDAL-
LIONS.
    617(TLS):22MAR74-304

REILLY, R. & G. SAVAGE. WEDGWOOD:
THE PORTRAIT MEDALLIONS.
617(TLS):22MAR74-304
REILLY, R.J. ROMANTIC RELIGION.
M.F. SLATTERY, 290(JAAC):SPRING
72-406
639(VQR):SPRING72-LXXVI
REIMAN, D.H., ED. SHELLEY & HIS
CIRCLE: 1773-1822. (VOLS 5&6)
G.M. MATTHEWS, 617(TLS):6SEP74-
948
REIMANN, H. HÖHERE SCHULE UND HOCH-
SCHULE IN DEN USA.
J. HERBST, 182:VOL25#17/18-588
REIMER, E. - SEE JOHN OF GARLAND
REINARTZ, M. GENESE, STRUKTUR UND
VARIABILITÄT EINES SOGENANNTEN
EHEBRUCHSCHWANKS.
E. MOSER-RATH, 196:BAND13HEFT1/2-
184
REINDORP, R.C. SPANISH AMERICAN
CUSTOMS, CULTURE & PERSONALITY.
D.F. BROWN, 399(MLJ):FEB72-113
REINER, E. LA PLACE DE L'ADJECTIF
ÉPITHÈTE EN FRANÇAIS.*
F.M. JENKINS, 545(RPH):AUG72-151
REINERT, H. REVIEW TEXT IN GERMAN
FIRST YEAR.
R.H. ESSER, 221(GQ):JAN72-210
REINFELD, F. COMPLETE BOOK OF CHESS
OPENINGS.
617(TLS):22FEB74-193
REINGOLD, N. - SEE HENRY, J.
REINHARDT, S. STUDIEN ZUR ANTINOMIE
VON INTELLEKT UND GEFÜHL IN MUSILS
ROMAN "DER MANN OHNE EIGENSCHAF-
TEN."
A. HOLMES, 220(GL&L):APR73-266
G.P. KNAPP, 72:BAND210HEFT1/3-
170
REINHOLD, H., ED. CHARLES DICKENS.*
J.M. BLOM, 433:JUL72-375
A. MAACK, 430(NS):SEP72-554
REINHOLD, M. HISTORY OF PURPLE AS
A STATUS SYMBOL IN ANTIQUITY.*
A. ERNOUT, 555:VOL46FASC1-169
REINMUTH, O.W. THE EPHEBIC INSCRIP-
TIONS OF THE FOURTH CENTURY B.C.
D.M. LEWIS, 123:DEC73-254
REISCHAUER, E.O. JAPAN.
M.J. MAYO, 293(JAST):NOV71-157
REISS, A.H. CULTURE & COMPANY.
E.L. KAMARCK, 59(ASOC):FALL-
WINTER73-92
REISS, E. THE ART OF THE MIDDLE ENG-
LISH LYRIC.
639(VQR):AUTUMN72-CXXIX
REISS, H. - SEE KANT, I.
REISS, T.J. TOWARD DRAMATIC ILLU-
SION.
R.C. KNIGHT, 208(FS):JUL73-326
H.C. KNUTSON, 188(ECR):SPRING72-
67
REIZOV, B.G. SUR LES LITTÉRATURES
EUROPÉENNES.
FR. DE LABRIOLLE, 535(RHL):MAY-
JUN72-544
RELA, W. GUÍA BIBLIOGRÁFICA DE LA
LITERATURA HISPANO AMERICANA, DES-
DE EL SIGLO XIX HASTA 1970.
D.W. FOSTER, 263:APR-JUN73-199
"RELIEF & REHABILITATION OF WAR VIC-
TIMS IN INDOCHINA."
W. SHAWCROSS, 453:18JUL74-16

REMARQUE, E.M. SHADOWS IN PARADISE.
G. EWART, 364:OCT/NOV72-146
REMY, Y. & A. LE GRAND MIDI.
S.G. STARY, 207(FR):FEB72-709
"THE RENAISSANCE."
J.K. GADOL, 551(RENQ):WINTER72-
470
RENARD, C. - SEE STENDHAL
RENARD, J. OEUVRES. (VOL 1) (L.
GUICHARD, ED)
H. GODIN, 208(FS):APR73-224
RENARD, J-C. LE DIEU DE NUIT.
617(TLS):19JUL74-771
RENAULT, F. LAVIGERIE, L'ESCLAVAGE
AFRICAIN ET L'EUROPE (1873-92).
H. DESCHAMPS, 69:JAN72-68
RENAULT, M. THE KING MUST DIE. THE
CHARIOTEER. THE MASK OF APOLLO.
H. KENNER, 441:10FEB74-15
RENAULT, M. NORTH FACE.
441:10NOV74-38
RENAULT, M. THE PERSIAN BOY.*
B.F. DICK, 569(SR):AUTUMN73-864
J.N. HARTT, 639(VQR):SUMMER73-
450
H. KENNER, 441:10FEB74-15
S. MARCUS, 231:MAR74-89
RENDEL, M. THE ADMINISTRATIVE FUNC-
TIONS OF THE FRENCH CONSEIL D'ÉTAT.
M. ANDERSON, 208(FS):APR73-240
RENDELL, R. THE FACE OF TRESPASS.
N. CALLENDAR, 441:2JUN74-20
617(TLS):5APR74-375
RENES, P.B. TEACHER TRAINING AT
BUTIMBA.
S. MILBURN, 69:JAN72-79
DE RENÉVILLE, J-R. AVENTURE DE L'AB-
SOLU.
J. CATESSON, 98:DEC72-1082
RENFREW, C. BEFORE CIVILIZATION.*
R. ATKINSON, 362:3JAN74-23
442(NY):7JAN74-72
617(TLS):22MAR74-302
RENNERT, M. CIRCLE OF DEATH.
N. CALLENDAR, 441:25AUG74-30
RENOIR, J. MY LIFE & MY FILMS.
P. ADAMS, 61:DEC74-127
R. GREENSPUN, 441:17NOV74-6
R. MAYNE, 362:5DEC74-746
RENVOIZE, J. CHILDREN IN DANGER.
D. THOMAS, 362:6JUN74-743
RENVOIZE, J. THE NET.
J. MELLORS, 362:1AUG74-156
617(TLS):4OCT74-1092
RENWICK, J. MARMONTEL, VOLTAIRE &
THE "BÉLISAIRE" AFFAIR.
H.T. MASON, 617(TLS):13DEC74-
1424
RENZULLI, L.M., JR. MARYLAND: THE
FEDERALIST YEARS.
F.A. CASSELL, 656(WMQ):OCT73-684
639(VQR):SUMMER73-CXXII
REPLOGLE, J. AUDEN'S POETRY.*
W. DAVIES, 447(N&Q):SEP72-345
M. SELETZKY, 38:BAND90HEFT3-412
"REPORT OF THE SECRETARY OF DEFENSE,
JAMES R. SCHLESINGER, TO THE CON-
GRESS ON THE FY 1975 DEFENSE BUD-
GET & FY 1975-1979 DEFENSE PRO-
GRAM."
M. KALDOR & A. COCKBURN, 453:
13JUN74-24

"REPORT OF THE SECRETARY TO THE COM-
MISSIONERS 1968-1969." [ROYAL
COMMISSION ON HISTORICAL MANU-
SCRIPTS, GREAT BRITAIN]
   M.H. ARNOLD, 14:JUL/OCT72-419
REPS, J.W. TIDEWATER TOWNS.
   F.D. NICHOLS, 656(WMQ):JUL73-540
   639(VQR):WINTER73-XLI
RESCHER, N. ESSAYS IN PHILOSOPHICAL
ANALYSIS.*
   J-G. ROSSI, 53(AGP):BAND54HEFT2-
   198
RESCHER, N. THE PRIMACY OF PRACTICE.
CONCEPTUAL IDEALISM.
   617(TLS):19APR74-412
RESCHER, N. SCIENTIFIC EXPLANATION.*
   H. LEHMAN, 486:JUN72-272
   E.P. MILLSTONE, 483:OCT72-380
   F. WILSON, 154:DEC72-655
RESCHER, N., ED. STUDIES IN THE
THEORY OF KNOWLEDGE.*
   K.T., 543:SEP71-146
RESCHER, N. WELFARE.
   D. WATSON, 518:JAN73-29
RESCHER, N. & A. URQUHART. TEMPORAL
LOGIC.
   K. FINE, 479(PHQ):OCT72-370
   A. MERCIER, 182:VOL25#1/2-5
RESENHÖFT. W. EXISTENZERHELLUNG DES
HEXENTUMS IN GOETHES FAUST (MEPHIS-
TO'S MASKEN) WALPURGIS).
   H. REISS, 220(GL&L):APR73-244
RESHETAR, J.S., JR. THE SOVIET POL-
ITY.*
   M. RUSH, 550(RUSR):JAN72-83
RESKE, H. TRAUM UND WIRKLICHKEIT IM
WERK HEINRICH VON KLEISTS.
   J. GEAREY, 222(GR):MAY72-232
RESPOSO, E.R.C. - SEE UNDER CASTRO
RESPOSO, E.R.
RESTAINO, F. J.S. MILL E LA CULTURA
FILOSOFICA BRITANNICA.*
   P. DUBOIS, 542:JUL-SEP72-389
RESTIF DE LA BRETONNE. LA VIE DE
MON PÈRE.* (G. ROUGER, ED)
   B. DIDIER, 535(RHL):MAR-APR72-
   318
RESTON, J., JR. THE AMNESTY OF JOHN
DAVID HERNDON.*
   42(AR):VOL32#3-502
RETI, L., ED. THE UNKNOWN LEONARDO.
   P. ADAMS, 61:DEC74-127
   K. CLARK, 453:12DEC74-12
   E. COCHRANE, 441:1DEC74-2
RETI, L. - SEE LEONARDO DA VINCI
REUCHLIN, J. HENNO - KOMÖDIE.
(H.C. SCHNUR, ED)
   F. RÄDLE, 52:BAND7HEFT1-83
REUTER, H.G. DIE LEHRE VOM RITTER-
STAND.
   G. VOLLMANN-PROFE, 224(GRM):
   BAND22HEFT4-436
REVEL, J-F. NI MARX NI JÉSUS.
   H.W. BRANN, 207(FR):APR72-1031
REVEL, J-F. ON PROUST.
   676(YR):AUTUMN72-X
REVERDIN, O., ED. POLYBE.
   O. MURRAY, 617(TLS):18OCT74-1158
REVERDIN, O. - SEE "ENTRETIENS SUR
L'ANTIQUITÉ CLASSIQUE"
REVERDY, P. NOTE ÉTERNELLE DU PRÉ-
SENT.
   617(TLS):24MAY74-566

REVERDY, P. SELECTED POEMS.*
   R.W. GREENE, 207(FR):DEC71-484
   R. PEVEAR, 249(HUDR):SPRING73-
   192
REVSON, P. SPEED WITH STYLE.
   R.W. CREAMER, 441:1DEC74-90
REVZINA, O.G. STRUKTURA SLOVOOBRAZ-
OVATEL'NYX POLEJ V SLAVJANSKIX
JAZYKAX.
   M. ONATZKY-MALINE, 353:15OCT72-
   126
REWALD, J. THE HISTORY OF IMPRES-
SIONISM.* (4TH ED)
   617(TLS):3MAY74-464
REX, J., ED. APPROACHES TO SOCIOL-
OGY.
   617(TLS):23AUG74-903
REX, J. SOCIOLOGY & THE DEMYSTIFICA-
TION OF THE MODERN WORLD.
   A. RYAN, 362:25JUL74-125
   617(TLS):23AUG74-903
REXROTH, K. & L. CHUNG, EDS & TRANS.
THE ORCHID BOAT.
   639(VQR):SUMMER73-CXI
REY, A. LA LEXICOLOGIE.*
   J. CHAURAND, 209(FM):JAN72-74
   J. DARBELNET, 207(FR):DEC71-493
REY, A. LES TROUBLES DE LA MÉMOIRE
ET LEUR EXAMEN PSYCHOMÉTRIQUE.
   Y. HATWELL, 542:OCT-DEC72-480
REY, P. THE GREEK.
   M. LEVIN, 441:28JUL74-20
REY, W.H. ARTHUR SCHNITZLER: "PRO-
FESSOR BERNHARDI."
   R.R. SCHLEIN, 406:SUMMER73-194
REY-COQUAIS, J-P. INSCRIPTIONS
GRECQUES ET LATINES DE LA SYRIE.
(VOL 7)
   D.J. GEAGAN, 24:FALL73-299
   E.W. GRAY, 303:VOL92-235
REY-DEBOVE, J., ED. LA LEXICOGRA-
PHIE.
   M. MATHIOT, 350:DEC73-961
REYCHMAN, J. & A. ZAJACZKOWSKI.
HANDBOOK OF OTTOMAN-TURKISH DIPLO-
MATICS. (T. HALASI-KUN, ED)
   R.A. ABOU-EL-HAJ, 318(JAOS):APR-
   JUN72-384
REYES, A. VIDA Y FICCIÓN.
   T.O. TAYLOR, 573(SSF):WINTER72-
   110
REYNA, F. CONCISE ENCYCLOPEDIA OF
BALLET.
   617(TLS):7JUN74-620
REYNOLDS, G. A CONCISE HISTORY OF
WATERCOLOURS.
   T. CROMBIE, 39:JUN72-520
   D. THOMAS, 135:APR72-290
REYNOLDS, G. NICHOLAS HILLIARD &
ISAAC OLIVER.
   T. CROMBIE, 39:JUN72-520
REYNOLDS, J. SEVEN DISCOURSES DE-
LIVERED IN THE ROYAL ACADEMY BY
THE PRESIDENT.*
   M.R. BROWNELL, 290(JAAC):WINTER
   72-269
REYNOLDS, R. TEXAS.
   R.A. WILSON, 584(SWR):SUMMER73-
   274
REZNIKOFF, C. FAMILY CHRONICLE.
   M. HINDUS, 390:NOV72-77
REZVANI. COMA.
   M. CAGNON, 207(FR):OCT71-211

REZVANI. LE RÉMORA.
B.L. KNAPP, 207(FR):OCT71-212
REZVANI. THÉÂTRE.
B.L. KNAPP, 207(FR):DEC71-485
RHEES, R. DISCUSSIONS OF WITTGEN-
STEIN.*
J.V.W., 543:DEC71-366
RHEES, R. WITHOUT ANSWERS.
P. WINCH, 536:JUN72-87
RHEIN, P.H. ALBERT CAMUS.*
H.T. MASON, 447(N&Q):SEP72-352
RHODES, D. THE EASTER HOUSE.
A. CHEUSE, 441:4AUG74-4
RHODIN, E. THE SINISTER AFFAIR.
M.P. WORTHINGTON, 329(JJQ):SUM-
MER74-430
RHYS, J. GOOD MORNING, MIDNIGHT.
A. BROYARD, 441:26MAR74-35
RHYS, J. TIGERS ARE BETTER LOOKING.
H. MOSS, 442(NY):16DEC74-166
G. STADE, 441:20OCT74-5
RIABCHIKOV, E. RUSSIANS IN SPACE.*
(N.P. KAMANIN, ED)
W. SHELTON, 550(RUSR):JUL72-303
RIBBANS, G. NIEBLA Y SOLEDAD.*
A. KENWOOD, 67:MAY73-155
205(FMLS):OCT72-385
RIBBAT, E. DIE WAHRHEIT DES LEBENS
IM FRÜHEN WERK ALFRED DÖBLINS.*
J. DUYTSCHAEVER, 221(GQ):JAN72-
144
A.W. RILEY, 405(MP):AUG72-83
K. SCHRÖTER, 222(GR):JAN72-72
RICARDO, C. MARCHA PARA OESTE.
(4TH ED)
R.E. POPPINO, 263:JUL-SEP73-332
RICARDOU, J. LE NOUVEAU ROMAN.
617(TLS):2AUG74-824
RICARDOU, J. RÉVOLUTIONS MINISCULES.
J. ALTER, 207(FR):DEC71-486
RICATTE, R., WITH P. CITRON & L.
RICATTE - SEE GIONO, J.
RICCI, J.F.A. - SEE BRENTANO, C.
RICE, D.T. ISLAMIC PAINTING.
K.M. AHMAD, 273(IC):OCT72-366
B.W. ROBINSON, 39:AUG72-169
RICE, E. JOHN FRUM HE COME.
442(NY):13MAY74-159
RICE, E. MOTHER INDIA'S CHILDREN.
D. JACOBSON, 293(JAST):AUG72-975
RICE, F.M. & B. ROWLAND. ART IN
AFGHANISTAN.
90:MAR72-198
RICE, H.C., JR. & A.S.K. BROWN, EDS
& TRANS. THE AMERICAN CAMPAIGNS
OF ROCHAMBEAU'S ARMY, 1780, 1781,
1782, 1783.*
B.B. PETCHENIK, 656(WMQ):JUL73-
544
H.F. RANKIN, 639(VQR):SPRING73-
299
RICE, L.A. HUNGARIAN MORPHOLOGICAL
IRREGULARITIES.
G.F. MEIER, 682(ZPSK):BAND25
HEFT4/5-438
RICH, A. DIVING INTO THE WRECK.*
W.H. PRITCHARD, 249(HUDR):AUTUMN
73-585
R. SMITH, 398:SPRING74-84
639(VQR):AUTUMN73-CXL
RICH, N. HITLER'S WAR AIMS.
N. ASCHERSON, 453:18APR74-3

RICH, V., ED & TRANS. LIKE WATER,
LIKE FIRE.*
A. ADAMOVICH, 32:DEC73-863
RICHARD, J-P. PROUST ET LE MONDE
SENSIBLE.
617(TLS):17MAY74-513
RICHARD, J-P. STENDHAL ET FLAUBERT.
R.M. CHADBOURNE, 207(FR):FEB72-
732
RICHARDS, A. HOME TO AN EMPTY HOUSE.
617(TLS):1FEB74-97
RICHARDS, D.A. THE COMING OF WINTER.
R. HUNT, 99:NOV/DEC74-23
RICHARDS, D.S., ED. ISLAM & THE
TRADE OF ASIA.
A.S. EHRENKREUTZ, 589:JAN73-176
M.N. PEARSON, 293(JAST):FEB72-
383
RICHARDS, F. & A.C. HOMONOVUS.
42(AR):VOL32#3-508
RICHARDS, I.A. BEYOND.
D. YOUNG, 441:26MAY74-15
RICHARDS, J. BUT DELIVER US FROM
EVIL.
617(TLS):6SEP74-959
RICHARDS, J.O. PARTY PROPAGANDA
UNDER QUEEN ANNE.
H.T.D., 566:AUTUMN72-46
L. HORSLEY, 402(MLR):APR73-389
RICHARDS, K. & P. THOMSON, EDS. THE
EIGHTEENTH-CENTURY ENGLISH STAGE.
C.T.P., 566:SPRING73-113
RICHARDS, K. & P. THOMSON, EDS.
NINETEENTH-CENTURY BRITISH THEATRE.
R. DAVIES, 637(VS):JUN72-488
G. ROWELL, 541(RES):MAY72-229
RICHARDS, N. OTIS DUNN, MANHUNTER.
N. CALLENDAR, 441:6OCT74-38
RICHARDS, S., ED. THE BEST SHORT
PLAYS 1971.
A. RENDLE, 157:SUMMER72-75
RICHARDSON, J. AN ESSAY ON THE THE-
ORY OF PAINTING.* (2ND ED)
M.R. BROWNELL, 290(JAAC):WINTER
72-269
RICHARDSON, J. LOUIS XIV.
617(TLS):26JUL74-808
RICHARDSON, J. ENID STARKIE.*
W.G. MOORE, 364(FEB/MAR74-113
442(NY):8APR74-142
RICHARDSON, J. STENDHAL.
J. BAYLEY, 453:18JUL74-3
P. SOURIAN, 441:18AUG74-10
RICHARDSON, J. - SEE VERLAINE, P.
RICHARDSON, J.A. MODERN ART & SCIEN-
TIFIC THOUGHT.*
A.C. BIRNHOLZ, 127:SPRING73-352
290(JAAC):SPRING72-407
RICHARDSON, N.J., ED. THE HOMERIC
HYMN TO DEMETER.
617(TLS):3MAY74-470
RICHARDSON, R. & J. CHAPMAN. IMAGES
OF LIFE.
617(TLS):26JUL74-812
RICHARDSON, R.G. LARREY.
617(TLS):19JUL74-764
RICHARDSON, S. PAMÉLA OU LA VERTU
RÉCOMPENSÉE. (L'ABBE PRÉVOST,
TRANS)
F. LAUGAA, 557(RSH):OCT-DEC72-
612

RICHARDSON, W. ANECDOTES OF THE
RUSSIAN EMPIRE.
   I. DE MADARIAGA, 575(SEER):APR73-
311
RICHEY, M.F. ESSAYS ON MEDIEVAL GER-
MAN POETRY.* (2ND ED)
   E.G. FICHTNER, 222(GR):JAN72-65
RICHLER, M. NOTES ON AN ENDANGERED
SPECIES.
   L. GRAVER, 441:2JUN74-42
RICHLER, M. ST. URBAIN'S HORSEMAN.*
   A. COOPER, 287:JAN72-25
   L. ROOKE, 376:JAN72-118
RICHLER, M. SHOVELLING TROUBLE.*
   K. MC SWEENEY, 529(QQ):WINTER72-
584
RICHLER, M. THE STREET.
   R. CONQUEST, 364:AUG/SEP72-155
RICHMOND, H.M. SHAKESPEARE'S SEXUAL
COMEDY.*
   J.B. FORT, 189(EA):OCT-DEC72-539
   A. HOBSON, 149:DEC73-403
   R. WARREN, 447(N&Q):APR72-155
RICHMOND, I. ROMAN ARCHAEOLOGY &
ART.* (P. SALWAY, ED)
   R.M. OGILVIE, 447(N&Q):JUN72-240
RICHMOND, I. - SEE COLLINGWOOD, R.G.
RICHTER, A. - SEE VERGIL
RICHTER, G.M.A. ENGRAVED GEMS OF
THE ROMANS.*
   J. BOARDMAN, 90:JAN72-35
RICHTER, G.M.A. A HANDBOOK OF GREEK
ART. (5TH ED)
   290(JAAC):WINTER71-274
RICHTER, G.M.A. KOUROI.* (3RD ED)
   M. ROBERTSON, 90:JAN72-35
RICHTER, G.M.A. THE PORTRAITS OF
THE GREEKS: SUPPLEMENT.
   R.M. COOK, 123:DEC73-290
RICHTER, G.M.A. THE SCULPTURE &
SCULPTORS OF THE GREEKS. (4TH ED)
   R. HIGGINS, 39:MAY72-426
RICHTER, H. DADA, ART ET ANTI-ART.
   S. FAUCHEREAU, 98:AUG/SEP72-752
RICHTER, H. VIRGINIA WOOLF.*
   S. PROUDFIT, 191(ELN):SEP72-61
"HANS RICHTER BY HANS RICHTER." (C.
GRAY, ED)
   C. MILES, 290(JAAC):SUMMER72-549
RICHTER, H.W. BRIEFE AN EINEN JUN-
GEN SOZIALISTEN.
   617(TLS):1NOV74-1238
RICKARD, P. A HISTORY OF THE FRENCH
LANGUAGE.
   S. ULLMANN, 617(TLS):15NOV74-
1292
RICKARD, P. LA LANGUE FRANÇAISE AU
XVIE SIÈCLE.*
   E. BAUMGARTNER, 545(RPH):AUG72-
146
RICKARD, P. - SEE PESSOA, F.
RICKARD, P. & OTHERS - SEE "MEDIEVAL
COMIC TALES"
RICKE, H. DER HARMACHISTEMPEL DES
CHEFRENS IN GISEH [TOGETHER WITH]
SCHOTT, S. ÄGYPTISCHE QUELLEN ZUM
PLAN.
   A.M. BADAWY, 318(JAOS):APR-JUN72-
305
RICKENBACKER, W.F. DEATH OF THE
DOLLAR.
   G. BARRACLOUGH, 453:27JUN74-14

RICKLEFS, M.C. JOGJAKARTA UNDER
SULTAN MANGKUBUMI, 1749-1792.
   617(TLS):20SEP74-1023
RICKMAN, G. ROMAN GRANARIES & STORE
BUILDINGS.*
   W. BULMER, 313:VOL62-205
RICKS, C., ED. ENGLISH DRAMA TO
1710.
   481(PQ):JUL72-628
RICKS, C. KEATS & EMBARRASSMENT.
   J. BAYLEY, 362:28MAR74-410
   K. MILLER, 453:30CT74-35
   617(TLS):26APR74-432
RICKS, C. TENNYSON.*
   P. DICKINSON, 364:DEC72/JAN73-
140
   W.D. SHAW, 637(VS):JUN73-467
RICO, F. LA NOVELA PICARESCA Y EL
PUNTO DE VISTA.
   J. JOSET, 556(RLV):1972/1-110
RICO, F. EL PEQUEÑO MUNDO DEL HOM-
BRE.*
   J.B. AVALLE-ARCE, 400(MLN):MAR
72-347
RICOEUR, P. FREUD & PHILOSOPHY.*
   D. IHDE, 258:MAR72-138
RICOEUR, P. THE SYMBOLISM OF EVIL.
   M. RYAN, 154:DEC72-666
RICONDA, G. SCHOPENHAUER INTERPRETE
DELL'OCCIDENTE.
   E. NAMER, 542:JUL-SEP72-396
RIDEOUT, R.W. THE PRACTICE & PRO-
CEDURE OF THE NATIONAL INDUSTRIAL
RELATIONS COURT.
   617(TLS):25JAN74-88
RIDER, W. AN HISTORICAL & CRITICAL
ACCOUNT OF THE LIVES & WRITINGS OF
THE LIVING AUTHORS OF GREAT-BRIT-
AIN (1762).
   617(TLS):26JUL74-810
RIDGE, A. THE MAN WHO PAINTED ROSES.
   617(TLS):9AUG74-851
RIDGEWAY, J. COCKLESHELL JOURNEY.
   617(TLS):7JUN74-620
RIDGEWAY, J. THE LAST PLAY.*
   J.P. DEGNAN, 249(HUDR):AUTUMN73-
574
RIDGEWAY, J. THE POLITICS OF ECOL-
OGY.
   H.B. HOUGH, 31(ASCH):WINTER73/74-
152
RIDGWAY, B.S. THE SEVERE STYLE IN
GREEK SCULPTURE.*
   290(JAAC):WINTER71-275
RIDLEY, C.P., P.H.B. GODWIN & D.J.
DOOLIN. THE MAKING OF A MODEL
CITIZEN IN COMMUNIST CHINA.
   R.W. WILSON, 293(JAST):AUG72-945
RIDLEY, F.F. REVOLUTIONARY SYNDICAL-
ISM IN FRANCE.
   J.T. JOUGHIN, 207(FR):DEC71-452
RIDLEY, J. GARIBALDI.
   A. LYTTELTON, 617(TLS):8NOV74-
1259
RIDLEY, J. THE LIFE & TIMES OF MARY
TUDOR.
   617(TLS):12APR74-387
RIDLEY, J. LORD PALMERSTON.
   W.D. JONES, 639(VQR):WINTER72-
142
   D. ROBERTS, 637(VS):MAR72-369
RIDLEY, M. FAR EASTERN ANTIQUITIES.
   P. STEINLE, 60:JAN-FEB73-68

RIDOLFI, R. DIALOGO DI UN ASTRO-
NAUTA E DI LUDOVICO ARIOSTO.
M. PUCCINI, 275(IQ):FALL/WINTER
72-147
RIEDEL, M. STUDIEN ZU HEGELS RECHTS-
PHILOSOPHIE.
W. SCHMIED-KOWARZIK, 53(AGP):
BAND54HEFT1-95
RIEDEL, W. DER NEUE MENSCH.*
I. SCHUSTER, 564:MAR72-72
RIEDER, H. WENZEL.
F.G. HEYMANN, 32:DEC73-834
RIEFENSTAHL, L. THE LAST OF THE
NUBA.
E. WELTY, 441:1DEC74-5
RIEFENSTAHL, L. DIE NUBA.
617(TLS):5APR74-355
RIEGER, D. JACQUES CAZOTTE.*
P. BROCKMEIER, 224(GRM):BAND22
HEFT2-210
VON RIEKHOFF, H. GERMAN-POLISH RELA-
TIONS, 1918-1933.*
E.D. WYNOT, JR., 497(POLR):
SPRING72-99
RIEMER, J., ED. JEWISH REFLECTIONS
ON DEATH.
J.M. CAMERON, 453:31OCT74-6
RIEMSCHNEIDER, K.K. BABYLONISCHE
GEBURTSOMINA IN HETHITISCHER ÜBER-
SETZUNG.
G. NEUMANN, 260(IF):BAND76-265
RIEPE, D. THE PHILOSOPHY OF INDIA &
ITS IMPACT ON AMERICAN THOUGHT.*
(M. FARBER, ED)
E. DEUTSCH, 318(JAOS):JAN-MAR72-
168
RIES, W. GERÜCHT, GEREDE, ÖFFENT-
LICHE MEINUNG.*
D.C.A. SHOTTER, 313:VOL62-224
RIESE, T.A. & D. RIESNER, EDS. VERS-
DICHTUNG DER ENGLISCHEN ROMANTIK.*
R. GERMER, 72:BAND210HEFT4/6-402
RIESE, W. PHYLOANALYSIS.
P. DUBOIS, 542:OCT-DEC72-480
RIESS, C. THEATERDÄMMERUNG ODER DAS
KLO AUF DER BÜHNE.
C. TRILSE, 654(WB):3/1972-177
RIFFATERRE, H.B. L'ORPHISME DANS LA
POÉSIE ROMANTIQUE.*
A.E. CARTER, 207(FR):DEC71-539
L.M. CELLIER, 546(RR):FEB72-61
RIFFATERRE, M. ESSAIS DE STYLIS-
TIQUE STRUCTURALE. (D. DELAS, ED
& TRANS)
K. BENNETTE, 207(FR):FEB72-763
J. CULLER, 208(FS):APR73-244
J. CULLER, 297(JL):FEB72-177
G. KIHLBERG, 597(SN):VOL44#1-159
J-M. KLINKENBERG, 556(RLV):
1972/6-668
K.A. KNAUTH, 72:BAND210HEFT4/6-
350
H. RÜCK, 430(NS):MAY72-301
RIFKIN, S. MC QUAID.
N. CALLENDAR, 441:24FEB74-41
RIGAUT, J. ÉCRITS.* (M. KAY, ED)
R. CARDINAL, 208(FS):JAN73-110
RIGBY, A. ALTERNATIVE REALITIES.
617(TLS):20SEP74-1022
RIGG, A.G. A GLASTONBURY MISCELLANY
OF THE FIFTEENTH CENTURY.*
J.R. SIMON, 189(EA):JAN-MAR72-81

RIGGS, D. SHAKESPEARE'S HEROICAL
HISTORIES.*
M. WEST, 128(CE):MAY73-1131
RIGGS, W.G. THE CHRISTIAN POET IN
"PARADISE LOST."*
D. BUSH, 401(MLQ):MAR73-78
R.H. SUNDELL, 568(SCN):FALL-
WINTER73-68
639(VQR):AUTUMN73-CLII
RIGHINI, V. LINEAMENTI DI STORIA
ECONOMICA DELLA GALLIA CISALPINA.*
A. ERNOUT, 555:VOL46FASC1-170
RIGHTER, A. JOHN WILMOT, EARL OF
ROCHESTER.
J. WILDERS, 447(N&Q):MAY72-193
RÍHOVSKÝ, J. DAS URNENGRÄBERFELD IN
OBLEKOVICE.
U. FISCHER, 182:VOL25#12-427
RIIS, P.J. SUKAS I.
O. AURENCHE, 555:VOL46FASC1-103
RIKHOFF, J. ONE OF THE RAYMONDS.
J.R. FRAKES, 441:24MAR74-38
RILEY-SMITH, J. THE FEUDAL NOBILITY
& THE KINGDOM OF JERUSALEM, 1174-
1277.
617(TLS):5APR74-367
RILLA, W. THE DISPENSABLE MAN.
A. BROYARD, 441:17APR74-35
N. CALLENDAR, 441:5MAY74-14
RILOVA, A.C. & D. SUTHERLAND - SEE
UNDER CENTENO Y RILOVA, A. & D.
SUTHERLAND
RIMANELLI, G. & R. RUBERTO, EDS.
MODERN CANADIAN STORIES.
F. COGSWELL, 268:JUL74-157
RIMBAUD, A. A SEASON IN HELL. THE
ILLUMINATIONS. (E.R. PESCHEL,
TRANS OF BOTH)
617(TLS):28JUN74-690
RINGBOM, H. STUDIES IN THE NARRA-
TIVE TECHNIQUE OF "BEOWULF" & LAW-
MAN'S "BRUT."*
K. REICHL, 72:BAND210HEFT1/3-180
RINGE, D.A. THE PICTORIAL MODE.*
R.B. STEIN, 401(MLQ):DEC73-473
RINGER, V. THE SECRETARY.
M. LEVIN, 441:28JUL74-20
VON RINTELEN, F-J. CONTEMPORARY GER-
MAN PHILOSOPHY & ITS BACKGROUND.*
P. EMAD, 613:SPRING72-150
T.E. HILL, 477:AUTUMN72-445
R. PANIKKAR, 258:MAR72-137
E. SCHAPER, 479(PHQ):APR72-171
VON RINTELEN, F-J. JOHANN WOLFGANG
VON GOETHE, SINNERFAHRUNG UND
DASEINSDEUTUNG.
P. SOMVILLE, 542:JUL-SEP72-355
RIPIN, E.M., ED. KEYBOARD INSTRU-
MENTS.*
H.M.S., 410(M&L):JAN73-71
"THE RISE & PROGRESS OF THE PRESENT
TASTE IN PLANTING PARKS, PLEASURE
GROUNDS, GARDENS, ETC."
R. EDWARDS, 39:JAN72-67
RISNER, R. THE PASSING OF THE NIGHT.
A. LEWIS, 453:7MAR74-6
RISSET, J.C. AN INTRODUCTORY CATA-
LOGUE OF COMPUTER SYNTHESIZED
SOUNDS.
J.W. BEAUCHAMP, 518:SPRING-
SUMMER/FALL-WINTER71-348
RIST, J.M. EPICURUS, AN INTRODUC-
TION.*
R.G. TANNER, 63:AUG73-178

RIST, J.M. STOIC PHILOSOPHY.*
  V. CAUCHY, 154:DEC72-611
RISTELHUEBER, R. A HISTORY OF THE
  BALKAN PEOPLES. (S.D. SPECTOR, ED
  & TRANS)
  W.S. VUCINICH, 32:MAR73-195
RITCHIE, C. THE SIREN YEARS.
  J.L. GRANATSTEIN, 99:NOV/DEC74-
  53
RITSOS, Y. GESTURES.
  C. TOMLINSON, 364:OCT/NOV72-125
RITTE, H. UNTERSUCHUNGEN ÜBER DIE
  BEHANDLUNG VON VOLKSDICHTUNGSSTOF-
  FEN IM WERK SELMA LAGERLÖFS.
  W. FRIESE, 224(GRM):BAND22HEFT1-
  100
RITTENHOUSE, J.D. MAVERICK TALES.*
  R.N. ELLIS, 649(WAL):FALL72-234
RITTER, A. THE POLITICAL THOUGHT OF
  PIERRE-JOSEPH PROUDHON.*
  A.B. SPITZER, 207(FR):OCT71-234
RITTER, F.L. MUSIC IN AMERICA.
  M. PETERSON, 470:JAN72-32
RITTER, G. THE SWORD & THE SCEPTRE.
  (VOLS 3&4)
  617(TLS):8FEB74-128
RITTER, J., ED. HISTORISCHES WÖRTER-
  BUCH DER PHILOSOPHIE.* (VOL 1)
  J. BERNHARDT, 542:JAN-MAR72-114
  H.W. BRANN, 258:DEC72-623
RITTER, J., ED. HISTORISCHES WÖRTER-
  BUCH DER PHILOSOPHIE. (VOL 2)
  H.W. BRANN, 258:DEC72-623
  A. STERN, 182:VOL25#22-776
RIVEL, C., WITH J.C. LAURITZEN.
  POOR CLOWN.
  617(TLS):29MAR74-348
RIVERS, C. APHRODITE IN MID-CENTURY.
  W. SHEED, 453:7MAR74-18
RIVERS, E.L. - SEE ALONSO, D.
RIVERS, E.L. - SEE GARCILASO DE LA
  VEGA
RIVERS, I. THE POETRY OF CONSERVA-
  TISM, 1600-1745.*
  C.T.P., 566:SPRING73-107
RIVIÈRE, J. CARNETS 1914-1917. (I.
  & A. RIVIÈRE, EDS)
  617(TLS):28JUN74-695
RIVIÈRE, P. MOI, PIERRE RIVIÈRE,
  AYANT ÉGORGÉ MA MÈRE, MA SOEUR ET
  MON FRÈRE... (M. FOUCAULT, ED)
  617(TLS):1FEB74-107
DE RIVOYRE, C. BOY.
  617(TLS):9AUG74-849
RIZZA, C. THÉOPHILE GAUTIER CRITICO
  LETTERARIO.
  M. COTTIN, 535(RHL):JUL-AUG72-
  728
RIZZARDI, A. IL PRIMO SHAKESPEARE:
  IL MITO, LA POESIA.
  E. NAMER, 542:APR-JUN72-174
RIZZI, A. THE ETCHINGS OF THE
  TIEPOLOS.
  A. FRANKENSTEIN, 55:MAR73-16
  G. KNOX, 90:DEC72-876
RIZZO, G. - SEE FENOGLIO, B.
RIZZO-BAUR, H. DIE BESONDERHEITEN
  DER DEUTSCHEN SCHRIFTSPRACHE IN
  ÖSTERREICH UND SÜDTIROL.
  G.F. MEIER, 682(ZPSK):BAND25
  HEFT1/2-163

RIZZUTO, A. STYLE & THEME IN REVER-
  DY'S "LES ARDOISES DU TOIT."
  M.A. CAWS, 546(RR):OCT72-241
  M. GUINEY, 399(MLJ):NOV72-471
  Y. SCALZITTI, 405(MP):FEB73-277
  205(FMLS):APR72-196
ROACH, J. PUBLIC EXAMINATIONS IN
  ENGLAND, 1850-1900.
  G.J. CLIFFORD, 637(VS):JUN72-502
ROACHE, J. RICHARD EBERHART.*
  J.E. HARDY, 27(AL):JAN74-623
  S. YATES, 502(PRS):FALL72-260
ROBB, D.M. THE ART OF THE ILLUMI-
  NATED MANUSCRIPT.*
  617(TLS):3MAY74-480
ROBBE-GRILLET, A. GLISSEMENTS PRO-
  GRESSIFS DU PLAISIR.
  617(TLS):26APR74-433
ROBBE-GRILLET, A. PROJECT FOR A
  REVOLUTION IN NEW YORK.* (FRENCH
  TITLE: PROJET POUR UNE RÉVOLUTION
  À NEW YORK.)
  B. STOLTZFUS, 207(FR):OCT71-213
ROBBE-GRILLET, A. LE VOYEUR.* (O.
  PUCCIANI, ED)
  R.L. ADMUSSEN, 207(FR):OCT71-296
ROBBINS, C., ED. TWO ENGLISH REPUB-
  LICAN TRACTS.
  P. LEGOUIS, 189(EA):APR-JUN72-
  323
ROBBINS, H. THE PIRATE.
  W. FEAVER, 617(TLS):25OCT74-1183
  G. LYONS, 441:27OCT74-50
ROBBINS, J.A., ED. AMERICAN LITER-
  ARY SCHOLARSHIP, 1970.
  W. FRIDY, 517(PBSA):JUL-SEP73-
  356
ROBBINS, W. THE AMERICAN FOOD SCAN-
  DAL.
  S.E. COHEN, 441:19MAY74-14
  G. GOLD, 441:23FEB74-29
ROBE, S.L., ED. MEXICAN TALES &
  LEGENDS FROM LOS ALTOS.*
  F. KARLINGER, 196:BAND13HEFT1/2-
  197
  S. KARSEN, 238:SEP72-598
  R.J. SMITH, 292(JAF):JAN-MAR72-
  84
ROBERT OF FLAMBOROUGH. LIBER POENI-
  TENTIALIS. (J.J.F. FIRTH, ED)
  J.W. BALDWIN, 589:OCT73-784
ROBERT OF GRETHAM. ROBERT DE GRETH-
  AM, "MIROIR OU LES ÉVANGILES DES
  DOMNÉES." (S. PANUNZIO, ED)
  I. SHORT, 545(RPH):MAY73-732
ROBERT, L. DIE EPIGRAPHIK DER
  KLASSISCHEN WELT.
  D.M. LEWIS, 123:MAR73-110
ROBERTS, B. SPACEWALKS.*
  K. MC SWEENEY, 529(QQ):SUMMER72-
  275
ROBERTS, D. ARTISTIC CONSCIOUSNESS
  & POLITICAL CONSCIENCE.*
  E.W. HERD, 67:NOV73-319
ROBERTS, D. THE RAGWOMAN OF THE
  SHAMBLES.
  A. RENDLE, 157:WINTER72-80
ROBERTS, J.G. MITSUI.
  K. COONEY, 441:17FEB74-4
  R. STORRY, 617(TLS):29NOV74-1340
ROBERTS, J.M. THE MYTHOLOGY OF THE
  SECRET SOCIETIES.
  W.K.B. STOEVER, 651(WHR):AUTUMN
  73-423

ROBERTS, K. BRUEGEL.
E. YOUNG, 39:AUG72-167
ROBERTS, K. THE CHALK GIANTS.
617(TLS):15MAR74-269
ROBERTS, L.P. THE CONNOISSEUR'S
GUIDE TO JAPANESE MUSEUMS.
P.M. SCULL, 57:VOL34#4-350
ROBERTS, P.C. ALIENATION & THE
SOVIET ECONOMY.*
R.M. FEARN, 550(RUSR):APR72-203
AP ROBERTS, R. THE MORAL TROLLOPE.
(BRITISH TITLE: TROLLOPE: ARTIST &
MORALIST.)
D. SKILTON, 637(VS):JUN72-485
D. SMALLEY, 445(NCF):SEP72-232
ROBERTS, W.D. DIDN'T ANYBODY KNOW
MY WIFE?
N. CALLENDAR, 441:20OCT74-42
ROBERTSON, A. THE CHURCH CANTATAS
OF J.S. BACH.*
J.A.W., 410(M&L):JAN73-93
ROBERTSON, A.H. HUMAN RIGHTS IN THE
WORLD.
617(TLS):25JAN74-83
ROBERTSON, A.H., ED. PRIVACY &
HUMAN RIGHTS.
617(TLS):25JAN74-83
ROBERTSON, A.S. ROMAN IMPERIAL
COINS IN THE HUNTER COIN CABINET.*
(VOL 2)
J.M.C. TOYNBEE, 123:DEC73-258
617(TLS):21JUN74-672
ROBERTSON, C.N., ED. ONEIDA COMMUN-
ITY.
K. SILBER, 182:VOL25#13/14-469
ROBERTSON, C.N. ONEIDA COMMUNITY:
THE BREAKUP, 1876-1881.
T. STOEHR, 125:JUN73-328
ROBERTSON, D.W., JR. ABELARD & HEL-
OISE.
639(VQR):SUMMER72-XCII
ROBERTSON, H. GRASS ROOTS.
R. COOK, 99:MAR74-41
ROBERTSON, J. TRANSITION IN AFRICA.
617(TLS):1MAR74-205
ROBERTSON, P. RELENTLESS VERITY.
617(TLS):12APR74-386
ROBERTSON, P. THE SHELL BOOK OF
FIRSTS.
617(TLS):15NOV74-1297
ROBERTSON, W. THE DISPOSSESSED
MAJORITY.
K. GLASER, 396(MODA):FALL73-414
ROBESPIERRE, M. LES DROITS ET
L'ÉTAT DES BÂTARDS. [TOGETHER WITH]
CARNOT, L. LE POUVOIR DE L'HABI-
TUDE. (L.N. BERTHE & M. DE LAN-
GRE, EDS)
J.I. SHULIM, 173(ECS):SUMMER73-
513
ROBICHEZ, J. LE THÉÂTRE DE MONTHER-
LANT.
617(TLS):4OCT74-1060
ROBIN, A. MA VIE SANS MOI [SUIVI DE]
LE MONDE D'UNE VOIX.
W. ALBERT, 207(FR):FEB72-710
ROBINETT, R.F. & R.C. BENJAMIN.
MICHIGAN ORAL LANGUAGE SERIES.
E. HATCH, 608:JUN73-178
ROBINS, R.H. DIVERSIONS OF BLOOMS-
BURY.
E.F.K. KOERNER, 269(IJAL):APR72-
151

[CONTINUED]

[CONTINUING]
J.D. MC CLURE, 35(AS):FALL-
WINTER70-278
K.M. PETYT, 297(JL):SEP72-311
ROBINS, R.H. A SHORT HISTORY OF
LINGUISTICS.*
K.E. ZIMMER, 206:JAN72-133
ROBINSON, D. THE PROCESS OF BECOM-
ING ILL.
M. ROCHE, 262:SUMMER72-202
ROBINSON, D.L. SLAVERY IN THE STRUC-
TURE OF AMERICAN POLITICS, 1765-
1820.*
A. ZILVERSMIT, 656(WMQ):JAN72-
186
ROBINSON, I. CHAUCER & THE ENGLISH
TRADITION.*
A.C. SPEARING, 382(MAE):1973/3-
282
ROBINSON, I. CHAUCER'S PROSODY.*
R.T. DAVIES, 541(RES):MAY72-190
J.B. FRIEDMAN, 301(JEGP):APR73-
238
F. PYLE, 382(MAE):1973/1-47
J.R. SIMON, 189(EA):JAN-MAR72-62
ROBINSON, J. BED/TIME/STORY.
A. GOTTLIEB, 441:27OCT74-42
C. LEHMANN-HAUPT, 441:11OCT74-37
ROBINSON, J. COLLECTED ECONOMIC
PAPERS. (VOL 4)
617(TLS):18JAN74-53
ROBINSON, J. & J. EATWELL. AN
INTRODUCTION TO MODERN ECONOMICS.
617(TLS):18JAN74-53
ROBINSON, J.O., COMP. AN ANNOTATED
BIBLIOGRAPHY OF MODERN LANGUAGE
TEACHING.*
D.L. LANGE, 399(MLJ):NOV72-461
ROBINSON, K. WILKIE COLLINS.
617(TLS):29NOV74-1347
ROBINSON, M.F. NAPLES & NEAPOLITAN
OPERA.*
W. DEAN, 415:MAR73-261
D.R.B.K., 410(M&L):APR73-232
ROBINSON, P.A. THE SEXUAL RADICALS.
J.D. UYTMAN, 479(PHQ):APR72-187
ROBINSON, R., ED. DEVELOPING THE
THIRD WORLD.
M. TAUSSIG, 293(JAST):MAY72-634
ROBINSON, R. & R. EDWARDS. THE ART
& SCIENCE OF CHESS.
617(TLS):1NOV74-1240
ROBINSON, T. THE SCHOOLE OF MUSICKE.
(D. LUMSDEN, ED)
I. HARWOOD, 415:MAY73-493
ROBINSON, T.M. PLATO'S PSYCHOLOGY.*
G. SANTAS, 482(PHR):APR72-244
ROBSON, J., ED. THE YOUNG BRITISH
POETS.
T. EAGLETON, 565:VOL13#1-76
ROBY, K.E. A WRITER AT WAR.
617(TLS):9AUG74-863
ROCERIC-ALEXANDRESCU, A. FONOSTATIS-
TICA LIMBII ROMÂNE.
G. FRANCESCATO, 353:1DEC72-124
ROCHE, D. L'EGLISE ROMAINE ET LES
CATHARES ALBIGEOIS.
A-L. LEROY, 542:JAN-MAR72-84
ROCHE, J. THE MADRIGAL.*
K.M.B., 410(M&L):JUL73-354
J. HAAR, 415:AUG73-799
ROCHE, K.F. ROUSSEAU.
617(TLS):23AUG74-903

ROCHER, R. LA THÉORIE DES VOIX DU
VERBE DANS L'ÉCOLE PĀṆINĒENNE (LE
14E ĀHNIKA).*
    C. CAILLAT, 343:BAND14HEFT2-165
EARL OF ROCHESTER. POEMS ON SEVERAL
OCCASIONS.
    G. MARSHALL, 568(SCN):FALL-WIN-
TER73-84
ROCHLIN, G. MAN'S AGRESSION.*
    617(TLS):29MAR74-317
ROCK, P. DEVIANT BEHAVIOUR. MAKING
PEOPLE PAY.
    617(TLS):5APR74-364
ROCK, P. & M. MC INTOSH. DEVIANCE
& SOCIAL CONTROL.
    617(TLS):3MAY74-473
ROCK, W.R. NEVILLE CHAMBERLAIN.
    D.R. NEAT, 577(SHR):SPRING72-204
ROCKEFELLER, J.D. 3D. THE SECOND
AMERICAN REVOLUTION.
    42(AR):VOL32#4-705
ROCKLAND, M.A. - SEE MARÍAS, J.
ROCKS, L. & R.P. RUNYON. THE ENERGY
CRISIS.*
    J.P. DEGNAN, 249(HUDR):AUTUMN73-
574
ROCKWELL, C. KAGOK.
    W. ADRIAANSZ, 187:MAY74-313
    B-S. SONG, 187:MAY74-315
ROCKWELL, J. FACT IN FICTION.
    617(TLS):23AUG74-902
RODERICK, C. - SEE LAWSON, H.
RODEWALD, D. ROBERT WALSERS PROSA.*
    G.B. PICKAR, 406:FALL73-309
RODGERS, A.D. THE HOUSING OF OGLE-
THORPE COUNTY, GEORGIA, 1790-1860.
    H. GLASSIE, 292(JAF):JUL-SEP72-
289
    M.B. LAPPING, 576:OCT72-246
RODGERS, W.R. COLLECTED POEMS.*
    J. SAUNDERS, 565:VOL13#4-74
RODGERS, W.R., ED. IRISH LITERARY
PORTRAITS.*
    639(VQR):AUTUMN73-CLX
RODINSON, M. ISLAM & CAPITALISM.
    E.W. SAID, 441:10NOV74-4
RODINSON, M. MOHAMMED.
    J.W. FIEGENBAUM, 390:AUG-SEP72-
76
RODIS-LEWIS, G. L'OEUVRE DE DES-
CARTES.
    H. DUFOURT, 542:OCT-DEC72-437
RODRÍGUEZ-ALCALÁ, H. HISTORIA DE LA
LITERATURA PARAGUAYA.
    A.W. ASHHURST, 238:DEC72-976
RODRÍGUEZ-MOÑINO, A. LA SILVA DE
ROMANCES DE BARCELONA, 1561.
    E. GLASER, 240(HR):AUTUMN72-469
RODWAY, A. THE TRUTHS OF FICTION.*
    M.C. BEARDSLEY, 128(CE):FEB72-
597
ROECKER, W.A., ED. STORIES THAT
COUNT.
    D.B. KESTERSON, 573(SSF):FALL72-
412
ROEMING, R.F., ED. GENERATING LIT-
ERARY APPRECIATION.
    J.M. ELLIS, 399(MLJ):OCT72-409
ROETHKE, T. STRAW FOR THE FIRE.*
(D. WAGONER, ED)
    J. LA BELLE, 639(VQR):AUTUMN72-
637
    D. PASCHALL, 569(SR):AUTUMN73-
859

ROETHLISBERGER-BIANCO, M. CAVALIER
PIETRO TEMPESTA & HIS TIME.
    A.S. HARRIS, 56:AUTUMN72-310
ROETT, R. THE POLITICS OF FOREIGN
AID IN THE BRAZILIAN NORTHEAST.
    D. CARNEIRO, 263:JAN-MAR73-113
ROGER, J. - SEE ROUSSEAU, J-J.
ROGER, J. & J-C. PAYEN, EDS. HIS-
TOIRE DE LA LITTÉRATURE FRANÇAISE.
(VOLS 1&2)
    M. BERTRAND, 207(FR):FEB72-757
ROGERS, E.F. - SEE HACKETT, J.
ROGERS, F.R. & P. BAENDER - SEE
TWAIN, M.
ROGERS, P. THE AUGUSTAN VISION.
    C. RAWSON, 617(TLS):4OCT74-1081
ROGERS, P. GRUB STREET.
    J. DIERICKX, 182:VOL25#9/10-290
    566:AUTUMN72-44
    676(YR):SPRING73-XVI
ROGERS, R. A PSYCHOANALYTIC STUDY
OF THE DOUBLE IN LITERATURE.
    R. CHRIST, 613:SPRING72-123
    F. CREWS, 191(ELN):SEP72-68
    J.J. PAPPAS, 177(ELT):VOL15#3-
232
ROGERS, T. THE CONFESSIONS OF A
CHILD OF THE CENTURY.
    S. O'CONNELL, 418(MR):WINTER73-
190
    E. ROVIT, 659:AUTUMN74-539
    639(VQR):AUTUMN72-CXX
ROGERS, T. - SEE BROOKE, R.
ROGERS, T.J. TECHNIQUES OF SOLIP-
SISM.*
    W. SCHUMANN, 222(GR):MAY72-230
ROGERS, W. LIFE ABOARD A BRITISH
PRIVATEER IN THE TIME OF QUEEN
ANNE. (R.C. LESLIE, ED)
    617(TLS):26JUL74-810
ROGERS, W.R. THE ONE-GALLUSED
REBELLION.
    H.C. BAILEY, 9(ALAR):APR72-153
ROGGERONE, G.A. LA VIA NUOVA DI
LEQUIER.
    E. NAMER, 542:JUL-SEP72-382
ROGIN, G. WHAT HAPPENS NEXT?
    J.C. OATES, 473(PR):WINTER73-143
ROGISSART, J. LE TEMPS DES CERISES.
    P. AUBERY, 207(FR):DEC71-487
ROH, F. & J. TSCHICHOLD, EDS. PHOTO-
EYE.
    617(TLS):19APR74-425
"THE ROHAN BOOK OF HOURS." (M.
MEISS & M. THOMAS, EDS)
    617(TLS):15MAR74-272
"THE ROHAN MASTER."*
    A. FRANKENSTEIN, 55:NOV73-46
ROHLFS, G. FROM VULGAR LATIN TO OLD
FRENCH.*
    J.R. ALLEN, 207(FR):FEB72-721
    F.J. BARNETT, 208(FS):JUL73-361
    R.A. HALL, JR., 215(GL):VOL12#3-
186
    C. RÉGNIER, 209(FM):JUL72-267
ROHLFS, G. GRAMMATICA STORICA DELLA
LINGUA ITALIANA E DEI SUOI DIALET-
TI.*
    I.P., 275(IQ):FALL/WINTER72-128
ROHMER, R. ULTIMATUM.
    T. ANGUS, 296:VOL3#3-114
ROHR, A. - SEE STAPFER, P.A.

ROHRER, C. FUNKTIONELLE SPRACHWIS-
SENSCHAFT UND TRANSFORMATIONELLE
GRAMMATIK.
U.L. FIGGE, 490:JUL-OCT72-434
H. WEBER, 343:BAND15HEFT2-128
G. WILLIAMS, 206:JAN73-427
ROHRER, C. DIE WORTZUSAMMENSETZUNG
IM MODERNEN FRANZÖSISCH.*
P.M. LLOYD, 545(RPH):NOV72-430
ROHWER, J. & G. HÜMMELCHEN. CHRON-
OLOGY OF THE WAR AT SEA 1939-45.
617(TLS):26JUL74-782
ROIPHE, A. LONG DIVISION.
W.H. PRITCHARD, 249(HUDR):SPRING
73-231
DE ROLA, S.K. - SEE UNDER KLOSSOWSKI
DE ROLA, S.
ROLFE, C.D. SAINT-AMANT & THE THE-
ORY OF "UT PICTURA POESIS."
W. BIESTERFELD, 182:VOL25#15/16-
554
ROLFE, S.E. & J.L. BURTLE. THE
GREAT WHEEL.
G. BARRACLOUGH, 453:27JUN74-14
A.L. MALABRE, JR., 231:JUL74-89
ROLLAND, H. LE MAUSOLÉE DE GLANUM.
A.L.F. RIVET, 313:VOL62-207
RÖLLEKE, H. - SEE VON DROSTE-HÜLS-
HOFF, A.
ROLLESTON, J. RILKE IN TRANSITION.*
K.S. WEIMAR, 221(GQ):NOV72-750
"THE ROLLING STONE READER."
A. NELSON, 441:14APR74-19
J. ROCKWELL, 441:8MAY74-37
"THE ROLLING STONE RECORD REVIEW."
(VOL 2)
J. ROCKWELL, 441:8MAY74-37
ROLOFF, D. GOTTÄHNLICHKEIT, VERGOTT-
LICHUNG UND ERHÖHUNG ZU SELIGEN
LEBEN.
R.T. WALLIS, 123:MAR73-49
ROLOFF, D. PLOTIN: DIE GROSSSCHRIFT,
III, 8; V, 8; V, 5; II, 9.*
A.H. ARMSTRONG, 123:MAR73-34
J.M. RIST, 303:VOL92-209
F.M. SCHROEDER, 487:SUMMER72-208
ROLOFF, H-G. STILSTUDIEN ZUR PROSA
DES 15. JAHRHUNDERTS.
O. REICHMANN, 433:APR72-235
ROLOFF, H-G. - SEE WICKRAM, G.
ROLPH, C.H. BELIEVE WHAT YOU LIKE.
617(TLS):25JAN74-85
ROLPH, C.H. KINGSLEY.*
N. THOMPSON, 99:FEB74-40
ROLPH, C.H. LIVING TWICE.
D.A.N. JONES, 362:10OCT74-481
P. WHITEHEAD, 617(TLS):22NOV74-
1306
"ROMAN ET LUMIÈRES AU XVIIIE
SIÈCLE."*
R. JOLY, 535(RHL):MAR-APR72-314
ROMANO, D. FLIGHT FROM TIME ONE.
617(TLS):15FEB74-163
ROMANO, F.R. - SEE CARRILLO Y SOTO-
MAYOR, L.
ROMANOV, A.I. NIGHTS ARE LONGEST
THERE.
R.M. SLUSSER, 32:DEC73-825
"THE ROMANTIC EGOISTS."*
H. BEVINGTON, 441:1DEC74-82
"ROMANTISME ET POLITIQUE, 1815-
1851."*
D.G. CHARLTON, 208(FS):OCT73-459
[CONTINUED]

[CONTINUING]
B. REIZOV, 535(RHL):MAY-JUN72-
534
DE ROME, C. ÉPÎTRE AUX CORINTHIENS.
(A. JAUBERT, ED & TRANS)
E. DES PLACES, 555:VOL46FASC2-
316
ROMEO, L. THE ECONOMY OF DIPHTHONGI-
ZATION IN EARLY ROMANCE.
L.F. SAS, 660(WORD):AUG70-286
ROMERALO, A.S. - SEE UNDER SÁNCHEZ
ROMERALO, A.
ROMERO, M.G. - SEE CUERVO, R.J.
DE ROMILLY, J. LA TRAGÉDIE GRECQUE.*
F. JOUAN, 555:VOL46FASC2-294
ROMMETVEIT, R. WORDS, MEANINGS, &
MESSAGES.
G.A. BORDEN, 480(P&R):SPRING72-
123
J. PRŮCHA, 353:15AUG72-99
ROMULO, C.P. CLARIFYING THE ASIAN
MYSTIQUE.
C. HOBBS, 293(JAST):FEB72-381
RONALD, D.W. & R.J. CARTER. THE
LONGMOOR MILITARY RAILWAY.
617(TLS):1MAR74-221
"EGON RONAY'S DUNLOP GUIDE."
617(TLS):17MAY74-534
RONCONI, G. - SEE BARBARO IL VECCHIO,
E.
RONNING, C. A MEMOIR OF CHINA IN
REVOLUTION.
R.F. SWANSON, 441:22SEP74-36
DE RONSARD, P. LES OEUVRES DE
PIERRE DE RONSARD.* (VOLS 7&8)
(I. SILVER, ED)
D. FENOALTEA, 207(FR):APR72-1063
DE RONSARD, P. SONNETS POUR HÉLÈNE.*
(M. SMITH, ED)
B. BRAUNROT, 207(FR):FEB72-744
L.W. JOHNSON, 551(RENQ):SPRING
72-94
R. KLESCZEWSKI, 72:BAND210HEFT
1/3-219
L. TERREAUX, 535(RHL):MAR-APR72-
303
RONSLEY, J. YEATS'S AUTOBIOGRAPHY.*
H. ADAMS, 219(GAR):FALL72-249
ROOKE, B.E. - SEE COLERIDGE, S.T.
ROOKE, L. LAST ONE HOME SLEEPS IN
THE YELLOW BED.
J.L. GREEN, 573(SSF):SUMMER72-
285
ROOKMAAKER, H.R. MODERN ART & THE
DEATH OF A CULTURE.
P. QUINLAN, 290(JAAC):WINTER71-
275
ROOM, A. PLACE-NAMES OF THE WORLD.
617(TLS):29MAR74-348
ROONEY, F. VALEDICTORY.
M. LEVIN, 441:13OCT74-20
ROOSEN-RUNGE, H. FARBGEBUNG UND
TECHNIK FRÜHMITTELALTERLICHE
BUCHMALEREI.
D.V. THOMPSON, 54:DEC72-539
ROOSEVELT, F.D. & W.C. BULLITT. FOR
THE PRESIDENT - PERSONAL & SECRET.*
(O.H. BULLITT, ED)
639(VQR):SPRING73-LXXVII
ROOT, W.P. STRIKING THE DARK AIR
FOR MUSIC.
W.H. PRITCHARD, 249(HUDR):AUTUMN
73-580

ROOTH, E. STUDIEN ZU DREI ADJEK-
TIVEN AUS DER ALTHOCHDEUTSCHEN
FRÜHZEIT, "ARUNDI, UNMANALOMI,
WIDARZOMI."
  W. FLEISCHHAUER, 301(JEGP):APR73-
  268
ROOTS, I., ED. CROMWELL.
  617(TLS):1MAR74-221
ROPER, L.W. F.L.O.
  P. GOLDBERGER, 441:3MAY74-43
  W.H. JORDY, 453:13JUN74-33
  E.R. LIPSON, 441:7APR74-6
  J. SEELYE, 617(TLS):8NOV74-1255
  E. WEEKS, 61:APR74-118
ROPER, R. ROYO COUNTY.*
  617(TLS):12JUL74-741
RORABACHER, L.E. MARJORIE BARNARD &
M. BARNARD ELDERSHAW.
  H.P. HESELTINE, 71(ALS):OCT74-
  444
ROREM, N. THE FINAL DIARY.
  M. STEINBERG, 441:17NOV74-6
VON ROSADOR, K.T. - SEE UNDER TET-
ZELI VON ROSADOR, K.
ROSALES, A. TRANSCENDENZ UND DIFF-
ERENZ.
  J.D.C., 543:DEC71-367
ROSBACO MARECHAL, E. LOS TIEMPOS
MÁGICOS.
  T. HOLZAPFEL, 238:MAY72-389
ROSCI, M. BASCHENIS, BETTERA & CO.
  E.H. RAMSDEN, 39:OCT72-363
ROSCOE, S. JOHN NEWBERY & HIS SUC-
CESSORS 1740-1814.
  617(TLS):3MAY74-469
ROSE, K.F.C. THE DATE & AUTHOR OF
THE "SATYRICON."
  P.G. WALSH, 123:DEC73-272
ROSE, L.A. AFTER YALTA.
  C.B. MARSHALL, 639(VQR):AUTUMN
  73-626
ROSE, L.A. DUBIOUS VICTORY.
  L.C. GARDNER, 441:17MAR74-16
ROSE, L.B. THE LAUNCHING OF BARBARA
FABRIKANT.
  M. LEVIN, 441:26MAY74-18
ROSE, M. GOLDING'S TALE.
  42(AR):SPRING/SUMMER72-241
ROSE, M. SHAKESPEAREAN DESIGN.
  T. HAWKES, 676(YR):SUMMER73-561
  639(VQR):SUMMER73-CXVI
ROSE, R., ED. ELECTORAL BEHAVIOUR.
  P. PULZER, 617(TLS):6DEC74-1366
ROSE, R. PEOPLE IN POLITICS.
  I. BULMER-THOMAS, 619(TC):VOL
  177#1043-50
ROSE, R. POLITICS IN ENGLAND TODAY.
  617(TLS):9AUG74-848
ROSE, S. THE CONSCIOUS BRAIN.
  R.M. RESTAK, 441:31MAR74-27
ROSEN, C. THE CLASSICAL STYLE.*
  B.H. HAGGIN, 569(SR):SPRING73-
  356
  M. PETERSON, 470:MAR72-23
  481(PQ):JUL72-602
  639(VQR):SUMMER72-CIX
ROSEN, J.N. L'ANALYSE DIRECTE.
  C. BARDET, 542:OCT-DEC72-481
ROSEN, K., ED. THE MAN TO SEND RAIN
CLOUDS.
  P. ADAMS, 61:JAN74-99
ROSEN, M. POPCORN VENUS.*
  J. WILSON, 441:24MAR74-6

ROSEN, R.S. E.T.A. HOFFMANNS "KATER
MURR."
  J.M. MC GLATHERY, 222(GR):NOV72-
  312
  S.P.S., 191(ELN):SEP72(SUPP)-166
ROSEN, S. G.W.F. HEGEL.
  617(TLS):30AUG74-922
ROSEN, S. NIHILISM.*
  B. MAGNUS, 543:DEC71-292
ROSEN, S. NONE SO DEAF.
  617(TLS):22FEB74-176
ROSENBAUER, H. BRECHT UND DER BE-
HAVIORISMUS.*
  H. SCHER, 406:SUMMER73-179
ROSENBAUM, S.P., ED. ENGLISH LITER-
ATURE & BRITISH PHILOSOPHY.
  P.K. ALKON, 566:SPRING73-115
ROSENBERG, B. & H. SILVERSTEIN, EDS.
THE REAL TINSEL.
  P. SCHJELDAHL, 441:8DEC74-36
ROSENBERG, B.A. THE ART OF THE AMER-
ICAN FOLK PREACHER.*
  F.E. MOORER, 400(MLN):DEC72-1007
  D.J. WINSLOW, 292(JAF):APR-JUN72-
  191
ROSENBERG, H. ACT & THE ACTOR.
  M. WEITZ, 473(PR):WINTER73-126
ROSENBERG, H. THE DE-DEFINITION OF
ART.
  P. RUTA, 58:SEP/OCT72-70
  M. WEITZ, 473(PR):WINTER73-126
ROSENBERG, H. DISCOVERING THE PRES-
ENT.
  J. ACKERMAN, 453:7FEB74-25
  K. BAKER, 441:3FEB74-10
  A. BROYARD, 441:5FEB74-41
ROSENBERG, H. WILLEM DE KOONING.
  A. BROYARD, 441:14OCT74-31
  C. ROBINS, 441:1DEC74-104
  442(NY):16DEC74-168
ROSENBERG, J. ON QUALITY IN ART.
  S. ALPERS, 54:MAR72-110
ROSENBERG, J. DOROTHY RICHARDSON.*
  442(NY):14JAN74-98
ROSENBERG, J., S. SLIVE & E.H. TER
KUILE. DUTCH ART & ARCHITECTURE
1600-1800.
  J. BRUYN, 54:JUN72-219
ROSENBERG, M. THE MASKS OF KING
LEAR.*
  T. HAWKES, 676(YR):SUMMER73-561
  C.C. HUFFMAN, 301(JEGP):OCT73-
  552
ROSENBERG, P. THE SEVENTH HERO.
  N. ANNAN, 453:27JUN74-6
  G. LEVINE, 441:21JUL74-1
ROSENBERG, S. NAKED IS THE BEST
DISGUISE.
  C. LEHMANN-HAUPT, 441:5JUN74-49
  442(NY):24JUN74-104
ROSENBERG, S.N. MODERN FRENCH "CE."
  R.A. HALL, JR., 350:MAR73-198
  R. LASSALLE, 209(FM):JUL72-267
ROSENBERGER, F.C., ED. RECORDS OF
THE COLUMBIA HISTORICAL SOCIETY OF
WASHINGTON, D.C., 1969-1970.
  639(VQR):SPRING72-LXVIII
ROSENBLUETH, A. MIND & BRAIN.*
  J.M.B., 543:JUN72-766
  R. PUCCETTI, 486:DEC72-567
  42(AR):SPRING/SUMMER72-249
ROSENBLUM, R. THE GOOD THIEF.
  N. CALLENDAR, 441:6OCT74-38

ROSENBLUM, R. THE MUSHROOM CAVE.*
617(TLS):1MAR74-219
ROSENBLUM, R. FRANK STELLA.*
J-C. LEBENSZTEJN, 98:MAY72-391
ROSENFELD, A.H. - SEE WHEELWRIGHT, J.
ROSENFELD, M. EDMOND JALOUX.
A. MC CONNELL, 50(ARQ):WINTER72-376
ROSENFELDT, N.E. KAPITALISMENS
GENESIS.
A.T. ANDERSON, 32:MAR73-162
ROSENFIELD, I. HOSPITAL ARCHITEC-
TURE.
S. CLIBBON, 46:AUG72-128
ROSENFIELD, J.M. & S. SHIMADA. TRA-
DITIONS OF JAPANESE ART.*
J. HILLIER, 135:JUL72-227
D. RHODES, 139:DEC71-65
ROSENGARTEN, T. - SEE SHAW, N.
ROSENGREN, I. SEMANTISCHE STRUK-
TUREN.*
J. SCHARNHORST, 682(ZPSK):BAND25
HEFT1/2-167
ROSENMAN, J., J. ROBERTS & R. PILPEL.
YOUNG MEN WITH UNLIMITED CAPITAL.
J. ROCKWELL, 441:22DEC74-10
ROSENTHAL, D.B. THE LIMITED ELITE.
H. SPODEK, 293(JAST):MAY72-708
ROSENTHAL, D.M., ED. MATERIALISM &
THE MIND-BODY PROBLEM.
W.D., 543:DEC71-376
J. KEKES, 154:JUN72-316
ROSENTHAL, E. THE ILLUMINATIONS OF
THE VERGILIUS ROMANUS.*
J. GUTMANN, 290(JAAC):SUMMER73-
558
ROSENTHAL, F. FOUR ESSAYS ON ART &
LITERATURE IN ISLAM.
R. ETTINGHAUSEN, 57:VOL34#4-353
ROSENTHAL, J. INDIANS.
E. BASTOW, 648:JUN72-55
ROSENTHAL, M.L. THE VIEW FROM THE
PEACOCK'S TAIL.*
639(VQR):WINTER73-XII
ROSKILL, M. VAN GOGH, GAUGUIN & THE
IMPRESSIONIST CIRCLE.*
H. DORRA, 54:DEC72-560
ROSKILL, M.W. DOLCE'S "ARETINO" &
VENETIAN ART THEORY OF THE CINQUE-
CENTO.*
A. PALLUCCHINI, 54:MAR72-95
ROSKILL, S. HANKEY. (VOL 3)
J. GRIGG, 362:27JUN74-838
617(TLS):31MAY74-583
ROSS, A. THE BRADFORD BUSINESS.
617(TLS):1MAR74-219
ROSS, A. IF I KNEW WHAT I WAS DOING.
N. CALLENDAR, 441:20OCT74-42
ROSS, A., ED. LIVING IN LONDON.
M-K. WILMERS, 617(TLS):27DEC74-
1456
ROSS, A., ED. LONDON MAGAZINE STOR-
IES.
V. CUNNINGHAM, 617(TLS):20DEC74-
1437
ROSS, A. THE TAJ EXPRESS.
S. CONN, 362:28NOV74-717
617(TLS):5APR74-371
ROSS, A.M. WILLIAM HENRY BARTLETT.
617(TLS):26APR74-432
ROSS, D. G. STANLEY HALL.
W.A. KOELSCH, 432(NEQ):SEP72-436

ROSS, D. A PUBLIC CITIZEN'S ACTION
MANUAL.
42(AR):VOL32#4-712
ROSS, D.J.A. ILLUSTRATED MEDIEVAL
ALEXANDER-BOOKS IN GERMANY & THE
NETHERLANDS.
G. DOGAER, 182:VOL25#13/14-449
J.B. FRIEDMAN, 301(JEGP):JAN73-
118
F.P. PICKERING, 402(MLR):JUL73-
685
K. VARTY, 382(MAE):1973/1-82
ROSS, D.O., JR. STYLE & TRADITION
IN CATULLUS.*
K.W. MILLS, 313:VOL62-214
ROSS, H.E. BEHAVIOUR & PERCEPTION
IN STRANGE ENVIRONMENTS.
J. REASON, 617(TLS):6DEC74-1362
ROSS, I.S. LORD KAMES & THE SCOT-
LAND OF HIS DAY.*
A.E. MC GUINNESS, 173(ECS):SUM-
MER73-514
ROSS, J. THE BURNING OF BILLY
TOOBER.
617(TLS):31MAY74-591
ROSS, J. & C. ROMANO. THE COMPLETE
PRINTMAKER.
A. FRANKENSTEIN, 55:MAR73-16
ROSS, J. & M. WATERFIELD. LEAVES
FROM OUR TUSCAN KITCHEN.
N. HAZELTON, 441:1DEC74-94
ROSS, J.F. PHILOSOPHICAL THEOLOGY.*
A. PLANTINGA, 482(PHR):OCT72-509
ROSS, J.J. THE APPEAL TO THE GIVEN.
W. EASTMAN, 154:DEC72-649
ROSS, R. FALLS THE SHADOW.
N. CALLENDAR, 441:31MAR74-41
ROSS, S. MORAL DECISION.
I.M. FOWLIE, 518:MAY73-20
ROSS, S.D. LITERATURE & PHILOSOPHY.
D.D. TODD, 648:OCT72-68
ROSS, S.D. THE SCIENTIFIC PROCESS.
J-J. DAETWYLER, 182:VOL25#1/2-9
ROSS-MACDONALD, M. EVERY LIVING
THING.
617(TLS):1NOV74-1240
ROSSELLI, J. LORD WILLIAM BENTINCK.
R. MITCHISON, 362:2MAY74-574
617(TLS):10MAY74-501
ROSSETTI, L., ED. BIBLIOGRAFIA DELL'-
UNIVERSITÀ DI PADOVA. (VOLS 1-3)
P. ZAMBELLI, 548(RCSF):JUL-SEP72-
342
ROSSI, P. PHILOSOPHY, TECHNOLOGY &
THE ARTS IN THE EARLY MODERN ERA.
S. DEVONS, 551(RENQ):SUMMER72-
243
ROSSI, P. & D. RADCLIFF-UMSTEAD.
ITALIANO OGGI.
G.P. ORWEN, 276:AUTUMN72-346
ROSSI, V. ANDRÉ GIDE.*
H.T. MASON, 447(N&Q):FEB72-73
RÖSSING-HAGER, M. WORTINDEX ZU
GEORG BÜCHNER.
P.M. DALY, 564:OCT72-224
H.J. SCHMIDT, 406:WINTER73-425
RÖSSING-HAGER, M., ED. WORTINDEX ZU
GOTTFRIED KELLER, DIE LEUTE VON
SELDWYLA.
P. OCHSENBEIN, 657(WW):NOV/DEC72-
430
ROSSITER, C. THE AMERICAN QUEST,
1790-1860.
C.N. DEGLER, 656(WMQ):JAN72-173

ROSSITER, J. THE MANIPULATORS.
N. CALLENDAR, 441:3FEB74-26
ROSSITER, S. BLUE GUIDE TO CRETE.
617(TLS):9AUG74-854
ROSSITER, S., ED. THE BLUE GUIDES:
LONDON.
617(TLS):15MAR74-273
ROSSKAM, E. ROOSEVELT, NEW JERSEY.
42(AR):SPRING/SUMMER72-243
ROSSNER, R. THE END OF SOMEONE
ELSE'S RAINBOW.
N. CALLENDAR, 441:21APR74-42
ROSSO, C. MONTESQUIEU MORALISTE.
R. SHACKLETON, 208(FS):APR73-210
205(FMLS):JUL72-289
ROSSO, C. - SEE BIONDI, C. & OTHERS
VAN ROSSUM-GUYON, F. CRITIQUE DU
ROMAN.
L.S. ROUDIEZ, 546(RR):FEB72-76
ROSTAND, C. LISZT.*
J.A.W., 410(M&L):JAN73-98
ROSTAND, R. THE KILLER ELITE.*
N. CALLENDAR, 441:11AUG74-12
ROSTAND, R. VIPER'S GAME.
N. CALLENDAR, 441:3NOV74-71
ROSTEN, L. DEAR "HERM."
A. CORMAN, 441:24MAR74-22
ROSTEN, N. OVER & OUT.
M. ELLMANN, 676(YR):SPRING73-461
ROSTENBERG, L. THE MINORITY PRESS
& THE ENGLISH CROWN, 1558-1625.
H.S. BENNETT, 354:SEP72-257
ROSTOW, E.V. PEACE IN THE BALANCE.*
P. SEABURY, 639(VQR):SPRING73-
269
D. YERGIN, 676(YR):SUMMER73-594
RØSTVIG, M-S. THE HAPPY MAN. (VOL
2) (2ND ED)
R. SHARROCK, 481(PQ):JUL72-629
ROSZAK, T., ED. THE DISSENTING ACA-
DEMY.
W.G. MOORE, 402(MLR):JAN73-134
ROSZAK, T. WHERE THE WASTELAND
ENDS.*
M. CURRAN, 128(CE):APR73-1017
H. LOMAS, 364:AUG/SEP73-130
ROSZKO, F.C. A CLASSICAL ARMENIAN
GRAMMAR.
R.J. JEFFERS, 318(JAOS):OCT-DEC
72-581
ROTBERG, R.I. & A.A. MAZRUI. PRO-
TEST & POWER IN BLACK AFRICA.
J. VAN VELSEN, 69:APR72-153
ROTERS, E. PAINTERS OF THE BAUHAUS.*
A.C. BIRNHOLZ, 290(JAAC):SUMMER
72-552
ROTH, B. & J. WEINSHEIMER. AN ANNO-
TATED BIBLIOGRAPHY OF JANE AUSTEN
STUDIES 1952-1972.
617(TLS):5APR74-376
ROTH, C. JEWISH ART. (REV BY B.
NARKISS)
R.J.L.W. THOMAS, 135:MAY72-65
ROTH, E. A TALE OF THREE CITIES.
G. VERMES, 32:JUN73-411
ROTH, G. & J. VARLOOT - SEE DIDEROT,
D.
ROTH, J. THE RADETZKY MARCH.
P. ADAMS, 61:JUL74-100
E. WIESEL, 441:3NOV74-70
617(TLS):28JUN74-687
ROTH, J.K. FREEDOM & THE MORAL LIFE.
M.B.M., 543:SEP71-136
ROTH, J.K. - SEE ROYCE, J.

ROTH, P. THE BREAST.*
P. BAILEY, 364:JUN/JUL73-153
S. O'CONNELL, 418(MR):WINTER73-
190
ROTH, P. THE GREAT AMERICAN NOVEL.*
R. GILMAN, 473(PR):3/1973-467
M. MUDRICK, 249(HUDR):AUTUMN73-
545
E. ROVIT, 659:AUTUMN74-539
R. SALE, 418(MR):AUTUMN73-834
ROTH, P. MY LIFE AS A MAN.
A. BROYARD, 441:23MAY74-45
R. DAVIES, 617(TLS):1NOV74-1217
M. DICKSTEIN, 441:2JUN74-1
C. NEWMAN, 231:JUL74-87
E. TENNANT, 362:5DEC74-752
R. TODD, 61:JUL74-92
M. WOOD, 453:13JUN74-8
442(NY):24JUN74-102
ROTHBERG, A. THE HEIRS OF STALIN.
B.M. COHEN, 584(SWR):AUTUMN73-
353
B. SCHERR, 32:MAR73-212
ROTHBERG, A. ALEXANDER SOLZHENITZYN,
THE MAJOR NOVELS.
H. MUCHNIC, 550(RUSR):OCT72-431
A.P. OBOLENSKY, 399(MLJ):DEC72-
533
ROTHE, H-J. & R. SZESKUS - SEE MEN-
DELSSOHN, F.
RÜTHEL, H.K. KANDINSKY, DAS GRAPH-
ISCHE WERK.
P. VERGO, 90:MAY72-342
ROTHENBERG, J. THE JEWISH RELIGION
IN THE SOVIET UNION.*
M. FRIEDBERG, 550(RUSR):JUL72-
301
ROTHENSTEIN, J. MODERN ENGLISH
PAINTERS.
J. DARRACOTT, 362:21FEB74-246
ROTHENSTEIN, W. & R. TAGORE. IMPER-
FECT ENCOUNTER. (M.M. LAGO, ED)
R.E. TEELE, 352(LE&W):VOL15#4&
VOL16#1/2-917
ROTHMAN, D.J. THE DISCOVERY OF THE
ASYLUM.*
J.M. HOLL, 656(WMQ):APR73-368
639(VQR):SPRING72-LXVIII
ROTHSCHILD, E. PARADISE LOST.*
R.J. BARNET, 453:2MAY74-33
C. DRIVER, 362:23MAY74-671
R. TODD, 61:JAN74-91
617(TLS):24MAY74-544
ROTIMI, O. THE GODS ARE NOT TO
BLAME.
A. RENDLE, 157:WINTER71-77
ROTMAN, B. & G.T. KNEEBONE. THE
THEORY OF SETS & TRANSFINITE NUM-
BERS.
P. SMITH, 316:SEP72-614
ROTROU, J. HERCULE MOURANT. (D.A.
WATTS, ED)
R.C. KNIGHT, 208(FS):JUL73-328
J. VAN BAELEN, 207(FR):MAY72-
1195
ROTSTEIN, A. & G. LAX, EDS. GETTING
IT BACK.
C. TAYLOR, 99:MAY/JUN74-28
ROTTENSTEINER, F., ED. VIEW FROM
ANOTHER SHORE.*
617(TLS):15FEB74-163

ROTTMANN, L., J. BARRY & B.T. PAQUET, EDS. WINNING HEARTS & MINDS.*
   E. BINNO & J. VALENTINE, 128(CE): APR73-1022
   J.W. HEALEY, 502(PRS):WINTER72/73-355
RÖTZER, H.G. DER ROMAN DES BAROCK 1600-1700.
   G. HOFFMEISTER, 406:FALL73-312
ROUBARD, J. MONO NO AWARE.
   M. CRANSTON, 207(FR):OCT71-214
ROUBARD, J. TRENTE ET UN AU CUBE.
   617(TLS):10MAY74-507
ROUBINE, J-J. LECTURES DE RACINE.
   C. CHANTALAT, 535(RHL):JUL-AUG72-710
   W.O. GOODE, 207(FR):MAY72-1194
ROUD, R. GODARD.
   L. RUSSELL, 376:JAN72-120
ROUDAUT, J., ED. POÈTES ET GRAMMAIRIENS DU XVIIIE SIÈCLE.
   G. LAFEUILLE, 481(PQ):JUL72-629
   R. MERCIER, 557(RSH):JUL-SEP72-454
ROUDIEZ, L. - SEE O'BRIEN, J.
ROUDIEZ, L.S. FRENCH FICTION TODAY.*
   639(VQR):WINTER73-XXV
ROUECHE, B. FERAL.
   M. LEVIN, 441:29DEC74-20
   442(NY):11NOV74-215
ROUGER, G. - SEE RESTIF DE LA BRETONNE
ROUGERIE, J. PARIS LIBRE 1871.*
   R. MERKER, 207(FR):MAY72-1172
ROUGIER, L. LA RELIGION ASTRALE DES PYTHAGORICIENS.
   P. AUBENQUE, 543:JAN-MAR72-62
ROUGIER, L. TRAITÉ DE LA CONNAISSANCE.
   R. BLANCHÉ, 316:MAR72-178
ROULET, E. SYNTAXE DE LA PROPOSITION NUCLÉAIRE EN FRANÇAIS PARLÉ.*
   U. EGLI, 343:BAND14HEFT1-12
   A.J. NADEN, 361:VOL28#3-286
ROUMAIN, J. EBONY WOOD.
   639(VQR):SPRING73-LXIV
ROUQUET, A. THE PRESENT STATE OF THE ARTS IN ENGLAND.*
   D. FITZ-GERALD, 90:SEP72-639
ROUQUETTE, J-M. PROVENCE ROMANE.
   617(TLS):4OCT74-1060
ROUSE, P., JR. JAMES BLAIR OF VIRGINIA.*
   R.P. THOMSON, 656(WMQ):OCT72-661
   639(VQR):SPRING72-LVIII
ROUSSEAU, G.S., ED. ORGANIC FORM.
   H.K., 125:OCT72-87
ROUSSEAU, G.S. & P.G. BOUCÉ, EDS. TOBIAS SMOLLETT.*
   D.K. JEFFREY, 125:JUN73-321
   A. PARREAUX, 189(EA):OCT-DEC72-565
ROUSSEAU, J-J. DISCOURS SUR LES SCIENCES ET LES ARTS [&] DISCOURS SUR L'ORIGINE ET LES FONDEMENTS DE L'INÉGALITÉ PARMI LES HOMMES. (J. ROGER, ED)
   D. FAYETTE-LEDUC, 542:JUL-SEP72-334
ROUSSEAU, J-J. ROUSSEAU RELIGIOUS WRITINGS.* (R. GRIMSLEY, ED)
   B.C. FINK, 207(FR):OCT71-264
   205(FMLS):JAN72-92

ROUSSEL, D. LES SICILIENS ENTRE LES ROMAINS ET LES CARTHAGINOIS À L'ÉPOQUE DE LA PREMIÈRE GUERRE PUNIQUE.*
   A.H. MC DONALD, 123:MAR73-104
   B.H. WARMINGTON, 303:VOL92-232
ROUSSEL, R. THE METAPHYSICS OF DARKNESS.*
   N. ALFORD, 376:APR72-125
   R. GILLESPIE, 454:FALL72-89
   L. GRAVER, 639(VQR):SPRING72-315
   E.K. HAY, 401(MLQ):MAR73-85
   M. LAINE, 529(QQ):AUTUMN72-421
   F.P.W. MC DOWELL, 481(PQ):OCT72-922
   W. MESSENGER, 648:OCT72-70
   J. MEYERS, 136:VOL4#1-72
   F.K. SCHNEIDER, 613:WINTER72-611
ROUSSOS, E.N. HO HĒRAKLEITOS STIS ENNEADES TOY PLŌTINOY.
   G.J.P. O'DALY, 303:VOL92-210
ROUTH, F. CONTEMPORARY BRITISH MUSIC.*
   P. EVANS, 415:MAY73-490
ROUTH, F. EARLY ENGLISH ORGAN MUSIC FROM THE MIDDLE AGES TO 1837.*
   J.A.C., 410(M&L):JUL73-347
ROUVIER-JEANLIN, M. LES FIGURINES GALLO-ROMAINES EN TERRE CUITE AU MUSÉE DES ANTIQUITÉS NATIONALES.
   S. MARTIN-KILCHER, 182:VOL25#23/24-881
ROVERI, A.M.D. I SARCOFAGI EGIZI DELLE ORIGINE ALLA FINE DELL'ANTICO REGNO.
   A.M. BADAWY, 318(JAOS):APR-JUN72-304
ROVIT, E. CROSSINGS.
   E. ROVIT, 659:AUTUMN74-539
ROWAN, J. THE SOCIAL INDIVIDUAL.
   617(TLS):15MAR74-252
ROWAN, S.A. THEY WOULDN'T LET US DIE.
   A. LEWIS, 453:7MAR74-6
ROWAT, D.C. THE OMBUDSMAN PLAN.
   G.B. MC CLELLAN, 99:MAY/JUN74-59
ROWDON, M. LORENZO THE MAGNIFICENT.
   617(TLS):14JUN74-632
ROWDON, M. THE SPANISH TERROR.
   617(TLS):11OCT74-1139
ROWE, C.J. THE EUDEMIAN & NICOMACHEAN ETHICS.
   F.E. SPARSHOTT, 487:AUTUMN72-300
ROWE, J. THE HARD-ROCK MEN.
   A.L. ROWSE, 617(TLS):22NOV74-1305
ROWELL, G. HELL & THE VICTORIANS.
   J.W. BURROW, 617(TLS):2AUG74-821
ROWELL, G., ED. LATE VICTORIAN PLAYS, 1890-1914.*
   P. NORDON, 189(EA):OCT-DEC72-575
ROWELL, G., ED. VICTORIAN DRAMATIC CRITICISM.
   205(FMLS):JAN72-93
ROWLAND, B. BLIND BEASTS.
   D.S. BREWER, 402(MLR):JUL73-630
   D.E. LAMPE, 191(ELN):MAR73-226
   P.W. ROGERS, 529(QQ):AUTUMN72-416
   A.M. WILSON, 382(MAE):1973/1-91
ROWLAND, B., ED. COMPANION TO CHAUCER STUDIES.*
   J.R. SIMON, 189(EA):JAN-MAR72-52

ROWLAND, B. & F. RICE. ART IN
AFGHANISTAN.
  J. HILLIER, 135:JUN72-151
ROWLAND, K.T. EIGHTEENTH-CENTURY
INVENTIONS.
  617(TLS):3MAY74-484
ROWLAND, K.T. THE GREAT BRITAIN.
  M.J. PHILP, 637(VS):MAR72-383
ROWLAND, T.H. DISCOVERING NORTHUM-
BERLAND.
  617(TLS):1FEB74-116
ROWLEY, G. PRINCIPLES OF CHINESE
PAINTING. (REV)
  W. WATSON, 90:MAY72-337
ROWLEY, N., COMP. LAW & ORDER IN
ESSEX, 1066-1874.
  D.J. JOHNSON, 325:APR72-451
ROWSE, A.L. THE ELIZABETHAN RENAIS-
SANCE.
  639(VQR):WINTER73-XXXVIII
ROWSE, A.L. SIMON FORMAN.
  617(TLS):7JUN74-604
ROWSE, A.L. SHAKESPEARE THE MAN.*
  G. STEINER, 442(NY):18MAR74-142
ROWSE, A.L. WINDSOR CASTLE.
  617(TLS):12APR74-387
ROWSE, A.L. - SEE SHAKESPEARE, W.
ROXAS, F. THE WORLD OF FELIX ROXAS.
  G.K. GOODMAN, 293(JAST):MAY72-
  743
ROY, C. LES SOLEILS DU ROMANTISME.
  617(TLS):9AUG74-847
ROY, D.T. KUO MO-JO: THE EARLY
YEARS.
  Y.J. CHIH, 318(JAOS):OCT-DEC72-
  584
  F.W. HOUN, 293(JAST):NOV71-193
ROY, P. PIERRE BOULLE ET SON OEUVRE.
  J-P. CAP, 207(FR):OCT71-242
"ROYAL ACADEMY EXHIBTORS, 1905-1970."
(VOL 1)
  617(TLS):5APR74-376
ROYCE, J. THE PHILOSOPHY OF JOSIAH
ROYCE. (J.K. ROTH, ED)
  L.B. CEBIK, 219(GAR):SPRING72-97
ROZA, R. ROGER MARTIN DU GARD ET LA
BANALITÉ RETROUVÉE.
  P. BRADY, 207(FR):MAR72-915
ROZANOV, V. DOSTOEVSKY & THE LEGEND
OF THE GRAND INQUISITOR.
  R. GREGG, 550(RUSR):OCT72-432
RUBEL, M., ED & TRANS. PAGES DE
KARL MARX POUR UNE ÉTHIQUE SOCIAL-
ISTE.
  J. BERNHARDT, 542:JUL-SEP72-385
RUBENSTEIN, H. INSOMNIACS OF THE
WORLD, GOODNIGHT.
  S. OLSON, 441:15DEC74-24
RUBIN, D.L. HIGHER, HIDDEN ORDER.
  O. DE MOURGUES, 208(FS):JAN73-58
RUBIN, J. THE BARKING DEER.
  M. LEVIN, 441:31MAR74-40
RUBIN, L.D., JR. THE WRITER IN THE
SOUTH.
  J.W. TUTTLETON, 676(YR):WINTER73-
  305
  639(VQR):WINTER73-XVIII
RUBIN, W.S. FRANK STELLA.
  J-C. LEBENSZTEJN, 98:MAY72-391
RUBINOFF, L. COLLINGWOOD & THE RE-
FORM OF METAPHYSICS.*
  P. JONES, 154:MAR72-126
  J. PASSMORE, 63:AUG73-175

RUBINOFF, L., ED. TRADITION & REVO-
LUTION.
  K. MC SWEENEY, 529(QQ):SUMMER72-
  284
RUCH, M. - SEE CICERO
RUCHAMES, L., ED. RACIAL THOUGHT IN
AMERICA: FROM THE PURITANS TO ABRA-
HAM LINCOLN.
  K.J. HANSEN, 529(QQ):AUTUMN72-
  429
RÜCKERT, G. MÖRIKE UND HORAZ.
  G. STORZ, 52:BAND7HEFT1-99
RÜCKERT, H. VORTRÄGE UND AUFSÄTZE
ZUR HISTORISCHEN THEOLOGIE.
  F.F. BRUCE, 182:VOL25#3/4-79
RUDÉ, G. THE HISTORY OF LONDON: HAN-
OVERIAN LONDON 1714-1808.*
  R.W. GREAVES, 481(PQ):JUL72-550
  R.C. MIDDLETON, 656(WMQ):JUL72-
  504
  G.B. NEEDHAM, 173(ECS):FALL72-
  132
  639(VQR):WINTER72-XXXII
RUDÉ, G. PARIS & LONDON IN THE
EIGHTEENTH CENTURY.
  J.J. HECHT, 481(PQ):JUL72-551
RUDENKO, S.I. FROZEN TUMBS OF
SIBERIA.* (M.W. THOMPSON, ED &
TRANS)
  R.D. BARNETT, 39:AUG72-168
  G.F. DALES, 318(JAOS):APR-JUN72-
  328
RUDHARDT, J. LE THÈME DE L'EAU PRI-
MORDIALE DANS LA MYTHOLOGIE
GRECQUE.
  F. VIAN, 555:VOL46FASC2-285
RUDLOFF-HILLE, G. SCHILLER AUF DER
DEUTSCHEN BÜHNE SEINER ZEIT.
  R. DAU, 654(WB):1/1972-187
  I. KOWATZKI, 221(GQ):NOV72-765
RUDNER, R. & I. SCHEFFLER, EDS.
LOGIC & ART.*
  L.A. ELIOSEFF, 290(JAAC):SPRING
  73-405
RUDNIK, R. IN THE HEART OF OUR CITY.
  R. PINSKY, 491:JAN74-241
RUDOLF, P.R. - SEE VON LANGENSTEIN,
H.
RUDOLPH, H. KULTURKRITIK UND KON-
SERVATIVE REVOLUTION.*
  V.O. DURR, 301(JEGP):JAN73-97
  W.E. YATES, 402(MLR):OCT73-950
RUDOLPH, P. THE ARCHITECTURE OF
PAUL RUDOLPH.
  R.R. BOSCH, 576:MAR72-73
RUDOLPH, R.S. WOOD COUNTY PLACE
NAMES.
  M. CARMONY, 424:MAR72-62
RUDORFF, R. BELLE EPOQUE.
  M. GREEN, 364:FEB/MAR73-144
RUDORFF, R. WAR TO THE DEATH.
  617(TLS):31MAY74-588
RÜEGG, R. HAUSSPRÜCHE UND VOLKSKUL-
TUR.
  R.L. WELSCH, 292(JAF):JAN-MAR72-
  96
RUELL, P. DEATH TAKES THE LOW ROAD.
  617(TLS):30AUG74-933
RUELL, P. RED CHRISTMAS.
  N. CALLENDAR, 441:3MAR74-33
RUELLO, F. LA NOTION DE VÉRITÉ CHEZ
SAINT ALBERT LE GRAND ET CHEZ
SAINT THOMAS D'AQUIN.
  J. JOLIVET, 542:APR-JUN72-174

RUESCH, H. BACK TO THE TOP OF THE
WORLD.*
P. CAMPBELL, 617(TLS):27DEC74-
1466
RUFFIN, E. THE DIARY OF EDMUND RUF-
FIN. (VOL 1) (W.K. SCARBOROUGH,
ED)
639(VQR):AUTUMN72-CXXXVI
RUFFNER, B. ALL HELL NEEDS IS WATER.
W. GARD, 584(SWR):SPRING73-V
RUGGERI, U. DISEGNI PIAZZETTESCHI.
G. KNOX, 90:MAR72-183
RUGGIERS, P.G. - SEE BARBI, M.
RUHMER, E., WITH OTHERS, COMPS. BAY-
ERISCHE STAATSGEMÄLDESAMMLUNGEN.
J. GAGE, 90:MAR72-185
RUIGH, R.E. THE PARLIAMENT OF 1624.*
A.J. LOOMIE, 613:AUTUMN72-477
RUIN, H. HÖJDER OCH STUP HOS IBSEN
OCH NÅGRA ANDRA.*
G.C. SCHOOLFIELD, 563(SS):WINTER
73-89
RUIZ-FORNELLS, E., COMP. A CONCOR-
DANCE TO THE POETRY OF GUSTAVO
ADOLFO BÉCQUER.
J.R. CHATHAM, 399(MLJ):DEC72-519
RUIZ IRIARTE, V. ESTA NOCHE ES LA
VÍSPERA. (J.S. MERRILL, ED)
J. ALMEIDA, 238:DEC72-984
RUIZ SALVADOR, A. EL ATENEO CIEN-
TÍFICO, LITERARIO Y ARTÍSTICO DE
MADRID (1835-1885).
I.M. ZAVALA, 402(MLR):JUL73-679
RUKEYSER, M. BREAKING OPEN.
617(TLS):29MAR74-339
RUKSER, U. BIBLIOGRAFÍA DE ORTEGA.*
G.C. RUMP, 182:VOL25#7/8-205
RULE, J.B. PRIVATE LIVES & PUBLIC
SURVEILLANCE.*
R. HOLBROOKE, 441:16JUN74-4
RUMPLER, H. DIE PROTOKOLLE DES
ÖSTERREICHISCHEN MINISTERRATES
1848-1867, EINLEITUNGSBAND.*
F.L. CARSTEN, 575(SEER):JAN73-
136
RUNDLE, B. PERCEPTION, SENSATION &
VERIFICATION.
J.W.R. COX, 518:JAN73-31
RUOTOLO, L.P. SIX EXISTENTIAL HER-
OES.
P.J. CONN, 31(ASCH):WINTER73/74-
160
RUPP, H. DEUTSCHE RELIGIÖSE DICH-
TUNGEN DES 11. UND 12. JAHRHUN-
DERTS. (2ND ED)
D. BLAMIRES, 402(MLR):JUL73-688
RUPP, H. & E. STUDER - SEE RANKE, F.
RUPPIN, A. ARTHUR RUPPIN: MEMOIRS,
DIARIES, LETTERS. (A. BEIN, ED)
M.I. UROFSKY, 390:OCT72-77
RUPPRICH, H. DIE DEUTSCHE LITERATUR
VOM SPÄTEN MITTELALTER BIS ZUM BAR-
OCK. (PT 1)
M.L. BAEUMER, 406:WINTER73-393
RUPPRICH, H. DIE DEUTSCHE LITERATUR
VOM SPÄTEN MITTELALTER BIS ZUM BAR-
OCK. (PT 2)
617(TLS):25OCT74-1187
RUPRECHT, E. & D. BÄNSCH, EDS. LIT-
ERARISCHE MANIFESTE DER JAHRHUN-
DERTWENDE, 1890-1910.
J. OSBORNE, 402(MLR):JAN73-237

RUSCH, J. DIE VORSTELLUNG VOM GOLD-
ENEN ZEITALTER DER ENGLISCHEN
SPRACHE IM 16., 17. UND 18. JAHR-
HUNDERT.
K. FAISS, 182:VOL25#21-735
RUSE, M. THE PHILOSOPHY OF BIOLOGY.
A. FLEW, 518:OCT73-25
RUSHING, J.G. MARY DOVE.
M. LEVIN, 441:17MAR74-38
RUSHMORE, R. THE SINGING VOICE.
A. BLYTH, 415:MAR73-263
RUSKIN, J. THE BRANTWOOD DIARY OF
JOHN RUSKIN. (H.G. VILJOEN, ED)
J.L. BRADLEY, 637(VS):DEC71-236
A.O.J. COCKSHUT, 541(RES):MAY72-
221
S.W. JACKMAN, 376:JUL72-148
RUSKIN, J. RUSKIN IN ITALY. (H.I.
SHAPIRO, ED)
C. GORDON-CRAIG, 648:JAN73-75
LORD RUSSELL OF LIVERPOOL. HENRY OF
NAVARRE.
H.H. ROWEN, 207(FR):OCT71-238
RUSSELL, A.K. LIBERAL LANDSLIDE.
617(TLS):1MAR74-202
RUSSELL, D.A. PLUTARCH.*
639(VQR):AUTUMN73-CLXI
RUSSELL, E.W. REPORT ON RADIONICS.
617(TLS):17MAY74-536
RUSSELL, F. SEASON ON THE PLAIN.
M. LEVIN, 441:16JUN74-29
RUSSELL, J. FRANCIS BACON.
D. SOUTHALL, 592:MAR72-139
RUSSELL, J.B. WITCHCRAFT IN THE
MIDDLE AGES.
L.F. BARMANN, 377:MAR73-38
R. CAVENDISH, 203:WINTER72-345
RUSSELL, J.R. CABU.
T. STURGEON, 441:8SEP74-39
RUSSELL, P. PAYSAGES LEGENDAIRES.
K. RAINE, 598(SOR):SPRING74-471
RUSSELL, R. BIRD LIVES!
V. THOMSON, 453:17OCT74-14
RUSSELL, R. THE HARPSICHORD & CLAVI-
CHORD. (2ND ED REV BY H. SCHOTT)
P. WILLIAMS, 415:OCT73-1013
RUSSELL, R. & K. ISLAM, EDS & TRANS.
GHALIB 1796-1869.* (VOL 1)
M. DEMBO, 318(JOAS):JAN-MAR72-
183
RUSSELL, R. & K. ISLAM. THREE MUG-
HAL POETS.
C.M. NAIM, 318(JAOS):JAN-MAR72-
127
RUSSELL, T. THE DIAMOND BESSIE MUR-
DER & THE ROTHSCHILD TRIALS.
J.W. BYRD, 584(SWR):WINTER73-99
"RUSSISCHE LITERATURSPRACHE IM 18.
JAHRHUNDERT."
D. TSCHIŽEWSKIJ, 72:BAND21OHEFT
4/6-480
RUSSO, J.P. ALEXANDER POPE.
U.C. KNOEPFLMACHER, 401(MLQ):
DEC73-448
P.M. SPACKS, 301(JEGP):OCT73-565
W.K. WIMSATT, 566:AUTUMN72-31
RUSSU, I.I. ELEMENTE AUTOHTONE ÎN
LIMBA ROMÂNĂ.*
K. KAZAZIS, 104:SUMMER72-322
RUTHERFORD, A., ED. BYRON: THE
CRITICAL HERITAGE.
J.D. BONE, 447(N&Q):AUG72-314
A.P. ROBSON, 637(VS):JUN72-475

313

RUTHERFORD, A. & D. HANNAH, EDS.
COMMONWEALTH SHORT STORIES.*
R.B.J. WILSON, 381:JUN72-221
RUTHERFORD, D. KICKSTART.
N. CALLENDAR, 441:22SEP74-41
617(TLS):18JAN74-61
RUTHERFORD, W.E. MODERN ENGLISH.
F. COMES DE MATOS, 399(ML,1):JAN
72-57
RUTLAND, R.A. - SEE MASON, G.
RUTLAND, R.A. & W.M.E. RACHAL - SEE
MADISON, J.
RUTSALA, V. THE HARMFUL STATE.
H. GREGORY, 502(PRS):SPRING72-87
RUTT, R., ED & TRANS. THE BAMBOO
GROVE.*
P.H. LEE, 293(JAST):FEB72-427
P.H. LEE, 318(JAOS):OCT-DEC72-
588
639(VQR):WINTER72-XXVI
RUTTEN, C. LES CATÉGORIES DU MONDE
SENSIBLE DANS LES ENNÉADES DE
PLOTIN.
A. DOZ, 542:JAN-MAR72-59
RUTTEN, M. DE INTERLUDIËN VAN KAREL
VAN DE WOESTIJNE.
L. GILLET, 556(RLV):1972/5-556
RUTTKOWSKI, W.V. DIE LITERARISCHEN
GATTUNGEN.
W. HEMPEL, 400(MLN):APR72-514
RUWET, N. INTRODUCTION À LA GRAM-
MAIRE GÉNÉRATIVE.*
W.G. MOULTON, 660(WORD):AUG70-
282
P.A.M. SEUREN, 353:FEB72-111
RYAN, A., ED. THE PHILOSOPHY OF THE
SOCIAL SCIENCES.
E. BARKER, 262:WINTER72-463
A. ROSENBERG, 486:SEP72-424
RYAN, C. A BRIDGE TOO FAR.
M. BLUMENSON, 441:8SEP74-1
A. FARRAR-HOCKLEY, 617(TLS):
1NOV74-1224
D. MIDDLETON, 441:18OCT74-45
E. WEEKS, 61:OCT74-115
442(NY):30SEP74-131
RYAN, R. RAVENSWOOD.
617(TLS):22MAR74-295
RYBACK, E. THE HIGH ADVENTURE OF
ERIC RYBACK.
T.J. LYON, 649(WAL):FALL72-233
RYCK, F. SACRIFICIAL PAWN.
N. CALLENDAR, 441:24FEB74-41
RYCK, F. UNDESIRABLE COMPANY.
N. CALLENDAR, 441:29SEP74-41
RYDER, F.G., ED. DIE NOVELLE.*
R.M. BROWNING, 399(MLJ):APR72-
259
L.D. WELLS, 221(GQ):NOV72-790
RYDER, J. THE CRY OF THE HALIDON.
N. CALLENDAR, 441:4AUG74-26
RYDER, J. TREVAYNE.*
617(TLS):6SEP74-960
RYDER, V. THE LITTLE VICTIMS PLAY.
617(TLS):1NOV74-1240
RYDING, W.W. STRUCTURE IN MEDIEVAL
NARRATIVE.
M.W. BLOOMFIELD, 589:JUL73-584
RYKEN, L. THE APOCALYPTIC VISION IN
"PARADISE LOST."*
J.R. SCRUTCHINS, 577(SHR):WINTER
72-95

RYKWERT, J. ON ADAM'S HOUSE IN PARA-
DISE.*
617(TLS):24MAY74-563
639(VQR):AUTUMN73-CLXXI
RYLE, G. COLLECTED PAPERS BY GIL-
BERT RYLE.*
T.A. GOUDGE, 154:DEC72-596
A.B.W., 543:MAR72-567
RYMER, J.M. [OR T.P. PREST] VARNEY
THE VAMPYRE.
N. KIRBY, 651(WHR):SPRING73-210
RYTZ, H.R. GEISTLICHE DES ALTEN
BERN ZWISCHEN MERKANTILISMUS UND
PHYSIOKRATIE.
R. HAUSWIRTH, 182:VOL25#9/10-316
RZEPIŃSKA, M. HISTORIA KOLORU W
DZIEJACH MALARSTWA EUROPEJSKIEGO.
(VOL 1)
M. RIESER, 290(JAAC):SUMMER73-
555

SAALMAN, H. MEDIEVAL CITIES.
G.L. HERSEY, 56:SUMMER72-180
SAALMAN, H. - SEE MANETTI, A.D.
SAAVEDRA, M.D. - SEE UNDER DE CER-
VANTES SAAVEDRA, M.
SABADINO DEGLI ARIENTI, G. ART &
LIFE AT THE COURT OF ERCOLE I
D'ESTE. (W.L. GUNDERSHEIMER, ED)
617(TLS):29MAR74-318
SABALIŪNAS, L. LITHUANIA IN CRISIS.*
E. ANDERSON, 550(RUSR):OCT72-433
A. POLONSKY, 575(SEER):JAN73-143
SABATIER, R. THE MATCH BOY.
617(TLS):11OCT74-1109
SABATIER, R. LES NOISETTES SAUVAGES.
617(TLS):7JUN74-619
SABATIER, R. THREE MINT LOLLIPOPS.
M. LEVIN, 441:3MAR74-28
SABBAH, G. - SEE AMMIANUS MARCEL-
LINUS
SABERWAL, S. THE TRADITIONAL POLITI-
CAL SYSTEM OF THE EMBU OF CENTRAL
KENYA.
B. BERNARDI, 69:JUL72-257
SABRI-TABRIZI, G.R. THE "HEAVEN" &
"HELL" OF WILLIAM BLAKE.
617(TLS):15FEB74-145
SACCHETTI, F. IL TRECENTONOVELLE.
(E. FACCIOLI, ED)
M.P., 228(GSLI):VOL149FASC465-
143
SACHS, A. JUSTICE IN SOUTH AFRICA.*
G.M. FREDRICKSON, 453:31OCT74-29
SACHS, A. PASSIONATE INTELLIGENCE.*
A. PARREAUX, 189(EA):OCT-DEC72-
562
SACHS, M., ED. THE FRENCH SHORT
STORY IN THE NINETEENTH CENTURY.
R. GODENNE, 556(RLV):1972/5-549
SACHSE, W.L., COMP. RESTORATION
ENGLAND 1660-1689.*
D. GREENE, 481(PQ):JUL72-515
SACKER, H. - SEE MUSIL, R.
SACKLER, H. THE GREAT WHITE HOPE.
A. RENDLE, 157:WINTER71-77
SACKVILLE-WEST, V. CHALLENGE.
J. VAIZEY, 362:28FEB74-280
617(TLS):15MAR74-253
SACOTO, A. EL INDIO EN EL ENSAYO DE
LA AMÉRICA ESPAÑOLA.
A. BORINSKY, 400(MLN):MAR72-384

SADDHĀTISSA, H. BUDDHIST ETHICS.*
C.S. PREBISH, 293(JAST):MAY72-
639
SADDLEMYER, A. - SEE SYNGE, J.M.
SADIE, S. HANDEL CONCERTOS.
P. DRUMMOND, 415:JUN73-601
SADKA, E. THE PROTECTED MALAY
STATES, 1874-1895.*
M. DEMBO, 318(JAOS):OCT-DEC72-
517
SADLER, A.L. - SEE "THE TEN FOOT
SQUARE HUT & TALES OF THE HEIKE"
SADLER, G., ED. THE BAROQUE OPERAT-
IC AIRS. (VOL 2: ANDRÉ CAMPRA.)
617(TLS):23AUG74-907
SADLER, G.E. - SEE MAC DONALD, G.
SÁENZ, G. IDEOLOGÍA DE LA FUERZA.
W.L. SIEMENS, 238:DEC72-976
ŞAFĀ, Z-O-L., ED. VARQA VA GOLSHĀH-
E 'AYYUQI.
M.A. JAZAYERY, 318(JAOS):JAN-MAR
72-130
SAGAN, F. LA CHAMADE. (K.I. PERRY,
ED)
B.M. POHORYLES, 207(FR):OCT71-
295
SAGAN, F. SCARS ON THE SOUL.
P. ADAMS, 61:MAY74-139
A. BROYARD, 441:15APR74-35
M. ENGEL, 441:14APR74-6
J. UPDIKE, 442(NY):12AUG74-95
SAGARRA, E. TRADITION & REVOLUTION.*
K. BULLIVANT, 402(MLR):APR73-465
G. FRIESEN, 400(MLN):APR72-526
SAGNES, G. L'ENNUI DANS LA LITTÉRA-
TURE FRANÇAISE DE FLAUBERT À LAFOR-
GUE (1848-1884).*
R. SWITZER, 207(FR):MAR72-921
SÁGVÁRI, A., ED. FORRÁSOK BUDAPEST
MÚLTJÁBÓL. (VOLS 1&2)
I. DEAK, 32:SEP73-644
SAÏDI, O. KITĀB AL-'UYŪN WA'L-
ḤADĀ'IQ FĪ AḤBĀR AL-ḤAQĀ'IQ. (VOL
4, PT 1)
J. VAN ESS, 182:VOL25#12-437
SAIDY, A. & N. LESSING. THE WORLD
OF CHESS.
M. WATKINS, 441:8DEC74-18
SAIL, L. OPPOSITE VIEWS.
617(TLS):8NOV74-1265
SAINE, T.P. DIE ÄSTHETISCHE THEODI-
ZEE.*
E.J. ENGEL, 301(JEGP):APR73-283
SAINI, B.S. BUILDING ENVIRONMENT.
617(TLS):26APR74-455
ST. AUBYN, F.C. STÉPHANE MALLARMÉ.
H.M. BLOCK, 207(FR):OCT71-255
ST. AUBYN, G. INFAMOUS VICTORIANS.
R.B. MARTIN, 637(VS):MAR72-395
ST. CLAIR, L. THE EMERALD TRAP.
N. CALLENDAR, 441:17FEB74-33
ST. CLAIR, S. FOLKLORE OF THE
ULSTER PEOPLE.
T. BROWN, 203:SUMMER72-169
ST. CLAIR, W. THAT GREECE MIGHT
STILL BE FREE.
S.V. PAPACOSMA, 32:JUN73-424
ST. CLAIR, W. - SEE TRELAWNY, E.J.
ST. GEORGE, G. RUSSIA.
617(TLS):8FEB74-140
MARQUISE DE ST. INNOCENT, O. OLGA.
J. KLEMESRUD, 441:17MAR74-36
ST. JOHN, J. TO THE WAR WITH WAUGH.*
617(TLS):4OCT74-1064

ST. JOHN-PARSONS, D., ED. OUR POETS
SPEAK.
W.P. ROOT, 491:OCT73-34
ST. JOHN-STEVAS, N. - SEE BAGEHOT, W.
SAINT-ÉVREMOND. TEXTES CHOISIS.
(A. NIDERST, ED)
R. ZUBER, 535(RHL):SEP-DEC72-
1101
DE SAINT-JEAN, R. JOURNAL D'UN
JOURNALISTE.
617(TLS):5APR74-360
DE SAINT-THOMAS, J. CURSUS THEOLO-
GICUS: DE GRATIA.
A. FOREST, 542:JAN-MAR72-75
SAINTE-BEUVE, C-A. CAHIERS I. (R.
MOLHO, ED)
617(TLS):29MAR74-314
SAINTENY, J. HO CHI MINH & HIS VIET-
NAM.
J. BUTTINGER, 676(YR):AUTUMN72-
138
SAINTY, J.C., ED. OFFICIALS OF THE
BOARDS OF TRADE 1660-1870.
617(TLS):26JUL74-808
SAISSELIN, R.G. THE RULE OF REASON
& THE RUSES OF THE HEART.
J. BARCHILON, 207(FR):DEC71-540
H.T. BARNWELL, 208(FS):JUL73-329
R.A. DELATTRE, 290(JAAC):WINTER
72-270
R. MITCHELL, 399(MLJ):APR72-250
SAITZ, R.L. & D. CARR. SELECTED
READINGS IN ENGLISH FOR STUDENTS
OF ENGLISH AS A SECOND LANGUAGE.
N. ARAPOFF-CRAMER, 608:JUN73-184
SAKALL, D. & A. HARRINGTON. LOVE &
EVIL.
P. ADAMS, 61:JUL74-100
SAKHAROV, A.D. SAKHAROV SPEAKS.
(H.E. SALISBURY, ED)
S.E. LURIA, 441:15SEP74-30
SAKOIAN, F. & L.S. ACKER. THE AS-
TROLOGER'S HANDBOOK.
617(TLS):11OCT74-1143
SAKSENA, S.K. ESSAYS ON INDIAN PHIL-
OSOPHY.*
P.J. WILL, 293(JAST):FEB72-428
SAKUMA, E. ONAME FŪDOKI.
A.M. LEVY, 424:DEC72-290
SAKUTARŌ, H. - SEE UNDER HAGIWARA
SAKUTARŌ
SALA, M. ESTUDIOS SOBRE EL JUDEO-
ESPAÑOL DE BUCAREST. PHONÉTIQUE
ET PHONOLOGIE DU JUDÉO-ESPAGNOL DE
BUCAREST.
H. KAHANE, 350:DEC73-943
SALA-MOLINS, L. - SEE EYMERICH, N. &
F. PEÑA
SALACROU, A. DANS LA SALLE DES PAS
PERDUS.
617(TLS):14JUN74-643
SALAMANCA, J.R. EMBARKATION.*
A. MACLEAN, 617(TLS):22NOV74-
1308
J. MELLORS, 362:5DEC74-753
E. ROVIT, 659:AUTUMN74-539
SALANI, T.P. - SEE UNDER POGGI SAL-
ANI, T.
SALCEDO-BASTARDO, J.L. HISTORIA
FUNDAMENTAL DE VENEZUELA. (2ND ED)
B.A. FRANKEL, 263:JAN-MAR73-97

SALDITT-TRAPPMANN, R. TEMPEL DER
ÄGYPTISCHEN GÖTTER IN GRIECHENLAND
UND AN DER WESTKÜSTE KLEINASIENS.
J.M. COOK, 123:MAR73-109
SALE, R. MODERN HEROISM.*
C. RICKS, 453:24JAN74-43
SALES, G.M. & G. THE CLAY-POT COOK-
BOOK.
N. HAZELTON, 441:1DEC74-96
SALIL, S.B., ED. TECHNOLOGICAL
CHANGE.
K. HUDSON, 637(VS):SEP72-94
SALINAS, P. LA VOZ A TI DEBIDA Y
RAZÓN DE AMOR. (J. GONZÁLEZ MU-
ELA, ED)
J. DÍAZ, 241:SEP72-77
SALINAS DE MARICHAL, S. EL MUNDO
POÉTICO DE RAFAEL ALBERTI.*
P.G. CASADO, 399(MLJ):FEB72-101
SALISBURY, C.Y. RUSSIAN DIARY.
E. WEEKS, 61:SEP74-100
SALISBURY, H.E. - SEE SAKHAROV, A.D.
SALKEY, A., ED. ISLAND VOICES.
K. CUSHMAN, 573(SSF):SPRING72-
209
SALKEY, A. JAMAICA.
617(TLS):25JAN74-77
SALM, P. THE POEM AS PLANT.
R.P. BAREIKIS, 481(PQ):JUL72-686
R.M. BROWNING, 221(GQ):NOV72-723
H.S. DAEMMRICH, 290(JAAC):SPRING
72-407
U.K. GOLDSMITH, 399(MLJ):DEC72-
515
H. HENEL, 406:WINTER73-419
H. REHDER, 301(JEGP):OCT73-591
SALM, P. THREE MODES OF CRITICISM.
(GERMAN TITLE: DREI RICHTUNGEN DER
LITERATURWISSENSCHAFT.)
E.T. LONG, 125:OCT72-70
M. ZUTSHI, 402(MLR):JAN73-225
SALMEN, W. & C. PETZCH, EDS. DAS
LOCHAMER-LIEDERBUCH.
J.A.W., 410(M&L):JUL73-367
SALMI, M. - SEE "THE GRIMANI BREVI-
ARY"
SALMON, E.T. ROMAN COLONIZATION
UNDER THE REPUBLIC.
J. PINSENT, 313:VOL62-179
SALOMON, J-J. SCIENCE & POLITICS.
617(TLS):19APR74-407
SALOMON, P. LE ROMAN ET LA NOUVELLE
ROMANTIQUES.
R. MERKER, 207(FR):FEB72-770
SALONEN, A. DIE HAUSGERÄTE DER ALT-
EN MESOPOTAMIER NACH SUMERISCH-
AKKADISCHEN QUELLEN. (PT 1)
R.S. ELLIS, 318(JAOS):APR-JUN72-
294
SALTARELLI, M. LA GRAMMATICA GENERA-
TIVA TRASFORMAZIONALE.
R.J. DI PIETRO, 276:AUTUMN72-335
SALTARELLI, M. A PHONOLOGY OF ITAL-
IAN IN A GENERATIVE GRAMMAR.
R.A. HALL, JR., 276:SUMMER72-267
H. STAMMERJOHANN, 399(MLJ):OCT
72-400
SALTER, C.L. - SEE HSIEH, C-M.
SALTONSTALL, R., JR. MAINE PILGRIM-
AGE.
C. LEHMANN-HAUPT, 441:18FEB74-23
SALTVEIT, L. - SEE SEIP, D.A.

SALUS, P. PĀNINI TO POSTAL.
G.F. MEIER, 682(ZPSK):BAND25
HEFT1/2-164
SALUS, P.H., ED. ON LANGUAGE.*
K.E. ZIMMER, 545(RPH):FEB73-592
SALVADOR, A.R. - SEE UNDER RUIZ SAL-
VADOR, A.
SALVADOR, H. LA EXTRAÑA FASCINACIÓN.
J. OTERO, 238:SEP72-597
SALVAT, H. L'INTELLIGENCE, MYTHES
ET RÉALITÉS.
D. MERLLIÉ, 542:OCT-DEC72-483
SALVESEN, A. STUDIES IN THE VOCABU-
LARY OF THE OLD NORSE ELUCIDARIUM.
W. LINDOW, 353:1OCT72-124
SALVINI, M. NAIRI E IR(U)ATRI.
G. BUCCELLATI, 318(JAOS):APR-JUN
72-297
SALVINI, R. MEDIEVAL SCULPTURE.
N. HALL, 135:FEB72-140
SALVUCCI, P. CONDILLAC FILOSOFO
DELLA COMUNITÀ UMANA.
E. NAMER, 542:JUL-SEP72-321
SALWAY, P. - SEE RICHMOND, I.
SALZER, F. & C. SCHACHTER. COUNTER-
POINT IN COMPOSITION.
S. PERSKY, 513:FALL-WINTER69-151
SALZMAN, E. TWENTIETH-CENTURY MUSIC.
D. STOCK, 513:FALL-WINTER69-141
SALZMANN, W. MOLIÈRE UND DIE LATEIN-
ISCHE KOMÖDIE.*
A. FUSS, 209(FM):JUL72-261
U. SCHULZ-BUSCHHAUS, 52:BAND7
HEFT1-90
SAMACHSON, D. & J. THE RUSSIAN BAL-
LET & THREE OF ITS MASTERPIECES.
R. BAKER, 151:SEP72-77
SAMANIEGO, F.M. FÁBULAS. (E. JAR-
EÑO, ED)
P. ILIE, 240(HR):SUMMER72-346
SAMARAN, C. & R. MARICHAL. CATALOGUE
DES MANUSCRITS EN ÉCRITURE LATINE
PORTANT DES INDICATIONS DE DATE,
DE LIEU OU DE COPISTE. (VOL 6)
J.J. JOHN, 589:JUL73-587
SAMARAS, Z. THE COMIC ELEMENT OF
MONTAIGNE'S STYLE.
F.S. BROWN, 207(FR):DEC71-526
W.G. MOORE, 402(MLR):APR73-405
SAMARDŽIĆ, R. MEHMED SOKOLOVIĆ.
B. KREKIĆ, 32:DEC73-845
SAMARIN, R., ED. SHAKESPEARE IN THE
SOVIET UNION.
M. RIESER, 290(JAAC):WINTER71-
270
SAMARIN, W.J. BASIC COURSE IN SANGO.
R. OHLY, 353:1JUL72-121
SAMARIN, W.J. THE GBEYA LANGUAGE.*
A GRAMMAR OF SANGO.
K.L. BAUCOM, 353:1JUL72-123
SAMBROOK, J. WILLIAM COBBETT.
617(TLS):18JAN74-41
SAMMONS, J.L. HEINRICH HEINE.*
E. SPEIDEL, 447(N&Q):AUG72-313
R.E. STIEFEL, 222(GR):MAR72-139
SAMONA, G. & OTHERS. PIAZZA SAN
MARCO.
J. MC ANDREW, 54:JUN72-212
SAMONÀ, G.P. G.G. BELLI.
P. GIBELLINI, 228(GSLI):VOL149
FASC466/467-400

SAMOYAULT, J-P. LES BUREAUX DU SEC-
RETARIAT D'ETAT DES AFFAIRES ETRAN-
GÈRES SOUS LOUIS XV.
481(PQ):JUL72-552
SAMPSON, A. THE SOVEREIGN STATE OF
ITT.* (BRITISH TITLE: SOVEREIGN
STATE.)
R. ATKEY, 99:MAY/JUN74-55
SAMPSON, G. STRATIFICATIONAL GRAM-
MAR.
D.G. LOCKWOOD, 361:VOL29#3/4-360
SAMUEL, E. THE MAN WHO LIKED CATS.
N. SHRAPNEL, 617(TLS):8NOV74-
1248
SAMUEL, E. - SEE VAN DOREN, M. & M.
SAMUEL
SAMUELS, C.T. THE AMBIGUITY OF
HENRY JAMES.*
R. FALK, 445(NCF):SEP72-224
D.K. KIRBY, 432(NEQ):MAR72-137
SAMUELS, E. - SEE ADAMS, H.
"THE SAN FRANCISCO EARTHQUAKE & FIRE
OF APRIL 18, 1906."
W. ZUK, 505:DEC72-96
SANCHEZ, J. - SEE CORNEILLE, P.
SANCHEZ, S. IT'S A NEW DAY.
W.P. ROOT, 491:OCT73-34
SANCHEZ, T. RABBIT BOSS.*
G. BURNSIDE, 441:10MAR74-26
617(TLS):1MAR74-219
SÁNCHEZ-ALBORNOZ, C. INVESTIGACIONES
Y DOCUMENTOS SOBRE LAS INSTITU-
CIONES HISPANAS.
K. KENNELLY, 589:JAN73-178
SÁNCHEZ DE BADAJOZ, D. RECOPILACIÓN
EN METRO (SEVILLA 1554).
C. STERN, 240(HR):WINTER72-85
SÁNCHEZ REGUEIRA, M. - SEE DE SOLÍS,
A.
SÁNCHEZ ROMERALO, A. EL VILLANCICO
(ESTUDIOS SOBRE LA LÍRICA POPULAR
EN LOS SIGLOS XV Y XVI).*
P.O. GERICKE, 545(RPH):NOV72-490
SAND, G. CORRESPONDANCE.* (VOL 7)
(G. LUBIN, ED)
T.G.S. COMBE, 208(FS):JUL73-345
SAND, G. CORRESPONDANCE.* (VOL 8)
(G. LUBIN, ED)
T.G.S. COMBE, 208(FS):JUL73-345
J. GAULMIER, 535(RHL):MAR-APR72-
330
SAND, G. ÉCRITS AUTOBIOGRAPHIQUES.
(VOL 2) (G. LUBIN, ED)
J. GAULMIER, 535(RHL):MAR-APR72-
327
SAND, G. LETTRES D'UN VOYAGEUR.
R. MERKER, 207(FR):MAR72-880
SAND, G. OEUVRES AUTOBIOGRAPHIQUES.
(G. LUBIN, ED)
R. MERKER, 207(FR):OCT71-259
SANDBY, W. THE HISTORY OF THE ROYAL
ACADEMY OF ARTS.*
D. FITZ-GERALD, 90:SEP72-639
SANDE, T., ED. THE NEW ENGLAND TEX-
TILE MILL SURVEY.
R.M. CANDEE, 576:DEC72-336
SANDER, A. MEN WITHOUT MASKS.
S. SONTAG, 453:18APR74-17
SANDER, L. PALÄOGRAPHISCHES ZU DEN
SANSKRITHANDSCHRIFTEN DER BERLINER
TURFANSAMMLUNG.
M.J. DRESDEN, 318(JAOS):APR-JUN
72-315

SANDERS, C.R. & K.J. FIELDING - SEE
CARLYLE, T. & J.W.
SANDERS, E. THE FAMILY.
T.R. EDWARDS, 473(PR):WINTER73-
153
42(AR):VOL32#3-505
SANDERS, M.K. DOROTHY THOMPSON.*
M. SCHORER, 27(AL):NOV73-472
SANDERS, R. REFLECTIONS ON A TEAPOT.
A.H. ROSENFELD, 390:OCT72-65
SANDERS, W. JOHN DONNE'S POETRY.*
C.F. WILLIAMSON, 541(RES):AUG72-
346
SANDERS, W. THE DRAMATIST & THE
RECEIVED IDEA.
R.E. LYNCH, 125:OCT72-77
SANDKÜHLER, B. DIE FRÜHEN DANTEKOM-
MENTARE UND IHR VERHÄLTNIS ZUR MIT-
TELALTERLICHEN KOMMENTARTRADITION.
R. CRESPO, 433:JUL72-371
SANDLER, I. THE TRIUMPH OF AMERICAN
PAINTING.
K. MOFFETT, 56:AUTUMN72-313
SANDMAN, J. FORDS EAT CHEVS.
D. DAYMOND, 296:VOL3#2-103
SANDULESCU, J. HUNGER'S ROGUES.
N. ROSTEN, 441:1SEP74-6
SANDVED, A.O. STUDIES IN THE LANGU-
AGE OF CAXTON'S MALORY & THAT OF
THE WINCHESTER MANUSCRIPT.*
B. CARSTENSEN, 38:BAND90HEFT1/2-
228
J.R. SIMON, 189(EA):JAN-MAR72-56
SANER, H. KANT'S POLITICAL THOUGHT.
617(TLS):20SEP74-1022
SANFAÇON, R. L'ARCHITECTURE FLAM-
BOYANTE EN FRANCE.*
M.F. HEARN, 589:OCT73-786
SANGHARAKSHITA, B. THE THREE JEWELS.
D.J. KALUPAHANA, 485(PE&W):APR72-
230
SANJIAN, A.K., ED & TRANS. COLO-
PHONS OF ARMENIAN MANUSCRIPTS,
1301-1480.
E.V. GULBEKIAN, 318(JAOS):APR-
JUN72-375
SANKEY, B. A COMPANION TO WILLIAM
CARLOS WILLIAMS'S "PATERSON."*
C. DOYLE, 376:JUL72-136
SANNES, G.W. AFRICAN PRIMITIVES.*
G.I. JONES, 69:JAN72-75
SANOUILLET, M. & E. PETERSON - SEE
DUCHAMP, M.
SANSOM, W. THE BIRTH OF A STORY.
E. FEINSTEIN, 364:AUG/SEP72-157
SANSOM, W. THE MARMALADE BIRD.*
E. FEINSTEIN, 364:FEB/MAR74-137
SANSOM, W. PROUST & HIS WORLD.*
A. BROYARD, 441:5AUG74-21
442(NY):19AUG74-91
SANSOM, W. A YOUNG WIFE'S TALE.
J. MILLER, 617(TLS):15NOV74-1278
SANSOT, P. POÉTIQUE DE LA VILLE.
P. CHARPENTRAT, 98:MAY72-482
SANTAYANA, G. LOTZE'S SYSTEM OF
PHILOSOPHY.* (P.G. KUNTZ, ED)
W.L. BLIZEK, 290(JAAC):WINTER71-
276
D.S. ROBINSON, 484(PPR):SEP72-
130
J.W. YOLTON, 154:JUN72-293

SANTINELLO, G. IL PENSIERO DI
NICOLO CUSANO NELLA SUA PROSPET-
TIVA ESTETICA.
E. NAMER, 542:JAN-MAR72-105
SANTINI, P.C. MODERN LANDSCAPE
PAINTING.*
A. FRANKENSTEIN, 55:FEB73-15
SANTORO, C. GLI UFFICI DEL COMUNE
DI MILANO E DEL DOMINIO VISCONTEO-
SFORZESCO (1216-1515).
V. ILARDI, 551(RENQ):SPRING72-71
SANTRAUD, J-M. LA MER ET LE ROMAN
AMÉRICAIN DANS LA PREMIÈRE MOITIÉ
DU DIX-NEUVIÈME SIÈCLE.
T. PHILBRICK, 27(AL):NOV73-456
SANTUCCI, A. - SEE VARI, A.
SANZENBACH, S. LES ROMANS DE PIERRE
JEAN JOUVE.
R.B. LEAL, 67:NOV73-312
SAPARINA, Y. CYBERNETICS WITHIN US.
E.A. SCHMERLER, 186(ETC.):SEP72-
322
SAPORETTI, C. ONOMASTICA MEDIO-
ASSIRA.
J.G. FUCILLA, 424:JUN72-138
SAPPENFIELD, J.A. A SWEET INSTRUC-
TION.
B. GRANGER, 165:FALL74-204
SAPPLER, P., ED. DAS KÖNIGSTEINER
LIEDERBUCH: MS. GERM. QU. 719
BERLIN.*
T.M. KINNEAR, 220(GL&L):JUL73-
367
SARAN, V. SINO-SOVIET SCHISM.
C.C. HOFFMEISTER, 517(PBSA):APR-
JUN73-216
SARBIEWSKI, M.K. DII GENTIUM. (K.
STAWECKA, ED & TRANS)
568(SCN):SUMMER73-61
SARGENT, T., ED & TRANS. THE HOMER-
IC HYMNS.
M. RUDICK, 651(WHR):SUMMER73-319
SARGESON, F. MAN OF ENGLAND NOW.
H.W. RHODES, 368:SEP72-259
SARMA, M.V.R. THE HEROIC ARGUMENT.*
I. SIMON, 541(RES):AUG72-348
SARMIENTO, E. CONCORDANCIAS DE LAS
OBRAS POÉTICAS EN CASTELLANO DE
GARCILASO DE LA VEGA.*
A. ESPANTOSO DE FOLEY, 240(HR):
SUMMER72-319
SARNACKI, J. - SEE MONDRAGÓN, M.
SARRAUTE, N. BETWEEN LIFE & DEATH.
M. MUDRICK, 249(HUDR):AUTUMN73-
545
SARRAUTE, N. DO YOU HEAR THEM.*
(FRENCH TITLE: VOUS LES ENTENDEZ?)
M. GROVES, 268:JAN74-59
R. MICHA, 98:APR72-295
M. MUDRICK, 249(HUDR):AUTUMN73-
545
SARTON, M. AS WE ARE NOW.*
442(NY):8APR74-141
617(TLS):9AUG74-849
SARTRE, J-P. BETWEEN EXISTENTIALISM
& MARXISM.
617(TLS):7JUN74-607
SARTRE, J-P. LE DIABLE ET LE BON
DIEU. (D.J. CONLON, ED)
J. CRUICKSHANK, 208(FS):JAN73-
101
F. FLAGOTHIER, 556(RLV):1972/5-
553
205(FMLS):JUL72-289

SARTRE, J-P. L'IDIOT DE LA FAMILLE.*
T.H. ADAMOWSKI, 454:FALL72-79
H. LEVIN, 322(JHI):OCT-DEC72-643
SARTRE, J-P. UN THÉÂTRE DE SITUA-
TIONS.
617(TLS):3MAY74-482
SARVIS, B. & H. RODMAN. THE ABOR-
TION CONTROVERSY.
617(TLS):8MAR74-240
SASEK, L.A. - SEE SMITH, W.
SASSOON, S. POET'S PILGRIMAGE.
(D.F. CORRIGAN, ED)
G. EWART, 364:DEC73/JAN74-138
SATCHELL, W. THE LAND OF THE LOST.
(K. SMITHYMAN, ED)
617(TLS):8MAR74-237
SATER, W.F. THE HEROIC IMAGE IN
CHILE.
617(TLS):3MAY74-472
SATOW, E. A DIPLOMAT IN JAPAN.*
M.V. LAMBERTI, 318(JAOS):JAN-MAR
72-154
SATTLER, A. DIE EUROPÄISCHEN GEMEIN-
SCHAFTEN AN DER SCHWELLE ZUR WIRT-
SCHAFTS- UND WÄHRUNGSUNION.
G. STRICKRODT, 182:VOL25#11-346
SAUER, C.O. SIXTEENTH CENTURY NORTH
AMERICA.
M.H. JACKSON, 656(WMQ):OCT72-660
SAUER, G. DIE NOMINALBILDUNG IM
OSTJAKISCHEN.
G. DÉCSY, 260(IF):BAND76-376
SAUERLÄNDER, W. GOTHIC SCULPTURE IN
FRANCE 1140-1270.* (GERMAN TITLE:
GOTISCHE SKULPTUR IN FRANKREICH
1140-1270.)
G. SCHMIDT, 683:BAND35HEFT1/2-
124
SAUL, O. THE DARK SIDE OF LOVE.
M. LEVIN, 441:17FEB74-32
ŠAUMJAN, S.K. PROBLEMS OF THEORETI-
CAL PHONOLOGY.*
E. FUDGE, 361:VOL30#2/3-243
K.H. SCHMIDT, 206:MAR72-304
SAUNDERS, G., ED. SAMIZDAT.
P. REDDAWAY, 453:12DEC74-36
SAUNERON, S. LE PAPYRUS MAGIQUE
ILLUSTRÉ DE BROOKLYN.*
P.J. PARSONS, 123:MAR73-96
DE SAUSSURE, F. COURS DE LINGUIS-
TIQUE GÉNÉRALE.* (FASC 1) (R.
ENGLER, ED)
M. LEROY, 343:BAND14HEFT1-17
DE SAUSSURE, F. COURS DE LINGUIS-
TIQUE GÉNÉRALE.* (FASC 2&3) (R.
ENGLER, ED)
M. LEROY, 343:BAND14HEFT1-17
L. SÖLL, 260(IF):BAND76-208
DE SAUSSURE, F. COURSE IN GENERAL
LINGUISTICS. (C. BALLY & A. SECHE-
HAYE, WITH A. REIDLINGER, EDS)
617(TLS):7JUN74-617
DE SAUZÉ, E.B., E.K. DAWSON & B.J.
GILLIAM. NOUVEAU COURS PRATIQUE
DE FRANÇAIS. (3RD ED)
P. SILBERMAN, 207(FR):OCT71-289
SAVAGE, C.W. THE MEASUREMENT OF
SENSATION.
A.J.W., 478:JAN72-80
SAVAGE, G. & H. NEWMAN. AN ILLUS-
TRATED DICTIONARY OF CERAMICS.
617(TLS):17MAY74-536

SAVAGE, M.R. & A.G. THOMPSON, COMPS.
THE TYNE, 1800-1850.
W.B. STEPHENS, 325:OCT72-543
SAVAGE, T. A STRANGE GOD.
M. LEVIN, 441:25AUG74-31
SAVARD, J-G. & J. RICHARDS. LES
INDICES D'UTILITÉ DU VOCABULAIRE
FONDAMENTAL FRANÇAIS.
R.E. BOSWELL, 399(MLJ):MAR72-193
SAVARESE, G. PRIMO TEMPO DEL DE
SANCTIS E ALTRI SAGGI.
P. SHAW, 402(MLR):JAN73-198
SAVELLI, A. NUOVISSIME INTERPRETA-
ZIONI ETRUSCHE.
A. ERNOUT, 555:VOL46FASC2-322
VON SAVIGNY, E. DIE PHILOSOPHIE DER
NORMALEN SPRACHE.*
R.S., 543:DEC71-373
SAVILLE, J. THE MEDIEVAL EROTIC
ALBA.
639(VQR):SUMMER73-CXVII
SAVONAROLA, G. IL PRIMO SAVONAROLA.
(G. CATTIN, ED)
617(TLS):29MAR74-318
SAW, R.L. AESTHETICS.
L.B. BROWN, 290(JAAC):SUMMER73-
543
SAW SWEE-HOCK. SINGAPORE POPULATION
IN TRANSITION.
T.E. SMITH, 302:JAN72-68
SAWA, T. ART IN JAPANESE ESOTERIC
BUDDHISM.
T. BOWIE, 127:SUMMER73-458
SAWYERR, H. GOD: ANCESTOR OR CREA-
TOR?
A.C. EDWARDS, 69:OCT72-358
SAX, J.L. DEFENDING THE ENVIRON-
MENT.
M. FROME, 44:JUN72-8
SAXTON, A. THE INDISPENSABLE ENEMY.
R.F. MC CLELLAN, 293(JAST):NOV71-
176
SAYCE, R.A. THE ESSAYS OF MONTAIGNE.
C. CLARK, 208(FS):APR73-190
SAYER, M. SAMUEL RENN.
617(TLS):23AUG74-907
SAYERS, J.E. THE FOUNTAIN UNSEALED.
617(TLS):11JAN74-38
SAYRE, K.M. CONSCIOUSNESS.*
J.R. LUCAS, 482(PHR):APR72-241
SAYRE, N. SIXTIES GOING ON SEVEN-
TIES.*
617(TLS):19JUL74-758
SAYWELL, J. QUEBEC 70.
R. SIMEON, 529(QQ):SPRING72-100
SCABINI, E. IL PENSIERO DI PAUL
TILLICH.
J.R., 543:DEC71-367
SCADUTO, T. MICK JAGGER.
J. ROCKWELL, 441:27JUL74-27
C. SYLVESTRE, 362:26SEP74-418
SCAGLIA, G. - SEE DI JACOPO, M.
SCALAMANDRÈ, R. UN POETA DELLA PRE-
RIFORMA.
J. PINEAUX, 535(RHL):MAY-JUN72-
507
SCALES, D.P. ALDOUS HUXLEY & FRENCH
LITERATURE.
P. VITOUX, 677:VOL3-334
SCAMMELL, M., ED. RUSSIA'S OTHER
WRITERS.
H. ERMOLAEV, 550(RUSR):JUL72-304

"SCANDINAVIAN POLITICAL STUDIES."
(VOL 3)
E. ANDERSON, 563(SS):SUMMER73-
264
SCANNELL, D. MOTHER KNEW BEST.
M-K. WILMERS, 617(TLS):27DEC74-
1456
SCANNELL, V. SELECTED POEMS.
A. CLUYSENAAR, 565:VOL13#2-72
SCANNELL, V. THE WINTER MAN.
R. GARFITT, 364:FEB/MAR74-103
617(TLS):25JAN74-77
SCARANO, E. DALLA "CRONACA BIZAN-
TINA" AL "CONVITO."
P.A.T., 228(GSLI):VOL149FASC466/
467-465
SCARBOROUGH, W.K. - SEE RUFFIN, E.
"DOMENICO SCARLATTI: COMPLETE KEY-
BOARD WORKS." (R. KIRKPATRICK, ED)
P.H.L., 414(MQ):OCT72-675
SCARR, D. THE MAJESTY OF COLOUR.
(VOL 1)
617(TLS):5JUL74-733
SCÈVE, M. MAURICE SCÈVE: OEUVRES
POÉTIQUES COMPLÈTES. (H. STAUB,
ED)
D. FENOALTEA, 207(FR):APR72-1063
SCHACH, P. - SEE SVEINSSON, E.Ó.
SCHACH, P. - SEE THÓRDARSON, A.
SCHACHERMEYR, F. PERIKLES.
J. BRISCOE, 123:DEC73-231
SCHACHT, J. & C.E. BOSWORTH, EDS.
THE LEGACY OF ISLAM. (2ND ED)
W.M. WATT, 617(TLS):15NOV74-1280
SCHACHT, R. ALIENATION.*
C. DYKE, 319:JAN74-127
SCHAEFER, H.W. COMECON & THE POLI-
TICS OF INTEGRATION.
P. MARER, 32:JUN73-399
SCHAEFFER, S.F. ANYA.
W. NOVAK, 441:20OCT74-36
SCHAEFFER, S.F. FALLING.*
R. HOWARD, 473(PR):3/1973-510
SCHÄFER, E. LAUDATIO ORGANI.*
S.J., 410(M&L):APR73-225
SCHÄFER, E. DAS VERHÄLTNIS VON ER-
LEBNIS UND KUNSTGESTALT BEI CATULL.
J-C. DUMONT, 555:VOL46FASC2-343
SCHÄFER, G.M. UNTERSUCHUNGEN ZUR
DEUTSCHSPRACHIGEN MARIENLYRIK DES
12. UND 13. JAHRHUNDERTS.
J.S. GROSECLOSE, 406:FALL73-307
SCHÄFER, J. WORT UND BEGRIFF "HUM-
OUR" IN DER ELISABETHANISCHEN
KOMÖDIE.*
V.B. HELTZEL, 570(SQ):FALL72-454
SCHAFER, S. THE POLITICAL CRIMINAL.
C. LEHMANN-HAUPT, 441:26FEB74-41
SCHÄFER, W.E. - SEE HEIDEGGER, W.
SCHAFER, W.J. & J. RIEDEL. THE ART
OF RAGTIME.*
F. CONROY, 441:3FEB74-4
SCHAFFER, B. THE ADMINISTRATIVE
FACTOR.
617(TLS):15MAR74-252
SCHAFROTH, H.F. DIE ENTSCHEIDUNG
BEI GRILLPARZER.
W. PAULSEN, 222(GR):NOV72-306
SCHALL, J. HUMAN DIGNITY & HUMAN
NUMBERS.
W.E.M., 543:MAR72-568

SCHALLÜCK, P., ED. GERMANY - CULTUR-
AL DEVELOPMENTS SINCE 1945.
J.A.A. TER HAAR, 221(GQ):MAY72-
546
SCHANE, S.A. FRENCH PHONOLOGY & MOR-
PHOLOGY.
V. HOŘEJŠÍ, 353:1DEC72-113
SCHANZE, H., COMP. INDEX ZU NOVALIS'
"HEINRICH VON OFTERDINGEN."
E. STOPP, 402(MLR):APR73-458
SCHANZE, H., ED. INDICES ZUR DEUT-
SCHEN LITERATUR. (VOLS 1&2)
M. ALFORD, 220(GL&L):JUL73-356
SCHANZER, G.O., COMP. RUSSIAN LITER-
ATURE IN THE HISPANIC WORLD.
L.S. THOMPSON, 263:APR-JUN73-200
SCHAPERA, I. RAINMAKING RITES OF
TSWANA TRIBES.
A. KUPER, 69:JAN72-67
SCHAPIRO, L. - SEE TURGENEV, I.S.
SCHAPIRO, M. WORDS & PICTURES.
H. ZERNER, 453:14NOV74-37
SCHARANG, M. CHARLY TRAKTOR.
617(TLS):2AUG74-839
SCHÄRER, K. THÉMATIQUE DE NERVAL.*
W. BEAUCHAMP, 546(RR):APR74-161
SCHARLEMANN, R.P. REFLECTION &
DOUBT IN THE THOUGHT OF PAUL TIL-
LICH.
H.F., 543:DEC71-368
SCHATOFF, M., COMP. HALF A CENTURY
OF RUSSIAN SERIALS: 1917-1968.*
(VOL 2) (N.A. HALE, ED)
W.S. SWORAKOWSKI, 550(RUSR):APR
72-204
SCHATOFF, M., COMP. HALF A CENTURY
OF RUSSIAN SERIALS: 1917-1968.*
(VOL 3) (N.A. HALE, ED)
W.S. SWORAKOWSKI, 550(RUSR):OCT
72-433
SCHATZMAN, M. SOUL MURDER.*
42(AR):VOL32#3-505
SCHAU, A. MÄRCHENFORMEN BEI EICHEN-
DORFF.*
J.F.F., 191(ELN):SEP72(SUPP)-145
SCHECHNER, R. ENVIRONMENTAL THEATER.
J. LAHR, 441:3MAR74-26
SCHECHTER, R.L. NEAR THE WALL OF
LION SHADOWS.
V.B. YOUNG, 577(SHR):WINTER72-97
SCHEICK, W.J. THE WILL & THE WORD.
R.D. ARNER, 165:FALL74-198
SCHEIMANN, E. SEX CAN SAVE YOUR
HEART.
M. DUMONT, 441:19MAY74-6
SCHELER, L. - SEE ELUARD, P.
SCHELER, M. RESSENTIMENT. (L.A.
COSER, ED)
W.H. WERKMEISTER, 319:JAN74-132
SCHELLING, F.W.J. GRUNDLEGUNG DER
POSITIVEN PHILOSOPHIE. F.W.J.
SCHELLING: BRIEFE UND DOKUMENTE.*
(VOL 2) (H. FUHRMANS, ED OF BOTH)
M. VETÖ, 319:APR74-265
SCHELLING-SCHÄR, E. DIE GESTALT DER
OTTILIE.*
E.A. BLACKALL, 405(MP):AUG72-76
J. MILFULL, 222(GR):JAN72-75
SCHENKER, A.M., ED. FIFTEEN MODERN
POLISH SHORT STORIES.*
S.S. BIRKENMAYER, 104:SUMMER72-
315

SCHEPPER, M.M-D. LE THÈME DE LA
PYTHIE CHEZ PAUL VALÉRY.
R. GEEN, 546(RR):FEB72-72
SCHER, L. FINDING & BUYING YOUR
PLACE IN THE COUNTRY.
S. STEPHENS, 441:8DEC74-41
SCHER, S.P. VERBAL MUSIC IN GERMAN
LITERATURE.*
H.R. VAGET, 680(ZDP):BAND91HEFT
2-309
SCHERER, G. & A. WOLLMANN. ENGLISCHE
PHONETIK UND PHONOLOGIE.
K. REICHL, 72:BAND210HEFT4/6-355
SCHERER, R. PHILOSOPHIES DE LA COM-
MUNICATION.
R. BLANCHÉ, 542:OCT-DEC72-483
SCHERNBERG, D. DIETRICH SCHERNBERG,
"EIN SCHÖN SPIEL VON FRAU JUTTEN."*
(M. LEMMER, ED)
K. SMITS, 67:MAY73-139
SCHERPE, K. WERTHER UND WERTHERWIR-
KUNG.*
S. ATKINS, 222(GR):NOV72-297
SCHEUERLE, W.H. THE NEGLECTED BRO-
THER.
G.B. TENNYSON, 445(NCF):JUN72-
117
SCHEURWEGHS, G., ED. ANALYTICAL BIB-
LIOGRAPHY OF WRITINGS ON MODERN
ENGLISH MORPHOLOGY & SYNTAX 1877-
1960. (VOLS 1&2)
A.R. TELLIER, 189(EA):OCT-DEC72-
532
SCHEVILL, I.M. MANUAL OF BASIC
SPANISH CONSTRUCTIONS.
J.L. BENBOW, 399(MLJ):APR72-269
R.A. FARLEY, 238:MAY72-398
SCHIB, K. JOHANNES VON MÜLLER, 1752-
1809.
H.S. OFFLER, 182:VOL25#12-439
SCHIBEL, W. SPRACHBEHANDLUNG UND
DARSTELLUNGSWEISE IN RÖMISCHER
PROSA.
M. WINTERBOTTOM, 123:DEC73-279
SCHICK, E.B. METAPHORICAL ORGANI-
CISM IN HERDER'S EARLY WORKS.
J.K. FUGATE, 301(JEGP):JAN73-89
R. MAYO, 125:JUN73-313
H.B. NISBET, 402(MLR):APR73-456
SCHICKEL, R. SECOND SIGHT.
R. CAMPION, 200:JUN-JUL72-373
SCHIEB, G. & T. FRINGS, EDS. HENRIC
VAN VELDEKEN: ENEIDE I, II.
C. MINIS, 433:OCT72-508
SCHIER, K., ED & TRANS. SCHWEDISCHE
VOLKSMÄRCHEN.
W.E. RICHMOND, 563(SS):SPRING73-
157
SCHIER, R.D. DIE SPRACHE GEORG
TRAKLS.*
B. KÖNNEKER, 224(GRM):BAND22
HEFT4-444
SCHIFF, G. JOHANN HEINRICH FÜSSLI.
617(TLS):24MAY74-564
SCHIFFER, S.R. MEANING.*
G.H. HARMAN, 311(JP):18APR74-224
R. KIRK, 518:MAY73-22
SCHIFFERLI, P. DAS WAR DADA.
S. FAUCHEREAU, 98:AUG/SEP72-752
SCHILLER, F. SCHILLERS WERKE. (VOL
17 ED BY K-H. HAHN; VOL 28 ED BY
N. OELLERS)
L.A. WILLOUGHBY, 220(GL&L):JAN73-
93

SCHILLER, F. WALLENSTEIN.* (S.
KIRSHNER, ED)
E. GRIEM, 399(MLJ):DEC72-518
SCHILLER, G. ICONOGRAPHY OF CHRIS-
TIAN ART. (VOL 1)
J. BECKWITH, 39:JAN72-66
SCHILLER, J.P. I.A. RICHARDS'
THEORY OF LITERATURE.*
P. LE BRUN, 541(RES):FEB72-103
SCHILPP, P.A., ED. THE PHILOSOPHY
OF KARL POPPER.
P. SINGER, 453:2MAY74-22
SCHINDLER, M.S. THE SONNETS OF
ANDREAS GRYPHIUS.*
H. BEKKER, 301(JEGP):JAN73-78
P.M. DALY, 564:JUN72-138
P. SKRINE, 402(MLR):APR73-448
J. STRELKA, 406:SUMMER73-185
SCHIØRRING, N., H. GLAHN & C.E. HAT-
TING. FESTSKRIFT JENS PETER LAR-
SEN.*
J.A.W., 410(M&L):APR73-224
SCHIROK, B. DER AUFBAU VON WOLFRAMS
"PARZIVAL."
D.G. MOWATT, 67:NOV73-313
SCHLACHTER, W. ARBEITEN ZUR STRUK-
TURBEZOGENEN GRAMMATIK AUF DER
GRUNDLAGE FINNISCH-UGRISCHEN UND
INDOGERMANISCHEN MATERIALS. (B.
COLLINDER, H. FROMM & G. GANSCHOW,
EDS)
W. ABRAHAM, 206:JUL72-588
R-P. RITTER, 260(IF):BAND76-228
SCHLAUCH, M. LANGUAGE & THE STUDY
OF LANGUAGES TODAY.*
E. TRAUGOTT, 405(MP):MAY73-375
SCHLAWE, F. DIE BRIEFSAMMLUNGEN DES
19. JAHRHUNDERTS.*
W. MARTENS, 72:BAND210HEFT1/3-
167
SCHLEE, T. - SEE BUSCH, W.
SCHLEGEL, A.W. VORLESUNGEN ÜBER DAS
AKADEMISCHE STUDIUM.
H. EICHNER, 564:JUN72-141
SCHLEGEL, F. FRIEDRICH SCHLEGEL'S
"LUCINDE" & THE FRAGMENTS.* (P.
FIRCHOW, TRANS)
R. IMMERWAHR, 301(JEGP):APR73-
287
SCHLEGEL, R. INQUIRY INTO SCIENCE.
W.F. BARR, 486:DEC72-555
SCHLEGEL, S.A. TIRURAY-ENGLISH
LEXICON.
G.F. MEIER, 682(ZPSK):BAND24
HEFT6-546
G.W. MOORE, 293(JAST):FEB72-466
SCHLEGEL, S.A. TIRURAY JUSTICE.
D.V. HART, 318(JAOS):OCT-DEC72-
559
G.W. MOORE, 293(JAST):FEB72-466
SCHLEINER, W. THE IMAGERY OF JOHN
DONNE'S SERMONS.*
T.O. SLOAN, 599:SPRING72-203
SCHLEMMER, O. MAN. (H. KUCHLING,
ED)
A.C. BIRNHOLZ, 290(JAAC):SUMMER
72-552
SCHLEPP, W. SAN-CH'Ü.*
J.I. CRUMP, 318(JAOS):OCT-DEC72-
550
SCHLERATH, B., ED. ZARATHUSTRA.
J. DUCHESNE-GUILLEMIN, 343:BAND
15HEFT2-221
SCHLERATH, B. - SEE LOMMEL, H.

SCHLESINGER, A.M., JR. THE IMPERIAL
PRESIDENCY.*
R. CUFF, 99:MAY/JUN74-58
C. SERPELL, 362:19SEP74-378
441:10NOV74-40
SCHLINK, W. ZWISCHEN CLUNY UND
CLAIRVAUX.
E. ARMI, 576:OCT72-240
D. VON WINTERFELD, 683:BAND35
HEFT1/2-118
SCHLÖSSER, A. & A-G. KUCKHOFF, EDS.
SHAKESPEARE JAHRBUCH. (VOLS 103-
106, 1967-1970)
V.B. HELTZEL, 570(SQ):FALL72-452
SCHLÖSSER, A. & A-G. KUCKHOFF, EDS.
SHAKESPEARE JAHRBUCH. (VOL 107,
1971)
V.B. HELTZEL, 570(SQ):FALL72-454
SCHLUETER, P. - SEE LESSING, D.
SCHMALZRIEDT, E. PERI PHYSEOS - ZUR
FRUHGESCHICHTE DER BUCHTITEL.
P.M. HUBY, 123:DEC73-206
SCHMIDT, D.A. ARMAGEDDON IN THE
MIDDLE EAST.
N. SAFRAN, 441:7APR74-10
SCHMIDT, F.W. ZUM BEGRIFF DER NEGA-
TIVITÄT BEI SCHELLING UND HEGEL.
M.H., 191(ELN):SEP72(SUPP)-177
SCHMIDT, H. NIKOLAUS LENAU.*
E. LOEB, 399(MLJ):NOV72-474
SCHMIDT, H-P. BRHASPATI UND INDRA.
L. ROCHER, 318(JAOS):JAN-MAR72-
167
SCHMIDT, J. HÖLDERLINS LETZTE HYM-
NEN.*
M.L. DAEUMER, 221(GQ):MAR72-355
C.H., 191(ELN):SEP72(SUPP)-162
SCHMIDT, J., ED. ÜBER HÖLDERLIN.
C.H., 191(ELN):SEP72(SUPP)-162
SCHMIDT, J.E. ENGLISH IDIOMS & AMER-
ICANISMS FOR FOREIGN STUDENTS, PRO-
FESSIONALS & PHYSICIANS. ENGLISH
WORD POWER FOR PHYSICIANS & OTHER
PROFESSIONALS.
S. COOPER, 583:WINTER72-207
SCHMIDT, K.O. MEHR MACHT ÜBER LEIB
UND LEBEN.
R. MALTER, 342:BAND63HEFT4-513
SCHMIDT, L. HINTERGLAS.
E. ETTLINGER, 203:WINTER72-340
SCHMIDT, L. HISTORISCHE VOLKSLIEDER
AUS ÖSTERREICH VOM 15. BIS ZUM 19.
JAHRHUNDERT.
A. CLOSS, 433:OCT72-513
SCHMIDT, L. VOLKSGESANG UND VOLKS-
LIED.*
H. BAUSINGER, 182:VOL25#11-378
SCHMIDT, M. DESERT OF THE LIONS.
T. EAGLETON, 565:VOL13#3-71
J. GALASSI, 491:NOV73-113
SCHMIDT, M. JOHN WESLEY. (VOL 2,
PT 2)
617(TLS):29MAR74-347
SCHMIDT, M. - SEE VON BIBERACH, R.
SCHMIDT, R. - SEE VAIHINGER, H.
SCHMIDT, S. ROBERT BLUM.
H.F. YOUNG, 182:VOL25#13/14-502
SCHMIDT, V. SPRACHLICHE UNTERSUCH-
UNGEN ZU HERONDAS.*
A.W. JAMES, 303:VOL92-202
SCHMIDT, V. DIE STRECKFORMEN DES
DEUTSCHEN VERBUMS.
M.H. FOLSOM, 353:1OCT72-116

SCHMIDT-RADEFELDT, J. PAUL VALÉRY
LINGUISTE DANS LES "CAHIERS."*
N. GUEUNIER, 209(FM):APR72-175
S. LOSEREIT, 430(NS):DEC72-740
N.C.W. SPENCE, 208(FS):OCT73-475
SCHMITGES, H. CASPAR CLEMENS PICKEL
1847 BIS 1939.
M. BRINGMANN, 182:VOL25#9/10-299
SCHMITT, C.B. CICERO SCEPTICUS.
F. LASSERRE, 182:VOL25#23/24-884
SCHMITT, C.B. A CRITICAL SURVEY &
BIBLIOGRAPHY OF STUDIES ON RENAIS-
SANCE ARISTOTELIANISM 1958-1969.*
M.A. DEL TORRE, 548(RCSF):OCT-
DEC72-469
SCHMITT, F.A. ALEXANDER VON BERNUS.
H.B. GARLAND, 182:VOL25#11-367
SCHMITT, G. SONNETS FOR AN ANALYST.
A. BROSTOFF, 398:WINTER74-281
SCHMITT, L.E., ED. KURZER GRUNDRISS
DER GERMANISCHEN PHILOLOGIE BIS
1500.* (VOL 1)
G. GEIL, 343:BAND15HEFT1-70
SCHMITT, L.E. - SEE MITZKA, W.
SCHMITT, R. MARTIN HEIDEGGER ON
BEING HUMAN.
J. HOPKINS, 321:WINTER72[VOL6#1]-
64
SCHMITT, R. DIE NOMINALBILDUNG IN
DEN DICHTUNGEN DES KALLIMACHOS VON
KYRENE.*
P. CHANTRAINE, 555:VOL46FASC2-
302
SCHMITT, W. KOMMENTAR ZUM ERSTEN
BUCH VON PSEUDO-OPPIANS KYNEGETIKA.
G. GIANGRANDE, 123:MAR73-86
SCHMITZ, J.H. THE ETERNAL FRONTIERS.
617(TLS):31MAY74-591
SCHMITZ, V.A. BILDER UND MOTIVE IN
DER DICHTUNG STEFAN GEORGES.
F. CRONHEIM, 402(MLR):JUL73-701
SCHMITZ-VALCKENBERG, G. GRUNDLEHREN
KATHARISCHER SEKTEN DES 13. JAHR-
HUNDERTS.
R.E. LERNER, 589:APR73-404
SCHMOLL, H. - SEE MAYSER, E.
SCHNAPP, F. - SEE HOFFMANN, E.T.A.
SCHNAUFER, A. FRÜHGRIECHISCHER
TOTENGLAUBE.
C. SOURVINOU-INWOOD, 303:VOL92-
220
SCHNEEDE, U.M. THE ESSENTIAL MAX
ERNST.
617(TLS):23AUG74-899
SCHNEEWIND, J.B. BACKGROUNDS OF ENG-
LISH VICTORIAN LITERATURE.
J. CLIVE, 637(VS):DEC72-243
SCHNEIDER, B. DIE MITTELALTERLICHEN
GRIECHISCH-LATEINISCHEN ÜBERSETZUN-
GEN DER ARISTOTELISCHEN RHETORIK.
D.C. INNES, 123:DEC73-151
SCHNEIDER, B.R., JR. THE ETHOS OF
RESTORATION COMEDY.*
A. BARTON, 677:VOL3-291
H. HAWKINS, 541(RES):MAY72-209
R.D. HUME, 481(PQ):JUL72-631
C. VISSER, 627(UTQ):WINTER73-170
SCHNEIDER, E.W. THE DRAGON IN THE
GATE.*
N. WHITE, 447(N&Q):NOV72-431
SCHNEIDER, G.D. WEST AFRICAN PIDGIN-
ENGLISH.
D. DE CAMP, 215(GL):VOL12#1-35
L. TODD, 361:VOL28#1&2-185

SCHNEIDER, H. DIE FRANZÖSISCHE KOM-
POSITIONSLEHRE IN DER ERSTEN
HÄLFTE DES 17. JAHRHUNDERTS.
H.M.B., 410(M&L):OCT73-463
SCHNEIDER, J-P. LES GOUFFRES DE
L'AUBE.
M. SCHAETTEL, 557(RSH):JUL-SEP72-
479
SCHNEIDER, K.L. & G. MARTENS - SEE
"GEORG HEYM"
SCHNEIDER, K.R. AUTOKIND VS. MAN-
KIND.*
R.C. WEINBERG, 44:JUN72-8
SCHNEIDER, L.A. KU CHIEH-KANG &
CHINA'S NEW HISTORY.
639(VQR):SPRING72-LXIV
SCHNEIDER, M. ETÜDEN ZUM LESEN
SPRACHLICHER FORMEN IN GOETHES
WILHELM MEISTER.*
E. BAHR, 406:FALL73-316
D.G. LITTLE, 402(MLR):JUL73-690
H. REISS, 220(GL&L):APR73-243
SCHNEIDER, M. & S. GAROFALO. CON-
VERSIAMO UN PO'.
P. ROSSI, 276:AUTUMN72-347
SCHNEIDER, P. LENZ.
617(TLS):14JUN74-643
SCHNEIDER, P., ED. SEIN UND SOLLEN
IM ERFAHRUNGSBEREICH DES RECHTES.
F. GILLIARD, 182:VOL25#23/24-853
SCHNEIDER, R. STÜCKE.
617(TLS):5APR74-359
SCHNEIDER, U. DIE FUNKTION DER
ZITATE IM "ULYSSES" VON JAMES
JOYCE.
H. BONHEIM, 52:BAND7HEFT2/3-338
SCHNITZLER, A. & O. WAISSNIX. LIEBE,
DIE STARB VOR DER ZEIT. (T. NICKL
& H. SCHNITZLER, EDS)
W. NEHRING, 221(GQ):JAN72-188
SCHNUR, H.C. - SEE REUCHLIN, J.
SCHNURR, W. JOHNNIE DEATH.
N. CALLENDAR, 441:12MAY74-18
SCHOBER, R. VON DER WIRKLICHEN WELT
IN DER DICHTUNG.
G. HAINSWORTH, 208(FS):OCT73-495
SCHOCK, R. LOGICS WITHOUT EXISTENCE
ASSUMPTIONS.
T. HAILPERIN, 316:JUN72-424
SCHOELLER, B. GELÄCHTER UND SPAN-
NUNG.*
C.P. MAGILL, 220(GL&L):OCT72-62
SCHOENBAUM, S., ED. RENAISSANCE
DRAMA. (NEW SER, VOL 3)
I. DONALDSON, 541(RES):NOV72-494
C.J. GIANAKARIS, 551(RENQ):SUM-
MER72-229
SCHOENBAUM, S. SHAKESPEARE'S LIVES.*
R.L. MONTGOMERY, 570(SQ):SPRING
72-209
R. SANER, 191(ELN):JUN73-296
S. WELLS, 447(N&Q):APR72-142
SCHOENSTEIN, R. WASTED ON THE YOUNG.
M. LEVIN, 441:23JUN74-35
SCHOFIELD, R.E. MECHANISM & MATER-
IALISM.
J.R.R. CHRISTIE, 481(PQ):JUL72-
585
P.M. HEIMANN, 479(PHQ):APR72-178
SCHOGT, H.G. LE SYSTÈME VERBAL DU
FRANÇAIS CONTEMPORAIN.*
R. POSNER, 545(RPH):AUG72-94
SCHOLEFIELD, A. LION IN THE EVENING.
M. LEVIN, 441:31MAR74-40

SCHOLEM, G. SABBATAI SEVI.*
C. OZICK, 441:24FEB74-27
617(TLS):20SEP74-1024
SCHOLES, R., ED. THE PHILOSOPHER-
CRITIC.
M.J. GALGANO, 125:OCT72-70
J. STOLNITZ, 290(JAAC):SPRING72-
407
SCHOLES, R. STRUCTURALISM IN LITERA-
TURE.
617(TLS):2AUG74-824
SCHOLES, R. & C.H. KLAUS. ELEMENTS
OF THE ESSAY.
S. GILL, 447(N&Q):AUG72-310
SCHOLES, R.J. PHONOTACTIC GRAMMATI-
CALITY.*
C.E. CAIRNS, 206:SEP72-135
SCHOLZ, M.G. BIBLIOGRAPHIE ZU WAL-
THER VON DER VOGELWEIDE.*
S.M. JOHNSON, 221(GQ):MAR72-372
SCHOLZ, U.W. STUDIEN ZUM ALTITALIS-
CHEN UND ALTRÖMISCHEN MARSKULT
UND MARSMYTHOS.
R.M. OGILVIE, 123:MAR73-73
SCHOLZ-MICHELITSCH, H. DAS ORCHES-
TER- UND KAMMERMUSIKWERK VON GEORG
CHRISTOPH WAGENSEIL.
A.H. KING, 182:VOL25#15/16-560
SCHON, D.A. BEYOND THE STABLE STATE.
639(VQR):SUMMER72-CV
SCHONBERG, H.C. GRANDMASTERS OF
CHESS.*
F. BRADY, 441:20JAN74-18
SCHÖNDÖRFFER, O. - SEE KANT, I.
SCHÖNE, A. ENGLISCHE NONSENSE- UND
GRUSEL-BALLADEN.
C. MIDDLETON & R.D. ABRAHAMS,
677:VOL3-262
SCHÖNFELDER, G. DIE MUSIK DER
PEKING-OPER.
C. MACKERRAS, 415:JUN73-604
L.E.R.P., 410(M&L):OCT73-480
SCHONHOVEN, K. DIE BAYERISCHE VOLKS-
PARTEI 1924-1932.
A.J. NICHOLLS, 617(TLS):8NOV74-
1264
SCHÖNI, U. HENRI-FRÉDÉRIC AMIEL.
E.T. DUBOIS, 182:VOL25#7/8-234
SCHOOLFIELD, G.C. RILKE'S LAST YEAR.
H.W. PANTHEL, 399(MLJ):APR72-264
SCHOP SOLER, A.M. DIE SPANISCH-
RUSSISCHEN BEZIEHUNGEN IM 18.
JAHRHUNDERT.
I. DE MADARIAGA, 575(SEER):JUL73-
474
"ARTHUR SCHOPENHAUER: GESPRÄCHE."
(A. HÜBSCHER, ED)
H.W. BRANN, 258:DEC72-629
SCHOTT, H. - SEE RUSSELL, R.
SCHOTT, R. AUS LEBEN UND DICHTUNG
EINES WESTAFRIKANISCHEN BAUERN-
VOLKES.
M. FORTES, 69:OCT72-342
SCHOTT, S. - SEE UNDER RICKE, H.
SCHOTT, W. - SEE WILLIAMS, W.C.
SCHRADER, E., ED. WORTINDEX ZU GOTT-
FRIED KELLER, DER GRÜNE HEINRICH.
(1ST DRAFT)
P. OCHSENBEIN, 657(WW):NOV/DEC72-
430
SCHRAG, O.O. EXISTENCE, EXISTENZ &
TRANSCENDENCE.
J.D.C., 543:JUN72-767
M.E. WILLIAMS, 154:SEP72-455

SCHRAG, P. THE DECLINE OF THE WASP.
H.A. LARRABEE, 432(NEQ):DEC72-
578
SCHRAG, P. THE END OF THE AMERICAN
FUTURE.
S.R. WEISMAN, 441:24MAR74-18
SCHRAG, P. TEST OF LOYALTY.
R.M. BROWN, 441:16JUN74-5
SCHRECKENBACH, H-J., ED. BIBLIOGRA-
PHIE ZUR GESCHICHTE DER MARK BRAN-
DENBURG. (PT 3)
T. KLEIN, 182:VOL25#9/10-318
SCHRECKER, J.E. IMPERIALISM & CHI-
NESE NATIONALISM.
D.D. BUCK, 293(JAST):NOV71-184
SCHREIBER, F.R. SYBIL.*
617(TLS):27SEP74-1046
SCHREIBER, M. KUNST ZWISCHEN ASKESE
UND EXHIBITIONISMUS.
617(TLS):25OCT74-1188
SCHREIBER, M. DIE UNVORSTELLBARE
KUNST - DIE STÄRKE DES SCHWACHEN
ALS POETISCHES PRINZIP.
A.J. GAIL, 657(WW):MAR/APR72-143
SCHREINER, P. - SEE LOENERTZ, R-J.
SCHREINERT, K. - SEE FONTANE, T.
SCHREMMER, E., ED. HANDELSSTRATEGIE
UND BETRIEBSWIRTSCHAFTLICHE KALKU-
LATION IM AUSGEHENDEN 18. JAHRHUN-
DERT DER SÜDDEUTSCHE SALZMARKT.
H.C. PEYER, 182:VOL25#7/8-246
SCHREYL, K.H., ED. JOSEPH MARIA
OLBRICH, DIE ZEICHNUNGEN IN DER
KUNSTBIBLIOTHEK BERLIN.
J. HERMAND, 182:VOL25#21-754
SCHRIER, W. CONTEST ORATORY.
G.R. CAPP, 583:SUMMER73-402
"SCHRIFTEN DER THEODOR-STORM-GESELL-
SCHAFT." (SCHRIFT 20/1971)
J. DE CORT, 556(RLV):1972/4-447
SCHRIJVERS, P.H. HORROR AC DIVINA
VOLUPTAS.*
N. AUSTIN, 24:FALL73-301
SCHRIMPF, H.J. - SEE MORITZ, K.P.
SCHRÖDER, R. NOVELLE UND NOVELLEN-
THEORIE IN DER FRÜHEN BIEDERMEIER-
ZEIT.*
M. SWALES, 402(MLR):JAN73-231
SCHRÖDER, W., ED. DER NIBELUNGE
LIET UND DIU KLAGE.
D.E. LE SAGE, 402(MLR):JAN73-210
SCHRÖDER, W. VELDEKE-STUDIEN.*
D.E. LE SAGE, 402(MLR):JAN73-213
SCHRÖDER, W., ED. WOLFRAM-STUDIEN.*
J.W. THOMAS, 133:1972/2-209
SCHROEDER, A. THE LATE MAN.
R. MC CARTHY, 150(DR):AUTUMN72-
494
VON SCHROEDER, L., ED. MAITRĀYAṆĪ
SAṂHITĀ DER MAITRĀYAṆĪYA ŚĀKHĀ.
(BK 1)
L. ROCHER, 318(JAOS):OCT-DEC72-
572
SCHRÖER, M.M.A. ENGLISCHES HANDWÖR-
TERBUCH.* (PTS 16-25) (P.L. JAE-
GER, ED)
H.H. MEIER, 182:VOL25#15/16-544
SCHRÖER, M.M.A. ENGLISCHES HANDWÖR-
TERBUCH.* (PT 26) (P.L. JAEGER,
ED)
H. KOZIOL, 430(NS):NOV72-683
H.H. MEIER, 182:VOL25#15/16-544
SCHROETER, L. THE LAST EXODUS.
P. REDDAWAY, 453:12DEC74-36

SCHROTH, R.A. THE EAGLE & BROOKLYN.
P. KIHSS, 441:7DEC74-27
SCHUBERT, G. & J. DANELSKI, EDS.
COMPARATIVE JUDICIAL BEHAVIOR.
T.R.F., 543:JUN72-767
SCHUBERT, H-J. DIE ERWEITERUNG DES
BIBELGOTISCHEN WORTSCHATZES MIT
HILFE DER METHODEN DER WORTBIL-
DUNGSLEHRE.
R. SCHMITT, 343:BAND14HEFT1-105
E. SEEBOLD, 260(IF):BAND76-324
SCHUBERT, M.H. - SEE WACKENRODER,
W.H.
SCHUCHARD, B. "VALOR."*
M. SANDMANN, 545(RPH):NOV72-504
SCHÜDDEKOPF, O-E. FASCISM.
S.J. WOOLF, 617(TLS):11OCT74-
1118
SCHUELER, H.J. HANS FALLADA.*
K.G. POLLARD, 220(GL&L):APR73-
267
SCHUHMANN, K. DIE GRUNDLAGE DER
WISSENSCHAFTLEHRE IN IHREM UM-
RISSE.
H. DECLÈVE, 154:SEP72-440
SCHULER, S. THE COMPLETE TERRACE
BOOK.
S. STEPHENS, 441:8DEC74-43
SCHÜLKE, U., ED. KONRADS BÜCHLEIN
VON DER GEISTLICHEN GEMAHELSCHAFT.
C. HALL, 221(GQ):JAN72-183
SCHULL, J. REBELLION.
D. HELWIG, 529(QQ):AUTUMN72-428
G.A. RAWLYK, 150(DR):SUMMER72-
325
SCHULLER, G.A. SAMUEL VON BRUKEN-
THAL.
H.F. YOUNG, 182:VOL25#3/4-125
SCHULMAN, E. A HISTORY OF JEWISH
EDUCATION IN THE SOVIET UNION.*
M. FRIEDBERG, 550(RUSR):JUL72-
301
SCHULTE-SASSE, J. DIE KRITIK AN DER
TRIVIALLITERATUR SEIT DER AUFKLÄ-
RUNG.
K.L. BERGHAHN, 406:FALL73-314
SCHULTE-SASSE, J. LITERARISCHE WER-
TUNG.*
A. CLOSS, 402(MLR):APR73-464
SCHULTHEIS, W. DRAMATISIERUNG VON
VORGESCHICHTE.*
H. MOENKEMEYER, 301(JEGP):JUL73-
411
M. MUELLER, 564:MAR72-64
SCHULTZ, H.S. JAMES MADISON.
D.O. DEWEY, 656(WMQ):JAN72-188
SCHULTZE, J. ART OF NINETEENTH-
CENTURY EUROPE.
R.M. BISANZ, 127:WINTER72/73-228
SCHULTZE, M., ED. DAS GROSSE KARL
VALENTIN BUCH.
617(TLS):26APR74-440
SCHULZ, A.S. FELSBILDER IN NORD-
AUSTRALIEN.
R. PITTIONI, 182:VOL25#19/20-701
SCHULZ, D. STUDIEN ZUR VERFÜHRUNGS-
SZENE IM ENGLISCHEN ROMAN (1660-
1760).
W. KLUGE, 430(NS):AUG72-496
SCHULZ, G. FASCHISMUS - NATIONAL-
SOZIALISMUS.
617(TLS):25OCT74-1188

SCHULZ, G., ED. NOVALIS.
W. KUDSZUS, 406:SPRING73-98
E. STOPP, 402(MLR):APR73-460
SCHULZ, G. DIE SCHILLERBEARBEITUN-
GEN BERTOLT BRECHTS.
H. HULTBERG, 301(JEGP):JAN73-103
E. SPEIDEL, 402(MLR):JUL73-707
G. STORZ, 182:VOL25#23/24-870
SCHULZ, M. & O. BASLER. DEUTSCHES
FREMDWÖRTERBUCH.
E. ÖHMANN, 439(NM):1972/3-270
SCHULZ, M. BLACK HUMOR FICTION OF
THE SIXTIES.
J. KLINKOWITZ, 659:SPRING74-271
SCHULZ, V. STUDIEN ZUM KOMISCHEN IN
SHAKESPEARES KOMÖDIEN.
M. PFISTER, 72:BAND210HEFT4/6-
377
SCHULZ-BEHREND, G., ED. THE GERMAN
BAROQUE.
G. HOFFMEISTER, 406:FALL73-305
SCHULZ-BEHREND, G. - SEE OPITZ, M.
SCHULZE, F. FANTASTIC IMAGES.
D.M. SOKOL, 127:WINTER72/73-228
SCHUMACHER, E.F. SMALL IS BEAUTI-
FUL.*
H. LOMAS, 364:OCT/NOV73-133
SCHUMANN, R. ROBERT SCHUMANN: TAGE-
BÜCHER. (VOL 1) (G. EISMANN, ED)
G.A., 410(M&L):JAN73-76
SCHUPPENHAUER, C. DER KAMPF UM DEN
REIM IN DER DEUTSCHEN LITERATUR
DES 18. JAHRHUNDERTS.*
T.K. THAYER, 221(GQ):NOV72-707
SCHÜRER, E. THE HISTORY OF THE JEW-
ISH PEOPLE IN THE AGE OF JESUS
CHRIST (175 B.C. - A.D. 135). (VOL
1) (G. VERMES & F. MILLAR, EDS)
617(TLS):30AUG74-927
SCHURHAMMER, G. FRANCIS XAVIER.
(VOL 1)
617(TLS):19APR74-420
SCHURIG-GEICK, D. STUDIEN ZUM MOD-
ERNEN "CONTE FANTASTIQUE" MAUPAS-
SANTS UND AUSGEWÄHLTER AUTOREN
DES 20. JAHRHUNDERTS.
E-M. KNAPP-TEPPERBERG, 224(GRM):
BAND22HEFT3-319
P.J. WHYTE, 208(FS):APR73-223
SCHURMANN, F. THE LOGIC OF WORLD
POWER.
D. SCHNEIDERMAN, 441:22SEP74-34
R. STEEL, 453:8AUG74-37
SCHÜRR, F. ERLEBNIS, SINNBILD,
MYTHOS.*
E. GLASER, 240(HR):SUMMER72-339
SCHÜSSLER, I. DIE AUSEINANDERSET-
ZUNG VON IDEALISMUS UND REALISMUS
IN FICHTES WISSENSCHAFTSLEHRE.
W.H. WERKMEISTER, 319:OCT74-537
SCHUSTER, I. & I. BODE, EDS. ALFRED
DÖBLIN IM SPIEGEL DER ZEITGENÖS-
SICHEN KRITIK.
617(TLS):26APR74-442
SCHUSTER, L.A. & OTHERS - SEE MORE,
T.
SCHUSTER, M., COMP. MOTION PICTURE
PERFORMERS.
J. SPEARS, 200:OCT72-501
SCHÜTRUMPF, E. DIE BEDEUTUNG DES
WORTES ETHOS IN DER POETIK DES
ARISTOTELES.*
B.R. REES, 123:MAR73-50

SCHUTZ, A. THE PHENOMENOLOGY OF
THE SOCIAL WORLD.*
K-P. MARKL, 111:20OCT72-24
SCHÜTZEICHEL, R. ALTHOCHDEUTSCHES
WÖRTERBUCH.*
M. KAEMPFERT, 680(ZDP):BAND91
HEFT3-416
K. OSTBERG, 260(IF):BAND76-341
D.A. WELLS, 182:VOL25#19/20-662
SCHUYLER, J. THE CRYSTAL LITHIUM.*
T. CLARK, 114(CHIR):VOL24#4-170
639(VQR):WINTER73-XIII
SCHWAB, F.M. DAVID OF AUGSBURG'S
"PATERNOSTER" & THE AUTHENTICITY
OF HIS GERMAN WORKS.*
H. MILNES, 589:OCT73-788
SCHWÄNKE, H.P. - SEE HALLIG, R.
SCHWARTZ, B. THE LAW IN AMERICA.
I.R. DEE, 441:1DEC74-12
SCHWARTZ, C. GERSHWIN.*
H. KELLER, 617(TLS):13SEP74-970
SCHWARTZ, D. SELECTED ESSAYS OF DEL-
MORE SCHWARTZ. (D.A. DIKE & D.H.
ZUCKER, EDS)
J.C. DE VANY, 590:FALL/WINTER
73/74-42
SCHWARTZ, E. ELECTRONIC MUSIC.*
P. GRIFFITHS, 415:JUN73-603
SCHWARTZ, E. THE FORMS OF FEELING.
D.J. GORDON, 676(YR):SUMMER73-
583
SCHWARTZ, H. IDÉOLOGIE ET ART ROMAN-
ESQUE CHEZ JULES BARBEY D'AURE-
VILLY.
U. SCHULZ-BUSCHHAUS, 72:BAND210
HEFT1/3-231
SCHWARTZ, K. JUAN GOYTISOLO.
O.P. FERRER, 399(MLJ):NOV72-456
SCHWARTZ, M.A. POLITICS & TERRITORY.
S.J.R. NOEL, 99:NOV/DEC74-40
SCHWARTZ, R.B. SAMUEL JOHNSON & THE
NEW SCIENCE.*
P.L. FARBER, 173(ECS):SUMMER73-
524
P.J. KORSHIN, 301(JEGP):JAN73-
137
C. MC INTOSH, 481(PQ):JUL72-708
SCHWARTZMAN, E. CAMPAIGN CRAFTSMAN-
SHIP.
639(VQR):AUTUMN73-CLXVII
SCHWARZ, A., ED. A TWISTER OF
TWISTS, A TANGLER OF TONGUES.
617(TLS):18OCT74-1163
SCHWARZ, B. MUSIC & MUSICAL LIFE IN
SOVIET RUSSIA 1917-1970.*
G.A., 410(M&L):OCT73-468
S. KREBS, 32:MAR73-204
R. WEITZMAN, 364:JUN/JUL72-140
SCHWARZ, D.W.H. SACHGÜTER UND LEB-
ENSFORMEN.*
J.L. FLOOD, 220(GL&L):OCT72-68
SCHWARZ, E. DAS VERSCHLUCKTE
SCHLUCHZEN.
L.S. PICKLE, 301(JEGP):APR73-295
G.L. TRACY, 406:FALL73-306
SCHWARZ, P.P. AURORA.
J.F.F., 191(ELN):SEP72(SUPP)-146
SCHWARZ, V., ED. DER JUNGE HAYDN.
J.A.W., 410(M&L):APR73-234
SCHWARZ, W.J. DER ERZÄHLER MARTIN
WALSER.*
J.J. WHITE, 402(MLR):OCT73-956

SCHWARZ, W.J. DER ERZÄHLER UWE JOHN-
SON.*
M. BOULBY, 221(GQ):JAN72-174
SCHWARZ-BART, A. A WOMAN NAMED SOLI-
TUDE.* (FRENCH TITLE: LA MULÂ-
TRESSE SOLITUDE.)
P. CRUTTWELL & F. WESTBURG,
249(HUDR):SUMMER73-419
J. MELLORS, 364:AUG/SEP73-150
SCHWARZ-BART, S. THE BRIDGE OF BE-
YOND.
P. THEROUX, 441:17MAR74-41
J. UPDIKE, 442(NY):12AUG74-96
SCHWARZBACH, B.E. VOLTAIRE'S OLD
TESTAMENT CRITICISM.
J.H. BRUMFITT, 208(FS):APR73-209
A.R. DESAUTELS, 207(FR):DEC71-
516
SCHWARZBAUM, H. STUDIES IN JEWISH &
WORLD FOLKLORE.
D. BEN-AMOS, 196:BAND13HEFT1/2-
186
SCHWARZENBERG, C. IL SINDACALISMO
FASCISTA.
S.J. WOOLF, 617(TLS):11OCT74-
1118
SCHWEBELL, G.C., ED & TRANS. CONTEM-
PORARY GERMAN POETRY.
P. BRIDGWATER, 220(GL&L):APR73-
270
SCHWEICKERT, A. HEINRICH HEINES
EINFLÜSSE AUF DIE DEUTSCHE LYRIK
1830-1900.*
O.W. JOHNSTON, 221(GQ):NOV72-757
SCHWEIKERT, U. JEAN PAUL.
191(ELN):SEP72(SUPP)-171
SCHWEIKERT, U. JEAN PAULS "KOMET."
M.H., 191(ELN):SEP72(SUPP)-171
N.H. SMITH, 182:VOL25#7/8-236
SCHWEIKERT, U. - SEE "LUDWIG TIECK"
SCHWEIKLE, G., ED. DICHTER ÜBER
DICHTER IN MITTELHOCHDEUTSCHER
LITERATUR.*
C. LOFMARK, 220(GL&L):JUL73-352
SCHWEINFURTH, U. & OTHERS. LAND-
SCHAFTSÖKOLOGISCHE FORSCHUNGEN AUF
CEYLON.
P. VOSSELER, 182:VOL25#7/8-253
DE SCHWEINITZ, K. GROWING UP.
D.C. ANDERSON, 441:10NOV74-47
SCHWEITZER, B. GREEK GEOMETRIC
ART.* (GERMAN TITLE: DIE GEO-
METRISCHE KUNST GRIECHENLANDS.)
J.L. BENSON, 54:SEP72-339
A.M. SNODGRASS, 123:DEC73-249
SCHWENGER, H. SCHRIFTSTELLER UND
GEWERKSCHAFT.
617(TLS):25OCT74-1188
SCIOLLA, G.C. LA SCULTURA DI MINO
DA FIESOLE.
A.M. SCHULZ, 54:JUN72-208
SCKOMMODAU, H. THEMATIK DES PARA-
DOXES IN DER AUFKLÄRUNG.
P-E. KNABE, 72:BAND210HEFT4/6-
470
SCOBEY, J. RUGS & WALL HANGINGS.
L.J. GARTNER, JR., 441:8DEC74-50
SCORTIA, T.M. EARTH WRECK.
T. STURGEON, 441:8SEP74-39
SCOT, J. HOMÉLIE SUR LE PROLOGUE DE
JEAN.* (É. JEAUNEAU, ED & TRANS)
P. LANGLOIS, 555:VOL46FASC1-100

SCOTT, A.C. THE THEATRE IN ASIA.
P. CROSSLEY-HOLLAND, 187:MAY74-326

SCOTT, B. IT'LL BE QUITE ALL RIGHT
ON THE NIGHT.
A. RENDLE, 157:AUTUMN72-84

SCOTT, D. BIG WALL CLIMBING.
617(TLS):27DEC74-1471

SCOTT, G. THE RISE & FALL OF THE
LEAGUE OF NATIONS.
617(TLS):29MAR74-312

SCOTT, J. SWEAT & STRUGGLE. (VOL 1)
P. BASKERVILLE, 99:NOV/DEC74-46

SCOTT, J. TREASURE FOR TREASURE.
N. CALLENDAR, 441:21JUL74-18

SCOTT, J.S., ED. A DICTIONARY OF
BUILDING.
B. BROWN, 617(TLS):15NOV74-1290

SCOTT, N.A., JR. NEGATIVE CAPABIL-
ITY.*
H.T. MASON, 447(N&Q):SEP72-350

SCOTT, N.A., JR. THREE AMERICAN
MORALISTS.
A. BROYARD, 441:8JAN74-37

SCOTT, P.G. TENNYSON'S "ENOCH AR-
DEN."
C. FALL, 637(VS):SEP72-110
M.G. WIEBE, 529(QQ):SPRING72-118

SCOTT, R. MUSCLE & BLOOD.
R. CONOT, 441:22SEP74-4

SCOTT, R.H.F. JEAN-BAPTISTE LULLY.*
P. HOWARD, 415:AUG73-798

SCOTT, V. & D. KOSKI. THE KREUTZMAN
FORMULA.
N. CALLENDAR, 441:1SEP74-14

SCOTT-STOKES, H. THE LIFE & DEATH
OF YUKIO MISHIMA.
H. CLURMAN, 441:29DEC74-6
C. LEHMANN-HAUPT, 441:17JUL74-41

SCOTT-SUTHERLAND, C. ARNOLD BAX.*
L.F., 410(M&L):OCT73-483
A. PAYNE, 415:AUG73-798

SCOTTI, M. - SEE FOSCOLO, U.

"SCOTTISH SHORT STORIES 1974."
J. MELLORS, 362:26SEP74-416

SCOUFOPOULOS, N.S. MYCENAEAN CITA-
DELS.
K. BRANIGAN, 303:VOL92-240

"THE SCRABBLE PLAYERS HANDBOOK."
M. WATKINS, 441:8DEC74-22

SCRIMIERI, G. SULLA MAGIA IN TOM-
MASO CAMPANELLA.
E. NAMER, 542:APR-JUN72-168

SCRIMIERI, G. TESTIMONIANZE MEDIE-
VALI E PENSIERO MODERNO.
E. NAMER, 542:APR-JUN72-177

SCULLARD, H.H. FROM THE GRACCHI TO
NERO.
J-C. RICHARD, 555:VOL46FASC1-167

SCULLARD, H.H. SCIPIO AFRICANUS.*
G.V. SUMNER, 487:SPRING72-106

SCULLARD, H.H. - SEE MARSH, F.B.

SCULLY, C., ED. UNIVERSITY OF LEEDS,
PHONETICS DEPARTMENT, REPORT NO. 2.
G.F. MAIER, 682(ZPSK):BAND25
HEFT6-544

SCULLY, V. AMERICAN ARCHITECTURE &
URBANISM.*
A. FEIN, 576:MAR72-71

SCUTT, R. & C. GOTCH. SKIN DEEP.
617(TLS):27DEC74-1462

SEABORN, G.J. TREATMENT OR TORTURE.
P. DUBOIS, 542:OCT-DEC72-484

SEABORNE, M., ED. THE CHANGING CUR-
RICULUM.
E.P. MAHONEY, 551(RENQ):WINTER
72-473

SEABORNE, M. THE ENGLISH SCHOOL.*
D.J. OLSEN, 637(VS):JUN72-496

SEABROOK, J. CITY CLOSE-UP.
J. MARSH, 97(CQ):VOL6#1-70

SEABROOK, J. THE EVERLASTING FEAST.
T.R. FYVEL, 362:27JUN74-840

SEABROOK, J. LONELINESS.
617(TLS):12APR74-384

SEABURG, C. & S. PATERSON. MERCHANT
PRINCE OF BOSTON.
E.C. KIRKLAND, 432(NEQ):JUN72-283
639(VQR):SPRING72-LVIII

SEAGER, R. TIBERIUS.
J-C. RICHARD, 555:VOL46FASC2-354

SEAMAN, D. THE BOMB THAT COULD LIP-
READ.
M. LEVIN, 441:27OCT74-56
617(TLS):30AUG74-933

SEAMAN, J.E. THE MORAL PARADOX OF
"PARADISE LOST."
I. SIMON, 541(RES):AUG72-348
G. STRINGER, 568(SCN):FALL-WIN-
TER73-69

SEARLE, C. THIS NEW SEASON.
617(TLS):11JAN74-38

SEARLE, E. LORDSHIP & COMMUNITY.
D. KNOWLES, 617(TLS):1NOV74-1236

SEARLE, H. & R. LAYTON. TWENTIETH-
CENTURY COMPOSERS. (VOL 3)
H. OTTAWAY, 415:MAY73-491
A.W., 410(M&L):APR73-229

SEARLE, J. THE LUCKY STREAK.
A. KRUSE, 581:JUN73-240

SEARLE, J.R. SPEECH ACTS.*
L. HOLBOROW, 393(MIND):JUL72-458
L. LINSKY, 269(IJAL):JAN72-58

SEARS, D.T.P. THE LARK IN THE CLEAR
AIR.
P. GROSSKURTH, 99:OCT74-47
R. HUNT, 198:SPRING74-82

SEARS, S. & G.W. LORD, EDS. THE
DISCONTINUOUS UNIVERSE.
M.A. CAWS, 188(ECR):WINTER72-318

SEARY, E.R. PLACE NAMES OF THE AVA-
LON PENINSULA OF THE ISLAND OF
NEWFOUNDLAND.*
N.H. MAC KENZIE, 529(QQ):WINTER
72-558
J.A. RAYBURN, 424:MAR72-63

SEATON, A. THE RUSSO-GERMAN WAR,
1941-45.*
R.L. GARTHOFF, 550(RUSR):JAN72-80

SEAVER, P.S. THE PURITAN LECTURE-
SHIPS.*
T. WERGE, 568(SCN):SPRING73-5

SEBALD, W.G. CARL STERNHEIM.*
D.G. DAVIAU, 222(GR):MAY72-234

SEBASTIAN, R. MEMOIRS OF A PAID
MOURNER.
M.P. WORTHINGTON, 329(JJQ):SUM-
MER74-430

SEBBA, G. DESCARTES & HIS PHILOSO-
PHY.
P-M.S., 542:APR-JUN72-189

SEBEOK, T.A., ED. CURRENT TRENDS IN
LINGUISTICS. (VOL 2)
V.M. SOLNCEV, 353:15JUN72-109

SEBEOK, T.A., ED. CURRENT TRENDS IN
LINGUISTICS. (VOL 5)
K.V. ZVELEBIL, 361:VOL30#1-79
SEBEOK, T.A., ED. PORTRAITS OF LIN-
GUISTS.*
R. AUSTERLITZ, 269(IJAL):JUL72-
212
SECK, A. DAKAR.
R.J.H. CHURCH, 69:OCT72-349
SECREST, M. BETWEEN ME & LIFE.
A. NIN, 441:24NOV74-32
SECRET, F. BIBLIOGRAPHIE DES MANU-
SCRITS DE GUILLAUME POSTEL.*
W.J. BOUWSMA, 551(RENQ):SUMMER
72-214
SEDAINE, M-J. LA GAGEURE IMPRÉVUE.
(R. NIKLAUS, ED)
J-P. DE BEAUMARCHAIS, 535(RHL):
MAR-APR72-311
W.D. HOWARTH, 208(FS):APR73-213
E. SHOWALTER, JR., 207(FR):MAY72-
1193
SEDANO, J.A. - SEE UNDER ASENJO
SEDANO, J.
SEDGWICK, R. THE HOUSE OF COMMONS
1715-1754.
H.L. SNYDER, 481(PQ):JUL72-552
VON SEE, K. DEUTSCHE GERMANEN-
IDEOLOGIE.*
H. RIDLEY, 402(MLR):APR73-468
VON SEE, K. GERMANISCHE HELDENSAGE.
D. BLAMIRES, 402(MLR):OCT73-931
E.A. PHILIPPSON, 301(JEGP):JAN73-
62
VON SEE, K. GERMANISCHE VERSKUNST.*
H. UECKER, 680(ZDP):BAND91HEFT3-
410
VON SEE, K. DIE GESTALT DER "HÁVA-
MÁL."
L.M. HOLLANDER, 301(JEGP):JAN73-
117
SEEBASS, G. BIBLIOGRAPHICA OSIAND-
RICA.
W. ULLMANN, 354:JUN72-148
SEEBASS, T. MUSIKDARSTELLUNG UND
PSALTERILLUSTRATION IM FRÜHEREN
MITTELALTER.
617(TLS):21JUN74-661
SEEBERGER, W. HEGEL, ODER DIE ENT-
WICKLUNG DES GEISTES ZUR FREIHEIT.
P. ARNAUD, 542:JUL-SEP72-373
SEEBOLD, E. VERGLEICHENDES UND
ETYMOLOGISCHES WÖRTERBUCH DER GER-
MANISCHEN STARKEN VERBEN.
H. PENZL, 350:MAR73-181
H. SCHMEJA, 343:BAND15HEFT1-76
SEEDMAN, A.A. & P. HELLMAN. CHIEF!
E. PERLMUTTER, 441:12JUL74-29
SEELYE, J. DIRTY TRICKS.
P. SHOWERS, 441:24FEB74-36
SEELYE, J. THE KID.*
E.L. BULOW, 649(WAL):SPRING72-76
SEELYE, J. MELVILLE.*
P. MC CARTHY, 594:SPRING72-98
SEELYE, J. THE TRUE ADVENTURES OF
HUCKLEBERRY FINN.
D.R. NOBLE, JR., 577(SHR):SPRING
72-207
SEFERIS, G. MERES TOU 1945-1951.
617(TLS):4JAN74-4
SEFERIS, G. A POET'S JOURNAL.
P. ADAMS, 61:JUL74-100
L. DURRELL, 441:7JUL74-6
442(NY):5AUG74-87

SEGAL, C. THE THEME OF THE MUTILA-
TION OF THE CORPSE IN THE "ILIAD."
J.B. HAINSWORTH, 123:DEC73-265
A. THORNTON, 67:NOV73-284
SEGALEN, V. RENÉ LEYS.
N. BLIVEN, 442(NY):9DEC74-189
SEGHERS, A. SONDERBARE BEGEGNUNGEN.
617(TLS):8MAR74-229
SEGNITZ, B. & C. RAINEY, EDS. PSYCHE.
N. BALAKIAN, 441:15FEB74-37
SEGRE, D.V. THE HIGH ROAD & THE LOW.
M. LIPTON, 617(TLS):2AUG74-830
SEIDE, G. REGIERUNGSPOLITIK UND
ÖFFENTLICHE MEINUNG IM KAISERTUM
ÖSTERREICH ANLÄSSLICH DER POLNIS-
CHEN NOVEMBER-REVOLUTION (1830-
1831).
C. MORLEY, 32:MAR73-184
SEIDENSTICKER, B. DIE GESPRÄCHSVER-
DICHTUNG IN DEN TRAGÖDIEN SENECAS.
R.J. TARRANT, 487:SUMMER72-194
SEIDMAN, H. BLOOD LORD.
J. PARISI, 491:SEP74-343
SEIFERT, W. DAS EPISCHE WERK RAINER
MARIA RILKES.
B-L. BRADLEY, 221(GQ):NOV72-760
SEIGEL, J.E. RHETORIC & PHILOSOPHY
IN RENAISSANCE HUMANISM.*
D. WEINSTEIN, 322(JHI):JAN-MAR72-
165
SEIGEL, J.P., ED. THOMAS CARLYLE:
THE CRITICAL HERITAGE.
J.L. BRADLEY, 677:VOL3-315
SEIP, D.A. NORWEGISCHE SPRACHGE-
SCHICHTE. (REV & TRANS BY L.
SALTVEIT)
S.R. SMITH, 563(SS):SPRING73-152
SEITZ, A. SÄMTLICHE SCHRIFTEN.
(VOL 3) (P. UKENA, ED)
P.V. BRADY, 220(GL&L):JUL73-352
"SEJARAH MELAYU OR MALAY ANNALS."
(C.C. BROWN, TRANS)
J.M. ECHOLS, 293(JAST):AUG72-989
SEKRECKA, M. LOUIS-CLAUDE DE SAINT-
MARTIN.
F.P. BOWMAN, 207(FR):FEB72-736
SELA, O. THE KIRIOV TAPES.
N. CALLENDAR, 441:24MAR74-41
SELBOURNE, D. THE DAMNED.
A. RENDLE, 157:WINTER71-77
SELBY, J. A SHORT HISTORY OF SOUTH
AFRICA.
617(TLS):15FEB74-165
SELDEN, M., ED. REMAKING ASIA.
R. TERRILL, 441:21APR74-14
453:21MAR74-40
SELDEN, M. THE YENAN WAY IN REVO-
LUTIONARY CHINA.
D.G. GILLIN, 293(JAST):MAY72-659
639(VQR):AUTUMN72-CXLV
SELLARS, W. SCIENCE & METAPHYSICS.*
J. KOPPER, 342:BAND63HEFT1-125
SELLEKAERTS, W., ED. INTERNATIONAL
TRADE & FINANCE.
A. WALTERS, 617(TLS):29NOV74-
1340
SELLERS, O.R. & OTHERS. THE 1957
EXCAVATION AT BETH-ZUR.
J.F. ROSS, 318(JAOS):APR-JUN72-
302
SELLHEIM, R. & F. MAASS - SEE EISS-
FELDT, O.

SELTZER, L.F.   THE VISION OF MEL-
VILLE & CONRAD.*
   E.K. HAY, 401(MLQ):MAR73-85
   P. MC CARTHY, 594:SPRING72-98
SELUCKY, R.   ECONOMIC REFORMS IN
EASTERN EUROPE.
   M. GAMARNIKOW, 32:SEP73-632
SELVON, S.   THOSE WHO EAT THE CASCA-
DURA.
   E. FEINSTEIN, 364:APR/MAY72-142
SELWYN, F.   CRACKSMAN ON VELVET.
   617(TLS):20DEC74-1437
SELZER, D.   ELSEWHERE.
   617(TLS):22MAR74-295
SEMAAN, K.I.   LINGUISTICS IN THE
MIDDLE AGES.
   D. COUTINHO, 353:1MAR72-97
SEMBDNER, H. - SEE FALK, J.D.
SEMENKO, I.M.   POĚTY PUŠKINSKOJ PORY.
   L.G. LEIGHTON, 104:SUMMER72-328
SEMERARI, G.   INTERPRETAZIONE DI
SCHELLING. (VOL 1)
   E. NAMER, 542:JUL-SEP72-395
SEMI, F.   CICERO MAIOR.
   R.G. PENMAN, 123:MAR73-81
SEMMEL, B.   THE METHODIST REVOLUTION.
   F.R. BARRY, 617(TLS):20DEC74-
   1447
SEMMEL, B.   THE RISE OF TREE TRADE
IMPERIALISM.
   D.O. HELLY, 637(VS):DEC71-232
SEMMEL, B. - SEE HALÉVY, E.
SEMPRUN, J.   THE SECOND DEATH OF
RAMÓN MERCADER.* (FRENCH TITLE:
LA DEUXIÈME MORT DE RAMÓN MERCADER)
   442(NY):7JAN74-75
SEMPRUN, J.   LE "STAVISKY" D'ALAIN
RESNAIS.
   T. ZELDIN, 617(TLS):11OCT74-1110
SEMYONOV, J.   PETROVKA 38.
   N. CALLENDAR, 441:8DEC74-44
SEN, L.K., V.R. GAIKWAD & G.L. VARMA.
PEOPLE'S IMAGE OF COMMUNITY DEVEL-
OPMENT & PACHAYATI RAJ.
   H.A. GOULD, 293(JAST):NOV71-216
DE SENANCOUR, E.P.   LIBRES MÉDITA-
TIONS: TROISIÈME VERSION. (B. LE
GALL, ED)
   R. GRIMSLEY, 208(FS):OCT73-456
SÉNART, P. - SEE DE CUSTINE, A.
"THE SENATE WATERGATE REPORT."
   A. COCKBURN, 453:28NOV74-8
SENCOURT, R.   T.S. ELIOT: A MEMOIR.*
(D. ADAMSON, ED)
   W.W. ROBSON, 473(PR):WINTER73-
   136
SENDER, R.J.   ENSAYOS DEL OTRO MUNDO.
   G.D. CARRILLO, 238:SEP72-593
SENDER, R.J.   EL REY Y LA REINA.
   M. PEDEN, 238:MAY72-386
SENECA.   THE ELDER SENECA: DECLAMA-
TIONS.
   617(TLS):9AUG74-864
SENESH, H.   HANNAH SENESH, HER LIFE
& DIARY.
   M.S. CHERTOFF, 287:MAY72-25
   A. MEGGED, 390:MAY72-71
VON SENGER, H.   KAUFVERTRÄGE IM TRA-
DITIONELLEN CHINA.*
   K. MÄDING, 318(JAOS):OCT-DEC72-
   583

SENGHOR, L.S.   ANTHOLOGIE DE LA NOU-
VELLE POÉSIE NÈGRE ET MALGACHE DE
LANGUE FRANÇAISE.
   J. DECOCK, 207(FR):OCT71-215
SENGLE, F.   BIEDERMEIERZEIT. (VOL 1)
   H. DENKLER, 680(ZDP):BAND91HEFT2-
   288
   C.P. MAGILL, 402(MLR):JUL73-696
   G. MÜLLER, 597(SN):VOL44#1-215
   J.L.S., 191(ELN):SEP72(SUPP)-133
SEN GUPTA, S.C.   AN INTRODUCTION TO
ARISTOTLE'S "POETICS."
   J.K. FEIBLEMAN, 290(JAAC):WINTER
   72-279
SENIOR, G. & G. HENNIN.   ST. HELENS
AS IT WAS.
   617(TLS):1FEB74-110
SENN, A.E.   THE RUSSIAN REVOLUTION
IN SWITZERLAND, 1914-1917.*
   P. AVRICH, 550(RUSR):JAN72-83
SENN, F., ED.   NEW LIGHT ON JOYCE
FROM THE DUBLIN SYMPOSIUM.
   M. BEJA, 329(JJQ):FALL73-65
SENNETT, T.   WARNER BROTHERS PRE-
SENTS.
   G. RINGGOLD, 200:OCT72-499
SEPHOJ, J.J.   L-ONE L-TWO N J C.
   639(VQR):SPRING72-XLVIII
"ANNE SERANNE'S GOOD FOOD WITH A
BLENDER."
   N. HAZELTON, 441:1DEC74-96
SERENY, G.   INTO THAT DARKNESS.
   L.S. DAWIDOWICZ, 617(TLS):27DEC
   74-1458
SERLE, G.   FROM DESERTS THE PROPHETS
COME.
   A. FROST, 71(ALS):MAY74-324
SERNET, C. - SEE TZARA, T.
SERPER, A.   RUTEBEUF POÈTE SATIR-
IQUE.*
   G. LAFEUILLE, 546(RR):OCT72-224
SERRANO, M.   THE SERPENT OF PARADISE.
   617(TLS):31MAY74-581
SERRANO-PLAJA, A.   "MAGIC" REALISM
IN CERVANTES.*
   U. WICKS, 454:FALL72-84
SERREAU, R.   HEGEL ET L'HÉGÉLIANISME.
   F. HEIDSIECK, 542:JUL-SEP72-375
SERRES, M.   LE SYSTÈME DE LEIBNIZ ET
SES MODÈLES MATHÉMATIQUES.*
   P. PARRINI, 548(RCSF):JUL-SEP72-
   351
SERUMAGA, R.   THE ELEPHANTS.
   A. RENDLE, 157:WINTER70-80
SERVAN-SCHREIBER, J-L.   THE POWER TO
INFORM.
   R. STEIN, 441:3MAR74-22
SERVICE, J.S.   LOST CHANCE IN CHINA.
(J.W. ESHERICK, ED)
   J.C. THOMSON, JR., 441:5MAY74-3
   453:4APR74-44
SESSIONS, R.   QUESTIONS ABOUT MUSIC.*
   E.T. CONE, 513:SPRING-SUMMER72-
   164
   M. PETERSON, 470:MAY72-32
SETH, R.   THE EXECUTIONERS.
   R.M. SLUSSER, 32:DEC73-825
SETH-SMITH, M.   STEVE.
   617(TLS):19APR74-415
ŠETKA, J.   HRVATSKA KRŠĆANSKA TER-
MINOLOGIJA.
   B. FRANOLIĆ, 361:VOL29#1-95
SETON, C.P.   THE HALF-SISTERS.
   M. ATWOOD, 441:5MAY74-7

328

SETTEMBRINI, L. OPUSCOLI POLITICI
EDITI E INEDITI (1847-51). (M.
THEMELLY, ED)
A. JUNKER, 182:VOL25#9/10-292
SETTGAST, E.E. & G.F. ANDERSON.
BASIC SPANISH.
S.R. WILSON, 238:MAY72-400
SETTLE, M.L. THE LONG ROAD TO PARA-
DISE.
T.A. SHIPPEY, 617(TLS):27DEC74-
1466
SEUREN, P.A.M. OPERATORS & NUCLEUS.*
W. ABRAHAM, 343:BAND14HEFT1-21
R. HUDDLESTON, 215(GL):VOL12#2-
96
V. RASKIN, 353:MAY72-89
"73: NEW CANADIAN STORIES."
M. LUND, 198:FALL74-105
SEVERIN, D.S. MEMORY IN "LA CELES-
TINA."*
H. SIEBER, 400(MLN):MAR72-353
P. SMYTH, 238:MAY72-383
SEVERINO, R. EQUIPOTENTIAL SPACE.*
G. BROADBENT, 46:JAN72-66
MADAME DE SÉVIGNÉ. CORRESPONDANCE.
(VOL 1) (R. DUCHÊNE, ED)
617(TLS):22MAR74-277
SEWALL, R.B. THE LIFE OF EMILY DICK-
INSON.
C. LEHMANN-HAUPT, 441:30DEC74-21
H. LEIBOWITZ, 441:22DEC74-1
SEWALL, S. THE DIARY OF SAMUEL
SEWALL, 1674-1729. (M.H. THOMAS,
ED)
A. WHITMAN, 441:26JAN74-29
SEWARD, D. THE MONKS OF WAR.
J.A. BRUNDAGE, 377:MAR73-42
ŠEWC, H. GRAMITIKA HORNJOSERBSKEJE
RĚČE.
Z. TOPOLIŃSKA, 279:VOL15-215
SEWTER, A.C. BAROQUE & ROCOCO.
E. LARSEN, 127:SUMMER73-474
639(VQR):AUTUMN72-CLVI
SEXTON, A. THE BOOK OF FOLLY.
617(TLS):15FEB74-148
639(VQR):SPRING73-LXI
SEXTON, A. TRANSFORMATIONS.*
W.P. ROOT, 491:OCT73-34
639(VQR):WINTER72-XXII
SEXTON, R.J. THE COMPLEX OF YVOR
WINTERS' CRITICISM.
D. DONOGHUE, 617(TLS):30AUG74-
917
SEY, K.B. & I. GEDAI. ÉREMKINCSEK.
L. HUSZÁR, 32:DEC73-843
SEYMOUR, C., JR. MICHELANGELO'S
DAVID.
H. VON EINEM, 683:BAND35HEFT4-
313
SEYMOUR, H. BASEBALL: THE GOLDEN
AGE.
639(VQR):WINTER72-XXXVI
SEYMOUR, J. THE COMPANION GUIDE TO
THE COAST OF NORTH EAST ENGLAND.
J. MAPPLEBECK, 362:27JUN74-842
617(TLS):5APR74-377
SEYMOUR, J. THE COMPANION GUIDE TO
THE COAST OF SOUTH WEST ENGLAND.
617(TLS):5APR74-377
SEYMOUR-URE, C. THE POLITICAL IM-
PACT OF MASS MEDIA.
617(TLS):15MAR74-252
SEYPPEL, J. T.S. ELIOT.
C.H. SMITH, 659:SPRING74-277

SGALL, P. & OTHERS. A FUNCTIONAL
APPROACH TO SYNTAX IN GENERATIVE
DESCRIPTION OF LANGUAGE.
W. ABRAHAM, 343:BAND14HEFT1-27
SHAARA, M. THE KILLER ANGELS.
P. ADAMS, 61:OCT74-118
T. LE CLAIR, 441:20OCT74-38
SHACKLE, G.L.S. KEYNESIAN KALEIDICS.
617(TLS):20SEP74-1022
SHACKLETON BAILEY, D.R. CICERO.*
E. RAWSON, 313:VOL62-216
SHADBOLT, T. BULLSHIT & JELLYBEANS.
M. BEVERIDGE, 368:MAR72-86
SHAFFER, J.A. REALITY, KNOWLEDGE &
VALUE.
A.T., 543:DEC71-368
SHAFFER, J.A., ED. VIOLENCE.*
R.E. SANTONI, 258:JUN72-299
SHAHN, B.B. BEN SHAHN.*
A. FRANKENSTEIN, 55:JAN73-13
SHAIN, M. SOME MEN ARE MORE PERFECT
THAN OTHERS.
C. MAC CULLOCH, 198:FALL74-102
SHAKESPEARE, W. MUCH ADO ABOUT
NOTHING. (C. HINMAN, ED)
J.K. WALTON, 402(MLR):JUL73-636
SHAKESPEARE, W. THE RIVERSIDE SHAKE-
SPEARE. (G.B. EVANS, TEXTUAL ED)
F.W. BATESON, 617(TLS):30AUG74-
921
S. BOOTH, 453:12DEC74-44
D. DONOGHUE, 441:7APR74-23
SHAKESPEARE, W. SHAKESPEARE'S
SONGS. (A. HARBAGE, ED)
T.R. WALDO, 570(SQ):SPRING72-212
SHAKESPEARE, W. SHAKESPEARE'S SON-
NETS.* (2ND ED) (A.L. ROWSE, ED)
G. STEINER, 442(NY):18MAR74-142
SHALES, T. & OTHERS. THE AMERICAN
FILM HERITAGE.
W. ALEXANDER, 385(MQR):SPRING74-
180
SHANIN, T. THE AWKWARD CLASS.
D. ATKINSON, 550(RUSR):OCT72-417
M. MC CAULEY, 575(SEER):APR73-
305
N.A. MOSCOWITZ, 32:SEP73-621
SHANLEY, J.L. - SEE THOREAU, H.D.
SHANNON, A. A DESCRIPTIVE SYNTAX OF
THE PARKER MANUSCRIPT OF THE ANGLO-
SAXON CHRONICLE FROM 734 TO 891.
A. CRÉPIN, 189(EA):JAN-MAR72-78
SHANNON, D. CRIME FILE.
N. CALLENDAR, 441:22SEP74-42
SHANNON, W.V. THEY COULD NOT TRUST
THE KING.
442(NY):4FEB74-111
SHAPCOTT, T.W. BEGIN WITH WALKING.*
J. TULIP, 581:JUN73-231
SHAPIRO, B.J. JOHN WILKINS, 1614-
1672.*
W.S. GREAVES, 551(RENQ):AUTUMN72-
371
SHAPIRO, C., ED. CONTEMPORARY BRIT-
ISH NOVELISTS.
D. HEWITT, 447(N&Q):SEP72-347
SHAPIRO, H. THIS WORLD.
J. KESSLER, 390:APR72-71
SHAPIRO, H.I. - SEE RUSKIN, J.
SHARAGIN, A. TUPOLEVSKAIA SHARAGA.
H. ERMOLAEV, 550(RUSR):JUL72-304
SHARF, A. BYZANTINE JEWRY FROM JUS-
TINIAN TO THE FOURTH CRUSADE.
C. ABRAMSKY, 303:VOL92-256

SHARMA, D. THE DIFFERENTIATION
THEORY OF MEANING IN INDIAN LOGIC.
A. KASHER, 353:1NOV72-88
B.K. MATILAL, 206:JUL72-578
W.H. MAURER, 318(JAOS):JAN-MAR72-
173
SHARP, C. CECIL SHARP'S COLLECTION
OF ENGLISH FOLK SONGS. (M. KAR-
PELES, ED)
W. MELLERS, 617(TLS):13DEC74-
1411
SHARP, C.H. TRANSPORT ECONOMICS.
617(TLS):15FEB74-165
SHARP, G. LASSUS & PALESTRINA.
J. ROCHE, 415:FEB73-149
SHARP, H.S. & M.Z. INDEX TO CHARAC-
TERS IN THE PERFORMING ARTS. (PT
3)
R. BAKER, 151:SEP72-78
SHARPE, T. PORTERHOUSE BLUE.
R. BLYTHE, 362:2MAY74-576
617(TLS):19APR74-409
SHARPS, J.G. MRS. GASKELL'S OBSER-
VATION & INVENTION.
G. HANDLEY, 447(N&Q):JUL72-280
L. JONES, 637(VS):JUN72-497
SHARROCK, R. & R. WILLIAMS, EDS.
THE PELICAN BOOK OF ENGLISH PROSE.*
S. GILL, 447(N&Q):AUG72-310
SHATTUCK, C.H. THE HAMLET OF EDWIN
BOOTH.
R. SPEAIGHT, 570(SQ):SPRING72-
210
SHATTUCK, R. PROUST.
617(TLS):17MAY74-513
SHAW, D. THE LEVY CAPER.
C. WELLES, 441:29DEC74-2
SHAW, D.L. A LITERARY HISTORY OF
SPAIN: THE NINETEENTH CENTURY.
R. GUTIÉRREZ GIRARDOT, 72:BAND
210HEFT4/6-473
SHAW, D.L. - SEE BAROJA, P.
SHAW, G.B. THE BODLEY HEAD BERNARD
SHAW.* (VOLS 1-3) (D.H. LAURENCE,
ED)
E. SALMON, 397(MD):SEP72-217
SHAW, G.B. THE BODLEY HEAD BERNARD
SHAW.* (VOL 4) (D.H. LAURENCE, ED)
E. SALMON, 397(MD):DEC72-332
SHAW, G.B. COLLECTED LETTERS, 1898-
1910.* (D.H. LAURENCE, ED)
T.F. EVANS, 571:WINTER72/73-227
M. MEISEL, 637(VS):JUN73-483
E. SALMON, 397(MD):DEC72-332
E. SHORTER, 157:WINTER72-73
S. WEINTRAUB, 579(SAQ):AUTUMN73-
607
SHAW, G.B. PASSION PLAY. (J.E.
BRINGLE, ED)
R. WEINTRAUB, 572:MAY72-81
SHAW, G.B. THE ROAD TO EQUALITY.*
(L. CROMPTON, WITH H. CAVANAUGH,
EDS)
R.F. DIETRICH, 572:JAN72-46
SHAW, G.B. SAINT JOAN. (S. WEIN-
TRAUB, ED)
D. SUTHERLAND, 571:SPRING72-196
SHAW, G.B. SAINT JOAN, A SCREEN-
PLAY.* (B.F. DUKORE, ED)
J-C. AMALRIC, 189(EA):OCT-DEC72-
574
SHAW, G.B. SHAW: AN AUTOBIOGRAPHY,
1898-1950.* (S. WEINTRAUB, ED)
J.S. COLLIS, 571:SPRING72-184

SHAW, G.B. BERNARD SHAW'S NONDRA-
MATIC LITERARY CRITICISM. (S.
WEINTRAUB, ED)
K.L. ROBY, 572:SEP72-119
"THE GEORGE BERNARD SHAW VEGETARIAN
COOK BOOK." (R.J. MINNEY, ED)
M.G.E., 571:WINTER72/73-233
SHAW, L.R. THE PLAYWRIGHT & HISTORI-
CAL CHANGE.*
W. SCHUMANN, 399(MLJ):DEC72-514
SHAW, N. ALL GOD'S DANGERS. (T.
ROSENGARTEN, ED)
P. ADAMS, 61:OCT74-119
H.J. GEIGER, 441:20OCT74-1
A. WHITMAN, 441:9NOV74-29
442(NY):18NOV74-234
SHAW, R.B., ED. AMERICAN POETRY
SINCE 1960.
R. FULLER, 364:FEB/MAR74-99
617(TLS):28JUN74-695
SHAW, S.J. BETWEEN OLD & NEW.
P.F. SUGAR, 32:JUN73-423
SHAW, S.J. THE BUDGET OF OTTOMAN
EGYPT 1005-1006/1596-1597.
J.E. MANDAVILLE, 318(JAOS):APR-
JUN72-376
SHAWCROSS, W. CRIME & COMPROMISE.
G. MIKES, 617(TLS):29NOV74-1348
442(NY):16SEP74-149
SHE, L. - SEE UNDER LAO SHE
SHEA, D.B., JR. SPIRITUAL AUTOBIOG-
RAPHY IN EARLY AMERICA.
B. LEE, 447(N&Q):OCT72-393
SHEAD, R. CONSTANT LAMBERT.
H. OTTAWAY, 415:NOV73-1123
617(TLS):11JAN74-29
SHEAFFER, L. O'NEILL: SON & ARTIST.*
M. HARTMAN, 31(ASCH):SPRING74-
318
SHEARS, S. CHILD OF GENTLE COURAGE.
617(TLS):30AUG74-933
SHEATS, P.D. THE MAKING OF WORDS-
WORTH'S POETRY 1785-1798.
617(TLS):1MAR74-206
SHEED, F. THE CHURCH & I.
W.F. BUCKLEY, JR., 441:8SEP74-2
SHEED, W. PEOPLE WILL ALWAYS BE
KIND.*
V. CUNNINGHAM, 362:7FEB74-183
268:JAN74-66
617(TLS):18JAN74-47
639(VQR):AUTUMN73-CXXXVI
SHEED, W. THREE MOBS.
442(NY):23DEC74-84
SHEEHAN, B.W. SEEDS OF EXTINCTION.
G.S. WOOD, 656(WMQ):OCT73-658
SHEEHAN, J. THE ECONOMICS OF EDU-
CATION.
617(TLS):15MAR74-259
SHELDON, R. - SEE SHKLOVSKY, V.
SHELDON, S. THE OTHER SIDE OF MID-
NIGHT.
N. CALLENDAR, 441:27JAN74-12
SHELDON, W.F. THE INTELLECTUAL
DEVELOPMENT OF JUSTUS MÖSER.
R. PASCAL, 220(GL&L):JAN73-177
SHELTON, A.J. THE IGBO-IGALA BORDER-
LAND.
G.I. JONES, 69:JUL72-250
SHELTON, J.C. PAPYRI FROM THE MICHI-
GAN COLLECTION.
J.D. THOMAS, 313:VOL62-190

SHELTON, R. THE TATTOOED DESERT.*
J.W. HEALEY, 502(PRS):SUMMER72-
183
SHENKEN, A. & M. BESNARD. AU FIL
DES JOURS.
B. EBLING, 207(FR):MAR72-876
SHEPARD, L. JOHN PITTS.*
V.E. NEUBURG, 354:MAR72-68
SHEPARD, R. MIME.
R.J. SMITH, 157:WINTER72-74
SHEPARDSON, M. & B. HAMMOND. THE
NAVAHO MOUNTAIN COMMUNITY.*
H. LANDAR, 269(IJAL):APR72-157
SHEPHERD, J.F. & G.M. WALTON. SHIP-
PING, MARITIME TRADE, & THE ECONOM-
IC DEVELOPMENT OF COLONIAL NORTH
AMERICA.
S. ENGERMAN, 656(WMQ):APR73-332
SHEPPARD, D. BUILT AS A CITY.
617(TLS):1MAR74-208
SHEPPARD, F. LONDON 1808-1870.
G.B. TENNYSON, 445(NCF):JUN72-
117
A.S. WOHL, 637(VS):MAR73-349
639(VQR):AUTUMN72-CXLVIII
SHEPPARD, R. ON KAFKA'S CASTLE.
R. PASCAL, 617(TLS):7JUN74-611
SHEPPARD, R., R. THREADGILL & J.
HOLMES. PAPER HOUSES.
S. STEPHENS, 441:8DEC74-41
SHEPPARD, T.F. LOUMARIN IN THE
EIGHTEENTH CENTURY.
481(PQ):JUL72-554
SHEPPERSON, W.S. RESTLESS STRANGERS.
R.B. PEARSALL, 649(WAL):SPRING72-
69
SHERATON, T. THE CABINET-MAKER &
UPHOLSTERER'S DRAWING-BOOK.* (C.F.
MONTGOMERY & W.P. COLE, EDS) THE
CABINET DICTIONARY.* (W.P. COLE &
C.F. MONTGOMERY, EDS)
N. GOODISON, 90:JAN72-37
SHERIDAN, R.B. THE DRAMATIC WORKS
OF RICHARD BRINSLEY SHERIDAN. (C.
PRICE, ED)
617(TLS):22FEB74-169
SHERK, R.K. THE MUNICIPAL DECREES
OF THE ROMAN WEST.
F.C. BOURNE, 24:SPRING73-116
SHERMAN, A. WHEN GOD JUDGED & MEN
DIED.
N. SAFRAN, 441:7APR74-4
SHERMAN, A.J. ISLAND REFUGE.
617(TLS):8FEB74-123
SHERMAN, C.R. THE PORTRAITS OF
CHARLES V OF FRANCE (1338-1380).*
R.H. RANDALL, JR., 54:SEP72-348
SHERMER, D. WORLD WAR I.
617(TLS):8FEB74-128
SHEROVER, C.M. HEIDEGGER, KANT &
TIME.
J.H., 543:DEC71-369
T. KISIEL, 484(PPR):JUN73-601
SHERRINGTON, R.J. THREE NOVELS BY
FLAUBERT.*
R. DEBRAY-GENETTE, 535(RHL):MAY-
JUN72-539
C. SMETHURST, 402(MLR):APR73-422
SHERRY, N. CONRAD'S WESTERN WORLD.*
N. ALFORD, 376:JAN72-127
E. GERVER, 150(DR):SUMMER72-295
L. GRAVER, 639(VQR):SPRING72-315
F.P.W. MC DOWELL, 481(PQ):OCT72-
922   [CONTINUED]

[CONTINUING]
W. MESSENGER, 648:OCT72-70
T.C. MOSER, 637(VS):JUN72-490
J.E. SAVESON, 447(N&Q):FEB72-76
C.T. WATTS, 541(RES):MAY72-237
SHERWIN, J.J. IMPOSSIBLE BUILDINGS.
D. ALLEN, 491:MAY74-103
J.J. MC GANN, 385(MQR):FALL74-
416
SHERWOOD, J. NO GOLDEN JOURNEY.*
P. DICKINSON, 364:FEB/MAR74-121
SHERWOOD, J.M. GEORGES MANDEL & THE
THIRD REPUBLIC.
J.P.T. BURY, 208(FS):APR73-241
SHESTOV, L. DOSTOYEVSKY, TOLSTOY &
NIETZSCHE.*
L.J. SHEIN, 104:SUMMER72-335
SHETTER, W.Z. THE PILLARS OF SOCI-
ETY.
L. GILLET, 556(RLV):1972/5-558
SHEVELOV, G.Y. TEASERS & APPEASERS.
M. SAMILOV, 575(SEER):JAN73-127
SHEWMAKER, K.E. AMERICANS & CHINESE
COMMUNISTS, 1927-1945.*
T. TSOU, 293(JAST):AUG72-937
SHIBA YOSHINOBU. COMMERCE & SOCIETY
IN SUNG CHINA.
R.M. HARTWELL, 293(JAST):NOV71-
180
SHIBLES, W.A. AN ANALYSIS OF META-
PHOR IN THE LIGHT OF W.M. URBAN'S
THEORIES.
V.A. KRAMER, 290(JAAC):WINTER72-
278
M. OPPENHEIMER, JR., 186(ETC.):
DEC72-438
SHIBLES, W.A. METAPHOR.
W. SCHLEINER, 149:DEC73-394
B.M.H. STRANG, 447(N&Q):SEP72-
344
SHILLONY, B-A. REVOLT IN JAPAN.
617(TLS):20SEP74-1023
SHILOAH, A. & B. BAYER, EDS. YUVAL.
(VOL 2)
D.W., 410(M&L):JAN73-82
SHIMANOV, G.M. NOTES FROM THE RED
HOUSE.
H. ERMOLAEV, 550(RUSR):JUL72-304
SHINAGEL, M., ED. A CONCORDANCE TO
THE POEMS OF JONATHAN SWIFT.
G.P. MAYHEW, 566:SPRING73-100
SHIPMAN, D. BRANDO.
W. FEAVER, 617(TLS):27DEC74-1471
SHIPPEY, T.A. OLD ENGLISH VERSE.
M. LARES, 189(EA):OCT-DEC72-533
SHIPTON, C.K. BIOGRAPHICAL SKETCHES
OF THOSE WHO ATTENDED HARVARD COL-
LEGE IN THE CLASSES 1764-1767.
J.A. SCHUTZ, 432(NEQ):DEC72-607
SHIRE, H.M. SONG, DANCE & POETRY OF
THE COURT OF SCOTLAND UNDER KING
JAMES VI.*
C.B. GULLANS, 551(RENQ):SPRING72-
97
SHIRLEY, J.W., ED. THOMAS HARRIOT.
617(TLS):16AUG74-886
SHIRLEY, R.W. THE END OF A TRADI-
TION.
R.L. SECKINGER, 37:MAR72-42
SHIVELY, D.H., ED. TRADITION &
MODERNIZATION IN JAPANESE CULTURE.
B. TETERS, 293(JAST):MAY72-678

SHIVERS, A.S. JESSAMYN WEST.
M.S. WILSON, 150(DR):SUMMER72-
320
SHKLAR, J.N. MEN & CITIZENS.*
P.H. MEYER, 546(RR):OCT72-234
SHKLOVSKY, V. ZOO, OR LETTERS NOT
ABOUT LOVE. (R. SHELDON, ED &
TRANS)
V. ERLICH, 32:MAR73-210
L.G. LEIGHTON, 550(RUSR):JUL72-
318
SHMUELI, A. KIERKEGAARD & CONSCIOUS-
NESS.
G.J. STACK, 484(PPR):DEC72-285
SHOGAN, R. A QUESTION OF JUDGMENT.*
A.T. MASON, 639(VQR):AUTUMN72-
584
SHORES, C.F. PICTORIAL HISTORY OF
THE MEDITERRANEAN AIR WAR. (VOL 3)
617(TLS):5JUL74-733
SHORES, D.L. A DESCRIPTIVE SYNTAX
OF THE PETERBOROUGH CHRONICLE FROM
1122 TO 1154.
R.D. STEVICK, 589:OCT73-789
T.M. WOODELL, 35(AS):SPRING-
SUMMER70-134
SHORT, I., ED. THE ANGLO-NORMAN
PSEUDO-TURPIN CHRONICLE OF WILLIAM
DE BRIANE.
617(TLS):29MAR74-320
SHORT, M. - SEE HOLST, G.
SHORT, P. BANDA.
J. BIDDULPH, 362:14FEB74-215
617(TLS):1MAR74-205
SHORT, R. AFRICAN SUNSET.
617(TLS):15FEB74-165
SHORTER, A. AFRICAN CULTURE & THE
CHRISTIAN CHURCH.
617(TLS):13SEP74-984
SHORTO, H.L. A DICTIONARY OF THE
MON INSCRIPTIONS FROM THE SIXTH TO
THE SIXTEENTH CENTURIES.
H-J. PINNOW, 361:VOL30#2/3-294
SHRADER, S. LEAVING BY THE CLOSET
DOOR.
E. LICHTENBERG, 114(CHIR):VOL23
#4&VOL24#1-212
SHRAKE, E. STRANGE PEACHES.
M. MUDRICK, 249(HUDR):AUTUMN73-
545
SHREVE, S.R. A FORTUNATE MADNESS.
M. LEVIN, 441:4AUG74-27
SHRIVASTAVA, G.N. THE LANGUAGE CON-
TROVERSY & THE MINORITIES.
S.G. BHATIA, 293(JAST):AUG72-977
SHUB, A. AN EMPIRE LOSES HOPE.
A. PARRY, 550(RUSR):JAN72-81
SHUKLA, R.L. BRITAIN, INDIA & THE
TURKISH EMPIRE 1853-1882.
617(TLS):11JAN74-34
SHULMAN, A.K. MEMOIRS OF AN EX-PROM
QUEEN.*
S. O'CONNELL, 418(MR):WINTER73-
190
SHUMAKER, W. THE OCCULT SCIENCES IN
THE RENAISSANCE.*
639(VQR):WINTER73-XXIV
SHUMAN, J.B. & D. ROSENAU. THE KON-
DRATIEFF WAVE.
G. BARRACLOUGH, 453:27JUN74-14
SHUMWAY, G.L., COMP. ORAL HISTORY
IN THE UNITED STATES.
W.W. MOSS, 14:JAN72-65

SHUNKOV, V.I. & OTHERS, EDS. PEREK-
HOD OT FEODALIZMA K KAPITALIZMU V
ROSSII.
O. CRISP, 575(SEER):OCT73-582
SHUPTRINE, H. & J. DICKEY. JERICHO.
E. WEEKS, 61:DEC74-125
SHUR, L.A., ED. K BEREGAM NOVOGO
SVETA.
G. JANECEK, 263:APR-JUN73-198
SHURR, W.H. THE MYSTERY OF INIQUITY.
W. BEZANSON, 27(AL):NOV73-463
SHUSTER, M.R. THE PUBLIC INTERNA-
TIONAL LAW OF MONEY.
617(TLS):25JAN74-83
SHUTTLE, P. WAILING MONKEY EMBRAC-
ING A TREE.
V. CUNNINGHAM, 362:7FEB74-183
617(TLS):15FEB74-149
SHVIDKOVSKY, O.A., ED. BUILDING IN
THE USSR, 1917-1932.*
A.C. BIRNHOLZ, 290(JAAC):WINTER
72-279
B.S. PUSHKAREV, 550(RUSR):APR72-
189
C. WOODWARD, 46:MAR72-196
SHYER, M. LOCAL TALENT.
M. LEVIN, 441:20OCT74-41
SIAUVE, S. LA DOCTRINE DE MADHVA.
W. HALBFASS, 318(JAOS):JAN-MAR72-
176
O. VON HINÜBER, 182:VOL25#22-774
SIAUVE, S. LES HIÉRARCHIES SPIRITU-
ELLES SELON L'ANUVYĀKHYĀNA DE MAD-
HVA.
O. VON HINÜBER, 182:VOL25#22-774
SIBLEY, F.N., ED. PERCEPTION.
D. LOCKE, 393(MIND):OCT72-627
A.R. WHITE, 479(PHQ):OCT72-368
SICHEL, E. MICHEL DE MONTAIGNE.
R.G. ZIBART, 399(MLJ):NOV72-469
SICHIROLLO, L. GIUSTIFICAZIONI
DELLA DIALETTICA IN ARISTOTELE.
J. MOREAU, 542:JAN-MAR72-55
SICHIROLLO, L. PER UNA STORIOGRAFIA
FILOSOFICA.
E. NAMER, 542:JAN-MAR72-52
SIDDIQI, M.Z. THE SOCIAL POSITION
OF WOMAN THROUGH THE AGES.
Z.Y.A. KHAN, 273(IC):OCT72-365
SIDDIQUI, I.H. HISTORY OF SHER SHAH.
K.A.S. LAL, 273(IC):JAN72-86
SIDEL, V.W. & R. SERVE THE PEOPLE.
H.J. GEIGER, 441:17MAR74-4
SIDER, R.D. ANCIENT RHETORIC & THE
ART OF TERTULLIAN.
P. COURCELLE, 555:VOL46FASC2-346
SIDNELL, M.J., G.P. MAYHEW & D.R.
CLARK - SEE YEATS, W.B.
SIDNEY, P. THE COUNTESSE OF PEM-
BROKES ARCADIA.
F.B. WILLIAMS, JR., 551(RENQ):
AUTUMN72-358
SIDNEY, P. MISCELLANEOUS PROSE OF
SIR PHILIP SIDNEY. (K. DUNCAN-
JONES & J. VAN DORSTEN, EDS)
617(TLS):22MAR74-288
SIDOROV, A.A. KNIGA I ZHIZN'.
J.S.G. SIMMONS, 78(BC):WINTER72-
569
SIDRAN, B. BLACK TALK.
Y. BADER, 290(JAAC):SUMMER73-561
V. THOMSON, 453:17OCT74-14

SIEGEL, J.E. RHETORIC & PHILOSOPHY
IN RENAISSANCE HUMANISM.
P. DAMON, 545(RPH):FEB73-626
SIEGEL, M.B. AT THE VANISHING
POINT.
E.W. JACOBS, 59(ASOC):SUMMER-
FALL73-302
J. JEDLICKA, 151:NOV72-84
SIEGEL, P.N. - SEE TROTSKY, L.
SIEGEL, R. THE BEASTS & THE ELDERS.
J. PARISI, 491:SEP74-343
617(TLS):29MAR74-339
SIEGEL, R.E. GALEN ON SENSE PER-
CEPTION.
E.D. PHILLIPS, 123:MAR73-90
SIFAKIS, G.M. PARABASIS & ANIMAL
CHORUSES.
C.J. HERINGTON, 487:AUTUMN72-292
SIGAL, L.V. REPORTERS & OFFICIALS.
J.C. THOMSON, JR., 441:17FEB74-
16
SIGAUX, G., ED. LA COMÉDIE ET LE
VAUDEVILLE DE 1850 À 1900.
F. BASSAN, 557(RSH):OCT-DEC72-
616
SIH, P.K.T., ED. TAIWAN IN MODERN
TIMES.
T-L. LEE, 396(MODA):FALL73-425
ŠIK, O. CZECHOSLOVAKIA.
J.M. MICHAL, 32:JUN73-409
SILESIUS, A. LE PÈLERIN CHÉRU-
BIQUE. (E. SUSINI, ED & TRANS)
M. DE GANDILLAC, 542:APR-JUN72-
181
SILK, M.S. INTERACTION IN POETIC
IMAGERY.
P. LEVI, 617(TLS):15NOV74-1292
SILKIN, J. AMANA GRASS.*
639(VQR):WINTER72-XXIII
SILKIN, J. OUT OF BATTLE.
639(VQR):WINTER73-XVII
SILKIN, J. THE PRINCIPLE OF WATER.
617(TLS):19JUL74-762
SILLITOE, A. BARBARIANS.
617(TLS):24MAY74-554
SILLITOE, A. THE FLAME OF LIFE.
R. DAVIES, 617(TLS):29NOV74-1336
J. MELLORS, 362:5DEC74-753
SILLITOE, A. MEN, WOMEN & CHILDREN.*
E. FEINSTEIN, 364:FEB/MAR74-137
M. LEVIN, 441:22SEP74-40
SILMAN, T. DIKKENS: OCHERKI TVOR-
CHESTVA.
H. GIFFORD, 155:JAN72-56
SILVA, C. JUICIO FINAL.
G. FIGUEIRA, 263:APR-JUN72-211
DE SILVA, D. - SEE UNDER STERNLICHT,
S.
DE SILVA, K.M., ED. HISTORY OF CEY-
LON. (VOL 3)
617(TLS):14JUN74-647
SILVER, D.J., ED. JUDAISM & ETHICS.
F. ARMENGAUD, 53(AGP):BAND54
HEFT1-103
SILVER, I., ED. THE CRIME-CONTROL
ESTABLISHMENT.
R. REEVES, 441:11AUG74-4
SILVER, I. THE INTELLECTUAL EVOLU-
TION OF RONSARD.* (VOL 1)
R.A. KATZ, 546(RR):APR72-156
L. TERREAUX, 535(RHL):MAR-APR72-
301

SILVER, I. THE INTELLECTUAL EVOLU-
TION OF RONSARD. (VOL 2)
617(TLS):9AUG74-852
SILVER, I. - SEE DE RONSARD, P.
SILVERBERG, R. DYING INSIDE.
617(TLS):15MAR74-269
SILVERBERG, R., ED. THE MIRROR OF
INFINITY.
J.R. CHRISTOPHER, 573(SSF):FALL
72-415
SILVERBERG, R. NEW DIMENSIONS IV.
T. STURGEON, 441:10NOV74-50
SILVERLIGHT, J. THE VICTORS' DI-
LEMMA.*
P. KENEZ, 550(RUSR):JAN72-101
SILVERMAN, A. FOSTER & LAURIE.
J. KAPLAN, 441:28APR74-32
SILVERMAN, J.H. - SEE MONTESINOS,
J.F.
SILVERMAN, K. - SEE MATHER, C.
SILVERSTEIN, A. & V.B. SLEEP &
DREAMS.
P. SHOWERS, 441:28JUL74-10
SILVERSTEIN, M. - SEE WHITNEY, W.D.
SIME, M. A CHILD'S EYE VIEW.
617(TLS):18JAN74-61
SIMENON, G. MAIGRET & THE MILLION-
AIRES.
N. CALLENDAR, 441:24NOV74-39
SIMENON, G. MAIGRET LOSES HIS TEM-
PER.
442(NY):4MAR74-114
SIMENON, G. THE VENICE TRAIN.
442(NY):19AUG74-92
SIMENON, G. WHEN I WAS OLD.
639(VQR):AUTUMN73-CLXI
SIMEON, R. FEDERAL-PROVINCIAL DIP-
LOMACY.
J.M. BECK, 150(DR):WINTER72/73-
676
A.C. CAIRNS, 529(QQ):AUTUMN72-
413
SIMMONDS, J.D. CHINA'S WORLD.
R.M. PFEFFER, 293(JAST):NOV71-
198
SIMMONDS, J.D. MASQUES OF GOD.*
J.J. SCANLON, 301(JEGP):OCT73-
561
SIMMONDS, J.D., ED. MILTON STUDIES.*
(VOL 2)
J. ARTHOS, 551(RENQ):SPRING72-
116
SIMMONDS, J.D., ED. MILTON STUDIES.
(VOL 4)
G. STACY, 568(SCN):FALL-WINTER73-
72
639(VQR):AUTUMN73-CLII
SIMMONS, E.J. TOLSTOY.*
D.H. STEWART, 651(WHR):AUTUMN73-
418
SIMMONS, J. LEICESTER PAST & PRES-
ENT. (VOL 2)
G.E. MINGAY, 617(TLS):8NOV74-
1246
SIMMONS, J., ED. TEN IRISH POETS.
617(TLS):30AUG74-932
SIMMONS, J.C. THE NOVELIST AS HIS-
TORIAN.
R.L. WOLFF, 617(TLS):13DEC74-
1404
SIMMONS, J.S.G. RUSSIAN BIBLIOGRA-
PHY, LIBRARIES & ARCHIVES.*
W.F. RYAN, 575(SEER):OCT73-598

SIMMS, W.G. THE WRITINGS OF WILLIAM
GILMORE SIMMS.* (VOL 3) (R. BUSH
& J.B. MERIWETHER, EDS)
M.J. SHILLINGSBURG, 219(GAR):
WINTER72-512
SIMON, A. DICTIONNAIRE DU THÉÂTRE
FRANÇAIS CONTEMPORAIN.
M. GUGGENHEIM, 207(FR):OCT71-280
SIMON, C. CONDUCTING BODIES.
T. BISHOP, 441:15SEP74-4
SIMON, C. ORION AVEUGLE. LES CORPS
CONDUCTEURS.
C. DU VERLIE, 430(NS):SEP72-543
SIMON, C.M. FAITH HAS NEED OF ALL
THE TRUTH.
E.B. FISKE, 441:16JUN74-8
SIMON, E. NEIDHART VON REUENTAL.*
H. REINITZER, 680(ZDP):BAND91
HEFT3-461
SIMON, G. CHURCH, STATE & OPPOSI-
TION IN THE USSR.
P. REDDAWAY, 453:12DEC74-36
617(TLS):2AUG74-836
SIMON, G. DIE ERSTE DEUTSCHE FAST-
NACHTSSPIELTRADITION.*
E. CATHOLY, 589:APR73-406
F. HARTWEG, 182:VOL25#23/24-866
W.F. MICHAEL, 221(GQ):MAY72-525
SIMON, G. DIE KIRCHEN IN RUSSLAND.
G. CODEVILLA, 32:JUN73-393
SIMON, H. SONGS & WORDS.
617(TLS):18JAN74-60
SIMON, I. NEO-CLASSICAL CRITICISM
1660-1800.*
O.F. SIGWORTH, 173(ECS):SUMMER73-
526
SIMON, I. THREE RESTORATION DIVINES.
A. PARREAUX, 189(EA):OCT-DEC72-
556
SIMON, J. INGMAR BERGMAN DIRECTS.*
639(VQR):WINTER73-XLII
SIMON, J., ED. FOURTEEN FOR NOW.
J.K. CRANE, 573(SSF):WINTER72-95
SIMON, J.K., ED. MODERN FRENCH
CRITICISM.
M.A. CAWS, 188(ECR):WINTER72-318
SIMON, M. L'ANGLICANISME.
J. GURY, 549(RLC):JAN-MAR72-139
SIMON, R. - SEE GAUBIL, P.A.
SIMON, Y. LES JOURS EN COULEURS.
C. DU VERLIE, 207(FR):FEB72-711
SIMON, Y. WORK, SOCIETY, & CULTURE.
(V. KUIC, ED)
D. GERMINO, 258:DEC72-625
E. MEAGHER, 396(MODA):WINTER73-
103
SIMÓN DÍAZ, J. LA BIBLIOGRAFÍA.
A. AYENSA, 263:JAN-MAR73-94
D.W. CRUICKSHANK, 402(MLR):JAN73-
201
SIMÓN DÍAZ, J. BIBLIOGRAFÍA DE LA
LITERATURA HISPÁNICA.* (VOL 8)
M. FRANZBACH, 224(GRM):BAND22
HEFT2-207
SIMÓN DÍAZ, J. IMPRESOS DEL SIGLO
XVII.
J.L. LAURENTI, 263:OCT-DEC73-459
H.C. WOODBRIDGE, 517(PBSA):APR-
JUN73-215
SIMONE, F., ED. DIZIONARIO CRITICO
DELLA LETTERATURA FRANCESE.*
G. HAINSWORTH, 208(FS):OCT73-491

SIMONS, A. & S. LAPHAM, JR., EDS.
THE EARLY ARCHITECTURE OF CHARLES-
TON.
M.B. LAPPING, 576:OCT72-246
SIMOV, P., ED & TRANS. FRENSKI PO-
ETI.
N. DONTCHEV, 535(RHL):MAR-APR72-
350
SIMPSON, B. LABOUR.
617(TLS):25JAN74-70
SIMPSON, C. THE LUSITANIA.*
H.M. ADAMS, 396(MODA):FALL73-423
SIMPSON, C.M. - SEE HAWTHORNE, N.
SIMPSON, D.H. MARIA FITZHERBERT &
ROBERT BURT, VICAR OF TWICKENHAM.
617(TLS):9AUG74-864
SIMPSON, E. - SEE DONNE, J.
SIMPSON, G. SIMPSON'S LETTERS TO
LONDON 1841-42. (J.S. GALBRAITH,
ED)
617(TLS):3MAY74-468
SIMPSON, H. SINGERS TO REMEMBER.
E. FORBES, 415:MAR73-263
SIMPSON, J., ED & TRANS. ICELANDIC
FOLKTALES & LEGENDS.
K.H. OBER, 301(JEGP):APR73-260
SIMPSON, J. THE WAY LIFE WAS.
A. BROYARD, 441:29AUG74-35
SIMPSON, J. - SEE PARTRIDGE, E.
SIMPSON, L. ADVENTURES OF THE LET-
TER I.*
M. BORROFF, 676(YR):AUTUMN72-81
T. EAGLETON, 565:VOL13#1-76
D. ETTER, 114(CHIR):VOL24#3-147
639(VQR):WINTER73-XII
SIMPSON, L. AIR WITH ARMED MEN.
C. TOMLINSON, 364:JUN/JUL72-160
SIMPSON, L. NORTH OF JAMAICA.*
P. STITT, 598(SOR):SPRING74-517
SIMPSON, L. THE PEACOCK PAPERS.
M. DIXON, 99:JUL74-36
L. RICOU, 296:VOL3#3-100
SIMPSON, L.P. THE MAN OF LETTERS IN
NEW ENGLAND & THE SOUTH.*
G. CORE, 385(MQR):FALL74-411
639(VQR):AUTUMN73-CXLV
SIMS, G. HUNTERS POINT.
617(TLS):18JAN74-61
SINARI, R.A. THE STRUCTURE OF
INDIAN THOUGHT.*
E. DEUTSCH, 318(JAOS):OCT-DEC72-
500
J.L. MEHTA, 485(PE&W):APR72-227
SINCLAIR, K.V., ED. TRISTAN DE NAN-
TEUIL, CHANSON DE GESTE INÉDITE.
W.G. VAN EMDEN, 208(FS):APR73-
187
W.M. HACKETT, 382(MAE):1973/2-
175
SINCLAIR, L. LEON TROTSKY.
L.K.D. KRISTOF, 32:DEC73-818
SINEL, A. THE CLASSROOM & THE
CHANCELLERY.
617(TLS):22MAR74-291
SINFIELD, A. THE LANGUAGE OF TEN-
NYSON'S "IN MEMORIAM."
C. FALL, 637(VS):SEP72-110
W. SLINN, 67:MAY73-118
SINGER, B.J. THE RATIONAL SOCIETY.*
H.A. LARRABEE, 432(NEQ):MAR72-
135

SINGER, I.B. A CROWN OF FEATHERS.*
D.A.N. JONES, 362:5SEP74-317
M. WOOD, 453:7FEB74-10
441:10NOV74-38
617(TLS):20SEP74-993
SINGER, I.B. ENEMIES, A LOVE STORY.*
S. O'CONNELL, 418(MR):WINTER73-
190
SINGER, K. MIRROR, SWORD & JEWEL.*
639(VQR):AUTUMN73-CLXVII
SINGER, L. BOCA GRANDE.
M. LEVIN, 441:8SEP74-43
SINGER, M.R. WEAK STATES IN A WORLD
OF POWERS.
D. YERGIN, 676(YR):SUMMER73-594
SINGH, G. EUGENIO MONTALE.
639(VQR):AUTUMN73-CLIII
SINGH, G. THE RELIGION OF THE SIKHS.
N.G. BARRIER, 293(JAST):AUG72-
1001
S.C. CRAWFORD, 485(PE&W):JUL72-
338
SINGH, H. GURU NANAK & THE ORIGINS
OF THE SIKH FAITH.*
S. LAVAN, 293(JAST):MAY72-711
C.S.J. WHITE, 318(JAOS):APR-JUN
72-320
SINGLETON, C.S. - SEE DANTE ALIGHI-
ERI
SINISGALLI, L. L'ELLISSE.
617(TLS):4OCT74-1090
SINITSYN, B.V. OCHERKI EKONOMIKI
YUZHNOI KOREI (1953-1964).
G. GINSBURGS, 293(JAST):MAY72-
693
SINNHUBER, K.A. GERMANY.
C. BAIER, 220(GL&L):OCT72-67
SINOR, D. INNER ASIA: A SYLLABUS.
I. DE RACHEWILTZ, 318(JAOS):JAN-
MAR72-162
"SIR GAWAIN & THE GREEN KNIGHT."
(B. RAFFEL, TRANS)
R.J. BLANCH, 72:BAND210HEFT1/3-
185
"SIR GAWAIN & THE GREEN KNIGHT."
(R.A. WALDRON, ED)
J.R. SIMON, 189(EA):JAN-MAR72-82
SIRCHIA, F. NICOLAI HARTMANN DAL
NEOKANTISMO ALL'ONTOLOGIA.
A. MARINI, 548(RCSF):APR-JUN72-
170
SIRKIS, N. REFLECTIONS OF 1776.
I.R. DEE, 441:1DEC74-18
SISAM, C. & K., EDS. THE OXFORD
BOOK OF MEDIEVAL ENGLISH VERSE.*
J. LAWLOR, 541(RES):AUG72-384
W. RIEHLE, 72:BAND210HEFT1/3-182
R.H. ROBBINS, 447(N&Q):OCT72-387
P.W. ROGERS, 529(QQ):SUMMER72-
269
J.R. SIMON, 189(EA):JAN-MAR72-84
SISKIND, J. TO HUNT IN THE MORNING.
617(TLS):26APR74-448
SISLER, R. THE GIRLS.
R.Y. WILSON, 99:FEB74-43
SISSMAN, L.E. PURSUIT OF HONOR.
M. BOWERS, 398:WINTER74-292
SISSON, C.H. THE CASE OF WALTER
BAGEHOT.
C.J. MYERS, 150(DR):AUTUMN72-505
SISSON, C.H. IN THE TROJAN DITCH.
D. DAVIE, 362:9MAY74-603
R. NYE, 617(TLS):29NOV74-1335

SISSON, C.J. THE BOAR'S HEAD THEA-
TRE. (S. WELLS, ED)
J.R. BROWN, 157:AUTUMN72-79
G. WICKHAM, 677:VOL3-271
SITTER, J.E. THE POETRY OF POPE'S
"DUNCIAD."*
R. HOTCH, 301(JEGP):OCT73-568
U.C. KNOEPFLMACHER, 401(MLQ):
DEC73-448
P.M. SPACKS, 481(PQ):JUL72-747
A. WILLIAMS, 566:SPRING72-78
SITWELL, O. QUEEN MARY & OTHERS.
BEFORE THE BOMBARDMENT. COLLECTED
STORIES.
617(TLS):26JUL74-805
SIVAN, E. L'ISLAM ET LA CROISADE.
R.S. HUMPHREYS, 318(JAOS):APR-
JUN72-391
SIVARAMAMURTI, C. SOUTH INDIAN
PAINTING.
H. GOETZ, 318(JAOS):OCT-DEC72-
504
SIWEK-POUYDESSEAU, J. LE PERSONNEL
DE DIRECTION DES MINISTÈRES.
E.N. SULEIMAN, 98:MAR72-274 [&
CONT IN 98:APR72-374]
SJÖBERG, Å.W. & E. BERGMANN. THE
COLLECTION OF THE SUMERIAN TEMPLE
HYMNS [TOGETHER WITH] GRAGG, G.B.
THE KEŠ TEMPLE HYMN.
W. HEIMPEL, 318(JAOS):APR-JUN72-
285
SJÖLIN, B. EINFÜHRUNG IN DAS
FRIESISCHE.*
E.G.A. GALAMA, 433:JUL72-377
A. SPENTER, 260(IF):BAND76-356
SJÖWALL, M. & P. WAHLÖÖ. THE ABOMIN-
ABLE MAN.*
N. CALLENDAR, 441:13OCT74-48
SJÖWALL, M. & P. WAHLÖÖ. THE LOCKED
ROOM.*
617(TLS):6SEP74-960
SKAGG, J.M., F. DOWNS & W. VIGNESS,
EDS. CHRONICLES OF THE YAQUI EX-
PEDITION.
W. GARD, 584(SWR):SPRING73-V
SKAGGS, M.M. THE FOLK OF SOUTHERN
FICTION.
C.C. HOLLIS, 578:SPRING74-134
M.T. INGE, 27(AL):MAY73-316
639(VQR):SUMMER73-CXIV
SKEET, I. MUSCAT & OMAN.
617(TLS):18OCT74-1170
SKELTON, R., ED & TRANS. ANTHOLOGIA
GRAECA.
C.A. TRYPANIS, 303:VOL92-212
SKELTON, R. THE WRITINGS OF J.M.
SYNGE.*
H. PYLE, 541(RES):MAY72-235
SKELTON, R. - SEE YEATS, J.B.
SKELTON, R.A. COUNTY ATLASES OF THE
BRITISH ISLES, 1579-1850. (VOL 1)
E.M. RODGER, 354:JUN72-150
SKELTON, R.A. MAPS.
R.O. LINDSAY, 656(WMQ):JUL73-543
SKILLEND, W.E. KODAE SOSÓL.
P.H. LEE, 318(JAOS):JAN-MAR72-
159
SKILTON, D. ANTHONY TROLLOPE & HIS
CONTEMPORARIES.
J.N. HUNTER, 637(VS):MAR73-354
SKINNER, B.F. ABOUT BEHAVIORISM.
C. LEHMANN-HAUPT, 441:29MAY74-33
J. WEIZENBAUM, 441:14JUL74-6

SKINNER, B.F. BEYOND FREEDOM & DIG-
NITY.*
H. LOMAS, 364:APR/MAY72-135
SKINNER, B.G. HENRY FRANCIS LYTE.
A. BELL, 617(TLS):13DEC74-1421
SKINNER, E.P. AFRICAN URBAN LIFE.
L. MAIR, 617(TLS):15NOV74-1279
SKINNER, G.W., ED. MODERN CHINESE
SOCIETY. (VOL 1)
617(TLS):25OCT74-1207
SKINNER, G.W. & W. HSIEH, EDS. MOD-
ERN CHINESE SOCIETY. (VOL 2)
617(TLS):25OCT74-1207
SKINNER, G.W. & S. TOMITA, EDS.
MODERN CHINESE SOCIETY. (VOL 3)
617(TLS):25OCT74-1207
SKINNER, M.L. THE FIFTH SPARROW.*
N. KEESING, 581:MAR73-86
SKLAIR, L. ORGANIZED KNOWLEDGE.
617(TLS):19APR74-407
SKLAIR, L. THE SOCIOLOGY OF PRO-
GRESS.
E. VALLANCE, 479(PHQ):JAN72-88
SKLAR, K.K. CATHARINE BEECHER.
P. ADAMS, 61:JAN74-99
617(TLS):25JAN74-82
SKLAR, L. SPACE, TIME, & SPACETIME.
R.G. SWINBURNE, 617(TLS):20DEC74-
1438
SKLAR, R. F. SCOTT FITZGERALD.
A. LE VOT, 189(EA):APR-JUN72-335
ŠKLOVSKIJ, V. LETTURA DEL "DECAM-
ERON."*
400(MLN):JAN72-161
SKOK, P. DICTIONNAIRE ÉTYMOLOGIQUE
DE LA LANGUE CROATE OU SERBE.
(VOL 1)
B. FRANOLIC, 361:VOL28#4-392
SKOVGAARD, J. A KING'S ARCHITECTURE.
617(TLS):15MAR74-272
SKRJABINA, E. SIEGE & SURVIVAL.*
(N. LUXENBURG, ED & TRANS)
A. PARRY, 550(RUSR):JUL72-319
SKRZYNECKI, P. HEAD-WATERS.
J. TULIP, 581:JUN73-231
SKUBISZEWSKI, P. CZARA WŁOCŁAWSKA.
P.B. GROSS, 182:VOL25#3/4-101
SKULTANS, V. INTIMACY & RITUAL.
617(TLS):22FEB74-188
SKURKA, N. & O. GILI. UNDERGROUND
INTERIORS.
S. STEPHENS, 441:8DEC74-43
SKUTCH, A.F. & A.B. SINGER. THE
LIFE OF THE HUMMINGBIRD.
G. GOLD, 441:19JAN74-29
SKVORECKY, J. L'ESCADRON BLINDÉ.
A. LIEHM, 98:OCT72-841
SKYTTÄ, K. PRESIDENTIN MUOTOKUVA.
P.K. HAMALAINEN, 32:JUN73-402
SLACK, C.W. TIMOTHY LEARY, THE MAD-
NESS OF THE SIXTIES & ME.
J. KRAMER, 441:11AUG74-3
SLADE, L. SLADE'S ANATOMY OF THE
HORSE.*
J. TULIP, 581:JUN73-231
SLADE, T. D.H. LAWRENCE.
E. DELAVENAY, 189(EA):JAN-MAR72-
172
S. GILL, 447(N&Q):FEB72-70
SLADEK, J. THE NEW APOCRYPHA.
617(TLS):5APR74-376
SLAGER, W.R. & OTHERS. CORE ENGLISH
ONE, TWO, THREE, & FOUR.
R. CRYMES, 608:JUN73-170

SLAPNICKA, H. DIE SOZIALISTISCHE
KOLLEKTIVPERSON.
W.E. BUTLER, 104:SPRING72-185
SLATE, S.J. SATAN'S BACK YARD.
M. LEVIN, 441:14JUL74-22
SLATER, E. THE NEW YORK TIMES BOOK
OF NEEDLEPOINT FOR LEFT-HANDERS.
L.J. GARTNER, JR., 441:8DEC74-49
SLATER, M., ED. THE CHRISTMAS BOOKS.
S. MONOD, 155:MAY72-122
SLATER, P. EARTHWALK.
S. SANBORN, 441:20JAN74-3
R. TODD, 61:JAN74-93
SLATER, W.J., ED. LEXICON TO PINDAR.*
A. URUŠADZE, 682(ZPSK):BAND25
HEFT4/5-444
SLATOFF, W.J. WITH RESPECT TO READ-
ERS.*
J. PINKERTON, 128(CE):FEB72-600
SLATTERY, M.F. HAZARD, FORM, &
VALUE.
M.C. BEARDSLEY, 290(JAAC):FALL72-
123
SLAVITT, D.R. ABCD.*
617(TLS):3MAY74-465
SLAVITT, D.R. ANAGRAMS.
L.T.L., 502(PRS):FALL72-276
639(VQR):WINTER72-XVI
SLAVITT, D.R. CHILD'S PLAY.*
L. SEARLE, 491:MAR74-353
639(VQR):SPRING73-LXII
SLAVITT, D.R. THE ECLOGUES & GEOR-
GICS OF VIRGIL.*
639(VQR):AUTUMN72-CXXV
SLAVITT, D.R. THE KILLING OF THE
KING.
G. LYONS, 441:27OCT74-50
SLAVUTYCH, Y. & OTHERS. PROFESSOR
J·B· RUDNYĆKYJ - SEXAGENARIUS
(1910-1970).
G.B. DROEGE, 424:SEP72-210
SLEEMAN, W.H. SLEEMAN IN OUDH.
(P.D. REEVES, ED)
D.M. SPENCER, 302:JUL72-222
SLEIGHT, J. & R. HULL. THE HOME
BOOK OF SMOKE COOKING.
617(TLS):8MAR74-245
SLESAR, H. THE THING AT THE DOOR.
N. CALLENDAR, 441:15DEC74-10
SLESINGER, T. ON BEING TOLD THAT
HER SECOND HUSBAND HAS TAKEN HIS
FIRST LOVER.
A. GOTTLIEB, 441:13OCT74-31
SLESSAREV, H. EDUARD MÖRIKE.
M.B. BENN, 402(MLR):JAN73-232
L. THOMAS, 220(GL&L):APR73-250
SLIMMING, J. MALAYSIA.
G.D. NESS, 293(JAST):MAY72-734
ŚLIWOWSKA, W. W KRĘGU POPRZEDNIKÓW
HERCENA.
A. GELLA, 32:DEC73-810
SLOAN, D. THE SCOTTISH ENLIGHTEN-
MENT & THE AMERICAN COLLEGE IDEAL.
G.W. PILCHER, 656(WMQ):JAN72-189
SLOAN, J.P. THE CASE HISTORY OF
COMRADE V.
E. ROVIT, 659:AUTUMN74-539
SLOAN, T.O. - SEE WRIGHT, T.
SLOANE, E. DIARY OF AN EARLY AMERI-
CAN BOY.
W. CHAPPELL, 441:3MAR74-12
SLOBIN, D.I. PSYCHOLINGUISTICS.*
P. FARB, 453:21FEB74-24
S.D. FISCHER, 206:NOV72-287

SLOCHOWER, H. MYTHOPOESIS.*
P. FINGESTEN, 290(JAAC):FALL71-
136
SLOMMA, H. SINN UND KUNST DER UNTER-
HALTUNG.
W. BEYER, 654(WB):7/1972-182
SLOTE, M.A. REASON & SCEPTICISM.*
G. HARMAN, 482(PHR):APR72-253
SLOTKIN, R. REGENERATION THROUGH
VIOLENCE.*
T. PHILBRICK, 27(AL):NOV73-454
M. ROGIN, 441:7JUL74-15
SLOTTMAN, W.B. & A.C. JANOS, EDS.
REVOLUTION IN PERSPECTIVE.
F.T. ZSUPPAN, 575(SEER):JUL73-
483
SLUTSKY, B. GODOVAYA STRELKA.
E. MORGAN, 617(TLS):11OCT74-1132
SMALL, N.J. SOME PRESIDENTIAL INTER-
PRETATIONS OF THE PRESIDENCY.
H.G. NICHOLAS, 447(N&Q):JUL72-
275
SMALLEY, D., ED. TROLLOPE: THE CRIT-
ICAL HERITAGE.
J.C. MAXWELL, 447(N&Q):FEB72-79
SMART, A. THE ASSISI PROBLEM & THE
ART OF GIOTTO.*
J. WHITE, 56:WINTER72-421
SMART, A. THE RENAISSANCE & MANNER-
ISM IN ITALY.*
639(VQR):SPRING72-LXXVI
SMART, N. THE PHENOMENON OF RELI-
GION.*
D. BASTOW, 518:OCT73-27
SMART, N. THE PHILOSOPHY OF RELIG-
ION.
G. SCHWARTZ, 485(PE&W):OCT72-485
SMELSER, M. THE WINNING OF INDEPEN-
DENCE.
I.D. GRUBER, 656(WMQ):JAN73-170
639(VQR):SPRING72-LXIV
SMERUD, W.B. CAN THERE BE A PRIVATE
LANGUAGE?
L. THIRY, 154:DEC72-662
SMIDT, K. MEMORIAL TRANSMISSION &
QUARTO COPY IN "RICHARD III."*
J.C. MAXWELL, 447(N&Q):APR72-146
SMIT, J.W. STUDIES ON THE LANGUAGE
& STYLE OF COLUMBA THE YOUNGER
(COLUMBANUS).*
R.E. REYNOLDS, 589:JAN73-179
P.G. WALSH, 123:DEC73-275
SMITH, A., ED. THE BRITISH PRESS
SINCE THE WAR.
W. HALEY, 617(TLS):30AUG74-931
SMITH, A. THE ESTABLISHED CHURCH &
POPULAR RELIGION 1750-1850.
E.P. BAKER, 203:SPRING72-78
SMITH, A. LECTURES ON RHETORIC &
BELLES LETTRES.* (J.M. LOTHIAN,
ED)
G. PHIFER, 583:FALL72-117
SMITH, A. TO CHINA & BACK.
617(TLS):29NOV74-1347
SMITH, A.B. IDEAL & REALITY IN THE
FICTIONAL NARRATIVES OF THÉOPHILE
GAUTIER.*
R.T. DENOMMÉ, 546(RR):OCT72-236
SMITH, A.C.H. ORGHAST AT PERSEPOLIS.
A. SEYMOUR, 364:FEB/MAR73-151
SMITH, A.D. THE CONCEPT OF SOCIAL
CHANGE.
617(TLS):10MAY74-505

SMITH, A.G.R. SCIENCE & SOCIETY IN
THE SIXTEENTH & SEVENTEENTH CEN-
TURIES.*
R.D. STOCK, 396(MODA):FALL73-439
SMITH, A.H. THE PLACE-NAMES OF
WESTMORLAND.* (PTS 1&2)
K.I. SANDRED, 597(SN):VOL44#1-
200
SMITH, A.H. THE SPREAD OF PRINTING
OUTSIDE EUROPE: SOUTH AFRICA.
R. CAVE, 503:SUMMER72-110
SMITH, A.J.M. TOWARDS A VIEW OF
CANADIAN LETTERS.
P. BUITENHUIS, 99:SEP74-50
SMITH, A.L., ED. LANGUAGE, COMMUNI-
CATION, & RHETORIC IN BLACK AMERI-
CA.
M. WAGNER, 583:SPRING73-304
SMITH, B. AUSTRALIAN PAINTING 1788-
1970.
A. MC CULLOCH, 381:SEP72-356
SMITH, B. & K. THE ARCHITECTURAL
CHARACTER OF GLEBE, SYDNEY.
617(TLS):24MAY74-549
SMITH, B.H. POETIC CLOSURE.*
A. MADSEN, 648:JAN73-68
M. PECKHAM, 223:MAR72-61
SMITH, C. EMMELINE, THE ORPHAN OF
THE CASTLE. (A.H. EHRENPREIS, ED)
481(PQ):JUL72-764
SMITH, C. - SEE "POEMA DE MIO CID"
SMITH, C., WITH M. BERMEJO MARCOS &
E. CHANG-RODRÍGUEZ, EDS. COLLINS
SPANISH-ENGLISH ENGLISH-SPANISH
DICTIONARY.*
205(FMLS):OCT73-380
SMITH, C.G. SPENSER'S PROVERB LORE.
J.C. MAXWELL, 447(N&Q):FEB72-80
B.A. MILLIGAN, 551(RENQ):SPRING
72-102
SMITH, C.W. THIN MEN OF HADDAM.
M. LEVIN, 441:5MAY74-57
SMITH, D. BLEEDING HEARTS...BLEED-
ING COUNTRY.*
R. SIMEON, 529(QQ):SPRING72-100
SMITH, D. GENTLE PATRIOT.
H.V. NELLES, 99:AUG74-25
SMITH, D.I.B., ED. EDITING EIGHT-
EENTH-CENTURY TEXTS.*
A. JOHNSTON, 677:VOL3-294
SMITH, D.I.B. - SEE MARVELL, A.
SMITH, D.J. CANAL BOATS & BOATERS.
617(TLS):15MAR74-273
SMITH, D.R. - SEE CONRAD, J.
SMITH, F. UNDERSTANDING READING.
S.E. LEGUM & B.A. CRONNELL, 350:
JUN73-523
SMITH, F. & G.A. MILLER, EDS. THE
GENESIS OF LANGUAGE.*
P. VAN BUREN & R.V. CLARK, 215
(GL):VOL12#2-112
SMITH, F.J., ED. PHENOMENOLOGY IN
PERSPECTIVE.
R.S., 543:JUN72-768
SMITH, G. A COLLECTION OF DESIGNS
FOR HOUSEHOLD FURNITURE.* (C.F.
MONTGOMERY & B.M. FORMAN, EDS)
N. GOODISON, 90:JAN72-37
SMITH, G. ARCHIBALD MAC LEISH.
R. ASSELINEAU, 189(EA):JUL-SEP72-
450
SMITH, G. - SEE HUXLEY, A.

SMITH, H. SHAKESPEARE'S ROMANCES.*
T. HAWKES, 676(YR): SUMMER73-561
639(VQR): SPRING73-LXVIII
SMITH, H.A. RETURN OF THE VIRGINIAN.
M. LEVIN, 441:7JUL74-19
SMITH, I.C. - SEE UNDER CRICHTON
SMITH, I.
SMITH, J. ENTERING ROOMS.*
R. GARFITT, 364:AUG/SEP73-124
SMITH, J. SHAKESPEARIAN & OTHER
ESSAYS.
F.W. BATESON, 617(TLS):30AUG74-
921
SMITH, J.A., ED. THE LIVING STREAM.
W. STUCK, 430(NS):JUL72-437
SMITH, J.B. MODERN FINNISH PAINTING.
F. CRICHTON, 39:MAY72-426
SMITH, J.C.D. A GUIDE TO CHURCH
WOODCARVINGS.
617(TLS):9AUG74-864
SMITH, J.H. CONSTANTINE THE GREAT.*
J.F. POWERS, 613:AUTUMN72-476
SMITH, J.H. FRANCIS OF ASSISI.*
441:10MAR74-32
SMITH, J.H., D. MAC MILLAN & V.A.
DEARING - SEE DRYDEN, J.
SMITH, J.R. & L.G., EDS. BEYOND
MONOGAMY.
M. HENTOFF, 453:8AUG74-36
SMITH, L. THE ORIGINAL.*
639(VQR):SUMMER72-CI
SMITH, L.B. HENRY VIII.
639(VQR):SPRING72-LX
SMITH, M. THE DEATH OF THE DETEC-
TIVE.
C. LEHMANN-HAUPT, 441:31JUL74-37
G. STADE, 441:23JUN74-6
442(NY):16SEP74-147
SMITH, M. THE LIVING LAND.
617(TLS):5JUL74-733
SMITH, M. - SEE DE RONSARD, P.
SMITH, M.A. FRANÇOIS MAURIAC.*
W. BUSH, 546(RR):DEC72-313
SMITH, M.G. CORPORATIONS & SOCIETY.
617(TLS):21JUN74-662
SMITH, M.G. - SEE MC CULLERS, C.
SMITH, M.L. - SEE UNDER LLEWELLYN
SMITH, M.
SMITH, N.A.F. VICTORIAN TECHNOLOGY
& ITS PRESENTATION IN MODERN BRIT-
AIN.
K. HUDSON, 637(VS):SEP72-91
SMITH, P.C. & E. WALKER. WAR IN THE
AEGEAN.
617(TLS):18OCT74-1159
SMITH, P.D., JR. TOWARD A PRACTICAL
THEORY OF SECOND LANGUAGE INSTRUC-
TION.
E.A. FRECHETTE, 399(MLJ):NOV72-
452
SMITH, P.M. CLÉMENT MAROT, POET OF
THE FRENCH RENAISSANCE.*
R.M. BURGESS, 551(RENQ):SPRING
72-91
T.C. CAVE, 208(FS):JAN73-53
L.K. DONALDSON-EVANS, 207(FR):
FEB72-751
M. QUAINTON, 402(MLR):JAN73-169
SMITH, R. BABE RUTH'S AMERICA.
R. ANGELL, 441:13OCT74-6

SMITH, R.B. LAND & POLITICS IN THE
ENGLAND OF HENRY VIII: THE WEST
RIDING OF YORKSHIRE, 1530-46.
D.S. BERKOWITZ, 551(RENQ):SUMMER
72-217
SMITH, R.H. OSS.
H.H. RANSOM, 639(VQR):WINTER73-
122
SMITH, S. SCORPION & OTHER POEMS.
T. EAGLETON, 565:VOL13#3-71
P. PORTER, 364:JUN/JUL72-144
SMITH, V. VALLE-INCLÁN: "TIRANO
BANDERAS."
205(FMLS):JUL72-290
SMITH, V.E. THE JONES MEN.
R. ELMAN, 441:29SEP74-4
442(NY):7OCT74-177
SMITH, V.L. ANTON CHEKHOV & THE
LADY WITH THE DOG.*
K. FITZLYON, 364:DEC73/JAN74-142
SMITH, W. EAGLE IN THE SKY.
R. BLYTHE, 362:4APR74-444
SMITH, W. THE POEMS OF WILLIAM
SMITH. (L.A. SASEK, ED)
M. CRUM, 541(RES):FEB72-111
J.A. FREEMAN, 568(SCN):FALL-
WINTER73-82
SMITH, W., JR. THE HISTORY OF THE
PROVINCE OF NEW-YORK.* (M. KAMMEN,
ED)
N. VARGA, 656(WMQ):JUL73-535
SMITH, W.J. NEW & SELECTED POEMS.*
T.H. LANDESS, 569(SR):WINTER73-
137
SMITH, W.J. - SEE "GRANGER'S INDEX
TO POETRY"
SMITHERS, D.L. THE MUSIC & HISTORY
OF THE BAROQUE TRUMPET BEFORE 1721.
617(TLS):20SEP74-995
SMITHSON, P. BATH.
H. CRALLAN, 46:JUN72-391
SMITHYMAN, K. - SEE SATCHELL, W.
SMITS, K. DIE FRÜHMITTELHOCHDEUT-
SCHE WIENER GENESIS.
P.F. GANZ, 382(MAE):1973/2-161
SMOLLETT, T. THE LETTERS OF TOBIAS
SMOLLETT, M.D.* (L.M. KNAPP, ED)
C. LAMONT, 541(RES):FEB72-82
G.S. ROUSSEAU, 405(MP):NOV72-163
SMOLLETT, T. THE LIFE & ADVENTURES
OF SIR LAUNCELOT GREAVES.
617(TLS):19APR74-410
SMOLAR, B. SOVIET JEWRY TODAY &
TOMORROW.
M. FRIEDBERG, 550(RUSR):JUL72-
301
L.H. LEGTERS, 32:MAR73-176
SMUTS, J.C. WALT WHITMAN.* (A.L.
MC LEOD, ED)
G.W. ALLEN, 27(AL):NOV73-465
SMYTH, J. LEADERSHIP IN WAR, 1939-
1945.
617(TLS):22NOV74-1311
SMYTH, W.R. THESAURUS CRITICUS AD
SEXTI PROPERTII TEXTUM.*
R.J. DICKINSON, 123:DEC73-173
SMYTHE, C. - SEE LADY GREGORY
SNELL, B. SZENEN AUS GRIECHISCHEN
DRAMEN.*
H. LLOYD-JONES, 123:DEC73-192
SNELLING, L. THE TEMPTATION OF
ARCHER WATSON.
M. LEVIN, 441:27OCT74-57

SNETHLAGE, J.L. KANT.
  R. MALTER, 342:BAND63HEFT1-130
SNOOK, I.A., ED. CONCEPTS OF INDOC-
TRINATION.
  I. GREGORY, 518:MAY73-25
SNOOK, I.A. INDOCTRINATION & EDUCA-
TION.
  I. GREGORY, 518:MAY73-25
SNOW, C.P. IN THEIR WISDOM.
  J.D. O'HARA, 441:27OCT74-7
  J.T. STORY, 362:10OCT74-482
  E. WEEKS, 61:DEC74-124
  617(TLS):11OCT74-1109
SNOW, C.P. LAST THINGS.*
  M. JONES-DAVIES, 189(EA):APR-JUN
72-331
SNOW, C.P. THE MALCONTENTS.*
  L.T. LEMON, 502(PRS):FALL72-266
SNOWDEN, F.M., JR. BLACKS IN ANTI-
QUITY.*
  P. MAC KENDRICK, 24:SUMMER73-212
SNOXALL, R.A., ED. LUGANDA-ENGLISH
DICTIONARY.
  K.L. BAUCOM, 353:1APR72-127
SNYDER, D.P. MODAL LOGIC & ITS
APPLICATIONS.
  M.J. CRESSWELL, 479(PHQ):OCT72-
369
  K.T., 543:DEC71-370
SŎ II-GYO. CHOSŎN WANGJO HYŎNGSAJ-
EDO ŬI YŎN'GU.
  W. SHAW, 293(JAST):FEB72-417
SOBEJANO, G. NOVELA ESPAÑOLA DE
NUESTRO TIEMPO.
  R. GUTIÉRREZ GIRARDOT, 72:BAND
210HEFT4/6-472
  G. ROBERTS, 238:SEP72-592
SOBEL, L.A., ED. RUSSIA'S RULERS.
  S.I. PLOSS, 550(RUSR):JUL72-320
SOBEL, R. THE ENTREPRENEURS.
  K. COONEY, 441:27OCT74-20
SOBELL, M. ON DOING TIME.
  R.H. ROVERE, 441:17NOV74-12
SOBLE, R.L. & R.E. DALLOS. THE IM-
POSSIBLE DREAM.
  C. WELLES, 441:29DEC74-2
SOBOL, K. BABE RUTH & THE AMERICAN
DREAM.
  R. ANGELL, 441:13OCT74-6
  C.M. CURTIS, 61:NOV74-110
SOBRINO, J., J.B. SILMAN & F. VER-
GARA. REPASO DE ESPAÑOL.
  F.M. WALTMAN, 238:SEP72-608
SODANO, A.R. - SEE PORPHYRY
SÖDERHJELM, J.O. KOLME MATKAA MOS-
KOVAAN.
  P.K. HAMALAINEN, 32:JUN73-402
SÖDERHOLM, T. THE END-RHYMES OF MAR-
VELL, COWLEY, CRASHAW, LOVELACE &
VAUGHAN.
  B. SUNDBY, 597(SN):VOL44#1-197
SOHN POW-KEY. HAN'GUK UI KO HWALT-
CHA: EARLY KOREAN TYPOGRAPHY.
  B.C. BLOOMFIELD, 354:SEP72-253
SOHN POW-KEY, KIM CHOL-CHOON & HONG
YI-SUP. THE HISTORY OF KOREA.
  B.H. HAZARD, 293(JAST):AUG72-905
SOLÁ, D.F. GRAMÁTICA DEL QUECHUA
DE HUÁNUCO.
  C.T. SNOW, 269(IJAL):OCT72-276
SOLDATI, M. THE MALACCA CANE.*
  G. EWART, 364:OCT/NOV72-146
SOLDATI, M. UN PRATO DI PAPAVERI.
  617(TLS):10MAY74-504

SOLER, A.M.S. - SEE UNDER SCHOP
SOLER, A.M.
SOLERI, P. ARCOLOGY.*
  J. COOK, 576:MAR72-73
SOLERI, P. THE SKETCHBOOKS OF PAOLO
SOLERI.
  J. COOK, 576:MAR72-73
  C.P., 505:MAR72-114
SOLIN, H. BEITRÄGE ZUR KENNTNIS DER
GRIECHISCHEN PERSONENNAMEN IN ROM.*
(VOL 1)
  D.J. GEORGACAS, 424:JUN72-152
  S.M. TREGGIARI, 487:SUMMER72-210
SOLIN, H. L'INTERPRETAZIONE DELLE
ISCRIZIONI PARIETALI.
  J.M. REYNOLDS, 123:MAR73-111
DE SOLÍS, A. VARIAS POESÍAS SAG-
RADAS Y PROFANAS. (M. SÁNCHEZ
REGUEIRA, ED)
  M.J. WOODS, 402(MLR):JAN73-206
SOLL, I. AN INTRODUCTION TO HEGEL'S
METAPHYSICS.*
  M. FOX, 154:SEP72-447
  R.J.G., 543:JUN72-768
SOLMI, S. POESIE COMPLETE.
  617(TLS):4OCT74-1090
SOLMSEN, FR. - SEE HESIOD
SOLOMON, E.A. AVIDYĀ - A PROBLEM OF
TRUTH & REALITY.
  W. HALBFASS, 318(JAOS):OCT-DEC
72-576
SOLOUKHIN, V. SEARCHING FOR IKONS
IN RUSSIA.
  N. LUPININ, 550(RUSR):OCT72-434
  639(VQR):SUMMER72-CVI
SOLT, M.E., ED. CONCRETE POETRY.
  J. VERNON, 651(WHR):WINTER73-101
SOLTIS, A. THE BEST CHESS GAMES OF
BORIS SPASSKY.
  617(TLS):1MAR74-221
SOLWAY, D. THE CRYSTAL THEATRE.
PAXIMALIA.
  D. BARBOUR, 529(QQ):WINTER72-569
SOLZHENITSYN, A. AUGUST 1914.*
(RUSSIAN TITLE: AVGUST CHETYRNADT-
SATOGO.)
  F.C. BARGHOORN, 639(VQR):SPRING
73-316
  M. EHRE, 114(CHIR):VOL24#3-153
  W.H. PRITCHARD, 249(HUDR):SPRING
73-225
SOLZHENITSYN, A. CANDLE IN THE
WIND.*
  617(TLS):22FEB74-187
SOLZHENITSYN, A. THE GULAG ARCHIPEL-
AGO, 1918-1956. (RUSSIAN TITLE:
ARKHIPELAG GULAG 1918-1956.)
  S.F. COHEN, 441:16JUN74-1
  G.F. KENNAN, 453:21MAR74-3
  C. LEHMANN-HAUPT, 441:13JUN74-47
  G. STEINER, 442(NY):5AUG74-78
  617(TLS):22FEB74-187
SOLZHENITSYN, A. LETTER TO THE
SOVIET LEADERS.
  S.F. COHEN, 441:16JUN74-1
  A.D. SAKHAROV, 453:13JUN74-3
SOLZHENITSYN, A. LA MAISON DE MAT-
RIONA.
  G. PANKOW, 98:FEB72-165
SOLZHENITSYN, A. NOBEL LECTURE.*
(F.D. REEVE, TRANS) THE NOBEL LEC-
TURE ON LITERATURE. (T.P. WHITNEY,
TRANS)
  639(VQR):AUTUMN73-CLXX

SOLZHENITSYN, A. WE NEVER MAKE MIS-
TAKES.
V.D. MIHAILOVICH, 573(SSF):WIN-
TER72-112
L. ROOKE, 376:JUL72-145
268:JAN74-72
"SOLZHENITSYN."
H. BEVINGTON, 441:1DEC74-82
SOMERS, D.A. THE RISE OF SPORTS IN
NEW ORLEANS, 1850-1900.
639(VQR):AUTUMN72-CXLIV
SOMERVILLE, E.O. & M. ROSS. THE BIG
HOUSE OF INVER. FRENCH LEAVE.
P. GROSSKURTH, 362:17JAN74-88
SOMMER, I.K. DIE CHRONIK DES STUTT-
GARTER RATSHERRN SEBASTIAN KÜNG.
H.H. HOFMANN, 182:VOL25#1/2-56
SOMMER, R. TIGHT SPACES.
L. DIETZ, 441:19MAY74-30
SOMMERS, J. YÁÑEZ, RULFO, FUENTES.
B.G. CARTER, 238:MAY72-393
SOMVILLE, L. DEVANCIERS DU SURRÉAL-
ISME.
R. GEEN, 399(MLJ):DEC72-513
SONDEREGGER, S. ALTHOCHDEUTSCH IN
ST. GALLEN.*
D.E. LE SAGE, 402(MLR):JAN73-211
W. SANDERS, 680(ZDP):BAND91HEFT3-
415
"THE SONG OF ROLAND." (R. HARRISON,
TRANS)
J.C. BEDNAR, 545(RPH):MAY73-746
SONKES, M. DESSINS DU XVE SIÈCLE:
GROUPE VAN DER WEYDEN.*
M. HUGGLER, 182:VOL25#13/14-495
SONNINO, L.A. A HANDBOOK TO SIX-
TEENTH-CENTURY RHETORIC.*
W.J. BRANDT, 206:SEP72-123
"SONNTAGE MIT LATEINISCHER LITERA-
TUR."
A. ERNOUT, 555:VOL46FASC2-341
SONSTROEM, D. ROSSETTI & THE FAIR
LADY.*
W.E. FREDEMAN, 405(MP):NOV72-149
SONTAG, F. HOW PHILOSOPHY SHAPES
THEOLOGY.
R.A. OAKES, 484(PPR):JUN73-599
L.J. SHEIN, 154:DEC72-669
SONTAG, S. DERNIER RECOURS.
N. KATTAN, 98:MAR72-290
SOPEÑA IBÁÑEZ, F. ARTE Y SOCIEDAD
EN GALDÓS.
R.M. FEDORCHEK, 238:SEP72-592
SOPHOCLES. ANTIGONE. (R.E. BRAUN,
TRANS)
H. LLOYD-JONES, 617(TLS):1NOV74-
1221
SOPHOCLES. ELECTRA.* (J.H. KELLS,
ED)
F. LASSERRE, 182:VOL25#21-766
SOPHOCLES. PHILOCTETES.* (T.B.L.
WEBSTER, ED)
P. PUCCI, 24:SUMMER73-197
SORABJI, R. ARISTOTLE ON MEMORY.
R.G. TANNER, 63:AUG73-180
SORELL, W. THE DANCER'S IMAGE.
J. GALE, 151:MAY72-116
SORLIN, P. LA SOCIÉTÉ FRANÇAISE.
D. JOHNSON, 617(TLS):27DEC74-
1468
SOROMENHO, F.C. - SEE UNDER CASTRO
SOROMENHO, F.
SORRELL, A. BRITISH CASTLES.
617(TLS):19JUL74-772

SŌSEKI, N. I AM A CAT.
A. CHAMBERS, 352(LE&W):VOL15#4&
VOL16#1/2-921
R. STORRY, 285(JAPQ):JUL-SEP72-
370
SOSKICE, J.M. CHAPTERS FROM CHILD-
HOOD.
617(TLS):1FEB74-104
SOTO, O.N. & C.D. MC VICKER. TEMAS
DE ARCINIEGAS.
D.H. DARST, 238:MAR72-201
J.M. YALDEN, 238:MAY72-402
SOTOMAYOR, L.C. - SEE UNDER CARRILLO
Y SOTOMAYOR, L.
"SOURCE DATA AUTOMATION EQUIPMENT
GUIDE."
B. MENKUS, 14:JAN72-65
DE SOUSA ANDRADE, J. SOUSÂNDRADE:
HARPA DE OIRO (1889-1899). (J.
MORAES, ED)
191(ELN):SEP72(SUPP)-209
DE SOUSA ANDRADE, J. SOUSÂNDRADE:
INÉDITOS. (J. MORAES & F.G. WIL-
LIAMS, EDS)
G. MOSER, 238:SEP72-597
191(ELN):SEP72(SUPP)-209
DE SOUSBERGHE, L. UNIONS CONSÉCU-
TIVES ENTRE APPARENTÉS.
P. SMITH, 69:JAN72-73
SOUSTER, R. THE YEARS.
Z.S. SOLECKI, 529(QQ):SUMMER72-
274
SOUTHALL, R. LITERATURE & THE RISE
OF CAPITALISM.
617(TLS):4JAN74-9
SOUTHAM, B.C., ED. CRITICAL ESSAYS
ON JANE AUSTEN.* JANE AUSTEN: THE
CRITICAL HERITAGE.
A.J. FRY, 433:APR72-241
SOUTHAM, B.C. A STUDENT'S GUIDE TO
THE SELECTED POEMS OF T.S. ELIOT.
W. STUCK, 430(NS):JUL72-436
"SOUTHEAST ASIA'S ECONOMY IN THE
1970'S."
42(AR):SPRING/SUMMER72-247
SOUTHERINGTON, F.R. HARDY'S VISION
OF MAN.
R.O. PREYER, 637(VS):JUN72-499
M. WILLIAMS, 541(RES):MAY72-231
SOUTHERINGTON, F.R. - SEE HARDY, T.
SOUTHERN, E. THE MUSIC OF BLACK
AMERICANS.
C. KEIL, 187:JAN74-165
M. PETERSON, 470:JAN72-32
SOUTHERN, R. THE VICTORIAN THEATRE.*
H. OREL, 637(VS):SEP71-93
SOUVARINE, B. STALIN.
H.F. FIRESIDE, 550(RUSR):OCT72-
414
"SOVIET INTELLIGENCE & SECURITY SER-
VICES, 1964-70."
R.M. SLUSSER, 32:DEC73-825
SOWDEN, H., ED. SYDNEY OPERA HOUSE
GLASS WALLS.
617(TLS):11OCT74-1143
SOWINSKI, B. GRUNDLAGEN DES STUDI-
UMS DER GERMANISTIK. (VOL 1)
I. RAUCH, 221(GQ):NOV72-784
SOYINKA, W. THE BACCHAE OF EURIP-
IDES.
617(TLS):1MAR74-214
SOYINKA, W. THE JERO PLAYS. CAM-
WOOD ON THE LEAVES.
617(TLS):8FEB74-138

SOYINKA, W. MADMEN & SPECIALISTS.
A. RENDLE, 157:SPRING72-81
SOZZI, G.P. GERMAIN NOUVEAU.*
L. FORESTIER, 535(RHL):MAR-APR72-
341
SPAAK, C. L'ORDRE ET LE DÉSORDRE.
D. O'CONNELL, 207(FR):MAR72-903
SPAAK, P-H. THE CONTINUING BATTLE.
G.C. MC GHEE, 639(VQR):SUMMER72-
455
SPACKS, B. THE COMPANY OF CHILDREN.*
G. MIRANDA, 448:FALL-WINTER71/72-
109
SPACKS, B. SOMETHING HUMAN.*
M. BORROFF, 676(YR):AUTUMN72-81
SPACKS, P.M. AN ARGUMENT OF IMAGES.*
U.C. KNOEPFLMACHER, 401(MLQ):
DEC73-448
D.B. MORRIS, 481(PQ):JUL72-748
R. PARKIN, 566:SPRING72-81
639(VQR):AUTUMN72-CXXVIII
SPADA, J. BARBRA - THE FIRST DECADE.
W. FEAVER, 617(TLS):27DEC74-1471
SPADA, M. FICTIONS D'EROS.
J. FOX, 208(FS):JAN73-105
SPADE, R. PAUL RUDOLPH. EERO SAAR-
INEN.
R.F. JORDAN, 46:FEB72-129
SPAE, J.J. JAPANESE RELIGIOSITY.
A. BLOOM, 485(PE&W):JAN72-108
C.H. POWLES, 293(JAST):NOV71-203
SPAETH, S.G. MILTON'S KNOWLEDGE OF
MUSIC.
D. SCOTT, 415:AUG73-800
SPAGNOLETTI, G. - SEE MARTELLO, P.J.
SPAHR, G. WEINGARTNER LIEDERHAND-
SCHRIFT.
H. TERVOOREN, 680(ZDP):BAND91
HEFT3-451
SPALDING, H.D., ED. ENCYCLOPEDIA OF
BLACK FOLKLORE & HUMOR.
J.W. BYRD, 584(SWR):WINTER73-103
SPANGENBERG, W. SÄMTLICHE WERKE.
(VOL 1) (A. VIZKELETY, ED)
J.E. ENGEL, 301(JEGP):JAN73-71
"SPANISH TIMES & BOOM TIMES."
T.M. PEARCE, 649(WAL):WINTER73-
309
SPANNEUT, M. LE STOÏCISME DES PÈRES
DE L'EGLISE: DE CLÉMENT DE ROME À
CLÉMENT D'ALEXANDRIE.
P-M. SCHUHL, 542:JAN-MAR72-65
SPARK, M. THE ABBESS OF CREWE.
P. ADAMS, 61:NOV74-123
G. ANNAN, 617(TLS):15NOV74-1277
G. STADE, 441:20OCT74-4
E. TENNANT, 362:14NOV74-649
M. WOOD, 453:28NOV74-29
SPARK, M. COLLECTED STORIES: 1.
R.A. JOHNSON, 573(SSF):SUMMER72-
289
SPARK, M. THE HOTHOUSE BY THE EAST
RIVER.*
E. FEINSTEIN, 364:AUG/SEP73-148
42(AR):VOL32#4-695
639(VQR):AUTUMN73-CXXXVII
SPARK, M. NOT TO DISTURB.*
M. PAGE, 648:APR73-11
SPARK, M. THE PUBLIC IMAGE.
E.C. BUFKIN, 219(GAR):SPRING72-
100
SPARKES, B.A. & L. TALCOTT. THE
ATHENIAN AGORA.* (VOL 12, PTS 1&2)
J.M. COOK, 123:MAR73-71

SPARKS, B.W. & R.G. WEST. THE ICE
AGE IN BRITAIN.*
R. PITTIONI, 182:VOL25#9/10-303
SPARKS, E.H. THE MUSIC OF NOEL
BAULDEWEYN.
J.A.C., 410(M&L):APR73-218
SPARROW, G. VINTAGE VICTORIAN MUR-
DER.
R.B. MARTIN, 637(VS):MAR72-395
SPÄTH, E. DRYDEN ALS POETA LAUREA-
TUS.
E. LEHMANN, 38:BAND90HEFT3-403
SPATT, B.M. A PROPOSAL TO CHANGE
THE STRUCTURE OF CITY PLANNING.*
D.K. SHIPLER, 44:MAR72-15
SPEAIGHT, R. SHAKESPEARE ON THE
STAGE.
617(TLS):8FEB74-138
SPEAR, A.T. BRANCUSI'S BIRDS.*
M.S. YOUNG, 39:APR72-341
SPEARING, A.C. THE GAWAIN-POET.*
S.S. HUSSEY, 447(N&Q):JUL72-273
D. MEHL, 72:BAND210HEFT1/3-183
D.D.R. OWEN, 205(FMLS):JAN72-79
F. RIDDY, 382(MAE):1973/1-96
A.V.C. SCHMIDT, 541(RES):MAY72-
192
639(VQR):WINTER72-XXX
SPEARING, R. H.H.
C. PALMER, 415:JUN73-604
SPEARS, M.K. DIONYSUS & THE CITY.*
J. GLOVER, 565:VOL13#3-68
D.E.S. MAXWELL, 402(MLR):JAN73-
163
SPECHT, E.K. SPRACHE UND SEIN.
P. WESLY, 206:JAN72-140
SPECTOR, S.D. - SEE RISTELHUEBER, R.
SPEER, A. INSIDE THE THIRD REICH.*
W. VON MOLTKE, 44:MAY72-8
SPEICHER, J. LOWER & LOWER.
M. MEWSHAW, 441:20JAN74-25
SPEIRS, J. POETRY TOWARDS NOVEL.*
E. BLOOM, 454:SPRING73-276
J. CURTIS, 648:JAN73-74
J.R.D. JACKSON, 627(UTQ):SPRING
73-289
G.B. TENNYSON, 445(NCF):DEC72-
365
SPEIRS, L. TOLSTOY & CHEKHOV.*
D. FANGER, 454:WINTER73-188
A.K. LOJKINE, 67:MAY73-161
H. PITCHER, 205(FMLS):JUL72-237
E. WASIOLEK, 594:SPRING72-86
SPELLERBERG, G. VERHÄNGNIS UND
GESCHICHTE.*
G. HOFFMEISTER, 221(GQ):JAN72-
134
P. SKRINE, 402(MLR):APR73-450
SPELLMAN, A.B. BLACK MUSIC.
V. THOMSON, 453:17OCT74-14
SPENCE, J. OBSERVATIONS, ANECDOTES,
& CHARACTERS OF BOOKS & MEN. (J.M.
OSBORN, ED)
T.A. BIRRELL, 433:JAN72-112
SPENCE, J.D. EMPEROR OF CHINA.
P. ADAMS, 61:JUN74-114
E. HAHN, 441:26MAY74-7
H.L. KAHN, 453:28NOV74-26
V.S. PRITCHETT, 442(NY):4NOV74-
201
T. SHABAD, 441:18JUL74-39
SPENCER, C. LEON BAKST.
J. RUSSELL, 441:1DEC74-55
617(TLS):22MAR74-300

SPENCER, C. NAHUM TATE.
J. BLACK, 677:VOL3-289
SPENCER, E. THE SNARE.
P. CRUTTWELL & F. WESTBURG,
249(HUDR):SUMMER73-421
SPENCER, J., ED. THE ENGLISH LANGU-
AGE IN WEST AFRICA.
W.E. WELMERS, 350:MAR73-215
SPENCER, M.C. THE ART CRITICISM OF
THÉOPHILE GAUTIER.*
G.M. ACKERMAN, 54:MAR72-103
H.L. BRUGMANS, 207(FR):OCT71-256
SPENCER, P. NOMADS IN ALLIANCE.
617(TLS):8FEB74-131
SPENCER, R. THE AESTHETIC MOVEMENT.
R. STUDING, 290(JAAC):WINTER72-
279
SPENCER, R.E. & R. AWE. INTERNATION-
AL EDUCATIONAL EXCHANGE.
C-Y. TO, 399(MLJ):FEB72-94
SPENCER, R.F., ED. RELIGION &
CHANGE IN CONTEMPORARY ASIA.
R.J. MILLER, 293(JAST):NOV71-173
SPENCER, S. THE SPACE BETWEEN.*
E. ROVIT, 659:AUTUMN74-539
SPENCER, S. SPACE, TIME & STRUCTURE
IN THE MODERN NOVEL.*
G. BRÉE, 659:WINTER74-154
J. KLINKOWITZ, 454:SPRING73-268
P. ROSENBLATT, 50(ARQ):WINTER72-
375
SPENCER BROWN, G. LAWS OF FORM.
L.L. WHYTE, 84:AUG72-291
SPENDER, S. THE GENEROUS DAYS.*
T. EAGLETON, 565:VOL13#3-71
SPENDER, S. LOVE-HATE RELATIONS.
I. EHRENPREIS, 453:14NOV74-32
J. EPSTEIN, 441:23JUN74-1
617(TLS):24MAY74-546
SPENGLER, W.E. DER BEGRIFF DES
SCHÖNEN BEI WINCKELMANN.
R.P. BAREIKIS, 481(PQ):JUL72-786
SPERBER, D. LE SYMBOLISME EN GÉN-
ÉRAL.
E. LEACH, 617(TLS):4OCT74-1074
SPERBER, R., ED. DAS FLUSSGEBIET
DES MAINS.
R. RIS, 343:BAND14HEFT2-216
SPERK, K., ED. MEDIEVAL ENGLISH
SAINTS' LEGENDS.*
T.P. DUNNING, 597(SN):VOL44#1-
188
M. GÖRLACH, 38:BAND90HEFT4-507
SPERRY, S.M. KEATS THE POET.
617(TLS):8FEB74-130
SPETTIGUE, D.O. F.P.G.: THE EURO-
PEAN YEARS.
L. MC MULLEN, 296:VOL3#2-98
SPEVACK, M. A COMPLETE & SYSTEMATIC
CONCORDANCE TO THE WORKS OF SHAKE-
SPEARE.* (VOLS 2-6)
K. WIKBERG, 597(SN):VOL44#1-173
SPEVACK, M. THE HARVARD CONCORDANCE
TO SHAKESPEARE.
S. BOOTH, 453:12DEC74-44
D. DONOGHUE, 441:7APR74-23
T.W. RUSSELL 3D, 231:OCT74-101
SPICER, D.G. THE BOOK OF FESTIVALS.
K.B. HARDER, 424:JUN72-150
SPICKER, S.F., ED. THE PHILOSOPHY
OF THE BODY.
W.A.D., 543:SEP71-143

SPIELBERG, P. TWIDDLEDUM TWADDLEDUM.
C. LEHMANN-HAUPT, 441:17OCT74-45
M. MEWSHAW, 441:13OCT74-26
SPIES, W. MAX ERNST, 1950-1970.
A. FRANKENSTEIN, 55:FEB73-15
SPILLER, J. - SEE KLEE, P.
SPILLER, R.E. & A.R. FERGUSON - SEE
EMERSON, R.W.
SPILLER, R.E. & W.E. WILLIAMS - SEE
EMERSON, R.W.
SPINK, I. ENGLISH SONG.
P. PEARS, 362:28MAR74-412
DE SPÍNOLA, A. PORTUGAL E O FUTURO.
K. MAXWELL, 453:13JUN74-16
SPINOZA, B. I PRINCIPI DI FILOSOFIA
DI CARTESIO E L'APPENDICE. (B.
WIDMAR, ED)
P. DI VONA, 548(RCSF):OCT-DEC72-
475
SPIRO, M.E. BUDDHISM & SOCIETY.
N.P. JACOBSON, 485(PE&W):JAN72-
110
F.K. LEHMAN, 293(JAST):FEB72-373
"SPITSBERG: MISSION FRANÇAISE 1966."
G.S. BOULTON, 182:VOL25#11-381
SPIVAKOVSKY, E. SON OF THE ALHAMBRA.
R.L. KAGAN, 551(RENQ):SUMMER72-
214
A.J.R. RUSSELL-WOOD, 400(MLN):
MAR72-354
SPOCK, B. RAISING CHILDREN IN A
DIFFICULT TIME.
B. DE MOTT, 61:APR74-108
J. O'REILLY, 441:14APR74-3
SPONGANO, R., ED. RISPETTI E STRAM-
BOTTI DEL QUATTROCENTO.*
M.M., 228(GSLI):VOL149FASC466/
467-460
SPONGANO, R., ED. STUDI E PROBLEMI
DI CRITICA TESTUALE. (FASC 1)
A. SCAGLIONE, 276:SUMMER72-250
SPÖRLEIN, B. DIE LEUGNUNG DER AUFER-
STEHUNG.
F.F. BRUCE, 182:VOL25#7/8-213
"SPRACHEN - ZUORDNUNG - STRUKTUREN."
G.F. MEIER, 682(ZPSK):BAND25
HEFT1/2-165
SPRAGUE, A.C. & J.C. TREWIN. SHAKE-
SPEARE'S PLAYS TODAY.*
R.M. BENDER, 191(ELN):SEP72-43
SPRAGUE, R.K. - SEE PLATO
SPREIREGEN, P.D. - SEE BLUMENFELD, H.
SPRIANO, P. STORIA DI TORINO OPER-
AIA E SOCIALISTA.
S.J. WOOLF, 617(TLS):18OCT74-
1152
SPRIEWALD, I. & OTHERS. GRUNDPOSI-
TIONEN DER DEUTSCHEN LITERATUR IM
16. JAHRHUNDERT.
M.L. BAEUMER, 406:WINTER73-393
SPRIGGE, E. SYBIL THORNDIKE CASSON.
R.J. SMITH, 157:WINTER71-74
SPRIGGE, E. THE LIFE OF IVY COMPTON-
BURNETT.*
J. GINGER, 364:JUN/JUL73-148
639(VQR):AUTUMN73-CLX
SPRIGGE, T.L.S. FACTS, WORDS &
BELIEFS.*
N.J. MOUTAFAKIS, 484(PPR):JUN73-
595
J.D. RABB, 154:SEP72-475
SPRINGER, J. THE FONDAS.*
W. FEAVER, 617(TLS):27DEC74-1471

SPRINGER, J. & J. HAMILTON. THEY
HAD FACES THEN.
W. FEAVER, 617(TLS):27DEC74-1471
SPRINGER, O. - SEE "LANGENSCHEIDT'S
ENCYCLOPAEDIC DICTIONARY OF THE
ENGLISH & GERMAN LANGUAGES"
SPROTT, S.E. - SEE MILTON, J.
SPRUNGER, K.L. THE LEARNED DOCTOR
WILLIAM AMES.
J. TANIS, 656(WMQ):JUL73-538
SPUFFORD, M. CONTRASTING COMMUNI-
TIES.
E. MILLER, 617(TLS):13DEC74-1422
SPULER, B. HISTORY OF THE MONGOLS.
N. POPPE, 293(JAST):AUG72-956
SPULER, B. THE MONGOLS IN HISTORY.
J.J. SAUNDERS, 550(RUSR):OCT72-
434
SPURLING, H. IVY WHEN YOUNG.
D.A.N. JONES, 362:21MAR74-372
617(TLS):22MAR74-284
SPYCHER, P. FRIEDRICH DÜRRENMATT.
G.L. ALLEY, 406:SUMMER73-211
H.M. WAIDSON, 301(JEGP):OCT73-
611
SQUAROTTI, G.B. & G. MARTIGNETTI -
SEE BARBERI SQUAROTTI, G. & G. MAR-
TIGNETTI
SQUIRE, G. DRESS & SOCIETY.
A. HOLLANDER, 441:25AUG74-2
442(NY):30SEP74-131
SQUIRE, G. DRESS ART & SOCIETY.
617(TLS):24MAY74-565
SQUIRES, R. ALLEN TATE.*
639(VQR):WINTER72-VIII
SQUIRES, R., ED. ALLEN TATE & HIS
WORK.*
639(VQR):SUMMER73-CXV
SRAFFA, P., WITH M.H. DOBB, EDS.
THE WORKS & CORRESPONDENCE OF
DAVID RICARDO. (VOL 11)
617(TLS):3MAY74-472
SREJOVIĆ, D. EUROPE'S FIRST MONU-
MENTAL SCULPTURE.
A. MC PHERRON, 32:DEC73-844
SROKA, M. - SEE BRZOZOWSKI, S.
STAAKS, W. FRENCH VERB USAGE.
E.M. FUGETT, 207(FR):FEB72-773
STAAL, J.F. WORD ORDER IN SANSKRIT
& UNIVERSAL GRAMMAR.*
W.P. LEHMANN, 545(RPH):NOV72-405
STAAR, R.F., ED. YEARBOOK ON INTER-
NATIONAL COMMUNIST AFFAIRS 1972.
L. BLIT, 575(SEER):JUL73-492
STABB, M.S. JORGE LUIS BORGES.
J. ALAZRAKI, 399(MLJ):APR72-247
M. MORELLO-FROSCH, 238:MAY72-388
STACEY, C.P., ED. HISTORICAL DOCU-
MENTS OF CANADA. (VOL 5)
P.B. WAITE, 150(DR):SUMMER72-315
STACHOWIAK, H. RATIONALISMUS IM
URSPRUNG.
P. SELIGMAN, 154:DEC72-608
STACK, C. ALL OUR KIN.
453:21MAR74-41
STACK, E.M. THE LANGUAGE LABORATORY
& MODERN LANGUAGE TEACHING. (3RD
ED)
P.W. O'CONNOR, 221(GQ):NOV72-793
STACK, G. BERKELEY'S ANALYSIS OF
PERCEPTION.
A.S.C., 543:DEC71-371

VON STACKELBERG, J. VON RABELAIS
BIS VOLTAIRE.*
J-R. ARMOGATHE, 535(RHL):MAY-JUN
72-518
K. BAHNERS, 430(NS):AUG72-494
STACKHOUSE, M. ETHICS & THE URBAN
ETHOS.
W. SWENSON, 185:JUL73-351
STACKPOLE, E.A. WHALES & DESTINY.
S.C. SHERMAN, 656(WMQ):OCT73-676
STADLER, U. DER EINSAME ORT.
K.F. OTTO, JR., 301(JEGP):JAN73-
79
P. SKRINE, 402(MLR):APR73-450
"MADAME DE STAËL ET L'EUROPE."
L.M. CELLIER, 546(RR):FEB72-52
M. GUTWIRTH, 207(FR):OCT71-261
"STAFF STUDY OF THE OVERSIGHT &
EFFICIENCY OF EXECUTIVE AGENCIES
WITH RESPECT TO THE PETROLEUM IN-
DUSTRY, ESPECIALLY AS IT RELATES
TO RECENT FUEL SHORTAGES."
E. ROTHSCHILD, 453:24JAN74-38
STAFFORD, J. OLDHAM AS IT WAS.
617(TLS):1FEB74-110
STAFFORD, W. SOMEDAY, MAYBE.*
G. BURNS, 584(SWR):SUMMER73-278
V. YOUNG, 249(HUDR):WINTER73/74-
721
STAHL, D. A SELECTED DISCOGRAPHY OF
SOLO SONG.
E. SAMS, 415:NOV73-1125
STAHL, E.L. & W.E. YUILL. GERMAN
LITERATURE OF THE EIGHTEENTH &
NINETEENTH CENTURIES.*
G. RODGER, 220(GL&L):APR73-271
STAHL, W.H., WITH R. JOHNSON & E.L.
BURGE. MARTIANUS CAPELLA & THE
SEVEN LIBERAL ARTS.* (VOL 1)
J.R.C. MARTYN, 67:MAY73-151
STAIRS, D. THE DIPLOMACY OF CON-
STRAINT.
J.W. HOLMES, 99:NOV/DEC74-55
R.F. SWANSON, 441:22SEP74-36
617(TLS):5JUL74-707
STALEY, A. THE PRE-RAPHAELITE LAND-
SCAPE.*
J. HOLLANDER, 231:SEP74-82
STALLIBRASS, A. THE SELF-RESPECTING
CHILD.
617(TLS):27SEP74-1046
STALLKNECHT, N.P. GEORGE SANTAYANA.
H.W. SCHNEIDER, 319:APR74-277
STALLWORTH, A.N. THIS TIME NEXT
YEAR.
M. ELLMANN, 676(YR):SPRING73-461
STALLWORTHY, J. THE APPLE BARREL.
HAND IN HAND.
617(TLS):9AUG74-852
STALLWORTHY, J. WILFRED OWEN.
J. BAYLEY, 617(TLS):15NOV74-1273
STALLYBRASS, O. - SEE FORSTER, E.M.
STAMBAUGH, J. NIETZSCHE'S THOUGHT
OF ETERNAL RETURN.*
E.J.M. WEST, 125:FEB73-197
STAMBOLIAN, G. MARCEL PROUST & THE
CREATIVE ENCOUNTER.*
A.H. PASCO, 114(CHIR):VOL24#4-
176
C. ROSENBERG, 50(ARQ):WINTER72-
377
STAMM, R. THE SHAPING POWERS AT
WORK.*
N.C. DE NAGY, 38:BAND90HEFT3-409

STANDIFER, J.A. & B. REEDER. SOURCE
BOOK OF AFRICAN & AFRO-AMERICAN
MATERIALS FOR MUSIC EDUCATORS.
A. REYES-SCHRAMM, 187:MAY74-321
STANFORD, A., ED. THE WOMEN POETS
IN ENGLISH.*
H. ZINNES, 598(SOR):SPRING74-525
639(VQR):SUMMER73-CXI
STANFORD, D., ED. WRITING OF THE
NINETIES.
N. ALFORD, 376:JAN72-125
STANFORD, W.B. TOWARDS A HISTORY OF
CLASSICAL INFLUENCES IN IRELAND.
M.L. CLARKE, 123:MAR73-78
STANFORD, W.B. & R.B. MC DOWELL.
MAHAFFEY.*
M.L. CLARKE, 123:DEC73-291
M.J. WATERS, 637(VS):DEC72-228
STANKIEWICZ, D. & D.S. WORTH. A
SELECTED BIBLIOGRAPHY OF SLAVIC
LINGUISTICS. (VOL 2)
M. SAMILOV, 575(SEER):JAN73-155
STANKIEWICZ, E. DECLENSION & GRADA-
TION OF RUSSIAN SUBSTANTIVES.
C.E. GRIBBLE, 215(GL):VOL12#2-
134
STANLEY, G.F.G. CANADA INVADED,
1775-1776.
C.P. STACEY, 99:MAY/JUN74-36
STANLEY, G.F.G. - SEE WILSON, C.
STANSKY, P. & W. ABRAHAMS. THE UN-
KNOWN ORWELL.*
W.R. STEINHOFF, 385(MQR):SPRING
74-178
STANWORTH, P. & A. GIDDENS, EDS.
ELITES & POWER IN BRITISH SOCIETY.
617(TLS):5JUL74-709
STANZEL, F. NARRATIVE SITUATIONS IN
THE NOVEL.
T. TANNER, 402(MLR):JAN73-159
STAPFER, P.A. PHILIPP ALBERT STAP-
FER: BRIEFWECHSEL 1789-91 UND
REISETAGEBUCH. (A. ROHR, ED)
F. JÉQUIER, 182:VOL25#7/8-244
STARCK, T. & J.C. WELLS. ALTHOCH-
DEUTSCHES GLOSSENWÖRTERBUCH (MIT
STELLENNACHWEIS ZU SÄMTLICHEN
GEDRUCKTEN ALTHOCHDEUTSCHEN UND
VERWANDTEN GLOSSEN). (PT 1)
D.H. GREEN, 402(MLR):JAN73-208
STARK, F.B., C.B. LINK & E.L. PACKER,
EDS. FLOWERS IN COLOUR. HOUSE
PLANTS IN COLOUR. FLOWERING TREES
& SHRUBS IN COLOUR. ROCK GARDENS
& WATER PLANTS IN COLOUR.
617(TLS):17MAY74-536
STARK, R. BUTCHER'S MOON.
N. CALLENDAR, 441:15SEP74-44
STARKE, P.H. ABSTRAKTE AUTOMATEN.
A. SALOMAA, 316:JUN72-413
STARKIE, E. FLAUBERT THE MASTER.
L. WELCH, 150(DR):WINTER72/73-
668
639(VQR):SUMMER72-XC
STARN, R. DONATO GIANNOTTI & HIS
EPISTOLAE.
F. GILBERT, 551(RENQ):SPRING72-
77
STAROBIN, J.R. AMERICAN COMMUNISM
IN CRISIS, 1943-1957.*
P.J. JAFFE, 550(RUSR):OCT72-435
639(VQR):AUTUMN72-CLII

STAROBINSKI, J. LES MOTS SOUS LES
MOTS.
L. WELCH, 290(JAAC):SPRING73-412
STAROBINSKI, J. 1789 LES EMBLÈMES
DE LA RAISON.
617(TLS):24MAY74-552
STAROBINSKI-SAFRAN, E. - SEE PHILO
STAROSTE, W. RAUM UND REALITÄT IN
DICHTERISCHER GESTALTUNG.
I.M. GOESSL, 406:SUMMER73-183
N.H. SMITH, 182:VOL25#1/2-42
STARR, C.G. ATHENIAN COINAGE, 480-
449 B.C.*
S.K. EDDY, 24:FALL73-308
J.F. HEALY, 123:DEC73-252
R.T. WILLIAMS, 487:WINTER72-411
STARR, C.G. EARLY MAN.
617(TLS):22MAR74-304
639(VQR):AUTUMN73-CLXVII
STARR, G.A. DEFOE & CASUISTRY.*
F. BASTIAN, 541(RES):NOV72-500
J.D. CROWLEY, 594:SPRING72-124
M. SCHONHORN, 481(PQ):JUL72-664
D.W. TARBET, 173(ECS):WINTER72/
73-274
STARR, K. AMERICANS & THE CALIFOR-
NIA DREAM, 1850-1915.*
H.N. SMITH, 639(VQR):SUMMER73-
464
STARR, P., WITH J.F. HENRY & R.P.
BONNER. THE DISCARDED ARMY.
G. BURNSIDE, 441:31MAR74-20
STARR, S.F. - SEE VON HAXTHAUSEN, A.
STARR, S.Z. COLONEL GRENFELL'S WARS.
639(VQR):SPRING72-LVIII
STATES, B.O. IRONY & DRAMA.*
B. BECKERMAN, 402(MLR):JAN73-142
J.H. WHEATLEY, 128(CE):FEB72-606
R.A. ZIMBARDO, 191(ELN):SEP72-70
STATIUS. STACE, "ACHILLÉIDE."* (J.
MEHEUST, ED & TRANS)
F. DELARUE, 555:VOL46FASC2-338
STATLER, O. SHIMODA STORY.*
S. CRAWCOUR, 285(JAPQ):JAN-MAR72-
100
STAUB, H. - SEE SCÈVE, M.
STAUFFACHER, W. CARL SPITTELER.
617(TLS):5APR74-373
STAVE, J. WÖRTER UND LEUTE.
R. GILL, 220(GL&L):JUL73-332
STAVELEY, G. BROKEN WATERS SING.
M.E. ACKERMAN, 649(WAL):SPRING72-
74
STAWECKA, K. - SEE SARBIEWSKI, M.K.
STEAD, C. THE LITTLE HOTEL.
S. MAITLAND, 362:18JUL74-93
617(TLS):24MAY74-545
STEADMAN, J.M. DISEMBODIED LAUGHTER.
639(VQR):SPRING73-LXV
STEADMAN, M. MC AFEE COUNTY.
K. HILL, 573(SSF):SUMMER72-283
STEANE, J. THE NORTHAMPTONSHIRE
LANDSCAPE.
617(TLS):29MAR74-342
STEANE, J.B. THE GRAND TRADITION.
P. STEVENSON, 362:31OCT74-583
442(NY):23SEP74-146
617(TLS):26JUL74-788
STEARNS, R.P. SCIENCE IN THE BRIT-
ISH COLONIES OF AMERICA.
W.J. BELL, JR., 656(WMQ):JAN72-
163
S.A. SHAPIN, 481(PQ):JUL72-582
STEARNS, R.P. - SEE LISTER, M.

STEBLER, U. ENTSTEHUNG UND ENTWICK-
LUNG DES GEWISSENS IM SPIEGEL DER
GRIECHISCHEN TRAGÖDIE.
E.W. WHITTLE, 123:DEC73-277
STEEGMULLER, F. COCTEAU.*
Y. QUINTIN, 207(FR):MAR72-914
STEEGMULLER, F. STORIES & TRUE
STORIES.
M. GREEN, 364:DEC72/JAN73-145
STEEGMULLER, F. - SEE DUNCAN, I.
STEEL, D.J. SOURCES FOR SCOTTISH
GENEALOGY & FAMILY HISTORY.
M. MACLAGAN, 447(N&Q):JUL72-271
STEELE, J., ED. EASTERN EUROPE
SINCE STALIN.
617(TLS):13SEP74-983
STEELE, R. THE PLAYS OF RICHARD
STEELE.* (S.S. KENNY, ED)
M. JAMIESON, 157:WINTER71-68
C.A. ZIMANSKY, 481(PQ):JUL72-769
STEEN, S.W.P. MATHEMATICAL LOGIC.
J.L. BELL, 84:NOV72-363
STEENBERG, J. FREDENSBORG SLOT.
H. LUND, 90:FEB72-104
STEENE, B. THE GREATEST FIRE.
R.B. VOWLES, 301(JEGP):OCT73-585
STEENSMA, R.C. SIR WILLIAM TEMPLE.
D.R. NEAT, 577(SHR):FALL72-419
STEENSTRUP, J.C.H.R. THE MEDIEVAL
POPULAR BALLAD.
N. WÜRZBACH, 38:BAND90HEFT3-397
STEERS, J.A. THE COASTLINE OF SCOT-
LAND.
617(TLS):15MAR74-260
STÉFANINI, J. UN PROVENÇALISTE MAR-
SEILLAIS: L'ABBÉ FÉRAUD (1725-
1807).*
R.C. KELLY, 545(RPH):AUG72-142
STEFFENSEN, S. BERTOLT BRECHTS GE-
DICHTE.
J.K. LYON, 301(JEGP):JUL73-428
STEGAGNO PICCHIO, L. - SEE MOYA, M.
STEGMÜLLER, W. AUFSÄTZE ZU KANT
UND WITTGENSTEIN.
M. KLEINSCHNIEDER, 342:BAND63
HEFT2-281
STEGMÜLLER, W. PROBLEME UND RESUL-
TATE DER WISSENSCHAFTSTHEORIE UND
ANALYTISCHE PHILOSOPHIE. (VOL 2)
J.J. KOCKELMANS, 486:SEP72-397
STEGNER, W. THE UNEASY CHAIR.
T. BUCKLEY, 441:25APR74-43
M. COWLEY, 441:10FEB74-1
R. LYNES, 231:MAY74-90
E. WEEKS, 61:MAR74-95
442(NY):25MAR74-143
STEIN, A. INDIA & THE SOVIET UNION.
S.K. GUPTA, 550(RUSR):JAN72-102
STEIN, G. PREVIOUSLY UNCOLLECTED
WRITINGS. (R.B. HAAS, ED)
P. BEER, 617(TLS):8NOV74-1252
D. SUTHERLAND, 453:30MAY74-28
STEIN, G.P. THE WAYS OF MEANING IN
THE ARTS.
E. VIVAS, 290(JAAC):FALL71-117
STEIN, J.M. POEM & MUSIC IN THE
GERMAN LIED FROM GLUCK TO WOLF.
E. SAMS, 415:FEB73-146
H.E. SEELIG, 406:SPRING73-95
R.J. TAYLOR, 301(JEGP):JAN73-84
J.A.W., 410(M&L):APR73-230
STEIN, M.B. THE DYNAMICS OF RIGHT-
WING PROTEST.
D.P. MORTON, 99:APR74-34

STEIN, M.L. LOVERS, FRIENDS, SLAVES.
R. KOENIG, 441:29SEP74-36
STEIN, R.A. TIBETAN CIVILIZATION.
D. LANCASHIRE, 67:MAY73-164
STEIN, S. LIVING ROOM.
R. JAFFE, 441:19MAY74-38
C. LEHMANN-HAUPT, 441:10APR74-41
STEIN, W. CRITICISM AS DIALOGUE.*
A.J. FRY, 433:JAN72-113
STEINBACH, U. DĀT AL-HIMMA.
R. WIELANDT, 182:VOL25#5/6-167
STEINBERG, D.D. & L.A. JAKOBOVITS,
EDS. SEMANTICS.
J. LYONS, 402(MLR):JUL73-619
STEINBERG, D.J., ED. IN SEARCH OF
SOUTHEAST ASIA.
J.D. LEGGE, 293(JAST):MAY72-713
STEINBERG, E.R. THE STREAM OF CON-
SCIOUSNESS & BEYOND IN "ULYSSES."
J. NAREMORE, 329(JJQ):FALL73-62
STEINBERG, L. OTHER CRITERIA.*
A. FRANKENSTEIN, 55:JAN73-12
R. HOWARD, 139:DEC72-67
639(VQR):SPRING73-XCII
STEINECKE, H. HERMANN BROCH UND DER
POLYHISTORISCHE ROMAN.*
P. HASUBEK, 405(MP):AUG72-87
STEINECKE, H., ED. THEORIE UND TECH-
NIK DES ROMANS IM 19. JAHRHUNDERT.*
V. NEUHAUS, 680(ZDP):BAND91HEFT
2-286
STEINER, B.E. SAMUEL SEABURY, 1729-
1796.
G.E. HARTDAGEN, 656(WMQ):JUL73-
537
F.L. HOUGHTON, 70(ANQ):NOV73-47
STEINER, G. EXTRATERRITORIAL.
D. BARBOUR, 529(QQ):SUMMER72-255
H.A. BOSMAJIAN, 480(P&R):FALL72-
263
R.A. HALL, JR., 399(MLJ):NOV72-
455
H. LOMAS, 364:AUG/SEP72-144
A.H. ROSENFELD, 390:FEB72-70
STEINER, G. FIELDS OF FORCE.
C. LEHMANN-HAUPT, 441:1JUL74-27
D.K. MANO, 441:13OCT74-6
STEINER, G. IN BLUEBEARD'S CASTLE.*
D. BARBOUR, 529(QQ):SUMMER72-255
A.H. ROSENFELD, 390:FEB72-70
639(VQR):SPRING72-LII
STEINER, G. THE SPORTING SCENE.*
A. DICKINS, 364:AUG/SEP73-158
STEINER, G. - SEE FORSTER, G.
STEINER, J. DIE BÜHNENANWEISUNG.
P.V. BRADY, 220(GL&L):JUL73-327
STEINER, N.H. A CLOSER LOOK AT
ARIEL.*
617(TLS):12APR74-391
639(VQR):SUMMER73-CXX
STEINER, R. LE CHRISTIANISME ET LES
MYSTÈRES DE L'ANTIQUITÉ.
M. ADAM, 542:JAN-MAR72-65
STEINER, Z.S. THE FOREIGN OFFICE &
FOREIGN POLICY, 1898-1914.*
J.W. CELL, 637(VS):JUN72-481
STEINFELS, M.O. WHO'S MINDING THE
CHILDREN?
J. DASH, 441:21APR74-6
STEINHARDT, A. THUNDER LA BOOM.
J. SUSSMAN, 441:21APR74-39

STEINHOFF, H-H. BIBLIOGRAPHIE ZU
GOTTFRIED VON STRASSBURG.
W.T.H. JACKSON, 222(GR):NOV72-
310
J.W. MARCHAND, 301(JEGP):APR73-
262
STEINITZ, R., WITH E. LANG. ADVERB-
IAL-SYNTAX.*
R.R.K. HARTMANN, 353:MAY72-96
E. KOTTKE, 206:JAN73-422
STEINITZ, W. DIALEKTOLOGISCHES UND
ETYMOLOGISCHES WÖRTERBUCH DER OST-
JAKISCHEN SPRACHE.
G. GANSCHOW, 260(IF):BAND76-365
W. VEENKER, 343:BAND15HEFT1-32
STEINITZ, W. GESCHICHTE DES FINN-
ISCH-UGRISCHEN VOKALISMUS. (2ND
ED)
W. VEENKER, 343:BAND14HEFT2-207
STEINKRAUS, W.E., ED. NEW STUDIES
IN HEGEL'S PHILOSOPHY.
G. DI GIOVANNI, 154:MAR72-133
W.V. DONIELA, 63:AUG73-176
H.S. HARRIS, 484(PPR):DEC72-278
STEINMANN, A. & D.J. FOX. THE MALE
DILEMMA.
R. TODD, 61:NOV74-104
STEINMETZ, H., ED. LESSING - EIN
UNPOETISCHER DICHTER.*
H.B. GARLAND, 220(GL&L):OCT72-86
STEINWACHS, G. MYTHOLOGIE DES SUR-
REALISMUS ODER DIE RÜCKVERWANDLUNG
VON KULTUR IN NATUR.
J. THOMAS, 209(FM):JUL72-257
STEINWENTER, A. DIE STREITBEENDI-
GUNG DURCH URTEIL, SCHIEDSSPRUCH
UND VERGLEICH NACH GRIECHISCHEM
RECHTE.
D.M. MAC DOWELL, 123:DEC73-282
STELAND, D., ED. FRANZÖSISCHE LIT-
ERATUR. (VOLS 5&6)
M. LENTZEN, 72:BAND210HEFT4/6-
468
STELAND-STIEF, A.C. JAN ASSELIJN.
M. ROETHLISBERGER, 54:DEC72-553
STEMBER, S. THE BICENTENNIAL GUIDE
TO THE AMERICAN REVOLUTION.
A. WHITMAN, 441:20AUG74-39
STENDHAL. THE LIVES OF HAYDN, MOZ-
ART & METASTASIO BY STENDHAL
(1814).* LIFE OF ROSSINI. (R.N.
COE, ED & TRANS OF BOTH)
M.J.P. MATZ, 415:APR73-381
STENDHAL. LE ROUGE ET LE NOIR.
R. KEMPF, 98:OCT72-827
STENDHAL. LE ROUGE ET LE NOIR.*
(C. RENARD, ED)
J.L. SHEPHERD, 3D, 207(FR):FEB72-
767
STENDHAL. VOYAGES EN ITALIE. (V.
DEL LITTO, ED)
617(TLS):7JUN74-615
STENERSON, D.C. H.L. MENCKEN.*
C. BODE, 27(AL):MAR73-123
639(VQR):WINTER72-VIII
STENTEN, M. BABY.
617(TLS):2AUG74-839
STENTON, F.M. ANGLO-SAXON ENGLAND.
(3RD ED)
A.G. DYSON, 325:APR72-439
STENZEL, J. - SEE VON KLEIST, E.C.
STEPAN, A., ED. AUTHORITARIAN BRA-
ZIL.
617(TLS):8MAR74-242

STEPAN, A. THE MILITARY IN POLITICS.
639(VQR):SPRING72-LXXIII
STEPHAN, J.J. SAKHALIN.*
G.A. LENSEN, 293(JAST):NOV71-206
F. MC NEIL, 550(RUSR):JUL72-320
STEPHENS, A. RAINER MARIA RILKES
"GEDICHTE AN DIE NACHT."*
D. JOST, 182:VOL25#1/2-44
G.L. TRACY, 406:SUMMER73-188
STEPHENS, D., ED. WRITERS OF THE
PRAIRIES.
E. THOMPSON, 296:VOL3#3-98
STEPHENS, E.M. MY UNCLE JOHN. (A.
CARPENTER, ED)
617(TLS):20SEP74-1021
STEPHENS, M. THE QUESTION OF FLAN-
NERY O'CONNOR.
M.J. FRIEDMAN, 578:SPRING74-124
STEPHENS, R. THE ARABS' NEW FRON-
TIER.
617(TLS):11JAN74-34
STEPHENS, R.O. HEMINGWAY'S NONFIC-
TION.
B. ROUSE, 599:SPRING72-207
A. STEAD, 447(N&Q):FEB72-77
STEPHENSON, G. RUSSIA FROM 1812 TO
1945.*
M. KATZ, 104:SPRING72-154
STERN, F. THE FAILURE OF ILLIBERAL-
ISM.
M. JAY, 390:OCT72-72
STERN, G., G. MERKEL & J. GLENN -
SEE "LESSING YEARBOOK"
STERN, H.H., ED. LANGUAGES & THE
YOUNG SCHOOL CHILD.
M. PELZ, 430(NS):JUL72-431
STERN, J. BIBLE ET TRADITION CHEZ
NEWMAN.
J. GIBERT, 189(EA):OCT-DEC72-571
STERN, J.P. IDYLLS & REALITIES.*
M.B. BENN, 402(MLR):OCT73-948
D. JOST, 182:VOL25#3/4-92
205(FMLS):JUL72-290
STERN, M.H., COMP. AMERICANS OF
JEWISH DESCENT.
S.M. DUBOW, 14:APR72-225
STERN, R. AMERICAN ARCHITECTURE.
R. BANHAM, 54:DEC72-565
STERN, R. THE BOOKS IN FRED HAMP-
TON'S APARTMENT.*
617(TLS):5JUL74-707
STERN, R. OTHER MEN'S DAUGHTERS.*
J. MELLORS, 362:16MAY74-641
617(TLS):10MAY74-493
STERN, R.A.M. NEW DIRECTIONS IN
AMERICAN ARCHITECTURE.*
G.E. KIDDER SMITH, 576:MAR72-70
STERN, S. DER PREUSSISCHE STAAT UND
DIE JUDEN. (PT 3)
H.F. YOUNG, 182:VOL25#12-442
STERNBERGER, D. HEINRICH HEINE UND
DIE ABSCHAFFUNG DER SÜNDE.
617(TLS):25JAN74-65
STERNFELD, F.W., ED. A HISTORY OF
WESTERN MUSIC.* (VOL 5)
P. GRIFFITHS, 415:DEC73-1236
A.W., 410(M&L):OCT73-494
STERNFELD, F.W., ED. MUSIC FROM THE
MIDDLE AGES TO THE RENAISSANCE.
617(TLS):22MAR74-298
STERNFELD, W. & E. TIEDEMANN, EDS.
DEUTSCHE EXILLITERATUR 1933-1945.
(2ND ED)
H.F. PFANNER, 221(GQ):NOV72-775
[CONTINUED]

STERNFELD, W. & E. TIEDEMANN, EDS.
DEUTSCHE EXILLITERATUR 1933-1945.
(2ND ED) [CONTINUING]
  T.J. REED, 617(TLS):25OCT74-1199
  H. SAUTER, 52:BAND7HEFT2/3-308
STERNLICHT, S. JOHN WEBSTER'S IMA-
GERY & THE WEBSTER CANON. [TOGETH-
ER WITH] DE SILVA, D. WIT & THE
MORAL SENSE IN "VOLPONE" & THE
MAJOR COMEDIES.
  M. PFISTER, 72:BAND210HEFT4/6-
  382
STEVENS, G. SPEAK FOR YOURSELF,
JOHN.
  E. WEEKS, 61:JUN74-110
STEVENS, J. - SEE CHAMIER, G.
STEVENS, J.O. AWARENESS.
  R. WANDERER, 186(ETC.):DEC72-439
STEVENS, M. V. SACKVILLE-WEST.*
  B. BROPHY, 364:JUN/JUL73-138
  M. ROSENTHAL, 441:28JUL74-6
STEVENS, P. BREAD CRUSTS & GLASS.
  M. ESTOK, 150(DR):WINTER72/73-
  653
STEVENS, R.E., ED. RESEARCH METHODS
IN LIBRARIANSHIP.
  J.R.K. KANTOR, 14:JAN72-63
STEVENS, S. RAT PACK.
  M. LEVIN, 441:29DEC74-20
STEVENS, S.K., D.H. KENT & A.L.
LEONARD - SEE BOUQUET, H.
STEVENS, W. THE PALM AT THE END OF
THE MIND.* (H. STEVENS, ED)
  H. DAWSON, 301(JEGP):JUL73-463
STEVENS, W.B. COLLECTED POEMS OF
THE REVEREND WILLIAM BAGSHAW STEV-
ENS. (G. GALBRAITH, ED)
  P. MARAMBAUD, 189(EA):OCT-DEC72-
  566
STEVENS, W.B. A HISTORY OF GEORGIA.
  K. COLEMAN, 219(GAR):FALL72-401
STEVENSON, A. TRAVELLING BEHIND
GLASS. CORRESPONDENCES.
  S. CONN, 362:28NOV74-717
  617(TLS):19JUL74-762
STEVENSON, A.E. THE PAPERS OF ADLAI
E. STEVENSON. (VOL 1) (W. JOHNSON
& C. EVANS, EDS)
  W.C. HAVARD, 639(VQR):SPRING73-
  283
STEVENSON, C.H. THE SPANISH LANGU-
AGE TODAY.*
  E.P. HAMP, 269(IJAL):JAN72-79
STEVENSON, D. THE SCOTTISH REVOLU-
TION 1637-1644.
  617(TLS):8MAR74-234
STEVENSON, D.E. MRS. TIM FLIES HOME.
  M. LEVIN, 441:22DEC74-14
STEVENSON, L. THE PRE-RAPHAELITE
POETS.*
  639(VQR):SPRING73-LXXII
STEVENSON, L. SEVEN THEORIES OF
HUMAN NATURE.
  617(TLS):22NOV74-1310
STEVICK, P., ED. ANTI-STORY.*
  J.R. FRAKES, 573(SSF):FALL72-420
STEWART, C.W. THE LIFE OF BRIGADIER
GENERAL WILLIAM WOODFORD OF THE
AMERICAN REVOLUTION.
  639(VQR):AUTUMN73-CLVII
STEWART, G. & G. RAWLYK. A PEOPLE
HIGHLY FAVOURED OF GOD.
  J.M. BUMSTED, 529(QQ):WINTER72-
  556   [CONTINUED]

[CONTINUING]
  G.S. FRENCH, 656(WMQ):JUL73-524
STEWART, G.R. AMERICAN PLACE-NAMES.*
  F.G. CASSIDY, 424:JUN72-141
STEWART, J.I.M. THE GAUDY.
  617(TLS):25OCT74-1206
STEWART, J.I.M. THOMAS HARDY.*
  P. DICKINSON, 364:AUG/SEP72-149
  J. GINDIN, 639(VQR):WINTER72-152
  N. PAGE, 177(ELT):VOL15#2-175
  R.O. PREYER, 637(VS):JUN72-499
STEWART, J.I.M. SHAKESPEARE'S LOFTY
SCENE.
  K. MUIR, 447(N&Q):APR72-157
STEWART, P.R. IMITATION & ILLUSION
IN THE FRENCH MEMOIR-NOVEL, 1700-
1750.*
  R. DÉMORIS, 535(RHL):MAY-JUN72-
  516
  N. SUCKLING, 447(N&Q):JUN72-231
STEWART, R. THE APPARITION.*
  617(TLS):23AUG74-911
STEWART, R. BETHUNE.
  M. HORN, 99:SEP74-44
STEWART, W. HARD TO SWALLOW.
  J. ARMSTRONG, 99:NOV/DEC74-59
STICCA, S. THE LATIN PASSION PLAY.
  C. WITKE, 545(RPH):NOV72-459
STICHEL, R. STUDIEN ZUM VERHÄLTNIS
VON TEXT UND BILD SPÄT- UND NACH-
BYZANTINSICHER VERGÄNGLICHKEITS-
DARSTELLUNGEN.
  A. CUTLER, 589:OCT73-793
STICKLAND, I., ED. THE VOICES OF
CHILDREN 1700-1914.
  617(TLS):5APR74-376
STICKNEY, J.T. THE POEMS OF TRUM-
BULL STICKNEY. (A.R. WHITTLE, ED)
  639(VQR):WINTER73-X
STIEHL, U. EINFÜHRUNG IN DIE ALLGE-
MEINE SEMANTIK.
  C.V.J. RUSS, 402(MLR):OCT73-922
STIEHLER, G. DER IDEALISMUS VON
KANT BIS HEGEL.
  W. TEICHNER, 342:BAND63HEFT4-512
STILLINGER, J. THE HOODWINKING OF
MADELINE & OTHER ESSAYS ON KEATS'S
POEMS.
  M. ALLOTT, 677:VOL3-314
  S.M.S., 191(ELN):SEP72(SUPP)-54
STILLWELL, M.B. THE AWAKENING INTER-
EST IN SCIENCE DURING THE FIRST
CENTURY OF PRINTING 1450-1550.*
  M.B. HALL, 551(RENQ):SPRING72-75
STILLWELL, M.B. THE BEGINNING OF
THE WORLD OF BOOKS 1450 TO 1470.
  H. LEHMANN-HAUPT, 517(PBSA):JUL-
  SEP73-349
STIMPSON, C.R. J.R.R. TOLKIEN.*
  K. DUNCAN-JONES, 447(N&Q):SEP72-
  353
STIMSON, F.S. & R. NAVAS-RUIZ, EDS.
LITERATURA DE LA AMÉRICA HISPÁNICA.
  J.L. WALKER, 238:MAY72-397
STITES, R., WITH M.E. STITES & P.
CASTIGLIONE. THE SUBLIMATIONS OF
LEONARDO DA VINCI.
  H. WOHL, 127:WINTER72/73-246
STOBIE, M.R. FREDERICK PHILIP GROVE.
  L. MC MULLEN, 296:VOL3#2-98
STOCKENSTRÖM, G. ISMAEL I ÖKNEN.
  W. JOHNSON, 563(SS):SUMMER73-271
STOCKHAMMER, M. KANT DICTIONARY.
  V. ZEMAN, 342:BAND63HEFT3-392

STOCKHAMMER, M. PHILOSOPHISCH-
LITERARISCHE STUDIEN.
 K. OEDINGEN, 342:BAND63HEFT2-276
STOCKTON, D. CICERO.*
 J. HELLEGOUARC'H, 555:VOL46FASC2-
 343
STOJANOVIĆ, S. BETWEEN IDEALS &
REALITY.
 617(TLS):11JAN74-26
STOKER, J.T. - SEE MOLIÈRE, J.B.P.
STOKES, A. THE IMAGE IN FORM. (R.
WOLLHEIM, ED)
 J. GOLDING, 453:21MAR74-38
STOKES, M.C. ONE & MANY IN PRESOC-
RATIC PHILOSOPHY.*
 G. ANAGNOSTOPOULOS, 319:APR74-
 248
 G.B. KERFERD, 487:WINTER72-400
 C. MUGLER, 555:VOL46FASC2-292
STOKES, T. CRIMES OF PASSION.*
 W.H. PRITCHARD, 249(HUDR):AUTUMN
 73-580
STOLOFF, C. DYING TO SURVIVE.
 D. BLAZEK, 491:JUN74-167
 J.J. MC GANN, 385(MQR):FALL74-
 416
STOLOFF, C. STEPPING OUT.*
 B. HAMLIN, 448:SPRING72-97
STOLT, B. STUDIEN ZU LUTHERS FREI-
HEITSTRAKTAT.
 J. ERBEN, 680(ZDP):BAND91HEFT3-
 472
STOLTZ, J. TERRELL, TEXAS, 1873-
1973.
 W. GARD, 584(SWR):SUMMER73-272
STOLTZFUS, B. GIDE'S EAGLES.
 C.S. BROSMAN, 546(RR):FEB72-67
STOLZ, H., A. HERRMANN & W. MÜLLER.
BEITRAGE ZUR THEORIE DER SOZIAL-
ISTISCHEN ERZIEHUNG.
 S. BIRKNER, 654(WB):10/1972-182
STÖLZL, C. DIE ÄRA BACH IN BÖHMEN.
 S.Z. PECH, 32:DEC73-835
STONE, D., JR. FRANCE IN THE SIX-
TEENTH CENTURY - A MEDIEVAL SOCI-
ETY TRANSFORMED.
 I.D. MC FARLANE, 208(FS):JAN73-
 50
STONE, D.D. NOVELISTS IN A CHANGING
WORLD.
 R.B. HENKLE, 637(VS):DEC72-256
 L. STEVENSON, 445(NCF):SEP72-222
STONE, G. DARLING, I AM GROWING OLD.
 M. LEVIN, 441:12MAY74-14
STONE, G. THE SMALLEST SLAVONIC
NATION.*
 R. AUTY, 575(SEER):APR73-294
STONE, H. WORKBOOK OF AN UNSUCCESS-
FUL ARCHITECT.
 P. GOLDBERGER, 441:7JUL74-5
 617(TLS):15MAR74-272
STONE, M.E., ED & TRANS. THE TESTA-
MENT OF LEVI.
 S.P. BROCK, 318(JAOS):APR-JUN72-
 382
STONE, R. DOG SOLDIERS.
 C. LEHMANN-HAUPT, 441:31OCT74-45
 R. LOCKE, 441:3NOV74-1
 442(NY):16DEC74-166
STONE, R.K. MIDDLE ENGLISH PROSE
STYLE.
 P.J.C. FIELD, 589:JAN73-182
 R.M. WILSON, 382(MAE):1973/2-183

STONEHOUSE, B. ANIMALS OF THE ARC-
TIC.
 T.J. LYON, 649(WAL):FALL72-233
STONES, E.L.G., ED & TRANS. ANGLO-
SCOTTISH RELATIONS 1174-1328.
 J.R. SEWELL, 325:OCT72-539
STONEY, B. ENID BLYTON.
 R. DINNAGE, 617(TLS):27SEP74-
 1034
 W. FEAVER, 362:26SEP74-414
STORER, M.E. UN ÉPISODE LITTÉRAIRE
DE LA FIN DU XVIIE SIÈCLE.
 A. RAU, 78(BC):WINTER72-570
STORER, N.W. - SEE MERTON, R.K.
STOREY, D. PASMORE.
 P. BAILEY, 364:FEB/MAR73-157
 P. THEROUX, 441:17MAR74-40
 442:25MAR74-141
STOREY, D. A TEMPORARY LIFE.*
 A. BROYARD, 441:13AUG74-29
 M. LEVIN, 441:22SEP74-40
 J. MELLORS, 364:DEC73/JAN74-155
STOREY, W.G. THE "DE QUATUOR VIRTU-
TIBUS CARDINALIBUS PRO ERUDITIONE
PRINCIPUM" OF MICHAEL THE CARTHUS-
IAN OF PRAGUE.
 G. CONSTABLE, 589:JUL73-545
STORK, F.C. & J.D.A. WIDDOWSON.
LEARNING ABOUT LINGUISTICS.
 617(TLS):9AUG74-853
STORM, H. SEVEN ARROWS.*
 639(VQR):WINTER73-IX
STORM, T. & P. HEYSE. BRIEFWECHSEL.*
(VOL 2) (C.A. BERND, ED)
 A.F. GOESSL, 406:FALL73-318
 W. SCHUMANN, 221(GQ):MAR72-375
 J.W. SMEED, 220(GL&L):APR73-274
STORRER, W.A. THE ARCHITECTURE OF
FRANK LLOYD WRIGHT.
 617(TLS):23AUG74-899
STORY, J.T. CRYING MAKES YOUR NOSE
RUN.
 617(TLS):12APR74-396
STORZ, G. HEINRICH HEINES LYRISCHE
DICHTUNG.*
 J.L.S., 191(ELN):SEP72(SUPP)-154
STOTT, W. DOCUMENTARY EXPRESSION &
THIRTIES AMERICA.
 H. KRAMER, 441:20JAN74-4
 M. ORVELL, 31(ASCH):AUTUMN74-671
 617(TLS):14JUN74-635
STÖTZEL, G. AUSDRUCKSSEITE UND IN-
HALTSSEITE DER SPRACHE.
 K. BRINKER, 343:BAND15HEFT2-122
STOUT, J.A., JR. APACHE LIGHTNING.
 P. ADAMS, 61:NOV74-124
STOUT, R. PLEASE PASS THE GUILT.*
 617(TLS):30AUG74-933
STOUT, R. TOO MANY COOKS.
 N. CALLENDAR, 441:10FEB74-31
STOUTAMIRE, A. MUSIC OF THE OLD
SOUTH.
 G.W. WILLIAMS, 579(SAQ):WINTER73-
 163
STRACHEY, L. ERMYNTRUDE & ESMERALDA.
 G. MERLE, 189(EA):JAN-MAR73-157
STRACHEY, L. LYTTON STRACHEY BY HIM-
SELF. (M. HOLROYD, ED)
 G. MERLE, 189(EA):JAN-MAR72-175
STRAIN, J., ED. THE CONTRIBUTION OF
ANCIENT GREECE.
 D.R. JONES, 255(HAB):WINTER72-47

STRAINCHAMPS, E., ED. ROOMS WITH NO
VIEW.
L. SHERR, 441:24NOV74-34
STRAND, J. NOTES ON VALERIUS FLAC-
CUS' ARGONAUTICA.
F. LASSERRE, 182:VOL25#1/2-49
STRAND, M., ED. NEW POETRY OF MEXI-
CO.
C. TOMLINSON, 364:OCT/NOV72-125
STRAND, M. THE STORY OF OUR LIVES.*
L. LIEBERMAN, 491:AUG74-280
617(TLS):29MAR74-339
STRAND, M. - SEE ALBERTI, R.
"PAUL STRAND."
S. SONTAG, 453:28NOV74-35
STRANG, B.M.H. A HISTORY OF ENG-
LISH.*
A. BRUTEN, 541(RES):FEB72-62
J.C. MC LAUGHLIN, 297(JL):SEP72-
301
A. RYNELL, 597(SN):VOL44#1-180
A.R. TELLIER, 189(EA):JUL-SEP72-
432
STRANGE, A. ELECTRONIC MUSIC.
T. WELLS, 308:VOL15#1/2-274
STRASSER, S. THE IDEA OF DIALOGAL
PHENOMENOLOGY.
M.M. VAN DE PITTE, 154:SEP72-452
STRATFORD, J. THE ARTS COUNCIL COL-
LECTION OF MODERN LITERARY MANU-
SCRIPTS 1963-1972.
617(TLS):6SEP74-958
STRATFORD, P. - SEE "ANDRÉ LAUREN-
DEAU"
STRATHERN, A. & M. SELF-DECORATION
IN MOUNT HAGAN.
H. GLASSIE, 292(JAF):APR-JUN72-
202
T. HÅKANSSON, 592:MAR72-136
STRATMAN, C.J., D.G. SPENCER & M.E.
DEVINE, EDS. RESTORATION & EIGHT-
EENTH CENTURY THEATRE RESEARCH.
H.H. CAMPBELL, 517(PBSA):APR-
JUN73-200
G. MARSHALL, 568(SCN):SPRING73-
18
STRAUCH, D., ED. DAS OSTGÖTENRECHT
(ÖSTGÖTALAGEN).
G.W. WEBER, 182:VOL25#1/2-24
STRAUS, D. SHOWCASES.
H. BEVINGTON, 441:13OCT74-30
STRAUS, E.W., M. NATANSON & H. EY.
PSYCHIATRY & PHILOSOPHY.* (M.
NATANSON, ED)
A. HANNAY, 262:SUMMER72-208
P. SELIGMAN, 486:MAR72-99
STRAUS, R. ESCAPE FROM CUSTODY.
J. MC ELROY, 441:31MAR74-4
STRAUSS, L. XENOPHON'S SOCRATES.
C. MOULTON, 676(YR):AUTUMN72-127
H. NEUMANN, 319:APR74-252
STRAUSS, W.A. DESCENT & RETURN.*
J.C. IRESON, 402(MLR):OCT73-902
F.M. WEINBERG, 188(ECR):FALL72-
236
639(VQR):SUMMER72-CIV
STRAVINSKY, I. POETICS OF MUSIC.*
617(TLS):18OCT74-1171
STRAVINSKY, I. I.F. STRAVINSKIJ:
STAT'I I MATERIALY. (L.S. D'YACH-
KOVA, COMP; B.M. YARUSTOVSKY, ED)
F. STRAVINSKIJ: STAT'I, PIS'MA,
VOSPOMINANIJA. (L. KUTATELADZE,
[CONTINUED]

[CONTINUING]
COMP; A. GOZENPUD, ED)
R. CRAFT, 453:21FEB74-15
STRAVINSKY, I. THEMES & CONCLUSIONS.
J.A.W., 410(M&L):JAN73-83
STRAVINSKY, T. CATHERINE & IGOR
STRAVINSKY.*
J. NOBLE, 415:JUL73-700
STRAWSON, J. THE BATTLE FOR BERLIN.
617(TLS):4OCT74-1071
STRAWSON, P.F. THE BOUNDS OF SENSE.*
W. CERF, 393(MIND):OCT72-601
STRAWSON, P.F. FREEDOM & RESENTMENT.
L.J. COHEN, 617(TLS):28JUN74-685
STRAYER, J.R. THE ALBIGENSIAN CRU-
SADES.
F.L. CHEYETTE, 589:APR73-411
STRAYER, J.R. MEDIEVAL STATECRAFT
& THE PERSPECTIVES OF HISTORY.*
D.E. CAMPBELL, 207(FR):APR72-
1032
STRAYER, J.R. ON THE MEDIEVAL ORI-
GINS OF THE MODERN STATE.*
42(AR):VOL32#3-507
STRECH, H. THEODOR FONTANE: DIE
SYNTHESE VON ALT UND NEU.*
A.R. ROBINSON, 220(GL&L):JUL73-
318
STREET, M.M. WATCH-FIRES ON THE
MOUNTAIN.
W. MITCHINSON, 99:OCT74-41
STREET, P. ANIMAL REPRODUCTION.
617(TLS):30AUG74-936
STREETEN, P. THE FRONTIERS OF DEVEL-
OPMENT STUDIES.
617(TLS):21JUN74-662
STREETEN, P., ED. TRADE STRATEGIES
FOR DEVELOPMENT.
M. LIPTON, 617(TLS):2AUG74-830
STRELKA, J. DIE GELENKTEN MUSEN.
H.H. RUDNICK, 221(GQ):JAN72-131
K. WEISSENBERGER, 399(MLJ):NOV72-
459
STRELKA, J. VERGLEICHENDE LITERATUR-
KRITIK.*
A. CLOSS, 402(MLR):APR73-464
K. WEISSENBERGER, 52:BAND7HEFT
2/3-308
STRELKA, J., ED. YEARBOOK OF COM-
PARATIVE CRITICISM. (VOL 3)
S.L. GILMAN, 52:BAND7HEFT2/3-310
STRELKA, J. & W. HINDERER, EDS. MOD-
ERNE AMERIKANISCHE LITERATURTHEOR-
IEN.
H.D. OSTERLE, 222(GR):MAR72-147
STRICH, F. DIE MYTHOLOGIE IN DER
DEUTSCHEN LITERATUR VON KLOPSTOCK
BIS WAGNER.
B. BENNETT, 221(GQ):NOV72-684
STRICKER, D. LIEBE UND EHE. (W.W.
MOELLEKEN, ED)
C. HALL, 399(MLJ):MAY72-341
STRICKLAND, G. STENDHAL.
D. ELLIS, 362:5SEP74-316
STRICKLAND, M. THE BYRON WOMEN.
617(TLS):14JUN74-646
STRINDBERG, A. WORLD HISTORICAL
PLAYS.* (A. PAULSON, TRANS)
A.W. WONDERLEY, 222(GR):NOV72-
305
STRIZOWER, S. THE BENE ISRAEL OF
BOMBAY.
R.A. SCHERMERHORN, 293(JAST):
FEB72-436

349

STROHEKER, K.F. DER SENATORISCHE
ADEL IM SPÄTANTIKEN GALLIEN.
W.R. CHALMERS, 123:MAR73-104
STRÖMBÄCK, D., ED. LEADING FOLKLOR-
ISTS OF THE NORTH.
K.M. BRIGGS, 203:SUMMER72-162
STROMBERG, R.N. ARNOLD J. TOYNBEE.
A. TOYNBEE, 125:FEB73-171
STRONG, A.L. PLANNED URBAN ENVIRON-
MENTS.
D. DIMANCESCU, 505:FEB72-102
STRONG, R. SPLENDOUR AT COURT.
617(TLS):25JAN74-74
STRONG, R. VAN DYCK: CHARLES I ON
HORSEBACK.*
A.C. BIRNHOLZ, 290(JAAC):SUMMER
73-556
R. EDWARDS, 135:OCT72-138
A. FORGE, 592:NOV72-201
STROUD, D. GEORGE DANCE.*
J. HARRIS, 46:APR72-260
H. KALMAN, 576:MAY72-154
STROUD, J. IN THE SLEEP OF RIVERS.
T. PETROSKY, 398:WINTER74-297
STROUD, R.S. DRAKON'S LAW ON HOMI-
CIDE.*
C.W.J. ELIOT, 487:SPRING72-90
STROUSE, J., ED. WOMEN & ANALYSIS.
C. LASCH, 453:30CT74-12
E. LONG, 441:18AUG74-19
STRUEVER, N.S. THE LANGUAGE OF HIS-
TORY IN THE RENAISSANCE.*
D. WEINSTEIN, 322(JHI):JAN-MAR72-
165
STRUVE, G. RUSSIAN LITERATURE UNDER
LENIN & STALIN, 1917-1953.
E. RAIS, 550(RUSR):APR72-181
STRUVE, G. - SEE VALENTINOV, N.
STRUVE, W. DER ANDERE ZUG.
R.S., 543:MAR72-569
STRYK, L. AWAKENING.
J. PARISI, 491:SEP74-343
STRYKER, R.E. & N. WOOD. IN THIS
PROUD LAND.
H. KRAMER, 441:20JAN74-4
S. SONTAG, 453:18APR74-17
STUART, F., COMP. STORIES OF BRIT-
AIN IN SONG.
F. HOWES, 415:SEP73-903
STUART, J. COME BACK TO THE FARM.
J.R. LE MASTER, 50(ARQ):SPRING72-
91
STUART, R.C. THE COLLECTIVE FARM IN
SOVIET AGRICULTURE.
M. MC CAULEY, 575(SEER):OCT73-
619
STUART, W.B. GAMBLING MUSIC OF THE
COAST SALISH INDIANS.
M.I. ASCH, 187:JAN74-166
STUBBINGS, H.U. RENAISSANCE SPAIN
IN ITS LITERARY RELATIONS WITH
ENGLAND & FRANCE.*
C.V. AUBRUN, 240(HR):SUMMER72-
338
STUBBS, J. JOHN STUBBS'S "GAPING
GULF" WITH LETTERS & OTHER RELE-
VANT DOCUMENTS. (L.E. BERRY, ED)
B.W. BECKINGSALE, 447(N&Q):APR72-
159
STUBBS, J.C. THE PURSUIT OF FORM.*
J.H. MC ELROY, 50(ARQ):SPRING72-
89

"STUDI DI FILOLOGIA ROMANZA OFFERTI
A SILVIO PELLEGRINI."
T.G. GRIFFITH, 402(MLR):JUL73-
665
"STUDI DI STORIOGRAFIA ANTICA IN
MEMORIA DI LEONARDO FERRERO."
J-C. RICHARD, 555:VOL46FASC2-360
"STUDI LINGUISTICI IN ONORE DI VIT-
TORE PISANI."
J. GONDA, 353:10CT72-88
"STUDI MICENEI ED EGEO-ANATOLICI."
(FASC XV)
617(TLS):8MAR74-232
"STUDI SULLA DIALETTICA."
E. NAMER, 542:JAN-MAR72-69
"STUDIA ESTETYCZNE." (VOLS 5&6)
M. RIESER, 290(JAAC):WINTER71-
267
"STUDIA FRISICA: IN MEMORIAM PROF.
DR. K. FOKKEMA, 1898-1967 SCRIPTA."
E.G.A. GALAMA, 433:APR72-247
"STUDIES IN HONOR OF J. ALEXANDER
KERNS."
R. SCHMITT, 343:BAND15HEFT2-211
"STUDII CLASICE XII."
J. ANDRÉ, 555:VOL46FASC2-361
"STUDII CLASICE XIII."
A. ERNOUT, 555:VOL46FASC2-362
STUEWER, R., ED. HISTORICAL & PHIL-
OSOPHICAL PERSPECTIVES OF SCIENCE.*
R. ACKERMANN, 311(JP):18JUL74-
424
R.J.B., 543:SEP71-142
STUHLMANN, G. - SEE NIN, A.
STURDZA, I., R. VIANU & M. LĂZĂRES-
CU - SEE "FAIRY TALES & LEGENDS
FROM ROMANIA"
"STURLUNGA SAGA." (VOL 1) (J.H.
MC GREW, TRANS)
C.W. THOMPSON, 563(SS):WINTER73-
71
STURM, E. CRÉBILLON FILS ET LE
LIBERTINAGE AU XVIIIE SIÈCLE.
R. NIKLAUS, 535(RHL):MAR-APR72-
312
STURM, F. STIPULATIO AQUILIANA.
R. GANGHOFFER, 182:VOL25#23/24-
856
STURROCK, J. - SEE BUTOR, M.
STYAN, J.L. CHEKHOV IN PERFORMANCE.*
A.K. LOJKINE, 67:NOV73-329
205(FMLS):APR72-196
"STYLES IN 20TH-CENTURY PIANO
MUSIC."
M. DE VOTO, 513:FALL-WINTER69-
143
STYRON, W. IN THE CLAP SHACK.
B.H. FUSSELL, 249(HUDR):WINTER
73/74-753
I. MALIN, 578:SPRING74-151
SUÁREZ RADILLO, C.M. 13 AUTORES DEL
NUEVO TEATRO VENEZOLANO.
F. DAUSTER, 263:JUL-SEP73-345
SUBHAN, A. - SEE 'ALÎ KHÂN, Y.
SUCH, P. RIVERRUN.
E.J. DEVEREUX, 99:MAR74-38
H. PORTER, 296:VOL3#2-93
SUCKLING, J. SIR JOHN SUCKLING: THE
NON-DRAMATIC WORKS. (T. CLAYTON,
ED)
W. VON KOPPENFELS, 72:BAND210
HEFT4/6-384

SUCKLING, J. THE WORKS OF SIR JOHN
SUCKLING: THE PLAYS.* (L.A.
BEAURLINE, ED)
M. JAMIESON, 157:WINTER71-68
H. ZIMMERMANN, 72:BAND210HEFT4/6-
386
SUDHALTER, R.M. & P.R. EVANS, WITH
W. DEAN-MYATT. BIX.
J. WIDEMAN, 441:18AUG74-6
SUERBAUM, W. VOM ANTIKEN ZUM FRÜH-
MITTELALTERLICHEN STAATSBEGRIFF.
J. HELLEGOUARC'H, 555:VOL46FASC1-
167
SUGAR, P.F. & I.J. LEDERER, EDS.
NATIONALISM IN EASTERN EUROPE.
S.B. WINTERS, 497(POLR):WINTER72-
97
SUGIHARA, Y. & D.W. PLATH. SENSEI
& HIS PEOPLE.
O. CARY, 293(JAST):MAY72-686
SUGITA, G. - SEE UNDER GENPAKU SU-
GITA
SUHL, B. JEAN-PAUL SARTRE.*
J.L. CARAFIDES, 484(PPR):MAR73-
444
J. CULLER, 402(MLR):APR73-425
M. GUINEY, 399(MLJ):JAN72-61
E. MOROT-SIR, 546(RR):OCT72-242
SUKENICK, R. OUT.*
R. DE FEO, 249(HUDR):WINTER73/74-
776
E. ROVIT, 659:AUTUMN74-539
R. SALE, 418(MR):AUTUMN73-834
42(AR):VOL32#4-698
SULIMIRSKI, T. PREHISTORIC RUSSIA.
I. BOBA, 550(RUSR):OCT72-422
SULLIVAN, A.M. SELECTED LYRICS &
SONNETS.
M.E. MICHAEL, 590:SPRING/SUMMER
73-25
SULLIVAN, J., ED. G.K. CHESTERTON.
D.A.N. JONES, 362:25APR74-538
617(TLS):17MAY74-518
SULLIVAN, J. MAMA DOESN'T LIVE HERE
ANYMORE.
A. BROYARD, 441:4JUN74-41
SULLIVAN, J. - SEE CHESTERTON, G.K.
SULLIVAN, M. THE CAVE TEMPLES OF
MAICHISHAN.
N.T. PRICE, 57:VOL34#2/3-243
SULLIVAN, M. THE MEETING OF EASTERN
& WESTERN ART.
H. TREVOR-ROPER, 362:6JUN74-736
617(TLS):26JUL74-789
SULLIVAN, M.R. BROWNING'S VOICES IN
"THE RING AND THE BOOK."*
C. DAHL, 85:SPRING72-60
SULLIVAN, R. GOODBYE LIZZIE BORDEN.
P. ADAMS, 61:AUG74-91
SULLIVAN, W. CONTINENTS IN MOTION.
S.S. ODDO, 441:3NOV74-4
SULLIVAN, W. DEATH BY MELANCHOLY.*
N.K. BURGER, 579(SAQ):AUTUMN73-
613
SULLOWAY, A.G. GERARD MANLEY HOP-
KINS & THE VICTORIAN TEMPER.*
N. WHITE, 637(VS):JUN73-470
SULZBERGER, C.L. AN AGE OF MEDIOC-
RITY.*
J. EAYRS, 99:FEB74-39
SULZBERGER, C.L. THE COLDEST WAR.
C. JOHNSON, 441:18AUG74-14

SUMAROKOV, A.P. SELECTED TRAGEDIES
OF A.P. SUMAROKOV. (R. & R. FOR-
TUNE, TRANS)
A. DONSKOV, 104:SUMMER72-326
SUMMERFIELD, G., ED. WORLDS.
E. WELSH, 617(TLS):15NOV74-1290
SUMMERS, D. THE GREAT OUSE.
617(TLS):15MAR74-260
SUMMERS, H. START FROM HOME.
639(VQR):WINTER73-XIII
SUMMERS, J.H. THE HEIRS OF DONNE &
JONSON.*
R. FREEMAN, 541(RES):FEB72-70
P. LEGOUIS, 189(EA):JAN-MAR72-
163
SUMMERSON, J., ED. CONCERNING ARCHI-
TECTURE.*
S. OMOTO, 290(JAAC):WINTER71-266
SUMMERSON, J. THE LONDON BUILDING
WORLD OF THE EIGHTEEN-SIXTIES.
617(TLS):15MAR74-250
SUMMERSON, J. VICTORIAN ARCHITEC-
TURE.*
J. LEES-MILNE, 39:SEP72-254
J.F. O'GORMAN, 54:SEP72-366
SUMNER, W.L. THE ORGAN. (4TH ED)
P. WILLIAMS, 415:NOV73-1125
SUMNER-BOYD, H. & J. FREELY. STROL-
LING THROUGH ISTANBUL.
617(TLS):24MAY74-562
SUMPF, J. INTRODUCTION À LA STYLIS-
TIQUE DU FRANÇAIS.
J-M. KLINKENBERG, 209(FM):JUL72-
255
SUNDARAM, K. THE SIMHACHALAM TEM-
PLE.*
D.M. SPENCER, 318(JAOS):APR-JUN
72-322
SUNDBY, B. FRONT-SHIFTED "ING" &
"ED" GROUPS IN PRESENT DAY ENGLISH.
F.R. PALMER, 597(SN):VOL44#1-204
SUNDERLAND, J. CONSTABLE.
E. YOUNG, 39:AUG72-167
SUNY, R.G. THE BAKU COMMUNE 1917-
1918.*
A. WILDMAN, 550(RUSR):OCT72-413
SUPER, R.H. THE TIME-SPIRIT OF
MATTHEW ARNOLD.*
J.E. FREY, 637(VS):JUN72-494
SUPER, R.H. - SEE ARNOLD, M.
SUPPES, P. A PROBABILISTIC THEORY
OF CAUSALITY.
A.C. MICHALOS, 486:DEC72-560
SUPPES, P. STUDIES IN THE METHODOL-
OGY & FOUNDATIONS OF SERVICE.
H.D. LEVIN, 311(JP):28FEB74-112
"A SUPPLEMENT TO THE OXFORD ENGLISH
DICTIONARY."* (VOL 1) (R.W. BURCH-
FIELD, ED)
F.C. ROBINSON, 676(YR):SPRING73-
450
J.S. RYAN, 67:MAY73-167
639(VQR):WINTER73-XL
SURREY, S.S. PATHWAYS TO TAX REFORM.
B.I. BITTKER, 441:6JAN74-4
SURTEES, V. THE PAINTINGS & DRAW-
INGS OF DANTE GABRIEL ROSSETTI
(1828-1882).*
G. REYNOLDS, 39:JAN72-70
"'SUSANNAH,' AN ALLITERATIVE POEM OF
THE FOURTEENTH CENTURY."* (A.
MISKIMIN, ED)
H. BERGNER, 38:BAND90HEFT1/2-224
J.R. SIMON, 189(EA):JAN-MAR72-83

SUSINI, E. - SEE SILESIUS, A.
SUSINI, G. THE ROMAN STONECUTTER.
617(TLS):22FEB74-193
SUSSMAN, B. THE GREAT COVER-UP.
A. COCKBURN, 453:28NOV74-8
B. HUME, 441:8DEC74-5
SUTCLIFFE, A., ED. MULTI-STOREY
LIVING.
J. NAUGHTON, 617(TLS):23AUG74-
908
SUTER, R., ED. THE ISENBERG MEMOR-
IAL LECTURES 1965-1966.
A.S.C., 543:MAR72-570
SUTERA, O. VOCE DALLE PIETRE.
J.V. GRECO, 399(MLJ):MAR72-181
SUTHERLAND, C.H.V. ROMAN COINS.
M. GRANT, 617(TLS):27DEC74-1467
SUTHERLAND, D. ON, ROMANTICISM.
D.V.E., 191(ELN):SEP72(SUPP)-15
481(PQ):JUL72-634
SUTHERLAND, D.W. THE ASSIZE OF
NOVEL DISSEISIN.
617(TLS):25JAN74-85
SUTHERLAND, G. POLICY-MAKING IN ELE-
MENTARY EDUCATION 1870-1895.
617(TLS):1FEB74-98
SUTHERLAND, J. DANIEL DEFOE.*
M.G. MC CLUNG, 529(QQ):SPRING72-
114
M.E. NOVAK, 481(PQ):JUL72-665
SUTHERLAND, J. OXFORD HISTORY OF
ENGLISH LITERATURE.* (VOL 6: ENG-
LISH LITERATURE OF THE LATE SEVEN-
TEENTH CENTURY.)
P. DIXON, 447(N&Q):MAY72-195
E. SPÄTH, 38:BAND90HEFT1/2-235
SUTHERLAND, R. LARK DES NEIGES.
F. DAVIS, 150(DR):SUMMER72-329
SUTHERLAND, R. SECOND IMAGE.*
G.V. DOWNES, 376:APR72-123
SUTTON, A.C. WESTERN TECHNOLOGY &
SOVIET ECONOMIC DEVELOPMENT, 1917-
1930.
R.A. FFRENCH, 104:SPRING72-178
SUTTON, A.C. WESTERN TECHNOLOGY &
SOVIET ECONOMIC DEVELOPMENT 1930-
1945.*
V.G. TREML, 550(RUSR):JAN72-79
SUTTON, C. THE GERMAN TRADITION IN
PHILOSOPHY.
617(TLS):19APR74-412
SUTTON, D. - SEE FRY, R.
SUTTON, S.B. - SEE OLMSTED, F.L.
SUTTON, W. AMERICAN FREE VERSE.
J.C. DE VANY, 590:FALL/WINTER
73/74-42
SUTTON, W.A. THE ROAD TO WINESBURG.
G.T. TANSELLE, 27(AL):MAR73-126
SUŽIEDĖLIS, S., ED. ENCYCLOPEDIA
LITUANICA. (VOL 2)
G.B. FORD, JR., 575(SEER):JUL73-
493
SUZUKI, P.T. SOCIAL CHANGE IN TUR-
KEY SINCE 1950.
K.H. KARPAT, 318(JAOS):APR-JUN72-
374
SVAGLIC, M.J. - SEE NEWMAN, J.H.
SVEINSSON, E.Ó. NJÁLS SAGA.* (P.
SCHACH, ED & TRANS)
R.R., 502(PRS):FALL72-275
J. WILSON, 563(SS):WINTER73-67

SVENNEVIG, P. DANSKE KOMMISSIONS-
BETAENKNINGER, 1850-1970.
J.B. CHILDS, 517(PBSA):OCT-DEC73-
481
SWADOS, H. STANDING FAST.*
R. BROWN, 448:FALL72-82
SWAIN, J.O. JUAN MARÍN - CHILEAN.*
H. CASTILLO, 238:DEC72-974
SWALES, M. ARTHUR SCHNITZLER.*
F.J. BEHARRIELL, 301(JEGP):JUL73-
424
A. BURKHARD, 400(MLN):OCT72-799
SWAN, A.J. RUSSIAN MUSIC & ITS
SOURCES IN CHANT & FOLK-SONG.*
D. BROWN, 415:OCT73-1011
E.G., 410(M&L):OCT73-471
SWAN, B.F. THE SPREAD OF PRINTING
OUTSIDE EUROPE: THE CARIBBEAN AREA.
R. CAVE, 503:SUMMER72-110
SWAN, N. & D. WILTON, EDS. INFLA-
TION & THE CANADIAN EXPERIENCE.
R.C. MC IVOR, 529(QQ):SPRING72-
110
SWANBERG, W.A. LUCE & HIS EMPIRE.
639(VQR):WINTER73-XXIX
SWANN, B. & R. FELDMAN - SEE PICCOLO,
L.
SWANN, T.B. HOW THE MIGHTY ARE
FALLEN.
T. STURGEON, 441:8SEP74-39
SWANSON, D.C. A CHARACTERIZATION OF
THE ROMAN POETIC ONOMASTICON.
E.C. SMITH, 424:JUN72-149
SWANSON, D.R. THREE CONQUERORS.*
I. WILLIAMS, 637(VS):SEP72-113
SWANTON, M., ED. THE DREAM OF THE
ROOD.*
H. PILCH, 38:BAND90HEFT4-518
SWANTZ, M-L. RITUAL & SYMBOL IN TRA-
DITIONAL ZARAMO SOCIETY WITH SPEC-
IAL REFERENCE TO WOMEN.
T.O. BEIDELMAN, 69:OCT72-356
SWARNEY, P.R. THE PTOLEMAIC & ROMAN
IDIOS LOGOS.
A.K. BOWMAN, 487:WINTER72-415
SWEDENBERG, H.T., JR., ED. ENGLAND
IN THE RESTORATION & EARLY EIGHT-
EENTH CENTURY.
T.H. FUJIMURA, 125:JUN73-317
J.P. HUNTER, 566:AUTUMN72-36
568(SCN):FALL-WINTER73-96
SWEDENBERG, H.T., JR. - SEE DRYDEN,
J.
SWEE-HOCK, S. - SEE UNDER SAW SWEE-
HOCK
SWEENEY, C. BACKGROUND OF BAOBABS.
617(TLS):3MAY74-482
SWEENEY, J.J. SOULAGES.
617(TLS):4JAN74-16
SWEETMAN, D. PICASSO.
617(TLS):11JAN74-24
SWEETMAN, R. FATHERS COME FIRST.
617(TLS):18OCT74-1155
SWEETMAN, R. ON OUR KNEES.
P. HARDING, 159(DM):SUMMER72-132
SWEEZY, P.M. & H. MAGDOFF, EDS.
LENIN TODAY.
T. DEUTSCHER, 104:SPRING72-163
SWENSON, M., WITH L. SJÖBERG - SEE
TRANSTRÖMER, T.
SWERLING, A., ED. IN QUEST OF
STRINDBERG.
W. JOHNSON, 397(MD):DEC72-334

SWERLING, A. STRINDBERG'S IMPACT IN
FRANCE 1920-1960.
W. HOGENDOORN, 204(FDL):SEP72-
188
B.G. MADSEN, 563(SS):AUTUMN73-
401
205(FMLS):JUL72-290
ŚWIECHOWSKA, A. - SEE ZACHWATOWICZ,
J. & OTHERS
SWIFT, J. SWIFT'S "MISCELLANIES IN
PROSE & VERSE" (1711).
566:SPRING73-108
SWIGG, R. LAWRENCE, HARDY, & AMERI-
CAN LITERATURE.
G.A. PANICHAS, 149:SEP73-274
R.C. STEPHENS, 402(MLR):JUL73-
646
SWINBURNE, A.C. POEMS & BALLADS &
ATALANTA IN CALYDON. (M. PECKHAM,
ED)
L. ORMOND, 677:VOL3-321
J.F. STASNY, 399(MLJ):MAR72-178
SWINBURNE, A.C. SWINBURNE AS CRITIC.
(C.K. HYDER, ED)
C. DAHL, 637(VS):JUN73-480
SWINBURNE, R. THE CONCEPT OF MIR-
ACLE.*
G. SLATER, 479(PHQ):JAN72-89
SWING, T.K. KANT'S TRANSCENDENTAL
LOGIC.*
L. FUNDERBURK, 342:BAND63HEFT3-
389
SWINNERTON, F. ROSALIND PASSES.
442(NY):22APR74-153
SWINTON, G. SCULPTURE OF THE ESKIMO.
R.M. HUME, 99:JAN74-43
SWOBODA, K.M., ED. GOTIK IN BÖHMEN.
M.S. FRINTA, 32:SEP73-671
SYDENHAM, M.J. THE FIRST FRENCH RE-
PUBLIC 1792-1804.
617(TLS):9AUG74-862
SYKES, C. NANCY.*
639(VQR):SPRING73-LXXXI
SYLBERT, P. FINAL CUT.
M. WOOD, 453:31OCT74-39
SYLVESTER, D.W. ROBERT LOWE & EDU-
CATION.
617(TLS):2AUG74-837
SYLVESTER, R.S., ED. ST. THOMAS
MORE.
A. NOVOTNY, 182:VOL25#12-388
SYMCOX, G., ED. WAR, DIPLOMACY &
IMPERIALISM, 1618-1763.
617(TLS):13SEP74-984
SYME, R. EMPERORS & BIOGRAPHY.*
A. CHASTAGNOL, 555:VOL46FASC1-92
R.I. FRANK, 24:WINTER73-392
SYME, R. TEN STUDIES IN TACITUS.*
P.M. SWAN, 487:SPRING72-108
SYMINGTON, R.T.K. BRECHT UND SHAKE-
SPEARE.
G.L. TRACY, 564:MAR72-71
SYMMONS-SYMONOLEWICZ, K., ED & TRANS.
THE NON-SLAVIC PEOPLES OF THE SOV-
IET UNION.
M. FRIEDBERG, 32:DEC73-862
SYMONDS, J. THE SHAVEN HEAD.
S. MAITLAND, 362:12DEC74-786
SYMONS, J. BLOODY MURDER.
R. GADNEY, 364:APR/MAY72-144
SYMONS, J. MORTAL CONSEQUENCES.
R. HARRISON, 219(GAR):FALL72-384

SYMONS, J. NOTES FROM ANOTHER COUN-
TRY.
R. CONQUEST, 364:AUG/SEP72-155
SYMONS, J.M. MEYERHOLD'S THEATRE OF
THE GROTESQUE.
N.B. BEESON, 32:MAR73-203
N. MARSHALL, 157:SUMMER72-71
SYNGE, A., ED. STRANGERS' GALLERY.
617(TLS):30AUG74-928
SYNGE, J.M. LETTERS TO MOLLY.* (A.
SADDLEMYER, ED)
J.P. FRAYNE, 160:WINTER71/72-120
H. OREL, 397(MD):SEP72-213
R. SKELTON, 376:JAN72-131
639(VQR):SPRING72-LXII
SYRETT, H.C. - SEE HAMILTON, A.
SZABO, M.E. - SEE GENTZEN, G.
SZAFLIK, J.R. POLSKIE STRONNICTWO
LUDOWE PIAST, 1926-1931.
A.M. CIENCIALA, 32:MAR73-185
SZANTON, D.L. ESTANCIA IN TRANSI-
TION.
D.J. SCHEANS, 293(JAST):MAY72-
746
SZASZ, T.S. THE ETHICS OF PSYCHO-
ANALYSIS. THE SECOND SIN.
617(TLS):12APR74-384
SZASZ, T.S. THE MANUFACTURE OF MAD-
NESS.
R. DE SOUSA, 262:SUMMER72-187
SZCZELKUN, S.A. SURVIVAL SCRAPBOOK
3.
M. GREEN, 441:6OCT74-10
SZCZEŚNIAK, B.B. THE KNIGHTS HOSPI-
TALLERS IN POLAND & LITHUANIA.
K. GÓRSKI, 575(SEER):APR73-330
VON SZELISKI, J. TRAGEDY & FEAR.*
A. WACHTEL, 290(JAAC):FALL72-130
SZENDE, O. & M. NEMESSURI. THE
PHYSIOLOGY OF VIOLIN PLAYING.
O. HOLMES, 415:FEB73-149
SZLEZÁK, T.A. PSEUDO-ARCHYTAS, ÜBER
DIE KATEGORIEN.
F. LASSERRE, 182:VOL25#3/4-112
SZULC, T. INNOCENTS AT HOME.
442(NY):30SEP74-130

TACCOLA - SEE UNDER DI JACOPO, M.
TACK, A. RETURN OF THE ASSASSIN.
N. CALLENDAR, 441:19MAY74-42
TACKWOOD, L.E. & OTHERS. THE GLASS
HOUSE TAPES.
A. KOPKIND, 453:30MAY74-21
TADDEO, E. STUDI SUL MARINO.
D. CONRIERI, 228(GSLI):VOL149
FASC466/467-426
TADIÉ, J-Y. INTRODUCTION À LA VIE
LITTÉRAIRE DU XIXE SIÈCLE.
J.S.P., 191(ELN):SEP72(SUPP)-77
TADIÉ, J-Y. LECTURES DE PROUST.*
J. CRUICKSHANK, 208(FS):JUL73-
351
L.D. JOINER, 207(FR):MAR72-919
TAFURI, M. JACOPO SANSOVINO E L'AR-
CHITETTURA DEL '500 A VENEZIA.*
J. MC ANDREW, 54:JUN72-212
TAFURI, M., ED. SOCIALISMO, CITTÀ,
ARCHITETTURA URSS 1917-1937.
A.C. BIRNHOLZ, 54:SEP72-368
A. SENKEVITCH, JR., 576:MAR72-78

TAGLIACOZZO, G., WITH H.V. WHITE,
EDS. GIAMBATTISTA VICO.*
  T. BRUNIUS, 290(JAAC):FALL71-129
  R. PASOTTI, 321:WINTER72[VOL6#1]-
  77
  R.J. DI PIETRO, 206:JAN73-410
  L. POMPA, 483:APR72-162
TAGORE, R. THE CRESCENT MOON. GIT-
  ANJALI. LOVER'S GIFT & CROSSING.
  THE POST OFFICE. RED OLEANDERS.
  THE BROKEN NEST. HUNGRY STONES &
  OTHER STORIES. ONE HUNDRED POEMS
  OF KABIR.
  N.C. CHAUDHURI, 617(TLS):27SEP74-
  1029
TAHMANKAR, D.V. SARDAR PATEL.
  H. SPODEK, 293(JAST):FEB72-441
TAI CHÊN. TAI CHÊN'S INQUIRY INTO
  GOODNESS. (C-Y. CHENG, TRANS)
  S-H. LIU, 485(PE&W):OCT72-486
DE LA TAILLE, J. JACQUES DE LA
  TAILLE'S "LA MANIERE." (P. HAN,
  ED)
  S.L. BORTON, 207(FR):DEC71-529
TAIRA, K. ECONOMIC DEVELOPMENT &
  THE LABOR MARKET IN JAPAN.*
  M. BRONFENBRENNER, 293(JAST):
  MAY72-605
TAIT, V. A FAMILY OF BROTHERS.
  J.C. TREWIN, 157:AUTUMN72-77
TALBOT, G. TEN SECONDS FROM NOW.
  617(TLS):1FEB74-116
TALBOT, L. LA ROUE DU GOUVERNAIL.
  M. SCHAETTEL, 557(RSH):JUL-SEP72-
  481
TALBOTT, J.E. THE POLITICS OF EDU-
  CATIONAL REFORM IN FRANCE, 1918-
  1940.
  W.D. HALLS, 447(N&Q):FEB72-75
TALBOTT, S. - SEE KHRUSHCHEV, N.S.
"THE TALES OF ISE." (H.J. HARRIS,
  TRANS)
  A. CHAMBERS, 352(LE&W):VOL15#4&
  VOL16#1/2-921
TAMBIAH, S.J. BUDDHISM & THE SPIRIT
  CULTS IN NORTH-EAST THAILAND.*
  F.K. LEHMAN, 293(JAST):MAY72-724
  D.K. SWEARER, 318(JAOS):APR-JUN
  72-327
TAMBURINI, L. - SEE DE AMICIS, E.
TAMMUZ, B. CASTLE IN SPAIN.
  617(TLS):15FEB74-163
TAMUNO, T.N. THE POLICE IN MODERN
  NIGERIA.
  A.H.M.K-G., 69:JUL72-261
TANAKA, S. THE TEA CEREMONY.
  617(TLS):26APR74-434
TANG, A.M. LONG-TERM ECONOMIC & AG-
  RICULTURAL COMMODITY PROJECTIONS
  FOR HONG KONG, 1970, 1975 & 1980.
  J. WONG, 302:JAN72-73
"TANGLED HAIR" - SEE UNDER YOSANO
  AKIKO
TANN, J. THE DEVELOPMENT OF THE
  FACTORY.
  R.M. CANDEE, 576:DEC72-336
  D. HINTON, 135:MAR72-216
TANNENBAUM, E.R. FASCISM IN ITALY.
  617(TLS):25JAN74-87
TANNER, T. CITY OF WORDS.*
  L.J. CLANCY, 381:DEC72-494
  E. KREUTZER, 72:BAND21OHEFT1/3-
  198
  S. PINSKER, 594:FALL72-532

TANSELLE, G.T. GUIDE TO THE STUDY
  OF UNITED STATES IMPRINTS.*
  S.T. RILEY, 432(NEQ):SEP72-460
  H.C. WOODBRIDGE, 517(PBSA):JUL-
  SEP73-351
TAPIÉ, V-L. BAROQUE ET CLASSICISME.
  (2ND ED)
  P. CHARPENTRAT, 98:NOV72-997
TAPIÉ, V-L. FRANCE IN THE AGE OF
  LOUIS XIII & RICHELIEU. (D.M.
  LOCKIE, ED & TRANS)
  R.J. KNECHT, 617(TLS):6DEC74-
  1392
TAPPE, E.D. ION LUCA CARAGIALE.
  617(TLS):14JUN74-646
TARANOW, G. SARAH BERNHARDT.*
  J. SCARRY, 160:WINTER71/72-121
  E. WAGENKNECHT, 397(MD):DEC72-
  335
TARAPOREVALA, R.J. COMPETITION &
  ITS CONTROL IN THE BRITISH BOOK
  TRADE 1850-1939.
  617(TLS):15FEB74-164
TARGAN, B. LET THE WILD RUMPUS
  START.
  H. GREGORY, 502(PRS):SPRING72-87
  C. WATTS, 448:SPRING72-104
TARGET, G.W. THE PATRIOTS.
  R. DAVIES, 617(TLS):6DEC74-1361
TARI, M. - SEE UNDER MORIGUCHI TARI
TARN, J.N. FIVE PER CENT PHILAN-
  THROPY.
  F.M.L. THOMPSON, 617(TLS):2AUG74-
  823
TARN, J.N. WORKING-CLASS HOUSING IN
  19TH-CENTURY BRITAIN.
  H. HOBHOUSE, 637(VS):DEC72-254
TAROT, R. HUGO VON HOFMANNSTHAL.*
  E. WEBER, 301(JEGP):JAN73-100
  W.E. YATES, 402(MLR):APR73-470
TARPLEY, F. & A. MOSELEY, EDS. OF
  EDSELS & MARAUDERS.
  K.B. HARDER, 424:MAR72-70
TASCH, P.A. THE DRAMATIC COBBLER.
  K.A. BURNIM, 481(PQ):JUL72-642
  C. PRICE, 402(MLR):APR73-393
TASHJIAN, D. & A. MEMORIALS FOR
  CHILDREN OF CHANGE.
  H. KRAMER, 441:25AUG74-3
TASKER, J. - SEE LEAVIS, F.R.
TASSO, T. DISCOURSES ON THE HEROIC
  POEM. (M. CAVALCHINI & I. SAMUEL,
  TRANS)
  639(VQR):AUTUMN73-CLIII
TASSO, T. JERUSALEM DELIVERED.*
  (J. TUSIANI, TRANS)
  K.J. ATCHITY, 276:SUMMER72-257
  C.P. BRAND, 551(RENQ):SPRING72-
  89
TATARKIEWICZ, W. HISTORY OF AESTHET-
  ICS.* (VOLS 1&2) (J. HARRELL & C.
  BARRETT, EDS)
  M. RIESER, 290(JAAC):FALL72-129
TATE, A. THE SWIMMERS & OTHER SE-
  LECTED POEMS.*
  639(VQR):SUMMER72-CII
TATE, R. BIRDS OF A BLOODIED FEATH-
  ER.
  617(TLS):1MAR74-219
TATE, R.B. - SEE DEL PULGAR, F.
TATEO, F. - SEE PONTANO, G.
TATSUMI, O. - SEE UNDER OKABE TAT-
  SUMI

TAULI, V. INTRODUCTION TO A THEORY
OF LANGUAGE PLANNING.*
S. WYLER, 343:BAND14HEFT1-35
TAURO, A. - SEE "LA ABEJA REPUBLI-
CANA"
TAVANI, G. POESIA DEL DUECENTO
NELLA PENISOLA IBERICA.*
W. METTMANN, 240(HR):SUMMER72-
309
TAVERNE, D. THE FUTURE OF THE LEFT.
L. ABSE, 362:10JAN74-54
617(TLS):25JAN74-70
TAX, P.W. - SEE NOTKER DER DEUTSCHE
TAYLER, I. BLAKE'S ILLUSTRATIONS TO
THE POEMS OF GRAY.*
I.H.C., 191(ELN):SEP72(SUPP)-36
L.S. LUEDTKE, 173(ECS):SPRING73-
389
J. RIEGER, 481(PQ):JUL72-646
TAYLOR, A. THE COOL CHANGE.
J. SAUNDERS, 565:VOL13#3-75
TAYLOR, A.C., COMP. CURRENT RESEARCH
IN FRENCH STUDIES AT UNIVERSITIES
& UNIVERSITY COLLEGES IN THE
UNITED KINGDOM, 1970-71.*
R. MERCIER, 557(RSH):JUL-SEP72-
447
J. VOISINE, 549(RLC):APR-JUN72-
295
TAYLOR, A.J.P. BEAVERBROOK.*
639(VQR):SPRING73-LXXVII
TAYLOR, B. CONSTABLE.
P. ADAMS, 61:JAN74-99
TAYLOR, C. THE CAMBRIDGESHIRE LAND-
SCAPE.
617(TLS):5APR74-377
TAYLOR, C. DORSET.
A. CLIFTON-TAYLOR, 46:JAN72-66
TAYLOR, C. SNOW JOB.
R. BOTHWELL, 99:NOV/DEC74-59
TAYLOR, C.E. & R.E. SPURR, COMPS.
AERIAL PHOTOGRAPHS IN THE NATIONAL
ARCHIVES.
J.M. KINNEY, 14:JUL/OCT72-415
TAYLOR, C.M. - SEE ETHEREGE, G.
TAYLOR, D. AFTER THE FIRST DEATH.*
639(VQR):SUMMER73-CV
TAYLOR, D. AS TIME GOES BY.
P. ATKIN, 617(TLS):15NOV74-1290
TAYLOR, D.M. EXPLANATION & MEANING.
J.R. CAMERON, 479(PHQ):JAN72-72
R.L.M., 543:SEP71-136
E. PIVČEVIĆ, 393(MIND):JAN72-150
L. THIRY, 154:DEC72-664
TAYLOR, D.S., WITH B.B. HOOVER - SEE
CHATTERTON, T.
TAYLOR, E. THE SERPENT UNDER IT.*
617(TLS):31MAY74-591
TAYLOR, E.R. WELCOME EUMENIDES.*
639(VQR):AUTUMN72-CXXIV
TAYLOR, J. ALL THE WORKES OF JOHN
TAYLOR THE WATER-POET.
617(TLS):15FEB74-148
TAYLOR, J. SEEING A BEAR.
V. MC CABE, 649(WAL):SPRING72-75
TAYLOR, J. & A.H. NELSON, EDS. MEDI-
EVAL ENGLISH DRAMA.
R. EDWARDS, 651(WHR):AUTUMN73-
415
TAYLOR, J.A., ED. CLIMATIC RESOURCES
& ECONOMIC ACTIVITY.
617(TLS):16AUG74-886

TAYLOR, J.R. THE SECOND WAVE.
C. HARRISON, 157:WINTER71-75
M. PAGE, 397(MD):DEC72-331
TAYLOR, J.R. - SEE GREENE, G.
TAYLOR, L.E. PASTORAL & ANTI-PASTOR-
AL PATTERNS IN JOHN UPDIKE'S FIC-
TION.*
S.I. BELLMAN, 573(SSF):SUMMER72-
293
TAYLOR, O.R. - SEE DE VOLTAIRE,
F.M.A.
TAYLOR, P. THE COLLECTED STORIES OF
PETER TAYLOR.*
J. YARDLEY, 473(PR):2/1973-286
TAYLOR, P. PRESENCES.
B.H. FUSSELL, 249(HUDR):WINTER
73/74-753
42(AR):VOL32#4-700
639(VQR):SUMMER73-CXII
TAYLOR, P.S. GEORGIA PLAN: 1732-
1752.
T. REESE, 656(WMQ):OCT72-649
TAYLOR, R. GOOD & EVIL.
J. DONNELLY, 258:SEP72-446
J.J. THOMSON, 482(PHR):JAN72-113
TAYLOR, R., ED. THE ROMANTIC TRA-
DITION IN GERMANY.*
R.M., 191(ELN):SEP72(SUPP)-133
R. MOLLENAUER, 399(MLJ):APR72-
265
G. RODGER, 220(GL&L):JAN73-182
J. TRAINER, 402(MLR):JAN73-228
TAYLOR, R.J. THE ART OF THE MINNE-
SINGER.
H. LOMNITZER, 680(ZDP):BAND91
HEFT3-457
TAYLOR, R.J., ED. THE SUSQUEHANNAH
COMPANY PAPERS. (VOLS 10 & 11)
W.S. HANNA, 656(WMQ):JAN73-176
TAYLOR, S.W. & E. LUCIE-SMITH, EDS.
FRENCH POETRY TODAY.*
G. MERLER, 648:OCT72-60
TAYLOR, W., ED. RESEARCH PERSPEC-
TIVES IN EDUCATION.
617(TLS):8MAR74-231
TAYLOR, W.D. - SEE ANDERSON, S.
TAYLOR, W.L. A PRODUCTIVE MONOPOLY.
W. GRAEBNER, 432(NEQ):MAR72-139
TÊ-K'UN, C. - SEE UNDER CHÊNG TÊ-
K'UN
TEALE, E.W. A NATURALIST BUYS AN
OLD FARM.
E. WEEKS, 61:OCT74-116
TEBEAU, C.W. A HISTORY OF FLORIDA.
E.C. WILLIAMSON, 9(ALAR):APR72-
154
TEDESCO, N. LA CONDIZIONE CREPUSCO-
LARE.
400(MLN):JAN72-164
TEEPLE, G., ED. CAPITALISM & THE
NATIONAL QUESTION IN CANADA.
H.C. PENTLAND, 99:JAN74-26
TEETS, B.E. & H.E. GERBER, COMPS.
JOSEPH CONRAD.*
D.E. LEES, 445(NCF):DEC72-363
F.P.W. MC DOWELL, 481(PQ):OCT72-
922
TEEUW, A. & OTHERS. ŚIWARĀTRIKALPA
OF MPU TANAKUŇ.
J.M. ECHOLS, 318(JAOS):APR-JUN72-
361
TEEUW, A. & D.K. WYATT. HIKAYAT
PATANI.
W.R. ROFF, 293(JAST):NOV71-226

TEICH, M. & R. YOUNG, EDS. CHANGING
PERSPECTIVES IN THE HISTORY OF
SCIENCE.
617(TLS):26APR74-452
TEICHMAN, J. THE MIND & THE SOUL.
617(TLS):16AUG74-885
TEICHNER, W. DIE INTELLIGIBLE WELT.
W. STEINBECK, 342:BAND63HEFT4-
508
TEICHOVA, A. AN ECONOMIC BACKGROUND
TO MUNICH.
617(TLS):4OCT74-1071
TEIK, G.C. - SEE UNDER GOH CHENG
TEIK
TEILHARD DE CHARDIN, P. CHRISTIAN-
ITY & EVOLUTION.
441:14APR74-24
TEILHARD DE CHARDIN, P. HUMAN ENER-
GY. ACTIVATION OF ENERGY.
R.J. O'CONNELL, 613:SPRING72-151
TEJEIRA, V. MODES OF GREEK THOUGHT.
J.L. CARAFIDES, 484(PPR):JUN73-
600
Q. LAUER, 258:DEC72-634
TEKIN, T. A GRAMMAR OF ORKHON TUR-
KIC.
G.F. MEIER, 682(ZPSK):BAND25
HEFT6-542
TELLER, W. - SEE WHITMAN, W.
TEMKIN, O. GALENISM.
617(TLS):26APR74-451
TEMKIN, S. THE NEW WORLD OF REFORM.
617(TLS):1MAR74-218
"THE TEN FOOT SQUARE HUT & TALES OF
THE HEIKE." (A.L. SADLER, TRANS)
E.D. PUTZAR, 352(LE&W):VOL15#4&
VOL16#1/2-932
MADAME DE TENCIN. MÉMOIRES DU COMTE
DE COMMINGE. (J. DECOTTIGNIES, ED)
R. MERCIER, 557(RSH):APR-JUN72-
314
TENG, S.Y. THE TAIPING REBELLION &
THE WESTERN POWERS.
E. BOARDMAN, 293(JAST):FEB72-395
TENNYSON, C. & H. DYSON. TENNYSON,
LINCOLNSHIRE & AUSTRALIA.
P. COLLINS, 617(TLS):25OCT74-
1184
TEPLINSKY, L.B. 50 LET SOVETSKO-
AFGANSKIKH OTNOSHENII, 1919-1969.
O.M. SMOLANSKY, 32:MAR73-172
TEREJ, J.J. RZECZYWISTOŚĆ I POLI-
TYKA.
A.M. CIENCIALA, 32:MAR73-185
TERKEL, S. WORKING.
M. BERMAN, 441:24MAR74-1
A. BROYARD, 441:21MAR74-45 [&
CONT. IN] 441:22MAR74-43
B. DE MOTT, 61:AUG74-76
TERNES, E. GRAMMAIRE STRUCTURALE DU
BRETON DE L'ÎLE DE GROIX.
R.A. FOWKES, 350:MAR73-195
TERRACE, E.L.B. EGYPTIAN PAINTINGS
OF THE MIDDLE KINGDOM.*
H.S. SMITH, 90:APR72-249
TERRAS, V. BELINSKIJ & RUSSIAN LIT-
ERARY CRITICISM.
R. FREEBORN, 617(TLS):8NOV74-
1266
TERRELL, J.U. AMERICAN INDIAN AL-
MANAC.
639(VQR):WINTER72-XXXIII

TERRILL, R. R.H. TAWNEY & HIS
TIMES.*
J.M. CAMERON, 453:21MAR74-17
S. KOSS, 362:29AUG74-281
TERRY, J.H. & D.G.S. UPTON - SEE
CICERO
TERRY, P. - SEE "POEMS OF THE VIK-
INGS: THE ELDER EDDA"
TERRY, R.M. CONTEMPORARY FRENCH
INTERROGATIVE STRUCTURES.
A.W. GRUNDSTROM, 320(CJL):SPRING
71-154
D. STEAD, 207(FR):DEC71-494
TERWILLIGER, R.F. MEANING & MIND.
J.B. DALBOR, 480(P&R):WINTER72-
60
TESTA, A. THE DIALOGIC STRUCTURE OF
LANGUAGE.
K. TOGEBY, 545(RPH):MAY73-741
TESTA, A. MEDITAZIONI SU CAMPANELLA.
E. NAMER, 542:APR-JUN72-167
TESTARD, M. - SEE CICERO
TESTER, M. THE WIT OF THE ASQUITHS.
617(TLS):27DEC74-1471
TETEL, M. MARGUERITE DE NAVARRE'S
"HEPTAMERON."*
639(VQR):SUMMER73-CXVIII
TETEL, M. - SEE PIRANDELLO, L.
TETLOW, E. THE ENIGMA OF HASTINGS.
617(TLS):7JUN74-599
TETZELI VON ROSADOR, K. MAGIE IM
ELISABETHANISCHEN DRAMA.
R.H. ROBBINS, 72:BAND210HEFT4/6-
367
DEN TEX, J. OLDENBARNEVELT.
617(TLS):12JUL74-750
TEY, J. LA FILLE DU TEMPS.
M. POLLET, 189(EA):JAN-MAR72-66
THACKER, C. VOLTAIRE.
H.T. MASON, 208(FS):JUL73-333
THACKER, C. - SEE DE VOLTAIRE, F.M.A.
THACKRAY, A. ATOMS & POWERS.
J.R.R. CHRISTIE, 481(PQ):JUL72-
585
THACKRAY, R. INVESTIGATION INTO
RHYTHMIC ABILITIES.
E. SAMS, 415:AUG73-800
VON THADDEN, R. RESTAURATION UND
NAPOLEONISCHES ERBE.
J. VIDALENC, 182:VOL25#13/14-504
THADEN, E.C. RUSSIA SINCE 1801.*
A.E. ADAMS, 550(RUSR):JUL72-296
VAN THAL, H., ED. THE PRIME MINIS-
TERS. (VOL 1)
J. GRIGG, 362:17OCT74-512
VAN THAL, H. - SEE TROLLOPE, T.A.
THALHEIMER, R. REFLECTIONS.
A.W. MUNK, 484(PPR):MAR73-436
"THE THALIDOMIDE CHILDREN & THE LAW."
617(TLS):1FEB74-116
THALMANN, M. ROMANTIKER ALS POETO-
LOGEN.*
R. BELGARDT, 221(GQ):MAY72-526
THALMANN, R. & E. FEINERMANN. CRYS-
TAL NIGHT.
G. SALLOCH, 441:25AUG74-22
THARP, L.H. THE APPLETONS OF BEACON
HILL.
E. WEEKS, 61:JAN74-97
THATCHER, D.S. NIETZSCHE IN ENGLAND
1890-1914.*
E. DELAVENAY, 189(EA):JAN-MAR72-
183

[CONTINUED]

THATCHER, D.S. NIETZSCHE IN ENGLAND
1890-1914.* [CONTINUING]
S. DICK, 529(QQ):WINTER72-563
J. KLEINSTÜCK, 38:BAND90HEFT4-
547
A. KOLB, 637(VS):MAR72-390
THAVENIUS, J. KONKORDANS TILL HJAL-
MAR GULLBERGS LYRIK.
D. GUNDERSEN, 172(EDDA):1972/2-
124
THAYER, G. WHO SHAKES THE MONEY
TREE?
R. HOLBROOKE, 441:13JAN74-4
THAYER, H.S. MEANING & ACTION.*
G.M. BRODSKY, 543:DEC71-262
"THEATRE CHOICE (MODERN SHORT
PLAYS)."
A. RENDLE, 157:SUMMER72-75
THEEN, R.H.W. LENIN.
617(TLS):13SEP74-983
THEEN, R.H.W. - SEE VALENTINOV, N.
THEMELLY, M. - SEE SETTEMBRINI, L.
THEMERSON, S. SPECIAL BRANCH (A
DIALOGUE).
268:JAN74-70
THÉNEVIN, J. OCTOBRE À ANGOULÊME.
J.D. HUBERT, 207(FR):OCT71-216
THEOPHILUS. THEOPHILUS OF ANTIOCH:
"AD AUTOLYCUM."* (R.M. GRANT, ED
& TRANS)
J.N. BIRDSALL, 123:DEC73-273
THEOPHRASTUS. THE CHARACTER
SKETCHES. (W. ANDERSON, ED & TRANS)
M.D. MAC LEOD, 123:MAR73-26
THEOPHRASTUS. DE IGNE. (V. COUTANT,
ED & TRANS)
M.J. OSLER, 319:APR74-356
THEROUX, A. THREE WOGS.*
E. FEINSTEIN, 364:OCT/NOV73-154
639(VQR):SUMMER72-C
THEROUX, P. THE BLACK HOUSE.
C. LEHMANN-HAUPT, 441:11SEP74-49
J. MELLORS, 362:24OCT74-551
M. MEWSHAW, 441:8SEP74-18
617(TLS):4OCT74-1061
THEROUX, P. V.S. NAIPAUL.
T. HARRISON, 364:DEC72/JAN73-135
THEROUX, P. SAINT JACK.*
M. GREEN, 364:APR/MAY73-160
THEROUX, P. SINNING WITH ANNIE.
W.H. PRITCHARD, 249(HUDR):SPRING
73-234
THERRIEN, V. LA RÉVOLUTION DE GAS-
TON BACHELARD EN CRITIQUE LITTÉR-
AIRE.*
M.A. CAWS, 188(ECR):WINTER72-318
Y. SCALZITTI, 405(MP):NOV72-178
THÉVENIN, P. - SEE BOULEZ, P.
THIBAULT, G., J. JENKINS & J. BRAN-
RICCI. EIGHTEENTH CENTURY MUSICAL
INSTRUMENTS: FRANCE & BRITAIN.
617(TLS):12APR74-390
THIEBERGER, R. LE GENRE DE LA NOU-
VELLE DANS LA LITTÉRATURE ALLE-
MANDE.
P. BARBER, 222(GR):MAY72-236
THIEL, E. SACHWÖRTERBUCH DER MUSIK.
(2ND ED)
J.A.W., 410(M&L):OCT73-473
VAN THIEL, H. DER ESELROMAN.*
(VOLS 1&2)
H.J. MASON, 487:AUTUMN72-314
VAN THIEL, H. PETRON.
A. ERNOUT, 555:VOL46FASC2-345

THIEM, C. GREGORIO PAGANI.
P. CANNON-BROOKES, 90:APR72-250
THIERSTEIN, P. BAU DER SZENEN IN
DEN ARGONAUTIKA DES APOLLONIOS
RHODIOS.
G. GIANGRANDE, 123:DEC73-270
THIHER, A. CÉLINE.*
D. HAYMAN, 659:SPRING74-257
THIMONNIER, R. CODE ORTHOGRAPHIQUE
ET GRAMMATICAL.
J-M. KLINKENBERG, 209(FM):OCT72-
364
THIMONNIER, R. LE SYSTEME GRAPHIQUE
DU FRANÇAIS.
J-M. KLINKENBERG, 556(RLV):
1972/4-444
THIRKELL, A. MARLING HALL. MISS
BUNTING.
617(TLS):29MAR74-345
"THIS SIDE OF PARODIES."
R.R. LINGEMAN, 441:24FEB74-37
THOMAS. THE ROMANCE OF HORN. (VOL
2) (M.K. POPE, ED; REV & COMPLETED
BY T.B.W. REID)
J. MONFRIN, 545(RPH):FEB73-602
THOMAS, A. HOPKINS THE JESUIT.*
N. WHITE, 447(N&Q):NOV72-431
THOMAS, A. SONGS MY MOTHER TAUGHT
ME.*
R.M. BROWN, 296:VOL3#3-89
K. MULHALLEN, 99:MAY/JUN74-18
THOMAS, B. MARLON.
L. BRAUDY, 441:22SEP74-6
THOMAS, D. CHARGE! HURRAH! HURRAH!
617(TLS):18OCT74-1159
THOMAS, D. PRINCE CHARLIE'S BLUFF.
617(TLS):3MAY74-483
THOMAS, D. UNDER MILK WOOD/EN EL
JOVEN BOSQUE. (T. RAMOS OREA, ED
& TRANS)
R. VIDÁN, 202(FMOD):JUN72-350
205(FMLS):OCT72-385
THOMAS, D.D. CHRAU GRAMMAR.
F.E. HUFFMAN, 293(JAST):AUG72-
992
THOMAS, D.M. LOGAN STONE.
A. CLUYSENAAR, 565:VOL13#2-72
THOMAS, E. EVE ET LES AUTRES.
R. LORRIS, 207(FR):OCT71-217
THOMAS, E. LETTERS FROM EDWARD
THOMAS TO GORDON BOTTOMLEY.* (R.G.
THOMAS, ED)
W.J. KEITH, 627(UTQ):AUTUMN71-74
THOMAS, G. & M. MORGAN-WITTS. THE
SAN FRANCISCO EARTHQUAKE.
G. HASLAM, 649(WAL):SPRING72-70
THOMAS, G. & M. MORGAN-WITTS. VOYAGE
OF THE DAMNED.
D. SCHOENBRUN, 441:30JUN74-28
THOMAS, G.K. WORDSWORTH'S DIRGE &
PROMISE.
B.C.H., 191(ELN):SEP72(SUPP)-69
J.R.D. JACKSON, 627(UTQ):SPRING
73-289
THOMAS, H. CUBA.*
F.G. GIL, 639(VQR):WINTER72-134
THOMAS, H. EUROPE.*
J. LA PALOMBARA, 639(VQR):
AUTUMN73-621
THOMAS, H. GOYA: THE THIRD OF MAY,
1808.*
A. FRANKENSTEIN, 55:SUMMER73-78

THOMAS, J.D. A DESCRIPTIVE CATA-
LOGUE OF THE GREEK PAPYRI IN THE
COLLECTION OF WILFRED MERTON,
F.S.A. (VOL 3)
   H. CADELL, 555:VOL46FASC1-135
THOMAS, J.E. THE ENGLISH PRISON
OFFICER SINCE 1850.
   M. IGNATIEFF, 637(VS):JUN73-478
THOMAS, J-F. LE PÉLAGIANISME DE J-J.
ROUSSEAU.
   M. DAVID, 542:JUL-SEP72-336
THOMAS, J-F. LE PROBLÈME MORAL À
PORT-ROYAL.
   L. JERPHAGNON, 542:APR-JUN72-223
THOMAS, J.J. THE THEORY & PRACTICE
OF CREOLE GRAMMAR.*
   R.W. THOMPSON, 67:MAY73-163
THOMAS, J.W. MEDIEVAL GERMAN LYRIC
VERSE.*
   J.L. GRAY, 3D, 221(GQ):JAN72-185
THOMAS, L. THE LIVES OF A CELL.
   C. LEHMANN-HAUPT, 441:29JUL74-21
   J.C. OATES, 441:26MAY74-2
   J. UPDIKE, 442(NY):15JUL74-83
   C.H. WADDINGTON, 453:28NOV74-4
THOMAS, L. ARTHUR MC CANN & ALL HIS
WOMEN.
   M. LEVIN, 441:19MAY74-40
THOMAS, L. THE MAN WITH THE POWER.*
   M. LEVIN, 441:3NOV74-72
THOMAS, L. TROPIC OF RUISLIP.
   D. HARSENT, 617(TLS):1NOV74-1216
   J. MELLORS, 362:21NOV74-684
THOMAS, L.G. - SEE MORTON, A.S.
THOMAS, M. - SEE "THE GRANDES HEURES
OF JEAN, DUKE OF BERRY"
THOMAS, M.H. - SEE SEWALL, S.
THOMAS, O. METAPHOR & RELATED SUB-
JECTS.*
   R.J. MATTHEWS, 353:15OCT72-106
THOMAS, P. SEVEN LONG TIMES.
   P. ADAMS, 61:AUG74-91
   T. SELIGSON, 441:22SEP74-10
THOMAS, P.D.G. THE HOUSE OF COMMONS
IN THE EIGHTEENTH CENTURY.
   E.R. FOSTER, 656(WMQ):APR72-310
THOMAS, P.W. SIR JOHN BERKENHEAD
1617-1679.*
   I. ROOTS, 447(N&Q):MAY72-188
THOMAS, R. IF YOU CAN'T BE GOOD.*
   617(TLS):25JAN74-88
THOMAS, R. THE PORKCHOPPERS.
   617(TLS):6SEP74-960
THOMAS, R.H. & K. BULLIVANT. LITERA-
TURE IN UPHEAVAL.
   P. LABANYI, 617(TLS):25OCT74-
   1202
THOMAS, R.S. H'M.
   R. GARFITT, 364:AUG/SEP73-121
   J. MATTHIAS, 491:APR74-45
THOMAS, R.S. SELECTED POEMS 1946-
1968.
   J. FULLER, 362:7MAR74-310
   617(TLS):1MAR74-211
THOMAS, S. THE BRISTOL RIOTS.
   617(TLS):25OCT74-1208
THOMAS, T. THE FILMS OF GENE KELLY.
   617(TLS):19JUL74-760
THOMAS, T.M. INDIAN EDUCATIONAL
REFORMS IN CULTURAL PERSPECTIVE.
   C.S. BREMBECK, 293(JAST):AUG72-
   974

THOMAS, W.A. THE PROVINCIAL STOCK
EXCHANGES.
   617(TLS):16AUG74-883
THOMASIUS, C. DEUTSCHE SCHRIFTEN.
(P. VON DÜFFEL, ED)
   C.F.A. LANGSCHMIDT, 433:JAN72-
   110
THOMASON, R.H. - SEE MONTAGUE, R.
THOMPSON, C.W. VICTOR HUGO & THE
GRAPHIC ARTS (1820-1833).*
   A.G. ENGSTROM, 207(FR):DEC71-511
THOMPSON, D. THE EARLY CHARTISTS.
   P. HOLLIS,· 637(VS):DEC72-237
THOMPSON, E. TATTOO.
   H. BENNETT, 441:27OCT74-48
   C. LEHMANN-HAUPT, 441:25OCT74-43
THOMPSON, E.A. THE GOTHS IN SPAIN.
   J.N. HILLGARTH, 589:JUL73-591
THOMPSON, E.M. RUSSIAN FORMALISM &
ANGLO-AMERICAN NEW CRITICISM.
   V. ERLICH, 497(POLR):AUTUMN72-96
   R. SHELDON, 32:JUN73-430
   G.S. SMITH, 575(SEER):OCT73-600
THOMPSON, E.P. & E. YEO - SEE MAYHEW,
H.
THOMPSON, F.M.L. HAMPSTEAD.
   617(TLS):22MAR74-303
THOMPSON, G.H. THE FICTION OF E.M.
FORSTER.
   N. SHERRY, 447(N&Q):FEB72-74
THOMPSON, G.R. POE'S FICTION.*
   D.H. HIRSCH, 27(AL):NOV73-459
   639(VQR):SUMMER73-CXIV
THOMPSON, K. ACROSS FROM THE FLORAL
PARK.
   442(NY):30DEC74-63
THOMPSON, K. A DICTIONARY OF TWENTI-
ETH-CENTURY COMPOSERS 1911-1971.
   P. GRIFFITHS, 415:JUL73-701
   J.A.W., 410(M&L):JUL73-352
THOMPSON, K. THE TENANTS WERE COR-
RIE & TENNIE.*
   M. LEVIN, 441:24FEB74-39
THOMPSON, K.F. MODESTY & CUNNING.*
   R. BERRY, 677:VOL3-276
   J. BRITTON, 613:AUTUMN72-457
   K.M. LEA, 541(RES):MAY72-201
   V.K. WHITAKER, 191(ELN):DEC72-
   129
THOMPSON, K.F. WHITEHEAD'S PHILOSO-
PHY OF RELIGION.
   H.F., 543:MAR72-570
THOMPSON, L., ED. AFRICAN SOCIETIES
IN SOUTHERN AFRICA.
   A.M. KEPPEL-JONES, 529(QQ):SUM-
   MER72-279
THOMPSON, L.S. THE NEW SABIN. (VOL
1)
   617(TLS):23AUG74-910
THOMPSON, M.W. - SEE RUDENKO, S.I.
THOMPSON, N. THE ANTI-APPEASERS.
   J.M. MC EWEN, 529(QQ):AUTUMN72-
   434
THOMPSON, P. WILLIAM BUTTERFIELD.
   G.L. HERSEY, 676(YR):AUTUMN72-
   152
   J. LEES-MILNE, 39:AUG72-165
   R. PATTERSON, 637(VS):JUN73-479
   N. PEVSNER, 56:AUTUMN72-315
   G.B. TENNYSON, 445(NCF):JUN72-
   117
THOMPSON, R. WOMEN IN STUART ENG-
LAND & AMERICA.
   617(TLS):13SEP74-983

THOMPSON, T.W. WORDSWORTH'S HAWKS-
HEAD.* (R. WOOF, ED)
M. JACOBUS, 541(RES):FEB72-86
G.P. JONES, 447(N&Q):MAR72-115
K.K., 191(ELN):SEP72(SUPP)-69
639(VQR):WINTER72-XXXIV
THOMPSON, V.B. AFRICA & UNITY.
A.H.M. KIRK-GREENE, 69:JAN72-64
THOMPSON, W.I. PASSAGES ABOUT EARTH.
S. SANBORN, 441:31MAR74-33
F. ZINGRONE, 99:NOV/DEC74-33
THOMPSON, W.N. MODERN ARGUMENTATION
& DEBATE PRINCIPLES & PRACTICES.
R.W. BUCHANAN, 583:FALL72-115
THOMSEN, E. BAROKKEN I DANSK DIGT-
NING.
J. BANG, 172(EDDA):1972/3-182
THOMSEN, J.S., ED. VIRKELIGHEDEN
DER VOKSEDE.*
A. JØRGENSEN, 172(EDDA):1972/2-
119
THOMSON, A.J. & A.V. MARTINET. A
PRACTICAL ENGLISH GRAMMAR.
G. STORMS, 206:SEP72-145
THOMSON, B. THE PREMATURE REVOLU-
TION.
N.J. ANNING, 575(SEER):JUL73-470
THOMSON, D. AN INTRODUCTION TO
GAELIC POETRY.
617(TLS):10MAY74-507
THOMSON, D. WOODBROOK.
C. BLACKWOOD, 362:12DEC74-782
THOMSON, J.C., JR. WHILE CHINA
FACED WEST.
A.P.L. LIU, 318(JAOS):APR-JUN72-
347
THOMSON, J.M. RECORDER PROFILES.
E. GORDON, 415:MAR73-265
THOMSON, P. THE GROTESQUE.
205(FMLS):OCT72-381
THOMSON, R.M., ED. THE CHRONICLE OF
THE ELECTION OF HUGH, ABBOT OF
BURY ST. EDMUNDS.
617(TLS):21JUN74-680
THOMSON, R.W., ED & TRANS. THE
TEACHING OF ST. GREGORY.*
M. HEPPELL, 575(SEER):JUL73-473
THOMSON, R.W. - SEE ATHANASIUS
THORAVAL, J. & OTHERS. LES GRANDES
ETAPES DE LA CIVILISATION FRAN-
ÇAISE.
B. CAP, 399(MLJ):APR72-249
THORBURN, A. PLANNING VILLAGES.
M. DUNBAR, 46:DEC72-385
THORBURN, D. CONRAD'S ROMANTICISM.
442(NY):14OCT74-201
THÓRDARSON, A. THE SWORD. (P.
SCHACH, ED & TRANS)
E.S. FIRCHOW, 563(SS):SPRING73-
165
THORDARSON, B. LESTER PEARSON.
R. BOTHWELL, 99:NOV/DEC74-59
THOREAU, H.D. THOREAU'S WORLD.
(C.R. ANDERSON, ED)
M.I. LOWANCE, JR., 432(NEQ):
MAR72-144
THOREAU, H.D. WALDEN.* (J.L. SHAN-
LEY, ED)
M. FLAK, 189(EA):APR-JUN72-333
W.H. GILMAN, 432(NEQ):JUN72-300
THORESEN, L., WITH E.M. NATHANSON.
IT GAVE EVERYBODY SOMETHING TO DO.
R. ELMAN, 441:24MAR74-33

THORNBROUGH, E.L. T. THOMAS FOR-
TUNE.
639(VQR):AUTUMN72-CXXXVII
THORNTON, A. PEOPLE & THEMES IN
HOMER'S "ODYSSEY."*
N. AUSTIN, 24:SPRING73-92
M.M. WILLCOCK, 303:VOL92-188
THORNTON, M. JESSIE MATTHEWS.
E.S. TURNER, 617(TLS):25OCT74-
1191
THORNTON, P. - SEE ERIKSEN, S.
THORNTON, R.C. THE COMINTERN & THE
CHINESE COMMUNISTS, 1928-1931.*
S.R. SCHRAM, 32:DEC73-821
THORP, R. CIRCLE OF LOVE.
R. JAFFE, 441:19MAY74-38
THORPE, J. PRINCIPLES OF TEXTUAL
CRITICISM.*
J. FEATHER, 402(MLR):APR73-381
M. HANCHER, 290(JAAC):SPRING73-
414
THORPE, M., ED. CLOUGH: THE CRITI-
CAL HERITAGE.*
K. ALLOTT, 677:VOL3-320
ÞORSTEINSSON, B. ENSKA ÖLDIN Í SÖGU
ÍSLENDINGA.
B.E. GELSINGER, 589:APR73-417
THRAEDE, K. GRUNDZÜGE GRIECHISCH-
RÖMISCHER BRIEFTOPIK.*
G.O. ROWE, 24:FALL73-307
"THREE CONTEMPORARY JAPANESE POETS."
(G. WILSON & A. IKUKO, TRANS)
C. TOMLINSON, 364:OCT/NOV72-125
"THREE GENERATIONS OF TWENTIETH-
CENTURY ART."
T. LASK, 55:APR73-14
THULSTRUP, N. - SEE "KIERKEGAARDIANA"
THÜRMER, W. ZUR POETISCHEN VERFAHR-
ENSWEISE IN DER SPÄTESTEN LYRIK
HÖLDERLINS.
C.H., 191(ELN):SEP72(SUPP)-163
THUROT, F. TABLEAU DES PROGRÈS DE
LA SCIENCE GRAMMATICALE.* (A.
JOLY, ED)
G. LEPSCHY, 545(RPH):MAY73-742
R. POSNER, 208(FS):APR73-215
F. SOUBLIN, 209(FM):JAN72-63
205(FMLS):JAN72-94
THWAITE, A. INSCRIPTIONS.*
R. GARFITT, 364:AUG/SEP73-124
P. SMYTH, 491:DEC73-165
639(VQR):AUTUMN73-CXLI
THWAITE, A. NEW CONFESSIONS.
S. CONN, 362:28NOV74-717
617(TLS):21JUN74-667
THWAITE, A. POETRY TODAY 1960-1973.
617(TLS):26JUL74-796
THWAITE, A. WAITING FOR THE PARTY.
G. ANNAN, 362:1AUG74-155
A. LURIE, 453:28NOV74-39
442(NY):21OCT74-190
TIAMSON, A.T. MINDANAO-SULU BIBLIO-
GRAPHY.
D.V. HART, 293(JAST):NOV71-236
TIDYMAN, E. DUMMY.
P. ADAMS, 61:APR74-120
442(NY):11MAR74-136
453:21MAR74-40
TIDYMAN, E. GOODBYE, MR. SHAFT.
M. LEVIN, 441:3FEB74-30
TIDYMAN, E. LINE OF DUTY.
N. CALLENDAR, 441:29DEC74-21

TODD, A.C. & P. LAWS. INDUSTRIAL
ARCHAEOLOGY OF CORNWALL.*
J. THOMAS, 135:SEP72-62
TODD, C. VOLTAIRE'S DISCIPLE.
W. BIESTERFELD, 182:VOL25#15/16-
556
TODD, I. ISLAND REALM.
617(TLS):8NOV74-1269
TODD, L. PIDGINS & CREOLES.
R.B. LE PAGE, 617(TLS):6DEC74-
1360
TODD, R. WILLIAM BLAKE: THE ARTIST.*
D.V.E., 191(ELN):SEP72(SUPP)-37
481(PQ):JUL72-648
TODOROV, T. INTRODUCTION À LA LIT-
TÉRATURE FANTASTIQUE.* (GERMAN
TITLE: EINFÜHRUNG IN DIE FANTAS-
TISCHE LITERATUR.)
H. NOBIS, 490:JUL-OCT72-450
TODOROV, T. POÉTIQUE DE LA PROSE.
J. CULLER, 402(MLR):OCT73-900
TOELLNER, R. ALBRECHT VON HALLER.*
H. SCHIPPERGES, 182:VOL25#11-335
TOEPLITZ, J. HOLLYWOOD & AFTER.
617(TLS):16AUG74-882
TOFFLER, A. FUTURE SHOCK.*
E. BLENDON, 14:JAN72-62
W.P. IRVINE, 529(QQ):SUMMER72-
260
R.P.M., 543:DEC71-371
TOFT, J. THE HOUSE OF THE AROUSING.
D.J. ENRIGHT, 362:27JUN74-842
TOGHILL, J. THE BOAT OWNER'S MAIN-
TENANCE MANUAL.
617(TLS):5APR74-377
TOITA YASUJI. KABUKI, THE POPULAR
THEATER.*
E. PUTZAR, 352(LE&W):VOL15#4&
VOL16#1/2-927
TŌKEI, F. GENRE THEORY IN CHINA IN
THE 3RD-6TH CENTURIES (LIU HSIEH'S
THEORY ON POETIC GENRES).*
J. HERTZOG, 290(JAAC):SUMMER73-
560
M. LOI, 549(RLC):OCT-DEC72-606
TOKLAS, A.B. STAYING ON ALONE. (E.
BURNS, ED)
P. BEER, 617(TLS):8NOV74-1252
H. LEIBOWITZ, 441:3FEB74-1
V. THOMSON, 453:7MAR74-12
TOLCHIN, S. & M. CLOUT.
L. SHERR, 441:24NOV74-34
TOLIVER, H.E. PASTORAL FORMS &
ATTITUDES.*
J. BUXTON, 551(RENQ):AUTUMN72-
356
W. MC CLUNG, 191(ELN):JUN73-313
639(VQR):SPRING72-LVI
TOLLEY, K. YANGTZE PATROL.
W.R. BRAISTED, 293(JAST):AUG72-
939
TOLSTOY, I. TOLSTOY, MY FATHER.
E. STENBOCK-FERMOR, 550(RUSR):
APR72-204
639(VQR):SPRING72-LXII
TOMALIN, C. THE LIFE & DEATH OF
MARY WOLLSTONECRAFT.
P. BEER, 362:5SEP74-314
R. COBB, 617(TLS):6SEP74-941
TOMÁS, T.N., G. HAENSCH & B. LECHNER
- SEE UNDER NAVARRO TOMÁS, T., G.
HAENSCH & B. LECHNER

TOMIAK, J.J. THE SOVIET UNION.
J.H. HIGGINSON, 575(SEER):JUL73-
491
TOMKINS, C. LIVING WELL IS THE BEST
REVENGE.
D. AARON, 639(VQR):WINTER72-157
TOMLIN, E.W.F. JAPAN.
639(VQR):AUTUMN73-CLXVII
TOMLIN, E.W.F. THE LAST COUNTRY.
D.J. ENRIGHT, 362:21MAR74-374
617(TLS):26APR74-434
TOMLINSON, C. THE WAY IN.
617(TLS):8NOV74-1265
TOMLINSON, C. WRITTEN ON WATER.*
J.E. CHAMBERLIN, 249(HUDR):SUM-
MER73-395
G. EWART, 364:DEC72/JAN73-132
J. GALASSI, 491:NOV73-113
TOMMASEO, N. RACCONTI BIBLICI E
MEDITAZIONI SUI VANGELI.* (G. GAM-
BARIN, ED)
W.T.S., 191(ELN):SEP72(SUPP)-200
TOMMASOLI, W. MOMENTI E FIGURE
DELLA POLITICA DELL'EQUILIBRIO
(FEDERICO DA MONTEFELTRO E L'IM-
PRESA DI RIMINI).
L.F. SMITH, 551(RENQ):SPRING72-
67
TOMORY, P. THE LIFE & ART OF HENRY
FUSELI.*
T. LASK, 55:APR73-50
TOMPKINS, P. SECRETS OF THE GREAT
PYRAMID.
617(TLS):8FEB74-139
TOMSICH, J. A GENTEEL ENDEAVOR.*
C.E. CLARK, JR., 432(NEQ):MAR72-
131
TONELLI, G. A SHORT-TITLE LIST OF
SUBJECT DICTIONARIES OF THE SIX-
TEENTH, SEVENTEENTH & EIGHTEENTH
CENTURIES AS AIDS TO THE HISTORY
OF IDEAS.*
G. BARBER, 208(FS):JUL73-319
C. CESA, 548(RCSF):JAN-MAR72-105
G. GAWLICK, 53(AGP):BAND54HEFT3-
312
W. GERBER, 322(JHI):JAN-MAR72-
177
R. VOITLE, 191(ELN):JUN73-303
TONGUE, R.L. FORGOTTEN FOLK-TALES
OF THE ENGLISH COUNTIES.
T. BROWN, 203:SPRING72-77
TONKIN, H. SPENCER'S COURTEOUS PAS-
TORAL.
D. HERRON, 67:NOV73-290
TOOK, B. & M. FELDMAN. ROUND THE
HORNE.
D. THOMAS, 362:19&26DEC74-846
TOOKER, E. THE IROQUOIS CEREMONIAL
OF MIDWINTER.
A.F.C. WALLACE, 292(JAF):JUL-SEP
72-286
TOOP, D., ED. NEW/REDISCOVERED
MUSICAL INSTRUMENTS. (VOL 1)
617(TLS):5JUL74-706
TOPKINS, K. & R. IL BOOM.
M. LEVIN, 441:12MAY74-12
TORMEY, A. THE CONCEPT OF EXPRES-
SION.*
J. BRUCE, 290(JAAC):SPRING72-394
A.S.C., 543:MAR72-571
A. SAVILE, 479(PHQ):OCT72-378
TÖRNQVIST, E. A DRAMA OF SOULS.*
P. LEWTON, 447(N&Q):SEP72-349

TORY, E.E. - SEE GIRAUDOUX, J.
TORY, G. CHAMP FLEURY.
    D. WILSON, 208(FS):JAN73-52
TOSCANO, M. DESIGNS IN DIPLOMACY.
    L. CALDER, 104:SPRING72-167
TOSCHI, P. BIBLIOGRAFIA DEGLI EX-
VOTO ITALIANI.
    R. WILDHABER, 182:VOL35#11-382
TOU, T-I. LI HUNG-CHANG NIEN (JIH)
P'U.
    Y-D.R. CHU, 293(JAST):FEB72-396
TOULMIN, S. HUMAN UNDERSTANDING.
(VOL 1)
    T.A. GOUDGE, 529(QQ):WINTER72-
    577
    D. HOLDCROFT, 518:OCT73-29
    R.M. MARTIN, 484(PPR):MAR73-441
TOULMIN, S. & J. GOODFIELD. MODELLE
DES KOSMOS.
    R. CADENBACH, 53(AGP):BAND54HEFT
    2-210
TOURAINE, A. PRODUCTION DE LA SOCI-
ÉTÉ.
    617(TLS):1FEB74-98
TOURAINE, A. VIE ET MORT DU CHILI
POPULAIRE.
    617(TLS):8FEB74-124
TOURNEBIZE, J-M. PASTELS AUVERGNATS.
    M. SCHAETTEL, 557(RSH):JUL-SEP72-
    483
TOURNIER, M. THE OGRE.*
    M. ELLMANN, 676(YR):SPRING73-461
    L.T. LEMON, 502(PRS):WINTER72/73-
    358
    42(AR):VOL32#3-496
TOURNIER, M. LE ROI DES AULNES.
    D. BOUGNOUX, 98:JUN72-527
    A. MARISSEL, 207(FR):OCT71-218
TOURNIER, M. VENDREDI OU LA VIE
SAUVAGE.
    D. BOUGNOUX, 98:JUN72-527
TOWLER, R. HOMO RELIGIOSUS.
    617(TLS):30AUG74-935
TOWNROE, P.M., ED. SOCIAL & POLITI-
CAL CONSEQUENCES OF THE MOTOR CAR.
    617(TLS):9AUG74-848
TOYNBEE, J.M.C. DEATH & BURIAL IN
THE ROMAN WORLD.*
    R.M. OGILVIE, 123:DEC73-259
    R.E.A. PALMER, 487:SPRING72-97
    L. RICHARDSON, JR., 24:SUMMER73-
    221
TOYNBEE, P. TOWARDS THE HOLY SPIRIT.
    617(TLS):1MAR74-218
TRACHTENBERG, I. SO SLOW THE DAWN-
ING.*
    639(VQR):SPRING73-LVII
TRACHTENBERG, M. THE CAMPANILE OF
FLORENCE CATHEDRAL.
    C. GILBERT, 56:WINTER72-427
TRACY, C. - SEE GRAVES, R.
TRACY, C. - SEE JOHNSON, S.
TRACY, D. THE ACHIEVEMENT OF BER-
NARD LONERGAN.*
    W.E.M., 543:MAR72-571
TRACY, D. HONK IF YOU'VE FOUND
JESUS.
    M. LEVIN, 441:18AUG74-20
TRACY, H. WINTER IN CASTILLE.*
    P. ADAMS, 61:FEB74-96
    442(NY):4FEB74-110
TRACY, J.D. ERASMUS.
    A. NOVOTNY, 182:VOL25#17/18-629

TRACY, T.J. PHYSIOLOGICAL THEORY &
THE DOCTRINE OF THE MEAN IN PLATO
& ARISTOTLE.*
    W. CHARLTON, 393(MIND):JAN72-148
TRAGER, F.N., ED. BURMA.
    D. GUYOT, 293(JAST):MAY72-722
TRAGER, H.G., ED. WE THE BURMESE.
    C. HOBBS, 293(JAST):AUG72-986
TRAHAN, E.W., ED. GRUPPE 47.
    F.D. HORVAY, 399(MLJ):OCT72-394
    J.J. WHITE, 220(GL&L):APR73-268
TRAINA, A. VORTIT BARBARE.*
    A. ERNOUT, 555:VOL46FASC1-162
TRAKL, G. DICHTUNGEN UND BRIEFE.*
(W. KILLY & H. SZKLENAR, EDS)
    B. KONNEKER, 224(GRM):BAND22
    HEFT4-444
    J. SCHMIDT, 190:BAND66HEFT2-207
TRAMONTANA, S. I NORMANNI IN ITALIA.
    H. WIERUSZOWSKI, 589:APR73-419
"THE TRANSLATOR'S NEW TESTAMENT."
    617(TLS):15FEB74-165
TRANSTRÖMER, T. NIGHT VISION.
    C. TOMLINSON, 364:OCT/NOV72-125
TRANSTRÖMER, T. TWENTY POEMS OF
TOMAS TRANSTRÖMER.
    W.P. ROOT, 491:OCT73-34
TRANSTRÖMER, T. WINDOWS & STONES.*
(M. SWENSON, WITH L. SJÖBERG, EDS
& TRANS)
    639(VQR):WINTER73-XVI
TRANTER, J.E. RED MOVIE.
    J. TULIP, 581:JUN73-231
TRAPP, E. DIGENES AKRITES.
    E. JEFFREYS, 303:VOL92-253
TRAPP, F.A. THE ATTAINMENT OF DELA-
CROIX.*
    R.N. BEETEM, 54:JUN72-223
    M. ROSENTHAL, 135:FEB72-138
TRASK, W.R., ED. CLASSIC BLACK
AFRICAN POEMS.*
    W.P. ROOT, 491:OCT73-34
TRAUTMANN, T.R. KAUṬILYA & THE
ARTHAŚASTRA.
    J.W. SPELLMAN, 293(JAST):AUG72-
    966
    L. STERNBACH, 318(JAOS):OCT-DEC
    72-498
TRAVAGLIA, S. LA NOZIONE DI POSSI-
BILITÀ NEL PENSIERO DI NICOLA
ABBAGNANO.
    B. MAIORCA, 548(RCSF):JAN-MAR72-
    113
"TRAVAUX LINGUISTIQUES DE PRAGUE."*
(VOL 3)
    W. THÜMMEL, 343:BAND14HEFT2-123
TRAVEN, B. THE REBELLION OF THE
HANGED.
    639(VQR):WINTER73-IX
TRAVERSO, L. SUL "TORQUATO TASSO"
DI GOETHE E ALTRE NOTE DI LETTERA-
TURA TEDESCA.
    E. NAMER, 542:JUL-SEP72-356
TREACY, E. SPELL OF STEAM.
    617(TLS):22FEB74-193
TREASE, G. LAUGHTER AT THE DOOR.
    E.S. TURNER, 362:19SEP74-379
TREASE, G. SAMUEL PEPYS & HIS WORLD.
    639(VQR):WINTER73-XXIX
TREFMAN, S. SAM. FOOTE, COMEDIAN,
1720-1777.
    L. HUGHES, 481(PQ):JUL72-680

TREFZGER, M. DIE NATIONALE BEWEGUNG
ÄGYPTENS VOR 1928 IM SPIEGEL DER
SCHWEIZERISCHEN ÖFFENTLICHKEIT.
    P. SALMON, 182:VOL25#13/14-508
TREIP, M. MILTON'S PUNCTUATION &
CHANGING ENGLISH USAGE.*
    M.A. DI CESARE, 551(RENQ):WINTER
    72-512
    A. WARD, 541(RES):FEB72-78
TREISTMAN, J.M. THE PREHISTORY OF
CHINA.
    W.A. FAIRSERVIS, JR., 293(JAST):
    AUG72-925
    639(VQR):SPRING72-LXXII
TRELAWNY, E.J. ADVENTURES OF A
YOUNGER SON. (W. ST. CLAIR, ED)
    M. JACOBUS, 617(TLS):27DEC74-
    1461
TRELAWNY, E.J. RECORDS OF SHELLEY,
BYRON & THE AUTHOR. (D. WRIGHT,
ED)
    617(TLS):18JAN74-61
TREMBLAY, B. CRYING IN THE CHEAP
SEATS.*
    W.P. ROOT, 491:OCT73-34
TREMBLAY, J-P. GRAMMAIRE COMPARA-
TIVE DU FRANÇAIS ET DE L'ANGLAIS
À L'USAGE DES ANGLOPHONES.
    T.A. SHEALY, 207(FR):MAR72-883
    A. VAN DEN HOVEN, 628:FALL72-114
TRENCH, C.P.C. THE WESTERN RISING.
    J.R.Y. KING, 325:APR72-447
TRENDALL, A.D. GREEK VASES IN THE
LOGIE COLLECTION.
    R.M. COOK, 123:DEC73-290
    B.A. SPARKES, 303:VOL92-251
TRENDALL, A.D. THE RED-FIGURED
VASES OF LUCANIA, CAMPANIA & SIC-
ILY.* (1ST SUPP)
    N.R. OAKESHOTT, 303:VOL92-249
TRENOWDEN, I. THE HUNTING SUBMARINE.
    617(TLS):11OCT74-1143
TREPTOW, O. JOHN SIBERCH. (ABRIDGED
& ED BY J. MORRIS & T. JONES)
    D.W. EVANS, 354:MAR72-60
VON TRESKOW, I. DIE JUGENDSTILPOR-
ZELLANE DER KPM.
    F-A. DREIER, 135:JUL72-226
"TRÉSOR DE LA LANGUE FRANÇAISE."
(VOL 1) (P. IMBS, GENERAL ED)
    G. ANTOINE, 209(FM):OCT72-345
TREVISAN, D. THE VAMPIRE OF CURITI-
BA & OTHER STORIES.*
    P. CRUTTWELL & F. WESTBURG,
    249(HUDR):SUMMER73-417
TREVOR, W. ELIZABETH ALONE.*
    A. BROYARD, 441:13MAY74-35
    M. LEVIN, 441:30JUN74-30
    J. MELLORS, 364:FEB/MAR74-132
TREVOR-ROPER, P. THE WORLD THROUGH
BLUNTED SIGHT.
    H.P. RALEIGH, 290(JAAC):WINTER71-
    265
TREW, A. KLEBER'S CONVOY.
    M. LEVIN, 441:28APR74-37
TREWIN, J.C. PETER BROOK.
    R. HAYMAN, 157:SPRING72-75
TREWIN, J.C. - SEE O'CASEY, E.
TREXLER, R.C. SYNODAL LAW IN FLOR-
ENCE & FIESOLE, 1306-1518.
    J. KIRSHNER, 589:JUL73-593
TRIBE, D. PRESIDENT CHARLES BRAD-
LAUGH M.P.
    R.N. PRICE, 637(VS):SEP72-108

TRICAUD, F. - SEE HOBBES, T.
TRICKETT, R. BROWNING'S LYRICISM.
    M. HANCHER, 677:VOL3-318
TRIGG, R. PAIN & EMOTION.*
    B.L., 543:SEP71-137
TRIGGER, B.G., WITH A. HEYLER. THE
MEROITIC FUNERARY INSCRIPTIONS
FROM ARMINNA WEST.
    B.G. HAYCOCK, 318(JAOS):APR-JUN
    72-307
TRILLIN, C. AMERICAN FRIED.
    N.W. POLSBY, 231:AUG74-92
    R.A. SOKOLOV, 441:2JUN74-10
TRILLING, L. MIND IN THE MODERN
WORLD.*
    639(VQR):AUTUMN73-CLXX
TRILLING, L. SINCERITY & AUTHENTI-
CITY.*
    J. GINDIN, 385(MQR):SUMMER74-302
    H. LOMAS, 364:FEB/MAR73-140
    R. SALE, 249(HUDR):SPRING73-241
    R.E. SPILLER, 27(AL):NOV73-482
    W.K. WIMSATT, 676(YR):SPRING73-
    431
    639(VQR):SPRING73-XC
TRILSE, C. - SEE HEINE, H.
VON TRIMBERG, H. "DER RENNER" VON
HUGO VON TRIMBERG. (G. EHRISMANN,
ED)
    M.O. WALSHE, 220(GL&L):JUL73-347
TRINGHAM, R. - SEE MASSON, V.M. &
V.I. SARIANIDI
TRINKAUS, C. IN OUR IMAGE & LIKE-
NESS.*
    J.H. GEERKEN, 319:OCT74-525
    J.W. O'MALLEY, 551(RENQ):WINTER
    72-446
    B. VICKERS, 541(RES):NOV72-474
    D. WEINSTEIN, 322(JHI):JAN-MAR72-
    165
TRINTERUD, L.J., ED. ELIZABETHAN
PURITANISM.
    L.F. BARMANN, 613:AUTUMN72-465
    C.H. GEORGE, 551(RENQ):WINTER72-
    476
TRIPP, R.P. WITH PEN OF TRUTH.
    R.D. RICHARDSON, JR., 651(WHR):
    AUTUMN73-427
TRIVERO, P.A. L'ATTIVITÀ TEATRALE A
TORINO FRA LE DUE GUERRE.
    L.M., 228(GSLI):VOL149FASC465-
    146
TRIVERS, H. THREE CRISES IN AMERI-
CAN FOREIGN AFFAIRS & A CONTINUING
REVOLUTION.
    639(VQR):WINTER73-XXXVIII
TRNKA, B. A PHONOLOGICAL ANALYSIS
OF PRESENT-DAY STANDARD ENGLISH.
(2ND ED) (T. KANEKIYO & T. KOIZUMI,
EDS)
    R.E. BUCKALEW, 215(GL):VOL12#3-
    190
TROFIMENKOFF, S.M. ABBÉ GROULX.
    R. COOK, 99:MAY/JUN74-31
TROLLOPE, A. CLERGYMEN OF THE
CHURCH OF ENGLAND.
    617(TLS):27SEP74-1045
TROLLOPE, A. THE NEW ZEALANDER.
(N.J. HALL, ED)
    M. HARRIS, 72:BAND210HEFT4/6-422
    R. AP ROBERTS, 445(NCF):MAR73-
    472
    354:SEP72-263

TROLLOPE, T.A. WHAT I REMEMBER.
(H. VAN THAL, ED)
617(TLS):19APR74-415
TRONSKAJA, M. DIE DEUTSCHE PROSA-
SATIRE DER AUFKLÄRUNG.
R. FIENHOLD, 654(WB):10/1971-187
TROST, S. DIE PERSÖNLICHKEIT IM
UMSCHWUNG DER POLITISCHEN MACHT
NACH BALZACS COMÉDIE HUMAINE.
G.R. BESSER, 546(RR):DEC72-308
TROTSKY, L. LENIN. (T. DEUTSCHER,
ED & TRANS)
A. ASCHER, 550(RUSR):APR72-205
TROTSKY, L. 1905.* (A. BOSTOCK,
TRANS)
D.A. DAVIES, 32:DEC73-817
TROTSKY, L. LEON TROTSKY ON LITERA-
TURE & ART. (P.N. SIEGEL, ED)
R. SHELDON, 550(RUSR):JAN72-101
TROTSKY, L. LEON TROTSKY SPEAKS.*
(S. LOVELL, ED)
M. MC CAULEY, 575(SEER):OCT73-
628
TROTSKY, L. THE YOUNG LENIN.* (GER-
MAN TITLE: DER JUNGE LENIN.) (M.
FRIEDBERG, ED)
B.D. WOLFE, 32:DEC73-816
TROTTER, B. TELEVISION & TECHNOLOGY
IN UNIVERSITY TEACHING.
R.C. ELLSWORTH, 529(QQ):SPRING72-
123
TROUP, S.B., ED. THE PATIENT, DEATH
& THE FAMILY.
M.G. MICHAELSON, 441:21JUL74-6
TROUSSON, R. ROUSSEAU ET SA FORTUNE
LITTÉRAIRE.
D. LEDUC-FAYETTE, 542:JUL-SEP72-
337
J. VOISINE, 549(RLC):APR-JUN72-
306
205(FMLS):APR72-196
TROUSSON, R. - SEE FOUGERET DE MON-
BRON, L-C.
TROUSSON, R. - SEE MERCIER, L-S.
TROUT, P. LA VOCATION ROMANESQUE DE
STENDHAL.
F.W.J. HEMMINGS, 205(FMLS):JUL72-
230
TROVAIOLI, A.P. & R.B. TOLEDANO.
WILLIAM AIKEN WALKER.
639(VQR):SPRING73-XCII
TROYAT, H. DIVIDED SOUL.*
A. DE JONGE, 453:18APR74-30
TROYAT, H. PUSHKIN.*
R.B. ANDERSON, 399(MLJ):DEC72-
532
617(TLS):7JUN74-605
TRUBETZKOY, N.S. INTRODUCTION TO
THE PRINCIPLES OF PHONOLOGICAL
DESCRIPTION. (H. BLUHME, ED)
PRINCIPLES OF PHONOLOGY.*
J. VACHEK, 353:JAN72-49
TRUCHET, J., ED. THÉÂTRE DU XVIIIE
SIÈCLE.
W.D. HOWARTH, 208(FS):OCT73-455
TRUDEL, M. THE BEGINNINGS OF NEW
FRANCE 1524-1663.*
T.J.A. LE GOFF, 99:APR74-18
TRUDGILL, P. SOCIOLINGUISTICS.
R. DAVIES, 617(TLS):15NOV74-1291
TRUFFAUT, F. - SEE BAZIN, A.
TRULLEMANS, U.M. HUELLAS DE LA PIC-
ARESCA EN PORTUGAL.
E. GLASER, 240(HR):SUMMER72-323

TRUNK, I. JUDENRAT.*
617(TLS):5APR74-355
TRUNZ, E., ED. STUDIEN ZU GOETHES
ALTERSWERKEN.
H. REISS, 402(MLR):OCT73-943
TRUNZ, E. & W. LOOS, EDS. GOETHE
UND DER KREIS VON MÜNSTER.
W.H. BRUFORD, 402(MLR):APR73-457
TRYON, D.T. CONVERSATIONAL TAHI-
TIAN.*
R.F. MARTIN, 399(MLJ):DEC72-531
TRYON, T. HARVEST HOME.*
617(TLS):1MAR74-219
TRYON, T. LADY.
M. LEVIN, 441:22DEC74-15
TRYPANIS, C.A., ED & TRANS. THE PEN-
GUIN BOOK OF GREEK VERSE.*
G. THANIEL, 487:SUMMER72-189
TRYTHALL, J.W.D. EL CAUDILLO.
F.J. MORENO, 399(MLJ):APR72-268
TSANOFF, R.A. CIVILIZATION & PRO-
GRESS.
H.W. SCHNEIDER, 319:JAN74-137
G. WILLIAMS, 484(PPR):MAR73-440
TS'AO CHAO. CHINESE CONNOISSEURSHIP,
THE KO KU YAO LUN. (P. DAVID, ED
& TRANS)
H. GARNER, 39:JUL72-56
T. LAWTON, 54:DEC72-534
B. NEAVE-HILL, 135:JAN72-62
R. POOR, 293(JAST):MAY72-643
M. SULLIVAN, 127:SUMMER73-462
TS'AO HSÜEH-CH'IN - SEE UNDER CAO
XUEQIN
TSCHIŽEWSKIJ, D., ED. PRAGER LIN-
GUISTISCHER ZIRKEL: LITERATURWIS-
SENSCHAFT.
A. SHUKMAN, 575(SEER):JUL73-494
TSE-TUNG, C. - SEE UNDER CHOW TSE-
TUNG
TSE-TUNG, M. - SEE UNDER MAO TSE-
TUNG
TSIAPERA, M. A DESCRIPTIVE ANALYSIS
OF CYPRIOT MARONITE ARABIC.
A.S. KAYE, 318(JAOS):OCT-DEC72-
536
TSIRPANLIS, C.N. A MODERN GREEK
READER FOR AMERICANS.
J.E. REXINE, 399(MLJ):NOV72-464
TSIRPANLIS, C.N. A SHORT HISTORY OF
THE GREEK LANGUAGE.
J.E. REXINE, 399(MLJ):DEC72-534
TSOU JUNG. THE REVOLUTIONARY ARMY.
E. WICKBERG, 318(JAOS):JAN-MAR72-
148
TSURUMI, K. SOCIAL CHANGE & THE
INDIVIDUAL.*
G.A. DE VOS, 318(JAOS):OCT-DEC
72-558
TSUZAKI, S.M. ENGLISH INFLUENCES ON
MEXICAN SPANISH IN DETROIT.
J. NICHOLS, 545(RPH):NOV72-437
TSVETAEVA, M.I. NESOBRANNYE PROIZ-
VEDENIIA. (G. WYTRZENS, ED)
R.M. HAGGLUND, 32:JUN73-427
TSVETAYEVA, M. SELECTED POEMS.
K. FITZLYON, 364:APR/MAY72-128
R.M. HAGGLUND, 32:JUN73-427
M. MESIC, 491:JUL74-232
E. MORGAN, 617(TLS):11OCT74-1132
D. WEISSBORT, 565:VOL13#3-51

TSVETKOVA, B. KHAIDUTSTVOTO V BŬL-
GARSKITE ZEMI PREZ 15/18 VEK.
(VOL 1)
T. STOIANOVICH, 32:DEC73-846
TUBACH, F.C. INDEX EXEMPLORUM.*
J.G. ALLEE, 292(JAF):JUL-SEP72-
276
TUBBS, C.R. THE BUZZARD.
617(TLS):13SEP74-984
TUCHMAN, B.W. NOTES FROM CHINA.*
W.O. DOUGLAS, 31(ASCH):SUMMER74-
490
TUCHMAN, B.W. STILWELL & THE AMERI-
CAN EXPERIENCE IN CHINA 1911-1945.
C.F. ROMANUS, 293(JAST):FEB72-
400
TUCK, A. RICHARD II & THE ENGLISH
NOBILITY.
617(TLS):10MAY74-494
TUCKER, H., JR. - SEE RANK, O.
TUCKER, R.C. STALIN AS REVOLUTION-
ARY 1879-1929.*
B. DE MOTT, 61:FEB74-87
C. HILL, 453:24JAN74-9
R. PIPES, 617(TLS):14JUN74-625
TUCKER, R.N. JAPAN: FILM IMAGE.
617(TLS):20SEP74-1021
TUCKER, S.I. ENTHUSIASM.
A. BRUTEN, 447(N&Q):OCT72-390
J.D. BURNLEY, 566:SPRING73-115
G. REEDY, 173(ECS):SUMMER73-529
V. SALMON, 402(MLR):JUL73-621
G. STACY, 568(SCN):FALL-WINTER73-
97
TUCKEY, J.S. - SEE TWAIN, M.
TUDESQ, A-J. LA DÉMOCRATIE EN
FRANCE DEPUIS 1815.
N. HAMPSON, 208(FS):OCT73-500
TUGAN-BARANOVSKY, M.I. THE RUSSIAN
FACTORY IN THE 19TH CENTURY.*
A.J. RIEBER, 550(RUSR):APR72-206
TUGGLE, W.O. SHEM, HAM & JAPHETH.
(E. CURRENT-GARCIA, WITH D.B. HAT-
FIELD, EDS)
639(VQR):AUTUMN73-CLVII
TULARD, J. LE MYTHE DE NAPOLÉON.
J. GURY, 549(RLC):APR-JUN72-308
TULARD, J. - SEE CAMBACÉRÈS
TULLY, A. THE SECRET WAR AGAINST
DOPE.
R. SHERRILL, 441:7JUL74-1
TUMINS, V.A. TSAR IVAN IV'S REPLY
TO JAN ROKYTA.
J.L.I. FENNELL, 551(RENQ):WINTER
72-481
W.F. RYAN, 575(SEER):APR73-306
TÜMMLER, H. GOETHE ALS KOLLEGE.
J. GÖRES, 182:VOL25#1/2-46
TUNLEY, D. THE EIGHTEENTH-CENTURY
FRENCH CANTATA.
L. SALTER, 617(TLS):27DEC74-1465
TUNSTALL, J., ED. THE OPEN UNIVER-
SITY OPENS.
617(TLS):1FEB74-116
TUPLIN, W.A. THE STEAM LOCOMOTIVE.
617(TLS):15NOV74-1297
TUPPER, E.F. THE THEOLOGY OF WOLF-
HART PANNENBERG.
617(TLS):2AUG74-836
TURCHI, M. RIFLESSI LETTERARI IN
ITALIA DELLA BATTAGLIA DI LEPANTO.
A.D.B., 228(GSLI):VOL149FASC466/
467-461

TURCO, L. THE WEED GARDEN.
R. DICKINSON-BROWN, 398:WINTER74-
286
TURGENEV, I.S. QUELQUES LETTRES
D'IVAN TOURGUÉNEV À PAULINE VIAR-
DOT. (H. GRANJARD, ED) LETTERS
TO AN ACTRESS. (N. GOTTLIEB & R.
CHAPMAN, EDS & TRANS)
P. WADDINGTON, 617(TLS):6DEC74-
1396
TURGENEV, I.S. SPRING TORRENTS.
(L. SCHAPIRO, ED & TRANS)
R. FREEBORN, 575(SEER):APR73-300
205(FMLS):OCT72-385
TURKI, F. THE DISINHERITED.
S. HASSAN, 453:14NOV74-45
TURLACH, M. KERALA.
T.P. THORNTON, 293(JAST):AUG72-
979
TURNBULL, C.M. THE FOREST PEOPLE.
V. CRAPANZANO, 473(PR):3/1973-
471
TURNBULL, C.M. THE MOUNTAIN PEOPLE.
V. CRAPANZANO, 473(PR):3/1973-
471
617(TLS):8FEB74-131
TURNBULL, H. THE GUITAR.
617(TLS):26JUL74-788
TURNBULL, P. EUGÉNIE OF THE FRENCH.
617(TLS):5JUL74-730
TURNELL, M. JEAN RACINE - DRAMATIST.
W.G. MOORE, 364:APR/MAY72-139
639(VQR):WINTER73-XXVI
TURNER, D. - SEE MANDER, J.
TURNER, E.G. GREEK MANUSCRIPTS OF
THE ANCIENT WORLD.
J.N. BIRDSALL, 354:MAR72-57
D. CRAWFORD, 303:VOL92-252
TURNER, E.G. GREEK PAPYRI.
H. CADELL, 555:VOL46FASC1-137
TURNER, E.G. - SEE "ENTRETIENS SUR
L'ANTIQUITÉ CLASSIQUE" (VOL 16)
TURNER, F. BETWEEN TWO LIVES.
P. COOLEY, 385(MQR):WINTER74-79
L. SEARLE, 491:MAR74-353
617(TLS):29MAR74-339
TURNER, F. CATHOLICISM & POLITICAL
DEVELOPMENT IN LATIN AMERICA.
639(VQR):SPRING72-LXXIV
TURNER, F. SHAKESPEARE & THE NATURE
OF TIME.*
M. GRIVELET, 189(EA):OCT-DEC72-
544
K. MUIR, 447(N&Q):APR72-157
K. TETZELI VON ROSADOR, 72:BAND
210HEFT4/6-379
J.K. WALTON, 541(RES):AUG72-338
TURNER, F.M. BETWEEN SCIENCE & RELI-
GION.
617(TLS):26APR74-453
TURNER, G. A TIME TO HEAL.
617(TLS):27SEP74-1048
TURNER, L. MULTINATIONAL COMPANIES
& THE THIRD WORLD.
M. LIPTON, 617(TLS):2AUG74-830
TURNER, M.R., ED. PARLOUR POETRY.
B. BROWN, 617(TLS):15NOV74-1291
P. VEYRIRAS, 189(EA):JAN-MAR72-
178
TURNER, M.R., ED. THE PARLOUR SONG
BOOK.*
B. BROWN, 617(TLS):15NOV74-1291
A. LAMB, 415:MAR73-264

TURNER, P. & R. WOOD. P.H. EMERSON.
M. HAWORTH-BOOTH, 617(TLS):
27DEC74-1457
TURNER, R.L. & D.R. A COMPARATIVE
DICTIONARY OF THE INDO-ARYAN LAN-
GUAGES.
M. MAYRHOFER, 343:BAND15HEFT2-
220
TURNER, V. DRAMAS, FIELDS, & META-
PHORS.
R. FIRTH, 617(TLS):13SEP74-965
TURNER, W.O. CALL THE BEAST THY
BROTHER.
M. LEVIN, 441:27JAN74-12
TURNER-WILCOX, R. A DICTIONARY OF
COSTUME.
G. SQUIRE, 157:WINTER71-76
TURNEY, C. BYRON'S DAUGHTER.*
A.L. RUOFF, 651(WHR):SUMMER73-
315
617(TLS):14JUN74-646
TURVILLE-PETRE, G. NINE NORSE STUD-
IES.
A.J. DEVERSON, 67:NOV73-328
J. SIMPSON, 203:WINTER72-342
TUSIANI, J. ITALIAN POETS OF THE
RENAISSANCE.
W.J. KENNEDY, 275(IQ):FALL/WIN-
TER72-138
TUSTIN, F. AUTISM & CHILDHOOD PSY-
CHOSIS.
617(TLS):15FEB74-154
TUTE, W., WITH J. COSTELLO & T.
HUGHES. D-DAY.
617(TLS):7JUN74-599
TUTEN, F. THE ADVENTURES OF MAO ON
THE LONG MARCH.
E. ROVIT, 659:AUTUMN74-539
TUTTLE, I. CONCORDANCE TO VAUGHAN'S
"SILEX SCINTILLANS."*
K.J. HÖLTGEN, 447(N&Q):MAY72-187
TUTTLE, W.M., JR., ED. W.E.B. DU
BOIS.
A. GAYLE, 31(ASCH):SPRING74-332
TUTTLETON, J.W. THE NOVEL OF MAN-
NERS IN AMERICA.*
N. BAYM, 301(JEGP):JAN73-149
G. CORE, 385(MQR):FALL74-411
D.K. KIRBY, 579(SAQ):WINTER73-
169
639(VQR):AUTUMN72-CXXXII
TUVILL, D. ESSAYS POLITIC & MORAL &
ESSAYS MORAL & THEOLOGICAL. (J.L.
LIEVSAY, ED)
I. RIBNER, 677:VOL3-286
TVARDOVSKY, A. TYORKIN & THE STOVE-
MAKERS.
617(TLS):30AUG74-932
TWAIN, M. MARK TWAIN'S FABLES OF
MAN.* (J.S. TUCKEY, ED)
G. ARMS, 27(AL):MAR73-122
TWAIN, M. MARK TWAIN'S "WHICH WAS
THE DREAM?" & OTHER SYMBOLIC WRIT-
INGS OF THE LATER YEARS. (J.S.
TUCKEY, ED)
C.M. BABCOCK, 186(ETC.):MAR72-
101
TWAIN, M. WHAT IS MAN? & OTHER
PHILOSOPHICAL WRITINGS. (P. BAEN-
DER, ED)
L.P. SIMPSON, 27(AL):JAN74-617

TWAIN, M. THE WORKS OF MARK TWAIN.*
(VOL 2: ROUGHING IT.) (F.R. ROGERS
& P. BAENDER, EDS)
639(VQR):WINTER73-XXIX
"THE TWELFTH ANNUAL REPORT OF THE
KEEPER OF PUBLIC RECORDS." [LORD
CHANCELLOR'S OFFICE, GREAT BRIT-
AIN]
M.H. ARNOLD, 14:JUL/OCT72-419
"200 YEARS."
I.R. DEE, ?441:1DEC74-12
TWYCROSS, M. . THE MEDIEVAL ANADYO-
MENE.
617(TLS):15MAR74-261
TWYMAN, M. PRINTING 1770-1970.*
G. WAKEMAN, 354:SEP72-258
TYDEMAN, W., ED. ENGLISH POETRY
1400-1580.
N.W. BAWCUTT, 447(N&Q):MAY72-198
TYLER, A. CELESTIAL NAVIGATION.
G. GODWIN, 441:28APR74-34
TYLER, A. THE CLOCK WINDER.*
639(VQR):AUTUMN72-CXX
TYLER, R. THE PROSE OF ROYALL TYLER.
(M.B. PÉLADEAU, ED)
G.T. TANSELLE, 165:SPRING74-83
TYLOVÁ, M. PUBLIKAČNÍ ČINNOST PRA-
COVNÍKŮ ÚSTAVU PRO JAZYK ČESKÝ
ČSAV ZA LÉTA 1963-1967.
J.P. LOCHER, 343:BAND14HEFT1-82
TYRMAND, L. THE ROSA LUXEMBURG CON-
TRACEPTIVES COOPERATIVE.
H.K. ROSENTHAL, 32:MAR73-182
TZARA, T. LA PREMIÈRE AVENTURE CÉL-
ESTE DE MONSIEUR ANTIPYRINE.
S. FAUCHEREAU, 98:AUG/SEP72-752
TZARA, T. PRIMELE POEME. (S. PANA,
ED) LES PREMIERS POÈMES. (C.
SERNET, ED & TRANS)
S. FAUCHEREAU, 98:MAY72-416

"UE-BUCH DER KLAVIERMUSIK DES 20.
JAHRHUNDERTS."
M. DE VOTO, 513:FALL-WINTER69-
144
"UN GENERAL ASSEMBLY: STUDY OF THE
PROBLEMS OF RAW MATERIALS & DEVEL-
OPMENT; NOTE BY THE SECRETARY GEN-
ERAL." "UN CONFERENCE ON TRADE &
DEVELOPMENT: PROBLEMS OF RAW MA-
TERIALS & DEVELOPMENT; NOTE BY THE
SECRETARY GENERAL OF UNCTAD."
E. ROTHSCHILD, 453:16MAY74-16
UCHIMURA, K. THE COMPLETE WORKS OF
KANZO UCHIMURA. (T. YAMAMOTO & Y.
MUTO, EDS)
KUNIMOTO YOSHIRŌ, 285(JAPQ):OCT-
DEC72-491
UČIDA, N. DER BENGALI-DIALEKT VON
CHITTAGONG.
T. RICCARDI, JR., 318(JAOS):OCT-
DEC72-579
UEDA, M. MATSUO BASHŌ.
T.T. TAKAYA, 399(MLJ):MAR72-179
UEDING, G. SCHILLERS RHETORIK.
H.B. GARLAND, 182:VOL25#7/8-237
F. PIEDMONT, 481(PQ):JUL72-761
E. SCHAPER, 402(MLR):OCT73-944
UEHLING, T.E., JR. THE NOTION OF
FORM IN KANT'S CRITIQUE OF AESTHET-
IC JUDGMENT.
W.H. WERKMEISTER, 319:JUL74-405

UIBOPUU, V. SIMILARKOMPARATIVE KON-
STRUKTIONEN IM FINNISCHEN UND EST-
NISCHEN, INSBESONDERE IN DER MOD-
ERNEN SCHRIFTSPRACHE.
A. RAUN, 361:VOL29#2-190
UITTI, K.D. LINGUISTICS & LITERARY
THEORY.*
G. CLERICO, 209(FM):JAN72-61
UITTI, K.D. STORY, MYTH & CELEBRA-
TION IN OLD FRENCH NARRATIVE POET-
RY 1050-1200.
617(TLS):29MAR74-320
639(VQR):AUTUMN73-CLII
UJFALUSSY, J. BÉLA BARTÓK.*
H. TISCHLER, 32:JUN73-438
J.S. WEISSMANN, 607:#99-20
UJVÁRY, Z. AZ AGRÁRKULTUSZ KUTATÁSA
A MAGYAR ÉS EURÓPAI FOLKLORBAN.
F.L. KRAMER, 292(JAF):JAN-MAR72-
96
UKENA, P. - SEE VON HUTTEN, U.
UKENA, P. - SEE SEITZ, A.
ULAM, A. THE FALL OF THE AMERICAN
UNIVERSITY.*
676(YR):WINTER73-VIII
ULAM, A.B. THE RIVALS.*
E.B. TOMPKINS, 550(RUSR):OCT72-
410
ULAM, A.B. STALIN.
P. AVRICH, 441:27JAN74-7
B. DE MOTT, 61:FEB74-88
C. HILL, 453:24JAN74-9
C. NEWMAN, 231:FEB74-83
R. PIPES, 617(TLS):14JUN74-625
ULČ, O. THE JUDGE IN A COMMUNIST
STATE.
J. ROHLIK, 377:MAR73-57
Z.L. ZILE, 32:JUN73-401
ULIBARRÍ, S.R. TIERRA AMARILLA.
T.A. SACKETT, 399(MLJ):DEC72-515
ULLAND, W. "JOUER D'UN INSTRUMENT"
UND DIE ALTFRANZÖSISCHEN BEZEICH-
NUNGEN DES INSTRUMENTENSPIELS.*
H-J. LOPE, 209(FM):JUL72-264
ULLMAN, B.L. & P.A. STADTER. THE
PUBLIC LIBRARY OF RENAISSANCE
FLORENCE.
C.H. CLOUGH, 402(MLR):OCT73-905
ULLMAN, P.L. MARIANO DE LARRA &
SPANISH POLITICAL RHETORIC.*
J. CASALDUERO, 546(RR):APR72-164
T.A. SACKETT, 238:MAR72-179
191(ELN):SEP72(SUPP)-214
ULLMAN, R.H. THE ANGLO-SOVIET
ACCORD.
T.C. FIDDICK, 32:DEC73-820
617(TLS):11JAN74-31
ULLOA, B. LA REVOLUCIÓN INTERVENIDA.
H.D. SIMS, 37:AUG72-39
ULLRICH, F.B.C. - SEE UNDER CRUCITTI
ULLRICH, F.B.
ULMER, K. PHILOSOPHIE DER MODERNEN
LEBENSWELT.
L. BRAUN, 182:VOL25#23/24-838
ULRICH, A. ANTON ULRICH HERZOG VON
BRAUNSCHWEIG UND LÜNEBURG, "HIM-
LISCHE LIEDER" UND "CHRISTFÜRST-
LICHES DAVIDS-HARPFEN-SPIEL.
M. BIRCHER, 400(MLN):OCT72-788
UMPIERRE, G. DIVINAS PALABRAS.
D. LING, 402(MLR):OCT73-919
DE UNAMUNO, M. DIARIO ÍNTIMO.
P. DESCOUZIS, 238:DEC72-968

DE UNAMUNO, M. TRES NIVOLAS DE
UNAMUNO.* (D. BASDEKIS, ED)
T.R. FRANZ, 399(MLJ):OCT72-401
UNBEGAUN, B.O. RUSSIAN SURNAMES.
W.F. RYAN, 575(SEER):JUL73-461
UNBEGAUN, B.O., WITH D.P. COSTELLO
& W.F. RYAN - SEE WHEELER, M.
UNDERWOOD, M. A PINCH OF SNUFF.
N. CALLENDAR, 441:18AUG74-24
UNDERWOOD, M. REWARD FOR A DEFEC-
TOR.*
N. CALLENDAR, 441:31MAR74-41
UNDERWOOD, P. A GAZETTEER OF SCOT-
TISH & IRISH GHOSTS.
617(TLS):15FEB74-162
UNGAR, F. - SEE KRAUS, K.
"LES UNIVERSITÉS DU LANGUEDOC AU
XIIIE SIÈCLE."
P. KIBRE, 589:APR73-422
UNSELD, S., ED. GUNTER EICH ZUM
GEDÄCHTNIS.
617(TLS):29MAR74-314
UNSELD, S. HERMANN HESSE.
617(TLS):15MAR74-254
UNSWORTH, B. MOONCRANKER'S GIFT.*
A. BROYARD, 441:15MAR74-37
G. GODWIN, 441:7APR74-31
J. MELLORS, 364:FEB/MAR74-134
442(NY):13MAY74-157
UNVERRICHT, H. GESCHICHTE DES
STREICHTRIOS.
R.F.T.B., 410(M&L):OCT73-478
UPADHYE, A.N., ED. SAPTAŚATĪSĀRA
WITH BHĀVADĪPIKĀ OF VEMA BHŪPĀLA
[ALONG WITH THE] CHAPPANNAYA-GĀHĀO.
E. BENDER, 318(JAOS):OCT-DEC72-
569
UPADHYE, A.N. & OTHERS, EDS. ŚRĪ
MAHĀVIRA JAINA VIDYĀLAYA SUVARNAM-
AHOTSAVA GRANTH.
E. BENDER, 318(JAOS):OCT-DEC72-
569
UPDIKE, J. BUCHANAN DYING.
I. EHRENPREIS, 453:8AUG74-6
A. SCHLESINGER, JR., 61:JUN74-54
442(NY):8JUL74-80
UPDIKE, J. MUSEUMS & WOMEN & OTHER
STORIES.*
S. O'CONNELL, 418(MR):WINTER73-
190
W.H. PRITCHARD, 249(HUDR):SPRING
73-234
UPDIKE, J. RABBIT REDUX.*
M. FELD, 364:OCT/NOV72-152
E. LYONS, 145(CRIT):VOL14#2-44
E. ROVIT, 659:AUTUMN74-539
639(VQR):SPRING72-XLVIII
UPDIKE, J. SEVENTY POEMS.
P. PORTER, 364:JUN/JUL72-144
URBAN, M. EMIL NOLDE - LANDSCAPES,
WATER COLOURS & DRAWINGS.*
P. VERGO, 90:AUG72-565
URBAN, R. HISTORISCHE UNTERSUCHUN-
GEN ZUM DOMITIANBILD DES TACITUS.
K.H. WATERS, 313:VOL62-225
URBAN, Z. POZAPOMENUTÁ TVÁŘ BOŽENY
NĚMCOVÉ.
M. SOUČKOVÁ, 32:JUN73-435
URBANSKI, E.S. HISPANOAMÉRICA.
M.A. LUBIN, 263:OCT-DEC73-453

URLSPERGER, S., ED. DETAILED RE-
PORTS ON THE SALZBURGER EMIGRANTS
WHO SETTLED IN AMERICA. (VOL 2)
(NEWLY ED BY G.F. JONES)
    M.L. BROWN, JR., 656(WMQ):JUL73-
    533
URLSPERGER, S., ED. DETAILED RE-
PORTS ON THE SALZBURGER EMIGRANTS
WHO SETTLED IN AMERICA. (VOL 3)
(NEWLY ED & TRANS BY G.F. JONES &
M. HAHN)
    M.L. BROWN, JR., 656(WMQ):JUL73-
    533
    L.L. TRESP, 219(GAR):WINTER72-
    521
URMUZ. PAGINI BIZARE.
    S. FAUCHEREAU, 98:MAY72-416
UROFSKY, M.I. A MIND OF ONE PIECE.
    639(VQR):WINTER72-XI
UROFSKY, M.I. & D.W. LEVY - SEE
BRANDEIS, L.D.
URQUIDI, V.L. & R. THORP, EDS. LAT-
IN AMERICA IN THE INTERNATIONAL
ECONOMY.
    M. LIPTON, 617(TLS):2AUG74-830
URWIN, D.W. WESTERN EUROPE SINCE
1945.
    R. MARX, 189(EA):JAN-MAR72-185
URZIDIL, J. THERE GOES KAFKA.
    E. SPEIDEL, 447(N&Q):FEB72-66
USHER, S. THE HISTORIANS OF GREECE
& ROME.*
    J.A. ALEXANDER, 24:SPRING73-110
USIGLI, R. TWO PLAYS.
    A. RENDLE, 157:SUMMER72-75
USSERY, H.E. CHAUCER'S PHYSICIAN.
    R.H. ROBBINS, 72:BAND210HEFT4/6-
    366
USSHER, R.G. - SEE ARISTOPHANES
"LES UTOPIES À LA RENAISSANCE."
    F. HEIDSIECK, 542:APR-JUN72-179

VÄÄNÄNEN, V. INTRODUCTION AU LATIN
VULGAIRE. (2ND ED)
    L. ROMEO, 545(RPH):MAY73-692
VÄÄNÄNEN, V. - SEE CASTRÉN, P. & H.
LILIUS
VACALOPOULOS, A.E. ORIGINS OF THE
GREEK NATION.* (VOL 1)
    D.M. NICOL, 303:VOL92-257
VACCARO, G. VOCABULARIO ROMANESCO
BELLIANO E ITALIANO-ROMANESCO.
    P. GIBELLINI, 228(GSLI):VOL149
    FASC466/467-400
VACULÍK, L. THE AXE.* (GERMAN
TITLE: DAS BEIL; FRENCH TITLE: LA
HACHE.)
    P. ADAMS, 61:FEB74-96
    A. LEIHM, 98:OCT72-841
VACULÍK, L. THE GUINEA PIGS.* (GER-
MAN TITLE: DIE MEERSCHWEINCHEN.)
    P. ADAMS, 61:FEB74-96
    J. MELLORS, 362:5DEC74-753
VAGET, H.R. DILETTANTISMUS UND
MEISTERSCHAFT.
    E. BAHR, 406:WINTER73-431
    L. DIECKMANN, 301(JEGP):APR73-
    286
    T.P. SAINE, 222(GR):MAR72-130
VAIHINGER, H. KOMMENTAR ZU KANTS
KRITIK DER REINEN VERNUNFT. (VOLS
1&2) (2ND ED) (R. SCHMIDT, ED)
    J. KOPPER, 342:BAND63HEFT2-277

VAIL, V. & K. SPARKS. MODERN GERMAN.
    R.L. KYES, 399(MLJ):APR72-263
VAISSE, P. - SEE DÜRER, A.
VAIZEY, J. THE HISTORY OF BRITISH
STEEL.
    C. STORM-CLARK, 362:8AUG74-188
VAKALOPOULOS, A. ISTORIA TOU NEOU
ELLINISMOU. (VOL 4)
    R. CLOGG, 617(TLS):19JUL74-767
VALDÉS, MARQUESA D. - SEE UNDER DE
CASA VALDÉS, MARQUESA
DE VALDÉS, J. DIÁLOGO DE LA LENGUA.
(J.M. LOPE BLANCH, ED)
    A. ESPANTOSO DE FOLEY, 240(HR):
    SPRING72-222
VALDÉS-CRUZ, R.E. LA POESÍA NEG-
ROIDE EN AMÉRICA.
    O. FERNÁNDEZ DE LA VEGA, 263:
    APR-JUN73-212
VALENCY, M. THE CART & THE TRUMPET.*
    K. BAKER, 584(SWR):SUMMER73-276
    H.F. FOLLAND, 651(WHR):AUTUMN73-
    411
VALENTIN, P. & G. ZINK, EDS. MÉL-
ANGES POUR JEAN FOURQUET.
    J.E. HÅRD, 597(SN):VOL44#1-207
    E. TERNES, 343:BAND15HEFT1-15
VALENTINE, L. & A. THE AMERICAN
ACADEMY IN ROME, 1894-1969.
    639(VQR):AUTUMN73-CLXXIII
VALENTINI, N. & C. DI MEGLIO. SEX
& THE CONFESSIONAL.
    P. HEBBLETHWAITE, 617(TLS):6DEC
    74-1365
VALENTINOV, N. DVA GODA S SITVOLIS-
TATI. (G. STRUVE, ED)
    R.D.B. THOMSON, 104:SUMMER72-338
VALENTINOV, N. [N.V. VOLSKII] THE
EARLY YEARS OF LENIN. (R.H.W.
THEEN, ED & TRANS) ENCOUNTERS
WITH LENIN.
    R.H.W. THEEN, 104:SPRING72-120
VALENTINOV, N. NOVAIA ECONOMICHES-
KAIA POLITIKA I KRIZIS PARTII
POSLE SMERTI LENINA. (J. BUNYAN &
V. BUTENKO, EDS)
    G. GUROFF, 550(RUSR):APR72-193
VALERIUS FLACCUS, G. C. VALERI
FLACCI, "ARGONAUTICON LIBRI OCTO."
(E. COURTNEY, ED)
    J. ANDRÉ, 555:VOL46FASC1-157
VALÉRY, P. ANALECTS. (S. GILBERT,
TRANS)
    M. GUINEY, 399(MLJ):FEB72-110
VALÉRY, P. LE CIMETIÈRE MARIN.
(G.D. MARTIN, ED & TRANS)
    205(FMLS):OCT72-386
VALÉRY, P. THE COLLECTED WORKS OF
PAUL VALÉRY.* (VOL 1) (J. MATHEWS,
ED; D. PAUL & J.R. LAWLER, TRANS)
    K. MC SWEENEY, 529(QQ):AUTUMN72-
    438
"PAUL VALÉRY." [YALE FRENCH STUDIES,
NO. 44]
    N. SUCKLING, 208(FS):JUL73-354
VALESIO, P. STRUTTURE DELL'ALLITTER-
AZIONE.*
    G.C. LEPSCHY, 206:MAR72-276
    R. STEFANINI, 545(RPH):NOV72-361
VALETTE, R.M. ARTHUR DE GOBINEAU
& THE SHORT STORY.*
    A.D. HYTIER, 546(RR):FEB72-65

VALGARDSON, W.D. BLOODFLOWERS.
E.J. DEVEREUX, 99:SEP74-48
E. KLEIMAN, 296:VOL3#1-103
K. THOMPSON, 198:SPRING74-89
VALGEMAE, M. ACCELERATED GRIMACE.*
R.B. PARKER, 397(MD):MAR73-457
VÁLI, F.A. THE TURKISH STRAITS &
NATO.
L.M. LEE, 32:MAR73-199
VALLA, L. DE VERO FALSOQUE BONO.
(M. DE PANIZZA LORCH, ED)
D. CECCHETTI, 228(GSLI):VOL149
FASC466/467-421
DEL VALLE-INCLÁN, R. PÁGINAS SELEC-
TAS.* (J. MICHEL, ED)
M.A. SALGADO, 241:MAY72-91
VALLEJO, A.B. - SEE UNDER BUERO
VALLEJO, A.
VALLÈS, J. LITTÉRATURE ET RÉVOLU-
TION. (R. BELLET, ED)
R. GALAND, 207(FR):FEB72-758
VALLIÈRES, P. WHITE NIGGERS OF
AMERICA.* (FRENCH TITLE: NÈGRES
BLANCS D'AMÉRIQUE.)
J. KRAFT, 454:FALL72-73
VALLONE, A. L'INTERPRETAZIONE DI
DANTE NEL CINQUECENTO.*
J. CHIERICI, 276:SPRING72-81
VALLOTTON, M. & C. GEORG. FÉLIX VAL-
LOTTON.
N. LYNTON, 592:JUL/AUG72-54
VAMBE, L. AN ILL-FATED PEOPLE.
639(VQR):AUTUMN73-CLXVII
VANBRUGH, J. THE RELAPSE. (B. HAR-
RIS, ED)
K. STURGESS, 566:AUTUMN72-10
VANBRUGH, J. THE RELAPSE. (C-A.
ZIMANSKY, ED)
P.E. PARNELL, 568(SCN):FALL-
WINTER73-91
K. STURGESS, 566:AUTUMN72-10
VAN CAMP, J. & P. CANART. LE SENS
DU MOT "THEIOS" CHEZ PLATON.
J-F. COURNILLON, 542:JAN-MAR72-
39
VAN CONANT, L.M. AGUSTÍN YÁÑEZ.
J.L. WALKER, 238:SEP72-599
VANCOURT, R. LA PENSÉE RELIGIEUSE
DE HEGEL.
J. GRANIER, 542:JUL-SEP72-376
VANDALKOVSKAIA, M.G. M.K. LEMKE.
P. SHASHKO, 32:DEC73-811
VANDENBOSCH, A. SOUTH AFRICA & THE
WORLD.
R. DALE, 396(MODA):FALL73-428
VAN DE PITTE, F.P. KANT AS PHILOSO-
PHICAL ANTHROPOLOGIST.
W.H. WERKMEISTER, 319:JUL74-405
VAN DER BEND, J.G. HET SPINOZISME
VAN DR. J.G. BIERENS DE HAAN.
P. SOMVILLE, 542:APR-JUN72-229
VAN DER EYKEN, W., ED. EDUCATION,
THE CHILD & SOCIETY.
617(TLS):8MAR74-231
VAN DER PAARDT, R.T. L. APULEIUS
MADAURENSIS, THE METAMORPHOSES.
F. DELARUE, 555:VOL46FASC2-339
VAN DER POST, L. A FAR-OFF PLACE.
617(TLS):6SEP74-945
VANDER VEER, G.L. BRADLEY'S META-
PHYSICS & THE SELF.*
A.S.C., 543:DEC71-373
P. DUBOIS, 542:JUL-SEP72-343
[CONTINUED]

[CONTINUING]
F. RESTAINO, 548(RCSF):JAN-MAR72-
107
VANDERWERTH, W.C., COMP. INDIAN
ORATORY.
J.E. CHAMBERLIN, 249(HUDR):WIN-
TER73/74-786
VAN DE VATE, D., JR., ED. PERSONS,
PRIVACY, & FEELING.
W.D., 543:DEC71-378
VANDEVIVERE, I. LA CATHÉDRALE DE
PALENCIA ET L'ÉGLISE PAROISSIALE
DE CERVERA DE PISUERGA.
M. HUGGLER, 182:VOL25#13/14-492
VANDIER, J. MANUEL D'ARCHÉOLOGIE
EGYPTIENNE. (VOL 5)
A.M. BADAWY, 318(JAOS):APR-JUN72-
302
VÁNDOR, G. A RÉMÜLET EJSZAKÁI.
G. MIKES, 617(TLS):29NOV74-1348
VAN DOREN, C. & R. MC HENRY, EDS.
WEBSTER'S AMERICAN BIOGRAPHIES.
R.G. DAVIS, 441:1DEC74-100
A. WHITMAN, 441:23NOV74-29
VAN DOREN, M. GOOD MORNING.
J. PARISI, 491:SEP74-343
VAN DOREN, M. & M. SAMUEL. THE BOOK
OF PRAISE. (E. SAMUEL, ED)
N.K. BURGER, 441:22DEC74-14
VAN DUSEN, R. CHRISTIAN GARVE &
ENGLISH BELLES-LETTRES.
H. STREITER-BUSCHER, 52:BAND7
HEFT2/3-328
VAN DUYN, M. MERCIFUL DISGUISES.*
617(TLS):29MAR74-339
VAN DUYN, M. TO SEE, TO TAKE.*
T.H. LANDESS, 569(SR):WINTER73-
137
VAN DYKEN, S. SAMUEL WILLARD, 1640-
1707.
E.B. HOLIFIELD, 656(WMQ):JAN73-
181
VAN EERDE, K.S. WENCESLAUS HOLLAR.*
J. HAYES, 90:MAR72-182
VAN KAMPEN, B. THE WAY TO A MAN'S
HEART.
H. FRANCIS, 157:WINTER72-83
VAN LAAN, T.F. THE IDIOM OF DRAMA.*
M. GRIVELET, 189(EA):OCT-DEC72-
534
VANN, J.D., ED. CRITICS ON HENRY
JAMES.*
D.K. KIRBY, 432(NEQ):DEC72-591
VAN NIEL, R. A SURVEY OF HISTORICAL
SOURCE MATERIALS IN JAVA & MANILA.
J.A. LARKIN, 293(JAST):FEB72-471
VAN PASSEL, F. L'ENSEIGNEMENT DES
LANGUES AUX ADULTES.
E.C. CONDON, 207(FR):MAR72-882
VAN RIPER, C. THE NATURE OF STUTTER-
ING.
L. ASHMORE, 583:WINTER72-205
VAN ROSSUM-GUYON, F. CRITIQUE DU
ROMAN.
J. STURROCK, 208(FS):JUL73-367
S. SULEIMAN, 207(FR):APR72-1049
J. VERRIER, 557(RSH):OCT-DEC72-
628
VAN ROY, E. ECONOMIC SYSTEMS OF
NORTHERN THAILAND.
J.A. HAFNER, 293(JAST):FEB72-463
VAN TIEGHEM, P. DICTIONNAIRE DE
VICTOR HUGO.*
A.R.W. JAMES, 208(FS):JAN73-84

VAN VOGT, A.E. THE DARKNESS ON
DIAMONDIA.
617(TLS):15MAR74-269
VAN ZANTEN, D.T., ED. WALTER BURLEY
GRIFFIN: SELECTED DESIGNS.
D.L. JOHNSON, 576:MAR72-69
VÁRADY, L. DAS LETZTE JAHRHUNDERT
PANNONIENS (376-476).
M.A.R. COLLEDGE, 123:DEC73-243
VARAH, C., ED. THE SAMARITANS IN
THE '70S.
617(TLS):18JAN74-46
VARELA, F. DISPERSOS E PELA PRIM-
EIRA VEZ EM LIVRO (POESIA - PROSA).
(V.D.V. DE AZEVEDO, ED)
191(ELN):SEP72(SUPP)-210
VAREY, J.E. PÉREZ GALDÓS: "DOÑA PER-
FECTA."
205(FMLS):JUL72-290
VAREY, J.E. & N.D. SHERGOLD. FUEN-
TES PARA LA HISTORIA DEL TEATRO EN
ESPAÑA. (VOL 3)
G. EDWARDS, 402(MLR):JUL73-675
VAREY, J.E., N.D. SHERGOLD & J. SAGE
- SEE VÉLEZ DE GUEVARA, J.
VARGA, J. JOBBÁGYRENDSZER A MAGYAR-
ORSZÁGI FEUDALIZMUS KÉSEI SZÁZA-
DAIBAN, 1556-1767.
P.S. ELEK, 32:SEP73-643
VARGAS LLOSA, M. GARCÍA MÁRQUEZ.
G. DARÍO CARRILLO, 263:APR-JUN73-
184
D.L. SHAW, 402(MLR):APR73-430
VARGISH, T. NEWMAN.*
D.J. DE LAURA, 637(VS):MAR72-371
VARGYAS, L. - SEE KODÁLY, Z.
VARI, A. IL PRAGMATISMO. (A. SAN-
TUCCI, ED)
G. LANARO, 548(RCSF):JUL-SEP72-
354
VÁRKONYI, P. MAGYAR-AMERIKAI KAPCSO-
LATOK, 1945-1948.
S.D. KERTESZ, 32:MAR73-194
VARLEY, H.P. IMPERIAL RESTORATION
IN MEDIEVAL JAPAN.*
C.J. KILEY, 293(JAST):FEB72-409
VARLEY, H.P., WITH I. & N. MORRIS.
SAMURAI.
293(JAST):NOV71-237
VARNEY, J. TART IS THE APPLE.
M. LEVIN, 441:20JAN74-24
VARRO. THE FARMER. (B. TILLY, ED)
617(TLS):1MAR74-221
VARVARO, A. BEROUL'S "ROMANCE OF
TRISTRAN."
T.B.W. REID, 208(FS):JUL73-317
VASARELY, V. PLANETARY FOLKLORE.
P. ADAMS, 61:MAR74-97
VASARELY, V. VASARELY III.
S. BANN, 617(TLS):13DEC74-1410
VASARI, G. LE VITE DE' PIÙ ECCEL-
LENTI PITTORI SCULTORI E ARCHI-
TETTORI NELLE REDAZIONI DEL 1550
E 1568. (R. BETTARINI, ED)
H. ZERNER, 54:SEP72-355
VASMER, M. SCHRIFTEN ZUR SLAVISCHEN
ALTERTUMSKUNDE UND NAMENKUNDE.
(VOL 1) (H. BRÄUER, ED)
H. BIRNBAUM, 279:VOL15-220
VASYL'KO, V.S., ED. LES' KURBAS.
R.M. BAHRIJ-PIKULYK, 104:SUMMER
72-342

VATTIMO, G. IL CONCETTO DI FARE IN
ARISTOTELE. (VOL 13, FASC 1)
M-A. VINCENT-VIGUIER, 542:JAN-
MAR72-54
VATTIMO, G. SCHLEIERMACHER FILOSOFO
DELL'INTERPRETAZIONE.
E. NAMER, 542:JUL-SEP72-395
VAUCAIRE, M. LA BIBLIOPHILIE.
D.M. SUTHERLAND, 208(FS):APR73-
238
VAUGHAN, A.T., ED. THE PURITAN TRA-
DITION IN AMERICA 1620-1730.
C. TICHI, 165:FALL74-196
VAUGHAN, R. ALL THE MOON LONG.
617(TLS):6SEP74-960
VAUGHAN, R. PHILIP THE GOOD.
CHARLES THE BOLD.
617(TLS):4OCT74-1091
VAUGHAN, T. & G.A. MC MATH. A CEN-
TURY OF PORTLAND ARCHITECTURE.
505:MAY72-146
VAUGHN, R.G. THE SPOILED SYSTEM.
R. CASSIDY, 441:10NOV74-16
DEL VAYO, J.A. - SEE UNDER ALVAREZ
DEL VAYO, J.
VÁZQUEZ, J.A. - SEE UNDER AMOR Y VÁZ-
QUEZ, J.
VÁZQUEZ AMARAL, J. THE CONTEMPORARY
LATIN AMERICAN NARRATIVE.
L. GONZÁLEZ-DEL-VALLE, 263:OCT-
DEC73-472
VÁZQUEZ CUESTA, P. & M.A. MENDES DA
LUZ. GRAMÁTICA PORTUGUESA. (3RD
ED)
A. YLLERA, 202(FMOD):JUN72-344
VEALE, E.M. - SEE JAMES, M.K.
VEATCH, H.B. FOR AN ONTOLOGY OF
MORALS.*
H. RUJA, 484(PPR):SEP72-127
VEATCH, H.B. TWO LOGICS.*
A. SCHEFFCZYK, 53(AGP):BAND54
HEFT3-294
VECCHIO, E.B. - SEE UNDER BARBARO IL
VECCHIO, E.
VECCHIOTTI, I. LA FILOSOFIA DI
TERTULLIANO.
M. SPANNEUT, 557(RSH):APR-JUN72-
301
VECSEY, G. ONE SUNSET A WEEK.
B. KREMEN, 441:22SEP74-5
A.H. RASKIN, 441:16AUG74-27
VECSEY, G., ED. THE WAY IT WAS.
R.W. CREAMER, 441:1DEC74-90
VEENKER, W. VERZEICHNIS DER UNGAR-
ISCHEN SUFFIXE UND SUFFIXEKOMBINA-
TIONEN.
I. FUTAKY, 343:BAND14HEFT2-208
DE LA VEGA, G. - SEE UNDER GARCILASO
DE LA VEGA
DE LA VEGA, G.L.L. - SEE UNDER LOBO
LASSO DE LA VEGA, G.
DE VEGA, L. - SEE UNDER LOPE DE VEGA
DE LA VEGA, R. & H.J. SANDKÜHLER,
EDS. MARXISMUS UND ETHIK.
R. MALTER, 342:BAND63HEFT2-275
VELDHUYZEN, M., ED. OUDE EN NIEUWE
HOLLANTSE BOERENLIETIES EN CONTRE-
DANSEN.
H.M. BROWN, 415:OCT73-1015
VÉLEZ DE GUEVARA, J. LOS CELOS
HACEN ESTRELLAS.* (J.E. VAREY,
N.D. SHERGOLD & J. SAGE, EDS)
R.W. TYLER, 238:MAR72-177

VELLAS, V. & OTHERS - SEE "THE NEW
TESTAMENT IN MODERN GREEK"
VENABLES, F., ED. THE EARLY AUGUS-
TANS.
566:AUTUMN72-48
VENDLER, H. YEATS'S VISION & THE
LATER PLAYS.
H. ADAMS, 219(GAR):FALL72-249
VENÈ, G.F. PIRANDELLO FASCISTA.
E. SACCONE, 400(MLN):JAN72-153
VENEZKY, R.L. THE STRUCTURE OF ENG-
LISH ORTHOGRAPHY.*
Z. ŠALJAPINA & V. ŠEVOROŠKIN,
353:JUN72-89
VENGEROV, S.A., COMP. RUSSKIIA KNI-
GI - S BIOGRAFICHESKIMI DANNYMI OB
AVTORAKH I PEREVODCHIKAKH (1708-
1893).
M. RAEFF, 104:SPRING72-150
VENKATASUBBIAH, H. THE ANATOMY OF
INDIAN PLANNING.
K. NAIR, 293(JAST):MAY72-755
VENN, J. SYMBOLIC LOGIC. (2ND ED)
A. CHURCH, 316:SEP72-614
VENTE, R.E. PLANNING PROCESSES:
THE EAST AFRICAN CASE.
F. STEWART, 69:JAN72-85
VENTRIS, M. & J. CHADWICK. DOCU-
MENTS IN MYCENAEAN GREEK. (2ND ED)
P. LEVI, 617(TLS):9AUG74-854
VENTURI, F. UTOPIA & REFORM IN THE
ENLIGHTENMENT.*
C.N. STOCKTON, 481(PQ):JUL72-588
VENTURI, R., D.S. BROWN & S. IZENOUR.
LEARNING FROM LAS VEGAS.*
L.B. HOLLAND, 676(YR):SPRING73-
456
VENTURINI, G. UN UMANISTA MODENESE
NELLA FERRARA DI BORSO D'ESTE:
GASPARE TRIBRACO.
L. PAOLETTI, 228(GSLI):VOL149
FASC465-115
VENTURINI, G. - SEE VERDIZZOTTI, G.M.
VERBEEK, E. THE MEASURE & THE
CHOICE.
L.C. MC HENRY, JR., 173(ECS):
WINTER72/73-257
G.S. ROUSSEAU, 481(PQ):JUL72-709
VERCRUYSSE, J. - SEE DE VOLTAIRE,
F.M.A.
VERDAN, A. LE SCEPTICISME PHILOSO-
PHIQUE.
V. CAUCHY, 154:DEC72-613
VERDIER, A. LA VIE SENTIMENTALE DE
LAMARTINE.
F. LETESSIER, 557(RSH):JUL-SEP72-
456
VERDIZZOTTI, G.M. LETTERE A ORAZIO
ARIOSTI. (G. VENTURINI, ED)
M.P., 228(GSLI):VOL149FASC465-
145
VERGHESE, C.P. PROBLEMS OF THE
INDIAN CREATIVE WRITER IN ENGLISH.
J.P. GEMMILL, 352(LE&W):VOL15#4&
VOL16#1/2-916
VERGIL. VIRGILE, "LA HUITIÈME BUCO-
LIQUE."* (A. RICHTER, ED & TRANS)
M.C.J. PUTNAM, 24:SUMMER73-207
VERGIL. P. VERGILI MARONIS "AENEI-
DOS" LIBER I. (R.G. AUSTIN, ED)
W.A. CAMPS, 313:VOL62-230
J. PERRET, 555:VOL46FASC2-334

VERHAAR, J.W.M., ED. THE VERB "BE"
& ITS SYNONYMS. (PT 4)
B. SAINT-JACQUES & E.G. PULLEY-
BLANK, 215(GL):VOL12#1-52
VERHEUL, K. THE THEME OF TIME IN
THE POETRY OF ANNA AXMATOVA.
S. DRIVER, 32:SEP73-662
J.B. WOODWARD, 550(RUSR):JUL72-
308
VERÍSSIMO, É. BRAZILIAN LITERATURE.
191(ELN):SEP72(SUPP)-202
VERKUYL, P.E.L. BATTISTA GUARINI'S
"IL PASTOR FIDO" IN DE NEDERLANDSE
DRAMATISCHE LITERATUUR.
P. SKRINE, 402(MLR):APR73-474
VERLAINE, P. POÈMES CHOISIS. (M.
GALLIOT, ED)
J.L. SHEPHERD, 3D, 207(FR):OCT71-
297
VERLAINE, P. SELECTED POEMS. (J.
RICHARDSON, ED & TRANS)
D. KELLEY, 617(TLS):15NOV74-1291
VERLAINE, P. SELECTED VERSE. (D-J.
GOURÉVITCH, TRANS)
E.M. ZIMMERMANN, 207(FR):DEC71-
488
VERLAINE, P. SOME POEMS OF VERLAINE.
(R.H. MORRISON, TRANS)
S.E. LEE, 581:SEP73-335
VERLINDEN, C. THE BEGINNINGS OF
MODERN COLONIZATION.
P. MARAMBAUD, 189(EA):JUL-SEP72-
451
VERMANDEL, J.G. THE CLAVERSE AFFAIR.
N. CALLENDAR, 441:30JUN74-33
VERMES, G. & F. MILLAR - SEE SCHÜRER,
E.
VERMEULE, C. NUMISMATIC ART IN
AMERICA.
W.H. GERDTS, 127:SUMMER73-470
VERNADSKY, G. & R.T. FISHER, JR. -
SEE PUSHHAREV, S.
VERNIÈRE, P. - SEE DIDEROT, D.
VERNIÈRE, P. & R. DESNÉ, EDS. DIX-
HUITIÈME SIÈCLE. (VOL 2)
E. GUITTON, 535(RHL):JAN-FEB72-
135
B.N. MORTON, 207(FR):OCT71-283
VERNIÈRE, P. & R. DESNÉ, EDS. DIX-
HUITIÈME SIÈCLE. (VOL 3)
A.J. BINGHAM, 207(FR):APR72-1057
J-L. LECERCLE, 535(RHL):JUL-AUG
72-718
VERNON, J. THE GARDEN & THE MAP.
F.D. MC CONNELL, 659:SUMMER74-
406
617(TLS):12APR74-389
VERSNEL, H.S. TRIUMPHUS.*
D. MUSTI, 313:VOL62-163
R.M. OGILVIE, 123:MAR73-75
VERVLIET, H.D.L. LIPSIUS' JEUGD
1547-1578.
K.C. SCHELLHASE, 551(RENQ):
SPRING72-86
VERVLIET, H.D.L. & H. CARTER, EDS.
TYPE SPECIMEN FACSIMILES II.
P. GASKELL, 78(BC):WINTER72-561
VERVLIET, H.D.L. & H. CARTER. TYPE
SPECIMEN FACSIMILES 16-18.
D. CHAMBERS, 503:SUMMER72-108
VERWEYEN, T. APOPHTHEGMA UND SCHERZ-
REDE.
R. TAROT, 52:BAND7HEFT2/3-318

VESAAS, T. 30 POEMS. (K.G. CHAPMAN,
ED & TRANS)
L. ASKELAND, 563(SS):WINTER73-81
VESCOVINI, G.F. STUDI SULLA PROS-
PETTIVA MEDIEVALE.
E. NAMER, 542:JAN-MAR72-91
VESELOVSKY, Z. ARE ANIMALS DIFFER-
ENT? (M. BOORER, ED)
617(TLS):22FEB74-191
VESEY, G.S., ED. UNDERSTANDING WITT-
GENSTEIN.
617(TLS):18OCT74-1161
VESTAL, B. JERRY FORD, UP CLOSE.
N. VON HOFFMAN, 453:19SEP74-17
VEYSEY, A.G., ED. GUIDE TO THE
FLINTSHIRE RECORD OFFICE.
617(TLS):14JUN74-647
VEYSEY, L. THE COMMUNAL EXPERIENCE.
P. DELANY, 441:13JAN74-36
VIALE, V. GAUDENZIO FERRARI.
T.S.R. BOASE, 54:MAR72-94
VIALLANEIX, P., ED. LAMARTINE.
D.J. MOSSOP, 208(FS):JUL73-344
G. VANWELKENHUYZEN, 549(RLC):
JAN-MAR72-148
VIALLANEIX, P. - SEE DE LAMARTINE,
A.M.L.D.
VIAN, B. THÉÂTRE INÉDIT.
B.L. KNAPP, 207(FR):OCT71-219
VIANSINO, G. INTRODUZIONE ALLO
STUDIO CRITICO DELLA LETTERATURA
LATINA.*
A. ERNOUT, 555:VOL46FASC1-160
VIARD, J. PHILOSOPHIE DE L'ART LIT-
TÉRAIRE ET SOCIALISME SELON PÉGUY.
LES OEUVRES POSTHUMES DE CHARLES
PÉGUY.*
R.J. NELSON, 207(FR):OCT71-248
VIARD, J. PROUST ET PÉGUY.
J.A. GRIEVE, 67:NOV73-309
VIARRE, S. LA SURVIE D'OVIDE DANS
LA LITTÉRATURE SCIENTIFIQUE DES
XIIE ET XIIIE SIÈCLES.
E. JEAUNEAU, 542:JAN-MAR72-68
"VIATOR." (VOL 3)
R.J.P. KUIN, 70(ANQ):NOV73-43
VICAIRE, P. - SEE PLATO
VICINUS, M., ED. SUFFER AND BE
STILL.*
O. BANKS, 637(VS):MAR73-369
G.B. TENNYSON, 445(NCF):DEC72-
373
VICKER, R. THE KINGDOM OF OIL.
N. SAFRAN, 441:7APR74-10
VICKERS, B. CLASSICAL RHETORIC IN
ENGLISH POETRY.*
W.J. ONG, 128(CE):FEB72-612
VICKERS, B., ED. SHAKESPEARE: THE
CRITICAL HERITAGE. (VOL 1)
617(TLS):5JUL74-704
VICKERS, B. TOWARDS GREEK TRAGEDY.
617(TLS):29MAR74-320
VICKERS, G. FREEDOM IN A ROCKING
BOAT.
A. BLACK, 479(PHQ):JAN72-87
VICKERS, G. MAKING INSTITUTIONS
WORK.
617(TLS):1FEB74-98
VICKERY, J.B. ROBERT GRAVES & THE
WHITE GODDESS.
R.H.C., 125:FEB73-201
639(VQR):WINTER73-XXV

VICKERY, J.B. THE LITERARY IMPACT
OF "THE GOLDEN BOUGH."
D. ALBRIGHT, 639(VQR):SUMMER73-
461
C. ROSSMAN, 329(JJQ):SUMMER74-
420
"G.B. VICO, AN INTERNATIONAL SYMPOS-
IUM."
E. NAMER, 542:JUL-SEP72-339
VIDAL, G. BURR.*
P.N. FURBANK, 362:21MAR74-372
A. SCHLESINGER, JR., 61:JUN74-54
617(TLS):22MAR74-281
VIDAL, G. MYRON.
P. ADAMS, 61:DEC74-127
C. LEHMANN-HAUPT, 441:26NOV74-43
R. MAZZOCCO, 453:14NOV74-13
C. SIMMONS, 441:3NOV74-6
VIDAL, P. LA CIVILISATION MÉGALITH-
IQUE DE BOUAR.
R. DE BAYLE DES HERMENS, 69:
JAN72-78
VIDAL, R. THE "RAZOS DE TROBAR" OF
RAIMON VIDAL & ASSOCIATED TEXTS.
(J.H. MARSHALL, ED)
W.H. LYONS, 402(MLR):OCT73-912
205(FMLS):JUL72-288
VIDALENC, J. LE PEUPLE DES CAM-
PAGNES.
J.J. BAUGHMAN, 207(FR):OCT71-236
VIDERMAN, S. LA CONSTRUCTION DE
L'ESPACE ANALYTIQUE.
O. MARCEL, 542:OCT-DEC72-485
VIDLER, A.R. A VARIETY OF CATHOLIC
MODERNISTS.
P. MARSH, 637(VS):MAR72-364
VIDMAN, L. ISIS UND SARAPIS BEI DEN
GRIECHEN UND RÖMERN.
J.G. GRIFFITHS, 123:DEC73-217
TRAN TAM TINH, 487:SPRING72-100
R.E. WITT, 313:VOL62-198
VIEN, N.K. TRADITION & REVOLUTION
IN VIETNAM. (D. MARR & J. WERNER,
EDS)
H. MITGANG, 441:24AUG74-23
DE VIENNE, L. SPIRITUALITÉ DE LA
VOIX.
M. CHASTAING, 542:OCT-DEC72-487
VIER, J. HISTOIRE DE LA LITTÉRATURE
FRANÇAISE, XVIIIE SIÈCLE. (VOL 2)
E. GUITTON, 535(RHL):JUL-AUG72-
715
R. MERCIER, 557(RSH):APR-JUN72-
311
VIETH, D.M. - SEE DRYDEN, J.
VIETH, D.M. - SEE WILMOT, J.
"VIEWS FROM THE REAL WORLD: EARLY
TALKS OF GURDJIEFF."
D.W. HARDING, 453:18JUL74-6
VIGNAUX, P. LA PHILOSOPHIE AU MOYEN
AGE.
A. FOREST, 542:JAN-MAR72-76
DE VIGNY, A. STELLO [&] DAPHNÉ.
(F. GERMAIN, ED)
P.W. LOCK, 207(FR):OCT71-260
DE VILALLONGA, J-L. FIESTA.
R. LORRIS, 207(FR):MAR72-904
VILAR, E. THE MANIPULATED MAN.*
I. BENGIS, 441:24MAR74-32
VILELA, A. LA CONDITION COLLÉGIALE
DES PRÊTRES AU IIIE SIÈCLE.
H. MUSURILLO, 613:AUTUMN72-467

VILJAMAA, T. NOUNS MEANING "RIVER"
IN CURTIUS RUFUS.*
   B. LOFSTEDT, 260(IF):BAND76-298
   P.G. WALSH, 123:MAR73-100
VILJOEN, H.G. - SEE RUSKIN, J.
"LA VILLA ROMANA."
   R.M. OGILVIE, 123:DEC73-290
VILLAS BOAS, O. & C. XINGU. (K.S.
BRECHER, ED)
   J. UPDIKE, 442(NY):16SEP74-140
   A. WHITMAN, 441:16FEB74-29
   453:7MAR74-29
MADAME DE VILLEDIEU. LES DÉSORDRES
DE L'AMOUR. (M. CUÉNIN, ED)
   F. LAUGAA, 557(RSH):JUL-SEP72-
   451
   J.W. SCOTT, 208(FS):JAN73-63
   C.G.S. WILLIAMS, 402(MLR):APR73-
   411
VILLGRADTER, R. DIE DARSTELLUNG DES
BÖSEN IN DEN ROMANEN GEORGE ELIOTS.
   P.W. SCHRAMM, 445(NCF):MAR73-488
VILLIERS, C. L'UNIVERS MÉTAPHYSIQUE
DE VICTOR HUGO.*
   Y. GOHIN, 535(RHL):MAR-APR72-325
   J. SEEBACHER, 208(FS):OCT73-463
DE VILLIERS, G. KILL KISSINGER.
   N. CALLENDAR, 441:10NOV74-45
VILLON, F. OEUVRES.* BALLADES EN
JARGON (Y COMPRIS CELLES DU MS. DE
STOCKHOLM). (A. LANLY, ED & TRANS
OF BOTH)
   B.N. SARGENT, 207(FR):DEC71-534
VILLON, F. OEUVRES. (A. MARY, ED)
   J. FOX, 208(FS):JAN73-48
   W.W. KIBLER, 207(FR):DEC71-535
DE VILMORIN, L. POÈMES.
   F. GALAND, 207(FR):OCT71-219
VINAVER, E. A LA RECHERCHE D'UNE
POÉTIQUE MÉDIÉVALE.*
   N.B. SPECTOR, 405(MP):FEB73-258
VINAVER, E. THE RISE OF ROMANCE.*
   R.W. ACKERMAN, 401(MLQ):MAR73-98
   M.W. BLOOMFIELD, 589:JUL73-584
   D.S. BREWER, 402(MLR):OCT73-885
   J.H. CAULKINS, 188(ECR):SPRING72-
   65
   R.T. DAVIES, 541(RES):NOV72-463
   E. PORTER, 382(MAE):1973/2-168
   639(VQR):SPRING72-LIII
VINAVER, E. - SEE MALORY, T.
VINCENT, G. LE PEUPLE LYCÉEN.
   D. JOHNSON, 617(TLS):6DEC74-1360
VINCENT, H.P. THE TAILORING OF MEL-
VILLE'S "WHITE-JACKET."*
   P. MC CARTHY, 594:SPRING72-98
VINCENT, J.C. THE EXTRATERRITORIAL
SYSTEM IN CHINA, FINAL PHASE.*
   J.F. MELBY, 318(JAOS):JAN-MAR72-
   143
DA VINCI, L. - SEE UNDER LEONARDO DA
VINCI
VINÇON, H. TOPOGRAPHIE.
   M.H., 191(ELN):SEP72(SUPP)-171
VINEA, I. OPERE I: POEZII.
   S. FAUCHEREAU, 98:MAY72-416
LE VINIER, G. - SEE UNDER GUILLAUME
LE VINIER
VINOGRADOV, V.V. ANNA AKHMATOVA.
   A. HAIGHT, 575(SEER):APR73-327
VINOGRADOV, V.V., ED. SLAVJANSKOE
JAZYKOZNANIE.
   H.D. POHL, 353:15OCT72-117

VINOGRADOV, V.V., V.G. BAZANOV &
G.M. FRIDLENDER, EDS. ISSLEDOVAN-
IIA PO POETIKE I STILISTIKE.
   J. BAILEY, 32:DEC73-851
VINOKUR, G.O. THE RUSSIAN LANGUAGE.*
(J. FORSYTH, ED)
   R.E. BEARD, 399(MLJ):DEC72-521
   G. HÜTTL-WORTH, 350:SEP73-738
   F.J. OINAS, 550(RUSR):APR72-206
   205(FMLS):JAN72-94
VINQUIST, M. & N. ZASLAW. PERFORM-
ANCE PRACTICE.
   M. PETERSON, 470:MAY72-32
VINTON, J., ED. DICTIONARY OF CON-
TEMPORARY MUSIC.
   J. ROCKWELL, 441:9AUG74-31
VINTON, J., ED. DICTIONARY OF TWEN-
TIETH-CENTURY MUSIC.
   R. MACONIE, 617(TLS):6DEC74-1395
VIRGIL - SEE UNDER VERGIL
VIRGILLO, C. - SEE MACHADO DE ASSIS,
J.M. & M. DE AZEREDO
VIRIEUX-REYMOND, A. PLATON OU LA
GÉOMÉTRISATION DE L'UNIVERS.
   P-M.S., 542:JAN-MAR72-52
VIRMAUX, A. ANTONIN ARTAUD ET LE
THÉÂTRE.
   H. BÉHAR, 535(RHL):JAN-FEB72-159
VIRTANEN, R. ANATOLE FRANCE.
   J. SAREIL, 546(RR):FEB72-66
VISCA, A.S. ASPECTOS DE LA NARRA-
TIVA CRIOLLISTA.
   G. FIGUEIRA, 263:JUL-SEP73-346
"THE VISCONTI HOURS."* (M. MEISS &
E.W. KIRSCH, EDS)
   M.V. ALPER, 58:NOV72-92
VISHNYAKOVA-AKIMOVA, V.V. TWO YEARS
IN REVOLUTIONARY CHINA, 1925-1927.
   L.O-F. LEE, 293(JAST):FEB72-399
VITAL, D. THE SURVIVAL OF SMALL
STATES.
   H. HANAK, 575(SEER):OCT73-613
VITALIS, O. - SEE UNDER ORDERIC VIT-
ALIS
VITERBO, J. - SEE UNDER JAMES OF
VITERBO
VITTORINI, E. WOMEN OF MESSINA. A
VITTORINI OMNIBUS.
   R. MITGANG, 441:21JUN74-41
   P. SOURIAN, 441:30JUN74-6
VIVA, O.C. - SEE UNDER COSTA VIVA, O.
VIVANTE, P. THE HOMERIC IMAGINA-
TION.*
   H. CLARKE, 290(JAAC):FALL71-142
   G.L. COOPER 3D, 399(MLJ):FEB72-
   100
VIVAS, E. CONTRA MARCUSE.*
   T.R. MACHAN, 290(JAAC):SPRING72-
   401
VIVIANI, A. DAS DRAMA DES EXPRES-
SIONISMUS.
   H. DENKLER, 221(GQ):JAN72-152
   H. WEGNER, 133:1972/3-324
VIVIER, O. VARÈSE.
   R.D.E.N., 410(M&L):OCT73-485
VIZKELETY, A. - SEE SPANGENBERG, W.
VLASTO, A.P. THE ENTRY OF THE SLAVS
INTO CHRISTENDOM.*
   M. SAMILOV, 575(SEER):JAN73-131
VLASTOS, G., ED. THE PHILOSOPHY OF
SOCRATES.*
   J.J.R., 543:SEP71-143
   R.A. SHINER, 154:JUN72-289

VLASTOS, G., ED. PLATO: A COLLEC-
TION OF CRITICAL ESSAYS. (VOL 1)
 D. GALLOP, 154:JUN72-292
 C. KIRWAN, 479(PHQ):OCT72-358
 C.J. ROWE, 303:VOL92-218
 L.S., 543:MAR72-572
VLASTOS, G., ED. PLATO: A COLLEC-
TION OF CRITICAL ESSAYS. (VOL 2)
 C. KIRWAN, 479(PHQ):OCT72-358
 L.S., 543:MAR72-572
VLASTOS, G. PLATONIC STUDIES.
 G.E.R. LLOYD, 617(TLS):23AUG74-
 905
DE VLEESCHAUWER, H.J. LE PROBLÈME
DU SUICIDE DANS LA MORALE D'ARNOLD
GEULINCX.
 A. DE LATTRE, 542:APR-JUN72-208
VLIET, R.G. ROCKSPRING.
 P. ADAMS, 61:JUN74-115
VOET, L. THE GOLDEN COMPASSES.
 J. DREYFUS, 617(TLS):9AUG74-860
DE VOGEL, C.J. PHILOSOPHIA..* (PT
1: STUDIES IN GREEK PHILOSOPHY.)
 W.N. CLARKE, 258:DEC72-633
 E.N. LEE, 319:JUL74-384
 A.A. LONG, 479(PHQ):OCT72-361
VOGEL, E.F. CANTON UNDER COMMUNISM.
 A.P.L. LIU, 318(JAOS):APR-JUN72-
 346
VOGEL, J.F. DANTE GABRIEL ROSSETTI'S
VERSECRAFT.
 W.V. HARRIS, 191(ELN):SEP72-60
 J. REES, 677:VOL3-321
 D. SONSTROEM, 637(VS):DEC72-235
VOGEL, L.E. ALEKSANDR BLOK: THE
JOURNEY TO ITALY.
 617(TLS):10MAY74-504
VOGEL, U. KONSERVATIVE KRITIK AN
DER BÜRGERLICHEN REVOLUTION.
 H. HIRSCH, 182:VOL25#17/18-631
VOGEL, V.J. THIS COUNTRY WAS OURS.
 J.E. CHAMBERLIN, 249(HUDR):WIN-
 TER73/74-786
VOGELGESANG, S. THE LONG DARK NIGHT
OF THE SOUL.
 H. MITGANG, 441:24AUG74-23
VON DER VOGELWEIDE, W. - SEE UNDER
WALTHER VON DER VOGELWEIDE
VOGLER, T.A. PRELUDES TO VISION.*
 D.V.E., 191(ELN):SEP72(SUPP)-15
 K. KROEBER, 191(ELN):DEC72-154
VOGT, H. NEUE MUSIK SEIT 1945.
 J.S. WEISSMANN, 415:MAY73-496
VOGT, H. VORSCHULERZIEHUNG UND
SCHULVORBEREITUNG IN DER DDR.
 F. LILGE, 32:SEP73-634
VOGT, H. - SEE BUCER, M. & T. CRAN-
MER
VOGT, P. GESCHICHTE DER DEUTSCHEN
MALEREI IM 20. JAHRHUNDERT.
 F. WHITFORD, 592:NOV72-200
VOICANA, M. & OTHERS. GEORGE ENESCU.
 F. CHAGRIN, 607:#103-48
VÖLGYES, I., ED. HUNGARY IN REVO-
LUTION, 1918-19.*
 P.F. SUGAR, 32:SEP73-645
VOLKE, W., ED. HÖLDERLIN.
 C.H., 191(ELN):SEP72(SUPP)-163
VOLKMANN, H-E. DIE DEUTSCHE BALTI-
KUMPOLITIK ZWISCHEN BREST-LITOVSK
UND COMPIEGNE.*
 C.W. SYDNOR, JR., 104:SPRING72-
 165

VOLLRATH, E. DIE THESE DER META-
PHYSIK.*
 J. SIMON, 342:BAND63HEFT2-261
VOLSKII, N.V. - SEE UNDER VALENTINOV,
N.
DE VOLTAIRE, F.M.A. CANDIDE, OU
L'OPTIMISME.* (C. THACKER, ED)
 C. TODD, 402(MLR):APR73-413
DE VOLTAIRE, F.M.A. THE COMPLETE
WORKS OF VOLTAIRE.* (VOL 2) (O.R.
TAYLOR, ED)ז
 J.H. BRUMFITT, 208(FS):JUL73-335
 J. VERCRUYSSE, 535(RHL):JUL-AUG
 72-720
DE VOLTAIRE, F.M.A. THE COMPLETE
WORKS OF VOLTAIRE.* (VOL 7) (J.
VERCRUYSSE, ED)
 J.H. BRUMFITT, 208(FS):JUL73-336
DE VOLTAIRE, F.M.A. HISTOIRE DE LA
GUERRE DE 1741. (J. MAURENS, ED)
 J.H. BRUMFITT, 208(FS):OCT73-453
VONNEGUT, K., JR. BREAKFAST OF CHAM-
PIONS.*
 M. MUDRICK, 249(HUDR):AUTUMN73-
 545
 E. ROVIT, 659:AUTUMN74-539
VONNEGUT, K., JR. SLAUGHTERHOUSE-
FIVE, OR THE CHILDREN'S CRUSADE.
(FRENCH TITLE: ABATTOIR CINQ OU
LA CROISADE DES ENFANTS.)
 D.J. GREINER, 145(CRIT):VOL14#3-
 38
 P-Y. PETILLON, 98:APR72-386
VONNEGUT, K., JR. WAMPETERS, FOMA &
GRANFALLOONS.
 N. BALAKIAN, 441:23AUG74-27
VORDTRIEDE, W., WITH G. BARTENSCHLA-
GER - SEE "CLEMENS BRENTANO"
VORONEL, A. & V. YAKHOT, EDS. I AM
A JEW. JEWISHNESS REDISCOVERED.
 P. REDDAWAY, 453:12DEC74-36
VORZIMMER, P.J. CHARLES DARWIN.
 F.B. CHURCHILL, 637(VS):DEC72-
 257
VOSS, B.R. DER DIALOG IN DER FRÜH-
CHRISTLICHEN LITERATUR.
 P.L. SCHMIDT, 490:JAN72-121
VOSS, E.G. MICHIGAN FLORA. (PT 1)
 R. MC VAUGH, 385(MQR):SPRING74-
 169
VOVELLE, M. PIÉTÉ BAROQUE ET DÉ-
CHRISTIANISATION EN PROVENCE AU
XVIIIE SIÈCLE.
 R. DARNTON, 453:27JUN74-30
VOZNESENSKY, A. TEN' ZVUKA.
 E. MORGAN, 617(TLS):11OCT74-1132
VREEDE-DE STUERS, C. GIRL STUDENTS
IN JAIPUR.
 R.G. BENNETT, 293(JAST):FEB72-
 442
VROOMAN, J.R. VOLTAIRE'S THEATRE.
 D.J. FLETCHER, 208(FS):JUL73-334
 H. LAGRAVE, 535(RHL):MAY-JUN72-
 525
 R. NIKLAUS, 402(MLR):APR73-412
VRYONIS, S., JR. BYZANTIUM.
 P. CHARANIS, 589:JUL73-597
VRYONIS, S., JR. THE DECLINE OF
MEDIEVAL HELLENISM IN ASIA MINOR &
THE PROCESS OF ISLAMIZATION FROM
THE ELEVENTH THROUGH THE FIFTEENTH
CENTURY.
 J.W. BARKER, 377:MAR73-43
 P. CHARANIS, 589:JUL73-597

VUILLEMIN, J. LE DIEU D'ANSELME ET
LES APPARENCES DE LA RAISON.
D. BURRELL, 319:APR74-256
VUKANOVICH, E. ZVUKOVAIA FAKTURA
STIKHOTVORENII SBORNIKA "SESTRA
MOIA ZHIZN'" - B.L. PASTERNAKA.
D.L. PLANK, 32:MAR73-211
VYGOTSKY, L.S. THE PSYCHOLOGY OF
ART.
H.S. DAEMMRICH, 290(JAAC):SUMMER
72-564
J.D. WEST, 32:MAR73-202

WAAG, A. & W. SCHRÖDER, EDS. KLEIN-
ERE DEUTSCHE GEDICHTE DES 11. UND
12. JAHRHUNDERTS.
D.A. WELLS, 182:VOL25#13/14-476
DE WAARD, C. - SEE MERSENNE, M.
WAARDENBURG, J-J. L'ISLAM DANS LE
MIROIR DE L'OCCIDENT. (3RD ED)
H.K. SHERWANI, 273(IC):APR72-179
WACKENRODER, W.H. WILHELM HEINRICH
WACKENRODER'S "CONFESSIONS" & "FAN-
TASIES." (M.H. SCHUBERT, ED &
TRANS)
A. ANGER, 406:SPRING73-92
W.J.L., 191(ELN):SEP72(SUPP)-184
WADDICOR, M.H. MONTESQUIEU ET LA
PHILOSOPHIE DU DROIT NATUREL.
J. MAYER, 557(RSH):APR-JUN72-318
WADDINGTON, C.H., ED. TOWARDS A
THEORETICAL BIOLOGY. (VOL 3)
M. RUSE, 486:MAR72-105
WADDINGTON, M. DRIVING HOME.*
M. ESTOK, 150(DR):WINTER72/73-
653
C. MAC CULLOCH, 198:FALL74-96
WADDINGTON, M. - SEE KLEIN, A.M.
WADE, I.O. THE INTELLECTUAL DEVELOP-
MENT OF VOLTAIRE.*
W.H. BARBER, 208(FS):OCT73-452
WADE, I.O. THE INTELLECTUAL ORIGINS
OF THE FRENCH ENLIGHTENMENT.*
V. BROMBERT, 249(HUDR):SUMMER73-
405
J. GUICHARNAUD, 676(YR):AUTUMN72-
106
H.L. STANSELL, 377:MAR73-52
R.S. TATE, JR., 481(PQ):JUL72-
589
A. VARTANIAN, 401(MLQ):DEC73-467
639(VQR):SUMMER72-CVI
WADE, J.D. AUGUSTUS BALDWIN LONG-
STREET. (M.T. INGE, ED)
M.E. BRADFORD, 577(SHR):SPRING72-
206
WADE, R.A. THE RUSSIAN SEARCH FOR
PEACE - FEBRUARY-OCTOBER, 1917.
R. PETHYBRIDGE, 575(SEER):APR73-
332
WADSWORTH, J.B., ED. THE COMEDY OF
EROS. (N.R. SHAPIRO, TRANS)
A. SCAGLIONE, 545(RPH):MAY73-748
WADSWORTH, J.E., ED. THE BANKS &
THE MONETARY SYSTEM IN THE U.K.
1959-71.
T.M. PODOLSKI, 182:VOL25#19/20-
653
WAEGER, G. DIE SÜNDENBOCKE DER
SCHWEIZ.
A. WAHL, 182:VOL25#1/2-57

WAGENHEIM, K. BABE RUTH.
R. ANGELL, 441:13OCT74-6
C.M. CURTIS, 61:NOV74-110
WAGENKNECHT, C. WECKHERLIN UND
OPITZ.
J.L. GELLINEK, 301(JEGP):APR73-
279
W. HOFFMANN, 224(GRM):BAND22HEFT
2-202
WAGENKNECHT, D. BLAKE'S NIGHT.
617(TLS):15FEB74-145
WAGENKNECHT, E. AMBASSADORS FOR
CHRIST.
R.S. KLEIN, 432(NEQ):DEC72-581
WAGENKNECHT, E. JAMES RUSSELL
LOWELL.*
S.J. HASELTON, 613:SUMMER72-307
C. PEROTIN, 189(EA):JUL-SEP72-
451
WAGNER, E. BETTER OCCASIONS.
H. KRAMER, 441:26MAY74-4
WAGNER, G. ON THE WISDOM OF WORDS.*
G.A. BORDEN, 480(P&R):WINTER72-
58
W. BRONZWAER, 206:MAY72-447
R. WANDERER, 186(ETC.):DEC72-434
WAGNER, H. LINGUISTIC ATLAS & SUR-
VEY OF IRISH DIALECTS. (VOLS 1&2)
K.H. SCHMIDT, 343:BAND15HEFT1-
100
WAGNER, H. LINGUISTIC ATLAS & SUR-
VEY OF IRISH DIALECTS. (VOL 3)
W. MEID, 260(IF):BAND76-316
K.H. SCHMIDT, 343:BAND15HEFT1-
100
WAGNER, H. & H. KOLLER - SEE LHOTSKY,
A.
WAGNER, H. & C. Ó BAOÍLL. LINGUIS-
TIC ATLAS & SURVEY OF IRISH DIA-
LECTS. (VOL 4)
W. MEID, 260(IF):BAND76-316
K.H. SCHMIDT, 343:BAND15HEFT1-
100
WAGNER, J. BLACK POETS OF THE
UNITED STATES.*
617(TLS):29MAR74-339
WAGNER, K.H. GENERATIVE GRAMMATICAL
STUDIES IN THE OLD ENGLISH LANGU-
AGE.*
H.E. BREKLE, 206:MAY72-449
K.R. GRINDA, 260(IF):BAND77HEFT1-
120
E.C. TRAUGOTT, 297(JL):SEP72-297
WAGNER, M. DIE LEXIKALISCHEN UND
GRAMMATIKALISCHEN ARAMAISMEN IM
ALTTESTAMENTLICHEN HEBRÄISCH.
S. MORAG, 318(JAOS):APR-JUN72-
298
WAGNER, R. EIN NÜCZ UND SCHONE LER
VON DER AYGEN ERKANTNUSS.
R. RUDOLF, 182:VOL25#21-737
WAGNER, R. SÄMTLICHE WERKE. (VOLS
14 & 30) (M. BECK & E. VOSS, EDS)
R. CRAFT, 453:31OCT74-11
WAGNER, R. WAGNER WRITES FROM
PARIS... (R.L. JACOBS & G. SKEL-
TON, EDS & TRANS) STORIES &
ESSAYS. (C. OSBORNE, ED)
617(TLS):29MAR74-347
WAGNER-RIEGER, R. WIENS ARCHITEKTUR
IM 19. JAHRHUNDERT.
J. MAASS, 576:MAY72-156
P.V., 90:JAN72-52

WAGONER, D. NEW & SELECTED POEMS.
  J.T. IRWIN, 569(SR):WINTER73-158
WAGONER, D. RIVERBED.*
  W.G.R., 502(PRS):SUMMER72-186
WAGONER, D. THE ROAD TO MANY A
WONDER.
  P. ADAMS, 61:JUL74-100
  S. BLACKBURN, 441:21APR74-36
WAGONER, D. - SEE ROETHKE, T.
WAHLHAUS, R. JEWISH GOURMET COOKING.
  617(TLS):31MAY74-592
WAHLOO, P. THE GENERALS.
  617(TLS):19APR74-409
WAHLSTRÖM, E. ACCENTUAL RESPONSION
IN GREEK STROPHIC POETRY.
  D.C. INNES, 123:MAR73-94
WAHTERA, J. THE HAPPENING.
  M. LEVIN, 441:1DEC74-78
WAIDSON, H.M. THE MODERN GERMAN
NOVEL, 1945-1965. (2ND ED)
  J.J. WHITE, 402(MLR):JUL73-711
WAIN, J. ARNOLD BENNETT.
  L. TILLIER, 189(EA):JUL-SEP72-
  443
WAIN, J. SAMUEL JOHNSON.
  J. CAREY, 362:21NOV74-678
  D. GREENE, 617(TLS):22NOV74-1315
WAIN, J. THE LIFE GUARD.
  J. MILLS, 648:JAN73-56
  P. YVARD, 189(EA):JUL-SEP72-448
WAIN, J. - SEE JOHNSON, S.
WAIS, K., ED. DER ARTHURISCHE ROMAN.
  H. NEWSTEAD, 545(RPH):FEB73-594
WAISSENBERGER, R. DIE WIENER SECES-
SION.
  N. POWELL, 90:JUN72-420
WAIT, R.J.C. THE BACKGROUND OF
SHAKESPEARE'S SONNETS.*
  I. BROWN, 157:WINTER72-72
WAITE, P.B. CANADA, 1874-1896.*
  K. MC NAUGHT, 150(DR):AUTUMN72-
  496
WAITH, E.M. IDEAS OF GREATNESS.
  W. FROST, 301(JEGP):JAN73-132
  R.D. HUME, 481(PQ):JUL72-635
  G.E. JOHNSON, 551(RENQ):WINTER72-
  510
  E. SPÄTH, 38:BAND9OHEFT4-530
  M. WEST, 128(CE):MAY73-1131
  566:SPRING73-108
WAITH, E.M. & J.D. HUBERT. FRENCH &
ENGLISH DRAMA OF THE SEVENTEENTH
CENTURY.
  G. MARSHALL, 568(SCN):SPRING73-
  19
WAKEFIELD, D. STARTING OVER.*
  J. MELLORS, 362:16MAY74-641
WAKEFIELD, D., ED. STENDHAL & THE
ARTS.
  617(TLS):3MAY74-464
WAKEFIELD, W.L. HERESY, CRUSADE &
INQUISITION IN SOUTHERN FRANCE
1100-1250.
  617(TLS):9AUG74-862
WAKELIN, M.F., ED. PATTERNS IN THE
FOLK SPEECH OF THE BRITISH ISLES.
  H. HARGREAVES, 541(RES):NOV72-
  460
  B.M.H. STRANG, 447(N&Q):JUL72-
  269
  205(FMLS):OCT72-384
WAKELYN, J.L. THE POLITICS OF A
LITERARY MAN.
  C.H. HOLMAN, 27(AL):JAN74-614

WAKEMAN, F., JR. HISTORY & WILL.
  617(TLS):15MAR74-251
WAKOSKI, D. GREED, PARTS 5-7.
  639(VQR):WINTER72-XXIII
WAKOSKI, D. GREED: PARTS 8, 9, 11.
  G. BURNS, 584(SWR):SUMMER73-278
  V. YOUNG, 249(HUDR):WINTER73/74-
  724
  639(VQR):AUTUMN73-CXL
WAKOSKI, D. THE MOTORCYCLE BETRAYAL
POEMS.*
  639(VQR):AUTUMN72-CXXIV
WAKOSKI, D. SMUDGING.*
  D. BLAZEK, 491:JUN74-167
  639(VQR):WINTER73-XIII
WALBANK, F.W. POLYBIUS.*
  F. LASSERRE, 182:VOL25#23/24-885
  A. MOMIGLIANO, 453:18JUL74-33
  639(VQR):AUTUMN73-CLXI
WALCOT, P. GREEK PEASANTS, ANCIENT
& MODERN.
  M. ALEXIOU, 303:VOL92-258
WALCOTT, D. ANOTHER LIFE.*
  T.R. EDWARDS, 453:13JUN74-37
  R. GARFITT, 364:DEC73/JAN74-124
  P. SMYTH, 491:DEC73-165
WALCOTT, F.G. THE ORIGINS OF CUL-
TURE & ANARCHY.
  J.E. FREY, 637(VS):JUN72-494
WALD, H. REALITATE SI LIMBAJ.
  A. TILMAN, 542:OCT-DEC72-487
WALDENFELS, B. DAS ZWISCHENREICH
DES DIALOGS.
  S.L. HART, 484(PPR):DEC72-291
  D. HOWARD, 182:VOL25#3/4-69
WALDER, D. THE SHORT VICTORIOUS
WAR.
  442(NY):21OCT74-191
WALDHORN, A. A READER'S GUIDE TO
ERNEST HEMINGWAY.
  A.K. LOSS, 27(AL):MAY73-309
WALDMAN, A. LIFE NOTES.
  G. MALANGA, 491:JAN74-236
WALDMAN, D. ELLSWORTH KELLY.
  A. FRANKENSTEIN, 55:MAR73-16
WALDMAN, M. THE LADY MARY.
  639(VQR):WINTER73-XXVIII
WALDRON, R.A. - SEE "SIR GAWAIN &
THE GREEN KNIGHT"
WALKER, A. IN LOVE & TROUBLE.
  M. WATKINS, 441:17MAR74-40
WALKER, A., ED. ROBERT SCHUMANN.*
  G.W. HOPKINS, 415:AUG73-797
  J.A.W., 410(M&L):JUL73-357
WALKER, A.A., COMP. OFFICIAL PUBLI-
CATIONS OF BRITISH EAST AFRICA.
(PTS 2-4) OFFICIAL PUBLICATIONS
OF SIERRA LEONE & GAMBIA. THE
RHODESIAS & NYASALAND: A GUIDE TO
OFFICIAL PUBLICATIONS.
  J.A. CASADA, 517(PBSA):APR-JUN73-
  207
WALKER, A.K. WILLIAM LAW.
  617(TLS):2AUG74-836
WALKER, B. THE DONKEY CART.
  617(TLS):5APR74-376
WALKER, B.G. CHARTED KNITTING PAT-
TERNS.
  M.W. PHILLIPS, 139:DEC72-66
WALKER, D. BLACK DOUGAL.
  N. CALLENDAR, 441:10MAR74-12
WALKER, D.P. SPIRITUAL & DEMONIC
MAGIC FROM FICINO TO CAMPANELLA.
  E. NAMER, 542:APR-JUN72-178

WALKER, E.C. WILLIAM DELL: MASTER
PURITAN.*
C.H. GEORGE, 551(RENQ):WINTER72-
476
WALKER, K.S. DANCE & ITS CREATORS.
R. BAKER, 151:SEP72-77
WALKER, T. GLOVES TO THE HANGMAN.*
R. GARFITT, 364:AUG/SEP73-123
WALL, D. VISIONARY CITIES.
W.J. MALACHER, 363:MAY72-102
C.P., 505:MAR72-114
WALL, R.E., JR. MASSACHUSETTS BAY.
R.C. SIMMONS, 656(WMQ):APR73-342
WALLACE, B. VILLAGE LIFE IN INSUL-
AR SOUTHEAST ASIA.
S.A. SCHLEGEL, 293(JAST):AUG72-
990
WALLACE, G.A. & A.D.M. WALKER, EDS.
THE DEFINITION OF MORALITY.
R.D.L., 543:DEC71-375
WALLACE, H.A. THE PRICE OF VISION.*
M. KEMPTON, 453:4APR74-24
WALLACE, I. THE FAN CLUB.
W. FEAVER, 617(TLS):25OCT74-1183
J. FLAHERTY, 441:16JUN74-24
WALLACE, M. A SHORT HISTORY OF IRE-
LAND.
617(TLS):18JAN74-45
WALLACE, W.A. CAUSALITY & SCIENTIF-
IC EXPLANATION.
617(TLS):26APR74-453
WALLER, B. BISMARCK AT THE CROSS-
ROADS.
617(TLS):9AUG74-862
WALLER, D.J. THE GOVERNMENT & POLI-
TICS OF COMMUNIST CHINA.
J.F. COOPER, 293(JAST):AUG72-943
WALLER, I. MEN RELEASED FROM PRISON.
J. HAGAN, 99:NOV/DEC74-36
WALLER, L. THE COAST OF FEAR.
M. LEVIN, 441:18AUG74-20
WALLER, R. BE HUMAN OR DIE.
617(TLS):19APR74-413
WALLERSTEIN, I. THE MODERN WORLD-
SYSTEM.
G. LENZER, 441:29DEC74-17
WALLIS, J. GRAMMAR OF THE ENGLISH
LANGUAGE. (J.A. KEMP, ED & TRANS)
S. POTTER, 402(MLR):JUL73-629
WALLMANN, J.M. JUDAS CROSS.
N. CALLENDAR, 441:4AUG74-24
WALLNER, B., ED. A MIDDLE ENGLISH
VERSION OF THE INTRODUCTION TO GUY
DE CHAULIAC'S "CHIRURGIA MAGNA."*
E.J. FREEMAN, 597(SN):VOL44#2-
441
WALLRAFF, C.F. KARL JASPERS.
J.D.C., 543:SEP71-137
H.W. HAMILTON, 479(PHQ):APR72-
169
WALPOLE, H. SELECTED LETTERS OF
HORACE WALPOLE.* (W.S. LEWIS, ED)
639(VQR):AUTUMN73-CLVII
WALPOLE, H. HORACE WALPOLE'S CORRES-
PONDENCE. (VOLS 9-11) (W.S. LEWIS
& OTHERS, EDS)
R.D. ALTICK, 639(VQR):AUTUMN72-
613
M. KALLICH, 481(PQ):JUL72-782
WALPOLE, H. HORACE WALPOLE'S CORRES-
PONDENCE. (VOLS 35&36) (W.S.
LEWIS, ED)
M. DRABBLE, 362:6JUN74-738
617(TLS):3MAY74-469

WALSER, M. THE UNICORN.
E. GLOVER, 565:VOL13#3-44
WALSH, D. LITERATURE & KNOWLEDGE.*
M.C. ROSE, 321:WINTER72[VOL6#4]-
317
WALSH, D.D. & H.G. STURM. REPASO.
(REV)
R.W. HATTON, 238:MAY72-401
WALSH, G. GENTLEMAN JIMMY WALKER.
H. MITGANG, 441:18DEC74-49
WALSH, J.E. THE HIDDEN LIFE OF
EMILY DICKINSON.
N.C. CARPENTER, 219(GAR):SUMMER
72-231
G. MONTERO, 502(PRS):SUMMER72-
178
F.L. MOREY, 613:AUTUMN72-454
WALSH, P.G. THE ROMAN NOVEL.*
A. CAMERON, 123:MAR73-44
WALSH, R. EACH MAN IN HIS TIME.
J. SAYRE, 441:15DEC74-22
M. WOOD, 453:31OCT74-39
WALSH, S. THE LIEDER OF SCHUMANN.*
P. HAMBURGER, 607:#100-31
WALTER, H-A. DEUTSCHE EXILLITERATUR
1933-1950. (VOLS 1, 2 & 7)
T.J. REED, 617(TLS):25OCT74-1199
WALTER, N. - SEE KROPOTKIN, P.A.
WALTERS, B. IMAGES OF STONE.
617(TLS):11OCT74-1119
WALTHER VON DER VOGELWEIDE. DIE
LIEDER. (F. MAURER, ED)
P.F. GANZ, 220(GL&L):JUL73-353
WALTON, C. DE LA RECHERCHE DU BIEN.
T.M. LENNON, 319:APR74-261
WALTON, J.K. THE QUARTO COPY FOR
THE FIRST FOLIO OF SHAKESPEARE.
J. FEATHER, 447(N&Q):APR72-148
J.B. FORT, 189(EA):OCT-DEC72-539
A. SMITH, 354:DEC72-354
WALTON, L. THE GALÁPAGOS KID.
639(VQR):WINTER72-XVIII
WALTON, P.H. THE DRAWINGS OF JOHN
RUSKIN.
D. THOMAS, 135:DEC72-291
WALZER, M., ED. REGICIDE & REVOLU-
TION.
R.M. ANDREWS, 441:9JUN74-3
617(TLS):26JUL74-808
WAMBAUGH, J. THE ONION FIELD.*
617(TLS):1NOV74-1220
"THE WANDERER."* (T.P. DUNNING &
A.J. BLISS, EDS)
K.R. GRINDA, 38:BAND90HEFT1/2-
216
WANDRUSZKA, U. FRANZÖSISCHE NOMI-
NALSYNTAGMEN.
M. SANDMANN, 72:BAND210HEFT4/6-
433
WANG, H. FROM MATHEMATICS TO PHIL-
OSOPHY.
617(TLS):24MAY74-567
WANG KUO-WEI. POETIC REMARKS IN THE
HUMAN WORLD (JEN CHIEN TZ'U HUA).
C.S. GOODRICH, 318(JAOS):OCT-DEC
72-589
WANG, L.J. & S.E. LE VOYAGE IMAGI-
NAIRE.
W.W. KIBLER, 207(FR):MAR72-879
WANG, W.S-Y. & A. LYOVIN, COMPS.
CLIBOC: CHINESE LINGUISTICS BIBLIO-
GRAPHY ON COMPUTER.*
G.F. MEIER, 682(ZPSK):BAND25
HEFT4/5-427   [CONTINUED]

WANG, W.S-Y. & A. LYOVIN, COMPS.
CLIBOC: CHINESE LINGUISTICS BIBLIO-
GRAPHY ON COMPUTER.* [CONTINUING]
293(JAST):MAY72-753
VON WANGENHEIM, G. DA LIEGT DER
HUND BEGRABEN UND ANDERE STÜCKE.
(H. BOEHNCKE, ED)
617(TLS):16AUG74-884
WANGERMANN, E. THE AUSTRIAN ACHIEVE-
MENT, 1700-1800.*
C.A. MACARTNEY, 575(SEER):OCT73-
606
WARBURTON, I.P. ON THE VERB IN
MODERN GREEK.
K. KAZAZIS, 350:SEP73-736
WARBURTON, T. FINSK DIKT I SVENSK
DRÄKT.
G.C. SCHOOLFIELD, 563(SS):WINTER
73-93
WARD, A.G. & OTHERS. THE QUEST FOR
THESEUS.*
J. POLLARD, 303:VOL92-219
WARD, B. & R. DUBOS. ONLY ONE
EARTH.* (SPANISH TITLE: UNA SOLA
TIERRA. FRENCH TITLE: NOUS N'AVONS
QU'UNE TERRE.)
H.B. HOUGH, 31(ASCH):WINTER73/74-
152
F.L. PHELPS, 37:SEP72-38
WARD, B., J.D. RUNNALLS & L. D'ANJOU,
EDS. THE WIDENING GAP.
M. LIPTON, 617(TLS):2AUG74-830
WARD, C. UTOPIA.
E. WELSH, 617(TLS):15NOV74-1290
WARD, H., WITH T. GRAY. BULLER.
E.S. TURNER, 362:7MAR74-310
WARD, H.M. "UNITE OR DIE."*
A.G. OLSON, 656(WMQ):JAN72-192
WARD, J.R. THE FINANCE OF CANAL
BUILDING IN EIGHTEENTH-CENTURY
ENGLAND.
617(TLS):16AUG74-883
WARD, J.W. RED, WHITE, & BLUE.
A. HOOK, 447(N&Q):NOV72-425
WARD, M. TO & FRO ON THE EARTH.
617(TLS):11JAN74-26
WARD, P. SABRATHA, A GUIDE FOR VISI-
TORS.
B.H. WARMINGTON, 123:MAR73-77
WARD, R.E. PRINCE OF DUBLIN PRINT-
ERS.
J. FREEHAFER, 566:AUTUMN72-51
WARD, W.A., ED. THE ROLE OF THE
PHOENICIANS IN THE INTERACTION OF
MEDITERRANEAN CIVILIZATIONS.
N. JIDEJIAN, 318(JAOS):APR-JUN72-
310
WARD-PERKINS, J.B. CITIES OF AN-
CIENT GREECE & ITALY.
617(TLS):19JUL74-768
WARDER, A.K. INDIAN BUDDHISM.
B.G. GOKHALE, 318(JAOS):OCT-DEC
72-503
C. MEADOWS, 293(JAST):AUG72-962
WARDHAUGH, R. INTRODUCTION TO LIN-
GUISTICS.
R.J. DI PIETRO, 351(LL):JUN72-
131
R.D. KING, 35(AS):FALL-WINTER70-
285
WARDLE, D. THE RISE OF THE SCHOOLED
SOCIETY.
617(TLS):8MAR74-231

WARDLE, D.B. DOCUMENT REPAIR.
G.M. CUNHA, 14:JUL/OCT72-420
WARDLE, R.M. HAZLITT.*
J.E.J., 191(ELN):SEP72(SUPP)-49
D. MAJDIAK, 301(JEGP):OCT73-572
639(VQR):SPRING72-LXI
WARDMAN, A. PLUTARCH'S LIVES.
617(TLS):19JUL74-772
WARDROPPER, B.W., ED. SPANISH POET-
RY OF THE GOLDEN AGE.
E.L. RIVERS, 400(MLN):MAR72-351
M.D. TRIWEDI, 238:SEP72-604
WARK, R.R. DRAWINGS BY FLAXMAN IN
THE HUNTINGTON COLLECTION.
S. SYMMONS, 90:MAR72-185
WARK, R.R. DRAWINGS FROM THE TURNER
SHAKESPEARE.
617(TLS):8MAR74-228
WARNER, D. & P. THE TIDE AT SUNRISE.
A. AUSTIN, 441:12AUG74-21
WARNER, G. IRAQ & SYRIA 1941.
E. KEDOURIE, 617(TLS):22NOV74-
1311
WARNER, J.A. THE QUIET LAND.
M.A. MOOK, 292(JAF):APR-JUN72-
198
WARNER, O. GREAT BATTLE FLEETS.
617(TLS):8MAR74-245
WARNER, O. THE LIFE-BOAT SERVICE.
617(TLS):12JUL74-742
WARNER, P. DERVISH.
617(TLS):15FEB74-165
WARNER, S.B. THE URBAN WILDERNESS.
639(VQR):SPRING73-LXXXIV
WARNER, V. THESE YELLOW PHOTOS.
J. SAUNDERS, 565:VOL13#3-75
WARNER, V. UNDER THE PENTHOUSE.
R. GARFITT, 364:OCT/NOV73-117
WARNERS, J.D.P. & L.P. RANK. BAC-
CHUS. (VOL 2)
J.W. BINNS, 402(MLR):OCT73-898
F.J. NICHOLS, 551(RENQ):WINTER72-
444
WARNKE, F.J. VERSIONS OF BAROQUE.*
R.M. HUEBERT, 568(SCN):FALL-
WINTER73-101
J.V. MIROLLO, 401(MLQ):DEC73-464
R.W. UPHAUS, 290(JAAC):FALL72-
138
WARNKE, M., ED. DAS KUNSTWERK ZWIS-
CHEN WISSENSCHAFT UND WELTANSCHAU-
UNG.
H. DIENHARD, 54:MAR72-113
WARNOCK, G.J. THE OBJECT OF MORAL-
ITY.
R. GRICE, 483:APR72-172
R.M. HARE, 536:DEC72-199
J. NARVESON, 393(MIND):APR72-288
T.D. PERRY, 185:JUL73-341
A. RALLS, 479(PHQ):JUL72-258
WARNOCK, R.G., ED. DIE PREDIGTEN
JOHANNES PAULIS.*
R.C.J. ENDRES, 221(GQ):MAY72-543
WARREN, P. MINOAN STONE VASES.
J.J. POLLITT, 318(JAOS):JAN-MAR
72-193
WARREN, R.P. HOMAGE TO THEODORE
DREISER.
J. GRIMSHAW, 598(SOR):SPRING74-
504
P. HIDALGO, 202(FMOD):JUN72-337
WARREN, R.P. OR ELSE.
A. BROYARD, 441:24OCT74-45

WARREN, R.P. JOHN GREENLEAF WHIT-
TIER'S POETRY.* MEET ME IN THE
GREEN GLEN.*
J. GRIMSHAW, 598(SOR):SPRING74-
504
WARREN, R.P. - SEE MELVILLE, H.
WARREN, W. BANGKOK.
M. SMITHIES, 302:JUL72-219
WARWICK, L. THEATRE UN-ROYAL.
617(TLS):17MAY74-536
WASHBURN, W.E., ED. PROCEEDINGS OF
THE VINLAND MAP CONFERENCE.
J.R. BLUNDEN, 656(WMQ):OCT72-648
WASHBURN, W.E. RED MAN'S LAND -
WHITE MAN'S LAW.
S. LORANT, 639(VQR):SUMMER72-472
F.P. PRUCHA, 656(WMQ):APR72-313
WASHINGTON, B.T. THE BOOKER T. WASH-
INGTON PAPERS. (VOL 3) (L.R. HAR-
LAN, ED) [ENTRY IN PREV WAS OF
VOLS 1&2]
J. WHITE, 617(TLS):15NOV74-1296
"GEORGE WASHINGTON: A BIOGRAPHY IN
HIS OWN WORDS." (R.K. ANDRIST,
ED)
639(VQR):AUTUMN73-CLVI
WASIOLEK, E. - SEE DOSTOEVSKY, F.M.
WASKOW, A.I. THE BUSH IS BURNING.*
J. RIEMER, 287:JAN72-24
WASSERMAN, E.R. SHELLEY.*
R.E. BARBIERI, 613:AUTUMN72-460
P.H. BUTTER, 677:VOL3-308
S.C., 191(ELN):SEP72(SUPP)-61
S. HALL, 577(SHR):SUMMER72-287
J.J. MC GANN, 405(MP):FEB73-253
G. MC NIECE, 50(ARQ):SUMMER72-
189
K. MC SWEENEY, 529(QQ):AUTUMN72-
437
J. RIEGER, 301(JEGP):JAN73-147
T. WEBB, 541(RES):NOV72-511
639(VQR):SPRING72-LVII
676(YR):AUTUMN72-VI
WASSERSTROM, W. THE LEGACY OF VAN
WYCK BROOKS.
J. LYDENBERG, 432(NEQ):JUN72-294
WASSILJEWA, I.S. PRODUKTIONSÄSTHET-
IK UND NUTZEFFEKT DER ARBEIT.
H. LETSCH, 654(WB):3/1972-172
WASSON, R.G. SOMA.*
S. KRAMRISCH, 57:VOL34#2/3-263
WÄSTBERG, P. - SEE BERGMAN, B. & H.
SÖDERBERG
WASWO, R. THE FATAL MIRROR.
G.L. LITT, 401(MLQ):JUN73-204
639(VQR):WINTER73-XXI
WATERER, J.W. SPANISH LEATHER.
E.A. ENTWISLE, 135:FEB72-138
F.L. MAY, 39:DEC72-566
WATERHOUSE, K. THE PASSING OF THE
THIRD-FLOOR BUCK.
617(TLS):25OCT74-1205
WATERMAN, J.T. PERSPECTIVES IN LIN-
GUISTICS. (2ND ED)
E.F.K. KOERNER, 215(GL):VOL12#2-
138
WATERMEIER, D.J. - SEE BOOTH, E. &
W. WINTER
WATERS, D.D. DUESSA AS THEOLOGICAL
SATIRE.
V.K. WHITAKER, 551(RENQ):AUTUMN
72-359

WATERS, F. RIVERS OF AMERICA: THE
COLORADO.
I.R. DEE, 441:8SEP74-30
WATERS, I. HENRY MARTEN & THE LONG
PARLIAMENT.
617(TLS):11JAN74-27
WATERSTON, E. SURVEY.
W.E. SWAYZE, 296:VOL3#1-112
WATKINS, C. INDOGERMANISCHE GRAM-
MATIK.* (VOL 3, PT 1) (J. KURY-
ŁOWICZ, ED)
P. KIPARSKY, 206:NOV72-277
WATKINS, D. COMPLETE METHOD FOR THE
HARP.
A. GRIFFITHS, 415:JUL73-703
WATKINS, F.C. THE DEATH OF ART.
C.S. BROWN, 577(SHR):FALL72-411
WATKINS, F.C. THE FLESH & THE WORD.*
G. LANGFORD, 594:FALL72-534
WATKINS, G. GESUALDO.
A. COLEMAN, 441:22SEP74-38
617(TLS):8MAR74-241
WATKINS, M. OTHER PLACES.
617(TLS):18JAN74-61
WATKINS, O.C. THE PURITAN EXPERI-
ENCE.
S. BERCOVITCH, 568(SCN):SPRING
73-1
WATKINS, R. & J. LEMMON. THE POET'S
METHOD. HAMLET. A MIDSUMMER
NIGHT'S DREAM. MACBETH.
617(TLS):20SEP74-1020
WATLING, J. BERTRAND RUSSELL.
J.M.B. MOSS, 479(PHQ):JAN72-66
WATLINGTON, P. THE PARTISAN SPIRIT.
H.M. IRELAND, 656(WMQ):JAN73-163
639(VQR):SUMMER72-XCIII
WATSON, A. JUAN DE LA CUEVA & THE
PORTUGUESE SUCCESSION.*
A.A. HEATHCOTE, 402(MLR):APR73-
428
205(FMLS):JUL72-290
WATSON, A. LAW MAKING IN THE LATER
ROMAN REPUBLIC.
617(TLS):30AUG74-927
WATSON, B. CHINESE LYRICISM.*
W. MC NAUGHTON, 352(LE&W):VOL15
#3-511
WATSON, B. - SEE "CHINESE RHYME-
PROSE"
WATSON, E.A.F. SPENSER.
T.L. STEINBERG, 568(SCN):FALL-
WINTER73-80
WATSON, F. THE YEAR OF THE WOMBAT.
N. ANNAN, 453:28NOV74-19
F. DILLON, 362:19SEP74-380
R. FULFORD, 617(TLS):20DEC74-
1436
WATSON, F.J.B. THE WRIGHTSMAN COL-
LECTION: GOLD BOXES. (VOLS 3&4)
A.K. SNOWMAN, 135:JAN72-63
WATSON, G. THE ENGLISH IDEOLOGY.*
P. PARRINDER, 111:18MAY73-159
WATSON, G. THE LITERARY THESIS.
I.D. MC FARLANE, 402(MLR):APR73-
380
WATSON, G., ED. THE NEW CAMBRIDGE
BIBLIOGRAPHY OF ENGLISH LITERA-
TURE.* (VOL 2)
R.D. HUME, 481(PQ):JUL72-517
WATSON, G., ED. THE NEW CAMBRIDGE
BIBLIOGRAPHY OF ENGLISH LITERA-
TURE.* (VOL 3)
D.J. GRAY, 637(VS):SEP71-87

WATSON, H. CLAUDEL'S IMMORTAL HER-
OES.
E. BEAUMONT, 208(FS):OCT73-468
WATSON, J.R. PICTURESQUE LANDSCAPE
& ENGLISH ROMANTIC POETRY.*
C. SALVESEN, 541(RES):FEB72-89
WATSON, L. THE ROMEO ERROR.
A. GAULD, 617(TLS):20DEC74-1438
WATSON, M.M. THE WEST AIN'T WHAT IT
WAS.
A. RENDLE, 157:WINTER72-80
WATSON, P.J., S.A. LEBLANC & C.L.
REDMAN. EXPLANATION IN ARCHAEOL-
OGY.
H.D. TUGGLE, 486:DEC72-564
WATSON, R. CHRISTMAS IN LAS VEGAS.*
M. BORROFF, 676(YR):AUTUMN72-81
WATSON, V. THE BRITISH MUSEUM.
617(TLS):12APR74-400
WATT, D. - SEE HUXLEY, A.
WATT, H. DON'T LOOK AT THE CAMERA.
E.S. TURNER, 362:11JUL74-60
617(TLS):19JUL74-760
WATT, W.M. THE MAJESTY THAT WAS
ISLAM.
C.F. BECKINGHAM, 617(TLS):1NOV74-
1237
WATTENBERG, B.J. THE REAL AMERICA.
S.R. WEISMAN, 441:29SEP74-27
WATTERS, P. DOWN TO NOW.*
639(VQR):SUMMER72-LXXXVIII
WATTERS, R. COLERIDGE.
J.R.D. JACKSON, 627(UTQ):SPRING
73-289
WATTS, A. CLOUD-HIDDEN, WHEREABOUTS
UNKNOWN.
R.C. ZAEHNER, 617(TLS):6DEC74-
1389
WATTS, A. IN MY OWN WAY.*
H. LOMAS, 364:DEC73/JAN74-132
639(VQR):SUMMER73-CXXI
WATTS, A.C. THE LYRE AND THE HARP.*
G. FIGGE, 38:BAND90HEFT1/2-208
WATTS, A.J. WARSHIPS & NAVIES RE-
VIEW. (2ND ED)
617(TLS):26JUL74-815
WATTS, D.A. - SEE ROTROU, J.
WATTS, E.S. ERNEST HEMINGWAY & THE
ARTS.*
R.I. JOHNSON, 290(JAAC):FALL72-
138
WAUGH, H. MIRROR, MIRROR.
V. CUNNINGHAM, 362:7FEB74-183
617(TLS):18JAN74-47
WAYMAN, A. THE BUDDHIST TANTRAS.
617(TLS):19APR74-406
WAYMENT, H.G. THE WINDOWS OF KING'S
COLLEGE CHAPEL, CAMBRIDGE.
G.W. THOMAS, 135:OCT72-138
617(TLS):22FEB74-174
WEALES, G. CLIFFORD ODETS, PLAY-
WRIGHT.*
G. LONEY, 397(MD):SEP72-212
WEALES, G. - SEE WYCHERLEY, W.
WEARING, J.P. - SEE PINERO, A.
WEATHERBY, H.L. CARDINAL NEWMAN IN
HIS AGE.*
M.E. BRADFORD, 396(MODA):SUMMER
73-308
WEATHERILL, L. THE POTTERY TRADE &
NORTH STAFFORDSHIRE 1660-1760.
J.V.G. MALLET, 39:JAN72-69

WEATHERS, W. MESSAGES FROM THE
ASYLUM.
N.A. BRITTIN, 577(SHR):SPRING72-
197
WEAVER, C.H. HUMAN LISTENING.
H.D. DOLL, 583:SUMMER73-400
WEAVER, H. & P.H. BERGERON - SEE
POLK, J.K.
WEAVER, K.D. LENIN'S GRANDCHILDREN.*
S.M. ROSEN, 550(RUSR):JUL72-321
WEAVER, M. WILLIAM CARLOS WILLIAMS.*
W. SUTTON, 27(AL):MAR73-130
WEAVER, R.M. LANGUAGE IS SERMONIC.
(R.L. JOHANNESEN, R. STRICKLAND &
R.T. EUBANKS, EDS)
G.P. MOHRMANN, 480(P&R):WINTER
72-63
WEAVER, W., JR. BOTH YOUR HOUSES.
639(VQR):SPRING73-LXXXVII
WEBB, A.N., ED. AN EDITION OF THE
CARTULARY OF BURSCOUGH PRIORY.
A.G. DYSON, 325:OCT72-538
WEBB, C. ORPHANS & OTHER CHILDREN.
442(NY):2SEP74-82
WEBB, E. SAMUEL BECKETT.*
J-J. MAYOUX, 189(EA):JUL-SEP72-
412
WEBB, F. BRANNINGTON'S LEOPARD.
M. LEVIN, 441:25AUG74-31
WEBB, W. & R.A. WEINSTEIN. DWELLERS
AT THE SOURCE.
S. SONTAG, 453:18APR74-17
WEBBER, J. THE ELOQUENT "I."*
R.L. COLIE, 627(UTQ):AUTUMN71-80
WEBER, A. & D. HAACK, EDS. AMERIKAN-
ISCHE LITERATUR IM 20. JAHRHUNDERT.
L. TRUCHLAR, 430(NS):NOV72-676
WEBER, B.J. THE CONSTRUCTION OF
"PARADISE LOST."
I. SIMON, 541(RES):AUG72-348
WEBER, D. HEIMITO VON DODERER.
P. MISSAC, 98:FEB72-140
WEBER, G.W. "WYRD."
H. BECKERS, 680(ZDP):BAND91HEFT3-
413
WEBER, G.W., JR. THE ORNAMENTS OF
LATE CHOU BRONZES.
617(TLS):2AUG74-838
WEBER, H. DAS ERWEITERTE ADJEKTIV-
UND PARTIZIPIALATTRIBUT IM DEUT-
SCHEN.
J.A. HAWKINS, 220(GL&L):JUL73-
363
B. NYBELIUS, 597(SN):VOL44#1-223
WEBER, J., COMP. HUGO VON HOFMANNS-
THAL BIBLIOGRAPHIE.
J.B. BERLIN & R.C. NORTON,
301(JEGP):OCT73-606
WEBER, H-D. ÜBER EINE THEORIE DER
LITERATURKRITIK.
R. MOLLENAUER, 301(JEGP):OCT73-
593
WEBER, M. 48 SMALL POEMS.
L. SEARLE, 491:MAR74-353
42(AR):VOL32#4-701
639(VQR):AUTUMN73-CXL
WEBER, N. THE LIFE SWAP.
M. SELIGSON, 441:2JUN74-44
WEBER, P. DAS MENSCHENBILD DES BÜR-
GERLICHEN TRAUERSPIELS.
W. RIECK, 654(WB):7/1972-177
WEBER, W. A HISTORY OF LITHOGRAPHY.
A. FERN, 54:SEP72-372

WEBRE, A.L. & P.H. LISS. AGE OF
CATACLYSM.
    A. HACKER, 231:SEP74-72
WEBSTER, B. ONE BY ONE.
    639(VQR):SPRING73-LVII
WEBSTER, C. - SEE HARTLIB, S.
WEBSTER, D. EARLY CANADIAN POTTERY.
    J. TROY, 139:OCT72-8
WEBSTER, D.H. & W. ZIBELL. IÑUPIAT
ESKIMO DICTIONARY.
    T.C. CORRELL, 269(IJAL):JAN72-76
WEBSTER, N. A BURIAL IN PORTUGAL.
    442(NY):16SEP74-151
WEBSTER, N.W. THE GREAT NORTH ROAD.
    617(TLS):15NOV74-1297
WEBSTER, P. THE MIGHTY SIERRA.
    T.J. LYON, 649(WAL):FALL72-233
WEBSTER, T.B.L. POTTER & PATRON IN
CLASSICAL ATHENS.*
    K. SCHEFOLD, 182:VOL25#11-369
WEBSTER, T.B.L. - SEE SOPHOCLES
WECHSBERG, J. THE GLORY OF THE
VIOLIN.*
    42(AR):VOL32#4-707
    442(NY):15APR74-152
WECHSBERG, J. THE OPERA.*
    A. BLYTH, 415:MAR73-263
    M.F.R., 410(M&L):JAN73-94
WEDDE, I. & F. TUQAN - SEE DARWISH,
M.
WEDDERBURN, D., ED. POVERTY, IN-
EQUALITY & CLASS STRUCTURE.
    617(TLS):5JUL74-709
WEEBER, R. EINE NEUE WOHNUMWELT.
    T. KNORR, 182:VOL25#13/14-472
WEEKLEY, I. THE MOVING SNOW.
    P. CAMPBELL, 617(TLS):29NOV74-
1336
WEEKS, E. MY GREEN AGE.
    C. LEHMANN-HAUPT, 441:12FEB74-37
WEES, W.C. VORTICISM & THE ENGLISH
AVANT-GARDE.*
    S. DICK, 529(QQ):WINTER72-563
    P. EDWARDS, 111:20OCT72-29
    W. MARTIN, 659:WINTER74-145
    H. WITEMEYER, 651(WHR):SPRING73-
205
WEESNER, T. THE CAR THIEF.*
    S. O'CONNELL, 418(MR):WINTER73-
190
WEGNER, W. DIE NIEDERLÄNDISCHEN
HANDZEICHNUNGEN DES 15. BIS 18.
JAHRHUNDERTS.
    617(TLS):25JAN74-73
WEHDEKING, V.C. DER NULLPUNKT.
    C. RUSS, 617(TLS):25OCT74-1204
WEIDHORN, M. DREAMS IN SEVENTEENTH-
CENTURY LITERATURE.
    R. ELLRODT, 189(EA):OCT-DEC72-
548
WEIDMAN, J. TIFFANY STREET.
    617(TLS):23AUG74-897
WEIERS, M. UNTERSUCHUNGEN ZU EINER
HISTORISCHEN GRAMMATIK DES PRÄK-
LASSISCHEN SCHRIFT-MONGOLISCH.
    J.C. STREET, 318(JAOS):APR-JUN72-
358
WEIGEL, H. DER TROJANISCHE KRIEG.
    J. BOARDMAN, 123:MAR73-83
WEIGHTMAN, J. THE CONCEPT OF THE
AVANT-GARDE.*
    R. NYE, 364:AUG/SEP73-128
WEIL, A. THE NATURAL MIND.*
    H. LOMAS, 364:JUN/JUL73-141

WEIL, E. PROBLEMES KANTIENS. (2ND
ED)
    J. KOPPER, 342:BAND63HEFT1-131
WEILER, G. MAUTHNER'S CRITIQUE OF
LANGUAGE.*
    R-M.G. OSTER, 399(MLJ):APR72-262
WEIMANN, R. LITERATURGESCHICHTE UND
MYTHOLOGIE.
    U. WEISSTEIN, 125:FEB73-186
WEIMANN, R. PHANTASIE UND NACHAH-
MUNG.
    U. ROISCH, 654(WB):4/1972-168
WEIMAR, K.S., ED. GERMAN LANGUAGE
& LITERATURE.
    617(TLS):23AUG74-912
WEIN, H. PHILOSOPHIE ALS ERFAHRUNGS-
WISSENSCHAFT.*
    H.H., 543:JUN72-769
WEINACHT, H. DIE MENSCHWERDUNG DES
SOHNES GOTTES IM MARKUSEVANGELIUM.
    F.F. BRUCE, 182:VOL25#13/14-461
WEINBERG, H.G., COMP. THE COMPLETE
"GREED."*
    C.P. REILLY, 200:JUN-JUL72-371
WEINBERG, K. ON GIDE'S "PROMÉTHÉE."
    G.W. IRELAND, 529(QQ):WINTER72-
553
WEINBERGER, O. RECHTSLOGIK.
    E. MORSCHER, 536:DEC72-209
WEINBROT, H.D., ED. NEW ASPECTS OF
LEXICOGRAPHY.
    S.I. TUCKER, 402(MLR):OCT73-887
WEINER, J. MANTILLAS IN MUSCOVY.*
    L.B. TURKEVICH, 238:MAY72-384
WEINGARTEN, R. LA MANDORE.
    617(TLS):24MAY74-555
WEINGARTNER, F.F. TONES IN TAIWAN-
ESE.
    T.M. CHENG, 361:VOL30#2/3-285
WEINREICH, O. DIE SUFFIXABLÖSUNG
BEI DEN NOMINA AGENTIS WÄHREND
DER ALTHOCHDEUTSCHEN PERIODE.
    H. TIEFENBACH, 182:VOL25#19/20-
665
WEINREICH, U. ERKUNDUNGEN ZUR
THEORIE DER SEMANTIK.
    G. FRITZ, 343:BAND15HEFT2-201
WEINRICH, H. PHONOLOGISCHE STUDIEN
ZUR ROMANISCHEN SPRACHGESCHICHTE.*
    G. LEPSCHY, 353:15AUG72-114
WEINRICH, P.H., ED. A SELECT BIBLIO-
GRAPHY OF TIM BUCK.
    W. RODNEY, 99:NOV/DEC74-50
WEINSTEIN, L. HIPPOLYTE TAINE.
    S.J. KAHN, 125:FEB73-206
WEINSTEIN, M.A. WILLIAM EDMOND-
STOUNE AYTOUN & THE SPASMODIC CON-
TROVERSY.*
    W. FRANKE, 38:BAND90HEFT1/2-259
WEINSTEIN, P.M. HENRY JAMES & THE
REQUIREMENTS OF THE IMAGINATION.*
    R. FALK, 445(NCF):SEP72-224
    D.K. KIRBY, 432(NEQ):MAR72-137
WEINSTOCK, H. MITTELENGLISCHES ELE-
MENTARBUCH.*
    K. DIETZ, 260(IF):BAND77HEFT1-
126
WEINTRAUB, S. JOURNEY TO HEART-
BREAK.* (BRITISH TITLE: BERNARD
SHAW 1914-1918.)
    S.P. ALBERT, 397(MD):SEP72-219
    639(VQR):WINTER72-VIII

WEINTRAUB, S. WHISTLER.
D. COOPER, 453:8AUG74-10
J. HOLLANDER, 231:SEP74-82
H. KRAMER, 441:3MAR74-1
442(NY):18FEB74-119
617(TLS):15MAR74-249
WEINTRAUB, S. - SEE SHAW, G.B.
WEINTRAUB, S. & P. YOUNG, EDS. DIR-
ECTIONS IN LITERARY CRITICISM.
J.M. PATRICK, 568(SCN):FALL-
WINTER73-86
WEIR, T. THE WESTERN HIGHLANDS.
617(TLS):8MAR74-245
WEISGAL, M. MEYER WEISGAL...SO FAR.
S. KREITER, 287:MAY72-24
M. SYRKIN, 390:APR72-65
WEISGERBER, J. HUGO CLAUS.
P. BRACHIN, 549(RLC):JAN-MAR72-
161
WEISGERBER, J.L. DIE NAMEN DER
UBIER.*
M. FAUST, 343:BAND14HEFT1-46
WEISGERBER, L. RHENANIA GERMANO-
CELTICA.
H. SCHMEJA, 343:BAND14HEFT1-102
K.H. SCHMIDT, 260(IF):BAND76-317
WEISHEIPL, J.A. FRIAR THOMAS
D'AQUINO.
D. KNOWLES, 441:17FEB74-24
WEISMAN, J. GUERILLA THEATER.
B.H. FUSSELL, 249(HUDR):WINTER
73/74-753
639(VQR):AUTUMN73-CXLII
WEISS, D. "NAKED CAME I."
C. CHAUMEIL, 189(EA):JAN-MAR72-
177
WEISS, E. JOHANNES R. BECHER UND
DIE SOWJETISCHE LITERATURENTWICK-
LUNG (1917-1933).
K. KÄNDLER, 654(WB):5/1972-183
WEISS, P. DISCOURSE ON VIETNAM.
NOTES ON THE CULTURAL LIFE OF THE
DEMOCRATIC REPUBLIC OF VIETNAM.
J.J. WHITE, 220(GL&L):JUL73-325
WEISS, P. HÖLDERLIN.
C.H., 191(ELN):SEP72(SUPP)-163
WEISS, P. PHILOSOPHY IN PROCESS.
(VOL 5)
J. COLLINS, 613:SUMMER72-315
H. RUJA, 484(PPR):SEP72-128
WEISS, P. TROTSKY IN EXILE.
A. RENDLE, 157:SPRING72-81
WEISS, T. THE BREATH OF CLOWNS &
KINGS.*
R.W. DENT, 551(RENQ):WINTER72-
506
WEISS, T. THE WORLD BEFORE US.*
J.T. IRWIN, 569(SR):WINTER73-158
WEISSBORT, D. THE LEASEHOLDER.
J. SAUNDERS, 565:VOL13#3-75
WEISSENBERGER, K. FORMEN DER ELEGIE
VON GOETHE BIS CELAN.*
J. STRELKA, 221(GQ):MAY72-536
WEISSKOPF, T. IMMANUEL KANT UND DIE
PÄDAGOGIK.*
H. OBERER, 53(AGP):BAND54HEFT3-
310
WEISSMAN, S., ED. BIG BROTHER & THE
HOLDING COMPANY.
A. COCKBURN, 453:28NOV74-8
WEITZ, J. MAN IN CHARGE.
L. SLOANE, 441:23DEC74-25

WEITZ, M., ED. PROBLEMS IN AESTHET-
ICS. (2ND ED)
J.B.L., 543:SEP71-144
WEITZMANN, K. STUDIES IN CLASSICAL
& BYZANTINE MANUSCRIPT ILLUMINA-
TION.* (H.L. KESSLER, ED)
O. DEMUS, 589:APR73-427
I. ŠEVČENKO, 32:MAR73-154
WEIZMANN, C. THE LETTERS & PAPERS OF
CHAIM WEIZMANN. (LETTERS, VOL 4)
(C. DRESNER & B. LITIVINOFF, EDS)
617(TLS):5APR74-356
WELCH, C. PROTESTANT THOUGHT IN THE
NINETEENTH CENTURY. (VOL 1)
M.E. MARTY, 125:JUN73-308
WELCH, J. WINTER IN THE BLOOD.
A. BROYARD, 441:30OCT74-49
R. PRICE, 441:10NOV74-1
R. SALE, 453:12DEC74-18
442(NY):23DEC74-84
WELCHER, J.K. & G.E. BUSH, JR., EDS.
GULLIVERIANA: I.
566:SPRING72-86
WELDON, F. FEMALE FRIENDS.
S. BLACKBURN, 441:10NOV74-18
WELK, L., WITH B. MC GEEHAN. AH-ONE,
AH-TWO!
E.E. MORISON, 441:20OCT74-22
WELLAND, D., ED. THE UNITED STATES.
617(TLS):22FEB74-181
WELLARD, J. THE FRENCH FOREIGN
LEGION.
E. O'BALLANCE, 617(TLS):13DEC74-
1425
WELLEK, A. WITZ, LYRIK, SPRACHE.*
M.B. BENN, 402(MLR):APR73-463
W. LOCKEMANN, 221(GQ):JAN72-176
WELLEK, R. DISCRIMINATIONS.*
W.H. CLARK, JR., 290(JAAC):
SPRING72-389
WELLER, B.U. MAXIMILIAN HARDEN UND
DIE "ZUKUNFT."
H. RIDLEY, 220(GL&L):JUL73-368
WELLERSHOFF, D. LITERATUR UND LUST-
PRINZIP.
617(TLS):31MAY74-582
WELLES, C.B. ALEXANDER & THE HELLEN-
ISTIC WORLD.*
T.S. BROWN, 24:SPRING73-112
G.L. CAWKWELL, 123:MAR73-103
W.S. THURMAN, 399(MLJ):FEB72-100
WELLESZ, E. & F.W. STERNFELD, EDS.
THE NEW OXFORD HISTORY OF MUSIC.
(VOL 7)
D. MATTHEWS, 617(TLS):6DEC74-
1395
WELLMAN, C. CHALLENGE & RESPONSE.*
A.S.C., 543:DEC71-373
R.E. CARTER, 529(QQ):SPRING72-
112
H. JACK, 154:MAR72-137
R.K. SHOPE, 311(JP):31JAN74-46
WELLMAN, M.W. THE KINGDOM OF MADI-
SON.
639(VQR):AUTUMN73-CLXVI
WELLS, C. HIJACK.
A. RENDLE, 157:WINTER72-80
WELLS, C.M. THE GERMAN POLICY OF
AUGUSTUS.
N. BROCHMEYER, 182:VOL25#21-758
WELLS, D. JANE.*
A. BROYARD, 441:7FEB74-41
M. DRABBLE, 441:13JAN74-7
WELLS, D.A. - SEE TIMBS, J.

WELLS, G.A. THE JESUS OF THE EARLY CHRISTIANS.
U. SIMON, 220(GL&L):OCT72-60
R.E. WITT, 303:VOL92-223
WELLS, H.W. TRADITIONAL CHINESE HUMOR.
J.C. WANG, 352(LE&W):VOL15#3-517
WELLS, S. - SEE SISSON, C.J.
WELSH, A. THE CITY OF DICKENS.*
W. BURGAN, 637(VS):SEP72-122
S. MONOD, 189(EA):JAN-MAR72-165
H. REINHOLD, 38:BAND90HEFT4-545
R. SCHROCK, 191(ELN):SEP72-57
R. WILLIAMS, 155:JAN72-53
WELTY, E. LOSING BATTLES.*
J. YARDLEY, 473(PR):2/1973-286
WELTY, E. ONE TIME, ONE PLACE.
639(VQR):SPRING72-LXXIV
WELTY, E. THE OPTIMIST'S DAUGHTER.*
P. BAILEY, 364(JUN/JUL73-153
R. DRAKE, 396(MODA):WINTER73-107
S. O'CONNELL, 418(MR):WINTER73-190
E. ROVIT, 659:AUTUMN74-539
J. YARDLEY, 473(PR):2/1973-286
639(VQR):AUTUMN72-CXX
WENDT, H. FROM APE TO ADAM.
639(VQR):WINTER73-XLIII
WENG, B.S.J. PEKING'S U.N. POLICY.
42(AR):SPRING/SUMMER72-246
WENGER, K. GOTTFRIED KELLERS AUSEIN-ANDERSETZUNG MIT DEM CHRISTENTUM.*
K.T. LOCHER, 301(JEGP):APR73-293
WENNER, J. LENNON REMEMBERS.
42(AR):SPRING/SUMMER72-243
WENSINGER, A.S. & W.B. COLEY - SEE LICHTENBERG, G.C.
WENTZLAFF-EGGEBERT, C. FORMINTER-ESSE, TRADITIONSVERBUNDENHEIT UND AKTUALISIERUNGSBEDÜRFNIS ALS MERK-MALE DES DICHTENS VON SAINT-AMANT.
J-P. CHAUVEAU, 535(RHL):MAY-JUN72-513
WENZEL, M. HOUSE DECORATION IN NUBIA.
J.M.R., 46:AUG72-127
WERBOW, S.N., ED. FORMAL ASPECTS OF MEDIEVAL GERMAN POETRY.
F. GOLDIN, 222(GR):NOV72-294
VAN DER WERF, H. THE CHANSONS OF THE TROUBADOURS & TROUVÈRES.*
J.A.W., 410(M&L):APR73-215
WERKMEISTER, W.H. HISTORICAL SPEC-TRUM OF VALUE THEORIES. (VOL 1)
D. WILLARD, 477:AUTUMN72-454
WERNER, M., ED. BEGEGNUNGEN MIT HEINE.
617(TLS):25JAN74-65
WERNER, O. EINFÜHRUNG IN DIE STRUC-TURELLE BESCHREIBUNG DES DEUT-SCHEN.* (PT 1)
I. GUENTHERODT, 133:1972/3-315
J.A. HAWKINS, 220(GL&L):JUL73-360
G.J. METCALF, 221(GQ):MAR72-380
WERTHEIMER, R. THE SIGNIFICANCE OF SENSE.
B. VERMAZEN, 311(JP):15AUG74-506
WESKER, A. LOVE LETTERS ON BLUE PAPER.
617(TLS):23AUG74-897
WESKER, A. THE OLD ONES.
617(TLS):22MAR74-300

WESLAGER, C.A. THE DELAWARE INDIANS.
Y. KAWASHIMA, 656(WMQ):JAN73-183
WESSÉN, E. DIE NORDISCHEN SPRACHEN.*
E. KOLB, 657(WW):NOV/DEC72-431
WESSEN, E. SCHWEDISCHE SPRACHGE-SCHICHTE.
P. OCHSENBEIN, 657(WW):JUL/AUG72-288
WESSON, R.G. THE SOVIET RUSSIAN STATE.
G. HODNETT, 32:JUN73-396
D. LANE, 575(SEER):JUL73-489
WESSON, R.G. THE SOVIET STATE.
G. HODNETT, 32:JUN73-396
WEST, D.J. & D.P. FARRINGTON. WHO BECOMES DELINQUENT?
617(TLS):1MAR74-208
WEST, J. RUSSIAN SYMBOLISM.*
G. IVASK, 550(RUSR):APR72-192
WEST, M. HARLEQUIN.
M. LEVIN, 441:27OCT74-56
442(NY):16DEC74-167
617(TLS):4OCT74-1092
WEST, M.L. SING ME, GODDESS.
J.B. HAINSWORTH, 123:DEC73-265
WEST, T. THE TIMBER-FRAME HOUSE IN ENGLAND.
A. CLIFTON-TAYLOR, 135:FEB72-139
WESTERBERGH, U., ED. GLOSSARIUM MEDIAE LATINITATIS SUECIAE. (VOL 1, FASC 3)
J. ANDRÉ, 555:VOL46FASC2-350
WESTERINK, L.G. - SEE ARETHAS
WESTERMANN, C. RECHT UND PFLICHT BEI LEONARD NELSON.
G. HENRY-HERMANN, 536:JUN72-95
WESTHEIMER, D. THE OLMEC HEAD.
P. ADAMS, 61:APR74-120
N. CALLENDAR, 441:7APR74-34
WESTLAKE, D.E. HELP I AM BEING HELD PRISONER.
M. LEVIN, 441:14JUL74-20
WESTLAKE, D.E. JIMMY THE KID.
M. LEVIN, 441:17NOV74-52
WESTON, J. GOAT SONGS.
639(VQR):SPRING72-XLIX
WESTON, J.C. - SEE MAC DIARMID, H.
VAN DE WETERING, J. THE EMPTY MIR-ROR.
A. BROYARD, 441:27FEB74-43
A. GOTTLIEB, 441:3MAR74-2
WETHERBEE, W. PLATONISM & POETRY IN THE TWELFTH CENTURY.
639(VQR):AUTUMN72-CXXIX
WETHERILL, P.M. THE LITERARY TEXT.
J. CULLER, 617(TLS):15NOV74-1292
WEYDT, G. HANS JACOB CHRISTOFFEL VON GRIMMELSHAUSEN.
G. HOFFMEISTER, 221(GQ):NOV72-746
WEYDT, G. NACHAHMUNG UND SCHÖPFUNG IM BAROCK.
W. BENDER, 224(GRM):BAND22HEFT2-205
M. FELDGES, 657(WW):JAN/FEB72-70
WEYDT, G., ED. DER SIMPLIZISSIMUS-DICHTER UND SEIN WERK.
I. SPRIEWALD, 654(WB):1/1972-190
WEYDT, H. ABTÖNUNGSPARTIKEL.*
H.W. FELTKAMP, 433:APR72-231
WEYEMBERGH-BOUSSART, M. ALFRED DÖB-LIN.*
J. DUYTSCHAEVER, 221(GQ):JAN72-144

383

WEYMAN, S. A GENTLEMAN OF FRANCE.
P.J. KEATING, 617(TLS):29NOV74-
1347
WEYMOUTH, L., ED. THOMAS JEFFERSON.
617(TLS):21JUN74-663
WHALEN, R.J. TAKING SIDES.
J. FALLOWS, 441:27OCT74-28
WHALLEY, J.I. ENGLISH HANDWRITING
1540-1853.*
C.G. HOLLAND, 325:APR72-449
WHALLON, W. FORMULA, CHARACTER, &
CONTEXT.*
G. FIGGE, 38:BAND90HEFT1/2-208
WHARTON, M.E. & R.W. BARBOUR. A
GUIDE TO THE WILDFLOWERS & FERNS
OF KENTUCKY.
R. MC VAUGH, 385(MQR):SPRING74-
169
"WHAT TO TELL YOUR CHILD ABOUT SEX."
D.C. ANDERSON, 441:10NOV74-47
WHATMOUGH, J. THE DIALECTS OF ANCI-
ENT GAUL.*
M. LEJEUNE, 343:BAND15HEFT1-97
WHEARE, K.C. MALADMINISTRATION &
ITS REMEDIES.
617(TLS):25JAN74-88
WHEAT, L.F. PAUL TILLICH'S DIALEC-
TICAL HUMANISM.
R.D.L., 543:DEC71-374
WHEATLEY, J. LANGUAGE & RULES.
J.R. CAMERON, 479(PHQ):JAN72-78
W.J. HUTCHINS, 361:VOL28#1&2-131
WHEATLEY, J.H. PATTERNS IN THACK-
ERAY'S FICTION.*
D.C. BRYANT, 480(P&R):WINTER72-
55
M.G. SUNDELL, 594:FALL72-513
WHEATLEY, P. THE PIVOT OF THE FOUR
QUARTERS.
W. EBERHARD, 293(JAST):MAY72-641
617(TLS):24MAY74-565
WHEELER, H., ED. BEYOND THE PUNI-
TIVE SOCIETY.
617(TLS):29MAR74-317
WHEELER, M. THE OXFORD RUSSIAN-
ENGLISH DICTIONARY. (B.O. UNBE-
GAUN, WITH D.P. COSTELLO & W.F.
RYAN, EDS)
T.F. MAGNER, 32:JUN73-431
WHEELER, R. VOICES OF 1776.
639(VQR):WINTER73-XXXV
WHEELER-BENNETT, J. KNAVES, FOOLS &
HEROES.
D.C. WATT, 617(TLS):6DEC74-1363
WHEELWRIGHT, E.L. & B. MC FARLANE.
THE CHINESE ROAD TO SOCIALISM.
O.E. CLUBB, 104:SPRING72-186
WHEELWRIGHT, J. COLLECTED POEMS OF
JOHN WHEELWRIGHT.* (A.H. ROSEN-
FELD, ED)
P. CHRISTENSEN, 598(SOR):SPRING
74-485
639(VQR):SUMMER73-CX
WHELPTON, B. PAINTERS' PARIS.
PAINTERS' PROVENCE.
B. SCOTT, 39:JUN72-521
WHINNEY, M. ENGLISH SCULPTURE 1720-
1830.
P. CANNON-BROOKES, 39:JUN72-522
WHINNEY, M. WREN.
J. SUMMERSON, 46:MAR72-196
A.A. TAIT, 90:SEP72-635
J. WILTON-ELY, 39:JUN72-516

WHITAKER, B. THE FOUNDATIONS.
T. MEDAWAR, 362:21MAR74-375
S.G. PUTT, 617(TLS):27DEC74-1470
WHITAKER, B. & K. BROWNE. PARKS
FOR PEOPLE.
E. BEAZLEY, 46:JAN72-66
WHITAKER, R.E.M. & A. HISS. ALL
ABOARD WITH E.M. FRIMBO.
O. JENSEN, 441:17NOV74-26
WHITAKER, V., ED. WINTER'S CRIMES 5.
617(TLS):25JAN74-88
WHITBREAD, K., COMP. CATALOGUE OF
BURMESE PRINTED BOOKS IN THE INDIA
OFFICE LIBRARY.
J.K. MUSGRAVE, 293(JAST):MAY72-
715
WHITBY, W.M. & R.R. ANDERSON - SEE
LOPE DE VEGA
WHITE, A. THE LONG FUSE.
442(NY):14OCT74-200
WHITE, A. PALACES OF THE PEOPLE.
R. BLETTER, 576:MAY72-157
WHITE, A.R. TRUTH.*
V. HOPE, 479(PHQ):OCT72-373
M.D.P., 543:SEP71-137
WHITE, C. DÜRER.
A. SMITH, 90:FEB72-102
WHITE, C. & K.G. BOON. REMBRANDT'S
ETCHINGS.
S.W. PELLETIER, 90:NOV72-796
WHITE, D.H. POPE & THE CONTEXT OF
CONTROVERSY.*
G.S. ROUSSEAU, 541(RES):AUG72-
362
WHITE, D.M. & A.C. SEWTER. I DISEG-
NI DI G.B. PIAZZETTA NELLA BIBLIO-
TECA REALE DI TORINO.*
G. KNOX, 90:MAR72-183
WHITE, E. FORGETTING ELENA.*
M. MUDRICK, 249(HUDR):AUTUMN73-
545
WHITE, E.W. ANNE BRADSTREET.*
P.N. CARROLL, 656(WMQ):OCT72-662
P. NICOLAISEN, 568(SCN):SPRING
73-9
A.H. ROSENFELD, 432(NEQ):JUN72-
308
WHITE, E.W. BENJAMIN BRITTEN.*
J. MICHON, 189(EA):OCT-DEC72-512
WHITE, H.B. COPP'D HILLS TOWARDS
HEAVEN.
R.W. DENT, 551(RENQ):WINTER72-
506
WHITE, J. THE DREAM MILLENNIUM.
T. STURGEON, 441:8SEP74-40
WHITE, J.D. THE LEIPZIG AFFAIR.
617(TLS):20DEC74-1437
WHITE, J.E., JR. NICOLAS BOILEAU.
F.R. FREUDMANN, 399(MLJ):OCT72-
398
WHITE, J.F. NEW FORMS OF WORSHIP.
E.J. SUTFIN, 363:MAY72-105
WHITE, J.M. THE MOUNTAIN LION.
P. COOLEY, 385(MQR):WINTER74-79
WHITE, J.T. THE SCOTTISH BORDER &
NORTHUMBERLAND.
J. MAPPLEBECK, 362:27JUN74-842
WHITE, K.D. A BIBLIOGRAPHY OF ROMAN
AGRICULTURE.* (E.J.T COLLINS, ED)
J. ANDRÉ, 555:VOL46FASC2-358
WHITE, K.D. ROMAN FARMING.*
P.A. BRUNT, 313:VOL62-153
WHITE, M. COOKING FOR CROWDS.
N. HAZELTON, 441:1DEC74-96

WHITE, M., ED. DOCUMENTS IN THE HIS-
TORY OF AMERICAN PHILOSOPHY.*
W. MAYS, 518:MAY73-28
WHITE, M. SCIENCE & SENTIMENT IN
AMERICA.*
W. MAYS, 518:MAY73-28
WHITE, P. THE COCKATOOS.
617(TLS):28JUN74-687
WHITE, P. THE EYE OF THE STORM.*
A. BROYARD, 441:2JAN74-35
J. GRANT, 99:MAY/JUN74-16
S. HAZZARD, 441:6JAN74-1
C. RICKS, 453:4APR74-19
J. SKOW, 231:MAR74-92
G. STEINER, 442(NY):4MAR74-109
E. WEEKS, 61:FEB74-94
WHITE, P.L. & D. ROBBINS, EDS. EN-
VIRONMENTAL QUALITY & FOOD SUPPLY.
J.L. HESS, 441:14AUG74-39
WHITE, P.L. & N. SELVEY, EDS. NU-
TRITIONAL QUALITIES OF FRESH
FRUITS & VEGETABLES.
J.L. HESS, 441:14AUG74-39
WHITE, R.J. FROM PETERLOO TO THE
CRYSTAL PALACE.
V.M. BATZEL, 637(VS):MAR73-365
WHITE, R.L. - SEE ANDERSON, S. & G.
STEIN
WHITE, T.D. THE DISTANCE & THE
DARK.*
J. MAC KILLOP, 268:JUL74-150
WHITE, T.D. THE RADISH MEMOIRS.
617(TLS):14JUN74-629
WHITE, T.H. THE MAKING OF THE PRESI-
DENT 1972.*
617(TLS):8MAR74-227
"WHITE PAPERS OF JAPAN, 1969-1970."
293(JAST):MAY72-754
WHITEBREAD, L.G., ED & TRANS. FUL-
GENTIUS THE MYTHOGRAPHER.
589:APR73-436
WHITEHEAD, F., A.H. DIVERRES & S.F.E.
SUTCLIFFE, EDS. MEDIEVAL MISCEL-
LANY PRESENTED TO EUGÈNE VINAVER
BY PUPILS, COLLEAGUES & FRIENDS.
A. GIACCHETTI, 545(RPH):AUG72-
178
WHITEHEAD, J. JOINER.
E. ROVIT, 659:AUTUMN74-539
J. YARDLEY, 473(PR):2/1973-286
WHITEHILL, W.M., ED. BOSTON PRINTS
& PRINTMAKERS 1670-1775.*
639(VQR):AUTUMN73-CLXXII
WHITELEY, W.H. SWAHILI.*
K. LEGÈRE, 682(ZPSK):BAND25
HEFT6-522
WHITELOCK, D., ED. SWEET'S ANGLO-
SAXON READER. (15TH ED)
C.A. LADD, 447(N&Q):APR72-140
WHITER, L. SPODE.
J.V.G. MALLET, 90:FEB72-104
WHITESIDE, D.T. - SEE NEWTON, I.
WHITING, C. FINALE AT FLENSBURG.
617(TLS):4JAN74-6
WHITLEY, J.S. & A. GOLDMAN, EDS.
AMERICAN NOTES FOR GENERAL CIR-
CULATION.
K.J. FIELDING, 155:SEP72-193
WHITMAN, W. SPECIMEN DAYS.
R.G. SILVER, 646(WWR):MAR72-31
WHITMAN, W. WALT WHITMAN'S CAMDEN
CONVERSATIONS. (W. TELLER, ED)
J. SEELYE, 31(ASCH):SPRING74-329

WHITNEY, M.S. CRITICAL REACTIONS &
THE CHRISTIAN ELEMENT IN THE
POETRY OF PIERRE DE RONSARD.
D. STONE, JR., 551(RENQ):WINTER
72-463
WHITNEY, M.S. - SEE DE MAGNY, O.
WHITNEY, W.D. WHITNEY ON LANGUAGE.
(M. SILVERSTEIN, ED)
H. HOIJER, 350:JUN73-517
T. PYLES, 35(AS):SPRING-SUMMER70-
108
WHITROW, M., ED. ISIS CUMULATIVE
BIBLIOGRAPHY.
S.A. SHAPIN, 481(PQ):JUL72-518
WHITSON, R.E. THE COMING CONVER-
GENCE OF WORLD RELIGIONS.
J.P. REID, 613:SUMMER72-318
WHITTAKER, C.R. - SEE HERODIAN
WHITTAKER, J. GOD TIME BEING.
W. CHARLTON, 123:DEC73-280
É. DES PLACES, 555:VOL46FASC2-
291
WHITTAKER, P. THE AMERICAN WAY OF
SEX.
M.S. KENNEDY, 441:29SEP74-30
WHITTALL, A. SCHOENBERG CHAMBER
MUSIC.
O. NEIGHBOUR, 415:JAN73-35
WHITTEMORE, E. QUIN'S SHANGHAI
CIRCUS.
J. CHARYN, 441:28APR74-7
WHITTEMORE, L.H. THE SUPER COPS.*
617(TLS):5APR74-376
WHITTEN, N.E., JR. & J.F. SZWED, EDS.
AFRO-AMERICAN ANTHROPOLOGY.
M.S. EDMONSON, 292(JAF):APR-JUN
72-189
WHITTET, G.S. LOVERS IN ART.
I. KOBERNICK, 290(JAAC):WINTER
72-279
WHITTICK, A. EUROPEAN ARCHITECTURE
IN THE TWENTIETH CENTURY.
617(TLS):24MAY74-552
WHITTING, P., ED. BYZANTIUM.
R. BROWNING, 123:DEC73-287
C. HEAD, 589:APR73-430
WHITTLE, A.R. - SEE STICKNEY, J.T.
WHITTLE, T. BERTIE.
J. MILLER, 617(TLS):20DEC74-1437
"THE WHOLE COSMEP CATALOG."
B. HENDERSON, 441:19MAY74-37
WHONE, H. THE HIDDEN FACE OF MUSIC.
617(TLS):24MAY74-555
"WHO'S WHO 1974."
617(TLS):17MAY74-523
"WHY BRITAIN NEEDS LIBERAL GOVERN-
MENT."
E. PYGGE, 617(TLS):4OCT74-1076
WHYTE, L.L. L'INCONSCIENT AVANT
FREUD.
Y. BRÈS, 542:OCT-DEC72-488
WIATR, J.J. NARÓD I PAŃSTWO.
F. GROSS, 32:MAR73-134
WIBBERLEY, L. THE LAST STAND OF
FATHER FELIX.
M. LEVIN, 441:22SEP74-41
WICKBERG, E. IN DARKEST ENGLAND NOW.
D. MARTIN, 617(TLS):18OCT74-1169
WICKE, C.R. OLMEC.
M. STIRLING, 37:FEB72-42
WICKES, G. AMERICANS IN PARIS.*
R. ASSELINEAU, 189(EA):JUL-SEP72-
453

WICKHAM, A. SELECTED POEMS.
J. SAUNDERS, 565:VOL13#4-74
WICKHAM, G. EARLY ENGLISH STAGES
1300 TO 1660.* (VOL 2, PT 2)
J.C. TREWIN, 157:SUMMER72-70
G.W. WILLIAMS, 579(SAQ):WINTER73-
177
WICKRAM, G. SÄMTLICHE WERKE. (VOLS
6&8) (H-G. ROLOFF, ED)
E. SOBEL, 301(JEGP):OCT73-587
WICKS, C.B. THE PARISIAN STAGE.
(PT 4)
J. DECOCK, 207(FR):MAY72-1190
WIDEMAN, J.E. THE LYNCHERS.*
E. ROVIT, 659:AUTUMN74-539
WIDENER, D. N.U.K.E.E.
M. LEVIN, 441:17MAR74-38
"WIDENER LIBRARY SHELFLIST 40: FIN-
NISH & BALTIC HISTORY & LITERA-
TURES."
J.E.O. SCREEN, 575(SEER):OCT73-
634
"WIDENER LIBRARY SHELFLISTS 26 & 27:
AMERICAN LITERATURE."
B. WILLIAMSON, 354:DEC72-349
"WIDENER LIBRARY SHELFLISTS 45 & 46:
SOCIOLOGY."
617(TLS):6SEP74-958
WIDENGREN, G. DER FEUDALISMUS IM
ALTEN IRAN.
M.J. DRESDEN, 318(JAOS):OCT-DEC
72-570
WIDERSZPIL, S. & OTHERS. SOCIOLOGIE
V ZÁVODĚ - SOCJOLOGIA W ZAKŁADZIE
PRACY.
A. MATEJKO, 497(POLR):SPRING72-
105
WIDICK, B.J. DETROIT.
639(VQR):WINTER73-XXXIX
WIDMAR, B. - SEE SPINOZA, B.
WIDMER, K. THE WAYS OF NIHILISM.*
P. MC CARTHY, 594:SPRING72-98
"WID'S YEAR BOOK: 1918-1922."
H. HART, 200:JUN-JUL72-372
WIDSTRAND, C., ED. CO-OPERATIVES &
RURAL DEVELOPMENT IN EAST AFRICA.
A.H.M. KIRK-GREENE, 69:JAN72-80
WIEBE, R., ED. STORIES FROM WESTERN
CANADA.*
P. POLSON, 648:JUN72-53
WIEBENSON, D. TONY GARNIER: THE
CITÉ INDUSTRIELLE.*
G.L. HERSEY, 56:SUMMER72-180
WIEBENSON, D. SOURCES OF GREEK
REVIVAL ARCHITECTURE.*
S. BOYD, 576:MAY72-153
WIECEK, W.M. THE GUARANTEE CLAUSE
OF THE U.S. CONSTITUTION.
C.T. CULLEN, 432(NEQ):SEP72-453
WIECZYNSKI, J.L. - SEE PLATONOV, S.F.
WIENER, J. THE WAR OF THE UNSTAMPED.
A.T. PEACOCK, 637(VS):SEP71-104
WIENER, J.H. A DESCRIPTIVE FINDING
LIST OF UNSTAMPED BRITISH PERIODI-
CALS 1830-1836.
A. HUTT, 78(BC):SUMMER72-280
WIENOLD, G. FORMULIERUNGSTHEORIE -
POETIK - STRUKTURELLE LITERATUR-
GESCHICHTE AM BEISPIEL DER ALT-
ENGLISCHEN DICHTUNG.
J.W. MARCHAND, 301(JEGP):APR73-
236
E.G. STANLEY, 182:VOL25#19/20-
673   [CONTINUED]

[CONTINUING]
J. TRABANT, 490:JUL-OCT72-441
WIENPAHL, P. ZEN DIARY.*
J.B.L., 543:SEP71-138
WIERENGA, L. LA TROADE, DE ROBERT
GARNIER.*
C.J. THIRY, 556(RLV):1972/3-330
WIERLACHER, A. DAS BÜRGERLICHE
DRAMA.*
D. KASANG, 597(SN):VOL44#1-211
WIERZBICKA, A. DOCIEKANIA SEMANTY-
CZNE.
E. POZNAŃSKI, 353:10CT72-79
VON WIESE, B., ED. DEUTSCHE DICHTER
DER MODERNE.* (2ND ED)
H. RIDLEY, 220(GL&L):APR73-256
VON WIESE, B., ED. DEUTSCHE DICHTER
DER ROMANTIK.
O. SEIDLIN, 301(JEGP):OCT73-594
VON WIESE, B. KARL IMMERMANN.*
P. HASUBEK, 680(ZDP):BAND91HEFT2-
292
VON WIESE, B. - SEE IMMERMANN, K.
VON WIESE, B. & R. HENSS, EDS. NA-
TIONALISMUS IN GERMANISTIK UND
DICHTUNG.*
H. RIDLEY, 402(MLR):JAN73-238
WIESE, H., COMP. EXLIBRIS AUS DER
UNIVERSITÄTSBIBLIOTHEK MÜNCHEN.
B. HUBENSTEINER, 182:VOL25#19/20-
642
WIESEL, E. NIGHT, DAWN, THE ACCI-
DENT.
617(TLS):15FEB74-149
WIESEL, E. THE OATH.*
E.B. FISKE, 441:16JAN74-37
E. ROVIT, 659:AUTUMN74-539
M. WOOD, 453:7FEB74-10
WIESEL, E. SOULS ON FIRE.*
A.J. RAWICK, 287:MAY72-27
WIESINGER, P. PHONETISCH-PHONOLO-
GISCHE UNTERSUCHUNGEN ZUR VOKALENT-
WICKLUNG IN DEN DEUTSCHEN DIALEK-
TEN.
E.H. ANTONSEN, 301(JEGP):JUL73-
433
W.G. MOULTON, 221(GQ):MAR72-377
E. SCHWARZ, 343:BAND15HEFT2-178
WIET, G. BAGHDAD, METROPOLIS OF THE
ABBASID CALIPHATE.
J. LASSNER, 318(JAOS):APR-JUN72-
395
WIGGINTON, B.E., ED. THE FOXFIRE
BOOK.
B.A. ROSENBERG, 219(GAR):SUMMER
72-226
WILBER, D.N. PERSEPOLIS.*
290(JAAC):WINTER71-276
WILBUR, R. OPPOSITES.
W.H. PRITCHARD, 249(HUDR):AUTUMN
73-588
WILCKE, C. DAS LUGALBANDAEPOS.
A. SALONEN, 182:VOL25#3/4-114
WILCOX, A.M.C. - SEE MAURIAC, F.
WILCOX, C. LONG WAY DOWN.
N. CALLENDAR, 441:28JUL74-14
WILCZYNSKI, J. THE ECONOMICS OF
SOCIALISM.*
L. GILL, 104:SPRING72-180
WILCZYNSKI, J. PROFIT, RISK & IN-
CENTIVES UNDER SOCIALIST ECONOMIC
PLANNING.*
A.H. SMITH, 575(SEER):OCT73-621

WILCZYNSKI, J. SOCIALIST ECONOMIC
DEVELOPMENT & REFORMS.*
B. MIECZKOWSKI, 104:SPRING72-183
WILD, C. REFLEXION UND ERFAHRUNG.
M.J.V., 543:JUN72-770
WILD, P. FAT MAN POEMS.
W.P. ROOT, 491:OCT73-34
WILDE, O. THE ARTIST AS CRITIC.*
(R. ELLMANN, ED)
K. CONNELLY, 97(CQ):VOL6#1-93
WILDE, O. THE PICTURE OF DORIAN
GRAY. (I. MURRAY, ED)
617(TLS):26JUL74-811
WILDE, O. THE PICTURE OF DORIAN
GRAY. (ADAPTED BY J. OSBORNE)
617(TLS):4JAN74-14
WILDE, W.H. ADAM LINDSAY GORDON.
A. MITCHELL, 71(ALS):MAY74-332
WILDEBLOOD, J. THE POLITE WORLD.
617(TLS):10MAY74-496
WILDEN, A. SYSTEM & STRUCTURE.
H.R. OBLIERS & G.C. RUMP, 182:
VOL25#7/8-206
WILDER, A. AMERICAN POPULAR SONG.*
R.I. SCOTT, 648:JAN73-86
WILDER, T. THEOPHILUS NORTH.*
441:10NOV74-39
617(TLS):12JUL74-741
WILDES, H.E. WILLIAM PENN.
A. WHITMAN, 441:14DEC74-27
WILDHAGEN, K. & W. HÉRAUCOURT. ENG-
LISCH-DEUTSCHES/DEUTSCH-ENGLISCHES
WÖRTERBUCH. (VOL 2: DEUTSCH-
ENGLISCH.) (2ND ED)
B. JACOBS, 75:3/1972-37
WILDING, M. ASPECTS OF THE DYING
PROCESS.*
C. HARRISON-FORD, 581:JUN73-167
WILDING, M. MILTON'S "PARADISE
LOST."*
R.E.C. HOUGHTON, 447(N&Q):OCT72-
400
WILDMAN, E. NUCLEAR LOVE.*
E. ROVIT, 659:AUTUMN74-539
WILES, M. THE REMAKING OF CHRISTIAN
DOCTRINE.
R.P.C. HANSON, 617(TLS):22NOV74-
1321
WILES, P.J.D. COMMUNIST INTERNATION-
AL ECONOMICS.
W.D. BOWLES, 32:MAR73-177
WILES, P.J.D., ED. THE PREDICTION
OF COMMUNIST ECONOMIC PERFORMANCE.*
J.R. MILLAR, 550(RUSR):APR72-207
WILEY, R.A. - SEE KEMBLE, J.M. & J.
GRIMM
WILHELM, K. CITY OF CAIN.
M. LEVIN, 441:10MAR74-10
WILK, M. ELIMINATE THE MIDDLE MAN.
N. CALLENDAR, 441:24MAR74-41
WILKEN, R.L. JUDAISM & THE EARLY
CHRISTIAN MIND.*
H. MUSURILLO, 613:SPRING72-148
WILKERSON, T.E. MINDS, BRAINS &
PEOPLE.
617(TLS):16AUG74-885
WILKES, P. THESE PRIESTS STAY.
E.B. FISKE, 441:16MAR74-29
WILKINS, B.T. HEGEL'S PHILOSOPHY OF
HISTORY.
617(TLS):18OCT74-1161

WILKINS, D.A. LINGUISTICS IN LANGU-
AGE TEACHING.
G.A. RUNNALLS, 402(MLR):JUL73-
623
J.H. SCHUMANN, 608:SEP73-330
WILKINS, N. - SEE DE MACHAUT, G.
WILKINSON, C.K. NISHAPUR.
617(TLS):11OCT74-1108
WILKINSON, G. TURNER'S EARLY SKETCH-
BOOKS, 1789-1802.
D. THOMAS, 135:AUG72-303
WILKINSON, H.C. BERMUDA FROM SAIL
TO STEAM.
617(TLS):15FEB74-155
WILKINSON, J. THE CONQUEST OF CAN-
CER.
617(TLS):18JAN74-48
WILKINSON, J.H., 3D. SERVING JUS-
TICE.
P. EDELMAN, 441:6OCT74-6
WILKINSON, L.P. THE "GEORGICS" OF
VIRGIL.*
B. OTIS, 487:SPRING72-40
WILKINSON, N. A BRUSH WITH LIFE.
G. WILLS, 39:MAR72-231
WILKINSON-LATHAM, R. BRITISH ARTIL-
LERY ON LAND & SEA, 1790-1820.
617(TLS):15FEB74-165
WILKINSON-LATHAM, R. CRIMEAN UNI-
FORMS. (VOL 2)
617(TLS):12JUL74-751
WILKS, J. & E. BERNARD.
617(TLS):5JUL74-733
WILLAN, A. ENTERTAINING MENUS.
N. HAZELTON, 441:1DEC74-94
WILLCOCK, M.M. A COMMENTARY ON
HOMER'S "ILIAD," BOOKS 1-VI.*
G.S. KIRK, 303:VOL92-186
WILLCOX, W.B. - SEE FRANKLIN, B.
WILLCOX, W.B., WITH OTHERS - SEE
FRANKLIN, B.
WILLE, K. DIE SIGNATUR DER MELAN-
CHOLIE IM WERK CLEMENS BRENTANOS.
J.F.F., 191(ELN):SEP72(SUPP)-141
WILLER, J. PARAMIND.
D. BARBOUR, 296:VOL3#2-109
WILLER, J. THE SOCIAL DETERMINATION
OF KNOWLEDGE.
H.F., 543:MAR72-574
WILLETT, F. AFRICAN ART.*
G.I. JONES, 69:JAN72-75
WILLETT, J. EXPRESSIONISM.*
V.H. MIESEL, 290(JAAC):WINTER71-
276
D. SCOTT, 220(GL&L):APR73-259
WILLETTS, W. CERAMIC ART OF SOUTH-
EAST ASIA.
M. MEDLEY, 39:FEB72-150
WILLIAMS, A. THE BERIA PAPERS.*
442(NY):7JAN74-75
WILLIAMS, A. & M.E. NOVAK. CONGREVE
CONSIDER'D.*
481(PQ):JUL72-659
WILLIAMS, A.M., ED. CONVERSATIONS
AT LITTLE GIDDING.
F.B. ARTZ, 551(RENQ):SPRING72-
115
WILLIAMS, B. & J.W. EHRLICH. A MAT-
TER OF CONFIDENCE.* A CONFLICT
OF INTEREST.
N. CALLENDAR, 441:12MAY74-18
WILLIAMS, C.B. STYLE AND VOCABU-
LARY.*
D. WOLFF, 38:BAND90HEFT1/2-156

WILLIAMS, C.E. THE BROKEN EAGLE.
R.H. THOMAS, 617(TLS):11OCT74-
1137
WILLIAMS, C.K. I AM THE BITTER
NAME.*
J. VERNON, 651(WHR):WINTER73-103
WILLIAMS, D. TROUSERED APES.*
J.M. LALLEY, 396(MODA):SPRING73-
200
WILLIAMS, E. EMLYN.*
P. ADAMS, 61:MAY74-139
H. EDWARDS, 441:2JUN74-46
442(NY):24JUN74-104
WILLIAMS, E.B. FROM LATIN TO PORTU-
GUESE. (2ND ED)
K. ADAMS, 353:1JUL72-108
WILLIAMS, G. AFRICAN DESIGNS FROM
TRADITIONAL SOURCES.
C. HARRISON, 592:JUL/AUG72-52
WILLIAMS, G. BIG MORNING BLUES.
D. WILSON, 617(TLS):6DEC74-1361
WILLIAMS, G. - SEE DICKENS, C.
WILLIAMS, G.M. FROM SCENES LIKE
THESE.
E.C. BUFKIN, 219(GAR):SPRING72-
100
WILLIAMS, G.W. - SEE "JACOB ECK-
HARD'S CHOIRMASTER'S BOOK OF 1809"
WILLIAMS, H.W., JR. MIRROR TO THE
AMERICAN PAST.
A. FRANKENSTEIN, 55:NOV73-46
WILLIAMS, I., ED. MEREDITH: THE
CRITICAL HERITAGE.
A.P. ROBSON, 637(VS):JUN72-475
WILLIAMS, I. - SEE FIELDING, H.
WILLIAMS, J. AUGUSTUS.*
J.N. HARTT, 639(VQR):SUMMER73-
450
S. O'CONNELL, 418(MR):WINTER73-
190
E. ROVIT, 659:AUTUMN74-539
617(TLS):11JAN74-25
WILLIAMS, J. STAGE LEFT.
S. KAUFFMANN, 441:10MAR74-6
WILLIAMS, J. STATE OF GRACE.*
42(AR):VOL32#4-696
WILLIAMS, J. & N. DEAN. BLUES &
ROOTS/RUE & BLUETS.
639(VQR):WINTER72-XXXIV
WILLIAMS, J.A. CAPTAIN BLACKMAN.
S. O'CONNELL, 418(MR):WINTER73-
190
E. ROVIT, 659:AUTUMN74-539
WILLIAMS, K. ACROSS THE STRAITS.
M. JONES, 362:25APR74-543
617(TLS):4JAN74-4
WILLIAMS, K., ED. BACKGROUNDS TO
EIGHTEENTH-CENTURY LITERATURE.
F. BRADY, 566:AUTUMN72-48
173(ECS):SPRING73-401
WILLIAMS, L.P., WITH R. FITZ GERALD
& O. STALLYBRASS - SEE FARADAY, M.
WILLIAMS, M. THOMAS HARDY & RURAL
ENGLAND.
P. DICKINSON, 364:AUG/SEP72-149
S. FAUCHEREAU, 98:DEC72-1105
S. HYNES, 401(MLQ):SEP73-325
W.J. KEITH, 637(VS):MAR73-367
W.F. WRIGHT, 502(PRS):WINTER72/
73-359
WILLIAMS, M. THE POETRY OF JOHN
CROWE RANSOM.
I. EHRENPREIS, 579(SAQ):WINTER73-
169

WILLIAMS, P. FIGURED BASS ACCOMPANI-
MENT.*
G.J. BUELOW, 414(MQ):APR72-308
WILLIAMS, R. THE COUNTRY & THE
CITY.*
H. LOMAS, 364:AUG/SEP73-130
J. MOYNAHAN, 639(VQR):AUTUMN73-
633
R. SALE, 249(HUDR):WINTER73/74-
704
WILLIAMS, R. THE ENGLISH NOVEL FROM
DICKENS TO LAWRENCE.*
R. VIDAN, 202(FMOD):JUN72-351
WILLIAMS, R. EUROPEAN TECHNOLOGY.
617(TLS):31MAY74-579
WILLIAMS, R. GEORGE ORWELL.*
K. MC SWEENEY, 529(QQ):SPRING72-
115
WILLIAMS, R.C. CULTURE IN EXILE.
W. LAQUEUR, 575(SEER):APR73-331
G. STRUVE, 32:MAR73-208
639(VQR):AUTUMN72-CXLVIII
WILLIAMS, R.D., ED. THE AENEID OF
VIRGIL. (BKS 7-12)
617(TLS):8FEB74-140
WILLIAMS, R.L. THE MORTAL NAPOLEON
III.
639(VQR):AUTUMN72-CXL
WILLIAMS, R.L. LE PRINCE DES POLÉ-
MISTES: HENRI ROCHEFORT.
K.M. OFFEN, 207(FR):MAR72-892
WILLIAMS, S. PHILOSOPHICAL LECTURES
ON THE CONSTITUTION, DUTY, & RELI-
GION OF MAN. (M. CURTI & W. TILL-
MAN, EDS)
H.W. SCHNEIDER, 319:JAN74-124
WILLIAMS, S.A. GIVE BIRTH TO BRIGHT-
NESS.
P.R. KLOTMAN, 659:SPRING74-283
WILLIAMS, T. EIGHT MORTAL LADIES
POSSESSED.
E. WHITE, 441:6OCT74-14
WILLIAMS, T. THE HAIR OF HAROLD
ROUX.
C. LEHMANN-HAUPT, 441:3JUN74-35
WILLIAMS, T.A. MALLARMÉ & THE LAN-
GUAGE OF MYSTICISM.*
R.G. COHN, 546(RR):DEC72-313
H.A. GRUBBS, 207(FR):OCT71-256
D.J. MOSSOP, 208(FS):JAN73-91
WILLIAMS, W.C. IMAGINATIONS.* (W.
SCHOTT, ED)
M. DOYLE, 648:JUN72-51
WILLIAMS, W.E. ALLEN LANE.*
M. GREEN, 364:AUG/SEP73-139
WILLIAMS-ELLIS, C. ARCHITECT ERRANT.
J. CLOAG, 46:JAN72-65
WILLIAMSEN, V.G. - SEE MIRA DE
AMESCUA, A.
WILLIAMSON, A. THOMAS PAINE.*
M. CUNLIFFE, 441:4AUG74-2
A. WHITMAN, 441:6JUL74-15
WILLIAMSON, D. THE REMOVALISTS.
A. KRUSE, 581:JUN73-240
WILLIAMSON, G. THE INGENIOUS MR.
GAINSBOROUGH.
639(VQR):SPRING73-LXXX
WILLIAMSON, H.N.H. FAREWELL TO THE
DON.* (J. HARRIS, ED)
P. KENEZ, 550(RUSR):JUL72-322
WILLIAMSON, H.R. KIND KIT.
I. BROWN, 157:WINTER72-72

WILLIAMSON, H.R. LORENZO THE MAG-
NIFICENT.
617(TLS):23AUG74-909
WILLIAMSON, H.R. CATHERINE DE'
MEDICI.*
617(TLS):19APR74-420
WILLIAMSON, J.V. & V.M. BURKE, EDS.
A VARIOUS LANGUAGE.*
P.W. ROGERS, 529(QQ):WINTER72-
559
WILLIAMSON, S.R. THE POLITICS OF
GRAND STRATEGY.*
R. BULLEN, 325:OCT72-545
"WILLING'S PRESS GUIDE."
617(TLS):17MAY74-534
WILLINGHAM, C. ETERNAL FIRE.
J. YARDLEY, 473(PR):2/1973-286
WILLINGHAM, C. RAMBLING ROSE.*
639(VQR):WINTER73-IX
WILLIS, A.J. & M.J. HOAD, COMPS.
PORTSMOUTH RECORD SERIES: BOROUGH
SESSIONS PAPERS 1653-1685.
M.H. PORT, 447(N&Q):SEP72-342
WILLIS, J. GENIESH.
S. CHEDA, 99:AUG74-41
WILLIS, J. DE MARTIANO CAPELLA
EMENDANDO.
J.R.C. MARTYN, 67:MAY73-151
WILLIS, J. & M. "...BUT THERE ARE
ALWAYS MIRACLES."
A. BROYARD, 441:4SEP74-47
WILLIS, J.H., JR. WILLIAM EMPSON.
D. HEWITT, 447(N&Q):SEP72-351
WILLIS, R. MAN & BEAST.
617(TLS):27SEP74-1046
WILLIS, T. DEATH MAY SURPRISE US.
617(TLS):4OCT74-1061
WILLMOTT, W.E. THE POLITICAL STRUC-
TURE OF THE CHINESE COMMUNITY IN
CAMBODIA.
R.J. COUGHLIN, 293(JAST):MAY72-
731
WILLMS, B. DIE ANTWORT DES LEVIA-
THAN.
J. FREUND, 98:JUN72-555
WILLOCK, C. THE FIGHTERS.
M. LEVIN, 441:26MAY74-19
WILLOW, M.E. AN ANALYSIS OF THE
ENGLISH POEMS OF ST. THOMAS MORE.
617(TLS):19JUL74-770
WILLS, G. BARE RUINED CHOIRS.
J.P. BOYLE, 396(MODA):SUMMER73-
305
W. SHEED, 453:7MAR74-18
WILLS, G. JADE OF THE EAST.*
M. CHOU, 60:MAR-APR73-64
WILLS, J.E., JR. PEPPER, GUNS &
PARLEYS.
C.R. BOXER, 617(TLS):13DEC74-
1422
WILMES, E. BEITRÄGE ZUR ALEXANDRIN-
ERREDE (OR. 32) DES DION CHRYSOS-
TOMOS.
É. DES PLACES, 555:VOL46FASC2-
316
WILMET, M. LE SYSTÈME DE L'INDICA-
TIF EN MOYEN FRANÇAIS.*
G. LAVIS, 556(RLV):1972/4-442
WILMOT, J. THE COMPLETE POEMS OF
JOHN WILMOT, EARL OF ROCHESTER.*
(D.M. VIETH, ED)
J. WILDERS, 447(N&Q):MAY72-193

WILMOT, J. & OTHERS. THE GYLDEN-
STOLPE MANUSCRIPT MISCELLANY OF
POEMS BY JOHN WILMOT, EARL OF
ROCHESTER, & OTHER RESTORATION
AUTHORS.* (B. DANIELSSON & D.M.
VIETH, EDS)
T.A. BIRRELL, 433:APR72-238
WILSHIRE, B. METAPHYSICS.
R.W. NEWELL, 479(PHQ):JAN72-72
WILSON, A. AS IF BY MAGIC.*
R. DE FEO, 249(HUDR):WINTER73/74-
780
E. FEINSTEIN, 364:AUG/SEP73-148
WILSON, A. THE CHARTIST MOVEMENT IN
SCOTLAND.
P. HOLLIS, 637(VS):DEC72-237
WILSON, A. THE WORLD OF CHARLES
DICKENS.*
D. DONOGHUE, 445(NCF):SEP72-216
M.A. FIDO, 637(VS):SEP71-101
WILSON, A.J. POLITICS IN SRI LANKA
1947-1973.
617(TLS):20SEP74-1023
WILSON, A.M. DIDEROT.*
L.G. CROCKER, 319:JAN74-120
G. MAY, 676(YR):AUTUMN72-113
I.H. SMITH, 67:NOV73-306
639(VQR):SPRING73-LXXX
WILSON, B.R., ED. RATIONALITY.*
E. BARKER, 262:WINTER72-463
WILSON, C. MAPPING THE FRONTIER.
(G.F.G. STANLEY, ED)
R.E. EHRENBERG, 14:JUL/OCT72-410
I. MC CLYMONT, 150(DR):SPRING72-
149
WILSON, C. THE MIND PARASITES.
R. HACK, 114(CHIR):VOL24#3-158
WILSON, C. NEW PATHWAYS IN PSYCHOL-
OGY.*
H. LOMAS, 364:AUG/SEP72-144
WILSON, C. PARLIAMENTS, PEOPLES &
MASS MEDIA.
M. HOPPÉ, 619(TC):VOL177#1043-47
WILSON, C. THE SCHOOLGIRL MURDER
CASE.
P. ADAMS, 61:JUL74-100
N. CALLENDAR, 441:21JUL74-18
442(NY):16SEP74-150
617(TLS):14JUN74-629
WILSON, C. STRANGE POWERS.
617(TLS):26APR74-456
WILSON, D. THE LONG MARCH.
639(VQR):AUTUMN72-CXLV
WILSON, D.C. - SEE UNDER CLARKE
WILSON, D.
WILSON, E. UPSTATE.
G.H. DOUGLAS, 502(PRS):SUMMER72-
174
WILSON, E. A WINDOW ON RUSSIA.*
C. BROWN, 473(PR):2/1973-311
K. FITZLYON, 364:APR/MAY73-157
WILSON, F. MUSCOVY.*
O.P. BACKUS 3D, 550(RUSR):JUL72-
322
WILSON, G. & A. IKUKO - SEE "THREE
CONTEMPORARY JAPANESE POETS"
WILSON, G.B.L. A DICTIONARY OF BAL-
LET. (REV)
617(TLS):10MAY74-508
WILSON, G.M., ED. CRISIS POLITICS
IN PREWAR JAPAN.*
H. FUKUI, 318(JAOS):OCT-DEC72-
547

WILSON, H. CLAUDEL'S IMMORTAL
HEROES.
L. RIESE, 397(MD):DEC72-342
WILSON, H.H. A SHOW OF COLOURS.
R.B.J. WILSON, 381:JUN72-220
WILSON, J. TRUTH OR DARE.*
N. CALLENDAR, 441:7APR74-35
WILSON, J.R.S. EMOTION & OBJECT.
N.F. BUNNIN, 518:MAY73-30
WILSON, K. MIDWATCH.
K. BREWER, 649(WAL):FALL72-236
P. COOLEY, 385(MQR):WINTER74-79
WILSON, K. THE OLD MAN & OTHERS.
ROCKS.
K. BREWER, 649(WAL):FALL72-236
WILSON, K.P., ED. CHESTER CUSTOMS
ACCOUNTS, 1301-1566.
H.S. COBB, 325:APR72-442
WILSON, L.G. CHARLES LYELL. (VOL 1)
R. FOX, 637(VS):JUN73-476
J. RODGERS, 676(YR):WINTER73-277
617(TLS):25JAN74-76
WILSON, M. THE LIFE OF WILLIAM
BLAKE. (NEW ED) (G. KEYNES, ED)
I.H.C., 191(ELN):SEP72(SUPP)-38
WILSON, M.R. COPTIC FUTURE TENSES.
V. DAVIS, 318(JAOS):JAN-MAR72-
192
WILSON, N.G., ED. AN ANTHOLOGY OF
BYZANTINE PROSE.
R. BROWNING, 303:VOL92-252
WILSON, R. SCOTCH.
617(TLS):11JAN74-38
WILSON, R. - SEE FERGUSON, O.
WILSON, R.M. THE LOST LITERATURE OF
MEDIEVAL ENGLAND.* (2ND ED)
H. BERGNER, 38:BAND90HEFT4-506
J.R. SIMON, 189(EA):JAN-MAR72-48
WILSON, R.R. INTERNATIONAL LAW &
CONTEMPORARY COMMONWEALTH ISSUES.
A-R. WERNER, 182:VOL25#13/14-466
WILSON, S., JR. THE VIEUX CARRE NEW
ORLEANS.
M.B. LAPPING, 576:OCT72-246
WILSON, S., JR. & L.V. HUBER. THE
CABILDO ON JACKSON SQUARE.
M.B. LAPPING, 576:OCT72-246
WILSON, S., JR. & B. LEMANN. NEW
ORLEANS ARCHITECTURE. (VOL 1)
M.B. LAPPING, 576:OCT72-246
WILSON, W. DETOUR.
N. CALLENDAR, 441:25AUG74-29
WILSON, W. THE PAPERS OF WOODROW
WILSON.* (VOLS 8 & 12) (A.S.
LINK & OTHERS, EDS)
R.L. WATSON, JR., 579(SAQ):WIN-
TER73-154
WILSON, W. THE PAPERS OF WOODROW
WILSON.* (VOLS 9-11) (A.S. LINK
& OTHERS, EDS)
F.C. ROSENBERGER, 639(VQR):
SPRING72-304
R.L. WATSON, JR., 579(SAQ):WIN-
TER73-154
WILSON, W. THE PAPERS OF WOODROW
WILSON. (VOL 15) (A.S. LINK, D.W.
HIRST & J.E. LITTLE, EDS)
H.W. BRAGDON, 639(VQR):SUMMER73-
472
WILSON, W.R. HOGEN MONOGATARI.
H.P. VARLEY, 293(JAST):FEB72-408
WIMBUSH, R., COMP. THE GRAMOPHONE
JUBILEE BOOK, 1923-73.
K. SPENCE, 415:OCT73-1016

WIMSATT, J.I. THE MARGUERITE POETRY
OF GUILLAUME DE MACHAUT.*
F.R.P. AKEHURST, 207(FR):DEC71-
537
S. SMITH, 399(MLJ):MAR72-192
WINCKEL, F. MUSIC, SOUND, & SENSA-
TION.
W. SLAWSON, 513:SPRING-SUMMER70-
143
WINCKELMANN, J.J. WRITINGS ON ART.
(D. IRWIN, ED)
D.E.L. HAYNES, 39:SEP72-252
WINCOTT, L. INVERGORDON MUTINEER.
617(TLS):13SEP74-983
WIND, E., WITH G.L. HARRISS - SEE
MC FARLANE, K.B.
WINDER, R.B. SAUDI ARABIA IN THE
NINETEENTH CENTURY.
A.M. ABU-HAKIMA, 318(JAOS):JAN-
MAR72-125
WINGATE, J. BELOW THE HORIZON.
A. MACLEAN, 617(TLS):13DEC74-
1420
WINGE, M. KRITIKHISTORIE.
H.B. JOHANSEN, 172(EDDA):1972/4-
253
WINIGER, J. DAS FUNDMATERIAL VON
THAYNGEN-WEIER IM RAHMEN DER PFY-
NER KULTUR.
W. KIMMIG, 182:VOL25#19/20-678
WINKLER, H.A. MITTELSTAND, DEMOKRA-
TIE UND NATIONALSOZIALISMUS.*
617(TLS):1FEB74-93
WINNER, T.G., ED. TVORCHESKIE RAB-
OTY UCHENIKOV TOLSTOGO V YASNOI
POLYANE.
C. BROWN, 617(TLS):27SEP74-1044
WINNETT, F.V. & W.L. REED, WITH
OTHERS. ANCIENT RECORDS FROM
NORTH ARABIA.
A. JAMME, 318(JAOS):OCT-DEC72-
519
WINSOR, D. THE DEATH CONVENTION.
617(TLS):31MAY74-591
WINSTON, G.P. JOHN FISKE.
R. FALK, 445(NCF):MAR73-497
WINTER, E. ENAMEL PAINTING TECH-
NIQUE.
A.H. SCHWED, 363:MAY72-102
WINTER, F.E. GREEK FORTIFICATIONS.
J.M. COOK, 123:DEC73-284
H. PLOMMER, 303:VOL92-241
WINTER, G. A COUNTRY CAMERA, 1844-
1914.
J.H. BRUNVAND, 292(JAF):JUL-SEP
72-290
WINTER, J.M. SOCIALISM & THE CHAL-
LENGE OF WAR.
F.M. LEVENTHAL, 617(TLS):6SEP74-
947
WINTERBOTHAM, F.W. THE ULTRA SECRET.
D. HUNT, 617(TLS):13DEC74-1425
D. KAHN, 441:29DEC74-5
R. LEWIN, 362:240CT74-542
442(NY):30DEC74-64
WINTERBOTTOM, M. PROBLEMS IN QUIN-
TILIAN.*
J. ANDRÉ, 555:VOL46FASC1-158
F.R.D. GOODYEAR, 123:MAR73-37
WINTERBOTTOM, M. - SEE QUINTILIAN
WINTERS, Y. FORMS OF DISCOVERY.
W.W. ROBSON, 97(CQ):VOL6#2-189

WINTERS, Y. UNCOLLECTED ESSAYS &
REVIEWS. (F. MURPHY, ED)
D. BROMWICH, 441:19MAY74-36
D. DONOGHUE, 617(TLS):30AUG74-
917
WINTERSCHEIDT, F. DEUTSCHE UNTER-
HALTUNGSLITERATUR DER JAHRE 1850-
1860.
D.L. ASHLIMAN, 221(GQ):NOV72-752
WINTON, C. SIR RICHARD STEELE, M.P.*
F. RAU, 224(GRM):BAND22HEFT1-102
WIORA, W. DAS DEUTSCHE LIED.*
P.H.L., 414(MQ):APR72-315
WIRGIN, J. SUNG CERAMIC DESIGNS.
S.G. VALENSTEIN, 57:VOL34#2/3-
241
WIRTH, G. HEINRICH BÖLL.
C.O. ENDERSTEIN, 221(GQ):MAR72-
364
WISBEY, R.A., ED. THE COMPUTER IN
LITERARY & LINGUISTIC RESEARCH.*
G.R. WOOD, 35(AS):FALL-WINTER70-
283
205(FMLS):OCT72-380
WISE, A. THE HISTORY & ART OF PER-
SONAL COMBAT.
E. ARGENT, 157:SPRING72-78
WISE, D. & T.B. ROSS. THE INVISIBLE
GOVERNMENT.
441:10FEB74-25
WISE, T.J., ED. THE ASHLEY LIBRARY.
W.B. TODD, 517(PBSA):APR-JUN73-
203
WISEMAN, T. THE MONEY MOTIVE.
C. LEHMANN-HAUPT, 441:12NOV74-43
WISSE, R. THE SCHLEMIEL AS HERO.
D. FUCHS, 659:AUTUMN74-562
A.H. ROSENFELD, 390:DEC72-71
WISSER, B. - SEE MOORE, G.E.
WISTRAND, E. OPERA SELECTA.
F. LASSERRE, 182:VOL25#9/10-309
WISTRAND, E. SALLUST ON JUDICIAL
MURDERS IN ROME.
G.M. PAUL, 487:SUMMER72-199
WISWELL, T. THE SCIENCE OF CHECKERS
& DRAUGHTS.
617(TLS):29MAR74-349
WITCOVER, J. WHITE KNIGHT.
639(VQR):AUTUMN72-CXXXVII
WITHERELL, J.W., COMP. MADAGASCAR &
ADJACENT ISLANDS: A GUIDE TO OFFIC-
IAL PUBLICATIONS. FRENCH-SPEAKING
WEST AFRICA: A GUIDE TO OFFICIAL
PUBLICATIONS.
J.A. CASADA, 517(PBSA):APR-JUN73-
208
WITHERELL, J.W., COMP. OFFICIAL PUB-
LICATIONS OF FRENCH EQUATORIAL
AFRICA, FRENCH CAMEROONS, & TOGO,
1946-1958.
J.A. CASADA, 517(PBSA):APR-JUN73-
207
WITHERELL, J.W. & S.B. LOCKWOOD,
COMPS. GHANA: A GUIDE TO OFFICIAL
PUBLICATIONS, 1872-1968.
J.A. CASADA, 517(PBSA):APR-JUN73-
208
WITHROW, W. CONTEMPORARY CANADIAN
PAINTING.*
M. WILLIAMSON, 96:OCT/NOV72-86
WITKE, C. LATIN SATIRE.
N. RUDD, 123:MAR73-42
WITKE, C. NUMEN LITTERARUM.
S. PRETE, 589:APR73-432

WITT, R.E. ISIS IN THE GRAECO-ROMAN
WORLD.
G.A. WELLS, 303:VOL92-223
WITTE, B. DIE WISSENSCHAFT VOM
GUTEN UND BÖSEN.*
K.H. ILTING, 53(AGP):BAND54HEFT
2-202
WITTGENSTEIN, L. CARNETS 1914-1916.
(G.G. GRANGER, ED) LEÇONS ET CON-
VERSATIONS SUR L'ESTHÉTIQUE, LA
PSYCHOLOGIE SUR LA CROYANCE RELIGI-
EUSE [TOGETHER WITH] CONFÉRENCE
SUR L'ÉTHIQUE.
J. BOUVERESSE, 98:MAY72-441
WITTGENSTEIN, L. LETTERS TO RUSSELL,
KEYNES & MOORE. (G.H. VON WRIGHT
& B.F. MC GUINNESS, EDS)
617(TLS):18OCT74-1161
WITTGENSTEIN, L. ON CERTAINTY.*
(G.E.M. ANSCOMBE & G.H. VON
WRIGHT, EDS)
A. PALMER, 393(MIND):JUL72-453
WITTGENSTEIN, L. PROTOTRACTATUS.*
(B.F. MC GUINNESS, T. NYBERG &
G.H. VON WRIGHT, EDS)
A.B.W., 543:MAR72-575
WITTIG, H-G. WIEDERGEBURT ALS RADI-
KALER GESINNUNGSWANDEL.
R. MALTER, 342:BAND63HEFT2-269
WITTIG, M. LE CORPS LESBIEN.
617(TLS):4JAN74-5
WITTKOWER, R. GOTHIC VERSUS CLASSIC.
617(TLS):11OCT74-1108
WITTKOWER, R. PALLADIO & ENGLISH
PALLADIANISM.
617(TLS):24MAY74-549
WITTKOWER, R. & I.B. JAFFE, EDS.
BAROQUE ART.
M.V. ALPER, 58:NOV72-92
H.F. EDWARDS, JR., 290(JAAC):
SUMMER73-557
E.M. TUFTS, 127:SUMMER73-472
WITTLIN, T. COMMISSAR.*
R.M. SLUSSER, 32:DEC73-825
WŁOSZCZEWSKI, S. POLONIA AMERYKAŃ-
SKA.
G.J. LERSKI, 32:SEP73-637
WODEHOUSE, P.G. AUNTS AREN'T GENTLE-
MEN.
R. USBORNE, 617(TLS):27DEC74-
1455
WODEHOUSE, P.G. BACHELORS ANONY-
MOUS.*
M. LEVIN, 441:4AUG74-27
WODTKE, F.W. - SEE BENN, G.
WOEHRLIN, W.F. CHERNYSHEVSKII.*
R.H.W. THEEN, 550(RUSR):APR72-
185
639(VQR):SPRING72-LXIV
WOGATSKY, K. ANGUS WILSON.
S. MONOD, 189(EA):JUL-SEP72-450
WOGATZKI, B. DER PREIS DES MÄD-
CHENS.
V. EBERSBACH, 654(WB):9/1972-152
WOHLGEMUTH-BERGLUND, G. WORT FÜR
WORT.*
H. GERMER, 221(GQ):MAR72-387
E.A. METZGER, 399(MLJ):FEB72-119
WÖHRMANN, K-R. HÖLDERLINS WILLE ZUR
TRAGÖDIE.
C.H., 191(ELN):SEP72(SUPP)-163
WÓJCIK, Z. DZIEJE ROSJI, 1533-1801.
B. DMYTRYSHYN, 32:MAR73-163

WOLD, R. "EL DIARIO DE MÉXICO."*
C. LEWIS, 399(MLJ):MAR72-183
R.M. REEVE, 238:SEP72-598
WOLF, C. THE QUEST FOR CHRISTA T.*
639(VQR):WINTER72-XIX
WOLF, D. DORIOT, DU COMMUNISME À LA
COLLABORATION.
J.C. CAIRNS, 207(FR):DEC71-449
WOLF, G. BESCHREIBUNG EINES ZIM-
MERS.
M. RESO, 654(WB):9/1972-186
WOLF, G., WITH J. DI MONA. FRANK
COSTELLO, PRIME MINISTER OF THE
UNDERWORLD.
E. PERLMUTTER, 441:30MAY74-41
WOLF, L. TEXTE UND DOKUMENTE ZUR
FRANZÖSISCHEN SPRACHGESCHICHTE 16.
JAHRHUNDERT.*
R. BAEHR, 430(NS):MAR72-178
WOLF, P. THE FUTURE OF THE CITY.
P. GOLDBERGER, 441:11NOV74-27
WOLFE, D.M. MILTON & HIS ENGLAND.*
639(VQR):SPRING72-LXI
WOLFENSBERGER, H. MUNDARTWANDEL IM
20. JAHRHUNDERT.*
W. SCHENKER, 343:BAND15HEFT1-89
WOLFF, A. UNREAL ESTATE.
B. KUTTNER, 441:28APR74-4
WOLFF, C. PSYCHOLOGIA RATIONALIS.
(J. ÉCOLE, ED)
C.A. CORR, 319:JAN74-113
WOLFF, E. CHOU TSO-JEN.
A.A. RICKETT, 651(WHR):WINTER73-
93
WOLFF, G. THE SIGHTSEER.
A. BROYARD, 441:11FEB74-39
M. MEWSHAW, 441:3MAR74-4
R. SALE, 453:27JUN74-24
R. TODD, 61:MAY74-129
617(TLS):13SEP74-969
WOLFF, H.J. "NORMENKONTROLLE" UND
GESETZESBEGRIFF IN DER ATTISCHEN
DEMOKRATIE.
D.M. MAC DOWELL, 123:DEC73-227
WOLFF, H.J. - SEE RABEL, E.
WOLFF, K.H. - SEE MANNHEIM, K.
WOLFF, L. - SEE HARTMANN VON AUE
WOLFF, P., ED. DOCUMENTS DE L'HIS-
TOIRE DE LANGUEDOC. HISTOIRE DE
LANGUEDOC.
J. MUNDY, 589:APR73-422
WOLFF, P. WESTERN LANGUAGES, A.D.
100-1500.
J. FELLMAN, 589:OCT73-795
WOLFF, R.L. STRANGE STORIES.
M. ALLOTT, 637(VS):DEC72-240
WOLFF, R.P. PHILOSOPHY.*
S. GOLDMAN, 480(P&R):SUMMER72-
192
WOLFF, T. - SEE PUSHKIN, A.S.
WOLGAST, E. DIE WITTENBERGER LUTHER-
AUSGABE.
W. ULLMANN, 354:JUN72-148
WOLITZER, H. ENDING.
A. BROYARD, 441:30JUL74-37
J.M. CAMERON, 453:31OCT74-6
M. LEVIN, 441:4AUG74-27
WOLKERS, J. TURKISH DELIGHT.
M. LEVIN, 441:8SEP74-43
WOLLASTON, N. ECLIPSE.
R. BLYTHE, 362:4APR74-444
M. LEVIN, 441:16JUN74-28
617(TLS):5APR74-375

WOLLHEIM, R. ART & ITS OBJECTS.*
P. CHARLSON, 262:AUTUMN72-346
WOLLHEIM, R. FREUD.
F. CIOFFI, 262:SUMMER72-171
WOLLHEIM, R. ON ART & THE MIND.
K. BAKER, 61:DEC74-114
WOLLHEIM, R. - SEE STOKES, A.
"WOLS: APHORISMS & PICTURES."
I. BREAKWELL, 592:MAR72-137
WOLTERSTORFF, N. ON UNIVERSALS.*
J. PERRY, 311(JP):2MAY74-252
J.F. ROSENBERG, 482(PHR):JUL72-
382
E. TOMS, 483:JUL72-281
WONDERS, W.C., ED. CANADA'S CHANG-
ING NORTH.
D. SWAINSON, 529(QQ):AUTUMN72-
409
WOOD, C. CHAUCER & THE COUNTRY OF
THE STARS.*
J.A.W. BENNETT, 627(UTQ):WINTER
72-174
WOOD, C. DICTIONARY OF VICTORIAN
PAINTERS.
D. COOMBS, 135:MAY72-63
WOOD, G.R. VOCABULARY CHANGE.
L. PEDERSON, 350:MAR73-184
WOOD, M.F. IN THE LIFE OF A ROMANY
GYPSY. (J.A. BRUNE, ED)
617(TLS):22MAR74-284
WOOD, N. CLEARCUT.
42(AR):SPRING/SUMMER72-250
WOOD, O.P. & G. PITCHER, EDS. RYLE.
A.G.N. FLEW, 479(PHQ):APR72-159
WOOD, P.H. BLACK MAJORITY.
W.D. JORDAN, 441:22DEC74-12
W.L. ROSE, 453:17OCT74-29
WOOD, R.E., ED. THE FUTURE OF META-
PHYSICS.*
D. MIELKE, 485(PE&W):APR72-236
WOOD, T. SOMEBODY ELSE'S SUMMER.
D. SPETTIGUE, 99:MAY/JUN74-20
WOODBRIDGE, K. LANDSCAPE & ANTIQUI-
TY.*
L. HERRMANN, 90:SEP72-636
WOODCOCK, G. DAWN & THE DARKEST
HOUR.
P.L. WILEY, 659:WINTER74-148
WOODCOCK, G. INTO TIBET.
P. HYER, 293(JAST):MAY72-696
WOODCOCK, G., ED. WYNDHAM LEWIS IN
CANADA.*
R. SMITH, 150(DR):SUMMER72-302
WOODCOCK, G., ED. MALCOLM LOWRY.*
A. HUTCHISON, 376:APR72-126
WOODCOCK, G. WHO KILLED THE BRITISH
EMPIRE?
J. VAIZEY, 362:21NOV74-683
WOODESON, J. MARK GERTLER.*
W.G. PLAUT, 99:AUG74-39
WOODFORD, J. THE VIOLATED VISION.
W.A. FULLER, 529(QQ):AUTUMN72-
410
WOODHAM-SMITH, C. QUEEN VICTORIA.
639(VQR):SPRING73-LXXX
WOODHEAD, A.G. THUCYDIDES ON THE
NATURE OF POWER.*
R. WEIL, 555:VOL46FASC1-118
WOODHOUSE, A.S.P. A VARIORUM COMMEN-
TARY ON THE POEMS OF JOHN MILTON.
(VOL 2) (D. BUSH, ED)
639(VQR):AUTUMN72-CXXXIII
WOODHOUSE, C.M. CAPODISTRIA.
R. CLOGG, 617(TLS):19JUL74-767

WOODHOUSE, J.R. ITALO CALVINO.
D.D., 275(IQ):FALL/WINTER72-125
WOODRESS, J. WILLA CATHER.*
E.A. BLOOM, 677:VOL3-332
WOODRESS, J., WITH T. LUDINGTON & J.
ARPAD, EDS. ESSAYS MOSTLY ON PER-
IODICAL PUBLISHING IN AMERICA.
J.D. HART, 27(AL):NOV73-483
I.H. HERRON, 584(SWR):AUTUMN73-
356
WOODRING, C. POLITICS IN ENGLISH
ROMANTIC POETRY.*
J.R.D. JACKSON, 191(ELN):SEP72-
53
J.R.D. JACKSON, 627(UTQ):SPRING
73-289
J.D. JUMP, 541(RES):MAY72-214
J.J. MC GANN, 405(MP):FEB73-255
WOODRUFF, D. THE LIFE & TIMES OF
ALFRED THE GREAT.
617(TLS):27SEP74-1048
WOODS, F.J. MARGINALITY & IDENTITY.
639(VQR):SPRING73-147
WOODS, J. TURNING TO LOOK BACK.*
D. ETTER, 114(CHIR):VOL24#3-147
WOODS, S. ENTER THE CORPSE.
N. CALLENDAR, 441:29DEC74-20
WOODS, S. YET SHE MUST DIE.*
N. CALLENDAR, 441:3MAR74-33
442(NY):4MAR74-114
WOODSIDE, A.B. VIETNAM & THE CHI-
NESE MODEL.*
J.K. WHITMORE, 293(JAST):NOV71-
231
"WOODSTOCK CRAFTSMAN'S MANUAL."
S. MAREIN, 139:OCT72-8
WOODWARD, C. PLANTATION IN YANKEE-
LAND.
P. CONLEY, 432(NEQ):DEC72-597
WOODWARD, C. SKIDMORE, OWINGS &
MERRILL.
R.F. JORDAN, 46:FEB72-129
WOODWARD, C.V. - SEE FITZHUGH, G.
WOODWARD, D.H. - SEE FLETCHER, R.
WOODWARD, J.B. LEONID ANDREYEV.*
P.M. AUSTIN, 104:SUMMER72-334
WOODWARD, M.C. - SEE UNDER COSSÍO
WOODWARD, M.
WOOF, R. - SEE THOMPSON, T.W.
WOOLF, L. THE JOURNEY NOT THE ARRI-
VAL MATTERS.*
G.W. LEEPER, 381:JUN72-235
WOOLF, R. THE ENGLISH MYSTERY PLAYS.
R. EDWARDS, 651(WHR):AUTUMN73-
415
639(VQR):AUTUMN73-CLII
WOOLHOUSE, R.S. LOCKE'S PHILOSOPHY
OF SCIENCE & KNOWLEDGE.*
M.R. AYERS, 483:JUL72-276
G. BRYKMAN, 542:APR-JUN72-214
R.R. COX, 481(PQ):JUL72-725
D. ODEGARD, 154:MAR72-123
J.W. YOLTON, 479(PHQ):JUL72-269
WOOLLEY, B. SOME SWEET DAY.
M. LEVIN, 441:19MAY74-40
WOOLMAN, J. THE JOURNAL & MAJOR
ESSAYS OF JOHN WOOLMAN.* (P.P.
MOULTON, ED)
J.C. DANN, 656(WMQ):JUL72-507
639(VQR):WINTER72-XI
WORCESTER, D.E. & W.G. SCHAEFFER.
THE GROWTH & CULTURE OF LATIN
AMERICA. (2ND ED)
B. NÚÑEZ, 263:JUL-SEP73-335

WORCESTER, G.R.E. THE JUNKS & SAM-
PANS OF THE YANGTZE.
293(JAST):AUG72-1000
WORDEN, B. THE RUMP PARLIAMENT 1648-
1653.
617(TLS):28JUN74-696
WORDSWORTH, D. JOURNALS OF DOROTHY
WORDSWORTH. (REV) (M. MOORMAN, ED)
B.C.H., 191(ELN):SEP72(SUPP)-63
WORDSWORTH, J. & B. DARLINGTON, EDS.
BICENTENARY WORDSWORTH STUDIES IN
MEMORY OF JOHN ALBAN FINCH.
J.R.D. JACKSON, 627(UTQ):SPRING
73-289
J.R. WATSON, 541(RES):NOV72-508
WORDSWORTH, W. THE PRELUDE. (J.C.
MAXWELL, ED)
B.C.H., 191(ELN):SEP72(SUPP)-66
"THE WORKING CLASSES IN THE VICTOR-
IAN AGE."
617(TLS):29MAR74-343
"WORKING CONDITIONS IN THE VICTORIAN
AGE."
617(TLS):29MAR74-343
"THE WORKS IN ARCHITECTURE OF JOHN
CARR."
617(TLS):22FEB74-193
WORLEY, R.B. THE WONDERFUL WORLD OF
W.A.C. BENNETT.
R.M. BURNS, 529(QQ):SPRING72-108
WÖRNER, K.H. STOCKHAUSEN.* (B. HOP-
KINS, ED & TRANS)
P. GRIFFITHS, 415:APR73-381
A.W., 410(M&L):JUL73-356
WORONOFF, J. ORGANIZING AFRICAN
UNITY.
A.H.M. KIRK-GREENE, 69:JAN72-64
"WORSHIP." [HYMNAL]
J. ROFF, 363:FEB72-79
WORTH, D.S., A.S. KOZAK & D.B. JOHN-
SON. RUSSIAN DERIVATIONAL DIC-
TIONARY.*
L. ĎUROVIČ, 279:VOL15-202
D. WARD, 297(JL):FEB72-196
WORTHAM, J.D. BRITISH EGYPTOLOGY
1549-1906.
T.G.H. JAMES, 39:OCT72-364
R.J.L. WYNNE THOMAS, 135:NOV72-
215
VAN DER WOUDE, S., ED. STUDIA BIB-
LIOGRAPHICA IN HONOREM HERMAN DE
LA FONTAINE VERWEY.
C.F. BÜHLER, 354:JUN72-154
D. CHAMBERS, 503:SUMMER72-112
WOUK, H. THE CITY BOY.
441:12MAY74-34
WOYTEK, E. SPRACHLICHE STUDIEN ZUR
SATURA MENIPPEA VARROS.
J. ANDRÉ, 555:VOL46FASC1-144
WRAGG, D.W. A DICTIONARY OF AVIA-
TION.
617(TLS):29MAR74-348
WRAGG, D.W. FLIGHT BEFORE FLYING.
617(TLS):19JUL74-772
WRAY, E., C. ROSENFIELD & D. BAILEY.
TEN LIVES OF THE BUDDHA.*
T. BOWIE, 127:SUMMER73-458
M. SMITHIES, 302:JUL72-220
WREN, M.C. THE WESTERN IMPACT UPON
TSARIST RUSSIA.
A.J. RIEBER, 550(RUSR):JUL72-323
WRENN, C.L. - SEE "BEOWULF"

YATES, W.E. NESTROY.
D. GRONAU, 182:VOL25#9/10-294
YEATS, J.B. THE COLLECTED PLAYS OF
JACK B. YEATS. (R. SKELTON, ED)
B. GUINNESS, 39:MAY72-422
"JACK B. YEATS 1871-1957: A CENTEN-
ARY EXHIBITION."
B. GUINNESS, 39:MAY72-422
YEATS, W.B. DRUID CRAFT, THE WRIT-
ING OF "THE SHADOWY WATERS."
(M.J. SIDNELL, G.P. MAYHEW & D.R.
CLARK, EDS)
G.B. SAUL, 397(MD):DEC72-343
G.C. SPIVAK, 481(PQ):APR72-493
YEATS, W.B. REFLECTIONS. (C. BRAD-
FORD, ED) LETTERS TO THE NEW
ISLAND.
M. SIDNELL, 627(UTQ):SPRING72-
263
YEATS, W.B. JOHN SHERMAN & DHOYA.*
(R.J. FINNERAN, ED) UNCOLLECTED
PROSE BY W.B. YEATS.* (VOL 1)
(J.P. FRAYNE, ED)
H. ADAMS, 219(GAR):FALL72-249
M. SIDNELL, 627(UTQ):SPRING72-
263
YEATS, W.B. & M. RUDDOCK. AH, SWEET
DANCER. (R. MC HUGH, ED)
M. SIDNELL, 627(UTQ):SPRING72-
263
"THE YELLOW BOOK."
617(TLS):29MAR74-344
YEN KENG-WANG. T'ANG-SHIH YEN-CHIU
TS'UNG-KAO.
L.Y. CHIU, 302:JAN72-75
YERBA, V.G. - SEE UNDER GARCÍA YER-
BA, V.
YESENIN, S. SERGEY YESENIN: OTCHEYE
SLOVO. (S. KOSHECHKIN, COMP)
G. MC VAY, 402(MLR):JUL73-717
YETIV, I. LE THÈME DE L'ALIÉNATION
DANS LE ROMAN MAGHRÉBIN D'EXPRES-
SION FRANÇAISE, 1952-1956.
C.Y. MEADE, 188(ECR):WINTER72-
334
YEVGEN'YEVA, A.P., GENERAL ED. SLO-
VAR' SINONIMOV RUSSKOGO YAZYKA.
W.F. RYAN, 575(SEER):JAN73-124
YEVTUSHENKO, Y. STOLEN APPLES.
E. MORGAN, 617(TLS):11OCT74-1132
A. RANNIT, 550(RUSR):JAN72-102
YGLESIAS, H. HOW SHE DIED.*
S. O'CONNELL, 418(MR):WINTER73-
190
YGLESIAS, R. HIDE FOX, & ALL AFTER.
639(VQR):SPRING72-XLIX
YING-MAO & OTHERS. THE POLITICAL
WORK SYSTEM OF THE CHINESE COMMUN-
IST MILITARY.
M. GOLDMAN, 293(JAST):MAY72-665
YIP, W-L. EZRA POUND'S "CATHAY."*
A. LONSDALE, 447(N&Q):SEP72-355
YNFANTE, J. LA PRODIGIOSA AVENTURA
DEL OPUS DEI.
J. GEORGEL, 98:FEB72-183
YOLTON, J.W. LOCKE & THE COMPASS OF
HUMAN UNDERSTANDING.*
J.J. JENKINS, 483:JAN72-82
D. ODEGARD, 482(PHR):APR72-250
YONG-SŎP, K. - SEE UNDER KIM YONG-
SŎP
YORK, A. THE CAPTIVATOR.
N. CALLENDAR, 441:24FEB74-41

YORK, A. THE EXPURGATOR.
N. CALLENDAR, 441:8DEC74-44
YOSANO AKIKO. TANGLED HAIR.* (S.
GOLDSTEIN & SEISHI SHINODA, TRANS)
[SHOWN IN PREV UNDER TITLE]
M. BROCK, 285(JAPQ):JAN-MAR72-
102
YOSHINOBU, S. - SEE UNDER SHIBA YOSH-
INOBU
YOST, C. THE CONDUCT & MISCONDUCT
OF FOREIGN AFFAIRS.*
676(YR):SUMMER73-XVI
YOST, N.S. MEDICINE LODGE.
K. PORTER, 650(WF):APR72-134
YOUNG, A. COMPLETE POEMS. (L.
CLARK, ED)
J. FULLER, 362:7MAR74-310
617(TLS):12APR74-393
YOUNG, A.N. CHINA'S NATION-BUILDING
EFFORT.
J.K. CHANG, 293(JAST):AUG72-942
639(VQR):AUTUMN72-CXLV
YOUNG, A.P. THE "X" DOCUMENTS. (S.
ASTER, ED)
R. LEWIN, 362:29AUG74-284
YOUNG, D. BOXCARS.
D. CAVITCH, 441:17NOV74-46
YOUNG, D. THE HEART'S FOREST.
639(VQR):SPRING73-LXVIII
YOUNG, E. THE CORRESPONDENCE OF
EDWARD YOUNG 1683-1765.* (H.
PETTIT, ED)
H. FORSTER, 78(BC):AUTUMN72-426
R.E. KELLEY, 481(PQ):JUL72-788
T. MILLS, 541(RES):NOV72-502
H. TROWBRIDGE, 191(ELN):MAR73-
229
YOUNG, G. TRACKS OF AN INTRUDER.
D. MILES, 293(JAST):MAY72-733
YOUNG, I. THE PRIVATE LIFE OF ISLAM.
617(TLS):21JUN74-665
YOUNG, I. THEODORE.
C.A. HUGHES, 381:SEP72-363
YOUNG, K. HARRY, LORD ROSEBERY.
H. D'AVIGDOR-GOLDSMID, 617(TLS):
1NOV74-1239
YOUNG, K. - SEE LOCKHART, R.B.
YOUNG, M., ED. POVERTY REPORT 1974.
617(TLS):16AUG74-878
YOUNG, M. & P. WILLMOTT. THE SYM-
METRICAL FAMILY.*
P. STARR, 441:3FEB74-23
442(NY):27MAY74-107
YOUNG, M.T. SAINT-EXUPÉRY: "VOL DE
NUIT."
A. ANTONINI, 535(RHL):JUL-AUG72-
741
YOUNG, P., ED. ATLAS OF THE SECOND
WORLD WAR.
617(TLS):8FEB74-128
YOUNG, P. - SEE HEMINGWAY, E.
YOUNG, P. & R. HOLMES. THE ENGLISH
CIVIL WAR.
617(TLS):19JUL74-764
YOUNG, T.D. & M.T. INGE. DONALD
DAVIDSON.
L. COWAN, 578:FALL74-146
L.A. LAWSON, 396(MODA):SPRING73-
208
YOUNG, V. ON FILM.*
639(VQR):AUTUMN72-CLVIII
YOUNG, W.C. AMERICAN THEATRICAL
ARTS.*
D. SHEPARD, 150:WINTER71/72-124

YOUNG, W.C., ED. DOCUMENTS OF AMERI-
CAN THEATER HISTORY. (VOLS 1&2)
617(TLS):12APR74-402
YOUNGREN, W.H. SEMANTICS, LINGUIS-
TICS & CRITICISM.
D.P. FUNT, 249(HUDR):AUTUMN73-
572
D.F. STALKER, 290(JAAC):FALL72-
139
YOUNGSON, A.J., ED. BEYOND THE
HIGHLAND LINE.
J.A. SMITH, 617(TLS):26JUL74-809
YOUNT, J. THE TRAPPER'S LAST SHOT.
M. WATKINS, 441:17FEB74-31
YOURCENAR, M. DENIER DU RÊVE.
B.J. BUCKNALL, 207(FR):MAR72-905
YOURCENAR, M. FEUX. SOUVENIRS
PIEUX.
M. RENAULT, 617(TLS):23AUG74-893
YOURCENAR, M. PRÉSENTATION CRITIQUE
DE CONSTANTIN CAVAFY (1863-1933).
H. IOANNIDI, 98:APR72-354
YOURCENAR, M. THÉÂTRE I.
B.L. KNAPP, 207(FR):FEB72-712
YPMA, E. - SEE JAMES OF VITERBO
YU, G.T. CHINA & TANZANIA.
L-S. TAO, 293(JAST):MAY72-668
L-S. TAO, 293(JAST):AUG72-947
YU-NING, L. - SEE UNDER LI YU-NING
YU-WEN, J. - SEE UNDER JEN YU-WEN
YÜCEL, T. L'IMAGINAIRE DE BERNANOS.*
N. GUEUNIER, 209(FM):JAN72-66
N. GUEUNIER, 535(RHL):MAR-APR72-
348
YUDKEVICH, L.G. LIRICHESKIY GEROY
YESENINA.
G. MC VAY, 402(MLR):JUL73-717
YUILL, P.B. HAZELL PLAYS SOLOMON.
617(TLS):25OCT74-1206
YŪJI, M. - SEE UNDER MURAMATSU YŪJI
YÜN-SHENG, H. - SEE UNDER HSÜEH YÜN-
SHENG
YUSHIN, P.F. SERGEY YESENIN.
G. MC VAY, 402(MLR):JUL73-717

ZAC, S. - SEE KANT, I.
ŽÁČEK, V. & OTHERS. DĚJINY JUGO-
SLÁVIE.
W.S. VUCINICH, 32:JUN73-420
ZACHWATOWICZ, J. & OTHERS. KATHEDRA
GNIEŻNIEŃSKA. (A. ŚWIECHOWSKA, ED)
J.I. DANIEC, 497(POLR):SUMMER72-
94
W.C. LEEDY, JR., 54:JUN72-204
ZAEHNER, R.C. EVOLUTION & RELIGION.
L.S. BETTY, 485(PE&W):JUL72-341
ZAEHNER, R.C. OUR SAVAGE GOD.
J.W. BOWKER, 617(TLS):22NOV74-
1321
ZAHRNT, M. OLYNTH UND DIE CHALKIDI-
ER.
F. LASSERRE, 182:VOL25#3/4-117
ZAIDI, S.M.H. THE VILLAGE CULTURE
IN TRANSITION.
J. ELLICKSON, 293(JAST):FEB72-
450
ZAIONCHKOVSKOGO, P.A., ED. SPRAVOCH-
NIKI PO ISTORII DOREVOLIUTSIONNOI
ROSSII.
C.C. HOFFMEISTER, 517(PBSA):JAN-
MAR73-84

ZAJADACZ, P. STUDIES IN PRODUCTION
& TRADE IN EAST AFRICA.
F. STEWART, 69:APR72-165
ZALUMS, E. WESTERN AUSTRALIAN GOV-
ERNMENT PUBLICATIONS, 1829-1959.
(2ND ED)
J.B. CHILDS, 517(PBSA):APR-JUN73-
205
ZAMBON, M.R. LES ROMANS FRANÇAIS
DANS LES JOURNAUX LITTÉRAIRES
ITALIENS DU XVIIIE SIÈCLE.
N. JONARD, 549(RLC):JUL-SEP72-
464
ZAMMIT, J.A., ED. THE CHILEAN ROAD
TO SOCIALISM.
617(TLS):8FEB74-124
ZAMPETTI, P. PAINTINGS FROM THE
MARCHES: GENTILE TO RAPHAEL.
D. THOMAS, 135:NOV72-214
ZANDVOORT, R.W. COLLECTED PAPERS II.
N.E. ENKVIST, 597(SN):VOL44#1-
206
ZANE, G. INDUSTRIA DIN ROMÂNIA ÎN
A DOUA JUMĂTATE A SECOLULUI AL
XIX-LEA.
P. EIDELBERG, 32:DEC73-843
ZANELLI, D., ED. FELLINI SATYRICON.
R. GOWER, 97(CQ):VOL6#1-59
ZANER, R.M. THE WAY OF PHENOMENOL-
OGY.
R.J. DEVETTERE, 258:SEP72-468
D.C. MATHUR, 484(PPR):MAR73-439
ZANETTE, E. PERSONAGGI E MOMENTI
NELLA VITA DI LUDOVICO ARIOSTO.
400(MLN):JAN72-162
ZANTS, E. THE AESTHETICS OF THE NEW
NOVEL IN FRANCE.
J. ALTER, 207(FR):FEB72-723
ZAOZERSKAYA, E.I. U ISTOKOV KRUP-
NOGO PROIZVODSTVA V RUSSKOY PROM-
YSHLENNOSTI.*
O. CRISP, 575(SEER):OCT73-582
ZAREMBA, E., ED. PRIVILEGE OF SEX.
W. MITCHINSON, 99:OCT74-41
ZARETSKY, I.I. & M.P. LEONE, EDS.
RELIGIOUS MOVEMENTS IN CONTEMPOR-
ARY AMERICA.
H. COX, 441:22DEC74-13
ŻARNOWSKI, J. POLSKA PARTIA SOCJAL-
ISTYCZNA W LATACH 1935-1939.
A.M. CIENCIALA, 32:MAR73-185
ŻARSKA, A., ED. LITERATURA ROSYJSKA.
(VOL 1)
W.K. KONDY, 550(RUSR):JUL72-324
ZARTMAN, I.W., ED. MAN, STATE & SOC-
IETY IN THE CONTEMPORARY MAGHRIB.
617(TLS):1FEB74-99
ZASLAVSKY, C. AFRICA COUNTS.
J. BERNSTEIN, 442(NY):14OCT74-
194
ZASSENHAUS, H. WALLS.
442(NY):4MAR74-113
ZAVADOVSKIJ, J.N. BERBERSKIJ JAZYK.
E.T. ABDEL-MASSIH, 353:1MAR72-
115
ZAVALA, I.M. IDEOLOGÍA Y POLÍTICA
EN LA NOVELA ESPAÑOLA DEL SIGLO
XIX.
E. GONZÁLEZ, 263:JUL-SEP73-347
ZAVALA, I.M. MASONES, COMUNEROS Y
CARBONARIOS.
191(ELN):SEP72(SUPP)-212

ZDRAVOMYSLOV, A.G., V.P. ROZHIN &
V.A. IADOV, EDS. MAN & HIS WORK.
(S.P. DUNN, ED & TRANS)
D. LANE, 575(SEER):OCT73-616
S.J. RAWIN, 550(RUSR):JAN72-103
VAN DER ZEE, J. THE GREATEST MEN'S
PARTY ON EARTH.
D. GODDARD, 441:5MAY74-52
442(NY):22JUL74-83
ZEHBE, J. - SEE KANT, I.
ZEIGLER, J.W. REGIONAL THEATRE.
617(TLS):22MAR74-300
ZELDIN, T. FRANCE 1848-1945.* (VOL
1)
R.M. ANDREWS, 441:24FEB74-6
D. JOHNSON, 617(TLS):27DEC74-
1468
ZELNIK, R.E. LABOR & SOCIETY IN
TSARIST RUSSIA.*
FR.-X. COQUIN, 104:SPRING72-156
T. EMMONS, 550(RUSR):JUL72-297
T.H. VON LAUE, 575(SEER):JAN73-
138
639(VQR):SPRING72-LXXII
ZEMAN, H. DIE DEUTSCHE ANAKREON-
TISCHE DICHTUNG.
R.H. SAMUEL, 67:MAY73-142
ZEMAN, J.J. MODAL LOGIC.
H.A. LEWIS, 518:OCT73-33
ZEMSKY, R. MERCHANTS, FARMERS, &
RIVER GODS.*
M.N. KAY, 481(PQ):JUL72-556
J.T. MAIN, 656(WMQ):JAN72-176
ZENKOVSKY, S. RUSSKOE STAROOBRIAD-
CHESTVO.
H.A. STAMMLER, 32:DEC73-802
ZENKOVSKY, S.A. - SEE CIŽEVSKIJ, D.
ZENKOVSKY, S.A. & D.L. ARMBRUSTER.
A GUIDE TO THE BIBLIOGRAPHIES OF
RUSSIAN LITERATURE.*
C.C. HOFFMEISTER, 399(MLJ):NOV72-
457
205(FMLS):APR72-196
ZÉPHIR, J.J. PSYCHOLOGIE DE "SALA-
VIN" DE GEORGES DUHAMEL.*
R.J. BOURCIER, 207(FR):OCT71-244
L.C. KEATING, 399(MLJ):APR72-251
J. ONIMUS, 535(RHL):MAR-APR72-
349
ŽEPIĆ, S. MORPHOLOGIE UND SEMANTIK
DER DEUTSCHEN NOMINALKOMPOSITA.
W. ABRAHAM, 343:BAND14HEFT1-78
D.J. ALLERTON, 297(JL):SEP72-321
H. VATER, 350:JUN73-484
ZÉRAFFA, M. ROMAN ET SOCIÉTÉ.*
C.A. PRENDERGAST, 208(FS):APR73-
236
ZERBE, J. HAPPY TIMES.* (TEXT BY
B. GILL)
617(TLS):12APR74-386
ZETT, R. BEITRÄGE ZUR GESCHICHTE
DER NOMINALKOMPOSITA IM SERBOKRO-
ATISCHEN.
E. DICKENMANN, 343:BAND15HEFT1-
109
ZETTERSTEN, A. A STATISTICAL STUDY
OF THE GRAPHIC SYSTEM OF PRESENT-
DAY AMERICAN ENGLISH.
H.J. NEUHAUS, 38:BAND90HEFT1/2-
195
A.H. ROBERTS, 350:JUN73-492
Z. ŠALJAPINA, 353:15OCT72-115

ZETTL, H. TELEVISION PRODUCTION
HANDBOOK. (2ND ED)
H. MIXON, 583:FALL72-109
ŽEŽELJ, M. TRAGAJUĆI ZA MATOŠEM.
R.S. BAUR, 72:BAND210HEFT1/3-238
ZIEGLER, F. - SEE BEKKER, C.
ZIEGLER, G. - SEE CURIE, M. & I.
ZIEGLER, J. ZUR RELIGIÖSEN HALTUNG
DER GEGENKAISER IM 4. JH. N. CHR.*
(K. KRAFT & J. BLEICKEN, EDS)
T.D. BARNES, 313:VOL62-200
J-P. CALLU, 555:VOL46FASC2-358
ZIEGLER, P. KING WILLIAM IV.
P. HONAN, 637(VS):JUN73-458
ZIERER, E. THE THEORY OF GRAPHS IN
LINGUISTICS.
W.J. HUTCHINS, 361:VOL28#4-380
ZIEROTH, D. CLEARING.
L. HICKS, 99:MAY/JUN74-20
ZIFF, L. PURITANISM IN AMERICA.*
D.L. PARKER, 165:FALL74-201
617(TLS):10MAY74-497
ZIGGELAAR, A. LE PHYSICIEN IGNACE
GASTON PARDIES, S.J. (1636-1673).
L.C. ROSENFIELD, 319:APR74-258
ZILO, G.C. DU PONT.
R. SHERRILL, 441:15DEC74-5
ZIMANSKY, C.A. - SEE VANBRUGH, J.
ZIMIN, A.A. ROSSIIA NA POROGE NOV-
OGO VREMENI (OCHERKI POLITICHESKOI
ISTORII ROSSII PERVOI TRETI XVI V).
J. FENNELL, 32:MAR73-157
ZIMMERLY, D. - SEE GOUDIE, E.
ZIMMERMAN, F.B. THE ANTHEMS OF
HENRY PURCELL.
W. SHAW, 415:JAN73-37
ZIMMERMANN, A. VERZEICHNIS UNGE-
DRUCKTER KOMMENTARE ZUR METAPHYSIK
UND PHYSIK DES ARISTOTELES AUS DER
ZEIT VON ETWA 1250-1350. (VOL 1)
W.A.W., 543:MAR72-576
ZIMMERMANN, G. ORDENSLEBEN UND
LEBENSSTANDARD.
H. SCHIPPERGES, 182:VOL25#19/20-
693
ZIMMERMANN, R. UNTERSUCHUNGEN ZUM
FRÜHMITTELENGLISCHEN TEMPUSSYSTEM.
U. FRIES, 72:BAND210HEFT1/3-173
ZIMMERMANN, R.C. DAS WELTBILD DES
JUNGEN GOETHE.* (VOL 1)
R. OTTO, 654(WB):4/1972-186
ZIMMERSCHIED, D. THEMATISCHES VER-
ZEICHNIS DER WERKE VON JOHANN
NEPOMUK HUMMEL.
J. SACHS, 415:SEP73-898
ŽINKIN, N.I. MECHANISM OF SPEECH.
G.F. MAIER, 682(ZPSK):BAND25
HEFT6-545
ZINNER, H. STÜCKE.
617(TLS):5APR74-359
ZINS, H. HISTORIA ANGLII.
L. KOCZY, 182:VOL25#5/6-189
ZIOLKOWSKI, T. FICTIONAL TRANSFIG-
URATIONS OF JESUS.*
W.E. BARRETT, 639(VQR):SUMMER73-
458
M. COOKE, 676(YR):SPRING73-469
ZIOLKOWSKI, T. - SEE HESSE, H.
ZIOMEK, H. - SEE LOPE DE VEGA
ZIPES, J.D. THE GREAT REFUSAL.*
S. MEWS, 221(GQ):JAN72-167
J. PURVER, 220(GL&L):OCT72-77
E. SHAFFER, 402(MLR):APR73-462

WITHDRAWAL